Urban Agenda

Urban Agenda

Collection Editors

Luis Hernández-Callejo
Sergio Nesmachnow
Pablo de Frutos Madrazo
Tigran Haas
Yu-Sheng Shen
Marcia Eugenio-Gozalbo

MDPI

Basel • Beijing • Wuhan • Barcelona • Belgrade • Novi Sad • Cluj • Manchester

Collection Editors
Luis Hernández-Callejo
Department of Agricultural and Forestry Engineering
Universidad de Valladolid
Soria
Spain

Sergio Nesmachnow
Instituto de Computación, Facultad de Ingeniería
Universidad de la República
Montevideo
Uruguay

Pablo de Frutos Madrazo
Department of Applied Economics
Universidad de Valladolid
Soria
Spain

Tigran Haas
Urban Planning & Urban Design
KTH Royal Institute of Technology
Stockholm
Sweden

Yu-Sheng Shen
Department of Earth and Life Sciences
University of Taipei
Taipei City
Taiwan

Marcia Eugenio-Gozalbo
Department of Didactics of Experimental and Social Sciences and Mathematics
University de Valladolid
Soria
Spain

Editorial Office
MDPI AG
Grosspeteranlage 5
4052 Basel, Switzerland

This is a reprint of the Topical Collection, published open access by the journal *Urban Science* (ISSN 2413-8851), freely accessible at: https://www.mdpi.com/journal/urbansci/topical_collections/220K1SRWWA.

For citation purposes, cite each article independently as indicated on the article page online and as indicated below:

Lastname, A.A.; Lastname, B.B. Article Title. *Journal Name* **Year**, *Volume Number*, Page Range.

ISBN 978-3-7258-6432-4 (Hbk)
ISBN 978-3-7258-6433-1 (PDF)
https://doi.org/10.3390/books978-3-7258-6433-1

Contents

Preface

This Reprint focuses on the growing importance of the Urban Agenda as a comprehensive framework for promoting sustainable, inclusive, and resilient urban development. Its scope spans a wide range of disciplines and perspectives, reflecting the complexity of cities and the diverse challenges they face. The aim of this Reprint is to gather high-quality scientific contributions that deepen our understanding of urban dynamics and offer practical insights for guiding future policy and decision-making.

The motivation for preparing this Reprint stems from the need to highlight emerging research that connects technological progress, social transformation, and environmental responsibility within the context of the Urban Agenda. As cities and territories continue to evolve, it becomes essential to provide an updated scientific overview that supports more equitable and future-oriented models of development.

This Reprint is addressed to researchers, practitioners, planners, policymakers, and all professionals engaged in urban studies and territorial transformation. It is also intended for those seeking a broader understanding of how integrated, multisectoral approaches can strengthen sustainability at local, regional, national, and international levels.

Luis Hernández-Callejo, Sergio Nesmachnow, Pablo de Frutos Madrazo, Tigran Haas, Yu-Sheng Shen, and Marcia Eugenio-Gozalbo
Collection Editors

urban science

Editorial

The Urban Agenda

Sergio Nesmachnow [1,*] and Luis Hernández Callejo [2]

[1] Instituto de Computación, Facultad de Ingeniería, Universidad de la República, Montevideo 11300, Uruguay
[2] Department of Agricultural and Forestry Engineering, University of Valladolid, Campus Duques de Soria, 42004 Soria, Spain; luis.hernandez.callejo@uva.es
* Correspondence: sergion@fing.edu.uy

1. Urban Agenda

The concept of Urban Agenda refers to a strategic document that establishes a policy framework aimed at guiding the development of modern cities in order to respond to relevant urban challenges, such as population growth, mobility, housing, waste management, climate change, and social inclusion [1] (United Nations, 2016).

The original idea of the Urban Agenda was to define a conceptual framework and collection of principles for sustainable urban development; thus, the initiative lacked a normative character. However, with the introduction of the New Urban Agenda, adopted in 2016 at the United Nations Conference on Housing and Sustainable Urban Development (Habitat III) in Quito, Ecuador [2] (UN-Habitat, 2018), member nations of the UN established a specific, concrete, and universal commitment to promote a new global model for sustainable urbanization. The New Urban Agenda established a global framework with standards and principles for urban planning, construction, development, and management, with the main goal of guiding sustainable urban development and fostering a more positive urban future. The specific focus was on the best practices for managing rapid urbanization, supporting the climate goals under the Paris Agreement, and achieving the Sustainable Development Goals (SDGs) defined in the 2030 Agenda for Sustainable Development, particularly SDG 11 ("Make cities and human settlements inclusive, safe, resilient and sustainable") [3] (United Nations, 2015).

The Urban Agenda constitutes a working method and a process for all actors, public and private, that intervene in cities and that seek equitable, fair, and sustainable development from their different fields of action. It is also considered as a frame of reference for urban areas, establishing a range of urban policies of a social, economic, and environmental nature, which can be put into practice by any municipality in a rural or urban environment and by any city, regardless of its location and size, and which concern the entire territory. Urban Agenda proposes the synergy of six main concepts—urban planning and design, urban resiliency, sustainable mobility, economic growth and innovation, governance and decentralization, and equity and inclusion—as shown in Figure 1.

The concept of urban planning and design goes beyond traditional approaches based on the physical layouts of locations; it is a strategic tool to shape cities according to key goals, such as building compact, socially inclusive, environmentally sustainable, resilient, and economically vibrant urban environments. This concept provides the spatial framework for the implementation and development of other broader goals of the Urban Agenda (equity, sustainability, and prosperity).

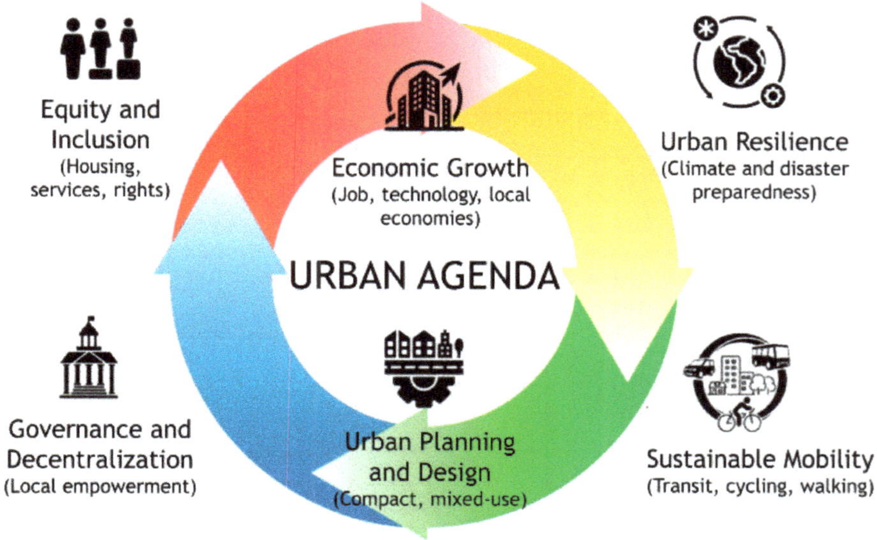

Figure 1. Synergy of the six main concepts of the Urban Agenda.

The concept of urban resiliency refers to the creation of cities that are able to anticipate, absorb, adapt, and recover from unforeseen environmental, economic, or social events. The main idea is to build strong and flexible urban environments that guarantee the continuity of public services, protecting lives and livelihoods, and building adaptive capacities for the future.

The concept of sustainable mobility encompasses several key issues related to the design and maintenance of proper transportation systems, following a people-centered paradigm to guarantee their affordability, accessibility, efficiency, safety, and environmental friendliness. Among the relevant key issues, prioritizing public transit, walking, and cycling is key to reducing dependence on private means of transportation and supporting compact, inclusive urban growth.

The concept of economic growth and innovation is focused on promoting and developing the role of cities as drivers of prosperity, productivity, and creativity, without compromising inclusiveness, sustainability, and resiliency. The main idea is to exploit the potential of cities as centers of economic dynamism to generate inclusive prosperity, foster entrepreneurship and technological innovation, and support sustainable industries, with a special focus on reducing inequalities and contributing to environmental and social wellbeing.

The concept of governance and decentralization proposes building effective, inclusive, transparent, and accountable institutions and empowering low-level local governments to allow for urbanization management following a democratic, participatory model. Decentralization is conceived as a key point, alongside coordination with national and global governments and initiatives, to fulfill the goals defined by the Urban Agenda.

Finally, the concept of equity and inclusion is horizontal to all other concepts. This refers to guaranteeing social justice, i.e., ensuring that all citizens have equal opportunities, rights, and access to city benefits, regardless of income, gender, age, ability, migration status, etc. This concept is key for addressing discrimination, poverty, and inequality so that cities become just, inclusive, and participatory environments. Under this concept, urbanization is conceived as a driver of inclusive development rather than exclusion or marginalization.

The New Urban Agenda is structured radially, considering five key elements or implementation pillars to develop the previous concepts: national urban policies, urban legislation, urban planning and design, local economy and finance, and local implementation. These pillars are meant to establish a paradigm shift, moving from traditional top-down approaches for urban planning and development to a new conception of cities, centered on the people, and adopting a holistic view of integral sustainable development. The New Urban Agenda pushes cities to move from a growth-first pattern to a people- and planet-centered urbanization model, adopting flexible, participatory, and inclusive planning strategies developed under an empowered, decentralized, and multi-level governance. Under this new paradigm, cities are conceived to be not reactive and fragmented, but integrated, proactive, and resilient. In this way, they can effectively respond to the main urban challenges, including rapid population growth, mobility, housing and urban infrastructure, climate change, and social inclusion.

The Urban Agenda is a relevant matter because without applying sustainable planning strategies, the rapid urban growth risks worsening inequality, congestion, pollution, and vulnerability to climate impacts. By shaping inclusive, green, and resilient cities, the Urban Agenda provides a blueprint for sustainable development at a global level.

2. Implementation, Practical Examples, and Relevance of Urban Agenda

The New Urban Agenda (New Urban Agenda) was never meant to stay abstract. It is framed to work across multiple, interconnected scales through which its pillars are translated into action.

The implementation of the New Urban Agenda pillars has been proposed at different levels:

- At a higher, global level, world institutions are meant to provide the overarching vision, and define the general frameworks and monitoring mechanisms for sustainable urbanization. The highest-level institution is the United Nations, which acts via relevant departments and programs, such as the United Nations Human Settlements Programme (UN-Habitat), the Department of Economic and Social Affairs (UN-DESA), and the United Nations Environment Programme (UNEP). Other important actors are multilateral development banks (e.g., the World Bank and regional banks), international non-governmental organizations, and academic networks.
- At the national level, national governments and organizations, such as ministries of finance, environment, housing, etc., planning offices, and other institutions in charge of urban development are responsible for framing the actions defined in the general frameworks into realistic national urban policies, taking into account the specific regulations, financing strategies, and institutional limitations.
- At the regional or metropolitan level, regional governments and municipalities are in charge of the coordination and management of urban–rural linkages, metropolitan regions, and cross-boundary systems.
- At the local or city level, the city authorities (city councils, municipal agencies) and relevant actors of the city, such as local businesses, academia, and civil society, work on specific implementation plans to define new models for governance, services, economic growth, and participation.
- Finally, at the community or neighborhood level, associations and movements such as social institutions, community-based organizations, societal and popular organizations, and cooperatives are involved to guarantee that all initiatives related to urban development are people-centered, inclusive, and equitable.

Relevant examples of specific actions to be undertaken at each level include the following: (at the global level) the global monitoring of high-level initiatives, the definition of global indicators, especially related to SDG 11: Sustainable Cities and Communities, and the creation of specific contents related to their paradigm and dissemination via open global knowledge-sharing platforms; (at the national level) the development of national urban policies aligned with sustainable development goals, the formulation of a legal basis for decentralization, fiscal transfers, and local empowerment, and the integration of the main pillars of the New Urban Agenda into national strategies and plans for infrastructure investment; (at the metropolitan level) the coordination and integration of metropolitan transportation systems, the definition of strategies for land use, housing, and environmental protection, and the promotion and development of economic clusters and innovation hubs; (at the city level) the implementation of participatory urban planning to ensure compact, mixed-use, and transit-oriented development, the creation of affordable housing and basic service delivery programs, and the development of green infrastructure, resilient buildings, and renewable energy; (at the community level) the implementation of programs for the community-driven upgrading of informal settlements, the promotion of participatory design in public spaces, parks, and transportation nodes, the inclusion of local forces in waste management, energy cooperatives, and microfinance, and the improvement of social cohesion through cultural, educational, and youth programs.

Some specific examples of the implementation of the Urban Agenda around the world include the following: the integration of public transportation and housing policies implemented in Bogotá, Colombia, built around the TransMilenio BRT system to promote accessibility and equity; the integrated and coordinated Urban Agenda for the EU initiative, focusing on the urban dimension and national policies and legislation through the use of specific working groups focused on affordable housing, sustainable mobility, and digital transition; the urban regeneration strategies developed in Nairobi, Kenya, to provide affordable housing, upgrade informal settlements, and undertake resilience planning; and the sustainable mobility policies developed in Toyama, Japan, to encourage walkable neighborhoods, accessible transit, and reduced carbon emissions.

3. Related Work

The fundamental criticisms of traditional top-down planning models are not new. In a seminal work, Jacobs (1961) exposed the main weaknesses of the rationalist urban planning approaches developed in the 1950s and 1960s. Jacobs criticized the privacy-oriented, automobile-dependent orthodox approaches and their management of green spaces. Instead, he proposed an innovative use of mixed-use streets, considering sidewalks and parks as the central components of the city. The use of valuable local knowledge and an organic view of urban complexity were also proposed to complement the design paradigm to create diverse, vital, and local communities. Although these criticisms were formulated decades before the New Urban Agenda was proposed, relevant comments were raised, which served as a foundation for proposing a sustainable means of urban development.

Another early work provided useful information for the characterization of urban environments. Sassen (1991) [4] developed a thorough analysis of three main global cities (New York, London, and Tokyo) and reviewed their role as economic centers in the era of globalization, but also their negative aspects as highly concentrated locations of economic power and inequality. Relevant outcomes from the analysis were considered to formulate the Urban Agenda recommendations regarding governance challenges and globalized urban economies.

In his article about urban informality, often referred to as one of the most influential works in critical urban studies, Roy (2005) [5] made strong criticisms of exclusionary urban planning models. Roy formulated informality as a structural condition of cities, especially when considering a Global South perspective. This concept influenced the New Urban Agenda and led to the proposal of a new paradigm of an inclusive and participative urban planning model. The comments about power, legality, and governance also influenced the New Urban Agenda's commitment to equity and transparency.

A few years before the proposal of the Urban Agenda, Glaeser (2011) [6] highlighted the role of cities as hubs of innovation, productivity, and human capital, providing some foundations for specific pillars included in the Urban Agenda proposal. The arguments about the economic, social, and environmental value of cities contributed to urbanization being positioned as a driving force for prosperity and sustainability, while recognizing the importance of density, connectivity, and human capital. Special recommendations were made for policymakers to avoid inequality and exclusion.

The flagship report by UN-Habitat (2016) [7] presented empirical evidence of the main urbanization trends, providing relevant input for the formulation of the New Urban Agenda. Existing urbanization models were characterized as non-sustainable and the need for new planning approaches that consider governance, finance, and social issues was acknowledged. The main considerations about urbanization and development from the report were crucial in defining the priorities of the New Urban Agenda.

The New Urban Agenda was proposed by the UN (2016) [2]. The formal global policy text was adopted at the UN Conference on Housing and Sustainable Urban Development (Habitat III) in Quito, Ecuador, consolidating more than twenty years of prior work regarding a new paradigm for sustainable urbanization. Key aspects, including sustainable development, housing, mobility, resilience, financing, and multi-level governance, were integrated according to the suggestions for urban interventions, in line with the 2030 Agenda and the SDG 11. At present, the New Urban Agenda is the primary normative framework shaping urban policies and urban strategies at global, national, and /local levels. An edited collection of articles and presentations at Habitat III was published by UN-Habitat (2018) [7], providing the view of scholars and practitioners on relevant subjects, such as urban planning, urban design, land use, and governance, under the New Urban Agenda. Both its theoretical development and the main concepts behind its practical implementations were covered in the collection, which aimed to provide useful hints about how to translate the general principles into local planning and real design practice.

The main concepts and perspectives of the recently proposed New Urban Agenda and its relationship with smart cities were presented in the compilation by Gil-Garcia et al. (2016) [8]. Several key elements were discussed, including innovative technologies, institutional frameworks, evaluation approaches, and case studies. The main focus of the study was to close the gap between theoretical models and real implementations and to demonstrate the need to align digital strategies with social goals. Special emphasis was placed on showing how smart urbanistic approaches help these proposals to reach their desired goals regarding sustainability, inclusion, efficiency, transparency, and participatory governance.

Regarding regional regulations and implementations, the Pact of Amsterdam (European Commission, 2016) [9] was formulated as the main document in the Urban Agenda for the European Union. The pact defines an operational, multi-level governance mechanism to include relevant urban priorities into the policies devised in Europe. The three core pillars of the Urban Agenda for the European Union are summarized in the slogan "better regulation, better funding, better knowledge". These pillars aim to improve the quality of life in urban areas by focusing on the development of effective policies tailored to the real needs of cities. A concrete implementation model at the regional level was proposed, based on discussion with supranational, national, and local actors.

The contributions from Japan and Germany towards urban sustainability were described in the compilation by Müller and Shimizu (2017) [10]. Specific case studies were described, showing approaches to the implementation of the New Urban Agenda concepts to deal with environmental challenges posed by rapid urbanization. The addressed issues included the application of sustainable practices, strategies for climate resilience, the creation of green infrastructure, and the development of urban ecosystem services. The empirical evidence and comparisons provide valuable insights into key concepts of the New Urban Agenda aiming to make cities more environmentally sustainable.

The role of new models for urban governance was discussed by Cruz et al. (2018) [11]. A review of relevant topics related to urban governance was performed, including sustainability, inclusion, politics of local government, and institutional innovation. Specific recommendations were formulated to define the major needs when developing effective urban policies under the New Urban Agenda. The article also helped to identify gaps between the ideal concepts formulated in the New Urban Agenda and the governance initiatives and implementations developed in the real world.

In the last five years, related works have reported a transition from the normative frame proposed by the New Urban Agenda toward concrete studies and applications. Special effort has been put into defining appropriate indicators to evaluate the effectiveness of implemented programs, the grade of success of governance policies, and financing opportunities, among other relevant issues. The incorporation of information and communication technologies into the novel paradigm of smart cities has been extensively studied too.

The United Nations has reviewed the regional implementations of the New Urban Agenda proposals. The review for Europe and North America (United Nations, 2022) [12] presented empirical evidence of the integration of New Urban Agenda concepts at the subnational and municipal levels. The overall conclusion was that disparities have emerged: whereas these proposals strictly followed the main New Urban Agenda concepts in high-income contexts and obtained good results, less promising outcomes were produced in poorer regions, especially regarding equity, decentralization, and the quality of urban services. The main suggestion was to strengthen regional institutions, since their robustness strongly conditioned the outcomes of New Urban Agenda initiatives. In turn, the 2022 World Cities Report (UN-Habitat, 2022) [13] focused on New Urban Agenda concepts related to urban resilience, equity, and future thinking. A data-driven analysis was conducted, and empirical evidence was presented about urban vulnerabilities and the role of policies to provide proper financing, planning, and governance to develop the New Urban Agenda as a key initiative towards SDG11. The reporting guidelines for 2024 (Urban Agenda Platform, 2024) [14] described practical outputs aiming to improve the quality and comparability of New Urban Agenda initiatives developed at national and local levels. Important subjects included how the applied indicators must be aligned with SDGs, the reliability of data-sources, and the need for precision when elaborating the reports.

Several articles have addressed of how crises reshape urban priorities. Specifically, the COVID-19 pandemic posed a real challenge to the new paradigm for urban development. During 2021–2023, several articles studied the way in which COVID-19 disrupted urban systems and the implications for the New Urban Agenda. Mouratidis (2021) [15] reviewed the impact of the pandemic on several aspects of urban quality of life, including mobility and access to public services, and Wolff and Mykhnenko (2023) [16] posed questions about the structural disruption of COVID-19 and possible adjustments. The main focus of these articles are resilience, public health, and how New Urban Agenda implementation must include adaptive planning strategies.

The transformative potential of a global Urban Agenda was studied by Espey et al. (2023) [17], studying how the New Urban Agenda is a useful tool to catalyze systemic changes. The analysis was influenced by the recent global shocks of the COVID-19 pandemic and climate change. From this perspective, Espey et al. concluded that local capacities must be strengthened, access to integrated funding instruments is crucial, and adaptive governance models are needed for the effective implementation of initiatives following the New Urban Agenda pillars. In a similar line of work, Badland et al. (2023) [18] introduced a framework for evaluating New Urban Agenda initiatives related to health, inclusion, and livability, implemented at the neighborhood level. The proposed framework considered a large number of spatial indicators, which were applied to provide information about the intervention in an effective way. This idea can be extended to other relevant goals of the New Urban Agenda related to mobility, sustainability, and equity.

In a recent article, Díaz-Sarachaga and Longo (2024) [19] surveyed a series of reports of New Urban Agenda development at the national level with the main goal of monitoring and reporting on the initiatives introduced by different countries. One of the most relevant results of the analysis indicated that some countries, including advanced economic nations, have not followed the templates for correct reports defined by the United Nations. In addition, important gaps were detected in relevant measurable indicators. The main conclusion was that more systematic strategies for monitoring and reporting are needed when putting into practice the main concepts of the New Urban Agenda.

Overall, recent articles have highlighted the importance of proper measurement and reporting for the correct evaluation of the implementation of New Urban Agenda initiatives. Clear and coherent monitoring and reporting frameworks and evaluation guidelines must be proposed and followed at the different implementation levels. Another relevant conclusion is that, besides the general concepts proposed in the New Urban Agenda, other concrete actions are needed for the initiatives to develop and achieve successful urban transformation. Among the main baseline actions that condition the effectiveness of New Urban Agenda initiatives are political commitment and the availability of funds, the development of capacities at the local and regional levels, and the integration of urban planning across different sectors and scales. These specific actions will help to effectively develop the New Urban Agenda to empower cities and increase their prosperity through inclusively and cross-sectorally designed plans committed to sustainability, equity, and resilience.

4. Articles Published in the Urban Agenda Topical Collection

This section presents a brief description of each article published in this Topical Collection. Articles are categorized into eight topics: governance, legislation, and citizen participation; sustainable mobility; urbanization housing and green spaces; nutrition and health; smart energies; smart tourism; and other topics (urban agriculture, climate change, smart waste management, and racial diversity).

4.1. Governance, Legislation, and Citizen Participation

The manuscript "A Qualitative Methodology for Identifying Governance Challenges and Advancements in Positive Energy District Labs" by Silvia Soutullo, Oscar Seco, María Nuria Sánchez, Ricardo Lima, Fabio Maria Montagnino, Gloria Pignatta, Ghazal Etminan, Viktor Bukovszki, Touraj Ashrafian, Maria Beatrice Andreucci, and Daniele Vettorato studies the implementation of Positive Energy District (PED) labs in Europe, which are specific urban areas meant to generate more energy than they consume. The article analyzes governance policies, the role of stakeholders, and factors hindering the development of PED labs via a qualitative methodology using data obtained by surveys and comparative case studies.

The main goal was to identify drivers of and barriers to its successful implementation and development. The main outcome is that not only is technical innovation required, but governance frameworks are also crucial (Soutullo, 2025).

The manuscript "Socio-Economic Feasibility for Implementation of Environmental Legislation along the Riparian Buffer Zones in Urban Rivers of Northern Tanzania" by Janeth Mwile Mwasenga and Ibrahimu Chikira Mjemah analyses how land use changes, economic pressures, and lack of enforcement affect the implementation of environmental legislation in Tanzania. The authors studied how socio-economic activities developed within the 60 m buffer zone of Tanzanian rivers. Using remote sensing and field interviews, the paper unpacks gaps in governance, compliance challenges, and community perceptions, advocating for policy coherence, capacity building, and socio-economic incentives. The relevant results relate urbanization with ecological threats and provide useful suggestions and recommendations to establish regional and national policies towards the sustainable management of these water resources (Mwasenga and Mjemah, 2023).

The manuscript "Enhancing Citizen Participation in Citizen-Centered Smart Cities: Insights from Two European Case Studies" by Idoia Landa Oregi, Silvia Urra-Uriarte, Itsaso Gonzalez Ochoantesana, Maite Anaya Rodriguez, and Patricia Molina-Costa examines how citizen participation was organized in two smart city projects in Europe (the URBANAGE and drOp projects). The authors acknowledged the relevant role of citizen participation in the paradigm shift towards citizen-centered smart cities under the New Urban Agenda guidelines to achieve resilience, inclusivity, and responsiveness to community needs. The study identifies procedural, structural, and awareness-related barriers to meaningful engagement, and proposes guidelines (e.g., participatory design, transparency, and feedback loops) to improve participation and equity (Landa et al., 2025).

4.2. Sustainable Mobility

The manuscript "The Impact of the COVID-19 Pandemic on the Public Transportation System of Montevideo, Uruguay: A Urban Data Analysis Approach" by Sergio Nesmachnow and Andrei Tchernykh applies urban data processing methods to open-source mobility and public transport data to assess the impact of the COVID-19 pandemic in Montevideo, Uruguay. Several key aspects were studied, including public transportation usage, shifts in mobility patterns, and the recovery of the public transportation system. The study provides useful lessons about the resilience of transport systems using a real case study and highlights the importance of multimodal transport and flexibility in operations (Nesmachnow and Tchernykh, 2023).

The manuscript "Pedestrian Flows Characterization and Estimation with Computer Vision Techniques by Federico Karagulian, Carlo Liberto, Matteo Corazza, Gaetano Valenti, Andreea Dumitru, and Marialisa Nigro describes a lightweight implementation for object detection and tracking to track pedestrian movements. The applied methodology uses the state-of-the-art YOLOv3 algorithm to analyze videos of walking patterns. The validation was performed using real videos taken in Piazza Duca d'Aosta, in Milan, Italia, recorded during different weekdays. Relevant outputs are generated, including densities, speeds, temporal patterns, etc. The proposed system contributes an innovative approach to gather real data to help public space design, safety, and mobility planning (Karagulian et al., 2023).

The manuscript "Assessment of Sustainable Mobility Initiatives Developed in Montevideo, Uruguay" by Sergio Nesmachnow and Silvina Hipogrosso evaluates several mobility initiatives (electric mobility, cycling infrastructure, and e-public transit) developed in Montevideo in the period 2020–2023. The study evaluates key Urban Agenda goals, including environmental impact, accessibility, and efficiency, and highlights successes and limitations, such as adoption rates and infrastructure gaps. The need for an integrated policy for the development of sustainable mobility initiatives is highlighted as one of the main conclusions of the analysis (Nesmachnow and Hipogrosso, 2024).

A computational intelligence approach, applied to analyze carbon intensity in the transport infrastructure sector of China, is presented in the manuscript "Carbon Intensity and Sustainable Development Analysis of the Transportation Infrastructure Industry in China: An MLP Network Approach" by Guandong Liu and Haicheng Xu. The goal of the study was to determine and evaluate the main factors that affect carbon intensity. Both traditional and newer indicators (including green revenue share and business model entropy) are considered in the study and a multi-layer perceptron machine learning model is applied. The model was trained and validated using a dataset from 20 Chinese transportation enterprises from 2018 to 2022. The results could identify thresholds for renewable energy capacity and the capital expenditure/revenue ratio. The obtained results are useful for formulating policies on decarbonization and investment, prioritizing industries that can benefit from adopting renewable energies, and targeting sectors that could apply circular economy initiatives (Liu and Xu, 2025).

4.3. Urbanization, Housing, and Green Spaces

The study reported in the article "A Partial Least Squares Analysis of the Perceived Impact of Sustainable Real Estate Design upon Wellbeing" by Anna Cortesi, Ioannis Vardopoulos, and Luca Salvati investigates how sustainable design features in real estate, including energy efficiency, green spaces, indoor environmental quality, and resource-saving technologies, are perceived to influence the comfort of occupants. The proposed model determines that sustainable design not only enhances environmental performance but also contributes positively to physical comfort, mental health, and overall quality of life. This is a relevant result for the New Urban Agenda paradigm, as it shows how sustainable housing and urban design can simultaneously address environmental goals and human-centered outcomes. Thus, it links green building practices to broader commitments to inclusivity, health, and quality of life in cities (Cortesi et al., 2022).

The manuscript "Urbanization and Land Use Planning for Achieving the Sustainable Development Goals (SDGs): A Case Study of Greece" by Dimitrios Kalfas, Stavros Kalogiannidis, Fotios Chatzitheodoridis, and Ermelinda Toska studied how urbanization quality, integrated land use strategies, and planning opportunities affect the attainment of SDGs in Greece. A quantitative survey was performed on 384 government leaders in Greece, analyzing relevant indicators regarding population growth, planning quality, level of infrastructure, environmental protection, the integration of land use strategies, and opportunities for urbanization and planning. The results highlight the importance of high-quality land use planning on achieving SDGs through the proper coordination of governance capacity, strategic policies, and regional initiatives. This case study is a practical demonstration of how governance, planning, and sustainable land use are central to driving inclusive, resilient, and sustainable urban transformation under the New Urban Agenda (Kalfas et al. 2023).

The manuscript "Comparison of Green Space Usage During COVID-19" by Humam Helmi, Can Kara, and Tuğşad Tülbentçi investigated how park usage and access changed due to the COVID-19 pandemic lockdowns in Northern Nicosia, Cyprus. Surveys and observational counts were conducted to gather relevant data. The main results indicate the shifts in usage frequency and duration, show which green spaces were more used, and reveal how accessibility and safety concerns shifted perceptions. The outcomes are useful for urban design, green areas, and park infrastructure planning decisions, as well as public health, which are all related to the resilience concept in the New Urban Agenda (Helmi et al., 2024).

The manuscript "Vulnerated Urban Areas under Regeneration: Strategies to Prevent Neighborhood Expulsion in Barcelona or How to Improve without Expelling?" by Gonzalo Piasek and Pilar Garcia-Almirall analyzes the negative social and urban effects of gentrification, especially in vulnerable neighborhoods of modern cities. Five case studies in Barcelona, Spain, are studied and regeneration programs are analyzed, applying mixed quantitative–qualitative methods and documenting displacement risk and household trajectories. Specific policy instruments (including social housing quotas, anti-displacement protections, and participatory regeneration) are proposed to reconcile physical improvements with social justice. The study offers valuable insights into the dynamics of gentrification, and how regeneration strategies could be more socially inclusive, contributing to the New Urban Agenda goals (Plasek and Garcia-Almirall, 2024).

The compendium presented in the manuscript "Trends, Methods, Drivers, and Impacts of Housing Informalities (HI): A Systematic Literature Review" by Rim Mrani, Hassan Radoine, Jérôme Chenal, and Alanda Kamana (2025) analyzes different types of housing informality, including unauthorized modifications, accessory dwelling units, squatting, etc., and their impact on urban landscapes. A holistic approach is applied to analyze economic, sociocultural, and regulatory factors and their impact on the subject, based on a study of 541 scientific peer-reviewed publications. The review provides helpful insights to understand the housing informality phenomenon under the New Urban Agenda paradigm and the proper governance and equality measures to address this issue (Mrani et al., 2025).

4.4. Nutrition and Health

A conceptual request for the development of a new transdisciplinary field is formulated in the manuscript "Towards a New Urban Health Science" by Franz Gatzweiler, Saroj Jayasinghe, José Siri, and Jason Corburn. The new concept of "urban health science" is proposed, which aims to integrate ecology, social determinants, and urban planning to properly address severe health challenges that are increasingly becoming a threat for people in modern cities. The definition of new indicators and cross-sectoral research are required to align city design with population health goals, following an approach that is highly relevant to the New Urban Agenda health commitments (Gatzweiler et al., 2023).

The manuscript "Sociodemographic Analysis of Disability in a Highly Depopulated Rural Region: The Case of Soria, Spain" by Juan R. Coca, Julio Fernández-Portela, Susana Gómez-Redondo, and Anabel Paramá-Díaz studied the difficulties faced by people with disabilities in very depopulated areas in terms of access to services and inclusion challenges. The authors explore how structural difficulties compromise the quality of life of disadvantaged citizens in comparison with those living in more populated regions. The main findings indicate that the distance from central services, severe budget constraints, and the absence of physical infrastructure are large barriers that lead to exclusion. In these contexts, usually the main form of assistance comes from informal social solidarity. Specific recommendations are provided about developing targeted mobility and service-delivery policies that are attentive to disability and geographies for improving inclusion (Coca et al., 2024).

The manuscript "Mapping Nutritional Inequality: A Primary Socio-Spatial Analysis of Food Deserts in Santiago de Chile" by Leslie Landaeta-Díaz, Francisco Vergara-Perucich, Carlos Aguirre-Nuñez, and Felipe Ulloa-Leon applies spatial analysis techniques combining census, retail location, and socioeconomic data to understand the influence of urban planning and socioeconomic factors on access to nutritious food and to identify "food deserts" (areas with low access to nutritious food) within Santiago de Chile. The study documents the spatial clustering of poor access to fresh food in peripheral districts and suggests targeted planning and market incentives (mobile markets and urban agriculture) to reduce nutritional inequality. The article presents the implications for public health, spatial planning, and food policy under the New Urban Agenda (Landaeta-Díaz et al., 2024).

The manuscript "Climate Change Awareness and Urban Food Choices: Exploring Motivations for Short Food Chain Engagement" by Elena Kokthi, Fatmir Guri, and Zenepe Dafku studies how awareness of climate change relates to the willingness of consumers to pay and engage in urban short food chains. Data from a survey in Tirana is examined and the results show that environmental motivations correlate with willingness to participate. However, relevant barriers are identified, including price, convenience, available information, and policy. Overall, the study finds that altruistic and ecological motivations matter, but also that demographics (education, gender, and family composition) modulate willingness to pay and participation. The article provides insights that could help to design food and nutrition policies that are sensitive to both climate and equity, according to the New Urban Agenda principles (Kokthi et al., 2025).

4.5. Smart Energies

The manuscript "Geographically Weighted Regression-Based Predictions of Water–Soil–Energy Nexus Solutions in Île-de-France" by Walid Al-Shaar, Olivier Bonin, Bernard de Gouvello, Patrice Chatellier, and Martin Hendel applies Ordinary Least Squares and Geographically Weighted Regression to predict the spatial potential of water–soil–energy nexus solutions, such as wastewater heat recovery, surface geothermal energy, and heat mitigation, using a case study in Île-de-France, France. The main results show that land use, population distribution, and impervious surfaces strongly influence deployment potential, while future land cover changes may limit some nature-based options. The study provides spatially explicit evidence to support sustainable urban planning, resilience strategies, and energy transition policies in line with the New Urban Agenda (Al-Shaar et al., 2022).

The manuscript "Biodiesel Production by Transesterification of Recycled Oil Catalyzed with Zinc Oxide Prepared Starting from Used Batteries" by Domenica Seminario-Calle, Melissa Ortega-Maldonado, Verónica Pinos-Vélez, Juan Cisneros, Andrés Montero-Izquierdo, Paulina Echeverría-Paredes, Paola Duque-Sarango, and Paúl Álvarez-Lloret describes an initiative based on circular-economy concepts for developing smart energies. The described project consists of recycling battery waste to produce ZnO catalysts for biodiesel synthesis. Via a laboratory study, the main results reported in the article show promising outcomes and suggest pathways to integrate waste valorization into urban energy and resource systems (Seminario-Calle et al., 2023).

4.6. Resilient Cities

The manuscript "Enumerating and Modelling the Seasonal alterations of Surface Urban Heat and Cool Island: A Case Study over Indian Cities" by Vinayak Bhanage, Sneha Kulkarni, Rajat Sharma, Han Soo Lee, and Shirishkumar Gedam analyzes seasonal changes in surface urban heat island and cool island effects using case studies in nine Indian cities. The study relates surface urban heat island magnitudes to vegetation gradient and urban surface temperatures. The applied regression models show that the vegetation gradient explains around 90% of surface urban heat island variations in pre-monsoon seasons and ~84% in winter, and that a drop of 0.1 in vegetation gradient corresponds to an increase of ~1.74 °C in surface urban heat island intensity. The findings imply that urban greening (vegetation coverage) and land cover planning are critical levers for mitigating seasonal heat stress under Indian climatic conditions.

In the manuscript "Developing Effective Project Management Strategy for Urban Flood Disaster Prevention Project in EDO State Capital, Nigeria" by Chima Ibeanu, Mazyar

Ghadiri Nejad, and Matina Ghasemi, data from interviews with state emergency management officials and surveys of both institutional staff and residents in Benin City, Nigeria, are used to identify effective project management strategies for urban flood prevention. The main result is that relevant strategies are establishing flood-warning systems, resilient infrastructure, and community programs using natural mitigation processes (watershed and land use planning); and establishing sustainable emergency planning that is strategic, inclusive, and maintained. The study underlines that project management for flood prevention needs to integrate structural (e.g., the development of drainage and resilient infrastructure), non-structural (e.g., warning systems and public awareness), and governance dimensions (coordination, stakeholder involvement, and laws/regulations) to reduce flood risk effectively (Ibeanu et al., 2022).

The manuscript "An Urban Density-Based Runoff Simulation Framework to Envisage Flood Resilience of Cities" by Naduni Wijayawardana, Chethika Abenayake, Amila Jayasinghe, and Nuwan Dias develops a runoff simulation framework to help design density-sensitive resilience strategies. A model that couples urban density metrics with hydrological modeling to assess flood resilience is presented. The developed tool is useful for planners evaluating density-related flood risk trade-offs and for resilience planning under the New Urban Agenda (Wijayawardana et al., 2023).

The manuscript "Mental Models for Assessing Impacts of Stormwater on Urban Social–Ecological Systems" by Caitlyn O'Connor and Phillip Levin uses stakeholder-elicited mental models to represent interactions among stormwater management, ecosystem services, and social outcomes. The main results of the analysis show how participatory modeling can reveal policy leverage points for integrated water governance in the context of the New Urban Agenda (O'Connor and Levin, 2023).

4.7. Smart Tourism

The manuscript "Impact of Tourist Areas on the Electrical Grid: A Case Study of the Southern Dominican Republic" by Miguel Aybar-Mejía, Randy Andrés, Alam Cabral-Soto, Carlos Montás, Wilmer-Johann Núñez-García, Elvin Arnaldo Jiménez Matos, Giuseppe Sbriz-Zeitun, and Deyslen Mariano-Hernández analyzes how tourism hotspots and demand spikes stress local grids. Specific measures are proposed and explored as a means of mitigation, including adaptive grid design, demand-side management, the integration of renewable energies and storage, and policy actions for tourism-sensitive energy planning. The study provides data-driven recommendations for resilient small-grid planning in tourist economies, linking urban energy resilience to economic activity, two relevant concepts in the paradigm of the New Urban Agenda (Aybar et al., 2023).

The review presented in the manuscript "A Bibliometric and Content Analysis of Sustainability and Smart Tourism" by Clara Madeira, Paula Rodrigues, and Monica Gomez-Suarez summarizes 104 documents published between 2015 and 2022 on the subject of sustainability and smart tourism, using data from the Web of Science. Growth trends are mapped to leading authors/journals/countries (notably China, Spain, Korea, Portugal), thematic clusters (smart tourism, sustainable tourism, innovation, smart cities), and methodological patterns. Key findings include the strong dominance of smart tourism terminology over sustainability in keywords, and significant collaboration among authors. The identified drawbacks are the gaps in empirical research, theory–practice links, and stakeholder diversity. The review aligns with the New Urban Agenda's emphasis on leveraging technology and innovation for sustainable service delivery and urban development and raises awareness about the need to integrate environmental, social, and economic aspects in tourism (Madeira et al., 2023).

4.8. Other Topics

Regarding urban agriculture, the manuscript "Assessing Citizens' Perceptions of Urban Agriculture and Its Contribution to Food Security—Worldwide Analysis and Specific Case Studies in Spain" by Ouiam Fatiha Boukharta, Leticia Chico Santamarta, Adriana Correa Guimaraes, and Luis Manuel Navas Gracia presents a global survey and case studies in Spain to investigate the attitudes of citizens towards urban agriculture, as well as its perceived benefits (food security and local consumption) and challenges. The survey finds generally positive perceptions about food security and social benefits but identifies barriers such as regulation and land access, recommending the integration of key concepts of the New Urban Agenda into urban planning policies. The study highlights the importance of awareness, integration during planning, and support for small-scale/local producers (Boukharta et al., 2025).

The relationship between waste, energy, and information systems is studied in the manuscript "Validating a Sustainable, Smart, and Circular City Architecture through Urban Living Lab Experiments" by Augusto Velasquez-Mendez, Jorge de Jesús Lozoya-Santos, and José Fernando Jiménez-Vargas. The article proposes an integrated architecture combining physical, digital, governance, and innovation layers to link waste, energy, and information systems. The proposal is validated through living-lab experiments (waste detection, IoT urban garden, etc.). Overall, the study shows how circularity, smart tech, and participatory governance are essential to circular urban transitions according to the New Urban Agenda concepts (Velásquez et al., 2025).

The manuscript "Defining the Organization of Municipal Solid Waste Management Based on Production Costs" by Massimo Beccarello and Giacomo Di Foggia analyzes how production costs can be used as the basis for defining the organizational models of municipal solid waste management systems in Italy. Using data on collection and treatment costs, the study identifies cost drivers and proposes efficiency benchmarks to optimize system design and governance. The authors argue that a cost-based organizational approach can enhance financial sustainability, transparency, and service quality, while supporting the broader transition toward circular economy goals. The study highlights the importance of cost transparency and organizational efficiency for local waste management services and contributes to sustainable urban metabolism, resource efficiency, and circular economy strategies central to the New Urban Agenda (Beccarello and Di Foggia, 2023).

The article "An Analysis of Urban Ethnic Inclusion of Master Plans—In the Case of Kabul City, Afghanistan" by Fakhrullah Sarwari and Hiroko Ono examines how the urban master plans of Kabul, Afghanistan, address—or fail to address—ethnic diversity and inclusion in the city. The study shows that, historically, planning practices have overlooked ethnic representation, reinforcing spatial and social inequalities across neighborhoods. Authors argue for more inclusive and participatory planning frameworks that recognize ethnic heterogeneity as a fundamental component of equitable and sustainable urban development. The study aligns directly with the emphasis of New Urban Agenda on inclusivity, reducing inequalities, and ensuring that marginalized groups are considered in urban policies (Sarwari and Ono, 2023).

5. Summary

Overall, the articles published in the Topical Collection "Urban Agenda" of the *Urban Science* journal collectively demonstrate the breadth and complexity of contemporary urban challenges and opportunities. Covering themes such as governance and citizen participation, sustainable mobility, housing and urban regeneration, nutrition and health, smart energy systems, smart tourism, and cross-cutting issues including climate change, waste management, and ethnic inclusion, the collection highlights the interdependence of the social, environmental, technological, and economic dimensions of urban development. The studies range from empirical case analyses to systematic reviews and methodological innovations, offering insights into both Global South and Global North contexts. A recurring emphasis is placed on inclusivity, resilience, and sustainability as guiding principles of the New Urban Agenda, while also underscoring the role of digital technologies, participatory governance, and circular economy approaches in shaping urban transformation. Taken together, these contributions provide a valuable knowledge base that bridges theory and practice, and they reinforce the need for integrated, multi-scalar strategies to advance equitable and sustainable urban futures. Table 1 provides an overall description of the articles published in this Topical Collection.

Table 1. Overall description of articles published in this Topical Collection.

Subject	Title	Author(s)/Year	Main Concepts
Governance, legislation, and citizen participation	Socio-Economic Feasibility for Implementation of Environmental Legislation along Riparian Buffer Zones in Northern Tanzania	Mwasenga and Mjemah (2023)	legislation, river buffers, enforcement, land tenure, community co-management
	Enhancing Citizen Participation in Citizen-Centered Smart Cities: Insights from Two European Case Studies	Landa et al. (2025)	citizen participation, smart cities, co-design, governance barriers
	A Qualitative Methodology for Identifying Governance Challenges and Advancements in Positive Energy District Labs	Soutullo et al. (2025)	Positive Energy Districts, governance challenges, regulatory barriers, stakeholder conflicts, financing, participatory frameworks.
Sustainable mobility	Impact of COVID-19 on Public Transport in Montevideo, Uruguay	Nesmachnow and Tchernykh (2023)	ridership collapse, resilience, contingency planning.
	Pedestrian Flows Characterization with Computer Vision Techniques	Karagulian et al. (2023)	pedestrian flows, artificial intelligence/computer vision, urban design, safety
	Assessment of Sustainable Mobility Initiatives in Montevideo, Uruguay	Nesmachnow and Hipogrosso (2024)	public transportation, cycling, electric mobility, policy coordination.
	Carbon Intensity of Transportation Infrastructure in China (MLP Analysis)	Liu and Xu (2025)	carbon intensity, infrastructure, transportation, decarbonization.
Urbanization, housing, and green spaces	Sustainable Real Estate Design and Wellbeing (PLS-SEM Analysis)	Cortesi et al. (2022)	sustainable housing, wellbeing, energy efficiency, indoor quality.
	Urbanization and Land Use Planning for Achieving SDGs: A Case Study of Greece	Kalfas et al. (2023)	land use planning, SDGs, governance, integrated strategies.
	Comparison of Green Space Usage During COVID-19	Helmi et al. (2024)	park use, pandemic, accessibility, urban design.
	Vulnerated Urban Areas under Regeneration: Strategies to Prevent Neighborhood Expulsion in Barcelona	Piasek and Garcia-Almirall (2024)	regeneration, gentrification, displacement, social housing.

Table 1. *Cont.*

Subject	Title	Author(s)/Year	Main Concepts
	Trends, Methods, Drivers, and Impacts of Housing Informalities: A Systematic Review	Mrani et al. (2025)	informal housing, drivers, impacts, policy agenda
Nutrition and health	Towards a New Urban Health Science	Gatzweiler et al. (2023)	urban health, transdisciplinary research, planning–health nexus.
	Sociodemographic Analysis of Disability in Rural Soria, Spain	Coca et al. (2023)	disability inclusion, depopulated areas, service access, equity.
	Mapping Nutritional Inequality: Food Deserts in Santiago de Chile	Landaeta-Díaz et al. (2024)	food deserts, access inequality, spatial analysis.
	Climate Change Awareness and Urban Food Choices: Short Food Chains	Kokthi et al. (2025)	climate awareness, local food systems, consumer behavior.
Smart energies	Geographically Weighted Regression-Based Predictions of Water–Soil–Energy Nexus Solutions in Île-de-France	Al-Shaar et al. (2022)	WSE nexus, GWR modeling, land use, population density, heat mitigation.
	Biodiesel Production with ZnO from Recycled Batteries	Seminario-Calle et al. (2023)	circular economy, biodiesel, recycling, smart energy.
	A Qualitative Methodology for Identifying Governance Challenges and Advancements in Positive Energy District Labs	Soutullo et al. (2025)	energy-positive districts, governance, regulation, innovation.
Resilient cities	Urban Density-Based Runoff Simulation Framework for Flood Resilience	Wijayawardana et al. (2023)	flood resilience, urban density, hydrological modeling.
	Enumerating and Modelling the Seasonal Alterations of Surface Urban Heat and Cool Island: A Case Study over Indian Cities	Bhanage et al. (2023)	SUHI, ΔNDVI, seasonal variation, urban greening, climate adaptation.
	Developing Effective Project Management Strategy for Urban Flood Disaster Prevention Project in Edo State Capital, Nigeria	Ibeanu et al. (2023)	flood prevention, project management, governance, resilient infrastructure, community engagement.
	Mental Models of Stormwater in Urban Social–Ecological Systems	O'Connor and Levin (2023)	stormwater, stakeholder engagement, social–ecological systems.
Smart tourism	Impact of Tourist Areas on the Electrical Grid: A Case Study of the Southern Dominican Republic	Aibar et al. (2023)	tourism energy demand, grid resilience, renewable integration, planning.
	A Bibliometric and Content Analysis of Sustainability and Smart Tourism	Madeira et al. (2023)	bibliometric review, smart tourism, sustainability gaps, innovation, global research trends.

Table 1. *Cont.*

Subject	Title	Author(s)/Year	Main Concepts
Other topics	An Analysis of Urban Ethnic Inclusion of Master Plans—In the Case of Kabul City, Afghanistan	Sarwari and Ono (2023)	ethnic inclusion, master plans, governance, participatory planning, equity.
	Defining the Organization of Municipal Solid Waste Management Based on Production Costs	Beccarello and Di Foggia (2023)	municipal waste management, cost analysis, governance, circular economy.
	Validating a Sustainable, Smart, and Circular City Architecture through Urban Living Lab Experiments	Velasquez et al. (2025)	circular cities, waste management, IoT, governance models.
	Urban Agriculture and Food Security: Citizens' Perceptions (Worldwide + Spain Case Studies)	Boukharta et al. (2025)	urban agriculture, food security, citizen attitudes.

Conflicts of Interest: The authors declare no conflict of interest.

List of Contributions:

1. Al-Shaar, W.; Bonin, O.; de Gouvello, B.; Chatellier, P.; Hendel, M. Geographically Weighted Regression-Based Predictions of Water–Soil–Energy Nexus Solutions in Île-de-France. *Urban Sci.* **2022**, *6*, 81. https://doi.org/10.3390/urbansci6040081.
2. Aybar-Mejía, M.; Andrés, R.; Cabral-Soto, A.; Montás, C.; Núñez-García, W.; Matos, E.; Sbriz-Zeitun, G.; Mariano-Hernández, D. Impact of Tourist Areas on the Electrical Grid: A Case Study of the Southern Dominican Republic. *Urban Sci.* **2023**, *7*, 32. https://doi.org/10.3390/urbansci7010032.
3. Beccarello, M.; Di Foggia, G. Defining the Organization of Municipal Solid Waste Management Based on Production Costs. *Urban Sci.* **2023**, *7*, 34. https://doi.org/10.3390/urbansci7020034.
4. Bhanage, V.; Kulkarni, S.; Sharma, R.; Lee, H.S.; Gedam, S. Enumerating and Modelling the Seasonal alterations of Surface Urban Heat and Cool Island: A Case Study over Indian Cities. *Urban Sci.* **2023**, *7*, 38. https://doi.org/10.3390/urbansci7020038.
5. Boukharta, O.; Chico Santamarta, L.; Correa Guimaraes, A.; Navas Gracia, L. Assessing Citizens' Perceptions of Urban Agriculture and Its Contribution to Food Security—Worldwide Analysis and Specific Case Studies in Spain. *Urban Sci.* **2025**, *9*, 150. https://doi.org/10.3390/urbansci9050150.
6. Coca, J.; Fernández-Portela, J.; Gómez-Redondo, S.; Paramá-Díaz, A. Sociodemographic Analysis of Disability in a Highly Depopulated Rural Region: The Case of Soria, Spain. *Urban Sci.* **2023**, *7*, 112. https://doi.org/10.3390/urbansci7040112.
7. Cortesi, A.; Vardopoulos, I.; Salvati, L. A Partial Least Squares Analysis of the Perceived Impact of Sustainable Real Estate Design upon Wellbeing. *Urban Sci.* **2022**, *6*, 69. https://doi.org/10.3390/urbansci6040069.
8. Gatzweiler, F.; Jayasinghe, S.; Siri, J.; Corburn, J. Towards a New Urban Health Science. *Urban Sci.* **2023**, *7*, 30. https://doi.org/10.3390/urbansci7010030.
9. Helmi, H.; Kara, C.; Tülbentçi, T. Comparison of Green Space Usage During COVID-19. *Urban Sci.* **2024**, *8*, 216. https://doi.org/10.3390/urbansci8040216.
10. Ibeanu, C.; Ghadiri Nejad, M.; Ghasemi, M. Developing Effective Project Management Strategy for Urban Flood Disaster Prevention Project in EDO State Capital, Nigeria. *Urban Sci.* **2023**, *7*, 37. https://doi.org/10.3390/urbansci7020037.
11. Jacobs, J. *The Death and Life of Great American Cities*; Random House: New York, NY, USA, 1961.

12. Kalfas, D.; Kalogiannidis, S.; Chatzitheodoridis, F.; Toska, E. Urbanization and Land Use Planning for Achieving the Sustainable Development Goals (SDGs): A Case Study of Greece. *Urban Sci.* **2023**, *7*, 43. https://doi.org/10.3390/urbansci7020043
13. Karagulian, F.; Liberto, C.; Corazza, M.; Valenti, G.; Dumitru, A.; Nigro, M. Pedestrian Flows Characterization and Estimation with Computer Vision Techniques. *Urban Sci.* **2023**, *7*, 65. https://doi.org/10.3390/urbansci7020065.
14. Kokthi, E.; Guri, F.; Dafku, Z. Climate Change Awareness and Urban Food Choices: Exploring Motivations for Short Food Chain Engagement. *Urban Sci.* **2025**, *9*, 142. https://doi.org/10.3390/urbansci9050142.
15. Landa, I.; Urra-Uriarte, S.; Gonzalez Ochoantesana, I.; Rodríguez, M.A.; Molina-Costa, P. Enhancing Citizen Participation in Citizen-Centered Smart Cities: Insights from Two European Case Studies. *Urban Sci.* **2025**, *9*, 140. https://doi.org/10.3390/urbansci9050140
16. Landaeta-Díaz, L.; Vergara-Perucich, F.; Aguirre-Nuñez, C.; Ulloa-Leon, F. Mapping Nutritional Inequality: A Primary Socio-Spatial Analysis of Food Deserts in Santiago de Chile. *Urban Sci.* **2024**, *8*, 129. https://doi.org/10.3390/urbansci8030129.
17. Liu, G.; Xu, H. Carbon Intensity and Sustainable Development Analysis of the Transportation Infrastructure Industry in China: An MLP Network Approach. *Urban Sci.* **2025**, *9*, 205. https://doi.org/10.3390/urbansci9060205.
18. Madeira, C.; Rodrigues, P.; Gomez-Suarez, M. A Bibliometric and Content Analysis of Sustainability and Smart Tourism. *Urban Sci.* **2023**, *7*, 33. https://doi.org/10.3390/urbansci7020033.
19. Mrani, R.; Radoine, H.; Chenal, J.; Kamana, A. Trends, Methods, Drivers, and Impacts of Housing Informalities (HI): A Systematic Literature Review. *Urban Sci.* **2025**, *9*, 101. https://doi.org/10.3390/urbansci9040101
20. Mwasenga, J.; Mjemah, I. Socio-Economic Feasibility for Implementation of Environmental Legislation along the Riparian Buffer Zones in Urban Rivers of Northern Tanzania. *Urban Sci.* **2023**, *7*, 73. https://doi.org/10.3390/urbansci7030073
21. Nesmachnow, S.; Hipogrosso, S. Assessment of Sustainable Mobility Initiatives Developed in Montevideo, Uruguay. *Urban Sci.* **2024**, *8*, 52. https://doi.org/10.3390/urbansci8020052
22. Nesmachnow, S.; Tchernykh, A. The Impact of the COVID-19 Pandemic on the Public Transportation System of Montevideo, Uruguay: A Urban Data Analysis Approach. *Urban Sci.* **2023**, *7*, 113. https://doi.org/10.3390/urbansci7040113.
23. O'Connor, C.; Levin, P. Mental Models for Assessing Impacts of Stormwater on Urban Social–Ecological Systems. *Urban Sci.* **2023**, *7*, 14. https://doi.org/10.3390/urbansci7010014.
24. Piasek, G.; Garcia-Almirall, P. Vulnerated Urban Areas under Regeneration: Strategies to Prevent Neighborhood Expulsion in Barcelona or How to Improve without Expelling? *Urban Sci.* **2024**, *8*, 118. https://doi.org/10.3390/urbansci8030118
25. Sarwari, F.; Ono, H. An Analysis of Urban Ethnic Inclusion of Master Plans—In the Case of Kabul City, Afghanistan. *Urban Sci.* **2023**, *7*, 3. https://doi.org/10.3390/urbansci7010003.
26. Seminario-Calle, D.; Ortega-Maldonado, M.; Pinos-Vélez, V.; Cisneros, J.; Montero-Izquierdo, A.; Echeverría-Paredes, P.; Duque-Sarango, P.; Álvarez-Lloret, P. Biodiesel Production by Transesterification of Recycled Oil Catalyzed with Zinc Oxide Prepared Starting from Used Batteries. *Urban Sci.* **2023**, *7*, 80. https://doi.org/10.3390/urbansci7030080.
27. Soutullo, S.; Seco, O.; Sánchez, M.N.; Lima, R.; Montagnino, F.M.; Pignatta, G.; Etminan, G.; Bukovszki, V.; Ashrafian, T.; Andreucci, M.B.; et al. A Qualitative Methodology for Identifying Governance Challenges and Advancements in Positive Energy District Labs. *Urban Sci.* **2025**, *9*, 288. https://doi.org/10.3390/urbansci9080288
28. Velasquez-Mendez, A.; Lozoya-Santos, J.; Jiménez-Vargas, J. Validating a Sustainable, Smart, and Circular City Architecture Through Urban Living Lab Experiments. *Urban Sci.* **2025**, *9*, 377. https://doi.org/10.3390/urbansci9090377.
29. Wijayawardana, N.; Abenayake, C.; Jayasinghe, A.; Dias, N. An Urban Density-Based Runoff Simulation Framework to Envisage Flood Resilience of Cities. *Urban Sci.* **2023**, *7*, 17. https://doi.org/10.3390/urbansci7010017.

References

1. United Nations Human Settlements Programme (UN-Habitat). World Cities Report 2016: Urbanization and Development—Emerging Futures. UN-Habitat. 2016. Available online: https://unhabitat.org/world-cities-report-2016 (accessed on 1 September 2025).
2. United Nations. New Urban Agenda. UN Conference on Housing and Sustainable Urban Development (Habitat III). UN-Habitat. 2016. Available online: https://habitat3.org/the-new-urban-agenda/ (accessed on 1 September 2025).
3. United Nations. Sustainable Development Goal 11: Make cities and human settlements inclusive, safe, resilient and sustainable. In *Transforming Our World: The 2030 Agenda for Sustainable Development*; United Nations: New York, NY, USA, 2015.
4. Sassen, S. *The Global City: New York, London, Tokyo*; Princeton University Press: Princeton, NJ, USA, 1991.
5. Roy, A. Urban informality: Toward an epistemology of planning. *J. Am. Plan. Assoc.* **2005**, *71*, 147–158. [CrossRef]
6. Glaeser, E. *Triumph of the City: How Our Greatest Invention Makes Us Richer, Smarter, Greener, Healthier, and Happier*; Penguin Press: London, UK, 2011.
7. UN-Habitat. *The Quito Papers and the New Urban Agenda*; Sennett, R., Burdett, R., Sassen, S., Clos, J., Eds.; Routledge: Abingdon, UK, 2018; ISBN 978-0815379294.
8. Gil-Garcia, J.; Pardo, T.; Nam, T. (Eds.) *Smarter as the New Urban Agenda: A Comprehensive View of the 21st Century City*; Springer International Publishing: Cham, Switzerland, 2016. [CrossRef]
9. European Commission. Pact of Amsterdam: Establishing the Urban Agenda for the EU. European Commission. 2016. Available online: https://www.urbanagenda.urban-initiative.eu/urban-agenda-eu (accessed on 1 September 2025).
10. Müller, B.; Shimizu, H. (Eds.) *Towards the Implementation of the New Urban Agenda: Contributions from Japan and Germany to Make Cities More Environmentally Sustainable*; Springer International Publishing: Cham, Switzerland, 2017; ISBN 978-3319613758.
11. da Cruz, N.; Rode, P.; McQuarrie, M. New Urban Governance: A Review of Current Themes and Future Priorities. *J. Urban Aff.* **2018**, *41*, 1–19. [CrossRef]
12. United Nations. Implementation of the New Urban Agenda in Europe and North America: A Review. 2022. Available online: http://urbanagendaplatform.org (accessed on 1 September 2025).
13. United Nations Human Settlements Programme (UN-Habitat). World Cities Report 2022: Envisaging the Future of Cities. 2022. Available online: https://unhabitat.org/world-cities-report-2022-envisaging-the-future-of-cities (accessed on 1 September 2025).
14. Urban Agenda Platform. New Urban Agenda Reporting Guidelines. 2024. Available online: https://www.urbanagendaplatform.org/sites/default/files/2024-05/NUA%20Reporting%20Guidlines.pdf (accessed on 1 September 2025).
15. Mouratidis, K. How COVID-19 reshaped quality of life in cities. *Land Use Policy* **2021**, *111*, 105772. [CrossRef] [PubMed]
16. Wolff, M.; Mykhnenko, V. COVID-19 as a game-changer? *Cities* **2023**, *134*, 104162. [CrossRef] [PubMed]
17. Espey, J.; Parnell, S.; Revi, A. The transformative potential of a Global Urban Agenda and its lessons in a time of crisis. *Urban Sustain.* **2023**, *3*, 15. [CrossRef] [PubMed]
18. Badland, H.; Villanueva, K.; Alderton, A.; Davern, M.; Goldfeld, S. An urban neighbourhood framework for realising progress towards the New Urban Agenda for equitable early childhood development. *Child. Geogr.* **2023**, *21*, 1087–1105. [CrossRef]
19. Díaz-Sarachaga, J.; Longo Sarachaga, J. Diagnosis on the implementation of the New Urban Agenda. *Glob. Sustain.* **2024**, *7*, e37. [CrossRef]

urban science

MDPI

Article

Façade Strategies for Climate Resilience: The Impact of Thermal Mass and Albedo on Urban Microclimates Across Different Climatic Zones

Noelia Alchapar [1,*], Emanuela Giancola [2], Gloria Pérez [3], Maira Terraza [1] and Cláudia Pezzuto [4]

[1] Institute of Environment, Habitat and Energy (INAHE-CONICET), CCT-Mendoza, Mendoza 5500, Argentina; mterraza@mendoza-conicet.gob.ar

[2] Department of Energy, CIEMAT, 28040 Madrid, Spain; emanuela.giancola@ciemat.es

[3] Eduardo Torroja Institute for Construction Science (IETCC), Spanish National Research Council (CSIC), 28033 Madrid, Spain; gperezaq@ietcc.csic.es

[4] Postgraduate Program in Urban Infrastructure Systems, School of Polytechnic, Pontifical Catholic University of Campinas (PUC-Campinas), Campinas 13087-571, SP, Brazil; claudiapezzuto@puc-campinas.edu.br

* Correspondence: nalchapar@mendoza-conicet.gob.ar; Tel.: +54-261-524-4310

Abstract: The intensification of thermal stress in cities due to urbanization and climate change underscores the urgent need to improve outdoor habitability. This study analyses the influence of three opaque façade technologies—traditional, lightweight and external thermal insulation composite systems—combined with two albedo levels (0.30 and 0.80), on summer outdoor conditions in Mendoza (Argentina), Madrid (Spain) and Campinas (Brazil). Using a calibrated microclimatic model with ENVI-met v5.6 software, a digital replica of a 10-storey urban canyon was simulated to generate 18 scenarios, assessing the effect of façade thermal mass and reflectivity on the urban microclimate. The results show that (i) scenarios that mainly affect air temperature (AT) are those that modify the thermal mass of the façade technologies. For example, traditional technology with a low albedo reduce maximum AT by up to 1.2 °C in Campinas, 0.89 °C in Mendoza, and 0.81 °C in Madrid compared to light technology with the same albedo level. (ii) Mean radiant temperature (MRT) increases significantly in scenarios involving lightweight façade by 4.53 °C in Madrid, 4.46 °C in Mendoza, and 3.39 °C in Campinas. Conversely, increasing façade albedo further amplifies MRT due to multiple reflections in urban canyons with increases of 6.50 °C in Campinas, 6.09 °C in Mendoza, and 5.33 °C in Madrid. The impact is more pronounced with traditional façades. (iii) Traditional façades and low-albedo ETIC systems experience the fewest hours of very high thermal stress (UTCI > 38 °C), whereas lightweight façades increase exposure to extreme heat. Overall, air temperature is primarily determined by façade thermal mass, mean radiant temperature by surface reflectivity, and thermal comfort by the combined effect of both. These findings confirm that high reflectivity can be counterproductive in dense urban canyons, emphasizing the importance of climate- and morphology-sensitive façade strategies for urban resilience.

Keywords: ENVI-met simulation; urban microclimate; façade thermal mass; albedo; mean radiant temperature; outdoor thermal comfort (UTCI)

1. Introduction

Urban agglomerations are undergoing significant transformations, marked by rapid urbanization, densification, and spatial expansion, alongside demographic shifts such as population aging and increased exposure to thermal stress driven by global warming [1]. These trends are evident in both developed and developing regions and pose considerable challenges for the future of the cities. The combined effect of heightened heat exposure and growing vulnerability—particularly among sensitive population groups—are likely to intensify thermal stress in the coming decades [2]. Urban populations growth has intensified land demand and accelerated the intensification of urban land use. These processes, often associated with greater impervious surface coverage and reduced soil permeability, contribute to elevated surface temperatures and exacerbate urban overheating and the urban heat island (UHI) effect [3]. The need to mitigate these impacts is reinforced by their direct consequences on human health, including higher heat-related mortality among vulnerable populations and in lower-income neighborhoods [4].

The interaction between urbanization—which amplifies the UHI effect—and climate change—which increases the frequency and intensity of heat waves—has been highlighted in numerous studies [5]. This interaction underscores the urgent need for targeted mitigation and adaptation strategies to improve urban environmental quality and resilience. This imperative has been recognized in both the European Union and the Southern Cone of Latin America, where urban areas are increasingly investing in evidence-based approaches to enhance thermal comfort and overall livability in public spaces [6].

Building more livable cities requires identifying thermal discomfort zones and establishing a quantitative basis for assessing the effectiveness of different mitigation strategies. In this regard, it is essential to evaluate and quantify pedestrian thermal comfort using thermal stress indices that integrate key environmental variables such as solar radiation, air temperature, wind speed, and humidity. These indices must also account for the specific characteristics of the urban fabric—including surface materials, vegetation density, building geometry, and shading elements—which directly affect the physiological responses of the human body. Among these indices, the mean radiant temperature (MRT) is a key microclimatic parameter for assessing outdoor thermal comfort [7]. Technically, MRT represents the uniform temperature of an imaginary enclosure in which a person would exchange the same amount of radiant heat as in the actual environment. Unlike air temperature alone, MRT accounts for the combined effect of shortwave and longwave radiation emitted and reflected by surrounding surfaces, thereby providing the equivalent temperature perceived by the human body after comprehensively considering all radiation influences [8]. MRT in urban environments depends on the thermal and radiative properties of exterior finishing materials, urban geometry [9,10], and vegetation cover [11]. Proper management of these factors is therefore essential to designing more comfortable and climate-resilient urban environments [12].

The Universal Thermal Climate Index (UTCI) is another widely used and robust tool for analyzing and managing outdoor thermal comfort. UTCI integrates air temperature, humidity, wind speed, and mean radiant temperature to comprehensively represent human thermal stress. Based on UTCI values, a thermal sensation scale is defined, categorizing different levels of stress from extreme cold to extreme heat [13].

In the urban environments, the main influence on MRT balance comes from longwave thermal radiation re-emitted by building surfaces-particularly façades and other vertical elements- toward the surrounding environment. The use of high-emissivity materials increases re-emitted thermal energy, thereby reducing surface temperatures. However, this re-emitted energy plays a critical role in raising ambient temperatures at the pedestrian level, intensifying thermal stress and reinforcing the UHI effect in densely built areas [14].

The albedo of urban surfaces also plays a significant role in shaping urban thermal comfort by determining the amount of reflected solar radiation [15]. High albedo materials reduce heat absorption by keeping surfaces cooler and lowering the emitted long-wave radiation [16]. For instance, studies by Alchapar et al. [17] in Latin American cities showed that every 10% increase in pavements and roofs albedo reduces air temperature by 0.5 °C in Mendoza, Argentina, and by 0.9 °C in Campinas, Brazil. However, when applied to façades, high albedo materials can lead to overheating within deep street canyons due to the increased mutual reflections between buildings. This process, referred to as the "Inter-Building Effect–IBE" by Pisello et al. ([18,19]), traps solar radiation at street level and increases the radiant load experienced by pedestrians. Consequently, while the use of high albedo urban materials is effective in lowering surface temperatures, its ability to reduce MRT and thermal stress is limited in dense, high-rise urban contexts.

Although the vertical surfaces of tall buildings can significantly alter urban radiation dynamics through absorption and re-emission and multiple reflections of solar energy, existing research often overlooks the impact of façade configurations on mean radiant temperature (MRT), surface heat flux, and the pedestrian-level radiative environment. While façades have been widely studied in relation to energy performance, passive solar control, and photovoltaic integration, their role in shaping the microclimatic balance and outdoor thermal comfort remains underexplored. In recent work, Kim et al. [13] analyzed the effects of variations in the emissivity and reflectivity of urban road and concrete pavements on the UTCI. However, the properties of building materials and green spaces were held constant, citing their limited feasibility for modification in real-world applications. Similarly, a review by Köker et al. [20] highlights the challenges for estimating the solar energy potential of urban façades through simulation compared to horizontal urban surfaces. Potential sources of error in façade modeling include shading from surrounding buildings and architectural elements such as overhangs and balconies, diffuse and reflected irradiance from the ground and adjacent structures, and variations in sky view factors due to complex urban morphologies. To address this research gap, a comparative study on the influence of different façade technologies in multi-story buildings on the urban microclimate and pedestrian thermal comfort across diverse climatic zones is of significant importance.

Among the innovative façade technologies, lightweight (dry) and modular systems are increasingly implemented in residential buildings worldwide. Over the past decade, lightweight construction has shown steady growth, driven by advantages such as faster construction timelines, greater design flexibility, and cost reductions resulting from shorter project durations. The global dry construction market is projected to reach USD 231.4 billion by 2028, with a compound annual growth rate (CAGR) of 5.7% between 2023 and 2028 [21]. This expansion is also evident in Latin America, particularly in Argentina, Chile, Mexico, and Colombia, where the region is expected to represent 14% of the global dry construction market by 2028 [22]. Lightweight construction technologies are promoted as more efficient and sustainable alternatives to traditional systems, primarily because of their high thermal resistance provided by materials such as polystyrene or polyurethane. However, these dry systems are characterized by low thermal inertia, which increases energy demand for heating and cooling [9,10]. This change in the energy balance of lightweight/dry envelopes alters the rate and manner in which building envelopes absorb and release energy to the external environment (e.g., street canyons). Several studies have reviewed the trends and challenges of dry construction technologies, consistently identifying low thermal inertia as a critical issue to be addressed in order to ensure both thermal comfort and energy efficiency in buildings [23].

Another well-established façade technology for multi-story buildings is the External Thermal Insulation Composite System (ETICS). This system provides a comprehensive solution for the thermal insulation of buildings and is applicable to both new constructions and retrofitting of existing structures. ETICS are characterized by a compact, waterproof, and breathable "sandwich" layer that adheres directly to the building façade. The fundamental principle of the system is the application of insulating material to the exterior façade surfaces, thereby enhancing the thermal performance of the building envelope while protecting it from external climatic conditions [24]. In terms of thermal inertia, ETICS display an intermediate behavior between lightweight and traditional technologies. While the external insulation layer substantially improves thermal resistance, it also reduces the capacity of the wall to store and release heat. Consequently, ETICS perform better than lightweight systems in moderating temperature fluctuations but fall short of the buffering capacity provided by traditional massive envelopes.

The primary objective of this study is to identify the most effective combinations of radiative and thermal properties for optimizing air temperature in opaque façades in optimizing outdoor air temperature (AT), mean radiant temperature (MRT), and urban thermal comfort,-assessed using the Universal Thermal Climate Index (UTCI)—during the summer months in three cities: Mendoza, Madrid, and Campinas. The analysis is based on a theoretical model developed with ENVI-met V.5.6. and considers three construction technologies with different thermal mass properties—lightweight or dry (L), traditional (T) and the ETIC system (S)—each evaluated in relation to two levels of albedo (0.3 and 0.8).

2. Methodology

2.1. Study Cities as Case Studies

This study focuses on the cities of Mendoza (Argentina), Madrid (Spain), and Campinas (Brazil) to examine how climatic and geographic variability across temperate and subtropical latitudes influences the performance of façades constructed with different building technologies. Figure 1 shows the geographical location of the three cities, while Table 1 summarizes their main characteristics [25,26].

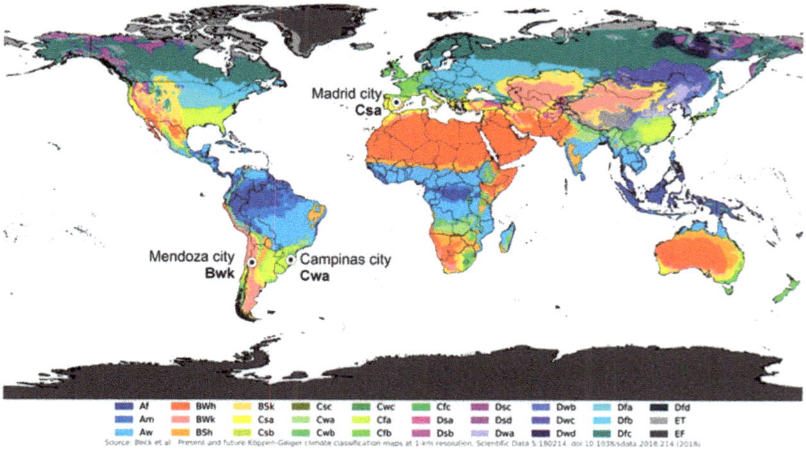

Figure 1. Location of the studied cities—Mendoza (Argentina), Madrid (Spain) and Campinas (Brazil) according to the Köppen climate classification [27].

Although Mendoza, Madrid, and Campinas all experience warm summers, their Köppen climate classifications [27] reveal fundamental differences in seasonal temperature and precipitation patterns. Mendoza (BWk) has a cold desert steppe climate, characterized by very low annual precipitation, warm summers, and distinctly cold winters. In contrast, Madrid (Csa) features a typical Mediterranean climate with hot, dry summers, mild and humid winters, and precipitation concentrated mainly in the transitional seasons. Campinas

(Cwa) presents a warm temperate climate with dry winters and hot summers; precipitation is concentrated in the warm season, while winters are milder and drier, without the cold conditions typical of steppe or desert climates. The three cities were selected to evaluate the impact of the façade technologies under diverse climatic conditions. The inclusion of desert steppe, Mediterranean, and warm temperate climates enables a comprehensive assessment of the façade performance across contrasting scenarios.

Table 1. Geographic and Climatic Conditions of the Evaluated Cities.

Characteristics	Mendoza, Argentina	Madrid, Spain	Campinas, Brazil
Location	32.86° S; 68.86° W 750 m a.s.l.	40.42° N; −3.70° E 680 m a.s.l.	22.53° S, 47.04° W 680 m a.s.l.
Population	2,043,540 hab.	3,460,491 hab.	1,139,047 hab.
Climate according to Köppen classification [27].	Desert with cold steppe, BWk	Typical Mediterranean, Csa	Warm temperate with dry winters and hot summers, Cwa
Maximum daily horizontal global radiation	1117 W/m^2	1011 W/m^2	1020 W/m^2
Mean wind speed (height: 10 m)	2.18 m/s (south)	2.61 m/s (south)	2.2 m/s (southeast)
Annual mean temperature	16.79 °C	14.72 °C	22.5 °C
Average minimum temperatures	−5 °C	−7.6 °C	12.4 °C
Average maximum temperatures	39 °C	40.4 °C	32.5 °C
Annual average relative humidity	60.32%	52.16%	69.0%
Annual average accumulated precipitation	220 mm	435 mm	1510 mm

2.2. Study Area and Theoretical Model

For this study, a single area was selected: a peripheral social neighborhood in Mendoza (32°54′48″ S, 68°50′46″ W), whose urban typology is representative of the three cities analyzed. The area features a regular urban layout with homogeneous building types. Residential buildings are typically one- or two-story single-family homes, forming a low-density urban fabric with rectangular blocks and street widths ranging from 16 to 20 m. The built-up area covers approximately 80% of the neighborhood, while urban vegetation accounts for 13%. The average building height is 3.2 m, resulting in a height-to-width (H/W) ratio between 0.15 and 0.19.

Regarding construction technology, the roofs are lightweight, with a wooden structure, ceramic tile covering, and expanded polystyrene insulation (U-value: 0.625 W/m^{2}K). The walls are traditionally constructed without thermal insulation, consisting of solid brick plastered on both sides (U-value: 1.07 W/m^{2}K). The vehicular pavements are asphalt.

The microclimate of the study area was simulated using ENVI-met v5.6, a robust and widely used tool in urban microclimate research and thermal comfort assessment. ENVI-met integrates wind dynamics, temperature and humidity profiles, vegetation, and radiative exchanges at high spatial resolution [28–32]. It allows for detailed estimation of Mean Radiant Temperature (MRT), a key variable in biometeorological indices such as the Predicted Mean Vote (PMV), Physiologically Equivalent Temperature (PET), and the Universal Thermal Climate Index (UTCI) [31]. ENVI-met has incorporated in version 5 advanced models for calculating MRT, notably the Indexed View Sphere (IVS) and Advanced Canopy Radiation Transfer (ACRT) modules. These modules account for short- and long-wave radiation fluxes using a six-directional measurement technique, improving upon the older Average View Factors (AVF) method that simplified secondary radiation exchanges [31,33]. Recent studies confirm the potential of these models, especially when applied with site-specific inputs and calibrated parameters such as surface albedo and cloud cover, highlighting the importance of empirical calibration for reliable simulations in complex urban morphologies [34]. Therefore, while ENVI-met enables robust analyses of thermal comfort and urban heat mitigation strategies, its application requires careful local calibration and validation with field measurements to ensure reliable results [31,33,34].

The model was comprehensively digitized to reflect the actual characteristics of the study area, including urban morphology, surface materials, and vegetation, all documented through field surveys. Surface materials were represented using the ENVI-met v5.6.1 standard database, with site-specific adjustments to the albedo of horizontal and vertical external surfaces. Vegetation was parameterized using the software's standard library, complemented by locally collected data. The microclimatic model was constructed as a 100 (x) × 80 (y) × 30 (z) grid with a resolution of 3.0 m (dx) × 3.0 m (dy) × 5.0 m (dz), covering a reference surface of 300 × 240 m.

To ensure simulation accuracy, a day with stable atmospheric conditions—free of precipitation and with minimal cloud cover—was selected to minimize external variability. Model calibration was conducted by comparing measured and simulated air temperatures recorded by a sensor installed within a central urban canyon. Although mean radiant temperature (MRT) was not directly validated through field measurements, it is considered representative, as the model incorporated critical input parameters such as albedo, material properties, and cloud cover, which are widely recognized as essential for accurate MRT estimation [31,34]. Microclimatic variables were collected at fixed station points (P1) in the central area of the study site (Figure 2) at pedestrian height (1.5 m). The measurement equipment used was a HOBO® H08-003-02 (Bourne, MA, USA, EE. UU.), with temperature accuracy of ±0.7 °C (from +21 °C) and humidity accuracy of ±5% (from +5 °C to +50 °C). Equipment was installed inside a radiation shield following WMO guidelines [35]. Figure 2 shows both the morphological configuration of the study area and the modeled section in ENVI-met. For calibration, the receptor was positioned at the exact location of the climate data logger (P1).

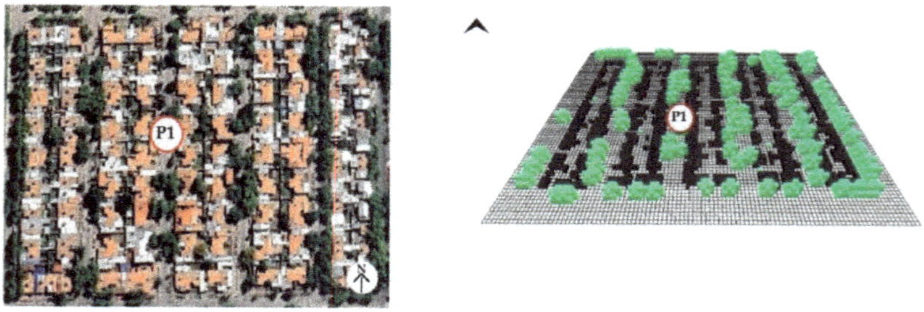

(**a**) (**b**)

Figure 2. Study area and P1 (data acquisition point/receptor), (**a**) aerial photographs, (**b**) study area digitalized with ENVI-met model (black volumes: buildings and green volumes: urban trees). Font: adapted from ENVI-met and Google Earth Pro.

The input climatic parameters correspond to the periods of highest solar radiation availability. Specifically, the analysis focused on 8 February for Mendoza, 23 August for Madrid, and 6 February for Campinas in 2024. These dates were selected as they represent typical summer climatic conditions for each respective location (Table 2).

Table 2. Input Data for the ENVI-met v.5.6 Model.

Parameters	Mendoza (February)	Madrid (August)	Campinas (February)
Average air temperature; °C	30.7	29.8	25.9
Maximum air temperature; °C	40.1	38.8	31.4
Minimum air temperature; °C	22.9	23.0	20.2
Thermal amplitude; °C	17.2	15.8	11.2
Average relative humidity; %	29.0	32.3	79.0
Average wind speed; m/seg	5.0	3.6	1.7
Maximum global solar radiation; W/m^2	1017	1011	941

Model Calibration

To ensure model stability, the ENVI-met simulation was run for two consecutive days (48 h). The results presented in Figure 3 correspond to the second day, when the model had reached steady-state conditions.

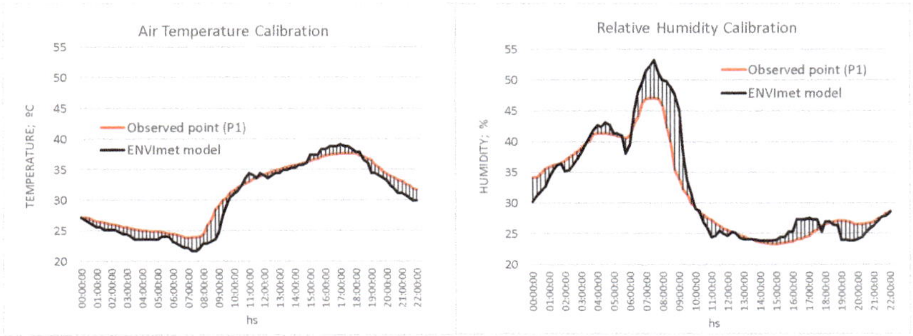

Figure 3. Calibration curves for air temperature and relative humidity of the ENVI-met model compared to fixed point. both at point P1.

Figure 4 presents a scatter plot comparing predicted and measured air temperature and relative humidity, along with the associated statistical metrics for the study area. The results indicate that the ENVI-met model performs well in estimating air temperature (Ta) and provides an acceptable fit for relative humidity (RH). For air temperature, the coefficient of determination was $R^2 = 0.91$, indicating a strong correlation with observed data. Errors were relatively low (RMSE = 1.46 °C, MAE = 1.20 °C), with a negative bias (MBE = −0.80 °C), reflecting a slight systematic underestimation. For relative humidity, the fit was somewhat lower ($R^2 = 0.84$), with RMSE = 3.04% and MAE = 2.00%, and a positive bias (MBE = 0.61%), indicating a minor overestimation. Overall, these results suggest that the model adequately reproduces the microclimatic conditions of the study area.

2.3. *Assessment of Different Scesnarios*

Once the model was calibrated and confirmed to reliably reproduce local climatic conditions, a new scenario was introduced. In this modified area, a simplified model was constructed with a typical building height of 30 m (≈10 stories) and no vegetation, allowing the isolation of the construction variable and maximizing façade exposure relative to the total envelope area. This configuration resulted in a sky view factor of 31% (Figure 5).

To evaluate the impact of different façade technologies on urban microclimatic performance in Mendoza, Madrid, and Campinas, 18 scenarios were analyzed. The variables considered were construction technology (traditional, lightweight, and ETIC system) and albedo level (0.3 and 0.8), applied across the three cities: Mendoza (BWk climate), Madrid (Csa climate), and Campinas (Cwa climate). The nomenclature (ID) of the scenarios is detailed in Table 3, while the construction specifications for each façade scenario are presented in Table 4.

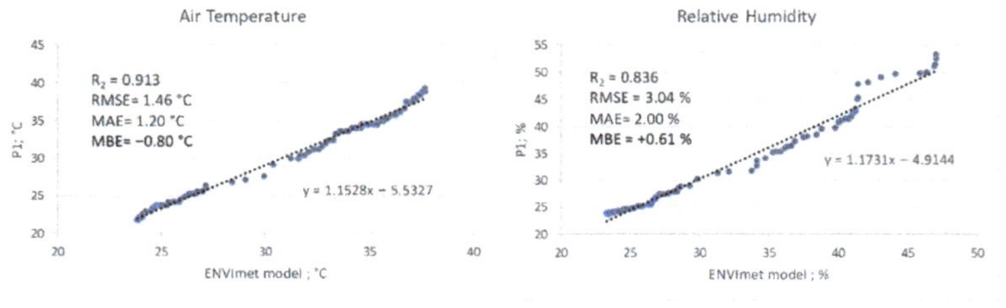

Figure 4. Scatter plot between predicted value (ENVI-met model) and measured value, both at point P1. Statistical calibration metrics: coefficient of determination (R^2); mean bias error (MBE); root mean square error (RMSE); mean absolute error (MAE).

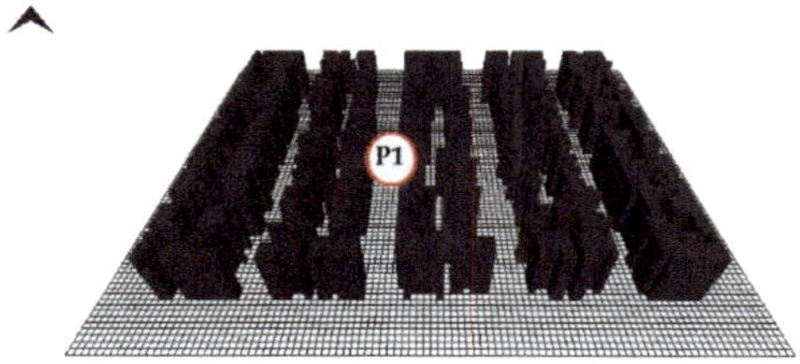

Figure 5. Study area in the ENVI-met v.5.6 model space with analysis scenario.

Table 3. Proposed scenarios for each of the three cities studied.

City	ID	Technology		
		Lightweight (L)	Traditional (T)	ETIC System (S)
Mendoza	Low Albedo	Men_L0.3	Men_T0.3	Men_S0.3
	High Albedo	Men_L0.8	Men_T0.8	Men_S0.8
Madrid	Low Albedo	Mad_L0.3	Mad_T0.3	Mad_S0.3
	High Albedo	Mad_L0.8	Mad_T0.8	Mad_S0.8
Campinas	Low Albedo	Cam_L0.3	Cam_T0.3	Cam_S0.3
	High Albedo	Cam_L0.8	Cam_T0.8	Cam_S0.8

Table 4 outlines the construction solutions for the façades, according to their radiative properties and thermal mass characteristics.

To evaluate the microclimatic impact of the thermal and radiative properties of different façade technologies within the study area, a comparative analysis was conducted across the climatic contexts of Mendoza, Madrid, and Campinas. Initially, the thermal performance of each technology was assessed individually in terms of thermal capacity (see Section 3.1). The thermal capacity of a material is a physical property that indicates the amount of thermal energy required to raise the temperature of a given quantity of that material by one degree Celsius (or Kelvin). In other words, it is a measure of a material's ability to store heat. This concept is closely related to the thermal inertia of materials, which requires more complex calculation models that consider the geometry of each component and boundary conditions, as the ENVI-met model does. The total thermal capacity per m^2

(C_{total}) of each studied technology is determined by the sum of the heat capacities per m^2 of its individual layers (C_i), according to the following formula:

Table 4. Thermal and radiative properties according to construction technology.

Traditional Technology (T)—Thickness: 0.18 m			
Properties	Stucco ext.	Solid Brick	Stucco Int.
* Thickness (e); meters	0.02	0.14	0.02
* Specific Heat (c); J/kgK	669	650	669
* Thermal Conductivity; W/mK	0.09	0.44	0.09
* Density (ρ); Kg/m^3	1920	1500	1920
Albedo	0.30/0.80		0.30/0.80
* Emissivity	0.90	0.90	0.90
Thermal Transmittance of the Component		1.07 W/m^{2}K	
Lightweight Technology (L)—Thickness: 0.12 m			
Properties	Cementitious board ext.	Isolant EPS	Cementitious board int.
* Thickness (e); meters	0.015	0.09	0.015
* Specific Heat (c); J/kgK	840	1500	840
* Thermal Conductivity; W/mK	0.2	0.07	0.2
* Density (ρ); Kg/m^3	620	400	620
Albedo	0.3/0.8		0.3/0.8
* Emissivity	0.94		0.94
Thermal Transmittance of the Component		0.623 W/m^{2}K	
Exterior Thermal Insulation System (S)—Thickness: 0.21 m			
Properties	Cementitious board ext.	Isolant EPS	Solid Brick int.
* Thickness (e); meters	0.015	0.05	0.14
* Specific Heat (c); J/kgK	840	1500	650
* Thermal Conductivity; W/mK	0.2	0.07	0.44
* Density (ρ); Kg/m^3	620	400	1500
Albedo	0.3/0.8		0.3/0.8
* Emissivity	0.94		0.9
Thermal Transmittance of the Component		0.782 W/m^{2}K	

* Default values. ENVI-met v.5.6 material library.

$$C_i = m_i \cdot c_i \quad (1)$$

where

C_i = heat capacity per m^2 of layer i (J/m^2·K);
$m_i = \rho_i \cdot e_i$ = mass per m^2 of the layer (kg/m^2);
ρ_i = density of the layer (kg/m^3);
e_i = thickness of the layer (m);
c_i = specific heat of the layer (J/kg·K).

Then, the total heat capacity per m^2 of technologies, C_{total} (J/m^2·K), is obtained by summing all layers:

$$C_{total} = \sum_{i=1}^{n} C_i = \sum_{i=1}^{n} (\rho_i \cdot e_i \cdot c_i) \quad (2)$$

This formula allows to calculate the total thermal mass of a composite wall per square meter, and find the most effective combinations of radiative and thermal mass properties. Secondly, various radiative and thermal properties façade configurations were simulated using ENVI-met software, and their influence on the urban environment was quantified through the parameters of mean radiant temperature (MRT) and outdoor air temperature (AT), as defined previously (see Section 3.2). Finally, to further understand the implications of façade technology selection, a thermal comfort analysis was conducted using the Universal Thermal Climate Index (UTCI) in the study cities (see Section 3.2.2. The objective of this analysis was to investigate how the different climatic characteristics (BWk for Mendoza, Csa for sMadrid, and Cwa for Campinas) interact with the thermal and radiative properties of façades and affect the perception of thermal stress, particularly under extreme heat conditions. The UTCI thermal stress categories considered in the analysis were interpreted as follows:

- Moderate heat stress: (26–32 °C);
- Strong heat stress: (32–38 °C);
- Very strong heat stress: (38–46 °C).

3. Results

3.1. Thermal Capacity of the Analyzed Technologies (C_{total})

Thermal inertia is the ability of a material to store and release heat. A material with high thermal inertia absorbs heat during the day and releases it slowly at night, helping to stabilize indoor temperatures. It is directly related to the total thermal capacity of the wall (C_{total}) that is the physical quantity used to quantify the effect of thermal inertia. Therefore, a wall with a higher C_{total} has greater thermal inertia and is more effective at damping temperature fluctuations.

Table 5 describes the distinctive thermal behavior of the three analyzed construction technologies, evaluated through their heat capacity per unit area (C_{total}). The traditional system (T) has a C_{total} of 187,840 J/(m^2·K), which means that raising the temperature of 1 m^2 of a traditional wall (18 cm thick) by 1 K requires approximately 187,879 J of thermal energy. These values demonstrate that traditional façade technology achieves the highest thermal inertia, making it ideal for damping daytime temperature fluctuations due to the high mass and density of its layers.

In contrast, the lightweight system (L) exhibits the lowest heat capacity, with a C_{total} of 69,624 J/(m^2·K), resulting in low thermal inertia. This technology prioritizes thermal insulation through the incorporation of a thick layer of expanded polystyrene (EPS), making it highly efficient at reducing heat transfer.

Finally, the External Thermal Insulation Composite System (S) achieves an optimal balance, combining significant thermal inertia (C_{total} = 174,312 J/(m^2·K)) due to its internal brick mass with superior insulation provided by an external EPS layer. This design allows the interior mass to regulate temperature while the insulation minimizes heat losses or gains, optimizing both comfort and energy efficiency.

The bar chart in Figure 6 describes the total thermal capacity per m^2 of each component by technology as calculated by Equation (1).

Table 5. Heat capacity per m^2 of technologies (C_{total}); J/m^2·K, according to construction technology.

Technology	Layer	e; m	ρ; kg/m^3	c; J/kg·K	C_i; J/m^2·K
Traditional (T)	Exterior Stucco	0.02	1920	669	25,670
	Solid Brick	0.14	1500	650	136,500
	Interior Stucco	0.02	1920	669	25,670
C_{total}		**0.18**			**187,840**
Lightweight (L)	Exterior Cementitious Board	0.015	620	840	7812
	EPS Insulation	0.09	400	1500	54,000
	Interior Cementitious Board	0.015	620	840	7812
C_{total}		**0.12**			**69,624**
Exterior Thermal Insulation Systems (S)	Exterior Cementitious Board	0.015	620	840	7812
	EPS Insulation	0.05	400	1500	30,000
	Interior Solid Brick	0.14	1500	650	136,500
C_{total}		**0.21**			**174,312**

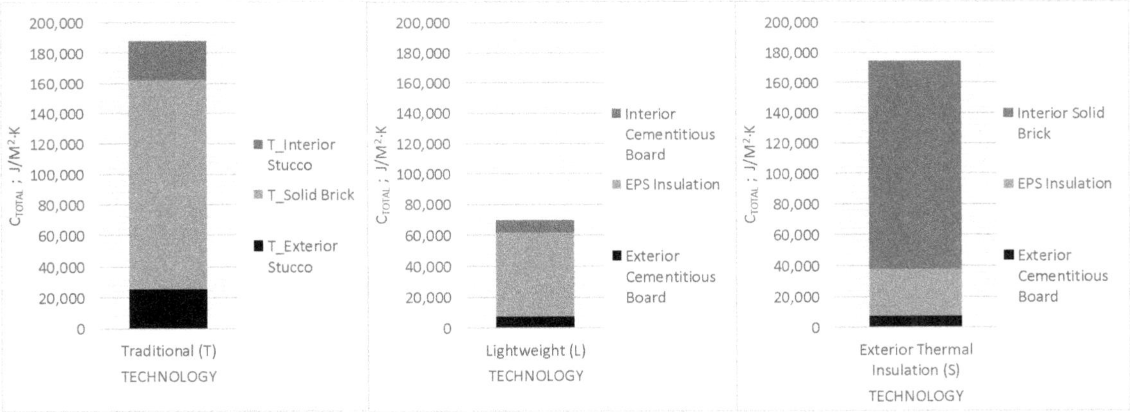

Figure 6. Heat capacity per m^2 of technologies (C_{total}); J/m^2·K.

3.2. Impact of Façade Technologies on Urban Environment

Table 6 presents the outdoor air temperature (AT) and mean radiant temperature (MRT) data for Mendoza, Madrid, and Campinas, considering different façade technologies (lightweight—L, traditional—T, and ETIC system—S) and albedo levels (0.3 and 0.8). The columns showing the maximum values of each variable (AT and MRT) are color-coded according to their range of behavior to facilitate analysis and highlight observable patterns.

Table 6 shows that the extreme values in the maximum AT column occur when the construction technology is varied (L0.3 vs. T0.3) across the three cities. In contrast, MRT is primarily influenced by surface albedo, with high-albedo façades producing higher MRT values than low-albedo ones (L0.3, T0.3, S0.3 vs. L0.8, T0.8, S0.8).

Figures 7 and 8 illustrate the urban microclimatic behavior in terms of air temperature and mean radiant temperature within the street canyon for the three study cities, across all 18 façade scenarios. Table 3 provides a detailed explanation of the nomenclature codes for each scenario.

Table 6. Air temperature (AT) and mean radiant temperature (MRT) at 1.5 m height for the analyzed scenarios in the three cities.

Scenarios		AT; °C			MRT; °C		
		Average	Maximum	Minimum	Average	Maximum	Minimum
Mendoza	Men_L0.3	30.9	37.57	23.89	34.14	69.33	20.33
	Men_T0.3	30.46	36.68	23.92	32.15	64.87	20.15
	Men_S0.3	30.58	36.99	23.89	32.81	66.29	20.28
	Men_L0.8	30.57	37	23.87	35.32	72.18	20.2
	Men_T0.8	30.41	36.57	23.93	34.69	70.96	20.21
	Men_S0.8	30.53	36.89	23.89	35.18	71.97	20.28
Madrid	Mad_L0.3	30.06	37.22	24.01	33.15	69.51	20.9
	Mad_T0.3	29.72	36.41	24.02	31.65	64.98	20.31
	Mad_S0.3	29.83	36.71	23.99	32.15	67.05	20.45
	Mad_L0.8	29.85	36.77	23.99	34.51	72.76	20.26
	Mad_T0.8	29.72	36.41	24.03	34.02	70.31	20.33
	Mad_S0.8	29.83	36.71	23.99	34.38	72.61	20.45
Campinas	Cam_L0.3	26.76	32.43	21.35	31.99	65.72	18.22
	Cam_T0.3	26.38	31.23	21.48	30.12	62.33	18.36
	Cam_S0.3	26.48	31.7	21.37	30.98	62.87	18.28
	Cam_L0.8	26.42	31.51	21.38	33.21	69.34	18.29
	Cam_T0.8	26.29	31.12	21.49	32.38	68.83	18.38
	Cam_S0.8	26.38	31.49	21.37	33.06	69.18	18.28

Color scale: minimun value → maximun value

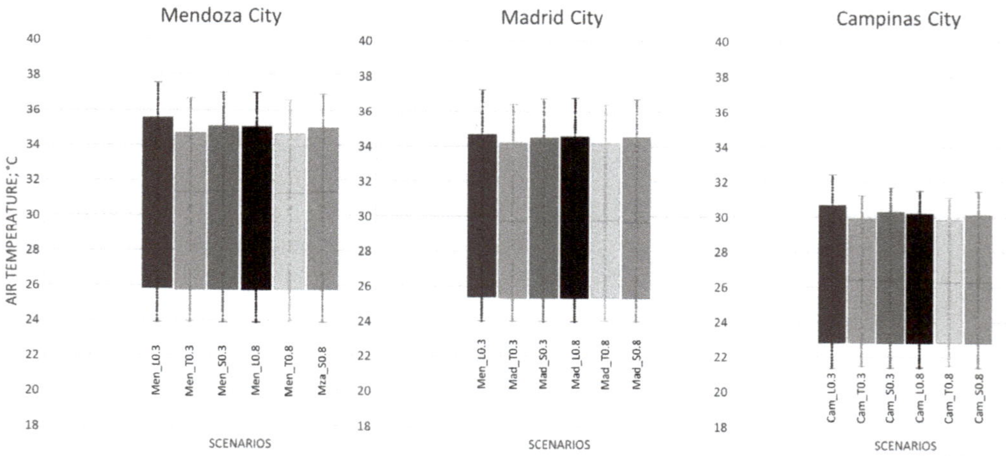

Figure 7. Air temperature at pedestrian level at 1.50 m for lightweight (L), traditional (T) technologies and Exterior Thermal Insulation System (S), according to albedo (0.3 and 0.8) for the cities of Mendoza (Men), Madrid (Mad) and Campinas (Cam).

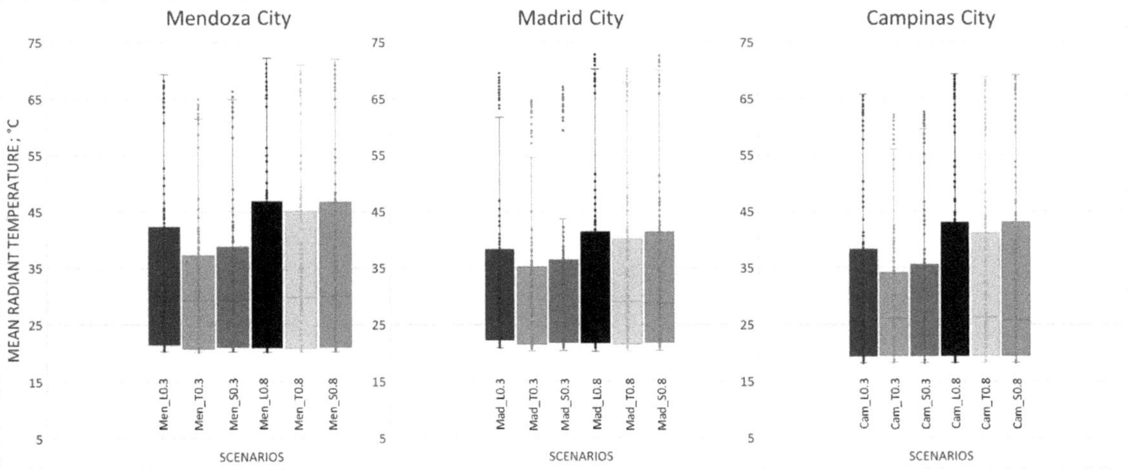

Figure 8. Mean radiant temperature at pedestrian level at 1.50 m for lightweight (L), traditional (T) technologies and Exterior Thermal Insulation System (S), according to albedo (0.3 and 0.8) for the cities of Mendoza (Men), Madrid (Mad) and Campinas (Cam).

3.2.1. Air Temperature (AT) and Mean Radiant Temperatures (MRT)

When evaluating the thermal behavior of the analyzed scenarios, it was observed that the MRT variable was highly sensitive to the three façade technologies (L, T, and S) and to both albedo levels (0.3 and 0.8) in façade technologies, compared to air temperature (AT). Next, consistent patterns were observed across cities:

- Air temperature (AT) in relation to technologies modification: traditional façades with low albedo (0.3) systematically presented the lowest maximum AT values, confirming the buffering effect of higher thermal inertia. In Campinas, for example, the maximum AT with traditional façades was 31.23 °C, while lightweight façades reached 32.43 °C—an increase of 1.2 °C. Similar, but smaller, differences were recorded in Mendoza (0.89 °C) and Madrid (0.81 °C) (T0.3 vs. L0.3). Lightweight façades, characterized by low thermal mass due to insulating materials such as polystyrene, responded more rapidly to diurnal variations. This accelerated heat release resulted in higher AT peaks and more pronounced daily fluctuations.
- Air Temperature (AT) in relation to albedo modification: regarding the impact of the radiative properties of façades, a lower influence on urban air temperatures was observed, compared to the effect of façade materials. Across the studied cities, increasing the albedo from 0.3 to 0.8 most significantly affected lightweight technologies. The greatest reductions in maximum AT occurred in Campinas, with decreases of 0.92 °C; in Mendoza and Madrid, average differences reached approximately 0.5 °C (L0.3 vs. L0.8) (Table 6 and Figure 7).
- Mean Radiant Temperature (MRT) in relation to technologies modification: lightweight façades with low albedo generate significantly higher MRT than other technologies, particularly in high-radiation contexts. The maximum differences between lightweight and traditional technologies reached 4.46 °C in Mendoza, 4.53 °C in Madrid and 3.39 °C in Campinas (L0.3 vs. T0.3). The increase is particularly pronounced in Mendoza and Madrid, cities characterized by high solar radiation and heliophany during the summer months (exceeding 1000 W/m^2). (Table 6 and Figure 8).
- Mean Radiant Temperature (MRT) in relation to albedo modification: high-albedo façades (0.8) amplified MRT due to multiple reflections within the deep canyon, a

phenomenon of radiative "trapping." Their interaction with solar altitude reinforced the effect of canyon geometry. Deep urban canyons in all study areas promoted higher maximum and average MRT values across the three cities, mainly due to inter-building radiation reflections (inter-building effect, [19]). Campinas was particularly affected because of its geographical position near the equator, where the sun strikes almost perpendicularly on horizontal surfaces, intensifying radiative load. Specifically, in Campinas, increasing façade albedo to 0.8 raised MRT by 6.50 °C for traditional technology (from 62.33 °C to 68.83 °C) and by 3.62 °C for lightweight technology (from 65.72 °C to 68.83 °C). In Mendoza, the maximum MRT difference was 6.09 °C for traditional façades (from 64.87 °C to 70.96 °C) and 2.85 °C for lightweight façades (from 69.33 °C to 72.18 °C). A similar trend was found in Madrid, with increases of 5.33 °C (from 64.98 °C to 70.31 °C) for traditional façades and 3.25 °C (from 69.51 °C to 72.76 °C) for lightweight façades (T0.8 vs. T0.3 and L0.8 vs. L0.3) (Table 6 and Figure 8).

Table 7 presents thermal maps of mean radiant temperature (MRT) distribution captured at the time of their maximum values (15:00 solar time) on the study days for each city. In these maps, black areas represent building footprints, while the color scale indicates MRT distribution and intensity, ranging from low temperatures (blue/green) to high temperatures (red/yellow).

Table 7. Distribution of mean radiant temperature for 18 analyzed scenarios at 15:00.

	Mendoza–Argentina		Madrid–Spain		Campinas–Brazil
Men_T0.3	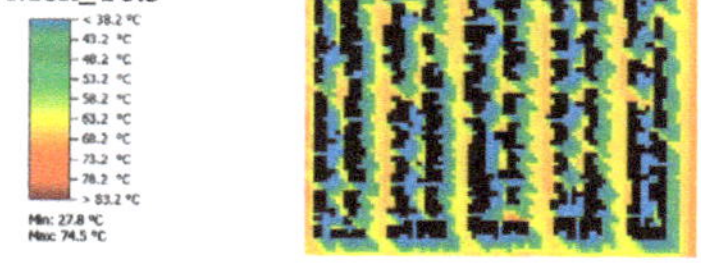	Mad_T0.3	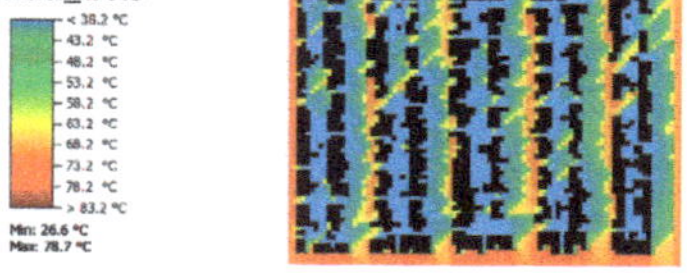	Camp_T0.3	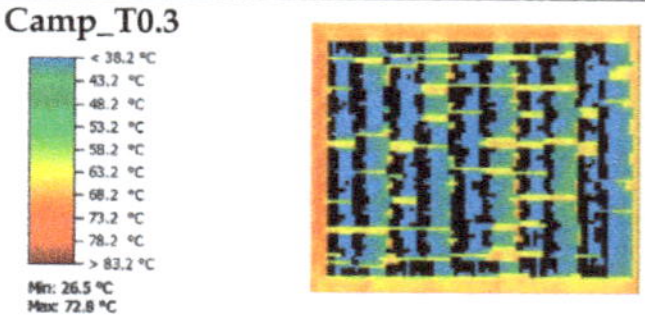
Men_T0.8	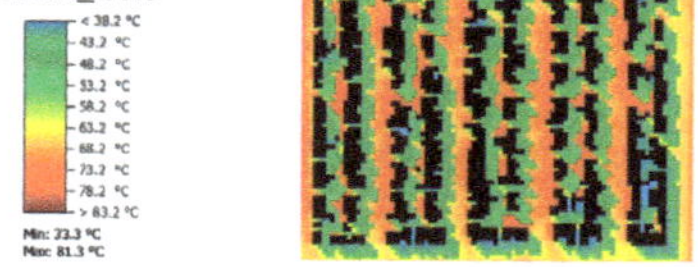	Mad_T0.8	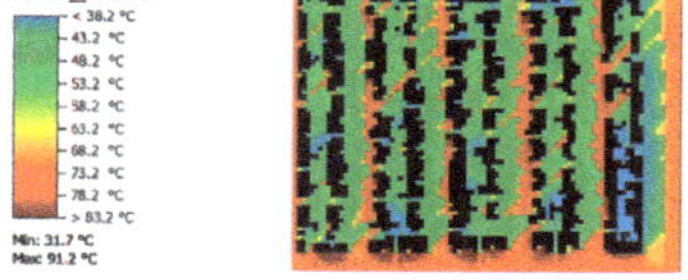	Camp_T0.3	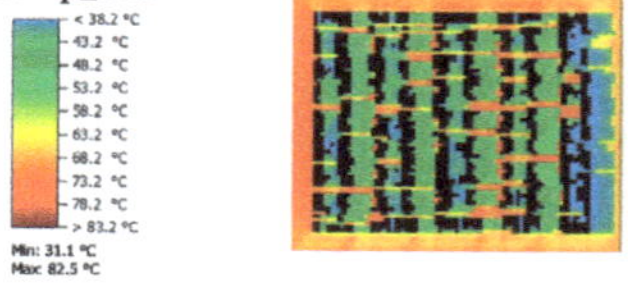
Men_L0.3	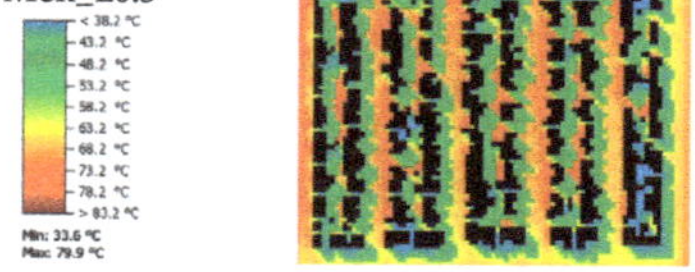	Mad_L0.3	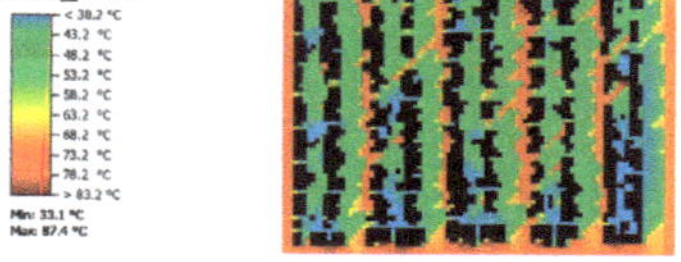	Camp_L0.3	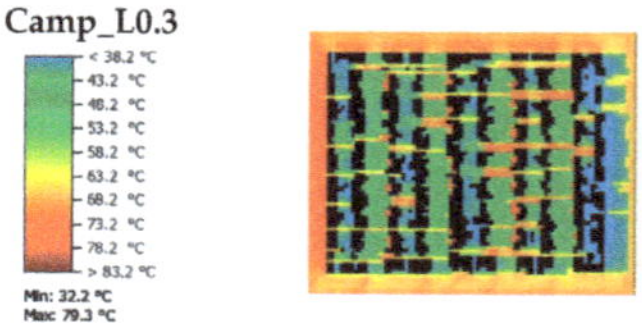
Men_L0.8	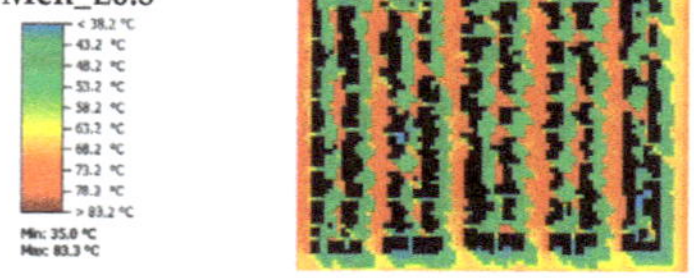	Mad_L0.8	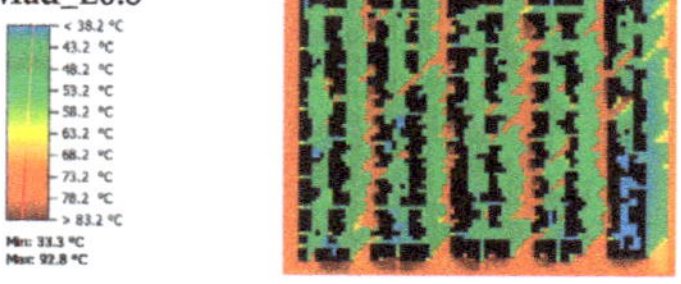	Camp_L0.8	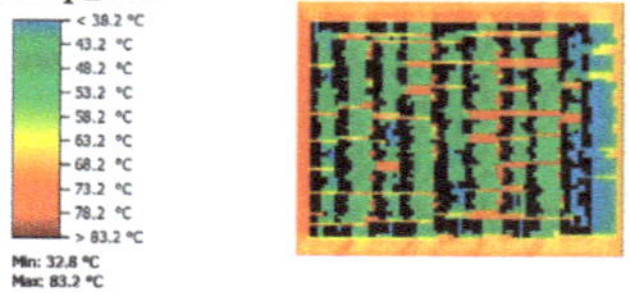

Table 7. *Cont.*

Mendoza–Argentina	Madrid–Spain	Campinas–Brazil

Men_S0.3

Mad_S0.3

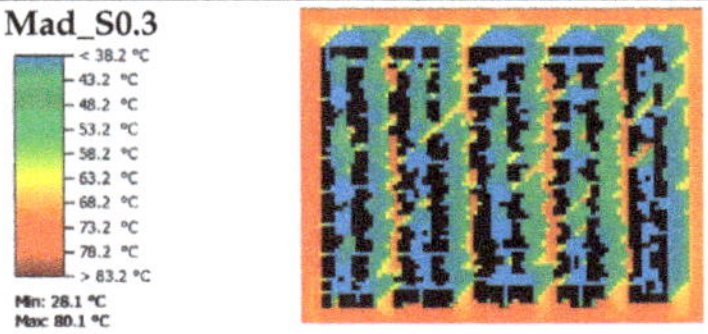

Camp_S0.3

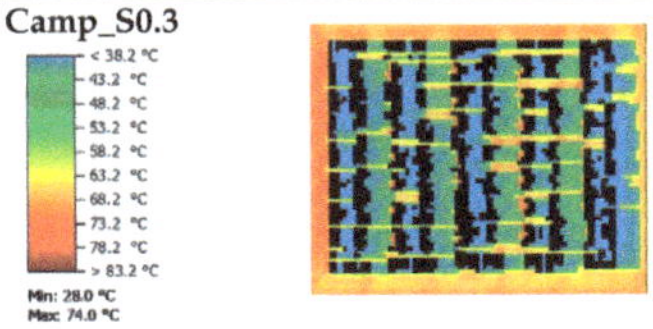

Men_S0.8

Mad_S0.8

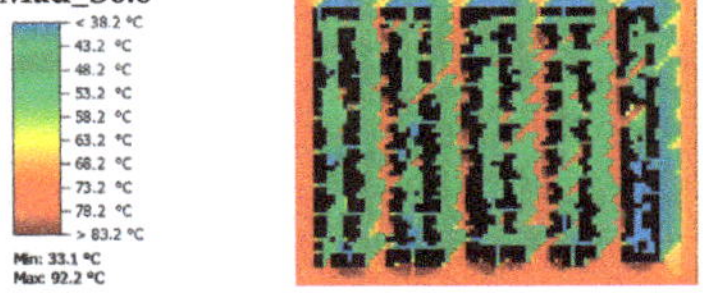

Camp_S0.8

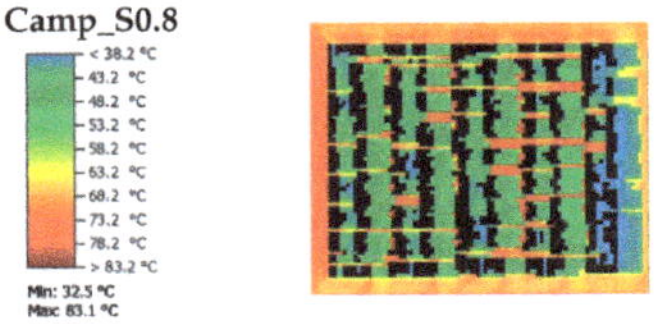

The orientation and extent of the shadow cones vary according to each city's latitude relative to the Equator. In Mendoza, shadows are compact and cast southward due to the high solar altitude angle (approximately 74° in February). Conversely, in Madrid, the shadow cones are much larger and oriented northward, owing to its northern latitude and lower solar altitude (61° in August). Finally, in Campinas, its proximity to the Equator results in shadows primarily cast westward, with a high solar altitude angle (84° in February). These spatial and temporal shading patterns, combined with façade reflectivity and thermal inertia, determine the net radiative load at pedestrian level and explain the observed variations in MRT and outdoor thermal comfort across cities (Table 7).

3.2.2. Thermal Comfort According to UTCI Index

Figure 9 illustrates the daily distribution of the Universal Thermal Climate Index (UTCI) for the different façade technologies across the three cities. Figure 10 presents the percentage of hours experiencing very strong heat stress for each technology and albedo level.

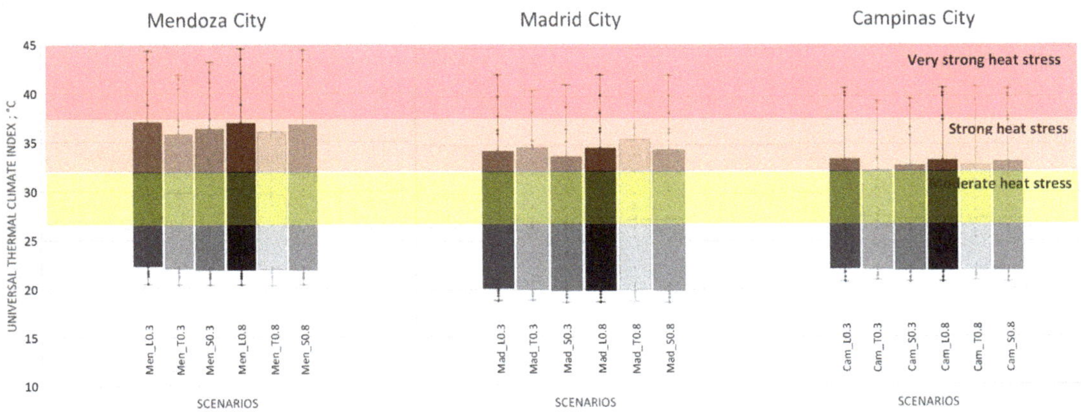

Figure 9. Universal thermal climate index at 1.50 m for lightweight (L), traditional (T) technologies and Exterior Thermal Insulation System (S), according to albedo (0.3 and 0.8) for the cities of Mendoza (Men), Madrid (Mad) and Campinas (Cam).

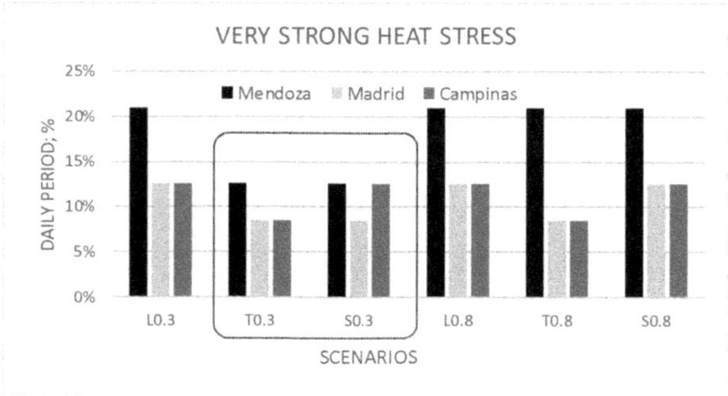

Figure 10. Daily percentage of hours within the very strong heat stress category (above 38 °C) according to the Universal Thermal Climate Index (UTCI) in the three cities studied (Mendoza, Madrid, Campinas), differentiated by façade scenarios: lightweight (L), traditional (T), and ETIC system (S), and by albedo levels: 0.3 and 0.8. Dotted box: It is highlighting the most effective technologies for the three analyzed climates.

This analysis aims to identify the combinations of façade technology and surface reflectance that are most effective in reducing heat stress. In Mendoza, the scenarios Men_T0.3 and Men_S0.3 (highlighted in Figure 10) exhibit the lowest percentage of hours under very strong heat stress, making them the most effective solutions for this climate. In Madrid, the most favorable configurations are Mad_T0.3, Mad_S0.3, and Mad_T0.8, which also show the lowest proportion of time under heat stress. In Campinas, the most efficient scenarios are Camp_L0.3 and Camp_L0.8, recording the fewest hours of very strong heat stress. This indicates that in warm-humid climates such as Campinas, thermal insulation is more critical than thermal mass, as the primary challenge is to limit sensible heat gains and prevent daytime overheating. In this context, lightweight systems with 9 cm of EPS insulation (C_i = 54,000 J/(m^2·K)) are adequate (Table 5).

By contrast, cities like Mendoza and Madrid, which experience large daily temperature ranges (>9 °C, see Table 3), benefit more from technologies with higher thermal mass. Both traditional façades (T, C_{total} = 187,840 J/(m^2·K)) and ETIC systems (S, C_{total} = 174,312 J/(m^2·K)) perform better. The higher heat capacity allows these systems to absorb incoming solar radiation during the day and release it gradually at night, dampening the thermal cycle within the urban canyon and reducing UTCI peaks. This buffering effect is particularly important in arid climates such as Mendoza, where intense solar radiation and low cloud cover amplify thermal contrasts.

Surface reflectance (albedo) plays a key role in high-thermal-mass technologies, while its effect is less pronounced in lightweight systems. Due to the rapid thermal response of low-mass façades, the influence of reflectance is short-lived and does not accumulate, limiting its impact on UTCI compared to massive constructions.

Specifically, in Mendoza, the percentage of time under very strong heat stress exceeds 21% for Men_L0.3, Men_L0.8, Men_T0.8, and Men_S0.8, with UTCI peaking at 44.98 °C. In Madrid, this percentage reaches 12.5% for Mad_L0.3, Mad_L0.8, and Mad_S0.8, with a maximum UTCI of 42.22 °C. In Campinas, time under very strong heat stress increases to 12.5% for Cam_L0.3, Cam_S0.3, Cam_L0.8, and Cam_S0.8, with maximum UTCI values of 40.94 °C (Figure 10).

4. Discussion

This study confirms that façade material properties—particularly thermal mass and albedo—are decisive in shaping microclimates within deep urban canyons. Traditional and ETIC systems, both with higher heat capacity, consistently buffered air temperature peaks and reduced UTCI exposure, especially in climatic locations with large diurnal ranges such as Mendoza. These findings are consistent with previous evidence on the benefits of thermal inertia for moderating microclimatic extremes ([36,37]), and reinforce its relevance as a passive cooling strategy in dense urban environment.

Lightweight façades, in contrast, showed limited capacity to regulate thermal conditions, producing higher MRT and longer periods of strong heat stress. This outcome echoes recent studies on the drawbacks of low-mass materials in outdoor comfort [13], highlighting the need to complement such systems with additional strategies. One promising approach is the integration of phase-change materials (PCMs), which have been shown to enhance the latent storage capacity of lightweight constructions [37].

The influence of façade reflectivity was even more critical. Increasing albedo from 0.3 to 0.8 systematically amplified MRT by more than 6 °C in deep canyons, despite negligible effects on air temperature. This pattern corroborates the "inter-building effect" described in ([18,19]) and recent reviews questioning the universal benefits of reflective materials [38,39]. While high-albedo surfaces are often promoted as urban cooling solutions [40], the results here demonstrate that, under specific morphologies, they can exacerbate pedestrian radiant stress. Alternative innovations, such as retro-reflective materials designed to redirect solar gains away from pedestrian zones may offer more effective solutions [41]. Evidence from previous studies ([39–42]) suggests that multi-strategy approaches outperform isolated interventions in mitigating urban heat and improving outdoor comfort. Overall, these findings emphasize that façade strategies cannot be generalized. Instead, they must be tailored to climate and morphology, integrating recent material innovations to mitigate unintended consequences and improve outdoor thermal comfort.

5. Conclusions

The results of this study confirm that the thermal performance of opaque façades in deep urban canyons is strongly determined by their thermal capacity and surface reflectivity. Traditional façades, with the highest heat storage capacity (C_{total} = 187,840 J/(m^2·K)), consistently achieved the lowest maximum air temperatures and MRT values across the three cities. In Campinas, for instance, maximum AT decreased by 1.2 °C compared to lightweight façades (31.23 °C vs. 32.43 °C), while MRT differences reached 3.39 °C (62.33 °C vs.
65.72 °C). Similar patterns were observed in Mendoza (ΔAT = 0.89 °C; ΔMRT = 4.46 °C) and Madrid (ΔAT = 0.81 °C; ΔMRT = 4.53 °C).

The ETIC system (C_{total} = 174,312 J/(m^2·K)) showed intermediate but robust behavior, balancing the buffering effect of thermal mass with the insulating performance of EPS. By contrast, lightweight façades (C_{total} = 69,624 J/(m^2·K)) systematically recorded the highest MRT and UTCI peaks, particularly in high-radiation climates such as Mendoza and Madrid, confirming their vulnerability due to low thermal inertia.

Albedo played a secondary role in AT modulation but had a decisive impact on MRT. Increasing surface reflectivity from 0.3 to 0.8 raised maximum MRT by up to 6.50 °C in Campinas (T0.3 = 62.33 °C vs. T0.8 = 68.83 °C), 6.09 °C in Mendoza (64.87 °C vs. 70.96 °C), and 5.33 °C in Madrid (64.98 °C vs. 70.31 °C). These increases, driven by multiple reflections and the inter-building effect, intensified radiant heat loads at pedestrian level, demonstrating that highly reflective façades can worsen thermal stress in tall, dense canyons.

Thermal comfort analysis further confirmed these trends. In arid and continental climates with large diurnal temperature ranges (Mendoza, Madrid), traditional and ETIC façades with low albedo minimized exposure to very strong heat stress (>38 °C), while lightweight façades prolonged it. In Campinas, a warm-humid climate, insulation proved more relevant, making lightweight façades comparatively effective in reducing sensible heat gains.

Overall, the study demonstrates that façade strategies cannot be generalized. Thermal mass is the primary determinant of AT, surface albedo governs MRT, and UTCI outcomes result from the combined influence of both. High reflectivity, often considered a universal cooling solution, may instead exacerbate thermal discomfort in dense urban morphologies. Climate- and morphology-sensitive façade design—favoring systems with higher thermal inertia and carefully selected albedo—represents a more reliable pathway to enhancing outdoor habitability and urban resilience.

Author Contributions: Conceptualization: N.A., E.G., G.P. and C.P.; methodology: N.A., E.G., C.P.; validation: N.A., C.P. and M.T.; investigation: N.A. and E.G.; resources: C.P., E.G. and G.P.; data curation: N.A. and M.T.; writing—original draft preparation: N.A. and E.G.; writing—review and editing: E.G., G.P. and N.A.; visualization: C.P., N.A. and M.T.; supervision: G.P.; project administration: G.P. and E.G.; funding acquisition: C.P. and G.P. All authors have read and agreed to the published version of the manuscript.

Funding: This work was supported by URBAN-TherCOM Project (Grant PID2020–114873RA-C33) and mateMAD Project (Grant PID2020-114873RB-C31) both funded by MCIN/AEI/10.13039/501100011033. They also thank the support by the São Paulo Research Foundation (FAPESP) under grant #2023/09875-1 and #2024/01299-4, and National Scientific and Technical Research Council of Argentina (CONICET) under grant #TE_2023_1_1012613.

Data Availability Statement: This article is a revised and expanded version of a paper entitled "Façade Construction Technologies and Their Impact on the Urban Microclimate: A Comparative Study between the Cities of Madrid and Mendoza", which was presented at VII Ibero-American Congress of Smart Cities. ICSC-CITIES 2024 conference in San José, Costa Rica, in November 2024. The original contributions presented in this study are included in the article. Further inquiries can be directed to the corresponding author.

Acknowledgments: The support provided by the following institutions is gratefully acknowledged: Instituto de Medio Ambiente, Hábitat y Energía (INAHE-CONICET), CCT-Mendoza, Argentina; Departamento de Energía, CIEMAT, Madrid, Spain; Instituto Eduardo Torroja de Ciencias de la Construcción (IETCC), Madrid, Spain; and School of Polytechnic Postgraduate Program in Urban Infrastructure, Pontifical Catholic University of Campinas (PUC-Campinas), SP, Brazil.

Conflicts of Interest: The authors declare no conflicts of interest. The funders had no role in the design of the study; in the collection, analyses, or interpretation of data; in the writing of the manuscript; or in the decision to publish the results.

References

1. Broadbent, A.M.; Krayenhoff, E.S.; Georgescu, M. The motley drivers of heat and cold exposure in 21st century US cities. *Proc. Natl. Acad. Sci. USA* **2020**, *117*, 21108–21117. [CrossRef]
2. Schinasi, L.H.; Benmarhnia, T.; De Roos, A.J. Modification of the association between high ambient temperature and health by urban microclimate indicators: A systematic review and meta-analysis. *Environ. Res.* **2018**, *161*, 168–180. [CrossRef] [PubMed]
3. Sinsel, T.; Simon, H.; Broadbent, A.M.; Bruse, M.; Heusinger, J. Modeling the outdoor cooling impact of highly radiative 'super cool' materials applied on roofs. *Urban Clim.* **2021**, *38*, 100898. [CrossRef]
4. Klinenberg, E. *Heat Wave. A Social Autopsy of Disaster in Chicago*; The University of Chicago Press: Chicago, IL, USA, 2015; Available online: https://www.perlego.com/book/1853205/heat-wave-a-social-autopsy-of-disaster-in-chicago-pdf (accessed on 26 September 2025).
5. Cheval, S.; Amihăesei, V.-A.; Chitu, Z.; Dumitrescu, A.; Falcescu, V.; Irașoc, A.; Micu, D.M.; Mihulet, E.; Ontel, I.; Paraschiv, M.-G.; et al. A systematic review of urban heat island and heat waves research (1991–2022). *Clim. Risk Manag.* **2024**, *44*, 100603. [CrossRef]

6. Pörtner, H.; Roberts, D.C.; Adams, H.; Adelekan, I.; Adler, C.; Adrian, R.; Aldunce, P.; Ali, E.; Begum, R.A.; Bednar-Friedl, B.; et al. Technical Summary. In *Climate Change 2022–Impacts, Adaptation and Vulnerability*; Cambridge University Press: Cambridge, UK, 2023; pp. 37–118. [CrossRef]
7. Gál, C.V.; Kántor, N. Modeling mean radiant temperature in outdoor spaces, A comparative numerical simulation and validation study. *Urban Clim.* **2020**, *32*, 100571. [CrossRef]
8. Herrmann, J.; Matzarakis, A. Mean radiant temperature in idealised urban canyons—Examples from Freiburg, German. *Int. J. Biometeorol.* **2012**, *56*, 199–203. [CrossRef]
9. Pérez, G.; Martín-Consuegra, F.; de Frutos, F.; Martínez, A.; Oteiza, I.; Frutos, B.; Alonso, C. Analysis of the Optical Response of Opaque Urban Envelope Materials: The Case of Madrid. *Infrastructures* **2022**, *7*, 116. [CrossRef]
10. Alonso, C.; Martín-Consuegra, F.; Oteiza, I.; Asensio, E.; Pérez, G.; Martínez, I.; Frutos, B. Effect of façade surface finish on building energy rehabilitation. *Sol. Energy* **2017**, *146*, 470–483. [CrossRef]
11. Ali-Toudert, F.; Mayer, H. Numerical study on the effects of aspect ratio and orientation of an urban street canyon on outdoor thermal comfort in hot and dry climate. *Build. Environ.* **2006**, *41*, 94–108. [CrossRef]
12. Forouzandeh, A. Prediction of surface temperature of building surrounding envelopes using holistic microclimate ENVI-met model. *Sustain. Cities Soc.* **2021**, *70*, 102878. [CrossRef]
13. Kim, J.; Park, S.; Lee, G. Analyzing urban thermal comfort changes due to modifications in urban material properties in a large-scale new town: A CFD study based on the universal thermal climate index (UTCI). *Sustain. Cities Soc.* **2025**, *130*, 106627. [CrossRef]
14. Costanzo, V.; Evola, G.; Marletta, L. Energy savings in buildings or UHI mitigation? Comparison between green roofs and cool roofs. *Energy Build.* **2016**, *114*, 247–255. [CrossRef]
15. Banerjee, S.; Graces Ching, N.Y.; Yik, S.K.; Dzyuban, Y.; Crank, P.J.; Yi, R.P.X.; Chow, W.T.L. Analysing impacts of urban morphological variables and density on outdoor microclimate for tropical cities: A review and a framework proposal for future research directions. *Build. Environ.* **2022**, *225*, 109646. [CrossRef]
16. Levinson, R. Using solar availability factors to adjust cool-wall energy savings for shading and reflection by neighboring buildings. *Sol. Energy* **2019**, *180*, 717–734. [CrossRef]
17. Alchapar, N.L.; Pezzuto, C.C.; Correa, E.N.; Chebel Labaki, L. The impact of different cooling strategies on urban air temperatures: The cases of Campinas, Brazil and Mendoza, Argentina. *Theor. Appl. Climatol.* **2017**, *130*, 35–50. [CrossRef]
18. Pisello, A.L.; Castaldo, V.L.; Poli, T.; Cotana, F. Simulating the Thermal-Energy Performance of Buildings at the Urban Scale: Evaluation of Inter-Building Effects in Different Urban Configurations. *J. Urban Technol.* **2014**, *21*, 3–20. [CrossRef]
19. Pisello, A.L.; Taylor, J.E.; Xu, X.; Cotana, F. Inter-building effect: Simulating the impact of a network of buildings on the accuracy of building energy performance predictions. *Build. Environ.* **2012**, *58*, 37–45. [CrossRef]
20. Köker, N.I.; Manni, M.; Giorio, M.; Jelle, B.P.; Di Sabatino, M.; Lobaccaro, G. Defining challenges of solar irradiance modeling on façades in urban environments: A systematic review. *Energy Build.* **2025**, *347*, 116137. [CrossRef]
21. Grand View Research. *Modular Construction Market Size, Share & Trends Analysis Report By Product (Relocatable, Permanent), By Material (Wood, Steel, Concrete, Others), By Application, By Region, And By Segment Forecasts, 2023–2030*; Grand View Research: San Francisco, CA, USA, 2023.
22. Cardona, A.O. Construcción en seco steel framing ahorra 30% en los tiempos de edificación en obras. *La República*, Medellín, 2018. Available online: https://www.larepublica.co/especiales/especial-camacero/construccion-en-seco-steel-framing-ahorra-30-en-los-tiempos-de-edificacion-en-obras-2790535 (accessed on 26 September 2025).
23. Elsinger, D.; Fernández, A.; Garzón, B. Calculador Integral de Eficiencia Energética de la Envolvente Arquitectónica: CIDEE-EA. *Averma* **2020**, *24*, 77–88.
24. Saint-Gobain, W. Guía de Soluciones para Aislar Fachadas (SATE). 2020. Available online: https://www.es.weber/files/es/2019-11/FOL-ES-Weber-La-Guia-webertherm.pdf (accessed on 26 September 2025).
25. Lawrie, L.; Drury, B.C. Development of Global Typical Meteorological Years (TMYx). 2022. Available online: https://climate.onebuilding.org (accessed on 1 August 2025).
26. CEPAGRI. Climatologia Campinas-Centro De Pesquisas Meteorológicas e Climáticas Aplicadas à Agricultura. 2025. Available online: https://www.cpa.unicamp.br/graficos (accessed on 17 March 2025).
27. Peel, M.C.; Finlayson, B.L.; McMahon, T.A. Updated world map of the Köppen-Geiger climate classification. *Hydrol. Earth Syst. Sci.* **2007**, *11*, 1633–1644. [CrossRef]
28. Pezzuto, C.C.; Alchapar, N.L.; Correa, E.N. Urban cooling technologies potential in high and low buildings densities. *Sol. Energy Adv.* **2022**, *2*, 100022. [CrossRef]
29. Muniz-Gäal, L.P.; Pezzuto, C.C.; de Carvalho, M.F.H.; Mota, L.T.M. Urban geometry and the microclimate of street canyons in tropical climate. *Build. Environ.* **2020**, *169*, 106547. [CrossRef]
30. Tsoka, S.; Tsikaloudaki, A.; Theodosiou, T. Analyzing the ENVI-met microclimate model's performance and assessing cool materials and urban vegetation applications—A review. *Sustain. Cities Soc.* **2018**, *43*, 55–76. [CrossRef]

31. Sinsel, T.; Simon, H.; Ouyang, W.; dos Santos Gusson, C.; Shinzato, P.; Bruse, M. Implementation and evaluation of mean radiant temperature schemes in the microclimate model ENVI-met. *Urban Clim.* **2022**, *45*, 101279. [CrossRef]
32. Liu, Z.; Cheng, W.; Jim, C.Y.; Morakinyo, T.E.; Shi, Y.; Ng, E. Heat mitigation benefits of urban green and blue infrastructures: A systematic review of modeling techniques, validation and scenario simulation in ENVI-met V4. *Build. Environ.* **2021**, *200*, 107939. [CrossRef]
33. Aleksandrowicz, O.; Saroglou, T.; Pearlmutter, D. Evaluation of summer mean radiant temperature simulation in ENVI-met in a hot Mediterranean climate. *Build. Environ.* **2023**, *245*, 110881. [CrossRef]
34. Schöneberger, P.; Sinsel, T.; Ouyang, W.; Tan, Z.; Bruse, M.; Simon, H. Enhancing urban microclimate simulations: Validating ENVI-met's accuracy in modeling multi-directional radiative fluxes and mean radiant temperature in subtropical hong kong. *Build. Environ.* **2025**, *284*, 113475. [CrossRef]
35. World Meteorological Organization. *Instruments and Observing Methodos Report No. 81*; World Meteorological Organization: Geneva, Switzerland, 2006.
36. Elnaggar, S.A.; Omar, W.F.; Elsafty, M. A Review of the Role of Façade Materials in Mitigating the Urban Heat Island. *Sci. J. Fac. Fine Arts Alex. Univ.* **2022**, *10*, 1–14. [CrossRef]
37. Piselli, C.; Castaldo, V.L.; Pisello, A.L. How to enhance thermal energy storage effect of PCM in roofs with varying solar reflectance: Experimental and numerical assessment of a new roof system for passive cooling in different climate conditions. *Sol. Energy* **2019**, *192*, 106–119. [CrossRef]
38. Alchapar, N.L.; Correa, E.N. The use of reflective materials as a strategy for urban cooling in an arid 'OASIS' city. *Sustain. Cities Soc.* **2016**, *27*, 1–14. [CrossRef]
39. Abdelwahab, R.A.; Fekry, A.A.; Hamed, R.E.-D. The effective landscape design parameters with high reflective hardscapes: Guidelines for optimizing human thermal comfort in outdoor spaces by design -a case on hot arid climate weather. *Comput. Urban Sci.* **2025**, *5*, 28. [CrossRef]
40. Fahmy, M.; Ibrahim, Y.; Hanafi, E.; Barakat, M. Would LEED-UHI greenery and high albedo strategies mitigate climate change at neighborhood scale in Cairo, Egypt? *Build. Simul.* **2018**, *11*, 1273–1288. [CrossRef]
41. Huang, X.; Bou-Zeid, E.; Pigliautile, I.; Pisello, A.L.; Mandal, J. Optimizing retro-reflective surfaces to untrap radiation and cool cities. *Nat. Cities* **2024**, *1*, 275–285. [CrossRef]
42. Ibrahim, Y.; Kershaw, T.; Shepherd, P.; Coley, D. On the optimisation of urban form design, energy consumption and outdoor thermal comfort using a parametric workflow in a hot arid zone. *Energies* **2021**, *14*, 4026. [CrossRef]

urban science

MDPI

Article

Validating a Sustainable, Smart, and Circular City Architecture Through Urban Living Lab Experiments

Augusto Velasquez-Mendez [1,*], Jorge de Jesús Lozoya-Santos [2] and José Fernando Jiménez-Vargas [1]

1 PhD Program in Technological Innovation Management, Universidad de los Andes, Bogotá 111711, Colombia; fjimenez@uniandes.edu.co
2 Escuela de Ingeniería y Ciencias, Instituto Tecnológico y de Estudios Superiores de Monterrey, Monterrey 64700, Mexico; jorge.lozoya@tec.mx
* Correspondence: a.velasquezm2@uniandes.edu.co

Abstract: Rapid urbanization and climate change pressure cities to integrate sustainability, digitalization, and circular economy principles. Yet most existing approaches treat these agendas separately, leaving gaps in how urban infrastructures, governance, and data systems can jointly support circular transformations. This paper addresses this challenge by proposing and validating a Sustainable, Smart, and Circular City (SSCC) architecture that operationalizes the waste–energy–information nexus. The architecture is structured into seven interconnected layers—Physical, Digital, Analytical, Participatory Governance, Data Strategy, Innovation Management, and Assessment—and is tested through two integrated experiments in the Fenicia Urban Living Lab, Bogotá: (i) an AI- and drone-based system for waste detection and community reporting and (ii) a solar-powered IoT urban garden for environmental monitoring. These experiments demonstrate how digital twins, participatory governance, and multi-actor collaboration can activate circular strategies while enabling evaluation against international standards (ISO 37106, U4SSC, LEED). The results confirm that the SSCC model can transform siloed services into integrated, circular functions that enhance quality of life, productivity, and ICT-based sustainability. The originality of this study lies in validating an SSCC architecture that incorporates the waste–energy–information nexus across seven layers and demonstrates, through Urban Living Lab experimentation, how such an architecture can guide the transition from Smart Sustainable Cities to Circular Cities.

Keywords: sustainable smart circular cities (SSCCs); urban living lab (ULL); waste–energy–information nexus; circular economy; smart city architecture; digital twin; internet of things (IoT); artificial intelligence (AI)

1. Introduction

The increasing challenges of climate change, urbanization, and resource scarcity have led cities to adopt sustainable development. The smart sustainable city (SSC) model seeks to use digital technology to improve urban operations, reduce environmental impact, and boost quality of life [1,2]. While it has enhanced urban services, it is criticized for emphasizing technology, often ignoring systemic integration with circular resource flows and citizen participation [3,4].

In this context, the circular city has recently gained traction as an emerging urban typology that goes beyond efficiency to promote regenerative urban systems. A circular city aims to incorporate the principles of the circular economy—such as reuse, recycling, regeneration, and value retention—into the urban metabolism, for example, by reusing building materials, recycling plastics and metals, or converting organic waste into compost, thus enabling cities to function not only as consumers but also as producers of resources through closed-loop systems [5,6]. These principles closely align with those of the 2030 Agenda and Sustainable Development Goal 11, which call for inclusive, safe, resilient, and sustainable cities [3].

According to the United for Smart Sustainable Cities (U4SSC) initiative, this transition requires reconfiguring the SSC model by integrating circularity in urban assets, services, and governance frameworks. The U4SSC guide to circular cities proposes a four-step implementation framework: establishing a circularity baseline, assessing the potential of circular actions, applying enablers to catalyze change, and evaluating impacts [7]. This approach moves beyond abstract principles by providing tools and templates to identify actionable circular strategies within specific city infrastructures, supported by enabling conditions such as data governance, stakeholder engagement, and innovation ecosystems [7].

This paper uses the following working definition of a circular city: *"A circular city is an urban system that integrates circular economy principles into its physical infrastructure, services, and governance mechanisms, aiming to decouple urban growth from resource consumption and environmental degradation."* This definition aligns with the perspective of the U4SSC initiative, which highlights that circular cities encourage the regeneration of natural systems, the preservation of material value, and the implementation of closed-loop processes across urban assets and functions. Achieving this vision requires rethinking how cities produce, consume, and manage resources through circular economy strategies. It also involves leveraging enabling technologies and participatory governance to promote cross-sectoral circular practices [1,3,4].

Global initiatives have repeatedly highlighted the importance of aligning smart city innovation with sustainable urban development. The UN-Habitat World Cities Report emphasizes that digital transformation must go hand in hand with environmental and social progress to avoid increasing urban inequalities [8]. Similarly, the World Smart Cities Outlook 2024 points out that smart performance should be evaluated alongside sustainability outcomes, highlighting the need for integrated frameworks [9]. Comparative analyses, such as the multidimensional assessments of Taipei and Almaty, reveal an ongoing gap between smart indicators and actual sustainability performance [10]. Additionally, Shmeleva and Shmelev suggest multidimensional frameworks for assessing Smart Sustainable Cities, showing that integrated approaches are essential for capturing the complexity of urban transitions [11]. These insights highlight that, although considerable progress has been made in evaluating smart and sustainable cities separately, bridging the two remains a critical research challenge, which this paper seeks to address.

1.1. Problem Statement and Research Gaps

Despite the conceptual maturity in the literature, the practical implementation of circularity within smart sustainable city (SSC) architectures remains underdeveloped. This constitutes a fundamental problem facing cities: circular strategies are often disjointed, evaluation methods are limited, and comprehensive frameworks that connect the circular economy, digital infrastructure, and participatory governance are missing [1,3,4]. Addressing this problem motivates the purpose of this paper, which is to propose and validate an architectural model for a Sustainable, Smart, and Circular City (SSCC) that explicitly incorporates the waste–energy–information nexus.

Within this broader problem, three specific research gaps can be identified. First, the integration of circularity into the SSC paradigm remains unclear, as much of the literature treats circularity as a separate rather than an essential part of smart sustainable cities [1,3,5,6]. Second, the alignment between digitalization, circularity, and the energy transition is limited. While IoT, AI, and data analytics are recognized as enablers, their roles in actively supporting circular flows and resource regeneration are rarely incorporated into governance or design practices [1–4]. Third, systemic and measurable urban architectures are missing. Current models often focus on digital platforms or sector-specific solutions but fail to explain the interconnections between infrastructure, governance, and innovation ecosystems. Although the U4SSC framework provides a foundation, it still needs adaptation and validation through real-world testing, especially in Global South contexts [3,7]. These gaps highlight the core challenge that the SSCC architecture aims to address.

Despite these global efforts, studies still reveal a disconnect between smart and sustainable performance. The comparison between Taipei and Almaty shows how cities can improve smart infrastructure while falling short in sustainability outcomes, highlighting the absence of unified performance metrics [10]. Likewise, Shmeleva and Shmelev contend that only multidimensional frameworks can adequately capture the interaction among technological innovation, environmental sustainability, and social well-being [11]. These findings confirm that the lack of integrated approaches remains a key gap, emphasizing the need for models like the SSCC that explicitly link smart and sustainable dimensions.

1.2. Objectives

Building on the gaps identified above, this paper addresses the need to structurally embed circularity within the frameworks of sustainable and smart cities. It explores how cities can move beyond isolated technological or environmental interventions and adopt systemic architectures that support innovation and evaluation in the context of circular urban transitions. This objective is addressed through this specific research question:

How can a smart sustainable city architecture integrate the circular city components that enable innovation and evaluation in real urban contexts?

To address this question, this paper proposes and validates a Sustainable, Smart, and Circular City (SSCC) architecture that explicitly incorporates the waste–energy–information nexus. The architecture consists of seven interconnected functional layers—Physical, Digital, Analytical, Participatory Governance, Data Strategy, Innovation Management, and Assessment—and is tested in the Urban Living Lab of Fenicia, Bogotá. This case study demonstrates how circular strategies can be activated through digital twins, urban experimentation, and collaboration among multiple actors. The originality of this research lies in validating an SSCC architecture that not only operationalizes the waste–energy–information nexus across these seven layers but also provides empirical evidence of how such an architecture can support the transition from Smart Sustainable Cities to Circular Cities.

2. Materials and Methods

This research uses a qualitative and design-oriented methodology to examine how sustainable, smart, and circular city architectures can incorporate the cycles of waste, energy, and information through physical, digital, and social elements. The study is divided into two main phases: a conceptual overview based on literature and reference models, and an empirical validation through an urban living lab (ULL) case study.

The conceptual synthesis of the SSCC architecture was achieved through a structured review of international standards and academic reference models, highlighting commonalities and gaps in integrating smart and circular city dimensions. These insights were incorporated into a seven-layer architecture explicitly designed to include the waste–energy–information nexus. To ensure the design's validity, the architecture was repeatedly tested against empirical requirements from the Fenicia ULL, where multi-actor workshops, participatory feedback, and real-world constraints informed its operational feasibility. Internal validity was supported by aligning each layer with established frameworks and KPIs, while external validity was confirmed through two integrated experiments, demonstrating both the system's functionality and its adaptability to different contexts.

Figure 1 shows the method used in this study. It starts with creating a conceptual framework that combines parts from current sustainable, smart, and circular city models. Then, an empirical case study at Fenicia ULL is performed to test the proposed architecture. Data collection included two participatory experiments: (i) community- and drone-based waste reporting and (ii) IoT sensor monitoring in the urban garden for environmental factors. Although the dataset was limited, it was enough for initial testing, allowing AI-supported analysis, integration into a digital twin, and a readiness assessment. System behavior was also examined using participatory causal loop diagrams (CLDs), with evaluation metrics adapted from frameworks like LEED for Communities, focusing on waste, energy, and quality of life. This method enabled a systematic evaluation across different layers and a focus on the waste–energy–information nexus.

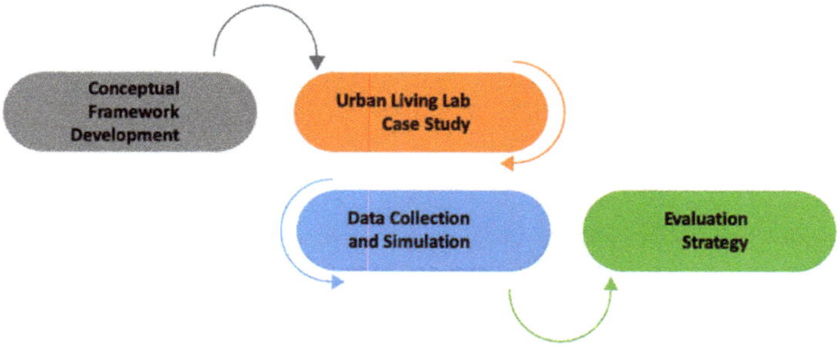

Figure 1. Methodological approach followed in this study.

3. Conceptual Framework Development

The first stage involved a structured review and synthesis of existing architecture models from smart, sustainable, and circular city paradigms. Key documents included international standards (e.g., ISO 37106:2021 [12]), technology integration frameworks (e.g., FIWARE, CPS/IoT architectures), and academic reference models. These models were compared and contrasted with the proposed SSCC architecture, highlighting complementarities, gaps, and opportunities for integration across physical infrastructure, sensor and data layers, digital modeling, governance, and assessment mechanisms.

3.1. Standards Based Foundations for Urban Architecture

The development of the SSCC architecture is based on international standardization efforts that aim to guide urban innovation toward sustainability, efficiency, and resilience. Two key references—the U4SSC initiative and the ISO 37106:2021 standard—provide structured pathways and operational models for the design and governance of smart sustainable cities.

The U4SSC initiative, coordinated by ITU, UNECE, and UN-Habitat, offers a four-step framework for implementing circular cities. This approach emphasizes: (1) establishing a baseline for urban circularity, (2) identifying and prioritizing circular actions across city assets and products, (3) deploying enablers to catalyze change, and (4) evaluating impacts using context-specific key performance indicators [7]. These steps are supported by tools and templates to streamline the assessment of urban circularity, covering areas such as energy, water, mobility, and waste.

Complementing this, ISO 37106:2021 introduces an operational model for digitally enabled smart cities, structured around four layers: (1) Leadership and governance, (2) Service and process integration (customer delivery), (3) Data and information management, and

(4) ICT infrastructure. This operational model supports horizontal integration across urban services and vertical coordination among governance, data strategy, and infrastructure. ISO 37106 encourages cities to move from siloed operations toward a "digital by default" service model, ensuring that urban processes are interoperable, citizen-centered, and responsive [12]. In practice, this shift enables urban services like integrated waste and water management platforms, mobility-as-a-service systems that combine different transport modes, energy efficiency initiatives linked to real-time consumption data, and participatory governance portals for citizen feedback. These services show how the model goes beyond simply applying technology to existing structures: it redefines how urban services are delivered, making them cross-sectoral, adaptable, and accountable. Figure 2 illustrates this transition, highlighting how siloed urban services are reorganized through governance changes that emphasize transparency, stakeholder collaboration, and integration of internal city systems.

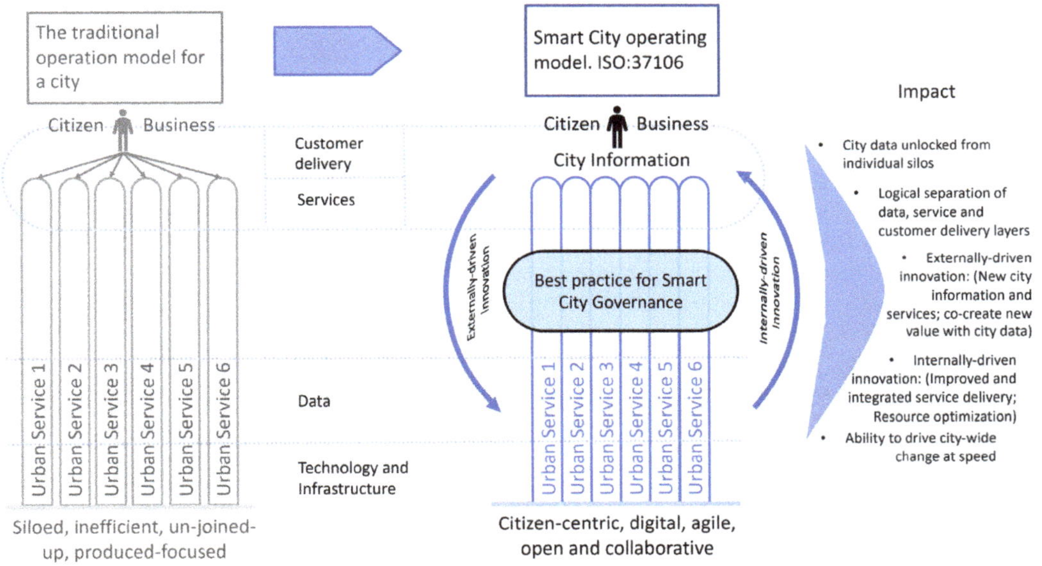

Figure 2. Transforming the city's operation model based on ISO 37106:2021.

Together, these frameworks outline both a strategic roadmap (U4SSC) and an operational architecture (ISO 37106) for implementing sustainable and smart urban systems. While U4SSC emphasizes sustainability transitions through circular actions, ISO 37106 concentrates on institutional transformation through digital capabilities. Their integration provides valuable guidance for constructing architectures that connect physical infrastructure, digital systems, and governance mechanisms—a foundational perspective for the SSCC model proposed in this study.

3.2. Academic Reference Models and Urban Architecture Definitions

The concept of smart city architecture in academic literature reflects a growing effort to organize urban complexity using clear frameworks. According to Anthopoulos [13], smart city architecture refers to *"the structured arrangement of digital and non-digital components that interact through services, data, and processes to support urban functionality"*. This definition highlights that architecture is not just a technological plan but a systemic setup of interconnected layers—physical, digital, social, and institutional—aligned with strategic urban goals.

Anthopoulos emphasizes two key roles of smart city architectures:

1. Operational integration, which ensures smooth interaction across physical infrastructure, data platforms, and user interfaces;
2. Strategic alignment, which connects technological deployments with urban priorities like resilience, inclusivity, and sustainability.

From an academic perspective, several reference models have been proposed to conceptualize smart city architectures. Anthopoulos' n-tier architecture model is one of the most influential, emphasizing a layered approach that includes data, infrastructure, interconnection, business, services, and user layers. This structure enables a modular and scalable design that supports both technological integration and governance needs [14].

Building on this vision, the Smart City Reference Architecture Model (SCRAM) proposed by Zygiaris [15] highlights the importance of planning ecosystems composed of green infrastructure, interconnected systems, instrumented platforms, applications, innovation layers, and governance. To integrate these two perspectives within our SSCC architecture, we adopt a layered approach where shared elements—such as data and infrastructure management, interconnection mechanisms, and governance functions—are aligned across both models. Key factors guiding this integration include interoperability standards (e.g., open APIs and data models), cross-cutting governance mechanisms that coordinate innovation and service delivery, and modular design principles allowing different layers to be adapted without disrupting the entire system. This approach ensures that both technological and governance aspects are incorporated while maintaining flexibility for validation through ULL experimentation.

Another perspective comes from enterprise architecture, as reviewed by Mamkaitis et al. [16], which applies the TOGAF Architecture Development Method (ADM) to classify smart city concerns into "why," "what," and "how." This framework helps organize technological and organizational processes in cities as enterprise-like systems, providing a structured approach for incremental development and integration [16].

Furthermore, the IDEAL-CITIES platform offers a trustworthy and secure framework designed for circular smart cities. Its architecture combines IoT, data security, resilience, and citizen participation into an operational backend made up of communication middleware, security mechanisms, and an application manager. It exemplifies how urban platforms can structurally embed circular economy and sustainability goals within smart city frameworks [17].

Additionally, there are some technical references like the FIWARE Reference Architecture, which proposes a modular, open-source model based on a Context Broker and the NGSI-LD data interface. It enables interoperability across domains—such as energy, mobility, and waste—by integrating IoT devices, open APIs, and semantic data structures [18]. In the SSCC architecture, energy is obtained from renewable sources at the community scale (e.g., solar modules in the urban garden), monitored through IoT sensors, and linked to demand management services. Waste is managed through participatory detection (community and drone imagery), classification using AI, and integration with municipal collection systems. These services are designed to be compatible with community needs by addressing daily concerns such as cleaner public spaces, efficient irrigation in the urban garden, and real-time feedback on service performance. Linking is achieved through the Context Broker, which enables waste, energy, and mobility data to flow across domains, supporting composite services like waste-to-alert systems or energy-to-irrigation control. Participation is integrated through Urban Living Labs (ULLs), where individuals contribute data, validate system outputs, and influence service design. Meanwhile, the Cyber–Physical System (CPS)/IoT Architecture outlined by NIST emphasizes the coordination between sensing, actuation, computation, and communication [19], providing the foundational layers that support this physical-digital integration in real-time.

Together, these models highlight a common goal: to develop layered, interoperable, and adaptable architectures that handle urban complexity. However, they differ in emphasis. Some models focus on technical integration (e.g., FIWARE, CPS), while others prioritize institutional coordination (e.g., enterprise architecture, SCRAM) or normative principles (e.g., Ideal Cities). These models also lay the groundwork for analyzing and designing smart city architectures that are adaptable, inclusive, and capable of evaluation.

The SSCC architecture discussed in this paper extends these traditions by explicitly incorporating circularity as an urban function, evaluation, and innovation management. The next section explains the structure and reasoning behind the SSCC model in detail.

3.3. *Proposed Architecture for Sustainable, Smart, and Circular Cities (SSCCs)*

The proposed SSCC architecture responds to the limitations and biases identified in existing smart city models. While useful, most current frameworks either focus on technological management without fully incorporating circularity and sustainability principles or emphasize governance without the operational mechanisms needed for systemic change.

Additionally, SSCC architecture responds to the fragmentation and siloed implementation often seen in urban technology strategies.

The model's structure was developed through a synthesis process involving the following:

- An analysis of international standards like ISO 37106 and the U4SSC implementation pathway.
- A critical review of academic models focusing on interoperability, adaptability, and governance alignment.
- The identification of three interconnected systemic components of a nexus: waste, energy, and information, which define the metabolic, energetic, and informational cycles that a circular smart city must manage.

In operational terms, the SSCC architecture addresses the three identified nexuses with specific mechanisms. Clean energy is produced from distributed renewable sources, such as solar panels in community facilities and microgrids, which are monitored through IoT sensors to ensure pollutant-free supply and efficient distribution. Different types of waste are managed through complementary flows: organic waste is processed into compost for urban agriculture, recyclable materials are redirected into municipal and community recycling streams, and residual waste is tracked for collection through participatory detection and AI-supported classification. Information generated across these processes—such as energy production, waste detection, and service usage—is collected via IoT devices and citizen reports, standardized through open APIs, and integrated into the digital twin (a *digital twin* is a virtual replica of urban systems that mirrors their physical, social, and environmental dynamics in real-time to enable monitoring, simulation, and decision support). This ensures that data not only documents performance but also actively supports decision-making and ongoing adaptation across the different layers of the architecture.

This resulted in organizing the SSCC architecture into four core functional layers called Urban Functions, supported by cross-cutting layers that ensure strategic alignment and assessability, as shown in Figure 3.

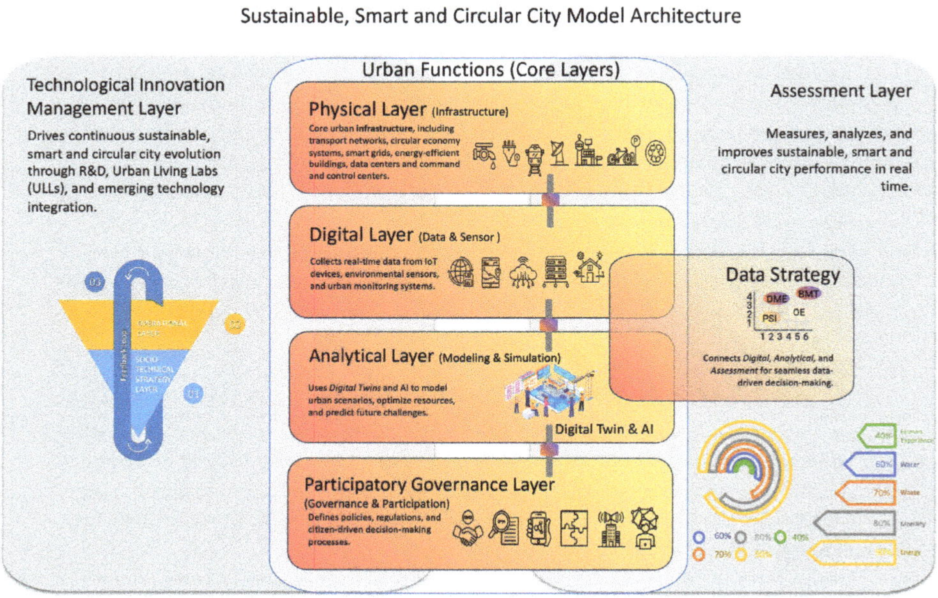

Figure 3. Sustainable, Smart and Circular City Model Architecture.

3.3.1. Urban Functions (Core Layers)

The SSCC model organizes the operational aspect of the city into four core layers, collectively known as Urban Functions. Each layer represents a key urban capability that supports the city's metabolism, manages urban services, and advances its transition toward sustainability and circularity. These functions are designed to be interoperable, not isolated, in line with the architectural principles outlined in ISO 37106 [12]. These layers form the structure of the city's operational dimension:

1. Physical Layer (Infrastructure Function):
   This layer encompasses the urban infrastructure systems that support the city's physical operations. It includes networks for energy, water, transportation, sanitation, and waste management, as well as essential digital infrastructure such as data centers and command-and-control centers. In the SSCC architecture, clean energy mainly originates from distributed renewable sources like solar panels on community facilities and microgrids, reducing dependence on fossil fuels and supplying pollution-free energy. Waste is managed through multiple streams: solid waste is reported via participatory methods and classified using AI; organic waste is composted in urban gardens; and recyclable materials (plastics, glass, metals) are diverted into municipal and community recycling processes. Data collected in this layer—such as real-time energy production, waste detection, and service usage—is made interoperable through IoT devices and open APIs, supporting higher layers of the architecture for monitoring, decision-making, and service enhancements. The Physical Layer serves as the tangible backbone of urban functionality and resilience, integrating civil and digital assets into a cohesive operational environment. Its inclusion addresses the need for physical–digital convergence and incorporates lessons from CPS and FIWARE architectures [13,16–18].
   Unlike traditional urban infrastructure, which is often linear and resource-intensive, the Physical Layer in a circular smart city features regenerative and interconnected systems. Energy networks prioritize renewable sources like solar microgrids, reducing

dependence on pollutants. Waste management shifts from end-of-pipe collection to infrastructure that supports sorting, recycling, and composting at various scales. Transportation is improved not only by roads and transit lines but also through shared electric fleets and smart charging stations. Additionally, digital infrastructure is designed to seamlessly integrate with physical assets, enabling real-time monitoring and optimization via IoT and digital twins. This redesign distinguishes circular smart cities from conventional urban areas by embedding circularity and intelligence directly into their infrastructure's design and operation.

2. Digital Layer (Sensing and Data Acquisition Function):
   The digital layer allows the city to perceive and record its state and processes. It includes IoT sensors, edge devices, user-reporting platforms, and telemetry systems that monitor key urban metrics like air quality, traffic flow, energy use, and public safety. Using standardized interfaces and real-time protocols (e.g., NGSI-LD), this layer gathers detailed data from the physical environment, ensuring observability and supporting situational awareness. Importantly, this online feature specifically applies to the Digital Layer and not the entire SSCC model. To prevent system failures, the layer has redundancy features such as distributed edge processing, local data buffering, and fallback procedures that enable services to keep running in degraded mode until connectivity is restored. Additionally, participatory reporting platforms provide an offline backup, ensuring critical information can still be gathered through community input. This design helps maintain system resilience even if parts of the digital infrastructure are temporarily offline. It thus serves as the essential input system for analysis and decision-support tools.
3. Analytical Layer (Modeling and Simulation Function):
   This layer defines the city's ability to model, simulate, and predict outcomes using real-time and historical data. It combines digital twin environments, AI-based analytics, scenario simulators, and system dynamics models to assess impacts, forecast demands, and evaluate urban policy options. By turning raw data into strategic insights, this layer supports evidence-based planning, operational improvements, and adaptive governance. It functions as the intelligence core of the SSCC architecture.
4. Participatory Governance Layer (Coordination and Co-decision Function):
   This layer organizes the institutional and collaborative processes through which the city involves stakeholders in co-design, oversight, and collective decision-making. It includes digital participation platforms, stakeholder engagement mechanisms, governance protocols, and interfaces for citizen science (e.g., ULLs) and deliberation. Its goal is to embed democratic legitimacy and local knowledge into the operation of all other layers, ensuring that the SSCC develops in a socially inclusive, accountable, and context-aware way.

These four layers interact dynamically, supported by the Innovation Management Layer, the Assessment Layer, and the Data Strategy.

3.3.2. Transversal Strategic Layers

Three more layers enhance strategic and operational consistency within the architecture:

1. Technological Innovation Management Layer:
   This layer acts as the engine of ongoing urban development. Operated through Urban Living Labs (ULLs), this layer supports experimentation, evaluation, and scaling of socio-technical innovations. It encourages collaboration among academia, public agencies, communities, and startups, and connects innovation directly to urban value creation.

2. Assessment Layer:
This layer supports dynamic monitoring and assessment of performance at all levels. It implements real-time and lagging KPIs within sustainable, smart, and circular city frameworks. In practice, evaluation combines live monitoring (through IoT data streams and dashboards) with structured self-assessments and progress reports created by various actors involved in service delivery. These reports may include institutional reviews, operator records, or participatory inputs when available, ensuring that information reflects both quantitative metrics and qualitative validation. Evaluation thus has a hybrid nature: automated indicators (e.g., ISO and LEED-based KPIs) are supplemented by reporting and review cycles from multiple stakeholders to ensure accuracy, transparency, and alignment with local priorities. The Assessment Layer facilitates adaptive governance by closing the loop between data collection, simulation, action, and learning. It primarily relies on KPIs for Sustainable Cities [20] and the Leadership in Energy and Environmental Design (LEED) rating systems [21], which measure improvements in urban services such as energy, water, waste, transportation, and human experience, in line with the UN Sustainable Development Goals.
3. Data Strategy Layer:
This transversal layer acts as a strategic enabler throughout the entire SSCC architecture. Instead of being merely a technical component, the data strategy is viewed as a socio-technical planning tool that guides how urban data is collected, integrated, managed, and used to create value across different domains. This layer defines three primary functions:
   (i) Data acquisition: ensuring participatory and interoperable data flows from three main sources—sensor and IoT networks capturing environmental, energy, and mobility data; citizen inputs via reporting platforms and mobile apps; and institutional records like municipal databases or operator reports. The collection process uses open standards (e.g., NGSI-LD), APIs, and interoperability protocols to ensure consistency and comparability;
   (ii) Data processing: supporting structured analytics through AI pipelines, edge–cloud architectures, and semantic alignment. This includes anomaly detection, combining diverse datasets, and preparing real-time inputs for the digital twin, ensuring data streams are reliable and usable across layers;
   (iii) Data application: converting insights into informed decisions, operational improvements, and co-creating public services. Examples include dynamic waste collection routes, adaptive urban garden irrigation, and citizen dashboards that foster transparency and participation.

   Within the SSCC model, the data strategy layer supports four value creation mechanisms: Decision-Making Enhancement (DME), Operational Efficiency (OE), Product and Service Innovation (PSI), and Business Model Transformation (BMT). It connects the digital, analytical, and assessment layers while also incorporating principles of inclusivity, ethics, and data justice [22]. This placement ensures that data does not just support city functions but actively drives urban transformation, linking sensing, modeling, participation, and evaluation within a unified and adaptable governance framework.

3.3.3. Comparative Positioning Within the Smart City Architecture Landscape

To evaluate the uniqueness and added benefits of the SSCC architecture, a comparative analysis was performed against a selection of leading smart city models. These include academic frameworks, institutional and enterprise models, and technology-centric platforms.

Each of these models provides valuable insights in areas such as interoperability, system integration, innovation support, or trust and security management.

However, the comparative review also highlights important gaps: most models lack built-in mechanisms for circularity, do not institutionalize innovation management, or treat evaluation as an external or ad hoc process. In contrast, the SSCC model positions sustainability, circularity, innovation, and evaluation as core architectural elements, implemented through clearly defined layers and interdependencies.

Table 1 summarizes the main differences and complementarities among these models, highlighting how the SSCC architecture builds on existing paradigms while addressing their structural limitations. This comparison supports the argument that the SSCC model provides a strong and scalable framework for managing complex urban transitions in a clear, participatory, and measurable way.

Table 1. Comparative positioning with key differences across models.

Model/ Framework	Main Focus	Key Layers/ Components	Circularity Integration	Evaluation Mechanisms
Anthopoulos n-tier	Layered architecture for ICT-enabled urban services and governance	Data, infrastructure, interconnection, business, services, users	Implied via sustainability, not explicit	Not central to model
Smart City Reference Architecture Model (SCRAM)	Innovation ecosystems and planning layers for smart cities	Green infrastructure, systems, platforms, apps, innovation, governance	Partially considered under sustainability goals	Implied via case studies and planning metrics
Enterprise Architecture (TOGAF-based)	Enterprise system modeling for incremental integration and governance	Business, application, data, technology (TOGAF ADM phases)	Not directly addressed	Enterprise KPIs and structured development phases
IDEAL-CITIES Framework	Secure and circular smart city architecture with IoT and citizen trust	Middleware, security layer, application manager, IoT/citizen interface	Explicit integration of circular economy principles	Security, trust, resilience metrics
FIWARE Architecture	Open-source, interoperable platform for smart cities with context data management	IoT agents, Context Broker (NGSI-LD), data/API management, digital twin integration	Dependent on use case; enables integration with circular services but not built-in	No inherent evaluation layer; depends on external dashboards or KPIs
NIST CPS/IoT Framework	Integration of cyber–physical systems with IoT for responsive, real-time city operations	Sensing, control, computation, communication, actuation	Not explicitly included; focus is on functional system interoperability and reliability	Focus on system performance, safety, and operational metrics; not sustainability KPIs
SSCC Architecture (Proposed)	Integration of sustainability, circularity, innovation and evaluation in urban systems	Physical infrastructure, Digital (sensors), Analytical (modeling/simulation), participatory governance, innovation management, data strategy, assessment	Core principle; waste-energy-information nexus articulated	Explicit assessment layer with sustainability and circular KPIs

4. Conceptual Framework for Transversal Layers: Integrating Innovation Management and Evaluation into the SSCC Architecture

The design of a Sustainable, Smart, and Circular City (SSCC) architecture requires cross-cutting components that support both innovation management and strong assessment mechanisms. While the core urban functions address the technological and participatory aspects of the system, these cross-cutting layers provide essential support for ongoing improvement and strategic alignment. In this section, we discuss two key cross-cutting layers: the Technological Innovation Management Layer and the Assessment Layer. Both layers build on our previous work on the Technological Innovation Model [23] and the multidimensional approach for assessing smart cities in developing countries [24].

4.1. Technological Innovation Management: Key Approaches

This layer provides the strategic and operational foundation for innovation management within the SSCC model. Based on the principles of Urban Living Labs (ULLs), it promotes collaborative, context-aware, and measurable urban innovation, addressing systemic urban challenges through co-creation, testing, and ongoing learning. The management of this layer is influenced by factors such as stakeholder engagement, institutional alignment, resource availability, and the maturity of tested solutions. Potential gaps—such as limited participation, weak institutional adoption, or barriers to scaling—are addressed through cycles of experimentation, feedback, and co-creation.

The innovation management model, as shown in Figure 4, integrated into this SSCC model layer, is structured around two interrelated domains.

Figure 4. Technological Innovation Management Layer.

Strategic Layer: Establishes the vision and governance structures for urban experimentation. It aligns technological interventions with sustainability goals, encourages stakeholder participation, and institutionalizes ongoing evaluation. It incorporates five socio-technical strategies [25]:

1. Enhancing civic engagement through digital and analog co-design mechanisms;
2. Facilitating physical and virtual testing environments;
3. Establishing adaptive governance for collaborative coordination;
4. Linking technologies with the dynamics of real urban life;
5. Ensuring integration of scalable, smart solutions grounded in local realities.

Operational Layer: Implements strategies through designated roles (coordinators, creators, enablers, providers, users) and feedback systems that link experimentation with measurable results. It uses platforms like digital twins to facilitate real-time learning and establishes KPIs for quality of life, productivity, and ICT-driven sustainability.

The layer is informed by empirical insights from the Fenicia ULL in Bogotá, a pilot that exemplifies urban innovation amid institutional fragmentation, limited digital infrastructure, and social complexity. In this context, the innovation model supports adaptive processes, stakeholder alignment, and the integration of smart solutions—especially around the waste–energy–information nexus.

Furthermore, the Technological Innovation Management Layer turns the SSCC into a dynamic innovation ecosystem, ensuring that urban transformation remains not only technological but also inclusive, participatory, and sustainable over time.

Orchestrating the SSCC Model Through the Technological Innovation Management Layer

The Technological Innovation Management (TIM) Layer is essential for orchestrating the SSCC model, acting as the catalyst for systemic change. Instead of viewing innovation as an external or spontaneous force, the SSCC framework treats it as a controlled and coordinated process that connects experimentation, stakeholder involvement, and iterative learning with urban planning and service design.

This orchestration aligns with and strengthens the implementation guidance of both ISO 37106 and the U4SSC framework in the following ways:

Alignment with ISO 37106: ISO 37106 defines an operational model that facilitates the shift from siloed, analog systems to integrated, data-driven, and citizen-centered cities. The SSCC's innovation layer addresses several key components of this transformation:

- "Leadership and governance" by establishing adaptive, multistakeholder governance through ULLs;
- "Service and process integration" by enabling testbeds that align services and innovation with community needs and local infrastructure;
- "Data and information management" through the use of platforms like digital twins, which enable real-time monitoring, traceability, and collaborative simulation;
- "ICT infrastructure" involves using participatory technologies to involve users in the innovation process, turning infrastructure into a civic asset.

Alignment with U4SSC Framework: The U4SSC methodology outlines four steps: (i) establishing baselines, (ii) identifying and prioritizing circular actions, (iii) deploying enablers, and (iv) evaluating impacts. The SSCC's innovation layer directly supports this pathway.

- As a platform for experimentation, it supports Step 2, which involves identifying circular actions that are locally feasible and impactful (e.g., waste-to-energy pilots);
- Through Urban Living Labs, it functions as a city enabler (Step 3), speeding up innovation adoption and local adaptation;
- By incorporating monitoring and assessment mechanisms, it lays the groundwork for Step 4, where urban impacts are evaluated and strategies are improved.

Regarding evaluation, the TIM Layer supports a phased and iterative process that begins with preparation (designing pilots and assessing readiness), moves through experimentation (ULL-based testing), and advances into operational deployment and scaling. Evaluation is guided by indicators from international standards (ISO 37120, LEED for Cities/Communities) and readiness frameworks (TRL, SRL, ORL), ensuring comprehensive coverage of technological, social, and organizational components. In this way, the TIM Layer coordinates innovation processes and aligns them with governance frameworks, while the Assessment Layer ensures that monitoring and validation are carried out systematically.

4.2. Smart Cities Assessment: Key Approaches

In developing countries, the assessment of smart cities has become increasingly important as cities adopt digital technologies to address major challenges like rapid urbanization, socio-economic inequalities, and sustainability. Implementing smart technologies in these regions holds the potential to greatly improve the quality of life and the efficiency of urban services, though it also presents unique challenges related to infrastructure and governance. According to Esashika [26], the evaluation of smart cities can be approached through several key frameworks. One approach focuses on ranking, comparing the performance of different cities using standardized indicators, while another assesses the maturity of smart cities by evaluating their level of technological adoption and public policy development. Additionally, the data-driven management approach emphasizes real-time management using big data, and the innovation ecosystem approach highlights collaboration among governments, academia, industry, and civil society to foster urban innovation.

These approaches, widely used worldwide, provide a solid foundation for evaluating the progress of smart cities. However, in developing countries, where social inequalities are greater and resources are scarcer, it is crucial to supplement these methods with an additional approach: Conscious and Inclusive Communities. This framework ensures that urban development is not only technologically advanced but also fair and participatory, focusing on the needs and realities of local communities as the core of the transformation process. Table 2 outlines the main features of each approach.

Table 2. Smart Cities Assessment.

Key Approach	Generalities
Ranking Approach	Based on rankings which compare the performance of cities based on standardized indicators such as mobility, governance, sustainability, and quality of life.
Maturity Approach	It classifies cities into stages, from early technology implementation to advanced integration of smart solutions.
Data-Driven Management Approach	Leverages technologies such as big data, IoT, and sensors to collect and analyze real-time data, optimizing urban services like mobility, waste management, and energy consumption.
Innovation Ecosystem Approach	Emphasizes collaboration between government, industry, and academia to drive urban innovation.
Conscious and Inclusive Communities Approach	Focused on ensuring that smart city development does not exacerbate social inequalities but instead promotes inclusion and equity.

The following section outlines these five key approaches, tailored to evaluating smart cities in developing countries, each providing a vital perspective for understanding and enhancing the urban transformation process in these areas.

4.2.1. Ranking Approach

The classification approach to smart city evaluation relies on the use of rankings, which compare the performance of cities based on standardized indicators such as mobility, governance, sustainability, and quality of life [27]. These rankings provide a quantitative snapshot of how cities perform in key areas of urban development, offering governments, policymakers, and stakeholders a clear view of where their cities stand in comparison to others. By identifying strengths and weaknesses in urban systems, this approach helps to pinpoint specific areas that require improvement, fostering more targeted policy interventions [28].

Several contemporary rankings evaluate smart cities, each with specific regional focuses and criteria. In Europe, the European Smart Cities Ranking by Giffinger et al. [29] continues to be influential, alongside the CITYkeys initiative, which prioritizes sustainability and innovation metrics [30]. Globally, the IMD Smart City Index (2023) and the Networked Society City Index by Ericsson [31] focus on holistic smart city metrics, including connectivity and citizen engagement. Other indices, such as the Smart City Index [32] and the IESE Cities in Motion Index 2023 [33], assess a city's performance across dimensions like mobility, governance, and quality of life, offering a comprehensive view of urban development.

In the context of developing countries, where cities often face significant disparities in infrastructure, technological capabilities, and governance, the classification approach serves as a particularly useful tool for benchmarking progress [28,34]. It allows cities to set clear, measurable goals and track their development over time relative to international standards. This is important for cities striving to enhance their global competitiveness while addressing critical challenges such as poverty, transportation inefficiencies, and energy shortages. Rankings also provide a means to promote transparency and accountability, as they allow citizens and stakeholders to assess the effectiveness of local governance based on visible, standardized criteria.

However, while the classification approach offers substantial benefits, it is not without challenges. In developing countries, there is often a lack of reliable and consistent data, which can undermine the accuracy and usefulness of rankings. Cities in these regions may struggle to collect the high-quality data necessary to measure performance across various indicators due to financial constraints, technical limitations, or insufficient administrative capacity. This data gap can lead to skewed or incomplete evaluations, potentially misrepresenting a city's actual progress or needs. Furthermore, the focus on measurable indicators can sometimes overlook critical qualitative aspects of urban life, such as social inclusion and community engagement, which are harder to quantify but equally essential to the success of smart city initiatives [35].

Despite these challenges, the classification approach remains a powerful tool for urban development in developing countries. It provides a structured, comparative framework that enables cities to benchmark their progress and set ambitious yet achievable targets. For governments, these rankings offer a roadmap to prioritize investments and reforms in areas where cities are lagging behind. Additionally, rankings serve as an important motivational tool, encouraging cities to improve their standing by implementing new policies, technologies, and governance strategies that address their specific shortcomings. The competitive nature of rankings can drive innovation, as cities seek to enhance their performance and visibility on a global stage [36].

In summary, the classification approach is highly valuable in promoting smart city development, especially in developing countries where the need for clear, actionable metrics is crucial. However, it must be adapted to the local context, with efforts made to improve data collection processes and account for qualitative dimensions of urban life. Despite its limitations, the visibility and accountability that rankings provide make them an indispensable tool for cities aiming to enhance their sustainability, governance, and overall quality of life.

4.2.2. Maturity Approach

The maturity approach evaluates a smart city's development by examining factors such as technological infrastructure, the adoption of public policies, and social engagement [37,38]. It classifies cities into stages, from early technology implementation to advanced integration of smart solutions. In developing countries, this approach helps cities identify strategic priorities, focusing on infrastructure and regulatory frameworks to advance towards higher levels of smart city development [35,39].

By assessing a city's technological readiness and governance capacity, the maturity approach provides a roadmap for policy and infrastructure improvements. Early-stage cities might prioritize basic infrastructure such as internet access and urban sensors, while more advanced cities could focus on smart transportation systems and real-time data analytics [40].

This approach is particularly valuable for developing countries, as it highlights developmental gaps and enables cities to set incremental goals aligned with their current capabilities. Policymakers can use this framework to understand which policies or interventions are needed to transition from one stage to the next, such as strengthening governance structures or enhancing public–private partnerships.

Despite its benefits, the maturity approach faces challenges, particularly in developing regions, where financial and resource constraints, along with political instability, can slow progress. For this reason, the approach advocates a phased, long-term strategy, ensuring cities gradually build the foundations for a more advanced smart city ecosystem.

Ultimately, the maturity approach remains an essential tool for guiding sustainable and inclusive urban growth. By understanding where a city stands in its development cycle, urban managers can make more informed decisions, allowing for targeted interventions and tailored strategies that address both technological and social needs.

4.2.3. Data-Driven Management Approach

The data-driven management approach leverages technologies such as big data, IoT, and sensors to collect and analyze real-time data, optimizing urban services like mobility, waste management, and energy consumption [41]. This approach enables cities to make informed and efficient decisions, adjusting operations dynamically to improve both service delivery and urban quality of life. In developing countries, data-driven systems present significant opportunities to enhance efficiency and transparency, addressing challenges such as congestion, pollution, and resource management [42].

By integrating real-time technologies, cities can optimize systems like traffic flow and energy use, becoming more responsive and adaptable [43]. This approach allows cities to bypass traditional urban management methods, streamlining processes and reducing inefficiencies. For example, real-time data on waste collection can optimize routes, lowering fuel costs, while smart meters can help reduce energy waste.

Despite its potential, technological infrastructure remains a key challenge in developing countries. The installation of sensors and data platforms requires substantial investment, and even where infrastructure exists, data processing capacity and skills gaps may limit effectiveness. Data privacy and security concerns also arise, particularly in regions with weak regulations, where there is a risk of data misuse or dependency on large technology firms.

Nevertheless, the benefits of data-driven management for improving urban efficiency, cost savings, and citizen engagement are substantial. It offers cities the ability to monitor and adjust their operations in real-time, fostering sustainable urban growth and better meeting the needs of the population [44]. While challenges remain, data-driven approaches represent a crucial step toward smarter, more responsive cities, especially in developing countries.

4.2.4. Innovation Ecosystem Approach

The innovation ecosystem approach, based on the Triple Helix model, emphasizes collaboration between government, industry, and academia to drive urban innovation. Over time, this model evolved into the Quadruple Helix, adding civil society as a crucial pillar, recognizing the role that citizens play in shaping city development [45]. By involving a broad spectrum of stakeholders, the model ensures that smart city solutions are not only technologically advanced but also aligned with the needs of the local population [46].

In developing countries, where technological and socio-economic barriers often exist, this approach is particularly important. Collaboration between sectors helps cities overcome challenges related to infrastructure, governance, and economic development. Governments provide regulatory support, industries offer technologies, academia supplies research, and civil society ensures inclusivity. Urban Living Labs (ULLs) exemplify this approach by engaging stakeholders—including citizens—in the testing and implementation of smart technologies, ensuring that innovations benefit all segments of the population, particularly the marginalized [47].

The innovation ecosystem approach operates on the principle that no single sector can address urban challenges alone. By fostering collaboration, it offers a holistic framework where each actor contributes unique capabilities to create sustainable and innovative solutions [48]. It also promotes the democratization of innovation, ensuring that citizens actively participate in the development of technologies that shape their cities.

However, the approach's success depends on effective coordination among stakeholders, which can be hindered by institutional silos, misaligned incentives, or a lack of trust. Cities must therefore promote inclusive governance frameworks that encourage open communication and shared accountability.

This approach is justified by its ability to create locally relevant and adaptable solutions, ensuring that smart city initiatives in developing countries become catalysts for broader transformation, not isolated experiments. The emphasis on collaborative learning ensures that smart city technologies are not only cutting-edge but also socially relevant and scalable to diverse urban contexts.

The innovation ecosystem approach is vital for developing smart cities, particularly in developing regions where challenges demand a collective effort. By fostering cooperation between government, industry, academia, and civil society, cities can co-create solutions that are inclusive, innovative, and sustainable, ensuring that technologies address the real needs of the communities they serve.

4.2.5. Conscious and Inclusive Communities Approach

The Conscious and Inclusive Communities approach, proposed as an original contribution of this study, focuses on ensuring that smart city development does not exacerbate social inequalities but instead promotes inclusion and equity [49–51]. This approach emphasizes the importance of involving local communities in all phases of smart city projects, from planning and implementation to governance. In developing countries, where inequalities are often deeper, this approach ensures that smart technologies address the real needs of marginalized populations, fostering urban development that is inclusive, culturally aware, and socially sustainable [50–52].

While other approaches prioritize technology, innovation, and institutional maturity, the Conscious and Inclusive Communities framework centers on people and communities as the core of the urban development process. The premise is that technology alone cannot solve urban problems unless the needs, active participation, and inclusion of citizens are considered [53,54]. The approach aims to mitigate urban inequalities, particularly in developing contexts, where smart city solutions, if not designed inclusively, risk worsening social divides. This approach ensures that the benefits of smart development reach all sectors of the population, especially the most vulnerable communities, which are often ignored in urban transformation processes [53,55].

The Conscious and Inclusive Communities framework promotes equitable and participatory development by fostering platforms where citizens are not only recipients of technology but co-creators of solutions [51]. Conscious inclusion ensures that residents can express their needs, participate in decision-making, and ensure that urban development respects their interests, identities, and cultures [53,56]. Moreover, cities that empower their communities through active and conscious participation are more resilient to challenges such as social, economic, or environmental crises. This approach highlights the importance of aligning urban development with local realities, drawing on the knowledge and adaptability of communities to create solutions that truly reflect their needs [51,56].

The justification for this approach is grounded in the need to overcome criticisms of traditional smart cities, which often prioritize technological infrastructure and economic efficiency over social contexts or the needs of the population [57]. As noted by scholars, one of the key criticisms of traditional smart city projects is their tendency to focus on technology without addressing the human element of urban life [57]. The Conscious and Inclusive Communities approach responds to these critiques by ensuring that technological solutions promote equitable and participatory development, rather than exacerbating social inequalities.

In developing countries, where inclusion and equity are not optional but essential for the success of any smart city project [28], this approach ensures that smart cities improve quality of life not just for the wealthiest or most connected sectors but for all citizens. This is particularly important for the disadvantaged communities, which are often the most affected by technological changes if they are not involved in the process from the start. By embedding inclusion and equity as central pillars of smart city development, the Conscious and Inclusive Communities framework ensures that cities become more just and resilient.

Furthermore, this approach complements the other evaluation frameworks—Classification, Maturity, Data-Driven Management, and Innovation Ecosystems—by ensuring that smart city assessments also measure their social impact and their capacity to include all citizens, regardless of socio-economic status. While the other approaches offer useful models for measuring and managing smart cities, they do not explicitly address the critical issues of social equity and participation. The Conscious and Inclusive Communities framework fills this gap, providing a more holistic view of urban development that goes beyond technological innovation to focus on social well-being.

Finally, the Conscious and Inclusive Communities approach promotes a broader vision of smart cities. True urban intelligence does not only lie in technological efficiency but in a city's ability to create a just, inclusive, and resilient society. The success of a smart city should not be measured solely by its ability to innovate, but by its capacity to improve the lives of all its citizens, ensuring that no one is left behind. This approach calls for a more inclusive evaluation of smart city initiatives, where success is defined not just by innovation metrics but by the social, economic, and cultural progress of the entire population.

4.2.6. Multidimensional Evaluation Framework

To effectively evaluate smart city initiatives, especially in the context of developing countries, a multidimensional framework is necessary. Such a framework must be attuned to local specificities and capable of supporting both strategic alignment and operational performance. The assessment model must, therefore, be flexible enough to accommodate diverse urban realities while enabling decision-makers to understand how digital, participatory, and innovative elements influence sustainable development outcomes.

The Assessment Layer is designed to align with the strategic objectives previously used in evaluating urban experiments within the ULL framework, specifically: quality of life, productivity, and ICT sustainability. These objectives ensure continuity and coherence across the SSCC evaluation structure and support the comparability of performance results over time and among initiatives. Consistent with the guiding principles of the SSCC model, this layer also emphasizes the interconnectedness of waste, energy, and information, positioning performance assessment not as a final step but as a dynamic process that both reflects and guides the city's transition pathways.

The evaluation approach used is organized around three primary strategic perspectives, each corresponding to particular layers in the SSCC architecture.

(a) Data-Driven Management Approach: This emphasizes how cities utilize digital technologies to enhance decision-making and improve services. It aligns with the SSCC model in the Digital Layer, Analytical Layer, and Data Strategy.
Data-Driven Management enables cities to create dashboards and simulations that inform policy development.

(b) Innovation Ecosystem Approach: This perspective focuses on how smart city projects create environments that support socio-technical innovation, collaboration, and entrepreneurship. It aligns with the SSCC model in the Technological Innovation Management Layer.
Innovation Ecosystem supports experimentation and rapid prototyping in ULLs.

(c) Conscious and Inclusive Communities Approach: This perspective highlights community participation, equity, and stakeholder engagement. It directly connects to the Participatory Governance Layer. Inclusive Communities helps identify barriers to participation and guides the development of fair governance frameworks.

These three approaches create a comprehensive framework for assessing smart city performance. They help in developing KPIs that are not only technical or operational but also social and inclusive.

The assessment framework proposes a multidimensional and inclusive approach that combines both quantitative tools—such as KPIs based on available data like energy usage, waste generation, or transportation efficiency—and qualitative tools, including participatory methods like focus groups, interviews, and co-design workshops that capture citizens' perceptions and experiences.

This structure supports ex ante assessment (e.g., before deploying a digital platform or service), ongoing assessment (e.g., tracking the adoption and impact of a smart waste management system), and ex-post assessment (e.g., measuring social inclusion outcomes after a participatory mobility planning process).

The adapted model highlights the following attributes:

- Inclusivity: Tools that capture diverse voices and community perspectives.
- Adaptability: Suitability for different urban settings and scalable from pilot projects to city-wide programs.
- Co-creation: A focus on KPIs created through participatory processes.
- Digital transparency: Utilization of open data and digital platforms to foster trust and promote accountability.
- Learning and iteration: Feedback loops that allow cities to evolve through evidence and citizen input.

This Assessment Layer is further enhanced by incorporating evaluation methodologies and indicators from complementary sources. The Arc and LEED for Cities and Communities frameworks provide a strong structure for measuring performance through quantifiable scores in areas like energy, water, waste, transportation, and human experience. These are especially useful for benchmarking environmental and livability performance across urban systems [58]. Additionally, the Sustainable Cities Handbook [20] introduces context-sensitive KPIs relevant to the Global South, especially for waste management and energy use, which closely align with the SSCC model's focus on circularity and transition.

Furthermore, the Data Strategy Layer highlights the importance of aligning data collection and management processes with evaluative goals, enabling the strategic use of urban data to inform both the simulation (Analytical Layer) and participation (Governance Layer). Together, these sources help operationalize the Assessment Layer as a dynamic, evidence-based, and participatory tool, connecting strategic urban goals to concrete metrics for sustainable, smart, and circular city performance. Table 3 presents the proposed multidimensional evaluation KPIs. These KPIs are indicative and can be adjusted according to the requirements of each urban service.

Table 3. Multidimensional Evaluation KPIs.

Dimension/Layer	KPIs [1]		
Technological Innovation Management Layer	Number of ULL experiments conducted per year	Rate of innovation adoption in urban services	Socio—Technical Innovation Readiness (Technological—TRL, Social—SRL, Organizational—ORL, Scalability—ScR)
Physical Layer	Energy use intensity ($kWh/m^2/year$) [LEED]	Solid waste diverted from landfill (%) [LEED]	Access to public transportation within 800m (%) [Arc]
Digital Layer	Real-time sensor coverage (% urban space)	Open data availability index	IoT data quality compliance rate
Analytical Layer	Simulation-to-decision integration rate	Predictive modeling accuracy (by urban service)	Use of scenario planning tools in policy design
Participatory Governance Layer	Citizen engagement rate in decision-making (%)	Inclusion index (gender, age, income representation)	Co-creation sessions held per year
Data Strategy	Data governance maturity score	KPI alignment with strategic objectives	Stakeholder accessibility to performance dashboards
Assessment Layer	Overall SSCC performance score	Cross-dimensional KPI dashboard coverage (%)	Number of domains monitored in real-time (Energy, Water, Waste, Transportation, Human Experience)

[1] These KPIs are indicative and can be modified based on the requirements of each urban service.

While international frameworks like LEED and Arc offer a common structure for evaluation, their direct application in developing countries is often limited by regional factors such as data access, institutional capacity, and infrastructure gaps. To address this, the SSCC model adds more context-specific KPIs, especially from the Sustainable Cities Handbook, which focus on waste and energy metrics tailored to the Global South. As a result, the evaluation follows the same general framework as in developed countries but includes adjustments to account for local constraints and opportunities. Furthermore, the innovation ecosystem perspective is operationalized by connecting data on multi-actor collaboration (e.g., participation records, institutional partnerships, co-created services) with performance indicators. This approach ensures the evaluation not only measures infrastructure or environmental results but also explores how governance, community, and innovation ecosystems interact to support sustainable, smart, and circular transitions.

4.2.7. Operationalizing the SSCC Model Through the Assessment Layer

The Assessment Layer is a vital component that enables the operationalization of the SSCC model by turning its conceptual framework into a results-oriented system. This is accomplished through a set of multidimensional KPIs that facilitate ongoing monitoring, benchmarking, and strategic alignment. Its design aligns with major international standards and frameworks that support the development of smart, sustainable cities.

This layer aligns with and supports the implementation guidance of both ISO 37106 and the U4SSC framework in the following ways:

Alignment with ISO 37106: ISO 37106 provides a framework for local governments to develop smart city operating models that are agile, transparent, and citizen-focused. The SSCC Assessment Layer helps implement this in the following ways:

- Performance-based management: The layer creates a clear system of indicators linked to city goals (e.g., quality of life, sustainability), allowing municipalities to shift from reactive to data-driven decision-making.
- Evidence-based evaluation cycles: These support ongoing improvement loops, as required in ISO 37106, allowing for iterative assessment of pilots and programs, especially in ULLs.
- Stakeholder participation: Using qualitative methods (e.g., co-design sessions, inclusive metrics) ensures the integration of user feedback, supporting the standard's call for inclusive and transparent governance.
- Cross-silo integration: KPIs are connected to various SSCC layers (e.g., digital infrastructure, innovation management), encouraging interdepartmental alignment and shared accountability related to different urban services—key principles of ISO 37106.

Alignment with U4SSC Implementation Framework: The U4SSC initiative offers a circular city implementation guide based on a four-step approach: (i) establishing baselines, (ii) identifying and prioritizing circular actions, (iii) deploying enablers, and (iv) evaluating impacts. The SSCC Assessment Layer aligns accordingly.

- Baseline establishment: Using multidimensional KPIs enables cities to evaluate their current status in areas such as waste, energy, water, and mobility—reflecting U4SSC's Step 1.
- Action prioritization: By mapping indicators to strategic objectives (e.g., productivity, sustainability), this layer enables informed prioritization of circular and digital actions.
- Enabler integration: The Assessment Layer uses tools like data governance protocols and open dashboards, which are defined in U4SSC as enablers for scaling action.
- Impact measurement: It offers a framework for continuous outcome evaluation using internationally benchmarked indicators (LEED, Arc), directly addressing Step 4 of the U4SSC model.

The Assessment Layer not only adheres to the guidelines of ISO 37106 and U4SSC, but also acts as a bridge between the strategic vision of the SSCC model and its practical application, making urban innovation cycles measurable, repeatable, and adaptable to different urban contexts.

5. Results

This section outlines the main empirical findings from implementing the SSCC model in the Fenicia ULL. A key insight from the research is that experimenting in isolation—focused on just one urban service—would not be enough to confirm the integrated vision proposed by the SSCC architecture.

Instead of trying to optimize waste management, energy systems, or information flows separately, the SSCC model aims to show how these elements connect through physical, digital, and social infrastructure. As a result, two coordinated experiments were created and implemented to put into practice and test the waste–energy–information nexus in real urban environments.

- Experiment 1 focused on AI-driven waste management in the neighborhood, using drone imagery, smartphone data, and community reports to locate, classify, and address waste. In this pilot, the AI model was trained and validated specifically to detect plastic bottles, which served as a representative category of recyclable waste. Community members submitted geotagged photos via a mobile platform, along with brief descriptions to report waste observations. Reports were verified by cross-checking submissions with drone imagery and manual validation by researchers in the Urban Living Lab. Although limited to one waste type, this process showed how AI detection, participatory reporting, and verification can be combined to support urban waste management, while also emphasizing the need to expand classification to other categories in future iterations.

- Experiment 2 assessed the socio-technical innovation of an urban garden equipped with solar-powered IoT sensors to monitor irrigation needs and explore ways toward energy self-sufficiency. The sensors tracked soil moisture, air temperature, and solar radiation, sending data to a cloud platform for real-time monitoring. Community members participated in the system through workshops and demonstrations, providing feedback on usability and the relevance of the information produced. Sensor data verification involved comparing automated readings with manual soil checks conducted by researchers. Although the pilot did not advance to a fully automated irrigation system, it showed how IoT and renewable energy can support participatory monitoring and raise community awareness of sustainable practices.

While each experiment has individual value, it is only when they are considered together—sharing data infrastructure, involving the same communities, and feeding into a common digital twin—that the model's transformative capacity becomes clear. The shift from siloed urban services to an integrated, circular ecosystem, as proposed by the SSCC architecture, requires this cross-experiment coordination. This section examines how each experiment helps validate specific layers of the SSCC model and how their integration supports systemic urban transformation.

Following this reasoning, the connection between both experiments was intentionally designed to prevent fragmentation and instead show how different urban interventions can work together as parts of an integrated sustainable system. This integration was organized according to the layered structure of the SSCC model, allowing a thorough validation of the waste–energy–information relationship through five main dimensions.

1. Shared physical infrastructure: Both experiments operate within the same urban area—the Fenicia neighborhood—and are connected via a common digital twin platform that spatially integrates waste reporting data, sensor-based monitoring, and geolocated intervention results. The neighborhood thus serves as a central point for multiple urban functions.
2. Common technological innovation layer: The two experiments use complementary emerging technologies. The waste management pilot applies AI for image classification and geolocation, while the urban garden incorporates IoT sensors powered by solar panels to monitor irrigation cycles. Both are integrated into the digital twin and designed to feed real-time data into participatory decision-making workflows.
3. Participation and governance layer: Residents and local actors (government, academia, civic organizations, and startups) are involved in both initiatives. Community members report waste via mobile platforms and take part in workshops to co-design and evaluate the urban garden sensor system. This shared participation not only boosts legitimacy but also supports the model's focus on inclusive governance.
4. Assessment layer: Key performance indicators (KPIs) from both experiments were designed to follow international standards like ISO 37106, U4SSC, and LEED for Communities. Metrics such as energy self-sufficiency, quality of life, waste reduction, and citizen engagement were used to track progress and evaluate replicability.

5. Scalability and replication potential: The modular design of both pilots enables them to be adapted to other urban settings. More importantly, their integration within the SSCC framework shows how cities can move from isolated pilots to scalable, system-wide solutions that connect environmental, technological, and social areas.

Together, these elements strongly support the SSCC model's main idea: that sustainable urban change needs not just new technologies, but also their coordination within a shared system that can connect services, infrastructure, and governance. In practice, this means sustainable transformation happens through specific services—like AI-assisted waste detection, IoT-based environmental monitoring, and participatory reporting—that turn abstract ideas of circularity into practical improvements for communities. Artificial intelligence helps these services by enabling automated classification, geolocation, and real-time feedback, thus linking digital abilities with real service delivery.

The validation of the SSCC model does not depend on testing each architectural layer separately, but instead on observing how these layers work together and support each other in real urban settings.

Table 4 explains how each SSCC model layer was implemented through the integrated experiments. It shows how the Physical and Digital Layers supported data collection, the Analytical Layer turned data into insights, the Participatory Governance Layer connected communities, the Data Strategy Layer ensured data compatibility, the Technological Innovation Management Layer coordinated experimentation, and the Assessment Layer carried out evaluations.

Table 4. Empirical evidence from Integrated Experiments.

SSCC Model Layer	Empirical Evidence from Integrated Experiments	Evaluation Ratio
Technological Innovation Management Layer	Application of the ULL based socio-technical innovation model in both experiments, using iterative design, multi-actor coordination, and testing in real-life settings.	High. (Social Readiness) SRL 7/(Organizational Readiness Level) ORL 5—Strong socio-technical engagement, moderate institutional uptake. Validated through continuous feedback loops and alignment with ISO 37106 operational guidance.
Physical Layer	Infrastructure of the Fenicia neighborhood used for both experiments; urban garden equipped with solar-powered IoT sensors; drones for photogrammetry-based 3D modeling.	Moderate. Tested in limited urban assets; infrastructure performance assessed mainly via pilot IoT and drone applications. Technological Readiness Level (TRL 6–7)—IoT prototypes tested in real context; drones validated for 3D mapping.
Digital Layer	Citizen-generated images (via smartphones and drones); sensor data from humidity, temperature, and solar radiation modules; data structured via FIWARE Smart Data Models.	High. Real-time acquisition validated; TRL 7—Validated in operational environment; interoperability tested through FIWARE standards.
Analytical Layer	Digital twins developed for both experiments: one for spatial waste accumulation simulation, another for agro-environmental monitoring and energy analysis in the urban garden	Moderate–High. Functionality of digital twins validated for visualization and analysis; predictive capacities still limited due to small datasets.
Participatory Governance Layer	Co-design sessions, structured feedback loops, and community sensing strategies; ongoing involvement of citizens in reporting, validation, and scenario planning.	High. (Social Readiness) SRL 7; Active community participation and validation; alignment with U4SSC inclusivity.

Table 4. *Cont.*

SSCC Model Layer	Empirical Evidence from Integrated Experiments	Evaluation Ratio
Data Strategy	Operationalized across acquisition, processing, and application domains; integration via Orion Context Broker, QuantumLeap, CrateDB; value created through mechanisms: Decision-Making Enhancement (DME), Operational Efficiency (OE), Product and Service Innovation (PSI), and Business Model Transformation (BMT).	Moderate. Interoperability validated; value creation mechanisms partially demonstrated in pilots; comprehensive integration still pending scaling.
Assessment Layer	KPI tracking aligned with ISO 37106, U4SSC, LEED for Communities; measuring Quality of Life, Productivity, and ICT-based Sustainability.	Moderate–High. KPIs defined and applied; coverage of sustainability dimensions validated, though benchmarking limited to pilot scale.

Note: Evaluation ratios combine quantitative results (e.g., TRL, SRL, ORL) with qualitative scales (Low, Moderate, High) derived from readiness frameworks and empirical validation in the Fenicia ULL. They are intended to be indicative rather than definitive, reflecting the pilot nature of the experiments.

The coordinated implementation of waste management and urban garden experiments thus shows the shift from isolated urban services to interconnected, circular city functions.

5.1. Waste Management Experiment: Validating Integrated Urban Intelligence

This section introduces the first experiment conducted at Fenicia ULL, which focused on developing a cyber–physical system (CPS) for participatory urban waste management over a one-month period from May to June 2025. The CPS integrated three types of data sources: (i) drone imagery for aerial identification of waste hotspots, (ii) photos uploaded by community members via a mobile platform, and (iii) geotagged annotations by researchers. The AI module was specifically trained to detect plastic bottles as a representative recyclable waste category. The CPS utilized multiple SSCC layers by combining physical sensing (Digital Layer), AI-based classification (Analytical Layer), participatory reporting (Governance Layer), and iterative validation through the ULL (Innovation and Assessment Layers). In this way, the CPS enabled not only automated waste detection but also verification and feedback from multiple stakeholders, demonstrating the feasibility of integrating cyber systems into circular waste management practices.

Figure 5 depicts the digital twin architecture developed for the Fenicia ULL waste management experiment, which, as shown in Figure 6, includes spatial data generation, citizen input, artificial intelligence, and geovisualization to enable the detection, simulation, and strategic planning of street-level waste.

5.1.1. Objectives of the Waste Experiment

The main objective of this experiment was to design, deploy, and validate a participatory CPS capable of identifying, classifying, and responding to solid waste accumulation in urban public spaces. The system aimed to achieve the following:

- Integrate citizen-generated and drone-acquired imagery.
- Process visual data using an AI model for waste classification and localization.
- Input data into a digital twin for real-time spatial visualization.
- Establish feedback and response systems at the institutional and community levels.

This directly supports the SSCC model's goal of moving from isolated public services to integrated, data-driven urban functions.

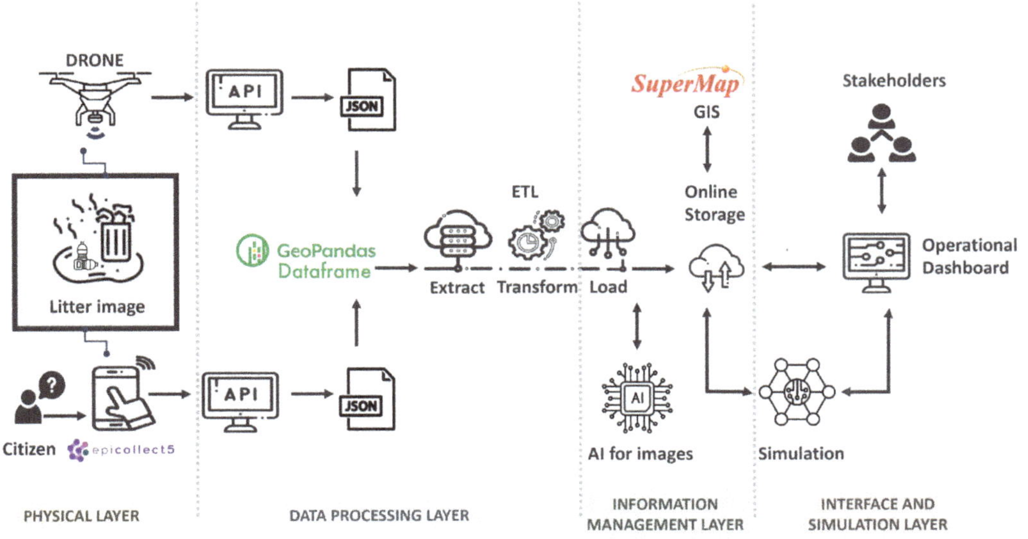

Figure 5. Digital Twin Architecture.

Figure 6. A neighbor taking a picture of litter using Epicollect 5, processed with AI, and visualized with a digital twin.

5.1.2. Methods and Implementation of the Waste Experiment

The system architecture consisted of the following:

1. A data collection interface through Epicollect5 v 86.2.1 for community members to geolocate and photograph waste incidents.
2. Drone flights to capture high-resolution aerial images.
3. A YOLOv5-based AI model trained to accurately detect different waste categories (100% precision; 81.1% recall).
4. A digital twin platform built with SuperMap GIS to visualize waste hotspots and aggregate temporal data.
5. A dashboard built with Grafana and FIWARE components (Orion Context Broker, QuantumLeap, CrateDB) to facilitate monitoring and data analysis.

Participation was encouraged through co-design sessions with residents, workshops with local government officials, and the incorporation of institutional responses from the UAESP (Bogotá's waste management authority).

5.1.3. Key Findings of the Waste Experiment

The main key findings are as follows:

- The system demonstrated low-latency information flows (<10 min) between data collection and visualization;
- Over 30 georeferenced reports were gathered from local residents using Epicollect5 v 86.2.1.
- The digital twin enabled multi-scalar decision-making, supporting both neighborhood-level response and institutional planning;
- The experiment confirmed the potential of open-source, low-cost architectures for smart waste systems in the Global South.

5.1.4. Validation and Contribution of the Waste Experiment

Table 5 presents the validation of the components in the experiment related to the SSCC model.

Table 5. Validation of SSCC Layers for Waste Experiment.

SSCC Model Layer	Validated Component in the Waste Experiment	Integration in Validation
Technological Innovation Management Layer	Iterative design under ULL principles; integration of academic, public, and community actors; real-environment testing of socio-technical system.	Integrated—Multi-actor coordination and iterative cycles connected to CPS deployment.
Physical Layer	Infrastructure of the Fenicia neighborhood used for experiment.	Non-integrated—Contextual infrastructure was used but not part of system-to-system integration.
Digital Layer	Image classification using YOLOv5 (100% precision, 81.1% recall); community sensing via smartphones; drone-based image acquisition.	Integrated—All digital inputs (AI, drones, smartphones) connected through data pipelines.
Analytical Layer	Real-time spatial modeling of waste hotspots; integration into SuperMap-based digital twin; dashboards built with Grafana and FIWARE stack.	Integrated—Outputs directly connected to Digital Layer inputs and governance dashboards.
Participatory Governance Layer	Community-generated data via Epicollect5 v 86.2.1; structured feedback mechanisms; institutional engagement with UAESP.	Integrated—Citizen reports and institutional validation linked to CPS workflows.
Data Strategy	Full data flow from acquisition (drones, smartphones) to processing (YOLOv5, FIWARE stack) and application (dashboard, institutional response); activation of value strategies: DME (waste hotspot detection and response planning), OE (automation of data capture and classification), and BMT (exploration of AI-based waste services as innovation layer for urban sanitation systems).	Integrated—Demonstrated end-to-end pipeline from collection to application.
Assessment Layer	KPIs aligned with ISO 37106, U4SSC, and LEED: improved cleanliness perception, reduced time-to-response, increased citizen engagement.	Partially Integrated—KPI tracking applied to outputs of Digital and Governance Layers, but limited to pilot scale.

The experiment's results clearly demonstrate progress toward the three strategic objectives outlined in the SSCC model.

1. Quality of Life: Enhancing urban cleanliness and citizen satisfaction through increased visibility of city efforts and community involvement.
2. Productivity: Improving waste collection processes and using spatial intelligence to support more efficient institutional planning.

3. ICT-Based Sustainability: Utilizing scalable, open-source technologies like FIWARE, Grafana, and SuperMap; focusing on interoperability and accessibility in low-resource urban environments.

While further iterations are needed to solidify the results, the pilot confirms the core ability of the SSCC architecture to support integrated, circular, and data-driven public service transformation. Although, the real-time visibility of waste flows combined with geospatial tagging offers key insights for resource planning and potential material recovery strategies.

5.2. *Urban Garden Experiment: Enabling Local Circularity and Energy-Aware Sensing*

This section examines the second experiment conducted within the Fenicia ULL, which centers on implementing an urban garden as a socio-technical platform for community engagement and assessing a solar-powered IoT system for environmental monitoring. This experiment highlights the integration of information, energy, and community participation.

Figure 7 displays the IoT FIWARE architecture for Fenicia ULL urban garden, including the smart data model. Figure 8 presents a 3D digital twin visualization of the urban garden and the solar-powered IoT system for environmental monitoring.

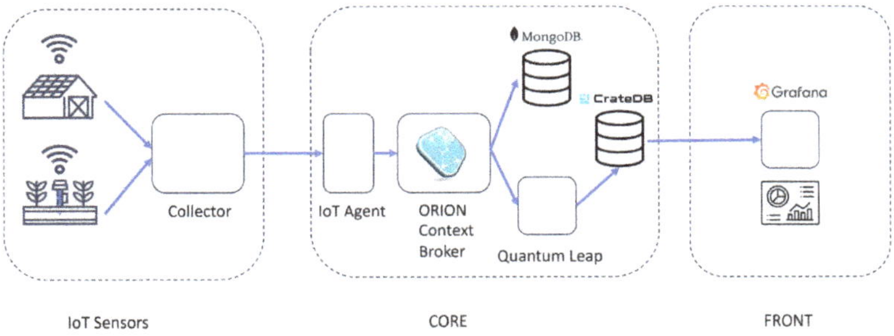

Figure 7. IoT FIWARE Architecture for Fenicia ULL Urban Garden.

Figure 8. Digital Twin 3D Visualization and solar-powered IoT system for Fenicia ULL Urban Garden.

5.2.1. Objectives of the Urban Garden Experiment

The urban garden experiment was designed to achieve the following objectives:

- Implement and verify a low-cost, energy-independent IoT system for environmental sensing (e.g., soil humidity, solar radiation, temperature) in urban agriculture.
- Visualize and control environmental conditions using digital twin technologies integrated with FIWARE and Smart Data Models.

- Evaluate the maturity of innovation across four complementary dimensions: Technological (TRL), Societal (SRL), Organizational (ORL), and Scaling (ScR).
- Facilitate knowledge transfer and community ownership through participatory design, dashboard interaction, and engaging stakeholders.

The pilot acts as a testing platform for integrating energy, information, and community management within a circular urban system.

5.2.2. Methods and Implementation of the Urban Garden Experiment

The experiment was designed using a layered socio-technical model organized into three main phases:

1. Technological Development: Solar-powered IoT sensors measured UV radiation, soil moisture, and temperature. The data were structured via NGSI-LD and processed using Orion Context Broker, QuantumLeap, and CrateDB, with visualization in Grafana and SuperMap digital twin. The FIWARE AgriApp Smart Data Model was adopted for semantic interoperability.
2. Participatory and Co-Design Activities: Workshops facilitated interface adaptation and data interpretation training. Community members proposed new sensor functions and dashboard designs.
3. Readiness Level Evaluation: A TRL-SRL-ORL-ScR framework was applied to assess the innovation's maturity and scalability, serving as a key component of the SSCC model's Assessment Layer.

5.2.3. Key Findings of the Urban Garden Experiment

The main key findings are as follows:

- The system demonstrated stable performance for over 30 days of continuous environmental data collection powered by the energy grid and solar energy;
- Participants showed strong acceptance and interest, especially when able to visualize data on dashboards and maps;
- The use of standardized data models and open-source platforms confirmed the feasibility of replicability and interoperability within smart territory frameworks;
- The project showed potential for future integration with organic waste reuse (e.g., composting) and closed-loop water-energy systems.

5.2.4. Validation and Contribution

Table 6 displays the validation of components in the experiment related to the SSCC model.

Table 6. Validation of SSCC Layers for Urban Garden Experiment.

SSCC Model Layer	Validated Component in the Waste Experiment	Integration in Validation
Technological Innovation Management Layer	Iterative prototyping within the ULL; validation from TRL 4 to TRL 7; use of open-hardware by startup ORUS.	Integrated—Orchestrated innovation cycles directly linked with TRL evaluation and ULL feedback.
Physical Layer	Urban garden space equipped with environmental sensors and autonomous solar energy system.	Integrated—Physical assets directly connected to digital sensing and analytical layers.
Digital Layer	Real-time sensor data acquisition (humidity, temperature, radiation); structured via Smart Data Models for agriculture.	Integrated—Sensor outputs connected to FIWARE context broker and data strategy workflows.

Table 6. *Cont.*

SSCC Model Layer	Validated Component in the Waste Experiment	Integration in Validation
Analytical Layer	Time-series dashboards (Grafana); data visualized in SuperMap digital twin for simulation of environmental trends.	Integrated—Outputs validated through visualization and simulation linked to Digital Layer inputs.
Participatory Governance Layer	Participatory design of interface; community training; co-creation of KPIs; involvement of Botanical Urban Garden of Bogotá (Jardin Botánico de Bogotá—JBB) and startup ORUS.	Integrated—Direct co-creation and feedback loops with institutional and community actors.
Data Strategy	End-to-end data integration using standardized models (FIWARE, NGSI-LD, AgriApp); activation of value strategies: DME (irrigation decisions), OE (sensor performance optimization), and PSI (co-designed services and visualizations with community and public actors).	Integrated—Demonstrated complete data pipeline from acquisition to application.
Assessment Layer	Full application of TRL, SRL, ORL, and ScR dimensions: TRL 7, SRL 7, ORL 5 (both ORUS and JBB), ScR 4.	Integrated—Multi-dimensional readiness evaluation embedded in the pilot validation.

The pilot confirms meaningful alignment with the SSCC strategic pillars:

1. Quality of Life: Promotes food sovereignty, environmental awareness, and access to green infrastructure.
2. Productivity: Facilitates data-driven irrigation, energy independence, and planning for crop cycles and climate adaptation.
3. ICT-Based Sustainability: Utilizes affordable sensing, solar power, open-source software, and standardized data to promote interoperability and replicability.

5.3. Integrated Validation of the SSCC Architecture: From Silos to Systemic Urban Services

The coordinated implementation of the waste management and urban garden experiments in the Fenicia ULL offers strong empirical support for the SSCC model as a layered and integrative urban framework. Each experiment, while separately addressing a specific issue—waste buildup and sustainable food production—was designed and carried out in a way that aligns with the main hypothesis of the SSCC framework: that sustainable urban transformation requires the integration of physical, digital, social, and data infrastructures to provide circular, intelligent, and participatory public services.

The articulation of both experiments reveals a shift from isolated service delivery to connected urban services.

- Shared Data Infrastructure: Both pilots used a common data ecosystem based on FIWARE standards, allowing interoperability and the creation of a unified digital twin platform that supports multisectoral monitoring.
- Community as a Cross-Cutting Actor: Residents participated in both waste reporting and the co-design of the urban garden sensing platform, demonstrating the potential of community engagement as a unifying element that enhances social legitimacy, responsiveness, and data quality.
- Strategic Alignment of KPIs: The evaluation of both experiments was conducted using KPIs focused on Quality of Life, Productivity, and ICT-based Sustainability, aligned with ISO 37106, LEED for Communities, and U4SSC frameworks. This confirms the feasibility of applying standardized, integrated evaluation tools across various urban functions.

- Operationalization of the Waste–Energy–Information Nexus: While the waste experiment concentrated on information-based planning for sanitation services and the garden experiment focused on decentralized energy and environmental sensing, their combined design envisions a future where waste reuse (such as composting and bioenergy) and energy-efficient irrigation are integrated into a closed urban metabolism.

Through the coordinated deployment of these experiments, all seven layers of the SSCC architecture were operationalized and evaluated, with clear results that demonstrate the feasibility of multisectoral integration; the adaptability of the architecture to local conditions; and the creation of measurable value via the data strategy layer, through DME, OE, PSI, and BMT mechanisms.

The transition from siloed service management to systemic, circular urban innovation is not only conceptually articulated but empirically validated through layered interaction. This positions the SSCC model as a scalable and evaluable framework capable of guiding urban transformations beyond pilot settings.

6. Discussion

The SSCC model introduced in this work provides a response based on both conceptual development and empirical validation. By designing and executing two integrated experiments in the Fenicia Urban Living Lab, we demonstrate how a layered urban architecture can support a systemic shift toward sustainable, smart, and circular cities.

The findings reveal that the SSCC model addresses three gaps identified in the literature. First, it demonstrates the conceptual integration of circularity into the SSC paradigm by embedding the waste–energy–information nexus into urban infrastructures. Second, it achieves operational alignment between digitalization, circularity, and energy transition through the use of AI, IoT, and FIWARE, illustrating how digital tools can strengthen circular strategies. Third, the SSCC architecture is shown to be modular, scalable, and evaluable, with all seven layers activated and validated against international standards (ISO 37106, U4SSC, LEED). Overall, these results highlight the potential of layered architectures to support systemic and measurable circular transformations in real-world settings.

An additional contribution involves integrating readiness frameworks (TRL, SRL, ORL, ScR) with KPI systems (ISO, U4SSC, LEED). This approach not only enables a comprehensive evaluation of the experiments but also enhances the model by aligning technical validation with international benchmarking standards.

While the Fenicia ULL provided a fertile environment to validate the SSCC model, the findings should be approached with caution regarding their generalizability. The layered architecture and its alignment with international standards (ISO 37120, ISO 37106, U4SSC, LEED) indicate that the conceptual framework can be applied across different contexts. However, specific experimental conditions—such as the scale of a neighborhood-level ULL, active participation of a local community, and the technological infrastructure in Bogotá—may limit direct transferability. Therefore, replicating this in other settings will require adjustments to fit the local environment, especially in larger metropolitan areas or cities with different governance structures and resource capacities. The validation presented here should be seen as a case study offering methodological insights and a replicable framework, but it needs further testing before broader use. Future research should replicate this case study in other urban areas to assess scalability and adaptability across various socio-technical and institutional conditions.

7. Conclusions

This study aimed to answer a key research question:

How can a smart sustainable city architecture integrate the circular city components that enable innovation and evaluation in real urban contexts?

This study aimed to validate a Sustainable, Smart, and Circular City (SSCC) model that integrates circularity into the smart sustainable city framework through layered architectures and Urban Living Lab experimentation. The results confirm that the proposed model offers both conceptual and practical benefits, supporting the transition from Smart Sustainable Cities (SSCs) to Circular Cities (CCs).

First, the research shows that the SSCC model provides a validated reference architecture. All seven layers—Physical, Digital, Analytical, Participatory Governance, Data Strategy, Technological Innovation Management, and Assessment—were activated and tested in real-world conditions. This thorough validation confirms the model's robustness and flexibility, demonstrating that layered architectures are effective tools for organizing complex socio-technical systems.

Second, the experiments demonstrate the feasibility of the SSC–CC transition. The waste–energy–information nexus serves as a clear link between the two paradigms, showing how circular practices (waste detection, participatory monitoring, resource optimization) can be incorporated into smart infrastructures supported by AI, IoT, and digital twins. This provides real-world evidence that transitioning to circularity is not just an ideal but also an achievable path when guided by systemic models.

Third, the research highlights the importance of ULLs in supporting sustainable urban transformation. The Fenicia ULL proved to be a productive environment for co-creation, validation, and iterative design, involving academic, government, community, and private stakeholders in experimentation. This demonstrates that ULLs can serve as both innovation testbeds and governance tools, bridging the gap between technological innovation and societal acceptance.

Fourth, the study makes a methodological contribution by integrating readiness frameworks with international KPI systems. This combined approach enables both systemic evaluation with standardized KPIs and context-aware validation through readiness levels, making the SSCC model adaptable to diverse urban settings, especially in developing countries where institutional and infrastructural challenges require flexible assessment methods.

Fifth, the validation confirms that the SSCC model is scalable and can be replicated. Although the experiments were conducted in Fenicia's pilot environment in Bogotá, the layered architecture provides a modular framework that can be adapted to other cities, especially in the Global South. By aligning with international standards and including context-sensitive indicators, the model shows potential to speed up circular transformations in various urban settings.

Finally, the study provides strategic recommendations for policy and practice. Sustainable transformation involves not only deploying digital technologies but also coordinating them across interconnected levels of governance, data, and community engagement. Future research should expand experiments beyond waste and urban gardens to include areas such as mobility, water, and food systems, thereby strengthening the evidence base for circularity across multiple urban sectors. Additionally, scaling the Assessment Layer will be essential to offer comparable, replicable, and actionable insights that can guide policy and planning at city, national, and international levels.

In summary, the SSCC model validated in this study provides both a conceptual breakthrough and a practical tool for guiding the transition from Smart Sustainable Cities to Circular Cities. By integrating innovative technologies, governance mechanisms, and participatory practices within a layered framework, the model shows that sustainable, smart, and circular transformations can be designed, evaluated, and scaled in real urban settings.

Overall, this research provides one of the first empirically validated pathways for progressing from Smart Sustainable Cities to Circular Cities, positioning the SSCC model as both a conceptual framework and a practical tool for systemic urban transformation.

7.1. Contributions to Theory and Practice

Theoretical Contribution: The model advances the conceptual integration of circularity into smart city research by proposing a systemic, architecture-based approach. The articulation of the waste–energy–information nexus introduces a new methodological perspective for analyzing urban metabolism.

Empirical Contribution: Using real-world experiments with ULLs shows that the SSCC model is not just a theoretical idea but also a practical framework. These experiments can be replicated by other cities, especially in the Global South.

Methodological Contribution: Combining ULL methodology with a layered architecture and multidimensional evaluation (TRL, SRL, ORL, ScR) offers a comprehensive approach to assessing the readiness and scalability of socio-technical urban innovations.

7.2. Limitations and Future Work

While the results are promising, several limitations still exist: Integration with waste-to-energy technologies (e.g., pyrolysis) remains in the proposal stage and requires future investment and pilot testing; long-term impacts on institutional decision-making and community behavior have not yet been assessed; and testing in other urban settings with different governance and infrastructure conditions has yet to be conducted.

Additionally, while the current implementation of the SSCC model in Fenicia has concentrated on validating the architecture through information flows, participatory sensing, and low-carbon energy monitoring, future phases will expand into the full operationalization of material circularity. This includes deploying waste-to-energy technologies (e.g., pyrolysis units), integrating composting processes linked to urban agriculture, and developing decentralized microgrids powered by renewable energy. These next steps are already part of the SSCC architecture's design logic and will be gradually implemented in the Fenicia ULL. In doing so, the model will fully meet the objectives of waste reduction, reuse, recycling, transformation, and energy transition outlined in this research.

This study did not measure the annual energy use, CO_2 emissions, or employment impact of the smart components used in the experiments. The devices employed—solar-powered IoT sensors, drones, smartphones, and pilot-scale dashboards—were designed to require minimal additional energy, with most of the monitoring infrastructure in the urban garden powered by autonomous solar systems. Although the potential systemic benefits of adopting circular practices are expected to outweigh the slight increase in the footprint of ICT devices, these assumptions were not tested directly here. Future research should include comparative evaluations of energy consumption, carbon emissions, costs, and employment effects, including possible rebound effects of AI and smart technologies, within the Assessment Layer of the SSCC model.

7.3. Final Reflection

In conclusion, the SSCC model, as validated through the experiments in Fenicia, offers a clear step toward reducing fragmentation in urban innovation. It demonstrates that sustainable, smart, and circular cities are not just ideals but also achievable realities when built on an architecture that combines people, data, and technology to promote collective well-being and planetary sustainability.

Author Contributions: Conceptualization, methodology, validation, formal analysis, resources, writing—original draft preparation, A.V.-M.; writing—review and supervision, J.d.J.L.-S. and J.F.J.-V. All authors have read and agreed to the published version of the manuscript.

Funding: This research received no external funding.

Data Availability Statement: The original contributions presented in this study are included in the article. Further inquiries can be directed to the corresponding author.

Acknowledgments: We acknowledge support given by researchers of Faculty of Engineering and Campus Management Office—Universidad de los Andes (Colombia), Progresa Fenicia Program (Colombia), Community of Fenicia (Colombia), researchers of Instituto Tecnológico de Monterrey (Mexico), Supermap GIS corporation (China), Universidad Pontificia Bolivariana (Colombia), ORUS Global corporation (Colombia) and SmartCity Colombia Foundation (Colombia). During the preparation of this manuscript, the author(s) used GenAI for the purposes of writing correction and style. The authors have reviewed and edited the output and take full responsibility for the content of this publication.

Conflicts of Interest: The authors declare no conflicts of interest.

References

1. Dindarian, A. Overview: The smart sustainable city initiatives and the circular economy. *Circ. Econ. Sustain.* **2022**, *1*, 369–384. [CrossRef]
2. Munonye, W.; Ajonye, G. Redesigning Urban Infrastructure for Circularity: The Role of Smart Cities in Reducing Waste. *J. Environ. Sci. Stud.* **2024**, *7*, 29. [CrossRef]
3. Brglez, K.; Perc, M.; Lukman, R. The complexity and interconnectedness of circular cities and the circular economy for sustainability. *Sustain. Dev.* **2023**, *32*, 2049–2065. [CrossRef]
4. Mylonas, G.; Kalogeras, A.; Petersen, S.; Munoz, L.; Chatzigiannakis, I. When Circular Economy Meets the Smart City Ecosystem: Defining the Smart and Circular City. In Proceedings of the 2024 IEEE International Smart Cities Conference (ISC2), Chon Buri, Thailand, 29 October–1 November 2024. [CrossRef]
5. Pegorin, M.; Caldeira-Pires, A.; Faria, E. Interactions between a circular city and other sustainable urban typologies: A review. *Discov. Sustain.* **2024**, *5*, 1–23. [CrossRef]
6. Blomsma, F.; Tennant, M.; Ozaki, R. Making sense of circular economy: Understanding the progression from idea to action. *Bus. Strategy Environ.* **2022**, *32*, 1059–1084. [CrossRef]
7. United Nations. *U4SSC: United 4 Smart Sustainable Cities: A Guide to Circular Cities*; UN: New York, NY, USA, 2020; ISBN 978-92-61-31171-1.
8. UN-Habitat. *World Cities Report 2022: Envisaging the Future of Cities*; UN-Habitat: Nairobi, Kenya, 2022. Available online: https://unhabitat.org/wcr/ (accessed on 25 August 2025).
9. UN-Habitat. *World Smart Cities Outlook 2024*; UN-Habitat: Nairobi, Kenya, 2024. Available online: https://unhabitat.org/world-smart-cities-outlook-2024 (accessed on 25 August 2025).
10. Shmelev, S.E.; Sagiyeva, R.K.; Kadyrkhanova, Z.M.; Chzhan, Y.Y.; Shmeleva, I.A. Comparative Sustainability Analysis of Two Asian Cities: A Multidimensional Assessment of Taipei and Almaty. *J. Asian Financ. Econ. Bus.* **2018**, *5*, 143–155. [CrossRef]
11. Shmeleva, I.; Shmelev, S. How sustainable is smart and how smart is sustainable? In *Sustainable Cities Reimagined*; Routledge: London, UK, 2019; pp. 213–234. [CrossRef]
12. *ISO 37106:2021*; Sustainable Cities and Communities—Guidance on Establishing Smart City Operating Models for Sustainable Communities. International Organization for Standardization: Geneva, Switzerland, 2021. Available online: https://www.iso.org/standard/82854.html (accessed on 16 February 2025).
13. Anthopoulos, L. *Understanding Smart Cities—A tool for Smart Government or an Industrial Trick*; Springer: Berlin/Heidelberg, Germany, 2017. Available online: https://link.springer.com/book/10.1007%2F978-3-319-57015-0 (accessed on 16 February 2025).
14. Anthopoulos, L. Defining Smart City Architecture for Sustainability. In *Environmental Science, Engineering*; IOP Press: Amsterdam, The Netherlands, 2015.
15. Zygiaris, S. Smart City Reference Model: Assisting Planners to Conceptualize the Building of Smart City Innovation Ecosystems. *J. Knowl. Econ.* **2012**, *4*, 217–231. [CrossRef]
16. Mamkaitis, A.; Bezbradica, M.; Helfert, M. Urban enterprise: A review of Smart City frameworks from an Enterprise Architecture perspective. In Proceedings of the 2016 IEEE International Smart Cities Conference (ISC2), Trento, Italy, 12–15 September 2016; pp. 1–5. [CrossRef]

17. Angelopoulos, C.; Katos, V.; Kostoulas, T.; Miaoudakis, A.; Petroulakis, N.; Alexandris, G.; Demetriou, G.; Morandi, G.; Waledzik, K.; Rak, U.; et al. IDEAL-CITIES—A Trustworthy and Sustainable Framework for Circular Smart Cities. In Proceedings of the 2019 15th International Conference on Distributed Computing in Sensor Systems (DCOSS), Santorini, Greece, 29–31 May 2019; pp. 443–450. [CrossRef]
18. FIWARE Organization. FIWARE for Smart Cities and Territories: A Digital Transformation Journey. Available online: https://www.fiware.org/wp-content/directories/marketing-toolbox/material/FIWAREBrochure_SmartCities.pdf (accessed on 16 February 2025).
19. Greer, C.; Burns, M.; Wollman, D.; Griffor, E. *Cyber-Physical Systems and Internet of Things*; National Institute of Standards and Technology—NIST: Gaithersburg, MD, USA, 2019. [CrossRef]
20. Smith, R.; Cadena, A.; Espinosa, E.; Quijano, N. Ciudades Sostenibles. Book. *Universidad de los Andes*. 2022. Available online: https://electricayelectronica.uniandes.edu.co/sites/default/files/proyectos/ebook_ciudades_sostenibles_uniandes.pdf (accessed on 17 February 2025).
21. U.S. Green Building Council. LEED certification. Available online: https://www.usgbc.org/leed/rating-systems/leed-for-cities-leed-for-communities (accessed on 17 February 2025).
22. Neira, T.; Vesga, R. Factores que afectan la generación de valor en la estrategia de datos de una organización. *RISTI. Iber. J. Inf. Syst. Technol.* **2024**, *72*, 137–157.
23. Velasquez-Mendez, A.; Lozoya-Santos, J.; Jimenez, J.F. Technological Innovation Management Model for Urban Living Labs in Smart Cities: Strategies for Urban Problem-Solving. In Proceedings of the 23rd LACCEI International Multi-Conference for Engineering, Education, and Technology: "Engineering, Artificial Intelligence, and Sustainable Technologies in service of society", Mexico City, Mexico, 16–18 July 2025.
24. Velasquez-Mendez, A.; Lozoya-Santos, J.; Jimenez, J.F. Assessing Smart Cities in Developing Countries: Multidimensional Approaches. In Proceedings of the VII Ibero-American Congress of Smart Cities ICSC-CITIES 2024, San Carlos, Costa Rica, 12–14 November 2024.
25. Velasquez-Mendez, A.; Lozoya-Santos, J.; Jimenez, J.F. Strategic Socio-Technical Innovation in Urban Living Labs: A Framework for Smart City Evolution. *Smart Cities* **2025**, *8*, 131. [CrossRef]
26. Esashika, D.S.S. Living Labs Contributions to Smart Cities from a Quadruple-Helix Perspective. Doctor's Thesis, Universidad de São Paulo, São Paulo, Brazil, 2020. [CrossRef]
27. Escolar, S.; Villanueva, F.; Santofimia, M.; Villa, D.; Toro, X.; López, J. A Multiple-Attribute Decision Making-based approach for smart city rankings design. *Technol. Forecast. Soc. Chang.* **2019**, *142*, 42–55. [CrossRef]
28. Tan, S.; Taeihagh, A. Smart City Governance in Developing Countries: A Systematic Literature Review. *Sustainability* **2020**, *12*, 899. [CrossRef]
29. Giffinger, R.; Fertner, C.; Kramar, H.; Meijers, E. *European Smart Cities Ranking*; Vienna University of Technology: Vienna, Austria, 2021.
30. Bosch, P.; Jongeneel, S.; Rovers, V.; Neumann, H.; Airaksinen, M.; Huovila, A. CITYkeys indicators for smart city projects and smart cities. *CITYkeys Rep. Eur. Comm.* **2017**. [CrossRef]
31. Ericsson. Networked Society City Index. *Ericsson*. 2016. Available online: https://mb.cision.com/Public/15448/2245037/938941 48bfbf1118.pdf (accessed on 17 February 2025).
32. IMD Smart City Index. IMD World Competitiveness Center. 2023. Available online: https://www.imd.org/smart-city-observatory/smart-city-index/ (accessed on 17 February 2025).
33. Berrone, P.; Ricart, J.E. *IESE Cities in Motion Index*; IESE Business School, University of Navarra: Pamplona, Spain, 2023.
34. Marchetti, D.; Oliveira, R.; Figueira, A.R. Are global north smart city models capable to assess Latin American cities? A model and indicators for a new context. *Cities* **2019**, *92*, 197–207. [CrossRef]
35. Sharifi, A. A critical review of selected smart city assessment tools and indicator sets. *J. Clean. Prod.* **2019**, *233*, 1269–1283. [CrossRef]
36. Fang, Y.; Shan, Z. How to Promote a Smart City Effectively? An Evaluation Model and Efficiency Analysis of Smart Cities in China. *Sustainability* **2022**, *14*, 6512. [CrossRef]
37. Aljowder, T.; Ali, M.; Kurnia, S. Development of a Maturity Model for Assessing Smart Cities: A Focus Area Maturity Model. *Smart Cities* **2023**, *6*, 2150–2175. [CrossRef]
38. Albino, V.; Berardi, U.; Dangelico, R.M. Smart Cities: Definitions, Dimensions, Performance, and Initiatives. *J. Urban Technol.* **2015**, *22*, 3–21. [CrossRef]
39. Angelidou, M. The Role of Smart City Characteristics in the Plans of Fifteen Cities. *J. Urban Technol.* **2017**, *24*, 3–28. [CrossRef]
40. Lee, J.; Hancock, M.; Hu, M. Towards an effective framework for building smart cities: Lessons from Seoul and San Francisco. *Technol. Forecast. Soc. Chang.* **2014**, *89*, 80–99. [CrossRef]
41. Kitchin, R. The real-time city? Big data and smart urbanism. *GeoJournal* **2014**, *79*, 1–14. Available online: http://www.jstor.org/stable/24432611 (accessed on 17 February 2025). [CrossRef]

42. Chuantao, Y.; Zhang, X.; Hui, C.; Jingyuan, W.; Daven, C.; Bertrand, D. A literature survey on smart cities. *Sci. China Inf. Sci.* **2015**, *58*, 1–18. [CrossRef]
43. Syed, A.S.; Sierra-Sosa, D.; Kumar, A.; Elmaghraby, A. IoT in Smart Cities: A Survey of Technologies, Practices and Challenges. *Smart Cities* **2021**, *4*, 429–475. [CrossRef]
44. Bibri, S. Data-Driven Smart Eco-Cities and Sustainable Integrated Districts: A Best-Evidence Synthesis Approach to an Extensive Literature Review. *Eur. J. Futur. Res.* **2021**, *9*, 1–43. [CrossRef]
45. Carayannis, E.; Campbell, D. Developed Democracies versus Emerging Autocracies: Arts, Democracy, and Innovation in Quadruple Helix Innovation Systems. *J. Innov. Entrep.* **2014**, *3*, 12. [CrossRef]
46. Appio, F.; Lima, M.; Paroutis, S. Understanding Smart Cities: Innovation Ecosystems, Technological Advancements, and Societal Challenges. *Technol. Forecast. Soc. Chang.* **2019**, *142*, 1–14. [CrossRef]
47. Puerari, E.; De Koning, J.I.J.C.; Von Wirth, T.; Karré, P.M.; Mulder, I.J.; Loorbach, D.A. Co-Creation Dynamics in Urban Living Labs. *Sustainability* **2018**, *10*, 1893. [CrossRef]
48. Soeiro, D. Smart cities and innovative governance systems: A reflection on urban living labs and action research. *Fenn.-Int. J. Geogr.* **2021**, *199*, 104–112. [CrossRef]
49. Supriyanto, E.; Saputra, J.; Rachmawati, M.; Nugroho, F. Community Participation-Based Smart City Development. In Proceedings of the First Multidiscipline International Conference, MIC 2021, Jakarta, Indonesia, 30 October 2021. [CrossRef]
50. Han, H.; Hawken, S. Introduction: Innovation and identity in next-generation smart cities. *City Cult. Soc.* **2018**, *12*, 1–4. [CrossRef]
51. Stratigea, A.; Somarakis, G.; Panagiotopoulou, M. Smartening-Up Communities in Less-Privileged Urban Areas—The DemoCU Participatory Cultural Planning Experience in Korydallos—Greece Municipality. In *Smart Cities in the Mediterranean*; Springer: Berlin/Heidelberg, Germany, 2017. [CrossRef]
52. Sepasgozar, S.; Hawken, S.; Sargolzaei, S.; Foroozanfa, M. Implementing citizen centric technology in developing smart cities: A model for predicting the acceptance of urban technologies. *Technol. Forecast. Soc. Chang.* **2019**, *142*, 105–116. [CrossRef]
53. Lee, J.; Babcock, J.; Pham, T.; Bui, T.; Kang, M. Smart city as a social transition towards inclusive development through technology: A tale of four smart cities. *Int. J. Urban Sci.* **2022**, *27*, 75–100. [CrossRef]
54. Kaluarachchi, Y. Implementing Data-Driven Smart City Applications for Future Cities. *Smart Cities* **2022**, *5*, 455–474. [CrossRef]
55. Bouzguenda, I.; Alalouch, C.; Fava, N. Towards smart sustainable cities: A review of the role digital citizen participation could play in advancing social sustainability. *Sustain. Cities Soc.* **2019**, *50*, 101627. [CrossRef]
56. Al-Saidi, M.; Zaidan, E. Understanding and Enabling "Communities" Within Smart Cities: A Literature Review. *J. Plan. Lit.* **2023**, *39*, 186–202. [CrossRef]
57. Cardullo, P.; Kitchin, R. Smart urbanism and smart citizenship: The neoliberal logic of 'citizen-focused' smart cities in Europe. *Environ. Plan. C Politics-Space* **2018**, *37*, 813–830. [CrossRef]
58. Arc for LEED. Available online: https://www.arc.gbci.org/arc-for-leed (accessed on 17 February 2025).

urban science

MDPI

Article

A Qualitative Methodology for Identifying Governance Challenges and Advancements in Positive Energy District Labs

Silvia Soutullo [1,*], Oscar Seco [1,*], María Nuria Sánchez [1], Ricardo Lima [2], Fabio Maria Montagnino [3], Gloria Pignatta [4], Ghazal Etminan [5], Viktor Bukovszki [6,7], Touraj Ashrafian [8], Maria Beatrice Andreucci [9] and Daniele Vettorato [10]

1 Renewable Energy Division, CIEMAT, 28040 Madrid, Spain; nuria.sanchez@ciemat.es
2 Laboratory for Energy Systems, IMPACT, HEPIA, University of Applied Sciences and Arts of Western Switzerland, 1202 Genève, Switzerland; ricardo.lima@hesge.ch
3 STeDI—Research Centre, The Cyprus Institute, 2121 Nicosia, Cyprus; f.montagnino@cyi.ac.cy
4 School of Built Environment, University of New South Wales (UNSW), Sydney 2052, Australia; g.pignatta@gmail.com
5 Austrian Institute of Technology (AIT), 1210 Vienna, Austria; ghazal.etminan@ait.ac.at
6 Advanced Building and Urban Design Ltd., 1139 Budapest, Hungary; bukovszki.viktor@abud.hu
7 School of Life Sciences, Technical University of Munich, 85354 Munich, Germany
8 Department of Architecture and Built Environment, Faculty of Engineering and Environment, Northumbria University, Newcastle Upon Tyne, Newcastle NE1 8ST, UK; touraj.ashrafian@northumbria.ac.uk
9 Department of Planning, Design, Technology of Architecture, Sapienza University of Rome, 00196 Rome, Italy; mbeatrice.andreucci@uniroma1.it
10 EURAC Research, Institute for Renewable Energy, 39100 Bolzano, Italy; daniele.vettorato@eurac.edu
* Correspondence: silvia.soutullo@ciemat.es (S.S.); oscar.seco@ciemat.es (O.S.)

Abstract: Governance challenges, success factors, and stakeholder dynamics are central to the implementation of Positive Energy District (PED) Labs, which aim to develop energy-positive and sustainable urban areas. In this paper, a qualitative analysis combining expert surveys, participatory workshops with practitioners from the COST Action PED-EU-NET network, and comparative case studies across Europe identifies key barriers, drivers, and stakeholder roles throughout the implementation process. Findings reveal that fragmented regulations, social inertia, and limited financial mechanisms are the main barriers to PED Lab development, while climate change mitigation goals, strong local networks, and supportive policy frameworks are critical drivers. The analysis maps stakeholder engagement across six development phases, showing how leadership shifts between governments, industry, planners, and local communities. PED Labs require intangible assets such as inclusive governance frameworks, education, and trust-building in the early phases, while tangible infrastructures become more relevant in later stages. The conclusions emphasize that robust, inclusive governance is not merely supportive but a key driver of PED Lab success. Adaptive planning, participatory decision-making, and digital coordination tools are essential for overcoming systemic barriers. Scaling PED Labs effectively requires regulatory harmonization and the integration of social and technological innovation to accelerate the transition toward energy-positive, climate-resilient cities.

Keywords: positive energy districts (PEDs); urban living laboratories (ULLs); urban energy transition; sustainable urban development; renewable energy integration

1. Introduction

To address the challenges generated by climate change and the rapid urbanization in densely populated regions, it is necessary to develop urban frameworks that allow reversing energy and environmental trends while reducing existing inequalities. A growing body of evidence indicates that even the most celebrated "frontrunner" cities are struggling to meet their own targets, revealing a persistent implementation deficit [1]. New urban models oriented toward a successful energy, economic, social, and environmental transition are needed [2–4]. Under this context, different governance initiatives are being proposed, mainly under two dominant theoretical paradigms of Transition Management and Polycentric Governance, which offer distinct yet complementary perspectives on how to conceptualize and organize the complex process of governing systemic change. The Transition Management approach provides a prescriptive, goal-oriented roadmap and governance frameworks such as the Climate City Contracts and local experimental governance setups [5]. On the other side Polycentric Governance offers a descriptive lens for understanding the multi-actor, multi-level reality in which any such roadmap must be navigated, as well as a way to address the key challenges in its implementation at the different scales: (i) stewarding capacity, (ii) unlocking capacity, (iii) transformative capacity, and (iv) orchestrating capacity [6].

Urban Living Laboratories (ULLs) represent one of the most interesting initiatives in the context of Polycentric Governance of urban climate transitions, which focuses on co-developing urban solutions in a multi-stakeholder dialog and under real conditions of use [7]. These labs represent a crucial step in learning how to design inclusive, sustainable, and climate-resilient urban environments [8], and embody an experimental governance model that facilitates the evaluation of different solutions in a real life, user centric setting, and the co-development of enhancements. Ultimately, they are designed to create a collaborative environment where various stakeholders can explore, develop, and experiment with solutions to urban challenges, all while involving local communities [9].

Their innovative approach to urban development and public–private partnerships steps beyond the traditional approach of implementing sandboxes and testbeds for innovative technologies in the urban fabric. It substantially underscores the need for adaptability, transparency, and informality in their processes, as well as the central role of citizens from the design to the uptake and evaluation phase. As a result of an appropriate setup, they can generate highly valuable insights that would inform decision making for city stakeholders. The innovation drivers in these projects stem from agglomeration effects and multi-actor engagement, where innovation activities cluster around living urban initiatives. However, these effects might not be evenly distributed, nor consistently beneficial for all participants [10]. The innovation process within ULLs is typically iterative, involving cyclical stages of development, testing, and refinement based on ongoing feedback and evaluation. There is a strong focus on learning and experimentation, with ULLs intentionally integrating processes of both research and innovation to generate new knowledge and effective solutions. Ultimately, urban living labs are designed to address a wide range of urban challenges, encompassing social, economic, and environmental issues that cities face on their path towards sustainable development. Authors explore the application of living labs to foster gendered energy technology innovation in impoverished urban settings [11], the establishment of new welfare spaces, and other social challenges [12,13].

Challenges and dilemmas associated with strategic urban experimentation have been assessed through a review of the literature on socio-technical systems, alongside insights from transdisciplinary research on living labs [14]. It has been envisaged the opportunity of combining the ULL approach with comprehensive urban transitional strategies, with the aim of functionalizing the ULL approach towards the achievement of specific socio-technical transitions in the urban environment, specifically supporting zero emission targets [15].

While much of the current literature and practical application of ULL originates from Europe, emerging experiences in Asia, the Americas, and Oceania demonstrate how these frameworks are adapted to these local socio-economic, climatic, and technological contexts. Initiatives such as the Urban Living Lab Center support low-carbon development by fostering capacity building and scaling urban innovations across sectors like energy, mobility, and digitalization. Through regional hubs in Asia, Africa, and Latin America, they promote collaborative urban transformation, linking training, research, and practical implementation [16].

In Asia, Japan's SolarEV City [17] integrates solar energy and electric vehicle infrastructures in dense urban areas, enhancing distributed energy storage and grid interaction [18]. Taiwan's initiatives in 'Smart Taipei' show the development of PED site-selection criteria tailored to local urban morphology and energy consumption patterns [19]. In South Korea, the Seongdaegol living lab, EnergyX DY-Building, and the Ulsan Hydrogen Town showcase different energy carriers (electric and hydrogen) within PED-like frameworks [20,21]. In China, smart city pilot policies have demonstrated significant progress in fostering green urban development through the deployment of digital infrastructures, industrial upgrading, and innovation-driven agglomeration effects, although regional heterogeneity persists due to variations in economic and technological capacity [22].

In the Americas, Canada offers well-documented cases such as the Drake Landing Solar Community, a district that achieves 100% solar space heating through seasonal thermal storage [23]. Montreal's Positive Energy District synergizes with Urban–Industrial Symbiosis principles [24], creating integrated energy flows between residential and industrial buildings [25]. West Five, an energy-positive community in Ontario, Canada, is designed to achieve net-zero energy by integrating residential, office, and retail spaces with renewable energy systems, including a micro-utility and solar PV installations. EVE Park initiative features 84 all-electric homes powered by solar energy and supported by battery storage systems, serving as a Canadian pilot for sustainable energy communities and innovative regulatory frameworks [26]. In Latin America, key examples of urban laboratories include Mexico City's Laboratorio para la Ciudad [27], which focuses on mobility and urban sustainability, and Chile's Laboratorio de Gobierno [28], dedicated to transforming public services through design thinking. Grassroots initiatives such as Arquitectura Expandida in Bogotá [29], community-led renewable energy projects like Argentina's Cauchari-Olaroz solar complex and Amazonian indigenous solar cooperatives [30], as well as Laboratorio Procomum in Brazil and Casa Gallina in Mexico City, add a cultural and environmental dimension to urban lab practices [31]. Together, these initiatives illustrate diverse approaches, ranging from government-led innovation to citizen-driven social experimentation.

Oceania hosts a growing number of urban living labs where innovative solutions for sustainable energy, mobility, and urban development are tested in real-world settings. These collaborative environments bring together government, academia, industry, and local communities to co-create and implement low-carbon urban systems. Projects such as CSIRO's Urban Living Labs [32], Monash University's Net Zero Precinct Living Lab [33], and the Lot Fourteen Innovation Hub [34] demonstrate the potential of precinct-scale innovation, integrating renewable energy, smart mobility, and circular economy principles, fostering partnerships between start-ups, research institutions, and public agencies to advance smart city technologies. Complementing these efforts, Australia's Regional Australia Microgrid Pilot Program (RAMPP) and Byron Bay's community microgrids reflect a resilience-driven approach, combining solar generation, energy storage, and community ownership in remote and regional areas [35]. Collectively, these living labs contribute to the region's transition towards energy-positive, climate-resilient urban environments.

Several urban strategies tailored to the local context can be assessed, creating a comprehensive map of solutions to tackle the climatic and energy challenges facing cities. Current literature presents various concepts related to climate-friendly neighborhoods, including Zero Emission Neighborhood [36], Nearly Zero Carbon Neighborhood [37], Net Zero Energy districts [38], Zero Energy District, Smart Energy Community, and Positive Energy District (PEDs) [39,40]. The latter concept, introduced by Set Plan Action 3.2 [41], encompasses three topics related to energy: flexibility, efficiency, and production [42]. The implementation, analysis, and optimization of innovative urban solutions in PEDs can highly benefit of the availability of flexible living laboratories, equipped to monitor and quantify urban fluxes, that would facilitate synergies among different urban factors such as energy, social, economic or governance [43], thus resulting into effective Positive Energy District Labs (PED Labs).

PED Labs are collaborative spaces where people work together to create neighborhoods that produce more renewable energy than they use over a year. These labs bring together researchers, city planners, businesses, and residents to test new ideas and technologies in real cities. Instead of focusing on traditional lab equipment, they prioritize teamwork and real-world experiments, like trying out solar energy systems or smart grids in actual urban areas. They also share lessons learned and help shape policies to make it easier for other cities to adopt similar solutions [44]. PED Labs use digital tools, like computer simulations or virtual models, to plan and test ideas before implementing them. While some PED Labs have physical locations, their main goal is to connect people and ideas, not just buildings. Virtual PED Labs [45] take this further by allowing remote collaboration and digital experiments, making it easier for experts worldwide to participate [46]. This virtual PED concept allows for expanding the area of energy generation and storage, as it is not subject to geographical boundaries, increasing its flexibility and autonomy through a greater number of energy market players involved [47].

Within this study framework, this paper tackles the lack of a consolidated definition of PED Labs and improves, through the reasoned selection of key practices, the overall approach to their adoption as a strategic tool to accelerate the deployment of effective PEDs. This work falls within the activities of Working Group 3 (WG3)—'PED Labs, Monitoring and Replication' of the COST Action CA19126 or Positive Energy Districts European Network (PED-EU-NET) [48]. Specifically, the process of reviewing existing concepts, projects, and facilities relevant to PED Labs, as well as mapping their current landscape, has been carried out in Task 3.1, resulting in the ability to position this concept in the international debate and generating key research questions related to its development and implementation across Europe and beyond.

Although the literature on PEDs and ULLs has expanded, significant gaps remain. Most research focuses on conceptual frameworks, technical definitions, and normative goals, while empirical insights on the specific implementation of PED Labs are limited. Existing case studies are scarce and often highlight best-case scenarios without critically analyzing their limitations, failures, or contextual challenges. As a result, how experimental, real-world PED Lab settings help overcome implementation barriers, and how these models can be transferred across diverse socio-economic, climatic, and regulatory contexts remains underexplored. The literature lacks comparative empirical studies, critical assessments of failures, detailed analysis of governance dynamics, and a consolidated definition or operational framework for PED Labs.

The main objective of this article is to identify the key aspects (challenges, barriers, stakeholders, and driving factors) that must be considered in the implementation process of PED Labs. To this end, a qualitative analysis based on surveys and subsequent analyses was conducted, addressing the following research questions:

- What are the current barriers to the implementation of PED-Labs?
- What are the drivers and incentive factors ('unlocking factors') that determine the "fertility of the soil" for PED-Lab initiatives?

- What processes and actors define the steps, power relationships, and subsidiarity in responsibilities and decisions within PED Lab initiatives?

The methodology applied in this study enables the identification of the main elements that define a PED Lab, the conditions for successful implementation, existing gaps, and the key actors involved at each stage of the process. The study also proposes a consolidated definition of PED Labs, maps their current landscape, and highlights key barriers, drivers, and stakeholder roles. By positioning PED Labs as strategic tools for energy transitions, the research addresses gaps in empirical evidence and governance analysis. This work contributes to the standardization of PED Lab models and offers practical guidance for cities, researchers, and practitioners aiming to implement or replicate such initiatives. Through a critical evaluation of existing efforts, it advances the understanding of PED Labs as catalysts for positive energy transitions in diverse urban contexts.

2. Methods

The qualitative analysis employed in this study aims to understand certain phenomena and characteristics related to PED Labs. A dynamic and flexible methodology was applied in phases: survey preparation, data collection, analysis, and interpretation of findings. The first step involved designing and administering structured questionnaires to expert focus groups. Data collection methods were subsequently defined through online questionnaires and group discussions, enabling the gathering of subjective and detailed insights through collective reflection on the topics discussed. Once the databases were created, the information was coded and processed, providing results on barriers, incentive factors, key stakeholders, and the characteristic facilities of these laboratories. This analysis allowed the current state of PED Labs to be mapped, identifying their strengths and weaknesses through a SWOT matrix, and addressing the proposed research questions. As a final outcome, a series of recommendations has been proposed to guide the development and future replication of PED Labs. These steps were essential to gather and synthesize practical knowledge, draw on diverse stakeholder experiences, and contribute to the conceptual development of the PED Lab model.

In parallel, a review of existing literature, EU-funded projects, and case studies was conducted to frame the PED Lab concept in a broader international and academic context. This ensured that findings from focus groups could be cross-referenced and validated against existing knowledge.

The entire methodology reflects an overview of an evolving field, where limitations relate mainly to the terminological ambiguity around PEDs and PED Labs across regions and disciplines, and the early-stage development of many initiatives. Additionally, participation in focus groups was voluntary, which may have introduced selection bias or incomplete coverage in the data collection. All participants are members of the COST Action CA19126 working groups.

Figure 1 presents a schematic representation of the participatory methodology implemented in this study, with each of the three main steps detailed in the subsequent subsections. The following sections of this article present the main results, answer the research questions posed in the introduction, propose recommendations, and outline the study's limitations.

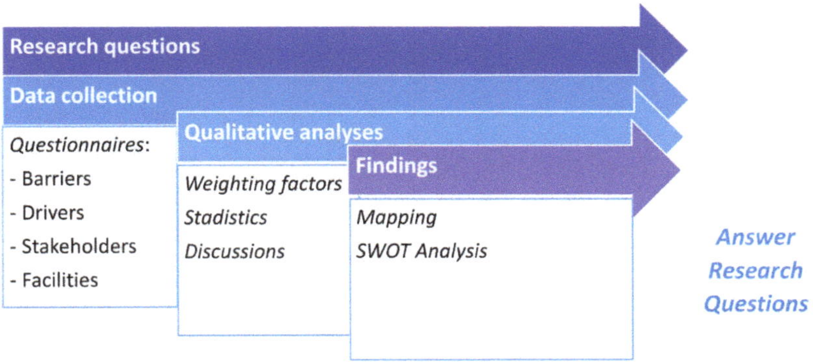

Figure 1. Diagram of the methodology implemented in this research.

2.1. Questionnaire Development and Data Collection

The generation of these questionnaires followed an iterative process based on literature and active participation of the WG3 expert group. The first step consisted of analyzing the experiences and outputs generated by different European projects on Smart Cities and Climate Neutral Cities, such as SINFONIA [49] or Cities4PEDs [50], and European initiatives like the CONCERTO Program [51] or the DUT partnership [52]. This process allowed for the development of several sets of questions about barriers, incentives, and stakeholders. Subsequently, several workshops were held within the activities of WG3 to update, adapt, and classify the questions proposed to the PED Lab concept. Numerous international initiatives have been working on Positive Energy Districts for years, although only recently has a database been developed to compile information on both PEDs and PED Labs [53]. This new PED database was created thanks to the collaboration between COST Action CA19126 [48], JPI Urban Europe [54], and Annex 83 of the EBC of the IEA [55]. Once the questions were adapted to the PED Lab environment, the questionnaires were presented to the WG3 expert group, gathering the necessary data to conduct this qualitative study.

The 30 PED laboratories registered in the Cost Action Database, located throughout Europe, were used as case studies for this research. (see Figure 2). This sample covers a wide range of European climates, encompassing regions from the south (Spain and Italy), the center (Netherlands and Belgium), and the north of Europe (Finland and Estonia). It also encompasses different contexts, such as social housing blocks, energy districts, and virtual laboratories. Identifying the main characteristics of these laboratories and evaluating the existing literature on these emerging urban concepts enabled the development of a series of questions for the questionnaires. These questions were selected to identify the key positive and negative factors influencing the implementation of PED Labs, according to the experience and opinions of the participants. More information about the questionnaires can be found in deliverable T3.1 of WG3 of Action Cost CA19126 [56].

The questions were initially coded around three thematic areas: (i) barriers to PED Lab implementation; (ii) drivers and unlocking factors enabling their success; and (iii) key stakeholders involved in their development and operation. Subsequently, another set of questions was designed and implemented, coded as facilities, with the objective of gathering information on the facility assets required for the operation of these laboratories.

To gather information on existing PED and PED Lab initiatives, several online workshops and interactive sessions were held with an average of twenty expert participants from the WG3—Task 3.1 network. The process was divided into two phases: (i) completion of online questionnaires using collaborative tools such as MURAL, and (ii) follow-up group discussions to validate and refine questionnaire results and build consensus.

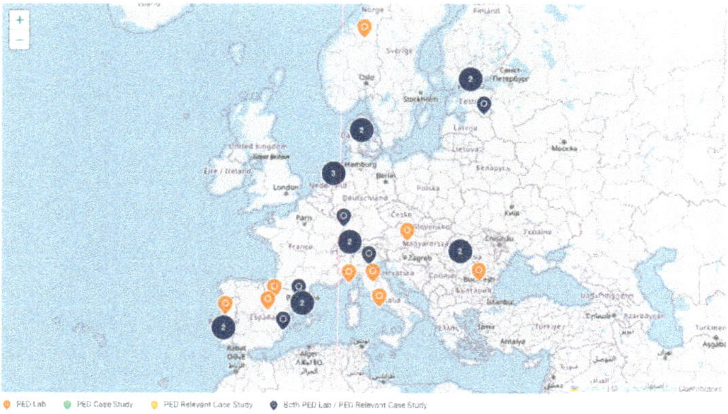

Figure 2. Map of PED Labs and PED Relevant Case Study distributed in Europe available in the Cost Action CA19126 Database [53].

To obtain relevance-weighted responses on these issues, participants were asked to:

- Approve and refine a proposed list of items in each of the three proposed thematic areas, suggesting groupings and modifications where necessary.
- Rate each item using a Likert scale from 1 (low relevance) to 5 (high relevance).
- Participate in facilitated discussions to interpret questionnaire results collectively and identify key learnings.

The qualitative analysis was structured around four main topics: barriers, drivers, stakeholders, and facilities, which were further divided into more specific categories. This coding of the questionnaire data allowed, on the one hand, the grouping of information to identify patterns or trends, and on the other, the development of a holistic understanding of these laboratories. Figure 3 shows the four topics coded in the questionnaires, schematically highlighting the key aspects to be considered within each.

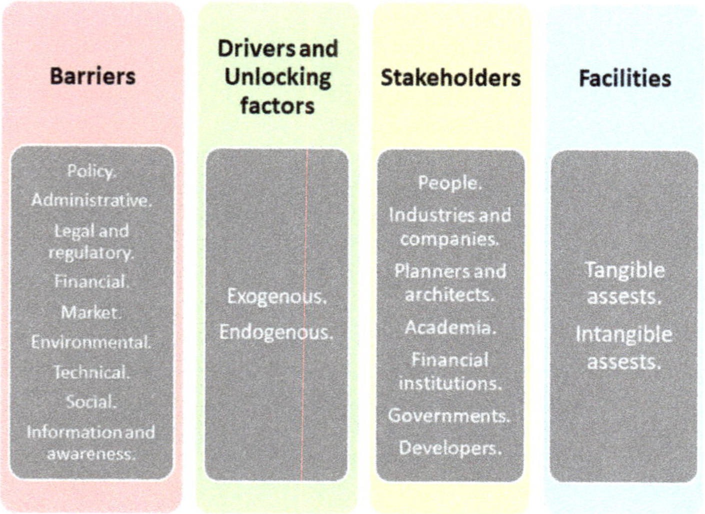

Figure 3. Scheme of the key aspects considered in the four thematic areas coded for the questionnaires.

2.1.1. Barriers

A series of questions was developed to identify the key aspects that hinder or block the implementation and development of PED Labs. These questions were formulated based on the existing literature on Smart Energy Cities projects [57–59] and were subsequently adapted, updated, and ranked based on feedback from a WG3 workshop involving eighteen experts from COST Action PED-EU-NET. In this workshop, it was assumed that the barriers to implementing a Smart Energy City are similar and scalable to those encountered in the PED Lab context. Nine categories of barriers (i.e., policy, administrative, legal and regulatory, financial, market, environmental, technical, social, and information and awareness) were proposed to the WG3 participants, resulting in fifty-one targeted questions.

2.1.2. Drivers and Unlocking Factors

Additional questions were designed to identify the key factors that drive the adoption of PED Lab initiatives or establish favorable conditions for their implementation and development. These questions were derived from the literature on Smart Cities and Urban Laboratories [60–62]. For analytical clarity and based on the area of action, the factors were classified into two categories, which are drivers and unlocking factors. Drivers are the key elements that motivate the initiation and execution of a laboratory, while unlocking factors are conditions that enhance or improve the initial environment, thereby facilitating the deployment of these urban laboratories.

2.1.3. Stakeholders and Processes

The successful implementation of PEDs requires the collaboration of diverse stakeholders, necessitating systematic methods for identifying and engaging these groups throughout different development phases. Cheng et al. [63] proposed a stakeholder mapping framework that addresses dynamic roles at the building, district, and city levels and suggests incorporating managerial tools into the PED development toolbox. Other interview-based studies have assessed stakeholders' perceptions regarding energy vulnerability mitigation through PEDs, thereby promoting a more inclusive transition in urban areas [64]. However, harmonizing design phases, stakeholder interests, and scales can be challenging due to their frequent intersections. In practice, these elements are interconnected at critical decision-making moments, known as "intervention points", where it is essential to identify the key stakeholders and the appropriate tools for engagement [65].

Similarly, further questions were sought to identify the main actors and processes involved at each stage of deploying PED Labs. In these questionnaires, six subsequent phases were identified: vision, decision, planning, execution, evaluation (check/act), and scaling and replication. Additionally, seven stakeholder groups were considered: people, industries and companies, planners and architects, academia, financial institutions, governments, and developers. The classification of stakeholders was built on the types of stakeholders commonly discussed in the PED literature. This follows either a taxonomical or functional approach. Taxonomical approaches identify stakeholder sectors, usually including community, market/private, policy/public sectors [66], in many cases supplemented by the research/academic sector [4]. The market sector can be broken down to energy providers, technology developers, while the community sector may include a citizen and an NGO subgroup [67]. The functional approach specifies roles justifying stakeholder engagement [68]. Property owners, energy system operators, potential local energy producers, and potential flexibility providers as key target groups to engage early on [69,70]; urban planners, representatives from different levels and departments of governments can act as important catalysts, and residents, researchers and technical experts are important to consult to ensure best fit and legitimacy in local contexts [71,72].

As the specific list of stakeholder types will vary from project to project [66], we opted for a taxonomical approach, using a functional approach to identify categories that will likely show different required levels of engagement, with the categories shown in Table 1.

Table 1. Stakeholder categories and actor types involved in the PED Lab implementation process.

Stakeholder Category	Stakeholder Type
Community	Residents, citizens, property owners, energy communities, and neighborhood organizations
Financial	Investors, banks, funding providers, and financial institutions
Industry	Technology providers, grid operators, energy providers, and private companies
Planning	Urban planners, architects, and consultants
Research	Universities, research institutions, and research-performing private companies
Policy	Local and national authorities, public administrations, and local and national governments
Developer	Real estate, asset, and portfolio developers and managers

2.1.4. Facilities

The design or replication of a PED Lab requires identifying the types of facilities necessary for its proper operation. Based on existing literature and the expertise of the participating professional group, this question was addressed by categorizing facilities into two groups: tangible and intangible assets. Tangible assets refer to elements that enable the physical transformation of a district (i.e., structures and infrastructure), while intangible assets relate to the transformation of non-physical components (i.e., society, knowledge, behavior, economy, or skills). Based on this, the questionnaire focused on three key aspects:

- The specific role of these facilities in the development of a PED Lab.
- Identification of tangible (hardware) and intangible (software) assets.
- Creation of a comprehensive list of facilities.

2.2. *Qualitative Analysis*

The second step involved a comprehensive qualitative analysis of the responses obtained from the questionnaires. Once the response database was generated, the data were systematically coded to identify convergence or divergence in expert opinion and to map the interconnections among barriers, drivers, and stakeholder roles. This process resulted in a classification of these laboratories' facilities based on tangible and intangible assets and stakeholder roles, as well as a SWOT matrix identifying the most positive and negative aspects of the implementation process. Other previous studies, also based on an approach using SWOT matrices, delve into identifying the key contextual factors for transforming districts in Latin America and the Caribbean [73].

These analyses were enriched by collaborative discussions held during multiple WG3 meetings under COST Action PED-EU-NET [48], ensuring that diverse perspectives were represented. This qualitative approach facilitated the identification of primary challenges faced by PED Labs and informed the subsequent development of targeted research questions.

2.3. *Findings*

The starting point for this methodology was the 30 relevant cases and laboratories from the Cost Action database [53], classified into four categories according to their implementation phase. An evaluation of their characteristics made it possible to identify the most relevant topics to be addressed in the questionnaires. Table 2 shows the classification of these laboratories and highlights some of their key characteristics.

Table 2. Classification of PED Labs and PED relevant cases from the Action Cost PED Database, indicating some of their peculiarities [53].

Phase	Number	Characteristics
Planning	12	Many of the PED Labs are planned within the framework of European projects targeting energy goals, climate neutrality, or inequality reduction. They leverage public–private partnerships and require more tailored regulations, broader stakeholder involvement and dissemination, and the simplification of certain administrative procedures.
Implementation	12	Several have been developed within European projects aimed at increasing energy efficiency and sustainability while reducing vulnerabilities. They leverage reduced material and technology costs and greater short-term stakeholder engagement. They require simpler, better-coordinated administrative procedures, more robust medium and long-term plans, and well-developed economic models.
Completed	1	Rehabilitated suburban area in Trento (Stardust project), which leveraged existing financing and economic models to improve energy efficiency and sustainability. It requires ongoing funding and stakeholder involvement to ensure the proper maintenance of the facilities in the future.
In Operation	5	Real, virtual, and semi-virtual laboratories (some also developed within European projects) operate through various funding sources. Require effective coordination, greater stakeholder engagement, and sustained funding to operate with updated facilities.

Once the surveys were developed, conducted, and processed, the final step of this methodology was to identify the main findings. To this end, the results were initially mapped to detect trends, peaks, or gaps, enabling the creation of categorized lists. The findings were then structured to highlight existing problems and challenges, as well as available resources and the essential requirements for the successful operation or replication of a PED lab. These aspects were organized using a SWOT matrix, which identifies strengths, weaknesses, opportunities, and threats. To develop this matrix, participants analyzed different laboratories listed in the COST Action CA19126 PED database [53], drawing on the collective experience and knowledge of professionals highly committed to PED initiatives across Europe. This database was specifically designed and developed to map PEDs, PED Cases, and PED Labs, supporting the identification of the most relevant characteristics of these urban structures and enhancing understanding of their development and operation.

3. Results

This section presents the outcomes obtained from the questionnaires, qualitative discussions, and WG3 workshops held in the framework of COST Action PED-EU-NET [49].

The first four Sections 3.1—3.4, present the details of the analysis performed on the identified barriers, drivers, unlocking factors, stakeholders, and facilities, respectively. The following Section 3.5 presents a SWOT analysis that synthesizes the internal strengths and weaknesses, as well as external opportunities and threats, associated with PED Lab development. Once all the information generated has been processed, and after a process of discussion and analysis, the research questions proposed are answered. These questions capture the main identified challenges and gaps and serve as a roadmap for future research on the implementation, evaluation, and replication of PED Labs.

3.1. Analysis of Barriers

Drawing on the survey data and collaborative discussions, the analysis categorizes the barriers that impede the successful implementation and development of PED Labs into distinct domains, offering an understanding of the challenges that must be overcome. In particular, nine categories are proposed within the group of blocking factors, such as

- *Policy*: Energy plans, governance body visions, or political commitment.
- *Administrative*: Coordination, public participation, dissemination, ownership or authorization procedures.
- *Legal and regulatory*: Regulations, instability, building codes, incentives or privacy protection.
- *Financial*: Cost, financial support, access to capital, economic crisis or risks and uncertainty.
- *Market*: Split incentives, energy price distortion, or energy market actors.
- *Environmental*: Lack of information or negative effects on the natural environment.
- *Technical*: Tested solutions, technical commitments, qualified personnel, computational scalability, grid instability or accurate urban models.
- *Social*: Inertia, interest, acceptance, engagement, rebound effect, attitudes, exclusion or lack of trust.
- *Information and awareness*: Insufficient information, awareness, perceptions or information asymmetry.

Analysis of these data reveals that administrative, legal, financial and some social factors pose significant challenges. Conversely, environmental factors, along with many technical and market factors, are perceived as less obstructive to the implementation of these laboratories. A more detailed analysis of the barrier code database highlights widespread concerns across almost all categories, identifying factors that delay or block implementation. Except for the Environmental topic, the other eight categories achieve average scores above 3 (on a scale from 1 and 5).

Figure 4 presents the questionnaire results on barriers, shown in a radar graph. On average, the highest-scoring category is Information and Awareness, followed by Financial and Social, with values above 3.6. The highest-scoring subcategory or question is 'Inertia' from the Social category, followed by 'Limited access to capital and cost disincentives' from the Financial category, both with values above 4. Conversely, the lowest-scoring subcategory or question is 'Negative effects of project intervention on the natural environment' from the Environmental category, followed by 'Hostile or passive attitude towards environmentalism' from the Social category, both scoring below 3.

To overcome the two main obstacles identified, a series of measures are proposed, recognizing that the contextual factors of each laboratory are key elements when selecting appropriate solutions. The barrier related to inertia can be reduced by increasing the engagement and active participation of technicians, citizens, and policymakers in laboratory activities through communication, information sharing, and capacity-building initiatives. Limited access to capital and financial instruments can be mitigated through new flexible economic models that combine public and private sponsorship to secure the necessary resources. Overcoming both barriers requires a shift in mindset to recognize and emphasize the benefits of integrated, efficient, and sustainable urban solutions that have already been successfully tested.

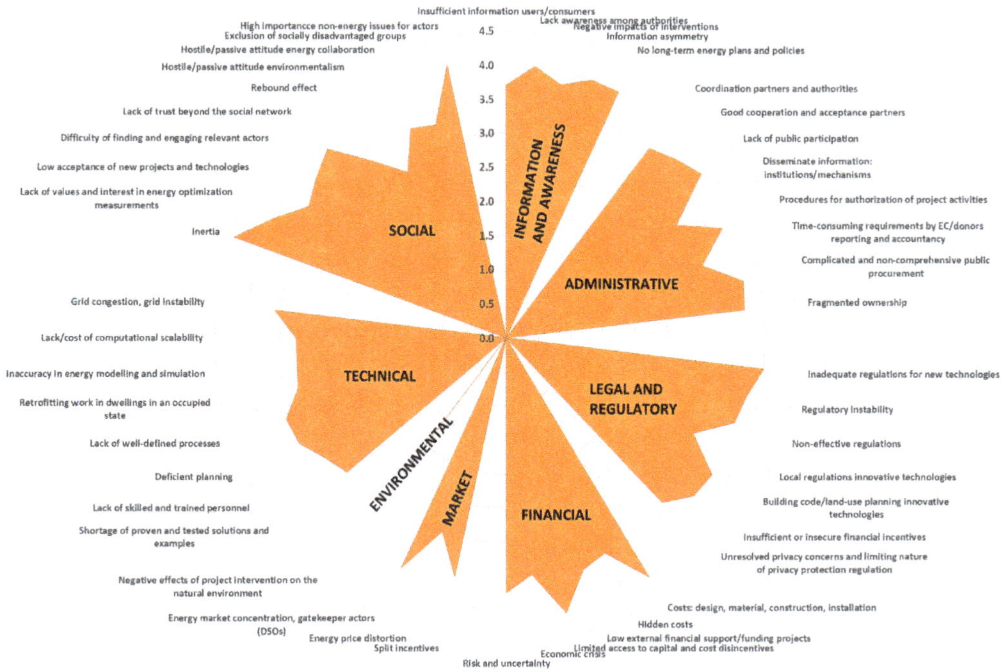

Figure 4. Radar graph showing the blocking factors weighted on a 1 to 5 Likert scale by the questionnaire participants.

3.2. Analysis of Drivers and Unlocking Factors

Two categories are defined for the group of driver factors, considering aspects such as

- Drivers: Climate change, urbanization trends, urban redevelopment, economic growth, market attractiveness, environmental quality, or energy autonomy.
- Unlocking factors: Technological improvements, innovative solutions, prefabricated packages, energy communities, prosumers, storage systems, decreasing cost, benefits, awareness, engagement, social acceptance, policy frameworks, funding, or multidisciplinary approaches.

Figure 5 presents the results of the questionnaires regarding driving factors. The statistical data for this code indicate that both Drivers and Unlocking Factors categories received averaged scores above 3, with values of 3.45 and 3.3, respectively, on a scale from 1 to 5. As illustrated in the radar graph the factors that most enhance the implementation of a PED Lab, according to respondents, include 'Climate change mitigation', 'Energy autonomy and independence', 'Economic growth', 'Financial mechanisms', 'Strong existing local networks and associations', 'Improved local and national policy frameworks', 'Technological improvements for renewable energy systems (RES) production', and 'Energy efficiency and prefabricated packages for buildings', all scoring above 4.

Conversely, the aspects that contribute least to the implementation of these urban laboratories include: 'Rapid urbanization trend and need of urban expansions', 'Ability to predict benefits', 'Ability to predict the distribution of benefits and impacts', 'Social acceptance', and 'Dedicated change-agents among citizens', all scoring less than or equal to 3.5. To further incentivize these less influential aspects, a series of measures is proposed, recognizing that the contextual factors of each laboratory are key when selecting appropriate solutions. Controlled and efficient urban expansion is necessary, characterized by the rational use of resources and a sustainable land use index. Improving social acceptance requires involving citizens in the development of new urban models, fostering a sense of pride and ownership in these laboratories. The development of digital citizen platforms allows for the evaluation of different integrated urban scenarios, helping to highlight the associated benefits and predict potential negative impacts that can be avoided.

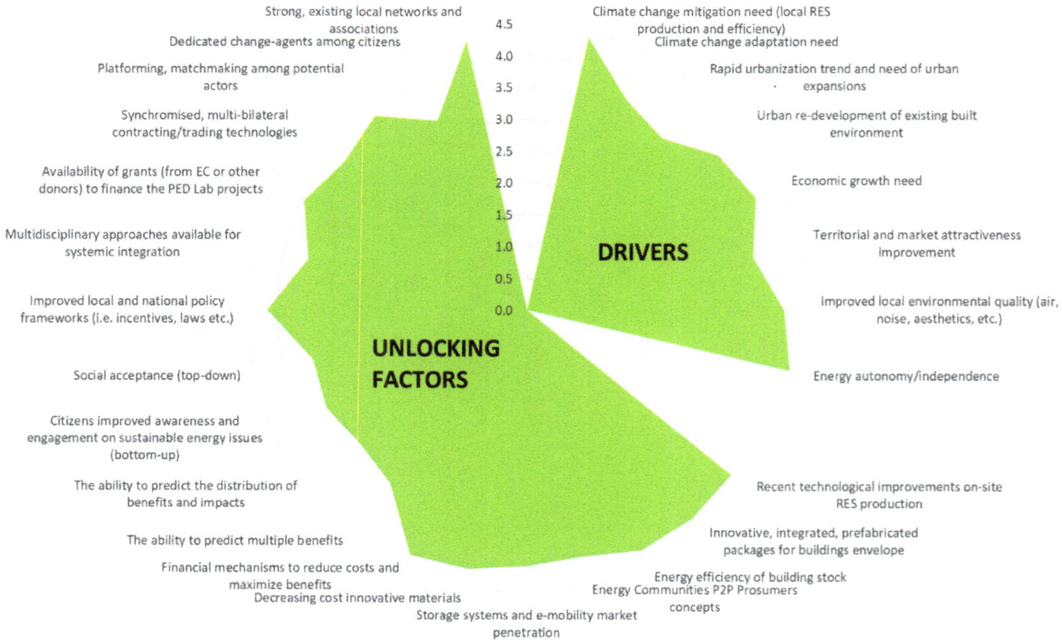

Figure 5. Radar graph showing the unlocking factors and drivers from 1 to 5 Likert scale by the questionnaire participants.

3.3. *Analysis of Stakeholders and Process Mapping*

The correct mapping of stakeholders requires identifying who will participate in each of the processes of these laboratories. Six phases are considered in the life cycle of a PED Lab: vision, decision, planning, implementation, check/act and upscale and replicate. Seven groups of stakeholders are proposed: people, industries and companies, planners and architects, academia, financial institutions, governments, and developers.

Figure 6 shows the influence of each stakeholder in the six proposed phases. As shown, the influence of each stakeholder varies throughout the implementation process, and it is important to note that some stakeholders may change their positions or reconsider their participation as they move from one phase to another. Analysis of the statistical values generated in this code shows average scores above 3 for both the phases and the stakeholder categories. In the phase category, average scores for all actors range between 3.6 and 3.8, with the highest values in the Vision phase and the lowest in the Plan and Check/Act phases. In the actor category, average scores throughout the process range between 3.3 and 4, with maximum values for Governments and minimum for Financial Institutions.

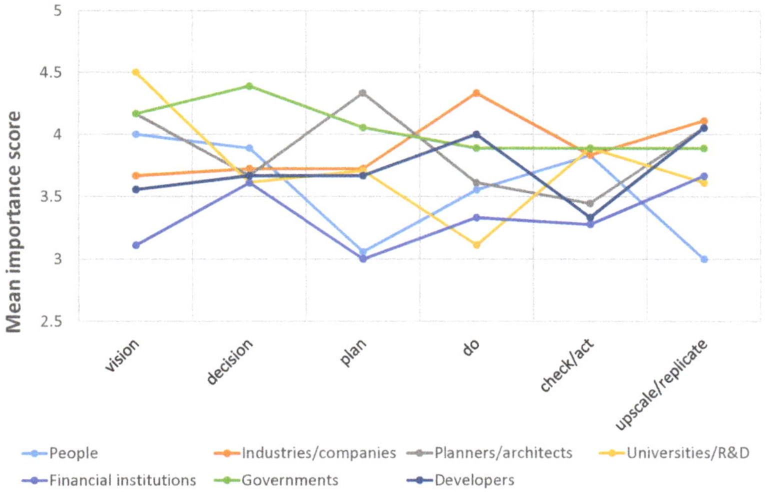

Figure 6. Line graph showing the stakeholders involved in each of the proposed processes, weighted from 1 to 5 by the questionnaire participants.

The distribution of stakeholder roles in each phase is as follows:

- *Vision phase*: The participation of universities and the R&D sector is determinant, along with that of the government and planners. Consulting with citizens is also a high priority.
- *Decision phase*: The government is the main actor, supported by citizens.
- *Plan phase*: In this phase, planners manage the process with support from the government, assisted by industry, universities, and developers.
- *Do phase*: Industry and developers are the primary actors operating within a framework promoted by the government. The role of financial institutions as investors also becomes prominent.
- *Check/Act phase*: All stakeholders must be involved in this phase in various capacities.
- *Upscale/Replicate phase*: This phase is linked to the 'do phase' and features a similar distribution of roles. Notably, the lack of citizen involvement in this phase is surprising.

The analysis of these aspects enables the formulation of practical recommendations to define a phase-based engagement strategy. The visioning phase is an open-ended discovery process where the PED Lab resembles a conventional laboratory, focused on research and innovation activities. The decision phase functions more as a participatory democratic process, emphasizing the involvement of public institutions and citizens, with activities focusing on deliberation and maximizing legitimacy. The planning phase is driven by planners, transforming the PED Lab into a participatory design/planning process, where the key activity is the synthesis of formal (expert) and tacit (citizen) knowledge strategies to frame and solve the PED challenge. The do phase is when technology developers take the lead, and the PED Lab becomes a sandbox to test, simulate or play out different PED configurations, identifying what works best in the local context. The check phase has no clear frontrunner; instead, co-leadership between research, policy, and private actors suggests a focus on sense making and translating previous findings into concrete actions across different domains such as new policies, installed technologies, and knowledge. Finally, the upscaling phase shows higher scores for the actors most involved in applying these findings to other projects. At this stage, the PED Lab consists of a series of strategizing activities, each leveraging the diverse stakeholder group and insights from earlier phases, focused on specific aspects of replication or upscaling. Citizens focus on expanding the PED's geographical or technical scope, technology developers on rolling out their products, developers on creating new PEDs elsewhere, and governments on establishing enabling frameworks to accelerate PED adoption.

3.4. Facilities Classification

Based on the responses from the expert panel, the facilities were classified according to tangible and intangible assets and the role of stakeholders in each phase. The following figure shows the classification of the facilities, highlighting when and where they are relevant in the implementation process.

Figure 7 effectively categorizes facilities into tangible and intangible assets, reflecting a holistic view of what is required to implement PED Labs. This dual categorization acknowledges that successful PED implementation relies not only on infrastructure and technology, but also on human, social, and institutional factors. The mapping of each facility across six implementation phases: Vision, Decision, Plan, Do, Check/Act, Upscale/Replicate, provides insight into the dynamic relevance of each asset type over time. For instance, intangible assets dominate the early stages, emphasizing the need for public awareness, fostering trust, and establishing robust legal frameworks. Conversely, technical systems become more critical in later action-oriented stages, during implementation and monitoring phases, ensuring that the necessary infrastructure is in place.

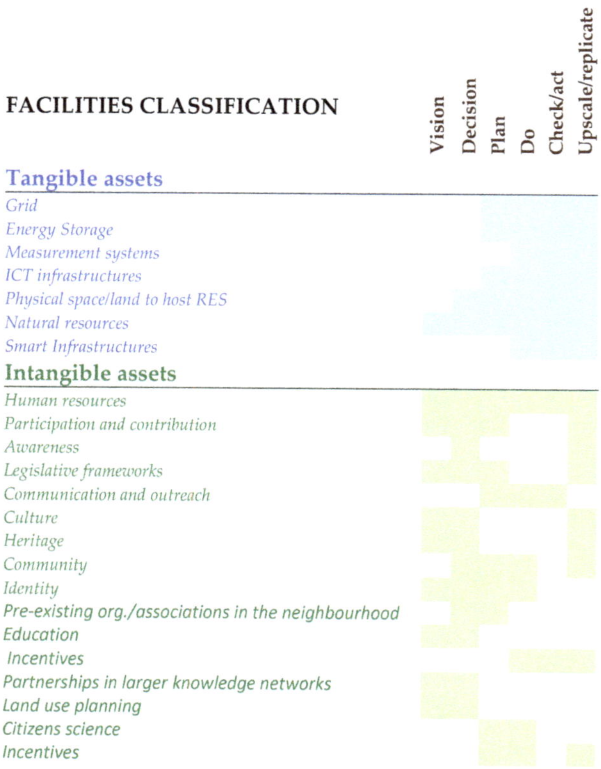

Figure 7. Classification of facilities to identify when and where they are relevant in the PED Lab implementation process.

The figure highlights the importance of intangible assets such as legislative frameworks, culture, education, and identity that are often underrepresented in technical planning. Their consistent presence across multiple stages suggests their foundational role in ensuring long-term behavioral change, social acceptance, and institutional resilience. This challenges traditional infrastructure-focused models by placing equal importance on intangible assets.

The matrix serves as a strategic planning tool, helping project teams and policymakers identify which facilities to prioritize at each stage and assess readiness and identify potential gaps. The early identification of gaps, such as weak community participation or insufficient legislative support, can inform corrective action before implementation begins.

The presence of certain assets in the final stage (Upscale/Replicate) reveals which elements are essential for expanding PED Labs beyond pilot projects. This includes assets such as participation, culture, community, and incentive mechanisms. Their enduring relevance suggests that sustainable upscaling depends on long-term investments in capacity building and institutional frameworks.

The diverse nature of the assets implies that PED Labs cannot be realized through isolated efforts. Successful implementation requires coordinated input from engineers, urban planners, social scientists, policymakers, educators, and citizens, encouraging collaborative governance models. Finally, the figure provides actionable insights for policymakers and funding bodies. It highlights critical leverage points, assets that support multiple phases, and thus offers guidance on where to prioritize investment. For example, strengthening education, legal frameworks, and community networks may yield system-wide benefits throughout the PED lifecycle. This enables more efficient resource allocation, better stakeholder coordination, and improved readiness for future scaling or replication.

3.5. SWOT Analysis

Once the key features, facilities, and main actors are identified, it is necessary to structure the results to highlight the available resources and necessary requirements for the successful operation or replication of a PED Lab. These aspects are structured in a SWOT matrix expressing the Strengths, Weaknesses, Opportunities, and Threats identified by the focus group. This analysis reflects the collective expertise and experience of practitioners actively and deeply engaged in PED initiatives across Europe. Figure 8 summarizes the main key elements of this SWOT matrix.

A major **strength** lies in the foundation of expertise many PED initiatives are built. Several teams already have extensive backgrounds in sustainability and smart energy systems, which naturally lends credibility and depth to PED-related projects. PED Labs also offers something cities rarely obtain: a chance to test strategies before fully committing to them. This ability to trial and adjust in real urban settings is crucial for reducing risk and improving outcomes. Another asset is the experience on the results of tested solutions, in other words, the availability of insights from earlier efforts, lessons learned, data collected, and relationships built, which accelerates future implementation. The practice of co-design, where solutions are shaped in collaboration with stakeholders, also stands out. It ensures that interventions resonate with those directly affected. Additionally, these labs serve as a platform for learning across projects and cities, encouraging replication and refinement.

Regarding the **weaknesses**, perhaps the most fundamental is the ongoing lack of a shared understanding of what exactly constitutes a PED Lab. This conceptual ambiguity can slow down coordination and dilute impact. Moreover, many projects suffer from limited or inconsistent engagement from key players. Without sustained buy-in from stakeholders, long-term implementation falters. In some cases, energy transition strategies are not aligned with urban planning processes, creating barriers to integrated solutions.

Regulatory support is often vague or missing entirely, especially at the district scale, where governance tends to be fragmented or absent. Time and resource constraints mean that many PED Labs are rushed into action without the chance to fully refine or tailor their interventions. Resource scarcity also extends to limited space, which constrains the development of renewable energy facilities. There is also the issue of insufficient communication between the many actors involved, with technical and social dimensions frequently handled in isolation rather than through a unified approach.

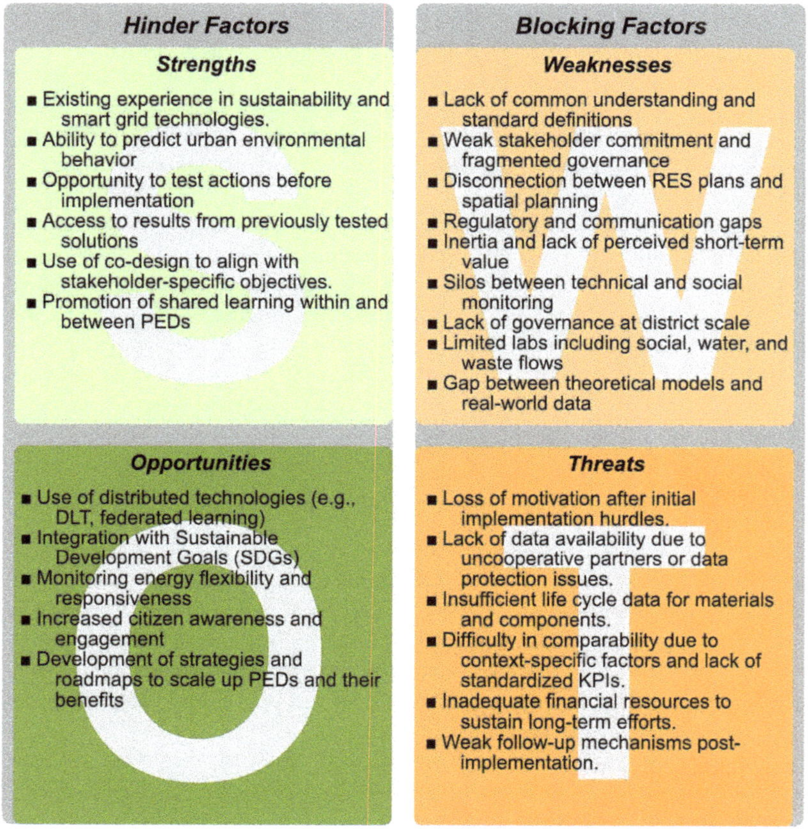

Figure 8. SWOT analysis summary based on the results obtained from the COST PED WG3 focus group.

Supporting the PED development, **opportunities** related to technological advancements, especially in decentralized systems, think block chain, edge computing, or federated data models, are becoming increasingly accessible. These can support the kind of distributed, flexible infrastructure PEDs require. At the same time, public awareness around energy and climate issues is rising. Citizens are more informed and, when engaged meaningfully, more willing to participate in transformative projects. This opens the door for labs to serve not only as technical platforms but also as civic spaces for dialog and innovation. The group also pointed to the opportunity to develop clear strategies and roadmaps to increase PED numbers and benefits.

Finally, several external **threats** were also pointed out. Starting is hard enough, but sustaining momentum is even harder. Many initiatives lose steam after the initial pilot phase, particularly when funding ends or partners drift away. Data privacy regulations and a lack of collaboration can limit access to the very information needed to evaluate and improve PED systems. Meanwhile, the variability in local conditions and the absence of standard performance metrics make it difficult to compare or benchmark results across contexts. This hinders the ability to build a robust evidence base. Finally, financial uncertainty remains a constant concern. Without long-term support and clear mechanisms for follow-up, even the most promising labs can stagnate or be dismantled before they reach maturity.

The four categories that make up this SWOT matrix allow highlighting the most general aspects to be considered in the implementation of a PED Lab. These elements complement other enquiries as that of Soutullo et al., 2020 [43]. However, it is important to keep in mind that these factors depend largely on the specific characteristics of each laboratory. While they provide useful insights, these factors should be carefully assessed against the specific context of the PED Lab to effectively support its successful deployment.

4. Discussion and Conclusions

Comparative international experiences show that PED Labs adapt their objectives and implementation strategies to reflect regional priorities and capacities. In Europe, they are primarily driven by policy frameworks and aligned with smart city and climate neutrality goals. In Asia, PED Labs often emerge from technology-driven urban experiments, integrating energy, mobility, and digital systems to foster innovation-led growth, with smart city initiatives supporting green urban development through digital infrastructure and industrial modernization. Across the Americas, PED-related efforts focus on combining renewable energy systems with innovative governance models and urban–industrial synergies. In Latin America, many initiatives arise from grassroots movements, blending social innovation with environmental sustainability and often emphasizing participatory approaches to urban development and energy transitions. In Oceania, PED Labs contribute to strengthening resilience in regional and remote communities by integrating renewable energy, energy storage, and community engagement. Despite these contextual differences, PED Labs face common challenges related to governance complexity, stakeholder coordination, and long-term sustainability, yet develop solutions shaped by local climate conditions, socio-economic realities, and technological readiness.

This study addresses a fundamental gap in the literature by clarifying the conceptual and operational contours of PED Labs, offering an empirically grounded framework to guide their implementation, evaluation, and replication. Through qualitative methodologies, stakeholder engagement, and cross-referencing with current European initiatives, the study identifies and analyzes the critical barriers, enablers, actors, and facilities critical to their deployment. Further analysis of the collected data highlights social and financial aspects as the most blocking factors. Nevertheless, climate change mitigation measures, strong local networks, and improvements in local and national policy frameworks are identified as the main drivers.

The implementation of PED Labs represents a significant step forward in the pursuit of sustainable, climate-resilient urban environments. Unlike traditional testbeds focused on isolated technology demonstrations, PED Labs operate as dynamic socio-technical systems. They integrate technological innovation with institutional, cultural, and community processes. This integrated perspective is reflected in the facility classification (Figure 7), where intangible assets, such as legislative frameworks, education, identity, and awareness, emerge as essential in early phases (e.g., Vision and Decision), while tangible infrastructures (i.e., ICT systems, energy storage, grid infrastructure) dominate implementation and upscaling phases. This finding underscores the need for holistic planning that incorporates both human and technical dimensions from the outset. PED Labs are not simply sites of technical innovation but key vehicles for co-producing knowledge, policy, and behavior change toward energy-positive urban futures.

Another key contribution of this research lies in its detailed mapping of stakeholder influence across the six phases of the PED Lab lifecycle. The stakeholder importance survey reinforces the importance of all the stakeholder groups, since neither received a score below 3. Interestingly, it shows different dominant actors in different phases. The mapping of stakeholders reveals the pivotal role of government actors and the importance of citizen involvement, particularly during the vision and decision phases. The analysis generated through this matrix supports the definition of a phase-based engagement strategy and, thus, the design concept of the PED Lab for each phase. Table 3 shows the dominant actors, the main facilities assets, and phase-based suggestions that outline engagement concepts at each phase of PED Labs.

Table 3. Specific roles of key Stakeholders, main facilities assets, and phase-based suggestions of PED Labs.

Phase	Dominant Actor	Main Facilities Assets	Engagement Concept
Vision	Research	Intangible	Citizen science, co-discovery
Decision	Policy and community	Intangible	Participatory democracy
Plan	Planning	Tangible and Intangible	Participatory planning and design
Do	Industry	Tangible	Citizen science, field testing
Check/Act	Industry, policy, research	Tangible	Sense making, site policy, and design recommendations
Upscale/Replicate	Industry, policy, planners, developers	Tangible and Intangible	Strategizing, general policy, market rollout recommendations

The participatory design of this study, leveraging input from the COST Action PED-EU-NET community, allows for a detailed exploration of these issues. Notably, the SWOT analysis reveals that while PED Labs benefit from accumulated technical expertise and increasing public interest in energy transition, they remain vulnerable to several risks. These include conceptual ambiguity, inconsistent stakeholder commitment, and funding discontinuity, factors that can undermine long-term impact if not addressed strategically.

Opportunities for the expansion and institutionalization of PED Labs are tied to the rapid evolution of decentralized energy technologies, increased digitalization, and the growing acceptance of collaborative governance models. Public awareness, growing civic interest, and emerging digital tools such as federated data platforms and smart simulations provide fertile ground for replication and upscaling. However, realizing this potential will require addressing structural weaknesses, particularly the absence of standardized frameworks and evaluation metrics.

The analysis of the data and the engagement concepts generated after the implementation of this methodology allows answering the three proposed research questions.

What are the current barriers to the implementation of PED-Labs?

This research identifies nine categories of factors that hinder the development of a PED Lab, including social, administrative, legal-regulatory, financial, and information-related factors. The qualitative analysis reveals that social and financial factors emerged as particularly obstructive, followed by administrative, regulatory, and legal, and information and awareness aspects. These findings reflect broader challenges in urban innovation, where multi-level governance and divergent stakeholder interests can create friction in implementation.

What are the drivers and incentive factors (unlocking) that determine the "fertility of the soil" for PED-Lab initiatives?

This research formulates forty-two questions related to unlocking and driving factors. The qualitative analysis identifies the need for climate change mitigation measures, the presence of strong local networks, and the improvement of local and national political frameworks as the primary aspects that most encourage the development of a PED Lab. Technological advancements and cost reductions in renewable systems also enhance the feasibility of PED Lab deployment. However, the absence of standardized governance models and common evaluation metrics continues to constrain the replicability and scalability of these initiatives across different urban contexts.

What processes and actors define the steps, power relationships, and subsidiarity in responsibilities and decisions within PED Lab initiatives?

In this work, seven groups of stakeholders have been identified that influence the achievement of urban laboratory objectives across the six proposed phases, depending on the activities required at each phase. Governments stand out as one of the main actors throughout the process.

The importance of collaborative governance is further reinforced by the classification of facilities and the interdependence of actors. While PED Labs thrive on cross-sectoral synergies, these are often undermined by fragmented practices and insufficient coordination. The classification framework developed in this research offers a practical tool to manage this complexity and ensure the timely mobilization of critical assets and actors.

Finally, this research affirms the pressing need for a shared conceptual and operational framework for PED Labs. The current diversity in definitions, approaches, and scopes across Europe and beyond creates barriers to comparison and replication. By distilling findings from focus groups, the literature review, and existing cases, this study contributes concrete parameters for future standardization, particularly in relation to stakeholder engagement, asset planning, and governance design.

PED Labs hold significant promise as instruments for achieving zero-emission targets and advancing broader urban sustainability agendas. Realizing this potential will depend on consolidating their conceptual foundations, embedding them within robust governance systems, and securing the long-term policy and financial commitments needed for impact.

5. Recommendations and Limitations

PED Labs emerge as viable platforms for conducting a variety of experiments towards PEDs, allowing for the analysis and validation of integrated solutions across similar or diverse urban contexts.

When implementing a PED Lab, the first recommendation is to establish a clear definition of what this type of urban laboratory is and what it entails. The initial concept is rooted in the Urban Living Lab concept combined with the Smart Energy City and Near Zero Energy Buildings frameworks, with a focus on the district scale and a robust monitoring component within controlled environments. This approach merges the capabilities of a living lab with sustainability and energy positivity objectives, enabling experiments to be conducted in real urban settings, and with a citizens' centric perspective, to validate innovative solutions on small and medium scales. However, stakeholder mapping is essential, as it reveals the dynamic roles of various groups throughout the six phases of a PED Lab's life cycle.

As a result of the application of this methodology, it was possible to answer the research questions formulated at the beginning of the study and to develop a series of recommendations for establishing effective PED Labs. These recommendations, along with suggested implementation mechanisms and expected outcomes, are listed in Table 4.

Table 4. Reasoned list of recommendations supporting the establishment of PED Labs.

Recommendation	Implementation Mechanism	Expected Effects
Prioritize stakeholder commitment and participation.	Develop tailored communication strategies for each stakeholder category, highlighting their specific value propositions	Balanced participation across stakeholder categories, embedding inclusion principles in PED Labs operations, and enhancing representativeness
Build coherent and inclusive governance at the district level, promoting citizen involvement in leadership wherever possible.	Design appropriate governance mechanisms through multi-stakeholder dialog. Identify and engage vulnerable and marginalized groups. Establish rules with PED Lab promoters to empower citizens.	More effective and impactful PED Labs, with inclusive governance and extended user-centered validation processes.
Focus on integrated, holistic district planning, incorporating other dimensions into the energy approach.	Establish a common planning tool at the district level as a PED Lab asset. Integrate energy dimension with mobility, services, zoning, and green infrastructure. Prioritize open source and open data systems to reduce barriers.	Consistent data collection, integration, and management. Holistic view of energy in district master planning. Open access to data and services.
Capitalize on favorable regulations through communication and action plans.	Map the existing regulatory landscape and promote strategies to activate supportive regulations via PED Lab governance.	Integration of the PED Lab into multilevel governance, accelerating the adoption of relevant energy and climate regulations.
Identify quick wins and short-term added value to motivate stakeholders.	Map project outputs and assets and identify those most suitable to deliver immediate value to stakeholders. Implement scaling-up actions on selected bundles.	Increased stakeholder engagement, reduced skepticism and disillusionment, and improved communication and dissemination through success stories.
Break down silos between technical, social, environmental, and political approaches	Provide tools for balanced dialog among stakeholders, introduce citizen science approaches and science-policy focus groups, and establish challenge-driven cross-disciplinary teams.	PED Labs are positioned as place-based open innovation platforms where diverse disciplines contribute to urban problem solving.
Leverage all available data providers, including citizen science, to bridge modeling with real-world applications.	Map data providers and develop value propositions to engage them in data sharing. Engage citizen science NGOs and pursue funding to increase high-quality citizen-sourced data generation.	Broader data sources, improved model validation, and enhanced citizens' involvement and awareness.
Further develop Information and Communication Technologies (ICT) in laboratory facilities.	Expand district ICT infrastructure through targeted projects, partnerships with technology providers, and the activation of underutilized assets (e.g., smart meters, home automation) with smart software solutions.	Improved data collection processes, greater data volume and coverage, and expanded opportunities for experimentation in PEDs.
Define reliable business models to test different scenarios, combining technologies and innovations	Integrate systemic business modeling as a core component of PED Labs. Engage stakeholders to align diverse interests and desired impacts in business model design.	Increased private sector interest, fairness embedded in co-designed models with vulnerable groups representatives, and greater acceptance and scalability.
Integrate PED Labs into urban strategies for achieving the UN SDGs	Develop a tool linking PED Lab outcomes to UN SDGs targets, demonstrating the contribution of PED solutions when fully deployed.	Enhanced contribution of PED Labs to local SDG agendas, and greater community mobilization toward sustainability goals

Table 4. *Cont.*

Recommendation	Implementation Mechanism	Expected Effects
Offer PED Labs as a platform to strengthen and scale PEDs	Design PED Labs as experimental open innovation, demonstrating how learning-by-testing reduces costs and improves acceptance and effectiveness.	Enhanced flexibility of PEDs through innovation and the establishment of continuous learning-by-testing cycles.
Manage the motivation cycle by design, including regular revamping actions and resource allocation	Incorporate regular motivation-boosting activities in PED Lab roadmaps and action plans, tailored for each category of stakeholder. Institutionalize stakeholder consultation about the motivation to stay engaged. Implement fair resource allocation mechanisms through inclusive governance, such as participatory budgeting.	Sustained interest and participation from diverse stakeholder groups, and fair resource allocation with greater benefits for citizens and underrepresented categories
Promote data sharing and prevent conflicts and a lack of cooperation by establishing clear rules and agreements	Co-design codes of conduct, engagement rules, and MoUs to establish the PED Lab as a trusted space and prevent conflicts over data sharing.	Smooth implementation of data sharing processes and mutually beneficial deals in data sharing among key providers.
Address sustainability from the early stages.	Integrate broad sustainability goals (social, economic, and ecological) into the PED Lab's design, development roadmap, and KPIs.	Strengthened role of PEDs in sustainability agendas and multilevel action plans.
Develop climate change, energy efficiency, renewable, social, and economic measures based on proven experiments.	Establish science-policy dialogs at the local level and support them with experimental roadmaps in PED Labs. Conduct joint planning and reviews to maximize their policy relevance.	PEDs become infrastructures supporting policy-science interfaces, improving the quality of local policies through continuous data availability and validation feedback.

Nevertheless, this methodology has several limitations, as only a limited number of laboratories in Europe were studied. Therefore, further analysis of PED Labs in different locations is necessary. Increasing the sample analyzed would reduce uncertainty in the results and build greater trust among governments, property owners, and residents. Another area for further development in this methodology is the evaluation of synergies between technologies and innovations, requiring the active engagement of all stakeholders. The results of this study support the co-design, co-experimentation, and evaluation of various technological combinations. In addition, deeper exploration of co-governance strategies is needed, since these approaches promote proactive innovation while ensuring that solutions remain fit for purpose. An information, training, and capacity-building plan should also be developed to improve the use of the generated knowledge. This would enhance the capacity of governments and decision-makers to rapidly implement inclusive technological, social, and economic measures that address urgent needs in urban settlements while driving systemic change to improve quality of life and environmental performance.

The research questions initially formulated and addressed through this methodology, along with the recommendations presented, are intended to guide future research, focusing on the most relevant aspects of PED Lab implementation: barriers, drivers, facilities, and stakeholder processes. However, further research is still needed, particularly to replicate these models in different contexts. Therefore, the design, implementation, and monitoring of additional PED Labs are essential to consolidate and validate the ideas presented in this research.

Author Contributions: Conceptualization, D.V., V.B., S.S., O.S. and G.E.; methodology, D.V., V.B., S.S., M.N.S. and O.S.; validation, S.S., M.N.S., G.P., R.L., F.M.M., V.B., T.A., M.B.A. and O.S.; formal analysis, S.S., M.N.S., G.P., R.L., F.M.M., T.A., M.B.A., V.B., D.V., G.E. and O.S.; investigation, D.V., V.B., S.S., M.N.S., G.P., R.L., F.M.M., T.A., M.B.A., G.E. and O.S.; resources, D.V., V.B., G.E., O.S., M.B.A. and S.S.; data curation, D.V., V.B. and S.S.; writing—original draft preparation, D.V., V.B., S.S., M.N.S., O.S. and G.E.; writing—review and editing, S.S., G.P., F.M.M., R.L., M.N.S., O.S., V.B., M.B.A. and T.A.; visualization, S.S., M.N.S. and O.S.; supervision, S.S., M.N.S. and O.S.; project administration, D.V., V.B., S.S., O.S. and G.E.; funding acquisition, M.B.A., O.S. and G.E. All authors have read and agreed to the published version of the manuscript.

Funding: This research was funded by COST (European Cooperation in Science and Technology) under the Action 19126 Positive Energy Districts European Network (PED-EU-NET), CA19126.

Institutional Review Board Statement: All consultations and surveys presented in this article have been carried out with experts who are part of the COST-Action PED-EU-NET, specifically with participants of the WG3 activities of this COST-Action. Participants are subject to the conditions set out in its Memorandum of Understanding.

Informed Consent Statement: The scientific results presented in this research have been carried out within the activities developed under the framework of the COST Action CA19126 working groups, whose participants are subject to the conditions set out in its Memorandum of Understanding.

Data Availability Statement: Data are available upon request.

Acknowledgments: This article/publication is based upon work from COST Action Positive Energy Districts European Network, CA19126, supported by COST (European Cooperation in Science and Technology).

Conflicts of Interest: Author Viktor Bukovszki was employed by the company Advanced Building and Urban Design Ltd. The remaining authors declare that the research was conducted in the absence of any commercial or financial relationships that could be construed as a potential conflict of interest. All authors are members of WG3 of the CA19126 PED-EU-NET.

References

1. Van der Heijden, J. When opportunity backfires: Exploring the implementation of urban climate governance alternatives in three major US cities. *Policy Soc.* **2021**, *40*, 116–135. [CrossRef]
2. Derkenbaeva, E.; Halleck Vega, S.; Hofstede, G.J.; Van Leeuwen, E. Positive energy districts: Mainstreaming energy transition in urban areas. *Renew. Sustain. Energy Rev.* **2022**, *153*, 11782. [CrossRef]
3. Sassenou, L.N.; Olivieri, L.; Olivieri, F. Challenges for positive energy districts deployment: A systematic review. *Renew. Sustain. Energy Rev.* **2024**, *191*, 114152. [CrossRef]
4. Turci, G.; Civiero, P.; Aparisi-Cerdá, I.; Marotta, I.; Massa, G. Transition Approaches towards Positive Energy Districts: A Systematic Review. *Buildings* **2024**, *14*, 3039. [CrossRef]
5. Doci, G.; Dorst, H.; Hillen, S.; Tjokrodikromo, T. Urban transition governance in practice: Exploring how European cities govern local transitions to achieve climate neutrality. *Front. Sustain. Cities* **2025**, *7*, 1559356. [CrossRef]
6. Yadav, A.; Anwer, N.; Mahapatra, K.; Shrivastava, M.K.; Khatiwada, D. Analyzing the Role of Polycentric Governance in Institutional Innovations: Insights from Urban Climate Governance in India. *Sustainability* **2024**, *16*, 10736. [CrossRef]
7. Voytenko, Y.; McCormick, K.; Evans, J.; Schliwa, G. Urban Living Labs for Sustainability and Low Carbon Cities in Europe: Towards a Research Agenda. *J. Clean. Prod.* **2016**, *123*, 45–54. [CrossRef]
8. Afacan, Y. Impacts of urban living lab (ULL) on learning to design inclusive, sustainable, and climate-resilient urban environments. *Land Use Policy* **2023**, *124*, 106443. [CrossRef]
9. Voorwinden, A.; Van Bueren, E.; Verhoef, L. Experimenting with collaboration in the Smart City: Legal and governance structures of Urban Living Labs. *Gov. Inf. Q.* **2023**, *40*, 101875. [CrossRef]
10. Bechtel, J.; Kock, A. The relevance of urban agglomeration micro-foundations for the emergence of innovation in living labs: A qualitative field study. *J. Clean. Prod.* **2023**, *427*, 139280. [CrossRef]
11. Mukama, M.; Kaviti Musango, J.; Smit, S.; Ceschin, F.; Petrulaityte, A. Development of living labs to support gendered energy technology innovation in poor urban environments. *Technol. Soc.* **2022**, *68*, 101850. [CrossRef]
12. Aernouts, N.; Maranghi, E.; Ryckewaert, M. (Eds.) *Towards a Definition of Socially-Oriented LivingLabs*, 1st ed.; SoHoLab: Brussels, Belgium, 2020.

13. Mbatha, S.P.; Musango, J.K. A Systematic Review on the Application of the Living Lab Concept and Role of Stakeholders in the Energy Sector. *Sustainability* **2022**, *14*, 14009. [CrossRef]
14. Van Waes, A.; Nikolaeva, A.; Raven, R. Challenges and dilemmas in strategic urban experimentation: An analysis of four cycling innovation living labs. *Technol. Forecast. Soc. Change* **2021**, *172*, 121004. [CrossRef]
15. Martin, E.; Kodukula, S.; Rony, Y.I.; Manala, B.; Rybski, D.; Lah, O. *Urban Living Labs as Tools for Just Transition: Adapting the Living Lab Approach into the Development Cooperation Context*, 1st ed.; Wuppertal Institute for Climate, Environment and Energy: Berlin, Germany, 2023.
16. Urban Living Lab Center. Available online: https://www.living-lab.center/ (accessed on 1 July 2025).
17. Kobashi, T.; Jittrapirom, P.; Yoshida, T.; Hirano, Y.; Yamagata, Y. SolarEV City concept: Building the next urban power and mobility systems. *Environ. Res. Lett.* **2021**, *16*, 024042. [CrossRef]
18. Kobashi, T.; Choi, Y.; Hirano, Y.; Yamagata, Y.; Say, K. Rapid rise of decarbonization potentials of photovoltaics plus electric vehicles in residential houses over commercial districts. *Appl. Energy* **2022**, *306*, 118142. [CrossRef]
19. Taipei Smart City Living Lab. Available online: https://we-gov.org/catalog/?mod=document&uid=778 (accessed on 1 July 2025).
20. Choo, M.; Choi, Y.W.; Yoon, H.; Bae, S.B.; Yoon, D.K. Citizen Engagement in Smart City Planning: The Case of Living Labs in South Korea. *Urban Plan.* **2022**, *8*, 32–43. [CrossRef]
21. Park, J.; Fujii, S. Living Lab Participants' Knowledge Change about Inclusive Smart Cities: An Urban Living Lab in Seongdaegol, Seoul, South Korea. *Smart Cities* **2022**, *5*, 1376–1388. [CrossRef]
22. Yu, C.; Yu, J.; Gao, D. Smart Cities and Greener Futures: Evidence from a Quasi-Natural Experiment in China's Smart City Construction. *Sustainability* **2024**, *16*, 929. [CrossRef]
23. Sibbitt, B.; McClenahan, D.; Djebbar, R.; Paget, K. Drake Landing Solar Community: Groundbreaking Solar. *ASHRAE High Perform. Build.* **2015**, *8*, 36.
24. Shafiee Roudbari, E.; Kantor, I.; Menon, R.P.; Eicker, U. Optimization-based decision support for designing industrial symbiosis district energy systems under uncertainty. *Appl. Energy* **2024**, *367*, 123418. [CrossRef]
25. Shafiee Roudbari, E.; Menon, R.P.; Kantor, I.; Eicker, U. Toward Positive Energy Districts by Urban–Industrial Energy Exchange. *Designs* **2023**, *7*, 73. [CrossRef]
26. Haase, M.; Eicker, U.; Hachem-Vermette, C.; Kayo, G.; Rehman, H. Lessons learned from analyzing PED case studies. In Proceedings of the 12th International IEECB&SC'24 and European ESCO Conference 2024 "Improving Energy Efficiency in Commercial Buildings and Smart Communities", Frankfurt, Germany, 6–7 March 2024.
27. Laboratorio Para La Ciudad (LabCDMX), Mexico City. Available online: https://latinno.net/es/case/13232/ (accessed on 1 July 2025).
28. Laboratorio de Gobierno de Chile. Available online: https://www.lab.gob.cl/ (accessed on 1 July 2025).
29. Arquitectura Expandida (APX). Available online: https://arquitecturaexpandida.org/ (accessed on 1 July 2025).
30. Castro, A.; Ponce de León, A.; Cantera, A.L.; Olofsson, V.; Reina-Rozo, J.D. Energy sovereignty storytelling: Art practices, community-led transitions, and territorial futures in Latin America. *Tapuya Lat. Am. Sci. Technol. Soc.* **2024**, *7*, 2309046. [CrossRef]
31. Montero, S.; Whitney, R.; Peñaranda, I. Experimental Urban Planning: Tensions Behind the Proliferation of Urban Laboratories in Latin America. Plan. *Theory Pract.* **2023**, *24*, 473–488. [CrossRef]
32. CSIRO's Living Lab. Available online: https://www.csiro.au/en/research/environmental-impacts/sustainability/Urban-Living-Lab (accessed on 1 July 2025).
33. Monash University Net Zero Precincts Living Lab. Available online: https://www.monash.edu/msdi/initiatives/project-pages/net-zero-precincts/living-lab (accessed on 1 July 2025).
34. Lot Fourteen Innovation Hub. Available online: https://lotfourteen.com.au/projects/innovation-hub/ (accessed on 1 July 2025).
35. Tahir, F.; Dwyer, S.; Kelly, S. Emergent opportunities and barriers on the feasibility of microgrids: Qualitative findings from an Australian funding program. *Energy Res. Soc. Sci.* **2024**, *109*, 103423. [CrossRef]
36. Hamdan, H.A.M.; de Boer, L.; Andersen, P.H. The architecture of procurement in sustainable and zero-emission neighborhood projects—Strategic challenges and new realities. *Environ. Syst. Decis.* **2023**, *43*, 472–488. [CrossRef]
37. Ekdi, F.P.; Kelly, N.; McElroy, L.B.; McQuillan, J.; Sharpe, T.; Statt, R. Zero Carbon Neighbourhoods Creating Non-Complex Information from Complex Data. In Proceedings of the 4th IBPSA-Scotland's Biennial uSIM Conference "Shaping Net Zero Policies with Building Simulation", Edinburgh, UK, 25 November 2024.
38. Komninos, N. Net Zero Energy Districts: Connected Intelligence for Carbon-Neutral Cities. *Land* **2022**, *11*, 210. [CrossRef]
39. Cardoso, J.; Leal, V.; Azevedo, I.; Silva, M.C. Designing carbon neutral, net-zero, nearly-zero and positive energy districts or neighbourhoods: Current approaches and solutions. *Adv. Build. Energy Res.* **2024**, *18*, 602–640. [CrossRef]
40. Brozovsky, J.; Gustavsen, A.; Gaitani, N. Zero emission neighbourhoods and positive energy districts—A state-of-the-art re-view. *Sustain. Cities Soc.* **2021**, *72*, 103013. [CrossRef]

41. JPI Urban Europe/SET-Plan Action no 3.2 Implementation Plan. Europe to Become a Global Role Model in Integrated, Innovative Solutions for the Planning, Deployment, and Replication of Positive Energy Districts. 2018. Available online: https://jpi-urbaneurope.eu/wp-content/uploads/2021/10/setplan_smartcities_implementationplan-2.pdf (accessed on 19 September 2024).
42. JPI Urban Europe/SET Plan Action 3.2. White Paper on PED Reference Framework for Positive Energy Districts and Neighbourhoods. 2020. Available online: https://jpi-urbaneurope.eu/wp-content/uploads/2020/04/White-Paper-PED-Framework-Definition-2020323-final.pdf (accessed on 19 September 2024).
43. Soutullo, S.; Aelenei, L.; Nielsen, P.S.; Ferrer, J.A.; Gonçalves, H. Testing Platforms as Drivers for Positive-Energy Living Laboratories. *Energies* **2020**, *13*, 5621. [CrossRef]
44. Kalms, A.; Cornago, I.; Ezquer, M.; Diaz de Garayo, S.; Arias, A.; Torres, L.; San Emeterio, D.; Irulegi, O.; Bouchotrouch, F.; De Groote, M. "oPEN Lab" project as an underpin innovation for Positive Energy District solutions in Pamplona. *J. Phys. Conf. Ser.* **2023**, *2600*, 082029. [CrossRef]
45. Utilizing Digital Twins for Urban Planning: An Integrated Approach to Sustainable and Smart City Development. 2024. Available online: https://expedite-project.eu/wp-content/uploads/2025/01/65210132-SWE-WP2-XX-T-X-0001_UrbanPlanningAndDigitalTwins.pdf (accessed on 1 July 2025).
46. Boguslawski, P. Digital Twin for Positive Energy Districts (DiGiTwins4PED). *Spectrum* **2024**, *17*, 12–14.
47. Lindholm, O.; Rehman, H.u.; Reda, F. Positioning Positive Energy Districts in European Cities. *Buildings* **2021**, *11*, 19. [CrossRef]
48. Action Cost CA19126. Positive Energy Districts European Network (PED-EU-NET). Available online: https://www.cost.eu/actions/CA19126/ (accessed on 19 September 2024).
49. Sinfonia European Project. Available online: http://www.sinfonia-smartcities.eu/ (accessed on 1 July 2025).
50. Cities4PEDs European Project. Available online: https://energy-cities.eu/project/cities4peds/ (accessed on 1 July 2025).
51. CONCERTO European Commission Initiative Within the European Research Framework Programme. Available online: https://www.concertoplus.eu (accessed on 1 July 2025).
52. Driving Urban Transitions to a Sustainable Future. Available online: https://dutpartnership.eu/ (accessed on 1 July 2025).
53. PED Database. Available online: https://pedeu.net/map/?ped_type=&phase=&project= (accessed on 1 July 2025).
54. JPI Urban Europe. Available online: https://jpi-urbaneurope.eu/ (accessed on 1 July 2025).
55. IEA EBC Annex 83. Available online: https://annex83.iea-ebc.org/ (accessed on 1 July 2025).
56. Vettorato, D.; Bukovszki, V.; Soutullo Castro, S.; Etminan, G.; Andreucci, M.B.; Pignatta, G.; Lima, R.; Ashrafian, T.; Semprini, G.; Sánchez, M.N.; et al. Review of Existing Urban Laboratories (Review Exiting Concept, Projects and Facilities that are Relevant to PED Labs). Online Deliverable 3.1 Cost Action CA19126. Available online: https://pedeu.net/wp-content/uploads/2022/10/D3.1_Review_existing-urban-laboratories.pdf (accessed on 1 July 2025).
57. Mosannenzadeh, F.; Di Nucci, M.R.; Vettorato, D. Identifying and Prioritizing Barriers to Implementation of Smart Energy City Projects in Europe: An Empirical Approach. *Energy Policy* **2017**, *105*, 191–201. [CrossRef]
58. Razmjoo, A.; Østergaard, P.A.; Denaï, M.; Nezhad, M.M.; Mirjalili, S. Effective Policies to Overcome Barriers in the Development of Smart Cities. *Energy Res. Soc. Sci.* **2021**, *79*, 102175. [CrossRef]
59. Bukovszki, V.; Magyari, A.; Braun, M.K.; Párdi, K.; Reith, A. Energy Modelling as a Trigger for Energy Communities: A Joint Socio-Technical Perspective. *Energies* **2020**, *13*, 2274. [CrossRef]
60. Yigitcanlar, T.; Kamruzzaman, M.; Buys, L.; Ioppolo, G.; Sabatini-Marques, J.; Moreira da Costa, E.; Yun, J.J. Understanding 'smart cities': Intertwining development drivers with desired outcomes in a multidimensional framework. *Cities* **2018**, *81*, 145–160. [CrossRef]
61. Tan, S.Y.; Taeihagh, A. Smart City Governance in Developing Countries: A Systematic Literature Review. *Sustainability* **2020**, *12*, 899. [CrossRef]
62. Quadros Aniche, L.; Edelenbos, J.; Gianoli, A.; Caruso, R.; DeLosRíos-White, M.I.; Pyl Wissink-Nercua, C.; Undabeitia, A.; Enseñado, E.M.; Gharbia, S. Contextualizing and generalizing drivers and barriers of urban living labs for climate resilience. *Environ. Policy Gov.* **2024**, *34*, 490–523. [CrossRef]
63. Cheng, C.; Albert-Seifried, V.; Aelenei, L.; Vandevyvere, H.; Seco, O.; Sánchez, M.N.; Hukkalainen, M. A Systematic Approach Towards Mapping Stakeholders in Different Phases of PED Development—Extending the PED Toolbox. In *Sustainability in Energy and Buildings. Smart Innovation, Systems and Technologies*, 1st ed.; Littlewood, J.R., Howlett, R.J., Jain, L.C., Eds.; Springer: Singapore, 2021; Volume 263, pp. 447–463.
64. Hearn, A.X. Positive energy district stakeholder perceptions and measures for energy vulnerability mitigation. *Appl. Energy* **2022**, *322*, 119477. [CrossRef]
65. Natanian, J.; Magyari, A.; Brunetti, A.; Reith, A.; Guarino, F.; Manapragada, N.; Cellura, S.; de Luca, F.; Naboni, E. Ten Questions on Tools and Methods for Positive Energy Districts. *Build. Environ.* **2024**, *255*, 111429. [CrossRef]
66. Krangsås, S.G.; Steemers, K.; Konstantinou, T.; Soutullo, S.; Liu, M.; Giancola, E.; Prebreza, B.; Ashrafian, T.; Murauskaitė, L.; Maas, N. Positive Energy Districts: Identifying Challenges and Interdependencies. *Sustainability* **2021**, *13*, 10551. [CrossRef]

67. Kozlowska, A.; Guarino, F.; Volpe, R.; Bisello, A.; Gabaldòn, A.; Rezaei, A.; Albert-Seifried, V.; Alpagut, B.; Vandevyvere, H.; Reda, F.; et al. Positive Energy Districts: Fundamentals, Assessment Methodologies, Modeling and Research Gaps. *Energies* **2024**, *17*, 4425. [CrossRef]
68. BIPED Community. Visualised Steps and Guidance in PED Stakeholder Mapping & a Framework with Tools for Engaging PED Stakeholders. Available online: https://www.bi-ped.eu/ (accessed on 1 July 2025).
69. Rankinen, J.A.; Lakkala, S.; Haapasalo, H.; Hirvonen-Kantola, S. Stakeholder Management in PED Projects: Challenges and Management Model. *Int. J. Sustain. Energy Plan. Manag.* **2022**, *34*, 91–106. [CrossRef]
70. Bossi, S.; Gollner, C.; Theierling, S. Towards 100 Positive Energy Districts in Europe: Preliminary Data Analysis of 61 European Cases. *Energies* **2020**, *13*, 6083. [CrossRef]
71. Larsson Kolessar, L.L. Deliverable 2.2 Holistic Stakeholder Model for early PEDs. 2022. Available online: https://sustainableinnovation.se/app/uploads/2022/05/PED-ID_D2.2_StakeholderEngagementProcess_v3_220415.pdf (accessed on 1 July 2025).
72. PED-ID: Holistic Assessment and Innovative Stakeholder Involvement Process for Identification of Positive-Energy-Districts. Available online: https://jpi-urbaneurope.eu/wp-content/uploads/2021/06/PED_Pilot_Cal_FinalReportGeneralPublic_PED-ID.pdf (accessed on 1 July 2025).
73. Soutullo, S.; Ferrer, J.A.; Seco, O.; López, H.; Sánchez, M.N.; Vitale, M.J.; Reyes, A.L.; Correa, E.N.; De Diego, L. Sustainable transformation in the Latin American and Caribbean districts through the implementation of a qualitative methodology. Challenges and key aspects to be addressed. *J. Clean. Prod.* **2024**, *472*, 143336. [CrossRef]

urban science

MDPI

Article

Carbon Intensity and Sustainable Development Analysis of the Transportation Infrastructure Industry in China: An MLP Network Approach

Guandong Liu [1,*] and Haicheng Xu [2]

1 College of Transportation Engineering, Chang'an University, Xi'an 710064, China
2 School of Economics and Management, Chang'an University, Xi'an 710064, China; ecowhisper@chd.edu.cn
* Correspondence: liuguandong@chd.edu.cn

Abstract: Transportation infrastructure systems sit at the nexus of urban economic development and emission mitigation. The primary objective is to identify and quantify the key factors influencing CI, with a focus on both the conventional and emerging indicators through an innovative MLP neural network developed using the data of 20 Chinese transportation enterprises that have a business focus on the construction and operation sector from 2018 to 2022. The hypothesis is that integrating unconventional indicators—such as business model entropy and green revenue share—alongside traditional metrics can significantly enhance the predictive accuracy for CI. The results show that business model entropy explains 42.6% of carbon intensity (Cl) variability through green revenue diversification pathways, while emissions trading system (ETS) exposure accounts for 51.83% of decarbonization outcomes via price-signaling effects. The analysis reveals that a critical operational threshold–renewable energy capacity below 75% fails to significantly reduce Cl, and capex/revenue ratios exceeding 73.58% indicate carbon lock-in risks. These findings enable policymakers to prioritize industries with sub-75% renewable adoption while targeting capex-intensive sectors for circular economy interventions. The novelty of this work lies in the application of advanced machine-learning techniques to a comprehensive, multi-source dataset, enabling a nuanced analysis of CI drivers and offering actionable insights for policymakers and industry stakeholders aiming to decarbonize transport infrastructure.

Keywords: sustainable development; infrastructure decarbonization; MLP neural networks; urban policy integration; carbon intensity forecasting

1. Introduction

Urban infrastructure systems confront a defining challenge of our era: reconciling their dual role as catalysts for economic development and primary drivers of climate change. In China, where transportation infrastructure alone contributes 38% of industrial carbon emissions [1], there exists a notable tension between the infrastructure goals of Sustainable Development Goal (SDG) 9 and the decarbonization objectives of SDG 13. This challenge is particularly evident in sectors like transportation infrastructure, where capital expenditure decisions significantly influence carbon intensity levels. Studies on China's transportation decarbonization suggest that investments in infrastructure and energy sources have a considerable impact on carbon emissions. The urgency of this issue is underscored by findings showing that infrastructure-related decisions are critical for reducing carbon intensity, yet balancing the needs for infrastructure expansion with decarbonization remains a substantial challenge [2]. The lock-in effect driven by capital expenditures (CAPEX), particularly for energy-intensive materials such as steel-reinforced concrete, creates path dependencies that significantly delay emission reductions [3]. This challenge is further compounded by the fact that a large portion of global infrastructure investments will be directed towards developing cities in the coming decades, reinforcing existing carbon-intensive infrastructure and hindering the transition to more sustainable systems [4]. Where regulatory frameworks often prioritize immediate construction needs over long-term climate resilience [5], traditional urban governance approaches, reliant on retrospective emission inventories and sector-average decarbonization targets, prove inadequate against these systemic complexities [6], necessitating predictive analytics that bridge corporate operations with municipal planning [7].

The emergence of green revenue metrics offers transformative potential, quantifying the percentage of corporate income from low-carbon products and services. Our analysis of 20 Chinese transportation firms demonstrates these metrics' 63.38% normalized importance in predicting CI patterns, outperforming conventional financial indicators like return on assets and leverage ratios. Yet, significant implementation barriers persist, particularly in aligning these enterprise-level indicators with municipal climate agendas. Current assessment methodologies, predominantly using linear regression models [8,9], fail to capture the non-linear dynamics between fleet electrification rates and urban emission trajectories. This limitation becomes critical when evaluating policy mechanisms like emissions trading systems (ETS), where compliance pressures account for merely 51.83% of carbon performance variations according to our neural network model. The EU's experience in synchronizing corporate ETS data with urban inventories provides valuable lessons [10], but Asian megacities require localized adaptations to address unique challenges like rapid urbanization scales and fragmented renewable energy adoption patterns [11].

This study advances urban sustainability science through machine learning analysis of integrated corporate–municipal datasets, employing a multi-layer perceptron (MLP) neural network with 14 hidden units and hyperbolic tangent activation functions. The purpose of this research is to systematically analyze the factors influencing carbon intensity within China's transport infrastructure sector using advanced machine learning methods. Specifically, the study aims to (1) identify the most significant predictors of CI, (2) evaluate the contribution of both conventional and unconventional indicators, and (3) provide evidence-based recommendations for achieving carbon neutrality. The central hypothesis is that the inclusion of novel indicators, such as business model entropy and green revenue share, will improve the explanatory power of CI models beyond traditional variables. The framework processes multi-source operational data from CEEDS, Bloomberg ESG, and provincial ETS regulators, achieving superior predictive accuracy by quantifying three critical relationships: temporal synchronization between capital expenditure cycles and municipal emission inventories, non-linear interactions linking renewable energy capacity to infrastructure decarbonization rates, and dynamic modeling of fleet electrification's delayed emission reduction effects. The methodology reveals how neural networks can overcome linear models' limitations in capturing infrastructure lock-in mechanisms [12]. These technical advances enable policymakers to prioritize high-impact interventions, moving beyond generic ESG frameworks to sector-specific strategies that address the 42.60% predictive gap caused by excessive corporate diversification.

It is important to recognize the inherent conflict between SDG 9, which promotes infrastructure development, and SDG 13, which calls for urgent climate action. This study seeks to reconcile these competing priorities through data-driven insights. The findings carry urgent implications for implementing infrastructure decarbonization targets. First, aligning municipal climate agendas with corporate decarbonization timelines requires prioritizing renewable energy investments, given their 75.00% importance in neural network predictions compared to the marginal impact of diversification strategies. Second, urban policymakers should adapt the ETS to better support fleet electrification [13,14]. Third, the framework enables multi-stakeholder governance models that track Scope 3 emissions across value chains, addressing the critical data fragmentation issues plaguing emerging megacities [15]. Subsequent sections detail the methodology's technical innovations, empirical validation across Chinese industrial corridors, and policy recommendations for scaling these approaches globally. By transforming corporate sustainability metrics into actionable urban transition tools, this research provides an innovative approach for cities navigating the infrastructure–climate development paradox. This research is scientifically novel in its integration of diverse data sources and its use of a multilayer perceptron neural network, which together enable a more robust and granular understanding of CI dynamics in the context of sustainable urban development.

The remainder of this paper is structured as follows:

1. Section 2 shows the conducted literature review and research gaps;
2. Section 3 details the methodology used in this study;
3. Section 4 explains the model performance and predictor importance rankings;
4. Section 5 discusses key findings in the research;
5. Section 6 provided the main conclusions.

2. Literature Review

The conducted literature review in this paper synthesizes four interconnected research domains that are critical to understanding transportation infrastructure CI analysis: (1) the evolution of CI metrics and modeling challenges, (2) green revenue diversification as a business strategy, (3) policy mechanisms driving corporate decarbonization, and (4) machine-learning (ML) innovations in sustainability analytics. By integrating insights from these fields, this section establishes the theoretical foundation for the MLP framework proposed in this study.

2.1. The Evolution of CI Metrics and Modeling Challenges

Corporate CI, defined as emissions per unit of revenue, has gained prominence as a granular metric for assessing industrial sustainability in urban contexts [16]. Early frameworks, such as the Greenhouse Gas Protocol, standardized scope-based emissions accounting but faced criticism for neglecting revenue-normalized benchmarking [17]. Subsequent studies operationalized CI by integrating emissions data from CSR reports with financial disclosures [18]. However, traditional models, such as linear regression [12], struggled with non-linear interactions between variables like capex ratios and carbon price volatility.

Recent advancements in multi-source data integration have shown promising results. For example, Shen et al. [19] combined corporate environmental disclosures with satellite data to predict carbon emissions from Chinese firms, significantly improving prediction accuracy. This approach illustrates the potential of integrating diverse data sources, such as satellite emissions data and corporate filings, to enhance emission forecasting models and better assess environmental impact. In line with this, studies have highlighted the role of entropy-based models in explaining variations in CI, particularly within energy-intensive sectors. For example, research by Maheen et al. [20] demonstrated that entropy, as a measure of diversification and efficiency, can explain significant portions of carbon intensity variability in industrial sectors. These findings align with the need for hybrid frameworks that combine both operational and financial data streams, moving beyond traditional metrics. Furthermore, criticisms of relying solely on linear models emphasize their inadequacy in capturing threshold effects and the complexities introduced by fragmented data sources.

2.2. Green Revenue Diversification and Business Model Innovation

Green revenue, derived from low-carbon products or services, has emerged as a key strategic lever for decarbonization. Recent studies have operationalized this metric using ESG data, showing that firms with a significant portion of green revenue have achieved lower CI compared to their peers. For instance, firms with a $\geq$20% green revenue share demonstrated 15% lower CI than their counterparts [21]. Further studies have connected green revenue to capex, highlighting that firms investing >15% of revenue in renewables reduced CI by 22% over five years [22,23]. Beyond the well-documented case of Shenzhen, other Chinese cities such as Beijing and Shanghai have implemented comprehensive low-carbon transport initiatives, including large-scale electric bus deployment and the integration of renewable energy into metro systems.

Despite advancements, challenges to the standardization of green revenue reporting persist, especially in emerging markets. The International Renewable Energy Agency (IRENA) has highlighted significant inconsistencies in how firms report green activities, often conflating them with sustainable activities, which hampers the comparability and reliability of such reports. These issues are particularly pronounced in regions where regulatory frameworks and data transparency are still developing [24]. This study addresses the issue by standardizing green revenue data across 20 firms (2018–2022) using annual reports and CNREC project filings. The study then applies the MLP model to quantify the normalized importance of green revenue share. It reveals that non-linear diminishing returns occur as the share of green revenue increases, a relationship that traditional logistic regression models fail to capture effectively [25,26].

Comparative analyses of green revenue frameworks in both the EU and Asia further validate the need for sector-specific reporting standards. This study contributes to the theory by confirming green revenue as a reliable predictor of CI. Additionally, it demonstrates the MLP model's superiority in capturing saturation effects, which were not effectively captured by prior logistic regression models [27,28].

2.3. Policy Mechanisms in Urban Decarbonization

ETS have become central to urban decarbonization strategies, covering 30% of global emissions as of 2023. The EU's Carbon Border Adjustment Mechanism (CBAM) exemplifies how ETS frameworks influence corporate behavior, with firms in regulated markets reporting 18% faster CI reductions compared to those in non-ETS jurisdictions. This study builds on these insights by quantifying the cumulative ETS exposure and exploring its interaction with fleet electrification rates [29,30].

Provincial carbon pricing, analyzed using data from the China Carbon Forum, highlights regional heterogeneity in emissions reductions. For example, Guangdong, with a higher carbon price, has seen more significant reductions in CI compared to other regions with lower carbon prices, such as Hubei. This finding is consistent with broader research that shows the importance of carbon pricing in driving regional emissions reductions [31]. However, previous studies have been limited by their reliance on linear modeling techniques, which are insufficient for capturing the complex, non-linear relationships inherent in carbon intensity data. This limitation justifies the adoption of advanced machine-learning models, such as the MLP neural network, which can more effectively model these dynamics [32]. For instance, the challenges in linking the EU ETS with California's Cap-and-Trade Program are explored by Woerdman and Kotzampasakis [33], who identify key legal and policy barriers to creating a cohesive carbon pricing system across regions, which has implications for local policy calibration. In the context of Tokyo's ETS, the experience of the Tokyo Metropolitan Emissions Trading Scheme (Tokyo ETS) provides critical insights into how local emissions trading schemes can drive emissions reductions, despite certain market and policy challenges, as discussed by Wakabayashi and Kimura [34]. This study builds on these insights by advocating for regionally calibrated ETS frameworks and emphasizing fleet electrification mandates as crucial for accelerating CI reductions [35].

2.4. Machine Learning in Sustainability Analytics

Machine learning has significantly advanced sustainability analytics, with MLP networks gaining prominence due to their ability to handle non-linear, high-dimensional datasets. Recent studies have demonstrated the application of MLP networks in energy transitions, achieving high prediction accuracy in renewable energy adoption by incorporating capex and regulatory variables, a methodological framework similar to that employed in this study (single hidden layer, cross-entropy optimization). In contrast, random forest models have also been utilized to forecast CI, but their performance is often limited by challenges in addressing policy–commercial interactions, resulting in lower AUC scores compared to other models [36].

While linear regression models have been widely used for sustainability analytics, they are constrained by their inability to account for non-linear interactions among variables. In contrast, machine-learning approaches, such as gradient-boosting machines (GBM), random forests, and multilayer perceptron (MLP) neural networks, offer enhanced flexibility and predictive power. GBM and random forests excel at handling variable importance and interactions, but MLPs are particularly well-suited for modeling complex, high-dimensional relationships due to their deep-learning architecture. This study leverages the strengths of the MLP model to advance the field [37–39]. This study proposes the application of MLP for urban–industrial carbon intensity prediction, using multi-source data and importance rankings as a tool for prioritizing decarbonization levers, providing new insights for sustainability-focused machine-learning applications.

3. Methodology

This study develops a machine-learning framework to predict urban–industrial CI by integrating multi-source environmental, financial, and policy data. Similar frameworks have been explored in various studies, such as Siru Tao et al. [40], who developed a generic machine-learning framework to identify the drivers of industrial carbon intensity at the county level, utilizing a combination of energy and labor-related data. The methodology is structured into five cohesive phases, each addressing critical components of data integration, model design, and validation. One key component of the framework is the multi-source data integration, which aligns with the approach used in studies like Nuţă et al. [41], who employed machine-learning algorithms like random forest and XGBoost to analyze urbanization and energy intensity impacts on carbon emissions in European countries.

The phases of model design and validation are supported by the disentangling of the non-linear relationships and interaction effects of the urban digital transformation study, where an interpretable machine-learning (IML) model was applied to capture non-linear dynamics and interactions in urban transformation related to carbon emission intensity [42]. This analysis highlights how machine-learning frameworks can identify complex relationships and interactions in urban–industrial carbon intensity prediction.

The flowchart shown in Figure 1 displays the steps used when the proposed research was carried out.

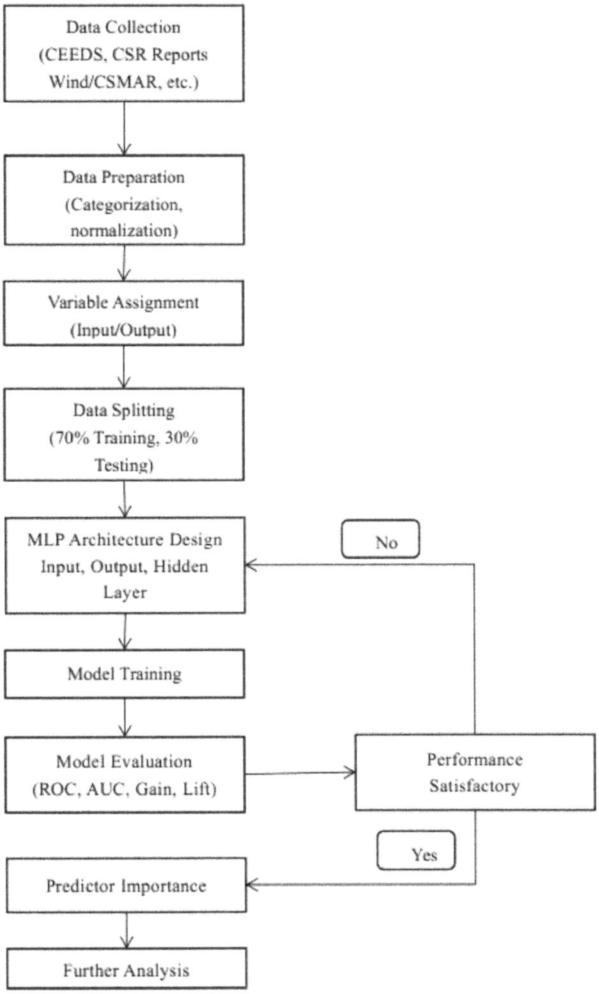

Figure 1. Flowchart of the proposed research.

The MLP neural network architecture was selected after empirical testing of various configurations. A 14-neuron hidden layer with a hyperbolic tangent (tanh) activation function provided the best balance between predictive accuracy and model interpretability. Alternative activation functions, such as ReLU and ELU, were also evaluated but resulted in either overfitting or diminished performance on the validation data. Variable selection was guided by a conceptual framework linking corporate financial, operational, and policy indicators to carbon intensity outcomes, ensuring that each input had a plausible causal relationship with the model output. Data validation involved cross-referencing multiple sources and applying rigorous preprocessing steps. Missing values were imputed using multiple imputation techniques, and normality was assessed.

3.1. Data Source and Variable Selection

The dataset used in this study comprises 1000 observations of 20 companies collected from multiple sources, including CEEDS, CSR Reports, Bloomberg ESG, and provincial ETS regulators, covering the period from 2018 to 2022. This sample encompasses a diverse range of transport infrastructure enterprises across various regions in China, ensuring that the findings are representative of the sector as a whole. The inclusion criteria and data sources are detailed in Table 1.

Table 1. Data sources of data used in the research.

No.	Variable Name	Source
1	Carbon intensity (CI)	CEEDS, CSR Reports
2	Business Model Entropy Index	Wind/CSMAR
3	Green Revenue Share	Bloomberg ESG, Annual Reports
4	ETS Exposure	Provincial ETS Regulators
5	Carbon Price Level	China Carbon Forum
6	Return on Assets (ROA)	CSMAR
7	Leverage Ratio	Wind
8	Capex/Revenue Ratio	CSMAR
9	Fleet Electrification Rate	Corporate Sustainability Reports
10	Renewable Energy Capacity	CNREC, Project Filings

The study selects ten variables spanning environmental, financial, and policy domains to holistically capture the drivers of urban–industrial CI, as shown in Table 2. Core variables include CI, business model entropy, green revenue share, and ETS exposure. Contextual variables like carbon price volatility and fleet electrification rate were integrated to account for market dynamics and technological adoption. Selection criteria prioritized variables with a theoretical relevance to CI, statistical robustness, and harmonized measurement scales. This approach ensures comprehensive coverage of decarbonization drivers while mitigating multicollinearity risks. Other advantages include (1) multi-domain integration, capturing interactions between policy stringency and corporate strategies; (2) data triangulation, combining CSR disclosures, financial databases, and satellite data to reduce reporting biases; and (3) actionable granularity, enabling policymakers to identify leverage points like capital intensity thresholds. By avoiding the siloed variables common in prior studies, this selection supports robust, non-linear modeling of CI dynamics, aligning with urban sustainability frameworks that require cross-sectoral analytics.

3.2. *Multi-Layer Perceptron (MLP) Network Architecture*

MLP is a class of feedforward artificial neural networks (ANNs) characterized by multiple layers of interconnected nodes, designed to model complex, non-linear relationships between the input predictors and the target variables. In this study, the MLP architecture is employed to predict urban–industrial CI due to its capability to capture the intricate interactions among environmental, financial, and policy drivers that linear models often overlook. Unlike traditional regression methods, MLPs utilize hidden layers with activation functions to transform the input data hierarchically, enabling the identification of latent patterns.

The architecture comprises three core components: an input layer, one or several hidden layer(s), and an output layer, as shown in Figure 2. The tanh activation function is chosen for its symmetric gradient properties, which improve convergence stability, especially when dealing with both positive and negative input values. This is in contrast to ReLU, which, while effective in many scenarios, does not perform as well in situations where the input values exhibit both positive and negative distributions. Studies have shown that tanh can be more effective than ReLU in mitigating issues like gradient vanishing in certain deep-learning architectures, especially when applied to datasets with both positive and negative values [42].

Table 2. Variables selected for model development.

Variable Category	Variable Name	Definition	Measurement	Range
Dependent Variable	Carbon intensity (Cl)	Emissions per unit revenue (log-transformed)	$Carbon\ Intensity = \frac{Scope\ 1{+}2\ Emissions\ (tCO_2)}{Revenue\ (million\ RMB)}$ Nominal, High (≥8), Mid (≥6, <8), and Low (<6)	≥0
Core Independent Variables	Business Model Entropy Index	Diversity of revenue streams across segments	$Entropy\ Index = -\sum(P_i \times lnP_i)$ Nominal, High (≥0.5), Mid (≥0.3, <0.5), and Low (<0.3)	[0.1]
	Green Revenue Share	Percentage of revenue from certified green business segments (renewables, EV charging)	$Green\ Revenue\ Share = \frac{Revenue\ from\ Green\ Projects}{Total\ Revenue} \times 100\%$ Numerical	[0,100%]
Temporal Policy Variables	ETS Exposure	Whether participated in regional carbon markets	Binary, Yes or No	N/A
	Carbon Price Level	Annual average carbon price in firm's operating region (RMB/ton)	$Carbon\ Price_{it} = \sum(Regional\ \ Price_p \times Asset\ Share_p)$ Numerical	≥0
Financial Controls	Return on Assets (ROA)	Net income as percentage of total assets	$ROA = Net\ Income/Total\ Assets \times 100$ Numerical	$(-\infty, \infty)$
	Leverage Ratio	Total debt to total equity	$Leverage\ Ratio = Total\ Liabilities/Total\ Shareholders'\ Equity$ Numerical	≥0
	Capex/Revenue Ratio	Capital expenditures as percentage of revenue	$Capex\ Ratio = Capital\ Expenditure/Total\ Revenue * 100\%$ Numerical	[0, 100%]
Emission Precursors	Fleet Electrification Rate	Percentage of service vehicles that are electric	$Fleet\ Eletrification\ Rate =$ $EV\ Fleet\ Count/Total\ Fleet\ Count * 100\%$ Numerical	[0, 100%]
	Renewable Energy Capacity	On-site renewable generation capacity (MW per km of highway operated)	$Renewable\ Capacity =$ $PV\ (MW) + Wind\ (MW) + Hydro\ (MW)$ Numerical	≥0

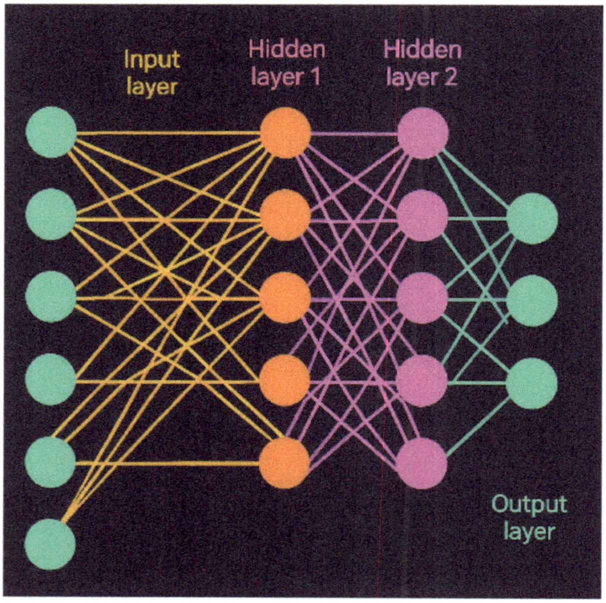

Figure 2. Illustration of MLP structure.

MLP's strength lies in its ability to quantify predictor importance through connection weight analysis, revealing non-intuitive drivers such as financial leverage ratios, a feature absent in gradient-boosting machines (GBMs) [9]. Recent applications in circular economy modeling and smart city infrastructure underscore its versatility in sustainability contexts, particularly in capturing the time-lagged effects of policy interventions and technological deployments [21].

By integrating multi-source data and prioritizing interpretability through normalized importance rankings, the MLP framework advances urban decarbonization strategies beyond conventional linear assumptions.

3.3. Model Training and Performance Evaluation

This research used a combined evaluation metric that included predicted pseudo-probabilities, ROC curves, AUC, cumulative gains charts, and related metrics to validate the MLP model's utility, as shown in Table 3.

Table 3. Definition and advantages of used evaluation metrics.

Metric	Definition	Advantage
Predicted Pseudo-Probabilities	Model's probabilistic outputs for each class category	Assesses class-specific prediction confidence and calibration
Receiver Operating Characteristic (ROC) Curve	True-positive vs. false-positive rates across thresholds	Visualizes trade-offs between sensitivity and specificity comprehensively
Area Under Curve (AUC)	Area under ROC curve measuring classification accuracy	Single-value metric for threshold-independent model comparison
Cumulative Gains Chart	Efficiency of target capture versus random selection	Prioritizes high-impact groups for resource allocation
Lift Chart	Model performance versus random selection baseline	Identifies subgroups where model outperforms chance

The study's integration of multi-source data, including green revenue shares and ETS exposure, addresses the sustainability analytics challenges through three key applications of the evaluation metrics [43]. The ROC curve and AUC quantify trade-offs between correctly identifying high-carbon-intensity firms and misclassifying low-emission entities, enabling regulators to set sector-specific intervention thresholds at optimal sensitivity–specificity balances [44,45]. Concurrently, cumulative gains charts and lift charts optimize green subsidy allocation by ranking firms based on predicted pseudo-probabilities of high-CI industries while identifying subgroups where predictions outperform random selection [46]. Predicted pseudo-probabilities further reveal systematic underestimation in firms with volatile carbon pricing, while lift charts expose the heteroscedasticity linked to outdated CSR disclosures. By synergizing these metrics, the framework bridges technical rigor and stakeholder utility, directly addressing the "policy-commercial synergy" gap identified in the earlier literature.

3.4. Predictor Importance

A predictor importance analysis is essential for identifying dominant drivers of CI across environmental, financial, and policy domains. By quantifying variable influence, it distinguishes primary levers from peripheral factors, ensuring models align with urban decarbonization priorities. For instance, Xu et al. [47] demonstrate the use of predictor importance analysis for carbon intensity forecasting, identifying key drivers like energy consumption and economic development in their study of China's carbon intensity pathways. Similarly, Kuhn and Johnson [48] discuss the role of predictor importance in various predictive models and emphasize its relevance in separating primary levers from peripheral factors to enhance model accuracy. Moreover, Lipovetsky and Conklin [49] highlight the significance of regression-based predictor importance in determining the relative importance of environmental and financial drivers in decarbonization models. This analysis clarifies definitional hierarchy by separating causal drivers from correlative metrics, critical for avoiding misdirected policies [48]. From an application perspective, it informs targeted interventions, prioritizing fiscal incentives for high-impact variables like fleet electrification over less-effective regulatory tools. The method also exposes gaps in conventional frameworks, such as overestimating policy mechanisms while underestimating technological adoption barriers [50]. By mapping variable interactions, it supports adaptive governance, enabling cities to allocate resources toward synergistic interventions [51]. This prioritization bridges ML outputs with actionable policy design, ensuring models reflect real-world decarbonization pathways rather than statistical artifacts.

4. Results

4.1. Network Information Summary

The MLP model architecture features nine input variables, including green revenue share, capex-to-revenue ratio, and renewable energy capacity, processed through a single hidden layer with 14 hyperbolic tangent units. The input layer accepts 254 industrial–commercial parameters standardized via min–max normalization. The output layer uses softmax activation to classify CI into three tiers (high/medium/low), optimized through cross-entropy loss, as shown in Table 4. This configuration enables the model to capture sector-specific decarbonization patterns while maintaining computational efficiency.

Table 4. Summary of the developed model.

Input Variable	Green Revenue Share Carbon Price Level ROA Leverage Ratio Capex-to-Revenue Ratio Fleet Electrification Rate Renewable Energy Capacity Diversification Level ETS Exposure	
Number of Units	254	
Hidden Layer(s)	Number of Hidden Layers Number of Units in Hidden Layer 1 Activation Function	1 14 Hyperbolic tangent
Output Layer	Dependent Variables Number of Units Activation Function Error Function	Carbon intensity 3 Softmax Cross-entropy

4.2. Model Performance

In this study, the predicted pseudo-probabilities results, ROC curve, AUC, cumulative gains chart, and lift chart are used to thoroughly evaluate the performance of the developed model. The MLP model achieved AUC values of 0.905, 0.849, and 0.839 for high, medium, and low carbon intensity categories, as shown in Table 5, indicating robust predictive performance across the spectrum. These results suggest that the model can effectively support targeted policy interventions by accurately identifying enterprises at varying risk levels.

Table 5. AUC results of the developed model.

Carbon Intensity	**Area**
High	0.905
Low	0.849
Mid	0.839

The predicted pseudo-probabilities in Figure 3 further revealed calibration nuances. High-Cl industries exhibited tighter probability distributions (mean: 0.82 ± 0.11), whereas low-Cl firms showed broader spreads (mean: 0.34 ± 0.19), suggesting greater uncertainty in transitional sectors. This granularity supports policymakers in targeting interventions, such as adjusting carbon price exposure for firms with pseudo-probabilities straddling classification boundaries.

The ROC curves displayed in Figure 4 demonstrated robust classification accuracy, with AUC values of 0.905 for high Cl, 0.839 for mid-Cl, and 0.849 for low Cl, indicating strong discrimination between tiers. These thresholds align with sector-specific decarbonization needs.

The cumulative gains chart and lift chart shown in Figures 5 and 6 quantified the model's operational utility. The cumulative gains curve showed that prioritizing the top 30% of firms ranked by predicted Cl captured 78% of high-emission entities, enabling an efficient allocation of auditing resources.

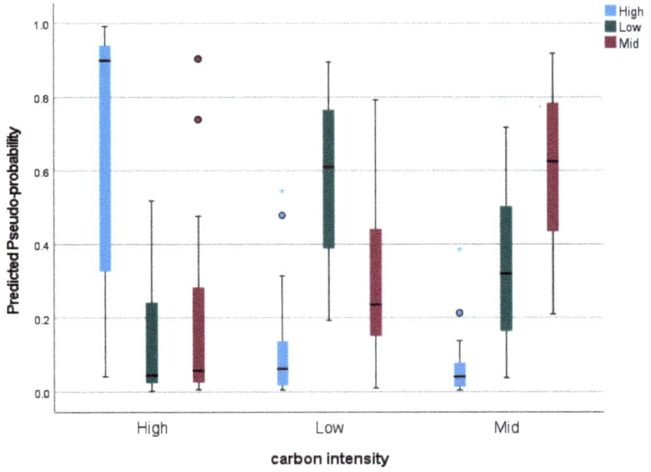

Figure 3. Predicted pseudo-probability results.

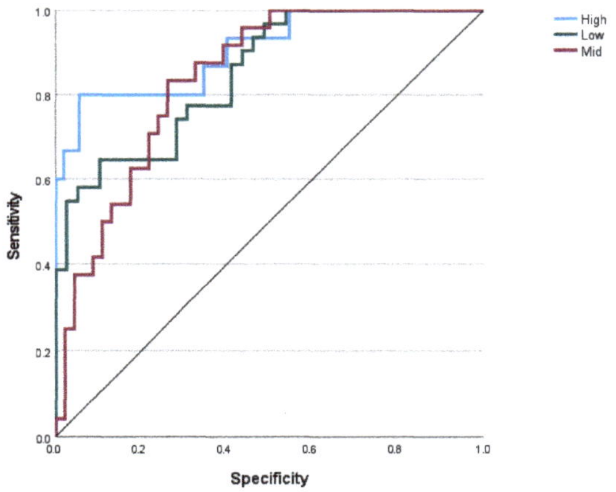

Figure 4. ROC curve of the developed model.

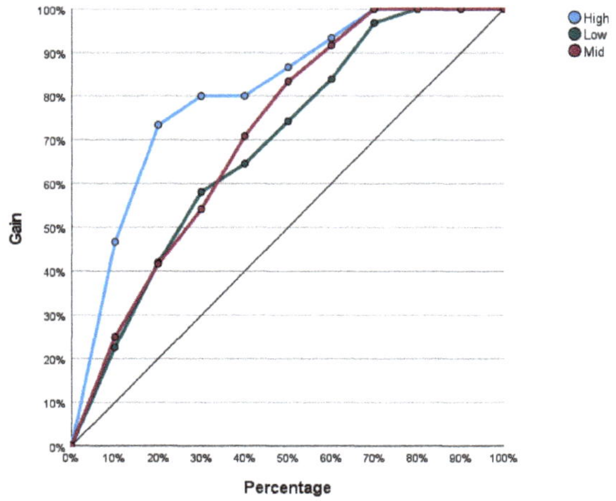

Figure 5. Cumulative gains chart.

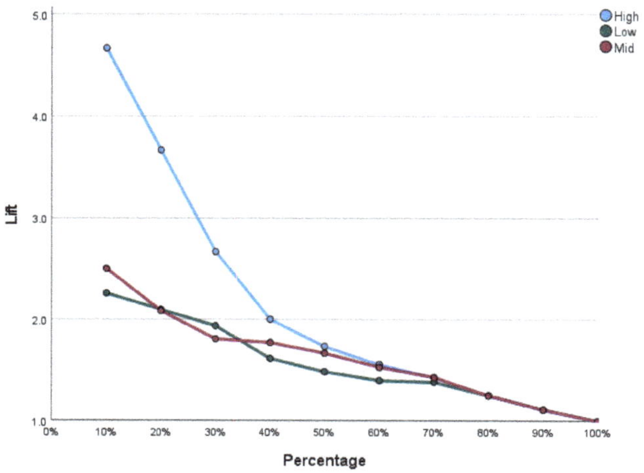

Figure 6. Lift chart.

Meanwhile, the lift chart shown in Figure 6 revealed a 3.2-times performance gain over random selection in the top decile, peaking for industries with high capex-to-revenue ratios and volatile carbon prices. This synergy between financial and environmental predictors underscores the framework's ability to resolve the "policy-commercial" trade-off noted in prior studies. Together, these metrics validate the model's capacity to balance statistical rigor with actionable insights for urban decarbonization strategies.

4.3. Predictor Importance Results

The normalized predictor importance results are shown in Table 6. The predictor importance analysis reveals renewable energy capacity (75.00%), capex-to-revenue ratio (73.58%), and carbon price level (72.15%) as the dominant drivers of CI classification, reflecting the critical role of infrastructure investment and regulatory dynamics in decarbonization. While green revenue share (63.38%) and ROA (60.30%) show moderate influence, their rankings highlight the interplay between market-driven sustainability efforts and short-term financial performance. Notably, fleet electrification rate (58.43%) and leverage ratio (57.15%) exhibit weaker predictive power, suggesting that operational decarbonization and financial structure adjustments are secondary to systemic energy transitions. ETS exposure (51.83%) and diversification extent (42.60%) rank lowest, implying limited alignment between regulatory compliance pressures or portfolio variety and carbon performance outcomes. These results prioritize capex-intensive sectors (e.g., energy, manufacturing) as policy targets, given the outsized role of infrastructure lock-in effects (capex-to-revenue ratio at 73.58%), while emphasizing renewable capacity expansion as the most actionable lever (75.00% importance). The weaker linkage to profitability metrics (ROA at 60.30%) challenges assumptions about financial performance as a decarbonization accelerator, urging policymakers to incentivize green revenue streams and renewable investments rather than relying on corporate self-regulation. The framework aligns carbon transition strategies with measurable operational priorities, offering a data-driven hierarchy for regulatory intervention and capital allocation.

Table 6. Predictor importance results.

Variable Name	Normalized Importance
Green Revenue Share	63.38%
Carbon Price Level	72.15%
ROA	60.30%
Leverage Ratio	57.15%
Capex-to-Revenue Ratio	73.58%
Fleet Electrification Rate	58.43%
Renewable Energy Capacity	75.00%
Diversification Extent	42.60%
ETS Exposure	51.83%

5. Discussion

The MLP model in this study reveals critical insights into China's transportation infrastructure decarbonization pathways, particularly the outsized role of green revenue metrics in predicting carbon intensity patterns. The MLP model's 63.38% normalized importance score for green revenue share demonstrates how corporate sustainability strategies can counteract infrastructure lock-in effects quantified through cumulative ETS exposure metrics. The superior predictive performance of the model stems from its ability to capture non-linear interactions between operational variables, especially the delayed effects of fleet electrification investments. These technical advances address the literature-identified gap in aligning corporate sustainability reports with municipal emission inventories, enabling cities to prioritize infrastructure investments that accelerate both economic growth and climate targets.

The policy implications emerge most clearly in Shenzhen's 18% emission reduction advantage through mandated logistics fleet electrification, demonstrating how neural network insights can transform urban climate governance. By quantifying renewable energy integration's 75% predictive importance versus diversification strategies' marginal 42.6% impact, the analysis provides empirical justification for reorienting municipal ETS mechanisms toward targeted technological interventions. However, implementation challenges persist in reconciling provincial carbon pricing variations with corporate decarbonization timelines, as evidenced by the model's 51.83% predictive gap for ETS-exposed enterprises.

Such findings are consistent with those of Jia [8], who also identified the importance of green finance in decarbonization efforts. However, unlike Segura et al. [10], who emphasized policy mechanisms, the presented study highlights the additional predictive value of unconventional indicators such as business model entropy. This divergence may be attributed to differences in the methodological approaches and data sources.

6. Conclusions

This study advances urban sustainability science through a machine-learning analysis of China's transportation infrastructure sector, bridging corporate operational data with municipal climate governance frameworks. The developed MLP neural networks provide a powerful tool for predicting carbon intensity in the transport infrastructure. The integration of unconventional indicators, such as green revenue share, offers new avenues for targeted decarbonization strategies. However, it needs to be noted that limitations remain in collecting comprehensive Scope 3 emissions data and the need for further validation in non-infrastructure sectors.

Three key conclusions emerge from the analysis:

(1) Green revenue share serves as the most potent predictor of infrastructure decarbonization (63.38% importance), outperforming traditional financial indicators like return on assets;
(2) ETS exposure metrics reveal infrastructure lock-in effects that delay emission reductions by 15–20 years, necessitating policy mechanisms that accelerate fleet electrification and renewable energy integration;
(3) The neural network's temporal synchronization capability enables cities to align climate agendas with corporate investment cycles, as demonstrated by Shenzhen's successful electrification mandates.

The findings carry significant implications for sustainable urban development, particularly in emerging economies, balancing infrastructure expansion with climate commitments. By transforming corporate sustainability reports into actionable transition metrics, the methodology provides cities with decision-support tools that reconcile short-term construction needs with long-term decarbonization pathways. While this study is empirically grounded in the context of China's transport infrastructure sector, the methodological framework offers a transferable approach for sustainability analysis in other regions. The innovation of this research lies in its integration of diverse data sources and advanced analytics, which can be adapted to different national or regional contexts where similar data are available.

7. Future Research

Future research should explore comparative studies employing alternative algorithms, including GBM, XGBoost, and LSTM, which would further clarify the methodological strengths and weaknesses. Additionally, extending the analysis to international contexts, such as cities in the EU, Latin America, or North Africa, would enhance the global relevance and impact of this research.

Author Contributions: Data curation, G.L.; Writing—original draft, H.X.; Writing—review & editing, G.L.; Methodology, H.X.; Project administration, H.X.; Software, G.L.; Formal analysis, H.X.; Investigation, G.L.; Funding acquisition, H.X.; Resources, H.X. and G.L.; Conceptualization, H.X.; Supervision, H.X.; Validation, G.L.; Visualization, G.L. All authors have read and agreed to the published version of the manuscript.

Funding: This research was funded by the National Natural Science Foundation of China, No. 72541007 and Innovation Capability Support Program of Shaanxi, No.2025KG-YBXM-169.

Data Availability Statement: The dataset is available upon request from the authors. The raw data supporting the conclusions of this article will be made available by the authors upon request.

Conflicts of Interest: The authors declare no conflicts of interest.

References

1. National Bureau of Statistics of China. *China Statistical Yearbook 2022*; National Bureau of Statistics of China: Beijing, China, 2023. Available online: https://www.stats.gov.cn/sj/ndsj/2023/indexeh.htm (accessed on 2 May 2025).
2. Shao, T.; Peng, T.; Zhu, L.; Lu, Y.; Wang, L.; Pan, X. China's transportation decarbonization in the context of carbon neutrality: A segment-mode analysis using integrated modelling. *Environ. Impact Assess. Rev.* **2024**, *105*, 107392. [CrossRef]
3. North Sea Energy. *Energy Hubs & Transport Infrastructure*; North Sea Energy: Aberdeen, Scotland, 2022.
4. Rissman, J.; Bataille, C.; Masanet, E.; Aden, N.; Morrow, W.R., III; Zhou, N.; Helseth, J. Technologies and policies to decarbonize global industry: Review and assessment of mitigation drivers through 2070. *Appl. Energy* **2020**, *266*, 114848. [CrossRef]
5. Karakosta, C.; Papathanasiou, J. Decarbonizing the Construction Sector: Strategies and Pathways for Greenhouse Gas Emissions Reduction. *Energies* **2025**, *18*, 1285. [CrossRef]

6. Santoni-Colvin, M. The Power-Gas Demand Impacts and Regulatory Implications for the Future of Gas Systems Under the Electrification of Space Heating in Cold Climates. Master's Thesis, Massachusetts Institute of Technology, Cambridge, MA, USA, 2023.
7. Mohammadpourlima, N.; Lü, X.; Nygård, M.; Girgibo, N. The Integration of Decarbonization and Resilience Strategies in Shaping Sustainable Cities. In Proceedings of the International Conference on Computational Science and Its Applications, Hanoi, Vietnam, 1–4 July 2024; Springer Nature: Cham, Switzerland, 2024; pp. 291–305.
8. Zeng, X.; Yu, Y.; Yang, S.; Lv, Y.; Sarker, N.I. Urban resilience for urban sustainability: Concepts, dimensions, and perspectives. *Sustainability* **2022**, *14*, 2481. [CrossRef]
9. Jia, Q. The impact of green finance on the level of decarbonization of the economies: An analysis of the United States', China's, and Russia's current agenda. *Bus. Strategy Environ.* **2023**, *32*, 110–119. [CrossRef]
10. Segura, S.; Ferruz, L.; Gargallo, P.; Salvador, M. Environmental versus economic performance in the EU ETS from the point of view of policy makers: A statistical analysis based on copulas. *J. Clean. Prod.* **2018**, *176*, 1111–1132. [CrossRef]
11. Hasnath, S.A. Megacities in developing Asia: Challenges and opportunities. In *The Elgar Companion to the Asian Development Bank*; Edward Elgar Publishing: Cheltenham, UK, 2024; pp. 167–176.
12. Darwish, D. Improving techniques for convolutional neural networks performance. *Eur. J. Electr. Eng. Comput. Sci.* **2024**, *8*, 1–16. [CrossRef]
13. Hou, X.; Lv, T.; Xu, J.; Deng, X.; Liu, F.; Lam, J.S.L. Electrification transition and carbon emission reduction of urban passenger transportation systems—A case study of Shenzhen, China. *Sustain. Cities Soc.* **2023**, *93*, 104511. [CrossRef]
14. Jiang, J.; Ye, B.; Ma, X.; Miao, L. Controlling GHG emissions from the transportation sector through an ETS: Institutional arrangements in Shenzhen, China. *Clim. Policy* **2016**, *16*, 353–371. [CrossRef]
15. Cao, D.; Puntaier, E.; Gillani, F.; Chapman, D.; Dewitt, S. Towards integrative multi-stakeholder responsibility for net zero in e-waste: A systematic literature review. *Bus. Strategy Environ.* **2024**, *33*, 8994–9014. [CrossRef]
16. O'Connor, E. Understanding Port Performance: An Examination of Challenges in the Contextualisation of Performance in Support of Policy Design in the Port Sector. Doctoral Dissertation, NUI Galway, Galway, Ireland, 2019.
17. Accounting, A.C. *The Greenhouse Gas Protocol*; World Resources Institute and World Business Council for Sustainable Development: Washington, DC, USA, 2004.
18. Fatima, K.; Azam, H.; Sulehri, F.A.; Bukhari, S.A.F.; Virk, H.K.U.R.; Geng, Y.; Ashraf, M.S. Sustainability Disclosures and Their Influence on Cost of Capital: A Comprehensive Bibliometric Study. *Bull. Bus. Econ. (BBE)* **2024**, *13*, 799–810. [CrossRef]
19. Shen, J.; Fu, X.; Guo, W. Corporate Carbon Emission Prediction Based on Multi-Source Data Fusion. In Proceedings of the 2024 4th International Conference on Artificial Intelligence, Robotics, and Communication (ICAIRC), Xiamen, China, 27–29 December 2024; IEEE: Piscataway, NJ, USA, 2024; pp. 144–147.
20. Maheen, R.; Cai, L.; Zhang, Y.S.; Zhao, M. Quantitative analysis of carbon dioxide emission reduction pathways: Towards carbon neutrality in China's power sector. *Carbon Capture Sci. Technol.* **2023**, *7*, 100112. [CrossRef]
21. Li, S.; Ao, X.; Zhang, M.; Pu, M. ESG performance and carbon emission intensity: Examining the role of climate policy uncertainty and the digital economy in China's dual-carbon era. *Front. Environ. Sci.* **2025**, *12*, 1526681. [CrossRef]
22. Wu, J.; Raghupathi, W.; Raghupathi, V. An Exploratory Study of the Association Between Green Bond Features and ESG Performance. *Sustainability* **2025**, *17*, 2094. [CrossRef]
23. Cai, Q.; Chen, W.; Wang, M.; Di, K. How does green finance influence carbon emission intensity? A non-linear fsQCA-ANN approach. *Pol. J. Environ. Stud.* **2024**, 1–7. Available online: https://www.pjoes.com/pdf-190658-115597?filename=How%20Does%20Green%20Finance.pdf (accessed on 2 May 2025). [CrossRef]
24. Network, S.B. Creating Green Bond Markets: Insights, Innovations, and Tools from Emerging Markets. 2018. Available online: https://policycommons.net/artifacts/1275089/creating-green-bond-markets/1861805/ (accessed on 2 May 2025).
25. Shi, Y.; Shen, Y.; Wu, H. Construction and research of regional green finance statistical model based on CVM-MLP neural network. In Proceedings of the 2021 2nd International Conference on Intelligent Computing and Human-Computer Interaction (ICHCI), Shenyang, China, 17–19 November 2021; IEEE: Piscataway, NJ, USA, 2021; pp. 188–193.
26. Shiran, G.; Imaninasab, R.; Khayamim, R. Crash severity analysis of highways based on multinomial logistic regression model, decision tree techniques, and artificial neural network: A modeling comparison. *Sustainability* **2021**, *13*, 5670. [CrossRef]
27. Okon, A.N.; Adewole, S.E.; Uguma, E.M. Artificial neural network model for reservoir petrophysical properties: Porosity, permeability and water saturation prediction. *Model. Earth Syst. Environ.* **2021**, *7*, 2373–2390. [CrossRef]
28. Mao, K.; Zhu, J.; Su, L.; Cai, G.; Li, Y.; Dong, Z. FinalMLP: An enhanced two-stream MLP model for CTR prediction. In Proceedings of the AAAI Conference on Artificial Intelligence, Washington, DC, USA, 7–14 February 2023; Volume 37, pp. 4552–4560.
29. Nikitas, A.; Kougias, I.; Alyavina, E.; Njoya Tchouamou, E. How can autonomous and connected vehicles, electromobility, BRT, hyperloop, shared use mobility and mobility-as-a-service shape transport futures for the context of smart cities? *Urban Sci.* **2017**, *1*, 36. [CrossRef]

30. Karmaker, S.C.; Sen, K.K.; Chapman, A.J.; Mohiuddin, G.; Saha, B.B. Innovation under Cap-and-Trade: How emission trading systems propel decarbonization. *Next Energy* **2025**, *7*, 100220. [CrossRef]
31. Green, J.F. Does carbon pricing reduce emissions? A review of ex-post analyses. *Environ. Res. Lett.* **2021**, *16*, 043004. [CrossRef]
32. Biørn, E. Estimating SUR system with random coefficients: The unbalanced panel data case. *Empir. Econ.* **2014**, *47*, 451–468. [CrossRef]
33. Kotzampasakis, M.; Woerdman, E. Linking the EU ETS with California's Cap-and-Trade Program: A law and economics assessment. *Cent. Eur. Rev. Econ. Manag.* **2020**, *4*, 9–45.
34. Wakabayashi, M.; Kimura, O. The impact of the Tokyo Metropolitan Emissions Trading Scheme on reducing greenhouse gas emissions: Findings from a facility-based study. *Clim. Policy* **2018**, *18*, 1028–1043. [CrossRef]
35. Wang, P.; Dai, H.C.; Ren, S.Y.; Zhao, D.Q.; Masui, T. Achieving Copenhagen target through carbon emission trading: Economic impacts assessment in Guangdong Province of China. *Energy* **2015**, *79*, 212–227. [CrossRef]
36. Rhafes, M.Y.; Moussaoui, O.; Raboaca, M.S. Machine learning models in renewable energy forecasting: A systematic literature review. *Indones. J. Electr. Eng. Comput. Sci.* **2025**, *37*, 1874–1886. [CrossRef]
37. Anupama, G.; Kesava Rao, V.V.S. Some objective methods for determining relative importance of financial ratios. *Int. J. Manag.* **2020**, *10*, 2019. [CrossRef]
38. Sun, Y.; Yang, Y.; Xiao, K. Leverage influence Chinese commercial banks and financial factors analysis based on artificial neural network research. In Proceedings of the 2021 6th International Symposium on Computer and Information Processing Technology (ISCIPT), Changsha, China, 11–13 June 2021; IEEE: Piscataway, NJ, USA, 2021; pp. 349–353.
39. Alrawashdeh, K.; Purdy, C. Fast activation function approach for deep learning based online anomaly intrusion detection. In Proceedings of the 2018 IEEE 4th International Conference on Big Data Security on Cloud (BigDataSecurity), IEEE International Conference on High Performance and Smart Computing,(HPSC) and IEEE International Conference on Intelligent Data and Security (IDS), Omaha, NE, USA, 3–5 May 2018; IEEE: Piscataway, NJ, USA, 2018; pp. 5–13.
40. Tao, S.; Wu, X.; Fang, K.; Lin, D. Identifying drivers of county-level industrial carbon intensity by a generic machine learning framework. *J. Clean. Prod.* **2024**, *454*, 142276. [CrossRef]
41. Nuţă, F.M.; Nuţă, A.C.; Zamfir, C.G.; Petrea, S.M.; Munteanu, D.; Cristea, D.S. National carbon accounting—Analyzing the impact of urbanization and energy-related factors upon CO_2 emissions in central–eastern European countries by using machine learning algorithms and panel data analysis. *Energies* **2021**, *14*, 2775. [CrossRef]
42. Wang, W.; Zhou, S.; Li, D.; Wang, Y.; Liu, X. Disentangling the non-linear relationships and interaction effects of urban digital transformation on carbon emission intensity. *Urban Clim.* **2025**, *59*, 102283. [CrossRef]
43. Yu, X.; Xu, Y.; Zhang, J.; Sun, Y. The synergy green innovation effect of green innovation subsidies and carbon taxes. *Sustainability* **2022**, *14*, 3453. [CrossRef]
44. Huang, Y. Government subsidies and corporate disclosure. *J. Account. Econ.* **2022**, *74*, 101480. [CrossRef]
45. Li, Z.; Zheng, C.; Liu, A.; Yang, Y.; Yuan, X. Environmental taxes, green subsidies, and cleaner production willingness: Evidence from China's publicly traded companies. *Technol. Forecast. Soc. Change* **2022**, *183*, 121906. [CrossRef]
46. Khosroshahi, H.; Dimitrov, S.; Hejazi, S.R. Pricing, greening, and transparency decisions considering the impact of government subsidies and CSR behavior in supply chain decisions. *J. Retail. Consum. Serv.* **2021**, *60*, 102485. [CrossRef]
47. Xu, G.; Yang, H.; Schwarz, P. Predicting China's carbon intensity through 2050: An integrated analysis method. *Clim. Dev.* **2023**, *15*, 292–303. [CrossRef]
48. Saarela, M.; Jauhiainen, S. Comparison of feature importance measures as explanations for classification models. *SN Appl. Sci.* **2021**, *3*, 272. [CrossRef]
49. Lipovetsky, S.; Conklin, W.M. Predictor relative importance and matching regression parameters. *J. Appl. Stat.* **2015**, *42*, 1017–1031. [CrossRef]
50. Liu, B.; Song, C.; Lai, M.; Chen, J.; Wang, Y.; Feng, Z. Deep decarbonization potential and implementation path under provincial differences in China's fleet electrification. *Sci. Total Environ.* **2024**, *946*, 174271. [CrossRef]
51. Biecek, P.; Burzykowski, T. *Explanatory Model Analysis: Explore, Explain, and Examine Predictive Models*; Chapman and Hall/CRC: Boca Raton, FL, USA, 2021.

urban science

MDPI

Article

Assessing Citizens' Perceptions of Urban Agriculture and Its Contribution to Food Security—Worldwide Analysis and Specific Case Studies in Spain

Ouiam Fatiha Boukharta [1,*], Leticia Chico Santamarta [1,2], Adriana Correa Guimaraes [1] and Luis Manuel Navas Gracia [1,*]

1 TADRUS Research Group, Department of Agricultural and Forestry Engineering, University of Valladolid, 34004 Palencia, Spain; lchico-santamarta@harper-adams.ac.uk (L.C.S.); adriana.correa@uva.es (A.C.G.)

2 Global Impact Department, Harper Adams University, Edgmond, Newport TF10 8NB, UK

* Correspondence: ouiamfatiha.boukharta@uva.es (O.F.B.); luismanuel.navas@uva.es (L.M.N.G.)

Abstract: There is growing worldwide concern about eating healthily and consuming local food. Consequently, urban agriculture has become a topical issue, especially in light of increasing demographics. The present article investigates and assesses how urban agriculture can be implemented to ensure greater food security and achieve sustainable development goals. The methodology consisted in distributing a worldwide survey, along with interviews with project managers of two urban agricultural practices in the cities of Valladolid and Segovia (Spain). The survey gathered 250 responses from nearly all continents, ensuring a diverse and global perspective and that most respondents were familiar with the concept of urban agriculture (80%) rather than food security (57.4%). The survey also revealed that 88.1% of respondents expressed their willingness to be engage in such projects. The interviews brought out a number of common points, such as ensuring that residents are properly aware about the value of integrating the food sector into cities and the benefits it provides, such as organizing activities and workshops, etc. However, promoting small organizations and start-ups linked to local production and consumption and integrating urban planning experts is crucial to ensure more resilient and sustainable cities. This research uniquely integrates quantitative survey data with in-depth qualitative case studies, linking global perceptions of urban agriculture and food security with local realities.

Keywords: urban agriculture; food security; sustainable development goals; survey; interviews; Spain

1. Introduction

Nowadays, it is extremely important to ensure sustainable urban food systems, given that urban areas are experiencing rapid population growth, intensive food commercialization and unhealthy nutritional patterns [1,2]. Indeed, the United Nations Human Settlements Programme estimates that 60% of the population will live in urban areas by 2030 [3,4], and where rapid urbanization and increasing industrial agricultural production exist, they have led to a growing disconnection between urban dwellers, their food sources and their connection with nature, distancing people from recent contact with each other [5,6]. Moreover, we live in a time of concern for people's mental health and well-being, as depression is now the leading cause of ill health and disability, with over 300 million people affected, according to the World Health Organization in 2017 [7,8]. However, there

 https://doi.org/10.3390/urbansci9050150

is a growing realization that connection with nature contributes significantly to our mental health and well-being [9].

Considering this current situation, policymakers and scientific researchers, therefore, see urban agriculture (UA) as a promising pillar of food security (FS) and urban resilience [9,10]. UA has been defined by the FAO as "the cultivation of plants and the raising of animals for food and other uses in and around cities, along with related activities such as production and delivery of inputs, processing and marketing of products" [11,12]. Based on this definition, we clearly understand that UA is the cultivation, processing and distribution of food products by growing plants in and around cities serving to feed local inhabitants [13–15]. It is also characterized by the systematic and extensive occupation of unused land in urban areas, with the establishment of individual, community or collective gardens and allotments [11,16].

The success of UA has been widely recognized for its benefits, which are aligned with aspects of sustainable development [5]. The social aspect includes social inclusion and integration, along with raising awareness; the environmental aspect relates to environmental protection, biodiversity preservation and climate regulation; and the economic aspect is linked to cost savings and healthy produce at a lower price [17,18]. Moreover, the successful implementation of UA is strongly linked to its positive perception by the public for those who live within urban areas and for the wider community in general [19]. UA contributes to several Sustainable Development Goals (SDGs), notably FS and improved nutrition (SDG 2), the promotion of sustainable and resilient cities (SDG 11) and the preservation of terrestrial ecosystems (SDG 15) [20,21]. Additionally, it also promotes sustainable consumption and, to a greater extent, production patterns (SDG 12), and it can strengthen social inclusion and equitable access to food resources (SDG 10) [22,23].

This research aims to achieve two objectives which, combined, are perfectly complementary and lead us to a main and comprehensive result. Firstly, a quantitative survey to provide an overview of perceptions of the role of urban agriculture in food security; secondly, an analysis of two qualitative case studies has been conducted in Spain to deepen this understanding by exploring in a more concrete and real way how urban agriculture is practiced and experienced at a local level. By combining these two approaches, the research allows us to capture global trends in perceptions of urban agriculture while grounding them in the lived experiences of project leaders in two Spanish cities, thus linking general attitudes to specific urban governance and implementation dynamics. Moreover, despite the growing number of research studies on urban agriculture and food security, a comprehensive understanding integrating both large-scale perceptions and site-specific case studies remains limited, and this is precisely where the present research makes a significant contribution, by providing a more qualified and comprehensive perspective on the role of urban agriculture in achieving sustainable food security.

This research paper is structured as follows: Section 2 presents the methodology used to carry out this study, including the implementation and distribution of the survey, as well as the approach taken in the interviews. Section 3 presents the results obtained from the two research sections, outlining the findings with diagrams and tables to make them more comprehensible, leading on to the Section 4, which is based on an evaluation of the results, drawing contrasts with the work of other researchers, followed by a series of conclusions and findings, together with recommendations for future studies.

2. Materials and Methods

The purpose of this investigation is to gain a precise understanding of the population's perception of UA, while establishing direct contact with project leaders to gain a more detailed insight into how such initiatives operate, the obstacles they face and their main challenges. To address our research problematics, a mixed-methods approach was adopted, involving different research methodologies, including a questionnaire survey and semi-structured interviews. The combination of these approaches enabled us to obtain a precise and in-depth understanding of the actual situation, featuring a comprehensive qualitative and quantitative analysis [24].

2.1. Theoretical Framework

This investigation has involved the integration of several theories that are essential for the proper performance of this research and for a complete and accurate assessment of our problematics. The survey comprised a series of questions that helped to better identify the population being evaluated, which allowed us to base our answers around this target population. Moreover, the development of the questions in relation to the adoption and influencing factors were underpinned by the Theory of Planned Behavior [25] and the COM-B model [26]. Regarding the interviews, the theory used was that of social practices [27]. It offered a very precise approach to understanding the behavior of individuals in the face of our problem, by examining the words of our participants. This theory allowed to better explore and evaluate the results through the responses collected, by assessing the participants' engagement in specific practices, their applications in their daily lives and how changes in materials, skills and meanings can influence their behavior. Analysis using Social Practice Theory shows how changes in practices can contribute to lasting changes in behavior and attitudes.

Besides the above-mentioned theories, a complementary analysis of the interview and survey data allowed us to provide an understanding of the psychological factors that influence individuals' behavior and attitudes in different contexts, as well as their decision-making in terms of actions, which will be further elaborated on and discussed in the following subsections [25,28].

2.2. Sampling Frame and Sampling Technique

The sample frame targeted individuals with direct or indirect involvement in UA, encompassing practitioners, researchers, policymakers and community members. Given the exploratory nature of the study, the selection process sought to capture a broad and diverse range of perspectives, ensuring the inclusion of both experienced and novice participants. This approach allows for a better understanding of the dynamics of the different contexts [29].

A random sampling method was used to maximize respondent diversity and avoid selection bias [30,31]. Although no strict stratification was applied, efforts were made to encourage responses from diverse demographic and professional groups to improve the robustness of the results. The survey was disseminated worldwide via our institutional and professional networks and our international research team, as well as our collaborators in several projects, enabling broad geographic and demographic coverage and diverse participation across all continents, offering a global visualization and perception of the worldwide perspective of urban agriculture and food security, not only at local and national levels, but also on an international scale. In addition, this approach involved voluntary participation while ensuring the representation of the various UA communities.

2.3. Data Collection and Administration

The survey was distributed between May and June 2022 in an online manner and at the national and international level, through our networks, via e-mail, colleagues and projects, etc., and its establishment was performed through the Google Form platform, for its efficiency, simplicity and feasibility. It should be emphasized that, given the purpose of this survey, no reliability analysis was applied, since such tests were not necessary and the questions were essentially descriptive and aimed at capturing perceptions, experiences and practices, rather than measuring hidden concepts or performing parametric analyses. The interviews, on the other hand, were conducted during the same period, focusing on two urban agricultural initiatives located in Spain, namely "Alimenta Conciencia" in the city of Segovia" and "Estrategia Alimentaria de Valladolid".

The questionnaire was completed in full anonymity, with respondents' consent and acceptance of the general rules prior to the start of the survey, regarding the use of data in this investigation. The interviews with the project leaders of both initiatives were recorded with their consent vocally (in Spanish), transcribed and professionally translated into English for in-depth interpretation of the results. These transcriptions were subsequently coded using NVivo 14 Software, which enabled to better structure the results, and thus obtain all the information needed for interpretation.

2.4. Content of the Questionnaire and Interviews

Different variables were defined and targeted to better understand the content of these questionnaires and interviews. Indeed, this theory, employed by Ajzen in 1991 [25], provides an in-depth understanding of human behavior, since it identifies three interdependent and identifiable dimensions: ability, opportunity and motivation, which are considered essential for the behavior to occur [26]. Ability refers to the skills and knowledge required by the individual; opportunity encompasses the environment and external conditions that enable the individuals to better identify themselves, while motivation includes intrinsic and extrinsic motivations. Consequently, this analysis provides a comprehensive basis for analyzing the behavior of the individuals concerned. Table 1 provides a more detailed explanation of each of these variables and presents some of the questions that were asked, both in the questionnaires and in the interviews:

Table 1. Main questions employed in the survey and throughout the interview.

Variable Name	Question Used in Survey	Question Used in Interview
Behavior (intention)	Would you support UA in your city?	Does your project aim to achieve objectives that are useful to residents and the city?
Behavior (Actual)	Have you ever been involved in some UA initiatives?	What is the current situation of your project? How is it going?
Attitudes	What do we mean by UA and FS?	What are the activities you are implementing in your UAP?
Subjective Norm	To what extent are the themes of UA and FS linked?	What should be the objectives of these urban agriculture projects to meet the needs of the inhabitants and their communities?
Project	Do you think your city needs the implementation of such initiatives?	What do you think makes this initiative successful?
Capability	Would you be interested in participating in such projects?	How do you try to promote your idea in your city? What method was the most effective?
Other motivation?	Would you like to tell us more about your thoughts/ideas on this subject?	What was your motivation for working on this project?

Table 1 provides a very clear explanation of the different variables highlighted in this research, as well as presenting the questions that were asked to our interviewees and survey respondents. We can clearly see that this is a very good method of bringing the two approaches together, ensuring that they are both brought coherently into one overall framework.

Besides the above series of questions, other aspects were addressed, such as the definition of "urban agriculture," "food security" and other aspects related to their integration with the SDGs, all through their own understanding, via a series of proposed answers.

Indeed, on the basis of their answers, we can better frame the population being assessed, better understand how they assimilate this knowledge and, therefore, better draw appropriate conclusions for our investigation. Furthermore, based on these responses, it would be more accurate to assess the current state of knowledge regarding the integration of the food sector in cities through UA, and thus, in the case of negative responses or lack of interest on the part of stakeholders, to determine what needs to be enacted to address this situation.

3. Results

The results obtained from the questionnaires and interviews are presented and explained in the following subsections, illustrated with tables and figures to make their understanding and interpretation more effective and straightforward.

3.1. Results from the Survey

As previously mentioned in the methodology, the survey was distributed using a random sampling method to ensure a representative sample. This multi-faceted distribution approach allowed us to reach a wide range of potential respondents from different professional backgrounds and geographical locations, with a total of 250 respondents from all over the world. This diversity ensures the robustness and generalizability of our results, as it encompasses the perspectives of individuals from different cultural, social and economic backgrounds.

3.1.1. Characteristic of the Respondents

Identifying the characteristics of the respondents was the first step in designing the median profile studied in this study. Indeed, Figure 1 clearly and easily presents all the details required about our respondents.

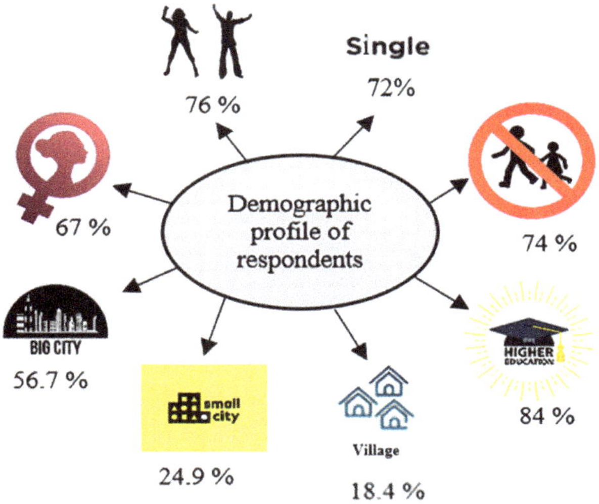

Figure 1. Characteristics of the survey respondents.

From Figure 1, it can be seen that the number of female respondents far exceeds the number of male respondents, with 67% female responses. Moreover, 72% of our respondents are single and in the 18–35 age range, and the majority have no children. In terms of place of residence, most of our respondents live in cities and only 18% live in villages. According to Figure 1, the demographic profile of the respondent appears to be that of a young, single woman without children, with a higher level of education and who lives in the city.

3.1.2. Geographic Distribution of the Respondents

Regarding the residence of our respondents, it should be noted that the survey was conducted on a global scale, bringing together participants from a variety of geographical regions. Figure 2, therefore, presents the geographical distribution of respondents to illustrate the geographic diversity of the sample and to support the global character of the study, rather than to perform a specific comparative country analysis.

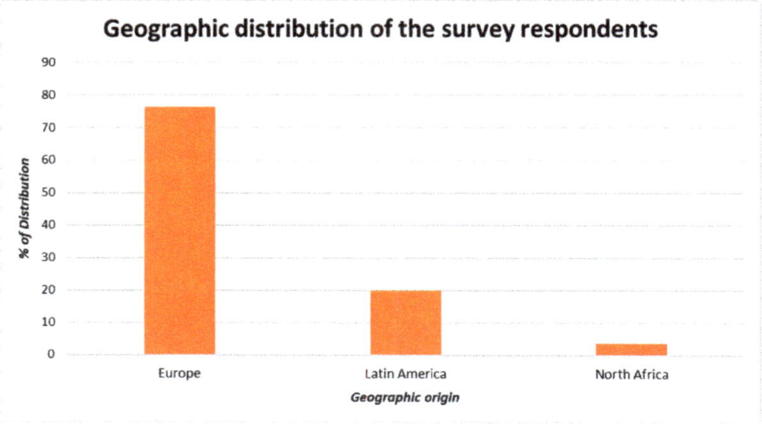

Figure 2. Percentage share of survey respondents' geographical distribution.

The results from Figure 2 show that 76.3% of responses came from European countries, including Spain, with the highest percentage of responses (20.4% out of 76.3%), followed by Ukraine, the United Kingdom, France and a few other countries from the rest of Europe. The second main category with participants who responded to our survey was from the Central American countries, mainly the Dominican Republic, with 20% of responses, and, finally, the third category was from North African countries, mainly Morocco, with 3.7% of responses. These results underline the broad geographical distribution of our survey (Figure 2).

3.1.3. Knowledge of UA and FS

In order to address our research question about the public's perception of UA and FS, numerous questions were asked to our interviewees, including their knowledge of UA and FS, the link between the two concepts and their importance in ensuring healthy and sustainable food systems, their willingness or not to support the implementation of these practices in cities and their level of interest in participating in such projects, etc. These findings are presented below:

- Definitions and concepts

One of the main questions asked to our respondents as part of the survey concerned their knowledge of UA and FS. Indeed, we presented a series of definitions relating to each of the two concepts, and they had to choose the right ones. According to the results obtained, 78.80% of responses concerning the definition of UA were correct, meaning, according to Olsson et al., in 2016: "an agricultural production system that is integrated into urban and peri-urban landscapes and is in line with the perspective of sustainable development" [32]. Regarding FS, only 57.40% of the population surveyed knew the correct answer, which is, according to Capone et al., in 2014, "having access for all people at all times to enough food to lead an active and healthy life" [33], while 42.60% had the wrong answer, thinking it was an international law or organization;

- Link between UA and FS

Respondents to this survey were asked a series of questions to better understand their perception of the link between UA and FS, along with their opinion on the importance of UAP in ensuring a sustainable food system. These findings will enable a better understanding of our audience's attitudes towards these two concepts, and will, therefore, allow to draw relevant conclusions. This information is presented in Figure 3.

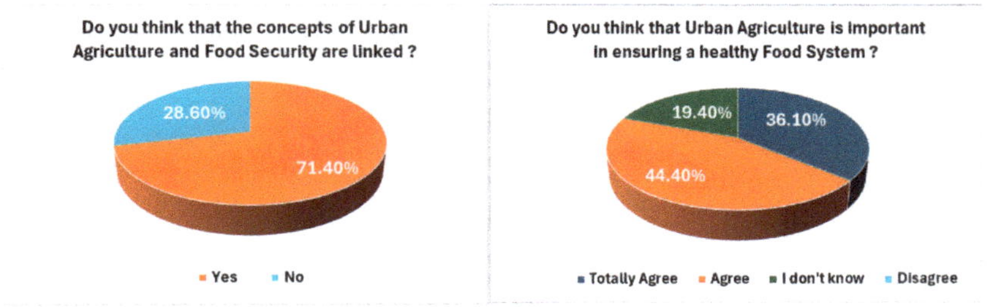

Figure 3. Urban agriculture and its link to food security (**left**); urban agriculture in ensuring a healthy and sustainable food system (in %) (**right**).

Regarding the link between UA and FS, Figure 3 shows that 71.40% of the respondents confirm agreement that both concepts are linked, while 28.60% believe that this link does not exist. Moreover, 80.50% of the respondents agree that this link will ensure a healthy and sustainable food system, while 19.40% disagree with this achievement. The percentages of disagreements present quite a small percentage compared to the majority, but this should still be considered and evaluated;

- Implementation of UA in cities

Another important aspect that needs to be addressed in this study is the integration of UA in cities and whether our respondents have ever participated in such projects. The results are presented in Figure 4.

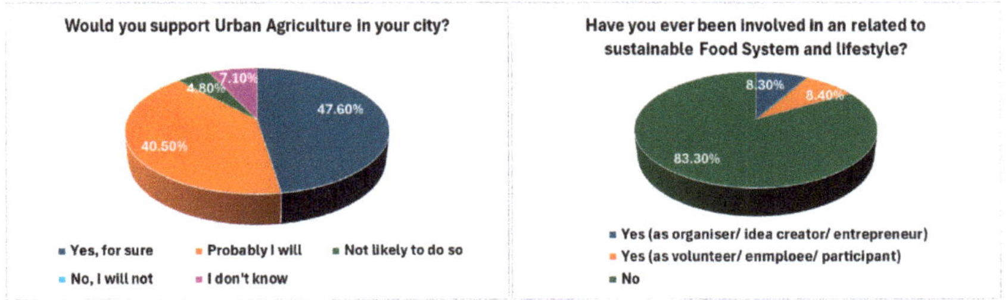

Figure 4. Supporting urban agriculture within cities (in %); involvement in urban agricultural practices and projects (in %).

Figure 4 shows that almost 47.60% of respondents are willing to support the inclusion of UA areas and practices in their city, and 40.50% are likely to do so (88.10% in total). However, 11.90% of respondents would not be ready to do so, which is a fairly low percentage compared to the rest of the responses. Moreover, Figure 4 shows that most of the responses would support the implementation of initiatives in their cities, but most of them have never been involved in an UA initiative.

Recognizing the differentiations of all the above-mentioned results enables greater understanding of the attitudes and multiple perspectives surrounding the involvement of UA in cities, allowing for better-informed decision-making and policymaking in this area.

3.2. Results from the Interviews

In order to make our results more concrete and realistic, we selected two UA initiatives from Spain, in order to evaluate their objectives, benefices, improvement and obstacles and, therefore, to draw conclusions and recommendations. The selection of the two urban agriculture initiatives was based on their compatibility with the objectives of our research problematics, respecting criteria that were aligned with our inquiries into the transition to sustainable food systems, as well as on the availability of relevant data and institutional contacts, which enabled an in-depth qualitative analysis. The following sections illustrate the previous points in further detail, enabling us to gain a better understanding of each of the two initiatives and to draw appropriate and relevant conclusions.

Interviews were carried out with the project managers of two initiatives, namely "Alimenta Conciencia" in the city of Segovia" and "Estrategia Alimentaria de Valladolid" in the city of Valladolid. These interviews allowed us to obtain a considerable amount of information about two projects in Spain, which allowed us to gain a general ideal about the situation in Spain, as well as gathering, through the project managers' own statements, information about the activities carried out, the objectives they would like to achieve and the obstacles they are encountering.

3.2.1. "Alimenta Conciencia" in Segovia City

Segovia is an active city in terms of health and equity, education and participation. To achieve a sustainable and healthy food system, Segovia's sustainable food strategy has the objectives of coordinating between the different administrations and promoting better administrative coordination

- Presentation of the initiative

The "Alimenta Conciencia" initiative was launched in 2019. However, due to the far-reaching effects of the COVID-19 pandemic, the expected timeframe for completion of the project was postponed from 2022 to the end of 2023. This delay was imposed due to major unexpected challenges posed by the pandemic, such as limited access to resources, restricted supply chains and the necessity to adjust project activities to ensure the safety of the participants. The interview was conducted with the coordinator of the "Alimenta Conciencia" project, who was very helpful and who agreed to answer to our questionnaire without any problem;

- Objectives and motivations

The main objectives of this initiative are to better know what is produced and consumed and how this affects the local economy and depopulation, as well as promoting a more sustainable, local, healthy and seasonal diet. Indeed, with the aim of combating food insecurity and promoting awareness, it was necessary to ask our interviewee about the motivation of creating and working on such an initiative. The motivations are therefore the following: "I am aware of the importance of food in this area", which means to ensure a sustainable development and: "I have a conception of the university academy as an information transfer", which means to contribute as much as possible to a better world for all, along with reconnecting people with nature and eating locally. Indeed, these statements by the project manager show and explain the reasons and motivations that led them to get involved and manage such urban agriculture projects, as well as the implementation and its benefits, something that allowed them to fight for its realization and thus have this motivation to implement it in the best possible way.

These challenging objectives are being achieved through a carefully designed framework, consisting of four key steps that are presented in the following Table 2:

Table 2. Four key steps to achieve the challenging goals of the "Alimenta Conciencia" initiative.

Key Steps	Explanation
Collaboration and Cooperation	Between all social actors involved in the project; strong cooperation and collaboration are needed; building a network of interconnected social actors
Increase organic production	Organic farming; eco-friendly environment; production of healthier food for consumers
Consumption	Encourage local consumption; priority given to products grown in the city or nearby "Km 0"; supports the local economy
Communication and education	Raise awareness and encourage inhabitants to adopt sustainable practices; organize educational activities

From Table 2, we can clearly see that the "Alimenta Conciencia" initiative has many objectives that can be classified into four aspects. Collaboration and cooperation are the first main step, which should be enacted among all the social actors involved in the projects, as the success of such an initiative depends on collective efforts, and meaningful engagement and partnerships are essential for the overall impact of the project. Next comes the step of increasing organic production, as it offers many benefits, including environmental sustainability, improved soil regeneration and healthier food production for consumers (Table 2). Then comes the consumption aspect, where this UA initiative encourages citizens to prioritize products grown in or near the city, known as "Segovia Eco Kilo 0", along with supporting the local economy, contributing directly to the livelihoods of local farmers and producers, sustaining rural communities and creating jobs. Finally, there is the communication and education aspect, which is considered a fundamental aspect and where the project aims to raise awareness and encourage people to adopt sustainable practices, ensuring a more sustainable and healthy future for current and future generations.

In terms of motivations, our interviewee mentioned that "I am aware of the importance of food in this area", which means helping to ensure sustainable development, and she also mentioned that she would like this to be available for "current and future generations". Indeed, these motivations are aligned with the objectives of sustainable development, in particular improving nutrition (SDG 2), the promotion of sustainable and resilient cities (SDG 11), the promotion of sustainable consumption (SDG 12), and being able to strengthen social inclusion and equitable access to food resources (SDG 10);

- Activities carried out

In order to promote a sustainable and healthy food system in and around the city of Segovia, "Alimenta Conciencia" is deeply involved with a series of actions and activities, which are presented with further details in Figure 5.

The "Alimenta Conciencia" initiative aims to implement actions and activities to ensure a more sustainable and healthier food system. This objective is being achieved through a number of activities shown in Figure 5. Indeed, the aforementioned initiative has established three local stores in Segovia, encouraging farmers in the province to sell their local produce in these stores, and encouraging consumers to avoid traveling to other distant markets, while still having access to healthy local groceries. In addition, "Alimenta

Conciencia" is committed to ensuring sustainable gastronomic tourism by organizing various awareness-raising activities to improve local knowledge, while encouraging local production and consumption. Finally, our interlocutor stressed that "it is necessary to carry out numerous educational activities with students to clarify the importance of healthy, local food" (Figure 5);

Figure 5. Activities realized in "Alimenta Conciencia" initiative.

- Main challenges and problems encountered

In addition to all the positive impacts that the "Alimenta Conciencia" initiative is bringing to the residents and the city of Segovia, it faces some challenges that are worth highlighting, and which are presented in Figure 6:

Main Challenges that "Alimenta Conciencia" initiative in Segovia has encountered	
Share knowledge	Knowledge-sharing towards urban agriculture and sustainable food systems is still a major challenge.
Lack of economic resources	Such initiatives are confronted with this problem, which represents first and foremost a problem of action.
Human factor	Lack of people willing to work on such projects, or people who are committed and not fully involved.
Geopolitical tensions	Conflicts between countries caused a global food crisis and led to an increase in product prices.

Figure 6. Main challenges that "Alimenta Conciencia" initiative in Segovia has encountered.

Figure 6 emphasizes that, in addition to the activities carried out, knowledge-sharing and a more positive attitude towards food systems are still a major challenge. Furthermore, our interviewee pointed out that "it's difficult to change people's consumption patterns, switching to the consumption of local and nearby products", which means that the "Segovia Eco Km0" is still a work in progress and should be further promoted and shared with everyone.

Regarding the problems encountered, our interlocutor emphasized the lack of economic resources, which the current and other similar initiatives face, and which is, above all, a problem in the conduct of action. Another important factor is the human factor; there is a lack of people willing to work on such projects or people who are committed and not fully involved. One other major aspect that was mentioned was the geopolitical tensions. Indeed, our interlocutor mentioned that "this has caused a global food crisis and led to an increase in product prices". It is currently necessary to find alternatives and create a healthy and comfortable environment to provide people with local produce (Figure 6).

3.2.2. "Estrategia Alimentaria de Valladolid" in Valladolid City

The city of Valladolid has developed a process of reflection on the local agri-food system. This process of research and reflection has led to a participatory process to draw up a food strategy for the city, which will then be translated into an action plan. Meanwhile, the strategy evaluated in this research study has entered its implementation phase, which is currently underway.

- Presentation of the initiative

The Valladolid City Council, the Entretantos Foundation and the University of Valladolid, joined in 2019 by the MercaOlid and VallaEcolid associations, launched the project "Estrategia Alimentaria de Valladolid" Project in 2016. Regarding the conducted interview, it was carried out with the Councilor of the Environment and the fourth Deputy Mayor of the Valladolid City Council (Ayuntamiento de Valladolid, in Spanish), to whom we would like to thank for the warm welcome and for answering all our interview questions in a smooth and efficient way. Moreover, the city of Valladolid and its surroundings have been developing a process of reflection on the local agri-food system over the last few years to start launching a participatory process for the development of a food strategy of its own and ensure new strategies such as "Valladolid's Agri-Food Strategy: participatory process";

- Objectives and motivations

According to our interviewee, the main aim of the "Estrategia Alimentaria de Valladolid" is to promote a space for collective processing of the food system, to work with other sectors for a more prolonged use of processed foods, along with broadening sales channels. Moreover, opening up a niche in catering with the possibility of developing new allergen-free products and innovation is considered one of the main objectives of these initiatives. Indeed, achieving these objectives would generate very positive learning, relationships and synergies for the local food system.

Regarding motivations, our interviewee mentioned many aspects, such as "People who work the land are the local producers of Valladolid and the surrounding area of Castilla y León and can develop their activities in a politically responsible manner". Indeed, this aspect is fundamental since farmers complain about this issue, and always mention that they wish to have more facilities from local authorities. Another aspect was mentioned: "People can have access to food close to their homes, without having to travel, called "Km 0"." Indeed, this aspect is nowadays necessary since ensuring local and closed products to the inhabitants is benefitting both the city and its inhabitants.

Furthermore, these objectives and motivations are entirely in line with a number of SDGs, which cover improving nutrition (SDG 2), promoting sustainable and resilient cities (SDG 11), fostering sustainable consumption (SDG 12) and strengthening social inclusion and equitable access to food resources (SDG 10);

- Activities carried out

The "Estrategia Alimentaria de Valladolid" is carrying out numerous activities to achieve its objectives and improve the progress of the project. Table 3 below gives a more detailed description of the activities carried out:

Table 3. Main activities realized at the "Estrategia Alimentaria de Valladolid".

Main Activities	Explication
Local markets	Organization of a local market once a month that brings together several local producers in the city of Valladolid.
Pedagogical activities	Organization of pedagogical activities within educational systems to ensure participation of children within dialogue about the importance of eating healthy and locally and also to show them how to plant a certain fruit or vegetable
Encourage local consumption	Organization of activities and workshops open to the public to explain the importance of eating locally for health and wellbeing, as well as to encourage people to start cultivating their own fruits and vegetables in their gardens and/or on balconies etc., if possible.

According to our interviewee, the main activity organized is the setting up of local markets. This market will connect the community by highlighting the diversity of the town's products, creating a thriving and dynamic local market for visitors and guests alike. Secondly, educational activities will be organized to highlight the importance of good nutrition. These activities will enable students to learn more about good nutrition and the positive impact it has on our well-being. To this end, a number of practical exercises are organized, such as practical advice on meat planning from experts, nutritional information and healthy cooking techniques and how these can improve our health and daily lives. The final main activity of "Estrategia Alimentaria de Valladolid" is to encourage local consumption in the community, supporting local businesses and raising awareness of the benefits of buying local produce. To achieve this, various events, open days and activities are organized to show the local population the positive impact on the environment and its impact on our daily lives (Table 3);

- Main challenges and problems encountered

Based on interviews with our initiative representative, it was possible to identify the main challenges facing the project during its implementation and progress. These aspects are further illustrated in the following Figure 7, which lists each challenge along with its explanation.

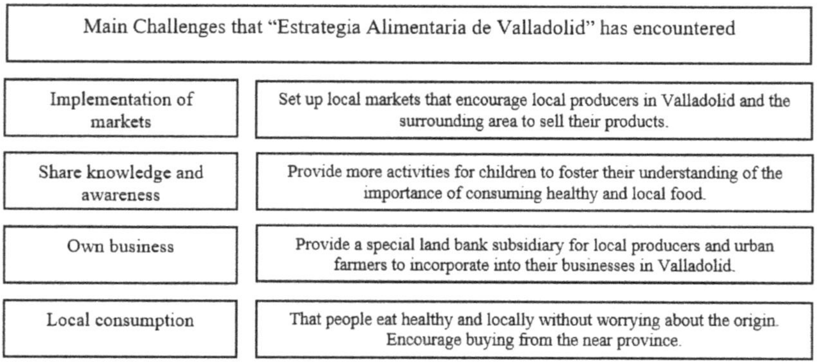

Figure 7. Main challenges that "Estrategia Alimentaria de Valladolid" has encountered.

Figure 7 clearly demonstrates that one of the major challenges of "Estrategia Alimentaria de Valladolid" is the creation of permanent local markets within the city where local farmers can sell their produce to local consumers. The project will also encourage them to open their own businesses in the city, securing land to make it easier for them to own property and start marketing to the community. Furthermore, the project seeks to organize more knowledge-sharing and awareness-raising activities, to emphasize the importance of local food and to encourage residents to buy at local markets, instead of traveling, and thus respect the "Km0" concept (Figure 7).

Regarding the challenges, the urban initiative "Estrategia Alimentaria de Valladolid" pointed out that it is very difficult to share knowledge with residents, to enable them to change their way of thinking about consumption and where they produce. Another aspect that was mentioned was increasing the number of participants in events and how to make these concepts more mainstream in cities, where one interviewee mentioned that "today we need more initiatives on UA and growing food in cities while consuming it, in order to make a change in citizens' daily diets" (Figure 7).

4. Discussion

This investigation focuses on two main research lines. The first one is related to the public's perception towards UA and its implementation, and the second was conducted through interviews with project managers. These investigations resulted in many findings that respond to our problematics. Indeed, from the in-depth analysis of the results presented above, there is clear evidence that there is an urgent need for action to create a healthy and sustainable urban environment that meets the needs of current and future generations.

The results of the survey brought the total number of respondents to 250 from all over the world, most of whom were women, living in cities, single and with university and higher education. In terms of their responses to the questions, one very impressive result is that the majority of respondents are familiar with the concept of UA, but this remains at a theoretical level, since when it comes to practical implementation, there is a notable lack of active engagement but the respondents are, nonetheless, interested. This is in line with the work carried out by Kirby et al., in 2021, in many European cities and in the United States, assessing the gap between theoretical knowledge of urban agriculture and practical commitment, where the results of their investigation revealed that many urban participants express a motivation to engage in these practices, but that structural obstacles or a lack of know-how limit their real involvement [34]. This can be considered along with the research carried out in Malaysia by Azmi et al. in 2024, highlighting the gap between theoretical knowledge of UA and practical engagement, which could an obstacle to future project implementation [35]. Another aspect is that most interviewees associate UA with sustainability and bio-products, which is correct, but less so with personal well-being and health issues, which is an essential aspect of UA, since it is seen as a public good for society rather than an individual good. This is fully in line with the work carried out in France by Boukharta et al. in 2023, underlining the impact that the implementation of urban agriculture projects has on both the population and the city, all linked to sustainable development and its goals, along with the connection that exists between these aspects [5]. Furthermore, Hallett's findings in 2013 also highlight the importance of implementing urban agriculture in cities, which guarantees a really important social impact in people's daily lives and for their psychological selves [36], something that was also founded in 2023 by Nicholas et al., thanks to an investigation carried out in Singapore, underlining the social benefits that urban agriculture brings to the population, such as creating new friendships and learning to communicate more effectively with people from different backgrounds, as well as the psychological benefits that enhance self-awareness, gratitude and stress reduction [37].

The survey results also showed that rural residents tend to be more familiar with agricultural concepts, as they are often directly involved in food production, and are aware of their daily benefits and advantages. Urban respondents, on the other hand, may not yet be fully aware of the need for this daily link, but the growing awareness and interest in urban agriculture and its influence on moral and physical well-being is now influencing their perception of its value; this finding has also been made by many researchers across different developed and developing countries [34].

Regarding FS, we can see that it is a term that is not well understood by our population, contrary to UA. Indeed, according to the survey outcomes, only half of the respondents understand exactly the definition of FS, something that attracts our attention in this research, since it is a term that should be very common, given its importance and usefulness in our daily life. These findings are in line with the work carried out by Gallegos et al. in 2023 in high income countries, notably Australia and the United States, and in 2017 by Arcari in Australia, which underlines the fact that the general public's understanding of FS is very limited and/or vague, and that it needs to be more effectively explained to the public at large [38,39]. Another important dimension underlining the results of this survey assessment through our respondents is the link between UA and FS, and most responses agree that the two concepts are linked and believe that this link will guarantee a healthy and sustainable food system. This was explained and proven by Siegner et al. in 2018, through a systematic review highlighting that UA and FS are complementary and that their link is really important for having access to food produced in urban areas [40,41], and also by Optiz et al. in 2016, who analyzed the existing link between the contribution of urban and peri-urban agriculture to food security in the Global North countries [42].

Secondly, from the interviews conducted with project managers from the Spanish urban initiatives "Alimenta Conciencia" in Segovia city and "Estrategia Alimentaria de Valladolid" in Valladolid city, it emerged that the two Spanish initiatives had several points in common and some differences that concern more ways of implementation and solving issues. Indeed, both initiatives are willing to implement UAP within the cities, while combating food insecurity and providing local produce from local farmers and local cultivation, without having the need to go far to other cities. This fact is totally aligned with the work carried out in Canada, United States and United Kingdom by Sonnino (2016) and in various American cities by Siegner (2018), which emphasizes the importance of UA in tackling food insecurity, and which links it directly to both local food production and the resilience of cities [40,43]. Another objective that has been mentioned by both initiatives' project managers is awareness, considering that it is the key to success of the progress of such an initiative. This progress should start with children, since they are the future generations, so they can influence their parents. This is related to the findings of Russ and Gaus carried out in the United States, underlining the importance of UA education in raising young people's awareness, commitment and understanding of the benefits to their moral and dietary health [44].

In terms of activities, the two initiatives have set up local markets, enabling local farmers to sell their produce directly to city consumers on the one hand, and allowing residents to buy their produce nearby on the other, thus supporting the local economy while eating healthily and properly. In 2001, Trobe carried out a study in the United Kingdom on the creation of local markets by urban farmers, and also found that most customers visit markets firstly out of curiosity, and then to buy fresh, healthy food, expressing a preference for organic produce [45]. Moreover, awareness-raising is a key activity that both initiatives and other similar ones carry out as much as possible in order to share knowledge about UA, FS and the importance of eating healthy, local food. A similar conclusion is drawn by Orsini: in urban gardens, children spend time playing and helping their parents grow plants, acquiring knowledge about agricultural practices and enabling an intergenerational transfer of knowledge [46]. These activities therefore encourage residents to consume locally, thereby contributing to making cities more resilient [47,48]. This is in line with the findings of Ferreira et al. regarding an investigation carried out in Portugal, who point out that UA and support for local consumption contribute to raising levels of food sovereignty and resilience, as well as implementing new strategies for education, participation and citizenship [49,50].

Many challenges have been mentioned in our analysis; sharing more knowledge is considered the main one for both initiatives, as well as organizing more activities and engaging as many participants as possible. In addition, another aspect is the economic one: the initiatives hope to receive more financial contributions in order to improve these projects and implement other related initiatives. Another aspect is to involve more participants in these UAP and to make them aware of the benefits of setting up urban farming areas in the city, thus ensuring more sustainable and resilient cities. Finally, both initiatives confirmed that they want to help people to open their own business, so that needs to be considered, as well as encouraging the km0 consumption, instead of having to travel to another city.

5. Conclusions

Urban agriculture has become a key research area and a sustainable solution due to its relevance to the current challenges of urbanization, continued population growth, drought and climate change [46,51]. A number of studies underline the importance of urban agriculture in reinforcing food security in urban areas, guaranteeing food self-sufficiency, reconnecting with nature and acquiring new knowledge in this field and, therefore, ensuring self-sufficient and resilient cities [52,53]. Integrating urban agricultural practices has thus been recognized as a strategic approach to promoting sustainable urban development, while encompassing its various objectives, including promoting food security and improved nutrition (SDG 2) and promoting sustainable and resilient cities (SDG 11) with the preservation of terrestrial ecosystems (SDG 15) [20,21]. Furthermore, the involvement of these urban practices within cities fosters sustainable consumption and, to a wider extent, sustainable production patterns (SDG 12) and strengthens social inclusion and equitable access to food resources (SDG 10) [22,23].

Through a survey distributed worldwide, this study assessed the public's perception of urban agriculture and food security, its implementation, integration and knowledge of the subject. Although the majority of respondents are young, urban and highly educated, the geographic diversity of the sample mitigates potential biases and provides valuable information on general perceptions of urban agriculture, particularly for this category, which represents the future generations. It would therefore be very interesting to hear from them in order to improve their knowledge on the subject. However, the fact that certain demographic groups are over-represented may limit the direct generalization of results to other populations with different demographic profiles, such as people with low levels of education or others who are not in this field. Regarding the interviews, they were conducted with two urban agriculture practices in Spain, namely "Alimenta Conciencia" and "Estrategia Alimentaria de Valladolid", both located in the Castilla y Leon region (Spain), in order to assess in a concrete and precise manner how these urban practices operate, the obstacles they face, their main challenges and limitations, etc.

Using this combination of approaches resides in the fact that, while the global survey identifies general trends and awareness gaps, the interviews provide concrete and complementary information in specific contexts. This dual approach is considered a strength, as it enables a broad, multi-angled understanding of key terms and thus addresses our problematic issues. Indeed, in this context, this mixed approach has shown that both the global survey and the local case studies indicate a common recognition and affirmation of urban agriculture as a valuable contributor to food security, given its various benefits linked to its role in improving access to fresh food, promoting social links between citizens, protecting the environment and so on. In addition, both approaches emphasize the need for local authorities to support these initiatives and back them up to ensure their long-term viability.

This qualitative and quantitative analysis highlighted a number of conclusions that should be emphasized, and which are as follows. First, education and awareness-raising initiatives are needed to highlight the importance of urban agriculture and its role in achieving food security. These could include school courses, community workshops and public open days to disseminate information and promote understanding among the population, and so on. Second, there should be encouragement of the creation of local stores by local producers, as their creation can make a significant contribution to the development of urban agriculture and the improvement of food security. To achieve this, it is important to ensure financial support, provide training and technical assistance and stimulate new calls for projects. Finally, expert urban planning is crucial to the successful integration of urban agriculture and the creation of sustainable urban environments. For this, urban planners need to draw on their expertise as well as that of architects, designers and other skilled professionals to integrate agriculture into urban spaces, as collaboration is essential to developing inclusive and sustainable urban plans.

Local authorities and urban planners have an important role in integrating urban agricultural practices in cities. Indeed, based on the results of this study, we recommend that municipal authorities and NGOs give high priority to supporting urban agriculture in land-use planning by allocating dedicated spaces, encouraging urban farming zones and community gardens. Moreover, they should provide support by offering technical training, facilitating access to funding and acting as intermediaries between local communities and public institutions, thus integrating urban agriculture into climate adaptation and food security plans, all aligned with the Sustainable Development Goals. Furthermore, the results underline that urban planners should implement participatory approaches and strategies that include urban agriculture professionals in the decision-making process, and design multifunctional green spaces that fulfill both an ecological and a food production function.

This study enabled us to gain a general understanding of people's perception of urban agriculture, its effects and its contribution to the population, as well as to deepen our understanding of this concept in relation to food security and self-sufficiency. Furthermore, the interviews highlighted several common points, such as the desire to ensure good education and awareness of the value of integrating the food sector into cities, as well as the appropriate organization of activities and workshops. It should be noted that the evaluation of these two urban agricultural practices provides lessons and a better understanding of the implementation of urban practices, not only in these cities, but also in other areas of Europe and the world, as the results of this investigation provide a better understanding of the changes that may have occurred in citizens' lives during the implementation of these initiatives, across all three dimensions of sustainable development—social, economic and environmental—while emphasizing their experiences and techniques as part of a collective learning process.

The responses from the interviews with the project managers of the two urban agriculture projects in Spain and the global pilot survey are positive in terms of knowledge of the subject, but the survey still needs to be developed to make it more accessible and understandable to all, particularly by encouraging small organizations and start-ups linked to local production. Finally, this investigation can be considered as a basis for future studies aimed at assessing the general public's perception of urban agriculture, as well as for conducting interviews with experts in the field, since this methodology allowed responses to our problematic, and could provide the basis for other investigations in Spain or worldwide.

Author Contributions: Conceptualization, O.F.B., L.M.N.G., L.C.S. and A.C.G.; methodology, O.F.B., L.C.S., A.C.G. and L.M.N.G.; software, O.F.B.; validation, O.F.B., L.C.S., A.C.G. and L.M.N.G.; formal analysis, O.F.B. and L.C.S.; investigation, O.F.B. and L.C.S.; resources, L.M.N.G. and L.C.S.; writing—original draft preparation, O.F.B.; writing—review and editing, O.F.B., L.C.S., L.M.N.G. and A.C.G.; visualization, O.F.B., L.C.S., A.C.G. and L.M.N.G.; supervision, L.C.S. and L.M.N.G.; project administration, L.M.N.G.; funding acquisition, L.M.N.G. All authors have read and agreed to the published version of the manuscript.

Funding: The present work is related to the FUSILLI Project, which is funded by the European Union's Horizon 2020 Research and Innovation program under the grant agreement No. 101000717 (https://fusilli-project.eu/) (accessed on 28 February 2025).

Data Availability Statement: Data are contained within the article. Our research study was conducted in full compliance with the University of Valladolid's Code of Ethics. The latest version of this code was approved by the Governing Council on 22 July 2022, which can be consulted at the following link: https://secretariageneral.uva.es/wp-content/uploads/III.6.-Codigo-Etico-de-la-UVa.pdf (accessed on 28 April 2025.). At the time this research was conducted, the approval processes followed were in accordance with all institutional requirements and regulations for studies involving human participants, including the Declaration of Helsinki. Moreover, informed consent was obtained from all participants through the online survey platform, where participants were informed that, by taking the survey, they indicated they had read and understood the data protection and consent statement and had agreed to participate. For focus groups and interviews, participants provided verbal consent after reviewing data protection information. All participants were informed of data confidentiality measures and their rights under GDPR requirements, including the right to withdraw from the study at any time without penalty. Data were anonymized during analysis and reporting to protect the participants' identities. In conclusion, all aspects of the research, including participant recruitment, informed consent procedures, data collection, anonymization and storage, were conducted in accordance with institutional ethical standards and European data protection regulations.

Acknowledgments: Ouiam Fatiha Boukharta has been financed under the call for the University of Valladolid's 2021 predoctoral contracts, co-financed by Banco Santander.

Conflicts of Interest: The authors declare no conflicts of interest. The funders had no role in the design of this study, in the collection, analysis, or interpretation of data, in the writing of the manuscript or in the decision to publish the results.

Abbreviations

The following abbreviations are used in this manuscript:

UA	Urban Agriculture
UAP	Urban Agricultural Projects
FS	Food Security
SDG	Sustainable Development Goal

References

1. Oliveira, G.M.; Vidal, D.G.; Ferraz, M.P. Urban lifestyles and consumption patterns. In *Sustainable Cities and Communities*; Springer: Cham, Switzerland, 2020; pp. 851–860.
2. Alemu, M.H.; Grebitus, C. Towards sustainable urban food systems: Analyzing contextual and intrapsychic drivers of growing food in small-scale urban agriculture. *PLoS ONE* **2020**, *15*, e0243949. [CrossRef]
3. Dogar, M.I.; Álvarez, G. United Nations Human Settlements Programme, Background Guide 2024. In Proceedings of the National Model United Nations, San Cristóbal Island, Ecuador, 22 November–1 December 2024.
4. UN-Habitat (United Nations Human Settlements Programme). Third United Nations Conference on Housing and Sustainable Urban Development (Habitat III), 44813 (August). 2011. Available online: https://unhabitat.org/habitat-iii (accessed on 2 November 2023).

5. Boukharta, O.F.; Pena-Fabri, F.; Chico-Santamarta, L.; Navas-Gracia, L.M.; Sauvée, L. Governance structures and stakeholder's involvement in Urban Agricultural projects: An analysis of four case studies in France. *Int. Food Agribus. Manag. Rev.* **2023**, *27*, 76–93. [CrossRef]
6. Santo, R.E.; Lupolt, S.N.; Kim, B.F.; Burrows, R.A.; Evans, E.; Evenson, B.; Synk, C.M.; Viqueira, R.; Cocke, A.; Little, N.G.; et al. Characteristics and growing practices of Baltimore City farms and gardens. *Urban For. Urban Green.* **2021**, *65*, 127357. [CrossRef]
7. Radfar, A.; Ferreira, M.M.; Sosa, J.P.; Filip, I. Emergent crisis of COVID-19 pandemic: Mental health challenges and opportunities. *Front. Psychiatry* **2021**, *12*, 631008. [CrossRef] [PubMed]
8. WHO, World Health Organization. *Guide for Integration of Perinatal Mental Health in Maternal and Child Health Services*; World Health Organization: Geneva, Switzerland, 2022.
9. Capaldi, C.A.; Passmore, H.A.; Nisbet, E.K.; Zelenski, J.M.; Dopko, R.L. Flourishing in nature: A review of the benefits of connecting with nature and its application as a wellbeing intervention. *Int. J. Wellbeing* **2015**, *5*, 1–16. [CrossRef]
10. Fei, S.; Wu, R.; Liu, H.; Yang, F.; Wang, N. Technological Innovations in Urban and Peri-Urban Agriculture: Pathways to Sustainable Food Systems in Metropolises. *Horticulturae* **2025**, *11*, 212. [CrossRef]
11. Caldas, E.; Jayo, M. Agriculturas urbanas em São Paulo: Histórico e tipología Agricultures urbaines à São Paulo: Histoire et typologie Urban agricultures in São Paulo: History and typology. *Confins* **2019**, *2*. [CrossRef]
12. FAO. *"Food Security," Policy Brief, Food Security*; FAO: Rome, Italy, 2007; pp. 1–4.
13. Mougeot, L.J. *Growing Better Cities: Urban Agriculture for Sustainable Development*; IDRC: Ottawa, ON, Canada, 2006.
14. Poggi, S.; Vinatier, F.; Hannachi, M.; Sanz, E.S.; Rudi, G.; Zamberletti, P.; Tixier, P.; Papaïx, J. How can models foster the transition towards future agricultural landscapes? In *Advances in Ecological Research*; Academic Press: Cambridge, MA, USA, 2021; Volume 64, pp. 305–368.
15. Martin-Moreau, M.; Ménascé, D. Urban agriculture: Another way to feed cities. *Field Actions Sci. Rep.* **2019**, *20*, 7–119.
16. Maćkiewicz, B.; Puente Asuero, R.; Garrido Almonacid, A. Urban agriculture as the path to sustainable city development. Insights into allotment gardens in Andalusia. *Quaest. Geogr.* **2019**, *38*, 121–136. [CrossRef]
17. Pradhan, P.; Subedi, D.R.; Dahal, K.; Hu, Y.; Gurung, P.; Pokharel, S.; Kafle, S.; Khatri, B.; Basyal, S.; Gurung, M.; et al. Urban agriculture matters for sustainable development. *Cell Rep. Sustain.* **2024**, *1*, 100217. [CrossRef]
18. Santo, R.; Palmer, A.; Kim, B. *Vacant lots to Vibrant Plots: A Review of the Benefits and Limitations of Urban Agriculture*; Johns Hopkins Center for a Livable Future: Baltimore, MD, USA, 2016.
19. Grebitus, C.; Chenarides, L.; Muenich, R.; Mahalov, A. Consumers' perception of urban farming—An exploratory study. *Front. Sustain. Food Syst.* **2020**, *4*, 79. [CrossRef]
20. Boukharta, O.F.; Huang, I.Y.; Vickers, L.; Navas-Gracia, L.M.; Chico-Santamarta, L. Benefits of Non-Commercial Urban Agricultural Practices—A Systematic Literature Review. *Agronomy* **2024**, *14*, 234. [CrossRef]
21. Lombardía, A.; Gómez-Villarino, M.T. Green infrastructure in cities for the achievement of the un sustainable development goals: A systematic review. *Urban Ecosyst.* **2023**, *26*, 1693–1707. [CrossRef]
22. Raja, S.; Caton Campbell, M.; Judelsohn, A.; Born, B.; Morales, A. *Planning for Equitable Urban Agriculture in the United States: Future Directions for a New Ethic in City Building*; Springer Nature: Berlin/Heidelberg, Germany, 2024.
23. Agyeman, J. *Introducing Just Sustainabilities: Policy, Planning, and Practice*; Zed Books Ltd.: London, UK, 2013.
24. Thurman, N. Mixed methods communication research: Combining qualitative and quantitative approaches in the study of online journalism. *SAGE Res. Methods Cases* **2018**. [CrossRef]
25. Ajzen, I. The theory of planned behavior. *Organ. Behav. Hum. Decis. Process.* **1991**, *50*, 179–211. [CrossRef]
26. Michie, S.; Van Stralen, M.M.; West, R. The behaviour change wheel: A new method for characterising and designing behaviour change interventions. *Implement. Sci.* **2011**, *6*, 1–2. [CrossRef]
27. Shove, E.; Watson, M.; Pantzar, M. *The Dynamics of Social Practice: Everyday Life and How It Changes*; Sage: London, UK, 2012; pp. 1–208.
28. Frost, N. *Qualitative Research Methods in Psychology: Combining Core Approaches 2e*; McGraw-Hill Education: Maidenhead, UK, 2021.
29. Button, C.; Seifert, L.; Chow, J.Y.; Araújo, D.; Davids, K. *Dynamics of Skill Acquisition: An Ecological Dynamics Approach*; Human Kinetics Publishers: Champaign, IL, USA, 2021.
30. Riyaz, A.; Musthafa, H.S.; Raheem, R.A.; Moosa, S. Survey sampling in the time of social distancing: Experiences from a quantitative research in the wake of COVID-19 pandemic. *Maldives Natl. J. Res.* **2020**, *8*, 169–192. [CrossRef]
31. Sarstedt, M.; Bengart, P.; Shaltoni, A.M.; Lehmann, S. The use of sampling methods in advertising research: A gap between theory and practice. *Int. J. Advert.* **2018**, *37*, 650–663. [CrossRef]
32. Olsson, E.G.; Kerselaers, E.; Søderkvist Kristensen, L.; Primdahl, J.; Rogge, E.; Wästfelt, A. Peri-urban food production and its relation to urban resilience. *Sustainability* **2016**, *8*, 1340. [CrossRef]
33. Capone, R.; El Bilali, H.; Debs, P.; Cardone, G.; Driouech, N. Food system sustainability and food security: Connecting the dots. *J. Food Secur.* **2014**, *2*, 13–22.

34. Kirby, C.K.; Specht, K.; Fox-Kämper, R.; Hawes, J.K.; Cohen, N.; Caputo, S.; Ilieva, R.T.; Lelièvre, A.; Poniży, L.; Schoen, V.; et al. Differences in motivations and social impacts across urban agriculture types: Case studies in Europe and the US. *Landsc. Urban Plan.* **2021**, *212*, 104110. [CrossRef]
35 Azmi, N.S.N.; Ng, Y.M.; Masud, M.M.; Cheng, A. Knowledge, attitudes, and perceptions of farmers towards urban agroecology in Malaysia. *Heliyon* **2024**, *10*, e33365. [CrossRef]
36. Hallett, S.; Hoagland, L.; Toner, E. Urban agriculture: Environmental, economic, and social perspectives. *Hortic. Rev.* **2016**, *44*, 65–120.
37. Nicholas, S.O.; Groot, S.; Harré, N. Understanding urban agriculture in context: Environmental, social, and psychological benefits of agriculture in Singapore. *Local Environ.* **2023**, *28*, 1446–1462. [CrossRef]
38. Gallegos, D.; Booth, S.; Pollard, C.M.; Chilton, M.; Kleve, S. Food security definition, measures and advocacy priorities in high-income countries: A Delphi consensus study. *Public Health Nutr.* **2023**, *26*, 1986–1996. [CrossRef]
39. Arcari, P. Normalised, human-centric discourses of meat and animals in climate change, sustainability and food security literature. *Agric. Hum. Values* **2017**, *34*, 69–86. [CrossRef]
40. Siegner, A.; Sowerwine, J.; Acey, C. Does urban agriculture improve food security? Examining the nexus of food access and distribution of urban produced foods in the United States: A systematic review. *Sustainability* **2018**, *10*, 2988. [CrossRef]
41. Horst, M.; McClintock, N.; Hoey, L. The intersection of planning, urban agriculture, and food justice: A review of the literature. In *Planning for Equitable Urban Agriculture in the United States: Future Directions for a New Ethic in City Building*; Springer: Cham, Switzerland, 2024; pp. 89–120.
42. Opitz, I.; Berges, R.; Piorr, A.; Krikser, T. Contributing to food security in urban areas: Differences between urban agriculture and peri-urban agriculture in the Global North. *Agric. Hum. Values* **2016**, *33*, 341–358. [CrossRef]
43. Sonnino, R. The new geography of food security: Exploring the potential of urban food strategies. *Geogr. J.* **2016**, *182*, 190–200. [CrossRef]
44. Russ, A.; Gaus, M.B. Urban agriculture education and youth civic engagement in the US: A scoping review. *Front. Sustain. Food Syst.* **2021**, *5*, 707896. [CrossRef]
45. Trobe, H.L. Farmers' markets: Consuming local rural produce. *Int. J. Consum. Stud.* **2001**, *25*, 181–192. [CrossRef]
46. Orsini, F.; Kahane, R.; Nono-Womdim, R.; Gianquinto, G. Urban agriculture in the developing world: A review. *Agron. Sustain. Dev.* **2013**, *33*, 695–720. [CrossRef]
47. Triboi, R.M. Urban Pastoralism around Bucharest: Between Preserving Livelihoods and Adapting to Pressure from Urban Sprawl. Martor. *Rev. D'anthropologie Du Musée Du Paysan Roum.* **2024**, *29*, 126–142. [CrossRef]
48. Yang, K. The paths to improve china's urbanization strategy. *Chin. J. Urban Environ. Stud.* **2021**, *9*, 2175001. [CrossRef]
49. Ferreira, A.J.; Guilherme, R.I.; Ferreira, C.S. Urban agriculture, a tool towards more resilient urban communities? *Curr. Opin. Environ. Sci. Health* **2018**, *5*, 93–97. [CrossRef]
50. Langemeyer, J.; Madrid-Lopez, C.; Beltran, A.M.; Mendez, G.V. Urban agriculture—A necessary pathway towards urban resilience and global sustainability? *Landsc. Urban Plan.* **2021**, *210*, 104055. [CrossRef]
51. Artmann, M.; Sartison, K. The role of urban agriculture as a nature-based solution: A review for developing a systemic assessment framework. *Sustainability* **2018**, *10*, 1937. [CrossRef]
52. Temesgen, H. Urban Agriculture for Food Security? A Qualitative Study in Addis Ababa, Ethiopia. Master's Thesis, University of Agder, Kristiansand, Norway, 2024.
53. Ajisope, T. Enabling Urban Agriculture in the Global North and South: A Comparative Study of the UK and Nigeria. Ph.D. Thesis, University of Salford, Salford, UK, 2023.

urban science

MDPI

Article

Climate Change Awareness and Urban Food Choices: Exploring Motivations for Short Food Chain Engagement

Elena Kokthi [1,*], Fatmir Guri [2] and Zenepe Dafku [2]

1 Department of Biotechnology and Food Science, Agricultural University of Tirana, 1001 Tirana, Albania
2 Department of Economics and Policies of Rural Development, Agricultural University of Tirana, 1001 Tirana, Albania; fatmirguri@ubt.edu.al (F.G.); zdafku@ubt.edu.al (Z.D.)
* Correspondence: ekokthi@ubt.edu.al

Abstract: This study explores the relationship between climate change awareness (CCA) and consumers' willingness to pay (WTP) for urban short food chains (USFC), focusing on the mediating role of biospheric, egoistic, and altruistic environmental concerns. A structured questionnaire was conducted with 230 respondents in Tirana, Albania, and the results were analysed using the PROCESS macro in SPSS 25.0. The findings reveal that CCA increases all three environmental concerns; however, only the altruistic concern significantly mediates USFC participation, particularly by limiting food waste (effect size = 0.502, $p = 0.002$). In contrast, egoistic concern negatively affects WTP, highlighting a value–action gap in sustainable behaviour. Reducing ultra-processed food consumption emerges as a key driver of engagement, linking personal and environmental health to local food choices. Gender moderates these relationships; despite showing high ecological concern, women express lower WTP due to household and budgetary considerations. Supporting the model, the survey data show that 88% of respondents are willing to pay a premium, typically 10–20% more, for food products from their preferred origin, and 88% are also willing to participate in the Tirana USFC initiative. The highest WTP (30%) is reported among highly educated women with children aged three to five. These findings highlight the need for targeted urban food policies that account for sustainability's psychological and demographic dimensions.

Keywords: CCA; urban short food chains (USFC); environmental concerns; food waste; ultra-processed food; gender

1. Introduction

While it contributes less to helping cities achieve food self-sufficiency, urban agriculture can set up a pathway to feed the citizens differently [1]. The 'in a different way' approach involves commercialising quality local products via short circuits, a sustainable model that significantly reduces the environmental footprint [2–8].

As a form of nature-based solution, urban agriculture contributes to climate adaptation by enhancing urban resilience, supporting biodiversity, and reducing food-related emissions [9–12]. Urban short food chains build on this foundation by reinforcing local food systems that reduce environmental impact and strengthen social cohesion and economic circularity within cities [13,14].

Urban short food supply chains (USFC) refer to localised food systems that shorten the distance between food producers and consumers within urban areas or their immediate surroundings. These systems typically involve direct sales models such as farmers' markets, community-supported agriculture, cooperatives, and urban food hubs, reducing intermediaries and increasing traceability [13,15,16]. Although some definitions emphasise direct producer–consumer interactions, recent research suggests that USFC can take multiple forms, including municipal food procurement, cooperative models, and urban food networks [13,17].

USFC aims to promote fresh, minimally processed food, enhance food security, and support local economies, aligning with urban agriculture's broader sustainability goals.

While USFCs are widely promoted as environmentally friendly alternatives, some scholars argue that their sustainability depends on the efficiency of their logistics [4,18–20]. Unlike large-scale food distribution networks that benefit from optimised transportation routes and economies of scale, USFC may increase per-unit emissions due to fragmented and non-optimized transport, mainly when deliveries involve multiple small-scale producers serving dispersed urban consumers [19]. This challenge suggests that, while USFC provides advantages regarding food quality, consumer engagement, and support for local economies, their environmental impact requires careful assessment, particularly in urban contexts where transport efficiency varies.

Building on this perspective, USFC emerges as a key mechanism for bridging the gap between food producers and urban consumers. By localising food production and minimising intermediaries, USFC aligns with the broader objectives of urban agriculture, fostering more direct and transparent food networks. However, the effectiveness of these systems depends not only on logistical efficiency but also on consumer engagement and the social acceptance of local food models.

Urban agriculture brings producers and consumers closer and encourages cities to reinvent and rethink their deep-rooted relationship with food. In this relationship, local products are essential to creating producer–consumer relations in a globalised agro-food system [20]. Their unique selling proposition is based on the localisation of production and the supply chain length in terms of the number of actors involved [1,13,15,16]. The direct contact and partnership between producers and consumers underscore the distinctive nature of these systems. However, these partnerships can only be established with a shared narrative among stakeholders regarding short food chains in urban areas, which rapidly evolve in the continuous industrialisation of a food system. Understanding the initiating factors is essential for building a collective story and creating sustainable partnerships, emphasising the need for collaboration.

Climate change awareness (CCA) is a powerful driver of sustainable food practices in this context. However, psychological and social factors such as environmental concern often moderate the transformation from awareness into action. Drawing on [21], this study investigates how different types of concern—biospheric, egoistic, and altruistic—mediate the link between CCA and participation in USFCs.

Despite growing interest in USFCs, there is limited understanding of how climate-related awareness translates into food behaviours in urban contexts, especially through the lens of concern types. Addressing this gap will contribute to designing more effective strategies that align environmental messaging with consumer motivations.

This research contributes to the existing literature by introducing a multi-pathway model that links climate change awareness (CCA) to engagement in urban short food chains (USFCs). It identifies the mediating role of three distinct types of environmental concern—biospheric, egoistic, and altruistic—in shaping sustainable food behaviours. Furthermore, the study explores key consumer drivers influenced by climate-related concerns, such as reducing food waste, preference for seasonal and local products, and avoiding ultra-processed foods. The remainder of this study is structured as follows: Section 2 outlines the theoretical framework, variables, and methodology. Section 3 presents the empirical analysis and findings. Section 4 offers a discussion of the results. Finally, conclusions and implications for policy and practice are presented.

2. Theoretical Framework and Methodology

2.1. Conceptual Framework and Hypotheses

Research shows that public CCA significantly influences consumer behaviour toward sustainable food practices, including participation in USFCs [13,16,22]. However, a gap between intention and action is often observed, motivating research into potential mediators such as environmental concern [23–25]. Schultz's (2001) environmental concern scale outlines three dimensions—biospheric, egoistic, and social-altruistic concern—which influence sustainable behaviour in distinct ways [21,26]. CCA is a significant predictor of biospheric concern, motivating individuals to prioritise ecological health and adopt sustainable consumption habits [27,28]. Personal benefits drive egoistic concern, while altruistic concern stems from a desire to help others and reduce environmental impact.

Research indicates that awareness of climate change is a significant predictor of biospheric concern, as individuals who are more informed about environmental issues are more likely to prioritise the planet's well-being and that of other living beings [21,29]. This heightened biospheric concern can lead to more sustainable consumption behaviours, such as increased participation in USFC, where the environmental impact of food choices is minimised [13,17,30]. Thus, the link between CCA and Biospheric Concern provides a foundation for promoting sustainable food systems through USFC. From this perspective, we suggest hypothesis H1, as presented in Table 1.

Table 1. Hypotheses linking CCA and environmental concerns to participation in urban short food chains.

Drivers	Pathway	Hypotheses
Biospheric concern	Path a_1: CCA → Biospheric Concern; Path b1: Biospheric Concern → USFC	*H1a: CCA positively influences biospheric concern*
		H1b: Biospheric concern positively affects participation in USFC
Egoistic concern	Path a_2: CCA → Egoistic Concern; Path b2: Egoistic Concern → USFC	*H1c: CCA positively influences egoistic concern*
		H1d: Egoistic concern positively affects participation in USFC
Altruistic concern	Path a3: CCA → Altruistic Concern; Path b3: Altruistic Concern → USFC	*H1e: CCA positively influences altruistic concern*
		H1f: Altruistic concern positively affects participation in USFCs

Source: authors' elaboration.

Similarly, studies have shown that CCA can also enhance egoistic concern as individuals become more aware of the potential impacts of environmental issues on their personal health, finances, and well-being [31–33]. This egoistic concern, in turn, can drive behaviours that align with personal benefits, such as participating in USFCs, which offer access to fresher, healthier, and potentially less contaminated food [34]. Moreover, the awareness of climate change fosters concern for the environment and highlights the personal advantages of sustainable practices; with this in mind, we suggest that CCA positively influences egoistic concern, subsequently enhancing participation in USFCs. See Table 1 for the suggested hypotheses and pathways.

CCA can significantly foster altruistic concern [28,35,36]. This concern, when embraced, often motivates actions that benefit the wider community and the environment. One such action is the support of the USFCs, which emphasise local, sustainable food production and reduce the environmental footprint [37,38]. Thus, an increased awareness of climate change issues can drive individuals to participate in USFC, driven by a sense of responsibility and concern for others' well-being. CCA positively impacts altruistic concerns and promotes engagement in USFC.

Finally, our research proposes a significant positive relationship between CCA and participation in USFCs, as illustrated in Figure 1 (Path c′: CCA → USFC). This relationship suggests that individuals more aware of climate change issues tend to perceive a greater personal responsibility to mitigate their environmental impact. This, in turn, leads to more sustainable consumption behaviours, such as buying locally produced food [25,39]. The importance of this direct relationship lies in its ability to independently motivate consumers to choose sustainable food practices, even without mediating specific environmental concerns such as biospheric, egoistic, or altruistic motivations [40,41]: see Figure 1a.

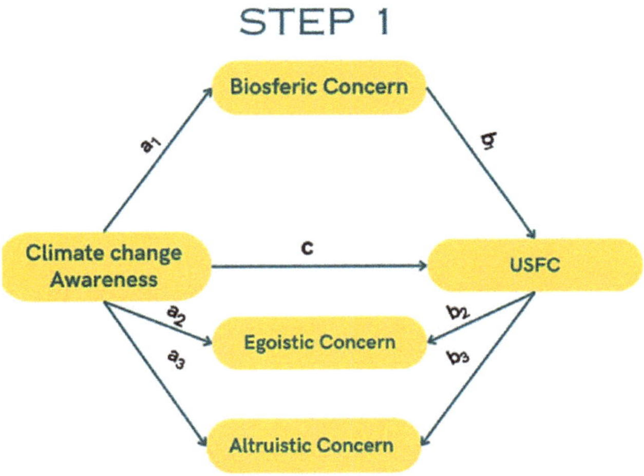

(a)

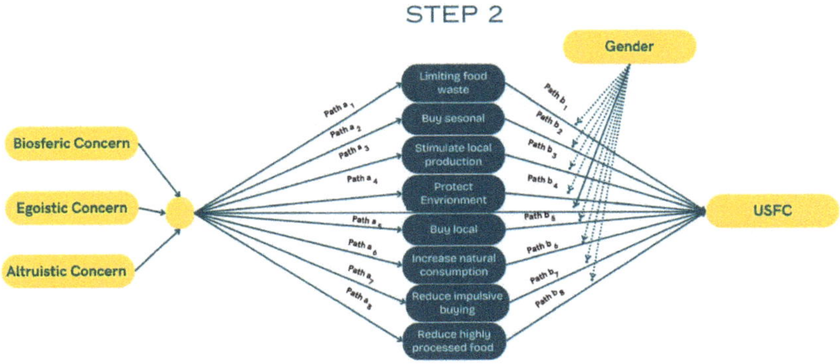

(b)

Figure 1. (**a**) Conceptual model illustrating the mediating role of biospheric, egoistic, and altruistic concerns in the relationship between climate change awareness and USFC engagement. Source: authors' elaboration. (**b**) The conceptual model illustrates the influence of biospheric, egoistic, and altruistic concerns on USFC engagement, mediated by specific sustainable behaviours. Source: authors' elaboration.

In the second step, climate change concerns are used as initiators to explore the possible pathways leading to willingness to participate in USFC (See Table 2 and Figure 1b).

USFC participation is often linked to eight key drivers of climate change concerns influencing consumer participation in USFCs. These drivers include limiting food waste [42–44], buying seasonal products [45,46], stimulating local production [2,47,48], protecting the environment, buying local products, increasing natural consumption, reducing impulsive buying, and reducing consumption of highly processed food.

Table 2. Possible pathways leading to willingness to participate in USFCs.

Drivers	Hypotheses	References
Limiting Food Waste	*H2.1: Climate Change Concern (CCC) → Limiting Food Waste → USFC*	[42–44,49,50]
Buying Seasonal Products	*H2.2: CCC → Buying Seasonal Products → USFC*	[2,48,51]
Stimulating Local Production	*H2.3: CCC → Stimulating Local Production → USFC*	[2,15,16,30]
Protecting the Environment	*H2.4: CCC → Protecting the Environment → USFC*	[46,52–54]
Buying Local Products	*H2.5: CCC → Buying Local Products → USFC*	[2,51]
Increasing Natural Consumption	*H2.6: CCC → Increasing Natural Consumption → USFC*	[47,48,52,55–58]
Reducing Impulsive Buying	*H2.7: CCC → Reducing Impulsive Buying → USFC*	[59–62]
Reducing Highly Processed Food Consumption	*H2.8: CCC → Reducing Highly Processed Food Consumption → USFC*	[63–65]

Source: authors' elaboration.

The hypotheses presented in Table 2 explore how the three climate change concerns (CCC) lead to consumer behaviours, such as limiting food waste, buying seasonal and local products, supporting local production, and engaging in environmentally protective actions, in alignment with USFC participation. Using the suggested framework, we comprehensively explore the distinct pathways through which different concerns affect consumer behaviour and provide critical insights into sustainable food systems supported by UFSC. The rest of the study is structured as follows: The second section presents the methodology. The third section presents the analysis of the results. The last section deals with the conclusions and discussions. The following section details the measurement and operationalisation of each variable proposed in the conceptual framework.

2.2. Questionnaire and Measurement of Variables

The instrument employed for this study is composed of four sections. In the first section, the demographic variables of respondents are collected. These variables, such as age, gender, household income, education, number of children, respective group age, etc., are crucial for understanding how different groups perceive and respond to environmental issues. See Table 3. The second section presents a question about CCA and environmental concerns (EC). The CCA is measured according to six statements as presented in Table 1: Are you aware of the danger of gas emissions from vehicles that harm people's health, etc.? The participants evaluated each statement with a five-point Likert scale (see Table 3). Environmental concern is explored using the [21] scale. The scale is made up of three subscales measuring the following factors: biospheric concern (e.g., "I am concerned about environmental problems because of the consequences for birds, plants, marine life, animals"), egoistic concern (e.g., "I am concerned about environmental problems because of the consequences for me"), and social–altruistic concern (e.g., "I am concerned about environmental problems because of the consequences for all people". Concerns are also measured using a five-point Likert scale (1 = not at all concerned, 5 = extremely concerned).

Table 3. Description of the variables considered in the study.

Category	Description
Socio-Demographic Characteristics	City (Tirana), age, gender, educational level, family income, parenthood status, number and age of children
Climate Change Awareness (CCA)	Awareness of air pollution, vehicle emissions, water pollution, chemical fertilizers, green space loss, and land degradation (1 = not informed, 5 = very informed)
Environmental Concerns	Concerns about environmental impact on plants, marine life, birds, animals, self, health, future, all people, and children (1 = not concerned, 5 = extremely concerned)
Sustainable Consumption and Food Preferences	Preferred food sourcing for school catering, willingness to pay more, motivations for paying more (e.g., limiting waste, seasonal food, reducing processed food), understanding of sustainable food consumption

Source: authors' elaboration.

Section three explores preferences for food origin and willingness to pay for sustainable food options. The questionnaire assessed consumer preferences for food sourcing locality, willingness to engage with municipal food programs, and willingness to pay (WTP) for locally sourced food in school catering. Respondents were asked where they preferred school food to come from, with options ranging from imports (EU and general), regional sources, national (Albania), and local (municipality level). Additionally, WTP was measured according to a yes/no question and percentage-based increase options (10%, 20%, 50%, or above 50%). To explore engagement with municipal-led food programs, respondents were asked whether they would support a system where school food is sourced from seasonal agricultural production under municipal oversight. These questions provide insights into consumer attitudes toward local and urban food networks, aligning with the study's focus on USFC. This study examines consumer engagement with localised food-sourcing practices as a proxy for participation in USFC. While not all models explicitly require direct sales, literature on urban food networks suggests that short supply chains in cities often involve intermediary-supported initiatives [48]. Therefore, our questionnaire assessed engagement with locally produced seasonal food rather than strictly measuring direct producer–consumer relationships.

This section asks respondents about their propensity to participate in UFSC and their motivations: see Table 3. Finally, the questionnaire assesses the respondents' understanding of sustainable food consumption.

2.3. Research Design and Sample

The questionnaire was distributed online using convenience sampling. A sample of 230 respondents was collected from October 2023 to January 2024 in Tirana, Albania. This city is the capital of and the largest city in Albania. The number of inhabitants in Tirana is forecast to increase from 891,526,560 in 2021 to 954,280 in 2031 (up to 30%) (INSTAT, 2020).

Table 4 shows the primary demographics of the participants in the survey. About 90% are women, and 96% of the respondents are parents, with the majority aged 26–45 (about 80%). This reflects how urban short food chains often attract individuals in their prime working years with greater purchasing power and autonomy over their food choices.

Table 4. Demographics.

Demographics	Value	Frequency	Frequency Percentage
Gender	Female	208	91%
	Male	20	9%
Age	18–25	6	2.6%
	26–35	110	47.8%
	36–45	78	33%
	46–55	30	13%
	Over 55	6	2.6%
Educational Level	Up to 9 years	4	1%
	12 years	14	5%
	University degree	108	47%
	Post-university degree	108	47%
Monthly incomes Eur	100–300	6	2.6
	301–600	24	10.4
	601–900	74	32.5
	1000+	124	53.8
Parent	Yes	220	95.7
	No	10	4.3
Number of children	1	102	44.3
	2	118	51.3
	3	10	4.3
	4	-	-
	Over 4	-	-
Children's age	6 months–3 years	56	24.3
	3 years–5 years	56	24.3
	5 years–12 years	64	27.8
	12–15 years	16	7
	15–18 years	38	16.5

Source: authors' elaboration.

The younger age group (18–25) is underrepresented (2.6%), likely due to their reliance on family-based food-purchasing decisions, reducing their direct participation in short food chains. Similarly, individuals over 55 (2.6%) may exhibit different consumption behaviours, preferring traditional food retail formats over short food chain initiatives. The majority are highly educated. These sample characteristics are linked with the higher propensity of women to respond to online questionnaires and their expertise in using online survey instruments. However, this population segment is interesting to explore, since they might serve as part of the Albanian urban community that can snowball the partnership process between the producers and parents. Half of the participants have two children, and it is interesting to consider whether this indicator impacts the parent's behaviour toward USFC participation. The predominance of women respondents and the high percentage of parents aged 26–45 could be considered a limitation due to potential sample bias, limiting the generalizability of the findings to a more diverse population. However, this also presents an opportunity, as the sample reflects a demographic with a keen interest in the topic and a higher propensity for engaging with online surveys, potentially providing rich insights into the behaviour and attitudes of this specific group. The Ethics Committee of the Agriculture University of Tirana, Albania, approved the questionnaire design and data collection process, ensuring compliance with ethical research standards.

2.4. Statistical Analysis

To achieve the study objectives, we applied a conditional process analysis that integrates mediation and moderation models [66–69]. The first model examines the mediating role of three environmental concerns (EC) types—biospheric, egoistic, and altruistic concerns—in the relationship between climate change awareness (CCA) and willingness to participate in USFCs. Mediation occurs when CCA influences EC, which in turn affects USFC participation. This model helps to identify which type of EC is most strongly affected by CCA and which EC type has the strongest effect on willingness to engage in USFC.

The second model incorporates moderation analysis, where demographic factors (e.g., gender) may influence the strength of the relationship between EC and USFC participation. Moderation implies an interaction effect, meaning that the predictor's effect (CCA or EC) on USFC participation can be enhanced, weakened, or even reversed depending on the moderating variable.

The PROCESS macro in SPSS was used to estimate these relationships, applying Model 4 for mediation and Model 5 for moderation, with bias-corrected 95% confidence intervals and bootstrapping to ensure robust estimations [66]. The equations for Model 4 and Model 5 are as follows:

Mediation model (Model 4—Step 1 Equation) (Figure 1a):

$$\text{M(Biospheric)} = \text{iM} + a_1(\text{CCA}) + \text{e}$$

$$\text{M(Egoistic)} = \text{iM} + a_2(\text{CCA}) + \text{e}$$

$$\text{M(Altruistic)} = \text{iM} + a_3(\text{CCA}) + \text{e}$$

$$\text{Y(USFC)} = \text{iy} + b_1(\text{Biospheric}) + \text{e}$$

$$\text{Y(USFC)} = \text{iy} + b_2(\text{Egoistic}) + \text{e}$$

$$\text{Y(USFC)} = \text{iy} + b_3(\text{Altruistic}) + \text{e}$$

$$\text{USFC} = b_1\text{EC} + c'\text{CCA} + e_2\text{USFC}$$

where:

EC represents environmental concerns (biospheric, egoistic, or altruistic)
CCA is climate change awareness
USFC is the willingness to participate in USFC
a Pathways captures the effect of CCA on EC
b Pathways captures the effect of EC on USFC participation
c' is the direct effect of CCA on USFC
e and e_2 are the error terms

Moderation model (Model 5—Step 2 Equation), See Figure 1b:

$$USFC = b_2EC + b_3(EC \times Moderator) + c'CCA + e_3USFC$$

where:

The interaction term EC × Moderator (e.g., gender) measures whether the strength of EC's effect on USFC participation changes based on the moderator, indicating the magnitude of the moderation effect.

The conceptual model integrates these variables by reducing their scales to regression scores, ensuring simplicity while retaining their statistical significance. Reliability tests (Cronbach's Alpha) confirmed high internal consistency for each construct: biospheric concerns (0.949), egoistic concerns (0.929), altruistic concerns (0.788), and CCA (0.947).

3. Results and Discussion

The study's findings on CCA among respondents are significant, revealing a high overall awareness level. A mean score of 4 on a 5-point scale indicates that respondents generally consider themselves well-informed about various environmental issues, underscoring the importance of the study's findings (See Table 5(1)). The highest mean score of 4.21 is related to awareness of the dangers of air pollution. This suggests that air pollution is particularly salient among the respondents, possibly due to visible effects such as smog or health advisories in Tirana City. Awareness of the environmental damage caused by chemical fertilisers and pesticides is also high, with a mean score of 4.17 (See Table 5(1)). This could be linked to increasing public discourse around sustainable agriculture and the push for organic products, highlighting conventional farming practices' environmental and health impacts. The score for awareness of water pollution dangers is 4.12, indicating a significant concern about water quality issues. Awareness of the dangers of insufficient green space and the degradation of cultivated land quality is lower, with mean scores of 4.03 and 3.86, respectively. This suggests that, while these issues are recognised, air and water pollution may take longer for the respondents to respond to. Overall, the high levels of awareness across these areas suggest a well-informed respondent group, particularly regarding issues that have immediate health implications or are frequently highlighted in public discussions on environmental sustainability.

Table 5. (1) Descriptive statistics of climate change awareness (CCA) items. (2) Descriptive statistics of environmental concern items across biospheric, egoistic, and altruistic dimensions. (3) Descriptive statistics of climate-driven motivations for participation in urban short food chains (USFCs).

(1)		
Question	Mean	StdD
Are you aware of the danger of vehicle gas emissions that harm people's health?	3.96	1.061
Are you aware that using chemical fertilisers and pesticides causes environmental damage?	4.17	0.952
Are you aware of the dangers of air pollution due to urbanisation?	4.21	0.881
Have you been informed about the dangers of water pollution?	4.12	1.046
Are you aware of the dangers of insufficient green space?	4.03	1.113
Have you been informed about the damage caused by the degradation of cultivated land quality?	3.86	1.214

Table 5. *Cont.*

(2)		
Concern for...	Mean	StdD
Plants	3.98	0.771
Aquatic life	4.01	0.778
Birds	3.92	0.831
Myself	4.55	0.660
My health	4.69	0.557
Children's health	4.78	0.479
My future	4.67	0.595
All individuals	4.59	0.640
(3)		
Driver	Mean	StdD
Buying locally produced foods to limit transportation	3.87	1.070
Increasing the consumption of natural foods	4.55	0.860
Promotion of local agricultural/livestock production	4.08	0.950
Purchase and consumption of seasonal foods	4.61	1.040
Reducing food waste	3.78	0.890
Reducing the consumption of highly processed foods	4.38	1.020
Reducing the excessive consumption that comes from impulsive purchases	4.15	1.010
The need to protect the natural environment	3.92	1.050

Source: authors' elaboration.

Table 5(2) presents the descriptive statistics for the environmental concern items measured across three dimensions: biospheric, egoistic, and altruistic. The results indicate that respondents most strongly expressed altruistic and egoistic concerns. Items such as *"Children's Health"* (M = 4.78, SD = 0.479), *"My Health"* (M = 4.69, SD = 0.557), and *"My Future"* (M = 4.67, SD = 0.595) received the highest average ratings, reflecting a strong egoistic orientation, where concern is linked to personal or familial well-being. This is closely followed by altruistic concern with *"All individuals"* (M = 4.59, SD = 0.640), suggesting a solid social responsibility toward others.

Conversely, biospheric concerns—related to non-human nature such as *plants* (M = 3.98), *aquatic life* (M = 4.01), and *birds* (M = 3.92)—show slightly lower mean values, though still relatively high. This distribution aligns with previous literature, suggesting that, while people acknowledge the importance of ecological well-being, personal and human-centred concerns often carry more weight in shaping behaviour [21,33]. As explored in our hypotheses, these findings are critical to interpreting the mediation effects of concern types in the pathway between CCA and participation in urban short food chains.

Parents' preference for food product origins indicates a strong inclination towards supporting local products, with 64% opting for those of Albanian origin and 32% preferring EU origin. However, the preference drops significantly to 13% when considering a narrower territory such as Tirana. This disparity might be attributed to concerns over product availability, quality, or perceived reliability from a smaller geographic area. Despite this, 88% of parents are willing to pay extra for food products from their preferred origin: they are typically willing to pay an additional 10–20%. This willingness to pay suggests a substantial market demand for origin-specific products driven by factors such as perceived quality, safety, and support for local economies. The same high level of willingness (88%) to participate in the USFC initiative of Tirana further underscores the community's commitment to supporting local food systems. About 10% of parents were uncertain, and only 2% were unwilling to participate. Surprisingly, there were no statistical differences in the mean of the WTP for the made-in-Albania label and the made-in-Tirana label. This contradicts the assumption that the WTP for Tirana agricultural products would be higher due to the narrower production area. Other studies have shown that the difference in WTP is even more remarkable when the local claim is expressed as 'small farm or territory'. The narrower the territory, the higher the WTP [70,71]. A well-defined origin increases the ability of the consumer to process the information coming from this information stimulus [72]. However, the present study has yet to support this result. One possible explanation is the parents' need for knowledge regarding the capacity of the territory of Tirana to provide agricultural and food products. The collective illusion that cities do not produce food continues; parents, as consumers, play a crucial role in shaping this perception. They do not associate Tirana with a specific agricultural production area. Additionally, the characteristics of the Tirana population play a role. In the last thirty years, Tirana has hosted Albanian individuals immigrating from different regions from north to south; 30% of the Albanian population moved toward Tirana. This trend persists; new parents come to Tirana with their existing territory associations. One study [73] shows that young Albanians are highly attached to and aware of national issues. However, a commonly shared story linked to Tirana's territory and agricultural products is needed in this case.

This study examines consumer preferences for local food sourcing in school catering, including urban-scale procurement. However, it does not explicitly differentiate short food supply chains based on the number of intermediaries. Future research should investigate consumer willingness to engage with short food supply chains (0 or 1 intermediaries) versus broader local food systems, ensuring a more precise distinction in food network structures.

The analysis of the demographics concerning motivation shows that gender, age, education and the age of the children significantly influence people's motivation to pay an additional price to participate in USFCs. This underscores the importance of understanding the demographics of the consumer base. Parents with higher education levels and children aged three to five years old express the highest WTP, 30%. Concerning the relationship with demographics, parents with two children (F value = 3.434; p value = 0.034), above five years (F value = 5.535; p value = 0.000), prefer made-in-Albania products over other options. Parents with children under five years of age prefer products of EU origin because they trust EU food safety institutions more than Albanian ones and because of the perception of high-risk food illnesses for that specific age [74,75].

The municipality of Tirana and the related stakeholders should play a crucial role in transforming citizens' perceptions of agriculture in urban areas and creating the city's food identity. The latter can be built by understanding the parents' primary motivations for participating in the USFC of Tirana.

In addition, an analysis of parents' understanding of sustainable consumption and whether it is associated with their willingness to pay shows that about 60% of the participants claim they understand the concept of sustainable consumption, while 40% still need to. Among those who understand, most link sustainable consumption to the energetic aspect, such as the balance of energy intake and expenditure, while 24% associate it with the environmental impact of consumption. Most respondents (around 35%) believe that food consumption is sustainable when the energy value of the food consumed is equal to the body's energy expenditure. This highlights a significant focus on the nutritional aspect of sustainability, indicating that many parents prioritise the balance between food intake and bodily energy needs. Interestingly, about 25% of respondents associate sustainable consumption with minimising the environmental impact of daily food consumption, showing an awareness of the broader environmental implications of their food choices. Approximately 15% of respondents consider zero food waste to be a critical component of sustainable consumption, which reflects an understanding of waste reduction as playing a part in sustainability efforts. Furthermore, around 12–15% of respondents link sustainable consumption to balancing plant and animal products in their diet and adjusting food costs to the family's financial capacity. These perspectives highlight a diverse understanding of sustainability, encompassing nutritional balance, economic considerations, and environmental impacts.

This analysis indicates that, while there is a substantial awareness of the energy balance aspect of sustainable consumption, there is also significant recognition of environmental impacts and waste reduction. Similarly, another factor that increases consumer interest in local products and USFC is the evolution of consumer preferences due to globalisation. Consumers, increasingly faced with uncertainty regarding the products they consume and their health effects, are considering alternatives, such as local or fresh products. These schemes are of particular interest to the agricultural systems of developing countries because they address the growing uncertainty of a specific segment of consumers concerning the food they consume [58,76].

Table 5(3) shows various motivations for participating in USFC and indicates that the most highly rated are 'Increasing the consumption of natural foods' and 'Purchasing and consuming seasonal foods', which score above 4.5. This high rating highlights the value and appreciation of fresh and seasonal products and natural foods. Other important motivations include promoting local agricultural/livestock production and protecting the natural environment, which scored around 4.1. This high rating suggests a strong concern for local economies and environmental sustainability. Conversely, 'Reducing food waste' and 'Reducing the consumption of highly processed foods' have slightly lower scores, indicating that, while these factors are essential, they may only be the primary motivators for some respondents. Exploring behavioural motivations within a rapidly evolving urban food environment—shaped by industrialisation, urbanisation, and the globalisation of food systems—provides valuable insights beyond pre-existing urban food chain structures. However, future research should further differentiate urban food chain mechanisms from broader short food supply chain engagement, ensuring a clearer understanding of consumer drivers and food system dynamics.

These motivations are critical components of the moderation mediation model used in the study, as they help us to understand the pathways through which climate change concerns and environmental awareness influence consumer behaviour and the willingness to engage with USFC. The analysis first investigates the direct and indirect effects of CCA on the willingness to pay (WTP) for USFC, as mediated by biospheric, egoistic, and altruistic concerns (see Table 6).

As shown in the methodology section, the second step involves analysing the impact of three types of environmental concern—biospheric, egoistic, and altruistic—on the willingness to pay (WTP) for USFC and the mediators linked to USFC.

CCA significantly increases biospheric, egoistic, and altruistic concerns. However, these concerns do not consistently translate into a willingness to pay for USFC. While CCA can increase concerns related to the environment, such as biospheric, egoistic, and altruistic concerns, these concerns do not always lead to actual behavioural changes, such as willingness to pay for USFC. This disconnect, often called the "value–action gap," is well-documented in environmental psychology [23,32,77,78]. It occurs because of various factors, such as financial constraints, perceived inconvenience [79,80], lack of trust [76], and competing priorities that can inhibit the translation of environmental concerns into actionable behaviours. Additionally, the perceived personal relevance and urgency of environmental issues may vary among individuals [79,81], contributing to inconsistent behavioural outcomes despite similar levels of concern.

Table 6. Impact of climate change awareness on environmental concerns and their mediation of willingness to pay for urban short food chains.

Hypothesis	Path	R-Squared	(Effect)	*p*-Value	Interpretation
H1a: CCA → Biospheric Concern	Path a_1	0.111	0.252	<0.001	CCA significantly increases biospheric concern
H1b: Biospheric Concern → USFC	Path b_1	0.036	0.028 (Indirect)	>0.05	No significant indirect effect on USFC participation
H1c: CCA → Egoistic Concern	Path a_2	0.041	0.113	0.003	CCA significantly increases egoistic concern
H1d: Egoistic Concern → USFC	Path b_2	0.036	−0.102 (Indirect)	<0.05	Egoistic concern negatively mediates the effect on USFC participation
H1e: CCA → Altruistic Concern	Path a_3	0.024	0.076	0.023	CCA significantly increases altruistic concern
H1f: Altruistic Concern → USFC	Path b_3	0.036	0.062 (Indirect)	0.044	Altruistic concern positively mediates the effect on USFC participation
Total Effect of CCA on USFC	Total Path	0.036	−0.141	0.16	No significant total effect of CCA on USFC participation
Direct Effect of CCA on USFC	Direct Path	0.036	−0.129	0.223	No significant direct effect of CCA on USFC participation
Interaction Effects	M1- Biospheric, M2- Egoistic, M3-Altruistic	-	Not significant	-	Interaction effects were not significant

Source: authors' elaboration.

Altruistic concern's significant positive mediation effect on USFC participation suggests that altruistic motivations can enhance engagement in sustainable practices. This finding aligns with the existing literature that emphasises the importance of social and ethical considerations in consumer decision making, particularly sustainability [36,82]. Individuals motivated by the well-being of others and the broader community can engage in behaviours supporting environmental sustainability, such as participating in USFC. Additionally, 90% of the respondents are female parents, which is significant, as studies have shown that women are often more engaged in sustainability issues due to their roles in household management and childcare, which heightens their concern for future generations and environmental health [83,84]. Conversely, egoistic concern has a significant negative mediation effect, indicating that higher egoistic concern may reduce willingness to pay for USFC (See Table 7). Egoistic concern focuses on personal benefits rather than collective or environmental well-being. This perspective often leads individuals to prioritise immediate personal gains, such as cost savings or convenience, over long-term environmental benefits [32,35]. As a result, individuals with higher levels of egoistic concern may be less willing to pay for sustainable options such as USFC, which often require higher upfront costs or sacrifices for convenience.

Table 7. Results of biospheric, egoistic, and altruistic concerns as drivers of USFC.

H	OV	R^2 (ECB)	Coefficient ECB	*p*-Value ECB	R^2 ECE	Effect ECE	*p*-Value ECE	R^2 (ECA)	Coefficient ECA	*p*-Value ECA
H2.1	Limiting Food Waste	0.090	0.349	<0.000	0.036	0.200	0.009	0.111	0.393	<0.0001
H2.2	Buying Seasonally	0.101	0.304	<0.000	0.110	0.287	<0.000	0.188	0.423	<0.0001
H2.3	Stimulating Local Produce	0.156	0.439	<0.000	0.088	0.304	<0.000	0.172	0.468	<0.0001
H2.4	Protecting the Environment	0.154	0.404	<0.000	0.097	0.294	<0.000	0.166	0.425	<0.0001
H2.5	Buying Local Products	0.065	0.280	0.000	0.034	0.188	0.010	0.096	0.345	<0.0001
H2.6	Increasing Natural Conservation	0.156	0.394	<0.0001	0.126	0.321	<0.0001	0.218	0.473	<0.000
H2.7	Reducing Impulsive Buying	0.074	0.301	0.000	0.086	0.299	<0.0001	0.113	0.377	<0.000
H2.8	Reducing Processed Food	0.136	0.415	<0.0001	0.156	0.406	<0.0001	0.230	0.546	<0.000
H2.9	WTP (Overall Model)	0.131	0.6520 (Direct effect)	0.092	0.146	0.3387 (Direct effect)	0.318	0.122	0.6520 (Direct effect)	0.092
	Limiting waste	-	0.502	0.002	-	0.448	0.006	-	0.502	0.002
	Buying Seasonal ly	-	−0.207	0.534	-	−0.236	0.476	-	−0.207	0.534
	Protecting the environment	-	−0.297	0.158	-	−0.213	0.306	-	−0.297	0.158
	Stimulating local production	-	0.067	0.775	-	0.047	0.837	-	0.067	0.775
	Increasing natural consumption	-	−0.663	0.022	-	−0.731	0.011	-	−0.663	0.022
	Reducing impulsive buying	-	−0.323	0.096	-	−0.291	0.120	-	−0.323	0.096
	Reducing processed food consumption	-	0.370	0.095	-	0.418	0.054	-	0.370	0.095
	Buying locally	-	0.000	1.000	-	−0.017	0.919	-	0.000	1.000
	Interaction (gender)	-	−0.730	0.021	-	−0.560	0.032	-	−0.730	0.021

Source: authors' elaboration. Outcome variable = OV, EC (biospheric) = ECB, EC (egoistic) = ECE, EC (altruistic) = ECA.

The finding that the overall and direct effects of CCA on urban short food chain participation are insignificant highlights the complexity of translating awareness into sustainable consumer behaviour.

The analysis reveals that biospheric concern (EC Biospheric) significantly and positively impacts several drivers of willingness to pay (WTP) for USFC. The most pronounced direct effects of EC Biospheric are seen in the stimulation of local production (effect size: 0.4389, $p < 0.000$) and protecting the environment (effect size: 0.403, $p < 0.000$). This underscores the potential for positive changes in the food system, offering an anticipatory pathway. Moreover, increasing natural consumption (effect size: 0.393, $p < 0.000$) and reducing processed food consumption (effect size: 0.414, $p < 0.000$) are also strongly influenced by EC Biospheric, further reinforcing the potential for a healthier and more sustainable food system. While the direct effect of biospheric environmental concern (EC Biospheric) on (WTP) is not significant (effect size: 0.717, $p = 0.093$), this study reveals the significant indirect effects of limiting food waste (effect size: 0.456, $p = 0.004$) on WTP, underscoring their importance in the context of USFC and making the audience feel informed and aware of these crucial factors.

Increasing natural consumption shows a significant negative mediation effect (effect size: −0.595, $p = 0.033$). Cognitive dissonance might play a role here [85]. Consumers already engaged in increasing natural consumption might feel they are contributing sufficiently to sustainable practices. Therefore, they might perceive less need to further engage in USFC initiatives, viewing them as an additional or redundant effort rather than a complementary one. This leads to a decreased willingness to pay for such initiatives, as people believe their existing actions are adequate. Second, the perceived costs and accessibility issues associated with natural products can contribute to this negative mediation effect. Even though consumers recognise the benefits of natural products, they may associate them with higher costs or limited availability, especially in urban settings. This perception can make them reluctant to pay more for USFCs, which might also be perceived as an expensive or less convenient option. Lastly, saturation and the prioritisation of concerns might be at play. Consumers who are highly focused on natural consumption may prioritise sustainability concerns, such as reducing plastic use or energy consumption, over supporting local food chains [86]. This prioritisation can result in a lower WTP for USFCs, as these consumers allocate their resources and efforts to other environmental areas they consider more impactful or immediate.

Gender significantly moderates the relationship between EC Biospheric and WTP, with an important negative interaction effect (effect size: −0.865, $p = 0.024$). Specifically, EC Biospheric negatively impacts WTP for females (effect size: −1.013, $p = 0.007$) but not for males (effect size: −0.148, $p = 0.227$). One possibility is that women, who constituted 90% of the sample, might have a more nuanced view of environmental concerns, potentially reflecting greater awareness of the complexity and challenges involved in sustainable practices. Women are often more directly involved in food purchasing and preparation and may thus be more cautious about changes that could affect household routines or budgets, especially in urban areas where time and resources are limited. Prior research suggests that women are more engaged in sustainable food networks and local food purchasing decisions.

The role of women in sustainable food networks, such as USFCs, as well as their influence on local food purchasing decisions, is becoming increasingly important within the discourse on food security and environmental sustainability [87–89]. Women's involvement is critical for ensuring food security at the household level and in advancing community sustainability efforts [87,90]. Women's participation in sustainable food networks is underscored by their unique purchasing behaviours and motivations [88,91–93]. Research shows that women tend to prioritise environmental and social considerations more strongly than men, making them more likely to purchase local and sustainably produced foods [94]. For example, studies highlight that women are often the primary decision makers regarding food purchases, which has a profound impact on family dietary diversity and overall nutrition [91,95]. Furthermore, women are increasingly aware of the social implications of their food choices, fostering more substantial support for local economies through informed purchasing decisions [96].

Women are also significantly involved in establishing and maintaining alternative food networks, which emphasize local food production and consumption. Their engagement in these networks often reflects a commitment to sustainable practices, community well-being, and ethical considerations in food sourcing [93,97,98]. For instance, initiatives such as food cooperatives, where women play a central role, enable collective action towards sustainable food sourcing while fostering community ties [98]. Such cooperative structures empower women through shared leadership and decision making and address barriers linked to individual purchasing power and access to sustainable food options [98]. In urban contexts, women's networks can enhance food security by enabling access to local and fresh produce while negotiating better purchasing conditions, such as buying on credit from informal vendors [88].

Women's active participation in urban sustainable food networks is critical for advancing environmental and social sustainability.

Our findings reveal that egoistic environmental concern (EC Egoistic) significantly influences various drivers of willingness to pay (WTP) for USFC. The largest direct effects of EC Egoistic are observed in reducing processed food consumption (effect size: 0.405, $p < 0.00$) and increasing natural consumption (effect size: 0.320, $p < 0.000$). Stimulating local production (effect size: 0.303, $p < 0.000$) and protecting the environment (effect size: 0.294, $p < 0.000$) are also significantly impacted.

Although the direct effect of EC Egoistic on WTP is not significant (effect size: 0.338, $p = 0.317$), significant indirect effects through limiting food waste indicate an important mediation pathway (effect size: 0.447, $p = 0.006$). Increasing natural consumption shows a significant negative mediation effect (effect size: −0.731, $p = 0.011$). Gender significantly moderates the relationship between EC Egoistic and WTP, with a notable negative interaction effect. An interaction effect is the combined effect of two or more variables on the dependent variable (WTP). Consumers' budget constraints may influence the negative mediation effect of increasing natural consumption on WTP for USFC, as natural or organic products are often perceived as more expensive [99]. Additionally, it is important to understand that urban lifestyle constraints, such as time and convenience, play a significant role in consumer choices [100]. Scepticism about the benefits of natural foods and these lifestyle constraints may deter consumers from opting for natural consumption despite potential benefits [101].

The analysis also uncovers the significant influence of altruistic concern (ECA) on various drivers of willingness to pay (WTP) for USFC. The highest direct effect is observed in reducing processed food (effect size: 0.545, $p < 0.000$) and increasing natural consumption (effect size: 0.472, $p < 0.000$). These results highlight the potential of altruistic concern. The overall model for WTP reveals a non-significant direct effect of altruistic concerns (effect size: 0.652, $p = 0.091$). However, the indirect effects achieved through various mediators are of paramount importance. Limiting food waste shows the highest positive indirect effects on WTP (effect size: 0.502, $p = 0.002$), indicating intense mediation. Increasing natural consumption has a significant negative mediation effect (effect size: −0.663, $p = 0.021$). Gender plays a significant moderating role, particularly for WTP (interaction effect size: −0.729, $p = 0.021$).

The findings of this study align with those of previous research on environmental concerns and sustainable food choices. Like [45,46], our results confirm that biospheric concerns strongly influence preferences for natural and minimally processed foods, reflecting a broader trend in sustainable consumer behaviour. Additionally, the indirect effect of limiting food waste as a driver of willingness to pay (WTP) for USFC reflects the conclusions of [44], who highlight food waste reduction as a critical component of sustainability in local food systems.

Moreover, our findings regarding the role of egoistic concerns in processed food reduction are consistent with [56], who found that personal health concerns significantly drive sustainable food choices. However, unlike studies that emphasise a strong direct effect of CCA on behaviour [102,103], our results indicate that CCA alone does not directly translate into WTP for USFC but operates through mediating factors. This suggests that awareness must be paired with targeted interventions to bridge the value–action gap, a finding that expands on other [104] work on consumer trust in short food supply chains.

The demographic challenge of urban food perceptions in Tirana also connects with the literature on urbanisation and food system restructuring [2,15]. Similarly to findings from [48], our results indicate that urban consumers often lack strong associations between their city and food production, reinforcing the need for a shared narrative to integrate urban agriculture into food policy discussions.

4. Conclusions

This study examined the role of environmental concerns, specifically, biospheric, egoistic, and altruistic concerns, in mediating the relationship between climate change awareness (CCA) and willingness to pay (WTP) for urban short food chains (USFC). The research aimed to understand how these environmental concerns shape consumer behaviour and engagement in sustainable food practices, particularly in urban settings such as Tirana, Albania. Our findings contribute to the growing literature on sustainable food systems and provide a nuanced understanding of the mechanisms that link environmental awareness to sustainable consumer behaviour. H1: CCA significantly increases biospheric concern: this hypothesis was supported, as CCA was shown to increase biospheric concern (Path a1) significantly. However, the indirect effect of biospheric concern on WTP for USFC was not significant (Path b1), indicating that, while individuals care about environmental issues, this concern does not always translate into actual behavioural change, confirming the existence of the value–action gap. Regarding H2: CCA significantly increases egoistic concern, and this hypothesis was also supported. Our findings indicate that CCA significantly increases egoistic concern (Path a2). Still, this concern negatively mediated the relationship between CCA and WTP for USFC (Path b2), which suggests that people with stronger egoistic concerns are less likely to engage in USFC, as they prioritise personal benefits over collective environmental outcomes. Moreover, concerning H3: CCA significantly increases altruistic concern; this hypothesis was supported, with CCA significantly increasing altruistic concern (Path a3). Additionally, altruistic concern positively mediates the relationship between CCA and USFC participation (Path b3), highlighting the importance of social and ethical motivations in promoting sustainable food choices.

The study's primary goal was to explore how environmental concerns mediate the relationship between climate change awareness and willingness to pay for USFC. Our results align with this goal, showing that environmental concerns are significant mediators, though the effect is more complex than previously assumed. Specifically, while biospheric and altruistic concerns positively influenced USFC participation, egoistic concerns had a negative mediating effect. This reinforces the idea that consumer behaviour is influenced by environmental awareness and personal values and priorities.

Our study also advances the conceptual model by demonstrating that CCA alone cannot translate directly into sustainable behaviours. Instead, increased awareness and targeted interventions, such as reducing impulsive buying and promoting local production, can foster engagement in sustainable food practices. These insights are crucial for informing future research and policy development, particularly in addressing the industrialisation of food systems and the rise of ultra-processed food consumption.

Another important finding is the significant role of gender in moderating the relationship between environmental concerns and WTP for USFC. Our study found that women, who made up 90% of the sample, exhibited a more substantial negative interaction effect with biospheric concerns, suggesting that women may be more cautious about adopting sustainable food choices due to constraints related to household responsibilities and urban lifestyles. This aligns with global trends recognising women's pivotal role in shaping food systems, particularly in sustainable food networks. Their involvement is critical for advancing food security and sustainability at the household and community levels.

Despite its valuable insights, this study has several limitations concerning sample composition. The sample was predominantly composed of women (90%) and parents (96%), mainly due to the distribution of the questionnaire through school networks and parent groups. While this allowed us to capture the views of a critical demographic segment, those primarily responsible for food purchasing and household nutrition, it limits the generalizability of the findings to the broader urban population. Future research should aim to include a more balanced representation of genders, age groups, occupational backgrounds (including those in environmental fields), and residential areas (urban vs. peri-urban/suburban) better to reflect the diversity of consumers in urban food systems. Expanding the demographic scope will help capture the full spectrum of motivations, barriers, and engagement strategies needed to promote USFC participation across various consumer segments.

This study underscores the need for policy interventions that bridge the gap between awareness and action. While CCA alone does not directly influence WTP for USFCs, policies can leverage behavioural nudges, financial incentives, and local food initiatives to encourage sustainable food choices. Strengthening urban agriculture in Tirana's food narrative and public procurement policies favouring local produce, educational programs, and incentives for urban farming could significantly enhance consumer engagement in USFCs.

Furthermore, our findings contribute to the broader discourse on the European Green Deal and its alignment with EU policies, particularly the Farm to Fork initiative. Future research should provide concrete policy recommendations tailored to the local context, addressing key barriers such as limited consumer awareness, logistical inefficiencies, and institutional fragmentation that may hinder the development of urban short food chains. Additionally, exploring the role of digital technology, such as online platforms, mobile applications, and traceability tools, can offer innovative pathways to enhance consumer engagement, improve transparency, and scale up participation in USFC initiatives in urban settings.

Author Contributions: Conceptualization, E.K. and F.G.; methodology, E.K. and Z.D.; software, E.K.; validation, F.G., formal analysis, E.K. and F.G. and Z.D.; investigation, E.K. and Z.D.; writing, E.K., F.G. and Z.D. All authors have read and agreed to the published version of the manuscript.

Funding: This study was conducted within the National Agency of Scientific Research and Innovation (NASRI) project. We would like to thank the NASRI for financing and contributing to this research.

Institutional Review Board Statement: This research was conducted following the ethical regulations of the Ethics Committee of the Agriculture University of Tirana. The Ethics Committee reviewed and approved the study protocol. All participants provided informed consent before they participated in the study. The study complies with all institutional and national regulations governing research with human subjects.

Informed Consent Statement: Informed consent was obtained from all participants before their involvement in the study. Participants were informed that their participation was voluntary and that they could withdraw at any time without consequence. The study involved completing a questionnaire, and participants were assured that their data would be kept confidential and used solely for research purposes. Anonymity was guaranteed, and no identifying information was collected or disclosed. Data privacy protocols were followed under the ethical guidelines of the Agriculture University of Tirana Ethics Committee.

Data Availability Statement: The data supporting this study's findings are available from the corresponding author upon reasonable request. Due to privacy and ethical restrictions, participants' data cannot be shared publicly. However, anonymised data can be provided to qualified researchers who meet the criteria for access to confidential information, which aligns with the guidelines set by the Agriculture University of Tirana Ethics Committee.

Acknowledgments: We express our sincere gratitude for the generous support of the National Agency for Scientific Research and Innovation (NASRI) in Albania, which enabled us to carry out this study. The financial support received for our project "Measuring Women's Social and Economic Impact as the Leading Actor for Poverty Reduction and Sustainable Development of Food Systems in Albani", based on Decision No. 10, date 21 July 2023, "On the approval of the financing of winning projects of the National Research and Development Program for the Period 2023–2024", is responsible for the significant success of the study.

Conflicts of Interest: The authors declare that they have no known competing financial interests or personal relationships that could have appeared to influence the work reported in this paper.

References

1. Hume, I.V.; Summers, D.M.; Cavagnaro, T.R. Self-sufficiency through urban agriculture: Nice idea or plausible reality? *Sustain. Cities Soc.* **2021**, *68*, 102770. [CrossRef]
2. Edwards-Jones, G. Does eating local food reduce the environmental impact of food production and enhance consumer health? *Proc. Nutr. Soc.* **2010**, *69*, 582–591. [CrossRef] [PubMed]
3. Guiné, R.P.F.; Bartkiene, E.; Florença, S.G.; Djekić, I.; Bizjak, M.Č.; Tarcea, M.; Leal, M.; Ferreira, V.; Rumbak, I.; Orfanos, P.; et al. Environmental Issues as Drivers for Food Choice: Study from a Multinational Framework. *Sustainability* **2021**, *13*, 2869. [CrossRef]
4. Hale, J.; Knapp, C.; Bardwell, L.; Buchenau, M.; Marshall, J.; Sancar, F.; Litt, J.S. Connecting food environments and health through the relational nature of aesthetics: Gaining insight through the community gardening experience. *Soc. Sci. Med.* **2011**, *72*, 1853–1863. [CrossRef]
5. Kropp, C.; Antoni-Komar, I.; Sage, C. *Food System Transformations: Social Movements, Local Economies, Collaborative Networks*; Critical Food Studies; Routledge: New York, NY, USA, 2021.
6. Marsden, T.; Banks, J.; Bristow, G. Food Supply Chain Approaches: Exploring their Role in Rural Development. *Sociol. Rural.* **2000**, *40*, 424–438. [CrossRef]
7. Owen, L.; Udall, D.; Franklin, A.; Kneafsey, M. Place-Based Pathways to Sustainability: Exploring Alignment between Geographical Indications and the Concept of Agroecology Territories in Wales. *Sustainability* **2020**, *12*, 4890. [CrossRef]
8. Pulighe, G.; Lupia, F. Food First: COVID-19 Outbreak and Cities Lockdown a Booster for a Wider Vision on Urban Agriculture. *Sustainability* **2020**, *12*, 5012. [CrossRef]
9. Awang, N. Fostering Empowerment of Urban Community Gardening Through Urban Agriculture Initiatives in Malaysia. *Int. J. Acad. Res. Bus. Soc. Sci.* **2024**, *14*, 3115–3124. [CrossRef]
10. Egerer, M.; Lin, B.B.; Kingsley, J.; Marsh, P.; Diekmann, L.; Ossola, A. Gardening Can Relieve Human Stress and Boost Nature Connection During the COVID-19 Pandemic. *Urban For. Urban Green.* **2022**, *68*, 127483. [CrossRef]
11. Faivre, N.; Fritz, M.; Freitas, T.; Boissezon, B.d.; Vandewoestijne, S. Nature-Based Solutions in the EU: Innovating With Nature to Address Social, Economic and Environmental Challenges. *Environ. Res.* **2017**, *159*, 509–518. [CrossRef]
12. Omondi, S.O.; Oluoch-Kosura, W.; Jirström, M. The Role of Urban-based Agriculture on Food Security: Kenyan Case Studies. *Geogr. Res.* **2017**, *55*, 231–241. [CrossRef]
13. Grando, S.; Carey, J.; Hegger, E.; Jahrl, I.; Ortolani, L. Short Food Supply Chains in Urban Areas: Who Takes the Lead? Evidence from Three Cities across Europe. *Urban Agric. Reg. Food Syst.* **2017**, *2*, 1–11. [CrossRef]

14. Mathew, R. Urban Agriculture: An Approach Towards Creating Sustainable Smart Cities: A Review. *Agric. Rev.* **2023**. [CrossRef]
15. Chiffoleau, Y.; Dourian, T. Sustainable Food Supply Chains: Is Shortening the Answer? A Literature Review for a Research and Innovation Agenda. *Sustainability* **2020**, *12*, 9831. [CrossRef]
16. Evola, R.S.; Peira, G.; Varese, E.; Bonadonna, A.; Vesce, E. Short Food Supply Chains in Europe: Scientific Research Directions. *Sustainability* **2022**, *14*, 3602. [CrossRef]
17. Doernberg, A.; Piorr, A.; Zasada, I.; Wascher, D.; Schmutz, U. Sustainability assessment of short food supply chains (SFSC): Developing and testing a rapid assessment tool in one African and three European city regions. *Agric. Hum. Values* **2022**, *39*, 885–904. [CrossRef]
18. Hesty, W.; Hidayati, F.; Noor, I. A Proposed Sustainable Model of Food Systems: Social and Environmental Welfare Impact. In Bogor, Indonesia. 2021. Available online: https://www.atlantis-press.com/article/125961283 (accessed on 20 February 2025).
19. Majewski, E.; Komerska, A.; Kwiatkowski, J.; Malak-Rawlikowska, A.; Wąs, A.; Sulewski, P.; Gołaś, M.; Pogodzińska, K.; Lecoeur, J.-L.; Tocco, B.; et al. Are Short Food Supply Chains More Environmentally Sustainable than Long Chains? A Life Cycle Assessment (LCA) of the Eco-Efficiency of Food Chains in Selected EU Countries. *Energies* **2020**, *13*, 4853. [CrossRef]
20. Malak-Rawlikowska, A.; Majewski, E.; Wąs, A.; Borgen, S.O.; Csillag, P.; Donati, M.; Freeman, R.; Hoàng, V.; Lecoeur, J.-L.; Mancini, M.C.; et al. Measuring the Economic, Environmental, and Social Sustainability of Short Food Supply Chains. *Sustainability* **2019**, *11*, 4004. [CrossRef]
21. Schultz, P.W. The Structure of Environmental Concern: Concern for Self, Other People, and the Biosphere. *J. Environ. Psychol.* **2001**, *21*, 327–339. [CrossRef]
22. Born, B.; Purcell, M. Avoiding the Local Trap: Scale and Food Systems in Planning Research. *J. Plan. Educ. Res.* **2006**, *26*, 195–207. [CrossRef]
23. Druen, P.B.; Zawadzki, S.J. Escaping the Climate Trap: Participation in a Climate-Specific Social Dilemma Simulation Boosts Climate-Protective Motivation and Actions. *Sustainability* **2021**, *13*, 9438. [CrossRef]
24. Kaçani, K.; Kokthi, E.; Lόpez-Bonilla, L.M.; González-Limόn, M. Social tipping and climate change: The moderating role of social capital in bridging the gap between aware-ness and action. *J. Int. Dev.* **2024**, *36*, 2537–2556. [CrossRef]
25. Kollmuss, A.; Agyeman, J. Mind the Gap: Why do people act environmentally and what are the barriers to pro-environmental behavior? *Environ. Educ. Res.* **2002**, *8*, 239–260. [CrossRef]
26. Helm, S.V.; Pollitt, A.; Barnett, M.A.; Curran, M.A.; Craig, Z.R. Differentiating environmental concern in the context of psychological adaption to climate change. *Glob. Environ. Change* **2018**, *48*, 158–167. [CrossRef]
27. Bamberg, S. How does environmental concern influence specific environmentally related behaviors? A new answer to an old question. *J. Environ. Psychol.* **2003**, *23*, 21–32. [CrossRef]
28. Howell, R.A. It's *not* (just) "the environment, stupid!" Values, motivations, and routes to engagement of people adopting lower-carbon lifestyles. *Glob. Environ. Change* **2013**, *23*, 281–290. [CrossRef]
29. Stern, P.C. New environmental theories: Toward a coherent theory of environmentally significant behavior. *J. Soc. Issues* **2000**, *56*, 407–424. [CrossRef]
30. Vittersø, G.; Torjusen, H.; Laitala, K.; Tocco, B.; Biasini, B.; Csillag, P.; de Labarre, M.D.; Lecoeur, J.-L.; Maj, A.; Majewski, E.; et al. Short Food Supply Chains and Their Contributions to Sustainability: Participants' Views and Perceptions from 12 European Cases. *Sustainability* **2019**, *11*, 4800. [CrossRef]
31. Franzen, A.; Vogl, D. Time Preferences and Environmental Concern: An Analysis of the Swiss ISSP 2010. *Int. J. Sociol.* **2013**, *43*, 39–62. [CrossRef]
32. Gifford, R. The dragons of inaction: Psychological barriers that limit climate change mitigation and adaptation. *Am. Psychol.* **2011**, *66*, 290–302. [CrossRef]
33. Gifford, R.; Nilsson, A. Personal and social factors that influence pro-environmental concern and behaviour: A review: Personal and Social Factors That Influence Pro-Environmental Behaviour. *Int. J. Psychol.* **2014**, *49*, 141–157. [CrossRef] [PubMed]
34. Vermeir, I.; Verbeke, W. Sustainable Food Consumption: Exploring the Consumer "Attitude–Behavioral Intention" Gap. *J. Agric. Environ. Ethics* **2006**, *19*, 169–194. [CrossRef]
35. Snelgar, R.S. Egoistic, altruistic, and biospheric environmental concerns: Measurement and structure. *J. Environ. Psychol.* **2006**, *26*, 87–99. [CrossRef]
36. Xu, Y.; Li, W.; Chi, S. Altruism, Environmental Concerns, and Pro-environmental Behaviors of Urban Residents: A Case Study in a Typical Chinese City. *Front. Psychol.* **2021**, *12*, 643759. [CrossRef]
37. Seyfang, G. *Community Currencies: A New Tool for Sustainable Consumptions? [Internet]*; Report No.: 06–09; University of East Anglia, The Centre for Social and Economic Research on the Global Environment (CSERGE): Norwich, UK, 2006. Available online: https://hdl.handle.net/10419/80270 (accessed on 1 January 2020).
38. Zepeda, L.; Nie, C. What are the odds of being an organic or local food shopper? Multivariate analysis of US food shopper lifestyle segments. *Agric. Hum. Values* **2012**, *29*, 467–480. [CrossRef]

39. Hines, J.M.; Hungerford, H.R.; Tomera, A.N. Analysis and synthesis of research on responsible pro-environmental behavior: A meta-analysis. *J. Environ. Educ.* **1987**, *18*, 1–8. [CrossRef]
40. Vermeir, I.; Verbeke, W. Sustainable food consumption among young adults in Belgium: Theory of planned behaviour and the role of confidence and values. *Ecol. Econ.* **2008**, *64*, 542–553. [CrossRef]
41. Wolf, J.; Moser, S.C. Individual understandings, perceptions, and engagement with climate change: Insights from in-depth studies across the world. *WIREs Clim. Change* **2011**, *2*, 547–569. [CrossRef]
42. Conrad, Z.; Blackstone, N.T. Identifying the links between consumer food waste, nutrition, and environmental sustainability: A narrative review. *Nutr. Rev.* **2021**, *79*, 301–314. [CrossRef]
43. O'Neill, K. Linking wastes and climate change: Bandwagoning, contention, and global governance. *WIREs Clim. Change* **2019** *10*, e568. [CrossRef]
44. Thyberg, K.L.; Tonjes, D.J. Drivers of food waste and their implications for sustainable policy development. *Resour. Conserv. Recycl.* **2016**, *106*, 110–123. [CrossRef]
45. Tobler, C.; Visschers, V.H.M.; Siegrist, M. Eating green. Consumers' willingness to adopt ecological food consumption behaviors. *Appetite* **2011**, *57*, 674–682. [CrossRef] [PubMed]
46. Tobler, C.; Visschers, V.H.M.; Siegrist, M. Addressing climate change: Determinants of consumers' willingness to act and to support policy measures. *J. Environ. Psychol.* **2012**, *32*, 197–207. [CrossRef]
47. Endrizzi, I.; Cliceri, D.; Menghi, L.; Aprea, E.; Gasperi, F. Does the 'Mountain Pasture Product' Claim Affect Local Cheese Acceptability? *Foods* **2021**, *10*, 682. [CrossRef]
48. Jarzębowski, S.; Bourlakis, M.; Bezat-Jarzębowska, A. Short Food Supply Chains (SFSC) as Local and Sustainable Systems. *Sustainability* **2020**, *12*, 4715. [CrossRef]
49. Iori, E.; Masotti, M.; Falasconi, L.; Risso, E.; Segrè, A.; Vittuari, M. Tell Me What You Waste and I'll Tell You Who You Are: An Eight-Country Comparison of Consumers' Food Waste Habits. *Sustainability* **2022**, *15*, 430. [CrossRef]
50. Liao, C.; Qiao, L.; Wang, X.; Lu, S. Exploring food waste prevention through advent food consumption: The role of perceived concern, consumer value, and impulse buying. *Front. Sustain. Food Syst.* **2022**, *6*, 988260. [CrossRef]
51. Dentoni, D.; Tonsor, G.T.; Calantone, R.J.; Peterson, H.C.; Dentoni, D.; Tonsor, G.T.; Calantone, R.J.; Peterson, H.C. The Direct and Indirect Effects of 'Locally Grown' on Consumers' Attitudes Towards Agri-Food Products. 2009. Available online: https://ageconsearch.umn.edu/record/59252 (accessed on 23 November 2020).
52. Bimbo, F.; Russo, C.; Di Fonzo, A.; Nardone, G. Consumers' environmental responsibility and their purchase of local food: Evidence from a large-scale survey. *Br. Food J.* **2020**, *123*, 1853–1874. [CrossRef]
53. Shen, M.; Wang, J. The Impact of Pro-environmental Awareness Components on Green Consumption Behavior: The Moderation Effect of Consumer Perceived Cost, Policy Incentives, and Face Culture. *Front. Psychol.* **2022**, *13*, 580823. [CrossRef]
54. Wells, V.K.; Ponting, C.A.; Peattie, K. Behaviour and climate change: Consumer perceptions of responsibility. *J. Mark. Manag.* **2011**, *27*, 808–833. [CrossRef]
55. Hughner, R.S.; McDonagh, P.; Prothero, A.; Shultz, C.J.; Stanton, J. Who are organic food consumers? A compilation and review of why people purchase organic food. *J. Consum. Behav.* **2007**, *6*, 94–110. [CrossRef]
56. Migliore, G.; Thrassou, A.; Crescimanno, M.; Schifani, G.; Galati, A. Factors affecting consumer preferences for "natural wine": An exploratory study in the Italian market. *Br. Food J.* **2020**, *122*, 2463–2479. [CrossRef]
57. Tandon, A.; Dhir, A.; Kaur, P.; Kushwah, S.; Salo, J. Why do people buy organic food? The moderating role of environmental concerns and trust. *J. Retail. Consum. Serv.* **2020**, *57*, 102247. [CrossRef]
58. Kokthi, E.; Kruja, D.; Guri, F.; Zoto, O. Are the consumers willing to pay more for local fruits and vegetables? An empirical research on Albanian consumers. *Prog. Agric. Eng. Sci.* **2021**, *17*, 19–27. [CrossRef]
59. Ericson, T.; Kjønstad, B.G.; Barstad, A. Mindfulness and sustainability. *Ecol. Econ.* **2014**, *104*, 73–79. [CrossRef]
60. Bahl, S.; Milne, G.R.; Ross, S.M.; Mick, D.G.; Grier, S.A.; Chugani, S.K.; Chan, S.S.; Gould, S.; Cho, Y.-N.; Dorsey, J.D.; et al. Mindfulness: Its Transformative Potential for Consumer, Societal, and Environmental Well-Being. *J. Public Policy Mark.* **2016**, *35*, 198–210. [CrossRef]
61. Fischer, D.; Stanszus, L.; Geiger, S.; Grossman, P.; Schrader, U. Mindfulness and sustainable consumption: A systematic literature review of research approaches and findings. *J. Clean. Prod.* **2017**, *162*, 544–558. [CrossRef]
62. Garg, R.; Bansal, S.; Rathi, R.; Bhowmick, S. Mindful consumption—A systematic review and research agenda. *J. Clean. Prod.* **2024**, *459*, 142373. [CrossRef]
63. Casas, R. Moving towards a Healthier Dietary Pattern Free of Ultra-Processed Foods. *Nutrients* **2022**, *14*, 118. [CrossRef]
64. Fardet, A.; Rock, E. Ultra-Processed Foods and Food System Sustainability: What Are the Links? *Sustainability* **2020**, *12*, 6280. [CrossRef]
65. Allaire, G.; Vandecandelaere, E. *Linking People, Places and Products: A Guide for Promoting Quality Linked to Geographical Origin and Sustainable Geographical Indications*, 2nd ed.; FAO: Rome, Italy, 2010.

66. Hayes, A.F. Partial, conditional, and moderated moderated mediation: Quantification, inference, and interpretation. *Commun. Monogr.* **2018**, *85*, 4–40. [CrossRef]
67. Hayes, A.F.; Montoya, A.K. A Tutorial on Testing, Visualizing, and Probing an Interaction Involving a Multicategorical Variable in Linear Regression Analysis. *Commun. Methods Meas.* **2017**, *11*, 1–30. [CrossRef]
68. Hayes, A.F.; Rockwood, N.J. Conditional Process Analysis: Concepts, Computation, and Advances in the Modeling of the Contingencies of Mechanisms. *Am. Behav. Sci.* **2020**, *64*, 19–54. [CrossRef]
69. Igartua, J.-J.; Hayes, A.F. Mediation, Moderation, and Conditional Process Analysis: Concepts, Computations, and Some Common Confusions. *Span. J. Psychol.* **2021**, *24*, e49. [CrossRef]
70. Deselnicu, O.C.; Costanigro, M.; Souza-Monteiro, D.M.; McFadden, D.T. A Meta-Analysis of Geographical Indication Food Valuation Studies: What Drives the Premium for Origin-Based Labels? *J. Agric. Resour. Econ.* **2013**, *38*, 204–219.
71. Stefani, G.; Romano, D.; Cavicchi, A. Consumer expectations, liking and willingness to pay for specialty foods: Do sensory characteristics tell the whole story? *Food Qual. Prefer.* **2006**, *17*, 53–62. [CrossRef]
72. Bytyçi, P.; Kokthi, E.; Hasalliu, R.; Fetoshi, O.; Salihu, L.; Mestani, M. Is the local origin of a food product a nexus to better taste or is just an information bias. *Int. J. Gastron. Food Sci.* **2024**, *35*, 100877. [CrossRef]
73. Dimitrova, R.; Musso, P.; Naudé, L.; Zahaj, S.; Solcova, I.P.; Stefenel, D.; Uka, F.; Jordanov, V.; Jordanov, E.; Tavel, P. National collective identity in transitional societies: Salience and relations to life satisfaction for youth in South Africa, Albania, Bulgaria, the Czech Republic, Kosovo and Romania. *J. Psychol. Afr.* **2017**, *27*, 150–158. [CrossRef]
74. Hida, L.; Karaulli, E.; Kokthi, E.; Hasani, A. The impact of origin in the selection of children's food-the-case of Albania and Kosovo. In Proceedings of the FIKUSZ 2021 XVI. Symposium for Young Researchers Budapest, Budapest, Hungary, 26 November 2021.
75. Karaulli, E.; Hida, L.; Kokthi, E.; Hasani, A. Will nutritionists reduce uncertainty in parents food choices? The case of baby food in Albania and Kosovo. In Proceedings of the FIKUSZ 2021 XVI. Symposium for Young Researchers Budapest, Budapest, Hungary, 26 November 2021.
76. Guri, F.; Kokthi, E.; Kelemen-Erdős, A. Consumers' Perceptions about Food Safety Issues: Evidence from Albania. In Proceedings of the 17th International Conference on Management, Enterprise, Benchmarking, Budapest, Hungary, 29–30 March 2019.
77. Balundė, A.; Perlaviciute, G.; Steg, L. The Relationship Between People's Environmental Considerations and Pro-environmental Behavior in Lithuania. *Front. Psychol.* **2019**, *10*, 2319. [CrossRef]
78. Agustin, M.G. Development and Validation of a Test to Measure Student's Climate Change Awareness (CCA) Toward Sus-tainable Development Goals. 19 November 2022. Available online: https://zenodo.org/record/7337032 (accessed on 24 July 2024).
79. Liu, Y.; Xie, C.; She, S. Perception of delayed environmental risks: Beyond time discounting. *Disaster Prev. Manag.* **2014**, *23*, 112–122. [CrossRef]
80. Smith, E.K.; Mayer, A. A social trap for the climate? Collective action, trust and climate change risk perception in 35 countries. *Glob. Environ. Change* **2018**, *49*, 140–153. [CrossRef]
81. Poortinga, W.; Demski, C.; Steentjes, K. Generational differences in climate-related beliefs, risk perceptions and emotions in the UK. *Commun. Earth Environ.* **2023**, *4*, 229. [CrossRef]
82. Chao, C.-M.; Yu, T.-K. How emotions and green altruism explain consumer purchase intention toward circular economy products: A multi-group analysis on willingness to be environmentally friendly. *Bus. Strategy Environ.* **2024**, *33*, 2803–2816. [CrossRef]
83. Khurana, T. Role of women in sustainability (1). In Proceedings of the 7th Asia Pacific Business Research Conference, Mumbai, India, 6–7 January 2020.
84. Low, B.S. Men, women, and sustainability. *Popul. Environ.* **1996**, *18*, 111–141. [CrossRef]
85. Watson, L.; Spence, M.T. Causes and consequences of emotions on consumer behaviour: A review and integrative cognitive appraisal theory. *Eur. J. Mark.* **2007**, *41*, 487–511. [CrossRef]
86. Beitzen-Heineke, E.F.; Balta-Ozkan, N.; Reefke, H. The prospects of zero-packaging grocery stores to improve the social and environmental impacts of the food supply chain. *J. Clean. Prod.* **2017**, *140*, 1528–1541. [CrossRef]
87. Roy, E.; Pusala, D. Role of Women and Youth in Food Security and Rural Livelihood. *Int. J. Agric. Ext. Soc. Dev.* **2020**, *3*, 68–70. [CrossRef]
88. Bowden, R.; Even-Zahav, E.; Kelly, C. Innovative Food Procurement Strategies of Women Living in Khayelitsha, Cape Town. *Urban Forum* **2018**, *29*, 315–332. [CrossRef]
89. Gamhewage, M.I.; Sivashankar, P.; Mahaliyanaarachchi, R.P.; Wijeratne, A.W.; Hettiarachchi, I.C. Women participation in urban agriculture and its influence on family economy—Sri Lankan experience. *J. Agric. Sci.–Sri Lanka* **2015**, *10*, 192–206. [CrossRef]
90. Doss, C.R. Women and agricultural productivity: Reframing the Issues. *Dev. Policy Rev.* **2018**, *36*, 35–50. [CrossRef]
91. Barak, F.; Efitre, J.; Odong, R.; Melgar-Quiñonez, H. Women's agency in nutrition in the association between women's empowerment in agriculture and food security: A case study from Uganda. *World Food Policy* **2023**, *9*, 228–249. [CrossRef]
92. L G, N.; N, P. Role of Women in Sustainable Agricultural Growth. In *A Modern Approach to AI-Integrating Machine Learning with Agile Practices*; Kappagantual, M., N, B., Babu, P.V., Eds.; QTanalytics: Delhi, India, 2024; pp. 125–133. Available online: https://qtanalytics.in/publications/index.php/books/article/view/410 (accessed on 17 March 2025).

93. Som Castellano, R.L. Alternative Food Networks and the Labor of Food Provisioning: A Third Shift? *Rural Sociol.* **2016**, *81*, 445–469. [CrossRef]
94. Chen, P.-J.; Antonelli, M. Conceptual Models of Food Choice: Influential Factors Related to Foods, Individual Differences, and Society. *Foods* **2020**, *9*, 1898. [CrossRef]
95. Shourove, J.H.; Meem, F.C.; Rahman, M.; Islam, G.M.R. Is women's household decision-making autonomy associated with their higher dietary diversity in Bangladesh? Evidence from nationally representative survey. *PLoS Glob. Public Health* **2023**, *3*, e0001617. [CrossRef]
96. Nakajima, M. Sustainable Food Consumption: Demand for Local Produce in Singapore. *Sustainability* **2022**, *14*, 12330. [CrossRef]
97. Bean, M.; Sharp, J.S. Profiling alternative food system supporters: The personal and social basis of local and organic food support. *Renew. Agric. Food Syst.* **2011**, *26*, 243–254. [CrossRef]
98. Plender, C. "It's a Co-op in Spirit, That's What It Is": Fostering Collaboration, Collectivity, and Egalitarianism in Food Cooperatives. *Krit. Etnografi Swed. J. Anthropol.* **2022**, *5*, 77–92. [CrossRef]
99. Yiridoe, E.K.; Bonti-Ankomah, S.; Martin, R.C. Comparison of consumer perceptions and preference toward organic versus conventionally produced foods: A review and update of the literature. *Renew. Agric. Food Syst.* **2005**, *20*, 193–205. [CrossRef]
100. Eisinger-Watzl, M.; Wittig, F.; Heuer, T.; Hoffmann, I. Customers Purchasing Organic Food—Do They Live Healthier? Results of the German National Nutrition Survey II. *Eur. J. Nutr. Food Saf.* **2015**, *5*, 59–71. [CrossRef]
101. Smith, T.A.; Huang, C.L.; Lin, B.-H. Does Price or Income Affect Organic Choice? Analysis of U.S. Fresh Produce Users. *J. Agric. Appl. Econ.* **2009**, *41*, 731–744. [CrossRef]
102. Fu, L.; Sun, Z.; Zha, L.; Liu, F.; He, L.; Sun, X.; Jing, X. Environmental awareness and pro-environmental behavior within China's road freight transportation industry: Moderating role of perceived policy effectiveness. *J. Clean. Prod.* **2020**, *252*, 119796. [CrossRef]
103. García-Salirrosas, E.E.; Escobar-Farfán, M.; Gómez-Bayona, L.; Moreno-López, G.; Valencia-Arias, A.; Gallardo-Canales, R. Influence of environmental awareness on the willingness to pay for green products: An analysis under the application of the theory of planned behavior in the Peruvian market. *Front. Psychol.* **2024**, *14*, 1282383. [CrossRef] [PubMed]
104. Bouman, T.; Steg, L.; Perlaviciute, G. From values to climate action. *Curr. Opin. Psychol.* **2021**, *42*, 102–107. [CrossRef]

urban science

MDPI

Article

Enhancing Citizen Participation in Citizen-Centered Smart Cities: Insights from Two European Case Studies

Idoia Landa Oregi [1,*], Silvia Urra-Uriarte [2,3], Itsaso Gonzalez Ochoantesana [1], Maite Anaya Rodríguez [1] and Patricia Molina-Costa [2]

[1] Faculty of Engineering, Mondragon Unibertsitatea, Loramendi 4, 20500 Mondragon, Spain; igonzalez@mondragon.edu (I.G.O.); manaya@mondragon.edu (M.A.R.)

[2] TECNALIA, Basque Research and Technology Alliance (BRTA), Astondo Bidea, Edificio 700, 48160 Derio, Spain; silvia.urra@tecnalia.com (S.U.-U.); patricia.molina@tecnalia.com (P.M.-C.)

[3] Department of Sociology and Social Work, Faculty of Social Sciences and Communication, University of the Basque Country (UPV/EHU), 48940 Leioa, Spain

* Correspondence: ilanda@mondragon.edu

Abstract: Citizen participation plays a critical role in the transformation towards citizen-centered smart cities, ensuring resilience, inclusivity, and responsiveness to community needs. Smart cities, while often associated with technological infrastructures and digital tools, also adopt a human-cepntered perspective that emphasizes the social and participatory dimensions of smart urban development. Engaging residents in these initiatives not only facilitates the acquisition of valuable insights but also strengthens the foundation for equitable urban development. However, the participatory process often encounters significant barriers that hinder its effectiveness, posing challenges to the creation of truly inclusive and citizen-centered smart cities. This paper analyzes the participatory processes and outcomes of two case studies, URBANAGE and drOp, both of which follow a Human-Centered Design approach and have implemented targeted actions to address participation challenges. This article explains the methodologies and processes followed in these projects and identifies key lessons learnt from their experiences and examining the impact of participatory processes on project outcomes. Lastly, it proposes practical guidelines to enhance the effectiveness of citizen involvement in future smart city initiatives. Despite their focus on different citizen groups and objectives, both case studies faced similar obstacles in fostering meaningful participation and awareness.

Keywords: human-centered design; participation; engagement; smart cities; co-creation; citizen

1. Introduction

Definitions of smart cities in scientific literature often focus on the role of information and communication technologies (ICTs). However, this heavy reliance on technology brings about the challenge of the digital divide, as it assumes that smart city residents possess a high level of technological literacy [1]. While smart cities are frequently associated with digital technologies, such as the collection of sensor data [2], their "smart" attributes also include broader concepts like awareness and self-sufficiency [3]. Consequently, a more human-centered perspective on smart cities is gaining traction [4], one that highlights the social dimensions of urban life and prioritizes the role of citizens at the core of smart city development [5]. This creates a more responsive city, complementing technological aspects with the city's capacity to listen, adapt, and co-evolve with its citizens through continuous feedback loops, participatory processes, and inclusive decision-making [6].

According to a perspective outlined in Cities and Citizens in 2033 [7], an intelligent city can be described as a smart ecosystem where individual intelligence extends beyond personal boundaries, permeating the entire urban community to enhance overall quality of life. This definition emphasizes the role of the community, not merely as a large group of service users and a source of data crucial to technological advancements, but as empowered individuals actively participating in the co-creation of the city they envision and require [8].

Citizen-centered cities are urban environments designed to prioritize the needs, aspirations, and well-being of their inhabitants, placing citizens at the core of decision-making and development processes [5]. Focusing on social well-being is a fundamental goal of citizen-centered cities, which aim to improve quality of life, well-being, and satisfaction in urban settings by designing spaces and solutions both for and with the people who live in or pass through them [9]. The creation of citizen-centered cities can be facilitated through participatory initiatives that promote active citizen participation. These initiatives provide significant benefits for individuals, communities, and authorities, such as adopting multi-directional problem-solving approaches, fostering community empowerment, strengthening social cohesion, building resilient communities, raising awareness, increasing accountability, encouraging inclusivity and diversity, and fostering innovative ideas (e.g., [5,10]) since they involve citizens all along the initiatives.

These cities are based on principles such as inclusivity, ensuring access to resources and opportunities for all residents regardless of background; sustainability, balancing economic growth with environmental stewardship to support long-term resilience, participatory governance, involving citizens in shaping policies and urban planning through co-creation and dialogue, and Human-Centered Design (HCD), making them adaptable to diverse needs of the community. By integrating these principles, citizen-centered cities strive to empower communities, build trust, and create vibrant, livable spaces that reflect the collective vision of their inhabitants.

However, implementing citizen participation initiatives is not without challenges. These processes often encounter internal and external barriers that can hinder their effectiveness. The main participation barriers identified in the literature include ensuring representativeness, addressing expertise gaps, mitigating political interference, managing power dynamics, overcoming time constraints, dealing with limited resources, and effectively leveraging technology [11–14]. These barriers often limit the success of a participatory process and while each of these barriers presents unique challenges, understanding them individually provides greater insight into how they limit participation and how they might be addressed. Representativeness is a challenge, as ensuring diverse and informed participation that reflects the entire community is difficult [13,15,16]. The expertise gap limits citizen contributions, as many lack the technical knowledge required for urban planning [12]. Political interference and a lack of systematic frameworks undermine genuine engagement and the collection of citizen input [16]. Power structures and institutional complexities create mistrust, reduce transparency, and hinder participation [10,16]. Time constraints and competing commitments make it hard for residents to engage actively [15]. Limited resources exacerbate disparities, with disadvantaged communities struggling to participate effectively [15]. Finally, a technology-first mindset prioritizes existing solutions over citizen-driven approaches, complicating data collection and integration [11,15].

Given the multifaceted nature of participation barriers, analyzing and evaluating these processes is essential for understanding their effectiveness. This analysis provides a critical feedback loop for policymakers, project designers, and urban planners, helping them refine participation frameworks to overcome these barriers. By examining both the processes and their outcomes, valuable insights can be gained to improve future participation initiatives and better align them with the needs and aspirations of communities. In this context, the study aims to explore two case studies that have tried to overcome the barriers of citizen participation through an HCD approach, by introducing how HCD can effectively address these barriers, offering a framework to foster greater citizen engagement and contribute to the creation of citizen-centered smart cities.

HCD provides an approach where the user, or in this case the citizen, becomes the central aspect of the process and its principal goal is to develop solutions that cater to their needs [17]. It is founded by five main principles [18]: understanding of people and environments, involvement of people through the process, user-centered evaluation, iteration, and multi-disciplinary skills. Understanding of people and environments focuses on empathizing and comprehending citizens' behaviors, needs, and contexts to ensure solutions are meaningful and relevant. The involvement of people through the process, fostered by collaborative and co-creation methodologies, emphasizes active citizen participation at every stage of design and decision-making. User-centered evaluation prioritizes iterative testing and feedback from citizens, ensuring that the solutions align closely with their needs. Iteration underlines the importance of refining solutions through repeated cycles of testing, feedback, and improvement, while respecting the timelines and resources available. Lastly, multi-disciplinary skills bring together diverse expertise and cross-domain interactions to address complex challenges from diverse perspectives and create comprehensive, citizen-centered solutions. By following these five main principles, every process creates solutions tailored to the community and their real needs, while also enabling the overcoming of barriers that hinder citizen participation [17].

Regarding participation barriers, the HCD approach's focus on inclusivity ensures that representativeness is prioritized, using methods to engage diverse community members and amplify the voices of underrepresented groups. Through its emphasis on empathy and co-creation, HCD bridges expertise gaps by enabling non-technical participants to contribute meaningfully, often translating complex concepts into accessible formats. The iterative and collaborative nature of HCD mitigates the effects of political interference and power imbalances by fostering transparency, trust, and shared ownership of the process. Additionally, HCD accommodates time and resource constraints by tailoring engagement methods to fit the realities of participants' lives, ensuring flexible and adaptable processes. Unlike a technology-first approach, HCD integrates technology as a tool rather than the driver, enabling solutions to emerge from citizen-driven insights and ensuring these tools support rather than hinder participation.

Considering this context, the primary objectives of this research are as follows:

- Objective 1: explore how HCD applies specifically to citizen participation in different smart city contexts.
- Objective 2: examine two case studies to examine the practical outcomes of such an application.

2. Materials and Methods

This study focuses on a qualitative perspective that includes the conduct of a descriptive–analytical method to collect and analyze data from two case studies [19] financed by Horizon Europe: URBANAGE and drOp. These two processes aim to regenerate neighborhoods by improving the quality of life of their citizens. Central to these case studies is a participatory approach, where citizens are not only beneficiaries but also active stakeholders in the regeneration process. Both processes emphasize co-creation among stakeholders, ensuring that solutions are developed collaboratively. The study examines how these case studies apply an HCD approach, examining the methodologies used, the challenges faced, and the outcomes achieved. Each case was independently examined and analyzed to gain a comprehensive understanding of the participatory processes involved. The methodological approach facilitated a detailed and exhaustive description of the cases, providing insight into the context and highlighting the particular characteristics of each case. Such an approach proved valuable for identifying challenges common to both phenomena and for assessing the applicability of this methodology across different cases.

2.1. Methodological Process

The methodological process followed in this study was structured in a sequence of four steps, as shown in Figure 1. It began with the definition of the study phenomena, establishing the thematic scope and research questions for both cases. This was followed by a detailed description of the two case studies, URBANAGE and drOp, focusing on their goals, implementation strategies, and outcomes. The two case studies were purposively selected for their citizen-centered approach to smart cities through a shared HCD framework, applied in contrasting contexts: one focusing on a digital tool for inclusive urban planning, the other on a methodology for renovating social neighborhoods, allowing for analysis of the framework's adaptability, scalability, and conceptual robustness. The results were then analyzed to identify commonalities and differences, extracting meaningful lessons from both cases. Finally, the findings were synthesized to draw broader conclusions, assess the methodology's validity, and propose directions for future research.

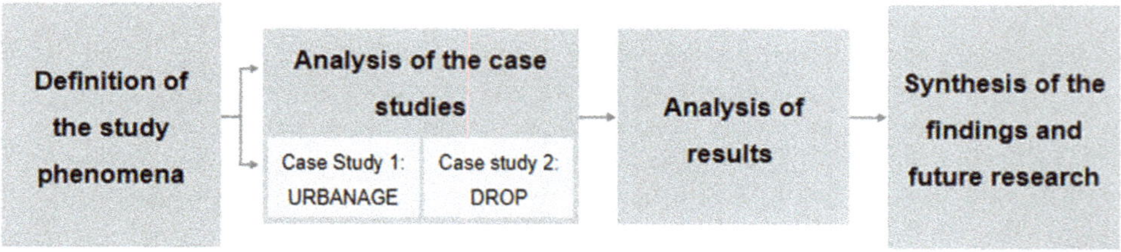

Figure 1. Methodological approach of the study.

2.2. Sample of the Study

In both projects, the sample of participants considered for analysis includes citizens who were part of the core working group, as well as civil servants from the respective municipal governments. Regarding the working groups of citizens, Figure 2 presents the demographic characteristics of each group.

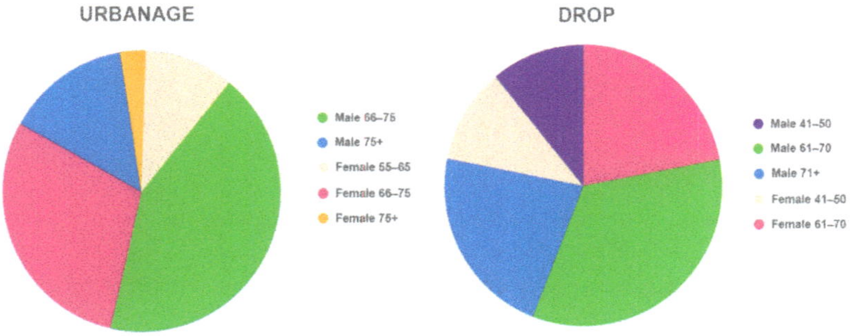

Figure 2. Citizen sample of both case studies.

2.3. Data Collection Methods

Understanding complex social phenomena requires both contextual depth and the voices of those directly involved. This study employs a qualitative methodological approach that combines three primary methods for data collection: a documental analysis, participatory observation and semi-structured interviews.

- Documental analysis: The documental analysis offers a comprehensive review of the literature, relevant reports, policy documents, and other written materials relevant to the cases under examination [20]. This method allows for the identification of key themes, and frameworks that shape the participatory processes under study. In this study, documental analysis was employed to examine the available documentation related to both processes. This approach allowed for a systematic and in-depth exploration of existing records, providing insights into the structure, development, and outcomes of each process.
- Participatory observation: Participatory observation is a method where the research team actively engages with the participants while simultaneously observing their interactions and behavior [21]. In this case, this method is used in the participatory workshops held in both projects to interact with and better understand participants and their demands.
- Semi-structured interviews: Semi-structured interviews were conducted with a range of key stakeholders, including practitioners, decision-makers, and community representatives. This approach was chosen to elicit in-depth, nuanced accounts that reflect diverse perspectives and firsthand insights [22]. Specifically, the interviews in both projects were conducted with both citizens and civil servants with the aim of evaluating their experience in the participatory process and its outcomes.

Together, these methods enable a rich and multidimensional understanding of the participatory mechanisms and their implications in practice [23]. This provides a robust foundation for assessing barriers to participation and strategies for enhancing citizen engagement in participatory initiatives.

2.4. Data Analysis

The collected data were analyzed using a thematic analysis approach, a widely used method in qualitative research that facilitates the identification, organization, and interpretation of patterns of meaning across a dataset [24]. This process entailed a systematic coding of qualitative data derived from the documentary sources, observation data and the interview transcripts to identify key themes and patterns related to the participatory processes. Particular attention was given to comparing and contrasting the two selected cases, with the aim of uncovering not only shared challenges and enabling factors but also case-specific dynamics that reflect contextual particularities. Through this comparative lens, the analysis sought to identify common barriers, emerging best practices, and innovative or unique approaches embedded in each participatory initiative. To enhance the credibility and rigor of the findings, triangulation was employed, cross validating the findings from documentary analysis, observation and interviews. This methodological strategy contributed to a more nuanced and trustworthy account of the participatory processes, grounded in both textual evidence and stakeholder perspectives.

3. Results

This section describes both case studies, highlighting the HCD process as key in overcoming participation barriers, outlining the actions taken in both of them as well as the results obtained.

3.1. Case Study Overview: URBANAGE & drOp

Both analyzed case studies employ a shared approach, prioritizing the involvement of their target groups at the core of the co-creation process. This method enables the effective allocation of resources, positioning the needs and concerns of the target audience at the forefront of the decision-making process.

URBANAGE aims to empower urban planners and policymakers to leverage innovative technologies in order to make more inclusive and data-driven decisions. This initiative seeks to cultivate the development of age-friendly cities by introducing a co-created decision-support ecosystem, which brings together key stakeholders, including public officials and end-users, particularly older adults. Through this collaborative process, URBANAGE has developed specialized tools rooted in cutting-edge technologies, tailored to the needs of Santander City in Spain.

Two innovative tools have been co-created and implemented in Santander as a result of the URBANAGE project. The first tool is an age-friendly route planner, specifically designed to cater to the needs of older adults. The second tool is a simulation platform for long-term urban planning, intended for civil servants. These tools exemplify the project's commitment to fostering inclusive and responsive urban planning practices.

The second case study discussed in this paper is drOp. The primary objective of drOp is to create an Integrated Renovation Methodology (IRM) designed to convert social housing districts into inclusive, smart neighborhoods. To accomplish this, the project adopts a human-centered approach and integrates advanced technologies to foster economic growth. This methodology is being implemented in a pilot case within the Santa Ana neighborhood of Ermua, Spain.

As an outcome of drOp, seven distinct initiatives have been developed in co-creation with citizens and are currently in the process of implementation. These initiatives are designed to contribute to the regeneration of the neighborhood through the enhancement of urban spaces, the strengthening of community ties, the promotion of economic development, and the advancement of social innovation, among other objectives.

This section gives an overview of both case studies (see Table 1), while the following sections explain each case in detail.

Table 1. Overview of the case studies.

	URBANAGE	**drOp**
General objective of the project	Assess the potential benefits, risks and impacts of implementing a long-term sustainable framework for data-driven decision-making in the field of urban planning for ageing well in cities	Design an integrated renovation methodology aimed at transforming neighborhoods through the combination of social innovation and local economic development
Duration of the project	February 2021–January 2024	October 2022–September 2025
Aim of the participatory process	Identify the needs and requirements of older people to use the city services and spaces and the challenges and the barriers civil servants find to reply to them	Identify the specific needs of the neighborhood and collaboratively co-create diverse solutions with its residents
Target audience	Older adults & civil servants	Entire neighborhood
Scale	City	Neighborhood
Geographical location	Santander	Santa Ana, Ermua
Results of the participatory process	The participatory process resulted in identifying the digital tools that could be useful for older adults in their daily lives and for civil servants to better plan age-friendly cities.	The participatory process resulted in the development and implementation of different initiatives

Both case studies follow an HCD approach. The main focus of the HCD approach is to engage users and stakeholders in the creation of solutions that address user needs while remaining practical and viable in the market [25]. This approach prioritizes designing products, services, spaces, or systems that genuinely respond to the preferences and needs of their target users, following four main stages (see Figure 3): understand, define, create and evaluate [17]. The process ultimately results in outcomes that are meaningful, effective, and feasible, aligning with user requirements. Each stage is divided into divergent and convergent sub-steps, where activities are guided by a human-centered perspective while accounting for real-world constraints such as time and resources [26].

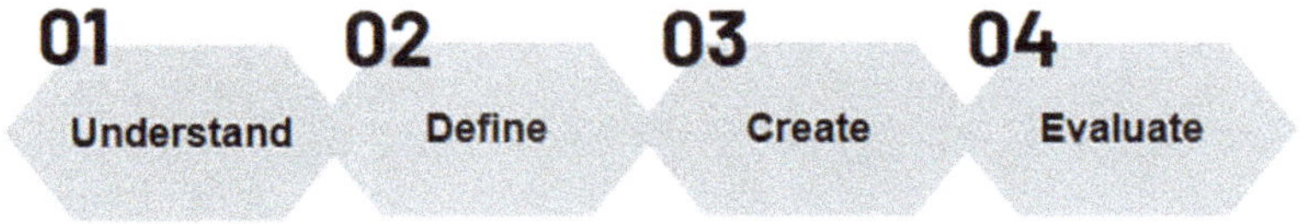

Figure 3. Phases of an HCD process.

Building on this process, the following sections examine each phase of the two case studies, detailing the steps undertaken and the key outcomes associated with each stage.

3.2. *Phase 1: Understand*

In the Understand stage, the emphasis lies in developing a grounded comprehension of the problem, the needs of the users, and the broader context in which the project unfolds. This involves careful exploration of stakeholders and communication strategies to ensure that the participatory process is inclusive, transparent, and meaningful from the outset. In the two case studies presented here, this phase was shaped by distinct but complementary approaches: in URBANAGE, it entailed identifying and mapping relevant stakeholders to support the design of age-friendly urban policies, while in drOp, it focused on establishing clear, accessible communication to facilitate residents' understanding and engagement. This section details the evaluation activities conducted during this phase in both cases and presents the main findings.

3.2.1. URBANAGE: Preparing the Participatory Process

This initial stage of URBANAGE laid the groundwork for subsequent focus group discussions and co-creation activities with end-users by establishing a comprehensive understanding of the relevant stakeholders for a project such as URBANAGE. It focused on identifying both those who can influence or contribute to the project and those whose needs and perspectives should be considered in the design and implementation of age-friendly urban policies.

URBANAGE targeted two main stakeholder groups: older adults and civil servants. To ensure inclusivity, older adult participants needed to reflect the diversity of ageing populations, considering factors such as age, gender, ability, digital literacy, socio-economic status, and, where applicable, race and ethnicity. For the civil servant group, representation across the domains outlined in the Global Age-Friendly Cities: A Guide was essential. This included professionals in urban planning, particularly those involved in outdoor environments, housing, and transport, as well as public servants in departments traditionally linked to older citizens, such as social services. Although the latter may not directly influence planning decisions, they provide essential insights into older adults' needs. Departments responsible for communication, citizen engagement, and information were also key, given their role in ensuring participatory and informed processes.

As a result, a stakeholder mapping was created. This stakeholder mapping process not only clarified the categories of actors to involve but also supported pilot sites in identifying the individuals and institutions most relevant to achieving URBANAGE's objectives. As an initial outcome, the mapping served as a strategic resource to guide inclusive engagement throughout the project's development.

3.2.2. drOp: Communicating the Participatory Process

This initial phase of drOp focused on ensuring effective and accessible communication with participants to support their meaningful involvement in the project. Recognizing that residents are experts in their lived experiences but may lack technical knowledge, the process prioritized clarity and inclusion. Planners and designers facilitated understanding by avoiding technical jargon and using diagrams, visuals, and illustrations to present the project's scope and potential outcomes in a comprehensible way.

To maintain transparency and engagement throughout the process, key decisions and updates were communicated through infographics distributed as printed pamphlets and displayed in the neighborhood office. These visual tools helped simplify complex content and foster a consistent flow of information with the community.

Additionally, AI-generated images depicting the neighborhood under various future scenarios—such as increased green spaces or the integration of smart technologies—supported residents in visualizing the implications of different planning decisions. By making the abstract tangible, these images enabled participants to better understand and contribute to shaping the project's direction.

As a result, the Understand phase effectively bridged the expertise gap between professionals and residents, enabling a more inclusive and informed participation process. Through accessible communication and visualization tools, participants were empowered to engage with the project from the outset, co-creating a shared vision for the future of their neighborhood.

3.3. Phase 2: Define

In the Define stage, the focus shifts to synthesizing the insights gathered during the initial phase in order to clearly frame the challenge and structure the participatory process. In the two case studies discussed here, this phase was approached through complementary strategies: in URBANAGE, it involved conducting focus groups to explore the barriers and motivations influencing older adults' civic participation, with particular attention to digital engagement; in drOp, it centered on the creation of a collaborative governance structure to support shared decision-making and sustained community involvement. This section describes the activities carried out in both contexts and presents the key findings emerging from this phase.

3.3.1. URBANAGE: Conducting Focus Groups

This second phase of URBANAGE focused on gathering diverse perspectives through focus group discussions held in Santander (see Figure 4). These sessions were designed to explore the needs, experiences, and attitudes of older adults, particularly regarding their engagement in civic activities and their interaction with digital technologies.

The main objective was to identify the motivations, challenges, and barriers that shape older adults' participation in public decision-making processes. Special attention was given to understanding how digital tools and gamification techniques could enhance their engagement, and which elements were perceived as most relevant and motivating in this context.

The process combined literature review, the development of a shared methodology and protocol, train-the-trainer workshops for local teams, and the execution and analysis of the focus groups. This ensured consistency across sites while allowing for the collection of locally grounded insights.

Figure 4. Overview of one of the focus groups [27].

As a result, the Define phase provided a nuanced understanding of the factors influencing older adults' civic engagement in different urban contexts. These insights are essential to tailoring participation strategies that are both inclusive and responsive to the needs and expectations of ageing populations, particularly in relation to digital inclusion and motivational approaches

3.3.2. drOp: Defining a Collaborative Structure

The second phase of drOp focused on establishing a collaborative framework to guide the participatory process. This framework, the Local Task Force (LTF), brought together community members, key stakeholders, the project team, and local authorities, structuring their involvement across three levels: a coordination structure, an executive commission, and an extended commission (see Figure 5). Each level represented different degrees of responsibility and engagement, ensuring balanced participation and shared decision-making.

Figure 5. Structure of the Local Task Force [28].

The LTF functioned as a local coalition dedicated to addressing neighborhood challenges through collective action. It provided a structured space for dialogue, promoted consensus-building, and acted as a mechanism for integrating bottom-up initiatives into formal planning processes.

As a result, the Define phase laid the institutional foundation for inclusive and transparent collaboration. By establishing a clear and participatory governance structure, it ensured that decision-making was informed by a wide range of perspectives, enhancing both the legitimacy and the effectiveness of the project.

3.4. *Phase 3: Create*

In the Create stage, the emphasis is placed on generating ideas and collaboratively developing potential solutions through co-creation sessions and iterative design processes. This phase foregrounds creativity, dialogue, and mutual learning to translate defined challenges into actionable outcomes. In the two case studies examined, this stage was shaped by distinct yet aligned practices: in URBANAGE, co-creation sessions facilitated collaboration between older adults and civil servants to define user requirements and develop practical tools tailored to age-friendly urban contexts; in drOp, the focus was on co-designing neighborhood projects with residents through flexible, context-sensitive sessions that encouraged open expression and collective prioritization. This section outlines the activities carried out during this phase and presents the main findings from each case.

3.4.1. URBANAGE: Holding Co-Creation Sessions

The third phase of URBANAGE centered on co-creation sessions designed to bring together older adults and civil servants in a collaborative environment to develop solutions tailored to the challenges identified in previous stages. These sessions supported the definition of user requirements, the refinement of use cases, and the development of practical tools such as data sources, visualizations, simulation models, and AI applications relevant to age-friendly urban environments.

The co-creation process unfolded in three sessions (see Figure 6). The first focused on gathering insights from older adults about their needs, challenges, and expectations in relation to accessible urban living. The second session engaged civil servants from pilot cities to assess the feasibility of the initial requirements, identify existing initiatives, and explore institutional capacities and constraints. The third session brought both groups together to prioritize user requirements, validate findings, and examine communication preferences and technical limitations.

Figure 6. Summary of the co-creation sessions in Santander [27].

As a result, the Create phase enabled a participatory and iterative design process that ensured solutions were both relevant to older citizens and feasible for local administrations. By fostering structured dialogue and negotiation, it reinforced shared ownership, improved the alignment between citizen needs and institutional capabilities, and laid the groundwork for inclusive and practical urban innovations.

3.4.2. drOp: Co-Creating the Neighborhood

The third phase of drOp focused on engaging residents and stakeholders in the design of neighborhood projects through co-creation sessions grounded in HCD principles. These sessions provided open and adaptable formats for dialogue, allowing participants to express their needs and aspirations freely (see Figure 7). The flexible design of the sessions ensured that they could be adjusted to participants' contexts, fostering genuine and sustained engagement.

Figure 7. Overview of some of the co-creation sessions [28].

Held within the neighborhood to guarantee accessibility, the sessions encouraged continuous resident involvement. Participants actively contributed to identifying, evaluating, and prioritizing the projects to be co-designed, ensuring that proposed initiatives reflected the everyday realities and desires of the community. In some sessions, digital tools were employed by facilitators to collect and manage data in real time. This approach enhanced efficiency, enabling residents to focus on content while reducing the need for extensive post-session processing.

As a result, the Create phase strengthened the participatory process by fostering meaningful collaboration between residents and project teams. It ensured that co-designed solutions were not only context-specific and inclusive but also grounded in local knowledge, reinforcing a sense of ownership and facilitating more effective implementation.

3.5. Phase 4: Evaluate

Finally, the Evaluate stage tests these solutions with users through usability testing, feedback loops, and iterative improvements, ensuring the designs are effective, feasible, and aligned with user needs before broader implementation. In URBANAGE, evaluation centered on user experience and impact assessment of co-created digital tools, with older adults and civil servants actively involved in a structured, multi-dimensional process. In drOp, the focus shifted toward assessing the participatory methodology as a foundational element of urban transformation, highlighting how citizens and civil servants perceived and experienced the process of co-creation. This section presents the evaluation activities conducted in both case studies and highlights the principal findings.

3.5.1. URBANAGE: Assessing the Outcome of the Project

The final phase of the URBANAGE project focused on evaluating the impact and relevance of the developed digital tools through a user-centered assessment approach. Aligned with the HCD principle of user-centered evaluation, this phase prioritized the active involvement of older adults and civil servants in validating project outcomes. By centering the lived experiences and expectations of these user groups, the evaluation process sought to ensure the solutions were both meaningful and applicable in real urban contexts. Through iterative feedback loops, collaborative validation mechanisms, and customized instruments for user input, the project aimed to enhance inclusivity, trust, and practical impact.

This evaluative process was integral to assessing the social dimension of two digital tools co-developed in Santander: an age-friendly route planner (see Figure 8) and a simulation tool for long-term urban planning (see Figure 9). While the technical dimension focused on the operability of these solutions, the social dimension explored their capacity to enhance public space engagement for older adults and decision-making for civil servants. The methodology was structured into three stages: baseline assessment, iterative testing, and final assessment; providing a systematic framework to track user perceptions and changes over time.

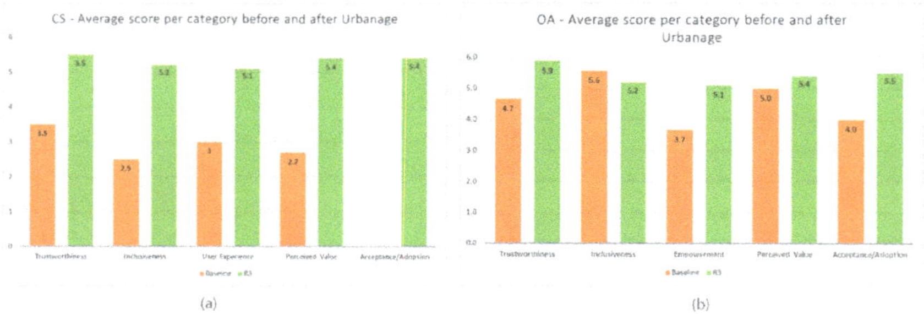

Figure 8. Comparison by category between the baseline and the final release of the age-friendly route planner, one of the digital tools developed by URBANAGE [27]; (**a**) civil servants; (**b**) older adults.

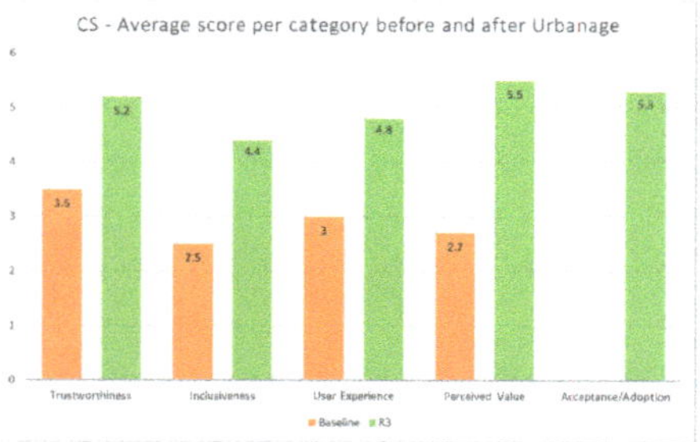

Figure 9. Comparison by category between the baseline and the final release of long-term urban planning tool, one of the digital tools developed by URBANAGE [27].

The evaluation criteria were drawn from theoretical models such as the Technology Acceptance Model and the Unified Theory of Acceptance and Use of Technology. Categories including Perceived Value, User Experience, Trustworthiness, Acceptance/Adoption, Inclusiveness, and Empowerment framed the assessment, ensuring a multidimensional understanding of user interaction with the tools. Data collection targeted both civil servants and older adults, employing surveys and guided workshops that accompanied each release of the tools.

The following figures reflect the change in the different categories of both older adults (OA) and civil servants (CS) experience after testing and using the urban digital tools developed through the URBANAGE project.

The results revealed significant improvements across most categories for both user groups, particularly in perceived value and trust. This underscores the positive influence of co-creation, with participants reporting a stronger sense of ownership and greater confidence in the tools' relevance and functionality. However, a marginal decline in the Inclusiveness category among older adults highlighted persistent challenges. Specifically, the digital format of the new tools did not align with the varied communication habits of some users, pointing to broader issues of digital accessibility and the need for context-sensitive solutions.

As a result, the evaluation stage confirmed the utility and acceptance of URBANAGE's digital tools while also underscoring the necessity of nuanced, inclusive design practices. More importantly, it revealed the added value of evaluating the participatory process itself—not merely the tools' outputs. The engagement and empowerment fostered through co-creation contributed directly to the quality and uptake of the final solutions. Thus, future initiatives would benefit from incorporating participatory process evaluation from the outset, enabling a deeper understanding of how stakeholder involvement influences outcomes and ensuring more robust, adaptable, and inclusive innovations in urban digital governance.

3.5.2. drOp: Assessing the Process

The evaluation phase of the drOp project was conceived as an integral component from the very outset, with the explicit goal of assessing not only the tools or outcomes but the participatory methodology itself. Building upon insights from precedent projects such as URBANAGE, drOp places particular emphasis on understanding the quality and effectiveness of its participatory strategies. Given that the project is still underway, the focus of the evaluation lies primarily in scrutinizing the engagement processes and participatory dynamics that underpin the transformation of the Santa Ana neighborhood in Ermua. This reflects a deliberate commitment to ensuring that participation is not merely instrumental but foundational to achieving inclusive and contextually grounded smart neighborhoods.

In the pilot case of Ermua, the evaluation centered on the participatory methodology employed throughout the co-creation process, rather than the final outcomes of the interventions. The methodology was designed to capture the perspectives and experiences of two principal stakeholder groups—citizens and civil servants—who were directly involved in the implementation and facilitation of the participatory process. To structure the evaluation, drOp adopted an analytical framework based on established theories in participation and social research, which allowed for a systematic exploration of three interrelated categories: Perceived Value, Acceptance, and Empowerment.

For civil servants, the evaluation focused on the perceived usefulness and ease of use of the participatory methodology (see Figure 10). Their input was gathered through targeted interviews aimed at understanding the practical aspects of its implementation and the kinds of support required to ensure effective application. The results revealed a high level of perceived usefulness, with moderate ease of use that improved significantly when facilitation support was available. This suggests that while the methodology was considered valuable for fostering citizen engagement, its successful deployment required structured guidance and capacity-building measures.

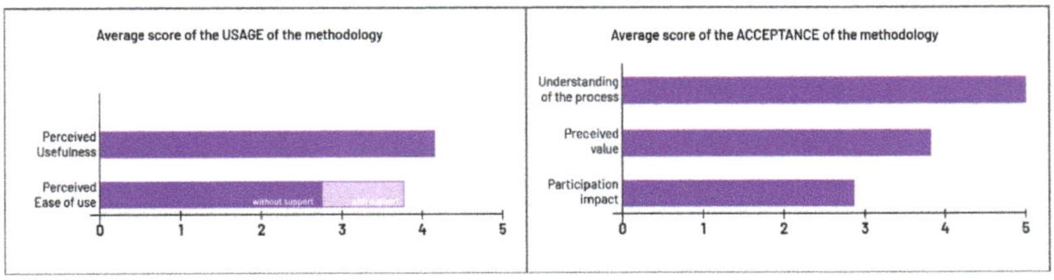

Figure 10. Average score of the assessment of the methodology developed in drOp [28].

Citizens were engaged through both surveys and interviews to explore their perceptions of the process and their evolving sense of empowerment. The assessment of Acceptance captured how participants understood the participatory process and how they perceived its value and potential impact. Participants reported a strong understanding of the process and high perceived value. However, the perceived impact of participation was more modest, not due to dissatisfaction with the results, but due to a shared perception that a broader engagement of the community would have led to greater transformation. This highlights a recurrent challenge in participatory design: translating individual satisfaction into collective impact through wider inclusion.

The following figures reflect the results in the different categories of both citizens and civil servants' experiences after being part of the participation process on the drOp project.

In terms of Empowerment, the evaluation documented a significant shift in the attitudes of citizens towards municipal-led initiatives (see Figure 11). At the beginning of the process, there was notable skepticism regarding institutional participation, despite strong community ties and a sense of belonging. Following their involvement in the co-creation activities, citizens demonstrated a more positive view of participatory governance and expressed a clear willingness to engage in similar processes in the future. This evolution illustrates how well-structured participatory approaches can serve as catalysts for reshaping perceptions and fostering greater civic trust.

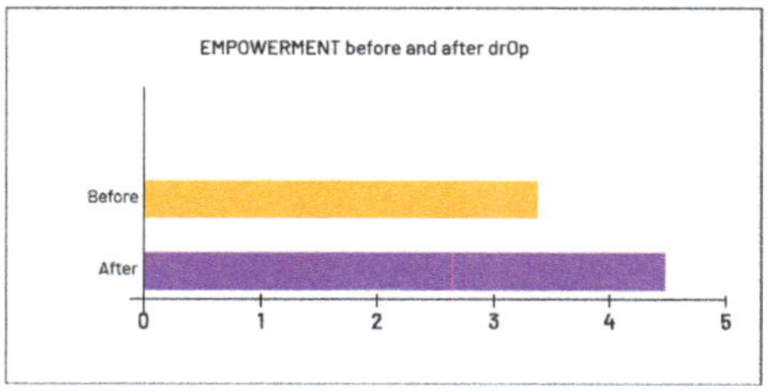

Figure 11. Average score of the empowerment of citizens before and after drOp [28].

The evaluation of the drOp methodology underscores the multifaceted value of participatory approaches in urban innovation. While civil servants recognized the methodology as a useful tool, and citizens appreciated its relevance and outcomes, the process also illuminated areas for refinement, particularly the need to broaden and diversify participation. Moreover, by foregrounding the participatory process as an object of evaluation, drOp contributes to a more nuanced understanding of the mechanisms that underpin meaningful citizen engagement. As such, this evaluative approach provides critical insights for future projects, reinforcing the need to embed participatory process assessment from the beginning to ensure adaptive, inclusive, and context-sensitive urban transformation.

4. Discussion

The discussion section delves into the application of an HCD approach in two distinct case studies: URBANAGE and drOp. Both projects are framed within the Horizon Europe funding framework, yet each represents a unique aspect of urban transformation, ranging from the creation of age-friendly cities to the renovation of social housing neighborhoods. While both initiatives share a common commitment to inclusivity, collaboration, and user-centered innovation, they each engage with different challenges and solutions within the broader context of urban development.

4.1. HCD for Age-Friendly Cities: Insights from URBANAGE

The URBANAGE project exemplifies how an HCD approach can enhance urban planning processes to create age-friendly cities. Rather than simply deploying disruptive technologies, the project integrates the principles of HCD to place the needs, challenges, and aspirations of older adults and public servants at the forefront of decision-making. By fostering an inclusive and participatory framework, URBANAGE ensures that technological solutions are grounded in the lived experiences and practical needs of the community, leading to more effective and sustainable urban transformations.

The process begins with the careful preparation of the participatory framework, which lays the foundation for meaningful engagement. Stakeholder mapping plays a critical role in identifying diverse participants, including older adults from various demographic and social backgrounds, as well as civil servants representing key domains such as urban planning, social services, and citizen engagement. This preparatory phase aligns with the

HCD principle of understanding users and their environment, ensuring that all relevant voices are included and their unique needs considered.

Focus groups represent the next stage of the process, providing an opportunity to explore the motivations, barriers, and perceptions of older adults regarding their participation in urban planning. These sessions delve into how gamification techniques and digital tools can enhance engagement, while also identifying factors that encourage or hinder involvement. The iterative design of the focus groups, including literature reviews, tailored protocols, and data analysis, reflects the HCD principles of fostering empathy and collaboration by deeply understanding the community's perspectives.

The co-creation sessions serve as the cornerstone of the URBANAGE methodology, enabling iterative dialogue and collaboration between older adults, civil servants, and project teams. Through multiple sessions, the project identifies user requirements, validates feasibility, and prioritizes solutions. The first session (CC1) focuses on older adults' needs and challenges, while the second session (CC2) gathers insights from civil servants on technical constraints and existing initiatives. The final session (CC3) brings these groups together, promoting mutual understanding, negotiation, and the refinement of user requirements. This structured yet flexible approach demonstrates the HCD principle of iterative problem-solving, ensuring that solutions are co-developed and validated by end-users.

URBANAGE highlights the value of HCD in integrating diverse perspectives and fostering a shared sense of ownership over urban planning initiatives. By combining participatory practices with advanced technologies like AI and simulation models, the project creates a decision-support ecosystem that is not only innovative but also deeply aligned with the needs of its stakeholders. This methodology underscores the transformative potential of HCD in driving inclusive, evidence-based urban planning for age-friendly cities.

4.2. HCD for Inclusive and Smart Neighbourhoods: Insights from drOp

drOp demonstrates the transformative potential of employing an HCD approach in urban renovation initiatives, where the focus is not solely on technological advancements but on creating resilient, inclusive, and adaptive neighborhoods. In this context, technology becomes an enabler of community-driven transformation, facilitating communication, collaboration, and informed decision-making, rather than dictating the direction of change. This aligns with the evolving notion of smart cities, where the emphasis shifts from technology-centric urbanization to a more people-centric approach that prioritizes the needs, aspirations, and agency of residents [5,29,30].

Through the integration of HCD principles, drOp illustrates how advanced technologies can be effectively embedded into urban renovation initiatives while respecting the lived experiences of the community. Smart technologies such as data collection tools, interactive digital platforms, and AI-driven simulations are used not to impose predetermined solutions but to foster dialogue and ensure that technological interventions are grounded in the real-world needs of the citizens [31]. For example, AI-generated models help residents visualize and understand potential changes to their environment, empowering them to participate actively in the decision-making process. These technologies are not the end goal but rather tools that support inclusive governance and co-creation, ensuring that the transformation of urban spaces reflects the values and priorities of the people who inhabit them.

Next, the establishment of an LTF underscores the importance of collaborative governance. By structuring decision-making processes across various levels and stakeholder groups, the project ensures that residents, local authorities, and experts work collectively toward shared goals. This approach aligns with the HCD principles of fostering multidisciplinary collaboration and empowering users, as residents are not only consulted but actively involved in shaping the project's direction. This decentralization of power is a key aspect of HCD, as it ensures that the solutions developed are deeply rooted in the local context and genuinely serve the people that are designed for [32]. The collaboration of diverse groups also fosters a culture of mutual respect and trust, further supporting the empowerment of users and the co-creation of meaningful, equitable solutions [26].

Finally, the co-creation sessions encapsulate the essence of HCD, offering open-ended, adaptable spaces for dialogue and collaboration. These sessions prioritize inclusivity and accessibility, ensuring that all voices are heard and valued. By employing digital tools to streamline data collection and analysis, the project demonstrates a commitment to efficiency without compromising the participatory ethos. Residents are empowered to evaluate and prioritize initiatives, ensuring that the outcomes reflect their needs and aspirations.

In essence, the drOp project exemplifies how HCD principles can be systematically embedded into smart city development, ensuring that technological advancements and social innovation are driven by the priorities of the community. This approach not only enhances the relevance and sustainability of the outcomes but also fosters a sense of ownership and agency among residents, paving the way for more inclusive and resilient urban environments.

4.3. Contrasting Approaches to HCD: Comparative Analysis of Both Case Studies

Both URBANAGE and drOp exemplify the transformative potential of HCD in fostering inclusive urban development, yet they approach their respective contexts with distinct focuses. URBANAGE centers its efforts on integrating advanced technologies into urban planning for age-friendly cities, emphasizing the importance of evidence-based decision-making rooted in the lived experiences of older adults and civil servants. In contrast, drOp is primarily concerned with renovating social housing districts into inclusive smart neighborhoods, placing a stronger emphasis on the participatory process itself as the project is still ongoing.

URBANAGE establishes a robust participatory framework through detailed stakeholder mapping, ensuring diverse representation from older adults and civil servants across relevant domains. It further explores motivations and barriers to engagement through focus groups, which delve into how digital tools and gamification can enhance participation. Co-creation sessions serve as the project's cornerstone, iteratively refining solutions based on user feedback and facilitating collaboration between stakeholders. This structured approach underscores URBANAGE's commitment to using HCD principles to co-develop innovative, evidence-based planning tools that reflect the community's needs and aspirations.

Conversely, drOp begins with an emphasis on clear communication to bridge knowledge gaps and foster transparency among residents. The use of visual aids, such as AI-generated images of potential neighborhood scenarios, allows participants to envision project outcomes, aligning with the HCD principle of understanding users and their environment. The establishment of an LTF ensures collaborative governance, empowering residents to actively participate in decision-making processes alongside local authorities and experts. Its co-creation sessions, designed for inclusivity and accessibility, focus on evaluating and prioritizing initiatives while employing digital tools to streamline data management. These mechanisms reflect drOp's dedication to refining the participatory process itself and fostering a sense of ownership among residents.

In summary, while both projects leverage HCD to ensure inclusivity and user-centered innovation, URBANAGE prioritizes integrating advanced technologies into urban planning outcomes, and drOp focuses on the participatory processes underpinning urban renovation. Together, they illustrate how HCD can be adapted to address diverse challenges in urban development, ensuring that technological advancements and social innovation are deeply rooted in the needs and aspirations of the community.

Despite their valuable contributions, both URBANAGE and drOp face certain limitations that may affect the broader applicability of their findings. In the case of URBANAGE, while the focus on evidence-based decision-making is commendable, the heavy reliance on technological solutions may not be universally adaptable, particularly in contexts where digital literacy is low or access to technology is limited. Furthermore, the ongoing nature of drOp means that its results are still in flux, and there is insufficient long-term data to fully evaluate the sustainability and success of its participatory frameworks. In practice, however, the insights gained from both projects could be applied by urban planners and policymakers seeking to integrate HCD into city development by ensuring that technological interventions are complemented with strong, inclusive participatory processes.

5. Conclusions

Although the methodologies of the two case studies differ, they both adhere to the core principles of Human-Centered Design (HCD). Each approach prioritizes the individuals affected by the issue, focusing on understanding their needs from the case studies inception and involving residents throughout the entire process. This approach ensures that the process is more attuned to the participants, enhancing the participatory experience and creating more customized solutions to the city's current challenges.

However, despite these efforts, several barriers to effective citizen participation remain. As identified in the literature, key challenges include ensuring representativeness, addressing expertise gaps, mitigating political interference, managing power dynamics, overcoming time constraints, dealing with limited resources, and effectively leveraging technology. While there is still considerable progress needed to fully overcome these obstacles, this paper outlines the key lessons learned from the development and evaluation of the two participatory processes. It also offers several guidelines for practitioners aiming to design genuinely citizen-centered smart cities that tackle these participation barriers head-on.

- **Ensuring Representativeness and Addressing Expertise Gaps.**

Both case studies adhere to the core principles of Human-Centered Design (HCD), prioritizing the individuals affected by the issue and involving residents throughout the entire process. This approach ensures that the process is more attuned to the participants, enhancing the participatory experience and creating more customized solutions to the city's current challenges. The URBANAGE evaluation highlighted that proactive engagement fosters trust and increases the likelihood of widespread adoption and perceived value. However, it also revealed a slight decline in inclusiveness among older adults due to the digital nature of the new tool, emphasizing the need to consider personal circumstances and context over chronological age. Providing training and educational resources can empower citizens with the knowledge and skills needed to participate effectively, further bridging the expertise gap.

- **Mitigating Political Interference and Managing Power Dynamics.**

Establishing a framework for sustained and multi-level engagement is crucial. This framework should be consistent and transparent, offering clear support and adequate resources. By co-creating a clear structure among all interested parties, defining the roles of each stakeholder, and outlining the decision-making process, the barriers related to power structures and political interference can be mitigated. The drOp evaluation showed that civil servants found the methodology highly useful, with ease of use improving when support was provided. Regular updates and assessment panels for discussion can also help maintain transparency and trust, reducing the influence of political interference and power imbalances.

- **Overcoming Time Constraints and Dealing with Limited Resources.**

To address time constraints and limited resources, it is essential to offer engagement activities that cater to the needs of the entire community. Creating a variety of participatory choices and activities allows citizens to contribute at different commitment levels. By consolidating discussions into fewer gatherings and adapting activities to the participants, the process becomes more efficient and practical, making better use of time and resources. The drOp evaluation indicated that while citizens valued the process and its outcomes, broader participation would have significantly enhanced the impact. Leveraging existing community spaces and resources can help minimize costs and logistical challenges, ensuring that participation is accessible to all.

- **Effectively Leveraging Technology.**

Technology should be an enabler of the process rather than the actual outcome. Integrating new technologies in citizen engagement requires a thoughtful approach, especially for individuals who are less digitally savvy. Clear communication about the added value of technology and its practical benefits can help build trust and acceptance among participants. The URBANAGE evaluation underscored the importance of addressing disparities in access to and use of digital technology. A dual-track policy that includes both digital and non-digital alternatives ensures inclusivity, preventing the exclusion of those who are unwilling or unable to adopt new technological tools. Providing technical support and training can also help bridge the digital divide, ensuring that all participants can engage effectively.

- **Transparency and Communication.**

Being transparent and clearly communicating the real impact of citizens' decisions is vital. A communication campaign throughout the process bolsters motivation and a sense of usefulness among participants. Clear, continuous communication in non-technical language ensures that the community feels included and valued. The drOp evaluation highlighted that citizens' perceptions of municipal-led initiatives evolved positively, with increased willingness to participate in future processes. Leaving room for feedback with every communication allows residents to share their input, increasing representativeness and reducing mistrust in the decision-making organs. Celebrating successes and acknowledging contributions can help maintain engagement and build a sense of community ownership over the process.

By addressing these barriers, practitioners can design genuinely citizen-centered smart cities that effectively tackle the obstacles to successful citizen participation. This holistic approach not only enhances the participatory process but also fosters a more inclusive, empowered, and resilient community.

Author Contributions: Conceptualization I.L.O. and S.U.-U.; methodology, I.L.O., I.G.O. and S.U.-U.; supervision I.G.O.; investigation, I.L.O., I.G.O., S.U.-U. and P.M.-C.; writing—original draft preparation, I.L.O. and S.U.-U.; writing—review and editing, I.L.O., I.G.O., S.U.-U., P.M.-C. and M.A.R. All authors have read and agreed to the published version of the manuscript.

Funding: This research was supported by funding from the URBANAGE project from the European Union's Horizon 2020 research and innovation programme under grant agreement No. 101004590 and the drOp project from the European Union's Horizon Europe research and innovation program under grant agreement No. 101080025.

Data Availability Statement: In the case of the URBANAGE project, the data supporting this study's findings are openly available in CORDIS—EU research results in the Impact Assessment report. In the case of the drOp project the datasets presented in this article are not readily available because they are part of an ongoing study. Requests to access the datasets should be directed to the authors.

Acknowledgments: We would like to thank all the participants involved in both case studies for their valuable contributions, as well as the members of the consortiums of both projects for their collaboration and support throughout the research process.

Conflicts of Interest: The authors declare no conflicts of interest. The funders had no role in the design of the study; in the collection, analyses, or interpretation of data; in the writing of the manuscript; or in the decision to publish the results.

Abbreviations

The following abbreviations are used in this manuscript:

HCD	Human-Centered Design
LTF	Local Task Force
CC	Co-Creation

References

1. Shin, S.Y.; Kim, D.; Chun, S.A. Digital Divide in Advanced Smart City Innovations. *Sustainability* **2021**, *13*, 4076. [CrossRef]
2. Mora, H.; Gilart-Iglesias, V.; Hoyo, R.P.-D.; Andújar-Montoya, M.D. A Comprehensive System for Monitoring Urban Accessibility in Smart Cities. *Sensors* **2017**, *17*, 1834. [CrossRef] [PubMed]
3. Simonofski, A.; Vallé, T.; Serral, E.; Wautelet, Y. Investigating context factors in citizen participation strategies: A comparative analysis of Swedish and Belgian smart cities. *Int. J. Inf. Manag.* **2021**, *56*, 102011. [CrossRef]
4. Lara, A.P.; Da Costa, E.M.; Furlani, T.Z.; Yigitcanlar, T. Smartness that matters: Towards a comprehensive and human-centred characterisation of smart cities. *J. Open Innov. Technol. Mark. Complex.* **2016**, *2*, 1–13. [CrossRef]
5. Lim, S.; Malek, J.A.; Hussain, M.Y.; Tahir, Z. Citizen participation in building citizen-centric smart cities. *Malays. J. Soc. Space* **2018**, *14*, 42–53. [CrossRef]
6. Sádaba, J.; Alonso, Y.; Latasa, I.; Luzarraga, A. Towards Resilient and Inclusive Cities: A Framework for Sustainable Street-Level Urban Design. *Urban Sci.* **2024**, *8*, 264. [CrossRef]
7. Jiménez, J. Ciudades y Ciudadanos en 2033. La transformación Urbana de España. Available online: https://www.pwc.es/es/publicaciones/espana-2033/assets/ciudades-y-ciudadanos-en-2033.pdf (accessed on 10 April 2025).
8. Sánchez-Teba, E.M.; Bermúdez-González, G.J. Are Smart-City Projects Citizen-Centered? *Soc. Sci.* **2019**, *8*, 309. [CrossRef]
9. International Guidelines on People-Centred Smart Cities | UN-Habitat. Available online: https://unhabitat.org/international-guidelines-on-people-centred-smart-cities (accessed on 10 April 2025).
10. Parekh, R.; Maleku, A.; Fields, N.; Adorno, G.; Schuman, D.; Felderhoff, B. Pathways to age-friendly communities in diverse urban neighborhoods: Do social capital and social cohesion matter? *J. Gerontol. Soc. Work.* **2018**, *61*, 492–512. [CrossRef]
11. Cao, H.; Kang, C.I. A citizen participation model for co-creation of public value in a smart city. *J. Urban Aff.* **2022**, *46*, 905–924. [CrossRef]
12. Wijnhoven, F.; Ehrenhard, M.; Kuhn, J. Open government objectives and participation motivations. *Gov. Inf. Q.* **2015**, *32*, 30–42. [CrossRef]
13. Thoneick, R. Integrating Online and Onsite Participation in Urban Planning: Assessment of a Digital Participation System. *Int. J. E-Plan. Res.* **2021**, *10*, 1–20. [CrossRef]
14. Kiss, B.; Sekulova, F.; Hörschelmann, K.; Salk, C.F.; Takahashi, W.; Wamsler, C. Citizen participation in the governance of nature-based solutions. *Environ. Policy Gov.* **2022**, *32*, 247–272. [CrossRef]
15. Maas, F.; Wolf, S.; Hohm, A.; Hurtienne, J. Citizen Needs—To Be Considered Requirements for Local Civic Participation Tools. *i-com* **2021**, *20*, 141–159. [CrossRef]
16. Wamsler, C.; Alkan-Olsson, J.; Björn, H.; Falck, H.; Hanson, H.; Oskarsson, T.; Simonsson, E.; Zelmerlow, F. Beyond participation: When citizen engagement leads to undesirable outcomes for nature-based solutions and climate change adaptation. *Clim. Change* **2020**, *158*, 235–254. [CrossRef]
17. Brown, T. Design Thinking. *Harvend Bus. Rev.* **2008**, *86*, 84.
18. *ISO 9241-210:2019*; Ergonomics of Human-System Interaction—Part 210: Human-Centred Design for Interactive. International Organization for Standardization: Geneva, Switzerland, 2019. Available online: https://www.iso.org/standard/77520.html (accessed on 10 April 2025).
19. Yin, R.K. *Case Study Research and Applications: Design and Methods*; Sage Publications: Thousand Oaks, CA, USA, 2017.
20. Bowen, G.A. Document analysis as a qualitative research method. *Qual. Res. J.* **2009**, *9*, 27–40. [CrossRef]

21. Musante, K.; DeWalt, B.R. *Participant Observation: A Guide for Fieldworkers*; AltaMira Press: Totnes, UK, 2010.
22. Clatworthy, S. Service Design Thinking. 2017. Available online: https://www.researchgate.net/publication/322733238_Service_design_thinking (accessed on 10 April 2025).
23. Sampieri, R.; Fernández, C.; Baptista, L. Metodología de la Investigación. Available online: https://apiperiodico.jalisco.gob.mx/api/sites/periodicooficial.jalisco.gob.mx/files/metodologia_de_la_investigacion_-_roberto_hernandez_sampieri.pdf (accessed on 10 April 2025).
24. Forbes, M. Thematic analysis: A practical guide. *Eval. J. Australas* **2022**, *22*, 132–135. [CrossRef]
25. Giacomin, J. What Is Human Centred Design? *Des. J.* **2014**, *17*, 606–623. [CrossRef]
26. Chen, E.; Leos, C.; Kowitt, S.D.; Moracco, K.E. Enhancing Community-Based Participatory Research Through Human-Centered Design Strategies. *Health Promot. Pract.* **2019**, *21*, 37–48. [CrossRef]
27. Deliverables | Urbanage. Available online: https://www.urbanage.eu/deliverables (accessed on 20 February 2025).
28. DROP. Knowledge—drOp. Available online: https://drop-project.eu/knowledge/ (accessed on 20 February 2025).
29. Webster, C.W.R.; Leleux, C. Searching for the real sustainable smart city? *Inf. Polity* **2019**, *24*, 229–244. [CrossRef]
30. Young, R.F.; Lieberknecht, K. From smart cities to wise cities: Ecological wisdom as a basis for sustainable urban development. *J. Environ. Plan. Manag.* **2019**, *62*, 1675–1692. [CrossRef]
31. Kopackova, H.; Komarkova, J. Participatory technologies in smart cities: What citizens want and how to ask them. *Telemat. Inform.* **2020**, *47*, 101325. [CrossRef]
32. Andreani, S.; Kalchschmidt, M.; Pinto, R.; Sayegh, A. Reframing technologically enhanced urban scenarios: A design research model towards human centered smart cities. *Technol. Forecast. Soc. Change* **2019**, *142*, 15–25. [CrossRef]

urban science

MDPI

Review

Trends, Methods, Drivers, and Impacts of Housing Informalities (HI): A Systematic Literature Review

Rim Mrani [1,2,*], Hassan Radoine [3], Jérôme Chenal [1,4] and Alanda Kamana [2]

[1] Urban and Regional Planning Community (CEAT), École Polytechnique Fédérale de Lausanne (EPFL), 1015 Lausanne, Switzerland; jerome.chenal@epfl.ch
[2] School of Architecture, Planning & Design (SAP+D), University Mohammed VI Polytechnic (UM6P), Ben Guerir 43150, Morocco; alanda.akamana@um6p.ma
[3] Citinnov, University Mohammed VI Polytechnic (UM6P), Rabat 11103, Morocco; hassan.radoine@um6p.ma
[4] Center of Urban Systems (CUS), University Mohammed VI Polytechnic (UM6P), Ben Guerir 43150, Morocco
* Correspondence: rim.mrani@epfl.ch

Abstract: This paper systematically reviews scientific papers to understand the primary forms of HI, why they arise, and how they affect the urban landscape. It addresses the question, "What are the key trends, drivers, and impacts of Housing Informality (HI), and what methods researchers use to study the latter?". Previous research addressed the trends, drivers, impacts, and methods individually, failing to adopt a holistic perspective that could clarify HI as a core scientific concept distinct from informal housing. Accordingly, this systematic literature review (SLR) explores 541 scientific peer-reviewed publications from Scopus, Web of Science, and Google Scholar. By utilizing a PRISMA framework, we reduced the number of documents to 27, which we thoroughly analyzed. The results highlight five main trends of HI around the globe: unauthorized modifications, informal market dynamics, Accessory Dwelling Units (ADUs), squatting, and unusual housing. These trends are induced by several economic and sociocultural drivers that address the gap between regulations and governance from one side and lived realities from another, resulting in economic, social, legal, health, and urban impacts.

Keywords: housing informality; urban housing; Global North–South

1. Introduction

Housing is more than a utility; it forms the basis for social inclusion and economic activity, which are vital for well-being [1–3]. It is a non-negotiable element of social security [4]. Accordingly, housing provision is still at the heart of modern human rights talk and has become a continuous part of international policy talks [5]. Both scholars and practitioners have acknowledged the strong relational position of safe and stable housing as essential to individual and community resilience [6], demarcating access to economic mobility pathways, public health outcomes, and socio-economic equity more broadly realized. Nonetheless, the global rapid urbanization processes come with unusual housing hurdles [7,8] and antagonisms with soaring prices, whilst a dearth of formal housing supply results in widening social disparities. Thus, exponential urban population growth outpaces formal housing stock availability [9] and stimulates land use changes, driving out-migration and sometimes outright expelling existing residents from their homes [10].

Urban housing systems must be elastic, accommodating various needs as they emerge [11]. In this context, the terrain of housing informalities (HI) is prominent—they are seen as both a sign of strain in urban housing gaps and an undermining of formal governance forces, and simultaneously a place from where interesting responses to unmet demands emerge. The flexibility, adaptability, and resourcefulness of informal housing practices—previously condoned as a "necessary evil"—are starting to be recognized for their ability to fill the gaps in formal housing systems [12]. However, scholarly discussion needs to differentiate between informal housing, which is typically associated with entire settlements developed without formal ownership or planning permissions [13], and housing informalities (HI), a completely distinct classification that covers various unregulated practices within formally recognized urban settings [14].

Informal housing is commonly linked to the Global South, where rapid urbanization and inadequate planning give rise to substantial informal settlements [15,16]. Such settlements are built beyond the purview of the law but eventually grow into established towns [17]. By contrast, housing informalities—the focus of this study—go beyond the zones of ownership and legality. This concerns unauthorized alterations and the informal use of the property in built-up areas otherwise governed by formal regulations. Crucially, these practices not only happen in the Global South, but are also more and more prevalent in high-income, highly-regulated cities. Cities in the Global North, including London, New York, and Sydney, have high housing affordability issues [18,19] where Accessory Dwelling Units (ADU) and sub-divided units (SDU) are emerging as semi-formal responses to stock deficiency, highlighting the housing informalities practices occurring across changing socio-economic landscapes [20,21].

This differentiation between informal housing and housing informalities (HI) is crucial for analyzing the changing landscape of urban informality [13,14]. They are tucked inside existing regulatory frameworks, but they remain non-conformist in a couple of dimensions, or they overexploit legal bounds to respond to the evolving needs of their dwellers [22,23]. Such informalities frequently result from regulatory blockades, economic outcasting, and sociocultural imperatives, making them a complicated and multi-pronged issue [24]. While informal settlements are commonly perceived as housing poverty and marginalized populations, HI can also result from urban densification [25], inward migration, and the failure of formal housing markets to produce reasonably priced and resilient forms of homes [26]. This complexity demands a deeper investigation of the root causes of HI, the methods used to analyze them, and the multiplicity of impacts they have on urban communities and landscapes.

The significance of research in HI is that it can take us beyond the formal housing and planning paradigms to open up spaces for re-imagining new possibilities towards urban resilience, adaptable housing, etc. Much of the work is on informal settlements. Still, this research extends its concerns into legal and planned urban landscapes regarding housing informalities—precisely where regulatory frameworks do not capture the nuances of contemporary transforming home needs [27]. This will help inform us on opportunities to explore how unauthorized alterations, uses of shared housing, and temporary structures operate within functionally informal contexts like those we identified in relatively high- and low-income contexts—thus providing a telling illustration of the creative strategies through which people and communities find their way in negotiating for space, legality, and survival inside existing formal housing markets.

This review is driven by the recognition that despite extensive research into discrete aspects of housing informality—from informal housing and unauthorized modifications to squatting—the body of knowledge is still disjointed. Earlier studies have tended to isolate these topics rather than analyze the combined effects of trends, research strategies, underlying causes, and consequences [24,26]. Here, we aim to close that gap by use of the following:

- Concept distinction. This explanation delineates informal housing, usually linked with complete settlements operating beyond formal legal frameworks, from housing informalities, which denote particular unregulated practices in regulated urban areas;
- Integrating multidimensional insights. This systematically synthesizes diverse aspects, such as market dynamics, regulatory challenges, socio-cultural drivers, and methodological approaches that previous research has treated separately;
- Emphasizing worldwide differences. The paper demonstrates that housing informalities extend beyond the Global South, emerging more frequently in high-income, tightly regulated urban centers and enriching the debate on housing issues;
- Informing decision-making in policy and practice. The review's integration of quantitative and qualitative perspectives creates a robust framework for guiding future urban planning, policy strategies, and academic debates on housing and informality.

This paper uses a systematic literature review (SLR) to explore and synthesize existing knowledge of housing informalities (HI). Based on an in-depth literature analysis, including key scholarly databases, we summarize trends, methods, and drivers of HI and impacts across sectors to comprehensively map current research on HI within urban settings. By doing so, we reveal some significant methodological lacunae in the literature, and suggest alternative directions for future research that can illuminate more comprehensively the socio-spatial (in)formality and its economic effects on housing informalities. Such quantitative and qualitative bridge-building contributes to broader debates on urban housing and informality, valuing HI not simply as a byproduct of socio-economic exclusion but as an essential and adaptive part of contemporary urban ecosystems. This research aims to answer a central question: "What are the key trends, drivers, and impacts of Housing Informality (HI), and what methods are used by researchers to study the latter?". This SLR thus incrementally informs our understanding of how formal governance and urban planning practices intertwine from informal housing dynamics to housing informalities practices. The study is structured in five sections. After this introduction, which depicts housing informalities practices and their relation to rapid global urban growth dynamics, Section 2 details the SLR steps through the PRISMA framework. Section three analytically presents both the quantitative and qualitative results. Section four extends the discussion to urban housing and development at large, while section five wraps up the study with a summary and key insights.

2. Materials and Methods

Following the PRISMA 2020 guidelines [28], this study applies a systematic literature review (SLR) methodology. Unlike primary research methods like field surveys or interviews, systematic reviews are a structured framework for analyzing previous studies. PRISMA enhances transparency, minimizes bias, and ensures a rigorous selection process in housing informality research. We extracted data from significant sources when collecting research papers, including Web of Science, Scopus, and Google Scholar. We limited ourselves to those three databases for their journals' scientific rigor and reputation. Moreover, we found that those databases cover the best of all the fields concerning housing informalities. Other sources were either repetitive or did not yield considerable results. To extract records from Google Scholar, for commodity reasons, we used Harzing's Publish or Perish free software (version: 8.10.4612.8838) to get all the papers corresponding to our search strings at once. We used Boolean operators to form our search queries using the study keywords. Before diving into the analysis, we subjected the gathered data to a stringent preparation process. Raw records were manually scrutinized and cleaned to remove errors, duplicated entries, and irrelevant variables. We standardized data formats across all sources, ensuring uniformity and quality, which paved the way for reliable quantitative and qualitative analyses. Data extraction from our selected databases took place on 10 May 2024.

Data collection process

Inclusion criteria:

Included keywords—Housing informality(ies), informality(ies) of housing and, informality(ies) in housing;

Language—Only papers published in English or French that are familiar to the authors and comprise most published materials within the scope of HI were considered.

Exclusion criteria:

Excluded keywords—informal housing, informal settlements, and slums. Publications mainly focus on informal settlements or slums;

Language—The exclusion criteria concern the use of languages other than English and French;

Papers published in conferences—Conference papers were also intentionally excluded to guarantee reliable and trustworthy references. All selected papers are original research or review publications that underwent peer review and are indexed in at least one of our chosen search engines and databases.

Screening: Three-step verification

After the first screening, we implemented a three-step verification that included a review of the title, the abstract, and the content to decide whether the papers were relevant. Reviewing titles and abstracts to judge relevance, a reviewer first screened the records. Afterward, a second reviewer independently re-evaluated the selection to confirm the decisions made. This independent verification process aimed to minimize bias, using Microsoft Excel for duplicate removal. As the PRISMA flow diagram expresses (Figure 1), this all-encompassing process ensures the papers selected to study for HIs are the most relevant.

We adopted a systematic method to evaluate bias risk in the studies included. For this review, we designed a tailored checklist that examined key elements in each study. The checklist aimed to ensure equitable data selection, confirm the clarity and consistency of outcome measures, assess the reports' comprehensiveness, and uncover potential conflicts of interest. Two independent reviewers conducted these evaluations to minimize subjective influence and ensure an objective, transparent assessment. We documented intervention characteristics and compared them with the predefined synthesis groups to determine eligible studies. Data for synthesis were prepared with precision in Microsoft Excel software (for Mac, version 16.72), using the number 1 to denote the availability of the items and 0 for their unavailability. We synchronized study measurements to develop a standardized dataset essential for meaningful comparisons and data merging.

Furthermore, we compiled the results into detailed tables and visual charts using Microsoft Excel software and online Google Sheets. Our approach involved comparing subgroups categorized by relevant study attributes and contextual factors, namely, scientific fields, interdisciplinary areas, research methods, geographical region, trends, drivers, and impacts, once again using the number 1 for the availability of the items and 0 for their unavailability, to gain insights into study variability. This strategy was aimed at investigating potential differences in the study findings. We also conducted sensitivity analyses to verify the stability of our overall results, confirming that our conclusions held even with the exclusion of specific studies or data elements. We carefully scrutinized the risk of bias from missing results by reviewing the published outcomes and double-checking the data extraction process, thereby reducing potential distortions from reporting biases. Ultimately, we assessed the overall certainty of the evidence through a systematic evaluation of study limitations, consistency, and precision, which provided a reliable measure of our confidence in the combined results.

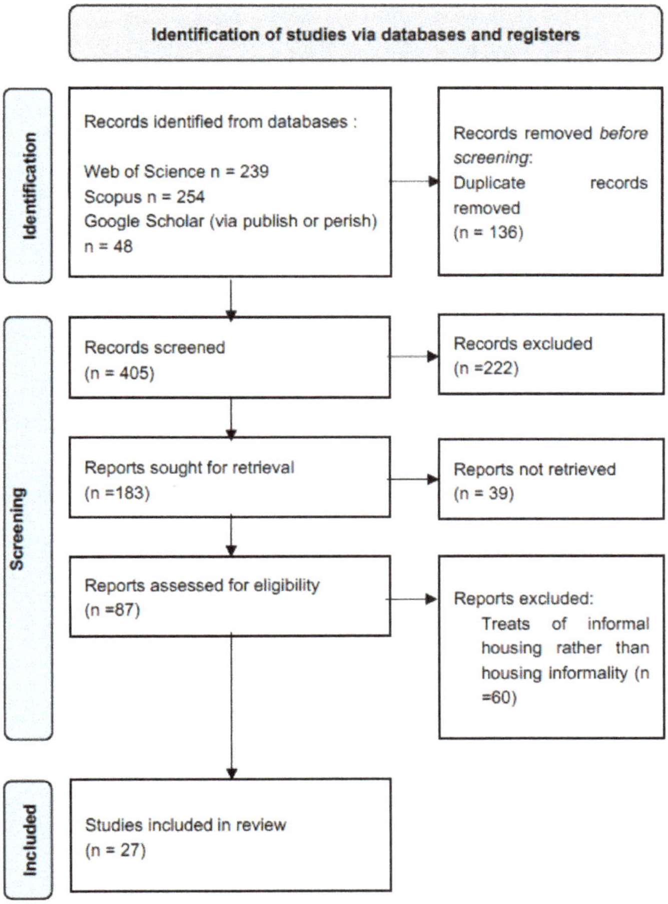

Figure 1. PRISMA 2020 flow diagram of the study.

3. Results

3.1. Quantitative Analysis

We scanned three essential academic databases to obtain different HI literature sources—Web of Science (WoS), Scopus, and Google Scholar. Up to 10 May 2024, we identified 541 publications in total (WoS $n = 239$; Scopus $n = 254$ and GS $n = 48$). To ensure each paper was original, our team created a Microsoft Excel process to identify and delete duplicates. Then, 136 repetitions were removed from the 541 papers returned; 405 unique entries remained to form an accurate dataset. Title and abstract evaluations were performed in the screening step to verify whether the investigations therein were related to the primary focus of this study, namely, that HI occurs within legally acknowledged systems. Then, 183 publications were finally selected after a painstaking selection process, focusing on their abstracts, in anticipation of comparing each research paper primarily concentrating on HI rather than having broader conceptions like informal housing, informal settlements, slums, or shantytowns generally. Accordingly, 87 articles were retained following a careful and demanding selection process for further study. Each of the 87 articles was thoroughly evaluated during the eligibility test to ensure they met the inclusion criteria. This phase involved corroboration to ensure that the materials focused on housing irregularities as stipulated in legally recognized frameworks. Sixty articles were rejected because they did not meet the requirements, especially those focused on informal settlements or slums. Ultimately, 27 publications meeting all the inclusion criteria were selected for review (see Table 1). These articles were selected based on their focus on housing irregularities and compliance with the established criteria, thus ensuring that high-quality, relevant literature will be reviewed. The table below presents 27 publications arranged chronologically—from the oldest to the most recent. Each entry has been assigned a code name (Paper *n*) to facilitate a systematic analysis of the key trends, methods, drivers, and impacts associated with urban housing informality. Two reviewers employed a standardized data extraction form to gather information from each report. They documented key study details such as the main fields, interdisciplinary areas, research methods, geographical region, trends, drivers, and impacts.

Table 1. List of the 27 selected records.

Ref	Paper Title	Authors	Journal	Publisher	Year
paper 1 [29]	Formal determinants of informal arrangements: housing and undocumented immigrants in Rotterdam	Jack Burgers	Journal of Ethnic and Migration Studies	Routledge	1998
paper 2 [26]	Augmented informality: South Africa's backyard dwellings as a by-product of formal housing policies	Charlotte Lemanski	Habitat International	Elsevier	2009
paper 3 [30]	Surviving in limbo: An insight into Slovenia's informal private rented housing sector	Richard Sendi, Barbara Černič Mali	Theoretical and Empirical Researches in Urban Management	JSTOR	2015
paper 4 [31]	A Hidden Informality? Informal Occupation in Milan: The Housing Needs and the Events of Protest	Nilva Karenina Aramburu Guevara	Journal of Studies in Social Sciences	Infinity Press	2016
paper 5 [24]	Backyard shacks, informality, and the urban housing crisis in South Africa: stopgap or prototype solution?	Turok, Ivan; Borel-Saladin, Jackie	Housing Studies	Routledge	2016
paper 6 [32]	Enumerating informal housing: A field method for identifying secondary units	Kathleen Kinsella	Canadian Geographer	Canadian Association of Geographers	2017
paper 7 [33]	Analytical investigation of urban housing typologies in twentieth century Istanbul	Elmira Ayşe Gür, Yurdanur Dülgeroğlu Yüksel	Archnet-IJAR: International Journal of Architectural Research	Emraldinsight	2019
paper 8 [34]	Cautious occupiers and restrained bureaucrats: Schwarzwohnen in the German Democratic Republic. Somewhat different from squatting	Udo Grashoff	Housing Studies	Routledge	2019

Table 1. *Cont.*

Ref	Paper Title	Authors	Journal	Publisher	Year
paper 9 [35]	In-formality in access to housing for Latin American migrants: a case study of an intermediate Chilean city	Yasna Contreras, Laura Neville, Rodrigo González	International Journal of Housing Policy	Routledge	2019
paper 10 [36]	Rent determinants of sub-divided units in Hong Kong	Ka Man Leung, Chung Yim Yiu	Journal of Housing and the Built Environment	JSTOR	2019
paper 11 [37]	Considering the camp: ambivalent geographies of mobile dwelling	Damian Collins, Laura Bates, Robin Kearns and Joshua Evans	Applied Mobilities	Routledge	2020
paper 12 [38]	Incremental housing: harnessing informality at Villa Verde	D O'Brien, S Carrasco, K Dovey	Archnet-IJAR: International Journal of Architectural Research	Emraldinsight	2020
paper 13 [39]	Real and fake data in Shanghai's informal rental housing market: Groundtruthing data scraped from the internet	Julia Gabriele Harten, Annette M Kim, J Cressica Brazier	Housing Studies	Routledge	2021
paper 14 [5]	Who feels secure in customary tenure and why? A triangular framework of perceived tenure security in China's small property right housing	Zhang, Mengzhu; He, Shenjing	Cities	Elsevier	2020
paper 15 [40]	Container housing: Formal informality and deterritorialized home-making amid bulldozer urbanism in Shanghai	Minhua Ling	Urban Studies	Sage	2021
paper 16 [22]	Hidden homes? Uncovering Sydney's informal housing market	Nicole Gurran, Madeleine Pill, Sophia Maalsen	Urban Studies	Sage	2021
paper 17 [20]	Urban informality in the Global North: (il)legal status and housing strategies of Ghanaian migrants in New York City	Mohammad Usman, Sabina Maslova, Gemma Burgessb	International Journal of Housing Policy	Routledge	2021
paper 18 [41]	Examining informal housing supply through rent gap analysis: An empirical study of sub-divided units in Hong Kong	K.M. Leung, Lennon H.T. Choy, K.W. Chau	Cities	Elsevier	2022
paper 19 [21]	Informalities as Resistance: Case Study of a Middle-Class Housing Neighborhood in Rabat, Morocco	Rim Mrani, Jerome Chenal, Hassan Radoine	Journal of Engineering and Architecture	American Research Institute for Policy Development	2022

Table 1. *Cont.*

Ref	Paper Title	Authors	Journal	Publisher	Year
paper 20 [42]	Struggles and opportunities at the platform interface: tenants' experiences of navigating shared room housing using digital platforms in Sydney	Zahra Nasreen, Kristian Ruming	Journal of Housing and the Built Environment	Springer	2022
paper 21 [19]	Breaking the rules? Informal housing, urban deregulation, and secondary dwellings in Australia	Pranita Shrestha, Nicole Gurran	European Urban and Regional Studies	Sage	2023
paper 22 [43]	Discounted housing? Understanding shared rental markets under platformisation	Nicole Gurran, Zahra Nasreen, Pranita Shrestha	Housing Studies	Routledge	2023
paper 23 [27]	Financing Housing Development in an Underdeveloped Financial Market: Learning from Developers' Financing Adaptations?	Kavaarpuo, Godwin; Mintah, Kwabena; Donkor-Hyiaman, Kenneth Appiah	Housing Policy Debate	Routledge	2023
paper 24 [44]	Migrants' perceived social integration in different housing tenures in urban China	Sainan Lin, Fulong Wu, Yu Wang, Zhigang Li	Geoforum	Elsevier	2023
paper 25 [18]	The regularity of informality: Reframing the formal-informal relationship with the help of informal housing in London	Emily Kelling	European Urban and Regional Studies	Sage	2023
paper 26 [45]	Boats as Housing in Oxford, UK: Trajectories of Informality in a High-Income Context	Jakub Galuszka	International Journal of Urban and Regional Research	Wiley-Blackwell	2024
paper 27 [46]	'In-betweenness': migrants experience accessing rental housing in the innerburbs neighborhoods of Santiago, Chile	Andrea Urbina Julio	Housing Studies	Routledge	2024

Our synthesis revealed clear and consistent trends across studies, which emerged despite variations in design and context. These patterns provide a strong basis for comprehending the central themes of the literature. Additionally, we identified meaningful differences in study outcomes through subgroup comparisons, highlighting that although contextual or methodological factors may influence results, the overall consistency is preserved. We found through sensitivity analyses that the synthesized findings were robust; variations in the data did not affect the overall conclusions, thus enhancing the evidence's credibility. Moreover, our assessment of reporting bias revealed that missing results had minimal impact, indicating that selective outcome reporting was not a significant concern. We carefully examined the risk of bias arising from missing results—reviewing the published outcomes and rechecking the data extraction process—and found no gaps, implying that selective outcome reporting was not problematic. Lastly, the thorough assessment of evidence certainty strongly permits high confidence in the review's outcomes.

3.1.1. Key Trends in Housing Informalities

Housing informalities (HI) can be classified into five key trends, each signifying a different response to regulatory and economic pressures. The first trend, Informal Market Dynamics, covers extra-legal housing practices such as informal housing tenure based on verbal agreements; migrants' housing dynamics, where legal obstacles lead to informal living situations; sub-divided units (SDUs), which result from partitioning legally recognized dwellings into unregistered rentals; shared housing without formal lease contracts; online rental platforms that enable short-term rentals outside regulatory oversight; and informal financing, including private loans or savings groups that sidestep traditional mortgages. Accessory Dwelling Units (ADUs), the second trend, are secondary residential units like backyard flats or garage conversions. While some are legal, many remain informal due to zoning restrictions. The third trend, unauthorized modifications, involves unapproved structural changes—such as adding floors or subdividing interiors—to meet space or income needs, often clashing with urban policies. Unusual housing is a movement that converts atypical structures, like container homes and boat houses, into residential spaces. Financial constraints, regulatory barriers, or personal preferences drive this trend.

On the other hand, squatting—the illegal occupation of land or buildings—has become a way to address housing shortages and challenge property laws in high-cost markets. These trends are part of housing informalities (HI), encompassing Informal Market Dynamics, Accessory Dwelling Units (ADUs), unauthorized modifications, and informal housing tenure. Migrants' housing dynamics, sub-divided units (SDUs), shared housing, online rental platforms, and informal financing are also central to these trends.

3.1.2. Subject Areas: Interdisciplinary Analysis

As illustrated in the bubble chart (Figure 2), the distribution and emphasis of research into housing informality among various academic disciplines set forth the disciplinary perspectives necessary for investigating HI, juxtaposing the proportion of research articles in each area. As the figure demonstrates, Legal Studies, Urban Studies, Sociology, and Housing Studies account for 100% of the studies selected. This strong presence reflects the importance of these fields in understanding and analyzing housing informalities (HI). Together, they highlight HI's complex and multi-dimensional nature.

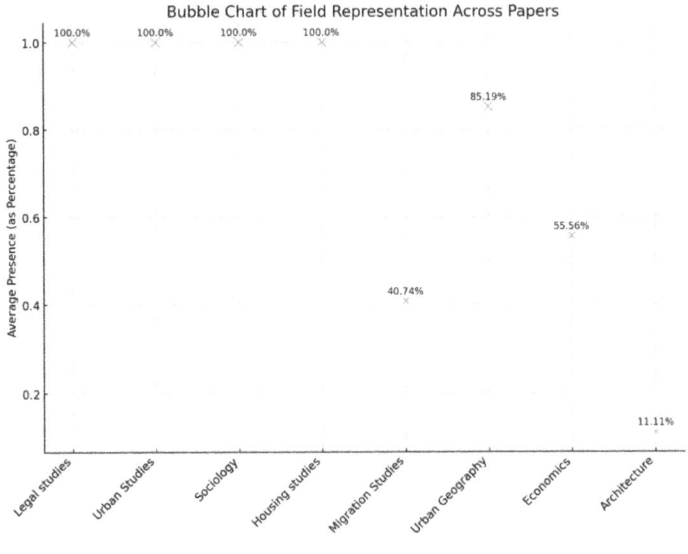

Figure 2. Bubble chart of subject areas of the papers that treat HI.

Legal Studies—A recurring field throughout the reviewed articles, demonstrating the legal dimensions inherent in many of the corresponding HI. Since HI typically exists outside the formal boundaries established by law or even in direct breach of it, investigating such phenomena usually entails, to some extent, examining legal systems, rules, and illegality itself. Legal Studies give us key perspectives on how these informal practices are regulated, fought over, or ignored in different jurisdictions, and underline the complexity of this relationship between law and housing.

Urban Studies—These are key to the analysis of HI, as these practices have been predominantly urban and interact with the major socio-economic forces reshaping urban forms. Indeed, as cities worldwide are increasingly going through rapid transformations, providing adequate housing, sustainable land use, and urban planning practices became essential issues, thereby rendering Urban Studies a crucial subject in understanding how HI gets established, adjusts, and influences the emergent qualities of urban landscapes. The universality of this subject in the literature illustrates that HI must be placed within broader urban development, governance, and sustainability debates.

Sociology—Sociology's prominent presence in the reviewed papers signals its critical contribution to understanding how HI are socially structured and, conversely, structure social relations and hierarchies. Using a sociological perspective, we can examine how communities manage informal settings, the social norms that shape housing practices outside formal regulations with an emphasis on family values, and how both collective and individual decision-making contribute to HI's lasting endurance.

Housing Studies—Housing Studies in all the papers considered for review underscore the natural and direct relationship with HI as a subfield within housing. Housing Studies examine how housing markets, policies, and functions interact across different parts of the world. This is essential to untangling how HI is situated within a larger context of defined urban systems and dynamics.

It investigates the changes in housing provision and the practices of living generated when formal housing responses no longer suffice, thereby revealing how HIs operate as reactions to—but also catalysts for transformation within—housing landscapes.

Urban geography appears in 85.19% of the reviewed papers, demonstrating its importance for the spatial analysis of HI and highlighting that locality is a prime factor when interpreting such phenomena. The geography in which practices are embedded profoundly impacts how HI can be realized due to substantial differences between different urban contexts. The attention to urban geography helps underscore how, even if certain informal practices may seem similar, the particular layout of city space, infrastructural requirements, and socio-spatial dynamics in which they occur will offer markedly different attributes and implications.

Economics featured in 55.56% of the studies, suggesting economic factors were significant reasons for housing informality. Economic analyses were peppered throughout more than half of the studies reviewed, indicating the centrality of housing affordability, income inequality, and market failures in catalyzing such conditions. Economic analysis sheds some light on why a community will use informal settlement, as the lack of formal housing options often forces this.

Migration Studies—More than a third of the reviewed papers (40.74%) focused on Migration Studies, suggesting a substantial overlap between migration itself and HI as an essential dimension of modern urban population mobility. The field of study represents a necessary link between migration patterns, which are frequently driven by socio-economic disparities and the lack of jobs/poverty, along with a quest for higher standards of living, on the one hand, and informal housing processes on the other. Migrants, especially those on the economic margin or uncertain of their legal status, are often forced into informal housing arrangements as they go through insecure urban areas. These crossroads highlight the dual potential of HI as a survival strategy and in response to broader socio-economic challenges confronting the migrant population.

Architecture—Surprisingly, only 11.1% of reviewed papers are about housing informality from an architectural perspective, which is paradoxical, since housing informality is related to architectural modifications in both the tangible and intangible realms. From the soft, imperceptible practices that suggest the use of changes to and perceptions of built spaces to direct physical transformations, housing informality is always tied in with architectural form and function. As such, these studies' failures to examine the architectural motives of HI prompt a pressing interrogation of how architectural practices produce (or inhibit) informal housing dynamics despite being at their core.

3.1.3. Regional Trends: A Comparative Analysis

To present a more rounded analysis of housing informalities (HI), it is necessary to unpack the Global North and South trends further. The global trend of these practices points to the phenomenon's universality, and highlights regional differences that influence informalities in housing.

Informal Market Dynamics

The bar chart above (Figure 3) shows that the most common studies were on Informal Market Dynamics (accounting for about 53% of total publications). This regards the dominance of market-oriented forces at the center of informalities in housing practices on a global scale, as people and societies strive to develop innovative alternative responses concerning housing beyond formal, regulated markets. A detailed exploration of the subtrends within Informal Market Dynamics illustrates how multifaceted this category is. While the largest subtrend associated with housing informality appeared to be geared toward discussions on informal housing tenure (71%), this underscores that issues with securing legal and stable accommodation are not just a phenomenon for specific countries in the Global South, but arise around the world [47]. In many cases, especially in rapidly urbanizing countries that struggle to accommodate socially marginalized groups, informal tenure systems play a significant role in offering shelter that the formal market is not able to provide [35,44,48]. It shows how the failure to secure formal housing leads many to act informally. The second axis is Migrants' Housing Dynamics (43%); migrants—who may be internal or external—repeatedly find themselves excluded from the formal housing systems by a web of legal, economic, and social obstacles. In the case of such amenities, potential migrants to the city may turn their attention to using urban housing markets (e.g., subletting or shared housing) as informal strategies in a densified built environment, which can be seen in cities like Hong Kong [36,41] and New York City [20].

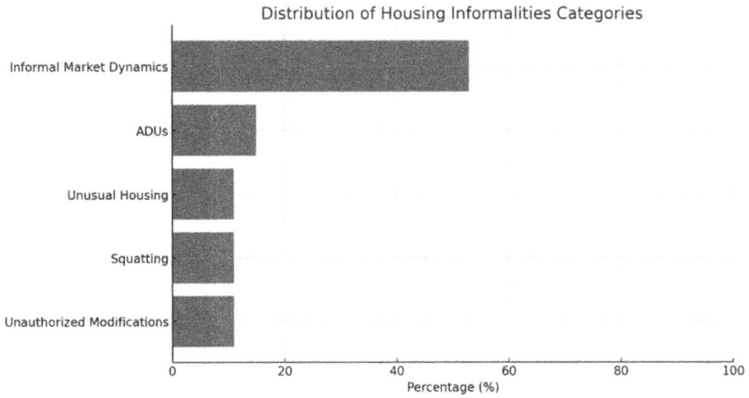

Figure 3. Bar chart of the global trends.

Furthermore, other adaptive strategies—particularly the use of sub-divided units (SDU) (14%)—are more prevalent in cities like Los Angeles and Sydney [22,42]. SDUs generally arise as under-the-table additions to existing homes, creating opportunities for flexible, affordable living in regions with sky-high housing prices [49]. Likewise, shared housing—representing 14% of the Informal Market Dynamics—is especially prominent in cities like London [18], where rising housing prices force residents to live together. SDU and shared housing also identify the functionality of how crushing competitive housing costs pushes marginalized residents to live informally off the books. Finally, the rise of online rental platforms (7%) in Informal Market Dynamics has emerged as a disruptive subtend in the latest developments. In cities like Sydney, platforms such as Gumtree have facilitated the formalization of housing through rentals that fall outside formal housing regulations by renting by item (bed or individual room) instead of dwelling [42], putting intense pressure on local supplies. Lastly, informal financing (7%) indicates the broader economic challenges faced in markets like Nigeria [6], where access to formal financial systems is limited, leading residents to utilize community-based finance saving or borrowing for housing requirements from informal lenders.

Adaptive Practices

ADU and Unauthorized Modifications

Accessory Dwelling Units (ADU), the second most common type of semi-formal homes in the dataset, account for about 15% of the reviewed papers. The push for ADU is one of the few bright spots in alleviating the housing shortages plaguing high-demand urban areas. Informally built backyards offer a flexible approach to meeting the growing need for affordable housing. They allow property owners to create living spaces without following conventional housing regulations. ADUs are a long-standing trend in some countries, such as Australia [19] and South Africa [24], responding to housing pressures and evading formal housing regulations. Although less studied (11%), unauthorized modifications are a similarly widespread form of adaptation, especially in the Global South [50,51]. This phenomenon is prominent where existing housing provisions do not correspond to the actual needs of the residents. Due to those diversified needs, they modify their formal houses at their own will without permission, as in the case of Turkey [33] and Morocco [21], for instance. In the construction arena, illegal changes in land use represent a continual contest between formal rules and regulations on one side, and urban life as city-dwellers live it on the other.

Alternative Housing

Unusual Housing and Squatting

On a global scale, the proportions of both unusual housing and squatting in the dataset are relatively high, at 11%; however, they remain marginalized from current discourses on housing informalities, reflecting their shallower academic coverage. Unusual housing is a phenomenon currently flourishing in certain zones across the planet, such as New Zealand and Oxford [45], characterized by various innovative and non-standard residential solutions that primarily differ from traditional housing standards. Such alternative strategies, including mobile dwelling camps, container housing, and boats, respond to the limitations of an increasingly restrictive local housing market and a growing demand for adaptable and affordable alternatives [4]. These examples illustrate how residents find and fit within crevices and non-regulated spaces when pursuing adequate housing rights. By comparison, squatting (a regular occurrence in places like Milan, Beijing, and former Eastern Germany) is a symbol of broader social exclusion and the housing crisis [52,53]. Squatting is seen in urban areas when impoverished people live in abandoned buildings by permission, to operate them, or otherwise—often as soon as a housing inventory and affordability crisis heightens the pressure on residential space [54,55]. This has a peculiar salience in the Global North, where political movements campaigning for housing rights are constrained severely by markets. In these areas, squatting begins to take the form of a practical approach to self-provision of housing, and also as a path through which to subvert official protocols—not just around what is legal or illegal, but about how the objectives of the right-to-housing and the urban process itself can be redirected.

Comparative insights: Global North vs. Global South

Despite vast geographical, economic, and cultural differences between the Global North and Global South, a cross-national comparison shows that housing informalities are born of shared necessity within an ever-changing economy, regulatory frameworks, and evolving social needs. However, not all adaptations are created equal. In the Global South, they are a response to either the absence or the failure of formal systems that cater to increasing urban populations [56]. This is where you find Informal Housing Tenure and unauthorized modifications—residents actively seeking to address challenges within formal housing systems. For their part, the informalities of the Global North—shared housing, ADU— are much more about navigating high-cost and over-regulated housing markets [18,19,22]. Destitute people hindered by the high cost of formal housing systems have instead improvised their solutions. The most prevailing trend, Informal Market Dynamics—seen equally in the Global North and Global South—reveals how informal housing practices emerge, catalyzed by market failures and affordability issues. Nevertheless, the shape these practices adopt (even if they do so as an ADU in the Global North or an unauthorized modification in the South) manifests the particular socio-economic and regulatory contexts of urban informality for housing. By considering the interrelations of housing informalities in their entirety, such a wide-angle approach enhances our understanding of the intricate strands that weave them together and, thus, how we might best address them via more informed policy interventions, as well as urban planning strategies relevant to both regional and global contexts.

3.1.4. Research Methods: A Comprehensive Overview

The multifaceted nature of the HI is such that addressing them necessitates using a combination of research tools. The methodological approaches found in this analysis highlight the dynamism involved in housing informality trends and the instruments used to study them. Figure 4, a stacked bar chart of primary research methods used across the trends covered in the dataset of this SLR, is given below.

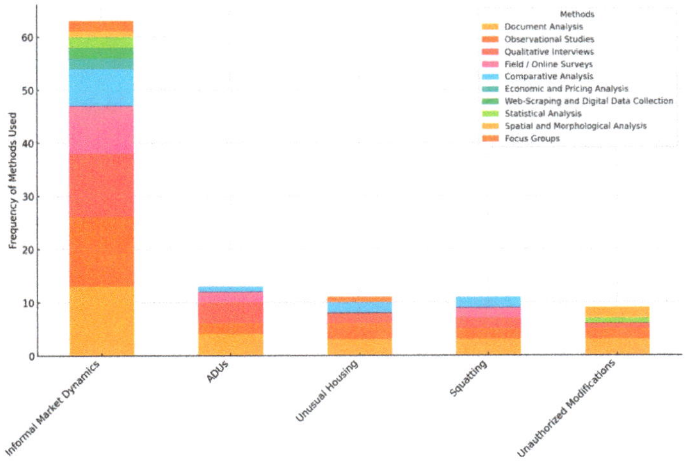

Figure 4. Stacked bar chart of method frequency according to each trend.

The co-occurrences shown in Figure 4 are empirical patterns drawn from the literature without evidence of causation. These patterns can be examined through various theoretical viewpoints to investigate how small-scale informality integrates with urban systems. For example, adaptive governance theories [57] emphasize how households and communities create innovative housing solutions when formal regulations are too restrictive or costly. Incremental urbanism [58] explores the gradual modifications—like unauthorized extensions—that residents implement to adjust their homes to changing family or economic circumstances. Furthermore, theories on informal housing [59,60] emphasize the interplay between formal regulations and socio-cultural norms, illustrating how activities in the "grey zone" emerge due to shortcomings in official housing policies. By connecting these phenomena to ongoing debates, we tie empirical observations—such as the significance of Informal Market Dynamics or the understudied practice of squatting—to broader understandings of how everyday agency, regulatory constraints, and market inefficiencies influence urban housing landscapes.

Informal Market Dynamics

Informal Market Dynamics is the most frequently studied and the most varied in terms of methodologies applied, making up the most significant portion of methodological applications across all datasets. Document analysis and qualitative interviews are essential for this trend, as they contain many historical and legal records pertinent to the study, as well as the lived experience of stakeholders within informal housing markets. All these methods are critical in unpacking the regulatory and socio-economic issues underpinning market-driven housing solutions in informal landscapes. Field/online surveys and economic and pricing analysis are the principal methods used to explore Informal Market Dynamics, which implies a quest for reliable data to identify economic forces underlying informal housing practices. Although much less commonly used, there is an emerging potential to use web-scraped live data from online platforms (e.g., Gumtree). This could offer an opportunity to get some insight into informal rental arrangements that fall under the radar of formal regulation. Accordingly, our methodological landscape within this trend highlights a holistic perspective on informal market dynamics in Global North and South contexts.

Adaptive Practices: ADUs and Unauthorized Modifications

Researchers take a relatively balanced approach in investigating Accessory Dwelling Units (ADU) and unauthorized modifications, with an inclination toward qualitative methods. Significantly, this section highlights the prominence of field/online surveys and, by implication, of direct engagement with property owners and residents involved in creating or adapting these informal spaces in response to formal housing shortages (field/online surveys; qualitative interviews). Spatial and morphological analysis have mainly been overlooked in the study of unauthorized modifications, a shortcoming that highlights a unique challenge with these interventions. Because common housing additions often result in substantial morphological changes, this oversight opens a promising avenue for research into unauthorized housing practices in regions like Morocco [21] and Turkey [33], where informal alterations abound. The rarely used Economic and Pricing Analysis of ADUs points to a more detailed examination of the economic costs associated with semi-formal housing outside these immediate neighborhoods, which could provide land markets in urban centers. By incorporating such analyses and data, researchers can more effectively quantify the economic scope of ADUs and grasp their trade-offs, most notably in high-demand urban housing markets like Los Angeles, Sydney, etc.

Alternative Housing: Unusual Housing and Squatting

The researchers in our reviewed papers mostly use qualitative approaches to study unusual housing and squatting through document analysis and qualitative interviews.

Comparative analysis and observational studies are also noticeable in both trends. This demonstrates an interest in comparative approaches on global scales to understand real-time adaptations of urban spaces. Yet, much of the research employed spatial and morphological analyses despite the effects of spatial change. This lack of consideration provides an area where future research could analyze how these informal practices affect the urban fabric, particularly in densified environments.

Furthermore, none of these trends feature economic and pricing analysis, suggesting that the broader market impacts (if any) on unusual housing and squatting are not being duly researched. Including economic data would help drill down into the affordability pressures driving people toward these alternative housing options, especially in expensive urban areas in both the Global North and South. The more frequent application of these under-used techniques would significantly improve our knowledge of these housing informality trends' socio-economic and spatiotemporal aspects.

The various methodologies applied across the trends in housing informality give an all-encompassing picture of the dynamics (socio-economic, legal, and spatial) at play. Nevertheless, the analysis exposes notable gaps in some trends (e.g., unauthorized modifications, unusual housing/squatting) mainly due to the less common usage of spatial and morphological analysis and Economic and Pricing Analysis. Focusing on these gaps also enables future researchers to more clearly explore how housing informalities practices mold to urban contexts and meaningfully stem from economic factors. Through expanding the methodological toolkit, researchers can bring an increasingly multi-faceted view to the study of housing informality, which is critical for evidence-informed policy and urban planning in Global North and South contexts.

3.2. *Qualitative Analysis*

Quantitative analyses are essential in understanding the statistical prevalence and distribution of trends within Housing Informalities (HI). Moreover, qualitative analysis allows for a more detailed exploration and new insights into the drivers, impacts, and/or context surrounding the HI phenomena. We also found that qualitative research can provide transdisciplinary insights into some of the intricate socio-economic, cultural, and regulatory dynamics surrounding HI, which quantitative data alone may not capture in all dimensions. Transitioning from the numerical characterization of trends to a thematic evaluation, in this part, we analyze the motivators, contexts, and macro socio-political mechanisms that facilitate HI across different geographies. This more nuanced approach offers more profound insights into HI, delivering significant gains in understanding how people and communities live in and through the housing informality landscapes. By interrogating these drivers, we hope to shed light on the multifaceted web of processes that underpin the longevity and changes of housing informality. In this context, we specifically examine the differences in these drivers across individual states. A study component aims to highlight the variations of these drivers and how they are manifested in different regions or communities.

3.2.1. Drivers: Thematic Assessment

Economic Drivers: Foundational Determinants Across Geographies

Among the various influences on housing informality, economic factors are the most widespread motivators of market-determined processes and informal practices across geographies. This is particularly notable in Informality Market Dynamics, ADU, and squatting/unauthorized modifications. Economic precarity and income inequality dominate housing affordability issues, which, in most cases, push individuals and households towards non-formal housing arrangements. The informal sector allows individuals who are otherwise boxed out by the formal housing sectors (due to lack of proper financial standing) to negotiate through these constraints. Of course, economic drivers do not act in a vacuum. They coincide with supply-side limitations, especially in high-demand urban locations where public housing is either absent or costly. For example, the emergence of Informal Market Dynamics within fast-growing urbanizing economies illustrates how market forces can lead to increased housing informality practices. These practices occur in the grey zones of economies, which are not addressed by formal regulations and offer a space for populations otherwise excluded from traditional housing markets. Likewise, Accessory Dwelling Units (ADU), a way to retrofit houses for housing shortages under informal economic arrangements, show where economic imperatives and legal circumvention intersect in highly regulated Global North housing markets.

Social and Cultural Drivers: Contextual Nuances in Housing Informality

A second layer of complexity arises with social and cultural determinants of informal housing. They talk about the patterns of behaviors at the community level, shared norms, and individual household strategies that work within, or are often are controversial in, the formal regulatory framework. This can especially be seen in phenomena like unauthorized modifications and squatting. People adapt what they are given into something that works for their community. Socio-cultural imperatives are a primary driver of extra-legal alterations in the case of unauthorized modifications, which typically occur through the renovation of formal housing units to accommodate multi-generational families living in or rented the property. Such adaptations are common in areas like Turkey and Morocco [21,33], where the presence of extended families and traditional cultural practices impact housing. In this light, squatting is understood as not only a reaction to housing exclusion on the part of individuals, but also more broadly as an action of city-wide resistance, as is the case in Milan [31] and East Berlin [34].

Vacant properties are targeted by squatters as a protest against unaffordable housing markets, exposing a broader contestation between citizens and urban governance frameworks. The Villa Verde housing project in Constitución, Chile, exemplifies how formal and informal practices can merge creatively. The incremental housing model in Villa Verde is a system wherein residents can finish their homes through informal building, starting with one slab and two perimeter walls, with the formal components pre-designed [38]. The project is a robust case in which informal strategies, enabled by the participatory and adaptable environment, give rise to self-regulating yet robust habitat alternatives. The participation in turn empowers the residents, making them content and at home, and also provides a means for informal practices with few aesthetic constraints determining architectural alignment. One of the reasons the Villa Verde project is so important is that it reveals how informal buildings can be incorporated into formal systems, providing a more versatile housing solution. This model is anchored in a participatory approach. The authors repeatedly call upon residents to attend workshops where they learn how to upgrade their homes [38], thereby setting up a structured but adaptable informal construction process. Residents also participate in the participatory process, creating a sense of community and developing local responsibility through an architectural coherence implementation strategy. The project of the architect Alejandro Aravena pointed out how informal construction can be combined with a formal system, opening the approach up for a more significant middle-class population.

Regulatory and Institutional Factors: Enablers and Constraints

The variable interplay of regulatory and institutional conditions is one of the most relevant topics across the housing informalities spectrum, from end to end. Human encounters with the built environment in a rule-governed world of formal housing regulations are, characteristically and crucially, spatially contingent on access to regulatory apparatus.

Informal practices fester when there is little or sporadic institutional oversight. In both the Global North and Global South, regulatory frameworks lag behind in adjusting to urbanization [61], and tend to exacerbate exclusionary housing markets. Weak regulatory environments lead to unregulated rentals, sub-divided units, or informal financing [27].

Nevertheless, online platforms such as Gumtree in Sydney may contribute to normalizing extra-legalized and informal rental arrangements, enhancing opportunities for speculative behaviors at the margins of more conventional housing market forms [42]. However, in the context of unauthorized modifications, the tight planning controls may also encourage homeowners to go around the formal system and carry out unpermitted changes of use in their homes. In addition to this, in some locations like New Zealand and Oxford, prime examples of unusual housing (such as container homes or dwellings on wheels) can appear as creative responses to the restrictions of regulation themselves [45], especially in markets where formal housing responses are falling behind widespread accumulation needs. As a result, the flexibility of housing informality solutions has become essential for many city dwellers who are not able to afford higher housing costs [6,14,20].

Demographic and Migration Dynamics: Migration as a Catalyst

Migration (internal and international) usually intersects with the informality of housing, given that migrant populations frequently lack access to formal housing markets due to legal, financial, or social restrictions. It is the archetype of informal housing for displaced or economically disadvantaged migrant workers, used in this case as a survival strategy (squatting and Informal Market Dynamics). The informal nature of housing stock in urban areas is further compounded by undocumented or precarious migrant populations, stimulating demand for affordable and adaptable options. This is the case for the SDU or shared houses that many migrants are turning to in cities like New York [20] and Hong Kong [36] to find alternative urban living accommodation.

Adaptability and Flexibility Needs: Drivers of Alternative Housing Forms

Adaptability and flexibility are other unique drivers strongly related to unusual housing and unauthorized modifications. The requirements for such models are grounded in economic realities and underlying consumer preferences for housing solutions that can change with life stages. Trends in unusual housing, like alternative containers or mobile dwelling homes, answer the need for adaptive-type solutions for different situations when traditional modes of housing are difficult or impossible to achieve. In this sense, the flexibility of more informal housing options is a key factor for many inhabitants, especially in cities with high housing prices. On the other hand, unauthorized modifications reflect a spatial adaptability situation wherein the formal housing provisions do not adequately serve the residents' needs. Residents can alter their homes to boost density, change spatial configurations, or monetize underused space without the time lag and expense of securing formal approvals. Therefore, the design of Villa Verde by Architect Aravena signifies how adaptability and flexibility should be institutionalized as an architectural model, thereby promoting the development from informality to formality through engaging people in self-help.

The qualitative analysis indicates that HI emerges via a multifaceted process, as economic drivers cannot be distilled into linear cause-and-effect processes but signify an array of financial, social–cultural regulatory, and demographic nexuses. The permutations of these drivers are unique to every place, generating an immense variety of housing informality types.

3.2.2. Complex Impacts: Dynamics Unfolded

Economic Impacts

The informal economy generated by housing informalities may significantly affect national and local economies. Informal Market Dynamics, ADU, squatting, and unauthorized modifications are all responses to the economic precarity found in the informal economy. They quickly become a parallel economy that allows for escaping moderating control instead of adhering to formal regulation, oversight, and taxation. While providing valuable housing alternatives, the shadow economy also leads to a considerable loss of tax revenue and increasing market distortions that affect the overall functioning of an economy. Informalities in housing practices continue to support the economy across various trends, even though all those earnings remain off-record. More specifically, in the case of informal housing tenure, migrants' housing dynamics, Sub-Divided Units (SDU), and shared housing, the rental markets represent an important area where rent is collected illegally by landlords who do not declare it. This deprives governments of much-needed tax revenue that funds urban development and the provision of formal dwellings [62]. In cities like Hong Kong [41], New York [20], and London [18], notable informal subletting also occurs, with SDU deeply entrenched in high-cost urban settings. These social housing dynamics are bolstered by online settlement platforms that allow units or properties to be rented, where unregulated rental activities bypass formal housing and tax policies.

Moreover, informal funding structures play a key role in financing building or adaptation in cases of housing informality. In countries such as Nigeria [63], other options include informal lending or community-based savings groups that provide capital for conversions/extensions within formally recognized housing frameworks (the financial transactions going untaxed and flowing entirely independently of the formal banking system). Profits from these informal lending systems are unrecorded, and the interest in this money circulation remains unaccounted for, increasing the size of the untaxed informal economy even further. In Turkey [33] and Morocco [21], unauthorized modifications involve an array of informal entrepreneurs—builders, contractors, and service providers—who make a living through illegal construction activities that tweak or extend formal housing units without official permits. Such changes, often conducted without inspection or oversight, generate massive potential revenues, but are tax-free. It makes the construction market a part of the informal sector, with all profits flying under the radar in the formal economy.

The housing informality sector is a country's most significant urban economy. However, as it does not go through formal channels, this severely handicaps the state's capacity to earn revenue from it, ensure its safety, or develop an attractive urban development strategy for future interventions. It simultaneously underscores the continual dilemma between the demands of systemically economically excluded groups and the authoritarian mechanisms that cannot provide shelter necessities.

Social Impacts

The social impacts of housing informality are multi-layered and weaved into the residents' experiences. Most commonly, these effects will be positive in some areas and harmful in others, depending on the type of housing trends. In Informal Market Dynamics, social impacts typically involve the development of close-knit neighborhoods in which residents pool resources together and generate informal support networks. But these communities can also suffer from social isolation, or even exclusion from the formal economy, depending on whether or not they are recognized and supported by the local governments. This juxtaposition underscores the tension between community solidarity and social exclusion. ADUs, by comparison, produce many positive social outcomes—they bring families together across generations, or create housing options for people who need them. They include a mix of residential types and create the opportunity for inter-generational living, better communities, and mixed-income neighborhoods.

Squatting, on the other hand, generates more contested social consequences. Squatting communities can create strong internal ties and resistance, but often are vilified and face legal challenges. This leads to a tense social landscape in which informal inhabitants struggle to position themselves within the larger cultural weave of an urban area. As previously mentioned, in Turkey or Morocco, informal modifications are non-authorized modifications that dwellings undergo to accommodate their social and family needs. These adaptations allow residents to establish multi-generational households, take in city renters, and form informal social networks that result in joint housing and economic advantages.

Legal and Regulatory Impacts: Navigating the Grey Zones

This issue of the interaction between non-conformal modes of dwelling and legal rules is crucial for urban governance. Housing informalities are often found in a legal grey zone or at the margins of formal systems; residents either bend regulations to inhabit legally permitted structures, or evade regulation altogether to gain access to housing. This common practice raises numerous legal and regulatory dilemmas for cities, as municipal laws do not recognize these informal arrangements. Legal and regulatory effects arise from the informal recognition of rental agreements, lack of tenure security, and building codes in Informal Market Dynamics. At worst, informal rentals, shared housing, and sub-divided units operate in a legal grey zone or the black market. This results in a precarious housing scenario with no legal backup if the tenant faces disputes or evictions. This raises a critical issue for cities: How do you regulate a housing market segment that lies (partly) beyond the formal and informal systems? Urban authorities face challenges in enforcing regulations, protecting tenants, or incorporating informal markets into more extensive housing strategies due to the absence of well-defined legal frameworks for such informal practices.

Squatting, by contrast, tends to operate completely separately from official legal channels [34]. It consists of living in a property, either vacant or abandoned, without permission, whereby one is directly testing the boundaries and limitations of real estate law. Of all the legal conflicts for cities, this may be one of the most straight-ahead battles, as municipalities are focused on removing squatters while also trying to address broader social concerns around housing rights versus property rights. This includes the contested legal nature of squatter settler residences in Milan [31], along with cases such as Beijing [5], where long-drawn-out lawsuits repeatedly arise between squatter's public estate owners and local authorities. This tension suggests the (in)capacity of (formal) legal systems to manage informalities in housing practices effectively. A primary issue from the side of cities is that informal housing elements point towards massive shortcomings in existing legal frameworks [64,65]. In addition, many regulatory mechanisms were developed when formal housing markets dominated, and have struggled to keep up with the informal nature of much housing practice. Therefore, the municipalities must respond by governing these practices using antiquated or overly rigid legal systems. Informal housing, including grey and fully extra-illegal practices, is still challenging to regulate since it concerns safety standards, urban planning policies, and the right to equal access to housing. With all these issues in perspective, cities need to develop new legal frameworks that reflect the nature of informalities in housing. Strategies that range from normalizing to regularizing and legalizing some elements of housing informality practices (like ADU or informal modifications) could be deployed as functional mechanisms for commodifying and formalizing these housing types within the rubric of more conventional urban governance. This will require establishing systemic connections between the formal and informal (subnational) systems that reshape the legal urban fabric into a more flexible and dynamic regulatory framework, leading to an environment that meets housing demands as much as possible, with minimal urban order/safety disruption.

Health and Safety Impacts: Immediate and Long-Term Concerns

In many cases of housing informality, regardless of type, one of the most common issues is related to health hazards caused by informality without compliance with formal building standards and health regiments. Factional disputes are one consequence of Informal Market Dynamics. For instance, without regulatory oversight, overcrowded living conditions can jeopardize safety. The informal rental units, sub-divided apartments, and unauthorized modifications often do not have proper ventilation, fire safety measures, or structural integrity, putting residents at risk. This is particularly true in rapidly urbanizing cities, where demand outpaces local government capacity to regulate health and safety construction procedures [66]. The health and safety impacts of ADU have been further removed, but they remain crucial. Without proper construction authorization, an unpermitted ADU can be built with insufficient plumbing or electrical infrastructure to support safe living. Hazardous indicators for squatters often emerge from living without key services such as clean water, electricity, and proper sanitation. Squatting communities usually reside in derelict or otherwise unsafe buildings, and corresponding residents occupy spaces where fires are far more likely to occur due to a slew of fire hazards. These health effects of squatting are further exacerbated by the fact that many people in these communities experience social exclusion, which prevents them from accessing essential services such as basic medical care.

Housing informality is also extensively entangled with a string of broad and different impacts—at an economic and social level, while equally at legal or health/urban development levels. The informal market dynamics are a potential threat and an opportunity for low-income groups, while ADU is an unregulated solution to low housing prices. Squatting and unauthorized modifications point to the tensions between informal residents and formal regulatory systems as residents struggle to retrofit their housing solutions within a restrictive legal system.

Ultimately, the consequences of housing informality are symptomatic of the underlying socio-economic setting that makes these practices possible. Policymakers and urban planners should implement more effective leverages by grasping the concrete issues of these impacts to enhance the resilience and adaptive capacity of informal housing communities and intervene in unsanctioned/insecure built solutions provided by deploying the necessary safety codes.

4. Discussion

Building on the synthesized results, this discussion section places the findings in the context of the existing literature. It interprets the trends and methodological insights while integrating an evaluation of the evidence's overall strength—considering factors such as consistency, reliability, and directness—and points out areas where further research may be needed. Housing informalities (HI) are complex, multi-scalar phenomena driven by the intersecting legal, economic, social, and spatial processes found in formal or informal land markets of both the Global North and South. In this systematic literature review (SLR), we selected 27 studies on HI to perform a comprehensive analysis, which contributes to obtaining an overall empirical understanding of the global research development related to housing informality. Through this discussion, we seek to synthesize these findings and situate them in the relevant academic debates—identifying central themes, methodological lacunae, and their implications for future urban planning and development practices, policy, and future architectural and urban research. This is supported by the trend that dominated the literature: the concept of Informal Market Dynamics. Informal housing markets in the Global North and South exist as mechanisms that stand as alternatives to market imperfections, regulatory constraints, and exclusion from socio-economic opportunities [67].

Nonetheless, even if the drivers of HI are standard, their implementation is context-specific, because it depends on urban configuration forms, legal provisions, and societal norms.

Why Housing Informalities Require a Refined Selection Process

Unlike the broad concept of "informal housing", which centers on settlements developed outside formal regulatory systems, "housing informalities" (HI) describe irregular, adaptive, or incremental practices within formally recognized frameworks of property ownership and governance. These might include unauthorized changes to legally owned homes, subdivided apartments, or semi-legal rentals in cities with functional zoning and infrastructural regulations. Studying HI demands a more precise research approach, excluding investigations into slums, shantytowns, or urban villages, where housing and land tenure exist largely outside official regulatory systems. This review highlights the often-overlooked yet growing forms of housing provision and livelihood strategies that bypass or adapt formal rules in both Global North and South contexts by concentrating on these embedded informal practices.

Beyond Conventional Boundaries

A strength of this review is that it illuminates the global scale of housing informalities, considering examples from across the globe—both in developed and developing countries. Housing violations are usually associated with the developing world, and mainly with slums or informal settlements [68–70]. Still, forms of this sort of informality can also be observed in rich countries, albeit under other guises [20,71], in situations such as when we see the explosion of ADU (Accessory Dwelling Units) and SDU (sub-divided units) in cities such as Los Angeles and Sydney without broad-based public consent or other significant regulatory changes that formally legitimize these housing types. Due to housing affordability challenges, informal housing practices may arise even in well-regulated, high-income nations. Rather than serving as an alternative to formal housing, housing informality should be re-envisioned as a parallel development model that adapts and evolves across diverse environments [72]. The unauthorized modifications in cities such as Rabat and Istanbul are clear examples of the ingenuity with which residents respond to failures in the formal housing supply prevailing in the Global South. In contrast, ADU and SDU developments across cities throughout the Global North suggest that many are articulating solutions that transcend hybridity, pushing standing regulatory envelopes. In examining the hybridization between traditional and modern forms in Moroccan housing, Pinson [73] shows how domestic spaces are mutated under socio-economic pressures.

Degree of Association Among the Five Major HI Trends

The analysis reveals a strong interconnection among the five key HI trends: unauthorized modifications, informal market activities, ADUs, squatting, and atypical housing. Each trend represents a distinct way of navigating or adapting to formal housing systems, yet they frequently share underlying causes such as affordability issues, regulatory gaps, and local cultural norms. For example, ADUs might start as a legally approved method to boost housing density, but eventually take on characteristics similar to unpermitted modifications—especially if homeowners expand structures without proper authorization. Likewise, unconventional housing options, such as container homes, can overlap with squatting when people occupy land or property without legal permission, highlighting the complex interplay in high-cost urban markets that drive residents toward unconventional solutions. Moreover, unregulated market dynamics—exemplified by informal financing and sub-leasing practices—can provide the hidden economic support that enables ADU construction and unauthorized alterations. Although these trends are frequently treated as isolated phenomena, they exist along a continuum of adaptive strategies addressing structural housing limitations. Appreciating these linkages offers a richer insight into how people combine multiple informal tactics to obtain shelter, thereby complicating the formulation of universal policies.

Visualizing the Interconnectedness of Trends, Methods, Drivers, and Impacts

We propose an alluvial diagram to understand better the complex relationship between trends in housing informality, the research methodologies used to study it, its underlying drivers, and its resulting impacts (Figure 5). This visualization is key to understanding the nested relationships between different dimensions of housing informalities and how they intersect across various contexts. This provides a visual aid to help examine how some trends are methodologically addressed, and what insights these methods provide concerning specific drivers and impacts. In contexts such as Turkey [33] and Morocco [21], unauthorized modifications are predominantly probed using qualitative methods, primarily via document analysis, qualitative interviews, and field/online surveys. Emphasis is often placed on these methods' social and cultural drivers, which sheds light on how community norms, family dynamics, and economic necessity influence informal practices within legally recognized housing frameworks.

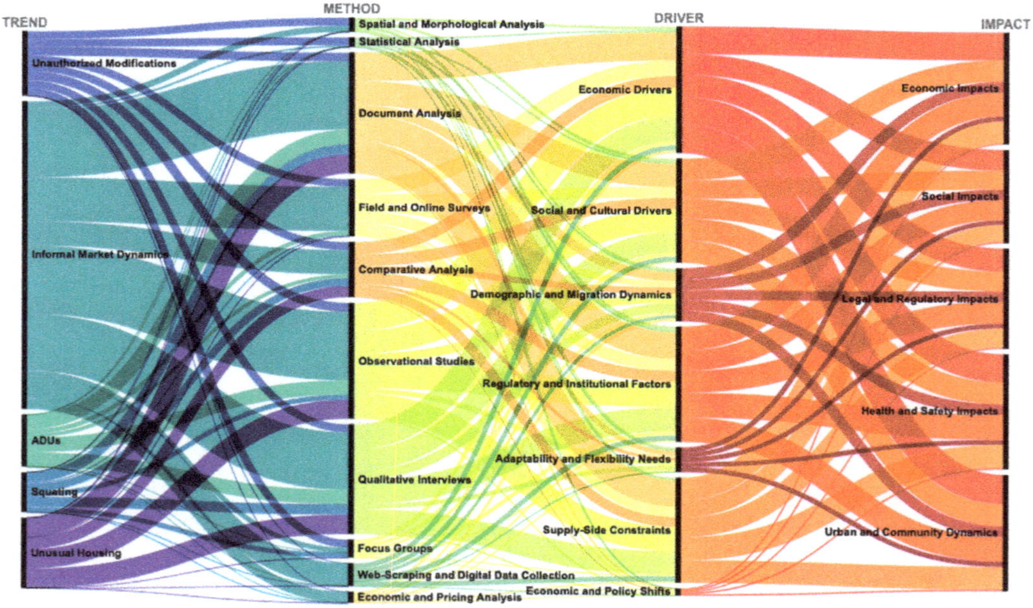

Figure 5. Alluvial diagram of methods used for each trend.

Furthermore, the diagram reveals that although unauthorized modifications have led to significant spatial changes, spatial and morphological analysis falls short as a tool for this purpose, marking a crucial research gap. This shortcoming leaves us with an incomplete understanding of these informal practices' architectural and urban effects, particularly their evolution over time into spatial forms. The diagram also shows that informal market dynamics and housing informality are the most widely studied trends, which correlate data and cross-research methods of economic and pricing analyses with web-scraping and digital data collection. This mix of methods also reflects the multi-faceted nature of informal markets and the underlying economic drivers, such as housing affordability crises, income inequality, market exclusion, etc. The over-representation of document analysis and field/online surveys within this trend clearly illustrates that understanding these informal markets requires a familiarity with historical/regulatory data and individuals' day-to-day challenges. In these cases, informal housing practices—such as sub-divided units (SDU) or unregulated rental markets—are reported to both exacerbate affordability pressures and provide adaptable yet fragile housing options for economically marginalized groups.

This visualization also highlights the relatively little-discussed trends like squatting and unusual housing despite [34] their prevalence in cities like Milan, Beijing, or Oxford. Observational studies and comparative analysis have traditionally focused on these types of housing informality [11,74,75], suggesting a call for more in-depth participatory research methodologies. The social and cultural drivers associated with these trends—socio-political resistance, squatting or adaptation needs, and unusual housing forms—are typically related to broader urban dynamics, as Figure 5 illustrates. However, no economic and pricing analysis is embedded into these trends, meaning the more significant implications for housing markets and urban affordability are not clearly understood, calling for further research.

Moreover, the visualization clearly shows how trends such as squatting and unusual housing receive extremely scarce attention, notwithstanding their high presence in cities like Milan, Beijing, and Oxford. Such forms of housing informality are usually studied through observational studies and comparative analysis, indicating the value of more immersive and context-sensitive research methodologies. The social and cultural drivers of these trends, e.g., socio-political resistance in squatting or adaptability needs in unusual housing forms, are closely linked to macro-urban processes at multiple scales, which we can visualize through the diagram (see Figure 5). Nonetheless, the absence of economic and pricing analysis in these trends implies a limited understanding of their broader effects on housing markets and urban affordability, which requires more research. Additionally, the diagram sheds light on the regulatory and institutional drivers and how these components affect informality in housing practices in different places. Trends such as ADU and unauthorized modifications can all be traced back to these drivers, indicative of strict or inflexible regulatory frameworks that typically turn residents toward informal solutions. ADU emerge as an innovation in the face of the failure of a formal dominant regulatory system, providing a living space within the existing property to satisfy housing demand, especially in the high-demand housing markets of the Global North. However, as the above diagram shows, research is disproportionately concentrated on document analysis and field surveys compared to economic analysis. This reduction suppresses our grasp of how ADU fits into the broader housing market ecosystem(s) and affordability. Ultimately, the diagram shows how these informal housing practices impact urban environments across a wide spectrum, from economic impacts to urban and community dynamics. It hints at their dual function within urban environments as challenges and opportunities. Similarly, unauthorized modifications and informal market dynamics are two scenarios that may have health and safety impacts (i.e., poor living conditions or regulatory non-compliance), but also encourage urban and community dynamics, which are more responsive and adaptable to change. One of the elements of informality that is not easy to quantify is social capital, which residents within HI often rely on. The figure thus highlights that the qualitative research methods are vital to thoroughly examining the socio-cultural implications of housing informalities.

Methodological Insights and Gaps: Toward a Comprehensive Research Framework

The methodological landscape of the reviewed studies demonstrates a rapidly evolving field in which various methods are used to characterize HI. The most common categories of methods applied in our mapping are document analysis, qualitative interviews, and field/online surveys, which are directly related to the socioeconomic and regulatory complexity encompassing housing informalities. Yet, the review also highlights key methodological deficiencies obscuring our view of HI. More sophisticated analyses like spatial and morphological analysis and economic and pricing analysis are significantly lacking in research on HI trends such as unauthorized modifications and unusual housing. Spatial and morphological studies, for example, are essential to grasping how informal practices change the urban fabric, often more radically [7], where unauthorized modifications or alternative housing solutions highly transform the physicality of cities. The lack of these methods within the reviewed studies poses a potential opportunity for future research to address the spatial impact of HI, especially within high-population-density urban areas, where such an implementation can drastically affect urban planning and infrastructure [76]. This, along with the infrequent use of economic and pricing analysis, suggest that HI is not as effectively assessed by strict economic or supply/chain mechanisms. While many may understand HI as a means to cope with economic precarity [77], these practices' more ambiguous and multifaceted relationships with other types of economies—embedded in formal housing markets, affordability, and urban inequality—remain under-theorized [78]. This would offer essential lessons in understanding the economic processes that allow informal housing markets to function—especially in cities with high demand, which are increasingly mixed up with formal housing systems [79].

Governance Gaps of Housing Informality

This study reveals a fundamental disconnect between formal governance structures—including regulatory rules, enforcement systems, and urban planning processes—and the everyday realities of households searching for shelter. In areas where institutional responses are lacking, or enforcement is inconsistent, a governance vacuum arises, leading to the rapid spread of unauthorized or unregulated modifications. The divergence between formal governance and the practical realities of housing amplifies several issues. Economically, low-income families that add unregulated extensions risk eviction or demolition. Socially and legally, communities dependent on informal financing or communal living may build closer ties, yet they remain vulnerable because their tenure is not legally secured. Health risks mount in overcrowded environments where sanitation, safety, and disease become serious concerns, while ad hoc urban expansions pressure infrastructure and alter urban morphology in unintended ways. Addressing these interlinked impacts requires policymakers and planners to align formal housing policies with residents' practices.

The Role of Socio-Cultural Factors in Shaping Housing Informality

One thing that stands out amidst this review is the relation between migration and housing informality. Migration (internal and international) is a key driver of housing informality, especially in urban contexts where legal, financial, or social circumstances prevent migrants from accessing formal markets with a framework for understanding the impact of migration on housing dynamics among migrants [80]. Migrants worldwide are often compelled to resort to informal solutions such as AUDS and SDU [71], shared accommodations, or squatting—a reality observed in cities like Hong Kong and New York City. Such a trend underscores the need to treat migration as an essential component of housing informality, especially in light of burgeoning global mobility and urbanization. Our findings from reviewed studies indicate that informality in housing is used for survival by the migrant population. However, our results also highlight the social and cultural complexity underlying everyday practices. An example pertains to unauthorized modifications, which are frequently motivated in Turkey and Morocco by socio-cultural forces, such as multi-generational family living, which require the adaptation of physical, formal housing units. These changes erode the divide between formal and informal housing, mirroring nuanced socio-cultural practices in determining urban housing dynamics.

Government Housing Policy and Its Role in Shaping Informal Housing

Another significant aspect of our analysis is how government housing policy influences and frequently limits the dynamics of housing informalities (HI). Since these policies are usually developed for fully regulated conventional markets, they often miss the adaptive strategies that define HI. This regulatory void fails to capture the myriad forms of informal market dynamics and adaptive approaches, and it may inadvertently promote them by imposing rigid standards misaligned with residents' actual circumstances. For example, in several cities, interventions intended to formalize informal settlements—via slum upgrading or ADU legalization—have met with mixed success. There are instances where these measures have increased housing security and safety; however, in other cases, heavy-handed enforcement has forced residents into riskier practices such as unauthorized modifications or squatting. These case studies demonstrate that while some government policies successfully incorporate informal practices into the formal sector, others restrict them and worsen housing vulnerability. Our critical review of these interventions underscores the need for a more flexible, integrative approach that aligns formal regulatory frameworks with residents' adaptive, often informal, strategies to secure shelter.

5. Conclusions

This SLR thoroughly interrogates the complex relationships shaping housing informalities practices (HI) in the Global North and South. It uncovers the universal nature of HI and region-specific expressions of it. The review also synthesizes comprehensive knowledge of HI trends, methods, drivers, and impacts, defining complex relationships within legally recognized frameworks and urban environments. Our results show that HI is not only present within the Global South, where much of the academic research on informal settlements and slums has focused. Instead, increased levels of ADU and SDU in high-income urban centers highlight how informal housing practices are not only resilient, but adaptively respond to affordability crises, regulatory barriers, and market failures also present in the Global North. The reconceptualization not only questions the conventional dichotomy between formal and informal housing; it also calls for a more flexible theoretical framework that would allow these practices to be understood as changing over time in different urban contexts.

Furthermore, it is critical to contextualize housing informality within socio-cultural and regulatory drivers. As evidenced in areas such as Turkey, Morocco, and South Africa, HI usually develops from incongruities between formal housing provisions and the realities experienced by residents who modify their homes for multigenerational living situations or economic or community reasons. Migration in the global south is also significant to urban housing informality. Migrant populations often experience legal, social, and financial barriers to obtaining access to formal housing, leading them to alternatives like shared or squatted accommodations. References to these findings raise a call for more context-aware urban policy-making that accounts for the sociocultural dimensions of HI and initiatives to bring communities into the planning process, in the hope of making urban development more inclusive and resilient.

Moreover, the results indicate that the interaction between formal/regulatory frameworks and informal housing practices needs to be rethought by urban planners and policymakers. Instead of criminalizing or excluding informality solutions from unilateral planning, cities should develop flexible alternatives for incorporating the informalities within the formal system. In some areas, ADUs are popular and effective; in others, support for incremental housing strategies, such as the Villa Verde project in Chile, is also a powerful tool enacted through local government regulations or zoning changes that codify it. Conversely, a heavy-handed regulatory response may worsen housing precarity, only pushing vulnerable populations further into the informal market. The second point involves the necessity of a more careful analysis of the economic effects of housing informality. Substantial reliance on informal practices leads to a legal grey zone, distorts markets, and can contribute to affordability pressures in incredibly dense urban environments. Economic analyses should be part of future efforts to identify HI's more significant monetary consequences, and guide policies focused on enhancing tenure rights, affordability, and the stability of national housing markets. This paper then sums up the diverse and complex character of housing informality, arguing for a comprehensive research agenda to bridge the spatial, economic, socio-cultural, and legal dimensions of informal housing behaviors. Addressing the identified methodological gaps and promoting cross-disciplinary collaborations, future research can also help inform more comprehensive urban policies, acknowledging and leveraging the adaptability of HI practices to be more inclusive and sustainable in both the Global North and the Global South.

Our review provides a broad perspective on the drivers, impacts, and typologies of housing informalities (HI); however, numerous areas still warrant deeper inquiry. One key area is the potential of emerging technologies—particularly AI-driven geospatial analysis—to improve the detection and mapping of informal housing. By integrating satellite imagery with machine learning algorithms, these tools could offer the more accurate tracking of unauthorized modifications and sub-divided units, thus facilitating precise policy interventions. Second, longitudinal studies are warranted to observe the temporal evolution of HI trends, and to investigate how economic fluctuations, migration flows, and regulatory adjustments influence the persistence or transformation of informal practices. Such investigations would help determine whether interventions (e.g., targeted upzoning or subsidy programs) facilitate the shift to formal compliance or push informal practices into new areas. Ultimately, evolving policy frameworks should incorporate informal housing solutions into governance structures, recognizing that many forms of informality are born not of outright illegality, but of a divergence between formal regulatory standards and lived realities. Strategies might involve legalizing certain unauthorized modifications under stringent safety criteria, supporting partial formalization via accessible financing, or co-designing solutions with community input. These research pathways can yield more nuanced, evidence-based strategies for aligning informality with broader urban development aims.

Author Contributions: Conceptualization, R.M.; methodology, R.M.; software, R.M.; validation, J.C., H.R. and A.K.; formal analysis, R.M.; investigation, R.M. and A.K.; data curation, R.M.; writing—original draft preparation, R.M.; writing—review and editing, A.K.; visualization, R.M.; supervision, J.C. and H.R.; project administration, R.M. All authors have read and agreed to the published version of the manuscript.

Funding: This research received no external funding.

Conflicts of Interest: The authors declare no conflicts of interest.

References

1. Hu, M.; Ye, W. Home Ownership and Subjective Wellbeing: A Perspective from Ownership Heterogeneity. *J. Happiness Stud.* **2020**, *21*, 1059–1079. [CrossRef]
2. Adedeji, A.; Olonisakin, T.T.; Buchcik, J.; Metzner, F.; Tsabedze, W.; Boehnke, K.; Idemudia, E.S. The multicultural conceptualization of well-being: The role of culture and circumstance in operationalizing well-being in South Africa: A mixed-methods approach. *BMC Public Health* **2023**, *23*, 2041. [CrossRef]
3. Gu, Y.; Zhu, X. Homeownership and household risky asset holdings: The moderating role of social security and the mediating role of subjective well-being. *Financ. Res. Lett.* **2024**, *66*, 105664. [CrossRef]
4. Hohmann, J.M. Resisting Dehumanizing Housing Policy: The Case for a Right to Housing in England. In *The Oxford Handbook of International Human Rights Law*; Oxford University Press: Oxford, UK, 2018. [CrossRef]

5. Zhang, M.; He, S. Who feels secure in customary tenure and why? A triangular framework of perceived tenure security in China's small property right housing. *Cities* **2020**, *107*, 102900. [CrossRef]
6. Chitengi, H.S. Regulations and housing informality in African cities: Appropriating regulatory frameworks to factors that influence resilience. *Hous. Soc.* **2018**, *45*, 14–41. [CrossRef]
7. van Doorn, L.; Arnold, A.; Rapoport, E. In the Age of Cities: The Impact of Urbanization on House Prices and Affordability. In *Hot Property: The Housing Market in Major Cities*; Springer: Berlin/Heidelberg, Germany, 2019; pp. 3–13. [CrossRef]
8. Tiwari, P.; Rao, J.; Day, J. Conceptualizing Housing for All. In *Development Paradigms for Urban Housing in BRICS Countries*; Springer: Berlin/Heidelberg, Germany, 2016; pp. 1–20.
9. Kamana, A.A.; Radoine, H.; Nyasulu, C. Urban challenges and strategies in African cities—A systematic literature review. *City Environ. Interact.* **2023**, *21*, 100132. [CrossRef]
10. Mwathunga, E.; Donaldson, R. Urban land contestations, challenges and planning strategies in Malawi's main urban centers. *Land Use Policy* **2017**, *77*, 1–8. [CrossRef]
11. van Niekerk, B. Housing as urbanism: A policy to discourage urban sprawl and provide well-located and affordable housing in South Africa. *Town Reg. Plan.* **2018**, *73*, 68–82. [CrossRef]
12. Agarwal, S.; Mandal, S.; Bajaj, D.; Agarwal, A.S.; Singh, T.P. Affordable Housing and its Sustainability-A review of Critical Success Factors (CSFs). In Proceedings of the 2021 9th International Conference on Reliability, Infocom Technologies and Optimization (Trends and Future Directions), ICRITO 2021, Noida, India, 3–4 September 2021. [CrossRef]
13. Recio, R.B.; Shafique, T. Reimagining (informal) housing futures in uncertain times. *Int. J. Hous. Policy* **2022**, *22*, 106–118. [CrossRef]
14. van Gelder, J.-L. Paradoxes of Urban Housing Informality in the Developing World. *Law Soc. Rev.* **2013**, *47*, 493–522. [CrossRef]
15. Kamete, A.Y. On handling urban informality in southern africa. *Geogr. Ann. Ser. B Hum. Geogr.* **2013**, *95*, 17–31. [CrossRef]
16. Cobbinah, P.B.; Finn, B.M. Planning and Climate Change in African Cities: Informal Urbanization and 'Just' Urban Transformations. *J. Plan. Lit.* **2022**, *38*, 361–379. [CrossRef]
17. Okyere, A.S.; Kita, M. Rethinking Urban Informality and Informal Settlements Growth in Urban Africa. *J. Sustain. Dev. Afr.* **2015**, *17*, 10–17.
18. Kelling, E. The regularity of informality: Reframing the formal–informal relationship with the help of informal housing in London. *Eur. Urban Reg. Stud.* **2023**, *31*, 425–436. [CrossRef]
19. Shrestha, P.; Gurran, N. Breaking the rules? Informal housing, urban deregulation, and secondary dwellings in Australia. *Eur. Urban Reg. Stud.* **2023**, *31*, 394–410. [CrossRef]
20. Usman, M.; Maslova, S.; Burgess, G. Urban informality in the Global North: (il)legal status and housing strategies of Ghanaian migrants in New York City. *Int. J. Hous. Policy* **2021**, *21*, 247–267. [CrossRef]
21. Mrani, R.; Radoine, H.; Chenal, J. Informalities as Resistance: Case Study of a Middle-Class Housing Neighborhood in Rabat, Morocco. *J. Eng. Archit.* **2022**, *10*, 2334–2994.
22. Gurran, N.; Pill, M.; Maalsen, S. Hidden homes? Uncovering Sydney's informal housing market. *Urban Stud.* **2021**, *58*, 1712–1731. [CrossRef]
23. Culwick, C.; Patel, Z. Building just and sustainable cities through government housing developments. *Environ. Urban.* **2020**, *32*, 133–154. [CrossRef]
24. Turok, I.; Borel-Saladin, J. Backyard shacks, informality and the urban housing crisis in South Africa: Stopgap or prototype solution? *Hous. Stud.* **2016**, *31*, 384–409. [CrossRef]
25. Todes, A.; Weakley, D.; Harrison, P. Densifying Johannesburg: Context, policy and diversity. *J. Hous. Built Environ.* **2018**, *33*, 281–299. [CrossRef]
26. Lemanski, C. Augmented informality: South Africa's backyard dwellings as a by-product of formal housing policies. *Habitat Int.* **2009**, *33*, 472–484. [CrossRef]
27. Kavaarpuo, G.; Mintah, K.; Donkor-Hyiaman, K.A. Financing Housing Development in an Underdeveloped Financial Market: Learning from Developers' Financing Adaptations? *Hous. Policy Debate* **2023**, *34*, 918–945. [CrossRef]
28. Page, M.J.; McKenzie, J.E.; Bossuyt, P.M.; Boutron, I.; Hoffmann, T.C.; Mulrow, C.D.; Shamseer, L.; Tetzlaff, J.M.; Akl, E.A.; Brennan, S.E.; et al. The PRISMA 2020 statement: An updated guideline for reporting systematic reviews. *BMJ* **2021**, *372*, n71. [CrossRef] [PubMed]
29. Burgers, J. Formal determinants of informal arrangements: Housing and undocumented immigrants in Rotterdam. *J. Ethn. Migr. Stud.* **1998**, *24*, 295–312. [CrossRef]
30. Sendi, R.; Mali, B.C.; Mali, B.Č. Surviving in limbo: An insight into Slovenia's informal private rented housing sector. *Theor. Empir. Res. Urban Manag.* **2015**, *10*, 19–39.
31. Karenina, N.; Guevara, A. A Hidden Informality? Informal Occupation in Milan: The Housing Needs and the Events of Protest. *J. Stud. Soc. Sci.* **2016**, *14*, 1–68.

32. Kinsella, K. Enumerating informal housing: A field method for identifying secondary units. *Can. Geogr.* **2017**, *61*, 510–524. [CrossRef]
33. Gür, E.A.; Yüksel, Y.D. Analytical investigation of urban housing typologies in twentieth century Istanbul. *Archnet-IJAR Int. J. Arch. Res.* **2019**, *13*, 93–111. [CrossRef]
34. Grashoff, U. Cautious occupiers and restrained bureaucrats: Schwarzwohnen in the German Democratic Republic. Somewhat different from squatting. *Urban Stud.* **2019**, *56*, 548–560. [CrossRef]
35. Contreras, Y.; Neville, L.; González, R. In-formality in access to housing for Latin American migrants: A case study of an intermediate Chilean city. *Int. J. Hous. Policy* **2019**, *19*, 411–435. [CrossRef]
36. Leung, K.M.; Yiu, C.Y. Rent determinants of sub-divided units in Hong Kong. *J. Hous. Built Environ.* **2019**, *34*, 133–151. [CrossRef]
37. Collins, D.; Bates, L.; Kearns, R.; Evans, J. Considering the camp: Ambivalent geographies of mobile dwelling. *Appl. Mobilities* **2020**, *5*, 21–38. [CrossRef]
38. O'Brien, D.; Carrasco, S.; Dovey, K. Incremental housing: Harnessing informality at Villa Verde. *Archnet-IJAR Int. J. Arch. Res.* **2020**, *14*, 345–358. [CrossRef]
39. Harten, J.G.; Kim, A.M.; Brazier, J.C. Real and fake data in Shanghai's informal rental housing market: Ground truthing data scraped from the internet. *Urban Stud.* **2021**, *58*, 1831–1845. [CrossRef]
40. Minhua, L. Container housing: Formal informality and deterritorialized home-making amid bulldozer urbanism in Shanghai. *Urban Stud.* **2021**, *58*, 1141–1157.
41. Leung, K.M.; Choy, L.H.T.; Chau, K.W. Examining informal housing supply through rent gap analysis: An empirical study of sub-divided units in Hong Kong. *Cities* **2022**, *126*, 103666. [CrossRef]
42. Nasreen, Z.; Ruming, K. Struggles and opportunities at the platform interface: Tenants' experiences of navigating shared room housing using digital platforms in Sydney. *J. Hous. Built Environ.* **2022**, *37*, 1537–1554. [CrossRef]
43. Gurran, N.; Nasreen, Z.; Shrestha, P. Discounted housing? Understanding shared rental markets under platformisation. *Hous. Stud.* **2023**, *39*, 3067–3091. [CrossRef]
44. Lin, S.; Wu, F.; Wang, Y.; Li, Z. Migrants' perceived social integration in different housing tenures in urban China. *Geoforum* **2023**, *139*, 103693. [CrossRef]
45. Galuszka, J. Boats as Housing in Oxford, UK: Trajectories of Informality in a High-Income Context. *Int. J. Urban Reg. Res.* **2024**, *48*, 126–144. [CrossRef]
46. Julio, A.U. 'In-betweenness': Migrants experience accessing rental housing in the innerburbs neighborhoods of Santiago, Chile. *Hous. Stud.* **2024**, 1–25. [CrossRef]
47. Newton, P.W.; Newman, P.W.G.; Glackin, S.; Thomson, G. Changing Attitudes to Housing and Residential Location in Cities: The Cultural Clash and the Greyfield Solution. In *Greening the Greyfields*; Springer: Berlin/Heidelberg, Germany, 2022; pp. 121–133.
48. Wenge, R.; Zhang, X.; Dave, C.; Chao, L.; Hao, S. Smart city architecture: A technology guide for implementation and design challenges. *China Commun.* **2014**, *11*, 56–69. [CrossRef]
49. Yang, Z.; Yang, H.; Wang, H. Evaluating urban sustainability under different development pathways: A case study of the Beijing-Tianjin-Hebei region. *Sustain. Cities Soc.* **2020**, *61*, 102226. [CrossRef]
50. Esmail, S.; Corburn, J. Struggles to remain in Kigali's "unplanned" settlements: The case of Bannyahe. *Environ. Urban.* **2020**, *32*, 19–36. [CrossRef]
51. Doe, B.; Peprah, C.; Chidziwisano, J.R. Sustainability of slum upgrading interventions: Perception of low-income households in Malawi and Ghana. *Cities* **2020**, *107*, 102946. [CrossRef]
52. Goodfellow, T. Urban Fortunes and Skeleton Cityscapes: Real Estate and Late Urbanization in Kigali and Addis Ababa. *Int. J. Urban Reg. Res.* **2017**, *41*, 786–803. [CrossRef]
53. John, S.; Mcgranahan, G.; Mkanga, M.; Ndezi, T.; Stephen, S.; Tacoli, C. The churn of the land nexus and contrasting gentrification processes in Dar es Salaam and Mwanza, Tanzania. *Environ. Urban.* **2020**, *32*, 429–446. [CrossRef]
54. Todes, A.; Kok, P.; Wentzel, M.; Van Zyl, J.; Cross, C. Contemporary South African Urbanization Dynamics. *Urban Forum* **2010**, *21*, 331–348. [CrossRef]
55. Chirisa, I.; Matamanda, A. Forces shaping urban morphology in Southern Africa Today: Unequal interplay among people, practice, and policy. *J. Urban. Int. Res. Placemaking Urban Sustain.* **2019**, *12*, 354–372. [CrossRef]
56. Olajide, O.A.; Agunbiade, M.E.; Bishi, H.B. The realities of Lagos urban development vision on livelihoods of the urban poor. *J. Urban Manag.* **2018**, *7*, 21–31. [CrossRef]
57. Ostrom, E. Beyond Markets and States: Polycentric Governance of Complex Economic Systems. *Am. Econ. Rev.* **2010**, *100*, 641–672. [CrossRef]
58. Hamdi, N. *The Placemaker's Guide to Building Community*; Routledge: Abingdon-on-Thames, UK, 2010. [CrossRef]
59. Roy, A. Urban Informality: Toward an Epistemology of Planning. *J. Am. Plan. Assoc.* **2005**, *71*, 147–158. [CrossRef]
60. Davis, M. *Planet of Slums*; Verso: London, UK, 2006.

61. Yussif, K.; Dompreh, E.B.; Gasparatos, A. Sustainability of urban expansion in Africa: A systematic literature review using the Drivers–Pressures–State–Impact–Responses (DPSIR) framework. *Sustain. Sci.* **2023**, *18*, 1459–1479. [CrossRef]
62. Scheba, A.; Turok, I.; Visagie, J. Inequality and Urban Density: Socio-economic Drivers of Uneven Densification in Cape Town. *Environ. Urban. ASIA* **2021**, *12*, S107–S126. [CrossRef]
63. Abubakar, I.R.; Aina, Y.A. The prospects and challenges of developing more inclusive, safe, resilient and sustainable cities in Nigeria. *Land Use Policy* **2019**, *87*, 104105. [CrossRef]
64. van Noorloos, F.; Kloosterboer, M. Africa's new cities: The contested future of urbanization. *Urban Stud.* **2018**, *55*, 1223–1241. [CrossRef]
65. Angelopulo, G. A comparative measure of inclusive urbanization in the cities of Africa. *World Dev. Perspect.* **2021**, *22*, 100313. [CrossRef]
66. Smit, W.; Parnell, S. Urban sustainability and human health: An African perspective. *Curr. Opin. Environ. Sustain.* **2012**, *4*, 443–450. [CrossRef]
67. Jimenez, E. Urban squatting and community organization in developing countries. *J. Public Econ.* **1985**, *27*, 69–92. [CrossRef]
68. Adegun, O.B. Exploring Just Sustainability in Re-Blocking Intervention in a Johannesburg Informal Settlement. *J. Asian Afr. Stud.* **2018**, *53*, 782–796. [CrossRef]
69. Visagie, J.; Turok, I. Getting urban density to work in informal settlements in Africa. *Environ. Urban.* **2020**, *32*, 351–370. [CrossRef]
70. Nuhu, S.; Munuo, N.; Mngumi, L. Governance challenges of regularization of informal settlements in peri-urban Tanzania: Perspectives from local stakeholders. *Int. J. Urban Sustain. Dev.* **2023**, *15*, 35–47. [CrossRef]
71. Chiodelli, F. The Dark Side of Urban Informality in the Global North: Housing Illegality and Organized Crime in Northern Italy. *Int. J. Urban Reg. Res.* **2019**, *43*, 497–516. [CrossRef]
72. Azunre, G.A. An Overlooked Phenomenon? Reflecting on Elite Housing Informality and its Potential Sustainability Implications. *J. Plan. Lit.* **2024**, *39*, 365–370. [CrossRef]
73. Pinson, D. Maroc: Un habitat «occidentalisé» subverti par la «tradition». *Maghreb Machrek.* **1994**, *143*, 190–203. [CrossRef]
74. Buyana, K. Keeping the doors open: Experimenting science–policy–practice interfaces in Africa for sustainable urban development. *J. Hous. Built Environ.* **2020**, *35*, 539–554. [CrossRef]
75. Akrofi, M.M.; Avogo, F.A.; Wedam, E.A. Sustainable urban development and the challenge of unauthorized buildings: Assessing demographic drivers in peri-urban areas of Ghana. *J. Hous. Built Environ.* **2019**, *34*, 571–598. [CrossRef]
76. Azunre, G.A.; Amponsah, O.; Takyi, S.A.; Mensah, H. Informality-sustainable city nexus: The place of informality in advancing sustainable Ghanaian cities. *Sustain. Cities Soc.* **2021**, *67*, 102707. [CrossRef]
77. Amoako, C.; Boamah, E.F. Build as you earn and learn Informal urbanism and incremental housing financing in Kumasi, Ghana. *J. Hous. Built Environ.* **2017**, *32*, 429–448. [CrossRef]
78. Sun, L.; Ho, P. Formalizing informal homes, a bad idea: The credibility thesis applied to China's "extra-legal" housing. *Land Use Policy* **2018**, *79*, 891–901. [CrossRef]
79. Guedes, R.; Iachan, F.S.; Sant'anna, M. Housing supply in the presence of informality. *Reg. Sci. Urban Econ.* **2023**, *99*, 103875. [CrossRef]
80. Brueckner, J.K. Urban squatting with rent-seeking organizers. *Reg. Sci. Urban Econ.* **2013**, *43*, 561–569. [CrossRef]

urban science

MDPI

Article

Comparison of Green Space Usage During COVID-19

Humam Helmi, Can Kara * and Tuğşad Tülbentçi

Faculty of Architecture, Near East University, via Mersin 10, Nicosia 99138, North Cyprus, Turkey; humam.helmi@neu.edu.tr (H.H.); tugsad.tulbentci@neu.edu.tr (T.T.)
* Correspondence: can.kara@neu.edu.tr

Abstract: The main aim of this paper is to evaluate park usage and accessibility in the northern part of Nicosia, Cyprus, and to compare the usage and accessibility before and after the COVID-19 pandemic. This study provides insights into how park usage changed due to the pandemic and lockdown measures, offering valuable information for urban developers on improving park safety and health standards during pandemic conditions. A total of 500 housing units were selected from among the Nicosia neighborhoods to assess changes in behavior and park usage pre- and post-pandemic. These data were analyzed using SPSS descriptive statistics, and field studies were conducted to identify key parks in Nicosia. The results indicate that parks offer a pleasant environment, with higher usage observed in the summer and spring seasons. However, a decline in park usage was noted during the pandemic, highlighting areas for enhancing safety and accessibility. Recommendations are made to assist urban developers in making informed decisions for future park improvements, as well as for further studies on this topic. This research aims to contribute to creating safer, more accessible parks for the residents of Nicosia.

Keywords: accessibility; usage; urban parks; COVID-19; before and after pandemic

1. Introduction

The coronavirus pandemic, also recognized as the COVID-19 pandemic, is an ongoing disease that started in 2019 (COVID-19) and produces a dangerous lung disorder also known as SARS-CoV-2. It was originally discovered in Wuhan, China, in December 2019. The World Health Organization stated that the epidemic was an worldwide public health emergency, and worry started in January 2020. It was classified as an emergency pandemic in March 2020. By December 2020, more than 67 million people had been infected, and more than 1.53 million deaths were officially stated regarding COVID-19 [1] Since the virus spreads through the air, public spaces faced massive shutdowns because of the fear of spreading the virus even more—only parks and some other similar public facilities remained open for use by locals during the pandemic [2]. Recently, there have been many studies concerning urban parks and how they affect the well-being of people, as well as regarding their psychological problems. Thus, this study focused mainly on Western nations—North America and Europe. This study recorded that urban environments and public areas do have effects on the psychological health and physical health of humans. Rapprochement between rustic and city areas has been studied, and the outcome has proven that people in city areas have more health risk issues than those in rustic regions [3]. The worry is steady and growing at a continuous rate because of the reality that urbanization is rising—it will increase by up to 12% by the year 2050 [4]. Overcrowded cities cause sound pollution and other types of contamination (e.g., water and/or air), which contribute to increasing risks to well-being and health safety levels for the residents of urban areas and also make the spread of a disease such as COVID-19 possible [5]. Research has also proved that people who are more open to natural surroundings will have better health and fewer health problems, causing them to have healthier bodies and better immune systems [6,7]. Thus, urban park spaces and how they are linked to people's health is an important issue to be inspected. More careful studies on the issue of COVID-19 can highly benefit all individuals, as it disturbs a great part of their lives [8].

The effect of parks on people is positively linked to preferable healthy lifestyles, but excuses can be made that park benefits and more profits are being restricted by multiple aspects. One of the tests stated that the dangers of spreading the virus in parks might be a serious issue, and most of the parks in Nicosia are considered to be unprepared for facing such a pandemic [9]. In this paper, we examine some of the signals around the usage of parks during COVID-19.

Analyzing social distancing, we argue that ensuring public access to nature should be an essential strategy of cities when coping with crisis, as is evident in the current situation and informed by historical insights.

This study aimed to calculate and study the usage of green areas and how they functioned during the COVID-19 pandemic in the center of the Nicosia region in Cyprus. This study aimed to measure the usage of green areas and parks in this zone and the parks' urban design in this district and application/usage. Calculating the accessibility and the usage of green areas will help us gain greater comprehension on how to improve these spaces in urban areas, which helps us to reach a higher level of quality of these parks while maintaining the health recommendation of social distancing and not spreading the virus.

This study can help people with power further progression in evolving city areas and especially in green spaces and urban parks. Moreover, this will aid in recording the problems individuals/residents have while using green areas and parks during a pandemic, like the absence of sitting zones and poor accessibility. This will help people with power to determine which factors of urban strategy and practice structures are extra significant for residents and to improve planning for urban parks, where children, their families, and local people can better and more efficiently use the parks' equipment and facilities. The core purpose of this study was to assess and compare the usage of parks before and after the pandemic.

2. Literature Review

2.1. Urban Parks and Health

The biosphere's metropolises are progressively overfilled and contaminated [10]. Urban parks deliver an extensive choice of ecological facilities that aid in fighting numerous city diseases and advance quality of life for urban inhabitants, especially in terms of their health. Such urban park areas are varied in scale, shelter, class fertility, ecological excellence, immediacy to community transportation, amenities, and facilities [11–13]. Public park areas contain reserves and parks, sporting grounds, and riparian areas—like river and stream banks, trails and greenways, public parks, road plants, and landscape upkeep areas—as well as fewer moderate places, like green alleyways, green walls, and graveyards [14]. Isolated natural areas contain private yards, common lands of residential houses, and company grounds.

Environmental facilities offered by urban parks not only assist the environmental integrity of cities but also protect the community health of city inhabitants. Urban green areas may clean the air, eliminate contamination, suppress noise, calm temperatures, prevent tempest water, and refill groundwater; furthermore, they can deliver nutrition [15,16]. For instance, vegetation in public areas might decrease airborne contamination by absorbing anything harmful that exists in the air [17]. Urban green and natural areas and city woods also modestly help with heat management by providing shade and cool areas, thereby decreasing the danger of temperature-related diseases for urban inhabitants [18,19].

Nonetheless, inside cities, urban parks are not equally spread. Park visitors can be biased based on salary, ethnic features, disability, gender, age, and additional axes of change [20,21]. In previous decades, the mixed availability of urban parks has been developed and documented as a subject of ecological fairness from the perspective of community well-being [22,23]. Studies have aimed to calculate the usage of city parks and natural areas, mainly parks; usage was qualified based on the sociodemographic characteristics of these places and in what way the absence of access affects community well-being. However, most of these studies have been conducted in Australia, the United Kingdom, and the United States

The reasons why urban parks and green areas are differentially spread in cities are diverse, based on the attitude toward a green plan, the area's history of land growth, developing philosophies about comfort and regeneration, and past class and ethnocidal disparity and state domination [24]. Frequently, descriptions are unified and found to support each other. For instance, the US's history of property growth is entangled with its past ethnocidal dominations and attitudes toward urban parkland use and design schemes.

In the United States, individuals of different racial backgrounds and lower-salary employees are more likely to inhabit city centers, where urban parks are scarce or poorly kept. Higher-income houses are frequently located on the outskirts of cities where the green zone is rich, well looked after, and well kept [25]. This ecological unfairness has developed significance, especially through grassland-gaining agendas and plans organize under-utilized city places for extra green areas. Restoring urban parks for groups of different racial backgrounds and/or lower-salary families will also generate green city areas. The creation of additional green areas will advance the appeal and community well-being and make the districts more desirable. In turn, housing prices will increase. This housing price growth will possibly lead to more dislocation and/or elimination of the very inhabitants that the urban parks and green areas were supposed to help. Students will also face higher rentals and therefore end up insecurely housed; individuals can be made to leave their neighborhoods, which results in fewer wanted districts and a park-shortage issue. This causes undesirable community health consequences; in addition to the sustained park shortage, this can also lead to dislocation as well as unwarranted relocations to undesirable locations in terms of public health [26].

Most studies on urban green areas and well-being focus on city gardens and natural zones [27,28]. Research connects the absence of gardens and parks to diminished well-being [29], such that the presence of natural zones defends well-being [30]. Moreover, natural areas and city gardens frequently serve as places for sports, which are also associated with improved well-being and reduction in numerous long-lasting illnesses [31,32]. Certainly, a great number of papers have demonstrated the connections between proximity to parks and engagement in physical exercise [33,34].

Researchers have focused on the connections between urban green areas (such as parks and gardens) and unhealthy weight issues [35]. Overweightness might be particularly damaging to children's well-being [36] as well as increases the chances of weight-related issues in adulthood [37]. While genetics play a role in weight-related issues [38], weight gain also stems from a person's exercise routine, and lower participation in sports seem to strongly affect the tendency to gain weight [39]. Children with access to gardens and recreational services are more likely to be active than kids who lack such access, and similar outcomes are shared in grownups [40,41].

For instance, Giles-Corti [42] discussed the importance of appeal and scale of the open zToe. Through statistical studies on ecological services in Perth, Australia, researchers found that city gardens inspire participation in sports and physical exercise when they are accessible and have certain attractive features (e.g., retail shops, trees, minor traffic, sidewalks) [43]. Veitch [44] examined the usage of city gardens in relation to physical activity in Australia before and after enhancements and discovered substantial increases in park usage after the enhancements.

Like physical health, mental health is empirically connected to green areas and urban parks [45]. The presence of city gardens decreases pressure and stress levels [46,47]. Urban parks and natural areas also give city inhabitants chances to interact with flora and fauna, to rest, and to experience solitude [48]. Going to parks revitalizes inhabitants and instills feelings of peace and calm [49].

2.2. Park Accessibility During the COVID-19 Pandemic

The COVID-19 epidemic caused the closure of entire cities in China and triggered public health actions across the globe as the virus spread. In Wuhan, where the virus first appeared, universities, roads, rail networks, and marketplaces were closed [50]. Similar protective actions were enacted in Hong Kong, Beijing, and Hubei Province to minimize the viral outbreak, as data on the virus continue to be collected [51].

The spread of the virus prompted the World Health Organization (WHO) on 30 January 2019 to declare that the COVID-19 pandemic (previously the coronavirus epidemic) constitutes a global public health emergency or a 'Public Health Emergency of International Concern' (PHEIC), which is defined as "an extraordinary event which is determined to constitute a public health risk to other States through the international spread of disease and to potentially require a coordinated international response". Potential risk factors include public concern over unexpected, uncommon, or unpredicted events; transportation guidelines for public well-being beyond the State's national boundaries; and the urgent need for global action.

In 2020, the novel COVID-19 epidemic prompted nations across the globe to engage in unprecedented actions of social distancing to control the spread of the virus. Such measures included school closures and urging people to stay home, centering around reducing the number of close physical interactions among people. This is widely regarded as one of the most effective approaches to keeping COVID-19 cases down [52,53].

At the same time, social distancing disrupted the everyday lives of entire populations wherever it was implemented [54]. Such large and unexpected disturbances to ordinary life are likely to influence people's health, especially for inhabitants of crowded cities with few urban parks and public spaces. For instance, older people, who are at the greatest danger of suffering from the deadly effects of COVID-19, also suffer from anxiety and unhappiness caused by social isolation [55,56].

Throughout these unusual conditions of public isolation, city landscapes offer opportunities for preserving health and well-being. The essence of this proposal is that in situations of voluntary social distancing, in which individuals are still permitted to go outside, urban green spaces can give individuals the opportunity to escape the confines of their households and benefit from a host of positive and healthy effects [57,58], including engaging in socially distanced interactions [59] and enjoying outdoor environments [60].

3. Study Area, Materials, and Methods

The study area included the central neighborhoods of northern Nicosia, Cyprus, covering approximately 112 square kilometers. This area was reported to have 51,386 inhabitants in 2011 and contain roughly 14,616 houses (see Table 1). A random sampling method was used with 500 houses across all the regions of Nicosia (see Figure 1). The number of survey participants in each region depended on the overall number of houses in the region, as specified in the table below.

Table 1. Questionnaire distribution table.

Neighborhood	Number of Houses Out of 14,616	Percentage	Number of Questionnaires Out of 500
ÇAĞLAYAN	366	2.5%	13
GÖÇMENKÖY	1013	6.9%	35
KIZILAY	1142	7.8%	39
KÖŞKLÜ ÇİFTLİK	996	6.8%	34
KUMSAL	558	3.8%	19
KÜÇÜK KAYMAKLI	3293	22.5%	112
MARMARA	937	6.4%	32

Table 1. *Cont.*

Neighborhood	Number of Houses Out of 14,616	Percentage	Number of Questionnaires Out of 500
TAŞKINKÖY	1191	8.14%	41
TAŞKINKÖY	1191	8.14%	41
YENİŞEHİR	1254	8.5%	43
SURLARİÇİ	1729	11.8%	58

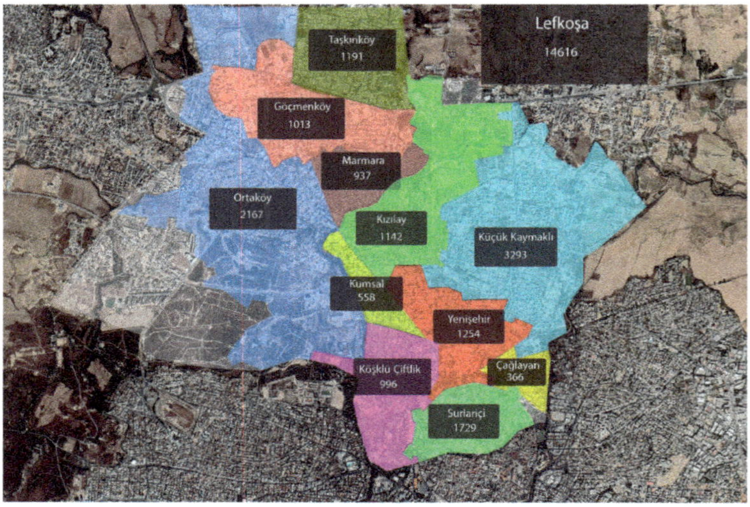

Figure 1. The distribution of the houses and the regions in Nicosia.

4. Results

4.1. The Usage of Park Areas

In this section, we compare the usage of urban green spaces before and after the pandemic and how this affected user behavior. Participants were asked a set of questions about their park usage before and after the pandemic in order to determine the time, purpose, and frequency of park usage, as well as which parks they mainly used. Figure 2 shows which parks the participants used during the pandemic, indicating which parks were most used.

The most used park is Kumsal Park (21%), followed by Barış ve Demokrası Park (19%), Belediye Park (14%), and Marmara Park (12%), with the remaining parks used 5–10%, as shown in the figure above. We can see that the most used parks are those near the city center, such as Kumsal, Belediye, and Barış ve Demokrasi Parks, mainly because they are easier to reach and have many surrounding activities, such as markets and coffee shops. They also do not require cars or other transportation to reach them, as most people can easily access them by walking. We asked the participants about how frequently they use the parks during the week before and after the pandemic, as shown in Figure 3.

It is clear that everyday park usage decreased before the pandemic, and monthly and weekly park usage increased after the pandemic; during the pandemic, people were not using the parks regularly due to accessibility problems caused by the lockdown. As a result, people's park usage decreased, and we found fewer people using the parks on a daily basis during the pandemic. However, we can see an increase in monthly usage of 12%, indicating that people still want to go to parks but experienced accessibility difficulties during the pandemic, so most of the park usage was among people living near parks

(5−10-minute walk), as they did not need transportation to reach the parks. People living farther away did not use parks during the pandemic.

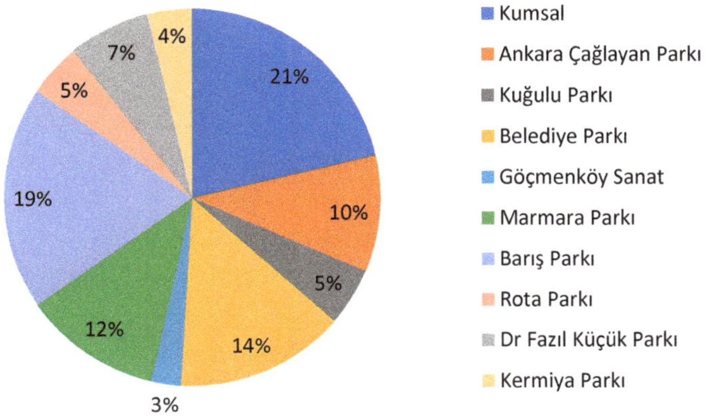

Figure 2. The parks that participants used.

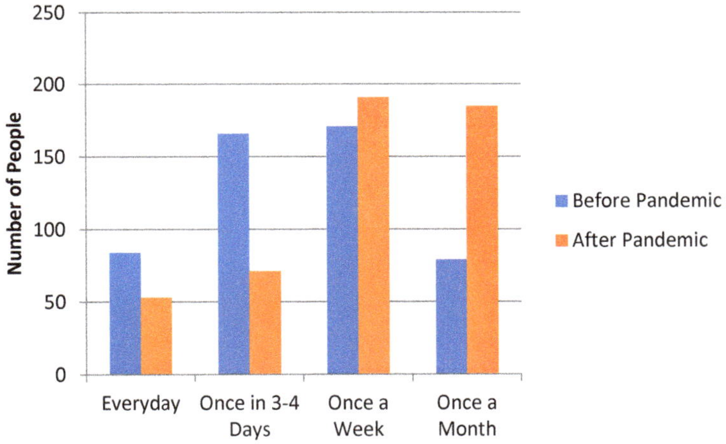

Figure 3. The difference in the usage before and after the pandemic.

Next, we asked participants about the times they mainly use the park and compared these before and after the pandemic, as seen in Figure 4.

There was a 22.4% decrease in evening-time users between 18:00 and 21:00 and a 22% increase in users between 12:00 and 14:00, which means that the majority of people were using the parks during the daytime during the pandemic due to the enforcement of lockdowns at night. Thus, peak hours before the pandemic were between 14:00 to 21:00 and 12:00 to 18:00 after the pandemic. Like most businesses, schools, and universities, parks were closed during lockdown, forcing most people to use the parks during the daytime, causing crowds in some cases, especially at park facilities providing sport equipment and children's playgrounds; too many people using the same equipment in a short amount of time might exacerbate the spread of COVID-19.

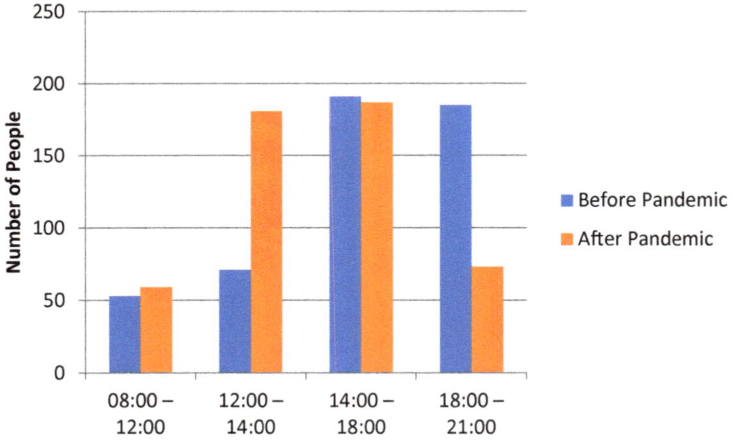

Figure 4. The difference is time usage before and after the pandemic.

In the next question, we asked about the purpose for which participants used parks before and after the pandemic to analyze if the pandemic changed their reasons for park usage. Figure 5 shows that the majority (36%) of participants visit the park for sitting and resting, with 32% using parks for sports and hiking, 21% to access children's playgrounds, 7% to access cafeterias and buffets, and 4% for other usage reasons.

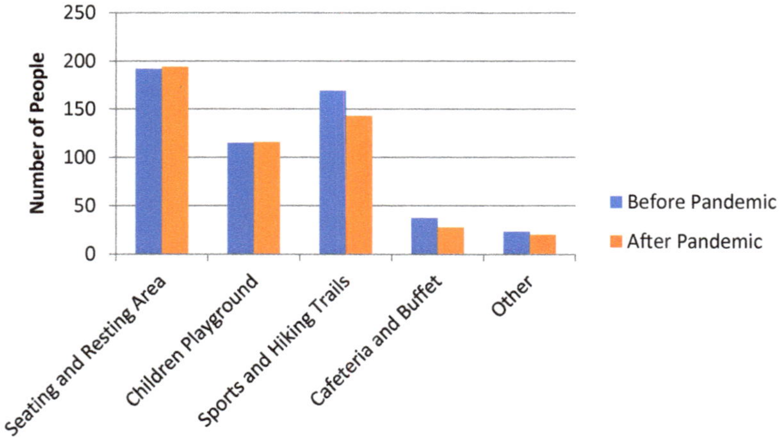

Figure 5. The difference in usage before and after the pandemic.

In Figure 5, the reasons for park usage before and after the pandemic can be seen as follows.

It can be seen that there are small changes in participants' park usage purposes, with an increase of 3% for sitting and resting and of almost 2% in children's playground access, as well as decreases of about 5% in sport equipment usage and 1.5% in cafeterias and buffet access; there was almost no changes in the other usages. Overall, we can say that there is not much difference regarding the reasons why people use parks before and after the pandemic.

4.2. Design and Improvements

In this part, the survey asked participants for their opinions on the parks and what kind of changes and improvements they want in parks, including what they are most concerned about when using parks. The participants had some ideas and opinions about how to improve the current parks.

In this part, we asked the participants about whether they think the usage of the parks increased or decreased during the pandemic; in Table 2, we can see the participants' responses and what they think about park usage during the pandemic.

Table 2. The participants' opinions about the usage of parks after the pandemic.

	Frequency	Percent
Increased	205	41
Decreased	295	59
Total	500	100

Table 2 shows that the majority (59%) of people think that park usage decreased during the pandemic because of the lockdown, while 41% think that park usage increased.

From this table, we can see that the participants see a decrease in park usage during the pandemic caused by the enforcement of lockdowns and accessibility problems, especially in areas that have no parks nearby, and thus, participants were required to travel some distance to reach the nearest park in their area; therefore, in addition to the lockdown, the lack of transportation resulted in a decrease in park usage.

In this question, we asked the participants what they would change or add to the parks, such as what kind of elements, facilities, and equipment they prefer, including the children's playground equipment, parking areas, medical stations, and so on. Figure 6 shows how participants answered this question.

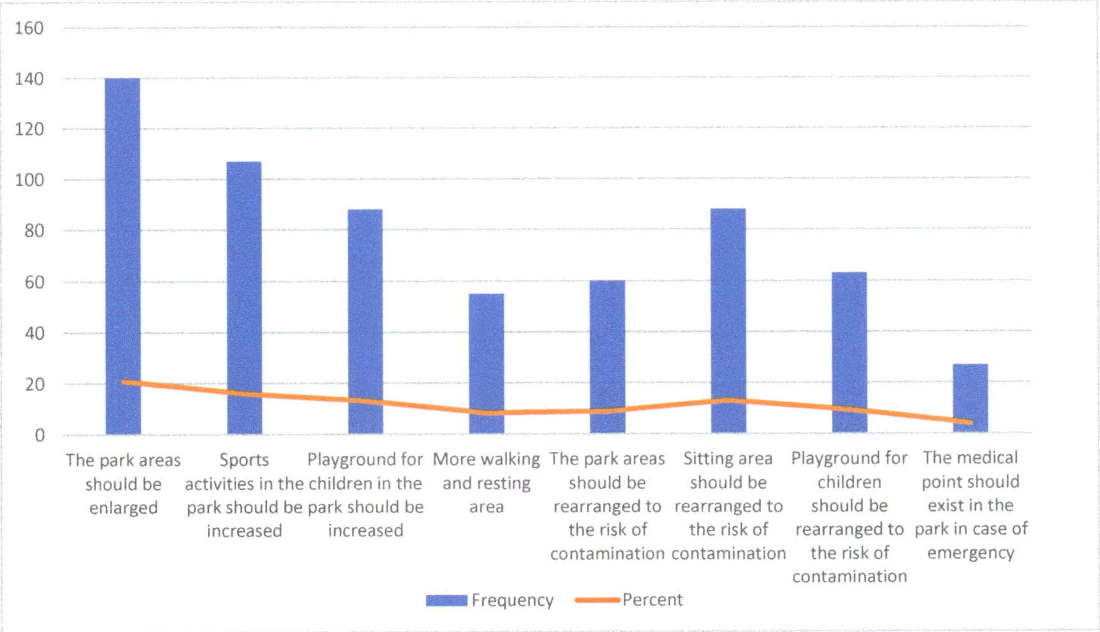

Figure 6. The participants' opinions of what should be changed in parks.

Figure 6 shows that the highest demand was for more parking areas (21%), followed by more sport activities (16%). Participants also expressed that children's playgrounds should be expanded and sitting areas should be rearranged to decrease the risk of contamination (13%); some participants also want children's playgrounds to be rearranged to decrease the risk of contamination (9.4%). This was followed by a demand for parking area to be rearranged to decrease the risk of contamination (9%); more walking and resting areas (8%); checkpoints at park entrances to check on facial masks (6%); and medical stations within the park in case of emergencies (4%).

The greatest demand is for more nearby parking lots, as most parks in Nicosia do not have any parking area for cars, meaning that visitors who drive to the parks usually have a hard time finding parking. Especially during the pandemic, people used their private cars to travel because of the lack of public transportation. The next greatest demand is for more sport activities; we can see that 28% of the people who use parks for sport activities noted that not all the parks have sport equipment, and those that do are very limited. The next greatest demand is a tie between an increase in children's playgrounds and the rearrangement of sitting areas. When it comes to children's playgrounds, these only exist in some parks and generally only allow for a very small number of users at one time. We can see that 23% of the people used parks for children's playgrounds during the pandemic, so having more playgrounds in parks will make it less crowded and increase availability to more people, thus making playgrounds safer to use during a pandemic. As for the rearrangement of sitting areas, most park benches allow two to three people to sit close together on them at the same time, so if they could be rearranged in a way to maintain social distancing, this will help the participants to use sitting areas more safely and be less likely to spread COVID-19. In the next table, we show both the rearrangement of children's playgrounds and parking areas at 9%. Existing children's playgrounds in parks are placed close to each other, condensing users to one place while the rest of the park remains empty and available, so spreading out the playgrounds across the park will help users to spread out and not gather in one area. This will help maintain social distancing and lower the transmission of COVID-19. When it comes to parking areas, people park their cars close to each other on the streets most of the time, so having less compact parking areas designed to maintain social distancing will provide safer park access. Next, 8% of the participants want more resting and walking areas, especially after the pandemic when users were not allowed to sit next to each other in order to maintain the social distancing rule. Thus, bench parks designed to allow two to three users now allowed only one to two users during the pandemic, which meant park users had very few sitting areas available for them; having more sitting places arranged in a way to maintain social distancing will help people sit in parks and use them safely, which is important, considering that 38% of people use parks for the purpose of sitting and resting. In total, 6% of participant felt the need for checkpoints to make sure people wear masks at all times and follow the social distancing rules because some people might not follow these rules and thus cause confusion in the parks. Lastly, 4% of people feel the need to include medical stations in parks for emergencies. To conclude, having larger parks with more sport equipment, larger children's playgrounds, and sitting areas arranged to lower the chances of people gathering at a single point will help users access parks safely while maintaining social distancing rules. Similarly, increasing socially distanced parking areas for people who come by car will also help people to access the parks more easily and create safer parks for everyone.

4.3. Children Usage

In this section, we asked the participants if they have children between the ages of 5 and 12 so we could study if there were any changes to the children's usage and behavior before and after the pandemic especially when 23% of the participants visit the parks because of children's activities and playgrounds; in Table 3, we can see the number of children in the participants' houses

Table 3. The number of participants' children between 5 and 12 years of age.

	Frequency	Percent
1 child	111	76
2 children	21	14.3
3 children	14	9.5
4+	0	0
Total	146	100

Table 3 shows that most have only one child between the ages of 5 and 12 at 76%, followed by two children at 14%, three children at 10%, and none with four children.

In the next question, we asked the participants about the children's usage and where they played before and after the pandemic. We can see the participants' answers for before and after the pandemic in Figure 7. Before the pandemic, most of the children played in their own house's yard at 36.8%, 35.2% at parks, 14.4% on streets and sidewalks, 12.8% in neighborhood yards, and 0.5% in open fields. After the pandemic, half of the children played in their house yard, followed by 35% for parks and streets, and for sidewalks, we have 9%, and 5% for neighborhood yards.

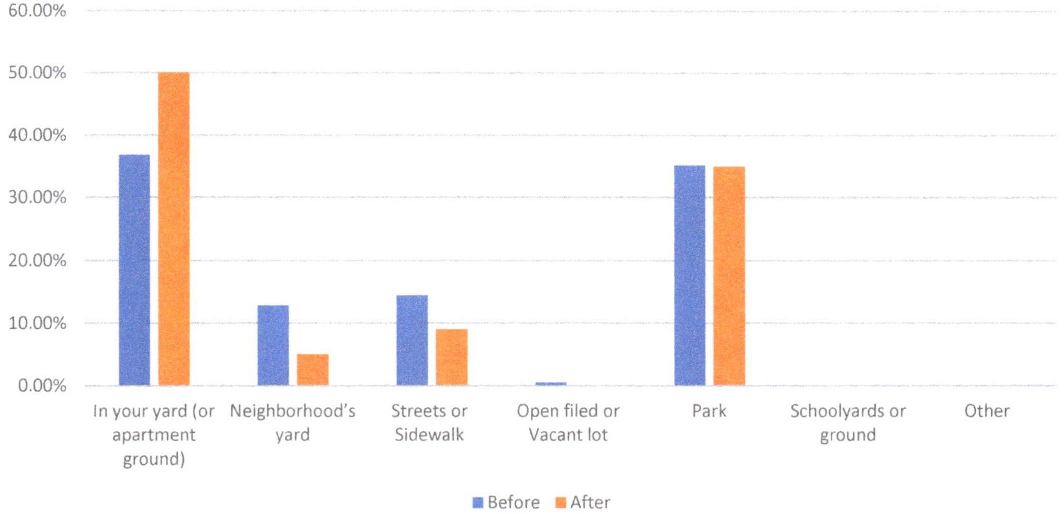

Figure 7. The difference in the places where children play before and after the pandemic.

From the figure above, we can see that most of the changes were concerned personal yards. During the pandemic, many preferred to use their house's yard for children to play in, and because of the lockdown, people could not leave their houses, so most of them turned to the house garden to play. Meanwhile, we see decreases in the use of neighborhood yards and streets and sidewalk because people were forbidden to leave their houses, but we see no increase or decrease in park usage so people preferred their garden and yard over the parks nearby because of the lack of children's playground and the fear of catching a COVID-19 infection so most park users during the pandemic were people who lived in an apartment that does not have private yards for their children.

Based on everything above, some recommendations for physical improvements, accessibility, and elements to enhance urban parks and public spaces, particularly green areas are presented as follows:

- Accessibility Improvements

Park designers should ensure that all pathways are wide, well maintained, and accessible for people with disabilities, including those using wheelchairs or strollers. Installing clear, multilingual signage that indicate park entrances, exits, restrooms, and features like playgrounds, sitting areas, and picnic spots are required Accessibility should be improved by ensuring that parks are connected to public transport routes, with bus stops or taxi stops areas close by, as well as accessible parking spaces close to park entrances with well-marked pedestrian pathways leading into the park.

- Physical Infrastructure

It is important to increase the number of sitting areas, benches, and shaded pavilions throughout the parks. This will improve the experience for people of all ages. Additionally, restroom accessibility is crucial, and restrooms should be clean and well distributed across various sections of the park for convenience. Energy-efficient, solar-powered lighting should be installed along pathways, in playgrounds, and in other key areas to allow for safe evening use and to support sustainable energy usage.

- Natural Elements and Landscaping

To improve comfort and environmental sustainability within parks, it is recommended to plant shade-providing trees, particularly around sitting areas and pathways. Utilizing native, drought-resistant, and low-maintenance plants and trees not only enhances the park's visual appeal but also supports local biodiversity. Additionally, incorporating natural or artificial water features, such as ponds, fountains, or small streams, will enrich a park's ambiance and benefit local wildlife. Establishing designated areas for community gardens or allotments encourages resident participation, fosters community interaction, and promotes local stewardship of green spaces.

- Recreational and Fitness Elements

To promote an active and inclusive environment, playground equipment fabricated from eco-friendly, durable materials should be installed. Separate zones should be designed catering to younger and older children and incorporating accessible play elements for children with disabilities. Additionally, outdoor gym stations should be equipped with simple fitness apparatuses, such as pull-up bars, benches, and balance beams, allowing adult visitors to engage in exercise at no cost. Dedicated walking, jogging, and cycling lanes should be established to encourage active use of the park while reducing potential conflicts between different user groups. Furthermore, maintaining well-kept areas for sports like basketball, tennis, soccer, and other group activities will foster community engagement and support physical fitness.

5. Conclusions

Many significant features around the accessibility and usage of urban parks are missing, such as easy access to the parks and their availability to the inhabitants of Nicosia. Many inhabitants suffer mobility problems or have difficulties reaching their local parks because of a lack of transportation or lack of parking areas, which means that the parks are not up to standard when it comes to accessibility and usage.

Additionally, many participants had problems with the sitting and relaxing areas, not because they were lacking but because of their design. Much of the seating requires people to sit close to each other, which was not allowed during the pandemic because of social distancing rules. Therefore, most park benches were only usable by a small number of participants, which creates a need for more well-designed seating areas that could be used safely during a pandemic.

Many people found they needed more parks near where they live. Many complaints were about the shortage of parks or the existing parks not being up to standard or not being used properly. Improving existing parks will reduce overcrowding and resolve accessibility issues for people who live far from their nearest park. This will generate healthier and more sustainable facilities with a lot of open places and parks near housing so people do not have to travel so far.

When it comes to the equipment and facilities in parks, many people commented on the lack of sport equipment and children's playgrounds. Therefore, providing more children's playgrounds and adding more sport equipment will solve the problem of too many users at the same facility. Designing parks so that multiple people can use the facilities at the same time while maintaining social distancing will help decrease health risk concerns and the spread of the COVID-19 virus.

The main objectives of this study were to identify the problems that participants faced while using their local parks during the pandemic and compare the usage and accessibility of Nicosia's parks before and after the pandemic. This will help decision-makers and authorities have a better understanding of the situation so they can implement better planning for the future and resolve current problems.

Author Contributions: Conceptualization, H.H. and C.K.; methodology, H.H. and C.K; software, H.H.; validation, H.H. and C.K.; formal analysis, H.H.; investigation, H.H.; resources, H.H., C.K., and T.T.; data curation, H.H. and C.K.; writing—original draft preparation, H.H., C.K., and T.T.; visualization, H.H.; supervision, C.K. and T.T. All authors have read and agreed to the published version of the manuscript.

Funding: This research received no external funding.

Data Availability Statement: Data can be made available upon reasonable request.

Conflicts of Interest: The authors declare no conflicts of interest.

References

1. Sun, J.; He, W.T.; Wang, L.; Lai, A.; Ji, X.; Zhai, X.; Li, G.; Suchard, M.A.; Tian, J.; Zhou, J.; et al. COVID-19: Epidemiology, evolution, and cross-disciplinary perspectives. *Trends Mol. Med.* **2020**, *26*, 483–495. [CrossRef] [PubMed]
2. Puglia, F.A.; Hills, A.; Dawoud, B.; Magennis, P.; Chiu, G.A.; Adams, A.; Ahmed, A.; Aiman, H.; Al-Harbawee, A.; Alderson, L.; et al. Management of oral and maxillofacial trauma during the first wave of the COVID-19 pandemic in the United Kingdom. *Br. J. Oral Maxillofac. Surg.* **2021**, *59*, 867–874. [CrossRef] [PubMed]
3. Mckenzie, T.L.; Cohen, D.A.; Sehgal, A.; Williamson, S.; Golinelli, D.; Lurie, N. Contribution of public parks to physical activity. *Am. J. Public Health* **2013**, *97*, 509–514.
4. United Nations, World Urbanization Process World Urbanization Prospects The 2014 Revision Economic and Social Affairs. 2014. Available online: https://population.un.org/wup/Publications/Files/WUP2014-Methodology.pdf (accessed on 20 April 2021).
5. Peen, J.; Schoevers, R.A.; Beekman, A.T.; Dekker, J. The current status of urban-rural differences in psychiatric disorders. *Acta Psychiatr. Scand.* **2010**, *121*, 84–93. [CrossRef]
6. White, M.P.; Alcock, I.; Wheeler, B.W.; Depledge, M.H. Coastal proximity, health, and well-being: Results from a longitudinal panel survey. *Int. J. Health Place* **2013**, *23*, 97–103. [CrossRef]
7. Tyrväinen, L.; Ojala, A.; Korpela, K.; Lanki, T.; Tsunetsugu, Y.; Kagawa, T. The influence of urban green environments on stress relief measures: A field experiment. *J. Environ. Psychol.* **2014**, *38*, 1–9. [CrossRef]
8. Saw, M.J.; Mavoa, S.; Villanueva, K.; Sugiyama, T.; Badland, H.; Kaczynski, A.T.; Owen, N.; Giles-Corti, B. Public open space, physical activity, urban design, and public health: Concepts, methods and research agenda. *Int. J. Health Place* **2015**, *33*, 75–82.
9. Bisht, S.S.; Mishra, V.; Fuloria, S. Measuring accessibility for inclusive development: A census sis-based index. *Soc. Indic. Res.* **2010**, *98*, 167–181. [CrossRef]
10. Blanco, G.; Lemus, J.A.; Grande, J. Retracted: Microbial pollution in wildlife: Linking agricultural manuring and bacterial antibiotic resistance in red-billed choughs. *J. Agric. Sci.* **2009**, *12*, 13–27. [CrossRef]
11. Dahmann, N.; Wolch, J.; Joassart-Marcelli, P.; Reynolds, K.; Jerrett, M. The active city? Disparities in the provision of urban public recreation resources. *Int. J. Health Place* **2010**, *16*, 431–445. [CrossRef]
12. Fuller, R.A.; Gaston, K.J. The scaling of green space coverage in European cities. Biology Letters. *J. Archit.* **2009**, *5*, 352–355.
13. Sister, C.; Wolch, J.; Wilson, J. Got green? Addressing environmental justice in park provision. *Geo J.* **2010**, *75*, 229–248. [CrossRef]
14. Roy, S.; Byrne, J.; Pickering, C. A systematic quantitative review of urban tree benefits, costs, and assessment methods across cities in different climatic zones. *Urban For. Urban Green.* **2012**, *4*, 351–363. [CrossRef]
15. Escobedo, F.J.; Kroeger, T.; Wagner, J.E. Urban forests and pollution mitigation: Analyzing ecosystem services and disservices. *J. Environ. Pollut.* **2011**, *159*, 2078–2087. [CrossRef]
16. Groenewegen, P.; van den Berg, A.; de Vries, S.; Verheij, R. Vitamin G: Effectsof green space on health, well-being, and social safety. *BMC Public Health* **2006**, *6*, 149. [CrossRef]

17. Nowak, D.J.; Crane, D.E.; Stevens, J.C. Air pollution removal by urban trees and shrubs in the United States. *J. Urban For. Urban Green.* **2006**, *4*, 115–123. [CrossRef]
18. Cummins, S.K.; Jackson, R.J. The built environment and children's health. *J. Pediatr. Clin. North Am.* **2001**, *48*, 1241–1252. [CrossRef]
19. Nowak, D.J.; Rowntree, R.A.; McPherson, E.G.; Sisinni, S.M.; Kerkmann, E.R.; Stevens, J.C. Measuring and analyzing urban tree cover. *J. Landsc. Urban Plan.* **1996**, *36*, 49–57. [CrossRef]
20. Byrne, J.; Wolch, J.; Zhang, J. Planning for environmental justice in an urban national park? *J. Environ. Plan. Manag.* **2009**, *52*, 365–392. [CrossRef]
21. McConnachie, M.M.; Shackleton, C.M. Public green space inequality in small towns in South Africa. *Habitat Int.* **2010**, *34*, 244–248. [CrossRef]
22. Dai, D. Racial/ethnic and socioeconomic disparities in urban green space accessibility: Where to intervene? *Landsc. Urban Plan.* **2011**, *102*, 234–244. [CrossRef]
23. Jennings, V.; Johnson-Gaither, C.; Gragg, R.S. Promoting environmental justice through urban green space access: A synopsis. *Environ. Justice* **2012**, *5*, 1–7. [CrossRef]
24. Byrne, J.; Wolch, J. Nature, race, and parks: Past research and future directions for geographic research. *Prog. Hum. Geogr.* **2009**, *33*, 743–765. [CrossRef]
25. Heynen, N.; Perkins, H.A.; Roy, P. The political ecology of uneven urban green space: The impact of political economy on race and ethnicity in producing environmental inequality in Milwaukee. *Urban Aff. Rev.* **2006**, *42*, 3–25. [CrossRef]
26. Bentley, R.; Baker, E.; Mason, K. Cumulative exposure to poor housing affordability and its association with mental health in men and women. *J. Epidemiol. Community Health* **2012**, *66*, 761–766. [CrossRef]
27. Bedimo-Rung, A.L.; Mowen, A.J.; Cohen, D.A. The significance of parks to physical activity and public health: A conceptual model. *Am. J. Prev. Med.* **2005**, *28*, 159–168. [CrossRef]
28. Kuo, F.E.; Sullivan, W.C.; Coley, R.L.; Brunson, L. Fertile ground for community: Inner-city neighborhood common spaces. *Am. J. Community Psychol.* **1998**, *26*, 823–851. [CrossRef]
29. Coutts, C.; Horner, M.; Chapin, T. Using geographical information system to model the effects of green space accessibility on mortality in Florida? *Go-Cart. Int.* **2010**, *25*, 471–484. [CrossRef]
30. Villeneuve, P.J.; Jerrett, M.; Su, J.G.; Burnett, R.T.; Chen, H.; Wheeler, A.J.; Goldberg, M.S. A cohort study relating urban green space with mortality in Ontario, Canada. *Environ. Res.* **2012**, *115*, 51–58. [CrossRef]
31. Centers for Disease Control and Prevention. Surgeon General's report on physical activity and health. *JAMA J. Am. Med. Assoc.* **1996**, *276*, 522. [CrossRef]
32. Woodcock, J.; Edwards, P.; Tonne, C.; Armstrong, B.G.; Ashiru, O.; Banister, D.; Beevers, S.; Chalabi, Z.; Chowdhury, Z.; Cohen, A.; et al. Public health benefits of strategies to reduce greenhouse-gas emissions: Urban land transport. *Lancet* **2009**, *374*, 1930–1943. [CrossRef] [PubMed]
33. Brownson, R.C.; Baker, E.A.; Housemann, R.A.; Brennan, L.K.; Bacak, S.J. Environmental and policy determinants of physical activity in the United States. *Am. J. Public Health* **2001**, *91*, 1995–2003. [CrossRef] [PubMed]
34. Sallis, J.F.; Floyd, M.F.; Rodrıguez, D.; Saelens, B.E. Role of built environments in physical activity, obesity, and cardiovascular disease. *Circulation* **2012**, *125*, 729–737. [CrossRef] [PubMed]
35. Ogden, C.L.; Carroll, M.D.; Flegal, K.M. High body mass index for age among US children and adolescents, 2003–2006. *J. Am. Med. Assoc.* **2008**, *299*, 2401–2405. [CrossRef]
36. Dietz, W.H. Health consequences of obesity in youth: Childhood predictors of adult disease. *Pediatrics* **1998**, *101* (Suppl. S2), 518–525. [CrossRef]
37. Freedman, D.S.; Mei, Z.; Srinivasan, S.R.; Berenson, G.S.; Dietz, W.H. Cardiovascular risk factors and excess adiposity among overweight children and adolescents: The Bogalusa Heart Study. *J. Pediatr.* **2007**, *150*, 12–17.e2. [CrossRef]
38. Stunkard, A.J. Genetic contributions to human obesity. *Res. Publ.—Assoc. Res. Nerv. Ment. Dis.* **1991**, *69*, 205–218.
39. Hill, J.O.; Peters, J.C. Environmental contributions to the obesity epidemic. *Science* **1998**, *280*, 1371–1374. [CrossRef]
40. Roux, A.V.D.; Evenson, K.R.; McGinn, A.P.; Brown, D.G.; Moore, L.; Brines, S.; Jacobs, D.R., Jr. Availability of recreational resources and physical activity in adults. *Am. J. Public Health* **2007**, *97*, 493–499. [CrossRef]
41. Timperio, A.; Salmon, J.; Telford, A.; Crawford, D. Perceptions of local neighborhood environments and their relationship to childhood overweight and obesity. *Int. J. Obes.* **2005**, *29*, 170–175. [CrossRef]
42. Giles-Corti, B.; Broomhall, M.H.; Knuiman, M.; Collins, C.; Douglas, K.; Ng, K.; Lange, A.; Donovan, R.J. Increasing walking: How important is the distance to attractiveness and size of public open space? *Am. J. Prev. Med.* **2005**, *28*, 169–176. [CrossRef] [PubMed]
43. Giles-Corti, B.; Donovan, R.J. The relative influence of individual, social and physical environment determinants of physical activity. *Soc. Sci. Med.* **2002**, *54*, 1793–1812. [CrossRef] [PubMed]
44. Veitch, J.; Ball, K.; Crawford, D.; Abbott, G.R.; Salmon, J. Park improvements and park activity: A natural experiment. *Am. J. Prev. Med.* **2012**, *42*, 616–619. [CrossRef]
45. Ernstson, H. The social production of ecosystem services: A framework for studying environmental justice and ecological complexity in urbanized landscapes. *Landsc. Urban Plan.* **2012**, *109*, 7–17. [CrossRef]
46. Ulrich, R.S. Natural versus urban scenes have some psychophysiological effects. *Environ. Behav.* **1981**, *13*, 523–556. [CrossRef]

47. Woo, J.; Tang, N.; Suen, E.; Leung, J.; Wong, M. Greenspace, psychological restoration, and telomere length. *Lancet* **2009**, *373*, 299–300. [CrossRef]
48. Fuller, R.A.; Irvine, K.N.; Devine-Wright, P.; Warren, P.H.; Gaston, K.J. Psychological benefits of green space increase with biodiversity. *Biol. Lett.* **2007**, *3*, 390–394. [CrossRef]
49. Kaplan, S.; Kaplan, R. Health, supportive environments, and the reasonable person model. *Am. J. Public Health* **2003**, *93*, 1484–1489. [CrossRef]
50. Allam, Z. How Cities and Architecture Respond to the Wuhan Coronavirus. Available online: https://www.archdaily.com/932840/how-cities-and-architecture-respond-to-thewuhan-coronavirus (accessed on 20 February 2020).
51. Buckley, C.; May, T. Effects of Coronavirus Begin Echoing Far from Wuhan Epicenter. Available online: https://www.nytimes.com/2020/01/25/world/asia/china-wuhan-coronavirus.html (accessed on 28 January 2020).
52. Gu, C.; Jiang, W.; Zhao, T.; Zheng, B. Mathematical Recommendations to Fight Against COVID-19. Available at SSRN 3551006 (2020). Available online: https://ssrn.com/abstract=3551006 (accessed on 21 August 2024).
53. Wilder-Smith, A.; Freedman, D.O. Isolation, quarantine, social distancing and community containment: A pivotal role for old-style public health measures in the novel coronavirus (2019-nCoV) outbreak. *J. Travel Med.* **2020**, *27*, taaa020. [CrossRef]
54. Fetzer, T.; Witte, M.; Hensel, L.; Jachimowicz, J.; Haushofer, J.; Ivchenko, A.; Caria, S.; Reutskaja, E.; Roth, C.; Fiorin, S.; et al. Global Behaviors and Perceptions in the COVID-19 Pandemic. 2020. Available online: https://poverty-action.org/global-behaviors-and-perceptions-covid-19-pandemic (accessed on 21 August 2024).
55. Hawkley, L.C.; Cacioppo, J.T. Aging and loneliness: Downhill quickly? *Curr. Dir. Psychol. Sci.* **2007**, *16*, 187–191. [CrossRef]
56. National Academies of Sciences, Engineering, and Medicine. *Social Isolation and Loneliness in Older Adults: Opportunities for the Health Care System*; National Academies Press: Washington, DC, USA, 2020.
57. Hartig, T.; Mitchell, R.; De Vries, S.; Frumkin, H. Nature and health. *Annu. Rev. Public Health* **2014**, *35*, 207–228. [CrossRef] [PubMed]
58. Markevych, I.; Schoierer, J.; Hartig, T.; Chudnovsky, A.; Hystad, P.; Dzhambov, A.M.; De Vries, S.; Triguero-Mas, M.; Brauer, M.; Nieuwenhuijsen, M.J.; et al. Exploring pathways linking greenspace to health: Theoretical and methodological guidance. *Environ. Res.* **2017**, *158*, 301–317. [CrossRef] [PubMed]
59. Jennings, V.; Bamkole, O. The relationship between social cohesion and urban green space: An avenue for health promotion. *Int. J. Environ. Res. Public Health* **2019**, *16*, 452. [CrossRef] [PubMed]
60. Weimann, H.; Björk, J.; Håkansson, C. Experiences of the urban green local environment as a factor for well-being among adults: An exploratory qualitative study in southern Sweden. *Int. J. Environ. Res. Public Health* **2019**, *16*, 2464. [CrossRef]

urban science

MDPI

Article

Mapping Nutritional Inequality: A Primary Socio-Spatial Analysis of Food Deserts in Santiago de Chile

Leslie Landaeta-Díaz [1,2], Francisco Vergara-Perucich [3,*], Carlos Aguirre-Nuñez [4] and Felipe Ulloa-Leon [3]

[1] Facultad de Salud y Ciencias Sociales, Universidad de Las Américas, Santiago 7500975, Chile; llandaeta@udla.cl
[2] Núcleo de Investigación en Nutrición y Ciencias Alimentarias, Universidad de las Américas, Santiago 7500975, Chile
[3] Núcleo Centro Producción del Espacio, Universidad de las Américas, Santiago 7500975, Chile; fulloal@externos.udla.cl
[4] Facultad de Ingeniería, Arquitectura y Diseño, Universidad San Sebastián, Santiago 7510157, Chile; carlos.aguirre@uss.cl
* Correspondence: jvergara@udla.cl

Abstract: This study investigates the socio-spatial distribution of food deserts in Santiago de Chile, aiming to understand how urban planning and socioeconomic factors influence access to nutritious food. Employing geospatial analysis techniques with data from OpenStreetMap and the 2017 Census, the research identifies areas within Santiago where access to healthy food is limited. The novelty of this study lies in its application of spatial autocorrelation methods, specifically Local Indicators of Spatial Association (LISA), to reveal clusters of nutritional inequality. The findings indicate significant concentrations of food deserts in both lower socioeconomic peripheral areas and, surprisingly, in some high-income central areas. These results suggest that both poverty and urban infrastructure, including car dependency, play critical roles in shaping access to healthy food. By highlighting over two million residents affected by food deserts, the study underscores the urgent need for integrated urban planning and public health strategies. This research contributes to the understanding of urban nutritional inequality and provides a replicable methodological framework for other cities. The implications extend beyond Santiago, offering insights into how urban design can be leveraged to improve public health outcomes through better access to nutritious food.

Keywords: food deserts; spatial epidemiology; urban planning; public health; nutrition

1. Introduction

Urban environments significantly influence dietary behaviours and nutritional outcomes, with various factors at play that can either promote or hinder healthy eating habits [1]. Urbanization is linked with changes in food availability, access, and consumption patterns that often lead to increased consumption of processed foods and decreased intake of fresh produce [2]. This shift contributes to higher rates of obesity and non-communicable diseases (NCDs) in urban areas compared to rural areas [1–3]. Urban residents often face barriers such as higher food prices and limited access to healthy food options, which can lead to poorer dietary outcomes [4]. Also, the availability of diverse food outlets and the physical accessibility of food stores significantly affect dietary behaviours in urban settings. Studies have shown that proximity to food stores that offer healthy food options is associated with better dietary habits [5]. Conversely, areas with limited access to healthy foods, known as food deserts, often have residents with poorer dietary outcomes.

Economic constraints are a critical factor influencing dietary choices in urban environments. Lower-income urban dwellers often opt for cheaper, energy-dense, but nutrient-poor foods due to financial limitations [1,3]. Interventions such as providing subsidies for healthy foods or implementing food pricing policies could potentially improve access to nutritious foods [1]. Cultural beliefs and social norms also play significant roles in shaping dietary behaviours in urban settings. These factors can influence food preferences and consumption patterns, which are important to consider when designing nutrition interventions [6]. Effective urban nutrition policies and interventions need to address the multifaceted nature of food environments. This includes enhancing the availability and affordability of healthy foods, regulating food marketing, and improving the overall quality of urban food environments [4,6]. Educational campaigns and community-based programmes can also play a role in promoting healthy dietary behaviours [5].

Developing and applying frameworks that consider the unique aspects of urban food environments in Low- and Middle-Income Countries (LMICs) can help in understanding and addressing the challenges faced by urban populations. Such frameworks should integrate various levels of influence, including individual, household, community, and policy factors [4,6]. From the perspective of the global obesity epidemic, considering the city as a nutritional space is a necessary shift that integrates urban planning with public health. One of the spatial manifestations of this gap between planning and nutrition is found in food deserts, defined as areas where access to healthy food is scarce or, quite simply, non-existent.

Food deserts significantly impact urban populations by limiting access to nutritious and affordable food, which can lead to poor dietary choices and increased health risks. Asakawa et al. [7] highlight that elderly residents in urban and rural areas suffer from poor nutritional conditions due to inadequate access to food and weak social ties, which disrupt healthy eating behaviours. Similarly, Frayne and McCordick [8] discuss the long-term health vulnerabilities of children in Southern African cities due to limited access to nutritious food, emphasizing the dire developmental consequences of malnutrition from an early age. Likewise, Karpyn [5] explores the relationship between the food environment and dietary outcomes in urban food desert communities, finding that perceptions of neighbourhood food availability and household food challenges significantly correlate with dietary outcomes. Bedore [9] provides a critical analysis of food deserts within the urban political economy, arguing that food deserts are not only about the availability of food but also about the choices and class relations that shape access to food in urban settings. Food deserts can exacerbate class disparities and limit individual autonomy and dignity by narrowing food choices for the underprivileged. Food deserts have a visible impact on urban populations, highlighting the importance of addressing food access, social ties, and the broader socioeconomic and environmental factors that contribute to food insecurity in cities. So far, the spatial visibility of food deserts is scarce in Latin America.

The study of food deserts from a geospatial perspective involves analyzing the spatial distribution of areas with limited access to affordable and nutritious food. Mack et al. [10] introduce a spatial optimization approach to locate urban gardens near food deserts, using Phoenix, Arizona, as a case study. Their paper highlights the use of maximal covering location models to propose alternative urban garden sites to improve food access. The methodology involves integrating census tract data with spatial analysis to identify potential sites for urban gardens, demonstrating how geospatial tools can be employed to address urban food access issues effectively. Jiao et al. [11] present a method to measure food access for different vulnerable population groups at a smaller geographic scale with various transportation modes. This study is set in Austin, Texas, and uses methods based on Geographic Information Systems (GIS) to quantify different transportation food access for different vulnerable groups at the block group level. By incorporating detailed mobility networks and classifying food establishments as healthy or unhealthy, this approach provides a nuanced understanding of food accessibility across different modes of transportation and for various demographic groups.

Sigalo et al. [12] explore the use of social media data, specifically geotagged Twitter data, to predict food deserts in the United States. This innovative approach leverages natural language processing techniques to analyze food-related tweets and assess their association with food desert status. By mapping tweets to their respective census tracts and analyzing the sentiment and nutritional content of food mentions, this study offers a novel method to identify and understand food deserts through the lens of social media. Most of these papers refer to census tracts as spatial units of analysis. Joyner et al. [13] employ a critical geographic approach to examine food apartheid in Salt Lake City, focusing on linking historical redlining maps with current food access issues. This study underscores the importance of considering historical and socio-political contexts in geospatial analyses of food deserts. These methodological contributions to spatial analyses of food deserts emphasize the importance of using diverse data sources, including census data, social relations, and cultural conditions, to enrich the analysis. Advanced GIS techniques and spatial optimization models are crucial for identifying the locations of potential urban gardens and analyzing the accessibility of food sources.

The nutritional challenges posed in the literature focus on the need for comprehensive strategies to address malnutrition and obesity in the context of Chile. Rodríguez-Osiac [14] highlights the significant challenge of obesity and related chronic diseases in Chile, noting the widespread consumption of processed and ultra-processed foods as major contributing factors. Furthermore, Rodríguez-Osiac [15] discusses the implementation of the NOURISHING framework in Chile, which categorizes actions to promote healthier eating across three domains: food environment, food systems, and behaviour change communication. However, there are gaps in the implementation of continuous public health communication, education, and fiscal measures, such as incentives for healthy and sustainable food production and taxes on unhealthy foods, to strengthen the implementation of healthy environments. This indicates a policy gap where economic tools could be leveraged to influence food affordability and purchase incentives, thereby supporting healthier dietary choices at the community level.

Santiago is a highly segregated and unequal city [16–19], whose spatial distribution patterns have already caused health problems [20–22] due to an urban and territorial planning model weakened by the prevailing deregulation model [23,24], with permissive urban and housing policies that contribute little to social cohesion [25–28]. The health problems associated with this urban model were already stressed during the new coronavirus pandemic. This article presents an exploratory study of the socio-demographic characteristics of households residing in food deserts in Santiago, Chile. This research applies a spatial epidemiology framework, which is a multidisciplinary field that examines the geographic distribution of diseases and their determinants, including demographic, environmental, and genetic factors [29]. It involves the use of geographic information systems and statistical methods to analyze and map disease patterns [30]. Pattern analysis is a key tool in this field, allowing for the evaluation of the spatial distribution of health outcomes [31]. The field also encompasses the study of spatial patterns in epidemic models, with a focus on the role of the force of infection [32]. The book Spatial Analysis in Epidemiology provides a comprehensive overview of the concepts and methods in this field [33]. This article uses a methodology infused by the methodological stance in spatial epidemiology aimed at articulating nutrition and urban planning.

To this end, data collection was conducted to visualize the territorial location of food deserts in the city, offering a replicable methodological approach for other cities through the use of OpenStreetMap data. A second phase of analysis examines the condition of food deserts to characterize the population living in these areas. The information and method developed in this research provide opportunities to reconsider urban planning tools, promoting better integration between urban planning and public health.

2. Materials and Methods

Spatial epidemiology is a multidisciplinary field that examines the geographic distribution of diseases and their determinants, including demographic, environmental, and genetic factors [29]. It involves the use of geographic information systems and statistical methods to analyze and map disease patterns [30]. Pattern analysis is a key tool in this field, allowing for the evaluation of the spatial distribution of health outcomes [31]. The field also encompasses the study of spatial patterns in epidemic models, with a focus on the role of the force of infection [32]. The book Spatial Analysis in Epidemiology provides a comprehensive overview of the concepts and methods in this field [33]. This article uses a methodology infused by the methodological stance in spatial epidemiology aimed to articulate nutrition and urban planning.

This article methodologically builds on spatial epidemiology to generate a unique map for the city of Santiago, the capital of Chile, one of the nations with the highest obesity rates, which increased by 23% between 2016 and 2024 (World Population Review, 2024). This database is composed of information obtained from georeferenced data from OpenStreetMap for the city of Santiago, Chile. Santiago, the capital of Chile (Figure 1), is the nation's largest city with a population of around 9 million, making it one of Latin America's most populous urban areas. Covering approximately 641 square kilometres, its metropolitan expanse extends to 15a,403 square kilometres. Santiago is administratively divided into 34 communes, each with its own municipal government, and the region is overseen by a regional governor. Geographically, it is situated in the central valley between the Andes mountains and the Coastal Range, with the Mapocho and Maipo Rivers running through it. As Chile's economic hub, Santiago generates a substantial portion of the national GDP, featuring advanced infrastructure and extensive public transport networks. Despite its economic strengths, the city faces significant socioeconomic disparities, with affluent areas contrasted by regions of poverty and limited access to services. Santiago's economy is diverse, with robust finance, retail, manufacturing, and service sectors.

Figure 1. Map of Santiago de Chile.

A search was conducted using specific parameters considered as spaces for the distribution of healthy foods for the specific case of Chile. These were under the general category of 'shops,' which were then specified using the keywords listed in Table 1, with those results. The map of resultant shops georeferenced are presented in Figure 2 marked by blue dots, while the division of comunas of Santiago (districts) is marked by magenta lines. The shops selected in OpenStreetMap were those indexed in the database as actually offering healthy food in Santiago. We excluded others that may provide a mix of fast food and healthy food, as well as restaurants, since these often offer a variety of food types. Additionally, we focused on identifying shops that sell food for preparation at home.

Table 1. Type of shops considered in the analysis.

Type of Shop	Count (n)
Convenience store	1282
Bakery	508
Supermarket	206
Greengrocer	109
Variety store	38
Herbalist store	13
Tea	10
Deli shop	9
Cheese store	3
Dairy shop	2
Farm products	2
Grocery store	2
Nutrition supplements	1

With the georeferenced points, a census layer was applied to characterize the blocks demographically and their socio-economic composition in establishing distances to these points. Different isochrones were determined to identify households that, due to their distance from food sources, can be considered to be located within food deserts. This determination was made using QGis software 3.4, employing the "union by proximity" function, applying a criterion of a maximum of 5 census blocks as a reference for direct proximity, from which distance measurement began. Although this is not a fixed measure due to the variation in shapes and sizes of blocks, the average is that if a household is 1500 m away from a store selling healthy products, it is considered a food desert.

Therefore, the spatial determination of food deserts is based on distance rather than subtraction. In other words, the farther a block is from healthy food supply points, the greater the probability of being a food desert. Once the most critical food desert areas were defined, these areas were characterized using information from the 2017 Census. After calculating the levels of access to healthy food facilities, we employed spatial autocorrelation analysis, specifically using Local Indicators of Spatial Association (LISA), to identify and cluster zones characterized by food deserts. LISA analyses spatial autocorrelation to uncover local variations in geographic patterns. Moran's I is a fundamental statistic in spatial analysis, particularly useful for understanding socio-spatial patterns within urban environments. It quantifies the extent of spatial autocorrelation, which refers to the degree to which similar values of a particular attribute—such as access to healthy food—are spatially clustered, dispersed, or randomly distributed across a geographic region. The statistic is calculated by comparing the value of the attribute at each location with the values at neighbouring locations, considering the spatial arrangement of those locations.

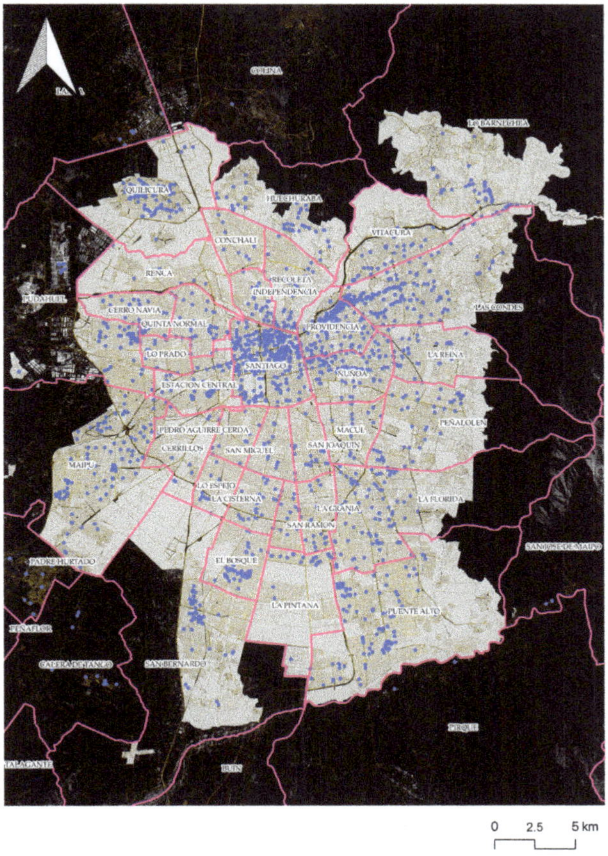

Figure 2. Shops indexed for the analysis.

The formula for Moran's I is as follows:

$$I = \frac{N \sum_{i=1}^{n} \sum_{j=1}^{n} w_{ij}(x_i - x)(x_j - x)}{W \sum_{i=1}^{n} (x_i - x)^2}$$

where N is the number of spatial units (e.g., neighbourhoods or census tracts); x_i and x_j are the values of the attribute at locations i and j, respectively; x is the mean of the attribute values; w_{ij} is the spatial weight between locations i and j, which defines the neighbourhood structure; and W is the sum of all spatial weights. A positive Moran's I indicates spatial clustering, meaning that similar values (e.g., areas with low access to healthy food) tend to be located near each other. This would suggest that food deserts are not randomly distributed but rather form distinct clusters in certain parts of the city. A negative Moran's I, on the other hand, indicates spatial dispersion, where areas with dissimilar values are located near each other. This would imply that regions with good and poor access to healthy food are interspersed. A Moran's I value near zero suggests randomness, indicating no significant spatial pattern in the distribution of the attribute.

While Moran's I provides a global measure of spatial autocorrelation across the entire study area, it does not reveal where these patterns occur locally. To address this limitation, LISA are used. LISA extends the analysis by calculating a local Moran's I value for each individual location within the study area. This localized analysis allows researchers to identify specific neighbourhoods or census tracts that contribute most to the overall spatial autocorrelation.

In the context of our research, LISA is particularly valuable for understanding spatial inequality related to food access. By identifying clusters of areas with low access to healthy food (food deserts), we can pinpoint regions where disparities in access are most pronounced. Visualizing these spatial relationships through LISA offers valuable insights into the complex factors that shape food environments and the well-being of communities within cities. After calculating the LISA values and identifying the High-High cluster, which represents areas with the highest potential for being food deserts, a socioeconomic characterization of these city zones was conducted. This characterization utilized data from the 2017 Census [34], the ISMT [35–37], and the 15-Minute City Index of Santiago [38–40]. The Socio-Material Territorial Index (ISMT) is a synthetic indicator used to stratify socioeconomic levels. It summarizes socio-material conditions based on four census variables: household head's education (79% variance), household overcrowding (7% variance), shared housing (3% variance), and housing material quality (11% variance), derived from Chile's 2017 Census. The 15-Minute City Index measures the accessibility of essential urban functions within a 15 min reach in Santiago. Using principal component analysis, it evaluates 28 functions—like services, education, and green spaces—highlighting areas with varying accessibility levels to guide urban planning towards more equitable, walkable neighbourhoods [41–43].

3. Results

The spatial distribution of food deserts in Santiago, as depicted in Figure 3, shows the levels of proximity from houses to healthy food points as indicated in the legend. The concentration of food deserts in specific areas suggests that residents in these neighbourhoods may experience greater challenges in maintaining healthy diets due to the lack of convenient and affordable access to fresh produce and other nutritious options. This can contribute to health disparities, including higher rates of obesity, diabetes, and other diet-related diseases. Nevertheless, there are also food deserts in peri-central areas such as San Miguel, San Joaquin, Macul, Lo Prado, and the severe case of Renca. Also, surprisingly, the high-income areas in Las Condes, Vitacura, and Lo Barnechea also show food deserts. These districts may have a factor of excessive dependence on cars, which may compensate the inaccessible presence of abundant healthy food supply.

Figure 4 presents a map illustrating the results of a LISA analysis conducted on the distribution of food deserts in Santiago. The map utilizes a colour scheme to represent the LISA results. Areas in red are classified as "High-High" clusters, indicating a statistically significant concentration of food deserts. These are neighbourhoods where the lack of access to healthy food is not only prevalent but also spatially clustered together. In contrast, areas in blue are classified as "Low-Low" clusters, signifying areas with good access to healthy food options that are also clustered together. The implications of this map are significant for understanding the spatial dynamics of food access in Santiago. The presence of High-High clusters (red areas) in the northeastern and southwestern peripheries of the city suggests that these areas are not only experiencing food deserts but are also spatially connected, forming larger zones of limited access to healthy food. This concentration of food deserts in specific geographic areas can exacerbate health disparities and perpetuate socioeconomic inequalities. Conversely, the Low-Low clusters (blue areas) indicate neighbourhoods with good access to healthy food options, often located in more affluent parts of the city. The "High-Low" category (yellow) highlights neighbourhoods lacking food access but adjacent to areas with better resources, while "Low-High" areas (orange) have good food access despite being near food deserts. This spatial pattern highlights the uneven distribution of resources and opportunities across Santiago, with some communities enjoying greater access to healthy food than others.

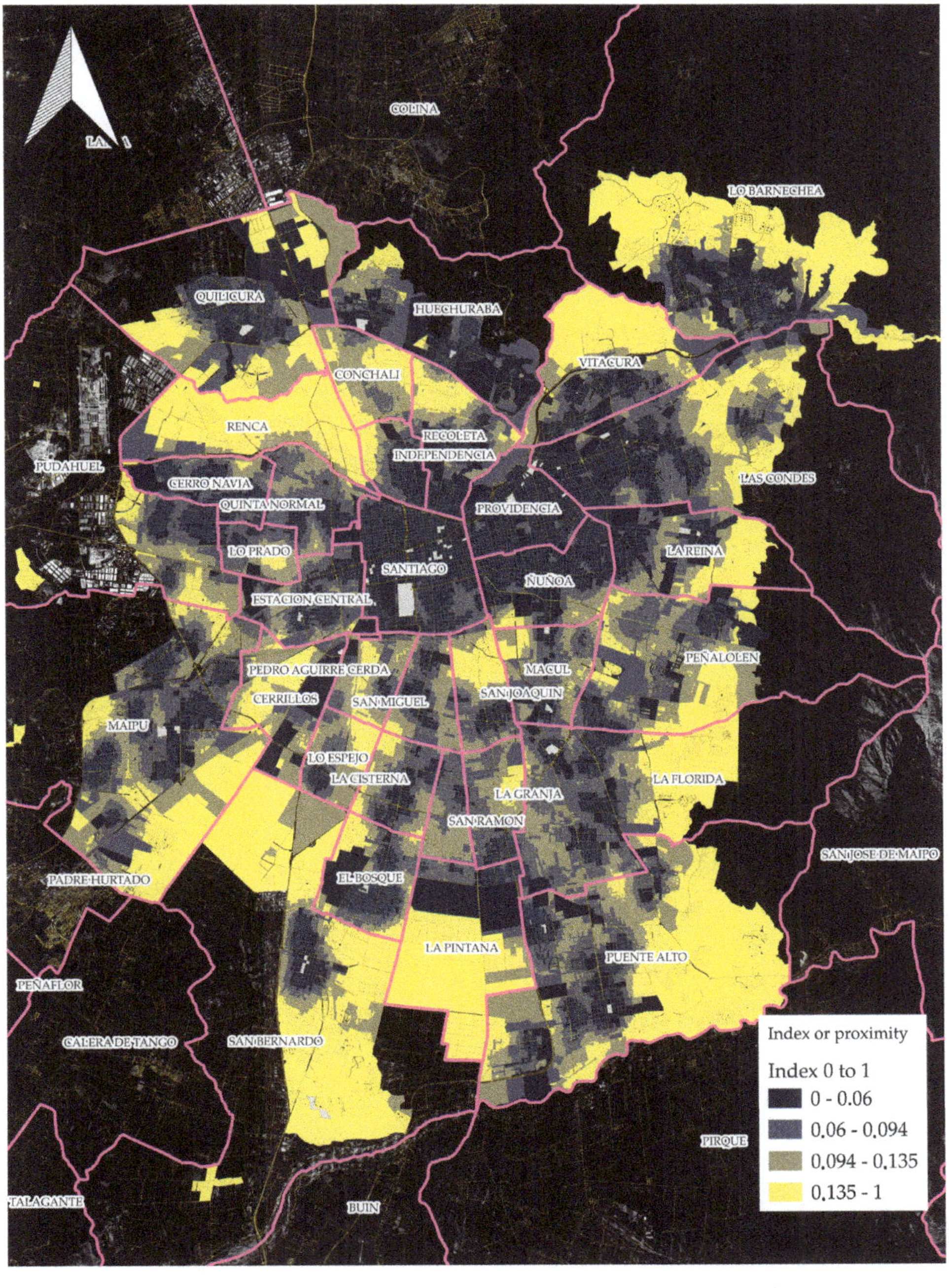

Figure 3. Map of food deserts in Santiago.

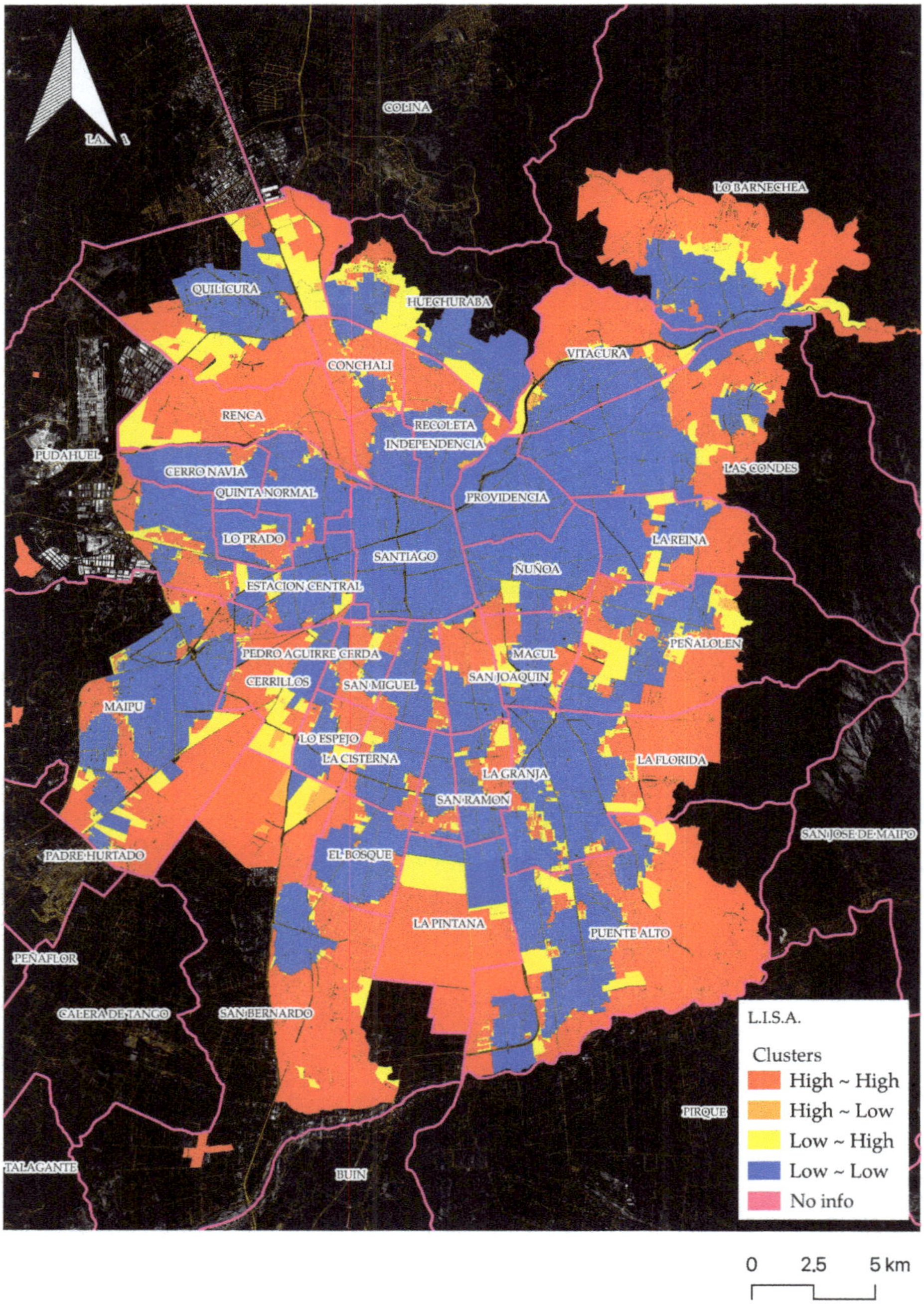

Figure 4. LISA of food deserts in Santiago de Chile.

Figure 5 shows the food deserts in relation to the location of healthy food suppliers. Tables 2 and 3 provide a statistical comparison of various socioeconomic and demographic indicators between food deserts (High-High LISA cluster) and food oases (Low-Low LISA cluster) in Santiago. The data reveal significant disparities between these two types of areas. Food deserts exhibit a higher index of distance to healthy food, indicating that residents in these areas have less access to nutritious options compared to those in food oasis. A food oasis is an area with abundant access to healthy, affordable food options, such as supermarkets, greengrocers, and farmers' markets. In contrast to food deserts, residents in food oases can easily obtain fresh produce and nutritious food, contributing to better dietary and health outcomes. This disparity is further reflected in the socioeconomic levels of the populations. Food deserts have a higher proportion of households in lower socioeconomic categories (C3, D, and E), while food oases are predominantly populated by households in higher socioeconomic categories (ABC1 and C2) defined by NRS social grades. The income distribution also differs significantly between the two areas. Food deserts have a substantially higher percentage of households with incomes below 40% of the median income, highlighting the concentration of poverty in these areas. In contrast, food oasis has a much lower percentage of households in this income bracket.

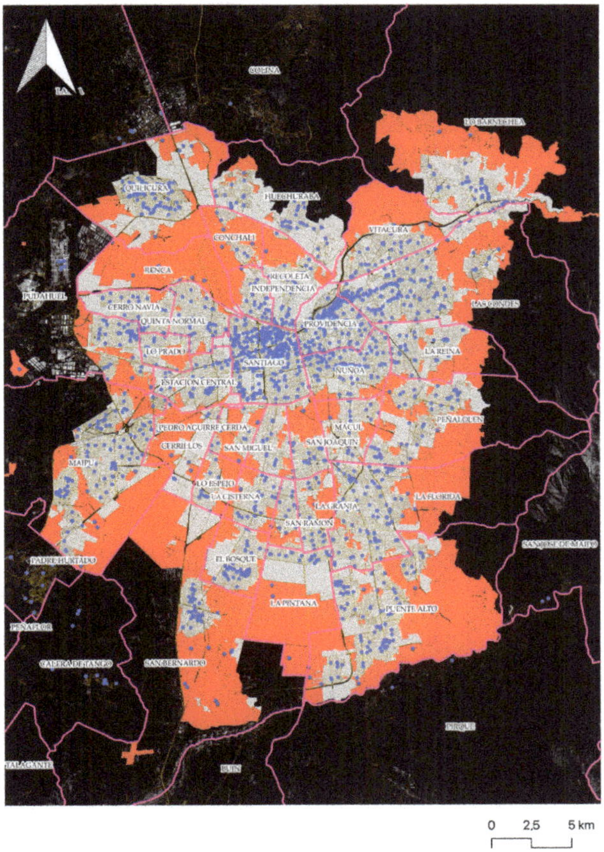

Figure 5. Clusters of food deserts (High~High in LISA) in Santiago in relation to shops indexed.

Table 2. Sociodemographic characterization of food deserts (High-High) based on LISA results.

Socioeconomic Level	ABC1	C2	C3	D	E	Total
Index of distance to healthy food	0.2209	0.2006	0.1619	0.1740	0.1313	0.1756
Mín. Index of distance to healthy food	0.1089	0.1086	0.1085	0.1086	0.1147	0.1085
Máx. Index of distance to healthy food	0.6862	0.8383	0.5977	1.0000	0.1548	1.0000
Std.Dev. index of distance to healthy food	0.1114	0.1349	0.0614	0.0815	0.0209	0.0870
household at 40% less incomes	0.0338	0.1238	0.3355	0.6270	0.6250	0.4837
Inmigrants	10,789	7912	12,454	43,954	-	75,109
Elderly over 65 years old	6545	16,765	35,738	130,784	-	189,832
Active population	71,987	157,285	302,726	869,638	17	1,401,653
Young 6 to 14 years old	16,669	29,499	47,411	149,973	-	243,552
Infants	7097	18,568	27,818	96,114	-	149,597
Women	55,615	119,309	223,151	648,265	8	1,046,348
Men	48,935	109,577	206,224	624,055	13	988,804
Population	104,615	229,133	429,572	1,272,863	42	2,036,225
Land Value (UF of 2018)	64.1866	30.1454	22.3622	17.0657	34.9342	21.3378
Socio-Material Territorial Index	0.9095	0.8632	0.8114	0.7552	0.4105	0.7853

Table 3. Sociodemographic characterization of food oasis (Low-Low) based on LISA results.

Socioeconomic Level	ABC1	C2	C3	D	E	Total
Index of distance to healthy food	0.0538	0.0563	0.0653	0.0674	-	0.0642
Mín. Index of distance to healthy food	0.0020	0.0018	0.0020	0.0019	-	0.0018
Máx. Index of distance to healthy food	0.1083	0.1085	0.1085	0.1085	-	0.1085
Std.Dev. index of distance to healthy food	0.0262	0.0283	0.0263	0.0247	-	0.0263
household at 40% less incomes	0.0434	0.1203	0.3373	0.6074	-	0.4215
Inmigrants	32,854	120,819	91,939	96,319	-	341,931
Elderly over 65 years old	36,437	112,609	92,981	190,452	-	432,479
Active population	187,821	728,445	645,857	1,121,921	-	2,684,044
Young 6 to 14 years old	23,146	73,184	86,056	179,059	-	361,445
Infants	18,976	58,950	56,260	117,134	-	251,320
Women	145,157	517,338	468,317	835,128	-	1,965,940
Men	124,966	472,326	435,439	803,490	-	1,836,221
Population	270,229	991,583	904,039	1,639,400	-	3,805,251
Land Value (UF of 2018)	67.5742	41.0489	24.2466	18.1708	-	26.2913
Socio-Material Territorial Index	0.9044	0.8711	0.8133	0.7598	-	0.8009

Tables 2 and 3 are structured to compare various socioeconomic and demographic indicators across different socioeconomic levels (ABC1, C2, C3, D, E) and the total population. It includes columns for each socioeconomic level and a Total column for aggregated data. Each row represents a specific variable, such as the Index of Distance to Healthy Food, Minimum and Maximum values of this index, Standard Deviation, percentage of households with 40% less income, number of immigrants, elderly population, active population, youth (6–14 years old), infants, women, men, overall population, land value (in UF of 2018), and the Socio-Material Territorial Index. Demographic differences are also evident. Food deserts have a higher proportion of elderly residents (over 65 years old) and a lower proportion of immigrants compared to food oasis. The working-age population (those aged 15–64) is more prominent in food oases, indicating a greater concentration of individuals currently employed or seeking employment compared to areas where a higher proportion of residents are of retirement age. Land values are 6% lower in food deserts compared to food oases, reflecting the economic disparities between these areas. The Total value of the Socio-Material Territorial Index, a composite measure of socioeconomic conditions, is also lower in food deserts, further emphasizing the disadvantaged position of these communities. Table 4 illustrates significant socioeconomic and demographic disparities between food deserts and food oases in Santiago. From Table 4, it can be seen that these areas have a lower active population, but also lower incomes, with land values 19% lower than in the food oases and a socio-material index that is also lower, albeit by 2%.

Table 4. Comparative differences between food deserts and food oasis in Santiago.

Comparative Factors	Food Oasis	Food Deserts	Differences
Index of distance to healthy food	0.0642	0.1756	1.7352
Mín. Index of distance to healthy food	0.0018	0.1085	59.2778
Máx. Index of distance to healthy food	0.1085	1.0000	8.2166
Std.Dev. index of distance to healthy food	0.0263	0.0870	2.3080
household at 40% less incomes	0.4215	0.4837	0.1476
Inmigrants	341,931.0000	75,109.0000	−0.7803
Elderly over 65 years old	432,479.0000	189,832.0000	−0.5611
Active population	2,684,044.0000	1,401,653.0000	−0.4778
Young 6 to 14 years old	361,445.0000	243,552.0000	−0.3262
Infants	251,320.0000	149,597.0000	−0.4048
Women	1,965,940.0000	1,046,348.0000	−0.4678
Men	1,836,221.0000	988,804.0000	−0.4615
Population	3,805,251.0000	2,036,225.0000	−0.4649
Land Value (UF of 2018)	26.2913	21.3378	−0.1884
Socio-Material Territorial Index	0.8009	0.7853	−0.0195

4. Discussion

The purpose of the study is to investigate the socio-spatial distribution of food deserts in Santiago de Chile, aiming to understand how urban planning and socioeconomic factors influence access to nutritious food. The results section of the study provides a detailed spatial analysis of food deserts in Santiago, utilizing georeferenced data from OpenStreetMap and census information to visualize and characterize these areas. The maps reveal a significant concentration of food deserts in the peripheries of the city, particularly in lower socioeconomic regions with less developed infrastructure. The LISA analysis further identifies clusters of high and low access to healthy food, indicating pronounced spatial inequality.

The spatial distribution of food deserts in Santiago underscores the city's socioeconomic disparities and urban planning challenges. The concentration of food deserts in the peripheries suggests that residents in these areas face significant obstacles in maintaining healthy diets due to the lack of convenient and affordable access to fresh produce and other nutritious options. This spatial pattern aligns with broader patterns of inequality observed in other studies about Santiago. Building on the work of Sabatini et al. [18] and Herrera-Marin et al. [19], which highlight Santiago's deep-seated segregation and the consequences of deregulated urban planning, this study empirically identifies and maps food deserts, revealing stark spatial patterns that confirm these earlier analyses. The results align with Mena et al. [21] and Vergara-Perucich et al. [20], who link poor health outcomes to the city's fragmented infrastructure, as the identified food deserts are concentrated in areas with inadequate urban amenities. Moreover, the findings resonate with Pradeilles et al. [3] and Cockx et al. [5] by illustrating how economic constraints limit access to nutritious food, particularly in lower-income areas. This research thus not only corroborates existing studies but also advances the understanding of Santiago's urban inequalities through the lens of nutritional access. The presence of food deserts in peri-central areas such as San Miguel, San Joaquin, Macul, Lo Prado, and Renca, as well as in high-income areas like Las Condes, Vitacura, and Lo Barnechea, suggests that food deserts are not solely a problem of poverty but also of urban planning and infrastructure. The unexpected presence of food deserts in high-income areas, as discussed in the paper, suggests a complex interplay of factors beyond mere economic capacity. The inference that these areas may exhibit an excessive dependence on cars to compensate for the physical inaccessibility of healthy food supply points is grounded in urban design and lifestyle patterns typical of affluent neighbourhoods. In these food deserts in high-income areas, residents often rely heavily on private vehicles, which can lead to the development of urban environments less conducive to walkability and local access to amenities, including food stores. This car-centric infrastructure might result in fewer local shops and supermarkets, creating pockets of inaccessibility despite wealth. In contrast, lower-income areas typically exhibit higher dependency on public transport or walking, making proximity to food sources more critical. This suggests that solutions to food deserts need to consider not only socioeconomic factors but also urban design and transportation infrastructure. Effective interventions need to consider the unique aspects of urban food environments, as suggested by Osei-Kwasi et al. [9]. This includes enhancing the availability and affordability of healthy foods, regulating food marketing, and improving the overall quality of urban food environments.

The results also align with the broader discussions on the need for comprehensive strategies to address malnutrition and obesity in urban settings, as highlighted by Rodríguez-Osiac [13]. The spatial characterization of food deserts in Santiago indicates a significant policy gap in urban planning and public health. The study suggests that urban planning tools need to be better integrated with public health initiatives to address the challenges of food deserts effectively. This could include the implementation of urban gardens, subsidies for healthy foods, and improved infrastructure to enhance access to nutritious food in underserved areas.

The study also highlights the importance of using diverse data sources and advanced GIS techniques to understand and address food access issues. The use of georeferenced data from OpenStreetMap and census information provides a robust methodological approach that can be replicated in other cities. This approach allows for a nuanced understanding of food deserts and the identification of areas most in need of intervention.

Future research should build on these findings to develop targeted interventions that address the specific challenges of food deserts in Santiago. This could include community-based programmes, educational campaigns, and policy measures aimed at improving access to healthy foods. The study provides a valuable framework for understanding the socio-spatial dynamics of food deserts and offers a replicable methodological approach for other urban settings.

5. Conclusions

The spatial representation of nutritional inequality in Santiago de Chile reveals a complex issue at the intersection of urban planning and public health. The identification of food deserts, areas with limited access to nutritious and affordable food, highlights a critical need for integrated strategies to address these inequities. This study shows that nutritional inequality is not just a reflection of economic disparities but is also deeply rooted in urban infrastructure and planning decisions. The concentration of food deserts in both peripheral and peri-central areas underscores the role of urban design in shaping access to essential services.

The findings that even high-income areas suffer from food deserts suggest that traditional measures of affluence and poverty are inadequate to fully understand this issue. The problem is embedded in the urban fabric, where infrastructure and urban design—or the lack thereof—play critical roles in determining access to healthy food.

Given these findings, several questions arise for further research. How can urban planning and public health policies be better integrated to address food deserts? What specific urban design features contribute to their creation in both low- and high-income areas? Additionally, how can transportation policies be adapted to improve access to healthy food in car-dependent neighbourhoods?

Further research should explore the effectiveness of interventions such as urban gardens, local food markets, and community-based programmes in reducing food deserts. Investigating the role of policy, including subsidies for healthy foods, taxes on unhealthy foods, and zoning laws that encourage the establishment of fresh food markets in underserved areas, could also provide valuable insights. Understanding the effectiveness of these strategies in other contexts will help tailor approaches to Santiago's unique urban environment.

Author Contributions: Conceptualization, F.V.-P. and L.L.-D.; methodology, F.V.-P.; software, F.V.-P.; validation, C.A.-N., L.L.-D. and F.U.-L.; formal analysis, F.V.-P.; investigation, F.U.-L. and F.V.-P.; resources, L.L.-D. and F.V.-P.; data curation, F.V.-P., C.A.-N. and F.U.-L.; writing—original draft preparation, F.V.-P.; writing—review and editing, L.L.-D.; visualization, F.V.-P.; supervision, C.A.-N. and L.L.-D.; project administration, L.L.-D.; funding acquisition, L.L.-D. and F.V.-P. All authors have read and agreed to the published version of the manuscript.

Funding: This research was funded by the National Agency of Research and Development of Chile (ANID), grant FONIS-SA23I0032 (SPATIAL FOOD EPIDEMIOLOGY: Geographically weighted modeling to identify urban determinants of nutritional health in the main cities of Chile). And the APC was co-funded by Universidad de Las Américas and ANID.

Data Availability Statement: All data has been presented in the main text.

Conflicts of Interest: The authors declare no conflict of interest.

References

1. Petermann-Rocha, F.; Martínez-Sanguinetti, M.A.; Villagrán, M.; Ulloa, N.; Nazar, G.; Troncoso-Pantoja, C.; Garrido-Méndez, A.; Mardones, L.; Lanuza, F.; Leiva, A.M.; et al. Desde una mirada global al contexto chileno: ¿Qué factores han repercutido en el desarrollo de obesidad en Chile? (Parte 1). *Rev. Chil. Nutr.* **2020**, *47*, 299–306. [CrossRef]
2. FAO; PAHO. *Panorama of Food and Nutrition Security in Latin America and the Caribbean*, 1st ed.; Food and Agriculture Organization of the United Nations and the Pan American Health Organization: Santiago, Chile, 2017; ISBN 978-92-5-130056-5. Available online: https://iris.paho.org/handle/10665.2/34500 (accessed on 24 July 2024).
3. Pradeilles, R.; Irache, A.; Wanjohi, M.N.; Holdsworth, M.; Laar, A.; Zotor, F.; Tandoh, A.; Klomegah, S.; Graham, F.; Muthuri, S.K.; et al. Urban Physical Food Environments Drive Dietary Behaviours in Ghana and Kenya: A Photovoice Study. *Health Place* **2021**, *71*, 102647. [CrossRef]
4. Hawkes, C.; Harris, J.; Gillespie, S. *Urbanization and the Nutrition Transition*; International Food Policy Research Institute: Washington, DC, USA, 2017.
5. Cockx, L.; Colen, L.; De Weerdt, J. From Corn to Popcorn? *Urbanization and Food Consumption in Sub-Saharan Africa: Evidence from Rural-Urban Migrants in Tanzania. SSRN J.* **2017**, *390*, 1–44. [CrossRef]
6. Westbury, S.; Ghosh, I.; Jones, H.M.; Mensah, D.; Samuel, F.; Irache, A.; Azhar, N.; Al-Khudairy, L.; Iqbal, R.; Oyebode, O. The Influence of the Urban Food Environment on Diet, Nutrition and Health Outcomes in Low-Income and Middle-Income Countries: A Systematic Review. *BMJ Glob. Health* **2021**, *6*, e006358. [CrossRef]
7. Karpyn, A.; Young, C.R.; Collier, Z.; Glanz, K. Correlates of Healthy Eating in Urban Food Desert Communities. *IJERPH* **2020**, *17*, 6305. [CrossRef]
8. Caro, S.; Carlos, J. Determinantes sociales y conductuales en salud nutricional: Evidencia para Chile. *Rev. Chil. Nutr.* **2015**, *42*, 23–29. [CrossRef]
9. Osei-Kwasi, H.A.; Laar, A.; Zotor, F.; Pradeilles, R.; Aryeetey, R.; Green, M.; Griffiths, P.; Akparibo, R.; Wanjohi, M.N.; Rousham, E.; et al. The African Urban Food Environment Framework for Creating Healthy Nutrition Policy and Interventions in Urban Africa. *PLoS ONE* **2021**, *16*, e0249621. [CrossRef]
10. Asakawa, T.; Iwama, N.; Tanaka, K.; Komaki, N. Food Deserts Issues in a Local City: Empirical Study in a Local City That Is Composed of Urban and Rural Area. *Ann. Jpn. Assoc. Urban Sociol.* **2016**, *2016*, 93–105. [CrossRef]

11. Frayne, B.; McCordic, C. Food Swamps and Poor Dietary Diversity: Longwave Development Implications in Southern African Cities. *Sustainability* **2018**, *10*, 4425. [CrossRef]
12. Bedore, M. Food Desertification: Situating Choice and Class Relations within an Urban Political Economy of Declining Food Access. *Stud. Soc. Justice* **2014**, *8*, 207–228. [CrossRef]
13. Rodríguez-Osiac, L.; Fernandes, A.C.P.; Mujica-Coopman, M.-F.; Caro-Moya, P.; Navarro-Rosenblatt, D. A Description of Chilean Food and Nutrition Health Policies. *Rev. Méd. Chile* **2021**, *149*, 1485–1494. [CrossRef] [PubMed]
14. Osiac, L.R.; Ortega, J.A.; Espinoza, P.G.; Carroza, M.B.; Castrol, P.E.; Figarir, A.M.; Medinas, F.R.; Bannout, M.A. Right to Food in the Chilean Constitution: Legal, Social and Nutritional Elements for a Proposal. *Rev. Medica Chile* **2022**, *150*, 1026–1035.
15. Correa-Parra, J.; Vergara-Perucich, F.; Truffello, R.; Aguirre-Núñez, C. Déficit de La Vivienda En El Gran Santiago: Evidencia Empírica Sobre Conflictos y Argumentos Para Repensar La Planificación Metropolitana. *Urbe. Rev. Bras. Gestão Urbana* **2023**, *15*, e20210251. [CrossRef]
16. Aguirre-Nuñez, C.; Ulloa-Leon, F.; Correa-Parra, J.; Vergara-Perucich, F. Socio-Spatial Analysis of Migrant School Students According to Bourdieu's Capitals in Santiago de Chile (2017–2020). *Heliyon* **2024**, *10*, e29884. [CrossRef]
17. Fuentes, L.; Rodríguez-Leiva, S. Young People's Access to Work and the City. Territorial Looks of Inequality and Segregation in Santiago, Chile [El Acceso de Los Jóvenes al Trabajo y La Ciudad. Miradas Territoriales de La Desigualdad y La Segregación En Santiago de Chile]. *Ciudad. Y Territ. Estud. Territ.* **2020**, *52*, 335–348. [CrossRef]
18. Sabatini, F.; Rasse, A.; Cáceres, G.; Robles, M.S.; Trebilcock, M.P. Promotores Inmobiliarios, Gentrificación y Segregación Residencial En Santiago de Chile. *Rev. Mex. Sociol.* **2017**, *79*, 229–260.
19. Herrera-Marin, M.-R.; Vergara-Perucich, F.; Aguirre-Nunez, C.; Godoy-Faundez, A. Discovering the Spread Patterns of SARS-CoV-2 in Metropolitan Areas. *Rev. Fac. Ing. Univ. Pedagog. Y Tecnol. Colomb.* **2023**, *32*, e16457.
20. Vergara-Perucich, J.F.; Correa-Parra, J.; Aguirre-Nuñez, C. The Spatial Correlation between the Spread of COVID-19 and Vulnerable Urban Areas in Santiago de Chile. *Crit. Hous. Anal.* **2020**, *7*, 21–35. [CrossRef]
21. Mena, G.; Martinez, P.P.; Mahmud, A.S.; Marquet, P.A.; Buckee, C.O.; Santillana, M. Socioeconomic Status Determines COVID-19 Incidence and Related Mortality in Santiago, Chile. *Medrxiv Prepr. Serv. Health Sci.* **2021**, *372*, eabg5298. [CrossRef] [PubMed]
22. Cociña, C. Housing as Urbanism: The Role of Housing Policies in Reducing Inequalities. Lessons from Puente Alto, Chile. *Hous. Stud.* **2021**, *36*, 1490–1512. [CrossRef]
23. Vicuña, M.; Orellana, A.; Truffello, R.; Moreno, D. Urban Integration and Quality of Urban Life: Dilemmas in Metropolitan Contexts [Integración Urbana y Calidad de Vida: Disyuntivas En Contextos Metropolitanos]. *Rev. INVI* **2019**, *34*, 17–47. [CrossRef]
24. Encinas, F.; Freed, C.; Aguirre-Nuñez, C.; Schueftan, A.; Vergara-Perucich, F.; Orellana, S. Individualism as Public Policy: The Incremental Housing Threatened by Energy Poverty; [El individualismo como política pública: La vivienda incremental amenazada por la pobreza energética]. *Rev. INVI* **2023**, *38*, 17–70. [CrossRef]
25. Contreras, Y.; Neville, L.; Gonzalez, R. In-Formality in Access to Housing for Latin American Migrants: A Case Study of an Intermediate Chilean City. *Int. J. Hous. Policy* **2019**, *19*, 411–435. [CrossRef]
26. Hidalgo Dattwyler, R.; Alvarado Peterson, V.; Rodriguez Negrete, L.; Paulsen Bilbao, A. Landscapes of progress: Economic growth and development facet in subsidized housing policies on santiago and valparaiso (1990–2016). *Revista* **2019**, *180*, 110–119.
27. Vergara-Perucich, F.; Fuster-Farfan, X.; Rubio, I.R.; Dattwyller, R.H.; Quiroz, S.R.; Alvarez, J.C.; Peterson, V.A.; Ruiz, O.M.; Vasquez, F.L. Informal housing and territorial organizations in Latin America. *Rev. Geogr. Norte Gd.* **2022**, *81*, 5–14. [CrossRef]
28. Elliott, P.; Wartenberg, D. Spatial Epidemiology: Current Approaches and Future Challenges. *Env. Health Perspect.* **2004**, *112*, 998–1006. [CrossRef]
29. Tatem, A.J. Innovation to Impact in Spatial Epidemiology. *BMC Med.* **2018**, *16*, 209. [CrossRef]
30. Yazici, M. Spatial Point Pattern Analyses and Its Use in Geographical Epidemiology. *Biostat. Biom. Open Access J.* **2017**, *1*, 1–5. [CrossRef]
31. Sun, G.-Q. Pattern Formation of an Epidemic Model with Diffusion. *Nonlinear Dyn.* **2012**, *69*, 1097–1104. [CrossRef] [PubMed]
32. Choi, M. Book Review: Spatial Analysis in Epidemiology. *Healthc. Inform. Res.* **2013**, *19*, 148. [CrossRef]
33. Mack, E.A.; Tong, D.; Credit, K. Gardening in the Desert: A Spatial Optimization Approach to Locating Gardens in Rapidly Expanding Urban Environments. *Int. J. Health. Geogr.* **2017**, *16*, 37. [CrossRef]
34. Jiao, J.; Urban Information Lab; School of Architecture; The University of Texas at Austin, Austin, Texas, USA. Measuring Vulnerable Population's Healthy and Unhealthy Food Access in Austin, Texas. *AIMS Public Health* **2016**, *3*, 722–732. [CrossRef]
35. Sigalo, N.; St Jean, B.; Frias-Martinez, V. Using Social Media to Predict Food Deserts in the United States: Infodemiology Study of Tweets. *JMIR Public Health Surveill.* **2022**, *8*, e34285. [CrossRef]
36. Joyner, L.; Yagüe, B.; Cachelin, A.; Rose, J. Farms and Gardens Everywhere but Not a Bite to Eat? A Critical Geographic Approach to Food Apartheid in Salt Lake City. *J. Agric. Food Syst. Community Dev.* **2022**, *11*, 1–22. [CrossRef]
37. National Institute of Statistics, Census, Santiago, Chile. 2017. Available online: http://www.censo2017.cl/ (accessed on 24 July 2024).
38. Truffello, R.; Flores, M.; Garretón, M.; Ruz, G. La Importancia Del Espacio Geográfico Para Minimizar El Error de Muestras Representativas. *Rev. Geogr. Norte Gd.* **2022**, *81*, 137–160. [CrossRef]
39. Correa, J.; Ulloa-Leon, F.; Vergara-Perucich, F.; Aguirre-Nuñez, C.; Truffello, R. Infrastructural Inequality: Exploring the Emergence of Digital Classes in the Metropolitan Area of Santiago, Chile. *Bull. Geogr.* **2023**, *62*, 107–122. [CrossRef]
40. Encinas, F.; Aguirre, C.; Truffello, R.; Hidalgo, R. Speculation, Land Rent and the Neoliberal City. Or Why Free Market Is Not Enough? *Rev. ARQ* **2019**, *1*, 2–15.

41. Ulloa-Leon, F.; Correa-Parra, J.; Vergara-Perucich, F.; Cancino-Contreras, F.; Aguirre-Nuñez, C. "15-Minute City" and Elderly People: Thinking about Healthy Cities. *Smart Cities* **2023**, *6*, 1043–1058. [CrossRef]
42. Correa Parra, J.; Vergara Perucich, F.; Aguirre Núñez, C. La Ciudad de 15 Minutos En Chile: Análisis Empírico Para Gran Santiago, Concepción y Valparaíso. *Cent. Visa Unit Main Page* **2022**, *15*, 17. [CrossRef]
43. Correa-Parra, J.; Vergara-Perucich, J.F.; Aguirre-Nuñez, C. Towards a Walkable City: Principal Component Analysis for Defining Sub-Centralities in the Santiago Metropolitan Area. *Land* **2020**, *9*, 362. [CrossRef]

urban science

Article

Vulnerated Urban Areas under Regeneration: Strategies to Prevent Neighborhood Expulsion in Barcelona or How to Improve without Expelling?

Gonzalo Piasek * and Pilar Garcia-Almirall

Barcelona School of Architecture, Polytechnic University of Catalonia, 08028 Barcelona, Spain; pilar.garcia-almirall@upc.edu
* Correspondence: gonzalo.piasek@upc.edu

Abstract: This article explores the negative effects of gentrification, especially in vulnerable areas of contemporary cities, by focusing on five case studies of the city of Barcelona. This relevant question is addressed here following a double strategy (quantitative and qualitative). In an attempt to engage on a debate around the scope and limitations of current urban regeneration interventions, the phenomenon of gentrification is quantified throughout time drawing from official statistics. At the same time, the voices of local entities' representatives are included to introduce a level of representation on the phenomenon. The results suggest that, even though urban regeneration strategies are absolutely necessary, especially in the more vulnerated areas, it is necessary to include more comprehensive approaches and tools that take into consideration not only the physical and urban effects of rehabilitation, but also the economic and social aspects. Thus, it may be necessary to engage in a more consequential discussion not only on how vulnerability and regeneration are theorized, measured and dealt with, but also on some less studied dimensions of the socio-urban phenomenon, such as the social capital and the social infrastructure of neighborhoods.

Keywords: urban regeneration; gentrification; social capital; social infrastructure

1. Introduction

Contemporary urban areas, their history and current state are not a consequence of chance or natural causes, but a result of struggles between different actors with interests and specific power to define rules and produce the cities through their interactions. According to Pírez [1], the city is a product of diverse processes, independent and still contradictory. Within this framework, economic actors are those whose activities answer to a logic of profit; political or governmental actors produce the city either in a direct or indirect way within the logic of power; actors determined by the logics of need (meaning their necessities are met outside the market or the public policy spheres) contribute via processes of self-production of the city; finally, actors moved by the logics of knowledge (scientific, technical, ideological) provide inputs that the three other actors take in order to define their own interventions. Thus, cities are a result of struggles and negotiations between these actors.

Since its very origin, sociology has studied the urban phenomenon, especially interested in the translation of social differences into the urban space. The Chicago School, especially from the 1920s and 1930s [2], is a necessary reference. From this framework on, one of the main concerns of urban studies would be around segregation, which is related to how social classes and groups are distributed among the urban space [3], as a materialization of social differences already present on a material level. Researchers have studied this phenomenon, contributing with very important findings that relate segregation to differences in income [4,5], while others have tried to disentangle the concept incorporating new variables, such as origin or ethnicity [6–8], which have also helped explain the formation of areas like ghettos [9]. This very clear separation of social groups, sometimes enclosed in specific areas of the cities or suburbs, is a tendency that is of course not new and has been addressed usually by promoting policies towards social mixture [10,11]. More recently, authors agree that COVID-19 has led to new forms of segregation [12] whose impacts researchers are still trying to understand fully [13]. With the end of the salary-centered society, in which having a job meant a more or less stable social integration, new patterns and forms of participation in society appeared, where one could actually be in "grey" areas or spaces "in between" the traditional poles of integration and disintegration [14]. Thus, the concept of vulnerability intends to capture these situations "in the middle", that are not explainable by the integration–disintegration binomial, but as a state of being "at risk of" [15] (disaffiliation, impoverishment, losing one's stability, etc.).

Throughout time, due to the specialization of different areas of the city as well as being a result of processes of segregation, some places, especially in old city centers, but also in suburbs or *banlieues* [16] faced processes of abandonment and/or change of functions that have put them at risk of becoming more and more relegated, becoming vulnerable neighborhoods [17]. There have been many efforts in academia to measure and identify the distribution of vulnerability throughout urban areas [18–24]. At the same time, there has been a very important debate on its very conceptualization, where some explain the fact that these are not vulnerable but vulnerated [25] emphasizing the fact that there is a responsibility that is not of residents themselves, but that should be found outside these areas, and that is related to other political and economic actors' responsibilities. However, no matter the definition that is adopted, at least two things related to this phenomenon are clear: first, the fact that urban vulnerability is a multidimensional phenomenon that incorporates not only economic, but physical and social dimensions [26]; secondly, the fact that these areas of the city represent a serious challenge to urban planners, which also needs to be addressed from a multidimensional perspective [27].

In Europe, in general, where most cities are old and dense, there is no much place for growth [28] because city limits are quite established, even after the processes of suburbanization. This means that it is not possible to grow via new construction, even when there is an increasing demand of new residents as well as a need to rehabilitate, resulting in a great deal of pressure on cities that makes access to housing more and more difficult. Thus, the intervention into the existing building stock is not important, but necessary, in order to improve the habitability conditions and the quality of life of residents, especially in vulnerated areas. This is the paradigm of regeneration, renovation and rehabilitation [29] which has changed over time and has become a parading for contemporary sensible sustainable intervention. When historicizing this process, a transition is observed from actions focused on improvement in the physical characteristics of the buildings to policies that gradually incorporate new perspectives and dimensions [30]. This evolution has led to programs with a comprehensive intervention will, encompassing previously unconsidered socioeconomic and/or structural aspects [31]. These modifications are not only theoretical, but are expressed through Conventions and Acts at a European level and will not be consolidated in Spain until after the 2008 crisis [32], especially with the enactment of the "3R-Law" (of rehabilitation, regeneration and urban renewal) in 2013 [33].

This work is written within the framework of two research projects [34,35] and a doctoral thesis, which have contributed with new tools towards the measurement and identification of vulnerable areas of the city. Within these frameworks, the main goal of the paper is to analyze how the intervention and improvement in vulnerable/vulnerated areas is being addressed, and whether an anti-speculative/anti-expulsion approach is a part of the discussion. The hypothesis is that gentrification is becoming a more and more relevant issue within urban regeneration actions, especially in lower-income areas of consolidated cities. This work will thus entail a double approach (quantitative and qualitative) that will focus on the analysis of specific vulnerated areas of Barcelona (selected from previous work), reflecting on the effects that existing tools of urban regeneration have had, whilst advocating for more comprehensive and humane ways of intervention that take into account not only the economic but also the "social gains" throughout the contemplation of the social infrastructure and social capital dimensions.

2. Theoretical and Analytical Framework

Within this research, the issue of gentrification [36,37] is a crucial point. Typically, when an area is improved, there is a risk of changing the population and altering the area's identity. This is mainly because improved spaces can undergo a valorization process, leading to increased prices, particularly in rent and local businesses [38,39]. This change in the residents' composition takes place when a certain area is "appropriated" by newcomers, usually of higher incomes, causing a more or less explicit expulsion of previous residents [40,41]. Aside from the resulting rise in prices, this phenomenon is also related to the potential presence of more vacation or tourist accommodations that can in turn place a significant strain on the rental market [42]. Thus, although there is quite a general agreement on the fact that gentrification and touristification have consequences of many kinds (cultural, economic, social, urban, etc.), their scope is something still under debate. There is also no agreement as to how gentrification should be measured and identified, mainly because it is only perceivable throughout time, making it harder to realize and prevent some of its negative effects. Some recent work suggests following the variables of rent, origin and job category [43] whilst others focus on gastronomic trends [44] and so on. What is clear is the fact that it entails a multidimensional phenomenon impacting not only on an economic but also a social level. This specific work intends to be a part of the ongoing discussion on the need to capture gentrification at an early stage, and will focus on specific vulnerated areas of the city of Barcelona.

At this point, it is also important to mention that gentrification is not only present at a local level but it is in fact a global phenomenon affecting most contemporary cities. However, its manifestations and responses vary widely across different contexts. For example, in the United States, gentrification often involves significant displacement of lower-income residents in cities like New York and San Francisco, which have implemented measures such as rent control and inclusionary zoning to mitigate its adverse effects. In the United Kingdom, gentrification has been closely linked to urban regeneration projects, particularly in cities like London. Policies like the New Deal for Communities and the Housing Market Renewal Initiative have aimed to revitalize deprived areas while attempting to balance economic growth with social equity [36]. Germany's approach to gentrification includes a strong emphasis on social housing and tenant protections. Berlin, for instance, has implemented measures such as rent caps and the prohibition of luxury renovations in specific areas. In Australia, cities like Sydney and Melbourne have seen significant gentrification, often linked to broader economic restructuring and globalization. Across these examples, the impacts of the implemented measures still continue to be debated.

Furthermore, this work aims to integrate some not-so-studied dimensions in urban research, mostly related to the characteristics of the built environment that may promote or defer processes of socialization, that can, in turn, translate into higher levels of civic engagement and/or participation. The first concept portraying the characteristics of the built environment is related to shared spaces, such as parks, bars, pedestrian streets, libraries, etc. and is usually defined as social infrastructure (SI) [45]. This author analyses how face-to-face interactions—at the school, the playground and the corner diner—can turn into the building blocks of all public life, directing planners' attention from grey or hard infrastructures "to a series of spaces and facilities—often overlooked and underfunded—that supports a robust public collective life in cities, and helps build into urban neighborhoods the capacity for all sorts of ways of being with others" [46]. It has become more important than ever to highlight the importance of ensuring very high standards of these shared spaces, especially when an urban area is being regenerated [47], due to its importance in social capital formation that can lead to community resistance to external threats, such as evictions.

The second concept, referring to everyday social interactions between residents, could be conceptualized as social capital (SC) [48]. Its differential degree can be explained in terms of its bonding and bridging forms, where the former entails strong relationships between individuals, and the latter is the case when these networks actually lead to higher levels of local organization and civic engagement. Thus, if higher levels of SC are desirable, given their effects on happy and healthy environments [49], there is still an underlying question related to vulnerable neighborhoods' ability to transform bonding into bridging forms of SC, which would speak of their power to stay cohesive and united amidst the different threats they may encounter (related to for example the visible and invisible forms of expulsion that will be explained later). The harm evictions can cause has been studied and it has been established that impacts are not only on the individual, but especially on the community level as a whole [50], showing how important it is not only to maintain but to find new ways to strengthen local social networks.

3. Materials and Methods

This manuscript focused on 5 neighborhoods (as can be seen in Figure 1), selected following multidimensional tools, given their interest as a representation of the spatialization of vulnerability in the city of Barcelona.

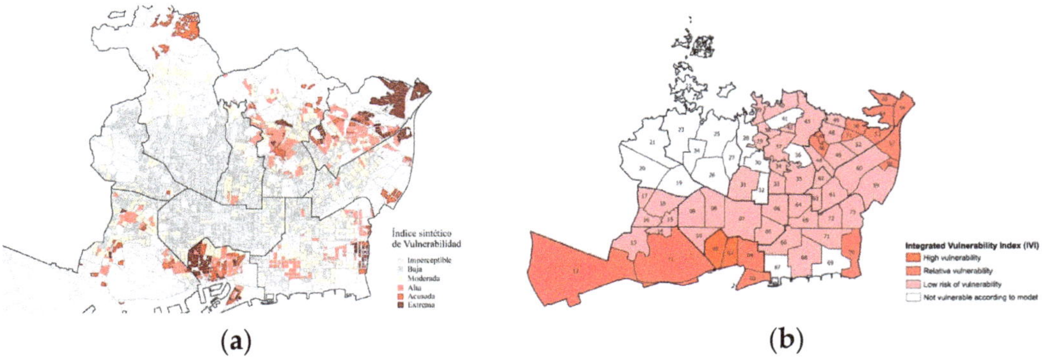

Figure 1. (**a**) Vulnerability index at a census section [22]; (**b**) Integrated Vulnerability Index at a neighborhood level [24].

The 5 selected case studies in Barcelona respond to previous work focusing on the identification of vulnerability [22], following a multi-scale and multi-disciplinary study, which incorporated some mapping of social, economic and urban indicators. The results were weighed following statistical tools, as well as a series of discussions maintained with a panel of experts in the field. This work has helped identify areas of the city with a higher concentration of multidimensional problems, which has in turn allowed the local administration to focus on specific areas, and design relevant programs and policies that adjust to these complex realities (as opposed to general interventions to which local communities have to adapt). The 5 neighborhoods that appeared to be at greater risk of vulnerability will be briefly introduced here in order to understand their relevance to this study's goal. However, a deeper analysis of their characteristics (in quantitative and qualitative terms) will be a part of this paper's Section 4.

La Barceloneta's origin is related to the economic activity of fishing in the middle of the XVIII century. Even though planned for a specific population (mostly low- and middle–low-income families), its particular location (right at the center of the city and in front of the sea), and the city's touristification process, have made this area especially attractive to private investment, resulting in a subdivision of most apartments, some renovations and a change of use (especially ground floors becoming commercial), which have made it almost impossible for old-renters to compete with newcomers, being directly or indirectly forced to leave their homes.

El Raval is also a neighborhood in the *Ciutat Vella* central district, which was born as a result of the extension of the walls of the old city. Although its first constructions could be traced to the XIV century, its growth and development was related to the early industrialization of XVIII century. From this time on, it has been home to low-income classes, especially immigrants from the Global South, that have endured big regeneration policies.

Trinitat Vella is a much younger neighborhood of the city and is a result of the "developmentalism" of the 1950s, when internal migrations resulted in a need for rapid housing which was met building big blocks in remote unconnected areas of the city that would little by little be incorporated into the urban fabric, mainly because of neighbor struggles.

Ciutat Meridiana's history is similar to *Trinitat Vella* and its blocks were built in the 1960s during the *Franco* dictatorship with no surrounding infrastructure or basic urban services, but with an added problem: it is quite inaccessible due to slopes, which has been its major neighbor concern.

Besòs i Maresme is also a result of the quick and massive construction of blocks of housing of the late 1950s and 1960s. The lack of basic urban services has been the center of neighbor demand. However, in recent years, its surrounding area has been facing a revitalization process that has started to bring pressure into this neighborhood.

For this paper, a double methodological strategy (quantitative and qualitative) was followed. It is essential to note that this division is theoretical, as both strategies contributed to a broader overarching strategy, as will be clear in the following section outlining the achieved results. As for the quantitative strategy, the intention was to characterize the case studies in relation to the effects that more or less recent urban interventions and trends have had at a local level, specifically in terms of rental prices (and other costs) and also on probable processes of resident expulsion. Thus, a series of indicators were selected following recent literature on the subject, with the intention to portray to what extent the neighborhoods are at risk of—or are already—experiencing gentrification and/or expulsion. An ad hoc database at a neighborhood level was built from available open-source official information portals [51–54]. Some indicators' behaviors were traced in time since complex dimensions such as gentrification demand a certain follow-up that a cross-sectional study cannot capture. As for the qualitative strategy, 13 interviews were conducted with local entities' representatives between 2021 and 2023, as well as with two housing policy technicians (See Table 1 for details).

Table 1. Interviewed entities from case studies.

Neighborhood *	Neighbor Association	Housing Related Entity
La Barceloneta	2	1
El Raval	2	2
Trinitat Vella	1	1
Ciutat Meridiana	1	1
Besòs i Maresme	1	1

* The 13 interviews associated with each case study were complemented with 2 interviews with local policy technicians that intervene in most neighborhoods.

As shown in Table 1, two types of local entities were consulted: those directly related to neighborhood issues and those focusing on housing. To maintain some degree of anonymity, their full descriptions are not provided here. However, it is noteworthy that some of these entities have a long history of local organization, advocating for the implementation of crucial policies concerning urban services, accessibility, social institutions and housing, some of them working very actively since their foundation during the second part of the last century. Others are especially active in the aftermath of the 2008 real-estate crisis, working locally to prevent evictions that would result in the erosion of the social fabric. As for the consulted technicians, they are specialists in either local housing and licensing or social programs.

The questions—full interview guide available in Appendix A—revolve around their representations on the phenomenon of urban regeneration, its scope, and its limits and opportunities, as well as its consequences on a local level. The selection of interviewees was made based on prior knowledge of these territories gained through the aforementioned research projects, as well as a result of "snowball effect" (where conversations with one social leader and/or representative would lead to another key actor). The interviews were recorded, transcribed and introduced into the *Atlas.ti* program [55] (8.4.3-1077 version), which is specialized software for qualitative data analysis. This permitted a better treatment of the information, allowing an identification of common, reiterated or opposite views on specific topics within the different interviewees. The analysis of discourse research technique [56] was followed, which is a practice commonly used in qualitative analysis with the intention of capturing the level of representation of a specific phenomenon, taking into account the power relations that are expressed via speech. The interviews were conducted until theoretical saturation of data, meaning that a new interview would not contribute any new relevant information.

In order to assess the quality of the research data that was produced for the purposes of this work—especially the qualitative data obtained from semi-structured interviews—specific actions were followed to guarantee that some degree of credibility, transferability, dependability, confirmability and authenticity [57] would be taken into account. The selection of interviewees, the construction of the interview guides and the strategies followed for data treatment incorporated these elements and also those present in another system, that are related to transparency, personal reflexivity and triangulation [58]. All in all, the design of the research strategy, the gathering of data, its treatment and dissemination have been carried out ensuring that data were of high quality, that the sources were respected and the results would be as transparent as possible.

4. Results

This section presents the results obtained throughout this research. It is divided into two different subsections that are very well connected to a third analysis section (see Figure 2). The next sections follow this structure: Gentrification: part of the problem of expulsion in Barcelona? Local strategies addressing the negative effects of gentrification; Incorporating the social capital and social infrastructure dimensions in anti-gentrification measures. The first topic is mostly related to the concept of gentrification and the threat of expulsion in vulnerated areas of Barcelona city, which are undergoing present or potential future valorization processes. Section 4.2 depicts some of the local strategies of Barcelona's administration and entities that aim to respond to urban problems that in turn also intend to tackle some of the negative effects of gentrification. Finally, the analysis aims to incorporate the variables of social capital and social infrastructure, suggesting that a comprehensive approach is needed (both for studying and intervening in vulnerated areas), in order to truly answer the need to improve habitability conditions and residents' quality of life, overcoming tools that have proven to have unwanted consequences which resulted in vicious cycles of impoverishment, expulsion and/or segregation.

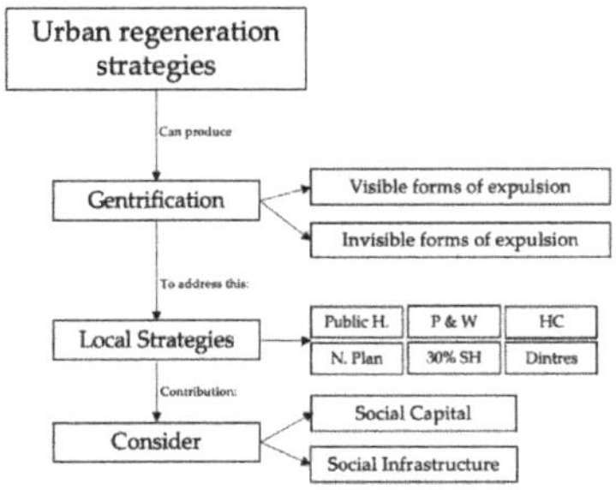

Figure 2. Organization of paper's results and analysis.

4.1. Gentrification: Part of the Problem of Expulsion in Barcelona?

The purpose of this subsection is to assess whether a gentrification process has been occurring or is likely to take place in the case studies. This analysis is intended to overcome traditional measures of urban poverty mostly related to income, that lead to not contemplating some neighborhoods as vulnerable/vulnerated, adopting a more comprehensive approach. Thus, some key indicators were traced in order to shed some light on the existing or potential changes in some of the economic and/or social trends. Starting from a recent work [24] where some physical characteristics were contemplated as a result of a factorial analysis, new variables like rent prices, household income and other dimensions related to the social profile and the commercial behavior of the area [59] were taken into account. Gentrification can be traced throughout a deep analysis of both a social and commercial change.

- Resident's profile change

Probable ongoing or future gentrification processes could be deduced by taking a look into whether some socio-demographic characteristics of the population change over time. Although the inhabitants register is a useful source of information, it does not inform about the reasons people move, where they come from and where they go to. Figure 3a shows the inner migration rate (people leaving their neighborhood by 1000 inhabitants), indicating that 2010 was a high peak in all cases, following the 2008 real-estate crisis. However, *Besòs-Maresme* in 2022 is almost at its 2010 level, above but still very close to *Barceloneta*, and they are almost as high as *Raval*, which has been systematically going down since 2010 (the tendency is related to its characteristic as a host location for immigrant newcomers). Figure 3b shows the same rate but considers new arrivals, where a similar trend is observed. In both figures, the percentages of these three case studies are way above the average of Barcelona city, which is very similar to those of *Trinitat Vella* and *Ciutat Meridiana*, and works as an indicator of the neighborhoods' dynamism.

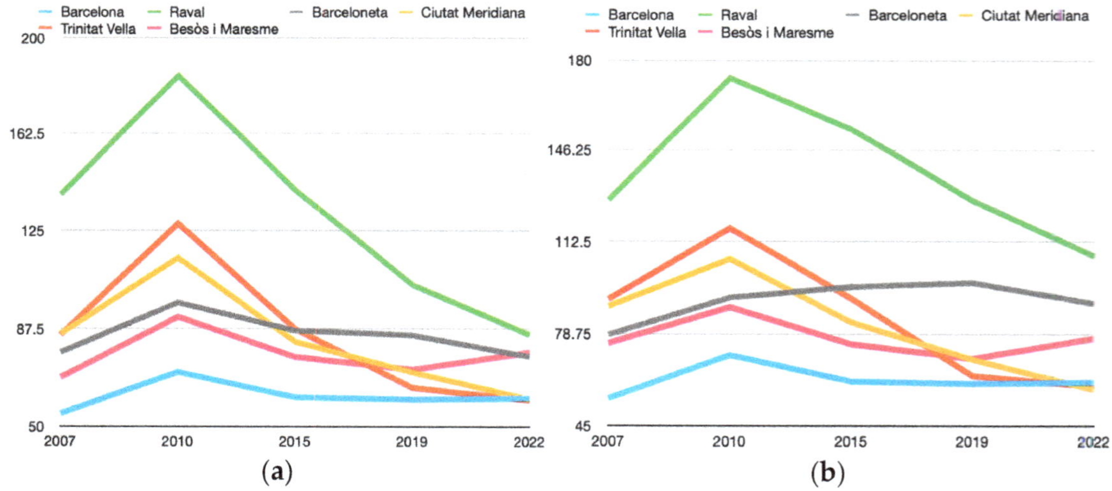

Figure 3. The 2007–2022 residential changes in the case studies: (**a**) change of residence (deregister); (**b**) change of residence (register). Source: Public Inhabitants Register.

Another important variable is age, which has also been studied in relation to gentrification trends [60]. Figure 4 portrays the percentage of young people in relation to the total population, showing that the *Barceloneta* case is most noticeable. Also, the case of *Besòs-Maresme* shows a positive trend in recent years and that of *Raval*, which seems to be slowing down, should also be followed closely.

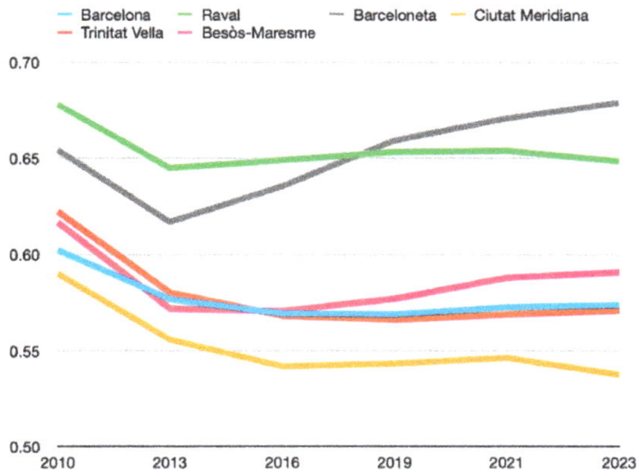

Figure 4. Age evolution in the case studies (2010–2021). Source: Barcelona Open Data.

This trend has been identified [61] in relation to digital nomads' (especially from European countries) residential choices as an indicator of the expulsion of older residents (as can be seen in Figure 5 portraying the concentration of high-income foreigners throughout the city). The combination of high-income immigration and a certain rejuvenation should raise some alarms as to profound socio-demographic ongoing changes.

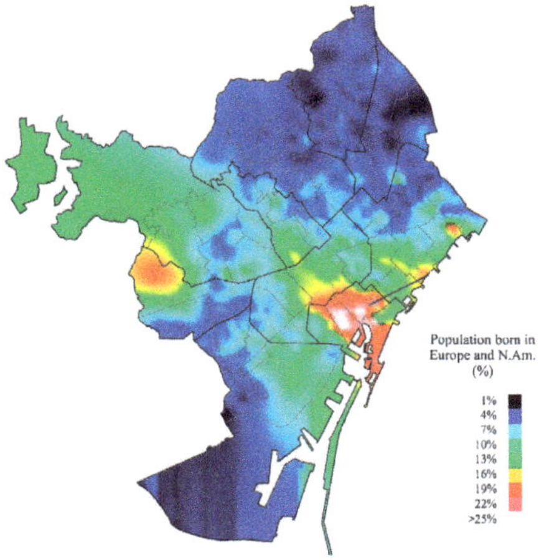

Figure 5. Population born in EU countries and USA. Source: adaptation from [61].

Another important variable is the education level of the population, a very good indicator of the individual cultural capital and a relevant agent of the processes of gentrification [62]. As can be seen in Figure 6, there is a general positive trend in Barcelona. However, the cases of *Barceloneta* and *Raval* are especially relevant in terms of the education level, but probably for different reasons. Although they are both part of the *Ciutat Vella* district—the most central and demanded one in terms of tourism—the rising level of education in *Raval* probably corresponds to immigrants' children that are the first generation to study at a higher level; *Barceloneta*'s improvement probably corresponds to the arrival of highly educated newcomers.

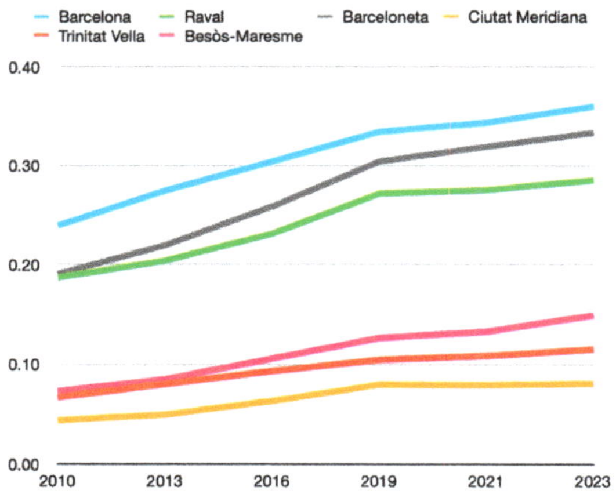

Figure 6. High education level (university) in the case studies (2010–2023). Source: Barcelona Open Data.

Another interesting approach is taking into account the number of people living in each dwelling: single occupancy of households between the ages of 18 and 64 years old [60]. Figure 7 shows how this indicator is over-represented in the case of *Raval* (which could be explained by the lack of information on overcrowded flats), and also of *Barceloneta* (more likely associated with small attractive apartments).

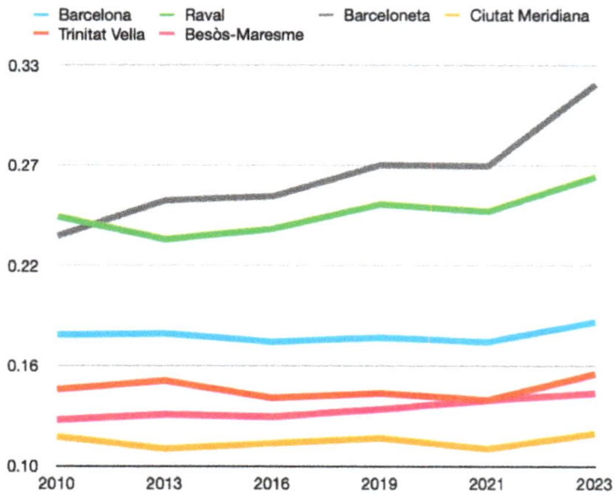

Figure 7. Dwelling's single occupancy in case studies (2010–2023). Source: Barcelona Open Data.

The number of years living in the same place is also an interesting piece of information. Figure 8a shows that neighborhood identity is something very important in Barcelona, related to its history where most neighborhoods used to be separate towns; Figure 8b shows which have been some of the most attractive areas of the city in past years (*Barceloneta*, *Raval* and *Besòs-Maresme*).

Up to this point, the analysis has shown there is an ongoing very real socio-demographic profile change in the case studies, especially perceptible for the neighborhoods of *Barceloneta*, *Raval* and *Besòs-Maresme*. This last one's behavior is probably less consolidated, meaning it should receive greater attention. These changes combined with touristification and real-estate market speculation could impact the sustainability of neighbor relationships and the thickening of social capital since expulsion (direct or indirect) can harm the social fabric, something which will be analyzed later.

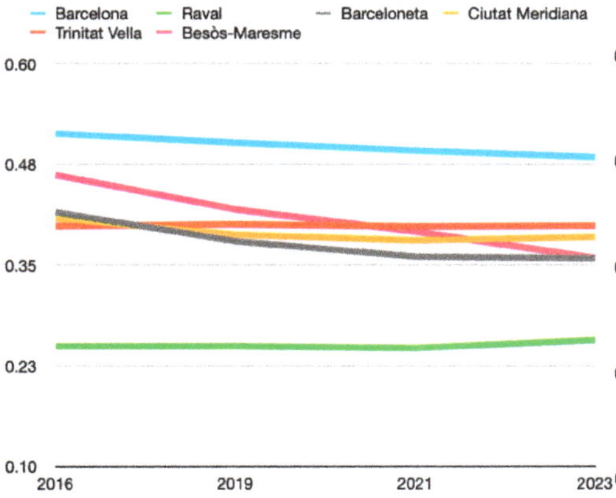

(**a**)

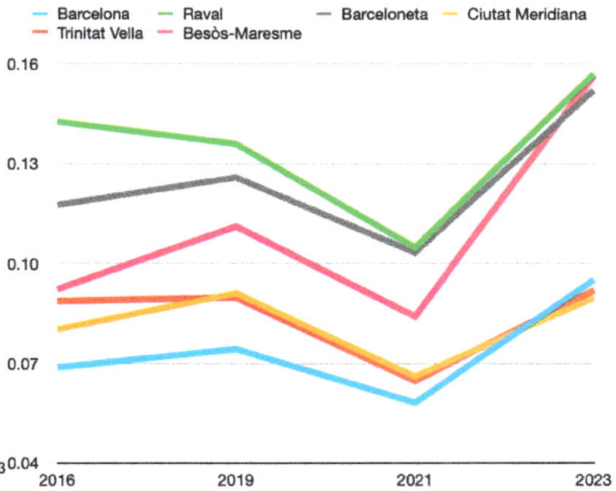

(**b**)

Figure 8. Years living in the same neighborhood. (**a**) more than fifteen years registered in the same neighborhood; (**b**) less than 1 year registered in the same neighborhood. Source: official register of inhabitants.

> "*Urbanism investment, in the end, is gentrifier itself. [...] The administration is one of the main gentrifying agents*" (Barcelona technician).

> "*Many very engaged female neighbors have encountered expulsion themselves at first hand, which made civic engagement strength to fade away*" (Barceloneta entity).

- Commercial profile change

Another very important question related to the topic of gentrification is the local economy: new social profiles demand and consume goods and services that are not necessarily the ones present at the territory before their arrival. Thus, one very visible consequence (and cause) of displacement is related to the mutation of local commerce, that, at the same time, has a direct effect on the urban landscape [63]. Table 2 shows the rise in the use of establishments for commercial activities between 2016 and 2019 in the case studies.

Table 2. Commercial activity in case studies (2016–2019 change).

Case Study	2016	2019	Change
Barcelona	60.265	80.553	134%
Raval	2.355	2.967	126%
Barceloneta	545	746	137%
Ciutat Meridiana	146	203	139%
Trinitat Vella	166	388	234%
Besòs-Maresme	462	609	132%

Source: Commerce, Restauration and Consumption Direction, Barcelona City Council.

Although some information on the type of activity is available (via the commercial census every 3 years), it does not specify the quality of establishments, whether they are "used" by residents or visitors, whether these correspond to old or new establishments, their importance on a local level, etc., making it necessary to incorporate some qualitative information: the idea of a certain commercial change was recurrent in the interviews, especially by older tenants referring to some kind of identity loss, especially since bars' and restaurant's terraces constitute very important spaces for socialization in the Spanish culture.

"The minute people with middle or high incomes arrive, this entails a whole new different type of economy takes place" (Besòs-Maresme entity).

4.1.1. "Visible" or Direct Displacement: Evictions

A quite striking thing is the fact that causes for evictions have been changing throughout recent years. Historically, Spain has been "a country of property owners" [64], meaning that access to housing used to be associated with buying a property. However, after the 2008 crisis, many evictions took place since Spanish people could not afford their mortgages. After the economic recovery, a new "generation rent" has begun to become the norm [65]. Thus, in recent years, non-payment of rent has become the main reason for eviction: in Barcelona only, from 2013 to 2021, 55,325 people were evicted, corresponding to an average of 6147 inhabitants each year, over 3.3% of the entire population [66]. Although it is difficult to gather data (especially at a disaggregated or neighborhood level), some entities have been collaborating with the local administration to map the eviction situation and identify possible concentrations [67]. This shared effort also allowed the identification of property owners who were more likely to evict: SAREB, Blackstone and Cerberus Capital Management (which are all legal persons, and control only a third part of the total households).

"An old lady living in a bank-owned apartment: in these cases, even politicians come help us stop the evictions" (Trinitat Vella entity).

"The existing support networks see themselves deteriorated because people are expelled, which complicates even more the associational life" (Barceloneta entity).

Even though eviction is a visible and direct form of expulsion, there are other forms whose low-visibility, silent—and because of that, also very intricate—processes can also lead to displacement. The role of SC and SI as barriers against this kind of threat is a part of the following section.

4.1.2. "Invisible" or Indirect Forms of Displacement

- Rise in rent prices

The rental market is an important indicator since more than 40% of housing in Barcelona corresponds to this segment (94% when focusing only on young people). As is clear in Figure 2a, the increase in rental prices in the last 20 years is significant, not only at a city level (that could be associated with economic trends and overall inflation), but it is specifically relevant in recent years in the case studies (see Figure 9b).

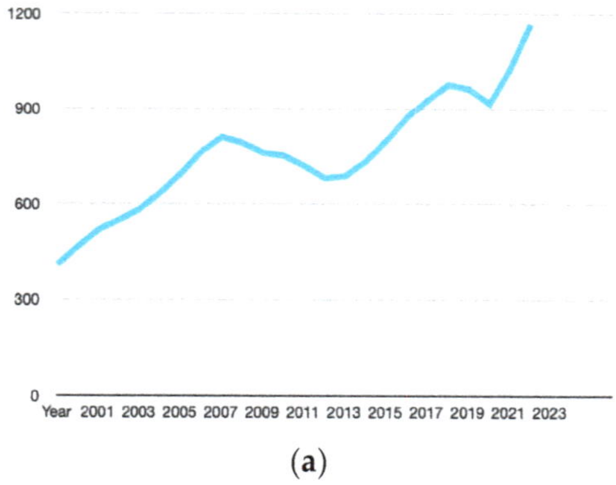

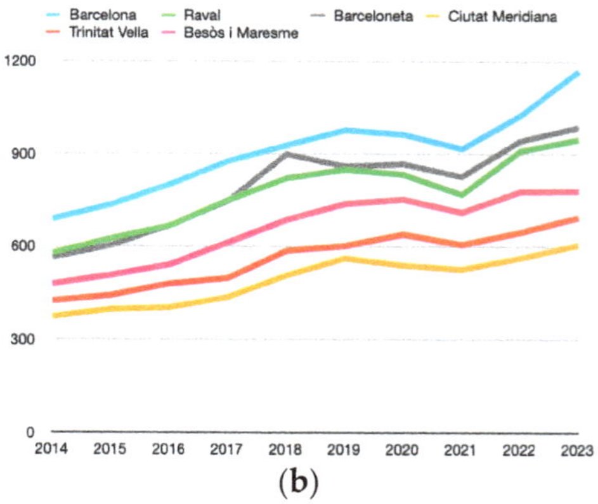

Figure 9. Changes in rent prices. (**a**) Average rent price per year in Barcelona (2000–2023); (**b**) average rent price per year in case studies and in Barcelona (2014–2023).

This situation has had direct consequences in terms of access to housing, especially for those mostly in need, and has been especially worsened by new market trends, such as the increasing number of temporary rentals (as opposed to long-term ones), and the rise in room rentals (as opposed to entire units), especially after COVID-19. Even though specific national housing norms aim to regulate the sector (actually, new national (*Ley de Vivienda* 12/2023) and local (rent regulation of February 2024) legislation was put forward recently) establishing minimum requirements for newly signed contracts—such as a 5-to-7-year minimum period of rent (depending on whether the property is owned by a natural or legal person)—new market trends and forms tend to "escape" from legislation, making it very hard to regulate contracts between private parties.

> "*The administration goes at a 10 km/h speed and the reality goes at 120 km/h, which is why we are always late*" (technician, Barcelona).

When looking into the quantity of contracts signed throughout the city in recent years, it is quite clear that, even considering the 2020 drop related to COVID-19, these seem to be going down (Figure 10a,b). However, the overall number of people living in the city has not changed much, suggesting that the housing offer is undergoing some kind of alteration that could be related to the aforementioned trends and the fact that official data cannot capture them entirely (at least, for the time being).

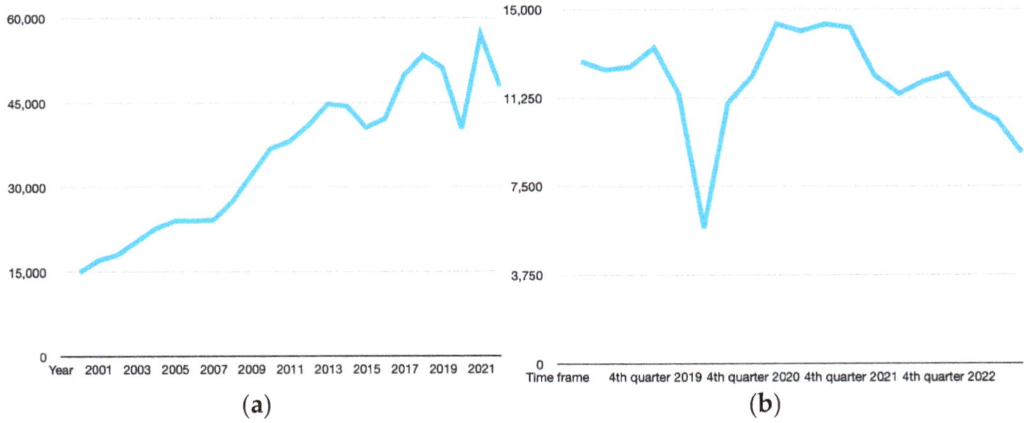

Figure 10. (**a**) Quantity of rent contracts in Barcelona (2000–2023); (**b**) quantity of rent contracts by quarter in Barcelona (2019–2023).

At the same time, accommodation offered to tourists also seems to be dropping when taking the August 2020 to August 2023 period into account (see Figure 11). This could be related to the Special Tourist Accommodation Plan (PEUAT), which was an instrument created to have some control over the increasing accommodation destined for touristic use. However, the presence of tourists in the city is still rising.

Thus, a relevant question is where this offer of accommodation is actually going (if, as has been said, tourist accommodation is being controlled and fewer long-term rent contracts are being signed). A possible answer could therefore be found in the increase in informality in the rental sector, suggesting a rise in temporary contracts (less than 1 year long and hence "escaping" from regulation), flat-sharing (where one person holds the contract and sub-lets the rooms) or even illegal tourist accommodation (since the aforementioned regulation establishes no new touristic rentals, especially in those areas at greater risk).

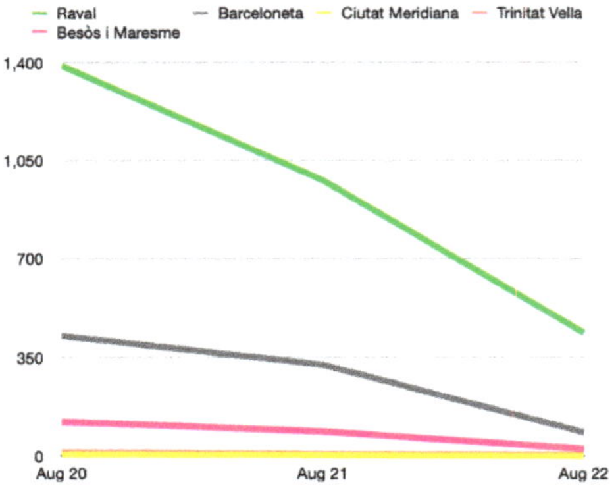

Figure 11. Housing offered to tourists (2020–2023).

What is even more worrying is the fact although income per capita seems to have followed a positive trend until COVID-19 (see Figure 12), the effort towards paying rent takes up most of this income in all case studies (see Table 3), even when the theoretical ideal percentage should be around 30%. A recent work [68] measured this in 2019 at a district level, showing similar results: the fact that the actual average effort in paying rent in the city was around 50%, and around (or higher than) 70% in vulnerable areas.

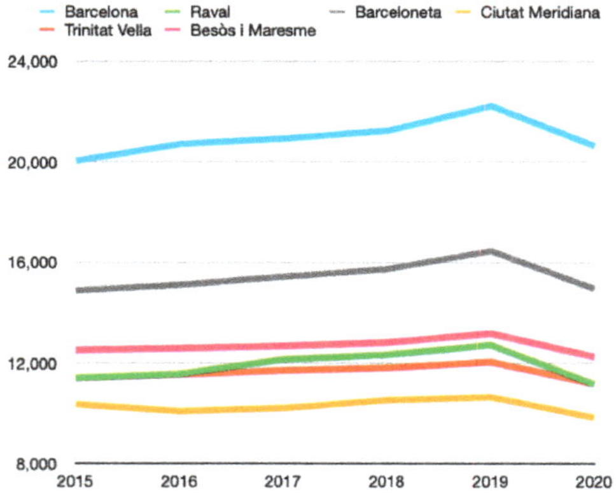

Figure 12. Income per household per neighborhood (2015–2020).

Table 3. Effort towards paying rent (2015–2020): relation between income and rent prices.

Neighborhood	2015	2016	2017	2018	2019	2020
Barcelona	44.0%	46.1%	50.2%	52.4%	52.8%	56.0%
Raval	65.8%	69.2%	73.9%	80.0%	80.2%	89.5%
Barceloneta	48.7%	53.0%	58.0%	68.6%	62.7%	69.7%
Ciutat Meridiana	46.0%	48.0%	51.2%	57.8%	63.3%	65.9%
Trinitat Vella	46.5%	49.8%	51.0%	59.5%	60.0%	68.6%
Besòs i Maresme	48.6%	51.6%	58.1%	64.2%	67.3%	73.7%

Source: Barcelona Statistics Department.

Another crucial point is that official statistics often fall short in fully capturing the complexities of real-world situations: non-registered residents, overcrowded flats, empty dwellings, second residences belonging to foreigners, apartments being exploited with other than residential use (commercial, sometimes illegal activities, etc.), are among the problems that were mentioned during the interviews. However, these are not usually captured by official data, making it very difficult to trace and tackle housing-related problems. This is why it is very important to implement qualitative strategies in order to truly capture the level of complexities that these issues entail.

> "*Against the idea that the neighborhood is conflictive because of its interculturality… the actual problem is with tourists and the competition for apartments, public space, consumption of goods and services*" (Raval entity).

> "*The pressure of tourism, everywhere but especially here, has had a direct impact on rent prices*" (Barceloneta entity).

> "*Sub-letting rooms with no contracts has become a common thing*" (technician, Barcelona).

- Overall increase in prices

Another very important problem also related to gentrification is not only the rise in rent prices but an overall increase in the cost of living, which can also result in a more silent form of expulsion. Again, it is not easy to trace price changes throughout time and throughout the different neighborhoods. Although it could be possible to choose some products or services and follow their behavior in order to account for this, a deeper analysis on the change in the commercial profile is probably more accurate and will be presented later.

> "*Recent changes in the neighborhood surrounding are attracting more fashionable and modern establishments*" (Besòs-Maresme entity).

> "*Many shops are aged; they close and these spaces are being exploited especially by newcomer immigrant population*" (Trinitat Vella entity).

These testimonies are particularly relevant, especially as the interviewees considered more "active" streets with shops related to safer environments, while streets with no commercial use seemed to be sometimes more abandoned and related to higher risks or danger. Thus, analyzing gentrification through the increase in rent prices and everyday costs but also tracking how these changes are lived and represented by residents is key, as these have an effect on the whole area's identity (commercial, but also social).

- Residential mobbing

Another very important situation that takes place, according to the interviewees, are situations of conscious neglect and abandonment of the dwellings by property owners. Aware of some of the market tendencies, they sometimes tend to speculate that higher benefits can be extracted from their properties, especially in vulnerated areas under renovation. Even though it is very difficult to obtain data that support these situations (that can go from not responding to renters' complaints, to not making necessary renovations, even threating tenants to increase rent prices, etc.), both the literature [69] and the interviews speak of these very unfair situations.

> "*People suffer pressure and harassment so they leave, with completely abandoned dwellings because the landlords do not fix or maintain them, with no elevators and deteriorated stairs*" (Barceloneta entities).

> "*Landlords as owners are obliged to maintain their property. Not doing so, passive mobbing, is a crime and can affect tenants even more than a more direct eviction*" (Raval entity).

By taking into account the behavior of some social and economic variables related to gentrification—and a more or less explicit threat of residential expulsion associated with it—it has become quite clear that not all case studies are affected in the same way. Centrality, attractiveness and tourism appear to be crucial dimensions that are not necessarily captured in depth by official statistics, making it necessary to develop other qualitative tools in order to fully understand the negative effects of undergoing valorization processes. In the following subsection, local strategies from the Barcelona case are presented.

4.2. Local Strategies Addressing the Negative Effects of Gentrification

So far, efforts have been made to capture the issues related to potential current or future gentrification processes in the case studies. At this point, it is also necessary to present the alternatives that the local administration together with local entities are putting forward in order to tackle some of the negative effects. This subsection presents some of the specific public programs and policies that are more or less related to the prevention of residents' expulsion and, at the same time, introduces the key role of local entities; the relevance of social capital and social infrastructure within the subject will be explained in the next section.

When some urban regeneration interventions prove to have negative impacts on the territories, driving up real-estate and other prices and expelling residents, at least two possible ways of action come into place. The first alternative is to leave things as they are, refraining from promoting any changes to break the apparent vicious circle where public actions may further harm the areas of intervention. A blind vote on the free market is probably not a valid way to go, when recognizing the fact that the starting point is already urban areas where spatialized forms of segregation and inequality are the norm. However, there is another way, which seems to be more suitable for a context in which access to adequate housing is at stake, forcing law-makers to implement strategies for the improvement of the existing tools and the creation of new ones aligned with the right to housing and the right to the city. A notable example of active involvement in the improvement and intervention of the real-estate market is the case of Barcelona.

- Public housing: having a big public residential stock would entail that the administration becomes a player that can compete with the private sector. However, the Spanish case is very different from other (especially Northern) European countries on this subject. Apart from being only 1.5%, "Official Protected Housing" (VPO in Spanish) has been predominantly developed for sale and not for rent and most of these dwellings will lose their protection status within the next 30 years. In spite of recent efforts from the municipal administration, the public building stock is definitely an unresolved matter [70] both in Spain and at the municipal level (taking into account the limited resources of the local administration and the fact that the housing law is a national one).
- Rehabilitation funds: the combination of old building stock, sometimes with patrimonial value, within a city with high levels of segregation—without mentioning the bureaucratic issues that public help entail and that is one of the main reasons for not reaching vulnerated areas—result in a very problematic situation in which a great deal of community organization is needed in order to go through any renovation. The result is that most granted subsidies end up in middle- or high-income neighborhoods [71] (when they are indeed put forward).
- The Neighborhood Plan: this very progressive and comprehensive policy is focused on the more vulnerated areas of the city and intervenes in multiple dimensions, including the urban and physical one. The work gained throughout some of its interventions has given place to the "High Complexity Dwellings" subsidies, which focuses on the recognition of social differences in the city and thus concentrates on buildings where ordinary economic help is not reaching.
- Some other specific policies such as the *Dintres* Plan (whose goal is to combat landlord harassment by imposing fines to prevent mobbing situations); the Preferential and Withdrawal Right (which establishes an obligation to inform the public administration before any property sale, allowing the municipality to buy before any other private actor); the compulsory 30% of social housing in all new buildings and/or big rehabilitations; the recent stimulus given to housing cooperatives; etc. All these do not seem to tackle the problem fully, as the housing crisis is bigger than ever. There is thus a need to further investigate the impact of these measures and at the same time come up with new valuation tools, indices or reference prices before and after any urban

intervention in order to identify and capture any surplus values that could result from public investment [72].

The analysis so far has provided a better understanding of the case studies, highlighting the changes they have experienced at various levels over past years and the consequent impacts on their characteristics and identity. At this point, it becomes clear that the value of regeneration and other urban interventions cannot be solely measured in economic terms, since their effects are multidimensional, which justifies the need to bring other (social) dimensions into the discussion.

5. Incorporating the Dimensions of Social Capital and Social Infrastructure Into the Analysis

At this point, it is important to realize that, while our focus may be on only a few case studies, the undergoing processes are assimilable to other Southern European cities (at the national or international level) and that the methodology and indicators selected—that were based on the recent literature—could be replicated in such contexts. The results here have shown that, despite the efforts of administration and entities, there are still very intricate problems associated with the risk of—or actual—gentrification and resident displacement, especially in those more central neighborhoods or areas undergoing processes of valorization, but also in some other areas of the city that have started to become attractive to real-estate investment. This entails there is a need to come up with more innovative tools to capture these dynamics and at the same time provide the city with more innovative solutions that leave no one behind. Thus, incorporating SC and SI, which are extensively studied and not necessarily captured by official surveys and censuses, could contribute to a more comprehensive study and planning of urban regeneration interventions. This section has been organized starting from the interviewee's views and ideas (see Figure 13).

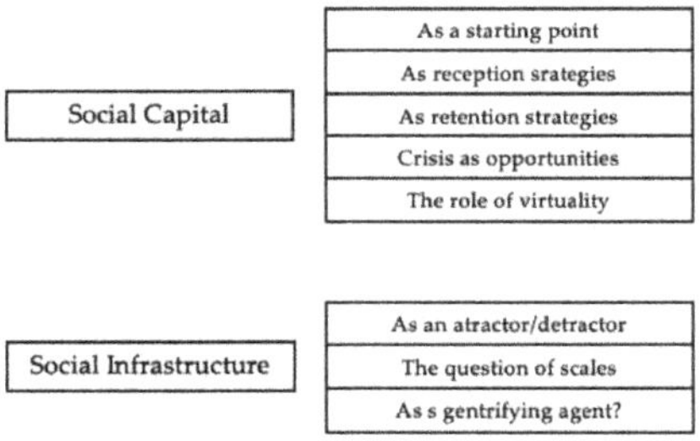

Figure 13. Social capital and social infrastructure for a comprehensive urban regeneration.

5.1. Social Capital

5.1.1. Social Capital as a Starting Point for Urban Renewal

As has been clear throughout this work, urban interventions can produce effects on the social and economic composition of the territories and generate—more or less visible or invisible, direct or indirect—forms of expulsion. Thus, an analysis on the social capital dimension might help shed some light on alternative ways of studying and addressing urban regeneration.

> *"The isolation due to highways favored proximity relations which makes this the most organized neighborhood, in terms of associations"* (Trinitat Vella entity).

> *"The few elder neighbors that still remain today have a sense of belonging that is very strong. The problem is they are less by the minute"* (Barceloneta entity).

The interviewees agreed upon the fact that the degree of organization is a key factor, to the point it can even define whether a specific policy or program is put forward or not, when the consulted technicians and representatives of local organizations referred to a certain need to lean on the communities when promoting any urban intervention. Actually, there is a recognized need to create social bonds where they do not exist, since experience has shown that, if there is no organization, no renovation/regeneration/rehabilitation is practicable at all. This idea was referenced at different scales: from housing interventions (bringing together horizontal property landlords was necessary when rehabilitating dwellings) to public space programs, concerning one or more building blocks (for the installation of elevators or the improvement of shared spaces such as parks).

> *"The different situations and places for informal relation between neighbors are the ones that are absolutely vital, functional and can generate stronger solidarities"* (Barceloneta entities).

> *"Self-management, which used to be the common thing, has been degrading and falling on less and less people, that are at the same time ageing. It is prone to disappear"* (Besòs-Maresme entity).

Taking into account the social capital component should entail things like mapping the level of association between neighbors before proposing any urban intervention, gathering residents and getting to know them in order to truly capture their needs and interests, building trust before any change in the urban landscape, communicating the alternatives for housing/neighborhood improvement and making the communities a central part of the programs in question, as co-designers and co-creators of the interventions. These kinds of situations where there is active citizen engagement—related to the bridging form of SC that was introduced in the theoretical section—have proven to have positive and long-lasting impacts, allowing a greater transformation of the environment and infrastructures. Thus, social capital gains and losses should be considered in any type of urban intervention. Some questions related to this issue are necessary: Is there a strong social fabric to rely on? Will the planned interventions be practicable, in relation to possible conflicts? What will the interventions imply in terms of potential valorization? What effects may the interventions have in terms of direct or indirect expulsion and breaking/strengthening of social ties?

5.1.2. Social Capital as Reception Strategies

Social capital, within the interviews, is also related to strategies for the adequate reception of new people arriving in the neighborhoods. These are especially relevant in vulnerated areas, where newcomers tend to be foreigners from the Global South, as is the case of *Raval*, but also of *Trinitat Vella* or *Ciutat Meridiana*. The role that public spaces play in creating positive "contexts of reception" for immigrants of such "arrival neighborhoods" has been studied as a key factor [73]. Within this context, some of the consulted entities' representatives mentioned there is a conscious effort in welcoming newcomers, making them feel a part of the social fabric. In vulnerated areas, where multiculturality tends to be the norm, co-operative and/or collaborative actions are not always easy to accomplish, especially when language and other cultural barriers operate strongly. In such cases, entities, social leaders and policymakers should act as facilitators, not concentrating on the differences, but drawing on common ground.

> *"We need to make newcomers get involved more in neighborhood related issues and implicate in its entities, which will at the same time make them feel it, live it and want to improve it"* (Trinitat Vella entitiy).

5.1.3. Social Capital as Retention Strategies

Apart from playing an important role in the reception of newcomers, social capital can also serve as a neighbor retainer, especially in the context of visible or invisible forms of expulsion that can impact negatively not only individually, but also collectively. Social capital is in this case a key dimension in urban regeneration since it would not only serve as a starting point, but as a mitigator of some of its possible negative effects. Neighbor network construction leading to collective action against the threat of expulsion has been proven to be a of absolute importance [74] and local examples of formal or informal neighbor organizations have been key in preventing further expulsion. Thus, taking this dimension into account by urban regeneration plans entails an active recognition of the existing social ties as well as the promotion of spaces for interaction, as will be seen when focusing on the role of social infrastructure.

> "*A hypothesis to be confirmed is whether strong proximity relations favor a sense of belonging, making even young people want to stay [in the neighborhood]*" (Trinitat Vella entitiy).

> "*There are networks of mutual support, related to the cultural element of the neighborhoods, that are informal yet entirely strong*" (Raval entity).

> "*At some level, you could think of the associational tissue as an element of attraction*" (Trinitat Vella entity).

5.1.4. Crisis as an Opportunity for Rapid Social Capital Generation

Recent crisis situations, such as the one during COVID-19, have had many impacts in different dimensions of everyday life. However, and at the same time, this situation has proven to what extent crises can have a potential to become true "sources" of social capital formation [75].

> "*This situation [COVID-19] has been a way for young people with a certain social consciousness, to quickly get involved for the first time because of their 'availability*" (Barceloneta entity).

> "*The pandemics has shown how very quickly people organize towards common goals*" (Ciutat Meridiana entity).

Although such crises are obviously undesirable, they can raise awareness of the importance of the local level and the power of bonding and bridging forms of social capital to counter external threats.

5.1.5. The Role of Virtuality in Social Capital Making

Recent work has highlighted the role of the internet in maintaining existing social ties and creating new ones [76]. In the interviewees' discourses it was quite clear that virtuality could become a means for socialization and social capital formation, especially when it was the only channel left (in relation to COVID-19 lockdown). Thus, the internet should be recognized as a valuable tool in social capital making and an effort should be made towards its democratization, especially within vulnerable populations, such as the elderly or people with lower education levels [77].

> "*Social networks, internet, are ways to mobilize an entire neighborhood*" (Barceloneta entity).

Within urban analysis, traditional statistical measures do not usually intend to capture this social capital dimension, showing less interest in the identification of the association levels between neighbors, even when these have proven to be very important. As has been explained here, to the point that some interventions do not even seem to be realizable without an active community; social capital also serves as a powerful resource in the reception and retention of population against the threat of expulsion; its development is stimulated during times of crises, mostly related to the concept of resilience [78]; virtuality seems also to be an important means. However, sometimes high levels of SC are not enough shield to resist external threats, especially when speculation in the form of very powerful actors is present in vulnerated territories. Thus, it is necessary to also focus on some characteristics of the built environment that can serve as a scenario for the formation and strengthening of SC. The concept of social infrastructure intends to capture the quality of these environments—places and spaces in which people meet, gather and interact—and where there is an opportunity for the formation of long-lasting social bonds. Where, why and how are these ties built? In shared spaces such as the stairs of the building, the terrace of the bar, the patio of the community school, even the pedestrian street.

5.2. Social Infrastructure

5.2.1. Social Infrastructure as an Enhancer of Social Interaction or Segregator

When attractive, of good quality and well-conceived, SI can become a key element in social capital formation. As an element of attraction, utilized and inhabited, it can promote the co-existence of people gathering in the same area; SI can also increase socialization, lead to trust building and network formation. In this sense, elements like parks, restaurants or streets can have a positive impact at a community level, as true enhancers of social interaction, bonding and civic engagement. Some examples of urban regeneration interventions in the case studies speak of a certain increase in the time spent outside the private spaces of home, where social interaction can happen, and have a long-lasting impact on the overall quality of the shared environment, an idea which has also been supported by research [46].

> *"At an urbanistic level, some things have had a positive effect on the neighborhood because these make you want to be outside, wander and stay in the street"* (Barceloneta entity).

> *"All public space interventions will, in the end, have positive effects in neighbor quality of life"* (Trinitat Vella entity).

However, and at the same time, inexistent or poorly planned shared spaces do not call for any kind of socializing which can in turn have negative social and physical effects, diminishing the opportunities for bonding and network building. In some cases, because of their poor planning, or even because there is no actual availability of space for social encounters to take place, SI can have serious social negative effects. Abandoned areas, poorly lit parks and streets that are too much vehicle oriented, are among the elements that can discourage social interaction, even aggravating pre-existing problems related to (dis)connection, (un)safety or (in)civism.

> *"The lack of spaces for interaction—other than the streets—do not stimulate the creation of a strong associational movement. There is no formal physical point of reference that can keep and stabilize ties"* (Barceloneta entity).

> *"Some public spaces should not be thought as a beautiful Barcelona catalogue model, but towards the concretion of very specific resident's needs and demands"* (Barcelona technician).

> *"Some areas [. . .] can turn into "no-land" areas"* (Barcelona technician).

The tension between SI as a promoter or discourager of social interaction also becomes very relevant when analyzing some transitional places, meaning areas that are affected by urbanistic planning or buildings that are emptied before their use changes. A good example of this situation in the case studies is the old prison in *Trinitat Vella* that was supposed to become a housing and commercial related project and was abandoned for a very long time, generating negative effects on the surrounding area, due to a progressive loss of local businesses and an abandonment of public spaces, since no intervention was planned for the transitional phase. This kind of situation needs to be taken into account, providing with solutions, even when these are not final.

5.2.2. SI and the Question of Scales

There is an ongoing debate on the very concept of social infrastructure, mostly related to its comprehensiveness. Which urban shared spaces—private, semiprivate or public—should fall under its definition and which ones should not? Can certain elements commonly associated with the private sphere (like dwellings or buildings) or the public one (like institutions or even streets) be a part of the definition? And also, is it possible to measure the degree of influence that each of these elements have on SC formation?

If a broader conceptualization is accepted, then housing-related elements, but also elements of the neighborhood level (such as parks, the presence of institutions like schools or sport facilities, the layout of streets, even the presence of some nature-related features that act as socialization promoters), would be taken into consideration when measuring the quality of SI, turning it into a multi-scale concept (with dwellings', cities', and in-between elements). This would entail that regeneration policies aiming at SC formation through SI should pay attention to many different variables from apparently different worlds, from local economy to family interaction at the school door, from library users to pedestrians and cyclists, which would turn any regeneration plan into a comprehensive one.

"Rehabilitation policies, when their true goal is to recuperate a certain degraded area, are accompanied by the improvement of not only the building, but also of the street. It makes more sense to intervene by whole areas, not unconnected pins" (Besòs-Maresme entity).

Thus, there is a need to increasingly recognize the value of SI elements in SC building [45]. Besides focusing on the physical improvement of streets, schools, restaurants or bars, the gains of investing in SI in social terms (not only economic ones) should also be considered. Thus, an integrated or comprehensive vision is necessary, where the focus not only revolves around creating diverse spaces for encounters that bridge differences, but also more socially homogenous places where affinity groups can share concerns, claims and interests [73].

5.2.3. Is SI a Gentrifying Agent?

An unresolved debate persists: whether to improve a vulnerated area (potentially causing unwanted effects related to valorization and population expulsion) or leaving things as they are (which may seem to protect residents, but can result in a greater abandonment of the area bringing further impoverishment and worsening pre-existing issues). Thus, regeneration is sometimes on the horns of a dilemma, especially in places where there is imminent or ongoing gentrification [79], as has been demonstrated for the cases of *Barceloneta*, *Raval* and *Besòs-Maresme*.

"Urbanism related investment is the greatest gentrifier and this is our biggest threat [especially when combined with] *degradation"* (Besòs-Maresme entity).

Also, the interviewed entities' representatives refer to a series of SI-related potentially exclusionary factors. Besides the risks associated with urban interventions leading to a potential rise in prices [41]—promoting social and commercial change that can in turn end up expelling residents—other situations related to the resident's representations of what the neighborhood means to them were added to the discussion.

"What is common? In vertical property, who's responsible for what happens between my door and the street door?" (Trinitat Vella entity).

"This neighborhood is somehow like a town, in the sense that people are from here feel like they belong" (Trinitat Vella entity).

"We feel we are a separated part from the rest of the city" (Ciutat Meridiana entity).

This apparent sense of belonging is related to what authors conceptualize as neighborhood pride [80], which is built throughout time and implies more or less strong links and relations between residents as well as those between residents with their environment. SI plays a crucial role not only in social capital building, but also in the identification of people with their known surrounding environment. Which brings us to the need to recognize the role of residents in the appropriation and shaping of their neighborhoods, within the city construction scheme presented at the beginning [1]. Whether the existing urban regeneration policies seek to accomplish higher levels of civic engagement towards the promotion of participating social infrastructures that are destined for resident's benefit and not a source of intended valorization and expulsion is perhaps one of the most important and unresolved issues.

6. Conclusions

This paper, written within two competitive projects, intended to be a part of an ongoing discussion on urban regeneration and its consequences. One of its main concerns has been to identify probable gentrification processes in five case studies. A series of indicators were taken into account in order to demonstrate whether gentrification is present and trace some of its associated impacts, mostly related to a possible identity change both economic and social. Gentrification can imply apparent improvement (because better levels of education, income or economic activity are desirable), but these cannot be at the expense of residents' lives, homes and businesses. Thus, researchers and policy makers need to generate innovative and comprehensive tools to understand but also tackle gentrification's negative effects urgently. At the same time, capturing the successful aspects of ongoing policies implies a question of measuring not only the economic but also the social gains of urban regeneration. In this sense, the incorporation of the SC and SI dimensions may be a part of the answer.

On a more methodological level, the mixed-method strategy followed here is susceptible of being replicated either in the same case studies in the near future or in other similar contexts. The first operation would allow the extraction of stronger conclusions related to probable gentrification processes (that a cross-sectional study cannot capture), whilst the second one could give a more complete picture of gentrification on a more general level. This is particularly important given that the phenomena affecting Barcelona are not isolated but respond to complex regional and global causes that also need to be traced [81].

Finally, urban regeneration seems to be an absolutely necessary strategy: a certain degree of intervention in the existing building stock and the neighborhood's environment is essential to answer some of the contemporary urban challenges, especially in vulnerated areas. Thus, we need to be able to control (some of) its effects and at the same time combat the negative impacts of gentrification. Before, during and after our interventions we need to be able to identify whether some sort of change in residential and/or commercial identity is expected (and act on it); also, we need to be able to identify whether the level of local association is affected (and in which direction) and which infrastructures are being offered for the purpose of social capital bridging and bonding forms. Taking these elements into account would entail more comprehensive, socially inclusive and just urban regeneration interventions for the benefit of all residents.

Author Contributions: Conceptualization, G.P. and P.G.-A.; methodology, G.P. and P.G.-A.; software, G.P.; validation, P.G.-A.; formal analysis, G.P.; investigation, G.P.; resources, G.P. and P.G.-A.; data curation, G.P.; writing—original draft preparation, G.P.; writing—review and editing, G.P. and P.G.-A.; visualization, G.P.; supervision, P.G.-A.; project administration, G.P.; funding acquisition, G.P. and P.G.-A. All authors have read and agreed to the published version of the manuscript.

Funding: This research was funded by the Spanish Research Agency (Agencia Estatal de Investigación AEI) grant number PID2022-142352OB-I00.

Data Availability Statement: All quantitative data was used from official and open sources. Qualitative data was a result of interviews, which cannot be published due to anonymity requests.

Conflicts of Interest: The authors declare no conflicts of interest. The funders had no role in the design of the study; in the collection, analyses or interpretation of data; in the writing of the manuscript; or in the decision to publish the results.

Appendix A

Full interview guide:

- Characteristics of the population

  Presentation of the person, institutional affiliation, origin.
  How would you describe a resident of this neighborhood?
  Can you identify one or more neighbor profile? Has this changed in the last years?
  How is the population that comes and goes, and what implications?
  Is there any population loss?
  What is the socioeconomic profile of the population? Is there any segregation?
  Do you consider that the population is generally different depending on the area?

- Characteristics of the buildings

What aspects would you highlight about the neighborhood? (positive or negative)
Currently, what main issues can you identify in the neighborhood?
What is the general state of the buildings in the neighborhood?
Are there areas considered good and bad? Why?
Are there vacant houses? And occupied ones? Are evictions taking place?
How is the rental market in the neighborhood (price, supply. . .)?
Who owns an apartment here, generally speaking?
Use of ground floors: commerce or housing.

- Urban regeneration and public spaces

Which are the main policies, programs, and laws you rely on to solve them?
Are you familiar with rehabilitation calls, the Pla de Barris, others?
What rehabilitation interventions have taken place recently? Impacts
Are there parks, green areas, facilities? (use of public areas, profile of users)
Are there architectural barriers in the neighborhood? Are there "black spots"?
And regarding commerce in the neighborhood, what trends/issues?

- Neighborhood and Associationism

How is the neighborhood organization? What are the main entities?
What social agents can you identify in the neighborhood? And leaders?
Would you say it is a neighborhood with a strong identity?
Are there places to talk about neighborhood issues? Which ones?
Cooperative housing experiences in the neighborhood?

- Vision about the future

What impact has the current COVID-19 crisis had?
What issues are you able to work on, and which ones are slipping away?
What vision do you have of the neighborhood in 10 or 20 years?

References

1. Pírez, P. Actores Sociales y Gestión de la Ciudad. 1995. Available online: https://www.researchgate.net/publication/274313532_Actores_sociales_y_gestion_de_la_ciudad (accessed on 26 March 2024).
2. Park, R.E. Human Ecology. *Am. J. Sociol.* **1936**, *42*, 1–15. Available online: http://www.jstor.org/stable/2768859 (accessed on 14 May 2024). [CrossRef]
3. Sun, C.; Shibuya, Y.; Sekimoto, Y. Social segregation levels vary depending on activity space types: Comparison of segregation in residential, workplace, routine and non-routine activities in Tokyo metropolitan area. *Cities* **2024**, *146*, 104745. [CrossRef]
4. OECD. *Metropolitan Areas*; OECD Regional Statistics; OECD Publishing: Paris, France, 2018. [CrossRef]
5. OECD. *Divided Cities: Understanding Intra-Urban Inequalities*; OECD Publishing: Paris, France, 2018. [CrossRef]
6. Frutos, T.; García, E. Diferenciación socio-espacial y segregación racial en España. *Barataria* **2016**, *21*, 91–109. [CrossRef]
7. Kauppinen, T.; van Ham, M. Unravelling the demographic dynamics of ethnic residential segregation. *Popul. Space Place* **2018**, *25*, e2193. [CrossRef] [PubMed]
8. Mateos Rodríguez, P. Segregación residencial de minorías étnicas y el análisis geográfico del origen de nombres y apellidos. *Cuad. Geogr.* **2006**, *39*, 83–101. Available online: https://revistaseug.ugr.es/index.php/cuadgeo/article/view/1502 (accessed on 14 May 2024).
9. Powell, R. Loïc Wacquant's 'ghetto': The case of Gypsy-Travellers in the UK. *Int. J. Urban Reg. Res.* **2013**, *37*, 115–134. [CrossRef]
10. Musterd, S.; Andersson, R. Housing Mix, Social Mix, and Social Opportunities. *Urban Aff. Rev.* **2005**, *40*, 761–790. [CrossRef]
11. Galster, G. Neighborhood Social Mix: Theory, Evidence, and Implications for Policy and Planning. In *Policy, Planning, and People: Promoting Justice in Urban Development*; Carmon, N., Fainstein, S., Eds.; University of Pennsylvania Press: Philadelphia, PA, USA, 2013; pp. 307–336.
12. Li, X.; Huang, X.; Li, D.; Xu, Y. Aggravated social segregation during the COVID-19 pandemic: Evidence from crowdsourced mobility data in twelve most populated U.S. metropolitan areas. *Sustain. Cities Soc.* **2022**, *81*, 103869. [CrossRef] [PubMed]
13. Heiki, L.; Aldrich, D.; Faiad, C.; Aoki, T.; Tseng, P.; Aida, J. The Role of Social Capital in Depression During the COVID-19 Pandemic. *Int. Perspect. Psychol.* **2024**, *13*, 68–78. [CrossRef]
14. Castel, R. *Las Metamorfosis de la Cuestión Social. Una Crónica del Asalariado*; Paidós: Buenos Aires, Argentina, 1997.
15. Beck, U. *Risk Society: Towards a New Modernity*; SAGE: London, UK, 1986.
16. Lauwe, P. Périphérie des villes et crise de civilisation. *Cah. Int. Sociol.* **1982**, *72*, 5–16. Available online: http://www.jstor.org/stable/40689992 (accessed on 14 May 2024).

17. Hernández Aja, A.; Alguacil Gómez, J.; Camacho Gutiérrez, J. La vulnerabilidad urbana en España. Identificación y evolución de los barrios vulnerables. *Empiria Rev. Metodol. Cienc. Soc.* **2014**, *27*, 73–94. [CrossRef]
18. Havard, S.; Deguen, S.; Bodin, J.; Louis, K.; Laurent, O.; Bard, D. A small-area index of socioeconomic deprivation to capture health inequalities in France. *Soc. Sci. Med.* **2018**, *67*, 2007–2016. [CrossRef] [PubMed]
19. Egea Jiménez, C.; Nieto Calmaestra, J.A.; Domínguez Clemente, J.; González Rego, R. *Vulnerabilidad del Tejido Social de los Barrios Desfavorecidos de Andalucía: Análisis y Potencialidades*; Centro de Estudios Andaluces: Sevilla, Spain, 2018. Available online: https://www.centrodeestudiosandaluces.es/datos/factoriaideas/ifo11_08.pdf (accessed on 14 May 2024).
20. Hernández-Aja, A.; Rodríguez Alonso, R.; Rodríguez Suárez, I. *Barrios Vulnerables de las Grandes Ciudades Españolas. 1991/2001/2011*; Spanish Ministry of Development: Madrid, Spain, 2018.
21. Fernández Aragón, I.; Ochoa de Aspuru Gulin, O.; Ruiz Ciarreta, I. Análisis de la desigualdad urbana. Propuesta de un Índice Sintético de Vulnerabilidad Urbana Integral (ISVUI) en Bilbao. *ACE Arch. City Environ.* **2021**, *15*, 9520. [CrossRef]
22. Garcia-Almirall, P.; Gemma, V.; Moix, B.M.; Ferrer Guasch, M.R.; Vima-Grau, S. *Estudi i Detecció a la Ciutat de Barcelona D'àmbits de Vulnerabilitat Residencial*; Ajuntament de Barcelona: Barcelona, Spain, 2017. Available online: http://hdl.handle.net/2117/114548 (accessed on 14 May 2024).
23. Hanoon, S.K.; Abdullah, A.F.; Shafri, H.Z.M.; Wayayok, A. Comprehensive Vulnerability Assessment of Urban Areas Using an Integration of Fuzzy Logic Functions: Case Study of Nasiriyah City in South Iraq. *Earth* **2022**, *3*, 699–732. [CrossRef]
24. Piasek, G.; Fernández Aragón, I.; Shershneva, J.; Garcia-Almirall, P. Assessment of Urban Neighbourhoods' Vulnerability through an Integrated Vulnerability Index (IVI): Evidence from Barcelona, Spain. *Soc. Sci.* **2022**, *11*, 476. [CrossRef]
25. Fajardo, G.; Merino, F.; Caraffa, M. *Innovación en el Acceso a la Vivienda: Masovería, Cesión de Uso y Cohousing*; CIRIEC: Valencia, Spain, 2022.
26. Temes, R. Valoración de la vulnerabilidad integral en las áreas residenciales de Madrid. *EURE (Santiago)* **2014**, *40*, 119–149. [CrossRef]
27. Ochoa-Ramírez, J.A.; Guzmán-Ramírez, A. La vulnerabilidad urbana y su caracterización socio-espacial. *Legado DE Arquitectura y Diseño* **2020**, *15*, 27. [CrossRef]
28. Martín-Consuegra, F.; Alonso, C.; Frutos, B. La regeneración urbana integrada y la declaración de Toledo. *Info. Cons.* **2015**, *67*, 2. [CrossRef]
29. Tejedor, J. Nuevo paradigma normativo sobre la ciudad: Retornando a la ciudad tradicional. *Info. Cons.* **2015**, *67*, 22. [CrossRef]
30. Montaner, J.M. Cap a una nova cultura de la rehabilitació a Barcelona. *Qüestions d'Habitatge* **2019**, *23*, 8–19. Available online: http://hdl.handle.net/2117/335652 (accessed on 15 May 2024).
31. Hernández-Aja, A.; Rodríguez-Suárez, I. De la rehabilitación a la regeneración urbana integrada. *Ciudades* **2017**, *20*, 1–20. [CrossRef]
32. Piasek, G.; Vima-Grau, S.; Garcia-Almirall, P. Brechas Y oportunidades en el diseño y la gestión de políticas de regeneración urbana. Estudio de 5 barrios vulnerables de Barcelona. *Inguruak* **2021**, *70*. [CrossRef]
33. 8/2013 National Spanish Law. Available online: https://www.boe.es/buscar/act.php?id=BOE-A-2013-6938 (accessed on 15 May 2024).
34. RE-INHABIT Project. Available online: https://vimac.upc.edu/es/re-inhabit/presentacion (accessed on 15 May 2024).
35. ENER-REGEN Project. Available online: https://futur.upc.edu/36993491 (accessed on 15 May 2024).
36. Lees, L.; Slater, T.; Wyly, E. *The Gentrification Reader*; Routledge: New York, NY, USA, 2010.
37. Smith, N. *The New Urban Frontier. Gentrification and the Revanchist City*; Routledge: New York, NY, USA; London, UK, 1996.
38. Hübscher, M. Gentrificación y Vulnerabilidad. Evaluación de Aspectos Sociales y Urbanísticos en Santa Cruz de Tenerife (Islas Canarias). In *Ciudades Medias y Áreas Metropolitanas. De la Dispersión a la Regeneración*; Abellán, F.C., Ed.; Ediciones de la Universidad de Castilla-la Mancha: Cuenca, Spain, 2018; pp. 633–651.
39. Lin, L.; Di, L.; Zhang, C.; Guo, L.; Di, Y. Remote Sensing of Urban Poverty and Gentrification. *Sustainability* **2021**, *13*, 4022. [CrossRef]
40. Janoshcka, M.; Hidalgo, R. *La Ciudad Neoliberal. Gentrificación y Exclusión en Santiago de Chile, Buenos Aires, Ciudad de México y Madrid. Santiago de Chile*; Pontificia Universidad Católica de Chile: Santiago, Chile, 2014.
41. Sorando, D.; Ardura, A. *First We Take Manhattan*; Catarata: Madrid, Spain, 2016.
42. Piñeira, M.J.; Fernández, A.; Mínguez, M.C. Vulnerability and Touristification, Who Are the Losers of the Urban Center? In *Sostenibilidad Turística: Overtourism vs. Undertourism*; Pons, G.X., Blanco-Romero, A., Troitiño-Torralba, L., Blázquez-Salom, M., Balears, I., Eds.; Societat d'Història Natural de les Balears: Palma, Spain, 2020.
43. Brown-Saracino, J. Explicating divided approaches to gentrification and growing income inequality. *Ann. Rev. Soc.* **2017**, *43*, 515–539. [CrossRef]
44. Lütke, P.; Jäger, E.M. Food Consumption in Cologne Ehrenfeld: Gentrification through Gastrofication? *Urban Sci.* **2021**, *5*, 26. [CrossRef]
45. Klinenberg, E. *Palaces for the People: How Social Infrastructure Can Help Fight Inequality, Polarization, and the Decline of Civic Life*; Crown Publishing Group: New York, NY, USA, 2018.
46. Latham, A.; Layton, J. Social infrastructure: Why it matters and how urban geographers might study it. *Urban Geogr.* **2022**, *43*, 659–668. [CrossRef]

47. Stender, M.; Nordberg, L. Learning from COVID-19: Social infrastructure in disadvantaged housing areas in Denmark. *Urban Plan.* **2022**, *7*, 432–444. [CrossRef]
48. Larissa, L.; Harlan, S.; Bolin, B.; Hacket, E.; Hope, D.; Kirby, A.; Nelson, A.; Rex, T.; Wolf, S. Bonding and Bridging: Understanding the Relationship between Social Capital and Civic Action. *J. Plan. Educ. Res.* **2004**, *24*, 64–77. [CrossRef]
49. How's Life? *OECD's Statistical Report.* 2015. Available online: https://www.oecd-ilibrary.org/economics/how-s-life-2015_how_life-2015-en (accessed on 4 July 2024).
50. Schwartz, G.; Leifheit, K.; Arcaya, M.; Keene, D. Eviction as a community health exposure. *Soc. Sci. Med.* **2024**, *340*, 116496. [CrossRef] [PubMed]
51. Open Data Barcelona. Available online: https://opendata-ajuntament.barcelona.cat/en/ (accessed on 15 May 2024).
52. Barcelona Statistics Department. Available online: https://ajuntament.barcelona.cat/estadistica/castella/index.htm (accessed on 15 May 2024).
53. Catalonia Statistics Department. Available online: https://www.idescat.cat/?lang=en (accessed on 15 May 2024).
54. Barcelona Online Data Portal. Available online: https://portaldades.ajuntament.barcelona.cat/es/ (accessed on 15 May 2024).
55. Atlas.ti software. Available online: https://atlasti.com/ (accessed on 15 May 2024).
56. Van Dijk, T.A. *News as Discourse*; Lawrence Erlbaum Associates, Inc.: Mahwah, NJ, USA, 1988.
57. Guba, E.G. Criteria for assessing trustworthiness of naturalistic enquiries. *Educ. Commun. Technol. J.* **1981**, *29*, 75–91. [CrossRef]
58. Treharne, G.; Riggs, D. Ensuring Quality in Qualitative Research. In *Qualitative Research in Clinical and Health Psychology*; Rohleder, P., Lyons, A., Eds.; Bloomsbury Publishing: London, UK, 2014.
59. López-Gay, A.; Sales-Favà, J.; Solana-Solana, M.; Fernánez, A.; Peralta, A. El avance de la gentrificación en Barcelona y Madrid, 2011–2019: Análisis socioespacial a partir de un índice de gentrificación. *Estud. Geogr.* **2021**, *82*, e084. [CrossRef]
60. López-Gay, A.; Ortiz-Guitart, A.; Solana-Solana, M. Vivienda, cambio poblacional y desplazamiento en un barrio en proceso de gentrificación. El caso de Sant Antoni (Barcelona). *EURE (Santiago)* **2022**, 48. [CrossRef]
61. Cocola-Gant, A.; López-Gay, A. Transnational gentrification, tourism and the formation of 'foreign only' enclaves in Barcelona. *Urban Stud.* **2020**, *57*, 3025–3043. [CrossRef]
62. Bridge, G. It's not Just a Question of Taste: Gentrification, the Neighbourhood, and Cultural Capital. *Environ. Plan. A Econ. Space* **2006**, *38*, 1965–1978. [CrossRef]
63. Hernández, A. De la Botiga a la Boutique. *URBS Rev. Estud. Urbanos Cienc. Soc.* **2016**, *6*, 79–99. Available online: https://dialnet.unirioja.es/servlet/articulo?codigo=5641798 (accessed on 26 March 2024).
64. Pareja-Eastway, M.; Sánchez-Martínez, M.T. El sistema de vivienda en España y el papel de las políticas ¿qué falta por resolver? *Cuadernos Económicos de ICE* **2015**, *90*, 149–174. Available online: https://www.revistasice.com/index.php/CICE/article/view/6111/6111 (accessed on 19 March 2024).
65. Byrne, M. Generation rent and the financialization of housing: A comparative exploration of the growth of the private rental sector in Ireland, the UK and Spain. *Hous. Stud.* **2020**, *35*, 743–765. [CrossRef]
66. Domingo, G.; Escorihuela, I. Qui Desnona a Barcelona? Anàlisi del Paper dels Grans Propietaris Privats en les Expulsions de la Ciutat. Observatori DESC. 2022. Available online: https://observatoridesc.org/sites/default/files/publication/files/informe_quidesnona_web.pdf (accessed on 26 March 2024).
67. Collaborative Eviction Map. Available online: https://cmmm-maps.eu/barcelona/ (accessed on 23 May 2024).
68. Arellano, B.; Roca, J. Informe Relatiu a la Valoració del Impacte de la Nova Proposta Normativa de Mesures Urgents per Millorar l'Accés a l'Habitatge Regulada al DLL 17/2019. 2020. Ajuntament de Barcelona. Available online: https://l1nq.com/4NtR8 (accessed on 19 March 2024).
69. Illa, M. *La Falsa Solució Turística: Concentració de Beneficis i Deute Social*; Observatori del Deute en la Globalització (ODG): Barcelona, Spain, 2019. Available online: https://l1nq.com/vvlg2 (accessed on 19 March 2024).
70. Navarro Soler, L.; Díez, O. La crisi de l'habitatge. Barcelona Metròpolis Dossier, 24 July 2021. Available online: https://www.barcelona.cat/metropolis/ca/continguts/la-crisi-de-lhabitatge (accessed on 16 May 2024).
71. Uzqueda, A.; Garcia-Almirall, P.; Cornadó, C.; Vima-Grau, S. Critical Review of Public Policies for the Rehabilitation of Housing Stock: The Case of Barcelona. *Buildings* **2021**, *11*, 108. [CrossRef]
72. Uzqueda Martínez, Á.L. La Intervención Pública en Rehabilitación y Regeneración Urbana en Barcelona: Caracterización de Claves Operativas y Metodológicas. Ph.D. Thesis, Technology of Architecture-Polytechnic University of Catalonia, Barcelona, Spain, 2024. [CrossRef]
73. Németh, J. Briding and Bonding. Public Space and Immigrant Integration in Barcelona's el Raval. In *Compation to Public Space*, 1st ed.; Mehta, V., Palazzo, D., Eds.; Routledge: London, UK, 2020. [CrossRef]
74. Alabart Vilà, A. Polítiques Urbanístiques i Moviment Associatiu Veïnal. *Barc. Soc. Rev. d'Inform. Estud. Soc.* **2010**, *19*, 87–97. Available online: https://ajuntament.barcelona.cat/dretssocials/sites/default/files/revista/revista-19-art7-politiques-urbanistiques-moviment-associatui-veinal.pdf (accessed on 23 May 2024).
75. Storr, V.; Haeffele, S.; Grube, L. Crisis as a Source of Social Capital: Adaptation and Formation of Social Capital during the COVID-19 Pandemic. *Cosm. Taxis* **2021**, *9*, 94. Available online: https://cosmosandtaxis.org/wp-content/uploads/2021/05/storr_et_al_ct_vol9_iss_5_6.pdf (accessed on 5 April 2024).
76. Pénard, T.; Poussing, N. Internet Use and Social Capital: The Strength of Virtual Ties. *J. Econ. Issues* **2014**, *44*, 569–595. [CrossRef]

77. Alessandrini, M. Getting Connected: Can Social Capital be Virtual? *Webology* **2006**, *3*, 1–8. Available online: https://www.webology.org/data-cms/articles/20200515034902pma33.pdf (accessed on 5 April 2024).
78. Manyena, S.B. The concept of resilience revisited. *Disasters* **2006**, *30*, 434–450. [CrossRef] [PubMed]
79. Domínguez-Mujica, J.; González-Pérez, J.M.; Parreño-Castellano, J.M.; Sánchez-Aguilera, D. Gentrification on the Move. New Dynamics in Spanish Mature Urban-Tourist Neighborhoods. *Urban Sci.* **2021**, *5*, 33. [CrossRef]
80. Renzaho, A.; Richardson, B.; Strugnell, C. Resident well-being, community connections and neighborhood perceptions, pride and opportunities among disadvantage metropolitan and regional communities: Evidence from the neighborhood renewal project. *J. Community Psychol.* **2012**, *40*, 871–885. [CrossRef]
81. Domínguez-Mujica, J. The Urban Mirror of the Socioeconomic Transformations in Spain. *Urban Sci.* **2021**, *5*, 13. [CrossRef]

urban science

MDPI

Article

Assessment of Sustainable Mobility Initiatives Developed in Montevideo, Uruguay †

Sergio Nesmachnow * and Silvina Hipogrosso

Engineering Faculty, Universidad de la República, Montevideo 11200, Uruguay; silvina.hipogrosso@fing.edu.uy
* Correspondence: sergion@fing.edu.uy

† This paper is an extended version of our paper published in VI Iberoamerican Congress on Smart Cities, ICSC-CITIES 2023.

Abstract: This article presents an assessment of sustainable mobility initiatives developed in Montevideo, Uruguay, in the period from 2020 to 2023. The significance of sustainable mobility is underscored due to its far-reaching implications for the environment, energy efficiency, and the overall quality of life of citizens. This study focuses on crucial aspects of four initiatives deployed in Montevideo in 2020–2023: electric mobility solutions using scooters, the development of infrastructure and services for urban cycling, the development of electric public transportation, and private electric transportation. Important results are obtained and commented on for each of the studied initiatives, regarding efficiency, environmental impact, accessibility, the quality of the service, and other relevant indicators. Based on the analysis, valuable knowledge is acquired to guide the future development of efficient and sustainable transportation modes in Montevideo, Uruguay.

Keywords: sustainable mobility; smart cities; case study

1. Introduction

In the last thirty years, there has been growing global recognition among cities regarding the significance of sustainable transportation to confront important urban mobility challenges and enhancing the well-being of citizens [1]. As a result, numerous noteworthy initiatives have been developed, including the encouragement of public transportation usage, the establishment of cycling and pedestrian infrastructures, the implementation of electric mobility solutions, and the integration of intelligent transportation technologies.

The study of sustainable mobility plays a vital role in the development of cleaner transportation methods and the assessment of their environmental impact [2]. The results from these studies help city planners and administrators optimize energy efficiency, improve connectivity and accessibility, ensure social equity, and promote healthier mobility alternatives and the integration of different modes of transportation. These endeavors align with urban planning strategies aimed at creating livable, resilient, and sustainable communities, ultimately enhancing the quality of life for citizens. Sustainable mobility is one of the sustainable development goals (SDGs). SDGs provide a framework for cities to prioritize sustainability in their development strategies, with specific targets. By embracing sustainable mobility initiatives, cities contribute to the advancement of these goals, fostering a more inclusive, resilient, and environmentally responsible urban environment. This integration of sustainable mobility practices not only improves the daily lives of residents but also contributes to broader global efforts toward a more sustainable future [3].

This article builds upon our initial study of sustainable mobility in Montevideo [4], exploring pertinent issues of sustainable mobility initiatives: the analysis of the unsuccessful implementation of an on-demand electric scooter (e-scooter) service, an in-depth analysis of the expansion of cycling infrastructure and services, an evaluation of newly deployed electric bus lines in the city, and the study of the development of private electric transportation. The main goal is to offer relevant insights and suggestions to inform the development of sustainable mobility options in Montevideo. This research is very relevant, considering that no global Sustainable Urban Mobility Plan has been proposed for Montevideo. The development of sustainable mobility has been performed through different initiatives, which are not always coordinated, under the Mobility Plan proposed for the city [5].

The key findings of the analysis reveal that sustainable mobility initiatives in Montevideo have progressed slowly, partly due to external factors and policy shortcomings. Efforts made in the development of electric bus lines and the expansion of urban cycling infrastructure have not reached a consolidated stage. The applied business model for the e-scooter service faced significant problems, particularly concerning safety, coverage, and affordability, that resulted in the discontinuation of the service. Furthermore, inadequacies in policy implementation and some externalities have hindered progress. Taxation, regulation, and subsides play critical roles in shaping the success of new business models [6]. Some externalities, like subsides, have a positive impact on the success of sustainable mobility initiatives, but regulations and taxation can affect or slow down their development.

The cycling infrastructure deployed between 2020 and 2023 extended the network, but several concerns still exist regarding connectivity, maintenance conditions, and intermodal connection. Montevideo is still way behind other Latin American cities in terms of the extent and quality of its bicycle network. The technical evaluation of electric buses in Montevideo indicates adequate operational efficiency and energy efficiency. However, the implemented electric lines do not provide service to the entire city, leaving important neighborhoods without access to electric public transportation benefits. Electric private transportation has developed quickly, and the forecasts are promising for the next decades.

This article has the following structure: The next section gives an overview of the key concepts of sustainable mobility and reviews the relevant literature on the subject. Section 4 outlines the applied methodology and details about the main features of the initiatives analyzed in this study. The analysis itself is presented in Section 5, along with relevant results and discussions. Finally, Section 6 summarizes the research findings, presents the conclusions drawn from this study, and outlines potential areas for future research.

2. Sustainable Mobility

Sustainability has emerged as a significant concern for contemporary society. It has evolved into a vital aspect for communities due to its direct impact on the quality of human life [7]. There is growing recognition of the central issues and threats posed by environmental problems, which further underscores the importance of sustainability.

Sustainability encompasses three main concepts: the environment, equity, and economics [8]. Recognizing the significance of these three dimensions allows for a holistic approach to sustainability. By considering the interconnections and interdependencies between these concepts, societies can strive towards a sustainable future that harmonizes environmental stewardship, social equity, and economic prosperity and perform specific actions in the present to preserve the environment for future generations [9]. Sustainability is within the broader concept of sustainable development, defined as the process of improving the quality of life of current and future generations by integrating economic growth, social inclusion, and environmental protection [10,11].

Among many other key aspects of sustainability, sustainable mobility plays a pivotal role in achieving the overall objectives of sustainability and sustainable development. The concept of sustainable mobility encompasses a range of strategies and guidelines aimed at fostering a transition in transportation systems towards more environmentally and socially conscious mobility options [1]. Sustainable mobility addresses the detrimental effects of conventional fossil fuel transportation on the environment, public health, and the general well-being of individuals, in line with SDG Target 11.2, to provide access to safe, affordable, accessible and sustainable transportation systems, specially focusing on the needs of vulnerable persons. This paradigm centers around the promotion of transportation methods that minimize energy usage, decrease greenhouse gas emissions, and prioritize the welfare of both individuals and communities.

Sustainable mobility plays a vital role in modern smart cities, as highlighted in recent research articles [12,13]. The paradigm is based on several key principles. These include the promotion and development of public transportation systems, the emphasis on active modes of transportation like walking and cycling, the incorporation of clean and energy-efficient technologies (e.g., electric vehicles), and the development of multimodal systems. Collectively, these principles represent a comprehensive approach to transportation that aims to reduce its impact on the environment, improve the quality of air, improve public health, and foster inclusive and livable communities. Achieving these goals requires a synergistic combination of technological advancements, policy measures and regulations, changes in behavior, and investments in infrastructure. From the perspective of citizens, the main purpose is to recognize and prioritize mobility as a valuable activity [1]. Simultaneously, the shift towards environmentally friendly cities and the adoption of decarbonized solutions and technologies for mobility contribute to the development of more livable communities. This development involves leveraging sustainable transportation solutions, particularly focused on bicycles and walking [14], and new urbanization models. Through this, cities can enhance their long-term economic and environmental resilience [15].

In particular, the socioeconomic aspect plays a crucial role in formulating effective mobility strategies that ensure equitable access to opportunities such as employment, education, culture, and recreation through public transportation. Sustainable mobility is closely connected to mitigating climate and environmental impacts, promoting energy efficiency, fostering innovative urban planning, and addressing several social–economic concerns like equity, safety, inclusion, health, and economic implications. By addressing these factors, sustainable mobility endeavors to enhance the overall quality of life of citizens.

3. Related Work

Many studies have studied sustainable mobility and its impacts in developed countries. Researchers have focused on assessing the environmental, economic, and equity-related consequences of sustainable mobility practices. Key factors, such as greenhouse gas emissions, air pollution levels, socioeconomic implications, and fairness, have been specifically analyzed in these studies, as evidenced by previous research conducted by Johnston et al. [16] and Ravagnan et al. [17]. By examining these aspects, researchers strive to gain a better understanding of the positive effects of sustainable mobility. These positive effects include reducing environmental harm, promoting economic well-being, and ensuring equitable access to transportation options for all members of society. Moreover, extensive analysis has been dedicated to evaluating the alignment of public transportation initiatives with sustainable development goals and exploring the contribution of smart city concepts to enhance the sustainability and appeal of public transportation systems, as highlighted by Bieliska et al. [18]. These studies have delved into the significant challenges, crucial problems, and associated benefits of sustainable mobility. The findings derived from these studies offer valuable insights that can be applied in the development of Mobility Plans and the design of sustainable public transportation systems, ultimately contributing to the realization of more sustainable and efficient transportation options. Previous research conducted by Miller et al. [19] has played a significant role in expanding the knowledge in this field.

In Latin America, several studies have focused on promoting sustainable mobility and reducing car dependence. Rodrigues et al. [20] developed an index to assess sustainable mobility in Brazilian cities in order to evaluate the adoption of sustainable transportation practices. In Colombia, Lyons [21] examined the effective implementation of sustainable mobility initiatives in Bogotá in order to reduce reliance on automobiles. Huertas et al. [22] developed a methodology for assessing sustainable mobility from relevant factors in Latin American countries. The methodology incorporated technological tools and considered economic, environmental, and social aspects. The approach was evaluated in a medium-sized city in Mexico, and the authors emphasized its replicability at a minimal additional cost in other cities. These studies in Latin America provide valuable insights into the efforts being made to promote sustainable transportation and reduce car dependency in specific urban areas.

Our article [23] developed a comprehensive study of sustainable public transportation initiatives implemented in Montevideo, Uruguay, until 2020. Quantitative (coverage, accessibility, and affordability) and qualitative indicators (public finance, integration, comfort, and pleasure) were computed for three sustainable mobility initiatives developed in Montevideo, providing an initial characterization of sustainable mobility and offering specific recommendations for developing sustainable Mobility Plans. A mobility analysis was conducted for a residential zone in the Parque Rodó neighborhood of Montevideo, Uruguay [24], employing the paradigm of Transit-Oriented Development (TOD) [25,26]. The research studied the inter-relationships between the urban environment, urban activities, and mobility indicators, with a particular focus on sustainable mobility. Various methods, including the analysis of urban data, conducting mobility surveys, and performing inspections of the infrastructure on-site, were utilized to assess the mobility demands, the use of different transportation modes, the land use patterns, and the condition of existing infrastructure for mobility within the study area [27,28]. The Parque Rodó neighborhood showed positive values for essential TOD indicators, indicating a solid base for the implementation of cleaner and environmentally friendly transportation systems. The study highlighted specific weaknesses and shortcomings, providing targeted recommendations to address these issues and enhance the overall sustainability of the transportation system in the area.

4. Description of the Studied Modes and the Applied Methodology

This section describes the studied sustainable transportation modes and outlines the methodology used for the analysis in the considered case study (Montevideo, Uruguay).

4.1. Overall Considerations

The description of the studied sustainable transportation modes was based on relevant articles from the related literature. In turn, the methodology employed for analyzing and assessing the technical viability of the studied sustainable transportation modes was based on studying the main aspects and issues identified as relevant in the related literature.

The main goal was to understand the reasons and factors that promote the use of the studied sustainable transportation modes, and also identify obstacles and opportunities for the development of each mode. For these reasons, each mode was analyzed considering some relevant factors that are common for them (e.g., environmental impact, economic cost, and travel time), and others that mainly apply to one or two of the studied transportation modes (e.g., operational and energy efficiency for electric public transportation).

The following subsections describe the factors considered in the analysis of each mode.

4.2. Electric Scooters

In the last ten years, electric scooters gained prominence in urban transportation. They provide a convenient and environmentally friendly option for short-distance commutes, particularly for the last-mile segment [29]. According to the National Association of City Transportation Officials (NACTO), shared e-scooters doubled the number of shared micromobility trips in the USA in 2018 [30]. E-scooters provide users with a self-sufficient transportation mode to replace walking and reduce travel time for their journeys [31]. E-scooters are also an alternative for short trips, reducing congestion and enabling public transportation to focus on longer trips [32]. The shared e-scooter service is highly appealing for users of other mobility services, such as car-sharing, that must perform trips of up to 3 km [33]. Furthermore, e-scooters act as a complement to existing public transportation systems, effectively providing feeder services, and as a connecting link between the (larger) public transportation network. Scientific publications and technical assessments from cities that have adopted shared e-scooters have identified relevant factors for this analysis. In this regard, the main methodological aspects to study are described next.

Characteristics of e-scooter users. Articles that have examined e-scooter services around the world have found that e-scooter users are predominantly male, young, from higher-income households, and possess higher levels of education [34,35]. Women tend to exhibit less interest in riding e-scooters [36], and have more safety-related concerns compared to men [37]. Regarding age, a younger age is a significant factor in e-scooter adoption [38]. Generally, e-scooter usage tends to decline as age increases [39]. However, older adults who initially try riding an e-scooter often become frequent users [36]. Although e-scooter usage patterns vary among different user groups, some users may rely on e-scooters as their primary mode of transportation, while others may use them occasionally for specific purposes, such as delivery operations [40] or as a recreational activity.

Characteristics of e-scooter trips. E-scooter trips vary across different cities and regions, depending on local factors such as infrastructure, regulations, and user preferences. However, some common characteristics have been found in related studies. E-scooter trips are typically short-distance journeys, i.e., last-mile trips. They are commonly used for distances within a few (3) km or less. E-scooter trips tend to be relatively short in duration, usually lasting between a few minutes to a maximum of half an hour, since they are primarily used for quick and convenient transportation over short distances. Studies also have shown that the length of e-scooter trips is influenced by the cost of the service [41].

Spatial distribution and service operation. The analysis of case studies showed that the majority of e-scooter trips predominantly take place in the city center and other central areas with high mobility demands [42]. E-scooters are predominantly found in areas characterized by high population density, abundant job opportunities, and a diverse range of activities. This operational strategy is rational as these areas experience higher usage rates, making them more profitable for businesses. However, the imbalanced distribution of shared e-scooters restricts access for a significant portion of the population [43], exacerbating transportation inequities rather than addressing existing shortcomings [44,45]. Certain barriers are associated with e-scooter services, including restricted deployment areas, limited availability of scooters at pickup points, technical problems, and high pricing.

Purpose of trips and peak usage. E-scooters are frequently used for a variety of purposes, including commuting to work or school, running errands, or leisure rides within urban areas. They are particularly popular for short and convenient trips within busy city centers. E-scooters are often also used for intermodal mobility, in combination with other modes of transportation, such as buses, trains, or bicycles, to complete a longer journey. E-scooters provide a convenient option for the last-mile connection between transit stops and final destinations [46]. The analysis of peak usage times indicated that e-scooters are commonly used during peak travel times (morning and evening commuting hour) as well as during lunch breaks and on weekends when people engage in leisure activities and social outings.

Safety. Safety is one of the main factors that deters potential riders from fully adopting shared e-scooters [36,37]. The feeling of insecurity primarily arise from interactions with motorized vehicles, urging a demand for better-separated infrastructure for micromobility and improved road conditions. Commuters who have not experienced e-scooters often feel negative perceptions regarding safety, due to a lack of familiarity with the operation of vehicles. Limitations imposed by certain characteristics of e-scooters, such as inconvenience in adverse weather conditions and being uncomfortable for long trips or when carrying goods, further discourage potential riders. Two controversial measures are the prohibition of riding on sidewalks when no specific infrastructure is available for e-scooters (forcing e-scooters to share the road with cars and other motorized vehicles), and the establishment of fixed parking locations that restrict the flexibility of door-to-door trips [47].

Cost-effectiveness and business model. In general, e-scooters tend to be more economical than public transportation and bicycle-sharing systems, particularly for short distances (e.g., 2 km). For example, a study developed in Chicago, USA, showed that e-scooters become expensive when the trip exceeds 1.5 km [48]. NACTO confirmed this result by indicating that shared scooter cost is significantly higher than that for shared bicycles, nearly doubling the price for an equivalent trip distance [30]. Additional limitations include the limited diversity of payment methods, the requirement of owning a smartphone for using the service, the lack of integration with smart cards used for public transportation, and inadequate information regarding the regulations for the service [49].

Environmental impact. E-scooters entered the mobility market as a sustainable transportation solution, which serves as a motivating factor for some users. However, studies that have applied Life Cycle Assessments have revealed various environmental concerns associated with e-scooters [50,51]. Based on current usage patterns and operational practices, there is a debate about if the e-scooter service leads to a reduction in environmental impact compared to the motorized transportation modes they replace [52]. Gebhardt et al. [53] found that the potential savings on greenhouse gas emissions when switching to e-scooters is low, 1.2% less than using gasoline cars, and that the reductions heavily depend on the usage patterns. Moreover, e-scooters can be more polluting than battery electric-powered cars, potentially steering the transportation system towards less sustainable mobility means.

Despite the reservations about the riding experience, economic cost, and safety, studies have shown that certain demographic groups, i.e., young people and those with medium–high incomes, are likely to overcome these concerns and become regular users of e-scooter systems [37,54].

4.3. Urban Cycling

Cycling has witnessed a substantial global increase over the past decade, and it is perceived as a viable and sustainable mode of transportation [55,56]. Several factors have contributed to the increase in cycling worldwide, including the development of dedicated bicycle lanes and paths, the implementation of bicycle-sharing systems, the adoption of new technologies and increased safety measures, and the promotion of active transportation by governments and organizations as a way to improve health and environmental awareness.

The surge and increased use of bicycles is a worldwide phenomenon. It has been observed in cities with a cycling tradition and in those where cycling was not previously a common mode of daily transportation. Notable samples include European cities, such as Amsterdam, London, Paris, and Vienna; North American cities, such as Chicago and Portland; and also Latin American cities, such as Bogotá, Rio de Janeiro, Santiago de Chile, Mexico City, and Buenos Aires [57]. Several relevant factors are considered in the related literature for the evaluation of cycling in smart cities, focusing on the development of cycling infrastructure, safety, accessibility, integration, environmental impact, and policy and regulations [58]. The main topics related to these factors are commented on next

Cycling infrastructure. The existence of cycling infrastructure is the primary factor often assessed to determine the effectiveness of strategies to promote cycling. Several infrastructure deployments are considered, including bicycle lanes, bicycle paths, parking facilities, workshops for self-maintenance, etc. The directness evaluates how efficient the cycling infrastructure is, in terms of providing convenient and time-saving routes for cyclists and minimizing detours and unnecessary diversions. It is also important to evaluate the proper integration of infrastructure with the urban environment, taking into account aesthetics and landscaping considerations. Another aspect to consider is the land uses of the surrounding areas, following the main concepts of TOD, to determine the bikeability of the zone [59] and the sustainability of the infrastructure [60]. It is crucial to evaluate the maintenance condition of cycling infrastructure, assessing the quality of the pavement, the implementation of regular maintenance practices, and the promptness of repairs.

Comfort and convenience. Relevant factors to evaluate comfort and convenience include the smoothness of bicycle lanes or paths, the provision of amenities (resting areas, bicycle parking), and the presence of facilities like bicycle-sharing or repair stations. The historical evolution of cycling infrastructure installation must be considered to determine if cycling is properly promoted and actively under development in the city. Evaluating the adaptability and the future growth is crucial for dynamic and well-planned cycling infrastructure, taking into account population growth in advance, ever-evolving mobility demands, and the existing options for expanding and modifying the existent infrastructure, in case it is needed. From the evaluation of the aforementioned factors, important outcomes are made available to policymakers, urban planners, and researchers to assess the effectiveness and quality of the cycling infrastructure. The resulting outcomes are very relevant to making informed decisions regarding the development and improvement of cycling infrastructure.

Safety. Safety is a major concern for cycling. The perceived risk of traveling alongside motor vehicle traffic is a significant obstacle to increased cycling participation [61]. Therefore, a crucial strategy for promoting cycling, particularly among vulnerable and risk-averse population segments, has been the establishment of dedicated off-road lanes for bicycles, mixed-use paths shared with pedestrians, and protected on-road cycling facilities that are physically separated from motor vehicles by barriers or buffer zones. This approach requires substantial investments in expanding and enhancing cycling infrastructure. The installation of clear signage and ensuring proper lighting and adequate visibility for both cyclists and motorists are relevant issues too [62]. In turn, ensuring appropriate width for cycling lanes and paths is important for accommodating cyclists comfortably and safely, allowing for overtaking and maneuvering, and reducing the risk of conflicts with other road users. Proper line width contributes to the overall effectiveness and usability of cycling infrastructure [63]. These factors play a crucial role in enhancing safety and communication between road users, contributing to a more efficient and secure cycling experience.

Cost-effectiveness. The cost-effectiveness evaluation must consider the financial investments required for planning, construction, and maintenance, in relation to the benefits and usage levels of the infrastructure [60,64]. Sophisticated and complete cost–benefit analyses for cycling infrastructure are relatively limited, and are less common than those for automobile and public transportation systems [65]. Key considerations for cost–benefit analyses involve assessing how a modification in cycling infrastructure affects factors such as cycling route preferences, transportation mode selection, potential destination choices, and the generation of new mobility demands. Additionally, it is important to evaluate the impact of the number of bicycles that will potentially use each link on a given or projected bicycle network [66]. To capture the influence of cycling infrastructure and the required investments, generalized cost models must be applied that take into account mode and route choice, and the main features of the studied area.

Connectivity and multimodality. Finally, it is crucial to evaluate the connectivity between vital destinations such as residential areas, business districts, education centers, parks, and public transportation hubs. The connectivity between key destinations is crucial for creating a comprehensive cycling network [64]. The evaluation involves assessing how well cycling infrastructure integrates with other transportation modes, particularly public transportation systems. Seamless transitions between cycling and walking, i.e., providing easy access to bicycle racks or sharing stations near bus stops or train stations, encourage combined bicycle and transit trips. This integration promotes the use of bicycles as a first-mile/last-mile solution, allowing commuters to conveniently switch between cycling and public transit for their daily journeys [67]. Additionally, providing adequate bicycle parking facilities at public transit stations is essential for encouraging and promoting multimodal transportation and enhancing the overall effectiveness of the cycling network. Moreover, evaluating and improving the integration of cycling infrastructure with key destinations extends beyond transportation hubs. It encompasses facilitating access to important locations such as schools, business districts, recreational areas, and residential neighborhoods. By providing safe and direct cycling routes to these destinations, cycling becomes a practical and attractive option for various purposes, including commuting, leisure, and social activities. The development of bicycle-sharing systems is another relevant factor to consider in modern cities to reduce the dependence people have on non-sustainable means of transportation [68], and also to increase livability and sustainability.

4.4. Electric Public Transportation

For the analysis of electric public transportation, the literature has identified several relevant factors related to sustainability, technology assessment, and operational strategies for a proper business model [69,70]. Manzolli et al. [71] concluded that the main lines of research on electric public transportation are related to the dimensions of environmental factors, economic factors, and the quality of the service; the efficiency and effectiveness of energy use; and fleet management and operation (scheduling, routing, and maintenance).

Environmental impact. It is important to evaluate the reduction in greenhouse gas emissions and air pollutants in comparison to traditional fossil fuel-powered buses [72]. This assessment should consider factors such as the source of electricity used for charging the buses and the overall lifecycle emissions associated with the manufacturing, operation, and disposal of the buses. Considering these factors provides a comprehensive understanding of the environmental benefits and sustainability of electric bus systems [73].

Cost-effectiveness. Another relevant factor is the economic feasibility of an electric public transportation system. The viability analysis of electric bus lines includes assessing the upfront costs of acquiring electric buses, installing charging infrastructure, and ongoing operational expenses. Additionally, considering factors such as potential savings on fuel costs and maintenance expenses over the lifespan of the buses is crucial [74].

Operational efficiency. To evaluate the operational efficiency of electric public transportation, it is necessary to analyze various factors, such as the energy consumption of vehicles; the efficiency of regenerative braking technologies; the distribution and accessibility of charging stations; the availability, charging speed, and energy efficiency of charging infrastructure; the operational range of vehicles regarding the considered line lengths; and the technology, energy storage capacity, and life of the battery installed on buses [75]. This evaluation helps ascertain the overall effectiveness and feasibility of electric buses in meeting transportation demands. By assessing these aspects, it becomes possible to gain insights into the operational performance and capabilities of electric bus systems [76].

Equity and accessibility. When assessing social equity and accessibility factors, it is important to analyze if the electric bus lines are effectively providing a proper mobility service to different communities, including suburban areas and neighborhoods with a lower socioeconomic reality [77]. This evaluation involves considering various aspects of accessibility, such as the location of bus stops, the frequency of the service, and the affordability of electric bus transportation across various demographic groups. By evaluating these factors, it becomes possible to determine if electric bus lines are providing equitable and accessible transportation options for all members of the community. The public perception of electric buses and their social acceptance play an important role in their adoption and success [78].

Passenger experience and comfort. Another important issue to consider is passenger experience and comfort when using electric bus lines. Several factors that contribute to overall satisfaction need to be assessed [79]. These factors include the existing noise and vibration levels, the capacity of vehicles (both for seated and standing passengers), the provision of air conditioning, and other comfort-related amenities. By understanding and analyzing these aspects, the evaluation allows one to determine if a positive and satisfactory travel experience is provided to commuters using electric bus services [80].

Integration. Finally, it is also important to assess the integration of electric bus lines with existing infrastructure by analyzing factors such as the compatibility of charging stations with the electrical grid, the availability of suitable depots, and the feasibility of integrating electric buses into existing maintenance and operational systems.

The mentioned factors are vital for assisting stakeholders in making well-informed decisions for implementing, operating, and optimizing electric public transportation systems. By considering these factors, stakeholders can maximize the benefits of electric buses and certainly contribute to the development of sustainable and efficient mobility. This analysis aids in identifying opportunities for improvement, addressing challenges, and guiding the development of strategies that align with sustainability goals and transportation objectives.

4.5. Electric Private Transportation

Several considerations described for electric public transportation are also important for electric private transportation. Additional factors include the economic analysis and the incentives and policies applied by the government. The main factors are described next.

Environmental impact. Those factors related to sustainability and environmental impact are crucial, especially considering that the number of private electric vehicles is several orders of magnitude higher than that of electric buses. Evaluating the overall reduction in emissions helps determine the environmental benefits of electric private transportation. Usually, Life Cycle Assessment methodologies are applied for a comprehensive evaluation of the environmental impact of electric vehicles [81]. These involve analyzing the environmental burdens associated with the production, use, and disposal of electric vehicles, including the extraction of raw materials, manufacturing processes, energy sources used in production, vehicle operation, and end-of-life management. The analysis considers emissions, energy consumption, and resource depletion, enabling a holistic understanding of the environmental footprint of electric private transportation [82].

Range and battery life. Considerations about range and battery life include the distance the vehicle can travel on a single charge and how long the battery retains its capacity over time [83]. These factors must be analyzed considering the particularities of the city, such as common-origin-destinations for trips, orography, and the quality of roads [84]. Both of them determine the practicality and usability of electric private transportation.

Charging infrastructure and support services. The availability and accessibility of charging infrastructure is essential for evaluating the development of electric private transportation. Factors to consider include the availability of charging stations, the charging speed, and the geographical location of charging points. The availability of different charging options (e.g., fast charging, level 2 charging) and the time required to fully recharge a vehicle influence the convenience and usability of electric private transportation. These factors help in determining whether the necessary infrastructure is in place to support electric private transportation, and it is a very relevant issue since the availability of private charging infrastructure influences the readiness to buy and use electric vehicles [85]. Regarding support services, the availability of maintenance and repair services and the support provided by manufacturers and dealerships are also very relevant.

Economic analysis. A proper cost–benefit analysis is crucial for understanding the financial implications of electric private transportation [86]. The main factors to evaluate include the purchase cost of electric vehicles, comparing them to conventional vehicles, and the potential savings in fuel and maintenance costs over the lifetime of vehicles [87].

Government incentives and policies. Assessing government incentives and related policies is also very relevant for a correct evaluation and development of electric private transportation [88]. Relevant factors to analyze, including financial incentives, tax credits, and the construction of dedicated infrastructure for electric vehicles, significantly influence the adoption and viability of electric private transportation [89].

By considering the described main factors, stakeholders can evaluate the feasibility, benefits, and challenges of electric private transportation and make informed decisions regarding its adoption, implementation, and development.

4.6. Methodology

The described factors were studied applying a methodology based on urban data analysis [90], considering several sources of data, both public and proprietary. A thorough review and analysis of existing information from the city administration, stakeholders, and transportation companies was performed. In turn, interviews with relevant actors were conducted. The data from our previous sustainable mobility survey [23] were also analyzed in the study of relevant factors. Comparative analyses were also are used as a main component of the applied methodology, and statistical analyses were applied, when corresponding. Finally, specific models were developed or adopted for the analysis of specific factors, such as business, energy efficiency, and environmental impact considerations.

5. Sustainable Mobility in Montevideo: Results and Analysis

This section discusses the results of the analysis conducted on the studied initiatives regarding sustainable mobility in Montevideo. The analysis was developed applying the methodology described in Section 4. Data processing was carried out using the high-performance computing platform of the National Supercomputing Center (Cluster-UY) [91].

5.1. Shared Electric Scooters in Montevideo

Uruguay introduced e-scooters as a mode of transportation six years ago (in 2018). Three companies introduced their services in Montevideo to offer and evaluate the reception of e-scooters. Whereas e-scooters offered a more environmentally friendly and user-friendly mode of transportation, the disadvantages outbalanced the perceived benefits for users. The e-scooter companies operated until 2019, and then made the decision to gradually discontinue their mobility services. The main features of the service were studied in our previous article [4], applying a quantitative approach considering various indicators. The analysis was complemented by several qualitative indicators to evaluate government regulations, subsidies and financial issues, the energy efficiency, and intermodal connectivity. The experience of shared e-scooters in Montevideo encountered significant challenges that hindered its operational success, as discussed in the following paragraphs.

Spatial distribution and socioeconomic characterization. The distribution of e-scooters in Montevideo reflected a common trend observed in many cities worldwide, where companies strategically deploy e-scooters in regions characterized by high economic indicators and income, densely populated areas, and areas with many job opportunities. In the case of Montevideo, the operational area of service for e-scooters was along the coast of Río de la Plata (the southern part of the city). This strategy aligns with profit objectives for companies, since these areas naturally have more potential users and experience higher utilization rates. However, in Montevideo, this concentration in specific areas caused an uneven e-scooter distribution, thereby restricting the accessibility for a significant number of citizens.

The Socioeconomic Level Index (INSE) [92] was used for the socioeconomic evaluation of neighborhoods in Montevideo. The INSE is a concise analytical instrument for assessing the economic situation of households, obtained through a short questionnaire [93,94]. The INSE classifies households based on their consumption capacity, ranging from 0 (representing the lowest socioeconomic level) to 9 (representing the highest socioeconomic level), to characterize neighborhoods according to their income levels. The mean value of the INSE in Montevideo is 4.5. The mean value of the INSE for neighborhoods served by the e-scooter service was 7.1 and all neighborhoods in the operation zone had larger INSE values than the mean value for Montevideo. Figure 1 clearly illustrates the trend, depicting the coverage area of the e-scooter service along the southern coast, which is predominantly inhabited by high-income residents. Darker shades of blue represent neighborhoods with a higher INSE value and lighter shades represent neighborhoods with lower INSE values.

Affordability. In line with the previous factor, the affordability of the system was also a problem for the consolidation of the e-scooter service. According to the average (time-based) fares for the e-scooter service, and considering a trip length of 12 min (the average travel time for using scooters), the cost of each trip is about UYU 60 (about USD 1.54, considering an average exchange rate of UYU 39 per USD in the period of 2019–2022). The cost of performing 45 trips (round trip for 22 or 23 business/education days in a typical working month) was UYU 2700, which represents 12.4% of an average low-income salary (UYU 21,744, USD 558) and 7.6% of an average medium-income salary (UYU 35,444, USD 908). In turn, the cost of performing 60 trips was 16.5% of an average low-income salary and 10.1% of an average medium income. These values are significantly higher than owning a standard or electric bicycle, or using public transportation (two trips per day), as shown in Figure 2. A standard bus ticket price using a smart card of the Metropolitan Public System was considered (USD 1.10). Costs for e-bicycles correspond to a national electric bicycle, assuming one battery charge (36 V, 7.8 A/280 W) per day and a battery life expectancy of two years. Bicycle costs correspond to a standard national/international bicycle. Both bicycle costs are pro-rated to the expected life of vehicles (five years).

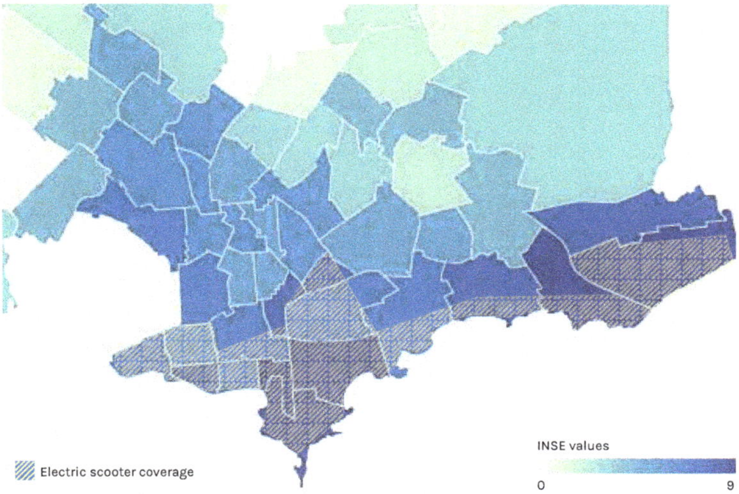

Figure 1. Coverage area of e-scooter service and INSE values for neighborhoods in Montevideo.

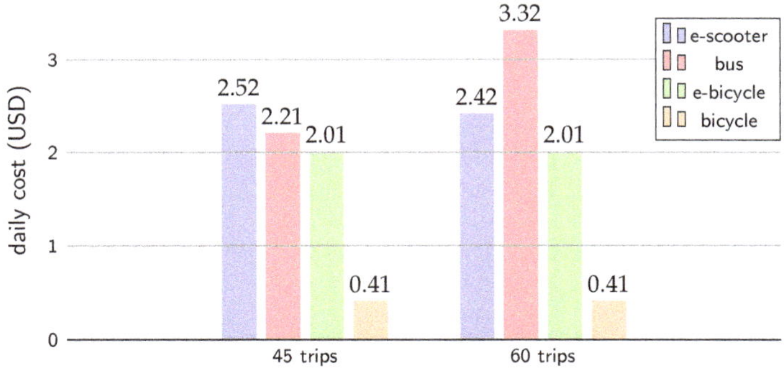

Figure 2. Cost comparison of the e-scooter service, bus, electric bicycle (e-bicycle), and standard bicycle in Montevideo. Comparisons are shown for common packages of 45 and 60 trips.

The cost of the e-scooter service was high, even prohibitive, for low-income citizens, especially considering that they are often used sporadically for rides and/or for first–last mile trips in multimodal mobility, which involves an additional cost (e.g., the cost of a bus ticket). Whereas e-scooters may be affordable for short trips for medium- and high-income citizens, the cost-effectiveness of the service diminishes for longer distances. As the fare charged users based on the distance traveled, the overall cost for longer trips became less favorable compared to other transportation modes, like buses, which offered flat-rate fares regardless of the distance traveled. The limited accessibility and affordability of the e-scooter initiative went against the principles of shared mobility, as it failed to provide a convenient and sustainable transportation option for a broad segment of the population.

Environmental impact. Important doubts were raised regarding the sustainability of e-scooters as an environmentally friendly mode of transportation in Montevideo. The practices employed by the e-scooter companies involved collecting scooters for charging and redistributing them using non-sustainable transportation (i.e., fuel-based) means.

Intermodal integration. In the case study of Montevideo, the limited coverage area for e-scooters created significant challenges in achieving meaningful intermodal integration. Users faced difficulties in efficiently combining e-scooters with other transportation modes, such as buses, to complete their journeys. This lack of integration hindered the overall effectiveness of e-scooters as an integral part of the transportation network. This limitation was an important drawback of the e-scooter service, since seamless intermodal transportation is a key component of a well-functioning urban transportation system.

Comfort. For trips outside the coastal promenade, users faced diverse topography, including hills and uneven terrain, which made longer rides less comfortable and physically challenging. Furthermore, users considered e-scooters to be inconvenient for long rides, or when they need to carry personal items. Inclement weather conditions, such as rain, strong winds, and extreme temperatures, have a notable impact on the usability of e-scooters, prompting users to choose more weather-resistant modes of transportation, such as buses.

User behavior and regulations. Other factors, such as the conduct of users of the e-scooter system while riding and parking vehicles, as well as their interaction with pedestrians and the environment, indicated the need for regulations to foster improved coexistence. The city government introduced specific measures to mitigate these concerns, including the definition of limited operational areas for e-scooters, the prohibition of riding e-scooters on sidewalks, the limitation of speed for e-scooters, and the enforcement of strict parking regulations. Other measures, such as mandating helmet usage and driver's licenses, were not effectively enforced during the brief period that the service was operating. These measures led to a significant decrease in user preference for e-scooters as a mean of transportation.

Commuting Travel Time. E-scooters were limited for long trips. When the distance grows, e-scooters became less suitable for commuting purposes [33,54]. In line with previous research that emphasized the ability of e-scooters to enhance travel time for trips, users in Montevideo perceived e-scooters as a viable option for trips up to 3 km. Beyond this, the comparatively low speeds of e-scooters in comparison to public buses impacted the overall travel time for commuters. Users found that e-scooters were not as time-efficient for longer journeys, diminishing their appeal as a primary means of daily transportation.

Safety. Consistent with findings in other zones of the city, the responses of commuters interviewed in the Parque Rodó neighborhood revealed that a prevailing sense of insecurity among riders is a notable impediment to the widespread adoption of e-scooters [4]. This insecurity primarily arises from interactions with motorized transportation means, underscoring the need for improved and segregated infrastructure and better road conditions to facilitate the growth of e-scooters for micromobility.

In conclusion, the unsuccessful implementation of a shared e-scooter service in Montevideo is attributed to a range of factors. Key issues included the limited spatial coverage of the service, the limitations for long trips, cost and comfort considerations, operational constraints, and regulatory challenges. Additionally, a lack of diverse payment methods, smartphone ownership requirements, poor integration with public transportation passes, and insufficient information regarding regulations hindered the adoption and usability of e-scooters. Collectively, these challenges hampered the viability and attractiveness of shared e-scooters as a sustainable mode of urban transportation in the city.

5.2. Urban Cycling

Urban cycling has been promoted as a healthy and sustainable transportation mode in Montevideo. The percentage of daily trips made by bicycle in Montevideo has shown a steady increase in the last decade, rising from approximately 1.5% in 2015 to less than 2% in 2017, out of a total of over three million trips daily. In 2022, a report from the city administration identified seven specific locations where bicycles accounted for as much as 4% of the total number of circulating vehicles [95]. The city boasts a bicycle population of over 300,000, owned by more than 100,000 individuals, with more than 80% of them relying on bicycles as their primary means of transportation. However, despite these promising statistics, the analysis reveals significant inconveniences that hinder urban cycling in Montevideo. These challenges include inadequate infrastructure, safety issues, poor connectivity, and a lack of modal integration, as described in the following subsections.

5.2.1. Infrastructure for Cycling

In the last decade, Montevideo took a commendable step towards improving its urban infrastructure by developing and expanding its bicycle network. This initiative exemplified the dedication of the city administration to promote sustainable mobility and offer its residents environmentally friendly and efficient transportation options. However, the cycling network deployed in the city has been inadequate to meet the escalating demands of a growing number of users. The survey of commuters in the Parque Rodó neighborhood [23] unveiled that a considerable portion of travelers are willing to transition from their current mode of transportation to cycling as a sustainable alternative.

Montevideo has implemented three types of cycling infrastructure that aim to enhance the safety and convenience of cyclists, namely the following:

- Bicycle lanes (*ciclovía*): these are designated sections of the road, typically a lane, exclusively dedicated to the circulation of bicycles.
- Bicycle paths (*bicisenda*): these are located on sidewalks, central flower beds, or landscaped areas; are separate from the road; and are exclusively designated for bicycle use.
- Streets with 30 km/h limits: This is when a speed limit of 30 km/h is enforced to promote coexistence with bicycles. Signage is installed to establish the priority of bicycles in the circulation.

From 2020 to 2023, significant progress was made in expanding the cycling network in Montevideo, in line with the goal of developing sustainable mobility and promoting cycling. However, certain aspects of the expansion of the cycling network require further attention. While progress has been made, the design of cycling lanes and paths has not yet met the established standards outlined in related studies, which play a crucial role in ensuring the safety and comfort of cyclists. Furthermore, the connectivity remains inadequate, with significant room for improvement.

In 2020–2022, new bicycle lanes were built on several important streets in the city:

1. In Luis Morquio (city center, Parque Batlle neighborhood), with a length of 0.5 km.
2. In Hocquart, from Arenal Grande to Bulevar Artigas (city center, La Comercial and Villa Muñoz neighborhoods), with a length of 1.4 km.
3. In Nueva Palmira, from Bulevar Artigas to Arenal Grande (city center, La Comercial and Villa Muñoz neighborhoods), with a length of 1.4 km.
4. In Isidoro de María, from Arenal Grande to General Flores (city center, Aguada neighborhood), with a length of 0.4 km.
5. In Luis Alberto de Herrera, from 8 de Octubre to Mazzini (city center, Parque Batlle neighborhood), with a length of 1.2 km.
6. In Belloni, from Perimetral to Instrucciones (north-east of the city, Villa Española neighborhood), with a length of 1.6 km.
7. In Cibils, from Route #1 to Tomkinson (west of the city, Las Torres and Paso de la Arena neighborhoods), with a length of 1.6 km.

In turn, new bicycle paths were built in other locations:

8. In Avenida Italia, from Gallinal to Albo (city center, Malvin, Buceo, and Parque Batlle neighborhoods), with a length of 5.9 km.
9. In Avenida Larrañaga, from the Hippodrome to Varela (north-east of the city, Ituzaingó and Villa Española neighborhoods), with a length of 2.5 km.
10. In Avenida Ricaldoni, from Vidiella to Morquio (city center, Parque Batlle neighborhood), with a length of 1.8 km.
11. In Bulevar Artigas, from Batlle Berres monument to Garibaldi (center to north of the city, Jacinto Vera neighborhood), with a length of 1.5 km.

12. In Avenida Larrañaga, from Varela to Joanicó (city denter, Larrañaga neighborhood), with a length of 1.9 km.
13. In Luis Alberto de Herrera, from Anador to Mazzini (city center, Parque Batlle neighborhood), with a length of 0.5 km.
14. In Cibils, from Ramírez to Route #1 (west of the city, Cerroa neighborhood), with a length of 2.6 km.

Finally, a new 30 km/h street was built in one location:

15. In Avenida Italia, from Gallinal to Bolivia (south-east of the city, Malvin and Portones neighborhoods), with a length of 1.5 km.

In 2023, a new bicycle lane was built on 18 de Julio, the main avenue of Montevideo, and San José street, connecting Plaza Independencia, the main square of the city where the House of Government is located, and the Obelisk, an emblematic monument located in Parque Batlle, the main central park of the city. This bicycle lane has a length of 3.5 km.

Figure 3 shows the current cycling infrastructure in Montevideo and the new infrastructure constructed between 2020 and 2023. Table 1 provides details on the length of the newly built bicycle infrastructure in Montevideo during the period 2020–2023, based on information provided by the Mobility Observatory from Intendencia de Montevideo [96].

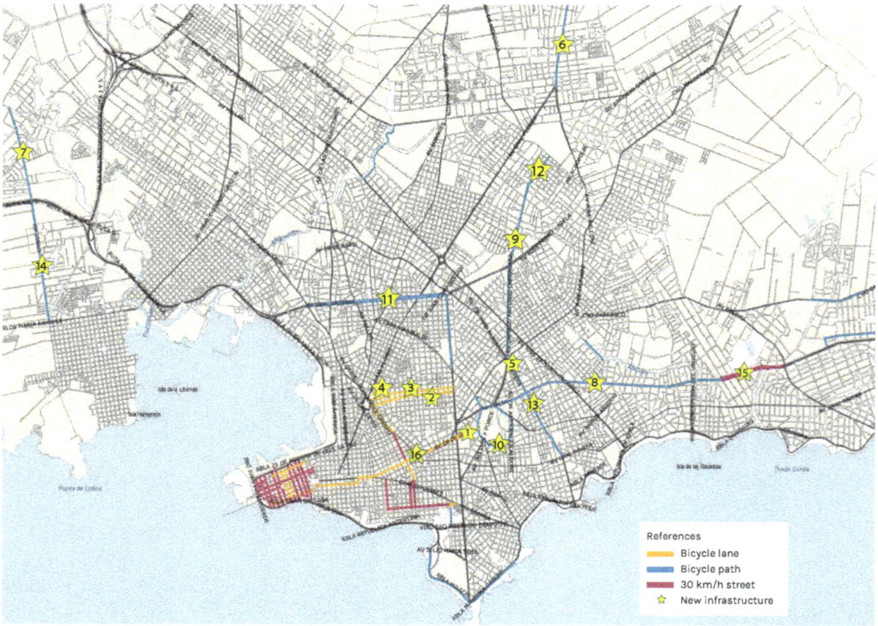

Figure 3. Infrastructure for cycling in Montevideo. Own design, base map from SIG Montevideo.

Table 1. Details of the cycling infrastructure in Montevideo (existing and built in 2020–2023).

Infrastructure Type	Existing (km)	New 2020–2023 (km)	Percentage	Over Total
bicycle lane	12.5	8.7	69.6%	0.32%
bicycle path	42.2	16.9	40.0%	0.98%
30 km/h street	16.6	1.5	9.0%	0.44%
total	71.3	25.8	32.6%	1.79%

The results in Table 1 show an important increase in bicycle lanes and paths in Montevideo in 2020–2023. The expansion of the bicycle network accounted for one-third of the

71.3 km within the city. However, this figure remains relatively small compared to the road network of Montevideo (3783 km) as shown in the last column in Table 1.

The cycling network in Montevideo accounts for a mere 1.79% of the road network. Furthermore, taking into account that 30 km/h streets are not considered fully safe for cycling because bicycles share the way with motorized vehicles without any physical separation, the percentage of dedicated cycling infrastructure is lower than 1.4%, which is a significantly low value in terms of built infrastructure specifically designed for cycling.

In comparison to other cities in the world, cycling infrastructure is significantly less deployed in Montevideo. For instance, Barcelona (Spain) has deployed an extensive network of dedicated paths for bicycles of more than 250 km, and the city has plans for 95% of its citizens to be within 300 m of a nearby bicycle path. Amsterdam (the Netherlands) provides over 500 km of infrastructure for bicycles, which has made cycling the first mode of transportation, accounting for a share of 36% and more than 700,000 daily bicycle trips. In Latin America, Bogotá (Colombia) has become a frontrunner in cycling infrastructure, offering an impressive length of 500 km of dedicated cycling infrastructure and a plan to expand the infrastructure to 800 km in two years. Buenos Aires (Argentina) has also made important advances, deploying over 250 km of cycling infrastructure that has contributed to the fast growth of cycling as a preferred transportation mode. Curitiba and Rio de Janeiro (Brazil), Mexico City, and Santiago de Chile have also made substantial investments in building and deploying cycling infrastructure. All of these cities are positioned ahead of Montevideo by a significant margin in terms of cycling infrastructure.

5.2.2. Safety and Maintenance

One of the most critical issues is ensuring adequate separation between cyclists and motorized vehicular traffic. Regrettably, this crucial safety measure is only implemented in a portion of the currently developed bicycle infrastructure. Protected cycling lanes separated from the roadway by physical barriers significantly reduce the risk of accidents and injuries for cyclists. The findings regarding lower risks on quiet streets and with cycling-specific dedicated infrastructure along busy streets provide support for the route-design approach commonly employed in countries in Northern Europe, where cycling is used as a primary mode of transportation [97]. Furthermore, it has been demonstrated that the risk of cyclist crashes and falls varies among different types of protected bicycle lanes. Specifically, bicycle lanes that feature a heavy separation from the road have been associated with a decreased risk, whereas other types of protected bicycle lanes are not effective at reducing the risk [98]. The safest options for cycling infrastructure are dedicated bicycle-only paths, which are separated from motorized traffic and exclusively designated for cycling, as well as cycle tracks, which are separate routes specifically designed for bicycles and not shared with motor vehicles. These types of infrastructure provide the highest level of safety for cyclists and they must be considered as the primary goal in extending the cycling network in Montevideo.

Ensuring appropriate lane widths for cycling infrastructure is another crucial factor to be addressed. Proper lane widths provide enough space for cyclists to maneuver and maintain a safe distance from other vehicles. Narrow lanes increase the risk of collisions, especially when vehicles invade the cycling lane. The recommended minimum width is typically 1.5 to 1.8 m for bicycle lanes. Wider bicycle lanes (e.g., 2 m or more) enhance safety and comfort, especially on high-volume or high-speed roads. On these heavy traffic roads, the construction of buffer zones between cyclists and motorized vehicles, which are not present in Montevideo, are are much needed on the main avenues (18 de Julio, Avenida Italia) and high-speed streets (Nueva Palmira, Hocquart, Fernández Crespo). The recommendation is wider (2.5 to 3 m) for physically separated cycling lanes.

Another relevant issue for safety is installing clear signaling, specifically designed for cyclists, to improve the guidance shown at intersections and areas where cyclists need to interact with motorized vehicles and pedestrians. Dedicated cyclist-specific signals are useful to indicate when it is safe for cyclists to proceed, helping to prevent conflicts and collisions with motorized traffic. By having separate signals that are positioned at appropriate heights and locations for cyclists, they are more likely to be noticed and acknowledged by all road users, reducing the risk of accidents. Cyclist-specific signals also increase the visibility of cyclists to other road users and improve the understanding of the intended actions to better comply with traffic regulations. Appropriate signals reduce ambiguity and confusion, ensuring that cyclists know when to stop, yield, or proceed, aligning their actions with the signals, and promoting a more orderly flow of traffic.

In general, there has been a satisfactory installation of signals in the cycling infrastructure deployed in Montevideo. However, newer infrastructures tend to have a higher number of clear, high-quality signals, whereas older bicycle lanes and paths often lack an adequate quantity of signals and they are not promptly replaced when damaged. Furthermore, the city lacks dedicated traffic lights installed for cyclists. Figure 4 presents two contrasting examples of adequate and inadequate signaling within the cycling infrastructure of Montevideo. In Figure 4b, although the bicycle path has the give-way signal for pedestrians, the adjacent street lacks any signal indicating the presence of the bicycle path.

(a) (b)

Figure 4. Examples of adequate and inadequate signaling within the cycling infrastructure of Montevideo (own photographs). (**a**) Bicycle path with proper signaling (location: 18 de Julio, aerial view). (**b**) Bicycle path without proper signaling (location: Avenida Italia).

Other specific issues have affected the normal safety of cycling infrastructure in Montevideo. For example, the bicycle lane on Avenida Italia has been used for driving cars and beacons have been installed along the lane. Cars and trucks are often parked in bicycle lanes, and large, city waste bins are even installed over bicycle lanes and paths.

The quality of the pavement in the cycling infrastructure is also very relevant. It is crucial to consider not only the pavement of bicycle lanes and paths, but also the overall condition of streets and roads where cycling infrastructure is absent. Unfortunately, many of these non-designated areas suffer from severe deterioration, creating hazardous conditions for cyclists during their commute. In this regard, three different situations happen in Montevideo. The new cycling infrastructure (constructed between 2020 and 2023) exhibits excellent or good quality pavement, well-maintained painting, and appropriate accessories. However, there have been reports highlighting specific cases of damaged pavement and poor signage. In turn, older bicycle lanes and paths experience infrastructure deterioration, faded painting, and inadequate signaling. Furthermore, numerous streets and avenues lacking dedicated cycling infrastructure, where cyclists must share lanes with other vehicles, suffer from poor pavement quality. This unfavorable condition presents challenges for cyclists traveling through such traffic routes, as exemplified in Figure 5.

(**a**) (**b**) (**c**)

Figure 5. Examples of different pavement maintenance conditions within the cycling infrastructure of Montevideo (own photographs). (**a**) Bicycle path with good quality pavement (location: 18 de Julio). (**b**) Bicycle path with deteriorated pavement (location: Avenida Italia). (**c**) Street with poor conditions for cycling (location: Bulevar Artigas).

5.2.3. Connectivity, Multimodality, and Socioeconomic Characterization

The cycling infrastructure in Montevideo is fragmented into multiple disconnected sub-networks, with several routes being significantly distant from the main core area. The construction of the bicycle lane on 18 de Julio in the last months of 2023 played a crucial role in connecting existing bicycle lanes and 30 km/h streets in the Downtown (Ciudad Vieja) area with the bicycle path in Parque Batlle, extending towards the east along Avenida Italia. This development served as a much-needed connection, facilitating smoother travel for cyclists. Currently, the most crucial connection that is needed is the construction of cycling infrastructure on Bulevar Artigas, spanning from Rambla to Nueva Palmira, to connect cycling infrastructures in the city center with those in the center–north. This infrastructure was approved in the participatory budget of the city government in 2013; however, it has yet to be built and deployed. Other bicycle lanes and paths in the west and in the north are very far away from the infrastructure deployed in the center. For example, the bicycle lane and bicycle path in Cibils (west of the city) would need 7.3 km of cycling infrastructure to be built to be connected with the nearest bicycle path in Bulevar Artigas. The bicycle path in Belloni (north of the city) would require building 2.3 km of cycling infrastructure to be connected with the nearest bicycle path in Larrañaga. Bicycle paths in Tajes and Camino Carrasco (east of the city) would need 1.9 km of cycling infrastructure to be built to be connected with the nearest 30 km/h street in Avenida Italia and Bolivia and would need 3.4 km to be built to be connected with the nearest bicycle path in Avenida Italia and Gallinal.

The absence of multimodal transportation in Montevideo is another significant issue of concern. Regarding cycling, buses are not designed for carrying and are not equipped to accommodate bicycles, and there is a lack of nearby parking infrastructure at major bus stations and terminals. These two main issues make it impossible for commuters to engage in multimodal trips, using a bicycle as either feeder or last-mile transportation options. This problem is particularly notable nearby main terminals where buses from medium or long distances end or pass through. Users must switch from medium- or long-distance buses to city buses, as there are no provisions for combinations with cycling. Moreover, the lack of safe and designated areas for bicycle parking creates a non-seamless transition between cycling and walking. Consequently, cyclists are compelled to use improvised parking locations on the street or in public places, which may lack essential safety measures. Overall, citizens rely on a single mode of transportation, mainly private cars or buses, which often leads to congestion, overcrowding, and the inefficient use of resources.

Regarding socioeconomic characterization and accessibility, cycling is significantly better than other sustainable transportation modes studied in this article.

5.2.4. Public Bicycles

A pilot plan for implementing a public bicycle-sharing service was developed by the city administration from 2015 to 2019. The system consisted of just 8 public bicycle stations located in Downtown (Ciudad Vieja) and 80 vehicles. Users of the service had to unlock bicycles and pay with a smart card of the Metropolitan Transportation System, and previous registration was required. The fist half-an-hour had no cost, and then the cost was proportional to the time until the vehicle was returned to a station. The system was not well received by citizens, although it was fairly used by tourists. The main issues were related to security; the registration process was reported to be unfriendly, and cases of vandalism were frequent. Despite an ambitious plan for extending the system to up to 60 stations in several neighborhoods and 600 vehicles, the system was discontinued in 2019.

The city administration has advertised the intention of reviving the public bicycle-sharing system in Montevideo to promote transportation equity, sustainability, and accessibility, learning from the past experience to create an improved and successful system [99]. However, up to March 2024, no public bicycle-sharing service is operating in Montevideo.

The factors discussed show that urban cycling in Montevideo is still in a developing stage. Overall, Montevideo has been classified as a city that is not very friendly to cyclists [100]. Despite its cost-effectiveness, and the increase in cycling trips due to the reduction in public transportation usage during the COVID-19 pandemic [101], there is progress to be made in establishing cycling as a prominent transportation mode in the city.

5.3. *Electric Public Transportation*

The environmental advantages and potential for reducing greenhouse gas emissions have propelled the global adoption of electric public transportation [102]. Numerous cities are embracing the transition of their public transportation systems to electric alternatives as part of their efforts to enhance sustainability and mitigate air pollution. Electric buses, in particular, have become a popular choice for electrifying public transportation fleets. With the demonstrated commitment of Uruguay to renewable energy and its substantial integration into the energy mix [103], there exists a distinct potential for the advancement of electric public transportation. The main advances and shortcomings of electric public transportation in Montevideo are described in the following subsections.

5.3.1. Development of Electric Bus Lines

Despite its acknowledged potential, the progress of electric public transportation in Montevideo has been limited. After the initial pilot plan using a single electric vehicle for various bus lines [4], there have been few significant advancements. By 2021, only one electric bus line had been fully deployed [23]. As of the year 2023, the bus company CUTCSA, which holds a large share of the public transportation in Montevideo, operates merely three electric lines: central line CE1 (formerly line CA1), differential line DE1 (formerly line D1), and line E14 (formerly line 14, but with a new route). CUTCSA has 20 electric vehicles in its fleet, all of them BYD model K9W. Smaller public transportation companies, namely COETC, COMESA, and UCOT, have incorporated a few Yutong model ZK 6128BEVG electric vehicles. COETC owns four buses, COMESA owns three buses, and UCOT owns three buses [104].

UCOT allocated two of its electric buses to serve line 316. However, in its more recent acquisitions in March 2023, UCOT opted to not incorporate new full-electric buses into its fleet, but hybrid buses instead. Enrique Garabato, UCOT Chief Technician, affirmed that "at present, the electric bus cannot fully substitute conventional gasoline or diesel buses, as it would need to offer an additional 30% range to be equally operational" [105]. In turn, as part of the pilot plan operated between 2020 and 2021, COMESA deployed electric buses on routes with fewer turns and complex maneuvers. COMESA assigned electric buses to several lines in Montevideo, among them lines 505, 524, 526, 538, 546, 582, and L24. Finally, COETC deployed electric buses to operate on central line CA1 and line 407. However, the company has not explored additional options for electric buses. Fernando Fernández, the President of COETC, stated that "an intermediate step exists: the hybrid bus" [105].

To expand the initial progress of electric public transportation in Montevideo, various alternatives have been explored. These include the establishment of a dedicated fund to encourage the acquisition of electric buses [106] and the introduction of a new financial program by the Ministry of Industry, Energy, and Mining. This program aims to develop tools to promote a smooth transition towards clean energy [107].

Regarding the three electric bus lines in operation, some advances and shortcomings are identified. The three lines enter Downtown and travel along 25 de Mayo Street, in line with the objective of creating an exclusive corridor for electric vehicles. Electric line E14 modifies the route of previous line 14, providing a faster trip from Downtown to Pocitos, Punta Carretas, and Parque Rodó. However, ten new bus stops were created, which do not include basic infrastructure for commuters (shelter, a bench, and signs).

5.3.2. Coverage, Accessibility, and Socioeconomic Characterization

Considering the standard technique of defining a buffer area delimited by parallel roads up to 300 m of the bus route to determine the acceptable walking distance accessible to the nearest bus stop [108], the coverage of electric lines is 11.7% of the total area of Montevideo. The accessibility calculation for bus stops on electric lines in Montevideo is 0.098, showing that there is significant room for improvement.

Regarding the socioeconomic characterization of electric public transportation in Montevideo, an analysis of the INSE values reveals that the three electric bus lines primarily prioritize offering mobility services to neighborhoods with higher socioeconomic index values, whereas peripheral neighborhoods are not included in the routes of the electric bus lines. The neighborhoods served by electric bus lines possess significantly higher INSE values compared to the average for Montevideo (up to 8.00 for electric lines E14 and DE1).

Figure 6 shows the routes of electric bus lines in Montevideo and the socioeconomic characterization of neighborhoods, clearly showing the discussed trend: electric lines serve the neighborhoods on the southern and eastern coasts, where citizens with high incomes live.

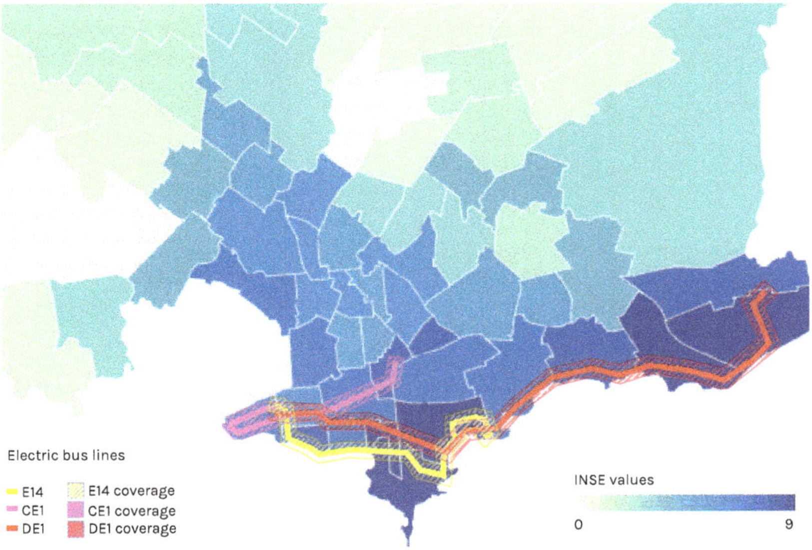

Figure 6. Electric bus lines and socioeconomic characterization of neighborhoods in Montevideo.

5.3.3. Operational and Energy efficiency

The average distance traveled by an electric bus in Montevideo is 161 km/day. A total of 73% of buses travel between 150 and 250 km per day, whereas 36% of travels are between 200 and 225 km [104]. However, except for DE1 (19.9 km), the route length of electric lines is significantly shorter than the average length for bus lines in Montevideo (16.7 km). The route for line CE1 is 7.0 km long, and the route for line E14 is 9.6 km long. At the end of the day, electric buses typically have a battery charge level between 50% and 60%. In 97% of cases, the electric buses arrive at their destination with at least 20% charge remaining in the battery, indicating the high level of adaptability of buses to the route and usage conditions.

Based on the study conducted by the Uruguayan government [104], the power consumption of electric buses varies between a minimum of 0.56 kWh/km and a maximum of 1.60 kWh/km. The average consumption is 1.11 kWh/km. Most of the operating units (75%) demonstrated an operational efficiency ranging from 0.9 kWh/km to 1.1 kWh/km. The number was 88% when extending the range between 0.7 kWh/km and 1.2 kWh/km. These are appropriate values for the operational efficiency of electric public transportation [109].

The energy efficiency of electric public transportation varies depending on several factors, including the bus model, the battery and engine technology, and the operational conditions. Common values for the energy efficiency of electric buses are between 0.8 and 1.5 kWh/km. This range is widely regarded as a favorable level of energy efficiency for electric buses: 0.8 kWh/km is considered appropriate for buses with a length of 12 m operating under typical daily conditions with an average temperature of 20 °C, encountering low traffic and operated by a skilled driver. Conversely, an energy efficiency of 1.5 kWh/km is considered reasonable for buses operating in winter with electric heating activated [110].

When compared to a diesel vehicle with a fuel efficiency of 2.51 km/L, the operation of electric buses results in a savings of over 615,000 L of fuel per year. The resulting energy difference, defined as the difference between the baseline diesel consumption and the current electricity consumption, is equivalent to 380 tons of oil. This value results in the avoidance of 1620 tons of CO_2 emissions in one and a half years. Additionally, the adoption of electric buses prevents the release of 344 kg of PM10, which represents about 5% of the total PM10 emissions generated by public transportation in Montevideo.

5.3.4. Passenger Comfort

To evaluate the passenger experience and comfort provided by electric bus lines, it is essential to analyze various factors, including noise, vibrations, seating capacity, air conditioning, and overall convenience and comfort for passengers. By understanding these factors, it becomes possible to ensure a satisfactory commuting experience for passengers.

Electric buses operating in Montevideo provide passengers with exceptional conditions that greatly enhance the commuting experience: a low level of noise, efficient air conditioning, and ample space for both seated and standing passengers. However, the experience of waiting for and boarding the electric buses is currently not satisfactory due to the inadequate infrastructure provided at several bus stops.

All the newly introduced bus stops (ten) for bus line E14 lack any form of infrastructure, such as shelters, seating benches, and information regarding the bus route and timetable. The bus stops lacking infrastructure are located in the Barrio Sur, Palermo, and Parque Rodó neighborhoods: Sarmiento between Patria and Maggiolo (in both directions), Rambla and Eduardo Acevedo (in both directions), Rambla and Barrios Amorín (in both directions), Rambla and La Cumparsita (in both directions), Ferreira Aldunate and Durazno, and Río Negro and Durazno. Six of these ten bus stops are situated along the promenade, directly facing the sea shore. This location poses significant challenges for passengers as it becomes exceedingly difficult to wait for the bus during rainy and windy weather conditions. Unlike the previously mentioned bus stops, lines CE1 and DE1 do not face a complete absence of infrastructure. This is because they utilize the existing bus stops from previous lines, namely D1 and CA1, which already have some form of infrastructure in place. Nevertheless, it is important to note that for many bus stops, the existing infrastructure is incomplete or damaged, and the availability of route and timetable information is limited to only a few stops. This situation represents a significant drawback of the electric bus lines, particularly taking into account that they have been in operation for over three years.

In summary, Montevideo has made gradual progress in promoting sustainable transportation through the implementation of electric bus lines. However, the city still has significant potential to proactively confront important issues in its goal of reducing greenhouse gas emissions, particularly related to public transportation. In this direction, the implementation of more electric bus lines will certainly allow for the expansion of the current transition from standard fossil fuel buses to more sustainable options. There is ample opportunity for strategic planning to extend the coverage of electric public transportation, ensuring that various parts of the city can benefit from the environmental advantages they provide. It is crucial to prioritize the inclusion of neighborhoods with medium and lower socioeconomic indexes to ensure a broader reach and enable a larger number of passengers to experience the benefits of sustainable and cleaner transportation.

5.4. Electric Private Transportation

The main factors described for the evaluation of electric private transportation are presented in the following subsections.

5.4.1. Electric Vehicle Market and Projections

By December 2023, the market of electric vehicles in Uruguay reached over 4000 vehicles. The introduction of electric cars in Uruguay began in 2015 with the sale of the Mitsubishi i-Miev model [111]. The progress was slow, but the market gradually expanded each year. In 2019, there were approximately 140 electric vehicles in circulation, which increased to 250 in 2020, then further grew to 800 in 2021, and reached 2000 in 2022 [112].

Based on data from the Uruguayan Association of Automotive Business (ACAU), the sales of new electric vehicles in Uruguay showed significant growth. In 2019, 160 new electric vehicles were sold. The number of new units increased to 300 in 2020, 697 in 2021, and reached 1044 in 2022. In 2023, 1887 new electric vehicles were sold [113], which was an an 80.92% increase in sales compared to the previous year. Out of the 1887 electric vehicles sold, 78.2% (1475 units) were in the car (648) and SUV (827) segments, representing a 72.9% increase over 2022 when both segments combined accounted for 853 vehicle sales. The number of SUVs quadrupled from 224 in 2022 to 827 in 2023 (43.8% of the electric vehicles sold). Figure 7 presents the number of new electric vehicles sold each year from 2020 to 2023.

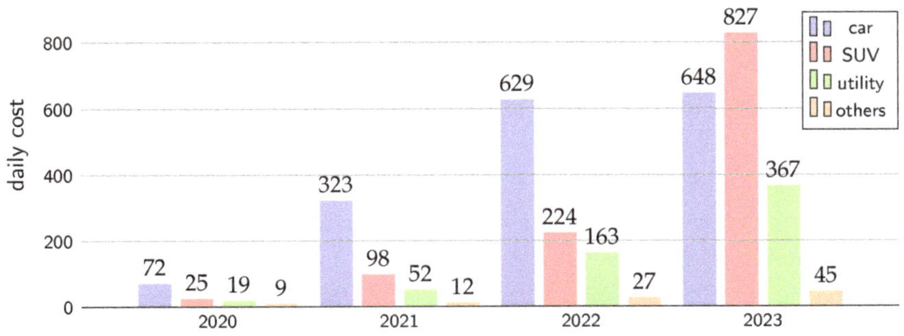

Figure 7. New electric vehicles sold in Uruguay by category, 2020 to 2023.

The growth of electric vehicles in Uruguay was higher than the increase in electric car sales worldwide, which averaged around 25% per year [114]. This trend is projected to continue from 2023 to 2030, indicating a sustained rise in the adoption of electric vehicles in Uruguay. Overall, in 2023 the number of electric cars was 3.2% of the total new car sales, which amounted to 58,367 new vehicles. Even though this number may seem relatively small, it represents a significant increase from previous years, where electric cars represented only 0.5% in 2020, 1.0% in 2021, and less than 2.0% in 2022. Table 2 reports the number of electric vehicles in Uruguay, the number of new vehicles sold each year, and the percentage increase compared to the previous year, covering the period from 2019 to 2023.

Table 2. Electric vehicles in Uruguay and new vehicles sold per year between 2019 and 2023.

Year	Electric Vehicles			
	Total	Increase	New	Increase
2019	140	-	160	-
2020	250	78.6%	300	87.5%
2021	~600	240.0%	697	132.3%
2022	~2000	333.0%	1044	49.8%
2023	+4000	>100.0%	1887	80.7%

Forecasts project that Uruguay will have around 82,000 electric vehicles in 2030. More optimistic projections suggest that the number of electric vehicles in circulation could reach 100,000 by 2030 [115]. This value would represent a significant share of the overall vehicle count in Uruguay, which is estimated to be between 450,000 and 500,000 units. The projected growth in the electric vehicle market of Uruguay aligns with global forecasts, which anticipate a 10–12% increase over the next four years [116].

Montevideo accounts for the highest demand for electric vehicles in Uruguay, representing 62% of the total market share. The ACAU concluded that "electric vehicles are establishing themselves in the market with great momentum, accompanying the global trend" [117]. According to studies by the United Nations Development Programme on the updated Nationally Determined Contributions, Chile, Colombia, Mexico, and Uruguay are the countries with the highest level of commitment to electric transportation in Latin America. These nations are leading the way in embracing and promoting electric mobility as part of their sustainable transport strategies. Uruguay has emerged as a frontrunner in electric car sales within the Latin American region. The country has been recognized for its notable achievements and advancements in promoting and selling electric vehicles, positioning Uruguay as a leader in the adoption of electric cars across Latin America [118].

In 2023, BYD sold the largest number of cars and SUVs. In cars, 72.7% of the vehicles sold (469 units) were produced by BYD. The best-selling model was BYD new e2 GS A/T (70 kW engine and 44.9 kWh battery) with 368 units sold, by far the most popular electric vehicle in the country. For SUVs, BYD sold 31.4% of the vehicles sold (260 units) in 2023, and the distance with competitors was not as large as in cars: 17.1% of the SUV sales (141 units) were from JAC and 16.8% (139 units) were from BMW. The best-selling model was BYD Yuan Plus EV480 GS A/T (150 kW engine and 60.5 kWh battery) with 226 units. Overall, BYD sold 951 units in 2023 (50.4%), far ahead of JAC with 219 (11.6%) and BMW with 148 (7.8%).

5.4.2. Environmental Impact

The environmental impact of electric vehicles in Uruguay has been analyzed in three scenarios, defined by Di Chiara et al. [119]:

- Reference scenario: assuming the trend of electric vehicles in 2021–2022.
- Energy efficiency scenario: assuming a positive result of existing energy efficiency policies in Uruguay for the promotion of electric vehicles, based on the government incentives described in Section 5.4.6.
- Sustainable development scenario: assuming a strong commitment towards reducing pollutant emissions to meet global climate goals in line with the Paris Agreement [116].

The environmental impact of electric vehicles is computed by applying the modeling for electromobility described by Di Chiara et al. [119] and the model for CO_2 avoided thanks to the use of electric vehicles developed by the MOVES project for Uruguay [120].

Electric vehicles do not emit CO_2 directly, but the emissions attributed to the electricity production used to charge the battery must be considered. In the case of Uruguay, the emissions associated with electricity generation are relatively low due to the highly clean electricity generation mix (more than 95% from renewable sources). A reference value for the emission factor for the electrical network is 13 tons of CO_2 per GWh [121]. It is also important to account for the CO_2 emissions associated with the extraction, transportation, manufacturing, and distribution of fossil fuels used in conventional vehicles. The reference values for CO_2 emissions are 0.21 kg/km for standard fuel-powered vehicles using either gasoline and gas oil, with an average performance of 12 to 14 km/L [122,123]. The estimation of the average distance traveled by private cars in Montevideo is 6370 km per year, based on data from the 2016 origin-destination survey for Montevideo [124]. Thus, an average medium-size electric vehicle for the Uruguayan market saves approximately 1.4 tons of CO_2 per year. The estimated overall reductions in CO_2 emissions with the use of electric cars (excluding motorcycles and buses) for the considered scenarios are as follows:

- Reference scenario: 8.479 tons of CO_2 in 2024 and 28.000 tons of CO_2 in 2030.
- Energy efficiency scenario: 8.479 tons of CO_2 in 2024 and 93.639 tons of CO_2 in 2030.
- Sustainable development scenario: 9.364 tons of CO_2 in 2024 and 219.383 tons of CO_2 in 2030.

According to the analysis by Tanco et al. [125], to fulfill the fundamental goal of achieving CO_2 neutrality by the year 2050, several milestones must be accomplished in Uruguay, including the following: all new passenger vehicles must be zero-emission by 2035, all new light-duty vehicles must be zero-emission by 2040, and new vehicles must also be zero-emission by 2045. This progression would result in more than half of the vehicles in Uruguay, including automobiles, SUVs, and utility and heavy-duty vehicles, being powered by non-fuel technologies by 2050. The reduction in emissions compared to 2021 is expected to begin from 2040, as older vehicles with low regulations will be gradually replaced by electric vehicles. The most favorable scenario (sustainable development scenario) predicts a CO_2-equivalent of 2065 kilotons in 2050, which is 42.9% lower than the reference scenario. In the current energy efficiency scenario, a CO_2-equivalent of 2540 kilotons is projected for the same year, representing a 29.8% reduction compared to the reference scenario. As part of the national strategy, Uruguay aims to achieve carbon neutrality by ensuring that the entire transportation sector emits only 1100 kilotons of CO_2-equivalent in 2050, taking into account the presence of CO_2-absorbing sources.

5.4.3. Range and Battery Life

The majority of the batteries used in electric vehicles in Uruguay use lithium-ion chemical combinations, which are widely available in the market. These combinations are the focus of extensive research and development, leading to significant improvements in battery performance. Lithium-ion batteries are known for their ability to provide high energy densities, making them a preferred choice for current electric vehicles.

According to the data provided by the Uruguayan Electricity Company UTE [126], the practicality and usability of electric private transportation in Montevideo is very high. The best-selling electric vehicle in the country, BYD model new e2 GS A/T, has a lithium battery of 44.9 kWh and an autonomy of 400 km. The second best, Changan E-STAR, has a lithium battery of 32.2 kWh and an autonomy of 300 km (New European Driving Cycle). The most sold SUV in the Uruguayan market, BYD Yuan Plus EV480 GS A/T, has a battery of 60.48 kWh and an autonomy of 300 to 400 km. The JAC e-S1 A/T has a battery of 30.2 kWh and an autonomy of 251 km. All other models currently sold in Uruguay use lithium or lithium-iron phosphate batteries and have an autonomy between 211 and 400 km. Considering that the estimated average distance traveled by private cars in Montevideo is 6370 km per year [124], i.e., less than 20 km per day, all electric vehicles in the market reach the required operating range for about a week, without the need to recharge in between.

Another important aspect related to sustainability is the reutilization and disposal of batteries. In this regard, there have been research initiatives for the reutilization of batteries used in electric vehicles in the country [127]. The Ministry of Industry, Energy, and Mining has allocated a portion of the Renewable Energy Innovation Fund to enhance its internal capabilities for better management of batteries and to encourage the adoption of technologies that promote reuse. This initiative aims to strengthen local capabilities to handle used batteries and foster the development of innovative technologies in this regard [128].

5.4.4. Charging Infrastructure and Support Services

The available charging infrastructure is crucial for the correct development of electric private transportation. It has been acknowledged that the primary barrier considered by users when it comes to adopting electric mobility is the availability of charging infrastructure [129]. Nearly half of the users surveyed take this concern into account [130]. This issue is closely related to the psychological barrier of the worry about running out of energy during a trip [131]. In this regard, UTE has deployed a network of charging stations in Montevideo, in other important cities in the country, and on the road network. As of December 2023, the charging infrastructure in Montevideo includes 25 locations with up to six charging connectors. Three standards are deployed: Mennekes type 2 (48 connectors), CCS2 (28 connectors), and CHAdeMO (2 connectors), for a total number of 78 charging connectors in the city, out of 288 in the country (also including 2 GB/T connectors). Regarding power, connectors with 7.7 KW, 22 kW, 43 kW, 50 kW, and 60 kW are available. The number of charging stations is deemed sufficient according to international standards, which suggest that there should be one charger available for every 10 vehicles.

At the end of 2018, the first public on-street charging station was inaugurated in collaboration between UTE and the Municipality of Montevideo (five chargers for electric taxis). In 2020, Uruguay had 66 electric charging points spread across the country, with a distance of 60 km between each point. The number of charging points increased to 115 in 2021 and to over 200 points in 2022. UTE has outlined its intentions to invest over USD 5 million for the expansion of the charging network in the country, in line with a national development plan for electric mobility [132]. An expansion plan will install 124 new charging points in the country, 100 of them for fast charging. The main goal of this initiative is to enhance the density of the electric charging infrastructure, aiming to establish a charging point every 50 km. This strategic approach aims to provide electric vehicle owners with greater autonomy and convenience while traveling within Uruguay.

Charging points in Montevideo operate in five charging modes:

- Slow: Conceived for emergency charging, using the standard electricity grid, alternate current, and a Schuko connector, with an associated power of 2.2 kW.
- Standard: Conceived for slow charging, using an Electric Vehicle Charging System, and alternate current, with an associated power of up to 7.4 kW. The estimated time for a full charge is between 5 and 8 h.
- Semi-fast: Conceived for moderate slow charging, using an Electric Vehicle Charging System, and alternate current, with an associated power of up to 22 kW. The estimated time for a full charge is between 1 and 3 h.
- Fast: Conceived for fast charging, using an Electric Vehicle Charging System, and alternate current, with an associated power of up to 43 kW. The estimated time for a full charge is one hour.
- Ultra fast: Conceived for moderate slow charging, using an Electric Vehicle Charging System, and direct current, with an associated power of up to 120 kW. The estimated time for a full charge is between 15 and 30 min.

Figure 8 presents the charging infrastructure for electric vehicles in Montevideo.

In 2020, Risso et al. [133] concluded that the charging infrastructure was adequate for the number of electric vehicles. However, it may not be sufficient to meet the anticipated demand in the near future based on the studied scenarios. Increasing the number of charging points was crucial to provide electric vehicle owners with convenient access to effectively meet their driving range needs. As a result of the expansion plan implemented between 2021 and 2023, the situation has improved. However, for certain growth scenarios, it will be necessary to further upgrade the infrastructure to accommodate mid- to long-term recharging requirements. Despite the substantial growth, the number of charging points in the country is still low (10% of the number of gas stations). This comparison highlights the need for further development and investment in charging infrastructure to bridge the gap and ensure sufficient coverage for electric vehicles across the country.

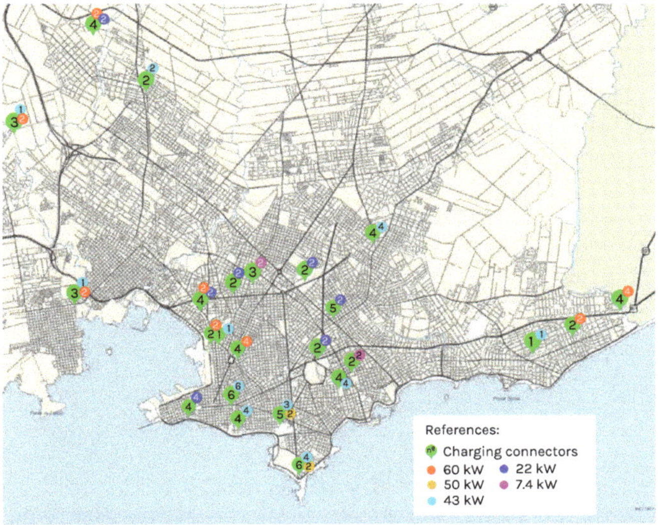

Figure 8. Charging infrastructure for electric vehicles in Montevideo (own design).

5.4.5. Economic Analysis

The average price of electric vehicles is USD 35,000 [113]. The BYD Seagull is the most affordable electric vehicle, with a price of USD 22,000. On the other end, BMW, Mercedes, and Tesla offer luxury electric vehicles for over USD 200,000. The best-seller BYD new e2 GS A/T costs USD 29,000. Prices decreased by 11.4% in 2023 compared to the previous year (USD 39,000), and the trend suggests that the value will continue to decline in the future.

Although the purchase cost of electric vehicles is higher than conventional vehicles in Uruguay (estimated average price of USD 29,000 [134]), the operating cost of electric vehicles is notably economical. Maintenance expenses are over three times cheaper than those for conventional vehicles. The maintenance of shock absorbers, tires, and brakes is similar, but other maintenance cost are significantly lower. Electric vehicles have fewer moving parts compared to conventional vehicles, primarily consisting of a motor with minimal components that operate continuously and smoothly. Thus, wear and tear are significantly reduced, and the stationary nature of batteries further contributes to their longevity.

The Director of Smart Projects in UTE, Eduardo Bergerie, commented that electric vehicles are more profitable in professional uses such as taxis [135]. For vehicles not used for business purposes, the estimated travel distance in Montevideo is between 6000 and 8000 km/year. For this short distance, an electric car is not the most cost-effective transportation mode, but it is preferred for a comfortable lifestyle, freedom of movement, and the inclination towards environmental consciousness, rather than as an economic decision.

The average expense for a charge to travel between 150 and 200 km is UYU 128 (USD 3.2), resulting in a cost of USD 0.18 per kilometer. The cost is even lower for users that install a charger at home and take advantage of multi-hour electricity tariffs provided by UTE, charging during the cheapest (valley) hours. The cost of domestic chargers in Uruguay ranges from USD 600 and the installation cost is approximately USD 1200 [136].

In terms of energy consumption, there is a notable disparity between electric vehicles and combustion vehicles, with a ratio of one to eight. This means that the distance traveled by a combustion car can be covered with only one-eighth of the energy consumed by an electric vehicle. The savings obtained from reduced operational costs quickly offset the higher initial investment required for purchasing an electric vehicle.

The reported numbers demonstrate the superiority of electric vehicles in terms of energy efficiency and overall cost-effectiveness, as they consume less energy per kilometer traveled compared to standard vehicles. Furthermore, the efficiency of electric vehicles can be further enhanced through advancements in battery technology and vehicle design.

5.4.6. Government Incentives and Policies

The government of Uruguay has been actively involved in promoting the electric mobility market through various measures and incentives:

- Uruguay has practically eliminated all taxes imposed on electric vehicles, with only the Value Added Tax remaining.
- Since 2011, electric vehicles have had a reduced Internal Specific Tax (IMESI) rate of 5.75% until 2021, and from then onward, it has been excempted (reduced to 0%). This substantial tax advantage contrasts with the tax rates imposed on combustion vehicles, which range from 23% to 46% for gasoline-powered vehicles.
- An additional tax benefit is the exclusion of the 23% import tariff (TGA).
- There is a reduction in the vehicle circulation fee. The value used for calculating the fee for electric vehicles excludes the Value Added Tax, and the applied percentage is reduced to half (2.5%) of the rate applied to combustion vehicles (5%).
- The government has introduced assistance programs aimed at promoting the use of electric vehicles in taxi, ride-hailing, and on-demand mobility services. These initiatives offer vehicle-specific discounts of up to USD 11,500.
- Decree 268/23 from the Executive Power has extended provisions that allow vehicles registered under the Investment Promotion Law to benefit from substantial tax reductions, encouraging the adoption of clean energy usage.

There is consistent adherence to the policy guidelines that various governments have been implementing for several years. In fact, since the inception of the initial incentive all the mechanisms aimed at promoting the adoption of electric vehicles have been preserved or enhanced, aligning with the environmental and energy objectives of Uruguay.

Other indirect initiatives and programs have been developed by the Uruguayan government to promote and foster electric private transportation:

- Support measures in the form of Energy Efficiency Certificates have been implemented since 2016. In 2022, the Vehicle Energy Efficiency Labeling Regulations were established, including significant advantages to the labeling system. Once the Ministry of Industry, Energy, and Mining establishes the regulations and the voluntary adoption period for vehicle importers concludes, prospective buyers of new vehicles will have access to an adhesive label displaying information such as fuel consumption per kilometer and CO_2 emissions, which are associated with the respective fuel types. For combustion vehicles, fuel consumption information will be indicated in km/L, while for electric and plug-in hybrid vehicles, consumption will be represented as km/kWh [137].
- From 2023 to 2025, private investors incorporating charging services are eligible for a 100% discount on the connection fee.
- The State Insurance Bank (Banco de Seguros del Estado, BSE) provides better insurance conditions and prices for electric vehicles in comparison to combustion vehicles.
- The government advanced on an ecosystem of capabilities for battery management.
- During the period between 2019 and 2022, the Subite Prueba initiative was developed. A one-month free trial of electric vehicles was offered to companies and institutions, who were encouraged to incorporate electric vehicles for urban cargo transportation and last-mile logistics. The vehicles were provided at no cost for a month-long trial period, allowing the beneficiaries to evaluate the benefits in their regular operations [138].

All the commented measures have contributed to promoting the integration of electric vehicles into the national vehicle fleet. The main efforts have been focused on two aspects. The first aspect is breaking down the cultural barriers and the distrust towards a new technology. The second is enabling the initial critical mass of vehicles, which creates the minimum viability conditions necessary for the development of an ecosystem encompassing workshops, technical services, insurance, spare parts, infrastructure, and other essential components. Without this ecosystem, the widespread adoption of electric mobility is not feasible [118].

6. Conclusions and Future Work

This article examined the recent progress made in implementing sustainable mobility initiatives in the public transportation of Montevideo, Uruguay. This study focused on the analysis of e-scooters, urban cycling, and electric public transportation. Important factors that contribute to the correct and sustainable development of the initiatives and the quality of service provided to commuters were assessed.

The main conclusion drawn from the analysis is that, despite the recent endeavors oriented to promote sustainable mobility in Montevideo, the developed initiatives have not consolidated yet. Specifically, the e-scooter business model encountered substantial challenges in Montevideo, mostly related to coverage, affordability, and safety, ultimately leading to the discontinuation of this service within the city. While there has been significant advancement in the establishment of urban cycling infrastructure between 2020 and 2023, it is important to acknowledge that the network in Montevideo still lags behind other capital cities in Latin America. Various challenges persist, including issues related to connectivity, the lack of intermodal connections, and maintenance conditions for bicycle lanes and paths. Although the operational efficiency of electric buses in Montevideo is commendable, only three electric bus lines have been implemented in the city. Furthermore, these electric bus lines predominantly serve the wealthier coastal neighborhoods, leaving a significant portion of the population without access to the benefits of electric public transportation.

Private electric transportation has developed steadily in the country, with an increasing number of vehicles and reasonable development of the ecosystem, including the charging infrastructure, services, and regulations. The anticipated environmental impacts are projected to be significant under different scenarios by 2030 and 2040. The Uruguayan government has developed a series of incentives and programs to promote electric public transportation, which have been positively received by the public. Nevertheless, there is a need to improve the infrastructure and guarantee the best conditions for the proper development of electric mobility in the near future. A comparison of the common factors analyzed for each sustainable mobility initiative is shown in Table 3.

Table 3. Comparison of common factors for each studied sustainable mobility initiative in Montevideo (references: ✓: good; ↗: rather good; ↘: rather bad; ✗: bad).

Factor	Initiative			
	E-Scooter	Bicycle	Electric Bus	Electric Vehicle
spatial distribution	✗	✓	✗	✓
safety	✗	✗	✗	↗
cost-effectiveness	✗	✓	✓	↘
environmental impact	↘	✓	✓	✓
infrastructure	✗	✗	↘	✓
comfort	✗	↘	✓	✓
accessibility	✗	✓	✗	✗
integration	✗	✗	✗	✗

The advancements made by Montevideo towards sustainable mobility are promising. However, it is crucial for both the city administration and the national government to demonstrate stronger commitment and collaboration to ensure the well-rounded and consistent development of integrated sustainable transportation solutions. The lack of an integrated Sustainable Urban Mobility Plan negatively affects the success of developing isolated, non-integrated initiatives.

The main focus for future work is on expanding this study to include other non-conventional sustainable transportation initiatives implemented in Montevideo. In this regard, that research effort should entail examining various initiatives involving private electric transportation, such as ride sharing and electric bicycles, shared electric cars, and electric cargo fleets, as well as exploring app-based electric mobility options. In order to gain a comprehensive understanding of the sustainable transportation panorama in Montevideo, it is important to analyze these additional aspects.

Author Contributions: Conceptualization, S.N.; methodology, S.N. and S.H.; software, S.N. and S.H.; validation, S.N. and S.H.; formal analysis, S.N.; investigation, S.N. and S.H.; resources, S.N. and S.H.; data curation, S.N. and S.H.; writing—original draft preparation, S.N. and S.H.; writing—review and editing, S.N. and S.H.; visualization, S.N. and S.H.; supervision, S.N.; project administration, S.N. All authors have read and agreed to the published version of the manuscript.

Funding: This research received no external funding.

Data Availability Statement: All relevant data is reported in the manuscript.

Conflicts of Interest: The authors declare no conflict of interest.

References

1. Marshall, S. The challenge of sustainable transport. In *Planning for a Sustainable Future*; Layard, A., Davoudi, S., Batty, S., Eds.; Spon: London, UK, 2001; pp. 131–147.
2. Gallo, M.; Marinelli, M. Sustainable Mobility: A Review of Possible Actions and Policies. *Sustainability* **2020**, *12*, 7499. [CrossRef]
3. Cirianni, F.; Leonardi, G.; Iannò, D. Operating and Integration of Services in Local Public Transport. In *Smart Innovation, Systems and Technologies*; Springer International Publishing: Cham, Switzerland, 2020; pp. 1523–1531. [CrossRef]
4. Hipogrosso, S.; Nesmachnow, S. Analysis of Sustainable Public Transportation and Mobility Recommendations for Montevideo and Parque Rodó Neighborhood. *Smart Cities* **2020**, *3*, 479–510. [CrossRef]
5. Intendencia de Montevideo. Plan de Movilidad. 2023. Available online: https://montevideo.gub.uy/sites/default/files/plan_de_movilidad.pdf (accessed on 12 March 2024).
6. Cirianni, F.; Leonardi, G. Analysis of transport modes in the urban environment: An application for a sustainable mobility system. In *The Sustainable City IV: Urban Regeneration and Sustainability*; WIT: Billerica, MA, USA, 2006. [CrossRef]
7. Robertson, M. *Sustainability Principles and Practice*; Routledge: Abingdon, UK, 2021.
8. Banister, D. The sustainable mobility paradigm. *Transp. Policy* **2008**, *15*, 73–80. [CrossRef]
9. Brinkmann, R. *Introduction to Sustainability*; Wiley-Blackwell: Hoboken, NJ, USA, 2021.
10. United Nations General Assembly. Report of the World Commission on Environment and Development: Our Common Future. 1987. Available online: http://www.un-documents.net/wced-ocf.htm (accessed on 1 August 2021).
11. United Nations General Assembly. Transforming Our World: The 2030 Agenda for Sustainable Development. 2015. Available online: https://sdgs.un.org/2030agenda (accessed on 1 May 2022).
12. Mavlutova, I.; Atstaja, D.; Grasis, J.; Kuzmina, J.; Uvarova, I.; Roga, D. Urban Transportation Concept and Sustainable Urban Mobility in Smart Cities: A Review. *Energies* **2023**, *16*, 3585. [CrossRef]
13. Müller-Eie, D.; Kosmidis, I. Sustainable mobility in smart cities: A document study of mobility initiatives of mid-sized Nordic smart cities. *Eur. Transp. Res. Rev.* **2023**, *15*, 36. [CrossRef]
14. United Nations. Report of the United Nations Conference on Housing and Sustainable Urban Development. 2016. Available online: https://www.un.org/sustainabledevelopment/cities/ (accessed on 1 August 2022).
15. Nundy, S.; Ghosh, A.; Mesloub, A.; Albaqawy, G.; Alnaim, M. Impact of COVID-19 pandemic on socio-economic, energy-environment and transport sector globally and sustainable development goal (SDG). *J. Clean. Prod.* **2021**, *312*, 127705. [CrossRef]
16. Johnston, R. Indicators for Sustainable Transportation Planning. *Transp. Res. Rec. J. Transp. Res. Board* **2008**, *2067*, 146–154. [CrossRef]
17. Ravagnan, C.; Rossi, F.; Amiriaref, M. Sustainable Mobility and Resilient Urban Spaces in the United Kingdom: Practices and Proposals. *Transp. Res. Procedia* **2022**, *60*, 164–171. [CrossRef]
18. Bielińska, E.; Hamerska, M.; Żak, A. Sustainable Mobility and the Smart City: A Vision of the City of the Future: The Case Study of Cracow (Poland). *Energies* **2021**, *14*, 7936. [CrossRef]
19. Miller, P.; de Barros, A.G.; Kattan, L.; Wirasinghe, S.C. Public transportation and sustainability: A review. *KSCE J. Civ. Eng.* **2016**, *20*, 1076–1083. [CrossRef]
20. Rodrigues, A.; Costa, M.; Macedo, M. Multiple views of sustainable urban mobility: The case of Brazil. *Transp. Policy* **2008**, *15*, 350–360.

21. Lyons, W. Sustainable transport in the developing world: A case study of Bogota's mobility strategy. In Proceedings of the International Conference on Sustainable Infrastructure 2017, New York, NY, USA, 26–28 October 2017.
22. Huertas, J.; Stöffler, S.; Fernández, T.; García, X.; Castañeda, R.; Serrano, O.; Mogro, A.; Alvarado, D. Methodology to Assess Sustainable Mobility in LATAM Cities. *Appl. Sci.* **2021**, *11*, 9592. [CrossRef]
23. Hipogrosso, S.; Nesmachnow, S. Towards a Sustainable Mobility Plan for Engineering Faculty, Universidad de la República, Uruguay. In *Smart Cities*; Springer International Publishing: Cham, Switzerland, 2021; pp. 199–215. [CrossRef]
24. Nesmachnow, S.; Hipogrosso, S. Transit oriented development analysis of Parque Rodó neighborhood, Montevideo, Uruguay. *World Dev. Sustain.* **2022**, *1*, 100017. [CrossRef]
25. Dittmar, H.; Poticha, S. Defining transit-oriented development: The new regional building block. In *The New Transit Town: Best Practices in Transit-Oriented Development*; Dittmar, H., Ohland, G., Eds.; Island Press: Washington, DC, USA, 2004.
26. Transportation Research Board. *Transit-Oriented Development in the United States: Experiences, Challenges, and Prospects*; National Acedemies Press: Washington, DC, USA, 2004. [CrossRef]
27. Massobrio, R.; Nesmachnow, S.; Gómez, E.; Sosa, F.; Hipogrosso, S. Public Transportation and Accessibility to Education Centers in Maldonado, Uruguay. In *Smart Cities*; Springer International Publishing: Cham, Switzerland, 2021; pp. 123–138. [CrossRef]
28. Massobrio, R.; Nesmachnow, S. Travel Time Estimation in Public Transportation Using Bus Location Data. In *Communications in Computer and Information Science*; Springer International Publishing: Cham, Switzerland, 2022; pp. 192–206. [CrossRef]
29. Smith, A. Electric Scooters Remain Prohibited in Toronto until Proper Regulations Developed. 2019. Available online: https://dailyhive.com/toronto/toronto-e-scooter-update-october (accessed on 23 September 2023).
30. National Association of City Transportation Officials. *Shared Micromobility in the U.S.: 2018*; National Association of City Transportation Officials: New York, NY, USA, 2018.
31. Kopplin, C.S.; Brand, B.M.; Reichenberger, Y. Consumer acceptance of shared e-scooters for urban and short-distance mobility. *Transp. Res. Part D Transp. Environ.* **2021**, *91*, 102680. [CrossRef]
32. Cao, Z.; Zhang, X.; Chua, K.; Yu, H.; Zhao, J. E-scooter sharing to serve short-distance transit trips: A Singapore case. *Transp. Res. Part A: Policy Pract.* **2021**, *147*, 177–196. [CrossRef]
33. Abouelela, M.; Al Haddad, C.; Antoniou, C. Are young users willing to shift from carsharing to scooter–sharing? *Transp. Res. Part D Transp. Environ.* **2021**, *95*, 102821. [CrossRef]
34. Reck, D.; Axhausen, K. Who uses shared micro-mobility services? Empirical evidence from Zurich, Switzerland. *Transp. Res. Part D Transp. Environ.* **2021**, *94*, 102803. [CrossRef]
35. San Francisco Municipal Transportation Agency. Powered Scooter Share Mid-Pilot Evaluation. 2019. Available online: https://www.sfmta.com/sites/default/files/reports-and-documents/2019/08/powered_scooter_share_mid-pilot_evaluation_final.pdf (accessed on 15 February 2024).
36. Nikiforiadis, A.; Paschalidis, E.; Stamatiadis, N.; Raptopoulou, A.; Kostareli, A.; Basbas, S. Analysis of attitudes and engagement of shared e-scooter users. *Transp. Res. Part D Transp. Environ.* **2021**, *94*, 102790. [CrossRef]
37. Sanders, R.; Branion, M.; Nelson, T. To scoot or not to scoot: Findings from a recent survey about the benefits and barriers of using E-scooters for riders and non-riders. *Transp. Res. Part A Policy Pract.* **2020**, *139*, 217–227. [CrossRef]
38. Wang, K.; Qian, X.; Fitch, D.T.; Lee, Y.; Malik, J.; Circella, G. What travel modes do shared e-scooters displace? A review of recent research findings. *Transp. Rev.* **2023**, *43*, 5–31. [CrossRef]
39. Zuniga, N.; Tec, M.; Scott, J.; Machemehl, R. Evaluation of e-scooters as transit last-mile solution. *Transp. Res. Part C Emerg. Technol.* **2022**, *139*, 103660. [CrossRef]
40. Castiglione, M.; Comi, A.; De Vincentis, R.; Dumitru, A.; Nigro, M. Delivering in Urban Areas: A Probabilistic-Behavioral Approach for Forecasting the Use of Electric Micromobility. *Sustainability* **2022**, *14*, 9075. [CrossRef]
41. Lazo, L. That Scooter Ride is Going to Cost You a Lot More. The Washington Post. 2019. Available online: https://www.washingtonpost.com/transportation/2019/10/18/that-scooter-ride-is-going-cost-you-lot-more/ (accessed on 23 September 2023).
42. Nikiforiadis, A.; Paschalidis, E.; Stamatiadis, N.; Paloka, N.; Tsekoura, E.; Basbas, S. E-scooters and other mode trip chaining: Preferences and attitudes of university students. *Transp. Res. Part A Policy Pract.* **2023**, *170*, 103636. [CrossRef]
43. Aman, J.J.C.; Zakhem, M.; Smith-Colin, J. Towards Equity in Micromobility: Spatial Analysis of Access to Bikes and Scooters amongst Disadvantaged Populations. *Sustainability* **2021**, *13*, 11856. [CrossRef]
44. Huo, J.; Yang, H.; Li, C.; Zheng, R.; Yang, L.; Wen, Y. Influence of the built environment on E-scooter sharing ridership: A tale of five cities. *J. Transp. Geogr.* **2021**, *93*, 103084. [CrossRef]
45. Hawa, L.; Cui, B.; Sun, L.; El-Geneidy, A. Scoot over: Determinants of shared electric scooter presence in Washington D.C. *Case Stud. Transp. Policy* **2021**, *9*, 418–430. [CrossRef]
46. Esztergár, D.; Tordai, D.; Lopez Lizarraga, J. Assessment of travel behavior related to e-scooters using a stated preference experiment. *Transp. Res. Part A Policy Pract.* **2022**, *166*, 389–405. [CrossRef]
47. Lo, D.; Mintrom, C.; Robinson, K.; Thomas, R. Shared micromobility: The influence of regulation on travel mode choice. *N. Z. Geogr.* **2020**, *76*, 135–146. . [CrossRef]
48. Smith, C.S.; Schwieterman, J. E-Scooter Scenarios: Evaluating the Potential Mobility Benefits of Shared Dockless Scooters in Chicago. Chaddick Institute Policy Series. 2018. Available online: https://trid.trb.org/View/1577726 (accessed on 23 September 2023).

49. Aman, J.; Smith, J.; Zhang, W. Listen to E-scooter riders: Mining rider satisfaction factors from app store reviews. *Transp. Res. Part D Transp. Environ.* **2021**, *95*, 102856. [CrossRef]
50. de Bortoli, A.; Christoforou, Z. Consequential LCA for territorial and multimodal transportation policies: Method and application to the free-floating e-scooter disruption in Paris. *J. Clean. Prod.* **2020**, *273*, 122898. [CrossRef]
51. Hollingsworth, J.; Copeland, B.; Johnson, J. Are e-scooters polluters? The environmental impacts of shared dockless electric scooters. *Environ. Res. Lett.* **2019**, *14*, 084031. [CrossRef]
52. Gebhardt, L.; Wolf, C.; Seiffert, R. "I'll Take the E-Scooter Instead of My Car"—The Potential of E-Scooters as a Substitute for Car Trips in Germany. *Sustainability* **2021**, *13*, 7361. [CrossRef]
53. Gebhardt, L.; Ehrenberger, S.; Wolf, C.; Cyganski, R. Can shared E-scooters reduce CO2 emissions by substituting car trips in Germany? *Transp. Res. Part D Transp. Environ.* **2022**, *109*, 103328. [CrossRef]
54. Baek, K.; Lee, H.; Chung, J.H.; Kim, J. Electric scooter sharing: How do people value it as a last-mile transportation mode? *Transp. Res. Part D Transp. Environ.* **2021**, *90*, 102642. [CrossRef]
55. Oviedo, D.; Sabogal-Cardona, O. Arguments for cycling as a mechanism for sustainable modal shifts in Bogotá. *J. Transp. Geogr.* **2022**, *99*, 103291. [CrossRef]
56. Zhao, C.; Nielsen, T.A.S.; Olafsson, A.S.; Carstensen, T.A.; Fertner, C. Cycling environmental perception in Beijing—A study of residents' attitudes towards future cycling and car purchasing. *Transp. Policy* **2018**, *66*, 96–106. [CrossRef]
57. Pucher, J.; Buehler, R. Cycling towards a more sustainable transport future. *Transp. Rev.* **2017**, *37*, 689–694. [CrossRef]
58. Karanikola, P.; Panagopoulos, T.; Tampakis, S.; Tsantopoulos, G. Cycling as a Smart and Green Mode of Transport in Small Touristic Cities. *Sustainability* **2018**, *10*, 268. [CrossRef]
59. Castañon, U.N.; Ribeiro, P.J.G. Bikeability and Emerging Phenomena in Cycling: Exploratory Analysis and Review. *Sustainability* **2021**, *13*, 2394. [CrossRef]
60. Candio, P.; Frew, E. How much behaviour change is required for the investment in cycling infrastructure to be sustainable? A break-even analysis. *PLoS ONE* **2023**, *18*, e0284634. [CrossRef]
61. Beck, B.; Perkins, M.; Olivier, J.; Chong, D.; Johnson, M. Subjective experiences of bicyclists being passed by motor vehicles: The relationship to motor vehicle passing distance. *Accid. Anal. Prev.* **2021**, *155*, 106102. [CrossRef] [PubMed]
62. van Lierop, D.; Soemers, J.; Hoeke, L.; Liu, G.; Chen, Z.; Ettema, D.; Kruijf, J. Wayfinding for cycle highways: Assessing e-bike users' experiences with wayfinding along a cycle highway in the Netherlands. *J. Transp. Geogr.* **2020**, *88*, 102827. [CrossRef]
63. Sanders, R. Perceived traffic risk for cyclists: The impact of near miss and collision experiences. *Accid. Anal. Prev.* **2015**, *75*, 26–34. [CrossRef] [PubMed]
64. Wysling, L.; Purves, R.S. Where to improve cycling infrastructure? Assessing bicycle suitability and bikeability with open data in the city of Paris. *Transp. Res. Interdiscip. Perspect.* **2022**, *15*, 100648. [CrossRef]
65. Liu, C.; Tapani, A.; Kristoffersson, I.; Rydergren, C.; Jonsson, D. Appraisal of cycling infrastructure investments using a transport model with focus on cycling. *Case Stud. Transp. Policy* **2021**, *9*, 125–136. [CrossRef]
66. Fonseca, F.; Ribeiro, P.; Neiva, C. A Planning Practice Method to Assess the Potential for Cycling and to Design a Bicycle Network in a Starter Cycling City in Portugal. *Sustainability* **2023**, *15*, 4534. [CrossRef]
67. Zuo, T.; Wei, H.; Chen, N.; Zhang, C. First-and-last mile solution via bicycling to improving transit accessibility and advancing transportation equity. *Cities* **2020**, *99*, 102614. [CrossRef]
68. Fishman, E.; Allan, V., Bike share. In *Advances in Transport Policy and Planning;* Elsevier: Amsterdam, The Netherlands, 2019; pp. 121–152. [CrossRef]
69. Conti, V.; Orchi, S.; Valentini, M.P.; Nigro, M.; Calò, R. Design and evaluation of electric solutions for public transport. *Transp. Res. Procedia* **2017**, *27*, 117–124. [CrossRef]
70. Mutavdžija, M.; Kovačić, M.; Buntak, K. Assessment of Selected Factors Influencing the Purchase of Electric Vehicles—A Case Study of the Republic of Croatia. *Energies* **2022**, *15*, 5987. [CrossRef]
71. Manzolli, J.; Trovão, J.; Antunes, C. A review of electric bus vehicles research topics—Methods and trends. *Renew. Sustain. Energy Rev.* **2022**, *159*, 112211. [CrossRef]
72. Sunitiyoso, Y.; Belgiawan, P.F.; Rizki, M.; Hasyimi, V. Public acceptance and the environmental impact of electric bus services. *Transp. Res. Part D Transp. Environ.* **2022**, *109*, 103358. [CrossRef]
73. Borén, S. Electric buses' sustainability effects, noise, energy use, and costs. *Int. J. Sustain. Transp.* **2019**, *14*, 956–971. [CrossRef]
74. Sánchez, J.T.; del Río, J.A.; Sánchez, A. Economic feasibility analysis for an electric public transportation system: Two cases of study in medium sized cities in Mexico. *PLoS ONE* **2022**, *17*, e0272363. [CrossRef] [PubMed]
75. Doulgeris, S.; Zafeiriadis, A.; Athanasopoulos, N.; Tzivelou, N.; Michali, M.; Papagianni, S.; Samaras, Z. Evaluation of energy consumption and electric range of battery electric busses for application to public transportation. *Transp. Eng.* **2024**, *15*, 100223. [CrossRef]
76. Cazuza, J.; Dias, T.; Nunes, M. Operational Performance Analysis of the Public Transport System over Time. *Infrastructures* **2023**, *8*, 82. [CrossRef]
77. Guo, Y.; Chen, Z.; Stuart, A.; Li, X.; Zhang, Y. A systematic overview of transportation equity in terms of accessibility, traffic emissions, and safety outcomes: From conventional to emerging technologies. *Transp. Res. Interdiscip. Perspect.* **2020**, *4*, 100091. [CrossRef]

78. Wang, N.; Pei, Y.; Wang, Y.J. Antecedents in Determining Users' Acceptance of Electric Shuttle Bus Services. *Mathematics* **2022**, *10*, 2896. [CrossRef]
79. Mouratidis, K.; Cobeña Serrano, V. Autonomous buses: Intentions to use, passenger experiences, and suggestions for improvement. *Transp. Res. Part F Traffic Psychol. Behav.* **2021**, *76*, 321–335. [CrossRef]
80. Kwon, Y.; Kim, S.; Kim, H.; Byun, J. What Attributes Do Passengers Value in Electrified Buses? *Energies* **2020**, *13*, 2646. [CrossRef]
81. Das, P.; Bhat, M.; Sajith, S. Life cycle assessment of electric vehicles: A systematic review of literature. *Environ. Sci. Pollut. Res.* **2023**, *31*, 73–89. [CrossRef]
82. Vilaça, M.; Santos, G.; Oliveira, M.; Coelho, M.; Correia, G. Life cycle assessment of shared and private use of automated and electric vehicles on interurban mobility. *Appl. Energy* **2022**, *310*, 118589. [CrossRef]
83. Alanazi, F. Electric Vehicles: Benefits, Challenges, and Potential Solutions for Widespread Adaptation. *Appl. Sci.* **2023**, *13*, 6016. [CrossRef]
84. Liu, X.; Zhao, F.; Geng, J.; Hao, H.; Liu, Z. Comprehensive assessment for different ranges of battery electric vehicles: Is it necessary to develop an ultra-long range battery electric vehicle? *iScience* **2023**, *26*, 106654. [CrossRef] [PubMed]
85. Patt, A.; Aplyn, D.; Weyrich, P.; van Vliet, O. Availability of private charging infrastructure influences readiness to buy electric cars. *Transp. Res. Part A Policy Pract.* **2019**, *125*, 1–7. [CrossRef]
86. Carlsson, F.; Johansson-Stenman, O. Costs and Benefits of Electric Vehicles: A 2010 Perspective. *J. Transp. Econ. Policy* **2010**, *37*, 1–28.
87. Lavee, D.; Parsha, A. Cost-benefit analyses of policy tools to encourage the use of Plug-in electric vehicles. *Transp. Res. Interdiscip. Perspect.* **2021**, *11*, 100404. [CrossRef]
88. Wappelhorst, S.; Hall, D.; Nicholas, M.; Lutsey, N. Analyzing Policies to Grow the Electric Vehicle Market in European Cities. International Council on Clean Transportation. 2020. Available online: https://theicct.org/sites/default/files/publications/EV_city_policies_white_paper_fv_20200224.pdf (accessed on 12 March 2024).
89. Åhman, M. Government policy and the development of electric vehicles in Japan. *Energy Policy* **2006**, *34*, 433–443. [CrossRef]
90. Massobrio, R.; Nesmachnow, S. Urban Mobility Data Analysis for Public Transportation Systems: A Case Study in Montevideo, Uruguay. *Appl. Sci.* **2020**, *10*, 5400. [CrossRef]
91. Nesmachnow, S.; Iturriaga, S. Cluster-UY: Collaborative Scientific High Performance Computing in Uruguay. In *Supercomputing*; Torres, M., Klapp, J., Eds.; Communications in Computer and Information Science; Springer: Cham, Switzerland, 2019; Volume 1151, pp. 188–202. [CrossRef]
92. Llambí, C.; Piñeyro, L. Índice de Nivel Socioeconómico, 2012: CINVE. Available online: https://cinve.org.uy/wp-content/uploads/2012/12/Indice-de-nivel-socioecon%C3%B3mico.pdf (accessed on 15 February 2024).
93. Perera, M.; Cazulo, P. Índice de Nivel Socioeconómico: Propuesta de Actualización, 2016: CINVE. Available online: https://portal.factum.uy/pdf/INSE_informe_2018.pdf (accessed on 15 February 2024).
94. Perera, M. Índice de Nivel Socioeconómico. 2018. Available online: http://www.ceismu.org/site/indice-de-nivel-socioeconomico-inse-2018/ (accessed on 12 August 2023).
95. El Observador. Bicicletas en Montevideo: "El Último Orejon Del Tarro" Que Gana Lugar Entre Contradicciones. Available online: https://www.elobservador.com.uy/nota/bicicletas-en-montevideo-el-ultimo-orejon-del-tarro-que-gana-lugar-entre-contradicciones-20227105107 (accessed on 16 March 2024).
96. Observatorio de Movilidad, Intendencia de Montevideo. Indicador INEX0103. Longitud de Ciclovías, Bicisendas y Zona 30. 2019. Available online: https://montevideo.gub.uy/sites/default/files/biblioteca/longitudcicloviasbicisendasyzona30_0.pdf (accessed on 24 September 2023).
97. Teschke, K.; Harris, M.; Reynolds, C.; Winters, M.; Babul, S.; Chipman, M.; Cusimano, M.; Brubacher, J.; Hunte, G.; Friedman, S.; et al. Route Infrastructure and the Risk of Injuries to Bicyclists: A Case-Crossover Study. *Am. J. Public Health* **2012**, *102*, 2336–2343. [CrossRef]
98. Cicchino, J.; McCarthy, M.; Newgard, C.; Wall, S.; DiMaggio, C.; Kulie, P.; Arnold, B.; Zuby, D. Not all protected bike lanes are the same: Infrastructure and risk of cyclist collisions and falls leading to emergency department visits in three U.S. cities. *Accid. Anal. Prev.* **2020**, *141*, 105490. [CrossRef]
99. El Observador. IMM Busca Retomar el Sistema de Bicicletas Publicas Que Dejo de Funcionar en 2019. 2021. Available online: https://www.elobservador.com.uy/nota/imm-busca-retomar-el-sistema-de-bicicletas-publicas-que-dejo-de-funcionar-en-2019-202192011340 (accessed on 24 September 2023).
100. Calone, D. Montevideo, Una Ciudad Poco Amigable Con Los Ciclistas. Available online: https://efe.com/deportes/2023-03-25/montevideo-una-ciudad-poco-amigable-con-los-ciclistas/ (accessed on 3 March 2024).
101. Nesmachnow, S.; Tchernykh, A. The Impact of the COVID-19 Pandemic on the Public Transportation System of Montevideo, Uruguay: A Urban Data Analysis Approach. *Urban Sci.* **2023**, *7*, 113. [CrossRef]
102. Krawiec, K.; Markusik, S.; Sierpiński, G. (Eds.) *Electric Mobility in Public Transport–Driving Towards Cleaner Air*; Springer International: Cham, Germany, 2021. [CrossRef]
103. Ardanche, M.; Bianco, M.; Cohanoff, C.; Contreras, S.; Goñi, M.; Simón, L.; Sutz, J. The power of wind: An analysis of a Uruguayan dialogue regarding an energy policy. *Sci. Public Policy* **2017**, *45*, 351–360. [CrossRef]

104. Comisión Técnica del Subsidio a la Compra de Ómnibus Eléctricos. Operación de Ómnibus Eléctricos Adquiridos a Través del Subsidio a la Compra Definido en el Art. 349 de la Ley 19.670. 2021. Available online: https://www.gub.uy/ministerio-industria-energia-mineria/sites/ministerio-industria-energia-mineria/files/documentos/noticias/Primer%20Informe%20anual%20buses%20el%C3%A9ctricos_2110.pdf (accessed on 23 September 2023).
105. Transporte Carretero. Informe Nueva Movilidad: U.C.O.T. 2021. Available online: https://www.transportecarretero.com.uy/noticias/energias-alternativas/informe/-nueva-movilidad-u-c-o-t-enrique-garabato-gerencia-de-talleres-aun-no-sustituyen/-al-omnibus-convencional-para-eso-se-necesitaria-un-30-mas-de-autonomia.html (accessed on 13 September 2023).
106. Portal Movilidad. Espera al Gobierno Nacional: Montevideo Contaría con Fondo Para Buses Eléctricos a Mitad de 2023. 2022. Available online: https://portalmovilidad.com/espera-al-gobierno-nacional-montevideo-contaria-con-fondo-para-buses-electricos/-a-mitad-de-2023/ (accessed on 12 August 2023).
107. Ámbito. El Parque de Buses. Available online: https://www.ambito.com/uruguay/el-parque-buses-electricos-aumento-al-35-n5681005 (accessed on 12 August 2023).
108. Zochowska, R.; Klos, M.J.; Soczówka, P.; Pilch, M. Assessment of Accessibility of Public Transport by Using Temporal and Spatial Analysis. *Sustainability* **2022**, *14*, 16127. [CrossRef]
109. Würtz, S.; Bogenberger, K.; Göhner, U.; Rupp, A. Towards Efficient Battery Electric Bus Operations: A Novel Energy Forecasting Framework. *World Electr. Veh. J.* **2024**, *15*, 27. [CrossRef]
110. Sustainable Bus. Electric Bus Range, Focus on Electricity Consumption. A Sum-Up. 2022. Available online: https://www.sustainable-bus.com/news/electric-bus-range-electricity-consumption/ (accessed on 12 August 2023).
111. Deloitte. Autos Eléctricos en Uruguay. Available online: https://www2.deloitte.com/uy/es/pages/manufacturing/articles/autos-electricos-industria-manufactura.html (accessed on 15 March 2024).
112. MIEM. Parque Automotor. Available online: https://www.gub.uy/ministerio-industria-energia-mineria/datos-y-estadisticas/estadisticas/parque-automotor (accessed on 15 March 2024).
113. ACAU. Sales Statistics of the Automotive Market. 2023. Available online: https://www.acau.com.uy/ (accessed on 1 March 2024).
114. EVs to Surpass Two-Thirds of Global Car Sales by 2030, Putting at Risk Nearly Half of Oil Demand, New Research Finds. Available online: https://rmi.org/press-release/evs-to-surpass-two-thirds-of-global-car-sales-by-2030-putting-at-risk-nearly-half-of-oil-demand-new-research-finds/ (accessed on 1 March 2024).
115. El Día. Circularán 100.000-Autos Electricos en 2030. Available online: https://eldia.uy/circularan-100-000-autos-electricos-en-2030/ (accessed on 12 March 2024).
116. International Energy Agency. Global EV Outlook 2023. 2023. Available online: https://www.iea.org/reports/global-ev-outlook-2023 (accessed on 8 March 2024).
117. Ámbito. Se Dispararon un 80.92% las Ventas de Vehículos Eléctricos en 2023. Available online: https://www.ambito.com/uruguay/se-dispararon-un-8092-las-ventas-vehiculos-electricos-2023-n5932476 (accessed on 15 March 2024).
118. Ámbito. Uruguay Lidera Las Ventas de Autos Eléctricos-en America Latina. 2023. Available online: https://www.ambito.com/uruguay/lidera-las-ventas-autos-electricos-america-latina-n5934595 (accessed on 15 March 2024).
119. Di Chiara, L.; Ferres, F.; Bastarrica, F. Impact of electromobility deployment scenarios in the power system of Uruguay by 2028. In Proceedings of the 2021 IEEE URUCON, Montevideo, Uruguay, 24–26 November 2021. [CrossRef]
120. Proyecto MOVES. ¿Cómo Calculamos el CO2 Evitado Gracias al Uso de Vehículos Eléctricos? 2023. Available online: https://moves.gub.uy/faq-items/como-calculamos-el-co2-evitado-gracias-al-uso-de-vehiculos-electricos (accessed on 12 March 2024).
121. MIEM. National Energy Balance. CO_2 Emission Factor. 2023. Available online: https://ben.miem.gub.uy/indicadores5.php (accessed on 12 March 2024).
122. IMM. Movility Observatory of Montevideo. Emissions of Pollutants by Type of Motorized Vehicle. Indicator INEX0401. 2023. Available online: https://montevideo.gub.uy/sites/default/files/biblioteca/emisionesdecontaminantesportipodevehiculomotorizadoo_1.pdf (accessed on 12 March 2024).
123. IMM. Movility Observatory of Montevideo. Emissions of Pollutants by Type of Motorized Vehicle. Indicator INEX0402. 2023. Available online: https://montevideo.gub.uy/sites/default/files/biblioteca/consumodeenergiaportipodevehiculoycombustible.pdf (accessed on 12 March 2024).
124. Mauttone, A.; Hernández, D. Encuesta de Movilidad Del área Metropolitana de Montevideo. Principales Resultados e Indicadores. 2017. Available online: http://scioteca.caf.com/handle/123456789/1078 (accessed on 20 August 2019).
125. Tanco, M.; Cavallieri, M.; Levy, M.; Rossi, S.; Jurburg, D. Impact of electric trucks in GHG inventory—A Uruguayan scenario study. *Transp. Res. Part D Transp. Environ.* **2023**, *117*, 103614. [CrossRef]
126. UTE. Vehículos Eléctricos. Available online: https://movilidad.ute.com.uy/vehiculos.html (accessed on 1 March 2024).
127. Bustillo, M.; Calvello, F.; Pérez, J. Estudio de Reutilización de Baterías de Vehículos Eléctricos. Engineering Faculty, Universidad de la República. 2023. Available online: https://hdl.handle.net/20.500.12008/3301 (accessed on 15 March 2024).
128. Mobility Portal Latinoamérica. Segunda Vida de Baterías de Vehículos Eléctricos: Ambiente Solicita Mayor Presupuesto Para Avanzar. 2023. Available online: https://mobilityportal.lat/segunda-vida-de-baterias-de-vehiculos-electricos-ambiente-solicita-mayor-presupuesto-para-avanzar (accessed on 12 March 2024).
129. Madina, C.; Zamora, I.; Zabala, E. Methodology for assessing electric vehicle charging infrastructure business models. *Energy Policy* **2016**, *89*, 284–293. [CrossRef]

130. United Kingdom Department For Transport. Annual Report and Accounts 2016/2017. 2017. Available online: https://www.gov.uk/government/publications/annual-report-and-accounts-2016-17 (accessed on 15 February 2024).
131. Kumar, R.; Chakraborty, A.; Mandal, P. Promoting electric vehicle adoption: Who should invest in charging infrastructure? *Transp. Res. Part E Logist. Transp. Rev.* **2021**, *149*, 102295. [CrossRef]
132. Uruguay Presidencia. UTE Invertirá Más de 5 Millones de Dólares en Nuevos Puntos de Carga Para Vehículos Eléctricos. 2023. Available online: https://www.gub.uy/presidencia/comunicacion/noticias/ute-invertira-5-millones-dolares-nuevos-puntos-carga-para-vehiculos (accessed on 15 March 2024).
133. Risso, C.; Vignolo, M.; Carriquiry, J.; Arismendi, F. An evaluation of the actual electric vehicles charging infrastructure in Uruguay and possible designing approaches. In Proceedings of the 2020 IEEE PES Transmission & Distribution Conference and Exhibition—Latin America (T&D LA), Montevideo, Uruguay, 28 September–2 October 2020. [CrossRef]
134. Autoblog. Precios Vigentes de Automóviles, SUVs, Utilitarios Livianos y Minibuses 0 km. 2024. Available online: https://www.autoblog.com.uy/p/precios-0km.html (accessed on 15 March 2024).
135. MIEM. Autos Eléctricos Son Más Rentables en Usos Profesionales Como el Taxi. 2023. Available online: https://www.eficienciaenergetica.gub.uy/ (accessed on 12 March 2024).
136. El Observador. Cuánto Cuesta Tener un Auto Electrico un Experto lo Responde. 2023. Available online: https://www.elobservador.com.uy/nota/cuanto-cuesta-tener-un-auto-electrico-un-experto-lo-responde-202310235034 (accessed on 15 March 2024).
137. Proyecto MOVES. Normativa de Etiquetado Vehicular. 2023. Available online: https://moves.gub.uy/iniciativa/normativa-de-etiquetado-vehicular/ (accessed on 12 March 2024).
138. MIEM. Subite Prueba: Beneficio Para Empresas e Instituciones Públicas o Privadas que Alquilen Vehículos Eléctricos. 2023. Available online: https://www.gub.uy/ministerio-industria-energia-mineria/comunicacion/convocatorias/subite-prueba-beneficio-para-empresas-instituciones-publicas-privadas (accessed on 12 March 2024).

urban science

Article

The Impact of the COVID-19 Pandemic on the Public Transportation System of Montevideo, Uruguay: A Urban Data Analysis Approach †

Sergio Nesmachnow [1,*] and Andrei Tchernykh [2]

[1] Facultad de Ingeníeria, Herrera y Reissig 565, Montevideo 11300, Uruguay
[2] CICESE Research Center, Ensenada 22860, Baja California, Mexico; chernykh@cicese.mx
* Correspondence: sergion@fing.edu.uy
† V Iberoamerican Congress on Smart Cities, ICSC-CITIES 2022.

Abstract: Urban mobility and strategies for public transportation play a vital role in promoting a more sustainable, accessible, and livable urban environment in smart cities. Data-driven decision making, multi-modal integration, and innovative means are key elements in developing effective public transportation. The COVID-19 pandemic had a significant impact on public transportation worldwide, including decreased travel, health and security concerns, and a shift in travel patterns. In particular, the use of public transportation reduced by up to 90% in developed countries. This article studies the mobility demands and patterns related to public transportation in Montevideo, Uruguay, amidst the COVID-19 pandemic. The study follows an urban data analysis approach, using open data from various sources, including citizen mobility, the public transportation system, COVID-19 case records, and economic indicators. The urban data methodology allows the deriving of significant findings, encompassing the assessment of trip reductions in Montevideo in March 2020 (71.4%, lower than similar cities in the world), the correlation between trip numbers and COVID-19 cases during the different pandemic waves, the recovery of public transportation usage, and the correlation with socio-economic indicators. These results offer valuable insights for quantifying and comprehending the behavior of citizens concerning public transportation throughout the COVID-19 pandemic, providing valuable understandings for policymakers and researchers to elaborate mobility strategies and policies.

Keywords: public transportation; COVID-19 pandemic; urban data analysis; mobility patterns; socio-economic analysis

1. Introduction

Urban transportation, i.e., the act of moving something (goods) or someone (people), and urban mobility, i.e., the ability of a person to freely move or be moved, constitute integral elements of the functional dimension of cities nowadays. Alongside other significant factors such as land use and urban planning, urban mobility plays a crucial role in shaping how citizens carry out their daily activities [1].

The advent of data-driven approaches fostered an enhanced paradigm referred to as Intelligent Transportation Systems (ITS). Data-driven approaches refer to methodologies and techniques that rely on the analysis and utilization of large volumes of data to derive insights, make informed decisions, and develop solutions for intelligent mobility. ITS leverage the power of data to uncover patterns, trends, and correlations, enabling administrators, organizations, and individuals to gain valuable insights and improve their decision-making processes. ITS encompasses advanced systems that integrate synergistic technologies to offer services to traffic operators and citizens. The primary objective of ITS is to develop coordinated and integrated mobility solutions that are smarter, safer, more efficient, and provide an enhanced user experience [2].

Urban mobility data play a crucial role in understanding mobility patterns, identifying anomalies and unusual movement behaviors, and conducting simulations of various realistic scenarios to assess the efficiency and quality of different means of transportation. The availability of real and synthesized mobility data has facilitated relevant studies in different domains: to enhance public transportation network designs, develop sustainable mobility initiatives, analyze and enhance the quality of service and user experience, identify stress conditions, predict traffic congestion, analyze public and private vehicle speeds, detect specific incidents, and assist in traffic engineering and traffic operation tasks [3–5]. By leveraging urban mobility data, researchers and practitioners can gain insights into the dynamics of transportation systems, optimize infrastructure and services, and improve the overall efficiency and effectiveness of urban mobility. The combination of real and synthesized mobility data offers a valuable resource for conducting comprehensive analyses and simulations, leading to more informed decision-making and better urban transportation management.

The COVID-19 pandemic had a profound impact on mobility worldwide, with significant disruptions observed across all modes of transportation. However, the impact was particularly prominent on public transportation systems. Among the most important consequences, the pandemic led to decreased ridership, significant operational changes, financial challenges, and an overall shift in travel patterns. All these issues hindered the primary objective of collective transportation (to provide accessible mobility to the public), since the efficiency of public transportation systems relies on the ability to transport large numbers of people and achieve economies of scale. The negative effects of the COVID-19 pandemic prompted a reevaluation of safety measures and future planning to ensure the continued provision of reliable and safe public transportation services.

Despite the implementation of various sanitary measures by governments and local administrations, the COVID-19 pandemic led to a substantial reduction in the number of trips taken on public transportation. This decline can be attributed primarily to the perception among citizens of a high risk of contagion when sharing a mode of transportation with others [6]. The decline in the number of trips on public transportation was significant, with reductions exceeding 90%, particularly in countries that implemented comprehensive lockdowns as a countermeasure. Despite the decrease in contagion levels in several countries, the recovery of public transportation ridership was not complete, i.e., a considerable number of passengers have opted for other means of transportation [7–9].

The analysis of urban mobility data plays a vital role in assisting public administrations and policymakers in enhancing public transportation systems [10]. Particularly during the COVID-19 pandemic, data analysis became even more critical as a tool for studying and understanding mobility patterns. Through a comprehensive analysis using relevant indicators, authorities were able to identify individuals who were compelled to travel despite sanitary measures, gain insights into their behavior, and appropriately size the public transport system to cater to their needs in such unique circumstances.

Following this line of research, this article contributes to the existing body of research by conducting a study that examines the demand and characterizes the mobility patterns of passengers of the public transportation system in Montevideo, Uruguay, during the COVID-19 pandemic. The study employs an urban data analysis approach to process and analyze openly available data pertaining to trips taken in the public transportation system of Montevideo. Furthermore, the study establishes correlations between the number of trips and COVID-19 statistics in the country. In addition to these datasets, other sources of data, such as geographical resources, socioeconomic information, and accessibility data, are also used to analyze several dimensions of the use of the public transportation system.

This article extends the previous conference article "Analysis of public transportation in Montevideo, Uruguay during the COVID-19 pandemic", presented in the V Ibero-American Conference on Smart Cities, Cuenca, Ecuador, 2022 [11]. The new content in this article includes: (i) an extended description of the methodology and the case study, including the description of the processing approach and its implementation; (ii) an evaluation of the performance of the developed computational tool; (iii) an expanded analysis of the mobility patterns for the case study during the COVID-19 pandemic, including the analysis of correlations in five different periods; and (iv) new studies to determine the correlation of mobility patterns with socio-economic information and accessibility characterization for neighborhoods of Montevideo.

The article is structured in the following manner. Section 2 introduces the problem of characterizing the public transportation usage during the COVID-19 pandemic and reviews related works. Section 3 describes the case study, the public transportation system in Montevideo, Uruguay, and the methodology and computational tools developed for the data analysis. The analysis of results obtained applying the proposed methodology is reported in Section 4. Section 5 presents the conclusions and formulates the main lines for future work.

2. Characterization of Public Transportation Usage during the COVID-19 Pandemic

This section focuses on describing the problem at hand and reviewing pertinent related works.

2.1. Description of the Problem

The addressed problem involves performing a characterization of the utilization of public transportation during the COVID-19 pandemic, specifically in a case study in Montevideo, Uruguay. The primary objective is to conduct a quantitative assessment of the reductions in public transportation usage following the declaration of the national sanitary emergency on 14 March 2020. Additionally, the study aims to characterize the mobility patterns of citizens using public transportation during different stages and waves of the pandemic, and understand how citizens resumed using public transportation as the sanitary conditions continually improved. Other relevant points of view are considered to characterize mobility patterns, taking into account different demographic groups, socio-economic information, and accessibility characterization for neighborhoods of Montevideo. The problem under investigation holds significant relevance, primarily due to two distinctive aspects of the case study conducted in Montevideo, Uruguay. These aspects are further elaborated upon in the subsequent paragraphs.

The first distinctive aspect is that in Montevideo, there exists a natural inclination among citizens to transition towards public transportation and other sustainable modes of transportation [12,13]. However, during the COVID-19 pandemic, this inclination experienced a significant reversal as citizens chose to rely on automobiles and other private transportation means for their commuting needs. This shift was driven by concerns regarding the perceived or suspected risk of contracting the virus through shared transportation, given the difficulty of maintaining the recommended social distance. Such a shift imply adverse implications for both sustainability and accessibility [7], leading to setbacks in sustainable mobility and exacerbating issues of equity and social exclusion. This phenomenon is not unprecedented, as safety considerations have long played a crucial role in shaping and influencing the mobility behavior of individuals [14].

The second interesting aspect of the problem and the addressed case study is that the approach taken by the Uruguayan government in managing the COVID-19 pandemic diverged from that of other countries. Instead of implementing strict lockdown measures, Uruguay adopted a model known as 'responsible freedom' or 'libertad responsable' in Spanish. Under this model, voluntary quarantine was encouraged, but people were not mandated to stay at home and mobility was not limited. The government implemented a meticulous tracking system for infected individuals, along with random COVID-19 testing. Measures such as promoting the use of face masks, public awareness campaigns emphasizing social distancing and social responsibility, and a reasonable reduction in social activities were also implemented. This model proved successful in maintaining control over infections, with several days during the initial months of the pandemic registering zero active cases [15]. The first wave of COVID-19 was thus delayed until mid-2021 when the influence of tourism and the resumption of social activities contributed to the spread of the virus. The situation returned to a state of normalcy in August 2021, only to be disrupted by the onset of the second wave fueled by the Omicron strain in the summer of 2022. However, the vaccination campaign progressed rapidly, with more than 50,000 shots administered per day, and the country ranked among the highest globally in terms of the percentage of vaccinated population [16]. By March 2022, the situation had once again stabilized, leading to the official declaration of the end of the sanitary emergency on 5 April 2022.

An approach applying data analysis to characterize the use of public transportation during the COVID-19 pandemic is valuable to provide relevant insights that can aid public administrations and transportation companies in future planning for incidents in public transportation. Some of the most relevant issues that can contribute to such planning include: (i) demand forecasting, considering the detected patterns and trends, to help optimizing resource allocation, scheduling, and capacity planning to align the service provision with the expected demand and avoid overcrowding or underutilization; (ii) route optimization, considering those most needed origins and destinations for trips, even in hard circumstances such as the pandemic, allowing companies to evaluate existing routes and focus on those that provide a solution to social needs for citizens that cannot afford private transportation; (iii) safety protocols and special allocation of resources for safety measures, by properly analyzing the impact of specific actions and regulations, providing helpful information to improve and refine safety protocols for future incidents or crises; and (iv) communication strategies and public awareness, considering relevant information about passengers behavior, preferences, and concerns during the pandemic, allowing to develop targeted strategies and public awareness campaigns to communicate important information, such as safety guidelines, service updates, and alternative transportation options during incidents or emergencies.

Overall, data analysis provides evidence-based insights that enable informed decision-making and future planning for incidents in public transportation. It helps authorities adapt and optimize services, enhance safety measures, communicate effectively with passengers, and ensure the resilience and sustainability of transportation systems in the face of future challenges.

2.2. Related Work

Several research articles have studied the demand for public transportation during the COVID-19 pandemic across different regions, including Europe, North America, and Asia. All these studies consistently found a significant decrease in the number of trips. However, the behavior of citizens varied depending on factors such as the presence or absence of lockdown measures and cultural influences [17]. For instance, studies reported a 59% reduction in Australian cities [18], a 60% decrease in Stockholm, Sweden [19], and a substantial 80% reduction (peaking at 90%) in Budapest, Hungary [20].

Wielechowski et al. [21] conducted a study in Poland, which confirmed significant variations in the reduction in public transportation usage based on the level of confinement and other policies implemented. Specifically, reductions ranging from 50% to 85% were observed in Warsaw when considering data from subway passengers. These findings were further supported by an online survey questionnaire, which indicated an average reduction of approximately 70% in public transportation usage [22]. In Gdansk, however, the use of public transportation experienced a more substantial decline, reaching up to 90%. Nevertheless, it is noteworthy that 75% of the individuals interviewed expressed their intention to resume using public transportation once the sanitary situation improved [9].

In the Netherlands, a study analyzing data from 2500 Dutch citizens from the Netherlands Mobility Panel revealed reductions in public transportation usage of up to 90% during the COVID-19 pandemic [7]. Among the various modes of transportation, public transportation experienced the largest decrease, surpassing the decline observed in other means of mobility, including private vehicles (both sustainable and non-sustainable options).

In North American countries, comparable reductions in public transportation usage were observed. In the United States, Lui et al. [8] conducted a study examining the impact of the pandemic on public transportation demand across more than 100 cities. They utilized data from a widely used navigation app and conducted statistical analyses, which revealed that communities with higher proportions of essential workers and vulnerable populations exhibited higher levels of demand for public transportation during the COVID-19 pandemic. The most substantial declines in public transportation usage were observed in the US Midwest region. A preliminary analysis indicated a similar trend for public transportation systems in Toronto and Vancouver, Canada. Palm et al. [23] conducted a survey involving 2753 citizens, reporting that 63% of respondents ceased using public transportation during the initial stage of the pandemic. However, when the study was replicated in March 2021 during the second wave of the pandemic, it was found that 70% of citizens who had previously stopped using public transportation had resumed its usage.

In Latin European countries, where there is a certain degree of similarity in citizen behavior compared to Latin American cities, researchers have examined different factors. Carteni et al. [24] conducted a study in Italy during the second wave of COVID-19, prior to widespread vaccination, to analyze the relationship between the spread of the virus and public transportation usage. The study found a high correlation, reaching up to 0.87, between the daily number of confirmed COVID-19 cases and the number of trips taken on public transportation 22 days prior. The authors concluded that the typical two-week quarantine measures, primarily focused on the incubation period, were insufficient as a comprehensive containment strategy. These measures may have led to a potential delay in identifying new cases and subsequently hindered the timely implementation of effective mitigation policies.

A study conducted by Rodríguez et al. [25] in Spain focused on examining the impact of the COVID-19 pandemic on both public and private mobility in Fuenlabrada, a mid-sized city near Madrid. The researchers utilized data from the public transportation smart card system and a Bluetooth traffic monitoring network, covering the period from February to September 2020. The findings revealed a significant reduction in both public and private mobility during the peak of the pandemic, with public mobility decreasing by 95% and private mobility by 86%. Similarly, Aloi et al. [26] conducted a study in the city of Santander, Spain, utilizing data from traffic counters, public transportation ITS, traffic control cameras, and environmental sensors. They observed comparable results, indicating a substantial decline in mobility during the pandemic. To gain initial insights into the extent of the decline in daily mobility and understand any changes in modal distribution and journey purposes, the authors recommended re-estimating the Origin–Destination trip matrices to align with the prevailing conditions during the COVID-19 pandemic. The re-estimation process facilitated an assessment of the reduction in daily mobility and provided valuable insights into shifts in transportation modes and travel purposes. These efforts served as a diagnostic tool to understand the evolving patterns of mobility during the pandemic. Aloi et al. also examined the effects of the pandemic on NO_2 emissions and traffic accidents. They found that the average overall mobility decreased by 76%, with public transportation demand experiencing a reduction of up to 93%. Additionally, there was a significant decrease in NO_2 emissions and traffic accidents, reaching reductions of approximately 60% to 67%.

Awad et al. [27] focused on investigating the behavior of users with regard to public transportation and shared mobility in Spain during the COVID-19 pandemic. A nationwide survey was implemented to gather information about preferences, frequency of trips according to the trip purpose, and willingness for changes, all regarding the COVID-19 pandemic. The main findings indicated a significant decrease in the use of public transportation; however, citizens expressed their willingness to continue using it provided that adequate sanitation measures were in place and without any increase in ticket prices compared to the pre-COVID-19 period.

The impact of the COVID-19 pandemic on public transportation systems in Latin America received relatively less attention in academic literature compared to other regions.

Andara et al. [28] conducted research examining the impact of the COVID-19 pandemic on mobility in eight large Latin American cities: Bogotá (Colombia), Buenos Aires (Argentina), Mexico City (Mexico), Santiago (Chile), Lima (Perú), and Brasilia, São Paulo, and Rio de Janeiro (Brazil). The study utilized mobility data from both public institutions (such as the IDB Invest Dashboard for mobility and traffic congestion) and private organizations (specifically the Moovit platform for public transportation usage), along with COVID-19 contagion data from Johns Hopkins Hospital University. The research developed models based on descriptive statistics to analyze the variations in motorized mobility during the period from March to September 2020. Regression models were employed to study traffic congestion and urban transportation. The main findings indicated that trips using private mobility means recovered at a faster rate compared to public transportation. This fact was attributed to the implementation of specific measures by municipal administrations for public services, as well as the concerns of citizens regarding the risk of infection associated with using public transportation. Additionally, the authors concluded that public transportation did not play a significant role in the spread of the pandemic in the cities under investigation.

Gramsch et al. [29] recently published a comprehensive analysis investigating the impact of a dynamic lockdown strategy on public transportation, specifically buses and metro, in Santiago, Chile. By utilizing a database of smartcard data capturing trips in 2019 and 2020, the authors conducted a comparative analysis to examine various indicators across different administrative divisions (municipalities) of the city. The key findings of the study revealed a significant 72% reduction in public transportation demand during periods of strict lockdown measures, while a 12% reduction was observed when the dynamic lockdown strategy was implemented. The research also highlighted the short-term effectiveness of lockdowns in reducing mobility. Furthermore, through a socio-demographic analysis, the study identified that lockdown measures had a greater impact on public transportation demand in municipalities with a higher proportion of elderly residents and households with higher incomes.

Other articles have focused on global mobility analysis. Puello [30] studied the transportation mode choice during the COVID-19 pandemic, from data surveyed in Santo Domingo, Dominican Republic. Results showed that the limited capacity, reduced safety, and no capacity of guaranteeing social distancing reduced public transportation usage and promoted a strong habit of commuting in private vehicles. Public transportation trips reduced between 40% and 50%. Mode captivity was also studied for public transportation users that had no access to alternative transportation means.

No studies have been published about the use of public transportation during the COVID-19 pandemic in Uruguay. This article contributes to this line of work by applying a data analysis approach to characterize mobility in the public transportation system of Montevideo during the COVID-19 pandemic.

A summary of related works is presented in Table 1. To date, there have been no published studies exploring the utilization of public transportation during the COVID-19 pandemic in Uruguay. However, this article aims to fill this research gap by employing a data analysis methodology to provide insights into the mobility patterns within the public transportation system of Montevideo during the pandemic. Through this study, valuable contributions can be made to enhance our understanding of how public transportation was affected and adapted during the challenging circumstances of the COVID-19 pandemic in Uruguay.

Table 1. Related works about mobility and public transportation reductions due to the COVID-19 pandemic.

Author	Year	Case Study	Contributions
De Vos [17]	2020	The Netherlands	effects of lockdown on mobility patterns
Beck, Hensher [18]	2020	Australian cities	59% reduction
Jenelius, Cebecauer [19]	2020	Stockholm, Sweden	60% reduction
Bucskyr [20]	2020	Budapest, Hungary	60% reduction
Wielechowski et al. [21]	2020	Poland	reductions of 50–85%
Kłos, Gutowski [22]	2022	Warsaw, Poland	reductions up to 90%
Palm et al. [23]	2021	Canada	63% reduction
de Haas [7]	2020	The Netherlands	reductions up to 90%
Liu et al. [8]	2020	USA	essential workers and vulnerable populations continued using public transportation
Carteni et al. [24]	2021	Italy	high correlation between reductions and COVID-19 cases
Rodríguez et al. [25]	2021	Spain	reduction up to 95%
Aloi et al. [26]	2020	Santander, Spain	reduction of 76%
Awad et al. [27]	2021	Spain	significant decrease but willingness to resume if adequate sanitation measures
Andara [28]	2021	Latin American cities	low recovering of public transportation
Gramsch et al. [29]	2022	Santiago, Chile	72% reduction
Puello [30]	2022	Dominican Republic	50% reduction

3. Description of the Case Study and Methodology for Analyzing Mobility and COVID-19 Data

This section describes the addressed case study and the methodology employed to analyze the public transportation system in Montevideo during the COVID-19 pandemic.

3.1. Description of the Addressed Case Study: Public Transportation in Montevideo, Uruguay

The public transportation system in Montevideo, Uruguay, serves as the most important means of commuting for residents and visitors alike. It comprises several modes of transportation, but the most used are buses (taxis and shared transportation are much less used). The Metropolitan Transportation System (STM) initiative is aimed at integrating and unify all public transportation services in Montevideo and its surrounding areas. The STM encompasses an extensive bus network, consisting of 145 primary bus lines that cover a wide range of routes throughout the urban area, over a thousand line variants, and an impressive number of around five thousand bus stops. These numbers are notably substantial for a city of the scale of Montevideo. The network of bus lines within the public transportation system in Montevideo is illustrated in Figure 1.

Buses in Montevideo generally operate on fixed schedules, with specific departure and arrival times for each route. During peak hours, buses tend to run more frequently to accommodate the higher demand. The schedules are accessible to the public and can be obtained from official sources or through online platforms.

As part of a series of efforts to enhance the efficiency, rationality, and safety in public transportation, the STM implemented a significant technological advancement in the last decade: the introduction of contactless electronic smart cards (STM cards) for ticket payment, eliminating the need for physical currency [31]. Commuters can purchase and recharge their STM cards, which are associated with the user identity. The data collected from STM cards play a crucial role in analyzing the performance of the system, understanding citizens' mobility patterns, and identifying specific problems that may impact the quality of service provided to the public. Essential information extracted from data collected by STM includes boarding stop, travel demand, bus line details, date and time of travel, ticket type, and user category, among others. These valuable data enable the computation of performance indicators, the identification of mobility patterns, and the categorization of mobility demands. Other new technologies, such as real-time bus tracking and digital information displays at bus stops, have been implemented to enhance the overall user experience and efficiency of the system.

Our research group has undertaken previous research endeavors [10,12,31–35] that involved the analysis of trip records within the Montevideo public transportation system. These studies also involved the integration of data from other sources, such as geospatial data and line information, to enhance the depth of analysis.

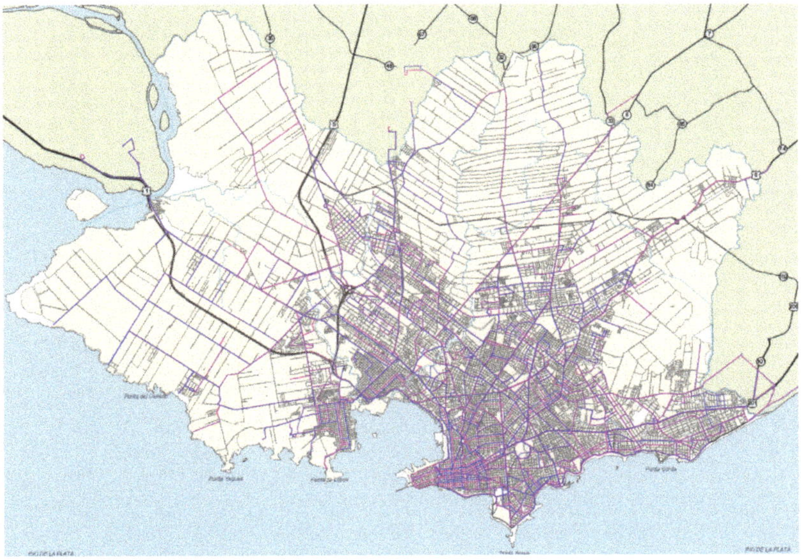

Figure 1. Network of bus lines of the public transportation system in Montevideo (data from sig.montevideo.gub.uy), accessed on 23 September 2023.

3.2. Sources of Data

Three main sources of data are applied for the characterization of mobility using public transportation. The first source of data is the open repository from the Uruguayan government, the National Open Data Catalog, available at https://catalogodatos.gub.uy/, accessed on 12 August 2023. The catalog provides access to various collections of data that are freely accessible. Relevant to the reported research, the catalog encompasses a dataset concerning bus trips obtained from the public transportation authorities in Montevideo. This dataset comprises comprehensive information regarding all trips undertaken within the public transportation system in Montevideo. It includes details such as the companies involved, specific bus lines, dates and times of trips, ticket categories, and other pertinent information like the originating bus stop and payment method (either smart card or cash). The dataset utilized for analysis covers a significant timeframe, from November 2019 to June 2022, encompassing the entire duration of the national health emergency caused by the COVID-19 pandemic. This extensive time range allows for a comprehensive analysis of the dynamics of the public transportation system throughout the entire period affected by the sanitary emergency.

The second source of data is the Geographic Information System provided by the Infrastructure for Spatial Data (IDE), from the national government, available at https://www.gub.uy/infraestructura-datos-espaciales/, accessed on 12 August 2023. Geographical information pertaining to the analysis was acquired from shapefiles that contained data on the locations of bus stops in Montevideo, as well as shapefiles containing polygons representing the neighborhoods within Montevideo. These shapefiles provided essential spatial data that facilitated the integration of geographical context into the analysis of the public transportation system in Montevideo during the pandemic.

Additionally, the third source of data is the freely accessible repository from the Uruguayan Interdisciplinary Group for COVID-19 Data Analysis (GUIAD-COVID-19) [36] and the Public Health Ministry. Specifically, the extracted data from this dataset consisted of the daily count of registered COVID-19 cases per department. This data source played a crucial role in incorporating information on the spread of the pandemic and its impact into the analysis.

All the source data and results of the analysis are available at https://github.com/nesmachnow/stm_covid_19, accessed on 30 August 2022.

3.3. Description of the Applied Methodology

The methodology employed in the study consisted of three main stages: data pre-processing, data processing utilizing parallel computing, and analysis of the obtained results. Each stage is described in detail in the following subsections.

3.3.1. Pre-Processing Stage

In this stage, the collected datasets were prepared for analysis. The data pre-processing phase encompassed several tasks, including data cleansing and the association of geographical locations with each recorded ticket sale in the trips dataset.

Geographical data from shapefiles, such as bus stop locations and neighborhood polygons, were processed and linked to the relevant data from the public transportation dataset. This task was accomplished by cross-referencing the shapefile containing the bus stop locations in Montevideo with the shapefile containing the polygons representing the neighborhoods in Montevideo. The cross-referencing process was carried out using the open-source, cross-platform desktop geographic information system application, QGIS. During this stage, a manual classification was conducted for bus stops located outside of Montevideo. These bus stops were categorized as either 'Canelones East' or 'Canelones West', based on their geographical location (Canelones is the department that surrounds Montevideo). By associating each ticket sale with its corresponding neighborhood and categorizing bus stops outside of Montevideo, the data were prepared for subsequent aggregation and analysis of the results.

Additionally, the COVID-19 infection data obtained from GUIAD-COVID-19 were organized and aligned with the corresponding time periods and geographical locations.

3.3.2. Data Processing Using Parallel Computing

The proposed study dealt with a substantial amount of data that required processing. The datasets pertaining to the analyzed period (2019–2022) exceeded 73 GB in size. Moreover, the study involved numerous operations that lent themselves well to parallel computing using the MapReduce paradigm. Several examples of such operations include grouping the data based on the day and neighborhood to analyze daily mobility patterns by neighborhood, transforming each trip into an integer to count the number of trips occurring each day, grouping the data by the day and user category, and grouping the data by the day and bus line. These operations could be effectively parallelized, allowing for efficient processing and analysis of the data. By dividing the data into smaller subsets and processing them using the computational power of multiple processors or computing units concurrently, the computational time for data analysis was significantly reduced.

3.3.3. Statistical Analysis of Data and Results

The concluding stage of the analysis encompassed the computation of pertinent metrics and the application of statistical and time series analysis techniques to the computed results. This stage involved deriving meaningful insights from the processed data by employing data visualization techniques and statistical methods and exploring temporal patterns. By conducting these analyses, the study aimed to uncover significant trends, relationships, significant correlations between variables, and patterns within the data, leading to a comprehensive understanding of impact of the COVID-19 pandemic on the utilization of the public transportation system in Montevideo.

Overall, the applied methodology allowed for the systematic processing and analysis of the collected data, enabling meaningful insights into the relationship between the COVID-19 pandemic and the usage of public transportation in Montevideo.

3.4. Resolution Approach

The development of the parallel algorithm for data processing involved several stages, which are outlined as follows:

1. Computation of daily trip count: A specific algorithmic approach was developed to calculate the number of trips per day. The primary objective was to examine how the onset of the pandemic and the declaration of the sanitary emergency influenced the mobility patterns and public transportation usage reduction. The trip data were partitioned by day to enable parallelization of the computation. A subsequent reduction function was applied in order to group the data by day.
2. Calculation of the correlation between COVID-19 cases and mobility patterns: Another algorithm was developed to determine the correlation between the reported number of COVID-19 cases and the mobility patterns using public transportation. The pandas library was utilized for this task, using the data obtained from the previous stage and the daily COVID-19 cases data. Through the application of statistical computations, the correlation between COVID-19 cases and trip data were calculated.
3. Analysis of mobility patterns: An analysis was conducted to examine the mobility patterns of citizens during the COVID-19 pandemic, considering factors such as neighborhood and socio-economic information, representative sampling of bus lines, and and discrimination by user category. The available data regarding public transportation usage was categorized based on the day and neighborhood, day and line number, and day and user category. Data analysis was conducted using the Pandas library. The objective of this analysis were to determine the mobility patterns during different stages of the COVID-19 pandemic and to identify the user categories that exhibited the highest dependence on public transportation, which was determined by assessing the correlation between COVID-19 cases and trips for each category.
4. Study of the recovery of the usage of public transportation system: The primary focus of this analysis was to study the recovery of the mobility during the COVID-19 pandemic, to pinpoint the periods and specific dates when citizens gradually resumed public transportation usage, reaching levels close to normal. By examining the fluctuations in the monthly average of daily trips over time, valuable insights were obtained regarding the progressive recovery of mobility.

Overall, the proposed stages of the parallel algorithm for data processing aimed to uncover valuable insights into the impact of the pandemic on the mobility patterns of citizens, the correlation between COVID-19 cases and trips, and the recovery of public transportation usage in Montevideo throughout the specified period.

3.5. Implementation Details

The proposed algorithms for data analysis were implemented using Scala [37], a flexible and powerful programming language over the MapReduce framework provided by Hadoop [38]. The choice of Scala was driven by its flexibility, robustness, and excellent interoperability, whereas the MapReduce framework was well-suited for handling the specific characteristics of the data processing problem. Both Scala and the Hadoop MapReduce framework are highly esteemed and widely adopted choices in the field of urban data analysis and big data processing.

For data storage purposes, the Hadoop Distributed File System (HDFS) was utilized. HDFS is specifically designed to be the storage system of Hadoop, employing data replication to ensure fault tolerance. HDFS provides the basis for developing a robust and efficient design for the data processing algorithm. In the event of a processing node failure, the data remains accessible on other configured nodes, guaranteeing availability. HDFS is optimized for storing vast amounts of data while maintaining multiple copies, ensuring both high availability and fault tolerance. Additionally, HDFS facilitates efficient data access, providing a substantial bandwidth. This enables MapReduce applications to effectively process large data volumes. Moreover, HDFS follows a write-once-read-many storage model, where input data are written only once and can subsequently be accessed and read multiple times when required.

The analysis of data and the obtained results was carried out utilizing Python, leveraging the efficiency and widespread usage of the Pandas and Matplotlib libraries. These tools are highly regarded in the field of data analysis, making them suitable choices for the task at hand.

4. Empirical Evaluation of the Case Study: Analysis of Results and Discussion

This section presents the findings from the experimental evaluation conducted to determine the impact of the COVID-19 pandemic and end mobility using the the public transportation system in Montevideo.

4.1. Computational Platform

The experimental evaluation was carried out on HPE Proliant servers with Xeon Gold 6138 processor, 40 cores and 120 GB of RAM memory, from the high performance computing platform of National Supercomputing Center (Cluster-UY), Uruguay [39].

Regarding the distributed implementation, the map processes were allocated 4 GB of physical memory and each one had a dynamic Java Virtual Machine (JVM) size of 3 GB. The reduce processes were assigned 8 GB of physical memory, with a dynamic JVM size of 6 GB. These values were determined in preliminary experiments conducted to determine the best parameters for an efficient use of the computational platform.

4.2. Computational Efficiency of the Parallel Distributed Approach

For the analysis of the computational efficiency of the parallel distributed approach, the maximum number of containers per node was set to 50. According to the recommendations and rules-of-thumb for the MapReduce implementation of Hadoop, the number of mappers is set automatically by the framework, according to the size of the input data, and the number of reducers to be used to perform the computations is to be between 1 and 87. Two experiments were carried out, the first with a volume of data of 7 GB (small instance) and the second with 73 GB (large instance). These experiments allow evaluating the computational efficiency and the scalability of the implemented approach for data processing.

Relevant metrics were considered in the analysis, including:

- TotalTime: the total time elapsed from the beginning until the end of the MapReduce job;
- CPUTime: the effective CPU usage time;
- TimeMaps: sum of the execution times of all the Map tasks;
- TimeReducers: sum of the execution times of all Reduce tasks.

Figure 2 presents the results of the computational efficiency evaluation, reporting the four execution time metrics for a different number of reducer processes.

The efficiency results in Figure 2 indicate that the number of reducers do not affect significantly the execution time for when processing 7 GB of data. The lowest overall execution times were computed using two and 60 reduce processes. Overall, the execution time required by mappers and reducers does not vary significantly when using more than three reduce processes. A larger overhead is also noticed when using from 7 to 87 reducers, but without impacting in the overall execution time. A similar result was obtained when processing 73 GB.

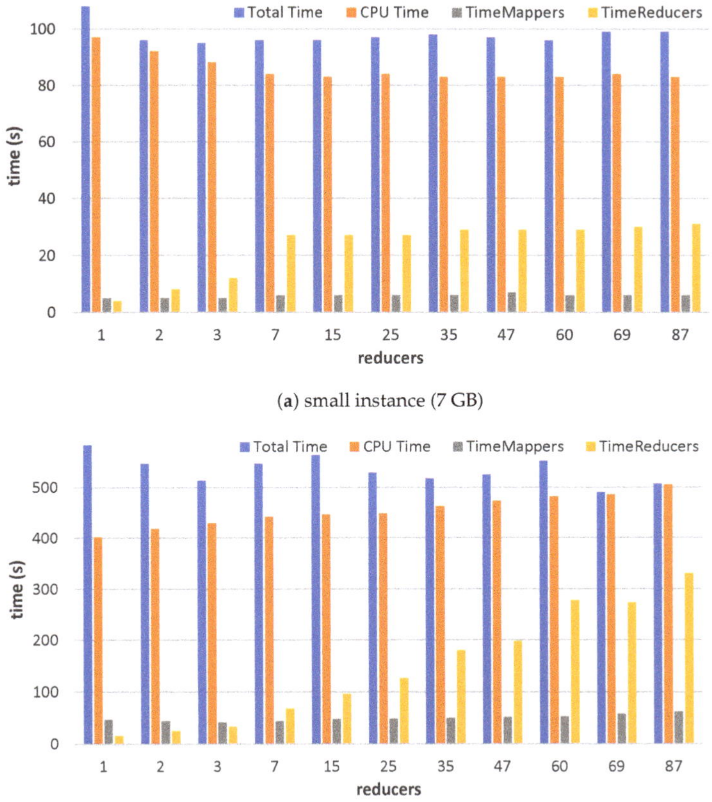

(**a**) small instance (7 GB)

(**b**) large instance (73 GB)

Figure 2. Computational efficiency of the proposed MapReduce implementation for data processing using different number of reducer processes.

The execution time values also demonstrate an excellent scalability of the implemented approach, since the average overall executions times only increased by a factor of five when increasing the size of the processed dataset in a factor of ten. This result indicates that the implemented MapReduce algorithm is able to properly adapt the data processing to take full advantage of the parallel capabilities offered by the high performance computing platform used.

Another interesting evaluation is the utilization of overlapping in the data processing workflow. This approach involves initiating the reducer tasks while the mapper tasks are still in progress, rather than waiting for the mappers to complete before starting the reducers. The analysis focused on observing the behavior and evaluate the overall execution time when the reducers start their work at different completion percentages of the mappers, specifically at 12%, 26%, 55%, and 89% of their progress. Additionally, a comparison is performed against the execution time without employing the overlapping technique. Figure 3 presents the execution time results for the considered overlapping percentages.

Based on the data obtained from Figure 3, the best performance was achieved when the reducers begins processing when the mappers have completed 87% of their tasks. Initiating the reducers earlier prolongs the execution time, since they lack sufficient data to process, resulting in idle time. However, without the implementation of overlapping, the overall execution time is also affected. As the mappers reach a significant completion percentage of their work, they start releasing resources, which are wasted if the reducers do not begin their tasks at that particular moment.

The configuration that obtained the best execution time results was used to perform the computation for all the analyses reported next.

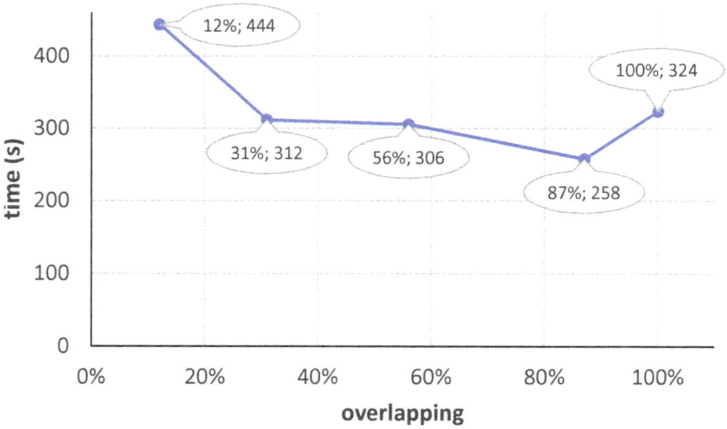

Figure 3. Execution time of the developed parallel MapReduce algorithm for different overlapping percentages.

4.3. Analysis 1: Impact of Declaring a State of Sanitary Emergency

The state of sanitary emergency was declared in 14 March 2020. This subsection analyzes the average number of trips for the public transportation system of Montevideo before and after that date. The baselines for the comparison are the month of November, 2019, and the period 1 March to 13 March 2020. The months between December and February are not fully representative of the mobility using public transportation in the city. The second term of public and private education ends in early December, significantly reducing the number of trips. In turn, the last week of December is Family Day (i.e., Christian Christmas) and New Year's Eve, and most activity in the city is reduced. January and February are the holiday months, and the number of people in Montevideo reduce significantly, since many people move to the Eastern seaside houses and resorts. The majority of educational activities, including schools, high schools, and universities, commenced on 2 March 2020. Under normal circumstances, bus trips experience a peak in March, with an average comparable to that of November.

A comparison of the average number of trips taken on the STM before and after the declaration of the sanitary emergency in Uruguay is depicted in Figure 4.

To account for the substantial difference in the number of trips between working days and weekends, Figure 5 illustrates a comparison of the average number of trips taken on the STM before and after the declaration of the sanitary emergency. The comparison is further differentiated to specifically examine the variations on working days and weekends.

Regarding the values reported in Figures 4 and 5, the dip observed at the beginning of the year is attributed to the seasonal nature of the data. As explained, January and February are typically holiday months, which results in a lower number of bus trips. However, the trend changes when most educational activities commenced on March.

Figure 4 provides a clear illustration of the decline in bus trips following the declaration of the sanitary emergency on 13 March 2020. The overall trips reduction amounted to 71.4%, compared to the daily trip count recorded from 1 March to 13 March. The same reduction was observed considering the trips performed in November, 2019 as a reference baseline. A contrasting situation is observed when analyzing weekdays and weekends separately. On weekends, Figure 5 shows that the reduction in weekend trips was more than a half (54.1%), which is partly attributed to the inherently lower number of bus trips typically taken during weekends. Consequently, the impact of the COVID-19 pandemic resulted in a relatively less significant reduction in weekend trips.

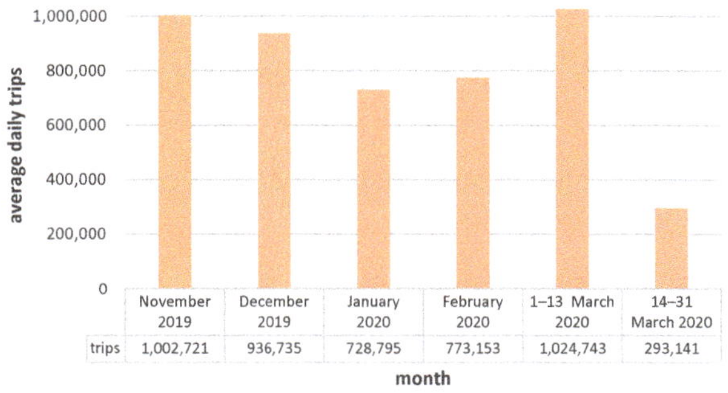

Figure 4. Time series of average daily trips before and after the sanitary emergency declaration (13 March 2020) in Montevideo, Uruguay (data from the period November 2019–March 2020).

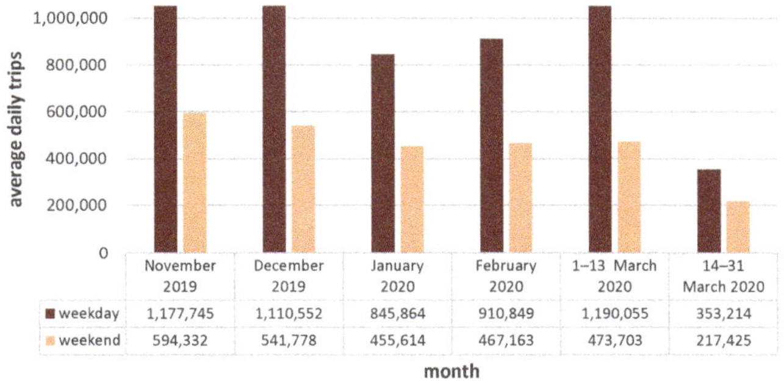

Figure 5. Time series of average daily trips in weekdays and weekends before and after the sanitary emergency declaration (13 March 2020) in Montevideo, Uruguay (data from the period November 2019–March 2020).

The documented reductions in public transportation trips in Montevideo are comparatively lower than those reported in similar cities across Europe and America. This outcome indicates that the responsible freedom model implemented in Montevideo effectively mitigated the perceived risk associated with public transportation trips, resulting in a lesser reduction when compared to other countries.

In the case study of Montevideo, the dependence on public transportation holds particular significance, as there are no alternative commuting options that are perceived as safer by passengers. In 2018, a shared bicycle public system was proposed for a limited area in Montevideo, but its operation was short-lived, and the service was discontinued in 2019. Despite some efforts to revive this system, none have succeeded in achieving their objectives. Therefore, the shared bicycle public system was not a viable commuting option during the COVID-19 pandemic. In 2019, a new form of mobility was introduced in Montevideo: shared e-scooters. Initially, the system gained popularity due to its novelty. However, users soon discovered several drawbacks associated with e-scooters, including a limited operational area, high costs, the risk of sharing roads with automobiles, a lack of available charged vehicles, and operational failures such as the use of non-sustainable methods (trucks) for arranging vehicles during the day. Unfortunately, the business model for e-scooters proved unsuccessful in Montevideo [12]. Private bicycles emerged as the only viable option for personal and safe transportation during the COVID-19 pandemic. However, they are not the preferred means of mobility in Montevideo, accounting for less than 15% of the modal share, mainly due to the lack of adequate cycling infrastructure in the city.

Since the declaration of the sanitary emergency, the utilization of public transportation exhibited a consistent upward trend, except in specific outbreak periods. A detailed analysis of the evolution is presented in the next subsection.

4.4. Analysis 2: Evolution of Public Transportation Usage during the COVID-19 Pandemic

Figure 6 illustrates the progression of the number of trips within the public transportation system in Montevideo from April 2020 to May 2022 (blue series), alongside the reported count of confirmed COVID-19 cases, as provided by GUIAD-COVID-19 and the Public Health Ministry (orange series).

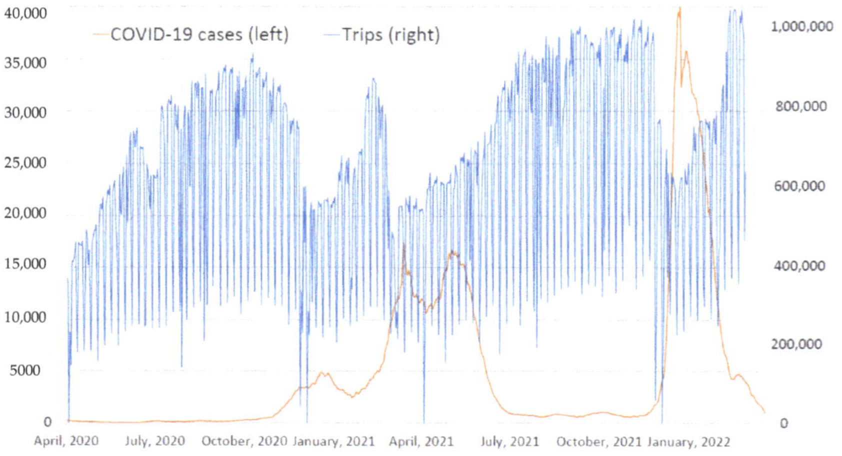

Figure 6. Number of confirmed COVID-19 cases and trips performed in the public transportation of Montevideo during the sanitary emergency period (April 2020–May 2022).

The moving average of the number of trips was studied to provide a clearer representation. This approach smooths the curve, filtering out the peaks caused by weekends and holidays, and provides a refined characterization of public transportation usage. Two periods were studied for defining the moving average: 14 and 21 days, according to the most generally accepted number of days for the contagious period for a person infected with COVID-19 (from two to four days before they develop symptoms, and for a period of two weeks afterward). The analysis showed a correct smoothness of the time series of trips, as shown in Figure 7 for the overall number of trips and for a representative neighborhood (Aguada). The curves showed almost no differences between the moving average values computed for 14 and 21 days. Thus, the moving average computed using the previous 14 data points in the series were considered in the following analysis.

Figure 8 presents a cleaner version of the number of trips in the public transportation system of Montevideo (moving average, blue curve) and the confirmed COVID-19 cases (orange series) from April 2020 to May 2002. Four special events (E1 to E4) are marked in the graphic, which are commented on next.

The relationship between public transportation mobility and the number of COVID-19 cases is clearly depicted in Figures 8 and 9. During periods of COVID-19 outbreaks, there was a noticeable decrease in the number of trips, which was subsequently followed by a gradual recovery as the number of cases declined. After an initial reduction of 70% in the first month and a half following the declaration of the sanitary emergency, the number of trips steadily rose until the end of 2020. Uruguay experienced a relatively milder initial phase of the pandemic compared to other countries, with several days even reporting no new cases. Consequently, citizens gradually resumed their use of public transportation. A slight increase in COVID-19 cases was observed in August 2020, resulting in a 10% reduction in public transportation usage (this situation is marked as event 'E1' in Figures 8 and 9). However, the first wave of the pandemic hit Uruguay in December 2020, with cases peaking at 5000. The outbreak led to a significant reduction of over 20% in public transportation usage (event 'E2' in Figures 8 and 9). In March 2021, cases decreased, and public transportation usage began to recover. However, a new outbreak happened in May 2021: the second wave, with over 15,000 COVID-19 cases. It caused a reduction of more than 40% in the number of trips (the valley marked as event 'E3'). Between August and December 2021, the number of COVID-19 cases significantly dropped, and public transportation usage returned to almost normal levels, over 800,000 daily trips on average. However, the third wave of the pandemic, caused by the highly contagious Omicron strain, started in January 2022. The third wave led to an exponential increase in infected individuals, reaching almost 40,000 confirmed cases by the end of January 2022. As a result, public transportation usage decreased significantly, dropping to approximately 50% of its usual level (event 'E4'). As COVID-19 cases declined, citizens quickly resumed their regular mobility patterns, leading to over 900,000 tickets sold in May 2022.

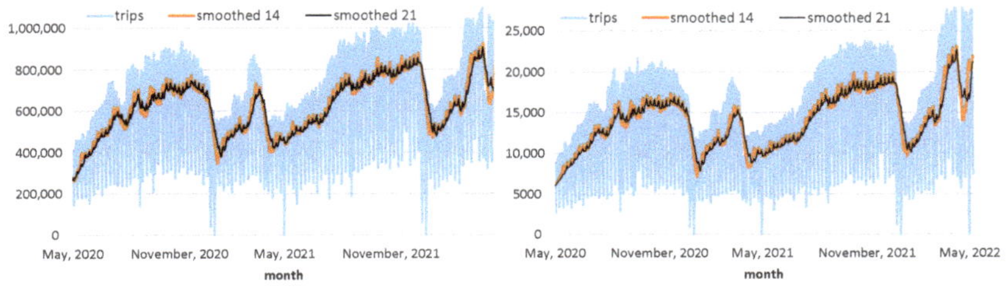

(a) Montevideo (b) Aguada neighborhood

Figure 7. Moving average analysis for trips in Montevideo and a representative neighborhood (Aguada). Light blue: trips, orange curve: average over 14 days, black curve: average over 21 days.

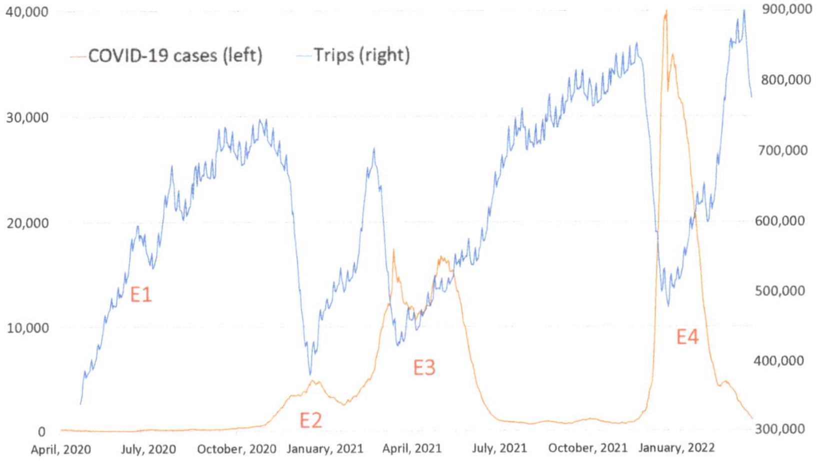

Figure 8. Number of trips and COVID-19 cases (smoothed, moving average).

Based on the reported results, five periods are identified in Figure 9 regarding the behavior of both COVID-19 cases and trips: a first period with few infections (gray background), the first wave (blue background), the second wave (green background), a second period with few infections (red background), and the third wave (yellow background). These periods are relevant to compute the statistical correlation between the studied time series.

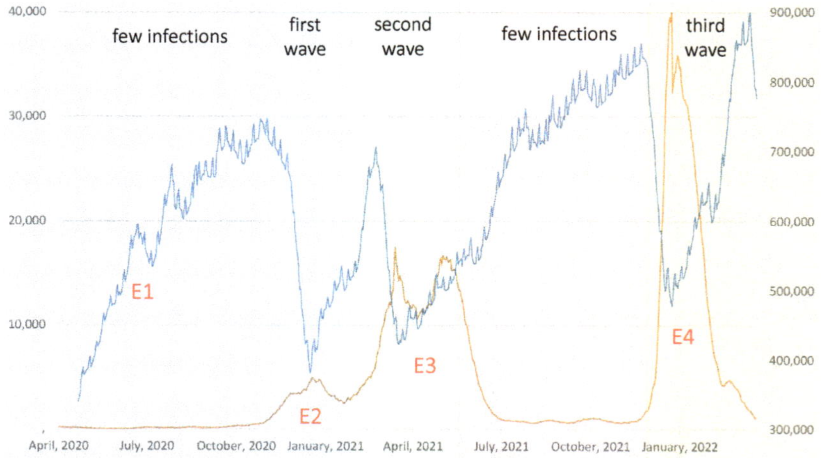

Figure 9. COVID-19 cases and trips performed in the public transportation of Montevideo during the sanitary emergency period (April 2020–May 2022)

Table 2 reports the Pearson correlation coefficient between the number of trips in the public transportation of Montevideo and the number of COVID-19 cases reported in the city for each of the five periods. The three COVID-19 waves are marked in gray and the higher values of the Pearson correlation coefficient are marked in bold font.

The Pearson correlation coefficient indicates a strong negative correlation between the two studied time series during the three COVID-19 waves (values up to −0.89378 for the first wave). As the number of COVID-19 cases experiences an upward trend, the use of public transportation exhibited a downward trend, and vice versa. The magnitude of −0.89378 suggests a high degree of linear relationship between the two variables. As the Pearson correlation coefficient evaluates linear relationships, the correlation coefficient closer to −1 indicate an inverse linear relationship. In the other periods, no correlation was detected, mainly because very few cases of COVID-19 occurred.

Table 2. Correlation between the number of trips in the public transportation system of Montevideo and the number of COVID-19 cases.

Period	Time	Pearson Coefficient
few infections 1	April–November 2020	0.67132
first wave	December 2020–February 2021	−0.89378
second wave	March–May 2021	−0.81794
few infections 2	June–November 2021	−0.43036
third wave	November 2021–February 2022	−0.85285

4.5. Analysis 3: Recovery of Public Transportation Usage

In Montevideo, Uruguay, the recovery of public transportation usage outpaced that of other capital cities worldwide. Table 3 presents the average number of daily trips for each month during the period when the public health emergency was in effect (from April 2020 to April 2022). It also includes the percentage compared to the average pre-COVID-19 pandemic trips (November 2019 and 1–13 March 2020).

Table 3. Recovery of the public transportation system in Montevideo.

2020								
pre-COVID-19	April	May	June	July	Aug.	Sept.	Oct.	Nov.
1,024,743	262,008	357,921	585,612	860,123	620,732	805,118	915,852	925,801
100.0%	25.6%	34.9%	57.1%	83.9%	60.6%	78.6%	89.4%	90.3%
2020	2021							
Dec.	Jan.	Feb.	March	April	May	June	July	Aug.
880,519	650,070	575,294	720,518	572,381	590,163	701,371	738,023	835,182
85.9%	63.4%	56.1%	70.3%	55.9%	57.6%	68.4%	72.0%	81.5%
2021				2022				
Sept.	Oct.	Nov.	Dec.	Jan.	Feb.	March	April	
925,830	996,702	992,601	990,924	602,185	712,046	1,050,306	1,082,415	
90.3%	97.3%	96.9%	96.7%	58.8%	69.5%	102.5%	105.6%	

The results presented in Table 3 demonstrate that following an initial sluggish period of two months after the declaration of the public health emergency, the number of trips in the public transportation of Montevideo experienced a rapid recovery. Within just four months (by July 2020), the system had regained 84% of its pre-COVID-19 reference value. Despite a slight decline in August 2020, the number of trips nearly reached pre-pandemic levels by November 2020, with a 90% recovery rate. However, the onset of the first major wave of COVID-19 cases in February 2021 led to a significant reduction of up to 56% in trip numbers. Once again, users gradually regained confidence in public transportation, resulting in a steady recovery until the second wave hit between April and June 2021, causing a decline in trips to 56% of pre-COVID-19 levels.

Following the first wave, the recovery of trip numbers was notably faster, reaching over 90% within just three months (by September 2021), and achieving a complete recovery in the latter months of 2021. The emergence of the third wave, specifically with the Omicron strain, led to a reduction in trip numbers to 59% in January 2022. However, the recovery was remarkably swift, surpassing the pre-COVID-19 value within only two months, by March 2022.

The presented results indicate that despite the initial decline in public transportation trips due to the rise in COVID-19 cases, citizens quickly regained their trust in the system. The recovery periods for trip numbers became progressively shorter with each wave and, in 2022, it took only around a month and a half to fully recover. This pace of recovery is notably faster compared to similar case studies reported worldwide [9,27,29]. These findings lead to the conclusion that the responsible freedom model implemented in Montevideo not only effectively mitigated the impact of the pandemic but also ensured a swift restoration of mobility patterns and the utilization of public transportation.

4.6. Analysis 4: Socioeconomic Characterization of Public Transportation Usage

The socio-economic context in Montevideo gave rise to diverse residential neighborhoods, each one with distinct characteristics. A relevant analysis to effectively characterize and understand the mobility patterns within the city is studying the correlation between trips originating from the different neighborhoods and their socio-economical level. This analysis provides valuable insights into the dynamics of movement between different locations in Montevideo.

For the analysis, the repository of trips was processed as follows. Given the absence of neighborhood information in the trips dataset, shapefiles containing bus stop locations and neighborhood polygons in Montevideo were processed. By determining the intersection between these shapefiles, the neighborhood corresponding to each bus stop was identified. This task was performed using the QGIS software. Subsequently, the trip dataset was grouped based on the neighborhood of each bus stop, and the Pearson correlation was calculated to assess the relationship between the number of trips originating from each neighborhood and the reported COVID-19 cases in the city.

The assessment of the socio-economic conditions in neighborhoods was conducted using the Socioeconomic Level Index (INSE) developed by Llambí and Piñeyro [40], and later updated by Perera and Cazulo [41] and Perera [42]. The INSE is a methodological tool used to assess the purchasing power or income of households. It relies on a set of indirect questions as a means to capture the information, considering the challenges associated with directly measuring or asking people about their income. By utilizing the INSE, households can be classified and segmented based on their consumption capacity, enabling a practical means to characterize the population according to their various income levels. The INSE defines 10 values for different geographical and administrative divisions, from 0 (lowest socio-economic level) to 9 (highest socio-economic level).

4.6.1. Reduction in the Number of Trips after the Declaration of the Sanitary Emergency

The reduction in the use of the public transportation system in Montevideo after the declaration of the sanitary emergency had a great dispersion. The minimum reduction was 63% for neighborhoods Casavalle and Casabó–Pajas Blancas. In turn, the maximum reduction was 89% for Parque Rodó neighborhood. The reduction is correlated with the INSE values. Neighborhoods exhibiting a weak correlation between the number of trips and COVID-19 cases are characterized by consistently low INSE values (2 or lower), with the exception of one neighborhood (La Blanqueada, with an INSE value of 6). Conversely, neighborhoods demonstrating a strong correlation between trips and COVID-19 cases tend to have higher INSE values (7 to 9). The Pearson correlation between the reduction in trips on public transportation and the INSE values is 0.7764, suggesting a reasonably high linear correlation between both variables. Figure 10 graphically presents the INSE values for the 63 neighborhoods in Montevideo (values between 0 and 9) and the reductions.

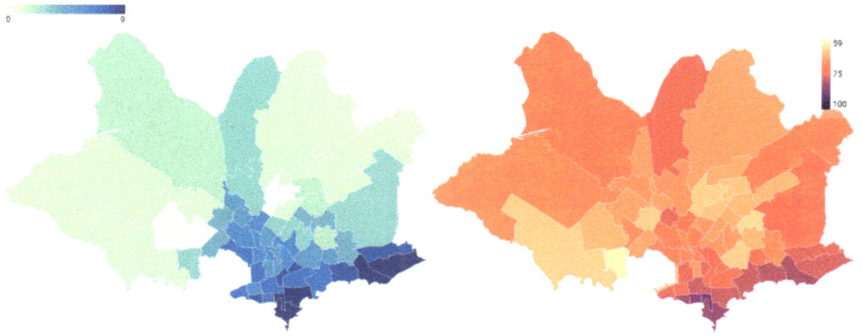

(**a**) Socioeconomic index (INSE) (**b**) Reduction in trips

Figure 10. Socioeconomic index and reduction in trips in the public transportation of Montevideo.

The choropleth maps in Figure 10 have a very similar structure, both with largest values of the reported indicators located along the southern seaside (in those neighborhoods where the wealthiest people live), and smaller values in peripheral neighborhoods of the city. The findings consistently indicate that residents in low-income neighborhoods had limited commuting options and were forced to rely heavily on public transportation, even in the hard circumstances of the COVID-19 pandemic. Individuals with low incomes often face limited mobility options and are more likely to rely on on-site manual labor jobs that are not compatible with the remote work paradigm. In contrast, individuals with higher incomes and greater purchasing power, living in neighborhoods with larger INSE values, significantly reduced their usage of public transportation, probably because they can afford other means of (private) transportation and/or they can perform their work from home.

The boxplots in Figure 11 clearly show the relationship between the socioeconomic level and the percentage of reductions. The observed reductions were significantly larger for neighborhoods with higher values of INSE, i.e., higher socio-economic conditions.

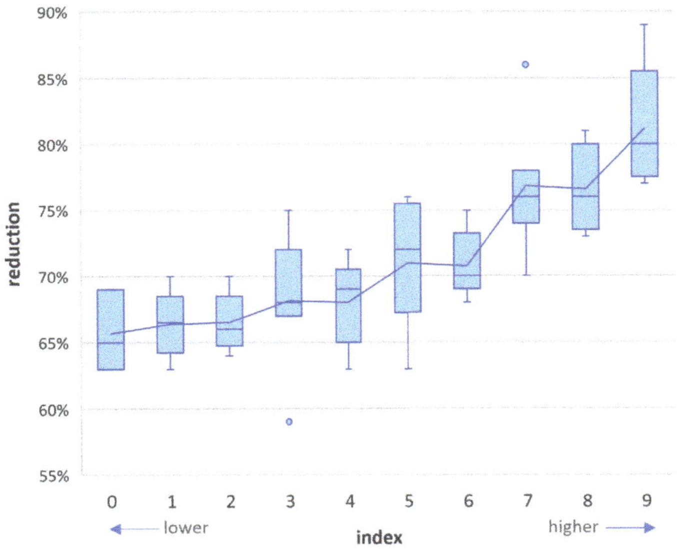

Figure 11. Boxplots summarizing the information of the results distributions for the reduction in trips on public transportation by neighborhood, grouped by socio-economic index.

4.6.2. Evolution and Recovery of the Use of Public Transportation System during the COVID-19 Pandemic

The analysis studies the correlation between the use of public transportation in Montevideo during the different stages of the COVID-19 pandemic and the socio-economic characterization provided by INSE values. The study is performed for the five periods identified in Section 4.4.

Figure 12 reports the Pearson correlation coefficient between the number of trips and the socioeconomic level of neighborhoods in Montevideo for the five periods studied. A consistent trend is detected for the three outbreak periods (waves), where the Pearson correlation coefficient was closer to -1 (linear inverse relationship) for neighborhoods with the highest INSE values, whereas the correlation for neighborhoods with lower INSE values had smaller coefficients (between -0.80 and -0.85). In the two periods with few infections, no relationship was detected.

An example of the different behavior of citizens regarding the use of public transportation system is shown in Figure 13. Trips for two representative neighborhoods in Montevideo are presented: Pocitos, a high-income neighborhood having the maximum INSE value (9) and a high negative correlation with the number of COVID-19 cases; and Casabó, a low-income neighborhood having the minimum INSE value (0) and a low correlation. The poverty index is almost 30% in Casabó, whereas a negligible value is reported for Pocitos (2%) [43]. Accessibility indexes are also significantly higher for Pocitos than for Casabó [44].

Results presented in presented in Figure 13 clearly show a noteworthy reduction in trips from the Pocitos neighborhood, associated with the special events and waves of the pandemic. The reduction in trips from Casabó neighborhood are not as significant. In the first wave, trips from Pocitos reduced up to 57.8%, while from Casabó only reduced 35.4%. A similar situation happened during the third wave of the COVID-19 pandemic: trips from Pocitos reduced by 55.3%, while from Casabó only reduced by 37.3%. The recovery rates were higher for Pocitos in both cases. Similar figures were obtained for other neighborhoods in each of the ten levels defined by the INSE indicator.

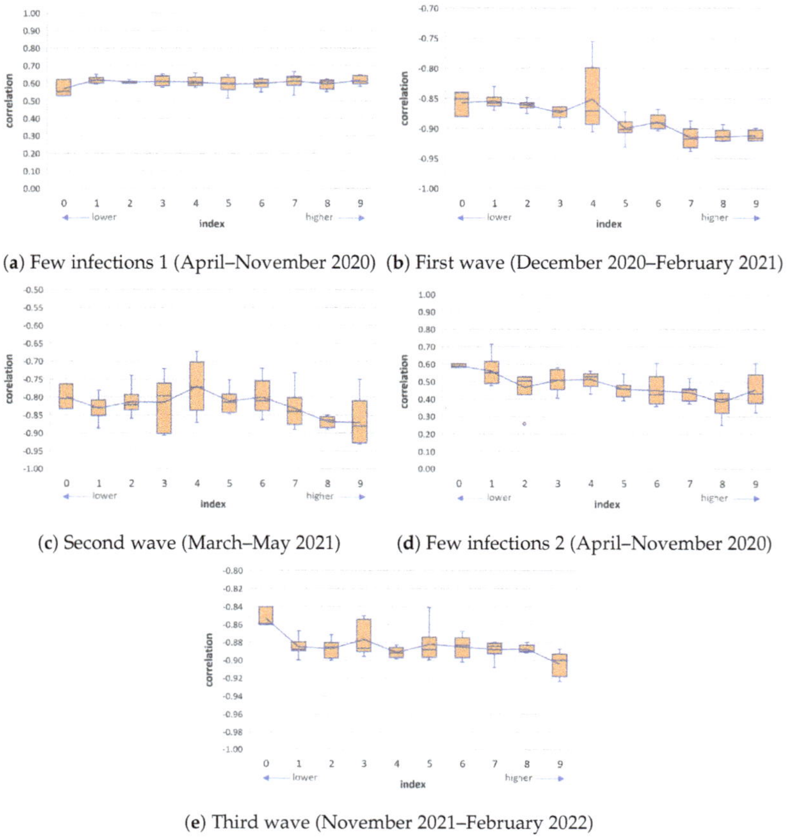

(**a**) Few infections 1 (April–November 2020) (**b**) First wave (December 2020–February 2021)

(**c**) Second wave (March–May 2021) (**d**) Few infections 2 (April–November 2020)

(**e**) Third wave (November 2021–February 2022)

Figure 12. Correlation between socio-economic index and the number of trips by neighborhood in the public transportation of Montevideo, for the five identified periods of the COVID-19 pandemic.

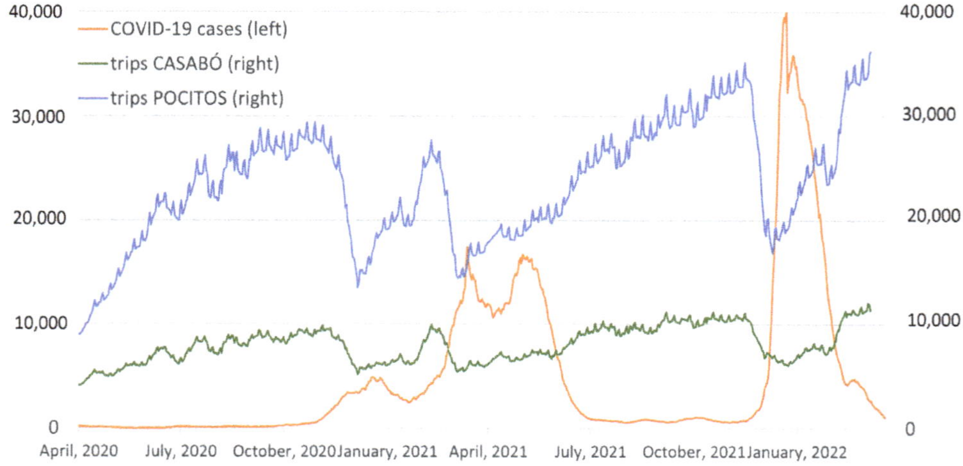

Figure 13. Comparison of trips from Pocitos (high INSE, high negative correlation) and Casabó (low INSE, low correlation) and COVID-19 cases.

4.7. Analysis 5: Mobility Patterns of the Elderly

Several articles has stated that the COVID-19 pandemics significantly changed the mobility patterns of the elderly, since restrictions excluded them from using public transportation [45–47]. Other factors were also relevant for the diminished number of trips of older adults using public transportation during the pandemic [48].

A specific analysis was conducted to examine the usage of public transportation by elders in Montevideo. The study utilized the information from the automated ticket sales system of the STM in Montevideo, which includes records for retired individuals (i.e., over 60/65 years old). Within this group, two types of tickets are sold: 'retired A' for those with the lowest economic income and 'retired B' those with a standard economic income. Table 4 presents the observed reduction in trips for both the 'retired A' and 'retired B' categories following the declaration of the sanitary emergency on 14 March 2020. Additionally, the reduction in trips for normal users tickets sold, corresponding to adults between 20 and 60 years old, is also provided to serve as a comparative baseline.

Table 4. Reduction in trips using public transportation in Montevideo for 'retired A', 'retired B', and normal users categories, following the declaration of the sanitary emergency on 14 March 2020.

Category	1–13 March	13–31 March	Reduction
retired A	40,041	9365	76.6%
retired B	14,383	3203	77.7%
normal users	541,259	181,378	66.5%

Results in Table 4 show that the reduction in public transportation usage by older individuals was 10% larger than for normal users. Despite that, the number of trips show that a significant share of the elder population (about one quarter) still relied on public transportation for commuting during the early days of the COVID-19 pandemics. This result is different to other reported reductions for countries like China [46], Iran [47], Italy [49], Korea [50], and the United Kingdom [51], where the mobility of older people using public transportation reduced to almost zero in the early stages of the COVID-19 pandemic, as a consequence of the very high perceived risk and the applied lockdown measures. No significant variations were detected in the reduction between the two studied 'retired' categories, suggesting that the economic factor did not play a significant role in that regard. The observed results can be reasonably attributed to the implementation of the 'responsible freedom' strategy by the Uruguayan government, as well as the remarkably low infection rates experienced in the initial days and months following the declaration of the sanitary emergency. As occurred for middle age adults, the perceived risk of using public transportation among older adults was not as high as in other countries. This is an important result, since maintaining mobility and social interactions have been recognized as crucial for older adults' health during the COVID-19 pandemic. This finding holds great significance as the preservation of mobility and social interactions has been acknowledged as critical for the health and well-being of older adults during the COVID-19 pandemic [48].

Figure 14 presents the evolution of public transportation usage for the three studied categories: retired A, retired B, and normal users (smoothed average values are reported).

The same trends are observed for the three categories regarding the initial reduction following the declaration of the sanitary emergency and the detected events related to the three waves of the COVID-19 pandemics. Furthermore, the recovery patterns follow a similar distribution too, with a less smooth recovery than for normal users, due to the larger number of tickets sold and the reduced mobility of the elderly in days with bad weather conditions. A sustained increment on public transportation usage is observed in the few infection periods identified in Figure 9 regarding the behavior of both COVID-19 cases and trips. The analysis suggests that the behavior of older people followed the same trend observed for normal users and other categories, without significant changes in the patterns of tickets sold. Overall, the number of trips recovered in May 2022 to up to 80% of the reference pre-pandemic value (March 2020), a similar value than for normal users.

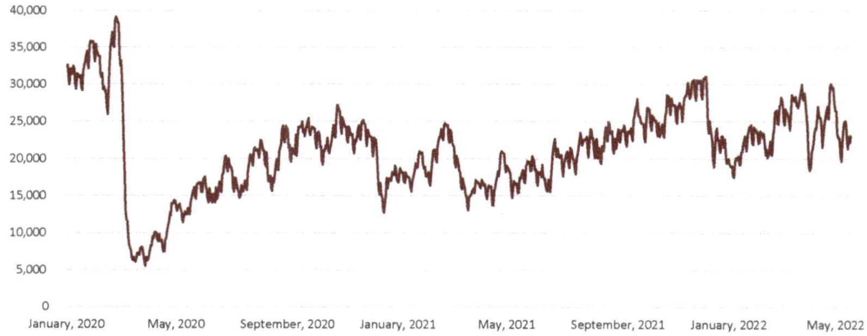

(**a**) Category: retired A

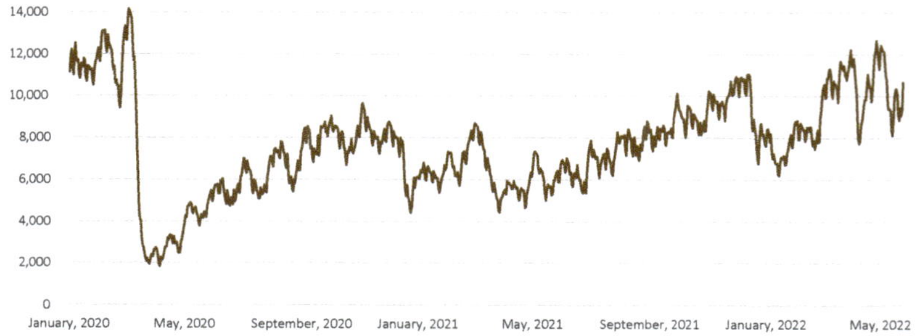

(**b**) Category: retired B

(**c**) Category: normal

Figure 14. Evolution of public transportation usage in Montevideo during the COVID-19 pandemic for retired and normal categories of users.

4.8. Summary of Results

The analysis allowed to determine several relevant results about public transportation usage in Montevideo during the COVID-19 pandemics. The main results are summarized next.

Regarding the impact of declaring a state of sanitary emergency, the analysis confirmed that the overall reduction on public transportation trips in Montevideo was 71.4%. The reduction was higher on working days (73.2%) than on weekends (54.1%). These reduction values were lower than for case studies in similar cities, e.g., 80–90% reduction in Budapest, Hungary [20], up to 85% in Warsaw, Poland [22], 90% in Gdansk, Poland [9], 90%

in cities in the Netherlands [7], 95% in Fuenlabrada, Spain [25], up to 93% in Santander, Spain [26], and more than 80% in major Latin American cities [28],

Regarding the evolution of public transportation usage during the COVID-19 pandemic, a negative correlation was found with the number of COVID-19 cases. The analysis identified four special events characterized by an increase in reported COVID-19 cases, as well as five distinct periods in the studied period, between April 20202 and May 2022. The negative correlation was particularly pronounced during the wave periods, namely the first wave (December 2020–February 2021) with a Pearson correlation coefficient of −0.89378, the second wave (March–May 2021) with a Pearson correlation coefficient of −0.81794, and the third wave (November 2021–February 2022) with a Pearson correlation coefficient of −0.85285. These coefficients indicate that as the number of COVID-19 cases increased, there was a corresponding decrease in public transportation usage, and vice versa.

Regarding the recovery of public transportation usage, Montevideo surpassed other similar capital cities worldwide. The number of trips in public transportation experienced a rapid rebound, with an impressive recovery rate. Within just four months after the declaration of the sanitary emergency in July 2020, the system had already regained 84% of its pre-COVID-19 trips. Although there was a slight decline in August 2020, the number of trips nearly reached pre-pandemic levels by November 2020, achieving a 90% recovery rate. Notably, the recovery of trip numbers after the first wave was significantly faster, surpassing 90% within three months and fully recovering in the latter months of 2021. A similar trend was detected after the second wave. Following the third wave, the recovery was remarkably swift, surpassing the pre-COVID-19 value within just two months, by March 2022. The recovery results indicate that despite the initial decline in public transportation trips due to the rise in COVID-19 cases, citizens swiftly regained their trust in the system. The recovery periods for trip numbers became progressively shorter after each new wave and, in 2022, only a month and a half was required to achieve full recovery. This recovery pace is significantly faster than the ones observed in similar case studies reported worldwide.

Finally, regarding the socioeconomic characterization of public transportation usage, different results were obtained for diverse neighborhoods of Montevideo. The reduction in trips after the declaration of the sanitary emergency was significantly lower in low-income neighborhoods (e.g., 63% in Casavalle and Casabó–Pajas Blancas) than in the wealthiest neighborhoods (e.g., 89% Pocitos and Parque Rodó). These results show that lower-income populations were more forced to continue using public transportation, due to limited alternative options for commuting.

The main findings obtained from this study provide valuable insights into the mobility patterns and public transportation usage in Montevideo during the COVID-19 pandemic. These findings offer important understanding for policymakers and researchers, enabling them to make informed decisions and develop effective strategies in response to similar challenges in the future.

5. Conclusions and Future Work

This article reported a study devoted to examine and characterize the utilization of the public transportation system in Montevideo, Uruguay, throughout the COVID-19 pandemic. The study adopts an urban data analysis approach, leveraging accessible open data on trips and relevant statistics related to the COVID-19 situation in Uruguay.

Several data sources were processed and studied applying a data analysis approach, to compute relevant indicators to characterize the public transportation usage. Trips data were correlated with the number of COVID-19 cases and socio-economic information to determine and analyze the different behavior of citizens.

The primary findings of the study reveal that the decrease in public transportation trips in Montevideo was 71.4%, which is noticeably lower compared to similar case studies. Additionally, a negative correlation was observed between the utilization of the public transportation system in Montevideo and the confirmed COVID-19 cases in Uruguay. Notably, the analysis of the correlation suggests that neighborhoods with a lower socioeconomic index, indicating lower-income populations were more reliant on the use of public transportation due to the lack of alternatives. Furthermore, the analysis of the recovery of public transportation trips indicates a swift rebound, surpassing the pace observed in other capital cities.

The obtained collective insights and results shed light on the mobility patterns and the usage of public transportation in Montevideo during the COVID-19 pandemic, providing valuable understanding for policymakers and researchers. The analysis made a concerted effort to address and mitigate the impact of various limitations. These included the heavy reliance on data availability and accuracy, the avoidance of bias by considering diverse population subsets and multiple geographical areas, and the consideration of external factors such as government regulations, work pattern changes, alternative transportation options, and individual preferences. However, establishing definitive causal relationships between the COVID-19 pandemic and the reduction in public transportation usage remains challenging due to subjective factors like the fear of infection and perceived risk associated with different modes of transportation, as well as specific economic factors. In terms of temporality, the study not only focused on the short-term effects of the pandemic on public transportation usage, but also considered potential long-term impacts and whether the observed changes in behavior persist beyond each immediate crisis or wave. It is crucial to recognize and address these limitations when interpreting the findings of the study to ensure the accuracy, validity, and the generalization of the results to other regions.

The main lines for future research include broadening the analysis to encompass additional categories such as age and tariff type. This expansion would provide a more comprehensive understanding of how different demographic factors influence public transportation usage during the COVID-19 pandemic. Another important direction for future work is to conduct a comprehensive analysis of the normalized post-COVID-19 situation, taking into account more recent trip data. These analyses would enable a more accurate assessment of the recovery and changes in public transportation patterns as the pandemic situation evolved and the everlasting impact on the behavior of citizens and their mobility habits. By considering these factors and incorporating updated data, further research can enhance the understanding of the long-term effects of the COVID-19 pandemic on public transportation and elaborate future mobility strategies and policies.

Author Contributions: Conceptualization, S.N. and A.T.; Methodology, S.N. and A.T.; Software, S.N.; Validation, S.N. and A.T., Investigation, S.N. and A.T.; Data curation, S.N.; Writing—original draft, S.N. and A.T.; Writing—review & editing, S.N. and A.T.; Supervision, S.N.; Project administration, S.N. All authors have read and agreed to the published version of the manuscript.

Funding: This research received no external funding.

Data Availability Statement: All the source data and results of the analysis are available at https://github.com/nesmachnow/stm_covid_19, accessed on 30 August 2022.

Conflicts of Interest: The authors declare no conflict of interest.

References

1. Cervero, R.; Guerra, E.; Al, S. *Beyond Mobility*; Island Press/Center for Resource Economics: Washington, DC, USA, 2017. [CrossRef]
2. Sussman, J. *Perspectives on Intelligent Transportation Systems (ITS)*; Springer Science + Business Media: Berlin/Heidelberg, Germany, 2005.
3. Hu, T.; Wang, S.; She, B.; Zhang, M.; Huang, X.; Cui, Y.; Khuri, J.; Hu, Y.; Fu, X.; Wang, X.; et al. Human mobility data in the COVID-19 pandemic: Characteristics, applications, and challenges. *Int. J. Digit. Earth* **2021**, *14*, 1126–1147. [CrossRef]
4. Huang, X.; Li, Z.; Jiang, Y.; Ye, X.; Deng, C.; Zhang, J.; Li, X. The characteristics of multi-source mobility datasets and how they reveal the luxury nature of social distancing in the U.S. during the COVID-19 pandemic. *Int. J. Digit. Earth* **2021**, *14*, 424–442. [CrossRef]
5. Nesmachnow, S.; Baña, S.; Massobrio, R. A distributed platform for big data analysis in smart cities: Combining Intelligent Transportation Systems and socioeconomic data for Montevideo, Uruguay. *EAI Endorsed Trans. Smart Cities* **2017**, *2*, 153478. [CrossRef]

6. Tirachini, A.; Cats, O. COVID-19 and Public Transportation: Current Assessment, Prospects, and Research Needs. *J. Public Transp.* **2020**, *22*, 1–21. [CrossRef] [PubMed]
7. de Haas, M.; Faber, R.; Hamersma, M. How COVID-19 and the Dutch 'intelligent lockdown' change activities, work and travel behaviour: Evidence from longitudinal data in the Netherlands. *Transp. Res. Interdiscip. Perspect.* **2020**, *6*, 100150. [CrossRef] [PubMed]
8. Liu, L.; Miller, H.J.; Scheff, J. The impacts of COVID-19 pandemic on public transit demand in the United States. *PLoS ONE* **2020**, *15*, e0242476. [CrossRef] [PubMed]
9. Przybylowski, A.; Stelmak, S.; Suchanek, M. Mobility Behaviour in View of the Impact of the COVID-19 Pandemic—Public Transport Users in Gdansk Case Study. *Sustainability* **2021**, *13*, 364. [CrossRef]
10. Massobrio, R.; Nesmachnow, S. Travel Time Estimation in Public Transportation Using Bus Location Data. In *Smart Cities*; Springer International Publishing: Berlin/Heidelberg, Germany, 2022; pp. 192–206. [CrossRef]
11. Collares, A.; Helal, D.; Nesmachnow, S.; Tchernykh, A. Analysis of Public Transportation in Montevideo, Uruguay During the COVID-19 Pandemic. In *Smart Cities*; Springer Nature: Cham, Switzerland, 2023; pp. 200–214. [CrossRef]
12. Hipogrosso, S.; Nesmachnow, S. Analysis of Sustainable Public Transportation and Mobility Recommendations for Montevideo and Parque Rodó Neighborhood. *Smart Cities* **2020**, *3*, 479–510. [CrossRef]
13. Hipogrosso, S.; Nesmachnow, S. A Practical Approach for Sustainable Transit Oriented Development in Montevideo, Uruguay. In *Smart Cities*; Springer International Publishing: Berlin/Heidelberg, Germany, 2022; pp. 256–270. [CrossRef]
14. Bohte, W.; Maat, K.; van Wee, B. Measuring Attitudes in Research on Residential Self-Selection and Travel Behaviour: A Review of Theories and Empirical Research. *Transp. Rev.* **2009**, *29*, 325–357. [CrossRef]
15. Taylor, L. Uruguay is winning against COVID-19. This is how [corrected]. *BMJ* **2020**, *370*, m3693. [CrossRef]
16. Costabel, M. Uruguay Emerges as a Rare Pandemic Winner in Latin America, 2021. *Foregn Policy* **2020**. Available online: https://foreignpolicy.com/2020/07/21/uruguay-coronavirus-pandemic-success-latin-america/ (accessed on 12 August 2023).
17. De Vos, J. The effect of COVID-19 and subsequent social distancing on travel behavior. *Transp. Res. Interdiscip. Perspect.* **2020**, *5*, 100121. [CrossRef]
18. Beck, M.; Hensher, D. Insights into the impact of COVID-19 on household travel and activities in Australia. *Transp. Policy* **2020**, *99*, 95–119. [CrossRef]
19. Jenelius, E.; Cebecauer, M. Impacts of COVID-19 on public transport ridership in Sweden: Analysis of ticket validations, sales and passenger counts. *Transp. Res. Interdiscip. Perspect.* **2020**, *8*, 100242. [CrossRef] [PubMed]
20. Bucsky, P. Modal share changes due to COVID-19: The case of Budapest. *Transp. Res. Interdiscip. Perspect.* **2020**, *8*, 100141. [CrossRef]
21. Wielechowski, M.; Czech, K.; Grzeda, Ł. Decline in Mobility: Public Transport in Poland in the time of the COVID-19 Pandemic. *Economies* **2020**, *8*, 78. [CrossRef]
22. Kłos, Z.; Gutowski, P. The Outbreak of COVID-19 Pandemic in Relation to Sense of Safety and Mobility Changes in Public Transport Using the Example of Warsaw. *Sustainability* **2022**, *14*, 1780. [CrossRef]
23. Palm, M.; Allen, J.; Liu, B.; Zhang, Y.; Widener, M.; Farber, S. Riders Who Avoided Public Transit During COVID-19. *J. Am. Plan. Assoc.* **2021**, *87*, 455–469. [CrossRef]
24. Cartenì, A.; Di Francesco, L.; Henke, I.; Marino, T.; Falanga, A. The Role of Public Transport during the Second COVID-19 Wave in Italy. *Sustainability* **2021**, *13*, 11905. [CrossRef]
25. Rodríguez, A.; Wilby, M.; Vinagre, J.; Fernández, R. Characterization of COVID-19's Impact on Mobility and Short-Term Prediction of Public Transport Demand in a Mid-Size City in Spain. *Sensors* **2021**, *21*, 6574. [CrossRef]
26. Aloi, A.; Alonso, B.; Benavente, J.; Cordera, R.; Echániz, E.; González, F.; Ladisa, C.; Lezama, R.; López, Á.; Mazzei, V.; et al. Effects of the COVID-19 Lockdown on Urban Mobility: Empirical Evidence from the City of Santander (Spain). *Sustainability* **2020**, *12*, 3870. [CrossRef]
27. Awad, S.; Julio, R.; Gomez, J.; Moya, B.; Sastre, J. Post-COVID-19 travel behavior patterns: Impact on the willingness to pay of users of public transport and shared mobility services in Spain. *Eur. Transp. Res. Rev.* **2021**, *13*, 20. [CrossRef]
28. Andara, R.; Ortego, J.; Gómez, M.; Ramírez, R.; Navas, L.; Vásquez, C.; Gaitán, M. Behavior of Traffic Congestion and Public Transport in Eight Large Cities in Latin America during the COVID-19 Pandemic. *Appl. Sci.* **2021**, *11*, 4703. [CrossRef]
29. Gramsch, B.; Guevara, C.A.; Munizaga, M.; Schwartz, D.; Tirachini, A. The effect of dynamic lockdowns on public transport demand in times of COVID-19: Evidence from smartcard data. *Transp. Policy* **2022**, *126*, 136–150. [CrossRef]
30. Puello, L. Impact of COVID-19 restrictions on mode use and mode captivity the city of Santo Domingo in Latin America. *Transp. Res. Interdiscip. Perspect.* **2022**, *13*, 100515. [CrossRef] [PubMed]
31. Massobrio, R.; Nesmachnow, S. Urban Mobility Data Analysis for Public Transportation Systems: A Case Study in Montevideo, Uruguay. *Appl. Sci.* **2020**, *10*, 5400. [CrossRef]
32. Denis, J.; Massobrio, R.; Nesmachnow, S.; Cristóbal, A.; Tchernykh, A.; Meneses, E. Parallel computing for processing data from Intelligent Transportation Systems. In Proceedings of the 10th International Supercomputing Conference in Mexico, Monterrey, Mexico, 25–29 March 2019; pp. 1–15.
33. Fabbiani, E.; Nesmachnow, S.; Toutouh, J.; Tchernykh, A.; Avetisyan, A.; Radchenko, G.I. Analysis of Mobility Patterns for Public Transportation and Bus Stops Relocation. *Program. Comput. Softw.* **2018**, *44*, 508–525. [CrossRef]

34. Massobrio, R.; Nesmachnow, S.; Tchernykh, A.; Avetisyan, A.; Radchenko, G. Towards a Cloud Computing Paradigm for Big Data Analysis in Smart Cities. *Program. Comput. Softw.* **2018**, *44*, 181–189. [CrossRef]
35. Massobrio, R.; Pías, A.; Vázquez, N.; Nesmachnow, S. Map-Reduce for Processing GPS Data from Public Transport in Montevideo, Uruguay. In Proceedings of the Simposio Argentino de Grandes Datos, 45 Jornadas Argentinas de Informática, La Plata, Argentina, 5–9 September 2016; pp. 41–54.
36. Grupo Uruguayo Interdisciplinario de Análisis de Datos. COVID Stats per Department. Available online: https://github.com/3dgiordano/covid-19-uy-vacc-data (accessed on 21 July 2022).
37. Odersky, M.; Spoon, L.; Venners, B. *Programming in Scala: [A Comprehensive Step-by-Step Guide]*; Artima Inc.: Walnut Creek, CA, USA, 2008.
38. White, T. *Hadoop: The Definitive Guide*, 4th ed.; O'Reilly: Beijing, China, 2015.
39. Nesmachnow, S.; Iturriaga, S. Cluster-UY: Collaborative Scientific High Performance Computing in Uruguay. In *Supercomputing*; Communications in Computer and Information Science; Springer: Berlin/Heidelberg, Germany, 2019; Volume 1151, pp. 188–202. [CrossRef]
40. Llambí, C.; Piñeyro, L. Índice de Nivel Socioeconómico. 2012. Available online: https://cinve.org.uy/wp-content/uploads/2012/12/Indice-de-nivel-socioecon%C3%B3mico.pdf (accessed on 30 August 2022).
41. Perera, M.; Cazulo, P. Índice de Nivel Socioeconómico: Propuesta de Actualización. 2016. Available online: http://ceismu.org/site/wp-content/uploads/inse-informe-final-28032016.pdf (accessed on 30 August 2022).
42. Perera, M. Índice de Nivel Socioeconómico. 2018. Available online: https://ceismu.org/site/wp-content/uploads/INSE-2018-documento-final.pdf (accessed on 30 August 2022).
43. CERES. La Delgada Línea de la Pobreza, 2020. Text in Spanish. Available online: https://ceres.uy/admin/uploads/slides/archivo_1667994302.pdf (accessed on 30 August 2022).
44. Perera, S.; Massobrio, R. Walking Accessibility to the Public Transport Network in Montevideo, Uruguay. In *Proceedings of the Smart Cities*; Communications in Computer and Information Science; Springer: Berlin/Heidelberg, Germany, 2023; pp. 17–30.
45. Lättman, K.; Olsson, L.E.; Waygood, E.O.D.; Friman, M. Nowhere to go–Effects on elderly's travel during Covid-19. *Travel Behav. Soc.* **2023**, *32*, 100574. [CrossRef]
46. Liu, Q.; Liu, Y.; Zhang, C.; An, Z.; Zhao, P. Elderly mobility during the COVID-19 pandemic: A qualitative exploration in Kunming, China. *J. Transp. Geogr.* **2021**, *96*, 103176. [CrossRef]
47. Shaer, A.; Haghshenas, H. Evaluating the effects of the COVID-19 outbreak on the older adults' travel mode choices. *Transp. Policy* **2021**, *112*, 162–172. [CrossRef]
48. Choe, E.Y.; Du, Y.; Sun, G. Decline in older adults' daily mobility during the COVID-19 pandemic: The role of individual and built environment factors. *BMC Public Health* **2022**, *22*, 2317. [CrossRef] [PubMed]
49. Guida, C.; Carpentieri, G. Quality of life in the urban environment and primary health services for the elderly during the Covid-19 pandemic: An application to the city of Milan (Italy). *Cities* **2021**, *110*, 103038. [CrossRef] [PubMed]
50. Park, B.; Cho, J. Older Adults' Avoidance of Public Transportation after the Outbreak of COVID-19: Korean Subway Evidence. *Healthcare* **2021**, *9*, 448. [CrossRef] [PubMed]
51. Reinhard, E.; Carrino, L.; Courtin, E.; van Lenthe, F.J.; Avendano, M. Public Transportation Use and Cognitive Function in Older Age: A Quasiexperimental Evaluation of the Free Bus Pass Policy in the United Kingdom. *Am. J. Epidemiol.* **2019**, *188*, 1774–1783. [CrossRef]

urban science

MDPI

Article

Sociodemographic Analysis of Disability in a Highly Depopulated Rural Region: The Case of Soria, Spain

Juan R. Coca [1,*], Julio Fernández-Portela [2], Susana Gómez-Redondo [3] and Anabel Paramá-Díaz [4]

[1] Social Research Unit on Health and Rare Diseases, Department of Sociology and Social Work, Faculty of Business and Labour Sciences of Soria, University of Valladolid, 42004 Soria, Spain
[2] Department of Geography, Faculty of Geography and History, Spanish Distance Learning University, 28040 Madrid, Spain; jfportela@geo.uned.es
[3] Social Research Unit on Health and Rare Diseases, Department of Pedagogy, Faculty of Education of Soria, University of Valladolid, 42004 Soria, Spain; susana.gomezr@uva.es
[4] GIR06—Psychological Research in the Digital Age, Faculty of Legal and Economic, Isabel I University, Sciences, 09003 Burgos, Spain; anaisabel.parama@ui1.es
* Correspondence: juanr.coca@uva.es

Abstract: European regions with a lower population density have greater structural difficulties in ensuring that the daily life of their inhabitants matches that of more populated regions. This problem persists in groups of people who present some type of disability. Soria (Spain) is one of such regions. It is considered the most depopulated region of Southern Europe. Therefore, the aim of this study was to analyse the reality of people with disabilities in one of the provinces with a lower population density. It also seeks to explore the relationship between the perceptions and the reality of the existing structure to infer the promotions or limitations of agency. To this end, we conducted a systematic review of the existing literature, a sociogeographic study of the study context, and a mixed investigation. The results show that the greatest problem lies in the cities and towns located far away from the capital city, causing budget cutbacks and, therefore, reducing the attention to the needs of people with disabilities. However, social solidarity has increased, which is perceived as greater social inclusion for this group.

Keywords: disability; depopulation; Southern Europe; social solidarity; mixed analysis

1. Introduction

Disability is a human reality that presents a large variety of faces and nuances; thus, we can assert that it is a biosocial phenomenon of great complexity due to the numerous aspects affected, which has generated the concept of the world of life. The idea of disability refers to the interaction between people who have some health problems and certain personal and environmental factors [1]. Thus, in order to approach this complexity, it is convenient to analyse the elements that constitute the sociotype of people with disabilities.

This concept implies the consideration of human relations and interactions among individuals of said group with their environment [2]. These authors based their study on the work of Berry [3] and reported that the term sociotype is an integrating concept that comprises internal and external factors, combining biological, psychological and social aspects.

Usually, it is considered that there are different types of disabilities, and these are usually limited to the following: auditory, intellectual, visual and physical. Moreover, they are also differentiated between congenital and acquired or unforeseeable disabilities [4]. Depending on the reality of each person and her/his limitations, the sociotype may be nuanced. In the present work, we performed a generic analysis of a person with a disability sociotype and how it is modulated by the sociogeographic context of depopulation.

The studies about the perception of people with disabilities toward areas with low population density are not frequent. The studies we found (Table 1) are mainly related to biomedical aspects: osteoporosis, obesity, cardiovascular diseases, etc. In our documentary analysis, we identified four articles with certain interest for our objectives. However, none of them were related to analyses of life perception. These studies analyse the importance of context in its relationship with disability, showing the relevance of social structure for our sociotype.

Table 1. Articles Related to Research.

	Title	Highlights	References
1	Contextual and mental health service factors in mental disorder-based disability pensioning in Finland—a regional comparison.	A lower risk of disability pensions was associated with contextual indicators of greater regional socioeconomic level. The authors found evidence of a significant regional variation related, at least partially, to the differences in the regional systems of mental health services and the treatment practices.	[5]
2	Associations of neighbourhood sociodemographic characteristics with depression and anxiety symptoms in old age: results from a five-wave study over 15 years	This article shows that urban areas with high density are associated with health problems such as depression and anxiety. In turn, these statistical associations were stable for 15 years. On the other hand, the authors assert that urban density is an important factor with a negative impact on mental health and older people.	[6]
3	Municipal unemployment and municipal typologies as predictors of disability pensioning in Norway: a multilevel analysis	People in municipalities with high unemployment rates were 7–17% more likely to acquire disability pensions. Of the total variability of disability pensions, 2.5% of men and 1.9% of women were between municipalities. The other municipal factors only showed mild influences. Conclusion: In addition to individual socioeconomic factors, contextual factors seem to be important determinants of disability pension rates.	[7]
4	Needs and ambitions in Swedish disability care.	In this study, the authors identified six characteristics to explain this variation: earlier presence of residential institutions, population density, human capital (age, education, employment, health), local culture, territorial surface and stable left-wing government. The results bolster a model of support to social care that responds to the needs of the population, although they also show accessibility problems. This means that spatial equity is violated. To sum up, the place of residence still matters.	[8]

Source: developed by the authors.

Berry [3] stated that the concept of sociotype is a conceptual framework that allows understanding the interactions between the social, cultural and environmental scopes. This framework influences the life-long growth, development and behaviour of a person, including his/her relationships, lifestyle and coping strategies. In this sense, it could be added that the sociotype is strongly related to agency (action capacity), which is influenced by the conditioning factors of each sociotype.

Margaret Archer established an analysis of the Social System based on two major dimensions: agency and structure. For this author, neither agency nor structure can separately determine human action. Human action requires the reflectivity that operates as a mediator between social structure and agency [9,10]. Therefore, this author considers that, at the internal level, there is a process that allows people to make decisions about their actions. Archer proposes a relationship between agency and structure through time [10]. In this sense, agency is related to structure and, lastly, the latter is also influenced by agency. Based on this idea, Archer considers that social agents are strongly related to structure, since these are the different existing social institutions.

The Archerian perspective, although useful, suffers from a certain subjectivism, as well as certain structuralism. Thus, it does not consider the phenomena of incorporation of people in their social environment, that is, the intermediate processes between the subjective elements and the objective–structural elements. In fact, Caetano [11] stated that Archer minimises social factors such as social origins, family socialisation, externality internalisation processes, the role of other structure–agency mediation mechanisms, and the persistence of social reproduction. However, Archer's perspective is sufficient to attain the objectives of the present study.

This work is focused on the concept of agency in people with disabilities and, more specifically, the perception and experience of this group in areas of low population density. This study is based on the premise that living in an area with a considerable demographic decline can substantially intensify the difficulties of a social group with a "low agency level" [12]. In this sense, we assert that the structure of the system influences the agency of people. Thus, the European regions with lower population density will have greater structural difficulties to ensure that the social agency of their inhabitants matches that of more populated areas. Furthermore, this problem is even greater in groups of people with disabilities.

Therefore, the present study is focused on one of the most depopulated territories of Southern Europe with the lowest population density: Soria (Spain). We begin by providing context for the province of Soria, highlighting its status as one of the most sparsely populated regions in all of Europe, and its prominent position within the group of sparsely populated regions in Southern Europe. As can be observed in Table 2 (where the most updated European data are shown, 2019), the greatest European depopulation is concentrated in the regions of said continent and in some of the regions that are not geographically located in the European continent (Guyane). According to Van Herwijnen et al. [13], many of the rural areas that suffer the most from demographic decline are located in Southern Europe. Some of these regions are Bulgaria, Greece, Il Mezzogiorno (Southern Italy), northeastern Spain and Portugal, as well as islands such as Sicily and Sardinia. However, the data about population density show that Soria is the most depopulated province of Southern Europe, although its depopulation level is somewhat stable.

Table 2. Population density in the most depopulated European regions.

Regions	2015	2016	2017	2018	2019
Soria	**8.9**	**8.8**	**8.7**	**8.7**	**8.7**
Licko-senjska zupanija	8.9	8.8	8.6	8.5	8.3
Oppland (statistical region 2016)	7.9	7.9	7.9	7.9	7.9
Innlandet	7.7	7.6	7.7	7.7	7.7
Hedmark (statistical region 2016)	7.5	7.4	7.5	7.5	7.5
Nordland	6.7	6.7	6.7	6.7	6.7
Troms (statistical region 2016)	6.6	6.6	6.6	6.6	6.6
Pohjois-ja Itä-Suomi	6.4	6.4	6.4	6.3	6.3
Norra Sverige	6.0	6.1	6.1	6.1	6.1
Sogn og Fjordane (statistical region 2016)	6.2	6.1	6.2	6.1	6.1
Mellersta Norrland	5.3	5.3	5.3	5.3	5.3
Västerbottens län	4.8	4.8	4.9	4.9	5.0
Nord-Norge	4.5	4.4	4.5	4.5	4.5
Kainuu	3.7	3.7	3.7	3.6	3.6
Iceland	3.3	3.3	3.4	3.5	3.6
Ísland	3.3	3.3	3.4	3.5	3.6
Guyane	3.2	3.2	3.3	3.3	3.4
Övre Norrland	3.4	3.4	3.4	3.4	3.4
Jämtlands län	2.6	2.6	2.6	2.7	2.7
Norrbottens län	2.6	2.6	2.6	2.6	2.6
Lappi	2.0	1.9	1.9	1.9	1.9
Finnmark (statistical region 2016)	1.7	1.6	1.6	1.6	1.6
Landsbyggd	1.2	1.2	1.2	1.3	1.3

Source: Eurostat—Population density by NUTS 3 region (data: person/km^2).

Next, we will elucidate the methodology employed to fulfill our objectives, followed by an exposition of the results derived from the application of this methodology. We will also offer a succinct section delineating the limitations we encountered during the study. Finally, we will expound upon the pivotal conclusions we have gleaned from our research endeavours.

2. Objectives

Through this research, we aim to gain insights into the challenges faced by individuals with disabilities residing in an extensively depopulated region. To accomplish this, we outline the following specific objectives:

O_1: analyse the social structure in the most depopulated region of Southern Europe and determine how it hinders or favours the study sociotype.

O_2: explore the relationship between the perceptions and the reality of the existing structure to infer the promotions or limitations of agency.

3. Methodology

This is an instrumental case study of the most depopulated province of Southern Europe. Following Stake [14], this study is instrumental for not being exclusively limited to the described area, since the aim is to extend it (as an operational model) to other areas of Southern Europe in demographic decline. In order to delve into the difficulties of people with disabilities in the most depopulated area of Southern Europe, at the beginning of 2020, a study was conducted in three different phases: documentary analysis, sociodemographic study and mixed investigation.

Bricout and Gray [15] stated that research requires a mixed approach, incorporating historical evidence, the analysis of those critical elements for the phenomenon under study, mixed-methods investigation, and repeated measures in adequate time intervals. Therefore, this multiple approach was selected for the present study.

3.1. Documentary Analysis

In the documentary study, which was carried out during April 2022, different information searches were conducted in different databases (specifically in Web of Science and SCOPUS), with the aim of performing a review of the articles published to date. Our analysis was based on the following searches: Disability + Europe + Depopulation = 1 paper; Disability + Europe + Society + Perception = 18 papers in WOS and 17 papers in SCOPUS (none of the articles mentioned low-population areas); Disability + Europe + "Low Population" = 2 papers in WOS and 0 in SCOPUS (1 related in Russian); Disability + Europe + "Population density" = 19 papers in WOS and 2 in SCOPUS (2 related); Disability + Europe + Population + Density = 100 papers in WOS and 24 in SCOPUS (1 related). This analysis was complementary to other studies conducted.

3.2. Sociodemographic Study

For the socio-geographic analysis, the demographic sources from the Spanish Institute of Statistics (INE) were used, specifically population censuses and registers of different years (https://www.ine.es/dyngs/INEbase/es/categoria.htm?c=Estadistica_P&cid=1254734710984 (accessed on 10 May 2023)). The population censuses are used in numerous countries for demographic studies [16–18]. To determine the historical evolution of the population of the province of Soria, from the year 1900 to the year 2021, the data of the censuses were used. The population censuses gather, analyse and publish the demographic, cultural, economic and social data of the inhabitants of the country, as well as the data of the different administrative divisions (regional, provincial, municipal. . ., etc.) related to a given date or period. They are carried out every ten years and were traditionally published in the years ending in 0. Thus, for the present study, we used the censuses of 1900, 1910, 1920, 1930, 1940, 1950, 1960 and 1970; after the 1970 census, the censuses began to be published in the years ending in 1. Therefore, the rest of the censuses used in this work were those of 1981, 1991, 2001, 2011 and 2021.

To build the population pyramids, which reflect the population structure by sex and age, we used the data from the Population Register of the province of Soria for January 2021. The Municipal Register is an administrative register that gathers the neighbours of a municipality and whose revision is the responsibility of the town halls, which are in charge of informing the INE about the monthly variations that occur in the data of their municipal registers.

The demographic information is completed with that provided by the INE through the 2012 Social Integration and Health Survey (https://www.ine.es/dyngs/INEbase/es/operacion.htm?c=Estadistica_C&cid=1254736176987&menu=resultados&idp=1254735573175 (accessed on 10 May 2023)), the survey of the Government of Castile and Leon (in the social services website) (https://serviciossociales.jcyl.es/web/es/servicios-sociales.html (accessed on 21 June 2023)), which shows the situation of people with disabilities in the autonomous community and the information related to the Social Action Centres (C.E.A.S.) obtained from the website of the Council of Soria (https://www.dipsoria.es/areas-diputacion/servicios-sociales/actividades-servicios-sociales (accessed on 06 July 2023)). With all this information, a series of cartograms were performed, which allowed for the visualisation of this information and showed its distribution throughout the territory, enabling comparisons among different geographic spaces. For the development of this mapping, we used ArcGis (ArcMap) software v.10.6. Maps of proportional symbols and choropleths were generated, which allowed representing zonal phenomena with absolute or relative values [19–21]. For the map of proportional symbols, i.e., the one related to the distribution of people with disabilities by Autonomous Community, the intervals were manually defined to better show the similarities/differences among the different Spanish regions. For the map of choropleths, that is, the one that presents the population density and variation, the colour palettes used allow identifying the existing similarities and differences among the municipalities of the province of Soria. For the graphs and tables, the Excel 2019 spreadsheet software was employed.

3.3. Mixed Investigation

In the quantitative study, an online questionnaire was developed, which gathered information about aspects related to mobility, specifically the state of the streets of their cities, as well as the accessibility to buildings and public transportation. The quantitative study presented difficulties and was completed by a small number of people. The reasons for this low response rate are analysed in the Limitations section. The questionnaire was responded to by 37 people (16 women and 21 men). Moreover, the number of responses from people over 60 years of age was also limited. Considering that, in the province of Soria in 2019, there were 6759 people with disabilities, the level of statistical significance of the data is low (the margin of error reached 16.07%, with 95% confidence interval). Of the analysed sample, 86.49% lived in the city of Soria, and 13.51% lived in the rest of the province; 22 people presented some administratively recognised disability, and 15 people did not have any type of administrative disability. The age of the participants is shown in Table 3. All this implies certain limitations in the quantitative data, granting them an illustrative character.

After determining these limitations in the quantitative information, these data were completed with a qualitative study. In this way, the study was completed and acquired greater depth, providing a complete and comprehensive view of the situation of this depopulated region. In this sense, the qualitative analysis was conducted based on a focal discussion group with 6 people who were strongly related to the scope of disability. All of these participants were workers in some association related to disability and had extensive knowledge on the reality of this issue in the province of Soria. The discussion group lasted two and a half hours and was conducted on 30 January 2020 at the campus of the University of Valladolid at Soria.

Table 3. Age distribution of the participants and the quantity of participants in the survey within each age category.

Age Group	Participants
20–30 years	6
30–40 years	7
40–50 years	13
50–60 years	8
60–70 years	2
More than 70 years	1
Total	37

Source: developed by the authors.

4. Results

4.1. Sociodemographic Analysis

4.1.1. Disability at the Regional Level

According to the data of the Spanish Secretariat of Social Services (2019), Castile and Leon was, in 2019, the fourth region in the whole of the Spanish territory with the largest number of applications to the system requesting autonomy and attention to dependency. The profiles of people who can enter this system are gathered in Article 2 of Law 39/2006, of 14 December, on the Promotion of Personal Autonomy and Attention to people in a situation of dependency, that is, those in a permanent state of dependency derived from age, disability or disease, and those with a lack or loss of physical, mental, intellectual or sensory autonomy.

Firstly, Andalusia is the region that recorded the largest number of applications (21.61%) of the total Spanish territory, followed by Catalonia and the Community of Madrid (17.97% and 11.94%, respectively). In the fourth place, Castile and Leon recorded 7.87% of applications, followed by the Community of Valencia, despite the fact that the population of the former (2,383,139) is 2.5 times smaller than that of the latter (5,058,138). After analysing the data as a function of the relationship between the number of applications and the total population of each Autonomous Community (AC), a significant change occurred: Castile and Leon was the region with the largest number of applications (5.95%), followed by Extremadura (5.16%) and La Rioja (4.86%).

The applications to the system requesting autonomy and attention to dependency are an indicator that shows, in part, the existing situation and the possible number of people who may have their disability legally registered. However, a more real view is provided by the Social Integration and Health Survey (2012), which shows the distribution, by autonomous communities and percentages, of disability in Spain, that is, of the people who have administratively recognised disabilities (Figure 1).

The largest number of people is concentrated in Andalusia, with a fifth of the Spanish total (20.96%), followed by Catalonia (15.37%), the Community of Valencia (11.30%) and the Community of Madrid (11.12%). These four regions combined gather over half of the people with disabilities in the whole of the country, specifically 58.75%. It is important to mention that these four communities are the most populated communities in Spain, and they gather 58.91% of all the inhabitants of the country; that is, there is a correspondence between the total population and people with disabilities. This is not the case for surface distribution, since all these people live in 29.8% of the Spanish territory. These communities are followed by Galicia (6.47%), the Canary Islands (4.78%), the Basque Country (4.86%) and Castile and Leon (4.52%). These are autonomous communities with smaller populations compared to the previous communities, and therefore, they show a smaller total number of people with disabilities. They are in an intermediate level between the most populated regions and the following group of territories with a smaller number of inhabitants and lower population with disabilities, such as Cantabria, the Balearic Islands, Extremadura and La Rioja (Figure 1).

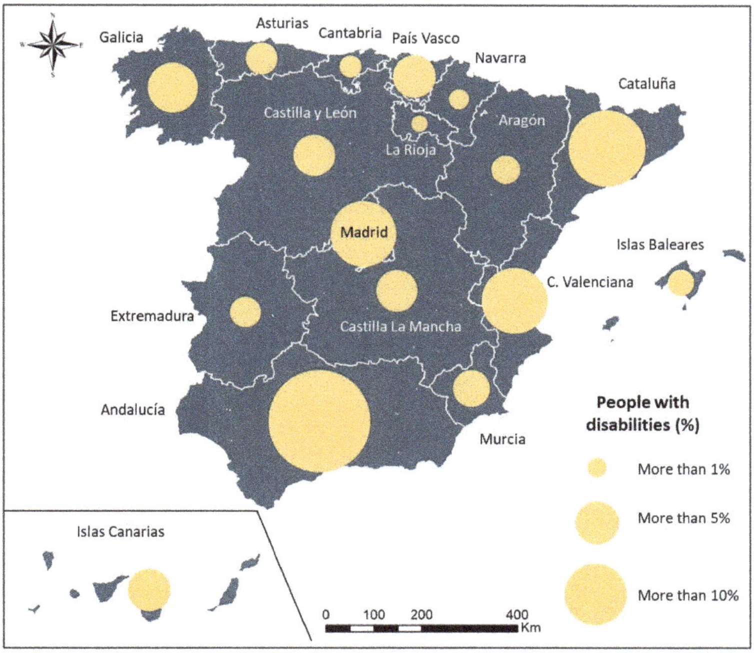

Figure 1. Distribution of people with disabilities obtained in the different regions of Spain. Date obtained from Social Integration and Health Survey (2012). Source: developed by the authors.

It is in the territory scope where problems emerge regarding accessibility to certain services and the lack of specialised equipment and centres required by this population group. A total of 41.25% of the population with disabilities is located in 70.2% of the Spanish territory, which coincides with the most aged regions, whose population is decreasing, presenting important structural problems.

Analysing the situation in Castile and Leon, the temporal data allow studying the evolution of the population with disabilities in this region. There are available data about the total number of cases between the years 2007 and 2018 (Government of Castile and Leon, 2018) by age groups and sex. In 2007, the number of cases was 152,037, whereas in 2018, the number of cases was 176,336; that is, an increase of 24,299 new cases of people with disabilities was recorded. These numbers indicate that 7.32% of the inhabitants of this Autonomous Community had some type of administratively recognised disability. The main cause that explains this increase is the ageing of Castile and Leon, which is a situation that implies the need for greater investment in daily social and care services. According to the data of the INE in 2018, the percentage of inhabitants aged 65 years and older in Spain was 19.07%, i.e., six points below the numbers of Castile and Leon, whose ageing data exceeded 25% of the population. Specifically, in this autonomous community, 25.06% of the population was over 65 years of age, which made it the second most aged region of Spain after Asturias (25.25%) and followed by Galicia (24.91%).

With respect to sex, the global difference between men and women was very small. In 2007, there were more women with disabilities than men, with percentages of 50.38% and 49.62%, respectively. However, in 2018, men represented 51.87% of people with disabilities, whereas women represented 48.13%. Regarding age groups, greater differences were found (Figure 2). In the older cohorts, the number of people with disabilities was larger. In this way, in the group of young inhabitants (0 to 14 years), the population with disabilities represented 2.26%, whereas for the group of 15–64 years, the population with disabilities represented 47.50%. More significant numbers were identified for the group that was

65 years and older, with more than half of the people with disabilities (50.24%), partly due to the characteristic ageing of the region of Castile and Leon, with an increasingly older and more dependent population that requires a series of care services. Within this last group, it is worth highlighting the difference between men and women in the cohort of 85 years and older. In this population group, there are twice as many women with disabilities compared to men: 10.52% of women versus 5.35% of men. The causes of this phenomenon are, as previously mentioned, the ageing of the population and the greater life expectancy of women, which makes them more numerous than men in this age group. With regard to the group of men, disability is more frequent in males than in females in practically the entire pyramid, from 0 to 79 years. The greatest differences are found in the group of 50–69 years, where the variation between men and women is over one point and, in some cases, it reaches almost one and a half points in favour of men, due to disabilities derived from certain jobs traditionally associated with men.

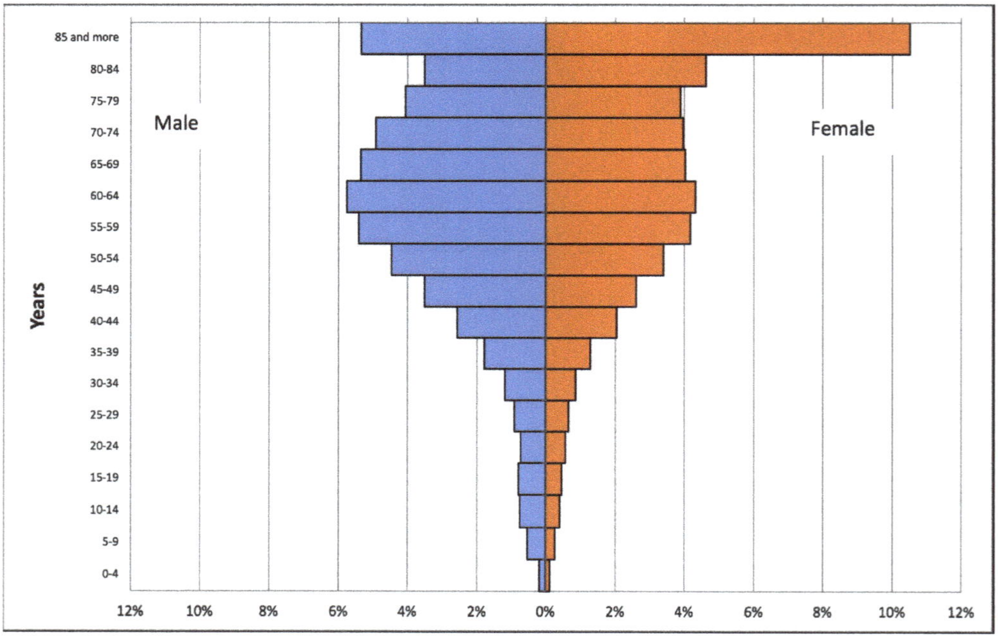

Figure 2. Population pyramid of people with disabilities in Castile and Leon in 2018. Source: Government of Castile and Leon. Developed by the authors.

According to the 2012 Social Integration and Health Survey conducted by the INE, the main limitation of this population group, both in the whole of Spain and in Castile and Leon, was being homebound, since over 50% of the people perceived it as a barrier to carry out their activities of daily living, mainly due to the maladaptation of buildings to their needs. It is worth pointing out the problems related to transportation, which is worse and less adapted in Castile and Leon, where 43.27% of people report encountering difficulties, compared to 29.87% of the population in the whole of Spain. Other important barriers are found in the realisation of cultural and leisure activities, with very high percentages, with the general Spanish population reaching 70% and that of Castile and Leon exceeding this percentage. The access to and mobility in buildings, as well as access to adequate employment, continue to present impediments for the daily living of people with disabilities. In regard to access to the Internet and social contact and support, the barriers have been practically removed.

4.1.2. The Local Context: Soria

The province of Soria presents sociodemographic characteristics that influence the economic scope and its territory. The evolution of the population between the years 1900 and 2020 shows a sharp decrease in the number of inhabitants from 150,000 in 1900 to merely 90,000 in 2020. That is, in absolute numbers, it has lost a total of 61,578 inhabitants, which poses a 40.93% lower population compared to the year 1900 (Figure 3). This decrease began in the mid-20th century, specifically in the decade of 1950–1960, when the process of rural flight took place, that is, the moving of the population from the rural areas to the urban areas, in search of new opportunities in the industrial and service sectors, due to the employment decline in agricultural activity as a consequence of the technical and technological reforms that occurred in the agricultural sector. The result of this change was the constant decrease in the population in the province, with people moving to industrial development areas such as those in Zaragoza and Valladolid, industrial promotion areas such as that in Burgos, the industrial regions of the Basque Country, and the Community of Madrid. The latter, in addition to being the capital of Spain, offered greater opportunities in the service sector.

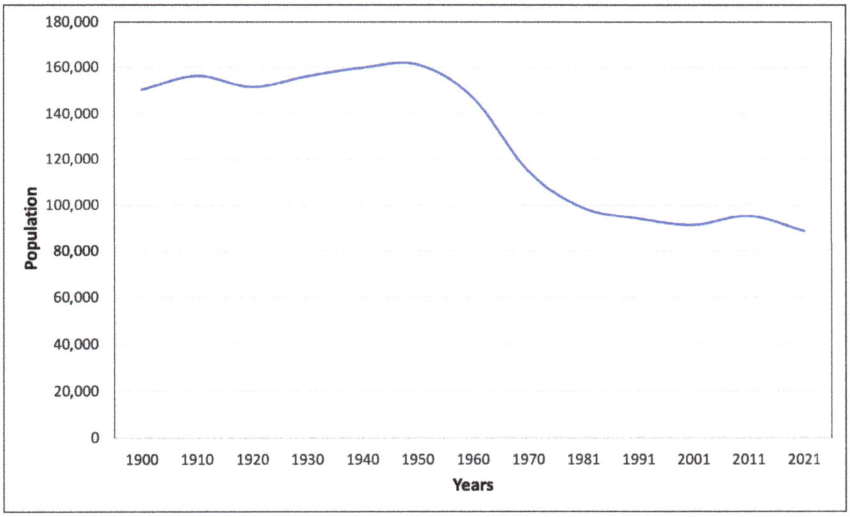

Figure 3. Evolution of the population in the province of Soria (1900–2021). Source: INE censuses. Developed by the authors. Note: Blue line shows the evolution of population during the 20th century and the beginning of the 21st century in the studied area.

The population decrease is associated with a decrease in population density, which has always been low, i.e., around 15 people per square kilometre (people/km^2) in the years that recorded the highest population in the province (1900–1950), decreasing to less than 10 people/km^2 from 1981 to 2020, with a population density of 8.62 people/km^2, thereby considering this territory as a demographic desert. Comparing these data for the year 2020 with those of Castile and Leon as a whole (25.42 people/km^2) and Spain (93.78 people/km^2), the numbers of the province of Soria are very low.

By municipality (Figure 4), of the 183 municipalities of the province, 153 (83.61% of the total) have a population below five people/km^2, of which 37 have less than one person/km^2. These numbers show the agonising situation of practically the entire province of Soria. The highest density is found in the city of Soria, with 146.64 people/km^2, which also concentrates 44.8% of the population of this province. The capital is followed by Salduero, with 56.44 people/km^2. In this case, this municipality has very little representation, as it has a very small population (152 inhabitants), distributed in a surface of only

2.69 km^2. The cases of Ólvega, San Leonardo de Yagüe and Almazán are more significant, with 37.23 people/km^2, 33.93 people/km^2 and 32.91 people/km^2, respectively; these localities have more than 1000 inhabitants each and operate as regional hubs, with a greater population concentration and greater development and economic diversity. Of the 183 localities of the province, only ten of them showed a population increase (Figure 4), whereas the other 173 presented a population decrease.

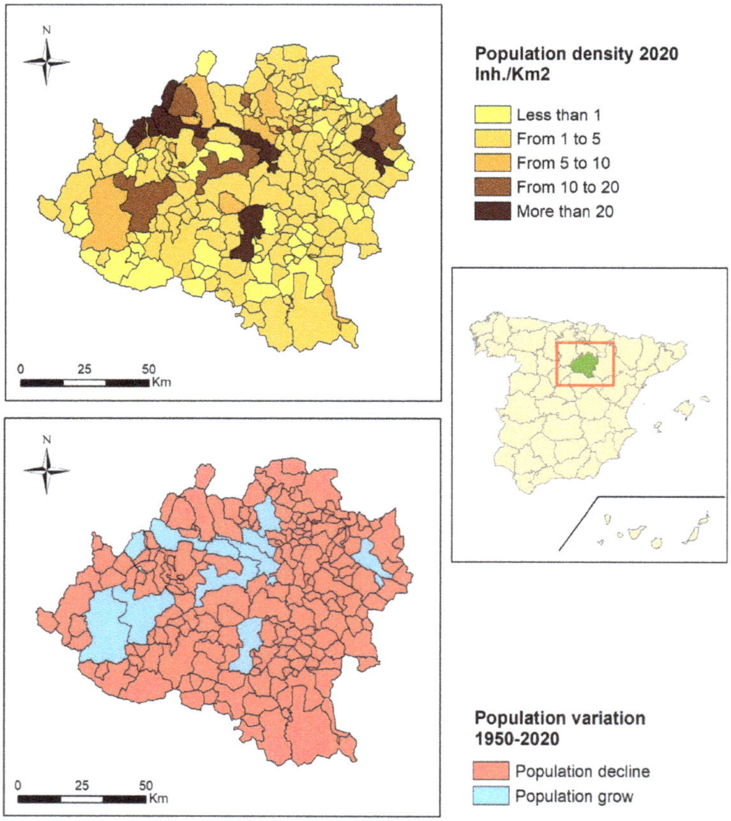

Figure 4. Population density in 2020 and Population variation (1950–2020) in Soria. Source: Continuous Census Statistics of the INE. Developed by the authors.

The structure by sex and age shows a very aged society due to the increase in the population over 65 years of age and the overageing of people over 84 years of age (population groups with a greater proportion of recognised disabilities). The birth rates decrease, the young population groups are increasingly narrower, as can be observed in the bottom of the population pyramid, and people are increasingly older (Figure 5).

The youngest group (0–14 years) represents 12.10% of the population, the age group of 15–64 years represents 62.32%, and the oldest group (65 years and older) represents 25.58%. The differences with Spain are great since, in the whole of the country, the percentage of the population aged 0–14 years is 14.40% and that of 65 years and older is 19.43%, which is also a worrying percentage since the ageing degree of the Spanish population is also high. Therefore, it is necessary to invest in social policies for the most disadvantaged population groups that are in full and constant growth.

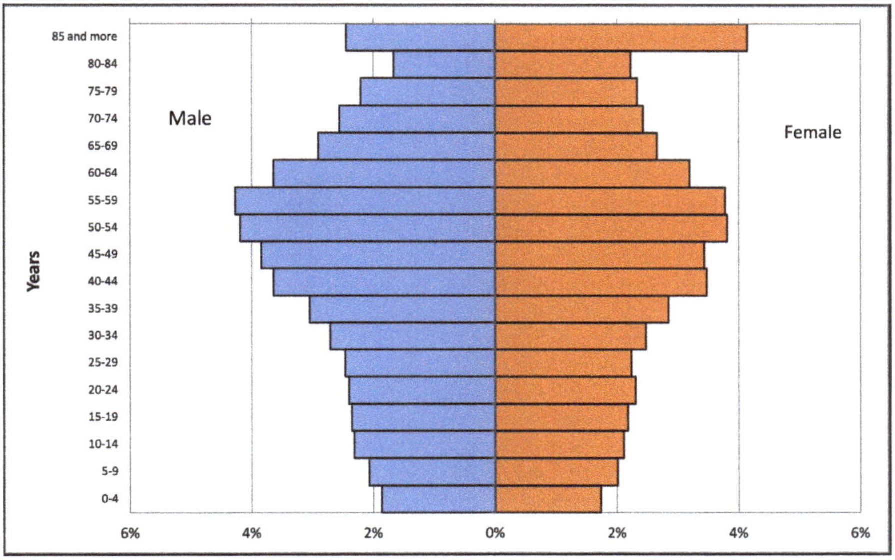

Figure 5. Population pyramid of the province of Soria in 2020. Source: Census of inhabitants of the INE. Developed by the authors.

The reality of disability in the province of Soria is influenced by its economic, social and demographic situation. As can be observed, the province of Soria presents an unbalanced population structure in terms of territory, characterised by a great degree of ageing, which influences the sociotype of people with disabilities. In fact, an important part of the sociotype of people with disabilities is constituted by older people (Figure 6).

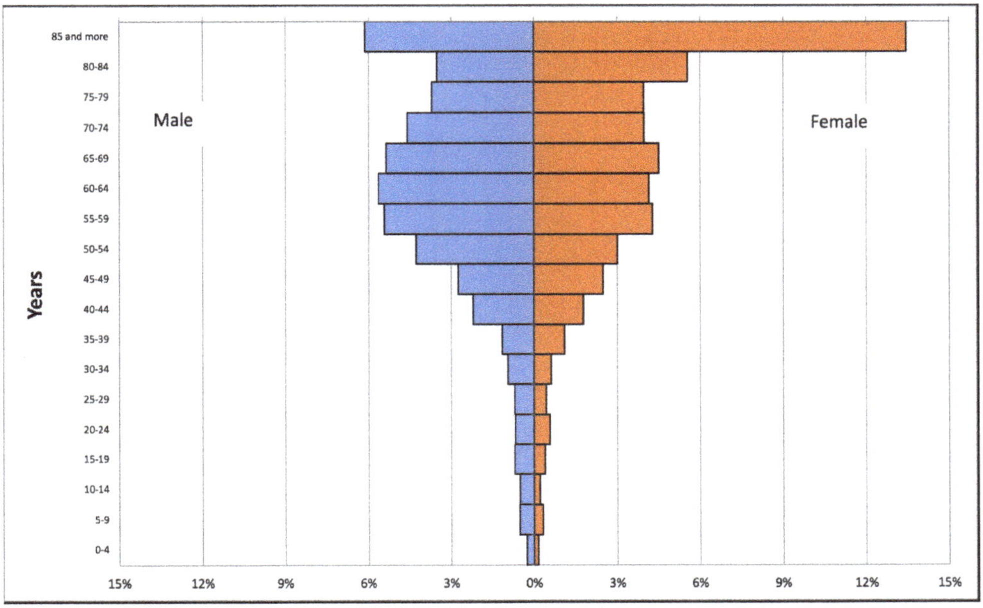

Figure 6. Population pyramid of people with disabilities (administrative) in the province of Soria. Source: Social Services of the Government of Castile and Leon, 2019. Developed by the authors.

In 2019, in the province of Soria, there were a total of 6759 people with disabilities, predominantly physical disabilities (64.90%), followed by intellectual disabilities (9.38%), mental disabilities (13.33%), visual disabilities (6.98%), and auditory disabilities (5.40%) (data from the Social Services of the Government of Castile and Leon, 2019). Cases of deaf-blind people have not been registered. Due to the important percentage of people with disabilities, this situation may lead the rest of the disabilities to remain invisible to some extent, or even marginalised in some cases by the administrations and social groups in the making of certain decisions that affect their daily living. According to the degree of disability, 51.16% range between 33 and 64% of disability, 27.05% range between 64 and 74%, and 21.79% have 75% or higher.

Figure 6 shows, as in the case of the situation of Castile and Leon, a sharp increase in adult people with disabilities, specifically from the age of 40 years, increasing year by year. It is worth highlighting the percentage of women aged 85 years and older, with 13.45% of all the people with disabilities, compared to 6.13% of men. Once again, this is due to the larger number of women in these age ranges. Therefore, the sociotype of people with disabilities is fundamentally represented by people over 50 years of age.

Regarding the place of residence, it is possible to distinguish those people who live in urban areas, that is, with populations of over 10,000 inhabitants, from those who live in rural areas. In the case of the province of Soria, the only locality with this characteristic is the city of Soria, with the other 182 municipalities belonging to the category of rural localities with less than 10,000 inhabitants. The urban habitat concentrates 48.54% of the people with disabilities, whereas the rural areas have the other 51.45%. The fact that over half of these people live in rural areas implies a series of associated problems, such as the scarcity of services and difficulties related to mobility. The smallest municipalities, i.e., those with less than 500 inhabitants, represent 89.62% of all the municipalities of the province, and these are the ones that report the largest number of problems. Thus, there are a total of 10 Social Action Centres (CEAS), which are shared among several municipalities and distributed throughout the entire province, and they struggle to alleviate this situation. In addition to these CEAS, social services are also provided by the town halls and associations of people affected by some disability, such as ASAMIS, ASOVICA-FADESS, Asociación Autismo Soria, FADISO (integrated by ALCER Soria, FRATER, ASPACE Soria and Parkinson Social), the Ande Soria Cultural Association, etc., which provide socio-healthcare attention to people with some type of disability.

4.2. Descriptive Quantitative Study

Based on the information reported by our informants, the general valuation of the situation is positive since 27 people valued this situation with a score of ≥5. This score is in disagreement with Figure 7, which shows a negative perception of accessibility in the towns and cities of residence.

In regard to accessibility to public buildings, 28 of the 37 participants gave a score of ≥5 to this parameter. Furthermore, over half of the participants (19 people) showed a positive perception toward accessibility to public buildings, with a score of ≥7. Only nine people gave a value of less than 5 to the accessibility to public buildings.

With respect to the valuation of the ease of access to public transportation, the responses were also generally positive, with 28 participants giving a score of ≥5.

The basic elements of accessibility of the province seem to be adequate, according to the perception of people related to disability. It would be convenient to delve into the understanding of accessibility through a more exhaustive, detailed and objective study, thoroughly analysing the situation of the streets, traffic signs, traffic lights, etc. In some cases, routine and everyday life affect our perception, which somehow alters our valuation.

The participants were also asked about the phenomenon of incorporating disability into the social structure. To this end, the informants were requested to value the following statement: "I consider that, in the locality where I live, people with disabilities are taken into account". The general perception of our informants was positive, with 24 people giving a score of ≥5 to this statement.

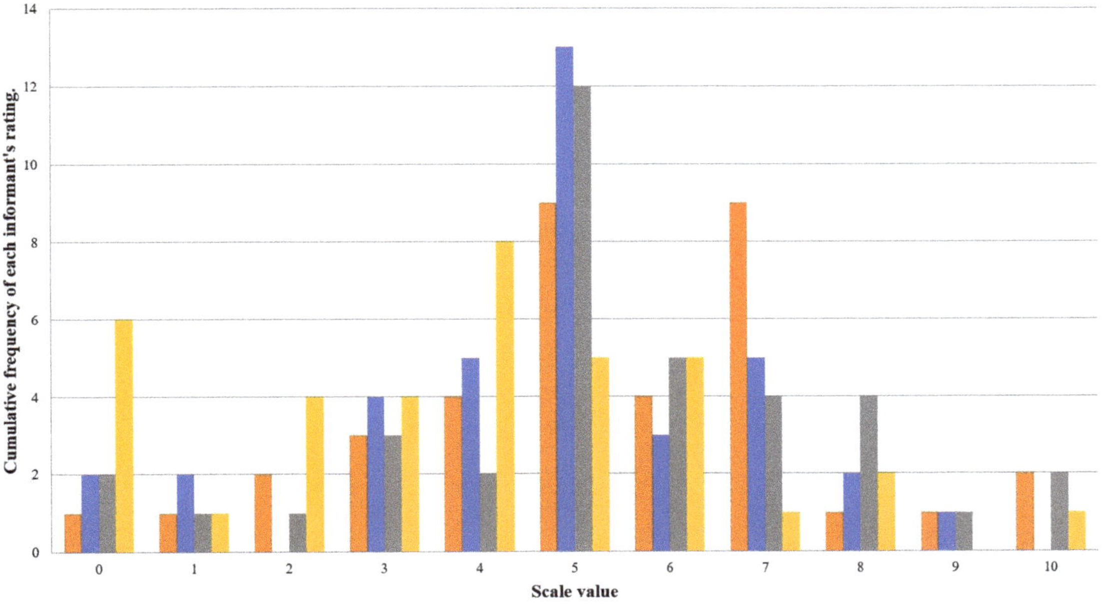

Figure 7. Comparison of the perception of the participants toward the work of the institutions [City Hall, County Council, Government of Castile and Leon, and Spanish Government] to address the problems of people with disabilities. Note: City Hall (orange), County Council (blue), Government of Castile and Leon (grey), and Spanish Government (yellow). Source: Developed by the authors.

Lastly, the participants were asked about their valuation of the information published by the media of the province. More specifically, we asked them to value from 0 to 10 whether the media, which reports on their province, addresses the problems of people with disabilities. In this case, the responses were less positive than the previous responses. In fact, eighteen people responded with a score of ≤5; nine, six and eight informants valued the information of the local media with a score of 3, 4 and 5 points, respectively. In this sense, it would also be convenient to thoroughly analyse the type of information that is presented about people with disabilities in the province.

Moreover, we considered that it would be important to know the perception of people affected by disability toward the political institutions (City Hall, County Council, Government of Castile and Leon, and Spanish Government). According to their responses (Figure 7), there was a clear difference between the valuation of the institutions that are closer to the citizens and the valuation of those that are farther away. It is not possible to establish a clear upward or downward tendency; thus, we decided not to incorporate this information. However, we could make some clarifying comparisons. Most of the participants (28 people) valued the work of the city hall with a score of 5 or higher. In the case of the County Council of Soria, the value was slightly lower (24 participants). For the Government of Castile and Leon, once again, 28 people valued the work of this institution with 5 or more points. Lastly, in the case of the Spanish Government, only 14 people gave a score of 5 or more points. It is also worth pointing out that nine informants valued the City Hall with 7 points, and eight people gave 4 points to the Spanish Government. In addition, six people considered that the Spanish Government did nothing and, therefore, gave it a score of 0.

The next step was to determine whether the closest political administrations (more specifically, the City Hall and the County Council) informed appropriately about the possible services they provide to improve the quality of life of people with disabilities. Therefore, it was important to ask the participants if they were well informed about the activities conducted by the closest institutions. In this case, 18 people gave a score of ≥ 5; thus, we could not consider that they generally felt well informed. In fact, on the other hand, 19 people had a negative perception, considering that these institutions do not inform adequately, valuing them with a score of ≤ 4. The data suggest that the local institutions need to improve their information means, although, as was previously mentioned, these data must be considered with caution, requiring further research and analyses in this respect.

After describing the perception of people related to disabilities toward the institutions, we focused our analysis on the situation of some services and the possibilities of improving the lives of people affected by disability. In this sense, we addressed the aspects related to employment, companies and the treatment in medical services. Thus, our aim was to obtain a general view of the reality of the social structure of the province regarding the analysed sociotype.

We began by approaching the collaboration and understanding the medical services offered to people affected by disability in the medical centres of the province. To this end, the participants were asked to provide their perception toward these aspects. The informants gave highly positive information in general lines. In fact, thirteen and seven people valued these interactions with a score of 8 and 5 points, respectively, whereas only four people reported a negative valuation.

With respect to the services aimed at people with disabilities, such as assisted housing and hospices, most of the responses were positive. In fact, 20 people gave a score of 5 or more points to such services, whereas 17 people had a negative perception toward them, with 11 people giving a score of 3 points to these services. The greatest problem was detected in the labour scope. In this sense, 25 people gave a negative valuation regarding the ease for people with disabilities to be employed. Moreover, eight people gave a score of 0 and 1 (four participants in each case). All this suggests that the institutions and companies have much work to do in this regard.

The abovementioned need for business effort became clear when we asked the informants whether employers were committed to people with disabilities. To this question, 25 people showed a negative perception (≤ 4) and, specifically, 13 participants gave a value of 3 points. This information suggests the existence of job integration barriers to people with disabilities in the province. This was subsequently corroborated in the qualitative study, where the representatives of the participating associations showed a clear concern about this issue. This negative impression of Sorian employers among the participants is complemented with the next aspect, which is related to the problem of equality in the conditions of access to employment. In fact, the informants showed a clear perception of inequality in the access to the job market. Thus, only nine people considered that the valuation of this parameter deserved a score of 5 or more points. This indicates the need for greater effort in this context in order to increase the levels of equality in the possibility of being employed.

4.3. Qualitative Analysis

The qualitative study demonstrated the difficulty in attending to people with disabilities in the province of Soria, mainly due to the lack of resources. This enables us to deduce the challenges individuals with disabilities may encounter in their capacity to engage in their activities and exercise their life choices (agency). This is, without a doubt, a discursive aspect that shows the existing problem in this region, according to the participants. I1 stated the following:

> *"I feel sad, because I could think of a lot of things to be improved, a lot of things to be done, but there are no technical, financial or human resources to provide assistance... So, I feel very sad and angry. But, anyways, I learned to control these feelings in time."*

I2 said: *"On my part, I believe that the most frustrating thing is the lack of sufficient services"*. In turn, I1 expressed the following: *"We also have the problem with subsidies, which are very scarce. The resources are the same in Soria City and in the rural area, that is, nothing."* The participants added that, due to these deficiencies, they had to move patients to hospitals of other provinces. Certainly, this factor significantly influences the potential for human connections with family and friends when one is admitted to a hospital. According to the participants, this generates a problem of estrangement in those affected: *"There is also the problem of estrangement. Of course, they spend 20 years in* [name of the association], *which is their family. And then we are forced to separate them from the association"*, which was endorsed by I3. In a different part of the debate, I4 stated:

> *"In relation to the state of the province, the bad things of the province (which I presume occur in all provinces), our people, the doctors, the lack of specialists and such... In the end, all of them have to flee the province.* [All informants repeated, of course!]. *In Valladolid, that is, inside the autonomous community, they created a team for orthoneuro-pediatric valuations; but for us, Valladolid is farther away from here than Madrid is. In the end, we all end up going to Madrid".*

Then, with respect to the actions carried out by the administration, I1 reported the following:

> *"The Administration, for example, if people with disabilities, any type of disability, have some type of service, is because us, the entities, are providing them. We are doing a great work for the Administration, because, if it weren't for the entities...".*

The participants presented numerous specific examples of streets, buildings or particular cases with accessibility problems. In this sense, they had a much more negative view of the context and of accessibility, compared to that shown by the participants in the quantitative study. For instance, I2 highlighted the need to increase the number of pictograms in the central area of the province to improve cognitive accessibility. I4 strongly asserted the following to support the idea of I2: *"People can't navigate here!"* I3 even stated, giving herself as an example, that older people find it very difficult to get an appointment in institutional buildings.

In contrast with this negative view, all participants stressed on solidarity and social advance. This aspect was pointed out as a factor of emotional and economic support for all entities. In this sense, I4 expressed the following:

> *"About Soria, I must highlight the solidarity of its people. In our case, for example, the hospice we are building is great. I mean, I believe that the people of Soria are giving more money than the Administrations. I think that the solidarity here is extraordinary, and that people respond to the problems".*

I4 and I3 stated that this is due to the small size of the city and the fact that *"we all know each other"*. In this sense, all participants underlined the importance of the educational centres and of the welcoming they receive in them. Thus, they believed that this factor is key to the inclusion and improvement of the lives of people affected by disabilities. However, despite the social advances, they considered that there is still much work to be done and that, for this reason, "they will fight on". This aspect was unanimous.

5. Discussion

This study shows the reality of disability in the province of Soria. This type of research is not frequent. In fact, Rodríguez-Soler et al. [22], in a bibliometric study on the rural depopulation in which they analysed 1150 articles between the years 1979 and 2018, did not mention the existence of studies related to disability in highly depopulated areas. This confirms, at least partly, our documentary study.

This province is the most depopulated territory of Southern Europe. Such depopulation is due to the fact that different social groups, such as single people, youth, women, and highly qualified people, among others, are more prone to moving to larger cities [23]. Thus, in regions such as Soria, there is a greater relative proportion of people with low education levels and older ages. This depopulation is forcing local services and businesses to terminate their activity due to a lack of demand [24]. This loss and its consequent lack of services and options has also been repeatedly reported by our informants in the qualitative analysis. In the quantitative analysis, the response was positive, although in this case it is important to be aware that most of the responses are from the capital, where the resources and services are concentrated. In line with this, Lewin et al. [8] stated that social care services respond to need/demand processes, although mechanisms of generation of these services also take place without the need for such demand. In fact, these authors linked the establishment of such services to political ideology, as well as to municipal characteristics. These elements, to some extent (although provisionally), can also be observed in the province.

The quantitative analysis shows several results of interest. Firstly, it seems that the needs of people with disabilities (mostly those of the capital) are covered. This fact could be related to the small relative size of the capital of the province (39,695 people according to the Municipal Census on 1 January 2022). This minimises some health problems related to the high population density [6]. Therefore, the problem would lie in the province itself, where the population nuclei are smaller and dispersion is greater. In this sense, the qualitative study clearly shows this fact and the assistance difficulties presented by the people who live in localities outside of the capital.

Thus, the people who live in the province would be in a situation of potential vulnerability in the face of cutbacks, for instance. In this sense, Sèpulchre [25] reported that the financial scope is fundamental for the development of measures of assistance to people with disabilities. For this reason, this author stated, according to the associative movement, that the action investment is lower than that indicated by the politicians, since the analysis of costs performed by the politicians does not consider the advantages of such actions. This is in line with our analysis, although it maintains the difficulty of attending to the needs of people with disabilities who live in the province. As was highlighted by Järkestig et al. [26], the cost reduction strategies derived from austerity policies also affected our sociotype, as it posed a substantial reduction in expenditures. Precisely, this fact is also perceived as an element of control reduction and of elections [27], as well as of the exclusion of participation in society [26]. In this sense, Järkestig et al. [26] and Hayes [28] asserted that austerity strategies must be understood as an ethical mechanism that excludes the most vulnerable social groups, which include our sociotype.

Moreover, different authors show that the context of depopulation has a negative effect on disability [5,7]. In the province of Soria, there are areas with a very high level of depopulation. According to the Spanish Federation of Municipalities and Provinces (FEMP), those municipalities with less than 1000 inhabitants have been established as municipalities at risk of disappearing. In the case of Spain, these represent 61.48% of all municipalities in the entire country. This percentage is considerably higher in the province of Soria, with 93.48%; that is, 172 of its 184 municipalities have less than 1000 inhabitants and would thus be at risk of disappearing, according to the FEMP. These numbers are worrying, since 64.13% of the Sorian municipalities have less than 100 inhabitants, which is a situation that has intensified and has a direct impact on the provision of essential services to the population, thereby making the lives of people with disabilities even harder in the rural areas. Indeed, structural challenges unquestionably impact the autonomy and the agency of individuals with disabilities. These limitations become more pronounced in sparsely populated regions characterized by service gaps and restricted life choices. This fact hinders the generation of community participation networks and, therefore, social inclusion [29]. To solve this problem, organisations related to disability try to promote mechanisms of approach for people in the capital to increase their community participation and socialisation. In essence, individuals with disabilities harness the power of collective action to amplify their agency through collaborative processes. However, these processes deteriorate the economic capacity of associations and, therefore, the possibility of carrying out activities of healthcare, improvement of quality of life, etc.

Another important aspect is related to the world of work. In this case, all the analyses conducted show that there is a problem in this sense and that, in addition, employers are not committed to the reality of our sociotype. Thus, the problem we are facing is that the State, taking into account the general demographic evolution and the relationships between unemployment and health [30], should be aware of this reality and develop strategies for the promotion of employment. Otherwise, no matter how many integration mechanisms are developed, these will not be complete [29]. This fact may also explain why the participants considered that the Spanish Government is one of the main political agents that care least about their needs.

6. Limitations and Opportunities

As was previously indicated, the quantitative analysis was limited due to two main reasons, although both are related to the lack of funding for the development of these works. It is known that gathering data face to face generates higher response rates, but they involve higher costs than the online format. On the other hand, older people do not usually agree to respond to online questionnaires or use social networks. Moreover, the analytical perspective used in the quantitative study was consultative and not exploratory. In fact, the aim of this study was to explore the subjective reality of people affected by disability, their assistance needs and the opinion of associative entities. Therefore, we did not focus our work on statistical precision but on the subjective and intersubjective perception of the participants.

The data that we have gathered originate from a modest sample size. However, it is worth noting that our approach in this quantitative study has been consultative rather than exploratory. Consequently, our emphasis has not been on achieving statistical precision, but on gaining insights into the subjective experiences of individuals affected by disability within a small, predominantly elderly population. This knowledge will serve as a foundational basis for conducting more intricate future studies in this domain and formulating practical recommendations for enhancement.

In view of this, the following are proposed as possible future lines of research:

1. Our first future line of research could be conducting a comprehensive investigation into the key determinants impacting the province of Soria, with a particular focus on the infrastructure network, including roads and public transport systems. We will explore their implications for land-use planning and accessibility to specialized facilities across various municipalities within the province. Additionally, we intend to create a geographical map that calculates distances and estimated travel times to the provincial capital, as well as other crucial urban centres in the surrounding area that serve as vital hubs for the local population.
2. A second future line of research could be studying the situation of other provinces in Spain which are in a similar situation of depopulation to Soria, such as the provinces of Teruel and Cuenca (Spain), in order to check whether there is a similar situation to that of Soria. This study would make it possible to establish similarities and differences between territories with a high level of depopulation and to be able to undertake measures to help alleviate the deficit.

7. Conclusions

1. In the province of Soria, there are localities with a very high depopulation level. These areas are located in the south of the province. In these localities, the possibility of increasing the difficulties that may be encountered by people with disabilities is greater than in other regions. This is also enhanced by the high centralism present in the province. In fact, most of the population is concentrated in the capital of the province.

2. The capital is not a city with great population density. This fact may be one of the elements that explain the positive view of the city. In this sense, the quantitative and qualitative analyses are in disagreement. The informants of the quantitative analysis perceive the city in a more positive manner than the participants in the qualitative analysis.
3. Social solidarity has increased, and this was perceived as a positive aspect. This fact improved, to some extent, the lives of people with disabilities and their social inclusion. The informants consider that there is much work to be done, although they also recognise that social exclusion has decreased.
4. The business sector and the political agents are perceived most negatively. The informants consider that there is no commitment to people with disabilities either on the part of employers or on the part of the government. For this, the State should be aware of the real existing needs in order to be able to implement integration mechanisms that provide solutions to this problem. This is one of the reasons why the informants consider the government to be one of the least committed agents to their problems. This allows confirming the need for further work to build a more equitable society, support the employment of people with disabilities and develop political mechanisms to improve the aspects that affect this sociotype.
5. In Soria, over 60% of its municipalities boast populations of less than 100 residents, predominantly situated in rural settings. This stark demographic distribution has had an adverse impact on the availability of essential services within these villages, subsequently exacerbating the challenges faced by individuals with disabilities in rural areas and limiting their agency.
6. Our investigation has substantiated our initial premise: residing in areas experiencing significant demographic decline can significantly magnify the hurdles encountered by specific social groups.

Author Contributions: Conceptualization, J.R.C. and A.P.-D.; methodology, J.R.C., J.F.-P., S.G.-R.; formal analysis, J.R.C. and A.P.-D.; data curation, J.R.C. and J.F.-P.; writing—original draft preparation, all authors; writing—review and editing, all authors. All authors have read and agreed to the published version of the manuscript.

Funding: This research received no external funding.

Data Availability Statement: The data reported here are available at request by scientific community members.

Conflicts of Interest: The authors declare no conflict of interest.

References

1. World Health Organitzation (WHO). Disability. Available online: https://www.who.int/health-topics/disability#tab=tab_1 (accessed on 7 April 2023).
2. Marijuán, P.C.; Montero-Marín, J.; Navarro, J.; García-Campayo, J.; del Moral, R. The "sociotype" construct: Gauging the structure and dynamics of human sociality. *PLoS ONE* **2017**, *12*, e0189568. [CrossRef] [PubMed]
3. Berry, E. The role of the sociotype in managing chronic disease: Integrating bio-psycho-sociology with systems biology. *Med. Hypotheses* **2011**, *77*, 610–613. [CrossRef] [PubMed]
4. Suriá, R. Análisis comparativo de la fortaleza en padres de hijos con discapacidad en función de la tipología y la etapa en la que se adquiere la discapacidad. *Anu. Psicol.* **2013**, *43*, 23–37.
5. Karolaakso, T.; Autio, R.; Näppilä, T.; Leppänen, H.; Rissanen, P.; Tuomisto, M.T.; Karvonen, S.; Pirkola, S. Contextual and mental health service factors in mental disorder-based disability pensioning in Finland—A regional comparison. *BMC Health Serv. Res.* **2021**, *21*, 1081. [CrossRef] [PubMed]
6. Motoc, I.; Timmermans, E.J.; Deeg, D.; Penninx, B.W.J.H.; Huisman, M. Associations of neighbourhood sociodemographic characteristic with depressive and anxiety symptoms in older age: Results from a 5-wave study over 15 years. *Health Place* **2019**, *59*, 102172. [CrossRef] [PubMed]
7. Reime, L.J.; Claussen, B. Municipal unemployment and municipal typologies as predictors of disabilitypensioninng in Norway: A multilevel analysis. *Scand. J. Public Health* **2013**, *41*, 158–165. [CrossRef] [PubMed]
8. Lewin, B.; Westin, L.; Lewin, L. Needs and Ambitions in Swedish Disability Care. *Scand. J. Disabil. Res.* **2008**, *10*, 237–257. [CrossRef]

9. Archer, M.S. *Structure, Agency and the Internal Conversation*; Cambridge University Press: Cambridge, UK; New York, NY, USA, 2003.
10. Archer, M.S. *Making Our Way through the World: Human Reflexivity and Social Mobility*; Cambridge University Press: Cambridge, UK; New York, NY, USA, 2007.
11. Caetano, A. Defining personal reflexivity: A critical reading of Archer's Approach. *Eur. J. Soc. Theory* **2017**, *18*, 60–75. [CrossRef]
12. Mitchell, D.T.; Snyder, S.L. Low-level agency. Disability, oppression and alternative genres of the human. In *Manifestos for the Future of Critical Disability Studies*; Routledge: New York, NY, USA, 2018; pp. 189–198.
13. Van Herwijnen, M.; Daly, G.; Iotzov, V.; ESPON EGTC; INOVA+. ESPON Fighting Rural Depopulation in Southern Europe. Transnational Observation. ESPON. Available online: https://www.espon.eu/sites/default/files/attachments/af-espon_spain_02052018-en.pdf (accessed on 19 May 2022).
14. Stake, R.E. *The Art of Case Study Research*; Sage: Thousand Oaks, CA, USA, 1995.
15. Bricout, J.C.; Gray, D.B. Community Receptivity: The Ecology of Disabled Persons' Participation in the Physical, Political and Social Environments. *Scan. J. Disabil. Res.* **2006**, *8*, 1–21. [CrossRef]
16. Shen, J.; Chu, D.; Zhang, Q.; Zhang, W. Developing a census data system in China. *Int. Stat. Rev. = Rev. Int. Stat.* **1999**, *67*, 173–186. [CrossRef]
17. Waldrop, J.; Long, J.F. A first look at the 21st Century: Census 2000. *Popul. Res. Policy Rev.* **2002**, *21*, 3–16. [CrossRef]
18. Howe, A. Revising long-established population estimates in Australia: Reasons, methods and implications. In *The Frontiers of Applied Demography*; Swanson, D.A., Ed.; Springer: Berlin/Heidelberg, Germany, 2017; pp. 409–429. [CrossRef]
19. Moreno Jiménez, A.; Buzai, G.D.; Fuensalida, M.; Claudia, B.; María Rosa, C.; Maria, V. *Sistemas de Información Geográfica: Aplicaciones en Diagnósticos Territoriales y Desigualdades Geoambientales*; Ra-Ma Editorial: Madrid, Spain, 2012.
20. Nielson, D. (Ed.) . *Geographic Information Systems (GIS): Tecniques, Applications and Technologies*; Nova Science Publishers, Inc.: Hauppauge, NY, USA, 2014.
21. Mohan, R.R.; Sharieff, A. *Geographical Information System: Theory & Practice*; Rawat Publications: Jaipur, India, 2018.
22. Rodríguez-Soler, R.; Uribe-Toril, J.; De Pablo, J. Worldwide trends in the scientific production on rural depopulation, a bibliometric analysis using bibliometrix R-tool. *Land Use Policy* **2020**, *97*, 104787. [CrossRef]
23. Meijer, M.; Syssner, J. Getting ahead in depopulating areas—How linking social capital is used for informal planning practices in Sweden and The Netherlands. *J. Rural Stud.* **2017**, *55*, 59–70. [CrossRef]
24. Lozano, A.; Jiménez-Bravo, D.; Pato, D.; Valera, A.; Luis, G. Voice Assistant and Route Optimization System for Logistics Companies in Depopulated Rural Areas. *Sustainability* **2020**, *12*, 5377. [CrossRef]
25. Sépulchre, M. Ensuring equal citizenship for disabled people: A matter of rights or a matter of costs? *Alter* **2020**, *12*, 114–127. [CrossRef]
26. Järkestig, U.; Melin, U.; Bergman, A.S. Strategies of austerity used in needs assessments for personal assistance—Changing Swedish social policy for persons with disabilities. *Eur. J. Soc. Work* **2021**, *24*, 380–392. [CrossRef]
27. Mladenov, T. What is good personal assistance made of? Results of a European survey. *Disabil. Soc.* **2020**, *35*, 1–24. [CrossRef]
28. Hayes, G. Regimes of austerity. *Soc. Mov. Stud.* **2017**, *16*, 21–35. [CrossRef]
29. Milner, P.; Kelly, B. Community participation and inclusion: People with disabilities defining their place. *Disabil. Soc.* **2009**, *24*, 47–62. [CrossRef]
30. Schuring, M.; Schram, J.L.D.; Robroek, S.J.W.; Burdorf, A. The contribution of health to educational inequalities in exit from paid employment in five European regions. *Scand. J. Work Environ. Health* **2019**, *45*, 346–355. [CrossRef]

urban science

MDPI

Article

Biodiesel Production by Transesterification of Recycled Oil Catalyzed with Zinc Oxide Prepared Starting from Used Batteries

Domenica Seminario-Calle [1,†], Melissa Ortega-Maldonado [1,†], Verónica Pinos-Vélez [1,2,*], Juan Cisneros [2], Andrés Montero-Izquierdo [1], Paulina Echeverría-Paredes [1], Paola Duque-Sarango [2,3] and Paúl Álvarez-Lloret [1]

[1] Grupo de Ingeniería de las Reacciones Químicas, Catálisis y Tecnologías del Medio Ambiente (IRCMA), Bioscience Department, Universidad de Cuenca, Víctor Manuel Albornoz, Cuenca 010107, Ecuador; domenica.seminario@ucuenca.edu.ec (D.S.-C.); isabel.ortega06@ucuenca.edu.ec (M.O.-M.); andres.montero@ucuenca.edu.ec (A.M.-I.); paulina.echeverria@ucuenca.edu.ec (P.E.-P.); paul.alvarez@ucuenca.edu.ec (P.Á.-L.)

[2] Departamento de Recursos Hídricos y Ciencias Ambientales, Universidad de Cuenca, Víctor Manuel Albornoz, Cuenca 010107, Ecuador; juan.cisneros@ucuenca.edu.ec (J.C.); pduque@ups.edu.ec (P.D.-S.)

[3] Grupo de Investigación en Recursos Hídricos (GIRH-UPS), Universidad Politécnica Salesiana, Campus El Vecino, Calle Vieja 12-30 y Elia Liut, Cuenca 010203, Ecuador

* Correspondence: veronica.pinos@ucuenca.edu.ec

† These authors contributed equally; thus, both share the first authorship.

Abstract: The consumption of batteries and cooking oil have been increasing. Most used batteries are disposed of incorrectly, leading to health and environmental problems because of their composition. In a similar form, cooking oil, once used, is often released by the discharge reaching the wastewater, polluting soil, and water, which affects its treatment. In Ecuador, these environmental passives are recollected and stored without further treatment, which is a temporary and unsustainable solution. To address this issue, the circular economy concept has gained increasing attention. In this study, zinc oxide was prepared from discarded batteries using the hydrometallurgical method to use as a catalyst; it achieved 98.49% purity and 56.20% yield and 20.92% of particles presented a particle size of 1–10 nm. Furthermore, the catalyst morphology was investigated in an SEM, which showed that particle size ranged from 155.69 up to 490.15 nm and spherical shapes. Due to its characteristics, the obtained catalyst can be used in the industry instead of the zinc oxide obtained by mining processes. These processes are known to produce heavy contamination in the ecosystems and human health. Additionally, a zinc oxide lifecycle in the environment was analyzed through a material flow analysis (MFA), taking into consideration two paths, one assuming the disposal of used batteries and the other assuming the recycling of zinc. Biodiesel was produced with a heterogeneous catalyst. This took place with a transesterification reaction with used cooking oil, ethanol, and zinc oxide (ZnO) as catalysts. The biodiesel obtained had the following characteristics: 37.55 kJg^{-1} of heating power, 0.892 gcm^{-3} of density, 4.189 mm^2/s of viscosity, 0.001% of water content, and a 70.91% yield. Furthermore, the energy consumption in biodiesel production was quantified, giving a total of 37.15 kWh. This kind of initiative prevents that waste from becoming environmental pollutants and potential health risks by giving them a second use as a resource. Moreover, turning waste into a valuable product makes the processes self-sustaining and attractive to be implemented.

Keywords: biodiesel; circular economy; discarded zinc batteries; used cooking oil; zinc oxide

1. Introduction

Most batteries, alkaline and Zn-C, which are used as power sources of energy for electronic devices, are not disposable. In recent years, in Ecuador, there has been an increase in battery consumption. A study in Ecuador in 2020 found that the national population of 16.8 million inhabitants consumes 17 million batteries, representing a per capita consumption of 1.06 $kghab^{-1}$. Only 1.53 million of these batteries were rechargeable (9.06%) [1]. It is estimated that 78.15% of the population dispose of batteries in common garbage, 6.08% burn or bury them, 5.95% keep them in their house, and only 8.21% deposit them in the proper collection center. This disposal practice leads to the accumulation of batteries in city landfills and results in pollution problems, particularly in water sources and soil, due to the leachates containing heavy metals [2–4].

The Ecuadorian Institute of Standardization (INEN) establishes that used batteries in Ecuador must be handed over to professionals authorized by the Ministry of Environment or AAAR (Responsible Environmental Enforcement Authority), according to the INEN 2534 standard. The process to be followed from collection to recycling is also outlined by the INEN [5]. However, unlike in Europe, where directives prohibit the disposal of batteries through incineration or dumping, there is no law in Ecuador prohibiting these methods [6]. In the city of Cuenca, although EMAC is the public company in charge of garbage collection, it lacks the initiative to collect batteries separately from other types of waste. In this regard, ETAPA EP (the public company responsible for water treatment and distribution) has assumed the responsibility of preventing batteries from contaminating drinking water sources and the wastewater treatment plant; however, its action is limited [7]. ETAPA EP collection points gather approximately 35–40 kg of batteries each month. After conducting a stabilization process, the batteries are confined [7]. This strategy entails logistical problems such as a lack of space and potential hazards, including the possibility of metal leaching due to flooding.

An effective waste management program should aim to provide batteries with a final treatment that needs to be environmentally sustainable and cost-effective. A typical alkaline battery comprises a zinc anode and a high-density manganese oxide cathode (MnO_2). In contrast, Zn-C batteries are predominantly made of zinc, followed by MnO_2. Then, from this composition, around 33% of zinc and 29% of manganese oxide can be recovered and used as raw material for industry [8]. Some authors have even succeeded in obtaining zinc oxide from Zn-C batteries. For instance, one study used sulfuric acid (H_2SO_4) for reductive leaching and selective precipitation with NaOH at pH 10 [9]. In contrast, another used an ionic liquid for battery leachate treatment [4]. Additionally, a third study employed solvent extraction, electrodeposition, and precipitation methods [10].

Currently, zinc oxide production mainly relies on chemical processes that utilize zinc as the raw material. Unfortunately, zinc is often mined alongside other metals, particularly lead, resulting in significant pollution with toxic metals in soil, water, and sediments from Pb-Zn mines [11]. Mining activities also lead to a substantial release of heavy metals into the environment, with zinc alone contributing up to 1.38×10^6 $kgyear^{-1}$ in close mining regions [12]. Such releases have been shown to cause freshwater and marine human toxicity, ecotoxicity, metal depletion, eutrophication, and soil damages [13]. Zinc is an essential element in the human body. Nevertheless, its excessive intake causes stomach cramps, nausea, and vomiting, and long-term exposure can affect cholesterol balance, immune system function, and fertility [12]. Additionally, heavy metals that incorporate into the soil can decrease pH, nutrients, and microbial diversity, rendering them unsuitable for agriculture since they leach into water bodies [12,14]. China, the biggest supplier of zinc in the world, has several regions next to mines with contaminated soil and water, leading to health issues for residents [12]. Poland has also contaminated allotment gardens in closed Zn and Pb mines, with the concentration of metals in soil and crops exceeding European Quality Standards, resulting in the integration of these contaminants into the food chain [14]. In Ecuador, mining areas have high concentrations of Zn in nearby rivers, with levels ranging from 513–2670 $mgkg^{-1}$. This is due to the discharge of waste generated during gold and silver extraction processes into the rivers, which carry heavy metals such as zinc [15]. Furthermore, ecosystem remediation from Zn-Pb mines can cost up to \$ 3.04×10^{10} [16].

Another common waste product is cooking oil. It is often taken to be inoffensive; nevertheless, its inadequate disposal can cause significant environmental harm. Typically, it is poured down the drain, leading to contamination of water bodies and wastewater treatment plants, negatively affecting the ecosystem and water treatment efficiency, respectively [17]. The oil forms a layer on the water that obstructs sunlight and limits oxygen absorption, leading to additional ecosystem damage. Additionally, removing oil from wastewater can be expensive [18]. In Ecuador, ~54 million liters of discarded oil are generated, and ~70% of this waste comprises vegetable oil [1]. ETAPA EP is responsible for collecting and managing this waste to avoid water contamination. Still, this action is limited to collecting and storing the oil and, in some cases, transferring it if an individual or institution requires it. Storing the oil is not a definitive solution because, in addition to the space problem, there is, as in the case of batteries, the danger of infiltration where the oil can leak [19]. However, there are ways to revalue this waste, such as producing biodiesel [20]. This is produced by transesterification, where used cooking oil triglycerides chemically react with alcohol to form fatty acid methyl esters [21], see Figure 1.

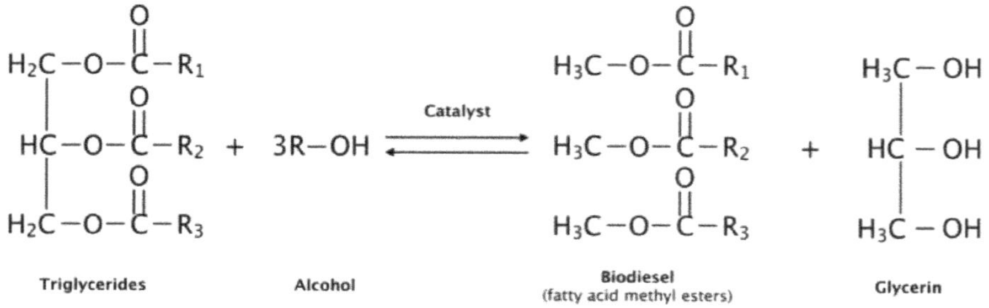

Figure 1. Transesterification reaction.

As shown in Table 1 (Inputs 1 to 4), biodiesel production has been extensively studied using homogeneous catalysts. This type of reaction is characterized by being fast, with a yield of over 90%. Nevertheless, it has disadvantages such as loss of catalyst and the need for neutralization. Table 1 also displays several investigations on biodiesel production utilizing different heterogeneous catalysts, along with 1% or less of the catalyst. The results indicate that the reaction is highly efficient, with the advantage of recovering the catalyst. Nevertheless, the reaction is a little slower in some cases due to diffusional mass problems. One of the catalysts used for the transesterification reaction is zinc oxide, indicated in Table 1 (Inputs 6 and 7). The use of discarded batteries' zinc oxide and used cooking oil for producing biodiesel can effectively reduce the amount of hazardous waste and its management costs [22]. Biodiesel is a great candidate to replace fossil fuels as a clean energy source due to its advantages. The main one is that the emission of CO_2, CO, unburned hydrocarbons, and particles is lower compared to fossil fuels. Likewise, the emission of SO_2 during the biodiesel combustion process is lower, due to low sulfur content in the biodiesel raw materials. These emission gases are the main cause of atmospheric pollution. Some other advantages include the fact that biodiesel can be produced from recycled oils and fats, can be used directly in diesel engines, and reduce the dependence on fossil fuels [23,24].

This research explores alternative processes that can properly revalorize waste municipal organic oil and batteries, which currently need to be managed appropriately. The proposed approach involves preparing the zinc oxide from discharged Zn-C batteries by a novel hydrometallurgical method and preparing biodiesel from cooking oil by catalyzed transesterification. Moreover, a material flow analysis (MFA) is developed to analyze the inputs, outputs, and storage of materials during 2022. This work evaluates a real sample of batteries and discarded oil deposited in municipal warehouses contributing to a circular economy, considering the real conditions in which these are delivered. For instance, discarded oil used in this study is a mixture of various sources from the entire city, such as fast-food stalls, local houses, restaurants, etc. In fast food stalls, a highly saturated oil, due to its reuse, is handed over for recycling.

Table 1. Transesterification condition's reaction to produce biodiesel with waste oil.

Input	Type of Oil	Catalyst		Oil/Alcohol	Reaction Time, min	Yield, %	Ref.
		Type	%				
1	Used Frying Oil from Sunflower	KOH	1	1:6	60	99.3	[25]
2	Waste Cooking Oil	KOH	0.5	1:6	60	93.13	[26]
3	Waste Municipal Organic Oil	KOH	1	1:6	90	93.31	[27]
4	Waste Municipal Organic Oil	NaOH	0.5	1:6	90	85.96	[27]
5	Waste Cooking Oil	CaO	1	1:8	90	96	[28]
6	Refined Palm oil	CaO-ZnO	7.5	1:30	120	86.99	[26]
7	Waste Cooking Oil	CFA/ZnO	0.5	1:12	180	98.14	[29]
8	Waste Cooking Oil	S–TiO_2/SBA-15	1	1:15	30	94.96	[30]

Ethanol was employed as the alcohol in all experiments.

2. Materials and Methods

2.1. Characterization and Pretreatment of Discarded Vegetable Oil

The discarded vegetable oil used in this study was sourced from a public company ETAPA EP in Cuenca, Ecuador. ETAP EP collects discarded oil from restaurants and households to store oil in an open pool. Before analysis, the sample of discarded vegetable oil was filtered through Whatman paper N_o. 40 using a glass funnel to remove residues. Next, filtered oil was washed with water at 80 °C, then left in a decanter. After removing the water from the decanter, the discarded vegetable oil was heated at 115 °C for 4 h to remove water. A pycnometer determined the density and Equation (1) was applied, where: ρm: sample density; m_0: empty pycnometer weight; m_1: weight of the pycnometer with water; m_2: weight of the pycnometer with sample; ρ_a: water density.

$$\rho = (m_2 - m_0)/(m_1 - m_0)\rho_a \tag{1}$$

The Ostwald procedure was used to measure the kinematic viscosity at 40 °C, with water as the reference liquid. The process involved placing 10 mL of distilled water in the Ostwald viscometer and immersing it in a container alongside a thermometer. The mixture was then heated until the liquid reached the upper limit A before being allowed to fall to the lower limit B, and the time taken was recorded alongside the temperature. The process was repeated with water at room temperature and the treated oil sample. The viscosity was calculated using the following Equation (2), where: μ: kinematic viscosity; ρ: density; n: dynamic viscosity.

$$\mu = \frac{\rho}{n} \tag{2}$$

The Karl Fischer titration method was employed to determine the water percentage in the sample. The sample was first weighed and then added to the equipment, where an iodine indicator was automatically added while stirring continuously. The platinum electrode determined the endpoint of the titration, and the percentage of water in the sample was displayed once all the water in the sample had been consumed.

2.2. Preparation of Zinc Oxide and Characterization

ETAPA EP provided Zn-C batteries, which were used in this study, see Table 2.

Table 2. Battery components.

Component	Percentage, %
Zinc (anode)	16.86
Manganese dioxide (cathode)	29.00

Table 2. *Cont.*

Component	Percentage, %
Carbon	5.71
Mercury	0.01
Cadmium	0.08
Ammonium chloride (electrolyte)	25.76
Plastic and others	22.76

Initially, only batteries in good condition, without rust or spills, were chosen. Subsequently, the batteries were disassembled. The zinc case and carbon rods were extracted by dismantling used batteries. The rods of carbon were immersed in nitric acid of 30% of concentration for 24 h, followed by washing until achieving a pH~7. Subsequently, the rods were dried at 110 °C for 12 h in an oven to eliminate any remaining water. A pyrometallurgical method was used to obtain zinc oxide [31] and to lixiviate the zinc case. To obtain 195.66 g of zinc chloride, 115.6 g of the zinc case was lixiviated at 100 °C for 60 min with 300 mL of hydrochloric acid of 37% concentration. Subsequently, 250 mL of sulfuric acid at 50% concentration was added. The solution was heated at 100 °C for an hour. In order to eliminate the impurities of the zinc sulfate, 500 mL of distilled water was added. The solution was boiled and filtered through Whatman No. 40 paper. The filtered solution was allowed to cool and stand at room temperature. Finally, crystals of sulfate of zinc (231.53 g) were obtained. To obtain zinc hydroxide (231.53 g) from the sulfate of zinc crystals, sodium hydroxide (Fisher Scientific, USA, assay ≥98.9%) solution of 30% of concentration was added until a pH of 6.5 was reached; as a by-product, sodium sulfate (341.46 g) was obtained. The subproduct, sodium sulfate, produced during the process is of a low concentration and not harmful to health, according to references [32,33]. The zinc hydroxide was recovered by filtration with Whatman paper No. 40, then dried at 100 °C for 1 h. Finally, zinc hydroxide was calcinated in a muffle at 900 °C for 6 h to obtain zinc oxide. The reactions that occurred are presented as follows.

$$ZnO + 2HCl \rightleftharpoons ZnCl_2 + H_20$$

$$ZnCl_2 + H_2SO_4 \rightleftharpoons ZnSO_4 + 2HCl$$

$$ZnSO_4 + 2NaOH \rightleftharpoons 2NaSO_4 + Zn(OH)_2 \downarrow$$

$$Zn(OH)_2 \rightleftharpoons ZnO + H_2O$$

In order to prepare the supported catalyst, zinc oxide (0.96 mg) was dispersed in water at 300 rpm. Then, a dry carbon rod (4.8 g) also recovered from the discarded batteries was impregnated with the oxide at 230 °C to evaporate all the solvent.

Scanning electron microscopy (SEM JEOL IT300) characterized the supported and unsupported zinc oxide characteristics to determine their superficial morphological and structural features. The zinc content was determined using atomic absorption with a graphite furnace (A. Perkin Elmer (Waltham, MA, USA) 3300 spectrometer AA with graphite furnace HGA 600). A structural characterization was held in an X-ray diffractor Bruker, Billerica, MA, USA, D2 Phaser, second generation.

2.3. Biodiesel Preparation and Characterization

The ethanol/oil ratio 6:1 was used for transesterification using both supported (ZnO-C) and unsupported catalysts (ZnO). The catalyst used were 5% $W_{ZnO}W_{solution}^{-1}$ or 1% $W_{ZnO-C}W_{solution}^{-1}$. The ratio of ethanol/oil and the amount of catalyst were established based on the studies shown in Table 1. To prepare the biodiesel, first ethanol (98%) and the catalyst (supported or unsupported) were mixed at 300 rpm, 60 °C for 20 min. Then, cleaned used oil was added and stirred for one hours. The resulting mixture was separated by decantation. After 3 h, the biodiesel was separated from the glycerin. The diesel was filtered by Whatman paper No. 42 and washed to recover the remaining catalyst. Finally, biodiesel was dried at 80 °C for 15 min. The process was repeated in triplicate for each catalyst type.

The entire process, from the disassembly of the batteries to the preparation of the zinc oxide and the cleaning of the used oil, through the transesterification reaction to obtain biodiesel, is shown in Figure 2.

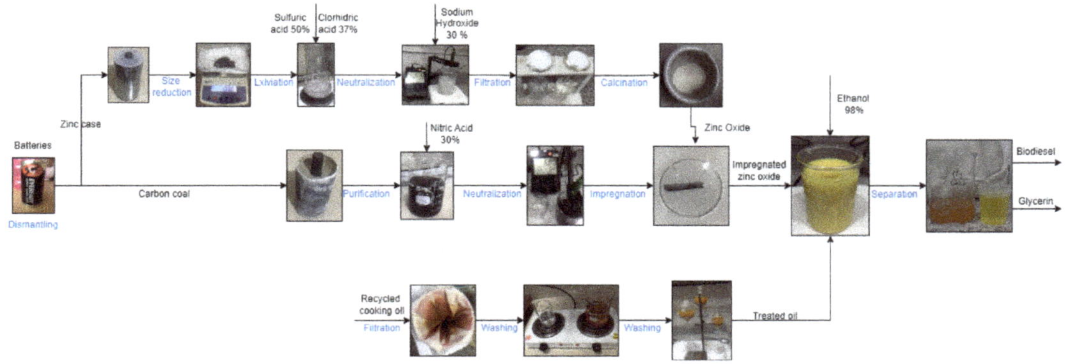

Figure 2. Catalyst obtention and transesterification reaction.

Biodiesel characterization involves the evaluation of five parameters: water content, specific heat capacity, density, viscosity, and reaction yield. The water content was obtained by injecting the sample into a Karl Fischer titrator. The specific heat capacity was achieved through a calorimetric pump. Density was measured by employing the pycnometer method. Viscosity was determined using the Ostwald method with an Ubbelohde viscometer, as described in Section 2.1. The reaction yield was calculated by analyzing the fatty acid methyl esters (FAMEs) for used oil and biodiesel samples. Derivatized samples were analyzed using gas chromatography to determine the concentration of the FAMEs of interest. All parameters were compared to three biodiesel standards: ASTM B 100, EN 590, and INEN 2489 [34–36].

2.4. Material Flow Analysis (MFA)

This analysis focuses on the study of a chemical element, compound, or material based on the law of conservation of mass. It aims to identify key aspects such as origin, volumes, generated waste, and emissions produced. Based on this, decisions can be made regard to resource, waste, and environmental management. In this case, the material to be analyzed is Zn-C batteries. For this purpose, an exhaustive search was conducted to gather information on the quantity of batteries from their commercialization up to their final disposal in the city of Cuenca in the year 2022. The choice of this particular year for analysis is due to the lack of available data on battery consumption between 2020 and 2021, which is attributable to the pandemic. Therefore, data on battery consumption were not collected until the year 2022, as provided by INEN. This information was used to identify flows, stocks, and processes. Once identified, the transfer coefficient was determined, which indicates the fraction of substance or material that enters and leaves a process. Equation (3) was used:

$$CT = \frac{Y1}{\sum X1} \tag{3}$$

where *CT*: transfer coefficient; *Y*1: process output mass; *X*1: process input mass.

This collected information was used to calculate the mass balance using STAN software. Mass flow data and transfer coefficients were entered into a flow diagram created in the software.

3. Results and Discussion

3.1. Zinc Oxide Characterization

3.1.1. Zinc Oxide Color, Purity, and Yield

A white powder of zinc oxide was obtained after applying the procedure mentioned in Section 2.2. Table 3 displays the results of the catalyst characterization. The purity of the zinc oxide was 98.49%, which is higher than the purity obtained in other studies that used the same hydrometallurgical method [31]. The color of the zinc oxide was white, and the yield obtained was 56.20% [31], which is similar to the yield obtained in this study (54.7%). However, when alkaline batteries were used, the yield was higher (66.42%) according to another study [37]. Finally, the nanometric scale fraction of the sample was 20.92%, indicating no uniform size.

Table 3. Zinc Oxide Characterization.

Characteristic	
Color	White
Purity, %	98.49
Particle size (1–10 nm), %	20.92
Yield, %	56.20

3.1.2. Zinc Oxide Particle Size

The catalyst morphology was investigated using scanning electron microscopy (SEM). Figure 3a displays the morphology of pure zinc oxide particles, while Figure 3b shows the supported zinc oxide. The size of pure ZnO particles ranged from 155.69 nm to 490.15 nm. The zinc oxide particles in Figure 3b exhibited spherical shapes with slight agglomeration deposited over the carbon support.

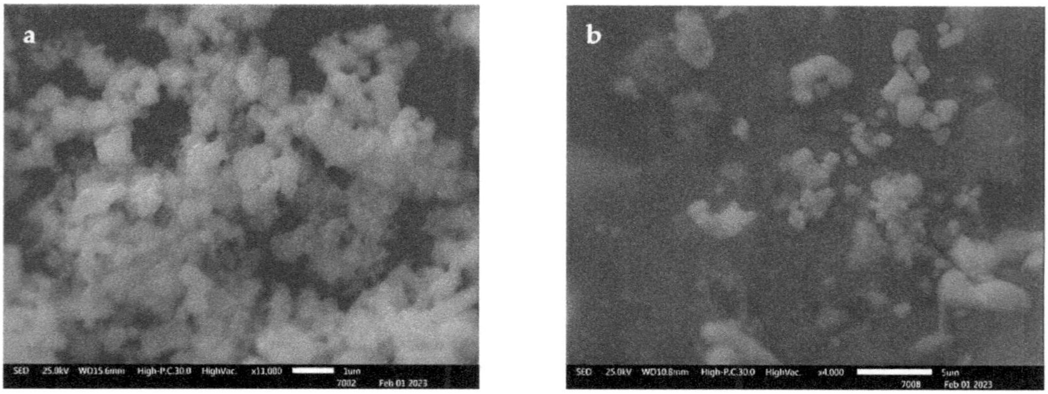

Figure 3. Scanning electron microscopy image of (**a**) zinc oxide particles, (**b**) zinc oxide particles supported in a carbon bar.

3.1.3. XRD Analysis

An structural characterization was held in a BRUKER D2 Phaser second generation X-ray diffractor. Figures 4 and 5 show the diffraction patterns obtained from both the carbon rod-impregnated ZnO and the ZnO−only sample. The presence of zinc oxide is verified in these two figures.

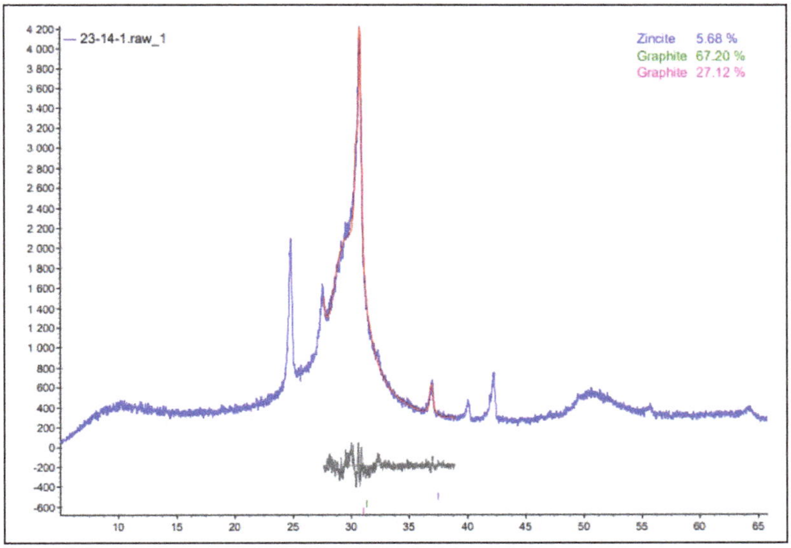

Figure 4. XRD of the ZnO−impregnated carbon bar sample.

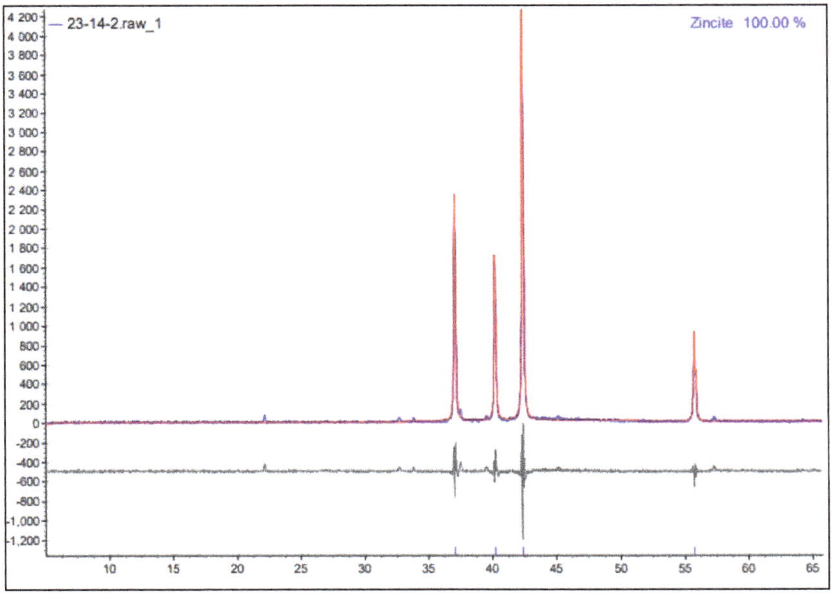

Figure 5. XRD of the ZnO sample. Samples in red and blue in gray the pattern.

The XRD pattern of the impregnated ZnO sample (Figure 4) revealed 5.68% ZnO. While the diffraction pattern of the sample of ZnO (Figure 5) presented a composition of 100% ZnO.

3.1.4. Pore Size and Surface Area

The values of pore volume and surface area are shown in Table 4.

Table 4. Results of coal analysis by BET method.

Description	Value
Surface area, m^2g^{-1}	1.93
Pore volume, cm^3g^{-1}	0.79

According to IUPAC, the pore distribution ranges from macro pores larger than 50 nm, mesopores between 2 to 50 nm, and micropores smaller than 2 nm. In this case, the coal falls under the category of mesopores; see Figure 6.

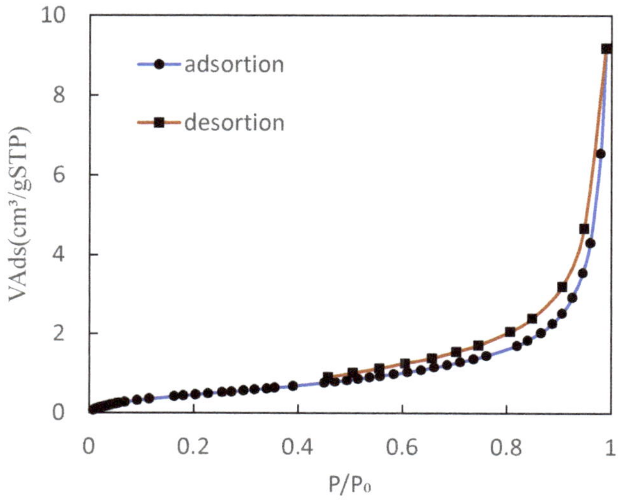

Figure 6. BET Isotherm of coal sample with impregnated ZnO catalyst.

3.2. *Material Flow Analysis (MFA)*

A material flow analysis was conducted to analyze the zinc oxide movement in the environment. Two diagrams are presented, one assuming the disposal of used batteries (refer to Figure 7), and the other assuming zinc recovery from used batteries (refer to Figure 8).

To conduct the MFA analysis, it was necessary to gather information on the inputs and outputs throughout the importation and commercialization to the final disposal of the batteries. The starting point was the quantity of batteries imported into Ecuador in 2022, which was 2170 tons, according to ITC [38]. According to INEC [39], 79.8% of discarded batteries was disposed of in the trash, 8.2% was burned, 5.6% was stored at home, 4.4% was left at collection centers, and 2% was given away or sold. It is worth noting that these data were collected at the national level, as no specific data were available for the city of Cuenca. Thus, this information was utilized under the assumption that the population of Cuenca exhibits the same consumption and disposal behavior as the national average.

According to Figure 7, after consumption, most of the batteries end up in landfill with 1731.66 t/y, and the rest of the batteries are incinerated or stored at home. EMAC EP is the company in charge of constantly monitoring the physical and chemical properties of the leachate produced at the Pichacay landfill in Cuenca, especially pH and heavy metals such as Zn. The pH can indicate the mobilization of dissolved inorganic species or ion concentrations. The landfill has two leachate zones: North 1 (LN1) and North 2 (LN2). According to the data provided by EMAC EP, the pH taken during 2022 in the LN1 zone ranges from 7.8 to 8.8. This is because the leachates in that zone run off from old and disused cells at the end of the methanogenic or maturation stage. Therefore, they usually have a pH higher than 7.5, as in LN1 [40]. On the contrary, the pH value is usually less than 6.5 when the leachate is young. In the case of the LN2 zone, the pH range is between 6.5 and 8.3. Therefore, an increase in pH may be because it has reached a state where there is a stabilization of the acid production processes [37].

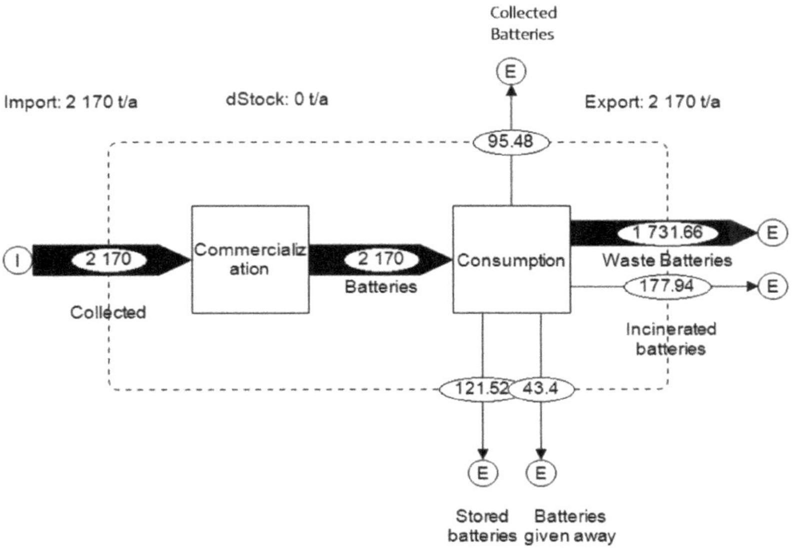

Figure 7. MFA of used batteries as disposal.

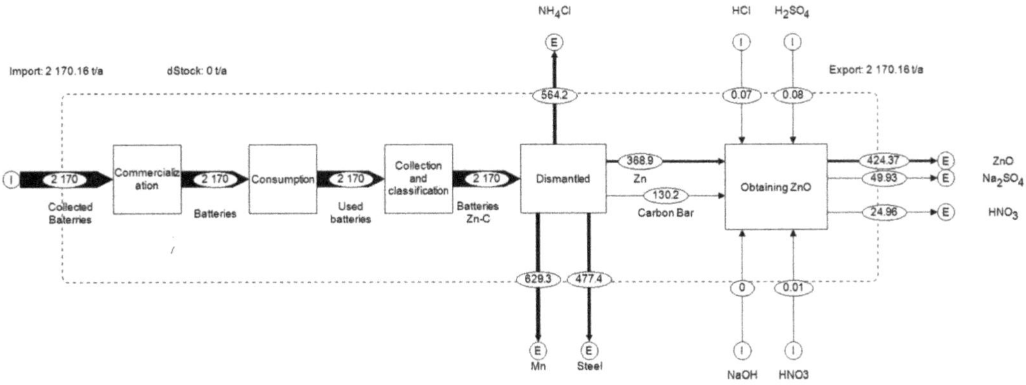

Figure 8. MFA of used batteries as a source of recycled metal.

The Zn concentrations measured in the LN1 and LN2 do not exceed 10,000 ug/L as seen in Table 5, thus remaining within the ranges regulated by the enforcement environmental entity. However, it is known that Zn accumulation can become toxic. Some symptoms of zinc poisoning include fever, breathing difficulty, nausea, chest pain, cough, gastric distress, dizziness, headaches, and loss of appetite. Furthermore, severe toxicity may cause copper deficiency anemia and hematological and neurological abnormalities [41,42].

Table 5. Zn concentration in leachates.

Metal	LN1, μgL^{-1}	LN2, μgL^{-1}	Standard, μgL^{-1}
Zn	500.89	1229	100.00

Zinc accumulation can be transferred by various means, such as water, soil, and plants. In turn, they can enter human bodies by food chains or by direct ingestion. This would pose a threat to human health [43]. The ingestion of very high doses of zinc can cause pulmonary lesions, necrosis in the bone marrow, liver, kidneys, and ocular lesions [37].

The data from the second MFA analysis are presented in Figure 8. The input data used were the same as in the first MFA. However, instead of the used batteries being discarded, incinerated, or stored at home after consumption, a process of recovery of zinc from the batteries was performed to obtain zinc oxide. In addition, we took advantage of the other components of the batteries to give them other uses. For this purpose, information was collected from each of the components of the battery, as shown in Table 2.

In this case, as shown in Figure 8, after storage, each component of the battery is separated. The different parts can be reused; for example, Mn can be used as an additive in ceramics. The amount of Zn was 369.9 t/y and the amount of carbon rod was 130.2 t/y. From this, the amount of ZnO that could be obtained was 424.37 t/y, thus enabling the recovery of a large part of the zinc compared to the number of batteries that ended up in the landfill. In addition to obtaining ZnO, $NaSO_4$ could also be obtained with 49.93 t/y and HNO_3 with 24.96 t/y. Therefore, these substances can be put to other uses instead of being disposed of. This whole process seeks to reuse all the components and substances produced both in the dismantling process and for obtaining ZnO.

This process aims to achieve the environmentally friendly recovery of metals, particularly zinc (Zn). This approach aims to minimize environmental and human health impacts, as evidenced by the reduced levels observed. Generally, the extraction of zinc is usually performed together with other metals, such as lead, which is known as one of the most toxic elements. Its extraction process is usually performed in an open pit. Therefore, there is a greater impact on the environment, especially due to the destruction of native flora and fauna. In addition, zinc must be separated from other materials, thus energy consumption is higher. Furthermore, smelting processes are carried out, in which harmful gases are produced, destroying the ecosystem through atmospheric pollution, and the solid waste generated ends up in the soil and in water sources [44,45].

3.3. Cooking Oil Processing and Characterization

The process for obtaining recycled cooking oil is provided by ETAPA EP, in which it is subjected to filtering, washing, and drying, as described in Section 2.1. The treated cooking oil was characterized to determine its density, viscosity, and water content. The results of the analysis are presented in Table 6. The density of the oil was found to be 0.9646 gcm^{-3}, which is consistent with the values reported in previous studies such as [46] (0.921 gcm^{-3}) and [47] (0.9119 gcm^{-3}). Furthermore, the density value is close to the ASTM D 1298 normative value of 0.96 gcm^{-3}. The viscosity of the oil was determined to be 50.9117 mm^{2}s^{-1}, which agrees with the viscosity values reported in similar studies, that is, (42.2 mm^{2}s^{-1}) [47] and (50 mm^{2}s^{-1}) [48]. The amount of water present in the sample was found to be 0.15%.

Table 6. Characteristics of recycled cooking oil.

Oil Characterization	
Density, gcm^{-3}	0.965
Viscosity, mm^{2}s^{-1}	50.912
Water amount, %	0.15

Figure 9 presents the results of fatty acids methyl esters (FAME) determined using GC-FID. The dominant fatty acid is C18:3 (α-linoleic acid), accounting for 30.54%. Therefore, all stoichiometric calculations were based on this fatty acid.

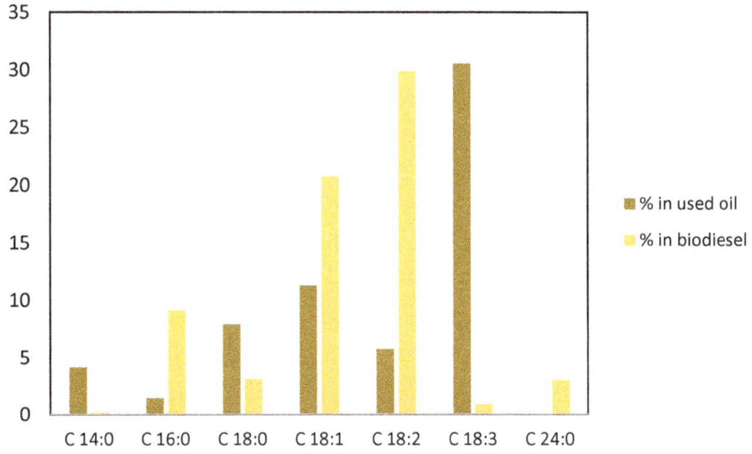

Figure 9. Fatty acids of used recycled cooking oil and biodiesel.

3.4. Biodiesel

In Figure 9 FAME composition is shown in percentage and g/mol. We can observe that the fatty acid in greater percentage is C18:2 (linoleic acid) accounting for 29.86%.

The results of the prepared biodiesel are shown in Table 7. The heating power for the prepared biodiesel is a little higher than values in other research, that is, between 35.9 kJg^{-1} to 37.26 kJg^{-1} [48,49]. This fact can be attributed to the catalyst, because zinc oxide boosts heating power in car engines [49]. The density obtained is within the range of 0.89 gcm^{-3} to 0.9 gcm^{-3}, as established by the INEN 148. The blank density was 0.93 gcm^{-3} in value, which is closer to the density of cooking oil. Therefore, without the use of the catalyst, the conversion was low. The viscosity obtained aligns with the ranges established by the INEN 2482, ASTM B 100, and EN 590 standards. The blank achieved higher viscosity than the norm, indicating that the transesterification was incomplete [50]. The water content is within the range of the INEN 2482, ASTM B 100, and EN 59 standards, demonstrating the effectiveness of the cooking oil drying process. The yield was 70.91%, surpassing the value of 49.78% registered in research that used the same catalyst [51]. However, compared to homogeneous catalysis that employed potassium hydroxide and calcium hydroxide, the achieved yield was lower, with yields ranging between 92% and 98% [28,52,53].

Table 7. Characteristics of biodiesel.

Biodiesel Characterization	
Heating power, kJg^{-1}	37.553
Density, gcm^{-3}	0.892
Viscosity, mm^2s^{-1}	4.189
Water amount, %	0.001
Yield, %	70.91

Despite obtaining better yields with other catalysts, zinc oxide is considered the most suitable catalyst for producing biodiesel due to its ability to reduce the time and temperature required for the synthesis [54]. Additionally, zinc oxide is a heterogeneous catalyst that can be easily recovered and does not require additional processes to neutralize the final product. Moreover, the performance can be improved by adding other catalytic phases [55].

Figure 10 presents the process of obtaining biodiesel from used oil using a recycled catalyst. In Cuenca, it is possible to collect ~38 kg of batteries and ~40 gallons of used vegetal cooking oil per month, from which 0.984 kg of zinc oxide and 886 L of biodiesel could be obtained. The process begins by disassembling the collected batteries, and the zinc plate is then leached with a mixture of acids. The resulting mixture is filtered, neutralized, and precipitated to recover the oxide. The recycled oil is then washed and filtered to remove impurities. The biodiesel is produced from the mixture of the resulting oxide, the prepared oil, and ethanol by transesterification. The final product is decanted to separate the biodiesel and glycerin.

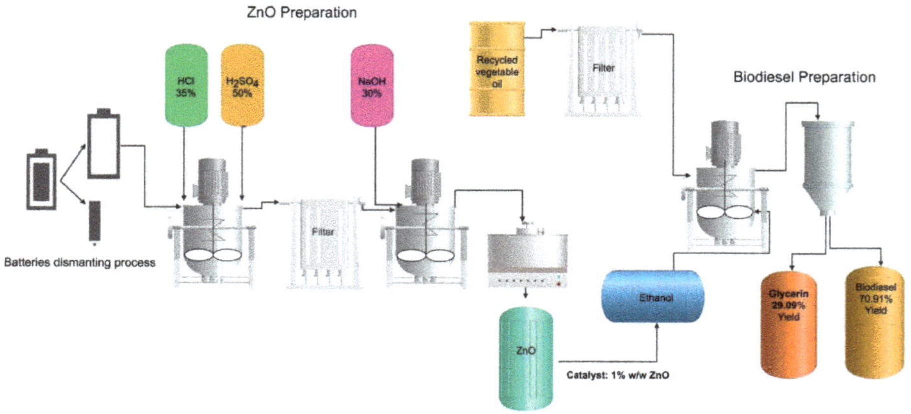

Figure 10. Scheme of the full process.

4. Conclusions

Obtaining biodiesel from recycled materials is a crucial step towards efficiently managing urban waste produced in Cuenca. If successful, this process could bring monetary benefits to ETAPA EP and promote the concept of a circular economy. This study transformed two wastes which are considered environmental liabilities into value-added products. Zinc oxide was obtained from zinc–carbon batteries, yielding 56% and a purity of 98%. A 5% zinc oxide catalyst was supported on a carbon rod, also recycled from the stack. The recycled oil was conditioned and characterized; it was determined that the fatty acid in major percentage was linoleic acid (18:2), 11.29%. The water amount was 0.15%, showing that the drying of the sample was effective. The density was 0.965 gcm^{-3} and the viscosity was determined to be 50.912 mm^2s^{-1}. Both parameters were within ASTM standards for recycled oils used to produce biodiesel. Better results for obtaining biodiesel with the pretreated vegetable oil and ethanol in a 6:1 ratio were obtained using the supported catalyst. The determination of the amount of water, viscosity, and density was the same as in the case of oil, obtaining the following values 0.005%, 0.892 gcm^{-3}, and 4.1887 mm^2s^{-1}, respectively. These parameters are within the ranges determined by biodiesel standards INEN 2482, ASTM B 100, and EN 590. The catalyst obtained favored the generation of biodiesel from recycled vegetable oil and ethanol. This was evidenced in the reaction yield since when using it, since a yield of 70.91% was obtained compared to the non-catalyzed blank where the yield was 0.5%. When comparing the yields between the catalyzed reactions, the yield and viscosity were not significantly different; the differences were found in terms of density. The supported catalyst allowed easier recovery of the catalyst.

The production of biodiesel involves several processes such as the production of zinc oxide, carbon treatment, and oil treatment. The energy consumption of each of the involved processes has been evaluated and quantified, resulting in an energy consumption of 32.9 kWh for obtaining the catalyst and 4.25 kWh for the oil treatment, thus obtaining the biodiesel sample through the reaction, which gives a total of 37.15 kWh.

Author Contributions: Conceptualization, V.P.-V. methodology, D.S.-C., M.O.-M. and V.P.-V.; software, D.S.-C. and M.O.-M.; validation, J.C.; investigation, D.S.-C. and M.O.-M.; resources, P.D.-S.; writing—original draft preparation, D.S.-C., M.O.-M. and V.P.-V., writing—review and editing, A.M.-I., J.C., P.Á.-L., P.D.-S., P.E.-P. and V.P.-V.; supervision, V.P.-V. All authors have read and agreed to the published version of the manuscript.

Funding: This research received no external funding.

Data Availability Statement: Not Applicable.

Conflicts of Interest: The authors declare no conflict of interest.

References

1. INEC. Información Ambiental en Los Hogares 2020. Available online: https://www.ecuadorencifras.gob.ec/documentos/web-inec/Encuestas_Ambientales/Hogares/Hogares-2022/MOD_AMB_HOGAR_ENEMDU_2022.pdf (accessed on 26 May 2023).
2. Ebin, B.; Petranikova, M.; Steenari, B.-M.; Ekberg, C. Investigation of Zinc Recovery by Hydrogen Reduction Assisted Pyrolysis of Alkaline and Zinc-Carbon Battery Waste. *Waste Manag.* **2017**, *68*, 508–517. [CrossRef]
3. Farzana, R.; Rajarao, R.; Behera, P.R.; Hassan, K.; Sahajwalla, V. Zinc Oxide Nanoparticles from Waste Zn-C Battery via Thermal Route: Characterization and Properties. *Nanomaterials* **2018**, *8*, 717. [CrossRef]
4. Mahandra, H.; Singh, R.; Gupta, B. Recycling of Zn-C and Ni-Cd Spent Batteries Using Cyphos IL 104 via Hydrometallurgical Route. *J. Clean. Prod.* **2018**, *172*, 133–142. [CrossRef]
5. INEN. Disposición de Productos Pilas y Baterias En Desuso, Requisitos. 2011. Available online: https://www.normalizacion.gob.ec/buzon/normas23/2534.pdf (accessed on 26 May 2023).
6. Abid Charef, S.; Affoune, A.M.; Caballero, A.; Cruz-Yusta, M.; Morales, J. Simultaneous Recovery of Zn and Mn from Used Batteries in Acidic and Alkaline Mediums: A Comparative Study. *Waste Manag.* **2017**, *68*, 518–526. [CrossRef]
7. Chicaiza, O. Programa de Gestión de Pilas Usadas. 2021. Available online: https://documentosboletinoficial.buenosaires.gob.ar/publico/PE-DIS-MAYEPGC-DGPOLEA-49-19-ANX.pdf (accessed on 26 May 2023).
8. Viswanathan, B. Chapter 12—Batteries. In *Energy Sources*; Viswanathan, B., Ed.; Elsevier: Amsterdam, The Netherlands, 2017; pp. 263–313. ISBN 978-0-444-56353-8.
9. Chen, W.-S.; Liao, C.-T.; Lin, K.-Y. Recovery Zinc and Manganese from Spent Battery Powder by Hydrometallurgical Route. *Energy Procedia* **2017**, *107*, 167–174. [CrossRef]
10. Tanong, K.; Tran, L.-H.; Mercier, G.; Blais, J.-F. Recovery of Zn (II), Mn (II), Cd (II) and Ni (II) from the Unsorted Spent Batteries Using Solvent Extraction, Electrodeposition and Precipitation Methods. *J. Clean. Prod.* **2017**, *148*, 233–244. [CrossRef]
11. Padoan, E.; Hernandez Kath, A.; Vahl, L.C.; Ajmone-Marsan, F. Potential Release of Zinc and Cadmium From Mine-Affected Soils Under Flooding, a Mesocosm Study. *Arch. Environ. Contam. Toxicol.* **2020**, *79*, 421–434. [CrossRef]
12. Zhang, X.; Yang, L.; Li, Y.; Li, H.; Wang, W.; Ye, B. Impacts of Lead/Zinc Mining and Smelting on the Environment and Human Health in China. *Environ. Monit. Assess.* **2012**, *184*, 2261–2273. [CrossRef] [PubMed]
13. Tao, M.; Zhang, X.; Wang, S.; Cao, W.; Jiang, Y. Life Cycle Assessment on Lead–Zinc Ore Mining and Beneficiation in China. *J. Clean. Prod.* **2019**, *237*, 117833. [CrossRef]
14. Ćwieląg-Drabek, M.; Piekut, A.; Gut, K.; Grabowski, M. Risk of Cadmium, Lead and Zinc Exposure from Consumption of Vegetables Produced in Areas with Mining and Smelting Past. *Sci. Rep.* **2020**, *10*, 3363. [CrossRef]
15. Oviedo Anchundia, R.; Moína-Quimí, E.; Naranjo-Morán, J.; Barcos-Arias, M. Contaminación Por Metales Pesados En El Sur Del Ecuador Asociada a La Actividad Minera. *Bionatura* **2017**, *2*, 437–441. [CrossRef]
16. Jia, Y.; Zhang, T.; Zhai, Y.; Bai, Y.; Ren, K.; Shen, X.; Cheng, Z.; Zhou, X.; Hong, J. Exploring the Potential Health and Ecological Damage of Lead–Zinc Production Activities in China: A Life Cycle Assessment Perspective. *J. Clean. Prod.* **2022**, *381*, 135218. [CrossRef]
17. Elgharbawy, A.S.; Sadik, W.A.; Sadek, O.M.; Kasaby, M.A.; Elgharbawy, A.S.; Sadik, W.A.; Sadek, O.M.; Kasaby, M.A. A review on biodiesel feedstocks and production technologies. *J. Chil. Chem. Soc.* **2021**, *66*, 5098–5109. [CrossRef]
18. Collin, T.; Cunningham, R.; Jefferson, B.; Villa, R. Characterisation and Energy Assessment of Fats, Oils and Greases (FOG) Waste at Catchment Level. *Waste Manag.* **2020**, *103*, 399–406. [CrossRef]
19. Chicaiza, O. Programa de Gestión de Aceite Vegetal. 2021.
20. Vásconez, L. Convenios en Cinco Ciudades del Ecuador Para Reciclar Aceites Usados. Available online: https://www.elcomercio.com/actualidad/ecuador/convenios-ciudades-ecuador-reciclar-aceites.html (accessed on 1 September 2021).

21. Bardhan, P.; Deka, A.; Bhattacharya, S.S.; Mandal, M.; Kataki, R. Chapter 18—Economical Aspect in Biomass to Biofuel Production. In *Value-Chain of Biofuels*; Yusup, S., Rashidi, N.A., Eds.; Elsevier: Amsterdam, The Netherlands, 2022; pp. 395–427. ISBN 978-0-12-824388-6.
22. Topi, D. Transforming Waste Vegetable Oils to Biodiesel, Establishing of a Waste Oil Management System in Albania. *SN Appl. Sci.* **2020**, *2*, 513. [CrossRef]
23. Neupane, D. Biofuels from Renewable Sources, a Potential Option for Biodiesel Production. *Bioengineering* **2023**, *10*, 29. [CrossRef]
24. Sheehan, J.; Camobreco, V.; Duffield, J.; Graboski, M.; Shapouri, H. *An Overview of Biodiesel and Petroleum Diesel Life Cycles*; National Renewable Energy Laboratory (U.S.): Golden, CO, USA, 2000; p. 60. [CrossRef]
25. Hamza, B.; Rouan, M.; Hammi, M.; Ziat, Y.; Chigr, M. Synthesis of Biodiesel by Transesterification of Used Frying Oils (UFO) through Basic Homogeneous Catalysts (NaOH and KOH). *Biointerface Res. Appl. Chem.* **2021**, *11*, 12858–12868. [CrossRef]
26. Sierra-Cantor, J.F.; Parra-Santiago, J.J.; Guerrero-Fajardo, C.A. Leaching and Reusing Analysis of Calcium–Zinc Mixed Oxides as Heterogeneous Catalysts in the Biodiesel Production from Refined Palm Oil. *Int. J. Environ. Sci. Technol.* **2019**, *16*, 643–654. [CrossRef]
27. Ramírez, J.; Buestán, L.; López-Maldonado, E.A.; Pinos-Vélez, V. Preparation and Physicochemical Characterization of Biodiesel from Recycled Vegetable Oil in Cuenca, Ecuador by Transesterification Catalyzed by KOH and NaOH. *Eng* **2023**, *4*, 954–963. [CrossRef]
28. Sipayung, R. Budiyono Optimization of Biodiesel Production from Used Cooking Oil Using Modified Calcium Oxide as Catalyst and N-Hexane as Solvent. *Mater. Today Proc.* **2022**, *63*, S32–S39. [CrossRef]
29. Yusuff, A.S.; Bhonsle, A.K.; Trivedi, J.; Bangwal, D.P.; Singh, L.P.; Atray, N. Synthesis and Characterization of Coal Fly Ash Supported Zinc Oxide Catalyst for Biodiesel Production Using Used Cooking Oil as Feed. *Renew. Energy* **2021**, *170*, 302–314. [CrossRef]
30. Hossain, M.N.; Siddik Bhuyan, M.S.U.; Md Ashraful Alam, A.H.; Seo, Y.C. Optimization of Biodiesel Production from Waste Cooking Oil Using S–TiO_2/SBA-15 Heterogeneous Acid Catalyst. *Catalysts* **2019**, *9*, 67. [CrossRef]
31. Chuquichanga, E.; León, D. Obtención de Óxido de Zinc a Partir de Pilas Zinc Carbono Desechables. Perú. 2019. Available online: http://repositorio.unac.edu.pe/handle/20.500.12952/4293 (accessed on 14 March 2023).
32. Samadhi, T. Environmental Impact of Sodium Sulfate Decomposition in Silicate Glass Manufacturing. Ph.D. Thesis, Alfred University, Alfred, NY, USA, 2003.
33. HERA. Cover Note of Sodium Sulfate. 2006. Available online: https://www.heraproject.com/files/39-f-06_sodium_sulfate_human_and_environmental_risk_assessment_v2.pdf (accessed on 26 May 2023).
34. INEN Biodiesel. Requisitos. 2013. Available online: https://www.normalizacion.gob.ec/buzon/normas23/2482.pdf (accessed on 26 May 2023).
35. ASTM Chapter 5 | Biodiesel. Available online: https://www.astm.org/mnl120170046.html (accessed on 4 January 2022).
36. EN Combustibles Para Automoción. Combustibles Par. Available online: https://www.une.org/encuentra-tu-norma/busca-tu-norma/norma/?c=N0052852 (accessed on 31 August 2022).
37. Alvarado, E.; GONZALES, K.; Mendoza, O. *Propuesta de un Método para la Recuperación de Zinc de Pilas Alcalinas Usadas bajo el Enfoque de Producción más Limpia*; Universidad de El Salvador: San Salvador, El Salvador, 2010.
38. ITC Trade Map—Estadísticas Del Comercio Para El Desarrollo Internacional de Las Empresas. Available online: https://www.trademap.org/Index.aspx (accessed on 2 March 2023).
39. INEC. Informacion Ambiental En Hogares 2022. Available online: https://www.ecuadorencifras.gob.ec/documentos/web-inec/Encuestas_Ambientales/Hogares/Hogares-2022/MOD_AMB_HOGAR_ENEMDU_2022.pdf (accessed on 1 March 2023).
40. Agbemafle, R.; Aggor-Woananu, S.E.; Akutey, O.; Bentum, J. Heavy Metal Concentrations in Leachates and Crops Grown Around Waste Dumpsites in Sekondi-Takoradi in the Western Region of Ghana. *Res. J. Environ. Toxicol.* **2019**, *14*, 16–25. [CrossRef]
41. Hussain, S.; Khan, M.; Sheikh, T.M.M.; Mumtaz, M.Z.; Chohan, T.A.; Shamim, S.; Liu, Y. Zinc Essentiality, Toxicity, and Its Bacterial Bioremediation: A Comprehensive Insight. *Front. Microbiol.* **2022**, *13*, 900740. [CrossRef]
42. Ryu, M.-S.; Aydemir, T.B. Chapter 23—Zinc. In *Present Knowledge in Nutrition*, 11th ed.; Marriott, B.P., Birt, D.F., Stallings, V.A., Yates, A.A., Eds.; Academic Press: Cambridge, MA, USA, 2020; pp. 393–408. ISBN 978-0-323-66162-1.
43. Kan, X.; Dong, Y.; Feng, L.; Zhou, M.; Hou, H. Contamination and Health Risk Assessment of Heavy Metals in China's Lead–Zinc Mine Tailings: A Meta–Analysis. *Chemosphere* **2021**, *267*, 128909. [CrossRef] [PubMed]
44. Du, B.; Zhang, H.; Ji, D.; Huang, Z.; Fangqun, G.; Zhou, J. Environmental Contamination and Health Risk Assessment to Toxic Elements in an Active Lead–Zinc Mining Area. *Expo. Health* **2022**, 1–12. [CrossRef]
45. Johansen, P.; Asmund, G.; Aastrup, P.; Tamstorf, M. *Environmental Impact of the Lead-Zinc Mine at Mestervig, East Greenland*; National Environmental Research Institute, University of Aarhus: Aarhus, Denmark, 2008.
46. López, L.; Bocanegra, J.; Malagón-Romero, D. Obtención de biodiesel por transesterificación de aceite de cocina usado. *Ing. Univ.* **2015**, *19*, 155–172. [CrossRef]
47. Rodriguez, D.; Riesco, J. Obtención de Biodiesel a Partir de Mezclas de Aceite de Cocina Usado y Aceite de Higuerilla Por Transesterificación. Available online: https://www.jovenesenlaciencia.ugto.mx/index.php/jovenesenlaciencia/article/view/1296 (accessed on 5 September 2022).

48. Tacias Pascacio, V.G.; Rosales Quintero, A.; Torrestiana Sánchez, B.; Tacias Pascacio, V.G.; Rosales Quintero, A.; Torrestiana Sánchez, B. Evaluación y caracterización de grasas y aceites residuales de cocina para la producción de biodiésel: Un caso de estudio. *Rev. Int. Contam. Ambient.* **2016**, *32*, 303–313. [CrossRef]
49. Gavhane, R.S.; Kate, A.M.; Pawar, A.; Safaei, M.R.; Soudagar, M.M.E.; Mujtaba Abbas, M.; Muhammad Ali, H.; Banapurmath, N.R.; Goodarzi, M.; Badruddin, I.A.; et al. Effect of Zinc Oxide Nano-Additives and Soybean Biodiesel at Varying Loads and Compression Ratios on VCR Diesel Engine Characteristics. *Symmetry* **2020**, *12*, 1042. [CrossRef]
50. Sánchez, E.M. Obtención de Biodiesel a Partir de Aceites Vegetales Empleando Catalizadores Sólidos Nanoestructurados. 2021. Available online: https://ria.utn.edu.ar/bitstream/handle/20.500.12272/5187/Tesis%20Doctoral%20-%20S%C3%A1nchez%20Faba%2C%20Edgar%20M.%20-%20UTN%20FRC.pdf?sequence=1&isAllowed=y (accessed on 24 March 2022).
51. Diaz, D.; Camargo, G.; Molano, M. Evaluación de Catalizadores de Óxido de Zinc y Su Actividad Catalítica En La Reacción de Transesterificación Para La Producción de Biodiésel. *Afinidad* **2008**, *65*, 299–305.
52. Fangfang, F.; Alagumalai, A.; Mahian, O. Sustainable Biodiesel Production from Waste Cooking Oil: ANN Modeling and Environmental Factor Assessment. *Sustain. Energy Technol. Assess.* **2021**, *46*, 101265. [CrossRef]
53. Sivarethinamohan, S.; Hanumanthu, J.R.; Gaddam, K.; Ravindiran, G.; Alagumalai, A. Towards Sustainable Biodiesel Production by Solar Intensification of Waste Cooking Oil and Engine Parameter Assessment Studies. *Sci. Total Environ.* **2022**, *804*, 150236. [CrossRef]
54. Dasta, P.; Pratap Singh, A.; Pratap Singh, A. Zinc Oxide Nanoparticle as a Heterogeneous Catalyst in Generation of Biodiesel. *Mater. Today Proc.* **2022**, *52*, 751–757. [CrossRef]
55. Guo, M.; Jiang, W.; Ding, J.; Lu, J. Highly Active and Recyclable CuO/ZnO as Photocatalyst for Transesterification of Waste Cooking Oil to Biodiesel and the Kinetics. *Fuel* **2022**, *315*, 123254. [CrossRef]

urban science

MDPI

Article

Socio-Economic Feasibility for Implementation of Environmental Legislation along the Riparian Buffer Zones in Urban Rivers of Northern Tanzania

Janeth Mwile Mwasenga [1,*] and Ibrahimu Chikira Mjemah [2]

[1] Department of Environmental Engineering and Management, College of Earth Sciences and Engineering, The University of Dodoma, Dodoma P.O. Box 11090, Tanzania
[2] Department of Geography and Environmental Studies, College of Natural and Applied Sciences, Sokoine University of Agriculture, Morogoro P.O. Box 3038, Tanzania; ichikira@gmail.com
* Correspondence: nsanyajanet@gmail.com

Abstract: The development of socio-economic activities within the 60 m buffer zone has imposed change on the characteristics of rivers in northern Tanzania, subjecting rivers to collateral and irreversible damage due to their prolonged exposure to anthropic activities. Time series satellite images were classified to analyze land use/cover (LULC) changes and anthropic development along the buffer zone from 2000 to 2020. Structured questionnaires were used to identify the encroachment factors and level of compliance with alleged environmental legislation. Furthermore, focus group discussions were used to acquire information on the concurrent barriers to environmental legislation implementation. The land use/cover change along the buffer zone showed that agriculture and artificial areas had a credible increase of about 43% and 30% from 2000 to 2020, respectively. Furthermore, forest and semi-natural areas decreased by 71% from 2000 to 2020, whereas wetlands decreased by about 2% within the same timeframe. On the other hand, artificial and agricultural areas increased by 24.5% and 19.5%, respectively. Forest and semi-natural areas decreased by about 44%, whereas wetlands and water showed a flimsy increase from 2000 to 2020. This trend shows that high land use/cover changes occurred along the riparian buffer zone. The results suggest that urbanization is the main driving force for riparian buffer zone encroachment, threatening ecological well-being and water resource sustainability in urban rivers. The findings of this study are useful for advancing regional and national policies and practices for sustainable water resource management.

Keywords: riparian buffer zone; rivers; encroachment; land use/cover; and anthropic activities

1. Introduction

Watersheds and rivers provide ecological features that are essential for community well-being from their hydrological services [1]. However, water resources are afflicted by the direct association between increased population and urban growth [2]. Africa is projected to have a high rate of urban residents worldwide, leaving Asia aside [3]. The high rate of increase in its urban population mirrors the demand for water for domestic, agricultural, and industrial uses, which might exceed the current supply capacity [4]. This phenomenon is expected to increase pressure on water resources, likely leading to the encroachment of riparian buffers, especially regarding urban rivers in sub-Saharan Africa.

In Tanzania, anthropic activities afflict the ecological functions of urban rivers in many dimensions. For example, the Msimbazi River in Dar es Salaam has an appreciable self-purification capacity; however, the pollution plight has overweighed this. Thus, rivers fail to maintain their functional attributes due to an inadequate or inefficient self-purification capacity [5]. Deforestation and river bank encroachment are the main agents of soil erosion, siltation, and even landslides in the middle section of the rivers [6].

Buffer zones are essential for conserving and safeguarding against protected areas or sensitive areas; in Tanzania, laws and policies have been set to protect riparian buffers. One among them is the Environmental Management Act of 2004 [7], which prohibits conducting human activities within 60 m of the water source [8]. There are increased socio-economic activities like agriculture within the 60 m strip of the riverbanks of Tengeru, Nduruma, Themi, and Maji ya Chai; this violation can be termed an act of encroachment.

One of the most pressing issues is the urban growth of Arusha city due to being a tourist hub that has attracted the population growth of rural dwellers and other dwellers in the country into the urban. Furthermore, population growth has been experienced in relative districts like Meru, which has led to the overexploitation of water resources. Economic water stress often increases due to population growth in urban areas. Since the water available is insufficient for economic use, urban dwellers extend to the nearby streams for easy access [9]. Rivers in the Arusha region pass through human settlements and downstream to areas with several human activities, including inefficiently treated effluent wastewater and inappropriate urban planning [10].

The practice of socio-economic activities in the buffer zones has affected the water quality, especially at the flood plains and downstream points of the rivers. Studies have shown fecal coliform in the Tengeru, Maji ya Chai, and Nduruma rivers beyond the permissible limit [10]. The report further showed high levels of electrical conductivity of up to 1722 μS/cm and BOD, nitrates, and total soluble phosphates levels of 10 mg/L, 50 mg/L, and 0.1 mg/L, respectively. These figures exceed the World Health Organization (WHO) standards, reflecting increased anthropic activities in urban rivers. The encroachment of riparian buffer zones also affects the stability of the river, water velocity, turbidity, and nutrient overloading, which are essential factors for the growth and breeding of amphibians and macroinvertebrates (Properties et al., 2015) [11].

Mckenzie et al. [12] warned that increased human activities along the riparian buffer zone could increase the impacts on water sources beyond the current knowledge. The aforementioned diverse pollutant sources and high populations along these rivers trigger the need to conduct a detailed analysis of the activities undertaken in riparian buffer zones. However, information on the levels of encroachment and the activities undertaken in the riparian buffer zone is scant or absent. Furthermore, the informed implementation of environmental legislation was envisaged to provide management needs for the sustainability of these rivers. Therefore, this paper aimed to quantify socio-economic development along the buffer zone and determine community compliance with the environmental legislation governing riparian buffer zones.

2. Material and Methods

2.1. The Study Area

The study focused on four rivers, Nduruma, Tengeru, Themi, and Maji ya Chai, located in the Arusha region of Tanzania (Figure 1). Tengeru, Nduruma, and Maji ya Chai are in the Meru district, while Themi is in the Arusha district. These rivers originate from the foothills of Mount Meru, which is the second-highest mountain in East Africa. These rivers join other rivers to form the Kikuletwa catchment in the Simanjiro district, which is situated in the northwestern part of the Pangani River basin, as documented by Kitalika et al., 2018 [10].

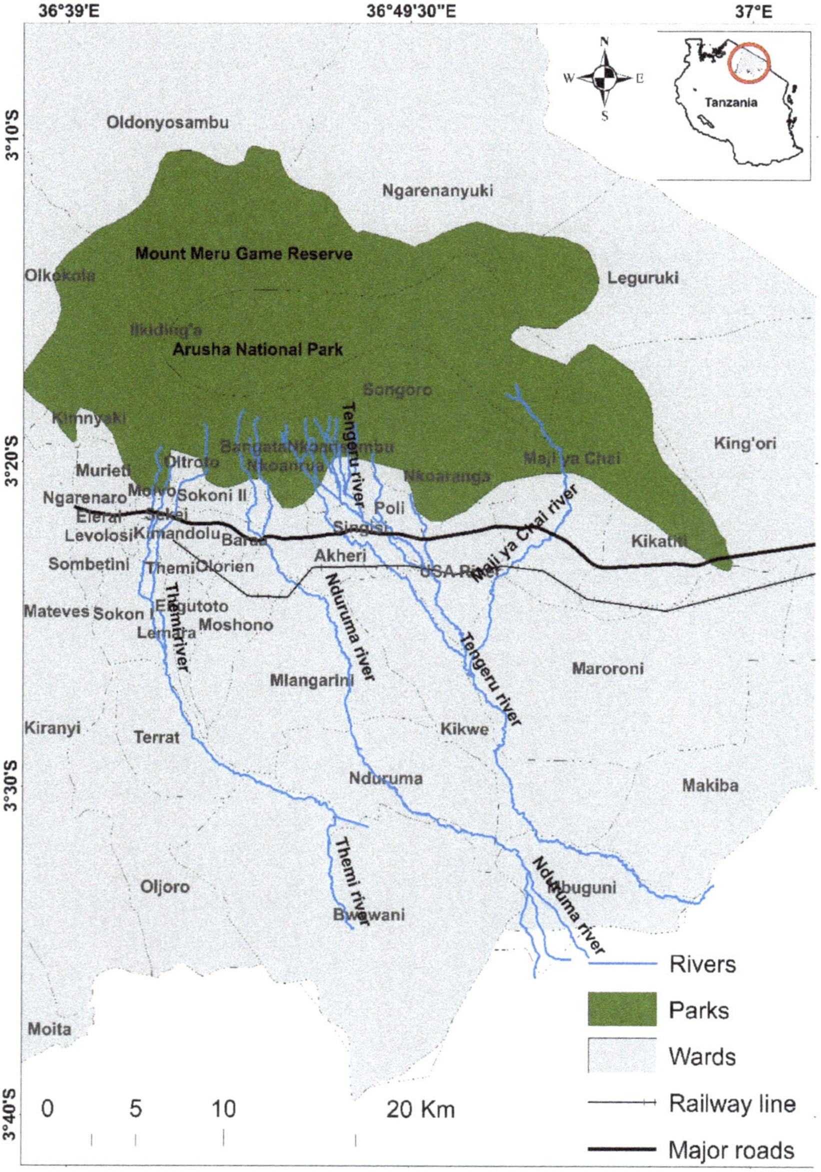

Figure 1. The study area.

Arusha city lies between latitudes 2° and 6° south and longitudes 34.50° and 38° east. The city lies below Mount Meru on the eastern edge of the eastern branch of the Great Rift Valley. Despite its proximity to the equator, the elevation of Arusha is approximately 1400 m (4600 ft), resulting in a temperate climate. By understanding the specific geographic and climatic attributes of Arusha and its surrounding regions, researchers and policymakers can better appreciate the environmental challenges and opportunities that are inherent in the area.

2.1.1. Climate

The study area was characterized by a mild, warm, and temperate climate that experienced an annual average temperature of 20 °C. There were two distinct wet seasons, October–December and February–June, that received an average rainfall of about 1717 mm. The highest average rainfall was observed in April. There were two distinct dry seasons in January and July–September. February was the hottest month, while July had the lowest average temperature of about 16.8 °C.

2.1.2. Socio-Economic Activities

Arusha City is famously known for its tourism industry, significantly contributing to its growth. Moreover, its proximity to the tourist attractions such as national parks and conservation areas has made Arusha a center for foreign interaction. Other socio-economic activities in Arusha include agriculture, livestock keeping, and small-scale industries [13]. Agriculture is currently leading, for it has threatened the ecosystem of riparian buffers due to its expansion from economically planned zones into protected zones which could be considered encroachment. The growth of industries has accounted for the increase in impervious areas, even in the regions to be protected and used for recharge purposes. In return, the rate of surface runoff has increased, as well as water stress, with a higher occurrence of floods due to a lack of flood attenuation.

2.2. Data Collection and Analysis

2.2.1. Data Acquisition

Time series satellite images from the years 2000, 2010, and 2020. Additionally, the river networks and shapefiles of this boundary were accessed from different sources (Table 1).

Table 1. Data used in this study.

Data Category	Description	Row/Path	Year	Data Source
Satellite image	Landsat 8 OLI-TRIS	168/062	2020	www.glovis.usgs.gov, accessed on 18 March 2022.
Satellite image	Landsat7 ETM+	168/062	2000	www.glovis.usgs.gov, accessed on 18 March 2022.
Satellite image	Landsat 7 ETM+	168/062	2010	www.glovis.usgs.gov, accessed on 18 March 2022.
Elevation	Digital Elevation Model	168/062	2022	www.glovis.usgs.gov, accessed on 20 March 2022.
Boundary	Tanzania District and Wards shape file	168/062	2022	www.nbs.go.tz, accessed on 23 January 2023.
River network	River network	-	2022	Pangani Basin Water Board

A survey was conducted on the respective riparian buffer to observe and identify the socio-economic activities in the buffer zones. The selected land use/cover classes followed the Corine land cover classification (Table 2). During this survey, 50–60 ground truthing points were collected to assess accuracy.

Structured questionnaires were used to gain information on the perception of the community regarding compliance and factors influencing the encroachment of buffer zones. A total of 195 were determined through the Taro Yamane Equation (1):

$$n = \frac{N}{1 + N * (e^2)} \tag{1}$$

where n is the sample size, N is the population, and e represents the acceptable sampling error. For example, the population size of Meru District used was 268,144, which was found according to the 2022 census.

Table 2. Description of land use classes.

Land Use Class	Description
Agricultural areas	Includes arable land, permanent crops, pastures, and heterogeneous agricultural areas.
Artificial Surfaces	Urban fabric, industrial, commercial and transport units, mine, dump and construction sites, artificial, non-agricultural vegetated areas.
Forest and semi-natural areas	Forest, shrub and/or herbaceous vegetation associations, and open spaces with little or no vegetation.
Wetlands	Inland wetlands and coastal wetlands
Water	Inland waters and marine waters.

A focus group discussion was held with experts from the Pangani Basin Water Board (PBWB), National Environment Management Council (NEMC), and Meru District Council. The aim was to identify the challenges hindering environmental law implementation. The discussion looked further into the impacts of encroachment, the recent efforts made by the organization to limit further encroachment activities, and factors influencing encroachment within the buffer zone.

2.2.2. Data Analysis

The acquired Landsat images were atmospherically and radiometrically corrected before classification. Quantum GIS was used to remove the scan lines in the Landsat 7 images using the provided supplementary data. Other image corrections, like contrast stretching, enhanced the color contrast in images before classification. Figure 2 presents the summary of the image classification workflow.

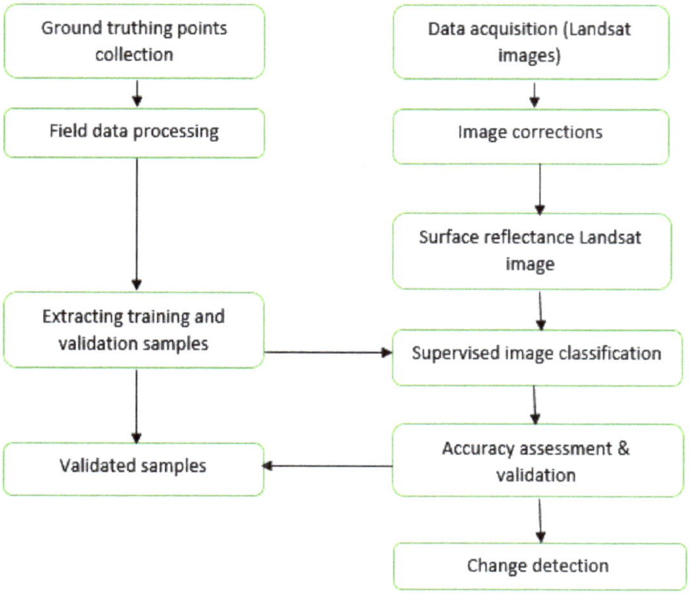

Figure 2. Remote sensing process flow chart.

The images were classified by supervised classification. Training samples for each class were allocated to the image; the training samples were combined to form a signature file that was used to perform a supervised classification by maximum likelihood. Satellite images of the year 2000, 2010, and 2020 were acquired from the United States Geological

Survey (USGS) website through USGS Global Visualization Viewer (GloVis) (https://glovis.usgs.gov/ (accessed on 18 March 2020)). Some of the satellite images had scanline errors, like Landsat 7 satellite images. These errors were corrected to remove the scan lines and prepare them for classification; this was conducted using a Quantum Geographic Information System (QGIS). Additionally, the pre- and post-processing of the images was conducted before and after classification.

An accuracy assessment was performed to determine the accuracy of the classification output. The *Kappa Coefficient* was used, and it was determined by using Equation (2).

$$Kappa\ Coefficient = \frac{N\sum_{i=1}^{m} CM_{ii} - \sum_{i=1}^{m} Ci_{corr}Ci_{pred}}{N^2 - \sum_{i=1}^{m} Ci_{corr}Ci_{pred}} \quad (2)$$

where N is the total number of selected classified pixels or points, m is the number of rows, CM_{ii} is the number of points that were correctly classified for a particular land use class and Ci_{corr} and Ci_{pred} were marginal totals for the row and column.

To determine the amount of *encroachment* (*% encroachment*), Equation (3) was used.

$$\%\ encroachment = \frac{Area\ of\ the\ buffer\ encroached}{Area\ of\ the\ 60\ metres\ buffer\ zone} \times 100\% \quad (3)$$

The structured questionnaires from Kobotoolbox were imported to R, where the statistical analysis of the factors influencing the *buffer zone*, the level of compliance with the regulations, the challenges encountered in implementing environmental legislation, and the relationship between these variables was performed.

Buffer zone analysis was performed upon the overlay of the rivers before a buffered shapefile was created; the shapefile was used as a clipping tool to determine the classes within the *buffer zone* and their respective areas. The buffer field was set at 60 m as stated in the Environmental Policy 2021, EMA, 2004, and the Water Resource Management Act, no 11 of 2009.

3. Results and Discussions

3.1. Accuracy of LULC Classification

The Kappa coefficient, overall accuracy, producer accuracy, and user accuracy for the satellite images of 2000, 2010, and 2020 were determined after the classification. The confusion matrix brought about the user accuracy (UA) and the producer accuracy (PA) for each class, as summarized in Table 3.

Table 3. User accuracy and producer accuracy for the years 2000, 2010 and 2020.

Land Use Classes	Years					
	2000		2010		2020	
	UA (%)	PA (%)	UA (%)	PA (%)	UA (%)	PA (%)
Agriculture areas	83.33	71.43	80	79	83.33	79.67
Water	80	100	100	100	100	100
Artificial Surfaces	80	100	80	100	83.33	100
Forest and semi-natural areas	75	85.71	100	100	90.91	66.67
Wetlands	75	66.67	80	50	81.82	81.82

The overall accuracy ranged from 81.48% to 85.37%, while the Kappa coefficient ranged from 0.8 to 0.83 (Table 4).

Table 4. Accuracy assessment.

	Accuracy Assessment	
Year	**Overall Accuracy (%)**	**Kappa Coefficient (%)**
2000	83.08	80.10
2010	85.37	83.24
2020	81.48	80.5

These values signify that the classification attained the minimum threshold required for land use/cover analysis and modeling [14]; thus, the results of this study were authentic, using minimum requirements for image classification accuracy [15].

3.2. Spatial and Temporal LULUC Changes

The changes in areas under each class are summarized in Table 5 and depicted in Figure 3. The observed changes across the three time periods show that the area of artificial areas continued to increase, from 157.86 in 2000 to 293.12 in 2010 and further to 452.23 km^2 in 2020. This increment suggests ongoing urbanization and development. Furthermore, the area of agricultural land also showed a steady increase, from 325.56 in 2000 to 481.80 in 2010 and further to 560.58 km^2 in 2020. This expansion indicates sustained agricultural activities and the potential expansion of farmland. Additionally, the changes in these classes signified an increase in population, increasing the demand for more food and shelter.

Table 5. A real change in LULC from 2000 to 2020.

Land Use Classes	Area (km2)			Change (%)		
	2000	**2010**	**2020**	**2000–2010**	**2010–2020**	**2000–2020**
Artificial areas	157.86	293.12	452.23	11.28	13.18	24.46
Agricultural areas	325.56	481.80	560.58	12.92	6.53	19.45
Forest and semi-natural areas	718.18	427.374	193.23	−25	−19.4	−44.4
Wetlands	4.73	3.852	0.261	0.319	0.298	0.357
Water	0.49	0.558	0.522	0.00426	−0.004	0.005

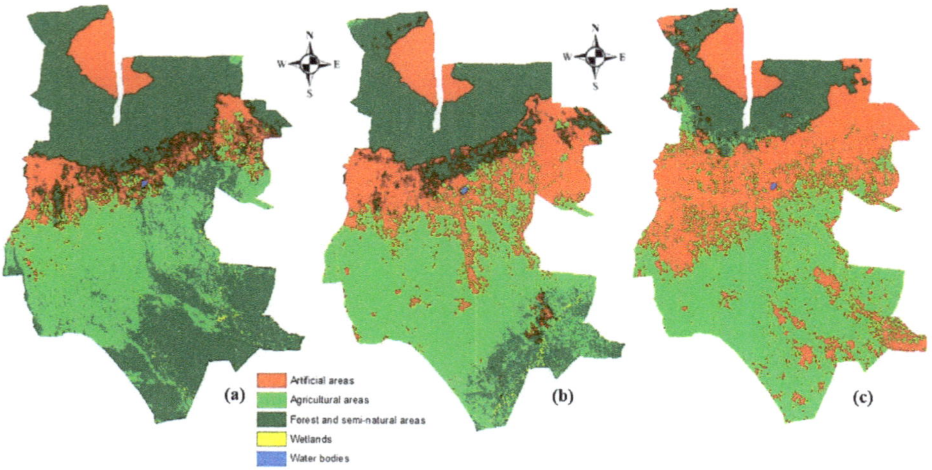

Figure 3. Classified land use/cover images for the years. 2000 (**a**), 2010 (**b**) and 2020 (**c**).

The forest and semi-natural areas decreased significantly from 718.18 in 2000 to 427.374 in 2010 and further to 193.23 in 2020. This decrease implies the substantial loss of natural and semi-natural habitats over these two decades. The area of wetlands decreased gradually from 4.73 in 2000 to 3.852 in 2010 and further to 0.261 in 2020; this trend highlights a continuing decline in wetland ecosystems. The decline in wetland ecosystems goes in tandem with a slight fluctuation in water. However, due to perennial rivers, the water area remained relatively stable over these years, with slight fluctuations from 0.49 in 2000 to 0.558 km^2 in 2010 and eventually to 0.522 km^2 in 2020.

Water showed a minimal change in its area between 2000 and 2020. However, there was a reduction in water between 2010 and 2020. In 2000, water and wetlands covered an area of about 0.4 km^2; a reduction of about 0.004% in water was observed in 2010, and an overall increment of about 0.005% was recorded between 2000 and 2020 for water and wetlands, respectively. This indicates no significant changes in water bodies during this decade. It is worth mentioning that a portion of water may be absorbed or obscured by the surrounding forest, shrub land or grassland. Conventionally, land that was initially occupied by forest and semi-natural covers may have been converted to agricultural areas and artificial surfaces. This trend is depicted in Figure 4.

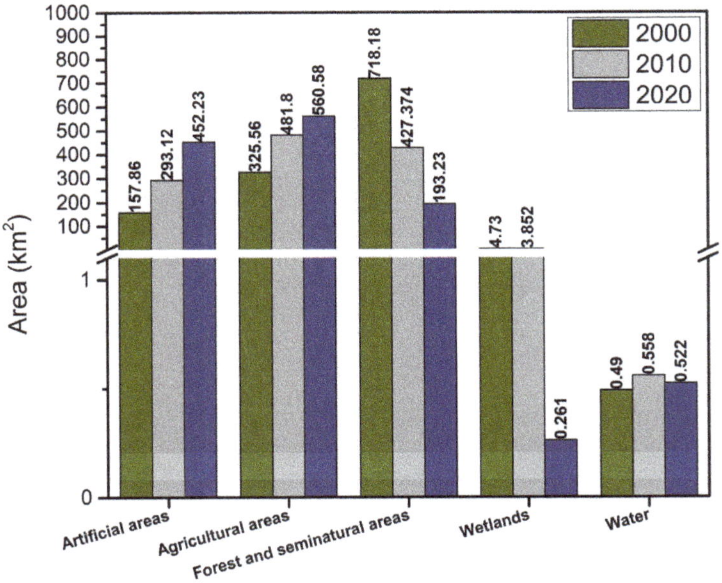

Figure 4. Change in the land use classes over the years 2000, 2010 and 2020.

There was a significant increase in artificial areas between 2000 and 2010, with a percentage change of 11.28% and an almost similar increment rate of 13.18% in the total area of the catchment between 2010 and 2020. This increase indicates rapid urbanization and infrastructure development during this period, albeit at a slightly increased rate compared to the previous decade. Furthermore, agricultural areas experienced a sharp increase, with a percentage change of 12.92% between 2000 and 2010 and expansion at a decreased rate of 6.53% between 2010 and 2020. These changes indicate expansion in agricultural activities and possibly an increased focus on food production during this period, probably exhausting most fertile areas in the previous decade.

Forest and semi-natural areas significantly declined between 2000 and 2010, with a percentage change of 25%. However, a similar decline with a comparatively reduced rate of 19.4% in forest and semi-natural areas was observed between 2010 and 2020. This indicated a substantial loss of forested and natural lands, possibly due to deforestation, urbanization, or land conversion for agricultural purposes. In line with this decline in forest and semi-natural areas, wetlands experienced a slight decrease, with a percentage change of 0.319% between 2000 and 2010. Furthermore, a flimsy increase of 0.298% was observed between 2010 and 2020; this indicates a minor loss of wetland habitats during this decade, indicating a strengthening of conservation strategies or encroachment of most wetlands.

Generally, between 2000 and 2020, there was a significant increase in artificial areas from 2000 to 2020 with a percentage change of 24.46%, which was relative to the total area. This indicates that urbanization and infrastructure development have expanded over the years. Agricultural areas have also experienced growth, with a percentage change of 19.45%, which is relative to the total area. This expansion suggests an expansion in agricultural activities and possibly increased food production. Furthermore, forest and semi-natural areas have shown a declining trend, with a percentage change of 44.4% relative to the total area. This indicates a significant reduction in forested and natural lands, possibly due to deforestation, urbanization, or the conversion of land for agricultural production. Additionally, wetlands have experienced a slight decrease, with a percentage change of 0.357%, which is relative to the total area. This suggests a minor loss of wetland habitats, which could impact the biodiversity and ecosystem services associated with wetland areas. In line with this, the area covered by water has remained relatively stable, with a small percentage change of 0.005% relative to the total area, indicating that there have been no significant changes in water bodies over the years.

Generally, the trends between 2000 and 2010 indicated rapid urbanization, moderate growth in agricultural areas, the significant loss of forest and semi-natural areas, a slight decrease in wetlands, and minor changes in water bodies. Between 2010 and 2020, these trends showed continued urban expansion at a slower rate, continued growth in agricultural areas but at a reduced pace, and a further decline in forest and semi-natural areas, including the significant loss of wetlands and relatively stable water bodies. These trends highlight the ongoing challenges of urbanization, deforestation, and land use changes, emphasizing the need for sustainable land management practices, conservation efforts, and the careful consideration of the environmental impact of human activities.

The land use/cover changes observed in the study area could have significant environmental, economic, and social implications, such as habitat loss, changes in ecosystem services, agricultural productivity, and urban development. Monitoring and managing these trends is important to ensure sustainable land use practices and minimize negative environmental and ecosystem impacts.

Previous studies in other Arusha City catchments have reported a similar agricultural land increment. Agricultural land was expected to increase by about 21.1% and 29.2% between 1985 and 2000 and from 1985 to 2015, respectively. This increase would likely continue for about 38.2% and 42.7%, from 1985 to 2030 and 1985 to 2050, respectively [16]. Similarly, the agricultural land on the slopes of Mount Meru were reported to increase from 46.85% to 50.42% between 1986 and 1996 and 42.8% between 1996 and 2006 [10]. The report further shows a general increase in the built-up area by 96.8 km^2 and 53.9 km^2 between 2006 and 2016, respectively. A large proportion of this increase was reported to align with a decrease in bushlands (from 31.5% to 24.19%), some of which could be found along the riparian buffer zone.

The reports show that urban growth in Arusha was approximately 287% from 1995 to 2015; the future projection shows an increment of 180% in the urban footprint by 2050 [17]. Kitalika et al. [10] reported that significant land use transitions from bushland and agricultural land into human settlements resulted from upgrading the conversion of Arusha town into a city status. A similar decrease in the forest was also reported in the northern [18–20], southern highlands [21], central regions, and coastal regions of Tanzania [22]. This indicates an increased pressure on water resources, predominantly urban rivers, which is likely to affect sustainability.

3.3. Socio-Economic Development along the Riparian Buffer Zones

Changes in land use/cover in the buffer zone are summarized in Table 6 and depicted in Figure 5. Between 2000 and 2020, the land cover in the buffer zone continuously showed persistent change as the driving factors exceeded the carrying capacity of the buffer zone. Within the buffer zone, there was an increase in artificial areas from 2.538 km^2 in 2000 to 8.361 km^2 in 2010 and, finally, 16.47 km^2 in 2020. This change was equivalent to 18.07% from 2000 to 2010, 25.06% from 2010 to 2020, and a total change of about 43.13% from 2000 to 2020. This change mirrored environmental destruction along the buffer zone, suggesting water quality and quantity change.

Table 6. Land use/cover changes within the buffer zone of Themi, Nduruma, Tengeru, and Maji ya Chai rivers.

Land Use Classes	Area (Km^2)			Change (%)		
	2000	2010	2020	2000–2010	2010–2020	2000–2020
Artificial areas	2.538	8.361	16.47	18.07	25.06	43.13
Agricultural areas	2.133	9.666	11.907	23.31	6.92	30.23
Forest and semi-natural areas	27.027	14.202	3.951	−39.63	−31.73	−71.36
Wetlands	0.639	0.09	0.009	−1.7	0.24	−1.94

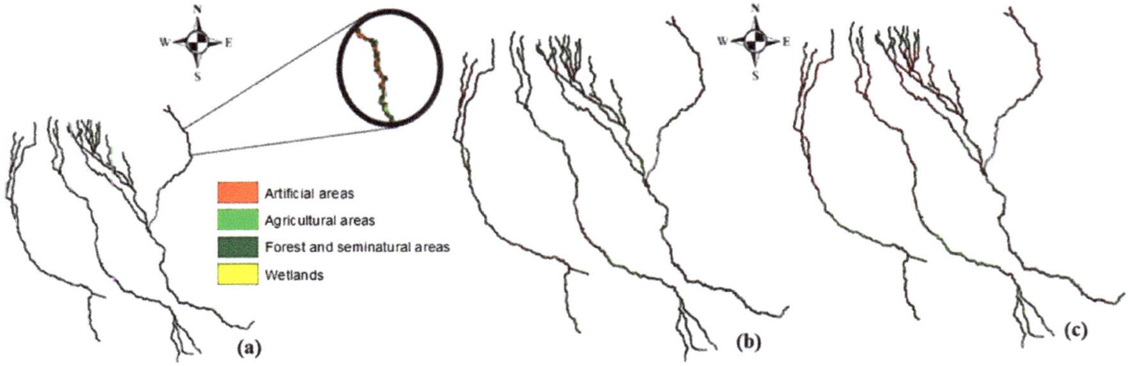

Figure 5. Buffer analysis of River Themi, Nduruma, Tengeru, and Maji ya Chai for the 2000 (**a**), 2010 (**b**), and 2020 (**c**).

On the other hand, there was an increase in agricultural areas by 7.533 km^2 from 2000 to 2010 and a slight decrease of 2.759 km^2 from 2010 to 2020. This change mirrored an equivalent increase of about 23.31% from 2000 to 2010, 6.92% from 2010 to 2020, and an overall increase of about 30.23% from 2000 to 2020.

There was a significant decrease in forest and semi-natural areas of 39.63% from 2000 to 2010 and a further shrinking in forest and semi-natural areas by 31.73%. This decrease was equivalent to a total decrease in forest and semi-natural areas by 71.36% from 2000 to 2020. Wetlands, on the other hand, showed a slight decrease of 1.7% from 2000 to 2010, a slight increase of about 0.24% from 2010 to 2020, and an overall shrinking of about 1.94% from 2000 to 2020.

The intermittent change that took place between the years 2000 and 2010 in LULC has been contemplated to be the result of a population increase, which intensified anthropic activities, thus, posing stress in areas once considered buffer zone. As the need for economic growth, food, and settlements increase, some classes tend to triumph over others in keeping up with the current demands. Land use classes that were part of the buffer zone ecosystem were converted into agriculture and artificial areas to suffice the community's needs and, thus, buffer zone encroachment.

These results are similar to those reported by [6] in the Bagmati River in the Kathmandu Valley. The general land cover in the Bagmati River showed that between 2006 and 2014, the vegetation and grassland class had a tremendous fall of 35.53% and 29.20%, respectively. Artificial areas, represented by built-up areas, increased by 14.82%, and road expansions increased by 0.37%, while open spaces and water bod stayed relatively constant. The hinted results are similar to the ones obtained in this study regardless of the difference in the description of land use classes. This phenomenon implies that the driving factors of encroachment in the buffer zones are almost the same, with the leading factor of encroachment being urbanization. The encroachment of smallholder farmers and the expansion of tea plantations were also reported in the Sigi sub-catchment [23].

3.4. Community Perception of the Factors Influencing River Buffer Zone Encroachment

The factors influencing river buffer zone encroachment include population growth, urbanization, poverty, water scarcity, and a shortage of fertile land and poverty. These are factors that other researchers in their studies have reprimanded; some of these factors exist in the respective study areas of Themi, Nduruma, Maji ya Chai, and Tengeru.

The existing encroachment factors at the site area are urbanization and poor urban planning, which contributes about 42%, water scarcity, which contributes 8.33%, and poverty, which contributes 16.67% (Figure 6). The urban growth rate before the enactment of EMA 2004 appeared to be low by 20% when compared to the current rate of 38.33%.

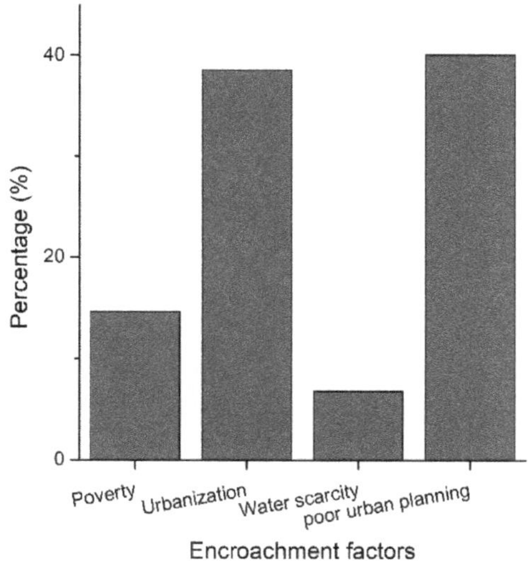

Figure 6. Factors influencing buffer zone encroachment.

The socio-economic activities in the selected case studies included agricultural activities such as maize plantations, floriculture, and olericulture. During the site survey, flower gardens were sported at Sekei near the river Themi and salad gardens on the river Nduruma's banks. About 46.67% of the respondents conducted agriculture-related activities, while 53.33% were involved in non-agricultural activities, including shopkeeping, lumbering, and garages along the buffer zone (Figure 7). Considering the nature of socio-economic activities performed in this area, it is evident that the increasing population led to economic water stress and thus forced peasants and other business owners to invade the restricted area for easy accessibility to water.

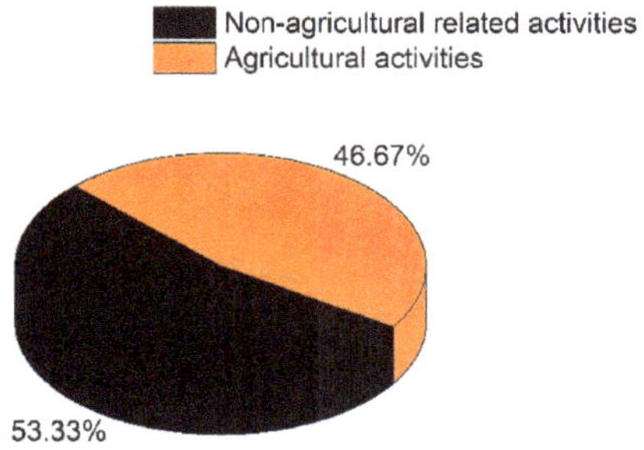

Figure 7. Socio-economic activities.

Studies indicate that urbanization is the major factor leading to the encroachment of the buffer zone in urban rivers [24]. Land use for the sake of residence and commercial purposes has become extremely lucrative such that it has infringed or constrained other important land use developments. Shrestha [6] reported that rapid urbanization has led to land scarcity with very high prices, which triggers people to encroach on the buffer zones. However, it is worth stating that the absence of the demarcation of the buffer zone of the river has not produced significant changes in the encroachment of the riparian buffer zones. These results have shown that the growth of urban areas has resulted in the shrinkage of forest and semi-natural areas and influenced the growth of built-up areas. This phenomenon can only imply that urbanization has subjected cities to land scarcity, thus invading buffer zones.

Level of Awareness and Compliance with Environmental Legislation

The results indicate that about 53.33% of the interviewed community members were aware of the regulations restricting the conduction of anthropic activities along the buffer zones. Furthermore, 46.67% of the community was unaware of the buffer zone regulations (Figure 8). Awareness is not adherence, and the level of adherence of the community to regulations governing the buffer zone was 70% adhered to, while those who did not adhere to these regulations comprised 30%.

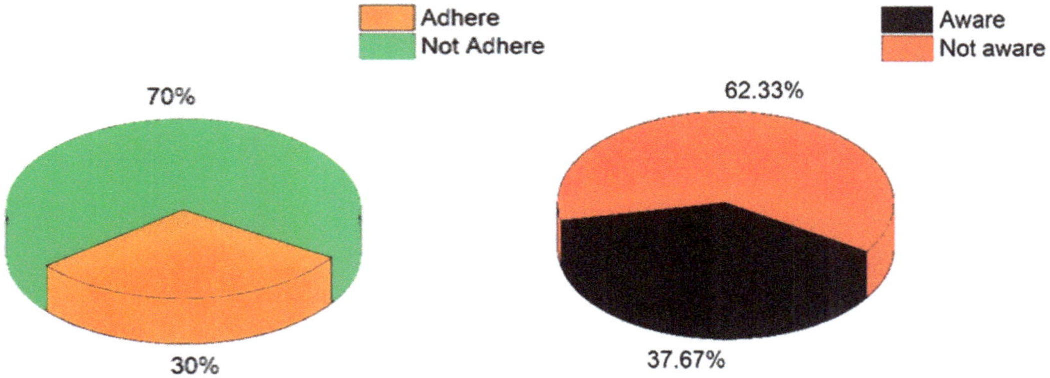

Figure 8. The level of compliance and the level of adherence to the environmental legislation.

In establishing the link between awareness and adherence, 76.9% of the community who responded to the survey and were aware of the buffer zone regulations did not adhere to the environmental legislation (Table 7). Furthermore, 76.7% of the community members were unaware of the environmental regulations and did not comply with the buffer zone regulations. This means that the level of awareness did not contribute to the adherence to environmental regulations in the study area.

Table 7. Level of awareness versus the level of adherence.

Level of Awareness	Level of Adherence (%)	
	Adhere	Do Not Adhere
Aware	23.1	76.9
Not aware	23.3	76.7

The results showed that a small proportion of community members established their residents within the river buffer zone before enacting the environmental management act, no 20 of 2004 [7]. However, a large proportion of the population established settlements along the river buffer zone, even after enacting the Environmental Management Act of 2004 (EMA, 2004). The results showed that 15%, 13.6%, and 37.5% of people aged 15–29, 30–44, and above 45 years had settled or dwelled in the area before enacting EMA, 2004. However, 75% of people aged 15–29 years, 86.4% aged 30–44 years, and 62.5% of those above 45 years started dwelling in the buffer zone after enacting EMA, 2004 (Table 8).

Table 8. Age versus settlement period.

Age (Years)	Settlement Period (%)	
	Before Enacting EMA, 2004	After Enacting EMA, 2004
15–29	15	75
30–44	13.6	86.4
Above 45	37.5	62.5

The link between education level and environmental legislation awareness showed a linear increase in awareness as the level of education increased. About 70% and 48.1% of those with no formal education and those with primary education were aware of the regulations. In contrast, the level of awareness increased to 70% for those with a university/college education (Table 9). This observation suggests that increasing awareness campaigns may reduce the rate of encroachment in riparian buffer zones.

Table 9. Level of education versus level of awareness.

Level of Education	Level of Awareness of the Environmental Legislation (%)	
	Aware	Not Aware
Not educated	30	70
Primary level	40	60
Secondary level	48.1	51.9
University level	70	30

The results indicate that most people aged 15–29 and 30–44 years were more aware of environmental legislation by 60% and 54.5%, respectively (Table 10). However, a significant proportion (40% and 45.5%) of this active group were still unaware of the environmental regulation governing the buffer zones of rivers. This trend implies the need for intensive sensitization for sustainable buffer zone management in the future. However, for the elderly under the category above 45 years, only 37.5% of people were aware, and 62.5% were unaware (Table 10). This triggers the need to extend sensitization training to the elderly group, which can be used to educate young ones in the villages.

Table 10. Age versus level of awareness.

Age (Years)	Level of Awareness (%)	
	Aware	Not Aware
15–29	60	40
30–44	54.5	45.5
Above 45	37.5	62.5

3.5. Community Perception of the Challenges Hindering the Enforcement of the Regulation Governing River Buffer Zones

Political intervention is where the politician protects the interests of those who elected them without considering the potential impacts that may be imposed on the environment. This challenge means there is a need to separate political interests from enforcing environmental legislation. Furthermore, the absence of demarcation along the buffer zones of rivers, especially urban rivers, resulted in some anthropic activities along the buffer zone. The installation of signs and symbols near river areas was not effectively implemented until recently when permanent river changes were observed to have signposts along the main roads.

An unawareness of environmental legislation is another challenge afflicting the buffer zones; most people are unaware of the environmental laws regarding the conservation of water resources and the need to leave a buffer zone, as presented in Table 10. Furthermore, land scarcity is one of the driving forces that has influenced society to encroach on buffer zones. Arusha city is under the pressure of development and is a center of tourist attractions that are prone to rapid growth and requires an increase in land. Therefore, buffer zones are the only sustainable fertile land for most low-income communities to conduct small-scale farming for income generation. Thus, river buffer zones and other open spaces succumbed to encroachment.

Climate change has greatly affected water availability for most domestic, agricultural, and industrial uses. Eventually, the community near rivers sought the most affordable and easily accessible water sources like river streams. Farmers and horticultural practitioners of the Nduruma River are famously known for the deviation of River streams for irrigation purposes into their farms, and the same case applies to the Tengeru River in Manyatta village. Furthermore, the recent rapid increase in population in the city has also led to an increased demand for development and other human needs. This increase in demand requires a large amount of land; thus, more interest is taken in open space areas like buffer zones.

Initiatives taken by the authorities include evacuation, especially in new developments apart from the existing ones. Another initiative was to charge fines for anthropic activities like sand mining or quarrying along the buffer zones. However, the plan was to install beacons for demarcating the buffer zones and inform the surrounding community that the law protected the buffer zone area. However, socio-economic activities that existed before the environmental legislation was allowed to occupy the buffer zones only if they were keen enough to protect the buffer zones against any environmental destruction. Since it has proved impossible to fully evacuate people from buffer zones since some of these areas have been leased to these people since colonial times; thus, these organizations have chosen to address this problem from different aspects.

3.6. Riparian Buffer Zone Encroachment as a Threat to Urban Rivers

Buffer zone encroachment is a challenge in many parts of the world. Abubakari and Romanus [25] reported the enormous encroachment of the Subin and the Aboabo Rivers buffer zones in Ghana. This study further showed that 33% of the structures along the riparian buffer zones of rivers were permanent, whereas 67% were temporary structures. In Nigeria, the encroachment of the buffer zone along the Ogun River by a built-up area increased from 34.1 Ha in 1964 to 123 Ha in 2008 [26]. A similar trend was reported in Sir

Lanka, where the Pinga Oya tributary in the upper Mahaweli River was reported to have encroached with 80% of the built-up area and in areas with a moderate population [27]. This report further showed high nutrient levels resulting from agricultural pollution. This trend signified that population pressure over water resources should be properly integrated into sustainable supply plans.

In India, the reports showed the encroachment of the Swarnrekha River and its tributaries in urbanized areas by about 0.73 km^2 within a 50 m buffer [28]. In Korea, the water quality in the Han River Basin was reported to decline due to increasing land development and natural activities in the watershed [29]. These reports indicate that increased anthropic activities such as urbanization and agriculture threaten water resources worldwide.

4. Conclusions

Regardless of the recently implemented efforts to limit encroachment activities, the incapacity to eliminate socio-economic activities along the riparian buffer zones threatens the sustainability of these rivers. The persisting increase in socio-economic activities like agriculture along buffer zones imperils the river ecosystems, guaranteeing little survival for aquatic biodiversity. Eutrophication is one of the existing impacts of agricultural activities, which is likely to create anoxic conditions and thus lead to the loss of aquatic biodiversity.

Increased artificial areas in buffer zones due to the collective demand for population growth and economic expansion affected river characteristics like river flow and flood attenuation. Rivers have become more susceptible to floods, stream perturbation, and sedimentation; far worse, some rivers are in the blink of disappearing due to drying. The corresponding increase in agricultural land and the built-up area in the buffer zone implies a significant decrease in forest cover and Shrub lands. Deforestation practices threatens the recharge capacity of rivers during dry seasons, considering the unreliable hydrologic patterns influenced by climate change. The removal of Shrub lands and forests threaten the disappearance of species like fig trees, alongside an increase in the sediment level and excess evapotranspiration from rivers. The surrounding community may also endure water stress scarcity in the near future.

An increase in fallow land impaired fertile soils by exposing them to active agents of soil erosion like wind and water. The loss of soil fertility succumbed the soil to stress from manure and chemical fertilizers. The soil has also accumulated a questionable number of pesticides and herbicides that are used to kill weeds and pests. Deteriorating soil quality has also affected the compactness of soil particles and, thus, increased sediments.

The authors recommend that water managers and decision-makers redefine the strategies that increase the effectiveness of governing buffer zones for sustainable management amid climate change. Further studies should focus on predicting future changes which could occur due to encroachment activities and the cost that the government will experience in remediating these changes if quick measures are not implemented. The economic feasibility of implementing EMA, 2004 should be reviewed to identify its areas of weakness and to recognize the areas that require re-enforcement.

Author Contributions: All authors contributed equally to this manuscript. All authors have read and agreed to the published version of the manuscript.

Funding: This research received no external funding.

Data Availability Statement: The National Bureau of Standards and Tanzania Meteorological Authority are the custodian of the raw data.

Conflicts of Interest: The authors declare no conflict of interest.

References

1. Lalika, M.C.S.; Meire, P.; Ngaga, Y.M.; Chang'a, L. Understanding watershed dynamics and impacts of climate change and variability in the Pangani River Basin, Tanzania. *Ecohydrol. Hydrobiol.* **2015**, *15*, 26–38. [CrossRef]
2. Thomas, K.J.; Zuberi, T. *Demographic Change, the IMPACT Model, and Food Security in Sub-Saharan Africa*; UNDP Regional Bureau for Africa Working Paper; UNDP: New York, NY, USA, 2012; pp. 1–23.
3. Parnell, S.; Walawege, R. Sub-Saharan African urbanisation and global environmental change. *Glob. Environ. Change* **2011**, *21*, S12–S20. [CrossRef]
4. Taylor, R.G.; Barrett, M.H.; Tindimugaya, C. Urban areas of Sub-Saharan Africa; weathered crystalline aquifer systems. In *Urban Groundwater Pollution*; Lerner, D., Ed.; Balkema: Boca Raton, FL, USA, 2003; pp. 155–179.
5. Mbuligwe, S.E.; Kaseva, M.E. Pollution and Self-Cleansing of an Urban River in a Developing Country: A Case Study in Dar es Salaam, Tanzania. *Environ. Manag.* **2005**, *36*, 328–342. [CrossRef]
6. Shrestha, S. Assessment of Bagmati River Encroachment through Application of GIS and Remote Sensing. Bachelor's Thesis, Pokhara University, Lekhnath, Nepal, 2015.
7. URT. *Environmental Management Act (EMA) No. 20 of 2004*; United Republic of Tanzania, Vice Presidents Office, Division of Environment: Dar es Salaam, Tanzania, 2004.
8. Tudor, F. Environmental Management Activities. *Qual. -Access Success* **2013**, *14*, 124–128.
9. Loewenson, R. Trends in Water Resources in East and Southern Africa. Training and Research Support Centre in the Regional Network for Equity in Health in East and Southern Africa (EQUINET). 2020; p. 17. Available online: https://equinetafrica.org/sites/default/files/uploads/documents/EQ%20ESA%20Trends%20in%20water%20resources%20May2020.pdf (accessed on 18 March 2023).
10. Kitalika, A.; Machunda, R.; Komakech, H.; Njau, K. Land-Use and Land Cover Changes on the Slopes of Mount Meru-Tanzania. *Curr. World Environ.* **2018**, *53*, 331–352. [CrossRef]
11. Emmanuel, H.; Peter, K.; Alex, W. Amphibian and Benthic Macro Invertebrate Response to Physical and Chemical Properties of Themi River, Arusha, Tanzania. *Res. Rev. J. Ecol. Environ. Sci.* **2015**, *3*, 38–50.
12. Mckenzie, J.M.; Mark, B.G.; Thompson, L.G.; Schotterer, U.; Lin, P.-N. A hydrogeochemical survey of Kilimanjaro (Tanzania): Implications for water sources and ages. *Hydrogeol. J.* **2010**, *18*, 985–995. [CrossRef]
13. de Bont, C.; Veldwisch, G.J.; Komakech, H.C.; Vos, J. The fluid nature of water grabbing: The on-going contestation of water distribution between peasants and agribusinesses in Nduruma, Tanzania. *Agric. Hum. Values* **2016**, *33*, 641–654. [CrossRef]
14. Ahmed, B.; Ahmed, R.; Zhu, X. Evaluation of Model Validation Techniques in Land Cover Dynamics. *ISPRS Int. J. Geo-Inf.* **2013**, *2*, 577–597. [CrossRef]
15. Jensen, J.R. *Introductory Digital Image Processing: A Remote Sensing Perspective*; Prentice-Hall Inc.: Hoboken, NJ, USA, 1996.
16. Msovu, U.E.; Mulungu, D.M.; Nobert, J.K.; Mahoo, H. Land Use/Cover Change and their Impacts on Streamflow in Kikuletwa Catchment of Pangani River Basin, Tanzania. *Tanzan. J. Eng. Technol.* **2019**, *38*, 171–192. [CrossRef]
17. Olarinoye, T.; Foppen, J.W.; Veerbeek, W.; Morienyane, T.; Komakech, H. Exploring the future impacts of urbanization and climate change on groundwater in Arusha, Tanzania. *Water Int.* **2020**, *45*, 497–511. [CrossRef]
18. Hemp, A. Continuum or zonation? Altitudinal gradients in the forest vegetation of Mt. Kilimanjaro. *Plant Ecol.* **2006**, *184*, 27–42.
19. Said, M.; Hyandye, C.; Mjemah, I.C.; Komakech, H.C.; Munishi, L.K. Evaluation and Prediction of the Impacts of Land Cover Changes on Hydrological Processes in Data Constrained Southern Slopes of Kilimanjaro, Tanzania. *Earth* **2021**, *2*, 225–247. [CrossRef]
20. Mmbaga, N.E.; Munishi, L.K.; Treydte, A.C. How dynamics and drivers of land use/land cover change impact elephant conservation and agricultural livelihood development in Rombo, Tanzania. *J. Land Use Sci.* **2017**, *12*, 168–181. [CrossRef]
21. Hyandye, C.; Martz, L.W. A Markovian and cellular automata land-use change predictive model of the Usangu Catchment. *Int. J. Remote Sens.* **2017**, *38*, 64–81. [CrossRef]
22. Ngondo, J.; Mango, J.; Liu, R.; Nobert, J.; Dubi, A.; Cheng, H. Land-Use and Land-Cover (LULC) Change Detection and the Implications for Coastal Water Resource Management in the Wami–Ruvu Basin, Tanzania. *Sustainability* **2021**, *13*, 4092. [CrossRef]
23. Yanda, P.; Munishi, P. *Hydrologic and Land Use/Cover Change Analysis for the Ruvu River (Uluguru) and Sigi River (East Usambara) Watersheds*; WWF/CARE International: Dar es Salaam, Tanzania, 2007.
24. Aabeyir, R.; Aduah, M.S. Assessment of encroachment of urban streams in Ghana: The case study of Wa Municipality. *J. Nat. Resour. Dev.* **2014**, *4*, 10–17. [CrossRef]
25. Abubakari, A.; Romanus, D.D. Impact of land use activities on Subin and Aboabo Rivers in Kumasi Metropolis. *Int. J. Water Resour. Environ. Eng.* **2012**, *4*, 241–251.
26. Adeofun, C.; Oyedepo, J.; Lasisi, T. An assessment of Urban encroachment on Ogun river bank protection zone in Abeokuta City, Nigeria. *J. Agric. Sci. Environ.* **2011**, *11*, 78–89.
27. Dissanayake, L. Stream corridor encroachment and its consequences: The case of Pinga Oya tributary in the upper Mahaweli River in Sri Lanka. *Model. Earth Syst. Environ.* **2021**, *7*, 1907–1916. [CrossRef]

28. Pandey, A.C.; Kumar, A. Spatio-temporal variability of surface water quality of fresh water resources in Ranchi Urban Agglomeration, India using geospatial techniques. *Appl. Water Sci.* **2015**, *5*, 13–26. [CrossRef]
29. Chang, H. Spatial analysis of water quality trends in the Han River basin, South Korea. *Water Res.* **2008**, *42*, 3285–3304. [CrossRef] [PubMed]

urban science

MDPI

Article

Pedestrian Flows Characterization and Estimation with Computer Vision Techniques

Federico Karagulian [1,*], Carlo Liberto [1], Matteo Corazza [1,*], Gaetano Valenti [1], Andreea Dumitru [2] and Marialisa Nigro [2]

[1] ENEA Research Centre Casaccia, Via Anguillarese 301, 00123 Rome, Italy
[2] Department of Civil, Computer and Aeronautical Engineering, Roma Tre University, Via Vito Volterra 62, 00146 Rome, Italy
* Correspondence: federico.karagulian@enea.it (F.K.); matteo.corazza@enea.it (M.C.)

Abstract: This work describes a straightforward implementation of detecting and tracking pedestrian walking across a public square using computer vision. The methodology consists of the use of the well-known YOLOv3 algorithm over videos recorded during different days of the week. The chosen location was the Piazza Duca d'Aosta in the city of Milan, Italy, in front of the main Centrale railway station, an access point for the subway. Several analyses have been carried out to investigate macroscopic parameters of pedestrian dynamics such as densities, speeds, and main directions followed by pedestrians, as well as testing strengths and weaknesses of computer-vision algorithms for pedestrian detection. The developed system was able to represent spatial densities and speeds of pedestrians along temporal profiles. Considering the whole observation period, the mean value of the Voronoi density was about 0.035 person/m^2 with a standard deviation of about 0.014 person/m^2. On the other hand, two main speed clusters were identified during morning/evening hours. The largest number of pedestrians with an average speed of about 0.77 m/s was observed along the exit direction of the subway entrances during both morning and evening hours. The second relevant group of pedestrians was observed walking in the opposite direction with an average speed of about 0.65 m/s. The analyses generated initial insights into the future development of a decision-support system to help with the management and control of pedestrian dynamics.

Keywords: pedestrian flow; pedestrian detection; pedestrian tracking; computer vision; convolutional neural networks

1. Introduction

Object detection represents one of the most important challenges in computer vision [1]. Targeting objects inside an image and classifying them based on a list of available classes is at the bottom of several applications, such as instance segmentation [2], image captioning [3], and object tracking [4]. The latter has recently received a great interest in the context of crowd dynamics [5–7], and it is the focus of the present work, in which the recognition of pedestrians is performed by means of video recording.

The fast development of deep-learning techniques observed in recent years has brought new insights into object detection, pushing it forward to a research hotspot [8]. Therefore, object detection is widely used in many applications, such as autonomous driving, robot vision, and video surveillance.

The increasing use of pedestrian facilities such as building complexes, shopping malls, airports, and train stations in densely populated cities demands pedestrian-flow data for planning, design, operation, and monitoring. When planning pedestrian facilities, quantities such as density and speed are commonly used to assess their safety and level of service [9]. Computer vision is a good methodology to automate density heat maps over an observation area. This facilitates the prompt localization of intervention areas at a resolution of meters, enabling the identification of the most frequent crowded hotspots. Finally, walking direction represents an important parameter to identify origin and destination areas, making it a valuable piece of information for mobility-management plans in crowded areas.

The present work was performed to implement a new sensing technology for crowded tracking over Centrale Station in the city of Milan, Italy. It is based on the previous work by Dumitru et al., 2023 [10], where similar techniques were applied over the same square. Here, we used a larger and homogeneous dataset to perform a deeper and more complete statistical analysis, allowing the daily and hourly profiles related to pedestrian presence in the study area to be reconstructed and the distributions of average speed and density to be estimated.

In addition, we also report a more detailed description of the methodology and of the weaknesses of the approach, at the same time removing uncertainties related to the analysis of different parameters on non-homogeneous datasets. In both works, the proposed technology is based on wireless cameras recording video streams to perform object detection through a computer-vision algorithm. The output of these elaborations was used to reconstruct the spatial distribution of pedestrian flows together with heat-density and speed maps.

The main contribution of this work is to assess the effectiveness and limitations of applying a tracking algorithm in a real-world pedestrian context for characterizing its dynamics by means of key quantities such as density, average speed, and direction [11–14].

In Section 2, the general used methodology is described for both the detection process and the tracking model, Section 3 presents the experimental setup, and Section 4 describes the metrics used to analyze the observed data, as well as results related to single steps of the recognition and tracking processes. In Section 5, general results are described, and conclusions close the paper in Section 6.

2. The Computer-Vision Model

2.1. The Detection Process

A common way to perform object detection is through a unique neural-network model (one-stage detector) implemented for image recognition. For the present work, detection and tracking of pedestrians through videos recorded from a fixed camera were implemented with the model YOLO (You Only Look Once), together with the neural network Darknet-53 [15,16]. The choice of YOLO was motivated by its execution speed, which makes it very convenient for processing videos of long duration.

With the introduction of convolutional neural networks (CNNs) in the field of image recognition, the YOLO network [15] was the first one-stage detector model for object detection within the deep-learning techniques. There are different versions of YOLO with very similar architectures and with the latest versions offering a reduced computing memory and higher average precision. For the present work, YOLOv3 was chosen because of its good speed performance in detecting objects compared to more recent versions of YOLO [17].

Although later versions of YOLO are characterized by improved performance in target detection together with higher computational speed and precision compared to YOLOv3, they also increase the algorithm complexity and memory consumption. Therefore, the choice of YOLOv3 was based on its maturity as an algorithm framework with a clear neural-network structure and real-time accuracy during online processing.

The YOLOv3 model applies a single neural network to the whole image, which is divided into a fixed number of smaller regions wherein identified objects are highlighted with a bounding box. The backbone of the YOLO architecture is represented by Darknet-53, consisting of a convolutional neural network (CNN) with a depth of 53 convolutional layers that act as a base for the object-detection network (Figure 1). The 53 layers are pre-trained during image classification using the COCO (common objects in context) dataset [18]. Down-sampling is applied to reduce the spatial dimension of the image to identify its structural features. Down-sampling of the image starts with 32 averaging filters (or kernels representing the weights of the neural-network layer) of 3 × 3 size that are doubled (32, 64, 128, 256, 512, 1024) at every convolutional layer and at each residual block. The residual block consists of skipping the training of one or two layers by means of skip connections or residual connections using an identity function in place of a non-linear activation function [19–21], such as the rectified-linear-unit (ReLU) function [22]. In other words, residual connections are used to allow the applied filters to directly access the next layer without passing through a non-linear activation function to avoid exploding gradients or vanishing gradients towards 0. As shown in Figure 1, each residual group has a bottleneck 1 × 1 filter, followed by a 3 × 3 filter, which is in turn followed by a residual skip connection. For the purpose of this work, we applied the weights used in the convolutional filters obtained in a recent paper that supplied trained configurations and weights, as well as the class names of the COCO dataset [18], on which the Darknet model was trained [23,24]. The convolutional filters slide all over the input layer to generate activation maps that are successively stacked together to form a convolutional layer. The ReLU is applied after each convolution to generate activation layers that are used to feed the next "stack" of layers. Basically, the ReLU function sets the threshold of all activation layers at 0.

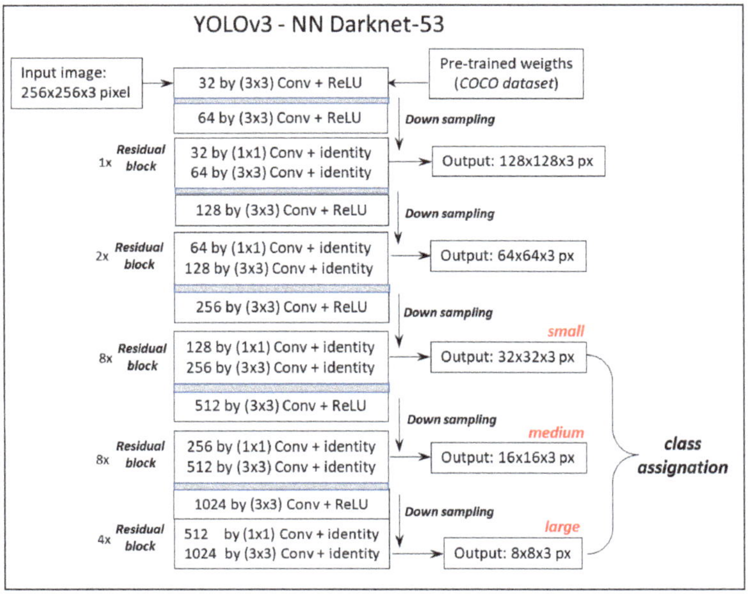

Figure 1. Schematic representation of the YOLOv3 model implemented with the neural network Darknet-53.

After every convolutional layer, a residual group consists of a series of repeated residual blocks as 1×, 2×, 8×, 8× and 4×. These refer to the number of times each layer of the sequence is repeated, and therefore they can be considered an indicator of the depth of the neural network. In the last three residual groups, the original input image becomes down-sampled at three different resolutions of 32 × 32, 16 × 16, and 8 × 8 pixels (small, medium, and large, respectively) to prevent the loss of low-level features and improve the ability to detect smaller objects (Figure 1). The use of residual blocks is aimed at avoiding saturation when increasing the number of convolutional layers [25]. The last step of the detection process consists of combining low-level features (8 × 8 pixels), detected in the last layers of the network, with high-level features (32 × 32 pixels), detected in the previous layers of the network [26], using a methodology similar to the feature-pyramid network (FPN), where large-scale features and medium-scale features are up-sampled to detect medium-scale objects and small-scale objects, respectively.

Compared to other R-CNNs (recurrent convolutional neural networks), YOLOv3 is definitely faster [16,27]. This is possible because YOLOv3 does not split the object-recognition process into multiple phases but rather produces a bounding box, inside which the probability and class of each object detected in the image are estimated. Despite the high speed in object detection, YOLO suffers from a reduced accuracy in localizing small-dimensional objects.

Three anchor boxes (or bounding boxes) are predicted for each layer, obtained from down-sampled features at three different resolutions of 32×32, 16×16, and 8×8 pixels, respectively. An anchor box is a bounding box of multiple aspect ratios pre-defined using the training dataset (COCO) by running a K-means partitioning algorithm among the possible available choices of identified objects. For each anchor box a prediction is made for (a) the centroid coordinates (*x*,*y*), as well as the width and height (*w* and *h*, respectively); (b) the objectness score $P(Object)$ to indicate whether the considered box contains an object (0 if it contains objects, 1 if it does not); and (c), the class probabilities, indicating which class the box belongs to (i.e., faces, cats, dogs, cups, etc.). Since the YOLOv3 model is trained with the COCO dataset, we can have up to 80 possible different classes to which objects can be assigned. However, the number of anchor boxes is reduced with the non-maximum-suppression algorithm (NMS, see below) to highlight the box that best overlays the detected object. The model also evaluates the accuracy of the dimension and localization of the bounding box with respect to the object itself. This is evaluated through the intersection over union (*IoU*) [28], defined as:

$$IoU_{pred}^{truth} = \frac{area(box(truth) \cap box(pred))}{area(box(truth) \cup box(pred))} \tag{1}$$

where IoU_{pred}^{truth} is the ratio between the extensions of the intersection and the union of the ground truth and the predicted box.

The computer-vision model identifies objects that are highlighted with bounding boxes. These boxes are represented by the coordinates of the object in the image over which the rectangular region is built through the hand choice of the aspect ratio as well as the hand choice of the possible labels of the bounding boxes. This process is carried out by manually tagging about 100 images to be used as the ground truth. A comparison is then carried out between the ground truth and the real person(s) belonging to the tagged test images. A detected person is linked to a particular ground-truth object if there is a minimum ratio of 50% between the overlap and the union of the detected bounding box with the ground-truth bounding box (see Equation (1)). Therefore, the ground truth refers to the bounding box defined around the real object (person). More precisely, ground-truth bounding boxes are a priori defined by specifying center coordinates and dimensions of the rectangular region enclosing the targeted objects. The image dataset is divided into a training set to train the object detector and a testing set to validate it. Both the training and testing sets consist of the actual images and the bounding boxes associated with the objects in the image.

IoU values close to 1 indicate a good correspondence between ground truth and prediction. This can also be considered an index to determine how much the ground-truth box overlaps with the anchor box. The probability that an object is enclosed within the bounding box is called the confidence score and is defined as:

$$Conf(Object) = P(Object) \times IoU_{pred}^{truth}, \tag{2}$$

where *P*(*Object*) is the a priori probability of finding the object in the box. As said above, for each grid scale the model predicts three anchor-bounding boxes, and therefore multiple anchor boxes could predict the same object. To overcome this issue, the non-maximum-suppression (NMS) algorithm is applied to remove possible duplicate results. Basically, this method determines the detection box characterized by the highest object-confidence score, higher than a given threshold, and adds it to the result while removing all other boxes with a lower *IoU*. Therefore, the final detection step assigns only one bounding box to each identified person, as shown in Figure 2. In the present work, a confidence-threshold value of 0.7 and an NMS threshold of 0.5 were chosen. The detection range is the result of fine tuning the computer-vision model to detect and track the largest number of targeted pedestrians over consecutive images. We have observed that an increase in detection range is not always followed by correct tracking of the targeted person. Therefore, a compromise was found between detection and tracking accuracy to build the time path of pedestrians. The obtained predicted bounding boxes correspond to the probability $Conf(person)$ that, for the detection of the pedestrian, the obtained object corresponds to the class of "*person*". Therefore, the individual bounding-box confidence prediction is defined as:

$$Conf(person) = P(person) \times IoU_{pred}^{truth} \quad (3)$$

where $P(Person)$ indicates the probability of finding a person within the bounding box.

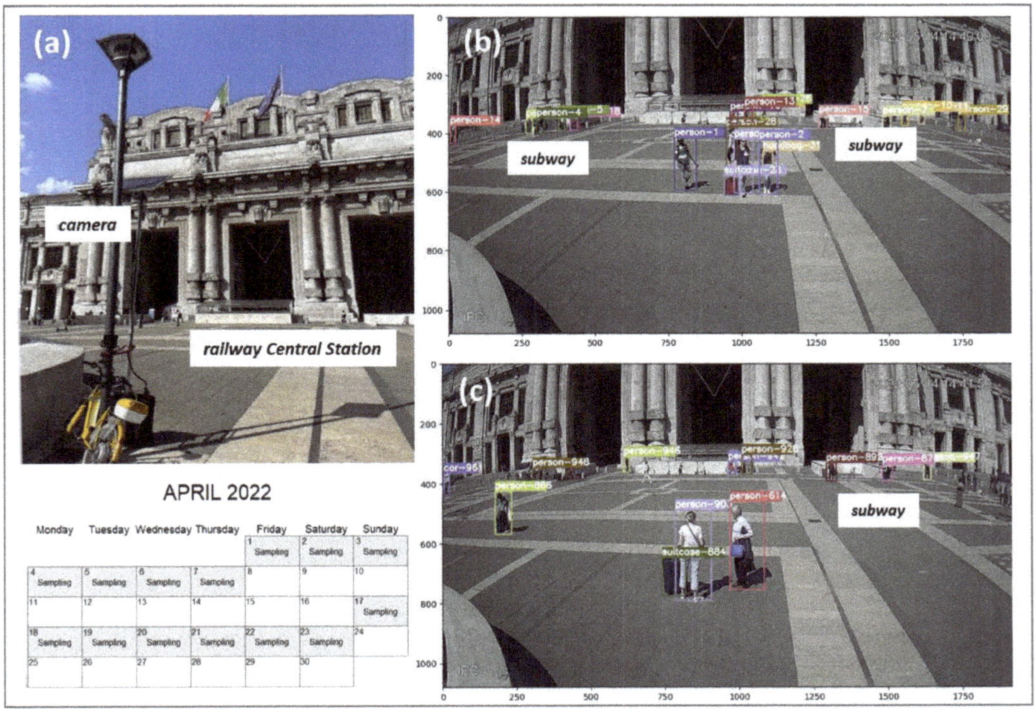

Figure 2. (**a**) Camera system for video collection located in the middle of the square Piazza Duca d'Aosta at Centrale Station in Milan, Italy. (**b**,**c**) Sample frames extracted from a video sequence. Bounding boxes indicate successfully detected people in the image within a time interval of 10 ms. Each bounding box is associated with a unique identifier.

2.2. Tracking Model

Object detection across frames in a video sequence raises the issue of performing multiple-object tracking (MOT). Tracking algorithms assign unique tracking IDs to every object found in each frame and try to maintain the same ID in subsequent frames using some sort of correspondence.

To track IDs assigned to pedestrians, we applied the SORT model as a tracking framework focusing on frame-to-frame prediction and association [29]. In this model, the inter-frame displacement of each object is approximated with a linear velocity independent of any other object in the video [30]. Tracking of a pedestrian is initialized when the correspondence between the real position of the pedestrian (ground truth) and its prediction is larger than a threshold value IoU_{min}. In that case, a tracker is initialized as a bounding box with an initial velocity set to zero. At each time step, a prediction is made for each target's bounding box considering previous steps. Trackers are usually terminated if the associated target is not detected in the subsequent frame. Figure 2b,c show an example of a detected person whose assigned ID was tracked along their trajectory while walking across Piazza Duca d'Aosta in front of Centrale Station in Milan. Figure 3 shows a typical case in which a detected ID is tracked in several consecutive frames until it disappears. For each ID, a time series is built, including the centroid of the detected person and the timestamp (Figure 4).

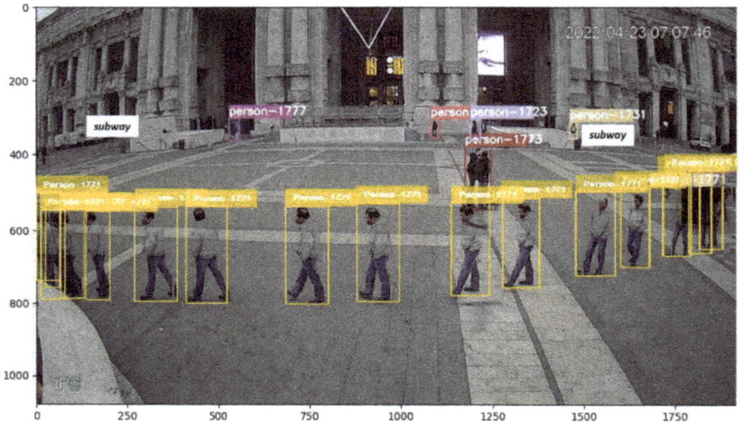

Figure 3. Example of a sequence of bounding boxes tracking a detected person with their ID maintained along the trajectory. For illustration purposes and clarity of the tracked path, only 2 frames per second are shown. Two entrance points of the subway are indicated. Axis labels refer to the pixel scale of the image.

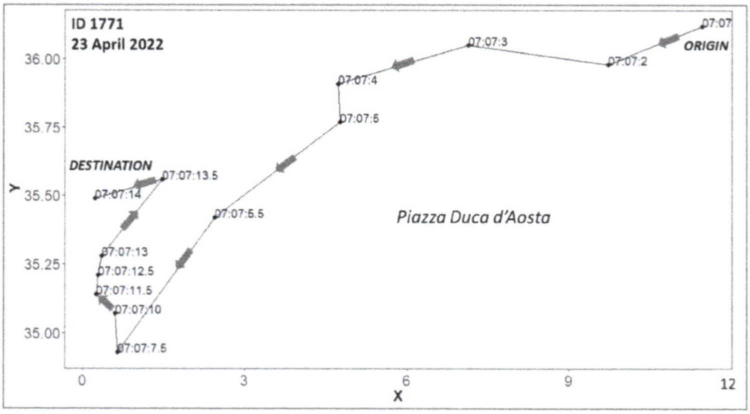

Figure 4. Example of a tracked ID along its trajectory. For illustration purposes and clarity of the tracked path, only 2 frames per second are shown. Axis labels refer to the metric system, epsg = 32,624.

To characterize the movement of a pedestrian walking across the square, it was necessary to switch from a 3D- to a 2D-view representation (from pixels to meters) and re-project the centroid coordinates to the metric system. This allowed us to observe the path followed by the tracked person at several timestamps. Figure 4 shows the trajectory followed by a tracked ID at a time resolution of 1 second. The sequence of the timestamps defines the position at the beginning of detection (origin) and the position at the end of detection (destination). The direction of each track was defined as the angle between its origin and destination.

3. Experimental Setup

As already stated, the study area chosen for our analysis was Piazza Duca d'Aosta in Milan, Italy, located in front of Milan Centrale Station. The area represents one of the strategic multimodal hubs of the city. With about 600 trains a day, Centrale Station is currently the second largest station in Italy in terms of size and traffic volume. Visited by more than 350,000 people per day, besides offering high-speed railway and lines to other European countries, the station is an interchange spot for buses, trams, trolleybuses, and two subway lines, as well as airport shuttles. The surrounding area hosts taxi and other mobility services such as bikes, scooters, and car sharing. The station has three large central entrance doors facing the main square, Piazza Duca d'Aosta, where two access points to the subway are located.

The dataset used to characterize pedestrian mobility over Piazza Duca d'Aosta consisted of a collection of videos recording the square with a strong perspective view, showing the flow of people around the main entrance of the station and the two access points of the subway (Figure 2a). For this purpose, a video-recording system was setup along one side of Piazza Duca d'Aosta facing the main entrance of Milan Centrale Station. The main purposes of this system were (a) to collect the video streaming coming from a camera adopting standard internet protocol, (b) to process a video stream by analyzing each frame, (c) to detect the presence of people within the frame, (d) to assign a unique identifier (ID) to each person, and (e) to track each person inside every video frame.

The camera was set up by the Azienda Mobilità Ambiente e Territorio (AMAT), with the purpose of acquiring the video stream from Piazza Duca d'Aosta and counting and analyzing the movements of pedestrians. Most of the video streaming was processed offline. The system was programmable remotely and could be controlled through a dedicated app [31]. The video stream was set to capture video in MP4 format in HD through an IP camera connected to a 4G router with a SIM card and a remotely reachable DDNS profile. The video stream had a frequency rate of 20 fps and was analyzed for a period of 14 days during the month of April 2022. The system power was supplied by an 80 W solar panel with a direct current of 12 V that was also charging a 12V, 75 Ah gel battery. The camera was mounted on the end of a telescopic pole that extended up to 4 m. The location of the camera was chosen to cover a wide view of Piazza Duca d'Aosta to detect and track pedestrians entering the station or accessing public transportation. Videos were recorded during 14 days, from 1 to 7 April and from 17 to 23 April 2022 between 07:00 and 20:00. We chose not to analyze any image during days with adverse weather conditions, since the number of people in the observation area was very low. Consequently, it was not possible to provide an estimation of the detection and tracking accuracy in those conditions. With respect to the previous work characterized by a similar methodology [10], this work is based on different dates, and the data collected for the analysis described in the following sections are more homogeneous, since the entire analysis was performed on the same dataset.

4. Metrics

To estimate the mean pedestrian speed, direction, and density over the study area, the capability to detect pedestrians in static images was assessed through the mean-average-precision (*mAP*) evaluation metric. As said above, a threshold value for the *IoU* of 0.5 was initially set to establish whether a pedestrian was detected or not, classifying the object as true positive (*TP*) or false positive (*FP*) in the case of *IoU* > 0.5 or < 0.5, respectively. If the ground truth was present in the image but the model failed to detect the object, it was classified as false negative (*FN*).

The average precision is usually defined as $AP = TP/(TP + FP)$. In general, the mean average precision at *IoU* = 0.5 (mAP_{50}) is calculated as the mean average precision of all the different classes of objects detected within a single image, based on the following expression:

$$mAP_{50} = \frac{1}{N}\sum_{i=1}^{N} AP_i \tag{4}$$

where N is the number of classes, which is equal to 80 in YOLOv3, and AP_i is the average precision for a single class of detected objects. The results, presented in Figure 5, showed a confidence score of about 67.6%. The *IoU* distribution showed a mean value of about 81%, whereas the mAP50 showed a mean value of about 61%.

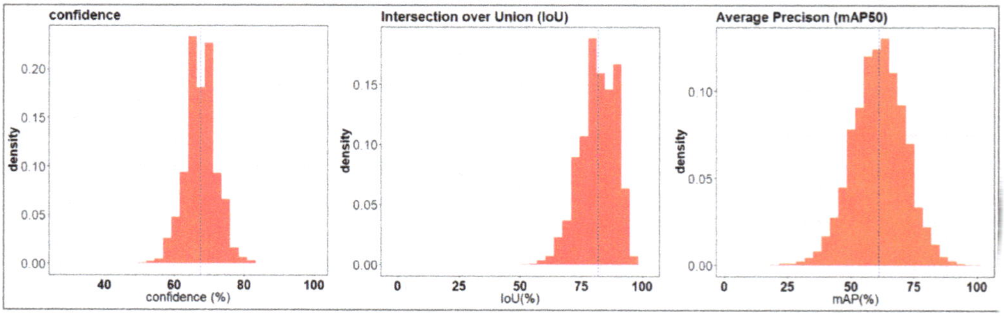

Figure 5. Distribution values obtained for 3 metrics used to evaluate the YOLOv3 model performance over the observations: confidence of the detection for the class "pedestrian" ($Conf(person)$), intersection over union (*IoU*), and mean average precision at *IoU* = 0.5 (mAP_{50}) for the class "pedestrian." Results refer to an observation period of 14 days during the month of April 2022. Blue dotted lines represent the mean value of the distributions.

Evaluation of multiple-object tracking was carried out with the standards Multiple Object Accuracy Tracking (*MOTA*) and Multiple Object Tracking Precision (*MOTP*) [32]. *MOTA* [33] is one of the most widely used metrics in object tracking. This metric matches the ground truth (*GT*) to predicted objects per detection. It considers the number of identity switches, false-positive (*FP*) detections, and false-negative (*FN*) detections across all video frames and is defined as:

$$MOTA = 1 - \frac{\sum_i FN_i + FP_i + MID_i}{\sum_i GT_i} \tag{5}$$

where *MID* is the mismatch error occurring when the object in the ground truth is erroneously associated with another object due to wrong tracking. Basically, *MOTA* measures the overall accuracy of both the tracker and the detection and can be considered a measure of the tracker's performance at detecting objects and maintaining their trajectories. In general, assuming that *MOTA* values are usually normally distributed, with a mean value larger than 80%, many of the objects are considered tracked. On the contrary, with a mean value between 20 and 80%, objects are considered partially tracked.

However, *MOTA* does not consider localization, which must be measured by a separate metric, such as Multiple Object Tracking Precision (*MOTP*) [33,34], which averages localization scores across all detections within a video and therefore estimates the accuracy of the detection model in localizing the object with respect to the ground truth:

$$MOTP = \frac{1 - IoU_{pred}^{truth}}{TM} \tag{6}$$

where *TM* is the total matches made between ground truth and the detection output. Basically, *MOTP* shows the ability of the tracker to accurately estimate object positions and, at the same time, to be consistent with trajectories. Well-performed tracking systems have a *MOTP* close to zero.

Figure 6 shows the distribution of *MOTA* and *MOTP* values obtained for all the pedestrians tracked during the detection process. A mean *MOTA* value of about 56% was observed. This indicates that most of the persons present in the videos were partially tracked [32]. On the other hand, the distribution of *MOTP* values showed a mean value of about 0.6, which, being close to zero, is an indication that the localization capability of the system was good.

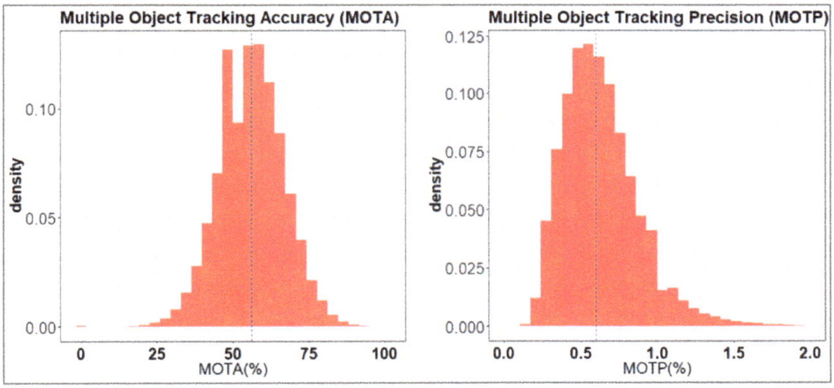

Figure 6. Distribution values obtained for two metrics used to evaluate tracking precision in the YOLOv3 model: Multiple Object Tracking Accuracy (*MOTA*) and Multiple Object Tracking Precision (*MOTP*). Results refer to an observation period of 14 days during the month of April 2022. Blue dotted lines represent the mean value of the distributions.

5. Image Processing

5.1. Speed and Direction

Statistical evaluations were performed after video processing with the computer-vision model, hereafter indicated as CV, to detect and track pedestrians in each frame of the recorded videos. As result, an extensive dataset of about 1.7 million images was gathered during 14 daily timeslots (07:00–22:00) from 1 to 7 April and from 17 to 23 April 2022. Raw data obtained from the CV model consisted of a time series of unique identification numbers (ID) assigned to people targeted in each frame. Raw data referred to a 3D view of the recorded image. Conversion of the coordinates into a 2D view with the ID position expressed in meters was performed using conversion factors dependent on the view angle of the camera, the viewpoint depth of the image, and the top-view dimensions of the observed square, Piazza Duca d'Aosta. The resulting 2D dimension of the observation area had a depth of 45 m and a width of 50 m.

The statistical analysis was structured in two steps: The first one consisted of the visualization of time profiles of the mean number of pedestrians in Piazza Duca d'Aosta during days and hours. The second one consisted of the analysis of the spatial distribution of pedestrian speed, direction, and density over the square by considering two well-defined timeslots: from 07:00 to 10:00 representative of the morning time window, and from 17:00

to 20:00 representative of the evening time window. Indeed, these are the most recurrent time slots of the week when people access the train station and the subway.

The cumulative number of pedestrians was estimated by adding the number of people detected and tracked at each hour of the day (Figure 7). A distinction was made for working days (Monday to Friday) and for the weekend (Saturday and Sunday) during evening and morning hours. The largest number of people was observed during morning hours and during weekdays (Figure 7a). The two-week sampling period highlighted Tuesday as the day with the largest number of people, whereas Sunday showed the lowest number. Analyzing the hourly profiles, a peak in the number of people was observed around 10:00–11:00 both on weekends and on working days (Figure 8b). Another peak was observed around 16:00 but only during working days. On the other hand, a larger number of people was observed around 21:00 during the weekend compared to working days.

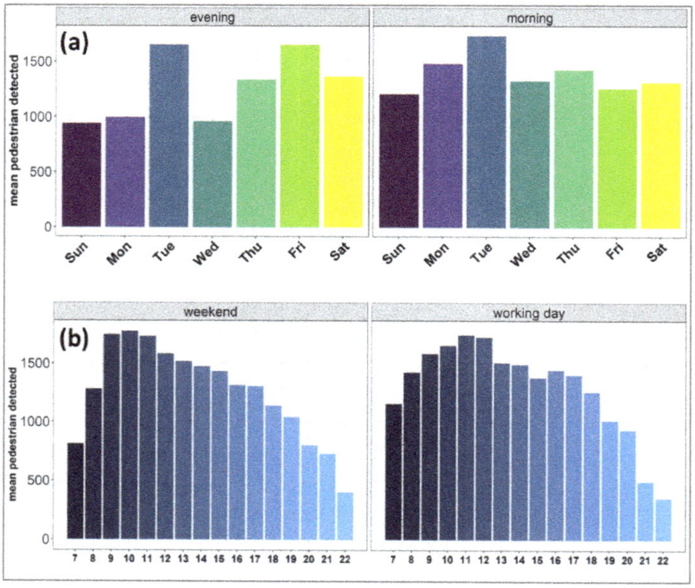

Figure 7. (**a**) Daily and (**b**) hourly profile of the mean (absolute) number of pedestrians in the observed target area.

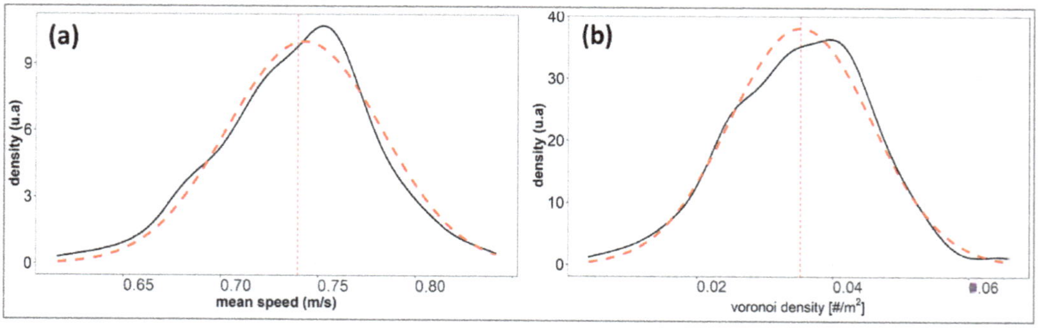

Figure 8. (**a**) Distribution of mean speed and (**b**) Voronoi density during the two-week observation period in April 2022. The ordinate axis label refers to the density distribution, expressed as arbitrary units. Colored dotted lines represent the modeled data distribution.

Pedestrian speed and direction were evaluated from the recurrence of the ID numbers assigned to each person together with the temporal sequence of their position. More precisely, for each ID, speed was estimated considering the distance between two consecutive positions of the pedestrian and the time intercurrent between them. Therefore, the resulting average speed of pedestrian i is defined as:

$$V^i = \frac{1}{N}\sum_t^N v_t^i = \frac{1}{N}\sum_t^N \frac{x_t^i}{\tau_t^i} = \frac{1}{N\tau}\sum_t^N x_t^i \quad (7)$$

where v_t^i is the instantaneous speed of pedestrian i at the timestamp t, N is the total of discrete uniform time interval τ, and, x_t^i is the space covered by pedestrian i at timestamp t.

In addition, it was possible to define the temporal distribution of mean speeds related to the overall study area by averaging for the entire pedestrian population the individual speeds at timestamp t:

$$V(t) = \frac{1}{P}\sum_i^P v_t^i = \frac{1}{P}\sum_i^P \frac{x_t^i}{\tau_t^i} = \frac{1}{P\tau}\sum_i^P x_t^i \quad (8)$$

where P is the total number of pedestrians at timestamp t.

Speeds were filtered to account only for moving individuals ($v > 0.3$ m/s) and to exclude bicycles and e-scooters ($v < 2.5$ m/s). Outputs were initially averaged every 15 minutes and then averaged by hour and by day. Daily and hourly profiles of the average speed did not show any significative trend, with the average value ranging from 0.71 to 0.79 m/s and a standard deviation of 0.2 m/s. Overall, speed distribution over the observation period showed a Gaussian shape centered at 0.74 m/s (Figure 8a).

Heat maps were generated to spatially represent pedestrian mean speed and density number. A square grid with a 2 × 2 m^2 cell area was overlaid on the observation area to achieve regular tessellation to visualize speed and density values in different parts of the square. This is a different approach with respect to a similar study [10], in which the Voronoi density was computed on the original Voronoi cells, with no reference to the regular grid used in the study.

Instantaneous speeds along each pedestrian trajectory were assigned to every crossed cell. For each cell, daily averages were computed from 30 minute speed averages. In addition, the direction of each trajectory was estimated from the angle, expressed as 0–360°, between the origin and the destination point of each pedestrian. Figure 9 shows that angles were mainly oriented towards two directions: one from the station or subway entrances toward the square (250° < *angle* < 280°) and one from the square towards the station or subway entrances (80° < *angle* < 120°) (Figure 9). Therefore, heat maps representing average speed and direction were filtered along these two main directions. The distribution of the angles shown in Figure 9 clearly indicates that the direction followed by the majority of pedestrians was the one from the station or subway entrances toward the square, with higher numerosity observed during the morning hours. However, to better understand and visualize the prevalent direction followed by pedestrians during the morning and evening hours, data clustering was carried out using the well-known K-mean methodology [35] to cluster the whole datasets of speeds and directions estimated during the observation period. The results (Figure 10 and Table 1) show that speed and direction could be grouped into two main categories. The largest numerosity of pedestrians fell within the same clusters during both morning and evening hours. During morning hours, the largest number of pedestrians was directed from the subway towards the square, with an average speed of about 0.77 m/s (Figure 10a), whereas a smaller number of pedestrians was directed towards the entrances to the subway and to the station at a speed of about 0.65 m/s (Figure 10a). On the other hand, during evening hours, the number of pedestrians moving towards the entrances of the subway and the station showed higher numerosity compared to the morning hours, with an average speed of 0.64 m/s (Figure 10b). However, during evening hours most pedestrians were also directed from the entrances to the subway towards the square at a speed of about 0.78 m/s (Figure 10b). It is important to point out that these results may also have been affected by the capability of the YOLOv3 model to better detect and track people along the direction of cluster 1 (see Table 1), therefore potentially resulting in the underestimation of the numerosity along the other directions.

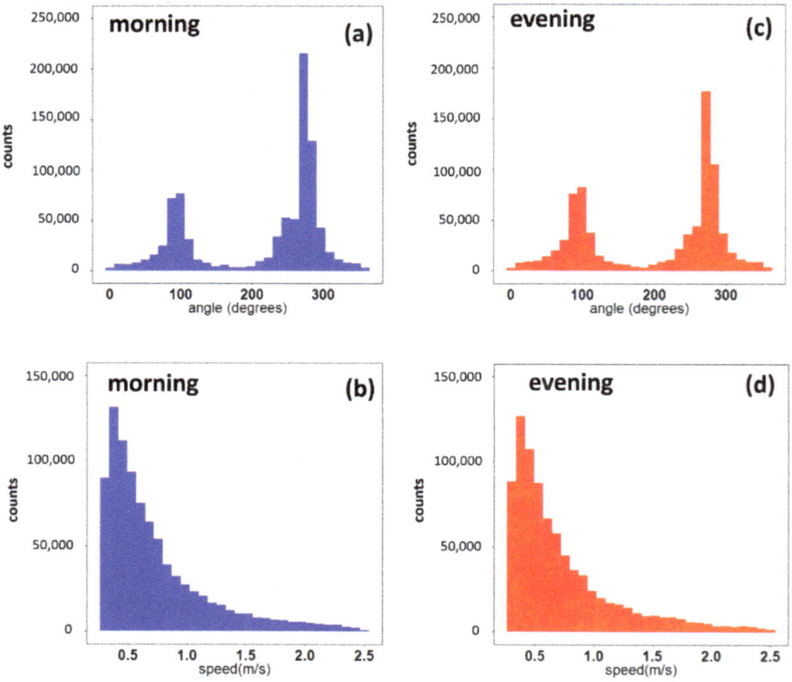

Figure 9. (**a**) Distribution of the angles followed by pedestrians during morning (from 07:00 to 10:00) and (**c**) evening hours (from 17:00 to 20:00) for the entire observation period. The 90° angle corresponds to 12:00. (**b**,**d**) Distribution of speeds during the same time windows.

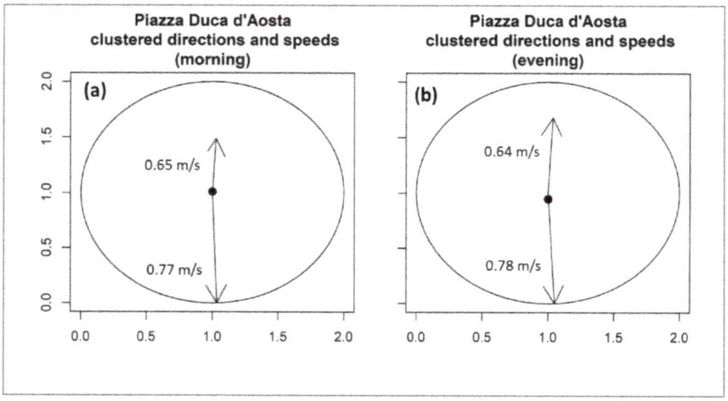

Figure 10. Clustered speed and directions in (**a**) the morning (from 07:00 to 10:00) and (**b**) the evening (from 17:00 to 20:00). The length of the arrows indicates the number of pedestrians for which speed and direction were weighted.

Table 1. Results obtained from clustering of directions during morning (from 07:00 to 10:00) and evening hours (from 17:00 to 20:00) for the entire observation period. The 90° angle corresponds to 12:00. The numerosity indicates the number of pedestrians classified within each cluster. The average speed for each cluster is also reported in table.

Morning				Evening			
Cluster	Angle (Degrees)	Numerosity	Speed (m/s)	Cluster	Angle (Degrees)	Numerosity	Speed (m/s)
0	272 ± 26	606,213	0.77 ± 0.4	0	273.0 ± 27	503,053	0.78 ± 0.5
1	86.6 ± 33	295,622	0.65 ± 0.4	1	86.8 ± 34	342,903	0.64 ± 0.4

Figures 11a and 12b clearly show that during morning and evening hours, pedestrians mainly used one of the subway entrances in the square when walking towards the station. On the other hand, during evening hours, Figures 11b and 12b clearly show that pedestrians used both subway entrances to leave and walk towards the square. In addition, as shown in Figures 11 and 12, peaks in speed were observed in the proximity of the subway entrances.

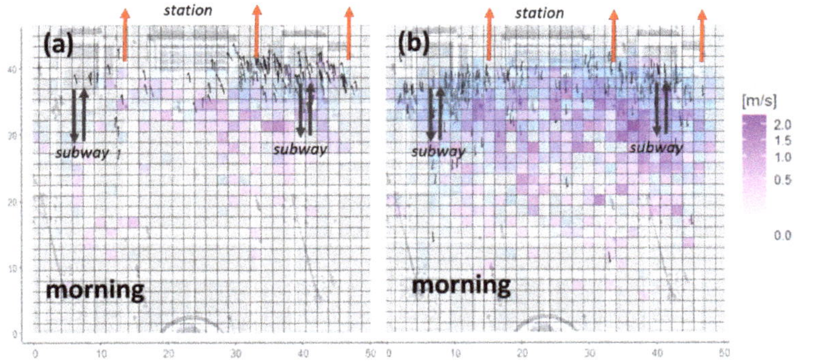

Figure 11. Heat map of speed across Piazza Duca d'Aosta during the morning (from 07:00 to 10:00) along the (**a**) entrance and (**b**) exit direction with respect to the station. Arrows indicate the ending point of a trajectory of a group of pedestrians together with its direction. Results are from two weeks of observations during the month of April 2022. Directions with high standard deviation were omitted. Red arrows indicate the entrances of the station. Grey arrows represent the access points of the subway.

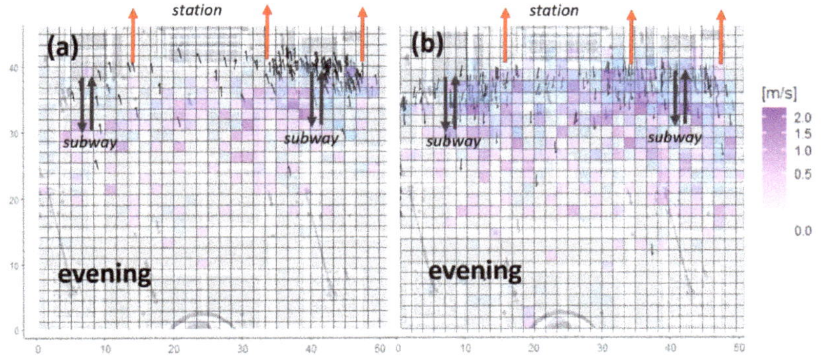

Figure 12. Heat map of speed across Piazza Duca d'Aosta during the evening (from 17:00 to 20:00) along the (**a**) entrance and (**b**) exit direction with respect to the station. Arrows indicate the ending point of a trajectory of a group of pedestrians together with its direction. Directions with high standard deviation were omitted. Red arrows indicate the entrances of the station. Grey arrows represent the access points of the subway.

5.2. Density Analysis

Estimation of pedestrian density was carried out using the Voronoi method. The Voronoi methodology assigns to every pedestrian a cell representing the closest area in order to calculate an arithmetic average of the perceived densities of each user and define the total crowding at a given time [10]. The method requires the Voronoi-cell diagram to be computed for the position of each pedestrian at each timestamp. Since the case study concerned an open area, the boundaries of a square roughly covering the study domain were intersected with the neighboring Voronoi cells to obtain finite areas. Voronoi cells are not of regular size, and they are built around each person by considering the near neighbors. Similar to the estimation of the spatial speed, a grid composed of square grid cells of 2 × 2 m^2 was overlaid on the observed area and intersected with the Voronoi cells. In a situation considered homogeneous, densities estimated with the Voronoi methodology do not show considerable variations; on the contrary, they are defined to highlight possible inhomogeneities in the density distribution. This latter condition was apparent during the whole observation period. Therefore, the Voronoi density was estimated considering the ratio between the number of people within each square cell and the total areas of the Voronoi cells intersecting the square cell itself. At timestamp t, the Voronoi density for each cell A_k of the regular square grid is defined as:

$$D_v^k(t) = \sum_i \frac{P_i^k(t)}{|A_i(t)|} \tag{9}$$

with

$$P_i^k(t) = \frac{|A_i(t) \cap A_k|}{A} \tag{10}$$

where $|A_i(t)|$ is the area of the i-th region obtained from the Voronoi tessellation on the basis of the pedestrian position $\vec{x}_i(t)$, $|A_k| = A$ is the area of each grid cell, and $P_i^k(t)$ is the normalized weight obtained by sectioning A on the basis of the intersection between the i-th Voronoi cell and the k-th grid cell.

To obtain a global-density indicator of the overall study area, the average space density at timestamp t can be estimated as:

$$\langle D_v \rangle_{space} = D_v^s = \frac{1}{N}\sum_{k=1}^{N} D_v^k(t) = \frac{1}{N}\sum_{k=1}^{N}\sum_i \frac{P_i^k(t)}{|A_i(t)|} = \frac{1}{NA}\sum_{k=1}^{N}\sum_i \frac{|A_i(t) \cap A_k|}{|A_i(t)|} \tag{11}$$

where N is the total number of grid cells. Finally, to aggregate the density indicators into time-average profiles, the following equation was used:

$$\langle D_v^s \rangle_{time} = \frac{1}{T}\sum_{t=1}^{T} D_v(t) = \frac{1}{NT}\sum_{t=1}^{T}\sum_{k=1}^{N}\sum_i \frac{P_i^k(t)}{|A_i(t)|} = \frac{1}{NAT}\sum_{t=1}^{T}\sum_{k=1}^{N}\sum_i \frac{|A_i(t) \cap A_k|}{|A_i(t)|} \tag{12}$$

where T is the number of discrete uniform timestamps.

Figure 13 shows the advantage of using the Voronoi-density approach rather than the standard density. The standard density is usually defined as the ratio between the number of people present in a cell and the cell area at a given time. However, the standard density shows higher variability in time with temporal spikes, highlighting the granularity of a single square cell in the temporal variation. Unlike the standard-density definition, the Voronoi method does not show strong oscillations when people enter or exit the measurement area, because in this case every individual produces a density distribution. This yields smoother temporal profiles compared to the standard density, allowing for a better visualization of the temporal variation of the density.

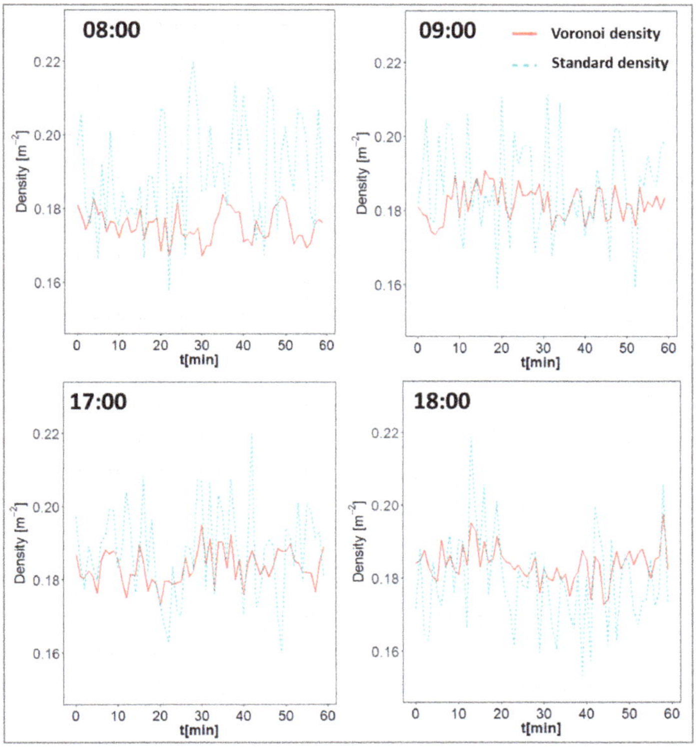

Figure 13. Time sequence of the Voronoi density and the standard density computed over a square cell in Piazza Duca d'Aosta with high occupancy during the day of 23 April 2022.

For each cell, daily Voronoi-density averages were computed from 15-minute density averages during the whole observation period. Data consistency was assured by averaging the total number of pedestrians crossing each cell within the same time range and by weighting the number of each ID included in the cell with the number of timestamps occurring every minute. This was fundamental to avoiding mismatches when averaging data from different time periods.

Having observed that only a portion of the square was mostly crossed by pedestrians during the observation time, spatial estimation of the Voronoi density was carried out on a square of reduced area. Figure 14 shows that the subway entrances as well the corridors in front of the entrance to the station were characterized by higher densities. This was observed both for morning and evening times. The highest density value observed during morning and evening hours was up to 0.16 person/m^2. This result is consistent with the time sequence of the Voronoi density shown in Figure 13. On the other hand, when considering the entire area of the square, the mean value of the Voronoi density was about 0.035 person/m^2, with a standard deviation of about 0.014 person/m^2 (Figure 8b). This value is consistent with the one found in the previous analysis carried out at the same location during a different time period [10]. Compared to typical results on vehicles, pedestrian densities estimated in this work showed very low variability. In the heat map of Figure 14, the density variability ranged from 0.02 person/m^2 to 0.16 person/m^2. Therefore, unlike the case of vehicles, the low value for the spread of density was not suitable for performing speed-density plots to estimate the relationship between walking speed and pedestrian density [36]. However, in another recent work [10], we estimated the speed–density relationship for the same pedestrian environment by taking advantage of a microscopic simulator.

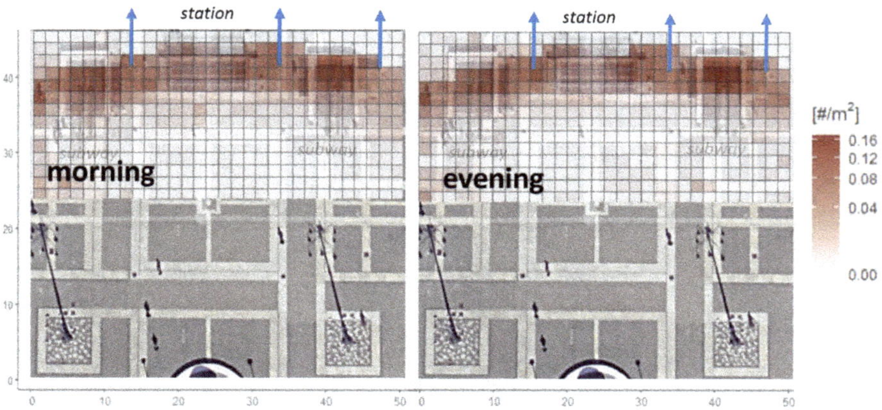

Figure 14. Heat map of the Voronoi density across Piazza Duca d'Aosta during the morning (from 07:00 to 10:00) and the evening (from 17:00 to 20:00) hours during the whole observation period and over the most crowed part of the square. Blue arrows indicate the entrances of the station.

From the daily profile shown in Figure 15a, low pedestrian density was observed during Saturday evening and Monday morning, whereas high density was observed during Monday evening and Tuesday morning. On an hourly basis, during the weekend, density values started decreasing during the evening from 20:00 to 22:00. On the other hand, during working days, no hourly trend was observed in the density, with only one peak around 14:00, and density values decreased during the evening from 20:00 to 22:00 (Figure 15b).

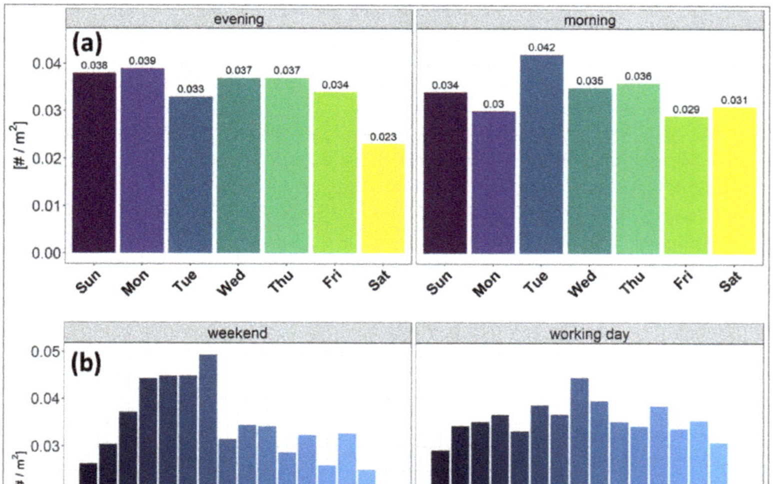

Figure 15. (**a**) Daily and (**b**) hourly profile of the mean Voronoi pedestrian density inside the observation area. Morning time ranges from 07:00 to 10:00, whereas evening time ranges from 17:00 to 20:00.

6. Conclusions

In this work, we illustrated the implementation of an algorithm of computer vision that analyzes images extracted from video frames recorded in front of the Centrale Station in Milan, Italy. The goal was to provide an estimate and a visual representation of speed, direction, and density of pedestrians walking across the square. Tracking and detection of pedestrians was achieved with discrete accuracy. The results clearly show that the main directions followed by pedestrians are linked to points of interest, such as the entrances to the subway and to the railway station. In addition, temporal characterization of pedestrian number and density highlighted the different pedestrian behavior during weekdays compared to weekends.

Even though it was not possible to experience high-flow conditions over the analyzed area, the system can be used offline in the preparedness phase, serving as a support to plan big events. Furthermore, the outcomes of this system can potentially provide useful information for commercial actors such as retailer or entertainment marketing statistics.

The present work highlights some strong points but also has some caveats. One strong point is represented by the value of an autonomous video-recording system: The self-sufficient operating mode does not need any connection to the power grid or any data transfer through a wired network. However, the configuration of the camera plays a key role in obtaining reliable and accurate data. Differences with respect to the results obtained in a previous similar work [10] are related to the different period of observation, when a lower number of pedestrians was detected. Moreover, more work needs to be performed to test the results with different settings of the camera in order to study the possible bias related to uneven spatial distribution of the detection and tracking performance.

Finally, data provided by the camera system and the methodology described in this paper can be useful for both mobility managers and security personnel. Detection and tracking of pedestrians are becoming a popular topic to control mass movements to ameliorate accessibility to public areas as well as to maintain a safe environment. Furthermore, the advancement of new high-performing versions of the YOLO tracking algorithm can significantly enhance the accuracy in estimating the key quantities required to characterize pedestrian-flow dynamics.

Author Contributions: Conceptualization, F.K., C.L., A.D. and M.N.; methodology, F.K., C.L., G.V. and M.N.; software, F.K. and A.D.; validation, F.K., C.L. and M.C.; formal analysis, F.K., C.L., A.D. and M.N.; data curation, F.K. and A.D.; writing—original draft preparation, F.K.; writing—review and editing, F.K., C.L. and M.C. All authors have read and agreed to the published version of the manuscript.

Funding: This research received no external funding.

Institutional Review Board Statement: Not applicable.

Informed Consent Statement: Pedestrian consent was waived due to the fact that images have been treated in order to guarantee at any stage of the data analysis the anonymity of each person involved. To inform pedestrians, a signpost indicating that the images were used in the framework of the research project CityFlows (https://cityflows-project.eu, accessed on 8 June 2023) has been placed below the camera.

Data Availability Statement: Data cannot be publicly shared.

Acknowledgments: The authors would like to thank AMAT—the Environmental Mobility and Territory Agency of Milan, Capgemini, and the project CityFlows for their support in developing and assessing the experimental framework.

Conflicts of Interest: The authors declare no conflict of interest.

References

1. Zou, Z.; Shi, Z.; Guo, Y.; Ye, J. Object Detection in 20 Years: A Survey. *arXiv* **2019**, arXiv:1905.05055. [CrossRef]
2. He, K.; Gkioxari, G.; Dollár, P.; Girshick, R. Mask R-CNN. *arXiv* **2018**, arXiv:1703.06870. [CrossRef]
3. Wu, Q.; Shen, C.; Wang, P.; Dick, A.; van den Hengel, A. Image Captioning and Visual Question Answering Based on Attributes and External Knowledge. *IEEE Trans. Pattern Anal. Mach. Intell.* **2018**, *40*, 1367–1381. [CrossRef] [PubMed]
4. Kang, K.; Li, H.; Yan, J.; Zeng, X.; Yang, B.; Xiao, T.; Zhang, C.; Wang, Z.; Wang, R.; Wang, X.; et al. T-CNN: Tubelets with Convolutional Neural Networks for Object Detection from Videos. *IEEE Trans. Circuits Syst. Video Technol.* **2018**, *28*, 2896–2907. [CrossRef]
5. Butenuth, M.; Burkert, F.; Schmidt, F.; Hinz, S.; Hartmann, D.; Kneidl, A.; Borrmann, A.; Sirmacek, B. Integrating pedestrian simulation, tracking and event detection for crowd analysis. In Proceedings of the 2011 IEEE International Conference on Computer Vision Workshops (ICCV Workshops), Barcelona, Spain, 6–13 November 2011; pp. 150–157.
6. Liberto, C.; Nigro, M.; Carrese, S.; Mannini, L.; Valenti, G.; Zarelli, C. Simulation framework for pedestrian dynamics: Modelling and calibration. *IET Intell. Transp. Syst.* **2020**, *14*, 1048–1057. [CrossRef]
7. Sundararaman, R.; De Almeida Braga, C.; Marchand, E.; Pettré, J. Tracking Pedestrian Heads in Dense Crowd. In Proceedings of the 2021 IEEE/CVF Conference on Computer Vision and Pattern Recognition (CVPR), Nashville, TN, USA, 20–25 June 2021; pp. 3864–3874.
8. LeCun, Y.; Bengio, Y.; Hinton, G. Deep learning. *Nature* **2015**, *521*, 436–444. [CrossRef]
9. Steffen, B.; Seyfried, A. Methods for measuring pedestrian density, flow, speed and direction with minimal scatter. *Phys. A Stat. Mech. Its Appl.* **2010**, *389*, 1902–1910. [CrossRef]
10. Dumitru, A.; Karagulian, F.; Liberto, C.; Nigro, M.; Valenti, G. Pedestrian analysis for crowd monitoring: The Milan case study (Italy). In Proceedings of the MT-ITS 2023 8th International Conference on Models and Technologies for Intelligent Transportation Systems, Nice, France, 14–16 June 2023.
11. Lu, Y.-J.; Tang, Y.-Y.; Pirard, P.; Hsu, Y.-H.; Cheng, H.-D. Measurement of Pedestrian Flow Data Using Image Analysis Techniques. *Transp. Res. Rec.* **1990**, *1281*, 87–96.
12. Jiao, D.; Fei, T. Pedestrian walking speed monitoring at street scale by an in-flight drone. *PeerJ Comput. Sci.* **2023**, *9*, e1226. [CrossRef]
13. Tokuda, E.K.; Lockerman, Y.; Ferreira, G.B.A.; Sorrelgreen, E.; Boyle, D.; Cesar-Jr., R.M.; Silva, C.T. A new approach for pedestrian density estimation using moving sensors and computer vision. *ACM Trans. Spat. Algorithms Syst.* **2020**, *6*, 1–20. [CrossRef]
14. Ismail, K.; Sayed, T.; Saunier, N. Automated Collection of Pedestrian Data Using Computer Vision Techniques. 2009. Available online: http://n.saunier.free.fr/saunier/stock/ismail09automated-tac.pdf (accessed on 8 June 2023).
15. Redmon, J.; Divvala, S.; Girshick, R.; Farhadi, A. You Only Look Once: Unified, Real-Time Object Detection. *arXiv* **2016**, arXiv:1506.02640. [CrossRef]
16. Redmon, J.; Farhadi, A. YOLOv3: An Incremental Improvement. *arXiv* **2018**, arXiv:1804.02767.
17. Nepal, U.; Eslamiat, H. Comparing YOLOv3, YOLOv4 and YOLOv5 for Autonomous Landing Spot Detection in Faulty UAVs. *Sensors* **2022**, *22*, 464. [CrossRef]
18. Lin, T.-Y.; Maire, M.; Belongie, S.; Bourdev, L.; Girshick, R.; Hays, J.; Perona, P.; Ramanan, D.; Zitnick, C.L.; Dollár, P. Microsoft COCO: Common Objects in Context. *arXiv* **2015**, arXiv:1405.0312. [CrossRef]
19. Kerner, B.S.; Rehborn, H.; Aleksic, M.; Haug, A. Recognition and tracking of spatial–temporal congested traffic patterns on freeways. *Transp. Res. Part C Emerg. Technol.* **2004**, *12*, 369–400. [CrossRef]
20. He, K.; Zhang, X.; Ren, S.; Sun, J. Deep Residual Learning for Image Recognition. *arXiv* **2015**, arXiv:1512.03385. [CrossRef]
21. Jastrzębski, S.; Arpit, D.; Ballas, N.; Verma, V.; Che, T.; Bengio, Y. Residual Connections Encourage Iterative Inference. *arXiv* **2018**, arXiv:1710.04773. [CrossRef]
22. Szandała, T. Review and comparison of commonly used activation functions for deep neural networks. In *Bio-Inspired Neurocomputing*; Bhoi, A.K., Mallick, P.K., Liu, C.-M., Balas, V.E., Eds.; Studies in Computational Intelligence; Springer: Singapore, 2021; Volume 903, pp. 203–224, ISBN 9789811554940.
23. Bochkovskiy, A.; Wang, C.-Y.; Liao, H.-Y.M. YOLOv4: Optimal Speed and Accuracy of Object Detection. *arXiv* **2020**, arXiv:2004.10934.
24. Wang, C.-Y.; Bochkovskiy, A.; Liao, H.-Y.M. Scaled-YOLOv4: Scaling Cross Stage Partial Network. In Proceedings of the IEEE/CVF Conference on Computer Vision and Pattern Recognition (CVPR), Nashville, TN, USA, 20–25 June 2021; pp. 13029–13038.
25. Balduzzi, D.; Frean, M.; Leary, L.; Lewis, J.P.; Ma, K.W.-D.; McWilliams, B. The Shattered Gradients Problem: If resnets are the answer, then what is the question? *arXiv* **2018**, arXiv:1702.08591. [CrossRef]
26. Zeiler, M.D.; Fergus, R. Visualizing and understanding convolutional networks. In Proceedings of the Computer Vision—ECCV 2014; Fleet, D., Pajdla, T., Schiele, B., Tuytelaars, T., Eds.; Springer International Publishing: Cham, Swirzerland, 2014; pp. 818–833.
27. Lin, T.-Y.; Goyal, P.; Girshick, R.; He, K.; Dollár, P. Focal Loss for Dense Object Detection. *arXiv* **2018**, arXiv:1708.02002. [CrossRef]
28. Rosebrock, A. Intersection over Union (IoU) for Object Detection. 2016. Available online: https://pyimagesearch.com/2016/11/07/intersection-over-union-iou-for-object-detection/ (accessed on 8 June 2023).
29. Bewley, A.; Ge, Z.; Ott, L.; Ramos, F.; Upcroft, B. Simple Online and Realtime Tracking. In Proceedings of the 2016 IEEE International Conference on Image Processing (ICIP), Phoenix, AZ, USA, 25–28 September 2016; pp. 3464–3468.

30. Kálmán, R. A new approach to linear filtering and prediction problems. *J. Basic Eng.* **1960**, *82*, 35–45. [CrossRef]
31. Dahua Products. Available online: www.dahuasecurity.com/products/All-Products/Network-Cameras/Consumer-Series/2MP/IPC-HFW1235S-W-S2 (accessed on 12 June 2023).
32. Bernardin, K.; Stiefelhagen, R. Evaluating Multiple Object Tracking Performance: The CLEAR MOT Metrics. *J. Image Video Process.* **2008**, *2008*, 1–10. [CrossRef]
33. Milan, A.; Leal-Taixe, L.; Reid, I.; Roth, S.; Schindler, K. MOT16: A Benchmark for Multi-Object Tracking. *arXiv* **2016**, arXiv:1603.00831. [CrossRef]
34. VisAI Labs. Evaluating Multiple Object Tracking Accuracy and Performance Metrics in a Real-Time Setting. Available online: https://visailabs.com/evaluating-multiple-object-tracking-accuracy-and-performance-metrics-in-a-real-time-setting/ (accessed on 22 February 2023).
35. Silgu, M.A.; Çelikoğlu, H.B. K-Means Clustering Method to Classify Freeway Traffic Flow Patterns. *Pamukkale J. Eng. Sci* **2014**, *20*, 232–239. [CrossRef]
36. Yang, X.; Zou, Y.; Chen, L. Operation analysis of freeway mixed traffic flow based on catch-up coordination platoon. *Accid. Anal. Prev.* **2022**, *175*, 106780. [CrossRef] [PubMed]

urban science

MDPI

Article

Urbanization and Land Use Planning for Achieving the Sustainable Development Goals (SDGs): A Case Study of Greece

Dimitrios Kalfas [1], Stavros Kalogiannidis [2,*], Fotios Chatzitheodoridis [3] and Ermelinda Toska [3]

[1] Department of Agriculture, Faculty of Agricultural Sciences, University of Western Macedonia, 53100 Florina, Greece; kalfdimi@otenet.gr

[2] Department of Business Administration, University of Western Macedonia, 51100 Grevena, Greece

[3] Department of Regional and Cross-Border Development, University of Western Macedonia, 50100 Kozani, Greece; fxtheodoridis@uowm.gr (F.C.); drdcbs00002@uowm.gr (E.T.)

* Correspondence: aff00056@uowm.gr

Abstract: Sustainable development has attracted the attention of social-economic, spatial well-being, and cultural continuity advocates across the world. However, the processes involved in land use as well as urban development have continued to affect the attainment of sustainable development. This study assessed the effects of urbanization and land use planning on achieving sustainable development goals. The data were collected using a survey questionnaire from 384 different government leaders in Greece. The study showed that the indicators of urbanization quality have a positive effect on sustainable development goals. It was revealed that there is a significant relationship between integrated land use strategies and sustainable development goals. The study showed that indicators of urbanization quality are very key to achieving different SDGs. This indicates that sustainable urbanization entails more than just converting agricultural land and forests without making any changes to them into cities, and it is equally one of the answers to the problem of the world's population growth if it is done with vision and dedication. The study clearly shows that integrated land use strategies are important in achieving the SDGs. In this case, land use planning is mostly a local effort, though some nations employ guiding land use plans created at the regional or inter-municipal level. Furthermore, urbanization opportunities and land-use plans have a great influence on the achievement of sustainable development goals. Notably, the goal of sustainable urban development is to make urban areas "sustainable" as well as to build or reinforce the city's sustainability-related economic, social, cultural, and environmental aspects. It then goes on to discover how to spread that idea and why it is important to be focused, using various definitions. The fundamental idea of sustainable urban development is then realized by reviewing the ideas and principles of sustainable development. Finally, some general recommendations are made regarding urban planning, sustainable urban development, and the significance of establishing the necessary conditions for its realization. Urban sustainability and proper use of land require structural changes as well as significant, fundamental shifts at all societal levels.

Keywords: sustainable development; urban development; urbanization; land use planning

1. Introduction

Land use and urbanization modifications caused by human factors are apparent everywhere. Important variables include direct drivers such as population expansion or infrastructure system modifications as well as indirect drivers such as energy transition processes. As a result, a wide range of land use disputes have arisen [1–3]. The negative implications of land use on combating climate change, protecting biodiversity, and sustaining vital ecosystem services are increasingly gaining prominence in political and scholarly discussions. In addition, cities have drawn increased attention as the locations of the primary issues with global sustainable development, as well as the locations of the solutions, as the percentage of the world's population living in urban areas has crossed fifty percent [4,5]. According to Nukala and Mutz (2015) [6], the post-2015 agenda must be meaningful for urban people, and the struggle for sustainable development will be won or lost in cities [7,8]. The adoption of sustainable development goals (SDGs) for cities marks a turning point in the understanding of their significance, not just as development sites but also as significant players in global governance and international politics [9–11].

Sustainable development is also affected by problems related to land usage [12,13]. The United Nations World Conference in Rio in 1992 established Agenda 21, which led to greater awareness of issues related to land use, urban growth, agriculture, and forestry and intensified debate during the next three decades. This also happened to a significant degree via bottom-up local efforts such as local Agenda 21 [3,12,14,15]. Modern normative discourses have been influenced by the UN-SDGs, which have resulted in a renewed drive for more sustainable land use. Compactness is the feature of urban form (shape, density, and land use) that limits the overexploitation of natural resources and enhances economies of agglomeration, with advantages for inhabitants in terms of closeness [16–18]. It is determined by the population and built-up area densities as well as the concentration of urban functions [4,11]. The UN SDGs are global development objectives, and specifications for regional and local levels are required in a multi-level governance structure. Further, the Territorial Agenda has made the initial moves on the European level, albeit they are not yet current [16,19]. National governments, including Greece, have also established sustainability policies and indicators at the national level. However, interpretations of international points of reference, particularly at the implementation level, vary from the basic spirit of UN goals [20,21].

The emergence of large-scale projects, such as the SDGs, was characterized by bottom-up procedures and a strong political determination to act. Regional and local governments, as well as the rural communities that surround them, adopt sustainability goals [8,22]. The performers require consistent political support as well as dependable help with day-to-day operations. Standards and legally enforceable recommendations that reinforce prior top-down techniques are critical components of supporting problem-solving implementation [23]. Spatial planning and regional development initiatives have received renewed attention during the last several years as means of resolving land use disputes and achieving sustainable land use. The new urban agenda and particular recommendations for urban and territorial planning, as well as scientific debate, all endorse this type of spatial governance as a significant and effective approach to addressing the issues related to sustainable land use [10,24,25].

This study's purpose was to assess the effect of urbanization and land use planning on achieving the SDGs. In addition, the study was particularly motivated by three different research questions (RQ):

RQ1: What are the different indicators of urbanization quality and their effect on the SDGs?
RQ2: What is the relationship between integrated land use strategies and SDGs?
RQ3: What is the effect of urbanization opportunities and land use planning on the attainment of the SDGs?

Furthermore, each research question's purpose relates to:

RQ1: To establish the different indicators of urbanization quality and their effect on SDGs.
RQ2: To examine the relationship between integrated land use strategies and SDGs.
RQ3: To explore the effect of the opportunities of urbanization and land use planning on the attainment of the SDGs.

Lastly, the study will considerably contribute to the current knowledge on the process of accomplishing the SDGs through proper land use planning and urbanization. Yet, the findings will generally assist policymakers in clearly comprehending how indicators of urbanization, integrated land use strategies, urbanization opportunities, and land use planning influence SDG achievement.

2. Literature Review

2.1. Theoretical Review

A constrained framework for understanding urban growth has been provided by neoclassical economic theory in particular. It basically presupposes the highly unregulated market of land, which is associated with high rent fees for urban land, and the framework also claims that location decisions undertaken by both private households and companies are a general reflection of the objective of attaining maximum utility, primarily through balancing space needs with the available financial budget and location preferences [26]. According to neoclassical economic theory, it could be reasonable to expect that groups with relatively high incomes would prefer residing outside of the city center where there are larger construction lots available, whereas low-income households or individuals may prefer staying close to the urban area so as to reduce transportation expenses [26,27]. The neoclassical monocentric model of urban spatial structure explains urbanization growth or general spatial expansion of cities using variables that include general demand for new residential and commercial land, rising disposable incomes, improvements in transportation systems, and dropping transportation costs [26,28]. Thus, the expanding physical footprint of urban centers and their corresponding declining density are usually caused by growth in population, rising affluence, and improved individual mobility as a result of the private motor vehicle's affordability [4].

Additionally, technical perspectives support the relevance of urbanization with regard to the geographical distribution of urban land uses in addition to economic theorizing [7,29]. Some attribute the pre-industrial city's compactness to the need to make the majority of excursions by foot or other equally sluggish forms of transportation. With the advent of quicker public transit systems and the private vehicle, this restriction was removed. This reasoning led to the conclusion that transportation technology was a factor in the physical expansion of cities [30]. Other technological advancements, such as computers, mobile phones, and increased internet use, may have had a great influence on the geographical decentralization of both people and their businesses, thereby creating the conditions for more terra firma types of urbanization.

2.2. Integrated Land Uses Strategies and SDGs

An approach to allocating land for various purposes that balances economic, social, and environmental interests at the national or subnational level is known as integrated land use planning [31]. Integrated land use strategies assist decision-makers and land users in deciding on the appropriate land use mix to eventually satisfy a variety of human requirements while protecting natural resources and ecosystem services. In order to reduce conflicting interests in land between different organizations, communities, and users, as well as between traditional right holders and public or private entities, land use planning is a well-established strategy [32]. Issues including population expansion, rising competition among varied players for scarce resources, land degradation, and unsustainable urban development are often addressed via integrated land use planning [33]. Land use planning faces extra challenges from climate change in addition to those posed by other factors. Incorporating climate change into all aspects of land use planning may help reduce climatic effects such as floods, droughts, water shortages, and heat stress, as well as lessen the likelihood of these hazards endangering valued assets. Sustainable land use planning may be helpful in preventing and lessening the effects of other natural catastrophes, both climate-related and not. Land-use planning is helpful, for instance, when snow avalanches occur, as in Switzerland and Austria, where zoning is utilized to limit new construction in avalanche-prone regions [34].

In other words, local and regional governments may guarantee that communities are equipped with built-in mechanisms to confront and mitigate such changes and strengthen their resilience to large climatic shifts [35]. Compared to conventional spatial planning, integrated land use planning demands a more strategic and long-term strategy to effectively acknowledge and address the implications of climate change. The vulnerability mapping of present and future climatic conditions should be incorporated into the knowledge base of the planning process in order to adequately account for climate change in land use planning. The most susceptible regions may be identified, and after discussion with stakeholders and agreement with the help of experts, alternate uses and spatially based adaptation methods can be chosen for those places (e.g., from biodiversity, forestry, and agricultural sectors).

Furthermore, planning tools can be used in a variety of ways to reduce climate risks, such as restricting development in hazard-prone areas, ensuring that the built environment can withstand a variety of natural disasters, preserving natural ecosystems that protect communities from hazards, promoting nature-based adaptation strategies, and informing stakeholders and decision-makers about risks and options [31,32]. Zoning, construction rules, and land use licenses are often used as precautions to prevent the exposure of important components to climatic threats [36]. Plans for afforestation and reforestation, the preservation and restoration of ecosystems, and the creation of rural or urban water retention zones are just a few examples of how integrated land use plans may affect land cover more broadly. The adoption of green, regret-free, and nature-based solutions should be prioritized wherever feasible in integrated land use planning's strategic recommendations. In this situation, a variety of co-benefits for the environment and society may be attained, such as the provision of ecosystem services, liveability and welfare, particularly in urban settings, and recreational possibilities [34].

2.3. *Indicators of Urbanization Quality*

Rapid social and economic development has been accelerated by urbanization, but it has also brought about a number of issues, including population density, traffic congestion, resource shortages, housing shortages, loss of biodiversity, and water pollution [29,37]. Urban sustainability is becoming more and more important to people. Realizing sustainable urban development entails paying critical attention to the different aspects of environmental conservation during the process of advancing urban growth. In this case, the different processes involved in enhancing urbanization, such as infrastructural growth and improving transportation, should not have any negative impact on the environment; otherwise, it would be hard to achieve the different goals of sustainable development [38,39]. Conflicts and interactions between these aspects emerge because cities are, to a greater extent, very complex ecosystems that are usually impacted by different forces of cultural, environmental, and social-economic dimensions [18,40].

Urbanization is necessary for humanity's sustainable development, and the degree of urbanization must be determined in light of the different aspects of sustainable development [10,30]. The rate and caliber of urbanization are very essential when determining the degree of sustainable urbanization, and this should also involve blending the processes of speed and quality [33,36]. The pace as well as the general quality of the entire process of urbanization ought to be reflected by pertinent, statistically calculable indicators in order to quantitatively define the phenomenon. A comprehensive analysis of economic, environmental, and social factors is required to identify various degrees of urbanization that are sustainable [37,41,42]. In order to categorize the research on indicators of sustainable urbanization, most studies show that indicators should include economic development, the standard of basic public services, environmental development, and urban-rural heterogeneity [26,43,44]. Kotsoni et al. (2017) evaluated urbanization based on different perspectives on city size and nature of existing infrastructure, public welfare, and integration of urban and rural areas, as well as the existing economic structure [29].

Barton (2021) noted that most urban areas are largely heterotrophic systems when viewed from the standpoint of ecological as well as environmental development, and they must depend on the natural environment for life support services. The key issues are those with the quality of the air and water and how they affect human disease and death [45]. Kotsoni et al. (2017) thought that industrial emissions, the rate of green space, the availability of water per capita, the rate of green space per capita, and the volume of total water per capita were some of the most important factors to consider in analyzing or assessing the forced interaction between urbanization and the environment [29].

Furthermore, Kleemann et al. (2017) suggested a set of metrics for measuring public welfare and living standards from the standpoint of fundamental public service quality [39]. Auzins et al. (2022) suggested traffic and accessibility signs [10,24]. Yet, indicators of mixed land use and land area were provided by Hameed (2021) [4], and an urban land use structure indicator was put out by Kleemann et al. (2017) [39]. Bibri et al. (2020) noted that based on the different perspectives of sustainable urbanization, ecological urbanization, and inclusive urban development, the majority of urbanization research indicators are normally related to economic growth, job creation, basic public service quality, environmental protection progression, urban-rural heterogeneity, as well as population growth [5,18,29].

2.4. Urbanization Opportunities and Land Use

Even utilizing modern geoinformatics and statistics techniques, just watching and quantifying the phenomenon of urban land use change is insufficient to completely comprehend it. As well, an explanation of its motivating factors is also required [12,36]. Nevertheless, Stepputat and Van Voorst (2016) emphasize that there is no grand theory of urbanization or comprehensive explanatory model of urban land use change that would allow for the interpretation and justification of actual findings [18]. Conversely, the social sciences and economics have provided several ideas that point to significant causes of human activities that consume land [16].

The land use planning process includes crucial elements such as social and economic assessments. Similar to many other projects, a land use project can only be carried out if the overall benefits exceed the total expenses [29,46]. Comparing social and economic analyses may reveal areas where new policies are required. In addition, other land resources may be destroyed or degraded as a result of certain land uses. Regardless of whether the procedure is environmentally sustainable, it is likely to proceed if the economic analysis demonstrates that the usage is beneficial from the perspective of a land user [47]. Further, economic analysis should consider the damage to land resources and the ensuing decrease in production [48]. Nevertheless, a significant number of land use planning initiatives have failed in the past due to inadequate consideration of social and economic factors throughout their design and implementation. As a result, it is critical to conduct suitable socio-economic analyses at all stages of the planning process when developing land use projects [21,35].

Recent research has substantially expanded our understanding of the origins and drivers of urban growth and land consumption, two critical environmental concerns [3]. On a larger scale, it is frequently capable of explaining the intensity of urban land use change; nevertheless, forecasting its spatial patterns remains a difficult challenge [3,39]. Due to this, spatially explicit land use models have been developed that describe the rates at which urban land use change occurs over time and the locations where it is most likely to occur [49]. Concretely, Solly, Berisha, and Cotella (2021) [50] have identified five categories of explanatory variables that are widely employed in models of urban land use change:

- Biophysical characteristics: These have an effect on the suitability of land tracts for the construction of structures or infrastructural facilities and may be the reason why certain places are not included in the development.
- Social variables represent household location choices. Examples include the neighborhood's ethnic diversity or economic level, as well as the presence of open green areas.
- Accessibility attributes are referred to as "proxies" for market access in economic considerations.
- Neighborhood interactions relate to a spatial autocorrelation between newly constructed regions and already established urbanized areas that have been observed. In contrast, it is unlikely that certain potentially incompatible land uses would be situated close to one another.

- Legally defining, or differentiating, the suitability of various land parcels has potential in spatial policy and planning. These regulations may be classified as "positive planning" if they determine whether a piece of land is suitable for a certain use or "negative planning" if their goal is to preserve present land uses.

As stated by Domingo, Palka, and Hersperger (2021), decentralized land use governance, in which many local governments have control over urban land use, is more likely to encourage urban sprawl because it increases the number of jurisdictions looking to convert land to urban uses to generate extra-budgetary income [51]. Furthermore, Metternicht (2017) revealed that exclusionary zoning laws, which are used by local governments to try to keep low-income populations out of their neighborhoods, are more likely to be tolerated in smaller towns [42]. These measures are motivated by suburban inhabitants' wishes to safeguard their housing investments and retain their social position [52].

2.5. Sustainable Development in Terms of Land Use and Urbanization

According to Dambeebo and Jalloh (2018), the transportation system is one of the primary factors affecting the environment in terms of congestion and air pollution [10]. This is particularly true when it is located close to an urban center. Similarly, Collier et al. (2020) noted that in land use planning, a new motorway or road attracts additional housing projects, businesses, and industries due to enhanced access, resulting in alterations to the land use pattern [53]. Nevertheless, Cotella et al. (2020) highlighted that the new transportation planning approach promotes noise-compatible land-use planning, which implies that urbanization is designed in such a way that air pollution is prevented [54].

Furthermore, while designing a motorway alignment, Zhang et al. (2022) prioritized the users' safety [12]. This priority can be accomplished by following the geometric design guidelines of the applicable national or international design standards for the particular road type. Similarly, this enables individuals and commodities to move about more effectively. In addition, urban land use must satisfy both present and future urban residents' requirements to be sustainable. Yet, residents nowadays are urging municipal leaders to modify land usage without jeopardizing future generations' needs [5,8]. Overall, urban land use planning and sustainable development are excellent principles, but putting them into practice is a crucial challenge. These should ideally be included in a comprehensive decision framework that acts as a roadmap for daily, individual, professional, or policy choices [16,29]. Finally, the New Urban Agenda highlights land, housing, land values, tenure security, and community development as essential elements of sustainable, inclusive cities, and these contribute to the promotion of the "land for people" phenomenon, as it is presented in Figure 1.

The idea of land covers both buildings and natural resources, making the whole built and natural world a part of it. The organizational systems for land management vary greatly across nations and areas throughout the globe and are a reflection of the local legal and cultural environments. In order to better assist the execution of land policy and sound governance, institutional structures may evolve over time. The land management activities in most countries may be categorized using the three components of land policies, land information infrastructures, and the different land administration functions that help promote a sustainable level of development. This land management paradigm and its related dimensions are well depicted in Figure 2 [34].

The national strategy for supporting goals relating to economic growth, social fairness and equality, and political stability includes land policy as one of its components [46]. Land policies are usually associated with different aspects of land markets, taxes on real estate, general management and control of land use, and the provision of land for minority groups [55,56]. The paradigm of land management encompasses the different tasks or activities involved in land administration that guarantee appropriate management of rights, constraints, duties, and dangers with respect to people's property, land, or natural resources [35,40].

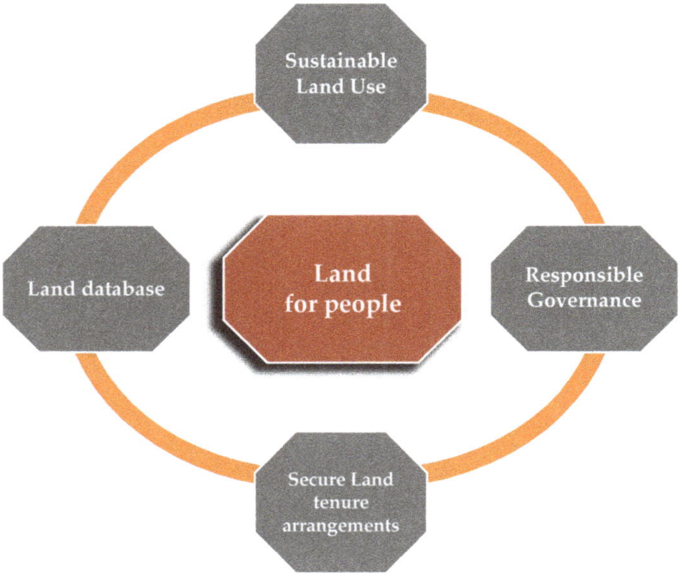

Figure 1. Aspects of Land Use Source.

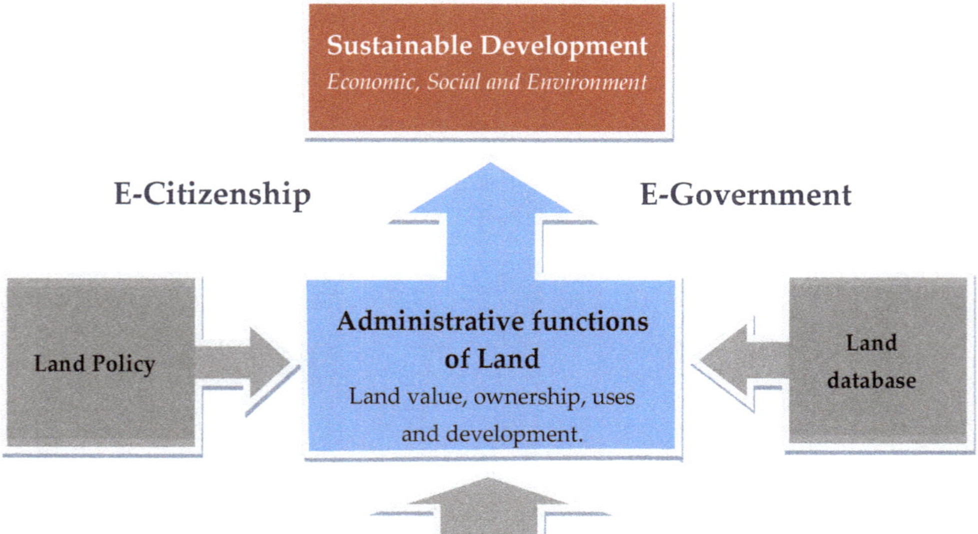

Figure 2. The land management paradigm.

Appropriate land information infrastructures serve as the foundation for and enable land administration activities. The organization of the land information area should integrate the constructed or artificial environment with the natural environment by primarily combining cadastral and topographic data that may also include topographical, environmental, and natural resource issues. The connections may be seen in the way that real conceptual, practical, and economic uses of land and assets affect their values. The potential future use of the property as defined by zoning, land use planning rules, or permit issuing procedures has an impact on land value as well [23,30].

2.5.1. Spatial and Land-Use Plans in Greece

Greece has the most diverse types of spatial designs of any OECD country, with 25 distinct kinds [28]. A 2014 change that has only been partially implemented as of 2016 further complicates the situation. An overview of the structure of land-use plans before and after the reform is given in the graphics on the preceding pages. There are a variety of reasons for the very vast number of spatial designs. While some of the current plans were already legally revoked, they continue to exist since they have not been updated. Several additional situations call for distinct sorts of plans, such as unique designs for various forms of urban growth [33].

The building code is a crucial regulation that governs many facets of construction activity, as it is in the majority of nations. Except when more explicit criteria have been set by a special plan covering the region, they are typically applied to all sorts of projects. Development in towns without a town plan and outside of them is governed by two significant ordinances. Municipalities interpret and implement national legislation established by the national government [41,54,57]. These decrees have a significant influence since they cover a considerable percentage of the country's territory while sometimes having lax enforcement. The kinds of land use that may be included in the various land-use plans are defined by another significant order. Even though this rule was eliminated with the most recent reform, it remains in effect for all outdated land-use plans until they are updated [58].

Municipalities have limited incentives to align their policies with those of the national government beyond what is legally required since land-use planning is almost solely the province of the national government, leaving little potential for coordination between levels of government [59]. One ministry is in charge of all land-use policies and develops strategic plans that serve as a roadmap for the whole government to promote horizontal coordination between the various departments of the national government [58]. Strategic plans are merely guiding tools with minimal enforcement measures; thus, it is up to each ministry to decide whether or not to implement them [28].

Finally, Greece's long-term environmental sustainability has been imperiled since 1950 as a result of the crucial economy's macroeconomic variables degradation as well as social and environmental changes [60,61]. According to Chatzitheodoridis et al., Greece is distinguished by the lack of a national urban strategy and a "non-planning" heritage, which is practiced mostly at the municipal level [62]. In addition, Greece's per capita land usage is somewhat lower than the OECD average. Nonetheless, between 2000 and 2012, the country recorded large gains in both its overall share of developed land and per-person land consumption [37]. During the same period, a significant suburbanization trend emerged, with the population decreasing in urban centers but increasing rapidly in the commuter zones of metropolitan regions. Chatzitheodoridis and Kontogeorgos have highlighted the relevance of the "umbrella function" of metropolitan units in promoting inter-municipal initiatives by developing a "metropolitan vision" [63]. However, outside of major metropolitan centers, Greece is distinguished by a very low proportion of developed and forested terrain [28].

2.5.2. Sustainable Development Goals of the United Nations

The United Nations (2017) noted that SDGs are easily attained across the world if only countries are able to follow the visions, guiding principles, and implementation goals associated with sustainable development [16]. The SGDs are largely guided by a shared vision that focuses on the development of highly resilient and sustainable cities as well as enhancing human settlements to improve standards of living and consequently promote prosperity for all. The process of achieving the SDGs requires strong or well-structured urban governance as well as long-term, comprehensive urban and territorial planning [64,65].

In order to create a more sustainable world, the SDGs advocate for the need to protect, restore, and promote the appropriate use of different terrestrial ecosystems, such as the battle against land and soil depletion and loss of biodiversity. The United Nations (2017) notes that when it comes to general production as well as consumption, the SDGs encourage the promotion of very strong infrastructures along with innovation and clean production [16,29]. The SGDs, especially Goal 6, help promote sustainable management of water resources and sanitation for all people, whereas Goal 13 highlights the need to address the different aspects of climate change and its repercussions [66]. The different SDGs, which are 17 in number, are presented in Table 1.

Table 1. The explanation of the different 17 Sustainable Development Goals (SDGs).

Goal	Description
No Poverty	This goal seeks to eradicate all forms of poverty, with a predicted 7% worldwide poverty rate in 2030.
Zero Hunger	This goal focuses on the elimination of hunger, malnutrition, and small-scale food producers' incomes, as well as improving agricultural practices.
Good Health and Well-Being	SDG 3 focuses on decreasing maternal mortality; eliminating substance abuse; and preventing deaths arising from pollution, among others
Quality Education	This goal seeks to guaranteeing access to quality and free education and promoting equitable and easy access to quality early childhood development.
Gender Equality	SDG 5 focuses on the general empowerment of women or girls, promoting gender equality.
Clean Water and Sanitation	This goal seeks to address water pollution, improve water usage efficiency, and safeguard the different water-dependent ecosystems, among others.
Affordable and Clean Energy	SDG Goal 7 focuses on enhancing the utilization of renewable energy, promoting and energy efficiency, etc.
Decent Work and Economic Growth	The objectives of SDG 8 include maintaining economic growth, enhancing economic productivity, and achieving full and productive employment.
Industry, Innovation, and Infrastructure	SDG Goal 9's focus on promoting dependable infrastructure for all, improving industrialization and technology, and supporting small-scale enterprises in developing nations.
Reduced Inequalities	SDG 10 focuses on income growth; social, economic, and political inclusion; better financial market and institution regulation, etc.
Sustainable Cities and Communities	SDG 11 encourages the employment of national urban policies, and the elimination of slums to improve people's standards of living or settlement.
Responsible Consumption and Production	SDG 12 focuses on promoting sustainable consumption and production patterns as well as addressing the effects of climate change on the environment.
Climate Action	SDG Goal 13 focuses on disaster preparedness, advocating for incorporation of climate policies into different national laws, and also increasing public awareness about climate change.
Life Below Water	SDG 14 focuses on protecting the marine and coastal ecosystems and protecting the fishing industry, among others.
Life on Land	This goal focuses on preserving forests and the different land ecosystems.
Peace, Justice, and Strong Institutions	This goal focuses on promoting peace and inclusion and advocating for justice for everyone, among others.
Partnership for the Goals	This last objective strives to support the SDGs' global collaboration and cooperation.

Sustainable development goals can easily be achieved through compact design, the avoidance of unplanned urban expansion, proper natural resource management, the general reduction of different greenhouse gas emissions or air pollution, and the promotion of disaster planning or crisis management [3,18]. It is important to note that land concerns are directly related to the maintenance and general promotion of the ecological as well as social functions of land, the avoidance of needless changes in land use, and the destruction of delicate and significant ecosystems [14]. The United Nations (2017) emphasizes that

SDGs must be achieved on a national and regional level and must be bolstered by legally enforceable targets for lowering land usage [16].

Planning, multilevel coordination, and collaboration are seen as essential tools for achieving the different SDGs. Long-term sustainable development goals have been hampered by fragmented sectoral programs and independent private ventures [10,67]. This is especially evident in secondary cities, where a lack of investment and gaps in development and infrastructure plans are endangering the provision of essential infrastructure and services [28]. Sectoral and spatial plans' cooperation and harmonization improve efficiency and synergy. According to Beriatos and Papageorgiou (2010), spatial planning is most successful as a participative, flexible, and ongoing process rather than a fixed blueprint [58]. The United Nations (2017) noted that there are several planning approaches that are tailored and can collectively act as the fundamental route to sustainable urban as well as territorial planning [16]. The need for planning activities is undeniable in general, even if the function of spatial planning techniques, particularly those linked to efficacy, is viewed in the scientific literature with more skepticism [27].

2.6. Research Hypothesis

Based on the literature reviewed in the previous sections, three research hypotheses were formulated as below:

Hypothesis (H1). *The indicators of urbanization quality have a positive effect on SDGs.*

Hypothesis (H2). *There is a significant relationship between integrated land uses strategies and SDGs.*

Hypothesis (H3). *Opportunities of urbanization and land use planning have a positive influence on the attainment of SDGs.*

3. Methodology

3.1. Research Design, Target Population, and Sampling Technique

The study utilized a cross-sectional research design and was therefore quantitative. The research design facilitated the collection and analysis of quantitative data to characterize a specific phenomenon based on the current trends, occurrences, and linkages between different variables. The cross-sectional survey research approach enabled the researcher to efficiently generalize the various study findings to a broader leadership population of Kozani city in Greece (Figure 3), which provided data on the study's subject.

Regarding the target population, the study targeted the different government leaders of Greece, as it is believed that they possess extensive knowledge of issues such as land use, urban planning, urbanization quality, and attainment of the different SDGs. Leaders were selected since they represent the people and are well versed in issues of urbanization, land use planning, and the achievement of sustainable development goals. It was prudent to use leaders as the study population since most of them are selected by the people and are residents of Greece, which would provide more reliable data to draw important conclusions for the study.

The population was chosen to establish the most appropriate sample for the study. Therefore, a sample size of 384 different Greek government leaders was selected based on a study population of 10,000 different government leaders across Greece. The sample size was calculated using Yamane's (1973) formula [68,69], as presented in Equation (1).

$$n = \frac{N}{1 + Ne^2} \quad (1)$$

Calculation of the minimum sample of respondents.

where:
n—is the sample size,

N—is the population,
e—is the level of significance, and
1—is the constant.

Using a 5% (0.05) level of significance

$$n = \frac{10,000}{1 + 10,000(0.0025)^2} \Leftrightarrow n = 384$$

where n = 384.

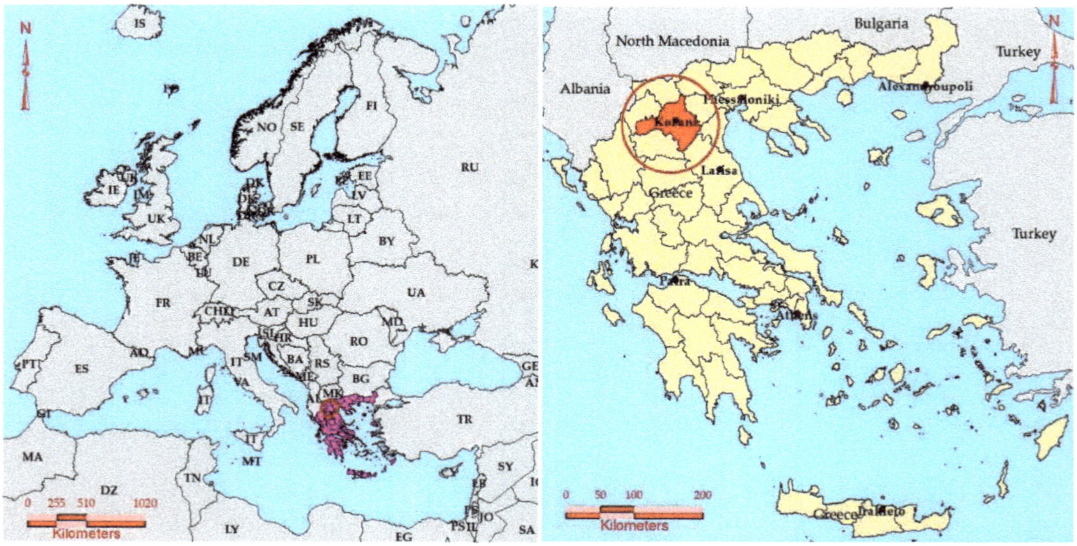

Europe | Greece, Kozani—study area

Figure 3. Maps of Europe, Greece, and Kozani.

This study utilized stratified and simple random sample methods that fall under probability sampling approaches. In this case, the aim sample was obtained by stratified sampling, and the final sample was drawn from the strata using a stratified random sampling technique. With stratification, the researcher divided subjects into subgroups called strata based on characteristics that they shared (e.g., gender, educational attainment, leadership position). Once divided, each subgroup is randomly sampled using another probability sampling method, which in this case was simple random sampling. Stratification in this study was so important since the leadership population was heterogeneous and a simple random sample would not have provided very accurate results without using stratified sampling techniques. Notably, simple random sampling has the advantage of yielding samples that are quite representative of the population.

3.2. Data Collection and Analysis

The authors adopted an online questionnaire to collect data from the leaders of Kozani, Greece. A survey questionnaire is one of the most straightforward and popular methods of collecting data. This is because it covers a large number of respondents rapidly, is less expensive, and allows respondents to freely reply to difficult questions without concern about the researcher's approval or rejection. Hence, an online survey questionnaire was employed to collect the most relevant information for evaluating how urbanization and land use planning assist in accomplishing the SDGs. For this study, well-formulated statements based on the various indicators of each independent variable as derived from the literature were used to measure each independent variable, and respondents were required to either strongly agree, agree, not sure, disagree, or strongly disagree with these statements. On the other hand, to measure the dependent variable, very specific statements relating to achieving the SDGs were developed and measured using a nominal scale. In this case, respondents would easily choose the best alternative among the presented aspects of the SDGs. Generally, the study was based on three major independent variables: indicators of urbanization quality, integrated land use strategies, and opportunities for urbanization and land use planning. Each of the independent variables was assessed based on well-constrained statements, and responses were based on a Likert scale of 1–5. 1—strongly disagree (SD), 2 is disagree (D), 3 is not sure, 4 is agree (A), and 5 is strongly Agree (SA). From each variable, a statement measurement on a Likert scale of 1–5 was picked and cross-tabulated with the different aspects of the SDGs. This would then help to provide the relationship between a particular independent variable and the dependent variable (achieving the SDGs). The description and measurement of the variables in this study are presented in Table 2.

Furthermore, the quantitative data collected from the selected study participants was coded and transferred to SPS for analysis. The results were presented in tables, and their interpretation was based on frequencies and percentages. The link between the research variables was established using Pearson's rank correlation test. Regression analysis was also utilized to ascertain how much urbanization and land use planning contribute to the accomplishment of the SDGs. In this case, a multiple regression model was employed (Equation (2)) to obtain the various predicted values [70–74].

Table 2. Variables, guiding question, and measurement.

Variable	Guiding Question	Measurement Statement	Measurement Scale
Dependent variable			
Achieving SDGs	What is the effect of urbanization and Land Use Planning on achieving SDGs.	1. Sustainable industrialization and improved technology 2. Reduced poverty in communities 3. Peace, equal justice and strong institutions 4. Strengthened climate action, and improved urban environment 5. Empowerment of women and girls to achieve gender equality 6. Enhanced shared prosperity of cities and regions 7. Others	Nominal scale
Independent Variables			
Indicators of urbanization quality,	RQ1: What are the different indicators of urbanization quality and their effect on SDGs?	1. Unplanned urbanization may lead to deforestation, or habitat loss, which may reduce biodiversity and change the ranges and interactions of many species. 2. Sustainable urbanization entails more than just converting agricultural land and forests without making any changes to them into cities. 3. Urbanization may be harmful to sustainable development if it is not properly controlled 4. Sustainable urbanization is one of the answers to the problem of the world's population growth if it is done with vision and dedication.	Likert scale

Table 2. *Cont.*

Variable	Guiding Question	Measurement Statement	Measurement Scale
Integrated Land use strategies,	RQ2: What is the relationship between integrated land uses strategies and SDGs?	1. Land use planning is mostly a local effort though some nations employ guiding land use plans created at the regional or inter-municipal level 2. The global approach to land management relies on effective governance structures. 3. Addressing sustainability challenges, such as poverty reduction, and sustainable energy greatly depends on proper land usage. 4. Land use planning promotes sustainable agriculture, which is also the first critical step towards achieving zero hunger. 5. Planning for land use may make sure that resources are utilized effectively, meeting people's demands while protecting their future resource availability.	Likert scale for each statement
Opportunities of urbanization, and land use planning	RQ3: What is the effect of urbanization opportunities and land use planning on the attainment of SDGs?	1. Land use planning promotes the quality use of land to accommodate changing human requirements while maintaining the long-term socioeconomic uses of the land. 2. Integrated urban planning is important in improving waste and water management, public transportation, and effective management of land 3. Land use planning guides on proper construction and maintenance of a city's infrastructure 4. Urban planning has an impact on infrastructure, transportation systems, and the layout of residential, commercial, and industrial districts, among other things	Likert scale for each statement

$$Y = \beta_0 + \beta_1 X_1 + \beta_2 X_2 + \beta_3 X_3 + \varepsilon \quad (2)$$

where:

Y—represents the achievement of SDGs,
β_0—is the constant coefficient of intercept,
X_1—represents the indicators of urbanization quality,
X_2—represent the integrated land use strategies,
X_3—represents the opportunities for urbanization and land use planning, and
ε—represents the error term in the multiple regression model.

The hypothesis of the study was tested, and the mode of accepting or rejecting the stated hypothesis was performed at the 0.05 level of significance.

Regarding ethical considerations, the researcher ensured that the Kozani local authorities were willing to participate in the study by obtaining their informed consent. In addition to this, the respondents' data was treated as confidential, personal, and private. The respondents were allowed to interpret the different opinion questions to answer queries, making it easier to get comprehensive replies to certain inquiries.

4. Results

This section presents the results obtained after analyzing the data collected from the selected respondents.

4.1. Demographic Characteristics

The results about the demographic characteristics of the selected respondents that participated in the study are presented in Table 3. The majority of the selected leaders

(61.4%) were male, with the remaining 38.5% representing females. Additionally, the majority of the respondents (56.8%) were between the ages of 31 and 40, with just 6% over the age of 50. The majority of the selected leaders (68.2%) had been in leadership for 5–10 years, with only 11.7% have been in leadership for less than 5 years.

Table 3. Showing participants' demographic information.

	Characteristic	Frequency	Percentage (%)
Gender	Male	236	61.4
	Female	148	38.5
Age bracket	Below 30 years	68	17.7
	31–40 years	218	56.8
	41–50 years	75	19.5
	Above 50 years	23	6.0
Years spent in leadership	Below 5 years	45	11.7
	5–10 years	262	68.2
	Above 10 years	77	20.1
	Total	384	100

Source: Authors' own work (2023).

4.2. Descriptive Analysis

The study sought to establish the effect of urbanization and land use planning on the achievement of the SDGs, and the findings on this variable are presented in Table 4. As shown by the results, 72.8% of the respondents agreed that unplanned urbanization may lead to deforestation or habitat loss, reducing biodiversity and changing the ranges and interactions of many species. In addition, the majority of the respondents (61.3%) agreed that sustainable urbanization entails more than just converting agricultural land and forests without making any changes to them into cities. Furthermore, 55.8% of the respondents believed that if urbanization is not properly controlled, it might be harmful to sustainable development. Lastly, more than half of the respondents (68.2%) agreed that, if done with vision and determination, sustainable urbanization is one of the answers to the problem of the world's population growth.

Table 4. Opinions on indicators of urbanization quality and their effect on SDGs.

Statement	SD %	D %	NS %	A %	SA %
Unplanned urbanization may lead to deforestation, or habitat loss, which may reduce biodiversity and change the ranges and interactions of many species.	7.2	10.4	3.5	72.8	6.1
Sustainable urbanization entails more than just converting agricultural land and forests without making any changes to them into cities.	3.4	2.7	7.8	61.3	24.7
Urbanization may be harmful to sustainable development if it is not properly controlled.	11.8	3.3	9.4	55.8	11.6
Sustainable urbanization is one of the answers to the problem of the world's population growth if it is done with vision and dedication.	10.3	4.7	1.5	68.2	15.3

Key: SD = strongly disagree, D = disagree, NS = not sure, A = agree, and SA = strongly agree; Source: authors' own work (2023).

The study also sought to explore the relationship between integrated land use strategies and SDGs, and the results are presented in Table 5. The results reveal that 73.6% of the respondents agreed that land use planning is mostly a local endeavor, though some nations employ guiding land use plans developed at the regional or inter-municipal level. Most of the respondents (55.3%) agreed that the global approach to land management relies on effective governance structures. Furthermore, 51.1% of the participants strongly agreed that addressing sustainability challenges, such as poverty reduction and sustainable energy, greatly depends on proper land usage. It was also agreed by 60.2% of the respondents that land use planning promotes sustainable agriculture, which is also the first crucial step towards achieving zero hunger. Finally, 64.2% agreed that planning for land use may make sure that resources are utilized effectively, meeting people's demands while protecting their future resource availability.

Table 5. Results on the relationship between integrated land use strategies and SDGs.

Statement	SD %	D %	NS %	A %	SA %
Land use planning is mostly a local effort though some nations employ guiding land use plans created at the regional or inter-municipal level.	4.7	6.7	5.4	73.6	9.6
The global approach to land management relies on effective governance structures.	7.9	8.6	15.4	55.3	12.8
Addressing sustainability challenges, such as poverty reduction, and sustainable energy, greatly depends on proper land usage.	6.9	6.6	5.2	30.2	51.1
Land use planning promotes sustainable agriculture, which is also the first critical step towards achieving zero hunger.	3.8	4.3	7.9	60.2	23.8
Planning for land use may make sure that resources are utilized effectively, meeting people's demands while protecting their future resource availability.	3.9	6.1	4.7	64.2	21.1

Key: SD = strongly disagree, D = disagree, NS = not sure, A = agree, and SA = strongly agree; Source: authors' own work (2023).

Correspondingly, the study investigated the effect of the opportunities of urbanization or land use planning on accomplishing the SDGs, and the results are presented in Table 6. In particular, 58.3% of the respondents agreed that land use planning promotes the quality use of land to accommodate changing human needs while preserving the land's long-term socioeconomic uses. It was acknowledged that 63.7% agreed that integrated urban planning is important in improving waste and water management, public transportation, and the effective management of land. Similarly, 61.0% of the respondents strongly agreed that land use planning guides the proper construction and maintenance of a city's infrastructure. Finally, it was revealed by a majority of the respondents (57.6%) that urban planning has an impact on infrastructure, transportation systems, and the layout of residential, commercial, and industrial districts, among other things.

Table 6. Showing the effect of opportunities of urbanization and land use planning on the attainment of SDGs.

Statement	SD %	D %	NS %	A %	SA %
Land use planning promotes the quality use of land to accommodate changing human requirements while maintaining the long-term socioeconomic uses of the land.	8.1	6.4	7.8	58.3	19.4
Integrated urban planning is important for improving waste and water management, public transportation, and the effective management of land.	3.0	6.2	5.6	63.7	21.5
Land use planning guides the proper construction and maintenance of a city's infrastructure.	1.9	14.7	6.8	15.6	61.0
Urban planning has an impact on infrastructure, transportation systems, and the layout of residential, commercial, and industrial districts, among other things.	1.6	8.7	10.8	57.6	21.3

Key: SD = strongly disagree, D = disagree, NS = not sure, A = agree, and SA = strongly agree. Source: authors own work (2023).

Finally, the respondents provided their opinions on the different aspects of the SDGs, whose results are presented in Figure 4. The results in Figure 4 indicate that SDGs are significantly more concerned with sustainable industrialization and improved technology (32.5%), followed by reduced poverty in communities (20.5%), strengthened climate action, and an improved urban environment (16%). Other participants (6%) highlighted aspects of SGDs, such as early childhood development, building resilience in agricultural practices, and enhancing resource efficiency and productive employment.

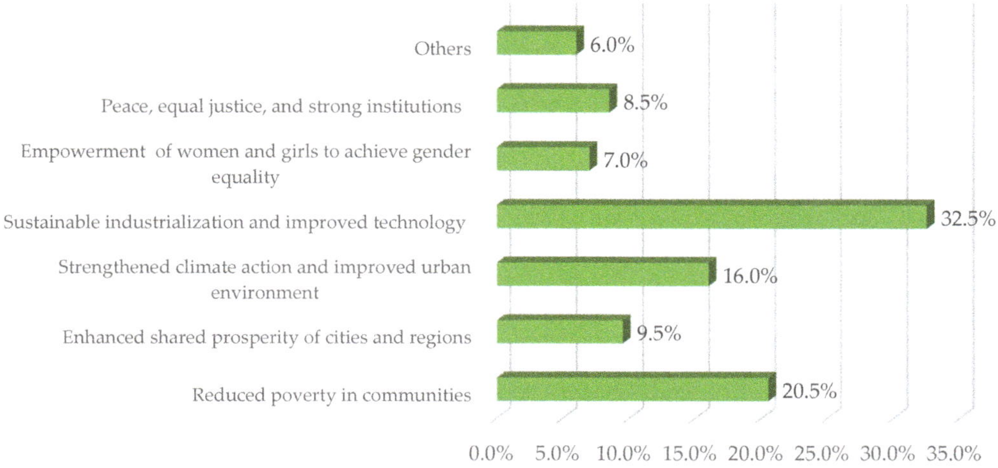

Figure 4. Aspects of SDGs.

4.3. Correlation Analysis

A correlation analysis was conducted to determine the relationship between study variables, and the results are displayed in Table 7. The findings indicate that indices of urbanization quality have a positive correlation with SDG achievement (r = 0.526), which is significant at 0.05. Hence, indicators such as population growth, urban leadership competency, and the quality of urban planning all have a significant influence on the possibility of meeting the SDGs. Further, integrated land use strategies showed a positive correlation with the achievement of the SDGs (r = 0.734), which was statistically significant at 0.05. Further, at a significance level of 0.05, there was a strong association or correlation between opportunities for urbanization and land use planning and the SDGs' accomplishment (r = 0.531).

Table 7. Cross-tabulation of aspects of urbanization, land use planning, and SDGs.

	Indicators of Urbanization Quality	**Integrated Land Use Strategies**	**Opportunities of Urbanization and Land Use Planning**	**Sustainable Development Goals**
Indicators of urbanization quality	1			
Integrated land use strategies	0.631 * 0.00	1		
Opportunities of urbanization and land use planning	0.913 * 0.02	0.708 * 0.000	1	
Sustainable Development Goals (dep.)	0.526 * 0.00	0.734 * 0.00	0.531 * 0.00	1 0.00

* Represent statistical significance at a 5% level of significance.

4.4. Results of Regression Analysis

A regression analysis was applied to determine the level to which indicators of urbanization quality, integrated land use strategies, urbanization opportunities, and land use planning predict the SDGs' success. The result of 0.791 of the multiple correlation coefficient (R) demonstrated a positive association between the three independent variables and the achievement of the SDGs. In addition, the value of R-Square confirms that indicators of urbanization quality, integrated land use strategies, urbanization opportunities, and land use planning result in an 83.6% shift in SDG achievement, as shown in Table 8.

Table 8. Model Summary.

Model	R	R Square	Adjusted R Square	Std. Error of the Estimate
	0.791	0.836	0.808	0.36421

Predictors: (constant): indicators of urbanization quality, integrated land use strategies, opportunities for urbanization, and land use planning.

The one-way ANOVA helped to find out whether the independent variables in this study were great or major predictors of the dependent variable (attainment of SDGs) or whether the linear regression model was well fitted with the data. As it is presented in Table 9, the findings F (3, 197) = 38.241, $p < 0.05$, indicate that the model and data are sufficiently matched.

Table 9. ANOVA analysis.

Model	R	Sum of Squares	df	Mean Square	F	Sig.
	Regression	42.137	3	17.102	38.241	0.017
1	Residual	4.102	381	0.046		
	Total	46.238	384			

Dependent Variable: SDGs; Predictors: (constant), indicators of urbanization quality, integrated land use strategies, opportunities of urbanization, and land use planning.

In addition, the different unstandardized coefficients of the model were examined to determine the effect of urbanization and land use planning on the attainment of the SDGs. As it is presented in Table 10, the beta coefficient of indicators of urbanization quality is 0.341, indicating that a unit change in indicators of urbanization quality results in a 34.1% change in SDGs. Furthermore, the beta coefficient of integrated land use strategies is 0.234, implying that any change in integrated land use strategies may lead to a 23.4% change in SDGs. Consequently, a unit change in urbanization and land use planning opportunities would result in a 26.1% shift in environmental sustainability.

Table 10. Regression coefficients.

Model	Unstandardized Coefficients		Standardized Coefficients	T	Sig.
	B	Std. Error	Beta		
(Constant)	0.836	0.196		2.438	0.026
Indicators of urbanization quality	0.341	0.103	0.397	3.736	0.002
Integrated Land use strategies	0.234	0.042	0.213	3.195	0.004
Opportunities of urbanization and land use planning	0.261	0.051	0.282	3.511	0.013

Dependent Variable: Achieving of SDGs.

In summary, the indicator of urbanization quality's p-value (0.002) was less than the significance level (0.05); hence, we accept hypothesis H1 that the indicators of urbanization quality have a positive effect on achieving the SDGs. Furthermore, the beta coefficient for integrated land use strategies was 0.23 and the p-value was 0.004, so we accept hypothesis H2 that there is a significant relationship between integrated land use strategies and SDGs. Yet, the p-value of opportunities for urbanization and land use planning was 0.013, indicating a substantial relationship between urbanization and land use planning opportunities and the SDGs. As a result, we accept Hypothesis H3, which states that opportunities for urbanization and land use planning have a positive influence on the attainment of the SDGs.

5. Discussion

This research examined the impact of urbanization and land use planning on achieving the SDGs, with a major focus on Greece. The results show that metrics of urbanization quality have a favorable impact on the SDGs. It was shown that integrated land use plans and the SDGs have a significant link. The research also indicated that urbanization possibilities and land-use plans have a significant impact on SDG achievement. It is also important to emphasize that the best land use choices are decided by weighing environmental, economic, and social factors [8,29]. While the literature has numerous theoretical land-use plan models, few studies focus on their actual application and distinctive difficulties in diverse locations, notably in Greece. Implementing an integrated land-use plan in a poor nation may be difficult due to a lack of data, political will, stakeholder engagement, and financial and human resources, according to the research. Previous land-use planning projects and studies addressed these issues in innovative ways, including the use of simpler models that needed less data, the importance of data collection, and the involvement of decision-makers throughout the process [66,75].

The study clearly shows that integrated land use strategies are important in achieving the SDGs. According to the literature, important components of the land use planning process include economic and social considerations. A land use project, similar to many others, can only be completed if the net benefits outweigh the net costs [29,42]. Combining social and economic evaluations may highlight areas that need new policy. In addition, some land uses may result in the destruction or degradation of other land resources. Whether or not the practice is environmentally sustainable, it is likely to move on if the economic analysis shows that it is advantageous from the viewpoint of a land user [43]. Economic analysis should also take into account the destruction of land resources and the subsequent decline in productivity [44]. This research emphasizes the need for strong governance institutions for a global approach to land management. Decentralization may be seen as a critical component in achieving the broader objective of sustainable development in this setting. This argument is particularly compelling when it comes to land use management and decision-making. Comprehensive planning, which merges policies and land-use regulations into a unified planning document that encompasses the whole jurisdiction, is another concept connected to integrated land-use management [5,54]. The presentation of political goals, objectives, problems, and preconditions should then be used to justify land use planning and more detailed land use laws. This also applies to public participation, which should be used to raise awareness of the importance of planning laws and enable communication between the government and the public on the management of natural resources and the overall urban and rural environment [35,76]. Moreover, a monitoring system is essential to making decisions on informal urban or rural growth in relation to overall land policies, such as via continuing updating of the large-scale topographic map base and suitable enforcement methods [7,10].

Moreover, communities with declining populations, or "shrinking towns", have economies that collapse due to concerns with unemployment and poverty, an aging workforce, vacant buildings, and the loss of historic sites. Similarly, Murray (2019) said that in order to compete with other jurisdictions for large economic development efforts such as new industrial facilities, office parks, or big-box regional retailers, local businesses and communities may suffer [30]. Furthermore, planners and supporters of smart growth frequently advocate for moderately high population density because of its alleged benefits, which include a smaller footprint of developed land, preservation of agricultural land and open space, more walking and less driving, support for public transportation, and more opportunities for social interaction [59]. The pressures placed on forest ecosystems near increasing urban areas cause problems for natural resource management. For outdoor recreation, city dwellers relocate to exurban areas. Another concern is the safety of people when they come into contact with wild animals, hazardous plants, and other outdoor risks. Urbanization trends may be harmful to the wellbeing of lower socioeconomic groups. Lower-income people may be disenfranchised as a result of "gentrification", or the movement of urban neighborhoods toward higher wages and more expensive housing [2,53]. The number of families that must use well water and septic systems grows as a consequence of land use rules that promote growth beyond the limits of water and sewage infrastructure.

Importantly, increased septic system use increases the risk of sewage backflow and seepage into water delivery systems, raising the possibility of long-term, undiscovered drinking water supply contamination. Finally, communities that want to protect agricultural land have a number of choices for controlling land use, which may help them achieve the SDGs by ensuring economic survival, food security, or maintaining rural beauty [4,39,46].

6. Conclusions

This study assessed the effect of urbanization as well as land use planning with regard to achieving sustainable development goals, with a focus on Greece. The study showed that indicators of urbanization quality, integrated land use strategies, and urbanization opportunities have a positive influence on the attainment of the different SDGs. The study showed that indicators of urbanization quality are very key to achieving different SDGs. This indicates that sustainable urbanization entails more than just converting agricultural land and forests without making any changes to them into cities, and it is equally one of the answers to the problem of the world's population growth if it is done with vision and dedication. The study clearly shows that integrated land use strategies are important in achieving the SDGs. In this case, land use planning is mostly a local effort, though some nations employ guiding land use plans created at the regional or inter-municipal level. The creation of a successful networking system may significantly increase, speed up, and optimize the process of information gathering, selection, and sharing while preventing redundancy and overlap. There is no way to create a comprehensive, sustainable land use plan for an area. At most, a regional plan may provide a broad overview of what has to be accomplished on a national level. Hence, each nation will need to customize its sustainable development plan in light of its unique issues, limitations, and comparative advantages. Regional plans must establish goals, pinpoint pertinent initiatives, evaluate how policies will affect the environment, look into ways to gather resources, and improve and promote engagement from all parties involved. Projects for land use planning shall not be promoted or carried out without expense. Hence, creating new funding sources to augment the national budget allocations should get top priority. New strategies for development, and by extension, for land use and management, are required by the difficult but generally accepted notion of sustainable land use planning. In this regard, it is necessary to manage the land and its associated resources from fresh angles. In order to accomplish sustainable land use planning development, policies, laws, objectives, and goals should be founded on local realities, customs, and natural resource management techniques. Prior to implementation, such policies and regulations should be evaluated for their effects on the environment and the socioeconomic system.

6.1. Recommendations

In order to promote proper land-use management, there is a need to incorporate the three domains of land policy, land information management, and land-use monitoring or enforcement, which could also help in achieving the SDGs. A system such as this, which incorporates monitoring and enforcement mechanisms, should promote sustainable growth while also giving people the fundamental tools for stopping and regulating unofficial urban expansion.

The lessons learned demonstrate that a radical departure from previous policies is required in order to adopt a new holistic approach to land use planning and management that is thorough, inclusive, and ecologically sustainable. This can greatly help the government achieve different SDGs in the shortest time possible.

Professionals with the necessary training who can function in the multisectoral setting of integrated natural resource management should be utilized in urbanization and land use planning. This can greatly enhance the process of attaining the SDGs.

In order to ensure that development is more comprehensive and global than local, a plan for an urban area should also take neighboring communities and land uses into account. This improves local social and economic activity while causing less environmental harm and achieving the SDGs.

There is a need to involve the population in different decision-making processes that aim at enhancing urbanization and land use. The population plays a key role in achieving proper land use and a high level of urbanization; hence, involving it in decision-making helps to achieve the SDGs.

In order to promote intra- and intergenerational fairness, sustainable land use planning integrates ecological, socioeconomic, political, and ethical concepts into the management of land for productive and other purposes.

In order to achieve equality and justice in regard to land use planning, it is also important to gather, analyze, and distribute timely and accurate data, as well as apply cutting-edge land assessment and evaluation technologies to provide solid scientific knowledge for optimal decision support when developing and executing policies and strategies to help in land use planning.

6.2. Limitations of the Study

There were methodological limitations in this study whereby, despite focusing on the entire country of Greece, the data was specifically collected from Kozani, and this would have affected the generalizability of the results. However, to address this limitation, we used government leaders as a sample size and then assumed that these represented different areas of Greece and not only Kozani.

6.3. Areas for Future Research

The findings suggest that future land development will be decided upon and governed by land use planning and policies. However, there is still much work to be done when it comes to debating informal urban expansion in Europe. Some European countries, particularly those in the south and east, are struggling in this area. As a consequence, future research should emphasize the various informal factors influencing overall sustainable development in Europe.

Author Contributions: Conceptualization, S.K. and F.C.; methodology, S.K. and D.K.; software, D.K.; validation, F.C. and E.T.; formal analysis, S.K.; investigation, S.K. and D.K.; resources, S.K., E.T. and D.K.; data curation, F.C. and E.T.; writing—original draft preparation, S.K.; writing—review and editing, D.K.; visualization, E.T. and D.K.; supervision, F.C.; project administration, F.C. and E.T.; funding acquisition, F.C. and E.T. All authors have read and agreed to the published version of the manuscript.

Funding: This research received no external funding.

Data Availability Statement: Data are available upon request.

Conflicts of Interest: The authors declare no conflict of interest.

References

1. Balk, D.; Tagtachian, D.; Jiang, L.; Marcotullio, P.; Cook, E.M.; Jones, B.; Mustafa, A.; McPhearson, T. Frameworks to envision equitable urban futures in a changing climate: A multi-level, multidisciplinary case study of New York City. *Front. Built Environ.* **2022**, *8*, 949433. [CrossRef]
2. Hoffmann, J. Demographic Change and Land Use. In *Sustainable Land Management in a European Context: A Co-Design Approach*; Weith, T., Barkmann, T., Gaasch, N., Rogga, S., Strauß, C., Zscheischler, J., Eds.; Springer International Publishing: Cham, Switzerland, 2021; pp. 63–74. ISBN 978-3-030-50841-8.
3. Surya, B.; Ahmad, D.N.; Sakti, H.H.; Sahban, H. Land Use Change, Spatial Interaction, and Sustainable Development in the Metropolitan Urban Areas, South Sulawesi Province, Indonesia. *Land* **2020**, *9*, 95. [CrossRef]
4. Hameed, A.A.S. Urban and Regional Planning Strategies to Achieve Sustainable Urban Development: (Subject review). *Int. J. Adv. Sci. Res. Eng.* **2021**, *7*, 22–27. [CrossRef]
5. Bibri, S.E.; Krogstie, J.; Kärrholm, M. Compact city planning and development: Emerging practices and strategies for achieving the goals of sustainability. *Dev. Built Environ.* **2020**, *4*, 100021. [CrossRef]

6. Nukala, R.B.; Mutz, D. Strategic Approach for Sustainable Land Use in an Emerging Country: Case of India. In Proceedings of the Annual World Bank Conference on Land and Poverty 2015, Washington, DC, USA, 23–27 March 2015; Deutsche Gesellschaft für Internationale Zusammenarbeit (GIZ) GmbH: Washington, DC, USA, 2015.
7. Comba, P.; Creaser, I.I.; Gahan, L.R.; Harrowfield, J.M.; Lawrance, G.A.; Martin, L.L.; Mau, A.W.H.; Sargeson, A.M.; Sasse, W.H.F.; Snow, M.R. Macrobicyclic chromium(III) hexaamine complexes. *Inorg. Chem.* **1986**, *25*, 384–389. [CrossRef]
8. Dolley, J.; Marshall, F.; Butcher, B.; Reffin, J.; Robinson, J.A.; Eray, B.; Quadrianto, N. Analysing trade-offs and synergies between SDGs for urban development, food security and poverty alleviation in rapidly changing peri-urban areas: A tool to support inclusive urban planning. *Sustain. Sci.* **2020**, *15*, 1601–1619. [CrossRef]
9. Gallardo, M.; Cocero, D. Using the European CORINE Land Cover Database: A 2011–2021 Specific Review. In *Sustainable Development Goals in Europe: A Geographical Approach*; De Lázaro Torres, M.L., De Miguel González, R., Eds.; Springer International Publishing: Cham, Switzerland, 2023; pp. 303–325. ISBN 978-3-031-21614-5.
10. Dambeebo, D.; Jalloh, C.A. Sustainable Urban Development and Land Use Management: Wa Municipality in Perspective, Ghana. *J. Sustain. Dev.* **2018**, *11*, 235. [CrossRef]
11. Almulhim, A.I.; Bibri, S.E.; Sharifi, A.; Ahmad, S.; Almatar, K.M. Emerging Trends and Knowledge Structures of Urbanization and Environmental Sustainability: A Regional Perspective. *Sustainability* **2022**, *14*, 13195. [CrossRef]
12. Zhang, S.; Guan, Z.; Liu, Y.; Zheng, F. Land Use/Cover Change and Its Relationship with Regional Development in Xixian New Area, China. *Sustainability* **2022**, *14*, 6889. [CrossRef]
13. Kalfas, D.G.; Zagkas, D.T.; Dragozi, E.I.; Melfou, K.K. An approach of landsenses ecology and landsenseology in Greece. *Int. J. Sustain. Dev. World Ecol.* **2021**, *28*, 677–692. [CrossRef]
14. Kalfas, D.; Zagkas, D.; Dragozi, E.; Zagkas, T. Estimating value of the ecosystem services in the urban and peri-urban green of a town Florina-Greece, using the CVM. *Int. J. Sustain. Dev. World Ecol.* **2020**, *27*, 310–321. [CrossRef]
15. Musakwa, W.; Niekerk, A. Van Implications of land use change for the sustainability of urban areas: A case study of Stellenbosch, South Africa. *Cities* **2013**, *32*, 143–156. [CrossRef]
16. United Nations. *Urbanization and Sustainable Development in Asia and the Pacific: Linkages and Policy Implications*; Economic and Social Commission for Asia and the Pacific: Bangkok, Thailand, 2017.
17. Cobbinah, P.B.; Erdiaw-Kwasie, M.O.; Amoateng, P. Rethinking sustainable development within the framework of poverty and urbanisation in developing countries. *Environ. Dev.* **2015**, *13*, 18–32. [CrossRef]
18. Stepputat, F.; Van Voorst, R. *Cities on the Agenda: Urban Governance and Sustainable Development*; Dansk Institut for Internationale Studier (DIIS), Ed.; DIIS Report: Copenhagen, Denmark, 2016; ISBN 8776057984.
19. Enemark, S. Integrated land-use management for sustainable development. *Proc. Jt. FIG Comm.* **2007**, *3*, 13.
20. Kalfas, D.G.; Zagkas, D.T.; Raptis, D.I.; Zagkas, T.D. The multifunctionality of the natural environment through the basic ecosystem services in the Florina region, Greece. *Int. J. Sustain. Dev. World Ecol.* **2019**, *26*, 57–68. [CrossRef]
21. Vlek, P.L.G.; Khamzina, A.; Tamene, L.D. *Land Degradation and the Sustainable Development Goals: Threats and Potential Remedies*; CIAT—International Center for Tropical Agriculture: Nairobi, Kenya, 2017.
22. Sharma, R.; Mina, U.; Kumar, B.M. Homegarden agroforestry systems in achievement of Sustainable Development Goals. A review. *Agron. Sustain. Dev.* **2022**, *42*, 44. [CrossRef]
23. Machingura, F.; Lally, S. *The Sustainable Development Goals and Their Trade-Offs*; Development Progress Case Studies: London, UK, 2017.
24. Auzins, A.; Brokking, P.; Jürgenson, E.; Lakovskis, P.; Paulsson, J.; Romanovs, A.; Valčiukienė, J.; Viesturs, J.; Weninger, K. Land Resource Management Policy in Selected European Countries. *Land* **2022**, *11*, 2280. [CrossRef]
25. ICLEI. *The Importance of All Sustainable Development Goals (SDGs) for Cities and Communities*; Urban Issues: Bonn, Germany, 2015.
26. Delphin, S.; Snyder, K.A.; Tanner, S.; Musálem, K.; Marsh, S.E.; Soto, J.R. Obstacles to the Development of Integrated Land-Use Planning in Developing Countries: The Case of Paraguay. *Land* **2022**, *11*, 1339. [CrossRef]
27. UN-Habitat. *A New Strategy of Sustainable Neighbourhood Planning: Five Principles—Note 3*; Urban Planning Discussion; UN-Habitat (United Nations Human Settlements Programme): Nairobi, Kenya, 2015.
28. OECD. Country fact sheet Greece. In *The Governance of Land Use*; OECD—Organisation for Economic Cooperation and Development, Ed.; OECD—Organisation for Economic Cooperation and Development: Washington, DC, USA, 2016; pp. 49–87.
29. Kotsoni, A.; Dimelli, D.; Ragia, L. Land Use Planning for Sustainable Development of Coastal Regions. In Proceedings of the 3rd International Conference on Geographical Information Systems Theory, Applications and Management—GISTAM, Porto, Portugal, 27–28 April 2017; Ragia, L., Rocha, J.G., Laurini, R., Eds.; SciTePress: Porto, Portugal, 2017; pp. 290–294.
30. Murray, S. *The Critical Role of Infrastructure for the Sustainable Development Goals*; Economist Intelligence Unit: New York, NY, USA, 2019.
31. Dang, A.N.; Kawasaki, A. A review of methodological integration in land-use change models. *Int. J. Agric. Environ. Inf. Syst.* **2016**, *7*, 1–25. [CrossRef]
32. Vale, D.S. Transit-oriented development, integration of land use and transport, and pedestrian accessibility: Combining node-place model with pedestrian shed ratio to evaluate and classify station areas in Lisbon. *J. Transp. Geogr.* **2015**, *45*, 70–80. [CrossRef]
33. SEV-BCSD. *Study on the UN Sustainable Development Goals in Greece the Business Perspective*; SEV-BCSD: Athens, Greece, 2017.

34. Enemark, S.; Williamson, I.; Wallace, J. Building modern land administration systems in developed economies. *J. Spat. Sci.* **2005**, *50*, 51–68. [CrossRef]
35. Keles, R. Sustainable urbanization and its policy implications. The case of Turkey. In *Interdependency between Agriculture and Urbanization: Conflicts on Sustainable Use of Soil and Water*; Camarda, D., Grassini, L., Eds.; CIHEAM: Bari, Italy, 2001; pp. 119–135.
36. UN-Habitat. *UN-Habitat's New Strategic Plan (2020–2023). The Role of Land and Property in Promoting Sustainable Urban Development*; Global Land Tool Network: Oslo, Norway, 2019.
37. Drosos, V.C.; Liampas, S.-A.G.; Farmakis, D.E. Zoning planning for sustainable development and exploitation of the mountainous areas. *Int. J. Soc. Sci. Humanit.* **2016**, *6*, 451–455. [CrossRef]
38. CDM Smith Inc. *India: Promoting Inclusive Urban Development in Indian Cities*; Ministry of Housing and Urban Poverty Alleviation: Honiara, Solomon Islands, 2013.
39. Kleemann, J.; Inkoom, J.N.; Thiel, M.; Shankar, S.; Lautenbach, S.; Fürst, C. Peri-urban land use pattern and its relation to land use planning in Ghana, West Africa. *Landsc. Urban Plan.* **2017**, *165*, 280–294. [CrossRef]
40. Azizi, P.; Soltani, A.; Bagheri, F.; Sharifi, S.; Mikaeili, M. An Integrated Modelling Approach to Urban Growth and Land Use/Cover Change. *Land* **2022**, *11*, 1715. [CrossRef]
41. Fu, S.; Zhuo, H.; Song, H.; Wang, J.; Ren, L. Examination of a coupling coordination relationship between urbanization and the eco-environment: A case study in Qingdao, China. *Environ. Sci. Pollut. Res.* **2020**, *27*, 23981–23993. [CrossRef]
42. Metternicht, G. *Global Land Outlook Working Paper. Land Use Planning*; United Nations Convention to Combat Desertification: Sydney, Australia, 2017.
43. Allen, C.; Smith, M.; Rabiee, M.; Dahmm, H. A review of scientific advancements in datasets derived from big data for monitoring the Sustainable Development Goals. *Sustain. Sci.* **2021**, *16*, 1701–1716. [CrossRef]
44. Osman, T.; Kenawy, E.; Abdrabo, K.I.; Shaw, D.; Alshamndy, A.; Elsharif, M.; Salem, M.; Alwetaishi, M.; Aly, R.M.; Elboshy, B. Voluntary Local Review Framework to Monitor and Evaluate the Progress towards Achieving Sustainable Development Goals at a City Level: Buraidah City, KSA and SDG11 as A Case Study. *Sustainability* **2021**, *13*, 9555. [CrossRef]
45. Barton, H. The Governance of Land. In *City of Well-Being*; Barton, H., Ed.; Routledge—Taylor & Francis Group: London, UK, 2016; pp. 237–247. ISBN 9781315438689.
46. ITAtech. *ITA Tech Guidelines on Monitoring Frequencies in Urban Tunnelling*; Châtelaine: Vernier, Switzerland, 2015.
47. IAI; INE; UNEP. *Urbanization, Global Environmental Change, and Sustainable Development in Latin America*, 1st ed.; Rodriguez, R.S., Bonilla, A., Eds.; Inter American Institute for Global Change Research (IAI): São José dos Campos, Brazil; Instituto Nacional de Ecología (INE): Mexico City, Mexico; United Nations Environment Programme (UNEP): Panama City, Panama, 2007; ISBN 978-85-99875-02-5.
48. Borrelli, P.; Robinson, D.A.; Fleischer, L.R.; Lugato, E.; Ballabio, C.; Alewell, C.; Meusburger, K.; Modugno, S.; Schütt, B.; Ferro, V.; et al. An assessment of the global impact of 21st century land use change on soil erosion. *Nat. Commun.* **2017**, *8*, 2013. [CrossRef]
49. Bell, K.P.; Irwin, E.G. Spatially explicit micro-level modelling of land use change at the rural–urban interface. *Agric. Econ.* **2002**, *27*, 217–232. [CrossRef]
50. Solly, A.; Berisha, E.; Cotella, G. Towards Sustainable Urbanization. Learning from What's Out There. *Land* **2021**, *10*, 356. [CrossRef]
51. Domingo, D.; Palka, G.; Hersperger, A.M. Effect of zoning plans on urban land-use change: A multi-scenario simulation for supporting sustainable urban growth. *Sustain. Cities Soc.* **2021**, *69*, 102833. [CrossRef]
52. UNIDO. *The 2030 Agenda for Sustainable Development: Achieving the Industry-Related Goals and Targets*, 1st ed.; United Nations—Department of Economic and Social Affairs, Ed.; United Nations—Department of Economic and Social Affairs: New York, NY, USA, 2015.
53. Collier, P.; Glaeser, E.L.; Venables, A.; Manwaring, P. *Urban Land Use Planning for Economic Growth*; IGC Cities That Work; International Growth Centre (IGC): London, UK, 2020.
54. Cotella, G.; Evers, D.; Rivolin, U.J.; Solly, A.; Berisha, E. *SUPER—Sustainable Urbanization and Land-Use Practices in European Regions*, 1st ed.; ESPON EGTC, Ed.; ESPON EGTC: Luxembourg, 2020; ISBN 978-29-197-9540-6.
55. Al-Hadad, B.M. Sustainable development in urban planning. In *First International Symposium on Urban Development*; Khoshnaw, F.M., Ed.; WIT Press: Koysinjaq, Iraq, 2013; pp. 227–233.
56. Weingaertner, C. Analysing Synergies between Urbanization and Sustainable Development: Developing a Draft Theory through Historical Pilot Studies. Ph.D. Thesis, KTH, Stockholm, Sweden, 2005.
57. Solly, A.; Berisha, E.; Cotella, G.; Janin Rivolin, U. How Sustainable Are Land Use Tools? A Europe-Wide Typological Investigation. *Sustainability* **2020**, *12*, 1257. [CrossRef]
58. Beriatos, E.; Papageorgiou, M. Towards Sustainable Urbanization and Spatial Planning of the Coastal Zone in Greece and the Mediterranean Basin. In Proceedings of the 46th ISOCARP Congress, Nairobi, Kenya, 19–23 September 2010; ISOCARP Institute, Ed.; ISOCARP Institute: Nairobi, Kenya, 2010; pp. 19–23.
59. Habitat for Humanity. *Housing and the Sustainable Development Goals: The Transformational Impact of Housing*; Habitat for Humanity: Atlanta, GA, USA, 2021.
60. Chatzitheodoridis, F.; Kontogeorgos, A.; Liltsi, P.; Apostolidou, I.; Michailidis, A.; Loizou, E. Women's Cooperatives in less favored and mountainous areas under economic instability. *Agric. Econ. Rev.* **2016**, *17*, 63–79.

61. Kalfas, D.; Chatzitheodoridis, F.; Loizou, E.; Melfou, K. Willingness to Pay for Urban and Suburban Green. *Sustainability* **2022**, *14*, 2332. [CrossRef]
62. Chatzitheodoridis, F.; Melfou, K.; Kontogeorgos, A.; Kalogiannidis, S. Exploring Key Aspects of an Integrated Sustainable Urban Development Strategy in Greece: The Case of Thessaloniki City. *Smart Cities* **2023**, *6*, 19–39. [CrossRef]
63. Chatzitheodoridis, F.; Kontogeorgos, A. Exploring of a Small-Scale Tourism Product under Economic Instability: The Case of a Greek Rural Border Area. *Economies* **2020**, *8*, 52. [CrossRef]
64. Nagy, S.; Somosi, M.V. The relationship between social innovation and digital economy and society. *Reg. Stat.* **2022**, *12*, 3–29. [CrossRef]
65. Panuccio, P. Smart Planning: From City to Territorial System. *Sustainability* **2019**, *11*, 7184. [CrossRef]
66. UN-Habitat. *Implementation of the New Urban Agenda in Europe and North America. A Review in Preparation for the Second Quadrennial Report (2022)*; UN-Habitat: Nairobi, Kenya, 2022.
67. Cox, L.; Hansen, V.; Andrews, J.; Thomas, J.; Heilke, I.; Flanders, N.; Walters, C.; Jacobs, A.S.; Yuan, Y.; Zimmer, A.; et al. *Land Use: A Powerful Determinant of Sustainable & Healthy Communities*; US Environmental Protection Agency: Boston, MA, USA, 2013.
68. Yamane, T. *Research Methodology/Sample Size*; University of Florida: Gainesville, FL, USA, 1973.
69. Singh, A.S.; Masuku, M.B. Sampling techniques & determination of sample size in applied statistics research: An overview. *Int. J. Econ. Commer. Manag.* **2014**, *2*, 1–22.
70. Kalogiannidis, S.; Kalfas, D.; Loizou, E.; Chatzitheodoridis, F. Forestry Bioeconomy Contribution on Socioeconomic Development: Evidence from Greece. *Land* **2022**, *11*, 2139. [CrossRef]
71. Kalogiannidis, S.; Kalfas, D.; Chatzitheodoridis, F.; Papaevangelou, O. Role of Crop-Protection Technologies in Sustainable Agricultural Productivity and Management. *Land* **2022**, *11*, 1680. [CrossRef]
72. Kalogiannidis, S.; Toska, E.; Chatzitheodoridis, F.; Kalfas, D. Using School Systems as a Hub for Risk and Disaster Management: A Case Study of Greece. *Risks* **2022**, *10*, 89. [CrossRef]
73. Kalogiannidis, S.; Kalfas, D.; Chatzitheodoridis, F.; Kontsas, S. The Impact of Digitalization in Supporting the Performance of Circular Economy: A Case Study of Greece. *J. Risk Financ. Manag.* **2022**, *15*, 349. [CrossRef]
74. Kalogiannidis, S.; Loizou, E.; Kalfas, D.; Chatzitheodoridis, F. Local and Regional Management Approaches for the Redesign of Local Development: A Case Study of Greece. *Adm. Sci.* **2022**, *12*, 69. [CrossRef]
75. Lynch, K. Sustainable Urbanisation. In *Global Environmental Issues*; Frances, H., Ed.; John Wiley & Sons, Ltd.: New York, NY, USA, 2012; pp. 201–235. ISBN 9781119950981.
76. UN-Habitat. *Sustainable Urbanization: Achieving Agenda 21*; UN-Habitat: Nairobi, Kenya, 2002.

urban science

MDPI

Article

Enumerating and Modelling the Seasonal alterations of Surface Urban Heat and Cool Island: A Case Study over Indian Cities

Vinayak Bhanage [1,2], Sneha Kulkarni [3,*], Rajat Sharma [4], Han Soo Lee [2,5] and Shirishkumar Gedam [1]

1 Centre of Studies in Resources Engineering, IIT Bombay, Powai, Mumbai 400076, India
2 Transdisciplinary Science and Engineering Program, Graduate School of Advanced Science and Engineering, Hiroshima University, Hiroshima 739-8529, Japan
3 Institute of Engineering Innovation, School of Engineering, The University of Tokyo, Tokyo 113-8656, Japan
4 School of Energy & Environment, Thapar Institute of Engineering & Technology, Patiala 147004, India
5 Centre for Planetary Health and Innovation Science, The IDEC Institute, Hiroshima University, Hiroshima 739-8529, Japan
* Correspondence: sneha.kulkarni@sogo.t.u-tokyo.ac.jp

Abstract: The present study has been carried out to analyze the seasonal variation of the Urban Heat and Cool Island over the nine developing cities of India. The magnitude of urban heat/cool island and vegetation gradient (ΔNDVI) were measured from the daytime satellite datasets. Results of this study show that during the pre-monsoon (March to May) season, the maximum magnitude of the Surface Urban Heat Island (SUHI) was experienced over Kolhapur city, whereas, in the winter, the highest intensity of SUHI was noticed over Pune city. Subsequently, outcomes also depict that the changes in ΔNDVI restrain the pre-monsoon means and the seasonal alterations in SUHI magnitude. However, during the winter (November to February) season, it is controlled by the temperature–vegetation conditions of the rural areas. For pre-monsoon and seasonal changes in SUHI, with the aid of ΔNDVI and the surface temperature of the urban area, regression equations were fitted for pre-monsoon and seasonal changes in SUHI, which explains nearly 90% of SUHI variation. Similarly, the variation of SUHI has been modeled for winter, which elucidates up to 84% of SUHI discrepancy. The study reveals that, on a seasonal scale, a decrement of 0.1 in seasonal ΔNDVI leads to an increase in the seasonal intensity of SUHI by 1.74 °C, which is quite a significant augmentation.

Keywords: MODIS; NDVI; seasonal variation; Surface Urban Heat Island; vegetation gradient

1. Introduction

Urbanization is the process where an increasing percentage of a population lives in cities and suburban areas. This process is often linked to industrialization and modernization, as many people shift from rural to urban areas [1]. These urban areas generate their climatic domain dissimilar from their surrounding rural area as they have different land surface properties, partitions of surface energy balance, urban geometry, soil moisture, vehicle density, etc. [2]. This disparity between the urban and rural areas in various physical and biophysical properties leads to a local scale modification of an urban climate. Though the overall spatial extent of the urban area is minimal, its entanglement is attached to half of the world's population living in the urban area [3]. The world's total urban area is expanding twice its population growth [4]. Hence, the modifications in the local climate generated by urban areas are imperative to understand its impact on climate and human health.

The phenomenon of the Urban Heat Island (UHI) is one of the best examples of modifying an urban climate mainly caused due to the process of urbanization. It mainly indicates the elevated temperatures in the urbanized area compared to the surrounding rural area [5]. Sometimes depending upon the response of local physical and biophysical factors to the existing climatic conditions leads to negative thermal alteration in the rural area; this phenomenon is known as the Urban Cool Island (UCI) [6]. These UHI and UCI reverberations are consequences of the disturbed cycles of the absorption and redistribution of incoming solar radiation by altered urban and rural surfaces. In the past, several studies have revealed that UHI/UCI can affect human health [6], economic growth [7], emission of greenhouse gases [8], stormwater runoff [9], rate of mortality [10], modification of local climate [11], etc. Thus, it is essential to comprehend the role of various parameters in the formation of UHI to design mitigation strategies to control the contribution of those factors in the development of the UHI/UCI.

Several studies found that alterations in vegetation strength, albedo, and partition of surface energy balance, sky view factor are the major driving factors that regulate the magnitude of the UHI [12–15]. In addition, previous research has shown that these parameters mentioned above can act as proxy variables to explain the phenomenon of UHI/UCI [16]. Most parameters associated with an urban area, such as the sky view factor and vehicle density, remain constant during the pre-monsoon and winter. In contrast, parameters, such as soil moisture, vegetation strength, etc., mainly influence the rural microclimatic conditions and induce alterations in the magnitude of the UHI/UCI concerning the season. Thus, it is essential to model the behavior of the UHI/UCI and quantify the seasonal changes in the magnitude of UHI/UCI related to those seasonally altered variables. To date, various models have been developed and introduced to study the phenomenon of UHI.

There are mainly three types of models viz. Numerical, Physical, and Empirical models to scale out and quantify the seasonal behavior and changes in the UHI/UCI. Each has its advantages and disadvantages. As we know, the spatial extent of the cities is much smaller than the grid size of the global climatic models, which are used as input to the numerical models. Therefore, it is challenging and computationally expensive to model other associated parameters to UHI/UCI. Subsequently, these models are developing continuously; hence, analyzing each parameter and behavior of UHI at stationary conditions is challenging. In earlier studies, physical models are mainly used for dispersion analysis, wind flow pattern, surface roughness analysis, etc. [17]. An approach to empirical modeling depends upon the statistical algorithm. These models mainly deal with an observed dataset. The only limitation of an empirical model is that they are restricted to a particular location. In UHI studies, among all the empirical models, the statistical model is commonly used to model and analyze the relationship of UHI with other physical and meteorological parameters. Several researchers have used this method to quantify and model the impact of UHI [5].

In the case of India, cities are mainly surrounded by agricultural fields, due to which higher albedo, emissivity, and rate of evapotranspiration have been observed over the rural area compared to the nearby urban area. This type of vegetation gradients and evapotranspiration between urban and rural areas leads to lowered surface temperature in rural areas. Throughout this process of evapotranspiration, vegetation releases water vapor into the atmosphere, which contributes to reducing the air temperature. On the contrary, impervious surfaces cover urban areas, such as conventional roofs, roads, and sidewalks. As a result of urban expansion, more vegetation is removed and replaced by more impervious surfaces (i.e., buildings and paving), actuating the reduction in the rate of evapotranspiration that promotes the incremental trends of the temperature inside the urban areas. The vegetation gradient between the urban and rural areas, which decides the magnitude of the UHI, is sensitive to seasonal variation and crop cycle. During the pre-monsoon season, less soil moisture, inactive agricultural practices, and deficient irrigation make rural land temporarily barren, which leads to having hotter surfaces in the rural areas, while due to enough irrigated parklands and roadside vegetation inside the cities makes it cooler than the surrounding rural area which may enhance the magnitude of UCI. Compared to the conditions mentioned above of the pre-monsoon season, in the winter, due to enough precipitation and agricultural practices, it shows the ideal the UHI case where urban areas are warmer than surrounding rural areas. According to [18], nearly all cities in India act as a UCI during the pre-monsoon season, which promotes a higher mortality rate due to the intense heat wave events in the rural areas near the urban vicinity. To resist such events, we need to quantify and understand the role of vegetation gradient between the urban and rural areas on a different spatiotemporal scale to model the behavior of the UHI. Several studies [19,20] have demonstrated the response of UHI and UCI with the rurally dominant parameters during the pre-monsoon and winter seasons. However, little attention has been paid to quantifying the seasonal changes in UHI/UCI associated with the seasonally altered parameters.

The phenomenon of the UHI is mainly divided into three types, i.e., Surface Urban Heat Island, atmospheric urban heat island, and sub-Surface Urban Heat Island. In this study, we mainly focused on the first type of heat island, known as the Surface Urban Heat Island. We will now indicate the Surface Urban Heat Island and surface cool island as the SUHI and SUCI, respectively. The SUHI/SUCI mainly deals with the differences between the urban and rural Land Surface Temperature (LST). In the past, several researchers [21–23] used the LST data obtained from the MODIS satellite has been used to quantify the phenomenon of SUHI. For the western part of the Indian region, Pandya et al. [24] evaluated the quality of LST obtained from the MODIS [24]. He found that LST obtained from the MODIS satellite is well correlated with the ground observation with the bias ranging from 0.7–7.6 °C with the correlation index >0.9. The MODIS LST product has been validated using ground-based measurements and other satellite-based LST products, and the results have shown good agreement with these independent datasets. Therefore, with the help of LST data obtained from the MODIS, this study aims to (1) Analyze and model the seasonal variation of the SUHI/SUCI based on the climatology of SUHI/SUCI; (2) Quantify the seasonal alteration of the SUHI/SUCI concerning seasonally altered parameters.

2. Study Area

The present study was carried out over nine developing cities in India (Figure 1). The population of each city is greater than 0.4 million [25]. These cities mainly span the four states of India, i.e., Maharashtra, Karnataka, Gujarat, and Andhra Pradesh. The physical and land surface characteristics of selected cities are different from each other. At the same time, the local climatic conditions of the cities are also different due to the variation in their topography and geographical location. These cities mainly fall under three climatic zones, i.e., hot and dry, hot and humid, and composite climate [26]. Due to the strong demand in the residential and industrial sectors, major cities, such as Hyderabad, Ahmadabad, Pune, Nashik, and Aurangabad, are seeing rapid urban development growth.

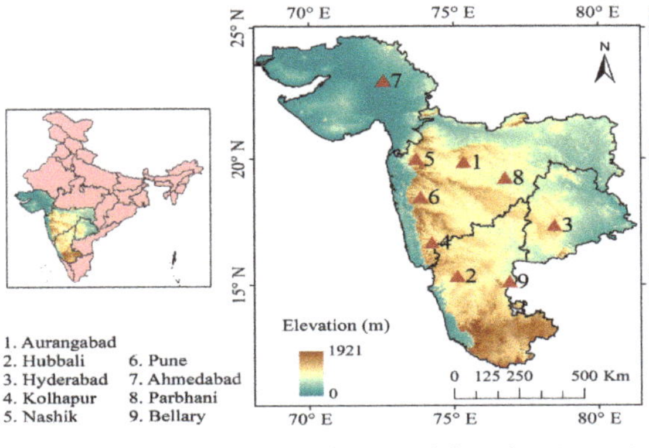

Figure 1. Locations of the selected cities and their elevation variations.

On the other hand, cities, such as Kolhapur, Parbhani, Bellary, and Hubbali, are surrounded by agricultural land where the urbanization rate is low compared to the larger cities. This study has been carried out for the seasons of the pre-monsoon (March, April, and May, MAM) and winter (November, December, January, and February, NDJF). The pre-monsoon and winter seasons have been defined based on the report published by the Indian Meteorological Department (IMD) [27]. Due to cloud cover, the MODIS datasets obtained during the monsoon season (June, July, August, and September, JJAS) did not meet the required quality standards. As a result, we have excluded the monsoon season from our analysis. The Climatological mean pre-monsoon surface temperature of the cities ranges between 39.44 °C to 45.68 °C, while during the winter season, it spans between 30.20 °C to 33.42 °C. The detail information about various physical and meteorological parameters is given in Table 1.

Table 1. Characteristics of selected nine cities of India.

Cities	Geographical Location	Population	Elevation (m)	Area (km^2)	Mean Premonsoon Surface Temperature (°C) (2006–2016)	Mean Winter Surface Temperature (°C) (2006–2016)
Aurangabad	19.87° N 75.34° E	1,508,000	568	139	45.68	31.18
Hubbali	15.36° N 75.12° E	944,000	671	404	42.96	33.32
Hyderabad	17.38° N 78.48° E	6,810,000	505	650	39.44	30.2
Kolhapur	16.7° N 74.24° E	549,236	546	120	41.53	32.05
Nashik	19.99° N 73.70° E	1,486,053	700	268	42.48	31.41
Pune	18.52° N 73.85° E	3,120,000	560	424	42.26	32.12
Ahmedabad	23.02° N 72.57° E	5,307,000	53	464	41.99	30.21
Parbhani	19.26° N 76.77° E	410,445	347	37.8	43.15	32.42
Bellary	15.13° N 76.92° E	3,070,000	485	89.9	43.46	33.42

3. Data and Methodology

3.1. Dataset Used

For this study, we analyzed data collected from MODIS-Terra, i.e., daytime eight-day composite data (MOD11A2) of Land Surface Temperature (LST) and monthly fused data (MOD13A3) of Normalized Difference Vegetation Index (NDVI). These datasets were obtained from the USGS website in a clear sky condition and further processed to maintain the images' quality and equal temporal granularity. In addition, MODIS quality control flags were used to check the quality of the datasets. As a part of pre-processing, the original projection of the datasets, i.e., sinusoidal, is converted to the geographical projection. We know that satellite datasets have their qualms depending upon many other factors. In 2002, Trishchenko et al. [28] studied the impact of the sensor's spectral response function on NDVI measurements to evaluate that it could result in their qualms between 0.02 to 0.06 in the absolute values for the NDVI estimated from the MODIS dataset. NDVI is mainly used to quantify vegetation vigor by measuring the difference between vegetation response within a near-infrared (NIR) and red (RED) channel of the electromagnetic radiation spectrum. It can be calculated by using the following equation:

$$\mathrm{NDVI} = \frac{\mathrm{NIR} - \mathrm{RED}}{\mathrm{NIR} + \mathrm{RED}} \quad (1)$$

In this formula, *NIR* is the reflectance value in the near-infrared band, and Red is the reflectance value in the red band. The values of NDVI range from −1 to 1. The values closer to 1 show higher vegetation vigor, while the measurements closer to −1 represent lower vegetation strength. Several researchers [29,30] conducted their study to compare the MODIS LST with the in situ and the LST retrieved from the other satellites. Their analysis found a good confirmation index between LST obtained from the MODIS and other sources over India and other parts of the world. The secondary data of population, which act as a proxy to various other parameters, such as anthropogenic heat and built-up area, were obtained from the 2011 Census Report, Government of India and utilized. The details about all the datasets and their sources are given in Table 2.

Table 2. Descriptions of the dataset used.

Parameter	Data	Temporal Resolution	Spatial Resolution	Period	References
Land Surface Temperature (Daytime)	MOD11A2	8 Day	1 km	2006–2016	https://lpdaac.usgs.gov/ (accessed on 11 September 2021).
NDVI	MOD13A3	Monthly	1 km	2006–2016	https://lpdaac.usgs.gov.modis (accessed on 11 September 2021).
Population	Census, 2011			2011	http://www.censusindia.gov.in (accessed on 12 August 2021).

3.2. Methodology

LST (8 days) and NDVI (monthly) data were obtained from 2006 to 2016 from MOD11A2 and MOD13A3, respectively. The temporal resolution of both datasets were not equal. Thus, the eight days of LST data were converted to the monthly mean datasets. In the further part, the monthly mean LST and NDVI datasets were converted to the seasonal mean datasets for the pre-monsoon (March to May) and winter (November to February) seasons. The quality of the MODIS datasets during the monsoon (June to September) season was not up to the mark due to the cloud cover; hence, we have not integrated the monsoon season for our analysis. Afterward, all the seasonal data were calculated over the nine developing cities of India for the 11 years, averaged out, and mean Climatological data were prepared for the pre-monsoon and winter. During the entire data pre-processing and preparation procedure, null values in the datasets were excluded. Figure 2 represents a general flow of data processing and methodology flow.

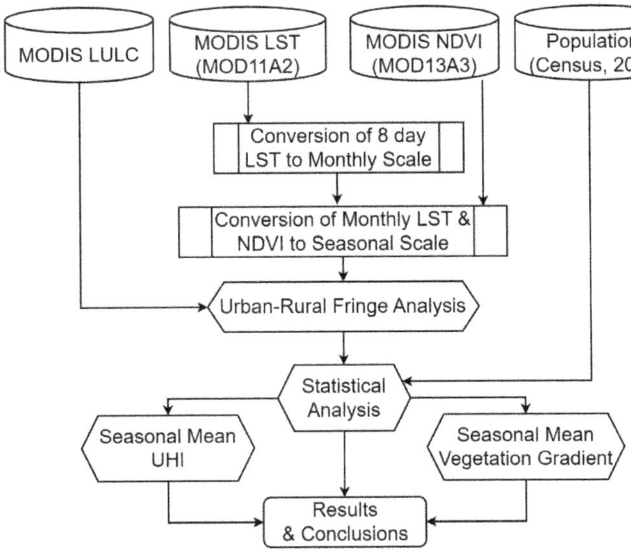

Figure 2. The General flow of methodology followed for this study.

3.2.1. Defining the Boundaries of the Urban and Rural Area

The UHI intensity mainly quantifies the difference in LST between urban and rural areas, so determining the urban and rural area boundary is essential. Urban area expansion is not restricted to municipal boundaries in cities, such as Ahmadabad and Pune. To mark these limits of urban–rural areas accurately, MODIS LULC data are used. Each city's buffer distance from the urban boundaries towards the rural region varies. The buffer distance for the smaller cities lies between 4–6 km, while due to the large urban sprawl, a larger buffer distance, i.e., 7–8 km, was considered for further evaluation. During this analysis, the buffer width is kept constant at 1 km.

3.2.2. Estimation of Surface Urban Heat Island (SUHI)

The method of urban–rural buffer analysis has been adopted to investigate the intensity of the UHI. In this method, the difference in mean LST between the urban and rural areas has been considered to calculate the SUHI magnitude (Equation (1). This method considers the averaged LST of rural buffer areas along each direction of the urban areas as its significant advantage.

$$\Delta T = Tu - Tr, \quad (2)$$

where,

ΔT: Surface Urban Heat Island Intensity (SUHII).
Tu: Mean Land Surface Temperature of the Urban Area.
Tr: Mean Land Surface Temperature of the Rural Buffer Area.

With the equation mentioned above (2) and the averaged LST data obtained for 2006–2016, SUHII for the nine cities has been calculated for both seasons, i.e., pre-monsoon and winter.

3.2.3. Evaluation of Urban-Rural Vegetation Gradient

A recent study documented that the amount of vegetation inside the city or around the rural area influences the magnitude of the SUHI [31]. However, the association between vegetation gradient and the UHI modification is still unexplored. Thus, it is essential to quantify this impact of the vegetation gradient on the SUHI. On a seasonal scale, the vegetation gradient between urban and rural areas alters due to meteorological changes affecting the cities' SUHII. Therefore, at a seasonal scale, it is necessary to elucidate the relationship between vegetation gradient and SUHII. During this study, the vegetation gradient was calculated with the help of averaged values of NDVI data obtained for 2006–2016. In this process, the urban–rural buffer analysis method was adopted to estimate the vegetation gradient over each city.

$$\Delta NDVI = NDVIu - NDVIr, \quad (3)$$

where,

ΔNDVI: vegetation gradient.
Tu: Mean NDVI of the Urban Area.
Tr: Mean NDVI of the Rural Buffer Area.

4. Results and Discussion

4.1. Seasonal Variation of SUHI

For the pre-monsoon and winter seasons, with the aid of 11 years of Terra MODIS LST datasets, the extensiveness of SUHI over the nine developing cities of India was calculated (Figure 3). The analysis shows that, during the pre-monsoon season, the maximum intensity of SUHI (1.47 °C) is observed over Kolhapur, while the minimum magnitude of SUHI (−0.85 °C) is observed over the city of Nashik. In the pre-monsoon season, out of the nine cities, four, viz. Parbhani, Hyderabad, Nashik, and Bellary, represent the Urban Cool Island (SUCI). This SUCI phenomenon mainly arises due to reduced vegetation and rising temperature in the adjacent rural part of the urban areas. Still, in the case of Hyderabad, no higher magnitude has been found in the vegetation of the urban area in both seasons. This phenomenon of the SUCI during the pre-monsoon and winter in Hyderabad may be the effect of a large water body in the middle of the town.

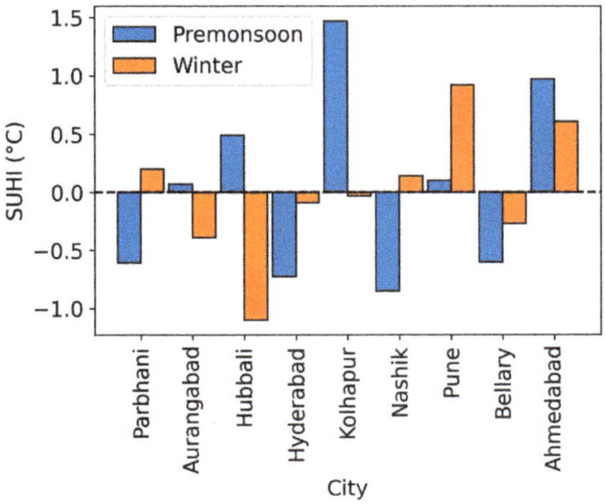

Figure 3. Patterns in the Surface Urban Heat Island (SUHI) over nine Different Cities in India during pre-monsoon (March to May) and winter season (November to February).

In the winter, the maximum intensity of the SUHI is found over Pune City (0.95 °C), followed by Ahmadabad (0.61 °C). Some cities, such as Aurangabad, Hubbali, Kolhapur, Hyderabad, and Bellary, show the negative behavior of the SUHI, i.e., the SUCI, during the winter season.

Figure 4 depicts that in the winter season, in cities experiencing the phenomenon of the SUCI, a negligible difference (−0.003 to −0.009) has been observed in ΔNDVI. On the other hand, cities with a higher magnitude of ΔNDVI represent the typical intensified profile of the UHI during the winter season. These seasonal alterations in the SUHI intensity may have occurred due to the seasonal changes in NDVI.

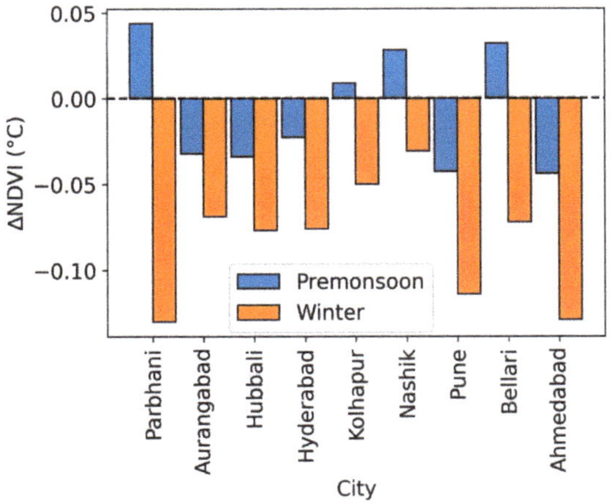

Figure 4. Seasonal Pattern of ΔNDVI over nine Different Cities in India.

4.2. Statistical-Based Modelling of Premonsoon and Winter SUHI

In the further part of the study, a statistical analysis was carried out to explore the association of the SUHI with other vegetation and climatic parameters on a different spatial and temporal scale, which may elucidate the spatial and seasonal variations in the SUHI.

To model the SUHI regression-based statistical model is developed for the pre-monsoon and winter seasons. A simple linear regression was performed between the SUHI and the other variables to identify the suitable forecaster. The other parameters were selected based on former literature and their physical significance to the phenomenon of the SUHI. To establish the SUHI model for the pre-monsoon and winter seasons, we mainly considered the five parameters, i.e., the mean land surface temperature of the urban and rural area, population, the vigor of vegetation in the rural part, and ΔNDVI. As we know, the total amount of incoming solar radiation is approximately equal for adjacent rural and urban areas. Still, the different land surface properties of the urban–rural area led to a difference in the magnitude of surface temperatures, which gave rise to the SUHI.

Thus, during this study, the LST of the urban and rural areas has been taken as a proxy variable to the land surface characteristics of the urban and rural areas, such as albedo, emissivity, heat capacity, etc. Various studies have been conducted, such as [32,33], to explain the negative relationship between temperature and vegetation. The vegetation in a particular territory keeps that area cool through evapotranspiration. Hence, the total amount of vegetation present in the urban and rural areas controls the temperatures of the respective area. It is considered one of the significant parameters that can pedal the magnitude of the SUHI. In addition, the disparity of vegetation strength between urban and rural areas can alter the natural cooling process of the environment, resulting in changes in the temperature difference between urban and surrounding rural areas. Besides these climatic and biophysical parameters, the population of the urban area is a significant factor that plays an essential role in the formation of SUHI. The more population in the urban area represents the high density of buildings, vehicles, roads, low sky view factor, and many industries. It creates more anthropogenic heat that gets discharged and trapped in the urban environment, making the urban area warmer. Hence, the population is also essential for modeling the SUHI effect. Figure 5 represents the correlation coefficient, i.e., R, between SUHI, and other predictors for the pre-monsoon and winter seasons.

During the pre-monsoon season, the significant relationship between ΔNDVI and the SUHI confirms that the difference in the vegetation vigor between urban and rural areas is one of the major factors responsible for developing the phenomenon of the SUHI in the pre-monsoon season. In addition, the association between population and surface temperature of the urban area reveals that an increase in the population of the urban area makes the city warmer. Compared to the pre-monsoon season, the association between the population and Tu becomes stronger during the winter, while the SUHI has the strongest association with Tr. It characterizes Tr as a controller of the SUHI effect for the winter season. Using the above analysis, we constructed the regression-based model for the SUHI during winter and pre-monsoon. We have mainly used three predictors to develop a model for the pre-monsoon season. Tu, population, and ΔNDVI. Likewise, the correlation analysis and the multivariate regression model (Equation (4)) also denotes the dominance of ΔNDVI during the pre-monsoon season. This regression model has a coefficient of determination (R^2) of 0.97 with $p < 0.0001$ and the Root Mean Square Error (RMSE) of 0.28 °C. The ΔNDVI as an alone predictor coefficient of determination (R^2) was 0.65; other variables were added to improve the model's predictability.

$$\text{SUHI in pre-monsoon} = 43.08 - 0.135\,(\text{Tu}) - 20.72\,(\Delta\text{NDVI}) - 0.00000025\,(\text{Population}) \quad (4)$$

During the winter, vegetation coverage in the surrounding rural area is a decisive factor controlling the magnitude of the SUHI. Initially, NDVIr as an alone predictor coefficient of determination (R^2) was 0.62. Thus, to perk up the model performance, additional predictors were added.

$$\text{SUHI in winter} = 107.96 - 0.37\,(\text{Tr}) + 11.08\,(\text{NDVIr}) \quad (5)$$

The model of the SUHI for a winter season has a coefficient of determination (R^2) of 0.89 with $p < 0.0001$ and the RMSE of 0.24 °C.

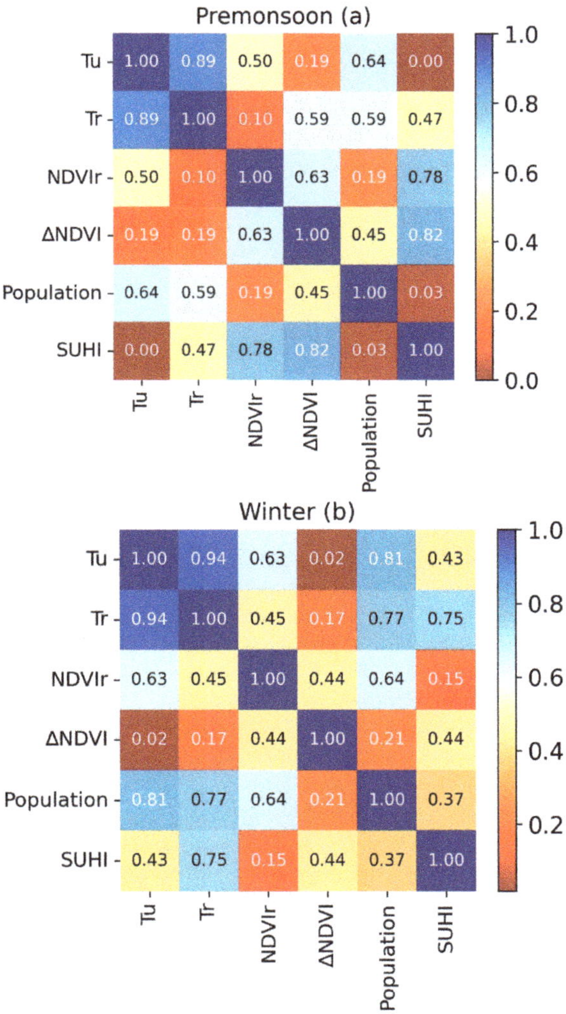

Figure 5. Coefficient of Correlation (R) analysis matrix between SUHI and other parameters for (**a**) Premonsoon and (**b**) Winter season.

4.3. The Relationship between ΔSeasonal SUHI and ΔSeasonal Change in Vegetation

The ΔSeasonal SUHI is obtained by calculating the difference between the mean of the pre-monsoon and wintertime SUHI. At the same time, the ΔSeasonal change in vegetation is retrieved by calculating the disparity of ΔNDVI between both seasons. Figure 6 elucidates the relationship between alteration in the seasonal NDVI and the difference between the seasonal SUHI. The negative affiliation with the correlation coefficient $R = -0.646$ ($p < 0.001$) at a 95% confidence level is found between seasonal change in Sthe UHI and seasonal variation in the difference between urban and rural vegetation. After observing the association between the ΔSeasonal SUHI and ΔSeasonal change in vegetation, it is required to find the significant controlling factors which decide the seasonal alterations in SUHI.

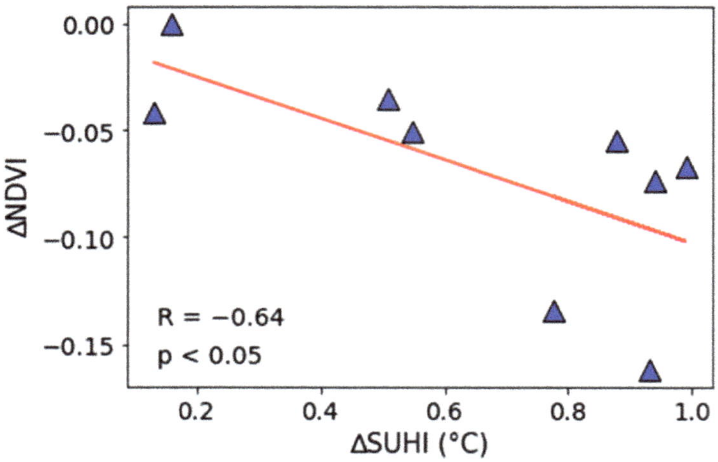

Figure 6. Association between seasonal alterations in ΔNDVI and ΔSUHI over 9 Different Cities in India.

Recently, a few studies noted that agricultural activities in rural areas tend to have more seasonal variation in the land surface properties than in the urban area [20,34]. It suggests that the magnitude of perturbations in LST due to land surface properties is greater over the rural area. Some studies explained that the population data as a proxy for the built-up area, anthropogenic heat, etc. [35]. Thus, to model the ΔSeasonal SUHI, we have used a multivariate regression method and considered three parameters viz. ΔSeasonal change in vegetation, ΔSeasonal rural LST, and population, which quantifies the seasonal change in SUHI, where

$$\Delta\text{Seasonal SUHI} = \text{SUHI winter} - \text{SUHI premonsoon} \quad (6)$$

$$\Delta\text{Seasonal change in vegetation} = \Delta\text{NDVI winter} - \Delta\text{NDVI premonsoon} \quad (7)$$

$$\Delta\text{Seasonal rural LST} = \text{LST of Rural Site (winter)} - \text{LST of Rural Site (premonsoon)} \quad (8)$$

The equation, "ΔSeasonal SUHI = −8.353 + (0.0142) × ΔSeasonal rural LST—(17.40) × ΔSeasonal change in vegetation", explains the changes in the seasonal SUHI with the coefficient of determination $R^2 = 0.68$ where the p-value < 0.005 for all the attributes of the equations. It indicates that a decrement in a ΔSeasonal change in vegetation by 0.1 leads to an increase in the ΔSeasonal SUHI by 1.74 °C, which is quite a significant augmentation if other variables remain constant. Hence, to reduce the intensity of the SUHI at a seasonal scale, it is necessary to reduce the magnitude of ΔSeasonal change in vegetation. The advantage of the above equation is that it can explain the ΔSeasonal SUHI variations of up to 68% over the nine cities in India using the readily available satellite data of NDVI and LST. We consider this equation true, at least for cities under study.

5. Conclusions

This study was mainly divided into two parts, i.e., (1) Assessment of the seasonal variation of SUHI and (2) the response of seasonal alterations in the SUHI to the seasonal variations in the vegetation strength. This study was performed over nine developing cities in India using satellite data for 2006–2016. These nine cities were chosen carefully based on their differences in (a) climatic zones, (b) geographical location, and (c) topographical characteristics.

In this study, during the pre-monsoon (March to May) and winter (November to February) seasons mean intensity of the SUHI and the ΔNDVI were derived for each city. A result shows that the SUHI's magnitude mainly depends upon the ΔNDVI. The positive values of ΔNDVI represent the phenomenon of the Urban Cool Island, where the city of Hyderabad was an exceptional case. In both the pre-monsoon and winter seasons, Hyderabad experiences the SUCI, which may be the effect of a large water body located in the middle of the city. It needs to be analyzed further to validate and quantify the impact of the water body on the SUHI.

Further statistical analysis between the SUHI and other studied variables shows that during the pre-monsoon season, ΔNDVI is the dominant factor which explains 97% of the SUHI with the RMSE of 0.28 °C, while in the winter season temperature of the rural region is the most significant parameter, which describes the 89% of the SUHI with the RMSE of 0.24°. The performed correlation and regression analysis confirms the sensitivity of each parameter to the mean seasonal SUHI so that one can concentrate on specific variables while designing the mitigation strategies for the SUHI. In the second part of the study, we quantified the response of the SUHI to the seasonal changes in vegetation strength. During this analysis, we found that an alteration in the ΔSeasonal change in vegetation explains 68% of the variation in the ΔSeasonal SUHI. As we know, the variation in vegetation strength during the winter and pre-monsoon seasons mainly depend upon the monsoon disparity. Thus, further exploration of seasonal changes in the magnitude of the SUHI and its association with the monsoon variation through its impact on seasonal vegetation strength needs to be evaluated.

Author Contributions: Conceptualization, V.B., S.K., H.S.L. and S.G.; methodology, V.B., S.K., H.S.L. and S.G.; software, V.B. and S.K; formal analysis, V.B., S.K. and R.S.; investigation, V.B., S.K., H.S.L., R.S. and S.G.; writing V.B. and S.K.; supervision, H.S.L. and S.G. All authors have read and agreed to the published version of the manuscript.

Funding: This work is a part of DST-INSPIRE program (DST/INSPIRE/03/2015/005692 IF160608).

Data Availability Statement: Not applicable.

Acknowledgments: V.B. and S.K. are thankful to the IIT Bombay for providing necessary facilities to carry out this research. All the authors are grateful to the editor and anonymous reviewers for their rigorous reviews, which greatly improved the quality of the manuscript. We are also thankful to R. Latha and B.S. Murthy for their support.

Conflicts of Interest: The authors declare no conflict of interest.

References

1. Urbanisation, Demographic Transition, and the Growth of Cities in India. Available online: https://www.theigc.org/sites/default/files/2016/11/Tumbe-2016-Working-paper.pdf (accessed on 15 February 2022).
2. Erell, E.; Pearlmutter, D.; Williamson, T. *Urban Microclimate: Designing the Spaces between Buildings*, 1st ed.; Routledge: Milton Park, UK; Philadelphia, PA, USA, 2011.
3. United Nations. *World Urbanization Prospects: The 2018 Revision*; United Nations: New York, NY, USA, 2018.
4. Angel, S.; Parent, J.; Civco, D.L.; Blei, A.; Potere, D. The dimensions of global urban expansion: Estimates and projections for all countries, 2000–2050. *Prog. Plann.* **2011**, *75*, 53–107. [CrossRef]
5. Oke, T.R. City size and the urban heat island. *Atmos. Environ. Pergamon Press* **1973**, *7*, 769–779. [CrossRef]
6. Heaviside, C.; Vardoulakis, S.; Cai, X.M. Attribution of mortality to the urban heat island during heatwaves in the West Midlands, UK. *Environ. Health* **2016**, *15*. [CrossRef]
7. Santamouris, M.; Cartalis, C.; Synnefa, A.; Kolokotsa, D. On the impact of urban heat island and global warming on the power demand and electricity consumption of buildings—A review. *Energy Build.* **2015**, *98*, 119–124. [CrossRef]
8. Sarrat, C.; Lemonsu, A.; Masson, V.; Guedalia, D. Impact of urban heat island on regional atmospheric pollution. *Atmos. Environ.* **2006**, *40*, 1743–1758. [CrossRef]
9. Li, H.; Harvey, J.T.; Holland, T.J.; Kayhanian, M. Erratum: The use of reflective and permeable pavements as a potential practice for heat island mitigation and stormwater management. *Environ. Res. Lett.* **2013**, *8*, 015023. [CrossRef]
10. Gasparrini, A.; Guo, Y.; Hashizume, M. Mortalité attribuable au froid et à la chaleur: Analyse multi-pays. *Environ. Risques Et Sante* **2015**, *14*, 464–465.
11. Lin, C.Y.; Chen, W.C.; Chang, P.L.; Sheng, Y.F. Impact of the urban heat island effect on precipitation over a complex geographic environment in northern Taiwan. *J. Appl. Meteorol. Climatol.* **2011**, *50*, 339–353. [CrossRef]

12. Spatio-Temporal Analysis of Urban Heat Island Effect For Different Land Use Land Cover Pattern Over Pune Metropolitan Region, India. In Proceedings of the AGU Fall Meeting Abstracts. Available online: https://ui.adsabs.harvard.edu/abs/2019AGUFMGC21I1384B/abstract (accessed on 9 August 2021).
13. Rakoto, P.Y.; Deilami, K.; Hurley, J.; Amati, M.; Sun, Q.C. Revisiting the cooling effects of urban greening: Planning implications of vegetation types and spatial configuration. *Urban. For. Urban. Green.* **2021**, *64*, 127266. [CrossRef]
14. Mariani, L.; Parisi, S.G.; Cola, G.; Lafortezza, R.; Colangelo, G.; Sanesi, G. Climatological analysis of the mitigating effect of vegetation on the urban heat island of Milan, Italy. *Sci. Total Environ.* **2016**, *569*, 762–773. [CrossRef]
15. Vinayak, B.; Lee, H.S.; Gedam, S.; Latha, R. Impacts of future urbanization on urban microclimate and thermal comfort over the Mumbai metropolitan region, India. *Sustain. Cities Soc.* **2022**, *79*. [CrossRef]
16. Bottayan, Z.; Kirsci, A.; Szegedi, S.; Unger, J. The relationship between built-up areas and the spatial development of the mean maximum urban heat island in Debrecen, Hungary. *Int. J. Climatol.* **2005**, *25*, 405–418. [CrossRef]
17. Kanda, M. Progress in the scale modeling of urban climate: Review. *Theor. Appl. Climatol.* **2006**, *84*, 23–33. [CrossRef]
18. Shastri, H.; Ghosh, S.; Paul, S.; Shafizadeh-Moghadam, H.; Helbich, M.; Karmakar, S. Future urban rainfall projections considering the impacts of climate change and urbanization with statistical–dynamical integrated approach. *Clim. Dyn.* **2019**, *52*, 6033–6051. [CrossRef]
19. Shastri, H.; Barik, B.; Ghosh, S.; Venkataraman, C.; Sadavarte, P. Flip flop of Day-night and Summer-Winter Surface Urban Heat Island Intensity in India. *Sci. Rep.* **2017**, *7*, 40178. [CrossRef] [PubMed]
20. Kumar, R.; Mishra, V.; Buzan, J.; Kumar, R.; Shindell, D.; Huber, M. Dominant control of agriculture and irrigation on urban heat island in India. *Sci. Rep.* **2017**, *7*, 14054. [CrossRef] [PubMed]
21. Barat, A.; Kumar, S.; Kumar, P.; Parth Sarthi, P. Characteristics of Surface Urban Heat Island (SUHI) over the Gangetic Plain of Bihar, India. *Asia-Pac. J. Atmos. Sci.* **2018**, *54*, 205–214. [CrossRef]
22. Pramanik, S.; Punia, M. Land use/land cover change and Surface Urban Heat Island intensity: Source–sink landscape-based study in Delhi, India. *Environ. Dev. Sustain.* **2020**, *22*, 7331–7356. [CrossRef]
23. Kumari, P.; Yadav, N.K.; Santra, A.; Upadhayay, U. Identification of urban Heat Islands from multi-temporal Modis land surface temperature data: A case study of the southern part of West Bengal, India. *Int. J. Eng. Sci. Res. Technol.* **2019**, 135–144.
24. Pandya, M.R.; Shah, D.B.; Trivedi, H.J.; Darji, N.P.; Ramakrishnan, R.; Panigrahy, S.; Parihar, J.S.; Kirankumar, A.S. Retrieval of land surface temperature from the Kalpana-1 VHRR data using a single-channel algorithm and its validation over western India. *ISPRS J. Photogramm. Remote Sens.* **2014**, *94*, 160–168. [CrossRef]
25. Census of India Census of India, 2011. *Econ. Polit. Wkly.* **2011**, *46*, 5.
26. Kottek, M.; Grieser, J.; Beck, C.; Rudolf, B.; Rubel, F. World map of the Köppen-Geiger climate classification updated. *Meteorol. Z.* **2006**, *15*, 259–263. [CrossRef]
27. A Technical Note on the Analysis of Modern Meteorological Gridded a Technical Note on the Analysis of Modern Meteorological Gridded Datasets Using Python. Available online: https://www.imdpune.gov.in/Reports/CRSResearchReports/TECHNICAL_REPORT_review.pdf (accessed on 22 November 2022).
28. Trishchenko, A.P.; Cihlar, J.; Li, Z. Effects of spectral response function on surface reflectance and NDVI measured with moderate resolution satellite sensors. *Remote Sens. Environ.* **2002**, *81*, 1–18. [CrossRef]
29. Singh, R.; Singh, C.; Ojha, S.P.; Kumar, A.S.; Kishtawal, C.M.; Kumar, A.S.K. Land surface temperature from INSAT-3D imager data: Retrieval and assimilation in NWP model. *J. Geophys. Res. Atmos.* **2016**, *121*, 6909–6926. [CrossRef]
30. Salama, M.S.; Velde, R.v.d.; Zhong, L.; Ma, Y.; Ofwono, M.; Su, B. Decadal variations of land surface temperature anomalies observed over the Tibetan Plateau by the Special Sensor Microwave Imager (SSM/I) from 1987 to 2008. *Clim. Change* **2012**, *114*, 769–781. [CrossRef]
31. Haashemi, S.; Weng, Q.; Darvishi, A.; Alavipanah, S.K. Seasonal variations of the surface urban heat Island in a semi-arid city. *Remote Sens.* **2016**, *8*, 352. [CrossRef]
32. Weng, Q.; Lu, D.; Schubring, J. Estimation of land surface temperature-vegetation abundance relationship for urban heat island studies. *Remote Sens. Environ.* **2004**, *89*, 467–483. [CrossRef]
33. Boegh, E.; Soegaard, H.; Hanan, N.; Kabat, P.; Lesch, L. A remote sensing study of the NDVI-T(s) relationship and the transpiration from sparse vegetation in the sahel based on high-resolution satellite data. *Remote Sens. Environ.* **1999**, *69*, 224–240. [CrossRef]
34. Zhou, D.; Xiao, J.; Bonafoni, S.; Berger, C.; Deilami, K.; Zhou, Y.; Frolking, S.; Yao, R.; Qiao, Z.; Sobrino, J.A. Satellite remote sensing of Surface Urban Heat Islands: Progress, challenges, and perspectives. *Remote Sens.* **2019**, *11*, 48. [CrossRef]
35. Zeug, G.; Eckert, S. Population growth and its expression in spatial built-up patterns: The sana'a, yemen case study. *Remote Sens.* **2010**, *2*, 1014–1034. [CrossRef]

urban science

MDPI

Article

Developing Effective Project Management Strategy for Urban Flood Disaster Prevention Project in EDO State Capital, Nigeria

Chima Ibeanu [1], Mazyar Ghadiri Nejad [2] and Matina Ghasemi [3,*]

1 Industrial Engineering Department, Girne American University, 99428 Kyrenia, Cyprus
2 Industrial Engineering Department, Cyprus International University, 99258 Nicosia, Cyprus
3 Business and Economic Department, Girne American University, 99428 Kyrenia, Cyprus
* Correspondence: matinaghasemi@gau.edu.tr

Abstract: Emphasizing the need to provide a coordinated flood management strategy in the country and avoid acting in an isolated way when it occurs, improving the attitude of flood control during floods, and controlling floods with comprehensive analysis are among the main purposes of the current study. In this study, the environment's physical, technological, social, economic, and political characteristics are considered to assess the urban flood risk. This study entails a discussion of flood hazard control in Benin City, the capital city of Edo State of Nigeria. The research methodology involves employing both interviews and questionnaire distribution. First, three key persons involved in flood control are interviewed at the State Emergency Management Agency (SEMA), which coordinates disaster risk reduction in the state, and then, the responses are classified into themes that are used to prepare the questionnaire to be distributed in four main regions. The questionnaires are distributed to the employees in institutions concerned with flood control and to the general population living in the region. Based on the obtained results from the interviews, some methods that could be applicable in controlling flooding in the region are listed. The results showed that the most important ones are flood warning systems, flood prevention through using the building resilient infrastructure and community programs, protection and mitigation through using natural processes, and strategic implementation of a flood emergency plan through sustainability.

Keywords: urban flood; disaster prevention; project management; flooding; Nigeria

1. Introduction

A flood is caused by a river, stream, or channel that overflows its banks and floods large areas of dry land. Changing weather patterns and global warming have led to more widespread flooding in urban areas [1,2]. When it comes to dealing with pollution, local governments in developing countries face huge obstacles and problems. Flooding in urban areas is a threat to the environment as well as human health and safety, especially in infrastructure and service delivery areas, which are critical to the long-term existence of cities [3,4]. As many people believe, the negative impact of flooding on the economy is not limited to the loss of customers and inventory. Even more harmful is the ripple effect that power and transportation disruptions have over a larger geographic area [5,6].

Flood is a global phenomenon that affects all aspects of human society due to its extent. Unsustainable human activities and climate events have the potential to derail the 17th UN Sustainable Development Goals, as they reverse the progress made possible through international cooperation and already achieved in eradicating extreme poverty and disease. Flooding is one of the key contributors to climate-related hazardous events that disproportionately affect poor countries due to their vulnerability. The International Federation of Red Cross and Red Crescent Societies conducted a study showing that flood disasters caused more deaths and injuries than any other natural or technological disaster between 1993 and 2002 [7,8]. There have been flood disasters in many different regions around Nigeria, as virtually every state has been affected by floods at some point in its history.

According to Hasson et al. [9], successful or sustainable flood protection project management can help reduce long-term flood losses and community suffering. The best or most sustainable project management strategies (PMS) to deal with the ongoing issue of floods are still being pursued by many countries and governments, especially those that are plagued by floods. This research aims to find ways to manage floods in order to minimize and even prevent the disasters in Nigeria as well as the problems and dangers these communities face as a result of floods. Benin City, the capital of Edo State in southern Nigeria, is considered as a case study. Due to the location, temperature, flora, and soils of Benin City, as well as the city's population numbers and settlement patterns of the city, the city is highly vulnerable to climate-related consequences such as floods and other natural disasters. Experimental field results are classified using a combination of primary and secondary data.

2. Literature Review

2.1. *Urban Flood Disaster*

Given the frequency of flooding, it is critical to consider physical hazards and socio-economic impacts during a thorough survey. Effective assessment of flood disasters, as well as other environmental disasters, can be made by examining the effects that disaster has had on past, present, and future events [10]. Flash floods and river floods are the two most common types of floods in the United States [11]. Depending on the amount of received rainfall, flash floods can occur within minutes or hours of heavy rainfall. However, these floods only last for a short time, and the entire region is not affected. River flooding is a natural and inevitable element of the river's life cycle and cannot be avoided. Floods caused by rivers may occur when rivers, streams, or water channels overflow their banks due to heavy rains upstream. In general, if there is significant rainfall upstream, river flooding may occur [12].

In a study, researchers summarized the main causes of floods as climate changes caused by high-level rainfall, temperature changes, and human activities such as construction works including water reservoirs, modification of canals, and changes in land use patterns, all of which have a combined impact on perennial flooding [13]. It is described as the change in the amount of precipitation that falls at a particular location over time, as measured by International Standard Time (IST) [14].

According to Alam [15], Dhaka in Senegal (Africa) has not yet completed the implementation of its city master plan (CMP), claiming that the city's development control laws are ineffective and the city's CMP has not yet been fully implemented. There was the following wave of land development by landowners, some of whom did not even seek plan clearance before commencing their projects, resulting in the distorting of the natural drainage setting and, as a consequence of the floods, a significant increase in flooding in the region. Furthermore, drainage restriction is another key element contributing to the recurrence of floods in the Dhaka metropolitan area. The tendency of blocking drainage systems, according to Alam [15], only serves to worsen the issue, which finally results in floods. He went on to remark that the city's poor drainage capacity is also a contributing element to the city's chronic flooding problems. This study revealed that drainage blockage and an insufficient drainage capacity to meet the city's rising population are important challenges in Edo State capital, Nigeria, and these issues are contributing reasons to the city's chronic flooding problems. Because of these circumstances, the Capital City Development Agency is obligated to destroy developments that hinder drainage systems in the vast majority of situations. In addition, there is a lack of coordination between flood prevention PMSs in the agencies while managing structural aspects of flood protection, and failures to include non-structural aspects of flood prevention projects, such as laws, public participation, awareness building, and appropriate plans, among other things. On the other hand, the literature on public engagement and awareness campaigns is severely lacking when it comes to the people of Edo State. Table 1 presents an overview of some recent flood disasters in Nigeria, as summarized by Ismail et al. [16].

Table 1. A review of some flood disaster cases in Nigeria.

Year	Location	Cause	Estimated Damage
2001	Abia, Adamawa, and Akwa-Ibom States	Rainfall	5000 people affected
2001	Zamfara State	Rainfall	12,300 people displaced
2005	Taraba State	Rainfall	50,000 people displaced
2008	Imo State	Rainfall	12,250 people displaced
2008	Edo State (Benin City)	Rainfall	20 houses collapsed and 4 dead
2008	Benue State	Rainfall	Destroyed 350 houses
2012	Plateau State	Rainfall leading to overflow of Lamingo dam	39 people dead, 200 homes submerged, 3000 people displaced

According to some of the world's top experts on project management, understanding an effective PMS and putting it into practice is vitally important to the success of any project [17]. According to the literature, project management has not been as effective as it might have been in terms of project delivery and improvement [8,18]. It was discovered that, even when initiatives were completed on time and under budget, the effects were, on average, less effective and less long-lasting [18].

A PMS is used in the managing of a project, as opposed to the concept of a "project strategy", which may be applied to a project in the management of the project, i.e., a high-level plan to achieve the project objectives [8]. Furthermore, it is said that the meaning of "strategy" varies depending on the academic and may vary from an overall strategy to a basic plan. According to academics, current literature has not yet embraced the merging of the concepts of "project management" and "strategic planning", even though they are both important. Despite this, the most important component of a PMS is to guarantee that the project achieves its objectives, is completed within financial constraints, and is completed on schedule, all of which contribute to the success of the project management process [19].

In their inquiry, Carvalho et al. [18] discovered a gap in the literature on the relationship between project success/failure and project management methodologies, which they filled. According to Newton [19], project management success has historically been defined as the achievement of project objectives in terms of money, time, and quality within the framework of a given project. Flood disaster management has three main steps: flood forecasting, runoff reduction, and flood peaks by volume reduction [20].

2.2. *Project Management Strategy for Urban Flood Disaster*

In order to evaluate the role of project management and its strategies for urban flood disasters, there are several studies that are considered here.

Kim et al. [21] emphasized improving developing countries' current management and laws and regulations. Later, Verweij et al. [22] illustrated that there is no sufficient single policy tool that can be considered to achieve success. In this regard, they proposed three useful combinations for policy instruments, including integrated contracting, project management, and non-government combinations. In another study, it was mentioned that not only decision-makers should monitor the processes, but also they should analyze the obtained results in this regard [23]. According to the study conducted by Komolafe et al. [24], all hydrological processes, advanced flood forecasting models, and flood risks should be discussed and investigated in an integrated manner, and mapping should be done more accurately and in more detail.

In 2016, Nkwunonwo conducted a study to identify cognitive limitations in flood management in Nigeria [25]. The author mentioned that Nigeria's main cause of floods is climate change and a lack of proper urban planning. According to the information obtained, between 1985 and 2014, the destructive effects of floods, which included a cost of 17 billion USD, affected 11 million people, including 1100 deaths.

Moreover, the findings of research considering the participants' point of view, conducted by Adelekan [26], showed that about 50% of the respondents to the questions had experienced at least a flood in their lives. This is while in Abeokuta or other places in Nigeria, more than 66% of these people did not anticipate the recurrence of floods in their minds and did not have the necessary preparation to deal with such an issue, while there was no warning before the flood occurred in these areas.

According to Adelekan and Asiyanbi [27], understanding the social aspects of risks is one of the most important pillars of risk management. According to them, urban management in the field of floods is often focused on quantitative studies regarding the vulnerability and flexibility of the flooded population; however, structural social actions are taken using these results. Therefore, the understanding level of the residents of flooded areas, their concerns, paradigm approach, and psychometrics have been investigated in that study [27].

3. Methodology

This section discusses the processes and methods that are used in the course of performing this study in order to achieve the objective of designing an effective PMS for flood protection projects in the Edo State of Nigeria. The qualitative data methodology is used extensively in this study, with a small amount of quantitative data included in the data analysis part in order to confirm a conclusion made during the interviews.

A purposive selection of participants is required for this study, which informed the decision to use the purposive sampling method, which included three key stakeholders in the flood prevention project in the state: a project manager, a principal town planning officer, and a senior government official in the flood prevention projects in Edo State capital. Semi-structured interviews were conducted with the three key stakeholders and questions to be asked were drawn from previous literature. The responses of these key persons were classified into themes and presented in a table. The most popular or most common themes were selected and these themes were used to construct a questionnaire that would be given to two groups of people, including the general population and employees of important organizations concerned with fighting flooding in the area. The responses from the two populations were compared and conclusions drawn from the results.

3.1. Primary Data

For this study, primary data in the form of interviews are collected and thoroughly examined. According to researchers, open-ended questions allow respondents to speak more freely from their point of view, while also allowing the interviewer to uncover new ways of comprehending and seeing the subject under conversation [28]. This is achieved by allowing important issues to be discussed that depart from the Interview guide.

The study begins with coding the transcribed interviews and categorizing them into the most significant themes, after which the most highlighted topics are selected to form the summary of results, as shown in the diagram below. Figure 1 illustrates the thematic analysis procedure for this study.

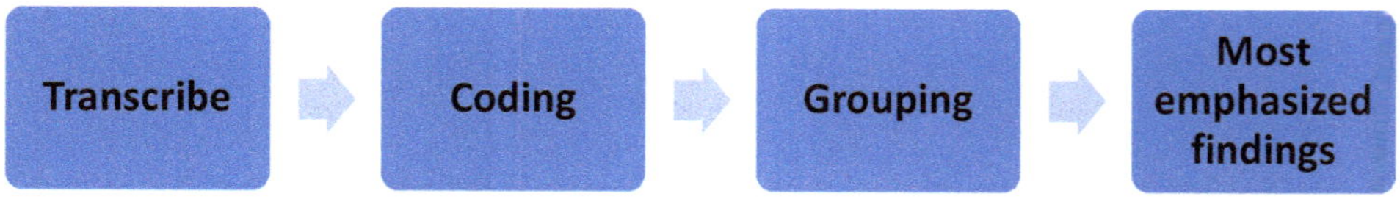

Figure 1. Thematic analysis procedure.

3.2. Validity and Reliability

Having confidence in a piece of research is important because it allows the public to have some trust in it, and it ensures that the measures used are as close to true measures as possible. Having confidence in the validity of a piece of research is also important because it informs the public whether or not what is measured is actually what is intended to be measured, and this is equally important. As a result, the deliverables of this project are evaluated by an expert in urban projects in this respect. Additionally, the supervisor of this study is active in confirming all of the sources of data obtained as well as the sort of data that is appropriate for the project's objective throughout the duration of the project. The conclusions from the interviews are further supported by a study from the Capital City Development Authority, which included an illustration of a drainage obstruction and statistical data on the consequences of floods.

3.3. Case Study

Benin City is the administrative and economic hub of Edo State, Nigeria, and is home to over a million people. This tropical urban community is characterized by its high humidity and temperature. It is comprised of three main local government areas: Oredo, Egor, and IkpobaOkha. The city of Benin is located on a short, key-shaped piece of land in West Africa that runs north to south. The land area is about 1125 km^2 and is located on relatively flat terrain at an elevation of averaging 200 m above sea level. It is situated between latitudes 6440 N and 6210 N and longitudes 5350 E and 5440 E [29]. Figure 2 shows the map of Edo State.

Figure 2. Map of Edo State.

The weather in Benin City is hot and humid most of the year. The wet season lasts from April to November, while the dry season lasts from December to early March. The temperature in Benin City is quite high, with an average daily temperature of around 28 degrees Celsius in the dry season and approximately 24 degrees Celsius in the wet season. The temperature range in the research region is rather minimal. During the rainy or wet season, Benin City and its surroundings get a lot of rain, particularly in the morning. Rainfall is present throughout the year, with an annual total of 2000–2300 mm and a monthly average of over 170 mm. This heavy rainfall is caused by significant evapotranspiration in the metropolitan region as a result of the high temperatures that have prevailed. In addition, high in the study region is relative humidity, which may reach up to 80 percent during the rainy season and 70 percent during the dry season in the summer [29].

Edo State has many unique relief zones, including the Northern Plateau, the Orle Valley, the Esan Plateau, the Benin lowlands, and swamp woods. It is composed of six sorts of physical elements that make up the landscape of Edo State. In Benin City, lowlands are found in a sandy coastal plain and alluvium clay, with some hills in the east, as well as in a sandy coastal plain. Slopes are filled in the direction of the southwest. The region is drained by the rivers Osse, Orhionmwon, and Ikpoba. In addition to having a huge flood plain throughout the River Osse's course, the other rivers are characterized by sharply incised valleys in their upper courses, which grow progressively wider as they flow into the River Ethiope in Delta State [30]. The Northern Plateau consists mostly of foundation rock, ranging in elevation from 183 to 305 m above sea level, with rare granite summits reaching beyond 610 m. Sandstone dominates the southern half of the mountain. The Afemai Hills rise to a height of 672 m above sea level, making them the highest point in the state. Orle Valley is created by an east–west river that cuts through the sandstone between the Northern Plateau and the Esan Plateau, resulting in the formation of a narrow gorge. The Plateau is drained by the rivers Owan and Orle, which flow west and east, respectively. The Esan Plateau, which extends from 213 to 305 m above sea level, is a continuation of the sandstone of the Northern Plateau [29].

4. Results

The obtained results are presented in three different categories of classification of experts' responses into themes, obtained responses from a questionnaire distributed to citizens, and obtained responses from a questionnaire distributed to employees of key organizations. Afterwards, comparing responses of the first and second surveys are presented.

4.1. Classification of Experts' Responses into Themes

Following the thematic analysis procedure, the responses from the interview of the key persons in the State Emergency Management Agency (SEMA), which coordinates Disaster Risk Reduction at the State level, are classified into themes based on keywords. The summary of the coding and classification is given in Table 2.

The interview responses from the key stakeholders, including a project manager, a principal town planning officer, and a senior government official in the flood prevention projects in Edo State capital, were classified into themes and presented in Table 2. These themes were arranged from the most popular to the least popular, which is simply the number of times one or more of the keywords associated with the themes were mentioned. The most popular themes (Themes 1, 2, 3, and 4) were selected to be scrutinized below.

Theme 1. Flood Warning system to ensure timely response against the threat of flood.

Edo State is widely known as an agricultural-based region and it is super dependent on seasonal characteristics of rainfall. In fact, recent studies have shown that rainfall variability is a real threat that cannot be ignored [31–33]. Agricultural growth has been largely affected by natural climate variability and extreme climate events like flooding, which have led to a massive decline in food productivity that has, in turn, caused food insecurity and poverty, especially in rural areas. The knowledge of this has prompted farmers to accept scientific forecasting as a way to access climate variability [32,33].

Theme 2. Flood prevention through using building resilient infrastructure and communities program.

Table 2. Summary of coding and classification of themes.

Theme Number	Themes	Keywords	Frequency (Number of Responses)
Theme 1	Flood warning system to ensure timely response against the threat of flood	Early warning systems; weather forecasts; access to information and warnings.	3
Theme 2	Flood prevention through using building resilient infrastructure and communities program	Floodproofing measures; improved traffic access; constructing dams, levees, bridges, and culverts.	3
Theme 3	Flood prevention, protection, and mitigation through using natural processes	Land use planning controls; catchment flood modeling; planting of shrubs and cover crops; construction of appropriate water channels.	3
Theme 4	Strategic implementation of flood emergency plan through sustainability	Maintenance of existing infrastructure; developing and improving maintenance structures.	3
Theme 5	Flood preparedness through understanding and awareness	Household emergency plan; access to information; understanding and awareness; educating citizens and stakeholders.	2
Theme 6	Flood mitigation through floodplain regulations	National flood insurance program; land use regulations; laws against deforestation; land zoning; subdivision regulations; development and redevelopment policies.	2
Theme 7	Flood prevention and mitigation through joint and coordinated action	Joint bodies; Government bodies and commissions; global water partnership; sustainable development goals; public awareness and public participation; flood insurance.	2
Theme 8	Flood prevention and mitigation through research, education, and exchange of knowledge	Research; research outputs from European countries; training and mentoring.	1
Theme 9	Flood prevention through water retention and non-structural measures	Water treatment plants; irrigation for farmlands.	1

The importance of building resilience, as part of disaster recovery strategies, reduce losses by ensuring the continuous provision of service, including shelter, health care, education, utilities, transportation, and other services [34]. Furthermore, it provides recommendations for future research into this area, including possible links between housing affordability challenges and physical environments. These issues are addressed by highlighting the opportunities for affordable housing development in urban areas, increasing population growth by reducing land use, expanding the public transit system, and decreasing air pollution. It provides information about how the implementation of an appropriate building design plan can lead to sustainable and affordable construction projects by focusing on several key areas [35]. Flood protection is achievable through enhancing resilience by strengthening physical environments that are essential in mitigating stormwater.

Theme 3. Flood prevention, protection, and mitigation through using natural processes.

Experience has shown that effective flood prevention and protection measures need to be taken in the watershed and that it is important to keep the interrelationships and interactions of the results of measures in mind. It is clear that there is a need to organize water management systems and improve forecasting, flood protection, and disaster relief measures based on the watershed. This can be carried out in cooperation with relevant institutions in the fields of hydrology and meteorology, emission reduction planning, water resource restoration, disaster management, and crisis prevention. In addition, there is a need for embedded technology. Flood prevention, safety, and mitigation require a very good mix of structural, preventive, and practical measures in all flood situations: building codes to keep systems out of flood-prone areas, proper land use, and designed floodplains with safety and control. Systems need to be developed in consideration of flood development plans, mitigation, early warning structures, careful verbal risk allocation, and flood preparedness [36–38]. In some cases, it is even advisable to change the sport and have unusually threatened housing.

Theme 4. Strategic implementation of flood emergency planning through sustainability.

As per the results of the study, comprehensive contingency plans must be organized at the local levels of the city to adequately and timely respond to floods and maintain operational popularity in all places where flooding can occur due to direct flooding, dams, dam failure, and various related problems and many others. To build the capacity and readiness of companies forced into the sport of flood protection.

4.2. Responses from Questionnaire Distributed to Citizens

Regarding the demographic characteristics, the results presented that of the total respondents, 83 were males and 125 of the respondents were females. This result represents a percentage of 39.9% and 60.1%, respectively. The majority of the respondents, 139, were less than 30 years old, while 41 were between 30 and 40 years of age, 21 were between 40 and 50 years old, and 7 of the respondents were between 50 and 60 years old. In terms of the relationship status of the respondents, 135 of the total respondents were single, 52 were married, 17 were currently divorced, and 4 chose not to identify within these categories. In terms of educational qualification, 11 of the respondents had a higher school diploma and below, 41 of them possessed an associate diploma, 85 possessed bachelor's degree from a university, 59 possessed postgraduate degrees, including M.Sc. and Ph.D., while 12 of them did not fall within these categories. This report shows that the majority of the respondents were educated, as a total of 69.3% possess at least a B.Sc. degree. Table 3 presents the information related to questionnaire distributions and retrieves in the three mentioned locations in this study.

Table 3. Questionnaires administered per area.

Location	Number of Questionnaires Distributed	%	Number of Questionnaires Retrieved	% of Questionnaires Distributed to Locations	% of Total
Upper mission/Lawani	75	25%	54	72%	26%
Ugbowo/UNIBEN Area	75	25%	52	69%	25%
Oba Market/Akpakpava area	75	25%	51	68%	24 5%
Murtala Mohammed Area (MMA)	75	25%	51	68%	24 5%
	300	100%	208		100%

At the state level, the State Emergency Management Agency (SEMA) is in charge of Disaster Risk Reduction (DRR). SEMA is tasked with administering policies that benefit the most vulnerable communities and areas. At local levels, SEMA has established volunteer schemes from local communities, such as the Emergency Management Vanguard (EMV), but the activities of these groups are unsustainable as they only engage in awareness campaigns during a disaster event. Moreover, they provide an immediate response to emergencies before the arrival of relevant agencies. The six managers that were interviewed in this study, were from the State Emergency Management Agency (SEMA) with headquarters in Benin City.

In terms of employment status, 49 of the respondents were self-employed, representing 23.6% of the sample population, 71 were currently employed, which represents 34.1% of the sample population, 59 were currently unemployed that represents the second largest group with 28.4%, while 29 of the respondents, 13.9%, were currently studying for their degrees.

From the obtained results, it can be concluded that the general population agrees with the key officers who were interviewed in the first part of the thesis. This is because the majority of the respondents in this study either agreed or strongly agreed with the points asked; 40.4% of the respondents agreed, while 13% strongly agreed with the point that flood warning systems are necessary for timely response in order to deal with the threat of flood. In total, 48.6% agreed and 13.8% strongly agreed that a flood warning system requires an effective forecast system through an experts forecasting team; 52.4% agreed and 21.6% strongly agreed that the main risk in the operating of early warning systems is the possibility of false alarms due to poor or too high forecasts. A total of 39.9% agreed and 31.7% strongly agreed with the point that flood prevention, safety, and mitigation require a very good mix of structural, preventive, and practical measures in all flood situations.

Furthermore, 47.6% agreed and 26.9% of the respondents strongly agreed that project management and other government institutions of Nigeria should collaborate to control the hazards of flooding. 37.5% and 35.6% agreed and strongly agreed that maintenance and improvement of current infrastructure are very important when dealing with flooding problems. Lastly, 45.2% and 23.1% agreed and strongly agreed that public awareness is necessary to combat flooding. From this result, it can be concluded that the general population is aware of the issue of flooding, its dangers, and control measures that must be put in place in order to address the issue.

The main responses obtained and concluded from the citizens are listed in the following:

- To deal with the threat of flood, a flood-warning system is necessary;
- A flood warning system requires an effective forecast system through an expert forecasting team;
- The main risk in the operation of early warning systems is the possibility of false alarms due to poor or too high forecasts.
- Collaboration of multiple institutions in Nigeria can plan measures related to restoration and environmental protection, which can also restore or protect these opportunities for weed growth and reduce flood risk;
- Climate forecasts are a major source of uncertainty, especially at the regional or local level, but other elements, including social and economic changes, are also important for climate resilience;
- A mix of structural, preventive, and practical measures in all flood situations, flood prevention, safety, and mitigation;
- Public awareness is necessary to combat flooding, as there may be a desire to adjust or even restrict the use, including industrial, agricultural, recreational, or personal use, to reduce potential damage;
- Floods occur when soil becomes saturated and its infiltration capacity is zero;
- Project management and other government institutions of Nigeria should collaborate to control the hazards of flooding;
- Maintenance and improvement of current infrastructure are very important when dealing with flooding problems;
- Taking Preventive measures for flooding hazards is inevitable to overcome flood management issues.

4.3. Responses from Questionnaires Distributed to Employees of Key Organizations

According to the results, 33 of the total respondents were male, while 17 were female; these figures represent 66% and 34% of the sample size, respectively. Only 3 of the respondents were less than 30 years old, with a percentage of 6%; 11 belonged to the category of 30 to 40, with 22%. A total of 21 and 15 were in the categories of 40 to 50 and from 50 to 60 years old, respectively, showing that most of the respondents were found to be between 40 and 50. In terms of the relationship status of the respondents, the majority of the respondents, 27 of them, were married, one was divorced, 17 were single, and 5 of them chose not to identify within these categories. In terms of educational qualification, 1 of the respondents had a higher school diploma and below, 11 of them possessed the associate diploma, 22 possessed bachelor's degree from a university, 15 possessed postgraduate degrees including M.Sc. and Ph.D., while 1 of them did not fall within these categories. This report shows that the majority of the respondents were educated, and a total of 74% possessed at least a B.Sc. degree.

After answering the questions, it can be concluded that the sample population has a similar level of understanding to the citizens of the area. This is because the responses were similar to the first survey conducted on the citizens, as the majority of them either agreed or strongly agreed with the points asked; 22% of the respondents agreed while 58% strongly agreed with the point that flood warning systems are necessary for timely response in order to deal with the threat of flood. Additionally, 22% agreed and 78% strongly agreed that a flood warning system requires an effective forecast system through an expert forecasting team. Further, 26% agreed and 62% strongly agreed that the main risk in the operating of early warning systems is the possibility of false alarms due to poor or too high forecasts, while 26% agreed and 66% strongly agreed with the point that flood prevention, safety, and mitigation require a very good mix of structural, preventive, and practical measures in all flood situations.

Furthermore, 42% agreed and 48% of the respondents strongly agreed that dealing with climate change and its adverse effects is necessary in order to control flooding; 30% and 62% agreed and strongly agreed that project management and other government institutions of Nigeria should collaborate to control the hazard of flooding. Lastly, 26% and 52% agreed and strongly agreed that public awareness is necessary to combat flooding.

The main responses obtained and concluded from the employees are listed in the following:

- To deal with the threat of flood, a flood-warning system is necessary for a timely response;
- Flood warning system requires an effective forecast system through an expert forecasting team;
- The main risk in the operation of early warning systems is the possibility of false alarms due to poor or too high forecasts;
- Collaboration of multiple institutions in Nigeria can plan measures related to restoration and environmental protection, which can also restore or protect these opportunities for weed growth and reduce flood risk;
- Climate forecasts are a major source of uncertainty, especially at the regional or local level, but other elements (including social and economic changes) are also important for climate resilience;
- Flood prevention, safety, and mitigation require a very good mix of structural, preventive, and practical measures in all flood situations;
- Floods occur when soil becomes saturated and its infiltration capacity is zero;
- Project management and other government institutions of Nigeria should collaborate to control the hazards of flooding;
- Maintenance and improvement of current infrastructure are very important when dealing with flooding problems;
- Taking preventive measures for flooding hazards is inevitable to overcome flood management issues.

4.4. Comparing Responses of the First and Second Survey

The results shown in Figure 3 are related to the responses given by the general population and the employees of key organizations. It is seen that there is a similarity in responses given by these groups. This result indicates that the general population understands the concept of flooding and what must be done in order to control or mitigate flooding in the area. This result also indicates that further education is not necessary on the concept of flooding, as the people already understand the concept. However, there is a general belief that the employees of these key organizations have a more detailed understanding of the concept of flooding, hence, their responses should be key in determining the factors or points to consider best for mitigating or controlling the impact of flooding in the area. From the results above, it is found that the following points have the highest percentage of people in agreement.

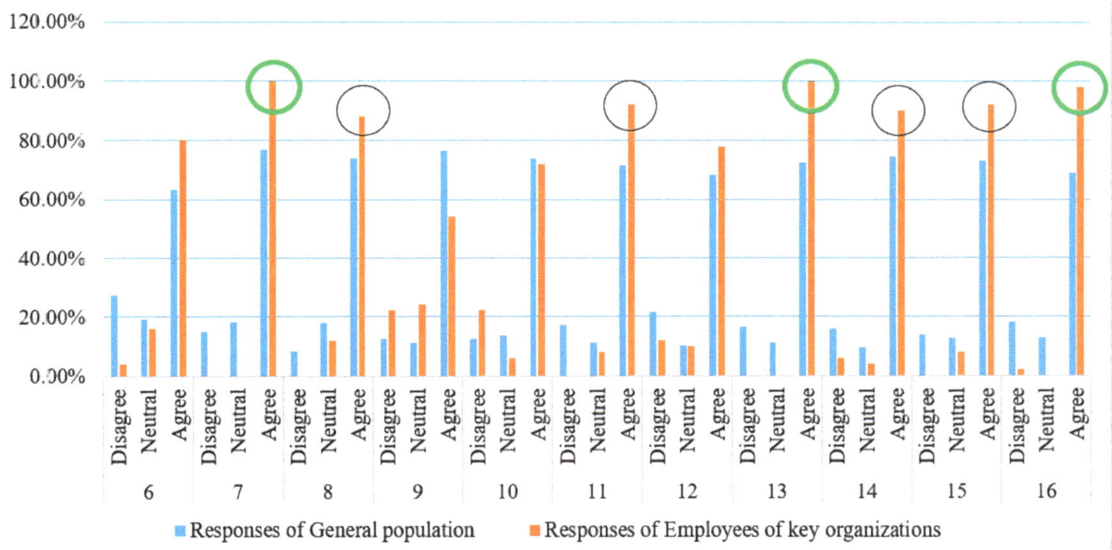

Figure 3. Summary of responses of the general population and employees of key organizations.

I. To deal with the threat of flood, a flood-warning system is necessary for a timely response.
II. The main risk in the operation of early warning systems is the possibility of false alarms due to poor or too high forecasts.
III. Flood prevention, safety, and mitigation require a very good mix of structural, preventive, and practical measures in all flood situations.
IV. Floods occur when soil becomes saturated and its infiltration capacity is zero.
V. Project management and other government institutions of Nigeria should collaborate to control the hazards of flooding.
VI. Maintenance and improvement of current infrastructure are very important when dealing with flooding problems.
VII. Taking Preventive measures for flooding hazards is inevitable to overcome flood management issues.

Of the four themes selected to conduct the survey, the results from the distribution of the questionnaire point to three themes: Theme 1, Theme 2, and Theme 4, which are the most important for combating flooding in the region. This is because points I and II reflect the ideas portrayed by Theme 1. Points III and VII reflect the ideas of Theme 2, while point VI reflects the ideas of Theme 4.

5. Discussion and Conclusions

Emphasizing the need to provide a coordinated flood management strategy in the country and avoid acting in an isolated way when it occurs, improving the attitude of flood control during floods, and controlling floods with comprehensive analysis are among the main purposes of the current study. In order to develop an effective project management strategy for urban flood disaster prevention in Edo State capital, Nigeria, interviews of key selected stakeholders were conducted to develop and suggest four themes as the most important strategies to implement productive project management procedures when combating flooding in the area. The themes emphasize establishing accurate flood warning systems to ensure timely response to flooding. In addition, flood prevention through using the building resilient infrastructure and communities program was seen as an important strategy to adopt. A resilient infrastructure includes the construction of dams, water treatment plants, and proper drainage systems. Dams are considered a resilient infrastructure and would be important in this area, and constant channeling of water from flooding to these water bodies could lead to even greater flooding caused by the overflowing of rivers to land. Policies that require proper land assessment before the construction of buildings and houses should be established. All these policies would work towards the common goal of fighting discriminatory use of land.

Strategic implementation of a flood emergency plan through sustainability is also crucial in this regard. It is considered one of the most important indicators for the purpose of this study. Plans to respond to floods in due time should be made at national and local levels and should be maintained in operational status everywhere flooding might occur. These plans must cover crisis management before, during, and after the occurrence of flooding.

Confinement plans should also be prepared beforehand for every floodplain basin in order to deal with any potential breach in any of the already established defense mechanisms. These plans would help deal with the spreading of the water across the flood plain either by retention or by control of flow. Evacuation plans should also be made to ensure the protection of lives and properties in case of any flood emergency. Finally, maintenance and sustainability are very important to any project. To this end, organizations should be set up or established strictly for the maintenance of already established structures and defense mechanisms. The employees of these organizations should be properly trained and well-maintained in order to ensure an effective organization of flood emergency operations.

In summary, in order to implement efficient project management strategies, countries and regions involved in flood disasters must consider the strategies from a holistic point of view. It means they have policies that cover all the management areas, namely integration, scope, time, cost, quality, communication, human resource, risk, procurement, and stakeholder management. If the related functional areas work in isolation, we cannot claim there is project management in the organization. The obtained themes present the importance of all the named management areas. They help the region to prevent and control flooding and, when it happens, decrease the negative impacts in practice.

6. Recommendation, Limitations, and Future Research

Flooding in Nigeria is largely caused by humans and worsened by human–nature interactions. Flooding is exacerbated by inadequate or non-existent drainage systems. Many neighborhoods lack a drainage infrastructure and depend on natural drainage ditches. Increased urbanization also means that more places are created with concrete, which cannot absorb water and so increases runoff. Another recognized reason is poor waste management. Flooding is exacerbated by citizens' bad attitudes toward garbage disposal and local authorities' failure to provide waste disposal services.

The absence of adequate legal and regulatory frameworks reflects the low priority accorded to controlling and managing floods in Nigeria. As a result, combining flood risk management with spatial design is the way to go. Historically, Nigeria has prioritized post-disaster flood response above flood management. Flood risk reduction and mitigation is now a national priority on the Nigerian government's disaster risk management agenda. The government does not lack research institutes and entities capable of developing a flood risk management plan. For instance, the National Emergency Management Agency has a planning section that works with flood data using a geographic information system.

Incidentally, there is still no efficient national early warning system for floods at the federal, state, and municipal levels. The Nigerian Meteorological Agency, for its part, forecasts seasonal rainfall, but communication remains a challenge. Integration and coordination are insufficient among current government organizations, which often carry out flood control initiatives without communicating with one another.

The government may continue to spend heavily on flood defenses that do not prevent floods, resulting in insufficient funding to deal with the aftermath. All players must be reoriented and engaged, and the boundaries of engineering techniques must be understood [1]. This should also entail marketing the advantages of mainstreaming resilience beyond the catastrophe management that underpins the new techniques [4]. This interaction should begin with an awareness of the elements behind the causes of flooding in Nigerian cities, as well as an appreciation of the uncertainty surrounding the causes of flooding. Green infrastructure and sustainable urban planning might potentially be linked with information and communication technology techniques. When flooding begins, citizens may utilize these to contact the appropriate authorities.

The current study, similar to other studies, has its limitations. The limitations include the small group of participants and stakeholders, which was raised due to the related organization selected as the case study; indeed, it only involved organizations in Edo State capital too. In addition, while there are many countries suffering from flood disasters in Africa, not just in Nigeria and in the small area where the study was conducted. In addition, more than the interviews, employing document analysis, or any previously published data could be helpful to obtain the themes.

This study has revealed and contributed to project management's body of knowledge about the structural and non-structural adaptive governance components that are critical to the successful and sustainable project management delivery of flood prevention projects in do State Capital and Nigeria in general. However, further research is needed on a number of critical issues (not emphasized in this project) such as financial mismanagement and efficient communication, and how they may affect the efficacy of flood prevention projects. Furthermore, research toward globally accepted criteria for successful flood projects will be necessary.

Author Contributions: Conceptualization, M.G.; methodology, M.G.N.; software, M.G.N.; validation, M.G.N.; formal analysis, M.G.N.; investigation, C.I.; resources, M.G.; data curation, C.I.; writing original draft preparation, C.I.; writing review and editing, M.G.; visualization, M.G.; supervision, M.G.N.; project administration, C.I. All authors have read and agreed to the published version of the manuscript.

Funding: This research received no external funding.

Institutional Review Board Statement: The study was approved by the Institutional Review Board of Girne American University, (Ref No.: 2021-22-Fall-0031).

Informed Consent Statement: Not applicable.

Data Availability Statement: Not applicable.

Conflicts of Interest: The authors declare no conflict of interest.

References

1. Wasko, C. Can temperature be used to inform changes to flood extremes with global warming? *Philos. Trans. R. Soc. A* **2021**, *379*, 20190551. [CrossRef] [PubMed]
2. Mariano, C.; Marino, M. Urban Planning for Climate Change: A Toolkit of Actions for an Integrated Strategy of Adaptation to Heavy Rains, River Floods, and Sea Level Rise. *Urban Sci.* **2022**, *6*, 63. [CrossRef]
3. Robati, M.; Rezaei, F. Applying the Sustainability Barometer Approach to Assess Urban Sustainability. *Urban Sci.* **2022**, *6*, 85. [CrossRef]
4. Bertilsson, L.; Wiklund, K.; de Moura Tebaldi, I.; Rezende, O.M.; Veról, A.P.; Miguez, M.G. Urban flood resilience—A multi-criteria index to integrate flood resilience into urban planning. *J. Hydrol.* **2019**, *573*, 970–982. [CrossRef]
5. Golabi, M.; Nejad, M.G. Intelligent and Fuzzy UAV Transportation Applications in Aviation 4.0. In *Intelligent and Fuzzy Techniques in Aviation 4.0*; Springer: Cham, Switzerland, 2022; pp. 431–458.

6. Vizvari, B.; Guden, H.; Nejad, M.G. Local search based meta-heuristic algorithms for optimizing the cyclic flexible manufacturing cell problem. *Ann. Optim. Theory Pract.* **2018**, *1*, 15–32.
7. Qureshi, M.I.; Qayyum, S.; Nassani, A.A.; Aldakhil, A.M.; Abro, M.M.Q.; Zaman, K. Management of various socio-economic factors under the United Nations sustainable development agenda. *Resour. Policy* **2019**, *64*, 101515. [CrossRef]
8. Anderson, D.K.; Merna, T. Project management strategy—Project management represented as a process based set of management domains and the consequences for project management strategy. *Int. J. Proj. Manag.* **2003**, *21*, 387–393. [CrossRef]
9. Hansson, K.; Danielson, M.; Ekenberg, L. A framework for evaluation of flood management strategies. *J. Environ. Manag.* **2008**, *86*, 465–480. [CrossRef]
10. Poff, N.L.; Matthews, J.H. Environmental flows in the Anthropocence: Past progress and future prospects. *Curr. Opin. Environ. Sustain.* **2013**, *5*, 667–675. [CrossRef]
11. Douben, K.J. Characteristics of river floods and flooding: A global overview, 1985–2003. *Irrig. Drain. J. Int. Comm. Irrig. Drain.* **2006**, *55*, S9–S21. [CrossRef]
12. François, B.; Schlef, K.E.; Wi, S.; Brown, C.M. Design considerations for riverine floods in a changing climate—A review. *J. Hydrol.* **2019**, *574*, 557–573. [CrossRef]
13. Bangalore, M.G.; Smith, A.; Veldkamp, T. Exposure to floods, climate change, and poverty in Vietnam. *Econ. Disasters Clim. Chang.* **2019**, *3*, 79–99. [CrossRef]
14. Igbinovia, S.O.; Orukpe, P.E. Rural electrification: The propelling force for rural development of Edo State, Nigeria. *J. Energy S. Afr.* **2007**, *18*, 18–26. [CrossRef]
15. Alam, M.J. "The organized encroachment of land developers"—Effects on urban flood management in Greater Dhaka, Bangladesh. *Sustain. Cities Soc.* **2014**, *10*, 49–58. [CrossRef]
16. Ismail, D.; Majid, T.A.; Roosli, R.; Ab Samah, N. Project management success for post-disaster reconstruction projects: International NGOs perspectives. *Procedia Econ. Financ.* **2014**, *18*, 120–127. [CrossRef]
17. Kaufmann, C.; Kock, A. Does project management matter? The relationship between project management effort, complexity, and profitability. *Int. J. Proj. Manag.* **2022**, *40*, 624–633. [CrossRef]
18. De Carvalho, M.M.; Patah, L.A.; de Souza Bido, D. Project management and its effects on project success: Cross-country and cross-industry comparisons. *Int. J. Proj. Manag.* **2015**, *33*, 1509–1522. [CrossRef]
19. Newton, R. *Project Management Step by Step: How to Plan and Manage a Highly Successful Project*; Pearson: London, UK, 2016.
20. Hossain, F.; Anagnostou, E.N. Assessment of current passive-microwave-and infrared-based satellite rainfall remote sensing for flood prediction. *J. Geophys. Res. Atmos.* **2004**, *109*, D07102. [CrossRef]
21. Kim, K.N.; Choi, J.H. Breaking the vicious cycle of flood disasters: Goals of project management in post-disaster rebuild projects. *Int. J. Proj. Manag.* **2013**, *31*, 147–160. [CrossRef]
22. Verweij, S.; Busscher, T.; van den Brink, M. Effective policy instrument mixes for implementing integrated flood risk management: An analysis of the 'Room for the River'program. *Environ. Sci. Policy* **2021**, *116*, 204–212. [CrossRef]
23. van Herk, S.; Rijke, J.; Zevenbergen, C.; Ashley, R. Understanding the transition to integrated flood risk management in the Netherlands. *Environ. Innov. Soc. Transit.* **2015**, *15*, 84–100. [CrossRef]
24. Komolafe, A.A.; Adegboyega, S.A.A.; Akinluyi, F.O. A review of flood risk analysis in Nigeria. *Am. J. Environ. Sci.* **2015**, *11*, 157–166. [CrossRef]
25. Nkwunonwo, U.C. A review of flooding and flood risk reduction in Nigeria. *Glob. J. Hum.-Soc. Sci. B* **2016**, *16*, 22–42.
26. Adelekan, I.O. Vulnerability assessment of an urban flood in Nigeria: Abeokuta flood 2007. *Nat. Hazards* **2011**, *56*, 215–231. [CrossRef]
27. Adelekan, I.O.; Asiyanbi, A.P. Flood risk perception in flood-affected communities in Lagos, Nigeria. *Nat. Hazards* **2016**, *80*, 445–469. [CrossRef]
28. Popping, R. Analyzing open-ended questions by means of text analysis procedures. *Bull. Sociol. Methodol.* **2015**, *128*, 23–39. [CrossRef]
29. Ikhile, C.I. Geomorphology and hydrology of the Benin region, Edo state, Nigeria. *Int. J. Geosci.* **2016**, *7*, 144–157. [CrossRef]
30. Alens, O.P. Assessment of the urban climate of Benin City, Nigeria. *J. Environ. Earth Sci* **2016**, *6*, 131–143.
31. Nicholson, S.E.; Selato, J.C. The influence of La Nina on African rainfall. *Int. J. Climatol.* **2000**, *20*, 1761–1776. [CrossRef]
32. Dore, M.H. Climate change and changes in global precipitation patterns: What do we know? *Environ. Int.* **2005**, *31*, 1167–1181. [CrossRef]
33. Ghasemi, M.; Nejad, M.G.; Alsaadi, N.; Abdel-Jaber, M.T.; Yajid, A.; Shukri, M.; Habib, M. Performance measurment and lead-time reduction in epc project-based organizations: A mathematical modeling approach. *Math. Probl. Eng.* **2022**, *2022*, 5767356. [CrossRef]
34. Ghasemi, M.; Nejad, M.G.; Aghaei, I. Knowledge management orientation and operational performance relationship in medical tourism (overview of the model performance in the COVID-19 pandemic and post-pandemic era). *Health Serv. Manag. Res.* **2021**, *34*, 208–222. [CrossRef] [PubMed]
35. Oluwasemire, K.O.; Stigter, C.J.; Owonubi, J.J.; Jagtap, S.S. Seasonal water use and water productivity of millet-based cropping systems in the Nigerian Sudan savanna near Kano. *Agric. Water Manag.* **2002**, *56*, 207–227. [CrossRef]
36. Arabian, M.; Ghadiri Nejad, M.; Barenji, R.V. Blockchain Technology in Supply Chain Management: Challenge and Future Perspectives. In *Industry 4.0*; Springer: Singapore, 2023; pp. 201–220.

37. Ghadiri Nejad, M.; Banar, M. Emergency response time minimization by incorporating ground and aerial transportation. *Ann. Optim. Theory Pract.* **2018**, *1*, 43–57.
38. Lallemant, D.; Hamel, P.; Balbi, M.; Lim, T.N.; Schmitt, R.; Win, S. Nature-based solutions for flood risk reduction: A probabilistic modeling framework. *One Earth* **2021**, *4*, 1310–1321. [CrossRef]

urban science

MDPI

Article

Defining the Organization of Municipal Solid Waste Management Based on Production Costs

Massimo Beccarello and Giacomo Di Foggia *

Department of Business and Law, University of Milano-Bicocca, 20126 Milan, Italy
* Correspondence: giacomo.difoggia@unimib.it

Abstract: A long-lasting dilemma on the efficient provision of services of general economic interest has become increasingly important in the waste management industry: competition or monopoly in municipal solid waste management. Previous literature has primarily examined the economics of scale and scope to provide an adequate response. Here, we contribute by investigating subadditivity in municipal solid waste management service costs. Subadditivity is a critical concept used to justify imperfect competition, which encourages natural monopolies where one producer will function more effectively than more firms. To test the hypothesis that a subadditivity in costs in waste management exists, we design a simulation based on empirical data for Milan, Italy. We compared the total production cost of the incumbent firm with the alternative hypothesis built by dividing the city into four areas and assigning each area to a different hypothetical firm. The results suggest that the existence of subadditivity results in 6% lower production costs, primarily stemming from business synergies, lower transactional costs, and optimization of productive resources and facilities. The evidence justifies, ceteris paribus, that the provision by a single firm is preferable to multiple firms in the analysis case. Implications for policies are straightforward. The one-fit rule approach fails to set the best condition for policymakers to create a level playing field transparently and efficiently for industry operators to perform efficiently.

Keywords: waste management; cost subadditivity; economies of scale; economies of scope; waste management chain; MSW

1. Introduction

Municipal solid waste management has become a major multidisciplinary topic and has gained even more traction in environmental economics [1,2] due to its prominent role in the transition toward circular cities. No wonder interest in how to identify the most cost-effective organizational forms has increased backed by circular economy targets.

Although it may appear linear, there are stages and coordination complexities that characterize it. A division into two consequential stages that differ technically and economically can be used to simplify understanding. First, at the waste collection stage, the separation of unsorted and sorted waste takes place. Second, the treatment and disposal stages are when recyclable waste is treated and residual waste is disposed of [3].

Concerning coordination complexities, one should note that waste management service contains a multitude of subservices, including waste collection, street sweeping, cleaning, on-demand, or residual waste disposal services; see Appendix A for a taxonomy of those considered in this paper.

The key question is: what is the most efficient industrial setting for this service? Economic theory suggests that competition is the first option, provided that certain conditions are met. A fair, competitive environment is also one of the main targets of European legislation on competition and public procurement; see, for example, the Directive 2014/24/EU on public procurement [4]. However, there may be exceptions to this principle, for example, in the case of benefits arising from the optimal scale of production in a particular industry.

We investigate whether the services of a single firm are socially preferable to those of several firms. We test this idea empirically by focusing on the production efficiency of waste management, considering possible subadditivity in production costs in the city of Milan, Italy. The analysis is developed by comparing a business-as-usual model in which waste management is provided by a single firm with an alternative scenario in which the city is divided into four areas and four firms provide the service in each of these areas.

We add to the literature on industrial production empirical evidence from a sector that is becoming increasingly important due to its relevance to the circular economy, particularly regarding the existence of subadditivity of costs.

The rest of this article is organized as follows: we review the relevant literature on economies of scale, subadditivity of costs, and waste management efficiency in Section 2. After that, in Section 3, some detailed information regarding the theory of cost subadditivity is provided together with the rationale for our hypothesis building and the research design. Section 4 contains the main empirical evidence. Section 5 discusses the main considerations and implications arising from the results obtained. Conclusions follow.

2. Literature Review

Given the convergence of various factors, such as public policies [5] and climate commitments, the need to provide public services in an economic and eco-efficient way is a focus in environmental economics [6,7]. Furthermore, the trend of the global economy is stressing industrial structures, especially in countries that depend on the import of raw materials. Several approaches have been used to investigate this sector. In this paper, we review some studies that have dealt with scale and scope dimensions since, to the best of our knowledge, additional studies are needed on subadditivity of costs—that is the purpose of this paper.

Efficient production size and scope and the environmental impact of firms are important for policy and market organization [8], and the number of relevant studies on the cost of waste management has increased [9–13]. The approaches used to estimate costs of waste management are often based on the unit cost method, benchmarking techniques, and cost estimation models using, for example, cost and production function analysis [14,15] and data envelopment analysis and stochastic frontier analysis [16].

Previous literature provides many insights into different technologies, scale economies, market forms, industries, and countries [17,18]. Scholars have also tried to empirically assess the impact of different regulated business models on waste management efficiency by focusing on the size of the territorial areas and municipalities [19,20]. For example, a recent paper analyzes municipalities that, like other production units, should be large enough to minimize average costs [21]. This is consistent with the fact that a renewed interest in decentralization has affected local public governance around the world [22], as well as at metropolitan scales [23]. Such studies can assess whether the scale of activities can explain performance in waste management [24].

Other studies focus on the cost structures of waste management [10], the relation with exogenous factors such as population density [25], the need to develop strategies to achieve sustainability targets [26], compliance with environmental legislation and costs [27], and zero waste management [28]. Similar approaches have been developed for other local environmental services, such as water, where studies suggest substantial cost benefits from the joint production of treated quality water [29] and potential benefits of appropriate scale and scope economies considering vertical and horizontal configurations of water industries [30]. The increasing pressure for cost efficiency has prompted governments to transfer some waste services to private firms [31], giving rise to the question of whether for-profit firms are compatible with outcomes that maximize social welfare [32].

Economic and political factors exert different impacts on waste management by private and public firms [33]. Private waste management operators are not necessarily better performers than public firms [34] because the profit maximization typical of private operators may clash with the social and environmental targets typical of public services. To this end, business models and waste management methods, such as the organization of collection services, have received limited attention [35], even if they have a significant impact [36]. Both controllable and noncontrollable factors can have a significant impact on costs [37].

Broadly speaking, a function is said to have subadditivity when the whole is less than the sum of two or more parts. This attribute is important in economies of scale when the combined operating costs of two enterprises are less than the sum of their individual operating costs [38]. Economies of scale take place when the average cost of production declines as production increases. Such a decline in average production cost can stem from, according to the sector, high fixed costs, lower input prices, or learning economies.

What characterizes economies of scale is that such relations typically operate over a range of output rather than for all possible output levels [39]. When economies of scale pertain to the firm's entire output rather than to a specific product, the cost savings resulting from making these products together include a variety of economies of scope. Concerning economies of scope, subadditivity of costs refers to a situation where the total cost of activities performed in combination is less than the total cost of activities performed separately due to synergies [40]. Indeed, multiple products show scope economies when the combined cost of producing them is lower when their production is organized jointly than when it is separate for each product or produced by more firms [41].

In a public service such as waste management that is made up of many services, it is reasonable to think that, based on economies of scale and scope, a logic of vertical integration is necessary, e.g., for transaction costs and information efficiencies. Economies of scale and scope also affect the public service delivery market structure debate. Specifically, fostering competition incentivizes operators to operate efficiently. However, competition in the market is not always the preferred configuration, as the production technology or the characteristics of the services produced can generate market failures. In some circumstances, existing production technology makes it more efficient to concentrate production on a single subject than a solution in which several firms carry it out. In such cases, the activity is configured as a natural monopoly. It is recognized that municipal waste services have typically been provided through natural or legal monopolies [15]. Indeed, services of general economic interest have general economic utility often subject to public service obligations. Market rules apply to firms responsible for managing such services as long as competition does not prevent them from accomplishing their tasks in the general interest, for example, in cases of imperfect competition [42]. Therefore, such services can be provided either by the state or by the private sector and by more firms that are part of public contracts or in a monopolistic manner.

Subadditivity of costs is a critical concept frequently used to justify imperfect competition, which encourages natural monopolies even if its analysis is challenging due to information asymmetry [43]. We help fill this gap by providing a detailed analysis of the cost production structure by empirically testing our idea using a specific business scenario.

3. Materials and Methods

Arguments for and against monopoly and competition in the provision of services embrace many perspectives [44,45]. Subadditivity assumes that the output level is produced at the lowest cost by a single firm [38]. Economies of scope and economics of scale are constrained types of subadditivity by comparing the costs of more firms that specialize in producing different outputs to one that produces two goods at comparable output levels. Taking an example of firms that produce individually, the production cost equals the sum of the costs incurred by each firm to produce a quantity q of product or service x. Equation (1) formalizes this concept, where Q stands for the quantity and i corresponds to one of the n firms existing in the industry. Equation (1) indicates that the production cost of the total quantity Q is the sum of the costs incurred by each firm to produce the share of Q, i.e., Q/n produced by each.

$$Production\ cost = \begin{cases} c_m(Q_x); one\ firm \\ \sum_{i=1}^{n} c_i\left(\frac{Q_x}{n}\right); n\ firms \end{cases} \quad (1)$$

{\displaystyle \sum _{i=1}^{n}c_{i}\;(Q_{i})}The hypothesis underlying the theory of subadditivity is resumed in Equation (2).

$$c_m(Q_x) \leq \sum_{i=1}^{n} c_i\left(\frac{Qx}{n}\right) \tag{2}$$

Natural monopolies stand out because marginal costs are typically small once an investment is made and because average costs decrease with increased output; if only one firm operates in the market, production costs may be lower than if there are competitors.

The standard average cost functions for one or more firms are shown in Figure 1. Subadditivity indicates that it is cheaper to produce the same production level when only firm one is producing. The existence of economies of scale is a sufficient but not required condition for monopolies to be sustainable. However, subadditivity is considered necessary even if there are insufficient conditions for a natural monopoly to be considered efficient.

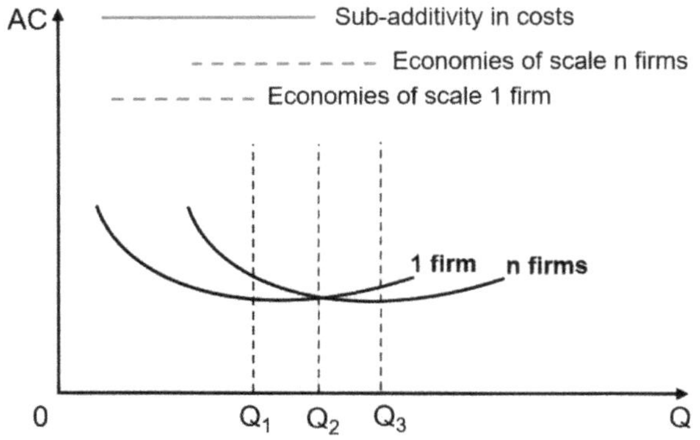

Figure 1. Average costs of one and multiple companies in a monopolistic market; Q = quantity of output; AC average cost.

We empirically tested whether starting from data on costs and waste production, Equation (3) H_0 is verified, i.e., if the service falls between 0 and Q_2 in Figure 1. In such a case, the collection of waste is configured as a natural monopoly due to economies of scale and above all, economies of density, which lead us to believe that the service costs are lower if the service is carried out by a single firm rather than by several firms. Beyond a certain level of output, in the case of Figure Q_2, more firms are able to operate more effectively.

In network services such as municipal solid waste collection, economies of density take on central importance. To ascertain the existence of a market failure, it is necessary to verify the conditions that make the collection phase a natural monopoly that cannot be contested.

A contestable natural monopoly, although not optimal, allows for eliminating the monopoly rents and can reach the most efficient allocation compatible with the cost coverage constraint in the absence of regulation. This result implies that in markets characterized by few irreversible costs and without other barriers to entry, competition in the market can produce results close to second-best efficiency even in the presence of natural monopolies. Furthermore, situations of market failure occur when the goods and services produced are public goods, such as waste management, because the market does not easily allow optimal production, given the difficulty in preventing free-riding behaviors.

Research Design

Our research question consists of testing the subadditivity of costs in waste management production costs in Milan. To contextualize the analysis, Table 1 presents contextual data regarding waste production.

Table 1. Background information regarding waste in the city of Milan.

Year	Inhabitants	Sorted Waste Tons	Waste Generated Tons	Sorted Waste %	Sorted Waste per Capita kg/Inhabitant	Waste per Capita kg/Inhabitant
2020	1,397,715	381,660	608,413	62.7	273.1	435.3
2019	1,406,373	433,404	707,507	61.3	308.2	503.1
2018	1,395,980	407,318	692,228	58.8	291.8	495.9

Source: Italian National Environmental Protection Institute.

The waste management incumbent runs the service both in the Municipality of Milan and in seventeen other towns in the Milan metropolitan area. Table 2 contextualizes the scope of the incumbent to carrying out the case study; indeed, the incumbent firms run the service in the Municipality of Milan and in seventeen other municipalities in the metropolitan area.

Table 2. Scope of analysis.

Variable	Total	Case Study
Number of Municipalities	18	1
Population	1844	1400
Area km^2	383	182
Workforce	3097	2444

Source: Own elaboration based on incumbent website.

Starting from the technical and economic data concerning the municipal waste collection service in Milan, we reclassified the cost of waste management to test our hypothesis. The cost reconstruction path started from information made publicly available by the Municipality of Milan, and the procedure for determining the values attributed to the activities refers to the accounting and technical documentation: the financial statements of the incumbent waste management firm, the indicators referring to the use and cost of personnel, and the indicators relating to the use of capital goods derived based on the service monitoring activity, as well as by analyzing the service contract.

Based on the above information, we estimated the costs classified as follows: collection, sweeping, other services, and on-demand. To verify the existence of subadditivity in the costs, starting from the accounting data, we estimated the overall costs, hypothesizing that four firms ran the service as in Figure 2. Therefore, the business-as-usual hypothesis foresees that the total quantity of the service that corresponds to the waste management service for the entire city of Milan was provided by a single operator, whereas the alternative hypothesis foresees that each of the four firms provide a fraction of the service provided the total quantity is the same.

Milan is divided into nine districts; we did not take into consideration a scenario with more than four firms, as the same organizational measures could not be guaranteed for each one. The hypothesis of mutual use of production inputs by different firms in the same operating area appears incompatible with adequate levels of effectiveness and efficiency. Given the characteristics of the service and the city of Milan, we simulated by assuming four firms corresponding to the four incumbent divisions. Geographically, in Figure 2 firm 1 runs the service in the northeast area of the city that is denoted as area 1, firm 2 runs the service in the southeast area, i.e., area 2, firm 3 runs the service in the southwest area that corresponds to area 3, and firm 4 runs the service in area 4 or the northwest side of the city. This is due to the inevitable duplication of costs deriving from fixed costs and investments necessary for the organization and provision of the service over reduced operating areas—the reduction of the functional area does not correspond to a proportional reduction in costs. Therefore, we assume that each firm independently carried out the service in the assigned areas. Table 3 provides information regarding the city of Milan and how it could be divided to allow multiple firms to run the waste management service.

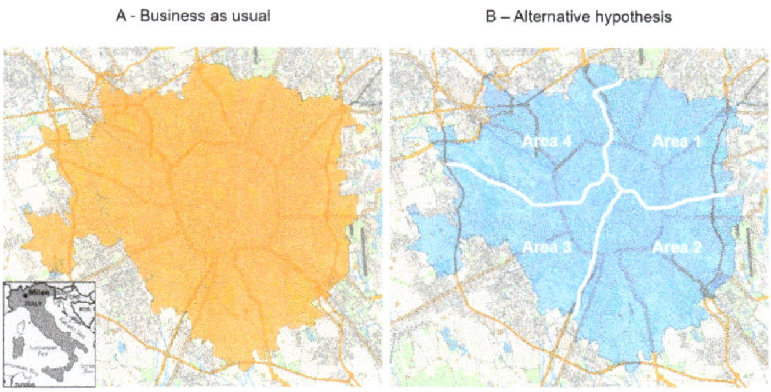

Figure 2. Approach for the alternative scenario. City of Milan, Italy. Inhabitants 2020: ~1.4 million, (metropolitan ~2.9 million). Elevation: 130 m above sea level. Area: 181.76 km^2. Subfigure; localization of the City of Milan.

Table 3. Reclassification of the city of Milan according to our scenario.

Administrative Units			Area 1		Area 2		Area 3		Area 4	
	km^2	Pop	km^2	Pop	km^2	Pop	km^2	Pop	km^2	Pop
District 1	9.7	98,679			4.8	49,339	4.8	49,340		
District 2	12.6	163,335	12.6	163,335						
District 3	14.2	145,328	14.2	145,328						
District 4	21	162,795			21	162,795				
District 5	29.9	127,280			29.9	127,280				
District 6	18.3	152,519					18.3	152,519		
District 7	31.3	177,731					20.4	115,525	11	62,206
District 8	23.7	188,650							23.7	188,650
District 9	21.1	190,058	10.6	95,029					10.6	95,028
Areas 1, 2, 3, 4 *			37.4	403,692	55.7	339,413	43.5	317,384	45.2	345,884
Milan	181.8	1,406,373								

Source: Elaboration based on data available online for the Municipality of Milan. * Our estimation. See Figure 3 for a map showing overlapping between municipalities and areas.

Figure 3 overlaps districts and business units that correspond to the areas used in the alternative hypothesis.

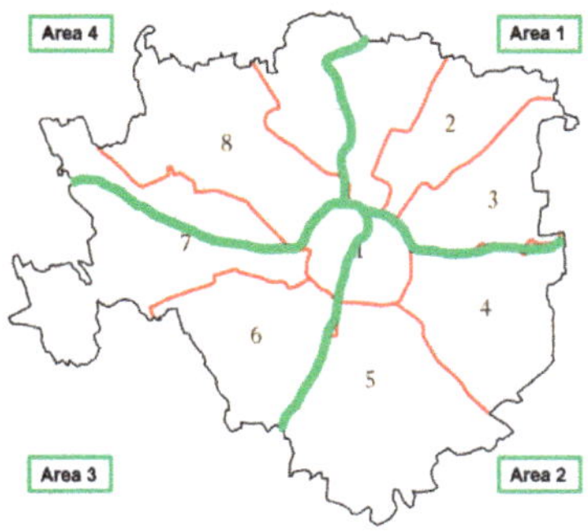

Figure 3. Districts and the four areas. In red nine districts, in green four areas.

From Table 3, the population of the four identified areas ranges from 0.31 to 0.4 million inhabitants, whereas the areas range from approximately 37 km^2 to slightly less than 56 km^2, from which we can derive population densities from 6 to 10 thousand inhabitants per km^2. We were able to divide the costs between the four firms considering the minimum organizational information for the performance of the service, inferable from the information in the documents used by the agency of the city of Milan. Appendix A summarizes the four types of services: collection, sweeping, other, and on-demand—more than fifty different subservices constitute the waste management service.

We define our hypotheses as follows:

$$Hypotheses: \begin{cases} H_0 = c_m(Q) \leq \sum_{i=1}^{4} c_i\left(\frac{Q}{4}\right) \\ H_1 = c_m(Q) > \sum_{i=1}^{4} c_i\left(\frac{Q}{4}\right) \end{cases} \quad (3)$$

Considering the hypothesis formalized in Equation (3), we developed our research question to verify H_0. In this paper, we focus on the production cost structure.

4. Results

Based on the above assumptions, a reasonable approximation of the total industrial cost of the individual activities that make up the waste management service was reconstructed. It should be noted that the total cost includes both the activities of collection and waste treatment and disposal. Table 4 shows the distribution and total cost according to the simulation designed to test our hypothesis.

Table 4. Business-as-usual and simulation.

	Costs and Resources	Workforce	Means	Production Cost
	Business-as-usual: incumbent			
c(Q)		2444	761	314,879,379
	Collection	999	248	157,821,729
	Sweeping	1378	498	141,086,581
	Other services	36	15	13,077,784
	On-demand	31	0	2,893,285
	Alternative hypothesis: firm 1/4			
$c_i\left(\frac{Qi}{n}\right)$	Collection	285	70	45,323,303
	Sweeping	390	141	40,399,649
	Other services	16	6	3,981,982
	On-demand	17	0	1,328,732
	Alternative hypothesis: firm 2/4			
$c_i\left(\frac{Qi}{n}\right)$	Collection	260	66	41,894,035
	Sweeping	348	128	36,385,046
	Other services	16	6	3,352,230
	On-demand	17	0	1,310,193
	Alternative hypothesis: firm 3/4			
$c_i\left(\frac{Qi}{n}\right)$	Collection	230	59	39,019,567
	Sweeping	328	128	35,136,937
	Other services	16	6	3,197,337
	On-demand	17	0	1,306,381
	Alternative hypothesis: firm 4/4			
$c_i\left(\frac{Qi}{n}\right)$	Collection	239	61	38,432,266
	Sweeping	343	118	34,649,655
	Other services	16	6	5,249,366
	On-demand	17	0	1,289,739
	Ttoal alternative hypothesis: Firms 1, 2, 3, 4			
$\sum_{i=1}^{4} c_i\left(\frac{Q}{4}\right)$		2555	795	332,256,419
	Collection	1014	256	164,669,171
	Sweeping	1409	515	146,571,287
	Other services	64	24	15,780,915
	On-demand	68	0	5,235,045

Note: reconstruction of costs to predict the total cost of service under the two hypotheses was possible by accessing information contained in the service contract between the Municipality of Milan and the incumbent, see Appendix B for parameters.

For each service contained in the service contract, all the production inputs, including staff, were allocated to one of the four actual business units. Differences in costs primarily derived from the fact that both staff and other production inputs would duplicate by dividing the service. This consideration is often omitted in economies of scale studies although it is of prominence.

Table 4 shows that the output level is produced at the lowest cost by a single firm providing imperfect competition, which encourages one producer since it probably functions more effectively than more firms. This can be examined by comparing workforce and production means. Regarding the workforce, our results suggest that a monopolist produced the same output as four firms, employing 4% fewer employees and requiring 9.5% fewer means of production.

Figure 4 compares the total production cost of waste management following our research design hypothesis. The production of a single firm is socially preferable in terms of production costs.

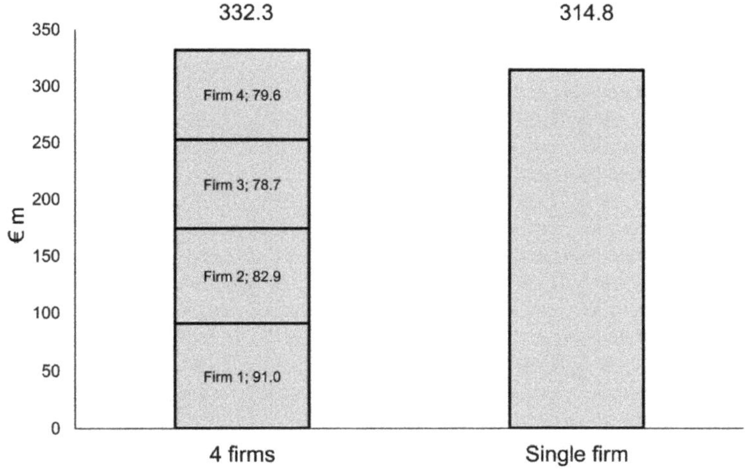

Figure 4. Simulation output of production costs.

We did not perform our simulation on more, smaller areas because the same organizational measures, such as the availability of operational areas functional to the service, could not be guaranteed in each area. The idea that different service managers share the same operational area seems incompatible with adequate levels of effectiveness and efficiency because of the duplication of costs deriving from the fixed costs and investments necessary for the organization and delivery of the service in reduced operational areas. The reduction in the operating area does not correspond to a proportional reduction in the costs. The simulation assumed that the firm that manages the waste management service provides the same services in each area.

5. Discussion

Starting from the fact that services of general economic interest can be provided either by the state or by the private sector and by more firms or by a monopolist, it is important to refer to the extent of imperfect competition and the structure of production costs to identify the best service provision industrial organization. Indeed, it is worth noting that economic theory foresees competition as the best option, provided that specific conditions are satisfied. Furthermore, a fair, competitive environment is also among the main targets of European legislation. As mentioned in the Introduction, however, we need to consider that such a principle can be derogated, e.g., following gains deriving from the optimal production size. A monopolistic structure in the municipal waste management service should be evaluated based on economies of scale, economies of scope, economies of density, morphological characteristics of the territory, relevant policies, and barriers to entry. The provision of the municipal solid waste management service must follow the technical and economic efficiency of the service, which, from the results, appears achievable through a single operator.

A single provider in a city like Milan is not in contrast with market principles. Indeed, competition is restricted when there is an intention to unduly favor or disadvantage certain economic operators; it follows that competition is not restricted by subadditivity of costs and other peculiarities of the sectors outside of public interest regulatory targets [46]. It seems that managing the entire municipal area by a single economic operator could positively affect the community, given the potential savings on the costs of managing the service. Considering the information in this study as a whole, we can verify that there are no substantial differences between the two management hypotheses regarding the activities of separate collection, separate collection of the organic fraction, separate collection of paper and cardboard, separate collection of glass, separate collection of plastic and metal packaging, street sweeping activities in general, and activities of emptying the bins—given that the quantity of the production factors, employed personnel, vehicles, and containers are proportional in the two scenarios analyzed in this article.

Furthermore, the results show that the activities that incur the highest costs are those related to collection, in particular, the sorting of bulky waste, durable goods, batteries, pharmaceuticals, exhausted toner cartridges, residual and sorted waste collection with dedicated containers, residual and sorted waste collection in cemeteries, the cleaning of markets, the collection and disposal of small items containing asbestos, the separate collection of used clothing, the separate collection of used oil and some sweeping activities such as cleaning the banks of watercourses, collecting leaves, cleaning tree rows and related areas, mowing and weeding sidewalks, washing tunnels, arcades, and underpasses of value. This is primarily due to the increase in personnel and vehicles to ensure service under the alternative scenario.

The contribution to the literature in the field of efficiency in the management of public services and in waste management consists of shedding light on concepts that are sometimes considered synonyms in studies aimed at evaluating the efficiency of public services: economies of scale and the subadditivity of costs, even if what emerged from the simulation may have some interpretative limitations. We start from the incumbent's financial and industrial data; therefore, some might object that it is impossible to calculate the costs of potential competitors based on the incumbent's costs. However, although this consideration might be worth noting, it does not override our hypothesis. The municipal waste management industry has a relatively rigid cost structure. Therefore, it is not wrong to assume that the cost structure of potential new entrants to the market may be similar to the cost structure of the incumbent, given that there are constraints concerning the quality of the service that imply a series of rigidities that the flexibility of the companies cannot overcome since this is, as mentioned, a market structure characterized by structural rigidity.

Based on the empirical evidence that emerged, we can deduce some implications for industrial policy and the governance of waste management services.

It is necessary to prepare regulatory measures and incentives to favor the aggregation of companies that do not reach a minimum efficient size. This concept is also critical considering the provisions of European legislation on public procurement, which is aimed at encouraging the participation of small and medium-sized enterprises. However, differently from other sectors where legislation is being more and more harmonized across countries, the number of non-harmonized laws in force across countries as well as their constant updates are prominent problems that make it difficult to obtain comparable information [47].

The results of this paper demonstrate that a market configuration that allows more companies to provide part of the municipal waste management service could worsen social well-being due to the increase in total production costs. However it should be noted that this consideration is not extendable in cities of different size or other organizational forms; for example, another study found that social welfare would increase if tenders' scope were reduced in terms of size [19]. Instead, another study based in Finland reported that switching from laissez-faire production to public procurement reduces the number of active firms on the local market, but results in a statistically significant and substantial decrease in prices [48], whereas an analysis of the city of Barcelona, where the city is divided in four areas, found that firms strategically manage quality performance and tend to deliver higher quality where they anticipate easier monitoring by the regulator [49], which can be thought of as a non-optimal condition given that quality of the service is not the same for citizens.

So, monopoly may be more efficient than competition when it comes to local service delivery, according to a study that found that municipalities that adopt an industrial organization strategy and create hybrid ownership firms benefit from market engagement and economies of scale due to monopoly production [50]. The above also impacts governance at the local level and, in particular, companies' organization and ownership structure. Typically, local authorities can entrust the management of local public services through three procedures: the first procedure consists of entrusting to third parties through public procedures following the provisions on contracts and service concessions, the second procedure involves the establishment of a mixed public–private company, and the third procedure consists of in-house management. EU jurisprudence also allows the so-called in-house provision of public services by the local authority under specific conditions, for which we refer to Article 106 of the TFEU. The optimal forms shall be selected considering reaching circular economy targets as the goal, given the positive impact on the economy [51,52].

6. Conclusions

As a service of general economic interest to which market rules apply, except where competition is contrary to the general interest, as in certain cases of imperfect competition, municipal waste management can be provided by several companies or by a single firm. As waste management is a strategic pillar of the circular economy, municipal waste management services must be organized to maximize the cost-effectiveness of their provision. Despite a remarkable body of economic literature, the results are heterogeneous due to different contexts, scholars' specializations, types of waste, and research approaches. Our results suggest the existence of subadditivity of costs, estimated at 6% lower production costs in the case of a single firm against a hypothetical market setting in which four firms separately provide a share of the service. Therefore, a municipal solid waste configuration with more companies simultaneously running the service in geographically divided areas could worsen social well-being due to the increase in total production costs.

Such efficiency gains come from synergies, lower transaction costs, and optimization of productive inputs and facilities. It must be taken into consideration that the results refer to a case study and similar conclusions can be drawn for cities with similar characteristics in terms of geographic, urbanistic, societal, and socio-economic conditions.

In addition, within the same framework, it is important to better understand the role of synergies in business models, particularly the implications of the size and scope of waste management firms given environmental targets. However, given that economies of scope favor large utilities, it is important to study the role of participation of small and medium-sized enterprises in the public procurement market due to the barriers that sometimes make it difficult for them to participate in tenders. We highlight that the 'one size fits all' approach is not the best way for policymakers to create a level playing field for businesses. The combination and trade-offs between economic efficiency targets and the implications of circular economy targets need to be clarified to better understand the main development drivers for generating growth opportunities for the benefit of society and the environment.

Author Contributions: Conceptualization, M.B. and G.D.F.; methodology, M.B. and G.D.F.; formal analysis, M.B. and G.D.F.; writing—review and editing, M.B. and G.D.F. All authors have read and agreed to the published version of the manuscript.

Funding: This research received no external funding.

Data Availability Statement: Publicly available datasets were analyzed in this study. Data on waste production and costs can be found at: https://www.catasto-rifiuti.isprambiente.it/index.php?pg=ru (accessed on 7 January 2023). Parameters are listed in Appendix B.

Conflicts of Interest: The authors declare no conflict of interest.

Appendix A

- Collection
  - Residual fraction of separate collection, separate collection of plastic and metal
  - Separate collection of organic fractions, separate collection of cardboard, separate collection of glass
  - Separate collection of bulky waste, waste collection and market cleaning, separate collection of used clothing
  - Separate collection of durable goods
  - Separate collection of batteries, separate collection of pharmaceuticals, separate collection of used toner cartridges
  - Recycling
  - Collection with dedicated containers
  - Collection in cemeteries
  - Asbestos collection and disposal
  - Separate collection of used vegetable oil
- Sweeping
  - Fine sweeping, global sweeping
  - Emergency response on public land
  - Hazardous waste collection
  - Roadside litter removal operations
  - Illegal dumping, cleaning of degraded areas
  - Massive sweeping
  - Sensitive areas—manual sweeping
  - Sensitive areas—mechanized sweeping
  - Sensitive areas—emptying litter bins
  - Area sweeping
  - Cleanup of municipal stream banks
  - Leaf collection
  - Cleaning tree rows and related areas
  - Mowing and weeding of sidewalks, parks: cleaning, dog areas, draining sumps
  - Galleries, porches, valuable areas
  - Emptying trash cans
- Other
  - Services at travel camps
  - City fairs, public events
  - Snow service
  - Purging and unclogging manholes
  - Cleaning of streambanks and embankments
  - Garbage collection service at municipal facilities
  - Cleaning of settling tanks
  - Bus toilets
  - Inspection of construction

- On-demand
    - Snow service
    - Pest and rodent control, installation of mobile signs, cleaning of weekly markets, after-events cleaning, cemetery waste disposal, miscellaneous emergencies, fountain cleaning, litter removal in public areas

Appendix B. Allocation of Resources on Services

Description	N	Area 1	Area 2	Area 3	Area 4
Residual fraction of separate collection, separate collection of plastic and metal	Staff	Scheme	Scheme	Scheme	Scheme
	Truck	Scheme	Scheme	Scheme	Scheme
Separate collection of organic fractions, separate collection of cardboard, separate collection of glass	Staff	Scheme	Scheme	Scheme	Scheme
	Truck	Scheme	Scheme	Scheme	Scheme
	Bins	∂ points	∂ points	∂ points	∂ points
Separate collection of bulky waste, waste collection and market cleaning, separate collection of used clothing	Staff	25%	25%	25%	25%
	Truck	25%	25%	25%	25%
Separate collection of durable goods	Staff	1dr-1wo	1dr-1wo	1dr-1wo	1dr-1wo
	Truck	1	1	1	1
Separate collection of batteries, separate collection of pharmaceuticals, separate collection of used toner cartridges	Staff	1 serv	1 serv	1 serv	1 serv
	Truck	1 serv	1 serv	1 serv	1 serv
Recycling	Staff	25%	25%	25%	25%
	Truck	1	1	1	1
Collection with dedicated containers	Staff	25%	25%	25%	25%
	Truck	25%	25%	25%	25%
	Bins	25%	25%	25%	25%
Collection in cemeteries	Staff	2	1	1	4
	Truck	2	1	1	4
	Bins	2	1	1	4
Asbestos collection and disposal	Staff	1dr-1wo	1dr-1wo	1dr-1wo	1dr-1wo
	Truck	1	1	1	1
Separate collection of used vegetable oil	Staff	1 driver	1 driver	1 driver	1 driver
	Truck	1	1	1	1
Fine sweeping, global sweeping	Staff	Scheme	Scheme	Scheme	Scheme
	Truck	Scheme	Scheme	Scheme	Scheme
Emergency response on public land	Staff	1dr-1wo	1dr-1wo	1dr-1wo	1dr-1wo
	Truck	1	1	1	1
Hazardous waste collection	Staff	1dr-1wo	1dr-1wo	1dr-1wo	1dr-1wo
	Truck	1	1	1	1
Roadside litter removal operations	Staff	1 driver	1 driver	1 driver	1 driver
	Truck	1	1	1	1
Illegal dumping, cleaning of degraded areas	Staff	1dr-1wo	1dr-1wo	1dr-1wo	1dr-1wo
	Truck	1	1	1	1
Massive sweeping	Staff	Scheme	Scheme	Scheme	Scheme
	Truck	Scheme	Scheme	Scheme	Scheme
Sensitive areas—manual sweeping	Staff	Scheme	Scheme	Scheme	Scheme

Description	*N*	**Area 1**	**Area 2**	**Area 3**	**Area 4**
Sensitive areas—mechanized sweeping	Staff	Scheme	Scheme	Scheme	Scheme
	Truck	Scheme	Scheme	Scheme	Scheme
Sensitive areas—emptying litter bins	Staff	Scheme	Scheme	Scheme	Scheme
	Truck	Scheme	Scheme	Scheme	Scheme
	Bins	∂ w/m	∂ w/m	∂ w/m	∂ w/m
Area sweeping	Staff	Scheme	Scheme	Scheme	Scheme
Cleanup of municipal stream banks	Staff	1dr-1wo	1dr-1wo	1dr-1wo	1dr-1wo
	Truck	1	1	1	1
Leaf collection	Staff	25%	25%	25%	25%
	Truck	25%	25%	25%	25%
Cleaning tree rows and related areas	Staff	1dr-2wo	1dr-2wo	1dr-2wo	1dr-2wo
	Truck	1	1	1	1
Mowing and weeding of sidewalks, parks: cleaning, dog areas, draining sumps	Staff	25% serv	25% serv	25% serv	25% serv
	Truck	25% serv	25% serv	25% serv	25% serv
Galleries, porches, valuable areas	Staff	1dr-1wo	1dr-1wo	1dr-1wo	1dr-1wo
	Truck	1	1	1	1
Emptying trash cans	Staff	Scheme	Scheme	Scheme	Scheme
	Truck	Scheme	Scheme	Scheme	Scheme
	Bins	∂ w/m	∂ w/m	∂ w/m	∂ w/m
Services at travel camps	Staff	1	1	1	1
	Truck	25%	25%	25%	25%
	Bins	25%	25%	25%	25%
City fairs, public events	Staff	1dr-1wo	1dr-1wo	1dr-1wo	1dr-1wo
	Truck	1	1	1	1
Snow service	Staff	m. sweeping	m. sweeping	m. sweeping	m. sweeping
	Truck	m. sweeping	m. sweeping	m. sweeping	m. sweeping
Purging and unclogging manholes	Staff	25%	25%	25%	25%
	Truck	25%	25%	25%	25%
Cleaning of stream banks and embankments	Staff	1dr-1wo	1dr-1wo	1dr-1wo	1dr-1wo
	Truck	1	1	1	1
Garbage collection service at municipal facilities	Staff	1 driver	1 driver	1 driver	1 driver
	Truck	1	1	1	1
Cleaning of settling tanks	Staff	1dr-1wo			
	Truck	1	1	1	1
Bus toilets	Staff	1dr-1wo	-	-	1dr-1wo
	Truck	1	-	-	1
Inspection of construction	Staff	25%	25%	25%	25%
On-demand					
Snow service	Staff	2	2	2	2
Pest and rodent control, installation of mobile signs, cleaning of weekly markets, after-events cleaning, cemetery waste disposal, miscellaneous emergencies, fountain cleaning, litter removal in public areas	Staff	1 serv	1 serv	1 serv	1 serv

Note: serv: for each of the services listed in the description cell, dr: driver, wr: worker, ∂ w/m: workers on means.

References

1. Di Foggia, G.; Beccarello, M. Market Structure of Urban Waste Treatment and Disposal: Empirical Evidence from the Italian Industry. *Sustainability* **2021**, *13*, 7412. [CrossRef]
2. Benito-López, B.; Moreno-Enguix, M.d.R.; Solana-Ibañez, J. Determinants of Efficiency in the Provision of Municipal Street-Cleaning and Refuse Collection Services. *Waste Manag.* **2011**, *31*, 1099–1108. [CrossRef] [PubMed]
3. Di Foggia, G.; Beccarello, M. The Impact of a Gain-Sharing Cost-Reflective Tariff on Waste Management Cost under Incentive Regulation: The Italian Case. *J. Environ. Manag.* **2020**, *265*, 110526. [CrossRef]
4. European Parliament. Directive 2014/24/EU of the European Parliament and of the Council of 26 February 2014 on Public Procurement and Repealing Directive 2004/18/EC Text with EEA Relevance. Official Journal of the European Union. Available online: https://eur-lex.europa.eu/legal-content/EN/TXT/?uri=celex%3A32014L0024 (accessed on 7 January 2023).
5. Sviták, J.; van Sinderen, J. Economic Impact of Competition Policy: A Look Beyond Consumer Surplus. *Economist* **2018**, *166*, 23–40. [CrossRef]
6. Llanquileo-Melgarejo, P.; Molinos-Senante, M. Assessing Eco-Productivity Change in Chilean Municipal Solid Waste Services. *Util. Policy* **2022**, *78*, 101410. [CrossRef]
7. Papcunová, V.; Vavrek, R.; Dvořák, M. Role of Public Entities in Suitable Provision of Public Services: Case Study from Slovakia. *Adm. Sci.* **2021**, *11*, 143. [CrossRef]
8. Llanquileo-Melgarejo, P.; Molinos-Senante, M. Evaluation of Economies of Scale in Eco-Efficiency of Municipal Waste Management: An Empirical Approach for Chile. *Environ. Sci. Pollut. Res.* **2021**, *28*, 28337–28348. [CrossRef]
9. Sarra, A.; Mazzocchitti, M.; Rapposelli, A. Evaluating Joint Environmental and Cost Performance in Municipal Waste Management Systems through Data Envelopment Analysis: Scale Effects and Policy Implications. *Ecol. Indic.* **2017**, *73*, 756–771. [CrossRef]
10. Pérez-López, G.; Prior, D.; Zafra-Gómez, J.L.; Plata-Díaz, A.M. Cost Efficiency in Municipal Solid Waste Service Delivery. Alternative Management Forms in Relation to Local Population Size. *Eur. J. Oper. Res.* **2016**, *255*, 583–592. [CrossRef]
11. Gullì, L.; Zazzi, M. Renewal Strategies for the Environmental Conversion of Crafts Districts in Italy. *Procedia Eng.* **2011**, *21*, 771–779. [CrossRef]
12. Bohm, R.A.; Folz, D.H.; Kinnaman, T.C.; Podolsky, M.J. The Costs of Municipal Waste and Recycling Programs. *Resour. Conserv. Recycl.* **2010**, *54*, 864–871. [CrossRef]
13. Da Cruz, N.F.; Simões, P.; Marques, R.C. Costs and Benefits of Packaging Waste Recycling Systems. *Resour. Conserv. Recycl.* **2014**, *85*, 1–4. [CrossRef]
14. Parthan, S.R.; Milke, M.W.; Wilson, D.C.; Cocks, J.H. Cost Estimation for Solid Waste Management in Industrialising Regions—Precedents, Problems and Prospects. *Waste Manag.* **2012**, *32*, 584–594. [CrossRef]
15. Carvalho, P.; Marques, R.C.; Dollery, B. Is Bigger Better? An Empirical Analysis of Waste Management in New South Wales. *Waste Manag.* **2015**, *39*, 277–286. [CrossRef] [PubMed]
16. Fried, H.O.; Lovell, C.A.K.; Schmidt, S.S. (Eds.) *The Measurement of Productive Efficiency and Productivity Growth*; Oxford University Press: New York, NY, USA, 2008. ISBN 978-0-19-518352-8.
17. Mmereki, D.; Baldwin, A.; Li, B. A Comparative Analysis of Solid Waste Management in Developed, Developing and Lesser Developed Countries. *Environ. Technol. Rev.* **2016**, *5*, 120–141. [CrossRef]
18. Wowrzeczka, B. City of Waste—Importance of Scale. *Sustainability* **2021**, *13*, 3909. [CrossRef]
19. Sarra, A.; Mazzocchitti, M.; Nissi, E. Optimal Regulatory Choices in the Organization of Solid Waste Management Systems: Empirical Evidence and Policy Implications. *Environ. Sci. Policy* **2020**, *114*, 436–444. [CrossRef]
20. Di Foggia, G.; Beccarello, M. Improving Efficiency in the MSW Collection and Disposal Service Combining Price Cap and Yardstick Regulation: The Italian Case. *Waste Manag.* **2018**, *79*, 223–231. [CrossRef]
21. Soukopová, J.; Nemec, J.; Matějová, L.; Struk, M. Municipality Size and Local Public Services: Do Economies of Scale Exist? *NISPAcee J. Public Adm. Policy* **2015**, *7*, 151–171. [CrossRef]
22. Bikker, J.; van der Linde, D. Scale Economies in Local Public Administration. *Local Gov. Stud.* **2016**, *42*, 441–463. [CrossRef]
23. d'Albergo, E.; Lefèvre, C.; Ye, L. For a Political Economy of Metropolitan Scale: The Role of Public–Private Relations. *Territ. Politi Gov.* **2018**, *6*, 182–198. [CrossRef]
24. Caldas, P.; Ferreira, D.; Dollery, B.; Marques, R. Are There Scale Economies in Urban Waste and Wastewater Municipal Services? A Non-Radial Input-Oriented Model Applied to the Portuguese Local Government. *J. Clean. Prod.* **2019**, *219*, 531–539. [CrossRef]
25. Mattson, J. Relationships between Density and per Capita Municipal Spending in the United States. *Urban Sci.* **2021**, *5*, 69. [CrossRef]
26. Beccarello, M.; Di Foggia, G. Sustainable Development Goals Data-Driven Local Policy: Focus on SDG 11 and SDG 12. *Adm. Sci.* **2022**, *12*, 167. [CrossRef]
27. Barchiesi, M.A.; Costa, R.; Di Pillo, F. The Link between the Compliance with Environmental Legislation on Separate Collection and the Municipal Solid Waste Costs. *Sustainability* **2022**, *14*, 5661. [CrossRef]
28. Hannon, J. Exploring and Illustrating the (Inter-)Disciplinarity of Waste and Zero Waste Management. *Urban Sci.* **2020**, *4*, 73. [CrossRef]
29. Worthington, A.C.; Higgs, H. Economies of Scale and Scope in Australian Urban Water Utilities. *Util. Policy* **2014**, *31*, 52–62. [CrossRef]

30. Saal, D.S.; Arocena, P.; Maziotis, A.; Triebs, T. Scale and Scope Economies and the Efficient Vertical and Horizontal Configuration of the Water Industry: A Survey of the Literature. *Rev. Netw. Econ.* **2013**, *12*, 93–129. [CrossRef]
31. Jacobsen, R.; Buysse, J.; Gellynck, X. Cost Comparison between Private and Public Collection of Residual Household Waste: Multiple Case Studies in the Flemish Region of Belgium. *Waste Manag.* **2013**, *33*, 3–11. [CrossRef]
32. Kinnaman, T.C. The Economics of Municipal Solid Waste Management. *Waste Manag.* **2009**, *29*, 2615–2617. [CrossRef]
33. Plata-Díaz, A.M.; Zafra-Gómez, J.L.; Pérez-López, G.; López-Hernández, A.M. Alternative Management Structures for Municipal Waste Collection Services: The Influence of Economic and Political Factors. *Waste Manag.* **2014**, *34*, 1967–1976. [CrossRef]
34. Bel, G.; Fageda, X. Empirical Analysis of Solid Management Waste Costs: Some Evidence from Galicia, Spain. *Resour. Conserv. Recycl.* **2010**, *54*, 187–193. [CrossRef]
35. Guerrini, A.; Carvalho, P.; Romano, G.; Cunha Marques, R.; Leardini, C. Assessing Efficiency Drivers in Municipal Solid Waste Collection Services through a Non-Parametric Method. *J. Clean. Prod.* **2017**, *147*, 431–441. [CrossRef]
36. Allesch, A.; Brunner, P.H. Assessment Methods for Solid Waste Management: A Literature Review. *Waste Manag. Res.* **2014**, *32*, 461–473. [CrossRef]
37. De Jaeger, S.; Rogge, N. Waste Pricing Policies and Cost-Efficiency in Municipal Waste Services: The Case of Flanders. *Waste Manag. Res.* **2013**, *31*, 751–758. [CrossRef] [PubMed]
38. Anand, J.; Kim, S. Sub-Additivity. In *The Palgrave Encyclopedia of Strategic Management*; Augier, M., Teece, D.J., Eds.; Palgrave Macmillan UK: London, UK, 2018; pp. 1674–1676. ISBN 978-1-137-00772-8.
39. Linden, G. Economies of Scale. In *The Palgrave Encyclopedia of Strategic Management*; Augier, M., Teece, D.J., Eds.; Palgrave Macmillan UK: London, UK, 2018; pp. 477–479. ISBN 978-1-137-00772-8.
40. Tirole, J. *The Theory of Industrial Organization*; MIT: Cambridge, MA, USA, 1988; ISBN 9780262200714.
41. Teece, D.J. Scope Economies. In *The Palgrave Encyclopedia of Strategic Management*; Augier, M., Teece, D.J., Eds.; Palgrave Macmillan UK: London, UK, 2018; p. 1537. ISBN 978-1-137-00772-8.
42. European Commission. Services of General Economic Interest. *EUR-lex* 2022. European Union. Available online: https://eur-lex.europa.eu/EN/legal-content/glossary/services-of-general-economic-interest.html (accessed on 7 January 2023).
43. Akan, M.; Ata, B.; Lariviere, M.A. Asymmetric Information and Economies of Scale in Service Contracting. *Manuf. Serv. Oper. Manag.* **2011**, *13*, 58–72. [CrossRef]
44. Bergendorff, H.; Larsson, T.; Näslund, R. The Monopoly v Competition Debate. *Telecomm. Policy* **1983**, *7*, 297–308. [CrossRef]
45. Caputo, M.R. Comparative Statics of a Monopolistic Firm Facing Price-Cap and Command-and-Control Environmental Regulations. *Energy Econ.* **2014**, *46*, 464–471. [CrossRef]
46. Joskow, P.L. Regulation of Natural Monopoly. In *Handbook of Law and Ecoonomics*; Polinsky, A.M., Shavell, S., Eds.; Elsevier: Amsterdam, The Netherlands, 2007; Volume 2, pp. 1227–1348. ISBN 1574-0730.
47. Di Foggia, G.; Beccarello, M. An Overview of Packaging Waste Models in Some European Countries. *Recycling* **2022**, *7*, 38. [CrossRef]
48. Meriläinen, J.; Tukiainen, J. Public Procurement versus Laissez-Faire: Evidence from Household Waste Collection. *CESifo Econ. Stud.* **2019**, *65*, 446–463. [CrossRef]
49. Bel, G.; Sebő, M. Watch Your Neighbor: Strategic Competition in Waste Collection and Service Quality. *Waste Manag.* **2021**, *127*, 63–72. [CrossRef] [PubMed]
50. Warner, M.E.; Bel, G. Competition or Monopoly? Comparing Privatization of Local Public Services in the US and Spain. *Public Adm.* **2008**, *86*, 723–735. [CrossRef]
51. Beccarello, M.; Di Foggia, G. Economic Analysis of EU Strengthened Packaging Waste Recycling Targets. *J. Adv. Res. Law Econ.* **2016**, *7*, 1930–1941.
52. Beccarello, M.; Di Foggia, G. Moving towards a Circular Economy: Economic Impacts of Higher Material Recycling Targets. *Mater. Today Proc.* **2018**, *5*, 531–543. [CrossRef]

urban science

MDPI

Review

A Bibliometric and Content Analysis of Sustainability and Smart Tourism

Clara Madeira [1,2,3,*], Paula Rodrigues [1,2] and Monica Gomez-Suarez [3]

[1] Faculty of Economics and Management, Universidade Lusíada–Norte, R. de Moçambique 21, 4100-346 Porto, Portugal
[2] COMEGI (Research Centre in Organizations, Markets and Industrial Management), R. da Junqueira 188-198, 1349-001 Lisboa, Portugal
[3] Department of Finance and Marketing Research, Universidad Autónoma de Madrid, Cantoblanco, 28049 Madrid, Spain
* Correspondence: clara-madeira@hotmail.com

Abstract: Sustainability and smart tourism are current hot topics in academic research. While these two concepts are complementary, their relationship has not been clearly outlined in the scientific literature. This bibliometric analysis aims to address this gap by examining the literature on sustainability and smart tourism. Specifically, this review has five objectives: (i) to document the size and growth of the literature on this topic, (ii) to identify the key authors, journals, and documents, (iii) to categorize the countries with the highest productivity rates, (iv) to highlight emerging topics and their relationship to the conceptual structure of each domain, and (v) to analyse the methodology approach. A total of 104 scientific documents were searched and analysed from the Web of Science Core Collection for the period 1900–2022 using R-Program and VOSviewer. The results indicate that there is an emerging knowledge base with main clusters identified in smart tourism, sustainable tourism, innovation, and smart cities. China, Spain, the Republic of Korea, Italy, Iran, and Portugal have demonstrated the highest rate of scientific production. This review provides valuable insights for both academics and practitioners seeking to expand their knowledge of sustainability and smart tourism research. It also offers new perspectives on the future development of these areas within the social sciences' academic literature.

Keywords: sustainability; smart tourism; smart cities; innovation; bibliometric review

1. Introduction

Research in the areas of sustainability and smart tourism has been a subject of interest in recent years [1,2]. Several explanations might be found for this increase of interest, including collaborations among scholars within the academic community resulting in academic contributions that can help to understand these fields [3]. Several published articles have presented bibliometric studies on both topics separately. Nevertheless, although a number of studies, such as [4–7], have shown the importance of smart technologies for sustainable tourism, to the best of the authors' knowledge, there are no bibliometric reviews relating to both fields together. Moreover, there is an absence of relational studies using social network analysis in the tourism domain [8]. For this reason, the purpose of this research is to fill this void, by examining how the research about sustainability and smart tourism has globally evolved.

Concerning the topic of sustainability, knowledge management [9], human resource management [10], tourism development [11], entrepreneurship [12], corporate governance and board attributes [13], socially responsible funds [14], and leadership [15] are distinct sub-disciplines analysed with this methodology.

Regarding smart tourism, bibliometric studies on this topic [16,17] have also been of interest for both academics and business practitioners, due to its capacity to provide useful information, timely data, and interconnectivity between tourism stakeholders [18]. As Celdrán-Bernabeu et al. [3] suggest, the interest in smart tourism as a research topic is growing within the academic community, and the collaborations established between researchers help to understand this field. For instance, Johnson and Samakovlis [16] examined the production of smart tourism knowledge and found that the most dominant authors within the authorship sub-clusters were Law, Leung [19], Lorenzo Cantoni, Ulrike Gretzel, Hannes Werthner, Chulmo Koo, and Namho Chung.

With respect to the emerging themes, the abovementioned authors analysed the keywords included in the papers and showed associations to terms, namely smart city, smart tourism, social media, and information technology.

This study aims to analyse the scientific production on sustainability and smart tourism. First, it covers the geographical and yearly distribution. Second, the main authors, articles, and top keywords are identified. Moreover, the clusters regarding the conceptual structure are shown. Then, a content analysis is performed to describe the theoretical or empirical nature of the most cited publications, featuring the major lines for future research within these fields and revealing the knowledge pillars of the respective concepts.

One of the main purposes of this study is to provide orientation and guidance to academics and practitioners who are developing their investigation within this field. Thus, this research increases their knowledge about the key scientific journals, authors, and articles shaping this topic. Moreover, these findings could also help scholars who are at an initial phase of their careers by listing the most prominent countries and institutions where they might develop their studies [20].

Hence, four research questions guided this systematic and bibliometric review of research on sustainability and smart tourism:

RQ1: How has scientific production on sustainability and smart tourism evolved geographically and yearly?
RQ2: Which authors, journals, and documents on sustainability and smart tourism have achieved the greatest scholarly impact?
RQ3: What is the conceptual structure of the knowledge base on sustainability and smart tourism?
RQ4: What are the gaps and directions for future research?

Regarding methodology, this study uses data derived from the database Web of Science (WoS) Core Collection, recognized as an important database used by tourism academics [21,22] and in interdisciplinary, international social science publications. The analysis and visualization process resorts to VOSviewer and R-Studio (Bibliometrics version 3.6.3). Through the application of a social network analysis (SNA), it was possible to identify collaborative networks specifically in sustainability and smart tourism, providing a deeper understanding of knowledge developing in the tourism domain [23]. Using several bibliometric indicators, this paper examines the main academic contributions in researching the relationship between sustainability and smart tourism.

This paper is organized as follows. In the next section, the theoretical framework is presented. Then, the methodology and the data collection process are introduced, followed by the presentation of the bibliometric review results that describe the state of the art of the studied topics. Additionally, through a social network analysis, two maps concerning the keywords and citation connections, respectively, are developed. The keyword analysis allowed us to identify four clusters. Finally, a content analysis and the main future research lines we identified based on the most cited articles of each conceptual cluster were elaborated.

2. Theoretical Framework

2.1. Smart Tourism

Smart is a current buzz term that cuts across many sectors and activities and is present on a daily basis. Gretzel, Werthner [24] (p. 559) described "Smart" as "a prefix to technological terms to indicate special capabilities, intelligence and/or connectivity, as in smart phone or smart card". It has also been associated with resource optimization through advanced technologies [25] or the interconnection and synchronization of different technologies [26]. The term "smart cities" has been widely used to describe different types of urban areas. As Harrison et al. [27] indicate, smart cities are urban areas that make use of operational data (e.g., traffic congestion data, power consumption statistics, etc.) and are capable of analysing this information and optimizing the city services in constant interaction with its inhabitants. These services have been made available to tourists, and one of the goals of smart cities is to be a smart tourism destination [28,29].

The constant development of information and communication technologies (ICTs) has challenged tourism practices and brought smartness into destinations. Several articles have been devoted to the analysis of smart tourism destinations [30–32]. Thus, Jovicic [33] (p. 278) defines a smart tourism destination as "a knowledge-based destination, where ICTs are used to provide a technological platform on which information and knowledge relating to tourism could be instantly exchanged". Following this trend, the European Union has promoted the "European Capital of Smart Tourism" initiative to reward and share the most exemplary European cities that implement tools, measures, and projects to develop smart tourism. The European Union [34] defines a smart tourism destination as "a destination that facilitates access to tourism and hospitality products, services, spaces, and experiences through ICT-based tools". Additionally, these practices must be centred around four key categories: sustainability, accessibility, digitalization, and cultural heritage and creativity.

2.2. Sustainability

Considering the different domains of sustainability that have been studied, one of the challenges is the lack of consistent definitions in the literature [35]. Based on a systems perspective, Ben-Eli [35] (p. 1340) offers the following definition of sustainability: "a dynamic equilibrium in the process of interaction between a population and the carrying capacity of its environment such that the population develops to express its full potential without producing irreversible adverse effects on the carrying capacity of the environment upon which it depends". According to the author, this definition portrays the idea of sustainability as a catalyst for creating a cohesive and functional balance between people, society, the economy, and the Earth's regenerative ecosystems, ensuring their ability to support life in the long term.

Many global organizations such as the OECD, the European Union, and the United Nations have been increasingly addressing this issue and warning multiple entities, governments, and populations on the consequences of their actions. International events such as the United Nations Conference on Sustainable Development organized in 2012 that addressed themes such as green and blue economies [36], the United Nations General Assembly in 2015 that provided a concrete goals agenda, and the Agenda 2030, in which the Sustainable Development Goals were defined [37] are examples of tangible steps that are being taken to promote sustainable practices.

In the scope of smart tourism, according to the European Union [34], sustainability goes beyond the societal equilibrium described by Ben-Eli [35] and includes various actions that should be taken in order to better manage the city resources, such as reducing seasonality and engaging locals and tourists in tourism activities. Climate change, the diversification and protection of local economies, the efficient management of natural resources based on more eco-friendly energies, and the city development are some of the concerns that should be considered by policymakers in the development of smart tourism practices.

2.3. Integrating Sustainability and Smart Approaches in Tourism

It is recognized that sustainability and smart approaches are closely related in the context of tourism [1,34], reinforced by the various definitions of smart tourism or smart cities encountered in academic papers that outline resource optimization [25,27], efficiency [35], competitiveness, and inclusiveness [18]. In fact, the smart tourism paradigm emphasizes the importance of efficient, responsible, and sustainable management of tourism resources as a crucial strategic goal for tourism destinations [6]. Inversely, the integration of big data and artificial intelligence into tourism services is also a key instrument to achieve sustainability [2]. Despite the conceptual connection between smart tourism and sustainability, there are several challenges that hinder their implementation, such as financial resources, incompatibility between market competitiveness and long-term growth, and even human behaviour (tourists, employers, and locals). These challenges, along with the complexity of both fields and the novelty of smart tourism, create a barrier to further empirical analysis into the relationship between sustainability and smart tourism. Therefore, more research is needed to explore the intersection of these topics in the scientific literature. According to Shen et al. [6], the merger of sustainable and smart strategies can be accomplished, for example, by encouraging suitable practices and involving tourists as co-managers, co-designers, and co-creators of tourism experiences. In addition, implementing eco-friendly practices, such as reducing plastic waste, conserving water and energy, and promoting local culture and products, can contribute to sustainability while also enhancing the tourist experience. Moreover, using technology to facilitate sustainable tourism, such as mobile apps that provide information on eco-friendly accommodations and activities, can also promote smart tourism.

3. Methods

3.1. Bibliometric and Content Analysis Methods

To understand the scientific production and the evolution over the last few years of sustainability and smart tourism, we performed a bibliometric analysis using bibliometrics and SNA. This approach has become popular to draw trends and deepen the understanding of emerging concepts [22,38]. Accordingly, its application seems to fit the objective of our research.

Bibliometrics applies mathematical and statistical methods to aggregated bibliographic data produced by other scientists within the field who express their opinions through citation, collaboration, and writing [39,40]. These methods represent a systematic, unambiguous, and replicable review process, while reflecting both quantitative and qualitative analysis [40–42].

Bibliometric tools withstand the measurement of publications and citations. While the former reflects productivity in quantifiable terms, the latter presents influence and quality of scientific production. These measures are analysed per author, per geographical area, and per time period. Moreover, the relevance of topics mentioned across the literature and the main methodological approaches of articles are determined through statistical analysis of keywords.

Subsequently, SNA is used to map bibliographic data, complementing bibliometrics. SNA facilitates the examination of various relationship structures and provides a straightforward interpretation of the corresponding interactions. Through mapping processes, it can measure relationships between nodes and understand how knowledge flows [42,43]. In addition, it identifies clusters that reflect strong groups within the networks [44]. Focusing these aspects, the main objective within SNA falls on the construction and analysis of networks.

In this study, we created a keyword co-occurrence network, which allows us to understand how the most relevant themes and core scientific knowledge around sustainability and smart tourism relate [45,46] and to identify the knowledge structure of the subject area [16]. The content analysis allows us to summarize the patterns in the literature by recognizing the "hot spots" and "blind spots" as well as complementing the previous selected methods [47,48]. Thus, the empirical investigation in this study endeavours to (i) understand the size and growth of scientific output in these topics, (ii) identify the most influential authors as well as the most productive countries, (iii) recognize core themes, (iv) uncover the main methodological approaches, and (v) recap the main future research guidelines.

To develop the bibliometric analysis, we used the Bibliometrix package (which offers resources to analyse and map bibliometric information) that works under the R-Program software (version 3.2.3). For SNA, we used VOSviewer (version 1.6.15) [49]. This method can reveal how scientific research in smart tourism and sustainability has contributed to theoretical discussions, methodological advancements, and practical implications in this field.

3.2. Data Collection

To sustain our bibliographic analysis, data from Web of Science [50] was collected. The search encompasses title, abstract, author keywords, and keywords plus and focuses this combination: "smart tourism" AND ("sustainability" OR "sustainable"). Additionally, only articles, book chapters, and reviews were considered.

All information published on WoS until the day of search, 19 December 2022, was considered. Hence, the database results in 104 articles from 2015–2022. The process to collect data is depicted in Figure 1.

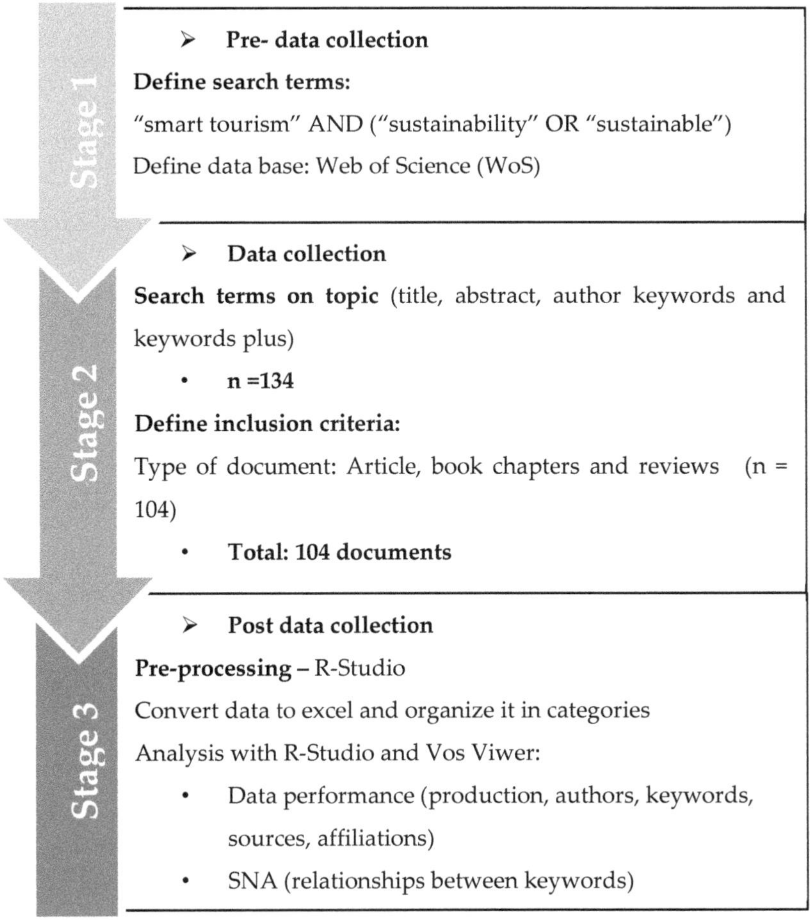

Source: Own elaboration.

Figure 1. Data acquisition and pre-processing for bibliometric analysis.

Note that, complementarily to the information from WoS, some qualitative categories, such as methodological approach, core themes, and future research lines, were assigned to each of the 104 articles after an attentive reading. All the data were then pre-processed for a better and more precise analysis.

The main indicators from the information retrieved from WoS show that the final database consisted of 104 documents from 52 different sources published between 2015 and 2022. Collaboration is predominant, with more than 90% of the documents having multiple authors. On average, each article is attributed to approximately 3 authors and has around 17 citations.

In the upcoming sections, a bibliometric review and content analysis will be conducted.

4. Results

4.1. Bibliometric Analysis

Figure 2 depicts the growth of scientific research on sustainability and smart tourism in cumulative terms from 2015 to 2022. It has been growing exponentially, especially from 2018 to 2020, but slightly decreased from 2020 to 2022. In fact, smart tourism has become a buzz term not only in academics but also in the media and the business world. In 2019, the European Union promoted a new initiative to find the "European Capital of Smart Tourism", recognizing exemplary European cities on practices of smart tourism.

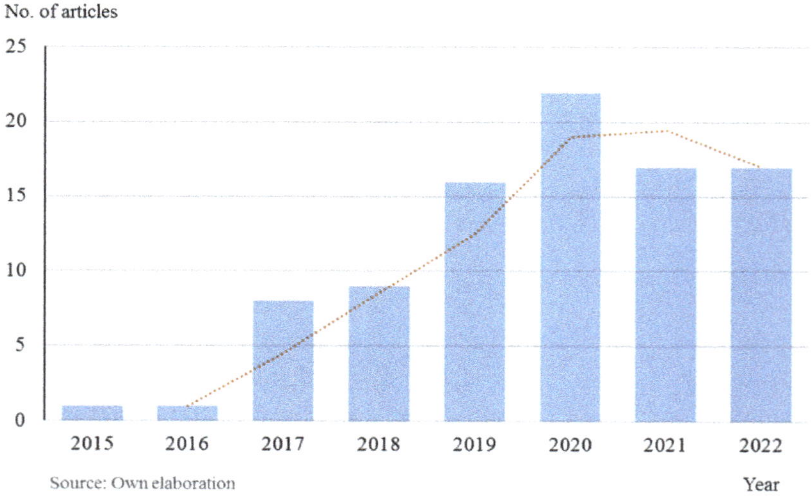

Figure 2. Annual scientific production, 2015–2022.

This might have raised awareness for the academy to explore the theme of smart tourism. Nonetheless, in 2020, the research might have shifted to other topics in the face of the consequences of the COVID-19 pandemic on tourism (which decreased significantly). Based on the data presented, it is perceived that the combination of sustainability and smart tourism is a relatively recent phenomenon on a global scale. This may be due to the fact that smart tourism is a new and developing field of research, with a focus on conceptual works that have yet to explore specific aspects of smart tourism, including sustainability. In order to find gaps in the literature related to sustainability and smart tourism, additional bibliometric statistics have been developed.

To gain insight into the geographic dissemination of the academic research, the overall distribution per continent is depicted on Figure 3 and the top 12 countries in Figure 4, based on the affiliation of all authors.

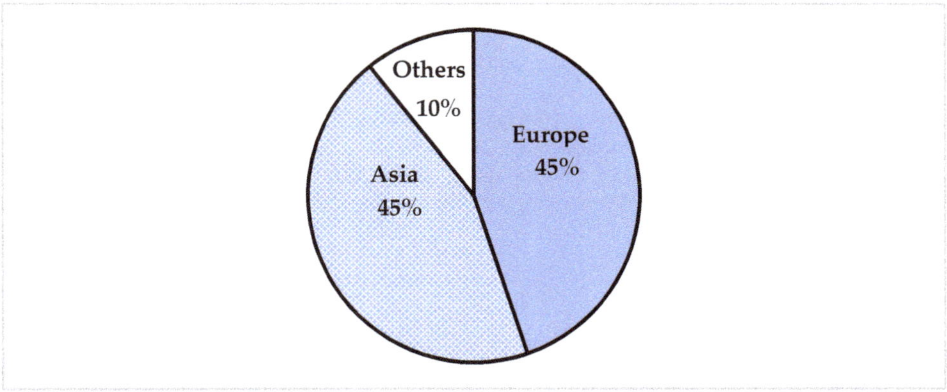

Source: Own elaboration.

Figure 3. Scientific production per continent (%), 2015–2022.

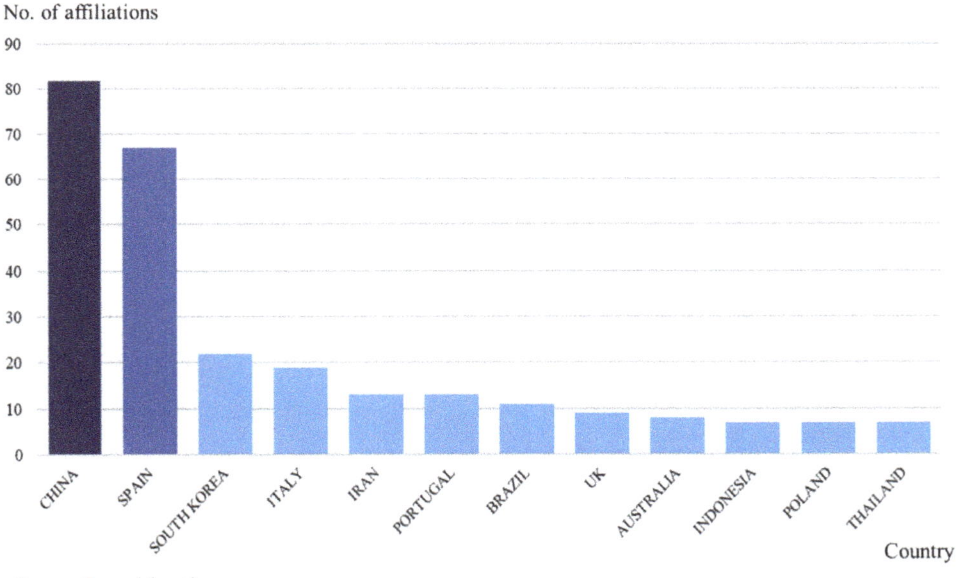

Source: Own elaboration

Figure 4. Scientific production per country, 2015–2022.

Crossing information from both figures, we note that the scientific literature is predominantly from Europe, where the Mediterranean region, including Spain, Italy, and Portugal, contributes the most, and Eastern Asia, strengthen by the production of China, mainly, and the Republic of Korea. Oceania, Africa, and the Americas are incorporated in "Others" (Figure 3), as they have individually a less significant proportion of article production. In this analysis, two clusters are identified: a group of Asian countries characterized by technologically integrated cities that relate to the smart concept and Southern Europe, which is highly dependent on tourism and not necessarily reputable for technological interconnectivity in its cities.

To show these differences, Table 1 presents aggregated indexes from (1) tourism, with the relative contribution of travel and tourism to employment and to GDP, data from 2019 retrieved from the World Travel and Tourism Council (WTTC) [51] Economic

Impact Reports; (2) technological development, with the 2022 Innovation Index from the World Intellectual Property Organization (WIPO) [52] and 2020 expenditures of research and development (R&D) in total gross domestic product (GDP) from the OECD [53] gross domestic spending on R&D; and (3) sustainability, through the 2020 Sustainable Development Goals Index (SDG), which tracks country performance on the 17 SDGs, as agreed by the international community in 2015 with equal weight to all 17 goals [54]. These measures show that Eastern Asian countries have a better performance in technology, while Southern Europe has a significant social-economic dependence on tourism, reflected in employment and GDP.

Table 1. Indicators of tourism, innovation, and sustainability.

	Tourism		Innovation and Technology		Sustainability
Country	**2019 T&T % of Total Employment**	**2019 T&T % of Total GDP**	**2022 Innovation Index**	**2020 R&D Expenditures % of Total GDP**	**2020 SDG Index**
China	10.3	11.3	55.3	2.1	73.9
Korea	4.8	4.2	57.8	4.5	78.3
Spain	14.6	14.3	44.6	1.2	78.1
Italy	14.9	13.0	46.1	1.4	77.0
Portugal	18.7	16.5	42.1	1.4	77.6

Source: Own elaboration.

In fact, regions such as Seoul in Korea; Beijing, Shenzhen, and Hong Kong in China; or Tokyo and Yokohama in Japan are internationally recognized for their smart cities, through the high investment in the IoT (Internet of things) towards the construction of infrastructure, housing, networks of transportation and services, and many others [53]. In Korea and Japan, governments have been investing in smart and eco-city projects from the early 2000s, while China has been adopting the latest smart technology for urban management [55]. On the other side, Southern Europe does not stand out in terms of high-tech urban structures in comparison with Northern European countries, such as Switzerland, the United Kingdom, and Sweden. Nonetheless, governments have been applying efforts in the development of smart systems in the scope of tourism [53].

Table 2 presents the top five articles based on the cumulative number of citations since their publication (higher than 50 citations). These articles have been published by authors from the two clusters identified in the previous section: Sun et al. [56], Pan et al. [57], and Shafiee et al. [58] from the Asian cluster, and Pencarelli [59] and Encalada et al. [60] from the European cluster. The document from Sun et al. [56] has an impressive mark of almost 500 citations. It conceptualizes "smart and connected communities" as a natural evolution of "smart cities" and presents a case study—TreSight—in Trento, Italy, that integrates the IoT and big data analytics for smart tourism and sustainable cultural heritage. It has become a guide and reference not only for scientific investigators but also for managers of city services.

Table 2. Most cited articles about smart tourism and sustainability, 2015–2022.

First Author, Year	Affiliation of First Author	Title	No. of Citations	Average No. of Citations/Year
Sun Y (2016) [56]	China	Internet of things and big data analytics for smart and connected communities	479	68.43
Pan SY (2018) [57]	Taiwan	Advances and challenges in sustainable tourism toward a green economy	149	29.80

Table 2. *Cont.*

First Author, Year	Affiliation of First Author	Title	No. of Citations	Average No. of Citations/Year
Pencarelli T (2020) [59]	Italy	The digital revolution in the travel and tourism industry	67	22.33
Shafiee S (2019) [58]	Iran	Developing a model for sustainable smart tourism destinations: a systematic review	62	15.50
Encalada L (2017) [60]	Portugal	Identifying tourist places of interest based on digital imprints: towards a sustainable smart city	55	9.17

Source: Own elaboration.

With respect to the scientific production per journal (Table 3), it is possible to observe that *Sustainability* attains a dominant position with its 38 published articles (37% of the total) and almost half a thousand citations. *IEEE Access* published one article that is currently the most cited of the database: "Internet of things and big data analytics for smart and connected communities" by Sun et al. [56]. The remaining 50 journals have a significantly lower output, averaging one paper per journal. Even though the number of articles is low, journals such as *Science of the Total Environment* (149), *Tourism Management Perspectives* (69), and *Journal of Destination Marketing & Management* (62) demonstrate a high rate of citations. One possible explanation for these results is the interdisciplinary nature of the topics covered across different academic fields (see Table 3). In terms of impact factor outlined in the 2021 Journal Citation Reports [61], *Science of Total Environment* is attached to the highest value (10.76) followed by *Tourism Management Perspectives* (7.61) and *Journal of Destination Marketing & Management* (7.16). Environmental sciences and business, management, and accounting are cross topics among the most relevant journals.

Table 3. Ranking of the five most productive and influential journals (sorted by citations), 2015–2022.

Journal	Publications	Citations	Impact Factor	Main Theme
Sustainability	28	492	3.89	Energy; environmental science; social sciences
IEEE Access	1	479	3.48	Computer sciences; engineering; material science
Science of the Total Environment	1	149	10.76	Environmental science
Tourism Management Perspectives	2	69	7.61	Business; management; accounting
Journal of Destination Marketing & Management	3	62	7.16	Business; management; accounting

Source: Own elaboration.

Next, the most frequent keywords (≥6 times) used by the authors of the collected scientific documents are listed in Table 4. This ranking is also observed through a word cloud (see Figure 5) that depicts the top 35 keywords, in which the size of each word reflects its frequency. Due to the high frequency of the term "smart tourism" (20%) among the 35 most used keywords, its relative size was reduced to make room for other keywords and to ensure a clear and comprehensive conceptual analysis of the word cloud. As expected, keywords such as "smart tourism" and "sustainability" dominate, which supports our selection of keywords in WoS. Nonetheless, it is interesting to note that the term "smart tourism" is much more frequent than "sustainability", reinforced by terms associated with smartness ("smart cities", "smart tourism destinations", "smart destinations", and "smart"). Additionally, it is possible to understand that keywords related to R&D and information and communications technology (ICT), such as "innovation", "technology", "smart", and "tourism intelligence", have a significant weight across the approached topics. Words related to management and politics, such as "governance", "co-creation", and "destination management", are relevant and reflect the political aspect involved in the construction of a smarter and more sustainable kind of tourism.

Table 4. Top keywords, 2015–2022.

Authors' Keywords	Number of Occurrences
Smart tourism	43
Smart tourism destination(s)	17
Sustainability	15
Tourism	15
Smart city(ies)	13
Sustainable tourism	11
Innovation	9
Smart destination(s)	9
Smart	7
Governance	6
Technology	6

Source: Own elaboration.

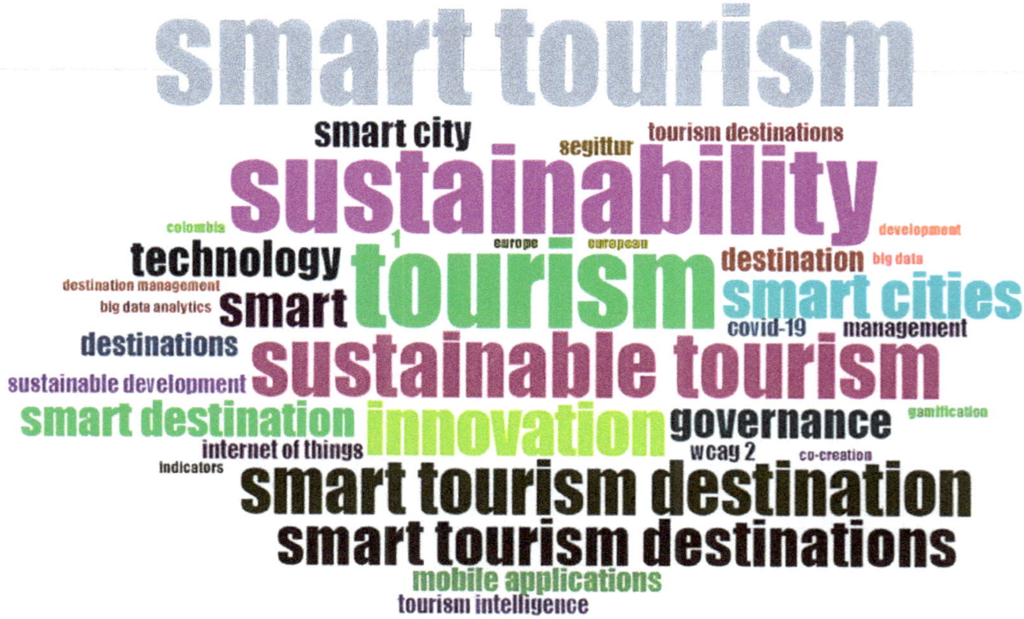

Figure 5. Word cloud.

4.2. Social Network Analysis: Co-Occurrence Network of Keywords

To analyse the main subjects of our database, we developed a keyword network with VOSviewer based on co-occurrences. This enables us to uncover links between concepts and to create a conceptual map. The attribute of occurrences indicates the number of documents in which a keyword occurs. Then, the map returns clusters that are shorter and somewhat isolated networks where nodes have a high number of interactions, more specifically, networks with densely connected groups of nodes with sparser connections between them. Descriptions of terminologies related to networks based in VOSviewer language [49,62] are presented in Table 5.

Table 5. Terminology of networks based in VOSviewer language.

Concepts	Description
Item or Node	The objects of interest. Items may for example be publications, researchers, or terms.
Link	A connection or a relation between two items.
Network	Set of nodes connected by their links.
Cluster/Community	Set of connected nodes included in a network. One node belongs to only one cluster.
Link strength (Link strength and total link strength are terms used in VOSviewer program)	Attribute of each link, expressed by a positive numerical value. In the case of co-authorship links, the higher the value, the higher the number of publications the two researchers have co-authored.
Weight Attribute: Total Link Strength	The cumulative strength of the links of an item with other items.

Source: Own elaboration.

Based on an initial set of 591 keywords (author keywords and keywords plus), the following criteria were applied to achieve the keyword co-occurrence network: (1) the full counting method, where each of the links has strength of one; (2) a minimum number of co-occurrences of six, meaning that each keyword belonged to at least six documents; and (3) association as the normalization method of the network layout [49]. The resulting network (Figure 6) was composed of 29 keywords and organized into four clusters identified by the VOSviewer algorithm, each named according to its main node: (1) smart tourism, (2) sustainable tourism, (3) innovation, and (4) smart cities (see Figure 6 and Table 6). Interestingly, certain themes such as technology and smart tourism destination were found to belong to different clusters (Table 6), specifically, smart tourism, sustainable tourism, and innovation clusters. This finding is consistent with previous analyses (e.g., Table 4), which identified smart tourism as the most frequently occurring term in our database.

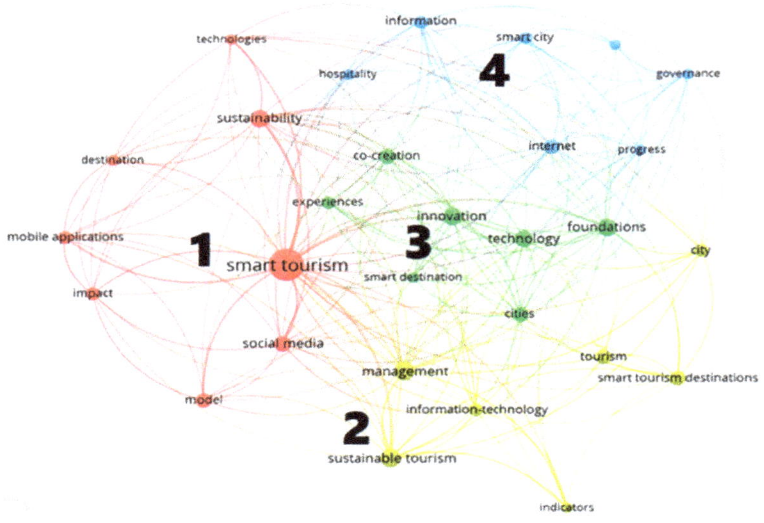

Source: Own elaboration (using VOSviewer)

1-Smart Tourism	2-Sustainable Tourism
3-Innovation	4-Smart Cities

Figure 6. Visualization of keyword co-occurrence network based on total link strength.

Table 6. Clusters identified in the keyword network.

Cluster No.	Colour	Name of Cluster	Number of Keywords
1	Red	Smart Tourism	8
2	Yellow	Sustainable Tourism	7
3	Green	Innovation	7
4	Blue	Smart Cities	7

Source: Own elaboration.

Table 6 presents a comprehensive summary of the conceptual network by identifying the four distinct clusters, each represented by a unique colour in the accompanying map in Figure 6, and the corresponding number of keywords. Each cluster in the network is characterized by a set of nodes and links, which are colour-coded to facilitate its visual identification. Smart tourism is highlighted in red, sustainable tourism in yellow, innovation in green, and smart cities in blue, respectively.

Considering the clusters identified through SNA (Figure 6 and Table 6), the next section will be devoted to the content analysis that will complement the information extracted above.

4.3. Content Analysis

This procedure is a highly flexible research method, enriching our analysis based on quantitative and statistical tools [48,63]. It is also considered a systematic and rigorous approach to analyse documents obtained for the bibliometric review [64], enabling the summary of trends and gaps in the most influential literature. Therefore, the most cited articles (a total of 20 articles with more than 20 citations) are identified. Then, a careful read of the title, its keywords, abstract, and article content were performed. This procedure allowed us to allocate each article to a thematic cluster. Table 7 provides information about the cluster identification, articles, methodology, and future lines of research.

Table 7. Analysis of the 20 most cited articles.

Cluster	Article	Methodology	Future Lines of Research
	Yoo et al. [7]	Empirical Quantitative	a. To carry out a follow-up study on actual users after a certain period, using the same model. b. Further studies should be carried out in other countries to determine whether the results vary based on network technology level, smartphone penetration rate, and cultural characteristics.
	Del Vecchio and Passiante [65]	Conceptual	*
	Ivars-Baidal et al. [66]	Conceptual and Empirical	a. This study proposes an indicator system for smart tourism destinations that could be applied in other contexts and help to develop more accurate tourism policies. b. Future studies must adjust the proposed indicators by enhancing psycho-econometric properties of some dimensions.
	Gretzel and Scarpino-Johns [67]	Conceptual	a. In practice, resilience management and smart tourism development are still disconnected, and merging the two would enable destinations to take advantage of their potential synergies. b. More critical studies are needed to reveal smart tourism management and governance vulnerabilities, implications, and traps. c. More technology-focused studies can also support the integration of smart tourism principles into its frameworks.

Table 7. *Cont.*

Cluster	Article	Methodology	Future Lines of Research
Sustainable Tourism	Mandic and Pranicevic [68]	Conceptual	a. The Interreg Italy–Croatia developed a data-based networking "Living Lab" that could guide researchers and practitioners on approaching a smart business ecosystem with creativity and innovation. b. There is a need to explore in depth the role of the ICT implemented in leading tourism destinations on new visitors' behaviours, decision making, and experiences. c. Since the role of smart governance in smart destinations has not been fully recognized by researchers, future studies should pay more attention to this dimension.
	Shafiee et al. [58]	Empirical Qualitative	a. To consider causal relationships and components from the model developed. b. Additionally, public governance of smart destinations' development could be better analysed, clarifying duties and political strategies.
	Pan et al. [57]	Conceptual	To evaluate policies, sector investments, and feedback mechanisms aimed at regulating corporate and tourist behaviours.
	Ribes and Baidal [69]	Conceptual	a. To validate the causal relationships inherent in the mechanisms found in the model. b. To analyse in depth the practical avenue of sustainability and smartness in order to mitigate the mere theoretical use of concepts such as smart destination that entail a great potential for the development of smart sustainability.
	Alfaro Navarro et al. [70]	Conceptual	This paper introduces an index to assess sustainable tourism at the European NUTS 2 level. Following the presented model, future works could: a. Extend environmental dimensions in the indicators by including subjective measures of aspects that have not been previously addressed. b. Conduct this study at micro levels, such as at NUTS 3 or cities.
	Pencarelli [59]	Conceptual	a. Integrating knowledge from various relevant fields is essential for research on smart tourism destinations, including information systems, travel behaviour, marketing, urban planning, destination management and governance, and the emerging fields of data sciences. b. To empirically examine and assess the potential practical impact of the digital revolution on tourists in the future. c. To evaluate the effect of the sharing economy on the value ecosystem within the tourism industry.
	Romão and Neuts [71]	Empirical Quantitative	a. To accurately identify distinct regional patterns of evolution and potential changes over time. b. To evaluate CO_2 emissions at a regional level and analyse spatial impacts of tourism on local ecosystems.
Innovation	Polese et al. [72]	Empirical Qualitative	a. Identify some key drivers that foster successful value co-creation and sustainability to enhance current insights on value co-creation and expose the various types of real user activities and collaborations. b. Integration of varied service theories is needed to establish a comprehensive meta-theory for service and value co-creation. c. Identifying the primary factors that drive value co-creation and innovation can promote an effective management for encouraging stakeholders' involvement and determining sustainable relationships, considering its complexity. d. The analysis focused solely on the perspectives of bed and breakfast (B&B) owners, thereby limiting the analysis to provider viewpoints. Future studies could investigate the opinions and behaviours of other smart tourism actors, such as travellers, to facilitate comparisons between managers' and users' perceptions, acceptance, and technology use.
	Battino and Lampreu [73]	Empirical Qualitative and Quantitative	*
	Kim and Kim [74]	Empirical Qualitative	a. Analyse which type of Internet connection, fixed or mobile, travellers tend to choose depending on the nature of their trip, the decision-making process, environments, and costs. b. To evaluate current methodologies that rely on survey-based data collection by studying consumer behaviour through analyses of mobile app reviews. c. Focus on analysing other technologies due to the potential for the platform provider to exert control over mobile technology, thereby influencing tourism planning governance and the competitiveness of tourism destinations.

Table 7. *Cont.*

Cluster	Article	Methodology	Future Lines of Research
Smart Cities	Tavitiyaman et al. [75]	Empirical Quantitative	a. Future works could collect data from the same destination (Hong Kong) during other periods, or from different destinations, and compare the results. In addition, the following could be considered: b. Other tourism stakeholders, such as governments, tourism policymakers, and tourism providers. c. Other criteria to visit future smart tourism destinations.
	Ma et al. [2]	Conceptual	a. An online tourism agency with big data marketing technology is an indispensable bridge between tourists and a tourism spot b. Consumer shopping behaviour and experience must be considered in business decisions. c. The altruistic preference between a tourism spot and an online tourism agency can promote environmental efficiency while bringing a better experience to tourists, which leads to a more sustainable development of tourism.
	Sun et al. [56]	Conceptual	*
	Encalada et al. [60]	Empirical Quantitative	a. Simply integrating technology within a tourism destination is not sufficient to make it "smart". To create an effective quality management evaluation system for tourist attractions, ICTs must be complemented with insights from experts such as government officials and researchers. b. Technology dependency is another concern to consider, highlighting the need to examine the outcomes of a digital split based on smart device access and affordable tourism infrastructure, and develop mechanisms to diminish the issue. c. Smart tourism could contemplate, among other strategies, the value in use, i.e., the value created by using data or technology instead of owning it, in order to mitigate digital footprints.
	Lee et al. [76]	Conceptual	a. Future studies could extend the components of the smart tourism city model.
	Sigalat-Signes et al. [77]	Conceptual	a. Further research could analyse quantitatively how smart a destination is, based on the perception of tourists and residents. b. To develop and extend information about smart tourism besides the private providers' view.

* The study does not present future lines of research. Source: own elaboration.

The next sections will show how each cluster identified with SNA will be complemented by the content analyses, including the sources identified and a brief description of the studies.

4.3.1. Cluster Smart Tourism

The first cluster in smart tourism covers studies about smart technology and its contribution to tourism [7,68]. Del Vecchio et al. [78] and Ivars-Baidal et al. [66] elaborate their research based on destinations' case studies, namely in Italy and Spain, respectively. Del Vecchio and Passiante [65] examined Apulia, Italy, and uncovered the impact of tourism on smart regional growth. Smart specialization "is a place-based strategy that invites the European regions to identify and follow a development path that is based on their specific vocations leverages the appropriate key enabling technologies, and focuses particularly on entrepreneurial development" [65] (p. 163).

Tourism represents a key industry for Apulia and should be approached strategically towards local growth and smart specialization. The researchers stress that the close relationship between a smart specialization strategy and tourism development will rely on the destination's capacity to capitalize on both the opportunities from ICT, fomenting its symbioses.

Additionally, Ivars-Baidal et al. [66] developed an indicator system in collaboration with INVAT.TUR, a public organization, to assess different smart tourism destinations of the Region of Valencia, Spain, regarding its policies. The authors provide a very useful tool that can be applied for tourism managers and governors that may adapt the suggested indicators in their own destinations. The work enhances the need to develop a strategic planning that should be inclusive of all stakeholders. Universal accessibility of destinations must be prioritized in future political actions. Moreover, sensorization may be improved to promote business connectivity. Finally, they find a gap concerning the impact of online marketing designed by the smart development on the tourist's experience.

The work of Gretzel and Scarpino-Johns [67] intersects the concepts of destination resilience and smart destination, which is an identified gap, so far, in the current studies. Moreover, it provided a model that may guide managers and policymakers in developing a more resilient and smart kind of tourism. This is sustained on five pillars: (1) sensing, (2) opening, (3) sharing, (4) governing, and (5) innovating. These are elements of smart tourism destination that should work synergistically, upgrading destination resilience.

Through an extensive literature review, Mandic and Pranicevic [68] assess the effect of ICTs on tourism destination appeal and draw implications for smart tourism development. These encompass six main aspects: attractions, public and private amenities, accessibility, human resources, image and character, and price. The authors conclude ICT impacts tourism management and travellers' experiences, providing a smart transition. Namely, there is impact on general tourism dynamics by promoting a process of co-creation, on travellers' decision making, on travel security, and on data privacy and access. Websites contribute significantly to boost exposure, influencing the image of tourism destinations, and to aggregate knowledge to tourists' decision making. Nonetheless, there are some negative factors associated with ICT on tourism, such as anxiety, addiction, and mindlessness. The authors assert that current and future destination management organizations should rely more on ICT and develop co-creation strategies.

Yoo et al. [7] added to the discussion by investigating the factors influencing the adoption of smart tourism applications that integrate game features. According to their study, these applications provide tourists with "emotional pleasure (through gaming elements) and cognitive information" [7] (p. 14). Furthermore, the authors emphasized gamification applied in the context of tourism to enhance the visitor's experience. They anticipate that the gaming attributes in gamified smart tourism applications differ from those found in conventional games.

4.3.2. Cluster Sustainable Tourism

The second cluster is centred on the modelling and conceptualization of sustainable tourism and provides theoretical and practical strategies to adapt and assess sustainable tourism.

Shafiee et al. [58] introduce a model for sustainable smart tourism destinations, which relies on meeting various criteria, including a significant Internet penetration rate, the adoption of ICT, the availability of smart infrastructure, the establishment of social networks, and the capacity to adjust to global shifts to ensure its successful execution.

Ribes and Baidal [69] examine the concepts of smartness and sustainability in tourism destinations from both theoretical and managerial viewpoints to develop an innovative model of smart sustainability. The authors find a strong correlation between these concepts, highlighting common elements such as long-term vision and planning, innovation, public–private cooperation, and stakeholders' involvement. In addition, they propose a synergistic model centred on smart sustainability, sustained on a public decision-making process that applies technology to support five pillars: planning and efficient resource management; monitoring, transparency, and participation; public–private cooperation, knowledge, and innovation; and communication, awareness raising, and the enhancement of the visitor experience. However, the model should not be interpreted linearly.

Likewise, through a cross-disciplinary perspective, Pan et al. [57] investigate tourism sustainability. The authors initially analyse the challenges and constraints of sustainability, such as energy and pollution, while also exploring fundamental concepts such as green infrastructure, agriculture, and smart technologies. They conclude that sustainable tourism management asks for an integrated and multidisciplinary approach, such as coordinating public policies and tourism strategies; incorporating local, national, and international governance; and promoting pioneering and green practices through environmental education.

Finally, the paper of Alfaro Navarro et al. [70] identified a gap concerning the analysis of sustainable tourism at a local level, hence, proposing an index to measure sustainable tourism at the European NUTS 2 level. Social and economic dimensions are the greatest players in the level of sustainability, but the environmental dimension has been growing substantially. Thus, regions that want to apply sustainable practices should focus first on environmental and then on social aspects. Germany stands out in social and environmental indicators, while Spain shows a good overall performance in each dimension. Alfaro Navarro et al. [70] challenge other investigators and practitioners to adapt the index at more micro levels, such as cities, and warn about the current lack of information to do so.

4.3.3. Cluster Innovation

The third cluster focuses on innovation and how it relates with smart and sustainable tourism. Pencarelli's research [59] explores the impact of technology in the tourism sector. One of the study's focal points examines the effects of the digital revolution on tourism, while another compares tourism 4.0 and smart tourism. The former refers exclusively to new ICTs, whereas the latter denotes the effective employment of these ICTs in a sustainable and long-term perspective toward the quality of life of tourists and locals. New ICTs have not only impacted business strategies but also visitors' participation in co-creation processes. Consequently, the authors argue that an optimal smart tourism approach should be based on sustainability, circular economy, quality of life, and social value. Additionally, they emphasize the need for co-creation strategies in both the physical and digital domains to enrich the tourist experience.

Ma et al. [2] focus on a transition from the traditional business model to a more sustainable approach. They discuss a low-carbon smart tourism strategy empowered by big data through an ideal system of supply chain of low-carbon tourism online-to-offline (O2O). This is based on a tourism spot that provides a low-carbon service while an online tourism agency provides big-data information. The performance is analysed in the decision modes centralized, decentralized, and altruistic. The last mode proves to be the best in achieving sustainability and supply chain coordination at the same time. The overall tourism experience can be consequently improved.

Polese et al. [72] and Kim and Kim [74] developed two qualitative studies. The first proposes an integrated model that combines service ecosystems and smart service systems to overcome some limitations inherent to these models when analysed independently. Polese et al. [72] delve into the key element steps for maximizing value co-creation and sustainability within the tourism industry and transitioning from innovation to social innovation. The authors emphasize the significance of ICT as an enabler of sustainable interactions between guests and hosts. The second draws attention to determining the contribution of mobile technology in attaining smart and sustainable tourism from the technological and consumer viewpoints. Kim and Kim [74] note the difficulty of evaluating the sequential relationship from mobile technology to mobility to sustainability, considering aspects such as the type of tourist, demographics, and geography. Nonetheless, the authors suggest that mobile technology advancements can offer tourists helpful information, contributing to efficient decision making and overall wellbeing.

On the other hand, Romão and Neuts [71] and Tavitiyaman [75] develop quantitative studies. Romão and Neuts' [71] research emphasizes the critical role of smart specialization in regional innovation strategies [79] and sustainable development. The authors analyse the use of territorial resources (natural and cultural) and other capital features in various European regions in the promotion of tourism specialization and performance through smart processes. The results indicate a gap in development among various countries in Europe, with tourism specialization failing to mitigate this issue. In light of the positive findings concerning the selected regions' CO_2 emissions, the authors recommend that technological and industrial development should prioritize energy-saving measures based on renewable sources. Tavitiyaman et al.'s [75] investigation aims to understand perceptions of tourists on tourism smart app attributes and how the use of those apps affects the perceived image of a destination and the tourists' future behavioural intention. Moreover, they analyse how information search moderates some of the identified relationships. The results pinpoint that the attributes smart information systems, smart sightseeing, e-commerce systems, and smart forecasting positively impact tourists' perceived destination image, which, in turn, increases their behavioural intention. Information search negatively moderates the relationship between smart app attributes and perceived destination image but positively moderates the relationship between perceived destination image and behavioural intention. Some practical implications are the development of smart tourism applications should be anchored on tourists' preferences and on the respective destination, and they should be regularly updated, reinforcing the destination image. Other stakeholders from public and private sectors should participate more in the development of smart tourist destinations.

4.3.4. Cluster Smart Cities

Lastly, the cluster of smart cities falls on the topics of smart communities [56,60], smart tourism cities [76], and on the transition from smart city to smart destination [56,77]. Lee et al. [76] explore, through a conceptual approach, the concepts and the components of smart cities (service, infrastructure, and land) and smart tourism (transportation, accommodation, gastronomy, attraction, and ancillary service), comparing both. Consequently, the authors converge the concepts, originating a new view on smart tourism cities. To improve the smart tourism experience, it is crucial that smart city elements should be integrated throughout the whole travelling process, before, during, and after. In addition, there is a need to aggregate all stakeholders' perspectives and interests (tourists, locals, and governments). Policies must follow both a rational and emotional approach, connecting efficiency in ICT to people's management. Some problems are discussed, namely regarding over-tourism and sustainability at environmental, social, and economic levels.

Encalada et al. [60] (p. 14) considered these challenges, including over-tourism, but also overpopulation in urban centres and suggest that for cities "becoming smart implies reinforcing a city's uniqueness rather than allowing it to become impersonal and homogenized". To fill a gap in the literature on the factors that shape the spatial distribution of visitors, the authors conducted a study that collected and analysed data from the social network *Panoramio* concerning tourist patterns in Lisbon in the period 2008–2014. Their research revealed patterns among tourists, including the most visited sights and their locations within the urban context, and explored how this related to various variables related to the city's tourism industry.

Besides Encalada et al. [60], two other works examine specific regions to sustain the concepts of smart city and its transition to smart destination. Sigalat-Signes et al. [77] analyses Gandia, Spain, aiming to understand how intermediate destinations such as this can evolve and transition to a smart tourism destination. This city appears to be transitioning to becoming a smart tourism destination but still lies in an initial phase of the smart model, based on six dimensions: population, environment, mobility, economy, quality of life, and governance. The authors suggest the human dimension is a main issue to guide cities in the direction of a smart management of tourism, including dialogue, participation, and a critical vision among the interest groups. It is recommended that, while tourism businesses should be flexible to technological advances, it also should be careful about its ICT governance since there is lack of knowledge about it.

In turn, Sun et al. [56] examine smart and connected communities (SCCs) that evolved from the concept of smart tourism. Through a case study, the authors present a project, Tresight, which provides a context-aware recommendation system that condenses opportunities and challenges of the IoT and big data analytics for the development of smart tourism and sustainable cultural heritage in Trento, Italy. It is based on FI-WARE technology, resorting to mobile crowdsensing and cyber-physical cloud computing, two of the most important IoT technologies identified in promoting SCCs. Moreover, Sun et al. [56] find that SCCs synergistically address liability, preservation, revitalization, and sustainability of a community, encompassing the goals of living in the present, planning for the future, and remembering the past of a community.

5. Future Research Directions

In this section, the lines of research of the 20 most cited articles that were used in the content analysis are summarized. These are the future lines of research that may be used for further research on the topics of smart and sustainable tourism, innovation, and smart cities. The future research areas are presented by cluster.

5.1. Research Agenda for Smart Tourism

Considering the studies covered in this cluster, the investigation of smart technology and its contribution to sustainable tourism offer several future lines of research. With respect to the investigation carried out by Yoo et al. [7] that examined some variables impacting the adoption of gamified smart tourism applications, the authors suggest for future research a follow-up study and the development of further investigation in other regions to verify whether the findings obtained vary depending on the level of network technology, the rate of smartphone penetration, and cultural traits. Ivars-Baidal et al.'s [66] research proposes an indicator system for smart tourism destinations that could be applied in other contexts (other regions, other types of destinations, etc.) and could help to develop more accurate tourism policies.

Based on the first trial to develop and apply the system, further studies should adjust the proposed indicators by enhancing psycho-econometric properties of some dimensions. Then, some comparative results could be drawn, leading to very interesting results. The work of Mandic and Pranicevic [68] presents the Interreg Italy–Croatia BLUTOURSYSTEM project developed by both researchers and practitioners to promote a big-data-based network "Living Lab". This project may guide future investigations and management plans on approaching a smart business ecosystem with creativity and innovation. The authors address two main gaps, concerning the necessity to examine in depth the role of the ICT implemented in leading tourism destinations on new visitors' behaviours, decision making, and experiences; and the understanding of smart governance on smart tourism. Finally, Gretzel and Scarpino-Johns [67] found some vulnerabilities concerning the development of resilient and smart tourism, for which they also developed a model. They state that both concepts (resilience and smart tourism) should be approached together. Additionally, more critical studies could be drawn to highlight smart tourism management and governance weaknesses and strengths. This could involve more technological-oriented studies to address any existing gaps and clarify what it is and how to achieve smart tourism [68].

5.2. Research Agenda for Sustainable Tourism

In relation to the second cluster, the authors provide some useful insights to perpetuate its advances so far. Shafiee et al. [58] and Ribes and Baidal [69], for example, suggest the further study of the causal relationships and components of the developed models of sustainable smart tourism destinations and smart sustainability, respectively. According to Ribes and Baidal [69], the practical application of the theoretical models and concepts such as smart destination should be fostered. This could be carried out through the deeper examination of the political, corporate, and investment attitude towards the smart development of destinations, as stated by both Pan et al. [57] and Shafiee et al. [58], and a greater integration between the economic, social, environmental, and technological strategies and substructures [58]. Alfaro Navarro et al. [70] provide an index to measure sustainable tourism at the European NUTS 2 level. Future researchers could apply this model, namely by incorporating subjective indicators of factors that were previously overlooked, particularly those related to the environment, extending the list of indicators. They could also analyse at micro levels, such as NUTS 3 or cities, even though the authors indicate a lack of information to do so. Thus, public organizations could also manage efforts to collect more useful and reliable information for smaller regional levels.

5.3. Research Agenda for Innovation

The research guidelines covered by the authors of this cluster highlight several aspects. First, the work developed by Pencarelli [59] suggests that smart tourism destinations might benefit from the integration of knowledge from other areas, such as information systems, travel behaviour, marketing, urban planning, etc. The authors also recommend to further investigate the impact of the digital revolution on tourists' behaviour, as well as the influence of the sharing economy on the value ecosystem. Polese et al. [72] suggest that to better understand and foster value co-creation it is vital to identify diverse types of real activities and cooperative efforts carried out by users. The authors also suggest that it is necessary to develop a general meta-theory for service and value co-creation, and this might be achieved through the integration of different service theories. Since the authors' research was conducted on B&B owners, merely considering the providers' viewpoint, additional empirical studies ought to be undertaken on tourists and other smart tourism systems in order to compare perspectives and assess the adoption of technology. Ma et al.'s [2] research reflects on the transition from the traditional approach to a more sustainable tourism model. They conclude that tourist behaviour and experience must be considered in the tourism market decisions. Moreover, an online tourism agency with big data marketing technology is an essential link between tourists and a tourism spot. In fact, tourism spots promote environmental efficiency and better tourist experiences and should be adapted if destinations want to achieve sustainability in the long term. In the investigation carried out by Kim and Kim [74], we verified that a possible avenue for future research relies on analysing what type of Internet is preferred by users (fixed vs. mobile), considering factors such as the nature of travel, the decision-making process, the environment, and the cost to the traveller. Another interesting potential study would be to examine other technologies in light of the potential that the platform player dominates the mobile technology. The output will be of interest to determine the governance of tourism planning and the competency of tourism destinations. The study by Romão and Neuts [71] points out the need for more precise identification of various regional evolution patterns and their expected time shifts, evaluating CO2 emissions at a regional level and analysing ecological footprints of tourism on the local biosphere. Lastly, the work of Tavitiyaman et al. [75] was based on tourists' perceptions on Hong Kong during an unstable political period of social unrest. Thus, the authors understand that future investigation could be replicated in a different political context and then compared with previous results. Moreover, the opinions of different stakeholders besides tourists could be explored, e.g., governments, tourism policymakers, and providers of tourism services. Other criteria to visit smart tourism destinations could be contemplated in future research.

5.4. Research Agenda for Smart Cities

In the last cluster, the smart cities, some future guidelines are pinpointed. Concerning the relevance of big data in the development of smart city services, Encalada et al. [60] suggest that future studies should integrate ICTs and complement with know-how by, for example, policymakers and investigators towards the promotion of a quality management evaluation mechanism regarding the tourist experience. Moreover, it is also recommended to analyse the consequences of a digital split based on smart device access and affordable smart tourism infrastructure in order to develop mechanisms that minimize this problem. Another area that deserves to be investigated in future relates to smart tourists and their massive digital footprints. It is important to develop studies that examine the value created by using data and technology instead of owning it. Lastly, Sigalat-Signes et al. [77] pinpoint that future research on the transition of a smart city into a smart destination could analyse quantitatively how smart a destination is, based on the perception of tourists and residents, and to extend information about smart tourism besides the private providers' view. Following the same idea, Lee et al. [76] suggest to other researchers to extend the components of the smart tourism city model.

6. Conclusions

This paper aims to provide a state of the art of the relationship between smart tourism and sustainability. Even though sustainability is a key area of smart tourism, the present study enabled us to conclude that the conceptualization of smart tourism is at an initial phase, following the approach of the better-known concept of the smart city, not developing yet with clarity sub-topics, such as sustainability, and how these relate and contribute to a smart course of action. Scientific research on these areas corroborates the underlined gap and propose a deep understanding of smart tourism either through an unambiguous theoretical approach or through the empirical analysis of diverse destinations and tourism contexts. Moreover, in the face of the social, economic, and environmental challenges of today and future generations, a sustainable perspective proves to be essential not only in tourism but in any business strategy. The results derived from this study have allowed us to answer all the research questions posed in the introduction.

Relating to RQ1, the descriptive analysis supported the answer to this question. The geographical distribution found that authors from European countries (Spain, Italy, and Portugal) and Asia (China and the Republic of Korea) have published the most documents on sustainable and smart tourism (90.0%) within the period of 2015–2022. This distribution is not surprising considering the relevance of tourism in the Mediterranean countries and the importance of technology in some Asian communities (e.g., Hong Kong and Seoul).

Regarding RQ2, the analysis of the articles with the most engagement (based on the number of citations) also validates this geographic clustering, which belongs to Sun et al. [56] and Pan et al. [57] from the Asian cluster, and Pencarelli [59] and Encalada et al. [60] from the European cluster. Considering the most prominent journals on sustainable and smart tourism, our findings demonstrate that *Sustainability* has the largest number of published articles. Despite the lower production of the remaining journals, it is important to notice the high rate of citations from *IEEE Access*, resulting from the most cited document of the database: "Internet of things and big data analytics for smart and connected communities" by Sun et al. [56].

Using a mapping process, the keyword co-occurrence network helped to find the current conceptual structure of research on the topic (RQ3). Furthermore, the content analysis of the most cited articles addressed the key research findings, methodological approaches, and proposed a future research agenda. Four relevant clusters were identified: (1) smart tourism, (2) sustainable tourism, (3) innovation, and (4) smart cities. Observing the relationship between the four clusters, a main conclusion is reached: sustainability and smart tourism are research topics that are highly interconnected with each other and with technology, innovation, and smart cities. Several articles highlighted the importance of technology and innovation on consumer experience as well as their contribution towards sustainability and smart tourism. However, there are other topics that should be explored such as the development of a more sustainable kind of tourism that focuses on an integrated and multi-disciplinary approach including several stakeholders (e.g., governments, citizens, and tourists) [57,66,76] and promoting green and innovative practices [2,57,70,71]. Another important contribution of this study is the recognition of research guidelines that might be useful for scholars that aim to develop these topics in the future (RQ4). Given the state of the topic's development, the clusters identified could be subject to a synthesis of substantive findings. Although the primary methodologies used in sustainability and smart tourism were highlighted in this research, verifying a balance between conceptual and empirical (quantitative and qualitative) studies, this should be examined more thoroughly.

The findings of this study have important implications for future research in the field of smart tourism and sustainability. Firstly, there is a need for further exploration of the interconnection between smart tourism, sustainability, innovation, and smart cities. This could involve examining how these concepts can be integrated into a co-creation approach involving multiple stakeholders, as well as exploring the development and implementation of green and innovative practices in tourism contexts. Secondly, there should be a more thorough examination of the balance between conceptual and empirical studies in sustainability and smart tourism. Finally, there is a need for a synthesis of substantive findings in the field, in order to provide a clearer understanding of the relationship between smart tourism and sustainability, a gap that this review tries to narrow. In summary, future research in this field should aim to develop a more comprehensive and multi-disciplinary approach to sustainability and smart tourism, while verifying the balance between conceptual and empirical studies and integrating substantive findings.

Nonetheless, this bibliometric study is not free of limitations. First, the social network analysis does not explore the content of the papers but classifies them according to categories to provide a general approximation of the scientific production in a given field of study. Thus, it is not always easy to classify articles into one category since it involves a certain degree of subjectivity. For this reason, the researchers pool their opinions before the final classification is made.

Second, even though we have tried to ensure that the searched keywords broadly represent the studied fields, there might be, on one side, important papers on the area that do not incorporate those exact keywords and, thus, are excluded from the database. On the other side, there might be non-relevant works in the final database since this systematic method does not measure the relative strength of the searched terms within the actual paper.

Third, citations may not reflect quality and might be, in fact, overestimated because of the underlying goals of citing each paper that are very particular to each author, the auto-citations, the frequency of citations by authors tends to increase for highly ranked journals, and a trend for earlier articles to have higher citation rates than more recent ones (due to being available for longer periods). To address this limitation, future studies could consider incorporating the Emerging Sources Citation Index or employing basic metric measurements to quantify pure bibliographic data.

Finally, only publications present in the WoS Core Collection were considered. However, we also performed an analysis using the Scopus database, and significant differences concerning the number of documents were not found. Future research should include documents from other databases.

Despite these limitations, the investigation provides a valid picture of the state of the art of smart tourism and sustainability, whose several categories can be scientifically extended or explored in more specific areas or time periods.

Author Contributions: Conceptualization: C.M., P.R. and M.G.-S.; data curation: C.M.; formal analysis: C.M.; investigation: C.M; methodology: C.M.; project administration: P.R. and M.G.-S.; software: C.M.; supervision: P.R. and M.G.-S.; visualization: C.M.; writing—original draft: C.M.; writing—review and editing: M.G.-S. and P.R. All authors have read and agreed to the published version of the manuscript.

Funding: This research received no external funding.

Data Availability Statement: Data supporting reported results are not available due to privacy restrictions.

Acknowledgments: This research is supported by national funds through FCT–Foundation for Science and Technology, I.P., Portugal under the project UIDB/04005/2020. The study was also conducted under the framework of the UAM research group TECHNOCONS "Consumer behavior and technology".

Conflicts of Interest: The authors declare no conflict of interest. The funders had no role in the design of the study; in the collection, analyses, or interpretation of data; in the writing of the manuscript; or in the decision to publish the results.

References

1. Li, Y.; Hu, C.; Huang, C.; Duan, L. The concept of smart tourism in the context of tourism information services. *Tour. Manag.* **2017**, *58*, 293–300. [CrossRef]
2. Ma, D.; Hu, J.; Yao, F. Big data empowering low-carbon smart tourism study on low-carbon tourism O2O supply chain considering consumer behaviors and corporate altruistic preferences. *Comput. Ind. Eng.* **2021**, *153*, 107061. [CrossRef]

3. Celdrán-Bernabeu, M.A.; Mazón, J.-N.; Ivars-Baidal, J.A.; Vera-Rebollo, J.F. Smart Tourism. Un estudio de mapeo sistemático. *Cuad. Turismo* **2018**, *41*, 107–138. [CrossRef]
4. González-Reverté, F.; Díaz-Luque, P.; Gomis-López, J.M.; Morales-Pérez, S. Tourists' risk perception and the use of mobile devices in beach tourism destinations. *Sustainability* **2018**, *10*, 413. [CrossRef]
5. Pradhan, M.K.; Oh, J.; Lee, H. Understanding travelers' behavior for sustainable smart tourism: A technology readiness perspective. *Sustainability* **2018**, *10*, 4259. [CrossRef]
6. Shen, S.; Sotiriadis, M.; Zhou, Q. Could smart tourists be sustainable and responsible as well? The contribution of social networking sites to improving their sustainable and responsible behavior. *Sustainability* **2020**, *12*, 1470. [CrossRef]
7. Yoo, C.; Kwon, S.; Na, H.; Chang, B. Factors affecting the adoption of gamified smart tourism applications: An integrative approach. *Sustainability* **2017**, *9*, 2162. [CrossRef]
8. Koseoglu, M.A.; Rahimi, R.; Okumus, F.; Liu, J. Bibliometric studies in tourism. *Ann. Tour. Res.* **2016**, *61*, 180–198. [CrossRef]
9. Sanguankaew, P.; Ractham, V. Bibliometric Review of Research on Knowledge Management and Sustainability, 1994–2018. *Sustainability* **2019**, *11*, 4388. [CrossRef]
10. Kainzbauer, A.; Rungruang, P. Science Mapping the Knowledge Base on Sustainable Human Resource Management, 1982–2019. *Sustainability* **2019**, *11*, 3938. [CrossRef]
11. Yoopetch, C.; Nimsai, S. Science Mapping the Knowledge Base on Sustainable Tourism Development, 1990–2018. *Sustainability* **2019**, *11*, 3631. [CrossRef]
12. Thananusak, T. Science Mapping of the Knowledge Base on Sustainable Entrepreneurship, 1996–2019. *Sustainability* **2019**, *11*, 3565. [CrossRef]
13. Zheng, C.; Kouwenberg, R. A Bibliometric Review of Global Research on Corporate Governance and Board Attributes. *Sustainability* **2019**, *11*, 3428. [CrossRef]
14. Fabregat-Aibar, L.; Barberà-Mariné, M.G.; Terceño, A.; Pié Dols, L. A Bibliometric and Visualization Analysis of Socially Responsible Funds. *Sustainability* **2019**, *11*, 2526. [CrossRef]
15. Hallinger, P.; Suriyankietkaew, S. Science Mapping of the Knowledge Base on Sustainable Leadership, 1990–2018. *Sustainability* **2018**, *10*, 4846. [CrossRef]
16. Johnson, A.-G.; Samakovlis, I. A bibliometric analysis of knowledge development in smart tourism research. *J. Hosp. Tour. Technol.* **2019**, *10*, 600–623. [CrossRef]
17. Zhang, Q.; Wang, Q.; Hao, J.-X.; Yu, Y. Mapping smart tourism research in China: A semantic and social network analysis using CiteSpace. In Proceedings of the 2016 13th International Conference on Service Systems and Service Management (ICSSSM), Kunming, China, 24–26 June 2016; IEEE: Manhattan, NY, USA, 2016.
18. Boes, K.; Buhalis, D.; Inversini, A. Conceptualising Smart Tourism Destination Dimensions. In *Information and Communication Technologies in Tourism 2015*; Tussyadiah AIe, I., Ed.; Springer International Publishing: Berlin/Heidelberg, Germany, 2015; pp. 391–403.
19. Law, R.; Leung, R.; Buhalis, D. Information technology applications in hospitality and tourism: A review of publications from 2005 to 2007. *J. Travel Tour. Mark.* **2009**, *26*, 599–623. [CrossRef]
20. Law, R.; Leung, R.; Buhalis, D. An Analysis of Academic Leadership in Hospitality and Tourism. *J. Hosp. Tour. Res.* **2010**, *34*, 455–477. [CrossRef]
21. De la Hoz-Correa, A.; Muñoz-Leiva, F.; Bakucz, M. Past themes and future trends in medical tourism research: A co-word analysis. *Tour. Manag.* **2018**, *65*, 200–211. [CrossRef]
22. Garrigos-Simon, F.J.; Narangajavana-Kaosiri, Y.; Lengua-Lengua, I. Tourism and sustainability: A bibliometric and visualization analysis. *Sustainability* **2018**, *10*, 1976. [CrossRef]
23. Köseoglu, M.A.; Okumus, F.; Putra, E.D.; Yildiz, M.; Dogan, I.C. Authorship trends, collaboration patterns, and co-authorship networks in lodging studies (1990–2016). *J. Hosp. Mark. Manag.* **2018**, *27*, 561–582. [CrossRef]
24. Gretzel, U.; Werthner, H.; Koo, C.; Lamsfus, C. Conceptual foundations for understanding smart tourism ecosystems. *Comput. Hum. Behav.* **2015**, *50*, 558–563. [CrossRef]
25. Gretzel, U.; Koo, C.; Sigala, M.; Xiang, Z. Special issue on smart tourism: Convergence of information technologies, experiences, and theories. *Electron. Mark.* **2015**, *25*, 175–177. [CrossRef]
26. Höjer, M.; Wangel, J. Smart sustainable cities: Definition and challenges. In *ICT Innovations for Sustainability*; Springer: Berlin/Heidelberg, Germany, 2015; pp. 333–349.
27. Harrison, C.; Eckman, B.; Hamilton, R.; Hartswick, P.; Kalagnanam, J.; Paraszczak, J.; Williams, P. Foundations for smarter cities. *IBM J. Res. Dev.* **2010**, *54*, 1–16. [CrossRef]
28. Tu, Q.; Liu, A. Framework of smart tourism research and related progress in China. In Proceedings of the International Conference on Management and Engineering (CME 2014), Shanghai, China, 24–25 May 2014.
29. Guo, Y.; Liu, H.; Chai, Y. The embedding convergence of smart cities and tourism internet of things in China: An advance perspective. *Adv. Hosp. Tour. Res.* **2014**, *2*, 54–69.
30. Baggio, R.; Del Chiappa, G. Real and virtual relationships in tourism digital ecosystems. *Inf. Technol. Tour.* **2014**, *14*, 3–19. [CrossRef]
31. Del Chiappa, G.; Baggio, R. Knowledge transfer in smart tourism destinations: Analyzing the effects of a network structure. *J. Dest. Mark. Manag.* **2015**, *4*, 145–150. [CrossRef]

32. Racherla, P.; Hu, C.; Hyun, M.Y. Exploring the role of innovative technologies in building a knowledge-based destination. *Curr. Issues Tour.* **2008**, *11*, 407–428. [CrossRef]
33. Jovicic, D.Z. From the traditional understanding of tourism destination to the smart tourism destination. *Curr. Issues Tour.* **2019**, *22*, 276–282. [CrossRef]
34. European Union. Smart Tourism Capital. 2019. Available online: https://smarttourismcapital.eu/downloads/guide-for-applicants.pdf (accessed on 12 September 2022).
35. Ben-Eli, M.U. Sustainability: Definition and five core principles, a systems perspective. *Sustain. Sci.* **2018**, *13*, 1337–1343. [CrossRef]
36. Atkisson, A.; Arnbom, T.; Tesar, C.; Christensen, A. Getting It Right in a New Ocean: Bringing Sustainable Blue Economy Principles to the Arctic. World Wide Fund for Nature. 2018. Available online: http://d2ouvy59p0dg6k.cloudfront.net/downloads/wwf_report_arctic_blue_economy_181018.pdf (accessed on 12 September 2022).
37. United Nations. What Are the Sustainable Development Goals? 2022. Available online: https://www.undp.org/sustainable-development-goals (accessed on 12 September 2022).
38. Milán-García, J.; Uribe-Toril, J.; Ruiz-Real, J.L.; de Pablo Valenciano, J. Sustainable Local Development: An Overview of the State of Knowledge. *Resources.* **2019**, *8*, 31. [CrossRef]
39. Pritchard, A. Statistical Bibliography or Bibliometrics? *J. Doc.* **1969**, *25*, 348–349.
40. Zupic, I.; Čater, T. Bibliometric methods in management and organization. *Organ. Res. Methods* **2015**, *18*, 429–472. [CrossRef]
41. Glänzel, W. *Bibliometrics as a Research Field: A Course on Theory and Application of Bibliometric Indicators*, 3rd ed.; Magyar Tudományos Akadémia, Kutatásszervezési Intézet: Budapest, Hungary, 2003.
42. Serrat, O. *Social Network Analysis*; Springer: Singapore, 2009. Available online: https://link.springer.com/chapter/10.1007/978-981-10-0983-9_9 (accessed on 30 November 2022).
43. Tabassum, S.; Pereira, F.; Fernandes, S.; Gama, J. Social network analysis: An overview. *Wiley Interdiscip. Rev. Data Min. Knowl. Discov.* **2018**, *8*, 1256. [CrossRef]
44. Kamińska, A. The application of methods of social network analysis in bibliometrics and webometrics. Measures and tools. 2018. *Nowa Biblioteka. Usługi Technol. Inf. Media* **2018**, *29*, 29–46.
45. Kovacs, A.; Van Looy, B.; Cassiman, B. Exploring the scope of open innovation: A bibliometric review of a decade of research. *Scientometrics* **2015**, *104*, 951–983. [CrossRef]
46. Su, H.-N.; Lee, P.-C. Mapping knowledge structure by keyword co-occurrence: A first look at journal papers in Technology Foresight. *Scientometrics* **2010**, *85*, 65–79. [CrossRef]
47. Sassmannshausen, S.P.; Volkmann, C. The scientometrics of social entrepreneurship and its establishment as an academic field. *J. Small Bus.* **2018**, *56*, 251–273. [CrossRef]
48. Gaur, A.; Kumar, M. A systematic approach to conducting review studies: An assessment of content analysis in 25 years of IB research. *J. World Bus.* **2018**, *53*, 280–289. [CrossRef]
49. van Eck, N.J.; Waltman, L. Software survey: VOSviewer, a computer program for bibliometric mapping. *Scientometrics* **2010**, *84*, 523–538. [CrossRef] [PubMed]
50. Ferreira, J.J.M.; Fernandes, C.I.; Ratten, V. A co-citation bibliometric analysis of strategic management research. *Scientometrics* **2016**, *109*, 1–32. [CrossRef]
51. World Travel and Tourism Council. Economic Impact Reports. 2021. Available online: https://wttc.org/research/economic-impact (accessed on 5 December 2022).
52. World Intellectual Property Organization (WIPO). Global Innovation Index 2022. In *What Is the Future of Innovation Driven Growth?* WIPO: Geneva, Switzerland, 2022. Available online: https://www.wipo.int/edocs/pubdocs/en/wipo-pub-2000-2022-en-main-report-global-innovation-index-2022-15th-edition.pdf (accessed on 5 December 2022).
53. OECD. *Main Science and Technology Indicators*; OECD Publishing: Paris, France, 2022; Volume 2022. [CrossRef]
54. Sachs, J.; Schmidt-Traub, G.; Kroll, C.; Lafortune, G.; Fuller, G.; Woelm, F. The Sustainable Development Goals and COVID-19. In *Sustainable Development Report*; Cambridge University Press: Cambridge, UK, 2020.
55. Joo, Y.; Tan, T.-B. Smart Cities in Asia: An Introduction. In *Smart cities in Asia*, 1st ed.; Joo, Y., Tan, T.-B., Eds.; Edward Elgar Publishing: Cheltenham, UK, 2020; pp. 1–17.
56. Sun, Y.; Song, H.; Jara, A.J.; Bie, R. Internet of things and big data analytics for smart and connected communities. *IEEE Access* **2016**, *4*, 766–773. [CrossRef]
57. Pan, S.-Y.; Gao, M.; Kim, H.; Shah, K.J.; Pei, S.-L.; Chiang, P.-C. Advances and challenges in sustainable tourism toward a green economy. *Sci. Total Environ.* **2018**, *635*, 452–469. [CrossRef] [PubMed]
58. Shafiee, S.; Ghatari, A.R.; Hasanzadeh, A.; Jahanyan, S. Developing a model for sustainable smart tourism destinations: A systematic review. *Tour. Manag. Perspect.* **2019**, *31*, 287–300. [CrossRef]
59. Pencarelli, T. The digital revolution in the travel and tourism industry. *Inf. Technol. Tour.* **2020**, *22*, 455–476. [CrossRef]
60. Encalada, L.; Boavida-Portugal, I.; Cardoso Ferreira, C.; Rocha, J. Identifying tourist places of interest based on digital imprints: Towards a sustainable smart city. *Sustainability* **2017**, *9*, 2317. [CrossRef]
61. Clarivate Analytics, C. Journal Citation Reports. 2022. Available online: https://clarivate.com/webofsciencegroup/solutions/journal-citation-reports/?gclid=CjwKCAiAkrWdBhBkEiwAZ9cdcNSY61X9Mo5l2fqVqk9FAQ8MIOm48TBHQUjn_mJvUsH24zAWMYvsJhoCLncQAvD_BwE (accessed on 1 November 2022).

62. van Eck, N.J.; Waltman, L. VOSviewer manual. In *Manual for VOSviewer Version*; Universiteit Leiden: Leiden, The Netherlands, 2011; Volume 1. Available online: https://www.vosviewer.com/documentation/Manual_VOSviewer_1.6.11.pdf (accessed on 7 December 2022).
63. White, M.D.; Marsh, E.E. Content analysis: A flexible methodology. *Libr. Trends* **2006**, *55*, 22–45. [CrossRef]
64. Krippendorff, K. *Content Analysis: An Introduction to Its Methodology*; Sage Publications: Thousand Oaks, CA, USA, 2018.
65. Del Vecchio, P.; Passiante, G. Is tourism a driver for smart specialization? Evidence from Apulia, an Italian region with a tourism vocation. *J. Dest. Mark. Manag.* **2017**, *6*, 163–165. [CrossRef]
66. Ivars-Baidal, J.A.; Celdran-Bernabeu, M.A.; Femenia-Serra, F.; Perles-Ribes, J.F.; Giner-Sanchez, D. Measuring the progress of smart destinations: The use of indicators as a management tool. *J. Dest. Mark. Manag.* **2021**, *19*, 100531. [CrossRef]
67. Gretzel, U.; Scarpino-Johns, M. Destination Resilience and Smart Tourism Destinations. *Tour. Rev. Int.* **2018**, *22*, 263–276. [CrossRef]
68. Mandic, A.; Pranicevic, D.G. Progress on the role of ICTs in establishing destination appeal Implications for smart tourism destination development. *J. Hosp. Tour.* **2019**, *10*, 791–813.
69. Ribes, J.F.P.; Baidal, J.I. Smart sustainability: A new perspective in the sustainable tourism debate. *Investig. Reg.* **2018**, *42*, 151–170.
70. Alfaro Navarro, J.L.; Andres Martinez, M.E.; Mondejar Jimenez, J.A. An approach to measuring sustainable tourism at the local level in Europe. *Curr. Issues Tour.* **2020**, *23*, 423–437. [CrossRef]
71. Romão, J.; Neuts, B. Territorial capital, smart tourism specialization and sustainable regional development: Experiences from Europe. *Habitat Int.* **2017**, *68*, 64–74. [CrossRef]
72. Polese, F.; Botti, A.; Grimaldi, M.; Monda, A.; Vesci, M. Social innovation in smart tourism ecosystems: How technology and institutions shape sustainable value co-creation. *Sustainability* **2018**, *10*, 140. [CrossRef]
73. Battino, S.; Lampreu, S. The role of the sharing economy for a sustainable and innovative development of rural areas: A case study in Sardinia (Italy). *Sustainability* **2019**, *11*, 3004. [CrossRef]
74. Kim, D.; Kim, S. The role of mobile technology in tourism: Patents, articles, news, and mobile tour app reviews. *Sustainability* **2017**, *9*, 2082. [CrossRef]
75. Tavitiyaman, P.; Qu, H.L.; Tsang, W.S.L.; Lam, C.W.R. The influence of smart tourism applications on perceived destination image and behavioral intention: The moderating role of information search behavior. *J. Hosp. Tour. Res.* **2021**, *46*, 476–487. [CrossRef]
76. Lee, P.; Hunter, W.C.; Chung, N. Smart Tourism City: Developments and Transformations. *Sustainability* **2020**, *12*, 3958. [CrossRef]
77. Sigalat-Signes, E.; Calvo-Palomares, R.; Roig-Merino, B.; Garcia-Adan, I. Transition towards a tourist innovation model: The smart tourism destination Reality or territorial marketing? *J. Innov. Knowl.* **2020**, *5*, 96–104. [CrossRef]
78. Del Vecchio, P.; Mele, G.; Ndou, V.; Secundo, G. Creating value from social big data: Implications for smart tourism destinations. *Inf. Process Manag.* **2018**, *54*, 847–860. [CrossRef]
79. Foray, D.; Goddard, J.; Beldarrain, X.G.; Landabaso, M.; McCann, P.; Morgan, K.; Nauwelaers, C.; Ortega-Argilés, R. *Guide to Research and Innovation Strategies for Smart Specialisations*; S3P-European Union: Brussels, Belgium, 2012.

urban science

MDPI

Article

Impact of Tourist Areas on the Electrical Grid: A Case Study of the Southern Dominican Republic

Miguel Aybar-Mejía *, Randy Andrés, Alam Cabral-Soto, Carlos Montás, Wilmer-Johann Núñez-García, Elvin Arnaldo Jiménez Matos, Giuseppe Sbriz-Zeitun and Deyslen Mariano-Hernández

Engineering Area, Instituto Tecnológico de Santo Domingo, Santo Domingo 10602, Dominican Republic
* Correspondence: miguel.aybar@intec.edu.do

Abstract: The growing integration of tourist areas and complexes increases the demand for electrical power systems. This increased demand may represent a vulnerability to voltage and frequency stability in electrical grids, where these parameters are essential for an optimal and continuous supply of electrical energy. The Dominican Republic has begun a tourist expansion process in areas that were previously not commercially exploited. Based on the factors mentioned above, this article's objective was to analyze the impact caused by the increase in electricity demand due to the tourism sector, using the Enriquillo Region of the Dominican Republic as a case study. The impacts of this expansion on the voltage profiles and the system's frequency were determined. The methodology consisted of obtaining information on the mathematical model of the system to evaluate the expansion plan for the study period and the projection of the demand of the grid. The complete system was modeled with this information, including expansion and possible renewable generators. Finally, the flow of charges was measured, and dynamic analysis was carried out. The quasi-dynamic and RMS/EMT simulations were carried out in the DIgSILENT software for this investigation. The results showed that the electrical system benefits stability and national standards. This is because the transmission lines reduced their loading by approximately 2.99% in 2032. As the years of study passed and the system load increased, the voltage in the bars of the 138 kV systems and generators did not exceed the range of ±5% established in the technical regulations of the Dominican electricity market.

Keywords: power flow; voltage profile; frequency control; renewal energy; DIgSILENT

1. Introduction

Today, the demand for electrical energy is seeing drastic increases [1]. Electricity is the heart of modern societies and economies, so its evolution brings with it the growth of power systems. Communities are expected to continue to increase their demand for electricity thanks to rising household incomes and the growing order and purchase of electrical devices with various applications, such as electric vehicles becoming more prevalent in homes and workplaces [2]. This situation forces electrical power systems to work to their limits and calls for reliable, stable, and quality systems that meet society's current and future demands. The electrical power systems provide consumers with the necessary electrical energy at the highest possible quality standards. For this reason, the stability of electrical power systems is critical [3,4].

Most tourism-related activities directly or indirectly require energy from fossil fuels or electricity, typically transformed from gas, coal, and petroleum [5]. The tourism industry typically involves high demands on energy use, living standards, and the environment. Moreover, population density and energy demand might shift significantly with the seasons [6]. While examining the impact of the energy systems of islands, tourism should be considered.

The number of rooms, usage patterns of visitors, building type and style, and maintenance of outside temperature are only a few variables that affect how much energy is needed in the tourism zone [7]. Several tourist destinations are found in distant locales that are far from the national electricity grids.

Globally, tourism is one of the sectors that contribute the most to the economies of many countries. According to [8], the tourism sector directly and indirectly contributes 270 million jobs and contributes more than USD 4.5 billion to the world's gross domestic product—a number given in 2020 by the World Travel and Tourism Council. In North, Central, and South America, 69.70 million tourist arrivals were registered for this year—an amount affected by the current global situation regarding SARS-CoV-2. In 2019, there were 219.30 million tourist arrivals [9]. This puts into perspective the relevance of the tourism sector in the Americas, through which nations' interest in promoting this sector can be understood and developed.

In the Dominican Republic, one of the sectors contributing the most to the national economy is tourism. According to the indicators presented by the Central Bank of the Dominican Republic [10], for 2019, the income was USD 7468.10, and the number of hotel rooms was 83,041.00, reflecting an increase of 21% in the number of available rooms and a 79% increase in economic income due to tourism compared to 2010.

The tourism industry has seasonal variations (summer and winter) in energy consumption, affecting the demand on the electrical grid [11]. The growth in demand due to the increase in the tourism sector in different countries causes the electrical distribution grid to work at or very close to its maximum capacity, producing power and energy losses in the system [12]. Similarly, it compromises the grid's stability, reducing its security and reliability.

Due to the economic importance of tourism and the close relationship that exists with the increase in electricity demand in countries [13], there is a growing need to analyze and project the medium- and long-term electricity demand in tourist areas [14], so as to be able to create more flexible electrical systems and ensure the technical capabilities to maintain the technical requirements for the generation, transmission, and distribution of the electricity grid.

Therefore, the study and planning of demand, voltage, and frequency stability is an important task to see the impact of tourist areas on the power grid. The voltage stability in a power supply is essential. The operating environment and load on the electrical grid are constantly changing. In order to improve the planning, design, operation, and economic aspects of the electric power grid, dynamic stability analysis is one of the most critical and practical approaches [15].

Following the development of global tourism, studies have attempted to analyze the stability of electric power systems—specifically, by applying frequency and voltage stability in areas where tourism is expected to expand.

Considering the above, this article aims to present a methodology for analyzing the impact caused by the increase in electricity demand due to the tourism sector. The Enriquillo Region, located in the southwestern Dominican Republic, was used as a case study.

The main contributions of this paper in this field of research are as follows:

- Evaluating the impact produced by the increase in electrical demand in the transmission lines on the frequency stability and system voltage, which impacts the quality of the energy service provided.
- Presenting some differences between the North American Reliability Corporation (NERC)'s primary international frequency regulations and the regulations applied in the Dominican Republic to maintain frequency stability.
- A methodological study with load profiles of areas used to evaluate the long-term impact of the power capacity by applying quasi-dynamic and RMS/EMT simulations using DIgSILENT software.

This article presents the methodology in Section 2. The topics concerning stability in the electrical grid are presented in Section 3. We then continue with the description of the case study in Section 4. Section 5 presents the results and discussion. Finally, Section 6 presents the conclusions and perspectives for future work.

2. Methodology

This article presents a methodology to evaluate tourism's impact on electrical systems, grid expansion, and the demand increase in the case study area. The impact of this expansion on the voltage profiles and the system's frequency is determined. The methodology consists of obtaining information on the mathematical model of the system to evaluate the expansion plan for the study period and the projection of the demand on the grid. With this information, the complete system is modeled, including expansion and possible renewable generators to consider. Finally, the flow of charges is measured, and dynamic analysis is carried out.

First, the necessary technical information was collected, which was obtained from the Dominican Electric Transmission Company (ETED), the electric power distribution company Edesur, and the National Energy Commission (CNE). The technical information on the generation technologies, transmission lines, and users connected to the grid was obtained from ETED and Edesur. This information was used to define the characteristic load profiles of the southern and hotel zones, while the data obtained from the CNE disclosed the system's trends.

The simulation defined two power demand profiles: The first profile was that of the southern zone. All measurement points were considered and used for the coordinate organism (OC-SENI) to establish present and future data. The second profile was that of the tourist areas and complexes, which served as a reference to simulate the behavior of the tourist sector. For the current load profiles, the electrical energy consumption obtained from the measurement points of the selected areas was used, estimating the average hours of all of the days of the month to determine the average behavior for a year. For future demand profiles, data on demand growth were used in the scenario forecast by the CNE until 2032.

Quasi-dynamic and RMS/EMT simulations were then performed in DIgSILENT. Quasi-dynamic simulation works well for planning studies where long-term load and generation profiles are established, and where grid evolution is modeled using variations and expansion stages [16]. The quasi-dynamic simulations were used to model the system's development during the analysis period, measuring variables such as line currents; line load; solar, wind, hydro, and conventional energy generation; and active, reactive, and apparent power in lines [17]. Regarding the RMS/EMT simulations, they were used to observe the system's behavior in the following situations: output of a generator with the capacity to activate the load shedding system, and input of the most significant load in a bus of the system. The bus bars' electrical frequency and voltage behavior were measured to validate whether they were within the stability margins. Finally, the results were analyzed, describing the behaviors in the simulations, and their relevance was verified in terms of the adverse effects that they could produce on the electrical power system. Figure 1 shows the methodology used for the study.

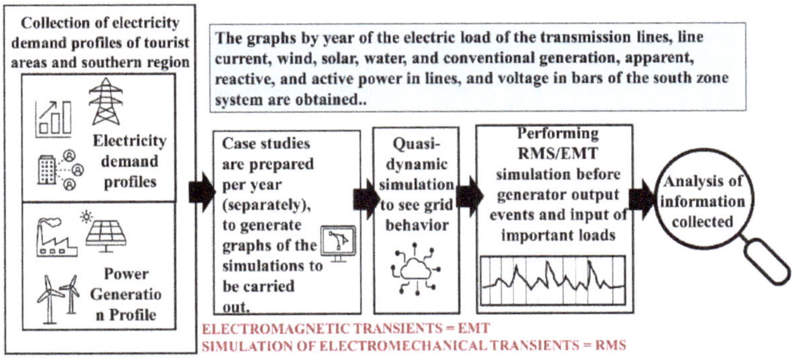

Figure 1. Methodology used.

3. Stability in Electrical Grids

Global electricity demand is expected to increase by more than 50% by 2030, according to the International Energy Agency [3]. Power systems must meet the voltage and frequency stability requirements to allow a level of reliability [18], but this is affected by the increase in demand caused by the rise in population, services, and tourist demand [19].

Grid stability should be maintained during normal and abnormal operations while minimizing system costs (both operating and long-term investment costs). This is why analysis and stability tools are used to understand how system behavior would be based on demand trends and, thus, to be able to propose solutions to possible system restrictions and operations. Some of the simulation tools that can be used for stability studies include GridLAB-D [20], PSS/E [21], OpenDSS [22], Siemens PTI PSS [23], and DIgSILENT PowerFactory [24].

Some studies that have analyzed how to maintain the stability of power systems using voltage and frequency variables as indicators of energy service quality are shown in Table 1.

Table 1. Studies of voltage and frequency stability in electrical power systems.

Ref.	Contributions	Limitations	Applied Software
[25]	FACTS control application to improve the stability of the electrical grid voltage	Does not cover frequency stability	Not specified
[26]	The control scheme for an MV-HVDC power system to improve stability	The study only focused on a multidimensional droop-based control strategy	DIgSILENT PowerFactory
[27]	The effect of voltage variation on frequency control was analyzed through phase loop dynamics	A unique problem arises in the frequency control structure when the voltage varies suddenly	MATLAB/Simulink
[28]	Proposed a controller for voltage and frequency called an automatic voltage regulator, which can be considered as a solution for tuning frequency	Unable to keep voltage and frequency balanced when connected to the grid	MATLAB/Simulink
[29]	Proposed a simple frequency controller that uses the inverter's output current as feedback to adapt its frequency	Existing schematics only focus on power and having an excellent transient response	MATLAB
[30]	Provides an introduction to the grid's control and stability of integrating renewable energies	The study was not detailed in the context of the electricity market	SimPowerSystems

Due to the increase in demand, electrical distribution grids are forced to operate at or near maximum capacity, which causes power and energy losses in the system, affecting the grid's stability and reducing its security and reliability [12].

Voltage stability refers to the ability of a system to maintain steady-state voltage while balancing active power. Table 2 presents the different types of voltage stability analysis and their interest times for analysis.

Table 2. Types of voltage stability analysis and their time responses.

Type	Time Responses
Stability against great disturbances	10 s to 10 min
Stability against small disturbances	Instant
Short-term stability	Several seconds
Long-term stability	Several seconds

Frequency stability refers to the ability of the system to maintain the balance of active power between generation and demand, and its objective is to keep the system frequency at its nominal value. Frequency stability may be required in transient instability and small disturbances. Table 3 shows the advantages and applications of some of the methods used for frequency stability.

Table 3. Methods of frequency stability.

Ref.	Method	Advantages	Application
[31]	Linear–quadratic control	Eliminates oscillation in three-phase investors, harmonic distortion and voltage degradation, and frequency in photovoltaic systems connected to the grid	Compensate the voltage on the line and optimize the energy flow to the loads
[32]	Sliding mode control	Guarantees stability and robustness against the uncertainties of the parameters	Used in nonlinear systems and operating systems with discrete timing
[33]	Robust control	Rectifies frequency fluctuations in investors connected to the grid	Maintain stability in the mode connected to the grid and current control in three-phase investors
[34]	P-Q control	Ensures a generation equally distributed between active power and reactive power	Control the frequency and voltage during shared loads
[35]	Predictive control of the model	The concepts in this management method are simple, and its controller is heuristic	Used when there are multiple input and output control problems

The NERC [36] presented a voltage stability control policy addressing voltage and frequency stability regulations.

4. Case Study

The Enriquillo Region is in the southwestern area of the Dominican Republic, formed by the provinces of Barahona, Pedernales, Independencia, and Bahoruco. The area occupied by these four provinces is 6961.43 km^2. The Enriquillo Region has five wind generation plants in two of its four areas: Barahona and Pedernales. Barahona has three plants, with a total installed capacity of 149.80 MW. At the same time, Pedernales has two plants, with a total installed capacity of 33.45 MW. Additionally, Barahona has a photovoltaic generation plant with an installed capacity of 25 MW, a thermal generation plant with an installed capacity of 51.80 MW, and a hydroelectric generation plant with an installed capacity of 7.50 MW (see Figure 2).

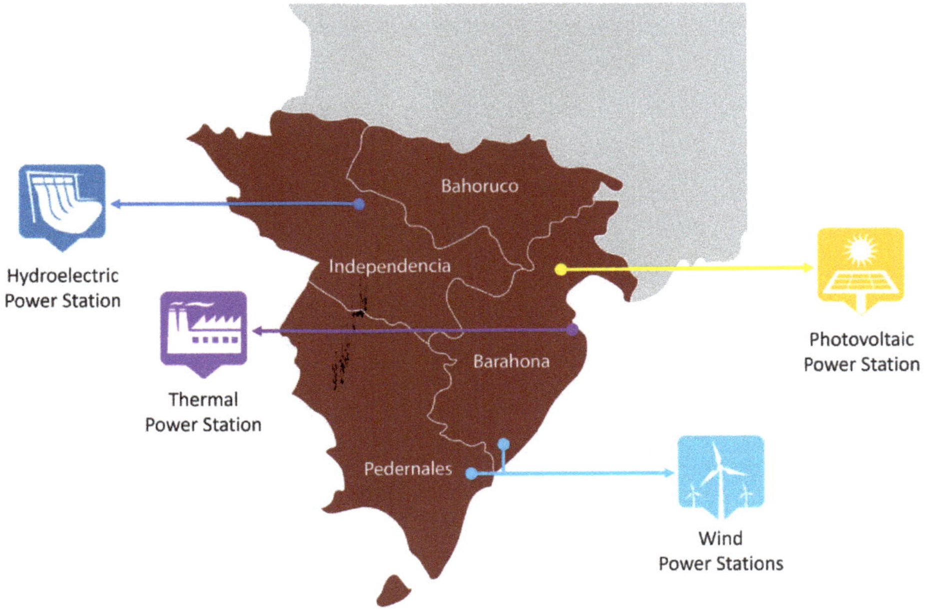

Figure 2. Location of the Enriquillo Region, Dominican Republic. Source: https://www.mapas.cne.gob.do/ (Accessed on 15 February 2023).

Table 4 presents the provinces, the type of generation, the capacity, and the year of implementation of the power plants that are part of the Enriquillo Region.

Table 4. Generation plants in the Enriquillo Region.

Province	Type of Generation	Generation Plant	Installed Capacity (MW)	Year of Initial Operation
Pedernales	Wind	Los Cocos I	25.20	2012
	Wind	Quilvio Cabrera	8.25	2011
Barahona	Photovoltaic	Canoa	25.00	2017
	Thermal power plant	Barahona-Carbón	51.80	2001
	Wind	Larimar I	49.50	2016
	Wind	Larimar II	48.30	2018
	Wind	Los Cocos II	52.00	2012
Independencia	Hydroelectric	Las Damas	7.50	1967
Bahoruco	-	-	-	-

The bus bar measurements of the electrical power flow of the southern zone are presented in Figure 3. In addition to considering the measurement points mentioned above, the measurement points of the tourist areas located in the eastern and northern parts of the country were considered as a reference for the impact on electricity demand caused by tourist areas, such as Guavaberry, Juan Dolio, Sosua, Cabarete, and Las Americas Airport.

Figure 3. Points of measurement of power flow and electricity demand in the southern part of the country.

Figure 4 shows the grid configuration in the simulated southern zone [17].

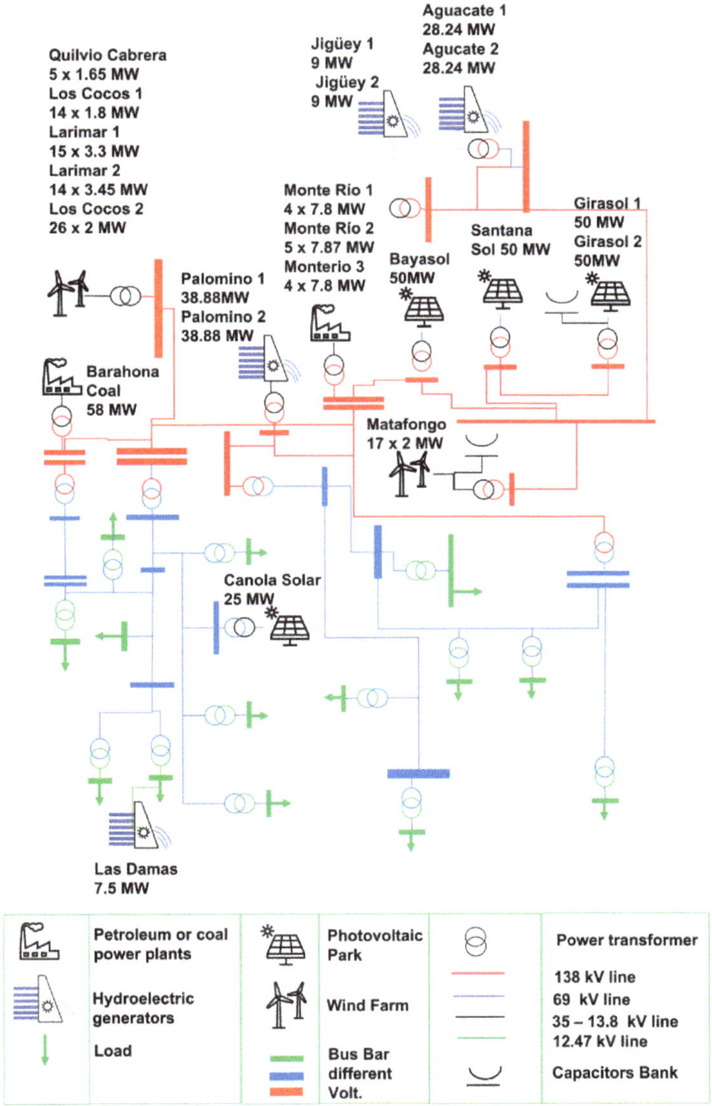

Figure 4. Grid section of the southern zone.

Figure 5 shows the average monthly demand registered in the southern zone for 2020, while Figure 6 shows the generation curves by source for the same area and year. Figure 6 shows the system's time demand; this peak is presented from the 20th hour. In contrast, photovoltaic solar generation presents its generation peak at 12–14 h. This difference is a challenge for the electrical system that could limit renewable generation. These data were essential for the simulation and scenarios presented in the Section 5.

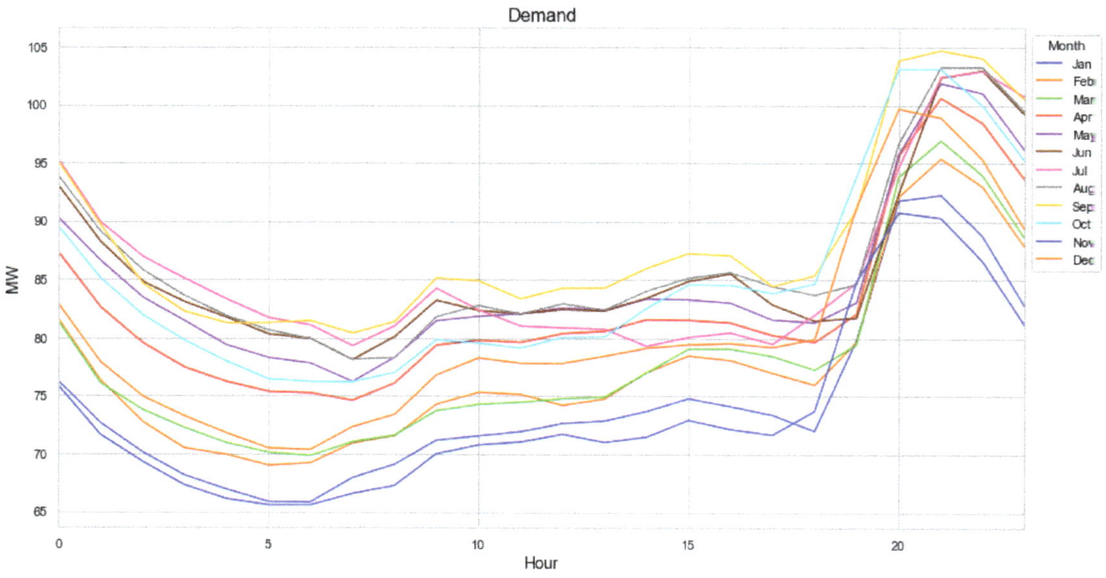

Figure 5. Average monthly demand in the southern zone.

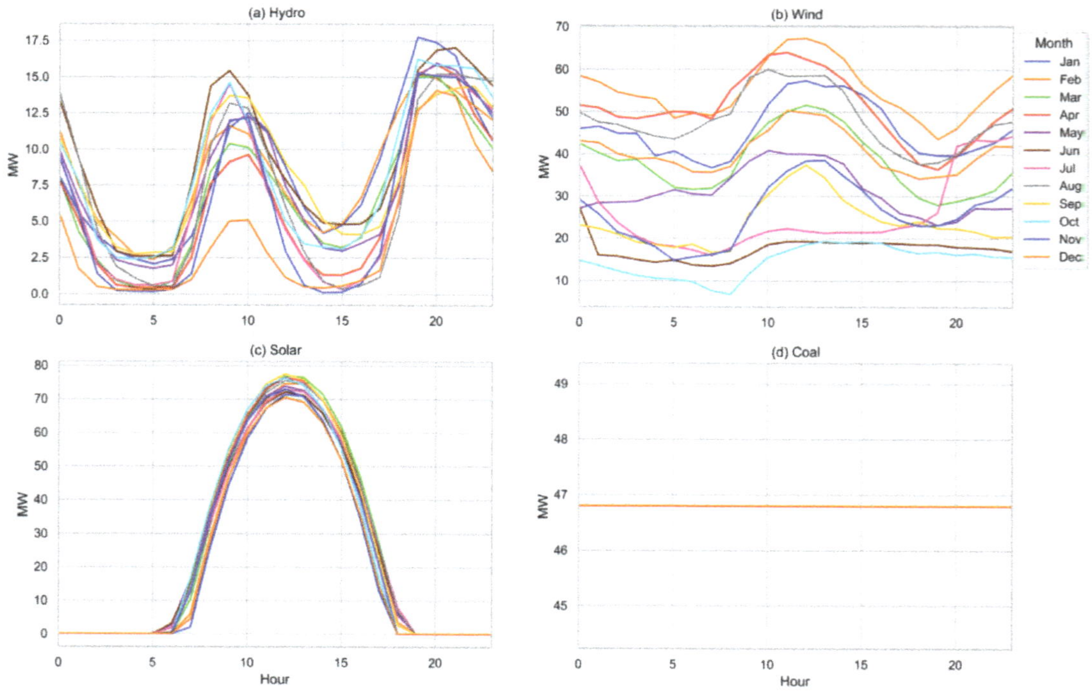

Figure 6. Generation curves by source: (**a**) hydro; (**b**) wind; (**c**) solar photovoltaic; (**d**) coal power plant.

Figure 7 presents the monthly generation curves for the year 2021 for technologies in the southern zone. For coal generation, the generation of electrical energy was constantly maintained; there were no ungathered outputs during the period observed. Wind generation in winter (from December until February) is where the most significant production was obtained. Photovoltaic solar generation remained constant, with variations in spring and in the summer presenting an increase in availability. Hydroelectric generation remained constant, experiencing decreases due to hydraulic resource management in winter due to a decrease in rainfall in the winter period. To maximize the value of the water, the hydro plant increases power generation during peak hours (18–23).

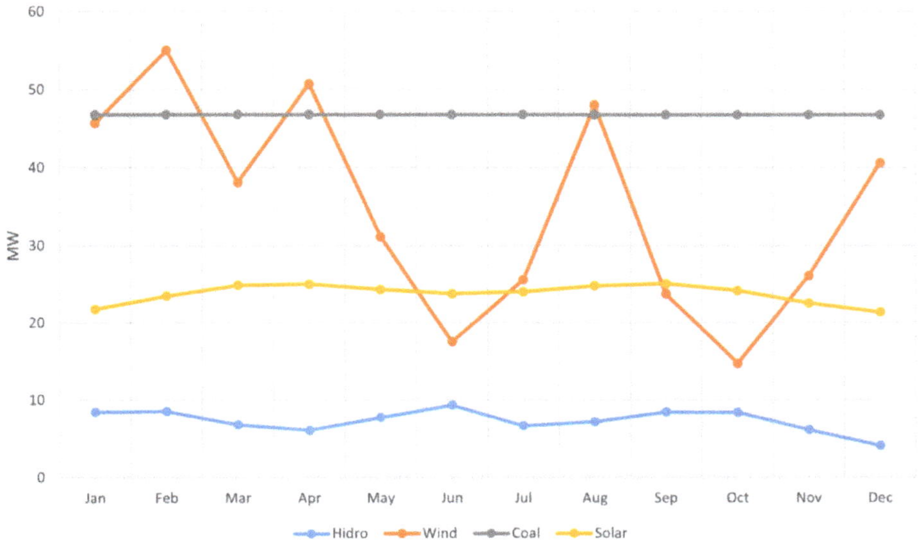

Figure 7. Monthly generation curves in the year 2021 for technologies in the southern zone.

The regulations for the primary frequency regulation are explained in Regulation of Law No. 125-01 [37]. Table 5 shows a comparison of international frequency stability standards with those of the Dominican Republic:

Table 5. Comparison of regulations on frequency stability.

Parameter	NERC	Dominican Republic
Active power between 1.5 and 10% of its value	√	√
Frequency insensitivity between 10 and 30 mHz	√	√
The dead band between 0 and 500 mHz	√	√
Frequency drop between 2 and 12%	√	√
Maximum justified delay (2 s)	√	
Activation time (30 s)	√	√
Distributed hydroelectric units for regulation		√

In resolution SI-060-2015-MEM, CC4.1.1 [38], it is explained that the regulation of voltages in 69 kV, 138 kV, or greater bus bars and generators must remain within the range of ±5%.

The power demand data per province are determined as the average of the maximum, average, and minimal demand in the daily dispatch program (PDD) [39]. The average power demand in the Enriquillo region in 2019 for the following provinces was Barahona 30.49 MW, Pedernales 1.97 MW, and Bahoruco 10.03 MW. The average power demand is from 11 a.m.–2 p.m., because in this area there are many solar photovoltaic components, and the grid is stressed more since the low demand is also affected by homes that install photovoltaic systems, which impacts the power demand.

According to [40], this area will have an annual growth of 3.41% in demand for electricity from 2021 to 2032. The analysis of the long-term demand for 2021 to 2024 was based on a single demand scenario with the annual energy projection obtained from the historical data of the actual demand supplied and forecast models based on the Box–Jenkins method. The Box–Jenkins method creates an autoregressive integrated moving average model and makes seasonal and trend adjustments [41] using the following function (Equation (1)):

$$Z_t = \delta + \theta_1 Z_{t-1} + \theta_2 Z_{t-2} + \theta_2 Z_{t-2} + \ldots + \varepsilon_t - \varnothing_1 \varepsilon_{t-1} - \varnothing_1 \varepsilon_{t-1} - \ldots \quad (1)$$

where

Z_t = the present stationary observation.

$Z_{t-1}, Z_{t-2}, \ldots, \varepsilon_{t-1}, \varepsilon_{t-2}, \ldots$ the past observations and forecasting error for the stationary time series.

ε_t = the present forecasting error.

In the expansion plan of the electric transmission system for 2021–2035 [26], it is explained that there will be a proliferation of non-conventional renewable energies in the electric power system without a specific insertion plan. This proliferation of non-conventional renewable energies causes much uncertainty about the definition of the optimal growth of the transmission grid. Due to the uncertainty caused, various scenarios in the areas most likely to carry out projects with more significant renewable potential were analyzed, along with the development of thermal generation projects near ports. This projection of power generation is why the country's future demand from 2017 to 2030 presents two possible scenarios:

Low growth: This scenario is based on the trend of the demand for electrical energy, which presents an average annual increase of 3.41%.

High growth: This alternative possibility considers a higher growth of the economic development of the country and a decrease in the energy not supplied, which presents a supply level of 100% by 2028.

Figure 8 presents the growth of demand considering a high-projection tourist area, while Figure 9 presents the growth of demand considering low demand growth in tourist areas. Both scenarios consider projections from other tourist sectors in the Dominican Republic. In both figures, a decrease in demand can be observed when the winter season begins. In addition, the cement plant executes its maintenance plan at the end of the year, reducing its electrical demand.

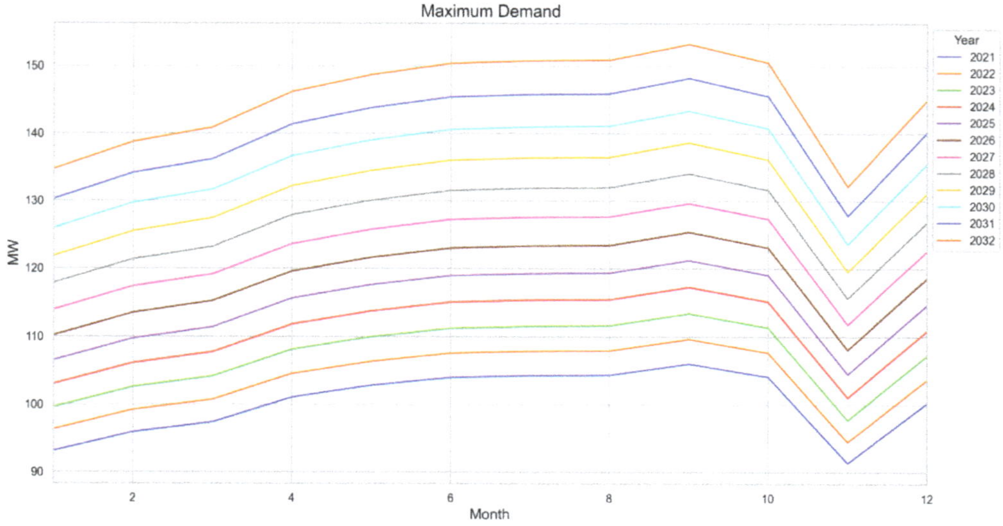

Figure 8. Growth of demand considering a high-projection future from 2017 to 2030.

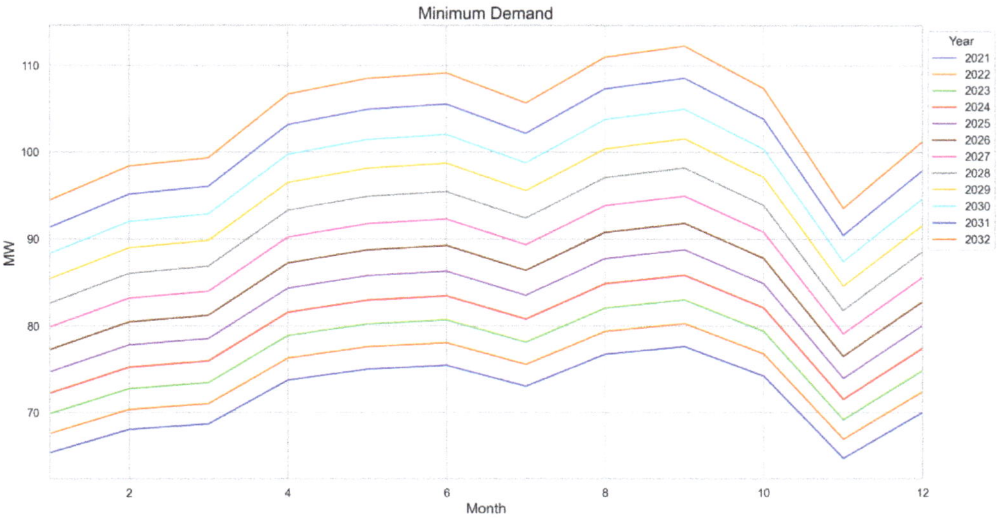

Figure 9. Growth of demand considering a low-projection future from 2017 to 2030.

5. Results and Discussion

In the Quasi-dynamic simulations, the following behaviors were identified:

Transmission lines reduced their load capacity by approximately 2.99%, which can be extrapolated to all of the regional lines. The evolution of the transmission line with the highest average load in the analysis period can be seen in Table 6. The southern region of SENI is purely an exporter of electrical energy. As mentioned, the lines connecting this area with the plant carry much power, especially when there is a good amount of Sun. With the increased local demand, the lines reduce their load level in this area. Generation is consumed locally; this behavior contributes to a longer useful life of the lines, alleviates grid congestion, allows for lower operating costs, improves grid reliability in the event of breakdowns or maintenance on adjacent lines, and reduces losses [30]. For this calculation, the security criterion was also taken (N-1).

Table 6. Transmission line evolution with a higher average load.

Years	Load (%)	Current (kA)
2021	31.022	0.152
2022	30.193	0.148
2023	29.435	0.144
2024	28.745	0.141
2025	28.196	0.138
2026	27.781	0.136
2027	27.501	0.135
2028	27.348	0.134
2029	27.324	0.135
2030	27.428	0.135
2031	27.664	0.137
2032	28.031	0.139

Table 7 shows that the highest- and lowest-voltage bus bars reduce their levels to more central values in the range that the regulations allow. Adjustment of the voltages above the acceptable range towards the safe area is achieved 10 years after the start of the study (2030).

Table 7. Evolution in bus bars of lower and higher average stress.

Years	Bar with Lower Average Voltage	Bar with Higher Average Voltage
2021	1.007	1.082
2022	1.007	1.079
2023	1.006	1.075
2024	1.006	1.071
2025	1.005	1.068
2026	1.005	1.064
2027	1.005	1.060
2028	1.004	1.056
2029	1.004	1.052
2030	1.003	1.047
2031	1.003	1.043
2032	1.003	1.037

The RSM/EMT simulations were performed assuming a failure at the AES Andres power plant, which supplies 300 MW to the electrical grid through two plants of 196.80 MW and 121.32 MW, representing 10% of the demand of the electrical system [27]; 300 MW represents approximately 10% of SENI's demand. Figure 10 shows the only demand from the southern zone, and compares the system's responses in 2021 and 2032—the years with the greatest and least impact, respectively.

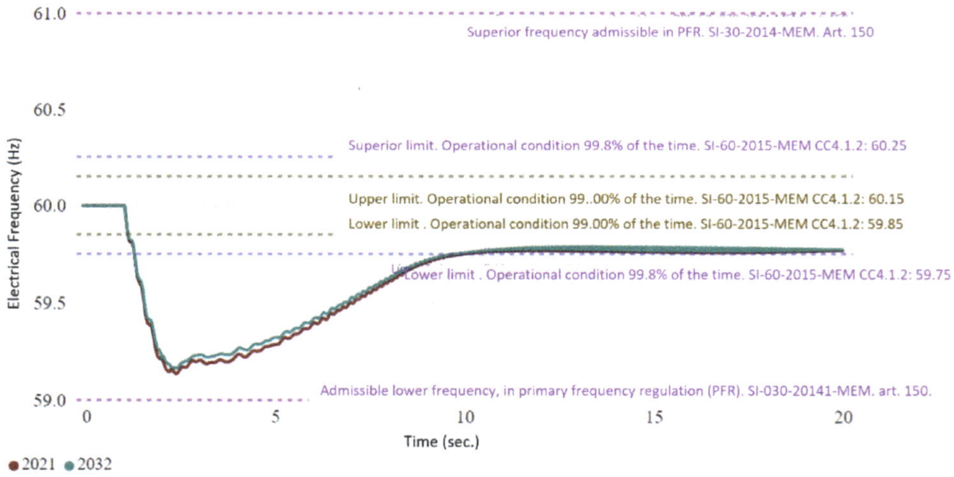

Figure 10. Electric frequency comparison slack bus between the years 2021 and 2032.

The simulation was carried out in a period of 20 s where, at the first second of starting, the electricity generator failed; the behavior of the system frequency can be visualized in the established period; this process was carried out for each year from 2021 to 2032.

Similarly, it can be seen that the frequency of the system reaches lower values in 2021 before the output of the power plant, reaching values of 59,135 Hz, while in 2032 minimum values of 59.165 Hz are reached, which represents an average difference of 0.0233% during the analysis period. After 3 s of analysis, primary regulation by raising the frequency to 59.768 for 2021 and 59.165 for 2032 presented a faster response in the latter. It should be noted that the frequency did not reach nominal values due to the lack of modeling of the secondary regulation, because it could not be observed in a 20 s time window but in minutes; this is an area that can be expanded in future research.

It is worth mentioning that the results obtained are shown to be outside the acceptable frequency ranges in the system operating conditions scenario, and that in the event of transients or faults that affect frequency stability, the primary regulation must come into play within 30 s of the event occurring, without leaving the established limits; this condition was fulfilled in the established analysis. These operating conditions show that even if a significant generator trips, the frequency can fluctuate and recover according to established regulations.

In the RSM/EMT simulations, the behavior of the electrical system in the region was analyzed in the face of the unexpected entry of a large load in the Pedernales area, which has the highest average annual demand for electricity. Figure 11 compares voltages in the system when a large power demand load enters during the analysis period. Currently, the southern zone is characterized by having a proven grid, with low demand and surplus generation. This causes the voltage to remain high in several areas of the southern zone, e.g., Substation Los Cocos and Barahona. With the increase in demand by 2031, voltage is normalized.

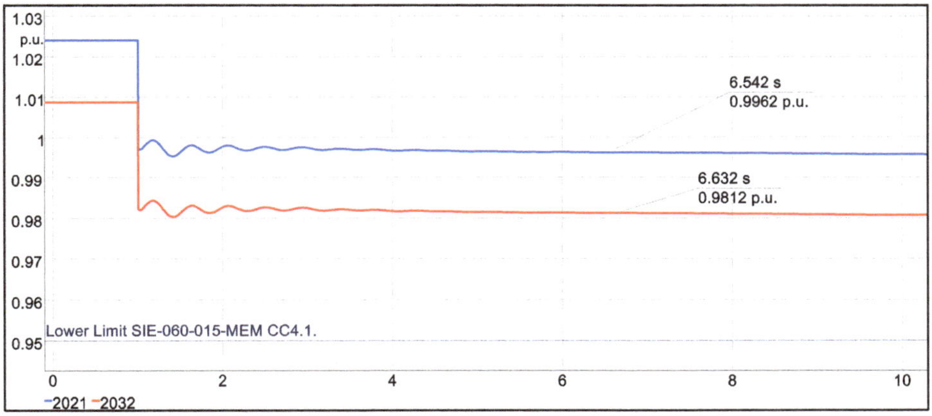

Figure 11. Comparison of voltages in the system when a large load enters between 2021 and 2032.

The voltage in the treated bus bar is above the upper limit of the norm, i.e., 1.05 p.u., while in 2032 it is within the allowed range. In both scenarios, the voltages in the bus bars oscillate before the entry of the most critical load in the Pedernales bus bar, tending to show more noticeable and more significant fluctuations in 2021, while in 2032 there are more damped oscillations (see Figure 12).

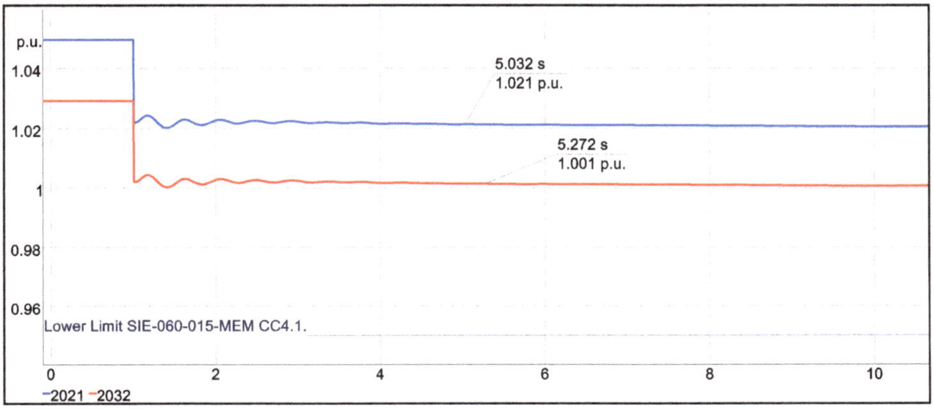

Figure 12. Comparison of voltage in the Pedernales bus bar before the entry of a large load.

Figure 13 shows a behavior similar to that in the bus bar. In both 2021 and 2032, it is observed that both voltages are identified above the allowed limits before the event. When the input event occurs, the voltage in 2021 remains outside the range. In 2032, this behavior does not take place, implying that the introduced load is crucial in maintaining the voltage within the range established by the norm. In both cases, the same thing happens as in the previous point—oscillations occur that are later corrected, with the one in 2021 being more pronounced.

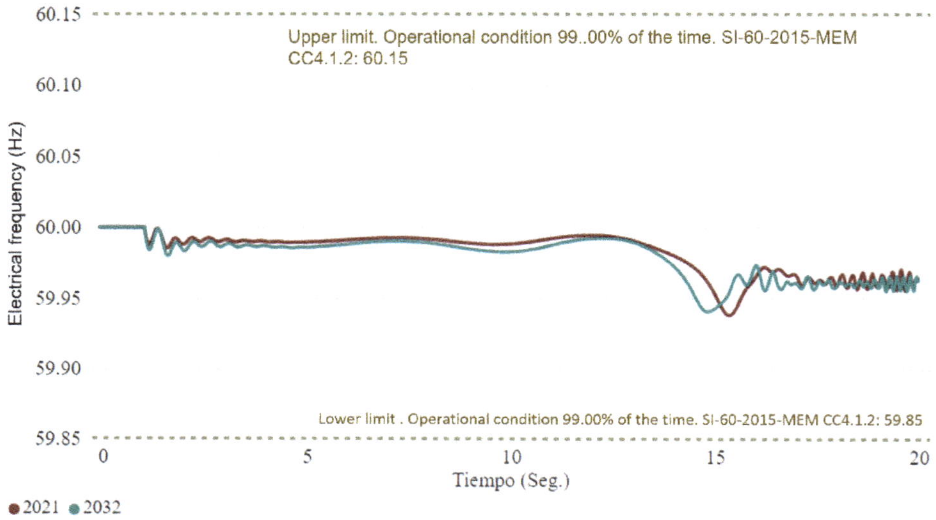

Figure 13. Frequency comparison in the system—load input in Pedernales, 2021 and 2032.

In the same way, an apparent variation in the electrical frequency is identified upon introducing the load in the Pedernales bus bar. For 2021 and 2032, oscillations are observed in the system. The apparent difference is that in 2021, there is a more pronounced disturbance in the frequency compared to 2032. It can also be observed that the frequency regulation starts working faster in 2032, i.e., 15 s after the event. In both cases, the frequency remains within the standard range, so this event does not compromise the electrical system.

6. Conclusions and Future Works

The stability control of interconnected national electrical systems at the voltage and frequency levels is a common problem that can be evaluated depending on the power system's complexity. The electrical demand that the tourist infrastructure can produce due to the growth of this sector in different regions of any country can affect the stability parameters of the power system, which can reduce the quality of energy service.

With the acquisition of data from the case study, it was possible to compare and evaluate the behavior of the current and projected energy demand due to growth according to the trend scenario of the electric power transmission company. It was also possible to simulate the necessary scenarios to conduct a technical analysis to reveal the system's behavior in the face of certain events.

In the simulation of a significant load connection event, the system maintained the voltage within the limits established by regulations, with a minimum value of 0.98 p.u. In the case of the simulation output of a large generator, the system's frequency remained above 59.90 Hz throughout the simulated period. The results of the simulations affirm that within the study time, the current system has sufficient capacity for the addition of electrical demand from the tourist facilities that are to be incorporated in the southern part of the country as part of a new tourism strategy that is to be developed. In addition, there is no need to implement techniques and/or methods for controlling voltage and frequency in the grid. With the quasi-dynamic simulations, it was possible to demonstrate that, as the years go by with the estimated growth, several parameters manage to change states from out of range to within range. The RMS/EMT simulations verified that in the face of events such as the output of a critical generator or the entry of a large load, the system does not present complications that put its continuous operation at risk.

One limitation of this methodology is not having adequate information about the grid model, the expansion of transmission lines, and the electric power generation system's features. This is crucial information that impacts the outcomes of the investigation.

For future work, conducting a stability study considering the intermittence of the connected renewable energies is recommended, to see how this affects the system's stability. In addition, scenarios should be implemented where unscheduled outputs of the generation plants are considered to observe the voltage and frequency profiles of the bus bars. Finally, a secondary regulation system should be implemented during the simulation of the generation profiles in the system.

The methodology used here can be applied to other electrical systems. It is necessary to have the model of the system to be analyzed, the expansion plan for transmission lines and electricity generation, and the demand forecast for the cases to be analyzed.

Author Contributions: Conceptualization, methodology, writing—review and editing, supervision: M.A.-M.; investigation, writing—original draft, software, formal analysis: R.A., A.C.-S., C.M. and W.-J.N.-G.; software, validation, formal analysis, supervision: E.A.J.M.; writing—review and editing: G.S.-Z., D.M.-H. and M.A.-M. All authors have read and agreed to the published version of the manuscript.

Funding: This research received no external funding.

Data Availability Statement: Data sharing not applicable.

Acknowledgments: We wish to thank the electricity generation company Haina (Egehaina) for information and support during the simulations using the DIgSILENT software, the Dominican Edesur Energy Distribution Company for the technical data on the demand for its circuits in the southern zone, and the Dominican Electrical Transmission Company (ETED) and the Energy Control Center (CCE) for the information on electric power flows and data on the transmission lines in the southern part of the country.

Conflicts of Interest: The authors declare no conflict of interest.

References

1. Li, X.; Ge, Y.Y.; Mao, X.; Xue, W.; Xu, N. Improved Energy Structure Prediction Model Based on Energy Demand Forecast. In Proceedings of the 2018 2nd IEEE conference on energy internet and energy system integration (EI2), Beijing, China, 20–22 October 2018; pp. 1–5. [CrossRef]
2. Patil, S.; Deshmukh, S.R. Development of control strategy to demonstrate load priority system for demand response program. In Proceedings of the 2019 5th IEEE International WIE Conference on Electrical and Computer Engineering, Bengaluru, India, 15–16 November 2019; pp. 1–6. [CrossRef]
3. IEA World Energy Outlook. 2020. Available online: https://www.iea.blob.core.windows.net/assets/a72d8abf-de08-4385-8711-b8a062d6124a/WEO2020.pdf (accessed on 19 February 2023).
4. Patel, T.; Parmar, M. (Special Issue for ITECE 2016) Power System Stability and Control. *Int. J. Adv. Res. Eng. Sci. Technol.* **2017**, *3*, 5. Available online: https://ijarest.com/index.php/ijarest/article/view/2019 (accessed on 1 February 2023).
5. Meo, M.S.; Chowdhury, M.A.F.; Shaikh, G.M.; Ali, M.; Masood Sheikh, S. Asymmetric impact of oil prices, exchange rate, and inflation on tourism demand in Pakistan: New evidence from nonlinear ARDL. *Asia Pacific J. Tour. Res.* **2018**, *23*, 408–422. [CrossRef]
6. Liu, Y.; Yu, S.; Zhu, Y.; Wang, D.; Liu, J. Modeling, planning, application and management of energy systems for isolated areas: A review. *Renew. Sustain. Energy Rev.* **2018**, *82*, 460–470. [CrossRef]
7. Suanpang, P.; Jamjuntr, P.; Jermsittiparsert, K.; Kaewyong, P. Autonomous Energy Management by Applying Deep Q-Learning to Enhance Sustainability in Smart Tourism Cities. *Energies* **2022**, *15*, 1906. [CrossRef]
8. Crús, A. El Turismo en el Mundo—Datos Estadísticos | Statista. Available online: https://es.statista.com/temas/3612/el-turismo-en-el-mundo/#:~:text=En%202021%2C%20seg%C3%BAn%20datos%20de,inicio%20de%20la%20pandemia%20de (accessed on 10 October 2021).

9. Statista Llegadas de Turistas Internacionales a América 1990–2020 | Statista. Available online: https://es.statista.com/estadisticas/632568/llegadas-de-turistas-internacionales-a-america/ (accessed on 10 October 2021).
10. Banco Central de la República Dominicana Estadísticas Sector Turismo. Available online: https://www.bancentral.gov.do/a/d/2537-sector-turismo (accessed on 30 December 2022).
11. Thomas, D.; Deblecker, O.; Ioakimidis, C.S. Optimal design and techno-economic analysis of an autonomous small isolated microgrid aiming at high RES penetration. *Energy* **2016**, *116*, 364–379. [CrossRef]
12. Jorge Eduardo Játiva Sierra. Impacto de la generación distribuida en la estabilidad del voltaje en los sistemas de distribucion, Universidad Politécnica Salesiana Sede Quito. 2020. Available online: http://dspace.ups.edu.ec/handle/123456789/19169, (accessed on 10 October 2021).
13. Stefánsson, Þ.; Sæþórsdóttir, A.D.; Hall, C.M. When tourists meet transmission lines: The effects of electric transmission lines on tourism in Iceland. *Energy Res. Soc. Sci.* **2017**, *34*, 82–92. [CrossRef]
14. Zhang, D.; Li, H.; Zhu, H.; Zhang, H.; Goh, H.H.; Wong, M.C.; Wu, T. Impact of COVID-19 on Urban Energy Consumption of Commercial Tourism City. *Sustain. Cities Soc.* **2021**, *73*, 103133. [CrossRef] [PubMed]
15. Refaat, S.S.; Abu-Rub, H.; Sanfilippo, A.P.; Mohamed, A. Impact of grid-tied large-scale photovoltaic system on dynamic voltage stability of electric power grids. *IET Renew. Power Gener.* **2018**, *12*, 157–164. [CrossRef]
16. GmbH, D. Quasi-Dynamic Simulation—DIgSILENT. Available online: https://www.digsilent.de/en/quasi-dynamic-simulation.html (accessed on 3 November 2022).
17. Organismo Coordinador del Sistema Eléctrico Nacional Interconectado de la República Dominicana (CO-SENI) Operación del Sistema Eléctrico Nacional Interconectado de la República Dominicana (SENI). Available online: https://www.dropbox.com/sh/rhs9u44j7z79u1k/AACEZm9U25eOQNY-XQiDQZMZa/UNIFILAR%20SENI?dl=0&subfolder_nav_tracking=1 (accessed on 9 November 2022).
18. Jabir, H.J.; Teh, J.; Ishak, D.; Abunima, H. Impacts of Demand-Side Management on Electrical Power Systems: A Review. *Energies* **2018**, *11*, 1050. [CrossRef]
19. Wu, Y.; Xin, B.; Zhu, H.; Ye, Z. Energy-Saving Operation Strategy for Hotels Considering the Impact of COVID-19 in the Context of Carbon Neutrality. *Sustainability* **2022**, *14*, 14919. [CrossRef]
20. Bharati, A.K.; Ajjarapu, V. SMTD Co-Simulation Framework with HELICS for Future-Grid Analysis and Synthetic Measurement-Data Generation. *IEEE Trans. Ind. Appl.* **2022**, *58*, 131–141. [CrossRef]
21. Lai, Y.; Hu, Y.; Li, W.; Liu, F.; Qie, Z.; Sun, Z. Research on Voltage Stability of Reactive Power Weak Support Regions in Countries along the Belt and Road Based on PSS/E. In Proceedings of the 2022 5th International Conference on Energy, Electrical and Power Engineering (CEEPE), Chongqing, China, 22–24 April 2022; pp. 235–239.
22. de Lima Vianna, P.; Viana, M.S.; Manassero, G.; Udaeta, M.E. A General Analysis of the Distributed Generation Impact on Electrical Energy Planning. In Proceedings of the 2018 53rd International Universities Power Engineering Conference (UPEC), Glasgow, UK, 4–7 September 2018; pp. 1–6.
23. Audring, D.; Kuri, A. Modelling and challenges of integration of large renewable power plants. In Proceedings of the 2021 56th International Universities Power Engineering Conference (UPEC), Middlesbrough, UK, 31 August–3 September 2021; pp. 1–6.
24. Al-Akayshee, A.S.; Kuznetsov, O.N.; Alwazah, I.; Deeb, M. Investigation of the Performance of Iraqi 400kV Electrical Network in DIgSILENT Power Factory. In Proceedings of the 2020 International Youth Conference on Radio Electronics, Electrical and Power Engineering (REEPE), Moscow, Russia, 12–14 March 2020; pp. 1–6.
25. Adetokun, B.; Muriithi, C. Application and control of flexible alternating current transmission system devices for voltage stability enhancement of renewable-integrated power grid: A comprehensive review. *Heliyon* **2021**, *7*, 7. [CrossRef] [PubMed]
26. Gu, M.; Meegahapola, L.; Wong, K.L. Coordinated Voltage and Frequency Control in Hybrid AC/MT-HVDC Power Grids for Stability Improvement. *IEEE Trans. Power Syst.* **2021**, *36*, 635–647. [CrossRef]
27. Mukherjee, N.; De, D.; Nandagaoli, N. Effect of sudden variation of grid voltage in primary frequency control application using converter based energy storage systems for weak grid systems. In Proceedings of the 2017 19th European Conference on Power Electronics and Applications (EPE'17 ECCE Europe), Warsaw, Poland, 11–14 September 2017; pp. P.1–P.10.
28. Bompard, E.; Mazza, A.; Toma, L. Classical grid control: Frequency and voltage stability. In *Converter-Based Dynamics and Control of Modern Power Systems*; Academic Press: Cambridge, MA, USA, 2021; p. 360, ISBN 978-0-12-818491-2. Available online: https://linkinghub.elsevier.com/retrieve/pii/B9780128184912000031 (accessed on 1 February 2023).
29. Ojo, Y.; Benmiloud, M.; Lestas, I. Frequency and voltage control schemes for three-phase grid-forming inverters. *IFAC PapersOnLine* **2020**, *53*, 13471–13476. [CrossRef]
30. Yan, L.; Xiaohui, Q.; Yongning, C.; Xinshou, T.; Sujuan, S.; Shenglun, Z.; Xiangmei, K.; Lei, S. Study on Requirement of Control and Stability with Renewable Energy Generation Grid Integration. In Proceedings of the 2019 IEEE 8th International Conference on Advanced Power System Automation and Protection (APAP), Xi'an, China, 21–24 October 2019; pp. 26–30.
31. Khamies, M.; Magdy, G.; Ebeed, M.; Kamel, S. A robust PID controller based on linear quadratic gaussian approach for improving frequency stability of power systems considering renewables. *ISA Trans.* **2021**, *117*, 118–138. [CrossRef] [PubMed]
32. Guo, J. Application of a novel adaptive sliding mode control method to the load frequency control. *Eur. J. Control* **2021**, *57*, 172–178. [CrossRef]
33. Dreidy, M.; Mokhlis, H.; Mekhilef, S. Inertia response and frequency control techniques for renewable energy sources: A review. *Renew. Sustain. Energy Rev.* **2017**, *69*, 144–155. [CrossRef]

34. Golpîra, H.; Seifi, H.; Haghifam, M.R. Dynamic equivalencing of an active distribution network for large-scale power system frequency stability studies. *IET Gener. Transm. Distrib.* **2015**, *9*, 2245–2254. [CrossRef]
35. Vazquez, S.; Rodriguez, J.; Rivera, M.; Franquelo, L.G.; Norambuena, M. Model Predictive Control for Power Converters and Drives: Advances and Trends. *IEEE Trans. Ind. Electron.* **2017**, *64*, 935–947. [CrossRef]
36. Counsil, W.E.C. Voltage Stability Criteria. Available online: https://www.wecc.org/Reliability/Voltage%20Stability%20Criteria%20May%201998.pdf (accessed on 10 October 2021).
37. Electricidad, S. de Reglamento para la Aplicación de la Ley General de Electricidad Número 125-01. 2012, 314. Available online: https://sie.gob.do/images/sie-documentos-pdf/leyes/LeyGeneraldeElecctricidadNo.125-01.pdf, (accessed on 10 October 2021).
38. *Superintendencia de Electricidad (SIE) Resolucion SIE-060-2015-MEM*; Distrito Nacional: Santo Domingo, Dominican Republic, 2015.
39. SENI, O.C. Informe Anual de Operaciones y Transacciones Económicas. 2020. Available online: https://www.oc.do/Informes/Administrativos/Informe-Anual/EntryId/175028 (accessed on 10 October 2021).
40. Roa, L.; Ogando, L.; LastNameSimó, A.; Aquino, F.; De La Cruz, S. Organismo Coordinador del Sistema Eléctrico Nacional Interconectado de la República Dominicana Para: Agentes del mem Preparado por: Gerencia de Operaciones Oc-Seni. Available online: https://www.oc.org.do/DesktopModules/Bring2mind/DMX/API/Entries/Download?Command=Core_Download&EntryId=160872&language=es-ES&PortalId=0&TabId=188 (accessed on 19 February 2022).
41. Lu, Y.; AbouRizk, S.M. Automated Box–Jenkins forecasting modelling. *Autom. Constr.* **2009**, *18*, 547–558. [CrossRef]

urban science

Opinion

Towards a New Urban Health Science

Franz W Gatzweiler [1,2,*], Saroj Jayasinghe [3,4], José G Siri [5] and Jason Corburn [6]

1 Institute of Urban Environment, Chinese Academy of Sciences, Xiamen 361021, China
2 United Nations University Institute in Macau, Macau SAR, China
3 Faculty of Medicine, University of Colombo, Kynsey Road, Colombo 00800, Sri Lanka
4 Faculty of Medicine, Sabaragamuwa University of Sri Lanka, Belihuloya 70140, Sri Lanka
5 Independent Researcher, Philadelphia, PA 19146, USA
6 School of Public Health & Department of City & Regional Planning, Center for Global Healthy Cities, UC Berkeley, Berkeley, CA 94720, USA
* Correspondence: franz@unu.edu; Tel.: +853-6801-7217

Abstract: The intensity and range of health challenges that people in cities are facing has increased in recent years. This is due in part to a failure to adequately adapt and respond to emergent and expanding global systemic risks, but also to a still-limited understanding of the profound impacts of complexity on urban health. While complexity science is increasingly embraced by the health and urban sciences, it has yet to be functionally incorporated into urban health research, policy, and practice. Accelerating urbanization in a context of escalating environmental constraints will require deeper engagement with complexity, yet also, paradoxically, much swifter, more effective, and more risk-averse decision-making. Meeting these demands will require adopting a science, policy and practice style which is integrative, inclusive, collaborative, systemic, fast, and frugal. We propose transformational shifts in scientific methodology, epistemological and ontological stances, types of rationality, and governance to shift researchers, policymakers, practitioners, and citizens towards a new, complexity-informed science of urban health.

Keywords: complex systems; urban health; inclusion; knowledge; rationality; governance

1. Introduction

While urban health scientists and decision makers have long acknowledged that cities are complex systems, inquiry and practice have yet to fully contend with the implications. We suggest here that approaching cities as complex systems will require significant, explicit changes to current research and practices for urban health. Failing to take such an approach contributes to data, decisions, and outcomes that perpetuate inequities, reduce freedoms, fail to adequately address environmental and ecosystem degradation, and contribute to suboptimal or declining health for the billions living in urban areas—particularly in times of global health crises, like those arising from climate change and the recent COVID-19 pandemic. As such, urban health should pursue a deeper, more pragmatic engagement with urban complexity science. This would help address the most urgent health and equity issues in cities, reduce the unintended consequences of urbanization—and of sustainable development itself—and strengthen competencies for governing complex urban systems.

Over the last several decades, various commissions and commentaries have called for more research on how city decision making and urban design influence population health and health equity, and for corresponding action [1–3]. These important reviews themselves build upon an older literature demanding that urban design, planning, and policy recognize the unique characteristics that contribute to well-being or ill health in urban settings [4–7]. This half-century of incremental work holds critical insights for urban health, yet there is still considerable scope to benefit from a new perspective on the interface between urban health science and policymaking that:

- acknowledges and prioritizes persistent inequities and recognizes their substantial origins in urban complexity;
- proceeds from a basic recognition that urban health is an emergent outcome of complex processes, and accordingly interrogates linear assumptions about health causation;
- adopts a multiscale perspective, considering how complex regional and global connectedness, networks, and flows impact urban health;
- focuses on ways to foster civic participation in urban goal setting, implementation, governance, monitoring, and communication;
- recognizes and works toward local resilience as an enabling framework for anticipating, responding to, and learning from health crises;
- places a greater emphasis on history and learning, especially from failed urban health experiments and under-appreciated successes;
- makes use of new digital tools and techniques.

Urban health scholars and practitioners have already, in many contexts, recognized that delivering more healthy, equitable, and inclusive cities depends on engaging more substantially with urban complexity, rather than attempting to simplify the irreducible. In fact, it is increasingly accepted that many negative health impacts in cities emerge due to the difficulty of perceiving, understanding, and governing urban complexity [8].

Important advances have been made in polycentric, participatory, reflexive, adaptive, and transdisciplinary research and policy styles, which can be viewed as attempts to engage with complexity and match complex decision-making situations with requisite governance institutions (e.g., structures, mechanisms, rules) [9]. Yet, recent times have also seen a reverse trend, towards more top-down/impositional and less bottom-up/consensual policy styles [10–12]; this trend has likely been accelerated by global health emergencies, risks, and disasters, and especially by the recent global COVID-19 pandemic [13].

This is not to say that more consensual policy styles are always 'better'. Rather, to effectively navigate an increasingly complex social, ecological, and technological urban environment, it is essential to have policy styles, participatory decision-making mechanisms, and governance capacities that match the constraints and opportunities imposed by complexity. The first law of cybernetics states that systems must have a number of control or response mechanisms equal to or greater than the number of potential disturbances the system faces [14]. Policymaking under complexity rarely obeys this law, usually due to the competing interest of creating more economically efficient outcomes.

Vatn [15] argues for the importance of matching policy regimes to complexity, noting that the latter conditions the very framework for decision choices. In contrast to simple modular systems, complex systems demand consideration of not only individual but social rationality, and not only instrumental but communicative rationality. In other words, they require that we consider not only the sum of progress toward individual goals but progress toward collective goals, and not only technical means of achieving outcomes but mechanisms that foster iterative, consensual understanding. Too often, institutional inertia causes science and policy to be based merely on individual rationality and instrumental types of human interactions, leading to cost-efficient but suboptimal choices and unintended negative consequences, particularly for complex issues such as urban sustainability and health. Mueller [16] traces "ubiquitous" policy failure to the false assumption that complex systems can be precisely determined, closely predicted and exactly controlled—a paradoxically simplistic acknowledgement of complexity that leads to overconfidence and unrealistic expectations.

Reservations against engaging more deeply with complexity are sometimes predicated on the perception that such engagement precludes timely and rigorous application of the scientific method. This is an especially poignant critique in the context of escalating challenges, where solutions are needed much faster than traditional science can typically provide them. Yet narrow decision-making based on linear assumptions often leads to calamitous outcomes in complex systems; in the words of Read [17] (often misattributed to Keynes), "It is better to be vaguely right than exactly wrong." Moreover, decision-making under complexity need not be fatally slow: there is a rich history of rapid, heuristic decision-making successfully applied to complex situations in health [18,19].

Decision-making guided by complexity science may also be perceived as lacking clarity (e.g., of goals, methods, or messages) and can accordingly give rise to mistrust. This is one reason why solutions to complex urban health issues usually depend on collective action; involving all relevant stakeholders across all pertinent scales increases the legitimacy of decisions, even where complexity imposes irreducible ambiguities.

Decision-makers themselves can impose additional barriers to engaging with complexity. For example, they may choose to persevere with an existing policy style or decision-making approach to maintain credibility and avoid the perception of unreliability—a behavior explainable through the lens of so-called 'sunk costs'. Complexity, often confused with 'complicatedness', can engender resistance based on the perceived costs of change—especially when changes might threaten policymakers' accustomed roles and positions. Vested interests will often prevent decision makers from making necessary changes to systems from which they benefit. These factors apply even where existing outcomes are globally suboptimal, and a complexity-informed approach would benefit the common good.

The challenge of systematizing complexity thinking in research, policy and practice is substantial. It calls for institutionalizing the participatory processes of knowledge-making within institutions that have consistently worked to isolate expert knowledge from the vagaries of dissent, populism, and politics. In grappling with the partiality of scientific knowledge and the inevitable uncertainty associated with complex reality, Jasanoff [20] made the case for 'technologies of humility'; methods—or better yet, institutionalized habits of thought—that seek to come to grips with the ragged fringes of human understanding: the unknown, the uncertain, the ambiguous, and the uncontrollable. Acknowledging the limits of prediction and control, technologies of humility confront head-on the normative implications of our lack of perfect foresight. They call for different capabilities and different forms of engagement between experts, decision-makers, and the public than have previously been considered needful in governance. They require not only formal mechanisms of participation but also an intellectual environment in which citizens are encouraged to bring their knowledge and skills to bear on the resolution of common problems.

In sum, it has become clear that informational and epistemological frameworks for policymaking must be adjusted in the face of complexity. In this commentary, we propose modifications to policymaking styles for urban health, elaborating on how complexity science and policy can be applied to urban health challenges to meet the demands of the 21st century.

2. Toward a New Urban Health Science

There is a long history of understanding and engaging with cities as complex systems. In the mid-19th century, Cerda [21] laid the groundwork for a science of cities on the basis of observations of geometry, form, and notions of mechanism at work. Geddes [22], half a century later, perceived cities as evolving from flows and networks. More recently, alongside significant advances in the field of complexity science, cities came to be seen as products of bottom-up, evolutionary, self-organizing processes, rather than top-down design [23,24].

Over the past decade, a new urban science has emerged which recognizes that cities are centers of complexity, encompassing multiple types of embedded, overlapping, and interacting systems [25–27]. Because this complexity is partly organized and partly emergent, cities are partly plannable and partly unpredictable and unplannable, depending on the physical and time scales of observation.

Urban health, defined here as the health of people living in cities and the complex state of the environments on which it depends, is no less subject to complexity than are cities themselves. Accordingly, to continue to safeguard and improve human health and the environment, especially in the context of escalating risks, the field of urban health will also have to come to grips with urban complexity. A new science for healthy cities would draw on lessons from the broader inquiry into urban complexity [28]. It would complement an understanding of urban health as the outcome of multiple social and environmental determinants, deepening the recognition of urban health as a product of the mutual interactions between humans and their environments—or, more broadly, as an emergent property of interacting socio-ecological-technological systems (SETS) [29,30].

The shift in focus from a multiple determinants perspective to one focusing on systemic interactions implies a corresponding change in the structure of the scientific enterprise; whereas the former can be studied by teams of researchers from multiple disciplines working in parallel, the latter requires consilience (converging evidence from many unrelated lines of inquiry) and the robust uptake of inter- and transdisciplinary inquiry [9,31,32]. This, in turn, requires a greater focus on participatory processes in order to ensure the multiple lines of evidence needed to generate new insights and inform policy and practice (among other benefits). In the words of Jane Jacobs [33], "Cities have the capability of providing something for everybody, only because, and only when, they are created by everybody."

By its nature, a complexity-informed science of urban health would encourage a focus on the upstream root causes of urban health and environmental challenges, allowing for a more efficient, proactive approach rooted in prevention, rather than the more typical reactive mode that endeavors to alleviate problems. Through its embrace of inclusive participation and a focus on systemic unintended consequences, it would also offer insights and incentives for addressing pervasive social, institutional, and health inequities in cities [34].

Critically, such an approach would also be better suited to understanding and finding solutions in the context of the characteristic hyperconnectivity of modern urbanization. As articulated by Batty [26], "In a world now dominated by communications ... it is high time we changed our focus from locations to interactions, from thinking of cities simply as idealized morphologies to thinking of them as patterns of communication, interaction, trade, and exchange; in short, to thinking of them as networks." Urban spaces feature exponentially accelerating connectivity. For example, modern transport systems enable rapid and thus more geographically extensive mobility, and thus larger numbers of potential person-to-person connections. The dense, intensely interconnected, rapidly changing milieux enabled by transport and other urban systems require governance responses that are equally fast, flexible, diverse, and multi-source, as has been observed for the special case of COVID-19 [35,36].

Urban connectivity is not limited to person-to-person interactions. Through systemic connections, urban complexity translates human activity into broad impacts on people and environments, solving some problems but also creating new 'wicked' challenges, themselves inextricably connected [37]. Thus, global urban systems have driven growth and development, raised life expectancy, and reduced poverty. However, urban growth is founded on—and has systematically degraded—the global ecosystems to which global networks of cities are connected and which provide the resources to build and feed cities and the sinks which absorb their wastes [38,39].

Thus, the better understanding of the city as a complex system eventually leads us to a firmer appreciation of the deep connections between cities and our planet. In the face of increasingly systemic global risks [13] and the increasing likelihood that we will collectively fail to achieve the United Nations Sustainable Development Goals (SDGs) [40] by 2030 [41], this understanding may also lead us to crucial new insights into how to define and pursue sustainability, drawing on lessons from complexity science and on our capacity for collective action and intelligence. It should also foster engagement with existing conceptual critiques of sustainable development [42–44]—in particular the ecological incoherence of the most widely visible measures of 'progress' [45]—fostering better outcomes by expanding the discourse of ideas.

3. Shifts to Enable a Complexity-Informed Approach to Urban Health

Based on long-standing observations by scientists, urban residents and other stakeholders, and decision makers, we propose *four critical shifts* to underpin a complexity-informed approach to urban health. These shifts have to do with (a) how we perceive the nature of the challenges we face (ontology) and our ability to have knowledge about them (epistemology); (b) the tools we use to derive that knowledge (methodology); (c) the way that we respond to and make decisions based on that knowledge (rationality); and (d) the way we organize our institutions to promote such an approach (governance).

1. **Nature and how we know it: shifting ontological and epistemological stances**

For close to half a millennium, the scientific method has been the primary basis for our claim to "know" reality, and thus the basis for evidence-informed decision-making. Indeed, Wilson observed that "with aid of the scientific method, we have gained an encompassing view of the physical world far beyond the dreams of earlier generations" [46]. Yet, this expanded view, and indeed the scientific method itself, has in some contexts been challenged as failing to represent a full or useful picture of real-world problems.

As classically applied, the scientific method tends to assume that natural processes are reducible to observable, testable cause-and-effect relationships among independent variables. It tends toward quantitative rather than qualitative analysis, discourages ambiguity, and perceives the analyst as an objective, unboundedly rational individual standing 'outside' the observed system. In philosophy this belief has been referred to as realism.

Reality, however, involves a host of complications: non-linear feedback relationships, multiway causality, emergent behavior, and the methods by which we observe or try to discover realty. The nature of human processes means that scientific production itself is subject to complex biases. It is therefore rarely helpful to ask which model is closest to one universal reality. What is more useful is to acknowledge that all models fail to completely account for the complexities of reality and that some models are more useful than others: model-dependent realism [47].

Thus, classical science often fails to produce actionable knowledge or meet societal needs. Models fail to reflect people's lived realities. Research cycles are consistently outpaced by events, institutional mechanisms for incorporating science into decision-making are underdeveloped, and scientific practice often fails to match the scope or complexity of societal challenges. Although overall trust in science is high—and in some contexts may even be higher in the context of the COVID-19 pandemic [47]—distrust often exists among groups or in contexts where science is perceived as producing evidence that diverges from lived realities or prescribing action that fails to address local priorities [48].

Addressing these issues requires shifting our understanding of the nature of reality and how we can know it. An alternate, more useful understanding of complex systems can be achieved by methodologies which are not less rigorous but more qualitative, allow ambiguity, and perceive complexity as emerging from the interactions among system components and with the broader environment—including interactions with the observer, who is thus internalized to the system. Such an approach suggests that the complex systems we observe and are part of are amenable to understanding and thus to forecasting and influence. A critical difference from the classical approach is the observation that science itself is not indifferent to changing environments and changing decision making situations [49].

Apart from model-dependent realism, another response has been to recognize the importance of a post-normal and mission-oriented approach to science [50,51]. While normal science claims its credibility from avoiding bias, post-normal science makes a conscious choice about the biases and values most appropriate to the task of guiding science to create knowledge for practice. It likewise embraces a broader section of society (an extended peer community) in the process of producing knowledge [52]. Among problems addressed by post-normal science are those relating to major technological hazards or environmental pollution. For such issues, ethical judgements and values play as important a role as formal analysis. Wider adoption of this epistemological stance—through conscious promotion by scientific authorities, in education, and in policy and practice—would improve our ability to meet increasingly complex challenges.

2. **Sharpening the tools of the trade: shifting scientific methodology**

To overcome persistent barriers to human understanding and effective practice, the scientific method, as typically implemented, must expand in its conceptualization and application to incorporate new methodologies; for example, systems approaches and transdisciplinary research are widely recognized as key methods for addressing complex challenges [9,29,53]. In the urban health context, Newell and Siri argue for the application of low-order system dynamics models in urban health policymaking [54].

Indeed, the practice of science is itself a complex system which would benefit from the insights of complexity science, continually adapting and honing its methods, rules, and perceptions to meet the enduring demands of a complex reality.

Similarly, to meet the demands of our new model-dependent realism, science must incorporate new domains of evidence, including practical and experiential knowledge and insights from the social sciences, and new partners from outside the science domain.

We have begun to see changes in the structure of science that would support methodological innovation. Indeed, "In every age, science is shaped around its leading problems, and it evolves with them" [55]. And thus, in the contextual shift from a 'small world on a big planet' to a 'big world on a small planet' [56], with vastly more (and more interconnected) people, cities, and other human artifacts, we have begun to see a softening of disciplinary boundaries and the appearance of hybrid scientific domains "in which consilience is implicit" [46], as well as the emergence of action-oriented, post-normal science in contexts where uncertainties are epistemological or ethical and decision stakes reflect conflicting purposes among stakeholders.

The continued expansion of novel, complexity-oriented methodologies will require explicit institutional and financial support as part of a project of field-building. It will require a serious effort by researchers to limit jargon and provide useful explanations and straightforward solutions for complex problems—without shortchanging irreducible complexity. Perhaps most of all, it will require an unflagging focus on the creation of actionable knowledge relevant to end users, given that the translation of knowledge into action is entirely dependent on societal trust in science.

Various resources are available to support this transition. To name just two, the International Science Council's global science programme on Urban Health and Wellbeing has over the last decade elaborated a systems approach to urban health and suggested actions for future research and action [57]. Meanwhile, the OECD has promulgated recommendations for supporting transdisciplinary research to address complex societal challenges, part of a wider, growing recognition of the value of this approach [9].

3. **Translating knowledge into justified action: shifting rationality**

When confronted with uncertainty (as opposed to calculable risks), limited time, data, and computational capacity—as is often the case in complex decision-making situations—traditional notions of rational action, premised on optimal decisions made under perfect information, are inaccurate and will typically fail to deliver desired outcomes. Rather, in such situations, ecological rationality, which accounts for context, and collaborative rationality, which seeks to progressively approach better answers through a process of co-discovery, should be favored.

Among other features, such rubrics may make use of heuristics to avoid the need for the explicit computation of probabilities and should be better adapted to the structure of their environment. In the shift from deterministic to probabilistic to heuristic decision-making, unrealistic assumptions of unbounded rationality and unlimited computational capabilities are increasingly relaxed. While heuristics are not a substitute for in-depth investigation, in an uncertain world, a simple heuristic—i.e., a fast, frugal, generally experience-based decision-making strategy that focuses on a small set of highly relevant predictors—can be more accurate than other decision-making strategies when action is urgently needed. Ecologically rational decisions can be achieved when heuristics are well-matched to their environments.

Heuristics have been promoted as one approach to managing complexity, for example, in the implementation of green infrastructure [58] and in data-driven urban design [59]. Critical systems thinking in ICT4S (Information and Communication Technology for Sustainability) requires a critical systems heuristics (CSH) approach, as demonstrated in Sidewalk Labs 'smart city' project in Toronto. CSH recognizes the limits of computational approaches in urban decision making and balances the tension between facts and values which must be taken into account and the notions of how people think human life should be organized [60]. Similar examples include the partial systems analysis of noise pollution reduction in a district of Beirut [61].

Another key element of rational decision-making in complex situations is collaboration among diverse partners. As is the case for methodological approaches to knowledge production, diversity in experiences, values, priorities, and background knowledge is critical to ensuring that decisions are both well-matched to needs and are likely to achieve the buy-in necessary for effective implementation.

All complex urban decision-making situations involve a range of interacting subjects and objects and diverse types of resources, including private, common pool and public goods and services. Adequate responses will incorporate a diverse set of methods based on different rationalities, accounting for both facts and values, as well as experiences and past knowledge of the past and future needs and aspirations.

4. Supporting a complexity-informed approach: shifting governance

When decision making strategies become more ecologically rational, and therefore, by definition, better matched to their social and biophysical environments, they will necessarily become more inclusive, deliberative, and reflexive. The norms and principles on which decisions are based should be adaptive and not persist irrespective of the circumstances under which they were formulated, which may have changed. In such contexts, governance for complex decision-making situations will be more robust and yet more flexible than structures based on individual rationality (i.e., based on an assumption of fixed principles and relationships).

Robust governance structures contribute to health-promoting urban complexity. They are adaptive insofar as they benefit from existing decision-making rules and strategies while retaining the capacity to change by learning. They are reflexive in the sense that they are able to change themselves in response to reflections on their own performance within the changing environments they operate in [62–64].

These shifts do not happen automatically and therefore we need substantially more research on the ways in which governance mechanisms and institutional structures interact with complex systems, as well as advocacy to promote those systems that generate healthy complexity (without creating unproductive chaos).

4. Conclusions

Urbanization continues to create a range of challenges and inequities which threaten health and wellbeing. A new urban health science is needed to understand why and how this is happening and to adequately and rapidly respond to systemic risks and prevent human disasters. The increasing complexity that comes with urbanization does not inexorably lead to an urban advantage.

The complexity of urban systems needs to be actively shaped; urban health challenges must be met with a diversifying array of human- and social capital supported by well-functioning and well-connected physical, institutional, and technological infrastructure.

In the practice of science, coping with complexity requires explicit efforts and investments into multidisciplinary, interdisciplinary, transdisciplinary, and mission-oriented science. Due to persistent incentive structures in science, specialized, narrow knowledge published in high-ranking journals is favored over more general and practical guides, reports or knowledge communication. These features of science practice lead to a fragmentation of knowledge and an increasing inequality of voices operating at the level of policymaking.

In terms of policy-making, coping with complexity requires more investments in the empowerment of the public, building social cohesion and participatory decision-making, not merely securing privileges and decision-making power. It requires leadership which does not shy away from complexity and is willing to address institutional and policy reforms which are tailored towards building collective action and the public good, also, or particularly, when that means that the political system needs to reform itself in order to better cope with complex decision-making situations.

In society, it means to actively engage in and with the urban health challenges that urban residents are confronted with, and for them to be part of the urban planning and design processes. It requires the articulation and recognition of people's visions of the city they need and want.

Bringing all of these required shifts together and building new interactions and alliances can be done by learning from cities in the real world which have grown and transformed successfully in response to the challenges they faced in the past. By exploring new possibilities and spaces provided by digitalization, today we are also able to take part in modelling, building and simulating healthy cities of and for the future. Complexity leadership theory [65], collaborative modelling and urban planning, citizen science, and creative collective intelligence [66] are examples which are part of a bundle of actions taking us forward to creating a new urban health science.

Author Contributions: All authors contributed equally to the manuscript. All authors have read and agreed to the published version of the manuscript.

Funding: This opinion piece is the outcome of the International Science Council's (ISC) global science programme on Urban Health and Wellbeing: A Systems Approach, which received funding by the Chinese Academy of Sciences, the Chinese Association of Science and Technology and the Xiamen City Bureau of Science and Technology.

Conflicts of Interest: The authors declare no conflict of interest.

References

1. Vlahov, D.; Freudenberg, N.; Proietti, F.; Ompad, D.; Quinn, A.; Nandi, V.; Galea, S. Urban as a Determinant of Health. *J. Urban Health* **2007**, *84*, 16–26. [CrossRef] [PubMed]
2. Rydin, Y.; Bleahu, A.; Davies, M.; Dávila, J.D.; Friel, S.; Grandis, G.D.; Groce, N.; Hallal, P.C.; Hamilton, I.; Howden-Chapman, P.; et al. Shaping Cities for Health: Complexity and the Planning of Urban Environments in the 21st Century. *Lancet* **2012**, *379*, 2079–2108. [CrossRef] [PubMed]
3. Giles-Corti, B.; Moudon, A.V.; Lowe, M.; Adlakha, D.; Cerin, E.; Boeing, G.; Higgs, C.; Arundel, J.; Liu, S.; Hinckson, E.; et al. Creating Healthy and Sustainable Cities: What Gets Measured, Gets Done. *Lancet Glob. Health* **2022**, *10*, e782–e785. [CrossRef] [PubMed]
4. Duhl, L.J. The Healthy City: Its Function and Its Future. *Health Promot. Int.* **1986**, *1*, 55–60. [CrossRef]
5. Harpham, T.; Lusty, T.; Vaughan, P. *In the Shadow of the City: Community Health and the Urban Poor*; Oxford University Press: Oxford, UK, 1988; ISBN 978-0-19-261698-2.
6. WHO Healthy Cities Project. *Promoting Health in the Urban Context*; WHO Healthy Cities Papers; World Health Organization: Geneva, Switzerland, 1988.
7. Stephens, C. Healthy Cities or Unhealthy Islands? The Health and Social Implications of Urban Inequality. *Environ. Urban.* **1996**, *8*, 9–30. [CrossRef]
8. Rybski, D.; González, M.C. Cities as Complex Systems—Collection Overview. *PLoS ONE* **2022**, *17*, e0262964. [CrossRef]
9. OECD Addressing Societal Challenges Using Transdisciplinary Research. *Technol. Ind. Policy Pap.* **2020**. [CrossRef]
10. Richardson, J. The Changing British Policy Style: From Governance to Government? *Br. Polit.* **2018**, *13*, 215–233. [CrossRef]
11. Zahariadis, N.; Petridou, E.; Exadaktylos, T.; Sparf, J. Policy Styles and Political Trust in Europe's National Responses to the COVID-19 Crisis. *Policy Stud.* **2021**, *44*, 46–67. [CrossRef]
12. Zahariadis, N.; Petridou, E.; Exadaktylos, T.; Sparf, J. (Eds.) *Policy Styles and Trust in the Age of Pandemics: Global Threat, National Responses*; Routledge: Abingdon, Oxfordshire, UK, 2022.
13. UNDRR. *Global Assessment Report on Disaster Risk Reduction 2022: Our World at Risk: Transforming Governance for a Resilient Future*; United Nations Office for Disaster Risk Reduction: Geneva, Switzerland, 2022.

14. Ashby, W.R. *An Introduction to Cybernetics*; Chapman and Hall: London, UK, 1956.
15. Vatn, A. *Institutions and the Environment*; Edward Elgar Publishing: Cheltenham, UK, 2005; ISBN 978-1-84720-121-8.
16. Mueller, B. Why Public Policies Fail: Policymaking under Complexity. *EconomiA* **2020**, *21*, 311–323. [CrossRef]
17. Read, C. *Logic: Deductive and Inductive*; D. Appleton: Boston, MA, USA, 1898.
18. Gigerenzer, G.; Todd, P.M.; Group, A.R. *Simple Heuristics That Make Us Smart*; Illustrated edition; Oxford University Press: New York, NY, USA, 2000; ISBN 978-0-19-514381-2.
19. Marewski, J.N.; Gigerenzer, G. Heuristic Decision Making in Medicine. *Dialogues Clin. Neurosci.* **2012**, *14*, 77–89. [CrossRef] [PubMed]
20. Jasanoff, S. Technologies of Humility. *Nature* **2007**, *450*, 33. [CrossRef] [PubMed]
21. Cerda, I. *Cerda: The Five Bases of the General Theory of Urbanization*; Soria y Puig, A., Ed.; Gingko Press Inc.: Madrid, Spain, 1999; ISBN 978-84-8156-065-7.
22. Geddes, S.P. *Cities in Evolution: An Introduction to the Town Planning Movement and to the Study of Civics.*; Williams: London, UK, 1915.
23. Portugali, J. *Self-Organization and the City*; Springer Series in Synergetics; Springer: Berlin, Heidelberg, 2000.
24. Batty, M. *Cities and Complexity: Understanding Cities with Cellular Automata, Agent-Based Models, and Fractals*; MIT Press: Cambridge, MA, USA, 2005; ISBN 978-0-262-02583-6.
25. Portugali, J.; Meyer, H.; Stolk, E.; Tan, E. (Eds.) *Complexity Theories of Cities Have Come of Age: An Overview with Implications to Urban Planning and Design*; Springer: Berlin, Heidelberg, 2012.
26. Batty, M. *The New Science of Cities*; MIT Press: Cambridge, MA, USA, 2013; ISBN 978-0-262-01952-1.
27. Bettencourt, L.M.A. *Introduction to Urban Science: Evidence and Theory of Cities as Complex Systems*; MIT Press: Cambridge, MA, USA, 2021; ISBN 978-0-262-04600-8.
28. Gatzweiler, F.W.; Reis, S.; Zhang, Y.; Jayasinghe, S. Lessons from Complexity Science for Urban Health and Well-Being. *Cities Health* **2017**, *1*, 210–223. [CrossRef]
29. Bai, X.; Surveyer, A.; Elmqvist, T.; Gatzweiler, F.W.; Güneralp, B.; Parnell, S.; Prieur-Richard, A.-H.; Shrivastava, P.; Siri, J.G.; Stafford-Smith, M.; et al. Defining and Advancing a Systems Approach for Sustainable Cities. *Curr. Opin. Environ. Sustain.* **2016**, *23*, 69–78. [CrossRef]
30. Meerow, S.; Newell, J.P.; Stults, M. Defining Urban Resilience: A Review. *Landsc. Urban Plan.* **2016**, *147*, 38–49. [CrossRef]
31. Lawrence, R.J.; Gatzweiler, F.W. Wanted: A Transdisciplinary Knowledge Domain for Urban Health. *J. Urban Health Bull. N. Y. Acad. Med.* **2017**, *94*, 592–596. [CrossRef]
32. Pineo, H.; Turnbull, E.R.; Davies, M.; Rowson, M.; Hayward, A.C.; Hart, G.; Johnson, A.M.; Aldridge, R.W. A New Transdisciplinary Research Model to Investigate and Improve the Health of the Public. *Health Promot. Int.* **2021**, *36*, 481–492. [CrossRef]
33. Jacobs, J. *The Death and Life of Great American Cities*; Vintage Books: New York, NY, USA, 1961.
34. Corburn, J. *Healthy City Planning: From Neighbourhood to National Health Equity*; Routledge: Oxfordshire, UK, 2013.
35. Jayasinghe, S. The COVID-19 Pandemic and Complexity Science: A Convergence of Earth Systems, Virus Species, the Urbanocene and Physical Hyper-Connectivity. *Univ. Colombo Rev.* **2020**, *1*, 5–15. [CrossRef]
36. Thoradeniya, T.; Jayasinghe, S. COVID-19 and Future Pandemics: A Global Systems Approach and Relevance to SDGs. *Glob. Health* **2021**, *17*, 59. [CrossRef]
37. Kearney, M. Astonishingly Hyperconnected. *Issues Sci. Technol.* **2022**, *38*, 77–80.
38. Scott, A.J.; Storper, M. The Nature of Cities: The Scope and Limits of Urban Theory. *Int. J. Urban Reg. Res.* **2015**, *39*, 1–15. [CrossRef]
39. Whitmee, S.; Haines, A.; Beyrer, C.; Boltz, F.; Capon, A.G.; de Souza Dias, B.F.; Ezeh, A.; Frumkin, H.; Gong, P.; Head, P.; et al. Safeguarding Human Health in the Anthropocene Epoch: Report of The Rockefeller Foundation–Lancet Commission on Planetary Health. *Lancet* **2015**, *386*, 1973–2028. [CrossRef] [PubMed]
40. *United Nations Transforming Our World: The 2030 Agenda for Sustainable Development*; United Nations: New York, NY, USA, 2015.
41. United Nations. World Moving Backwards on Sustainable Development Goals, Secretary-General Tells Economic and Social Council, Deploring 'Fundamental Lack of Solidarity'. *Meetings Coverage and Press Releases*, 22 March 2022.
42. Edwards, A.R.; McKibben, B. *Thriving Beyond Sustainability: Pathways to a Resilient Society*; Illustrated edition; New Society Publishers: Gabriola Island, BC, Canada, 2010; ISBN 978-0-86571-641-4.
43. McDonough, W.; Braungart, M.; Clinton, B. *The Upcycle: Beyond Sustainability—Designing for Abundance*, 1st ed.; North Point Press: New York, NY, USA, 2013; ISBN 978-0-86547-748-3.
44. Dernbach, J.C.; Cheever, F. Sustainable Development and Its Discontents. *Transnatl. Environ. Law* **2015**, *4*, 247–287. [CrossRef]
45. Hickel, J. The World's Sustainable Development Goals Aren't Sustainable. *Foreign Policy*, 30 September 2020.
46. Wilson, E.O. *Consilience: The Unity of Knowledge*; Reprint edition; Vintage: New York, NY, USA, 1999; ISBN 978-0-679-76867-8.
47. Hawking, S.; Mlodinov, L. *The Grand Design*; Bantam Books: New York, NY, USA, 2010.
48. *Wellcome Global Monitor Project Wellcome Global Monitor 2020: How Covid-19 Affected People's Lives and Their Views about Science*; Wellcome Trust: London, UK, 2020.
49. Bergeron, E. The Historical Roots of Mistrust in Science. *Human Rights*, 14 June 2021.
50. Funtowicz, S.O.; Ravetz, J.R. A New Scientific Methodology for Global Environmental Issues. In *Ecological Economics: The Science and Management of Sustainability*; Costanza, R., Ed.; Columbia University Press: New York, NY, USA, 1991.

51. International Science Council. *Unleashing Science: Delivering Missions for Sustainability*; International Science Council: Paris, France, 2021.
52. Kønig, N.; Børsen, T.; Emmeche, C. The Ethos of Post-Normal Science. *Futures* **2017**, *91*, 12–24. [CrossRef]
53. Ebikeme, C.; Gatzweiler, F.; Oni, T.; Liu, J.; Oyuela, A.; Siri, J. Xiamen Call for Action: Building the Brain of the City—Universal Principles of Urban Health. *J. Urban Health* **2019**, *96*, 507–509. [CrossRef]
54. Newell, B.; Siri, J. A Role for Low-Order System Dynamics Models in Urban Health Policy Making. *Environ. Int.* **2016**, *95*, 93–97. [CrossRef]
55. Funtowicz, S.; Ravetz, J.R. SCIENCE FOR THE POST-NORMAL AGE. In *The Postnormal Times Reader*; SARDAR, Z., Ed.; International Institute of Islamic Thought: Herndon, MV, USA, 2019; pp. 23–46. ISBN 978-1-56564-991-0.
56. Rockström, J.; Klum, M.; Miller, P. *Big World, Small Planet: Abundance within Planetary Boundaries*; Illustrated edition; Yale University Press: New Haven, CT, USA; London, UK, 2015; ISBN 978-0-300-21836-7.
57. UHWB. *Report of the Scientific Committee of the International Science Council's Programme on Urban Health and Wellbeing. An Interdisciplinary Science-Action Plan for Urban Health and Wellbeing in an Age of Complexity and Systemic Risks (2021–2025)*; Urban Health and Wellbeing Programme: Xiamen, China, 2021.
58. Aaltonen, M.; Sanders, T. Identifying Systems' New Initial Conditions as Influence Points for the Future. *Foresight* **2006**, *8*, 28–35. [CrossRef]
59. Mosler, S.; Hobson, P. Close-To-Nature Heuristic Design Principles for Future Urban Green Infrastructure. *Urban Plan.* **2021**, *6*, 67–79. [CrossRef]
60. Webb, A. The Heuristics of Agency: On Computation, Big Data Urban Design. *Int. Robot. Amp Autom. J.* **2019**, *5*, 121. [CrossRef]
61. McCord, C.; Becker, C. Sidewalk and Toronto: Critical Systems Heuristics and the Smart City. In Proceedings of the 6th International Conference on ICT for Sustainability, ICT4S 2019, Lappeenranta, Finland, 10–14 June 2019; Wolff, A., Ed.; CEUR-WS.org. 2019; Volume 2382.
62. El-Bastawissi, I.; Baba, N.E.; Khalil, S.; Hage, N.E.; Joumblat, R.; Gatzweiler, F. Partial Systems Analysis of Traffic Noise Reduction in Tarik al Jadidah, Beirut. *BAU J. -Creat. Sustain. Dev.* **2022**, 3, 9. [CrossRef]
63. Beck, U.; Giddens, A.; Lash, S. *Reflexive Modernization: Politics, Tradition and Aesthetics in the Modern Social Order*; Stanford University Press: Stanford, CA, USA, 1994; ISBN 978-0-8047-2472-2.
64. Dryzek, J.S. *Deliberative Democracy and Beyond: Liberals, Critics, Contestations*, 1st ed.; Oxford University Press: Oxford, UK, 2002; ISBN 978-0-19-925043-1.
65. Duit, A.; Galaz, V. Governance and Complexity—Emerging Issues for Governance Theory. *Governance* **2008**, *21*, 311–335. [CrossRef]
66. Arena, M.J.; Uhl-Bien, M. Complexity Leadership Theory: Shifting from Human Capital to Social Capital. *People Strategy* **2016**, *39*, 22–27.

urban science

MDPI

Article

An Urban Density-Based Runoff Simulation Framework to Envisage Flood Resilience of Cities

Naduni Wijayawardana [1,*], Chethika Abenayake [1,*], Amila Jayasinghe [1,*] and Nuwan Dias [2]

[1] Department of Town and Country Planning, University of Moratuwa, Moratuwa 10400, Sri Lanka
[2] Global Disaster Resilience Centre, University of Huddersfield, Huddersfield HD1 3DH, UK
* Correspondence: wijayawardanapnp.21@uom.lk (N.W.); chethika@uom.lk (C.A.); amilabj@uom.lk (A.J.); Tel.: +94-0112650921 or +94-772777236 (C.A.)

Abstract: Assessing the influence of urban density on surface runoff volume is vital for guiding the built-form expansions toward flood-resilient cities. This paper attempts to develop a spatial simulation framework to assess the impact of urban density on the level of surface runoff (SR), at the scale of the micro-watershed. This paper proposes a spatial simulation framework that comprehensively captures the influence of urban density dynamics over surface runoff. The simulation model consists of 13 proxies of urban density that are identified through a systematic literature review. The model is formulated through three case applications in Colombo, Sri Lanka; and validated statistically and empirically with reference to flooding events that occurred in 2021–2022. The possible planning interventions for reducing urban flooding are analyzed through an AI-based application of Decision Tree Analysis. The model results indicated that impervious coverage, open space ratio, and road density have the most significant impact on surface runoff volumes in selected micro-watersheds. The decision-making process for planning the built environment for reducing urban flooding is demonstrated by three possible density control options with a prediction accuracy of 98.7%, 94.8%, and 93.5% respectively. This contributes a novel framework to capture the density dynamics of built form in surface runoff simulations by three density areas (3Ds): density, diversity, and design; and to demonstrate the decision-making process for controlling the density of built form in reducing urban flooding.

Keywords: urban density; surface runoff; urban form; flood resilience; urban planning; systematic review

1. Introduction

Rapid urbanization generally increases the magnitude and frequency of flood events and exposes communities to increasingly severe floods. Urban flooding is a commonly found hazard that causes significant damage to property, people, and the environment due to high population density, service agglomeration, and impervious surfaces in urban areas [1,2]. Today more than 50% of the population is agglomerating into urban areas and flooding is the most frequently identified hazard. During the last twenty years (2000–2019), the number of significant flooding events reported more than doubled compared to the previous decade [3,4] (from 1389 events to 3254 events), while the number of storms with flood-related damages grew from 1457 to 2034. The recorded economic loss was USD 2.97 trillion [3]. As a result, most countries tend to make cities resilient to floods.

Even though flooding is a natural phenomenon, the risk factor enhances with community exposure and vulnerability [5]. When community agglomeration occurs with urbanization the risk of flooding increases [6]. Consequently, urban areas have become more vulnerable hotspots of extreme flooding events due to high-intensity developments. The urban form characteristics such as land use, density, type of buildings, street pattern, and building layout may have a significant impact on inundation flow, since they affect the discharging partition between each urban element, thus they affect flow depths and velocities [6,7]. As a result, urban watersheds have greater peak discharge rates than rural watersheds, which reduces the water storage capacity. The urban form densities may have more substantial damage on an equivalent exposed urban land unit [8]. As such, the impact of urban form density on flood damage is evaluated in this paper. The urban form density changes by anthropogenic activities which trigger the level of surface runoff (SR) and affect economic, social, physical, and environmental damage to the entire urban system. Hence, managing the level of SR due to urban form density can be manipulated as a decision-making tool for practitioners such as disaster managers, planners, developers, engineers, and government and non-government agencies in urban flood risk management.

Numerous factors cause the peak discharge of the urban catchment to increase SR according to principal studies. Among those various causative factors for flooding (i.e., high intensity of precipitation, topographic features of the catchment area, geological characteristics of the catchment area, type of vegetation cover, hydrologic conditions, and urban form density), the urban form density is the factor most responsible for greater peak discharge [9,10]. Further, SR controls how accumulated rainfall and discharge of runoff from the urban environment flows into the natural landscape through paving, residences, and building [11,12]. A series of studies have been performed that comprehensively explore the natural factors connected to SR in urban settings, according to recent literature. However, we still do not completely understand the dynamic and intricate aspects of urban form density with changing SR due to limited evaluation frameworks [13,14].

Anthropogenic activities play a significant role in increasing SR in urban catchment areas including reclamation of water retention areas, development activities in low-lying areas, unplanned urban development, infrastructural issues, and socio-economic factors that trigger urban flooding [15–18]. Accordingly, enhancing urban flood resilience is an important consideration for a more effective flood management strategy. A substantial number of studies illustrate that the level of SR significantly increases with high-dense urban form characteristics (i.e., building density, road density, land use, and built features) in particular, urban watershed areas [19]. There is a need to develop an accurate quantification mechanism to identify the relationship between urban form density and level of SR.

The high-density urban form indicates a high level of impervious surfaces which reduces the natural penetration capacity while decreasing the infiltration rate. That leads to peak runoff in the urban environment, which generally reduces hydrologic response time [6]. Eini et al., 2020 and Le et al., 2022 [18,20] explained how the growth of urban areas reduces the natural infiltration rate under different urbanization conditions. Eini et al., 2020 [20] investigated the sensitivities of urban flooding to urban land growth through the simulation of flood flows under different urbanization conditions. Consequently, urbanization causes increased SR that is unsuitable for addressing by urban drainage or canal discharge rates which reduce the time required to reach peak runoff and discharge. Urban densities are directly connected to the percentage of total impervious surface area, which indicates the geographical distribution of impervious surface among each kind of land use in a particular flood-affected urban watershed [13,21]. As a result, urban density is a broad concept that needs to be analyzed in its complex reality to change surface runoff in dynamic urban watersheds [22].

In such a context, the impact of built-form densities has a significant influence on increasing the level of SR under dynamic urban forms [18,23] because the built-up area or the building density increases the risk of urban flooding and waterlogging. Property, livelihood loss, and traffic delays due to urban flooding are also significant in urban areas as employment hubs with the agglomeration of economic properties of high value, which can be minimized by controlling the intensity of SR [4,24,25]. Even though existing studies evaluate the impact of urban flooding with natural parameters such as rainfall uncertainties, topo-geological conditions, land use changes, soil features, or hydraulic and hydrological perspectives to manage urban flooding at different spatial levels [1,2], how the urban form density factor alone impacts flooding in a dynamic urban environment has yet to be studied. Furthermore, the available knowledge merely explains how surface runoff depends on urban form densities at urban watershed scales which has become a critical challenge for decision-makers due to the limited availability and validity of accurate methods to predict future and existing flood situations. Consequently, there is a need to develop a novel theory-based quantification method to measure the impact of urban form densities on surface runoff, which will support decision-makers, urban planners, governmental and non-government agencies to make their decisions more strategically.

The primary aim of this study is to develop a spatial simulation framework to assess the impact of urban density on SR in urban watersheds' scale, under different urban form scenarios. The first objective of this study is to identify urban form-based proxies of urban density that are employed in quantifying SR. The second objective is to develop a conceptual framework to assess the influence of urban density on the level of SR at the urban watershed scale. Third, real ground validation of the developed conceptual framework will be performed under distinct urban form densities (i.e., at the urban watershed scale). Ultimately, the model output is expected to be developed as a planning guidance tool in process of decision-making.

1.1. Identifying the Urban Form-Based Proxies of Urban Density

Different studies argue that urban density has a significant influence on the change/ trigger runoff in a particular area, but there is no concern about what the most critical parameters are that influence SR due to the complexity of the urban environment [13,18]. One group of studies argued that the climate change impact is the key causative factor that changes the level of SR as per the environmental studies by focusing on rainfall intensity [1,3]. However, the impact of climate change will continue for a long time. Due to disparities in infrastructure expansion, urban density and land use varying, climatic conditions and the impact on the lengthy lifespan of the urban systems by increasing level of SR as the result of anthropogenic activities [18]. Urban flooding is the outcome of the interaction between hydrological and meteorological conditions, which are made worse by human activity in dense urban catchment areas [13,26]. As a result, studying the key causative proxies which trigger the level of surface runoff still remains an open-ended topic in the urban density-based literature.

As per the first objective, this research examined the urban density-based proxies which can be measured/quantified regarding the level of SR in the key literature by performing a systematic review. This systematic review is based on a 10-year time frame and makes a density classification that covers the overall urban form density factors by adapting predefined criteria (i.e., select the articles that have open access, density parameter data available at the local context, and the article relates to the urban planning subject field area, etc.). Table 1 indicates the identified density-based proxies that represent flood/runoff-based studies. As per the key outcome of the systematic review, there is no single agreement as to which urban density-based proxies have the highest impact that triggers the level of SR [14,27]. However, scholars come to grips with that, urban density has been well recognized in urban flood studies as a factor triggering the SR.

As shown in Table 1, previous studies have derived urban density-based proxies used to measure the level or change of SR by combining natural factors (i.e., precipitation change, soil characteristics, terrain conditions, type of vegetation cover, drainage condition) but no study focuses on the change of SR due to the variation of urban form density as a standalone indicator.

Table 1. Summary of density-based factors utilized to determine urban flooding by previous studies.

Identified Density-Based Proxies	[28]	[29]	[30]	[31]	[24]	[26]	[32]	[33]	[34]	[35]	[36]	[37]	[38]	[39]	[40]	[41]	[42]	[43]	[12]	[44]	[45]	[46]	[47]	[48]	[49]	[50]	[51]	[52]	[53]	[19]
Drainage Density	*	*				*			*			*	*	*		*										*				
Population Density			*	*	*		*	*								*				*				*	*				*	
Building Density			*	*				*		*						*						*	*		*	*	*			*
Building Height			*	*			*			*							*						*		*					
Green/Open Space Ratio			*					*								*	*	*							*					
Road/Street Density									*		*						*											*		
Accessibility/Access Road Width						*			*								*													
FAR										*		*			*		*		*											
Built Up/Ground Coverage Ratio (GCR)																*														
Impervious Surface Coverage/%						*										*					*	*					*			
Area of Building Footprints																	*													*
GSI																	*													
Plot Size			*							*							*													
Land Use			*			*					*										*				*					

* Factors mentioned in the relevant publication.

The systematic review observed three limitations based on the evaluation of proxies identified that affect SR. First, urban density is captured by several proxies/indicators in different studies but there is not any agreement on which indicator would represent runoff level the best. Second, the majority of surface runoff studies analyse the impact of riverine floods on the urban environment, not sudden urban floods that occur due to extreme precipitation and rapid expansion of imperviousness or urban densities. Urban flood studies show that SR increases due to urban development such as constructing and paving of roadways, which have a poorer capacity for absorption than earlier locations or natural fields. Rainfall runoff in urban settings can rise to six times more than in natural settings as a result. Third, the derived proxies are overlapping with urban form functionality that demands a quantification approach representing the impact on runoff with a strong conceptual framework. Hence, this research attempts to review the indicators of urban density that are being utilized in existing studies and identify the most influential indicator(s) that could better represent the impact of urban density on surface runoff, particularly referring to the micro-watershed level.

The following sections describe how the framework to quantify the impact of urban densities on SR at the urban watershed scale is developed with reference to existing theories, concepts, and models.

1.2. Framework to Assess the Influence of Urban Density Changes on the Level of SR

The second objective of this study is to develop a framework to identify the impact of urban density on the level of SR in the urban watershed scale. The theories, concepts, and models are identified by utilizing a theoretical and narrative review. Here, used three theoretical frameworks, the Pattern of Natural Movement, the Theory of Urban Maturation Process, and the Rational Method.

The theory of natural movement describes how space changes as a result of economic activity. Here, a well-known feature along the street network is a structural component of the urban form and building densities. The built-form densities were established when the first wave of urban growth was brought about by economic activity agglomerations. Second, there is a rise in the demand for property near economic centers, and property rights are important in that regard [54]. The development of built-form density, diversity of activities, and economic agglomeration are all seen to contribute to the long-term growth of cities. Here, the land subdivision, as observed in smaller plot systems, is thought to facilitate these processes [22].

Theoretical justifications for the use of plot systems in several domains that analyze cities in light of this concept are a component of this process. At this time, the parcel size becomes smaller [54]. Consequently, as people move to such urban centers, the natural characteristics there suffer severe anthropogenic damage, and the building density rises [55]. This tendency is facilitated by a wider segmentation of urban land into small plots, as mentioned in urban morphological studies [56]. With the elements of accessibility and rising density in urban areas, road networks play a vital role in the subdivision of land parcels [55]. When impermeable surfaces quickly encroach on the natural environment fast floods occur while limiting the penetration rates. This is a widespread phenomenon that occurs in urban watershed environments where small land parcels, high building density, and increasing imperviousness prevent rainwater from flowing.

As per the Theory of the Urban Maturation Process, urban form densities develop or increase with special integration and land use mix. This explains why city/urban form has different stages (i.e., beginning, developing, developed) that enhance when in combination with built form density, special integration with spatial structure, and city functions indicated by a mix of land use [57]. This is developed based on Hillier's (1999) spatial configuration idea with the combination of urban form features [57]. As a result, it theoretically defines interdependency between spatial structure (i.e., shape), degree of urban density, and degree of functional mix in the natural urban environment. Consequently, the functional mix indicates the land use density and density determined by building density. When the urban area becomes mature step by step, the density of the urban form increases due to the high level of accessibility and land use mix [13]. That leads to rise in SR and flooding because of highly dense urban clustering of activities (i.e., city function) and natural land conversion to the built environment (i.e., city spatial structure). In the end, it can be agreed that the planning process in a new town develops in combination with urban density, city functions, and special structure. To make flood-resilient cities, planning processes incorporate with control/management of SR with the previous concept (refer to Figure 1).

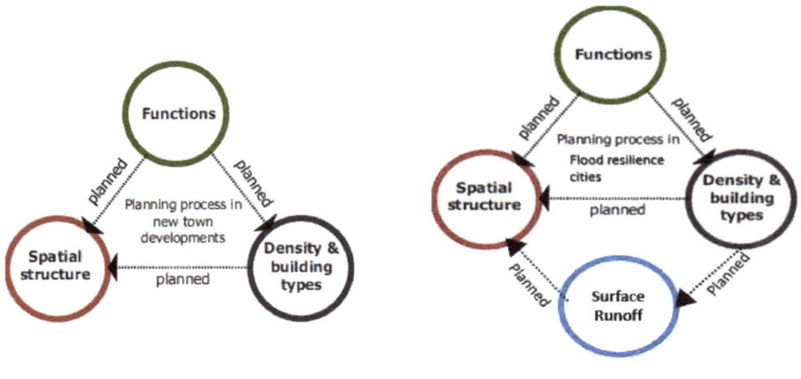

(a) (b)

Figure 1. Planning process in new town development combined with urban density, city functions, special structures, and surface runoff; (**a**) Planning process in new town development, (**b**) Planning process in new town development with SR.

The Rational Method illustrates how a natural system exists by balancing the water (rainfall) in an area with runoff water, among rainfall intensity and catchment area features [58]. The Rational Method assumes that rainfall intensity and catchment area act as a uniform feature, and the runoff coefficient changes with the land use type of built-form density in an area. However, recent studies argue that the runoff coefficient cannot be a standard value that should change with land use and the urban density of an area [56,58]. Based on that assumption this study will evaluate the change of runoff coefficients under different urban densities and their impacts on SR. Here, the authors argue that the SR should change based on the change of runoff coefficient with urban density features linked with the theory of natural moment and urban maturation process.

Concepts

In order to develop the conceptual framework, this study used a concept of urban density categorization which represents spatial variations. Here, the city concepts identified through the narrative review conducted focus on urban water management strategies practiced under different urban contexts.

There are several ways to quantify density, including building density, built-up coverage, land-use intensity, and spaciousness [8,59]. Among those several approaches, no specific measure best represents the urban density at the local or urban watershed scale due to urban form complexity. However, the majority of scholars agree that density is an important element of the entire urban form, which changes with anthropogenic activities [14,59]. A notion as conceptually complicated as density has several interconnected aspects [22,57]. It is feasible to quantify the elements in a certain area physically and geographically, but it is also possible to evaluate them using features of the individual or group [60]. Other aspects of urban form, such as land use, accessibility, utilities, and neighborhood characteristics, are also intimately related to urban density. In such a context, urban density is likely an arrangement of physical components [59]. Therefore, in urban planning and development, density has been used as a tool to assess urban density, spatial diversity, and design elements.

Here adapted to the "3D" model—density, diversity, and design—introduced by Cervero and Kockelman (1997) [61] to capture the variations of urban forms. This is a broad concept that comes under travel demand and transportation studies which also incorporate into urban planning studies [62]. Here they argued that entire urban density can be made with the combination of three factors: proxies of urban density, proxies of urban diversity, and proxies of urban design [63,64]. To attain these goals, new urbanists, neo-traditionalists, and other designers advocate for altering the built environment's three dimensions, or the 3Ds: density, diversity, and design [63]. This concept is able to accomplish the primary aim of this study by using the component analysis approach to evaluate the relative importance of each proxy as well as their combined effects. Table 2 indicates the definitions of each dimension.

Table 2. Definition for dimensions in 3Ds.

Dimension	Description with Candidate Variable
Density	This variable represents a ratio between the total amount of gross area and the area of a parcel upon which a building is located. Ex: Population density of the area, building density of the area, road density of the area, FAR (Floor Area Ratio).
Diversity	This variable represents variation or diversity in horizontal or vertical space in a particular area. Ex: Building height, level of accessibility, land use mix, plot size, built up coverage
Design	The variables or elements introduced that minimize or maximize impact. Ex: Green/open space ratio, access road width, impervious surface coverage, drainage density

Source: Compiled by author.

The conceptual framework of this study was developed based on the discussed theories and two concepts (i.e., 3Ds of urban form categorization and concepts of urban water management strategies).

1.3. The Proposed Conceptual Framework

The second objective of this study is to evaluate the impact of density-based urban form proxies on SR quantify under three broad density clustering approaches which come under 3Ds of urban forms, as proxies of urban density, proxies of spatial diversity, and proxies of urban design. Here it is expected to evaluate the most influencing proxies or groups of proxies on SR at the urban watershed scale. After identification of the most influencing indicator that would represent the level of SR at best, at the urban watershed scale can be developed as a planning and decision-making tool for making future cities resilient to flooding. Figure 2 represents the conceptual framework for this study. The next section explains the methods and materials utilized in the quantification process.

2. Materials and Methods

2.1. Overall Methodology

First, the variables to quantify urban form density as per the above-developed conceptual framework were defined. Second, a runoff simulation model for model formulation and validation was selected. Third, the selection of case study areas was carried out based on urban densities in urban morphology. After that, model formulation and validation were carried out with basic statistical analysis as well as decision tree analysis to measure the prediction probability and the level of accuracy of the pre-developed theoretical framework with real ground verifications. Below Figure 3 indicates the methodological flow chart.

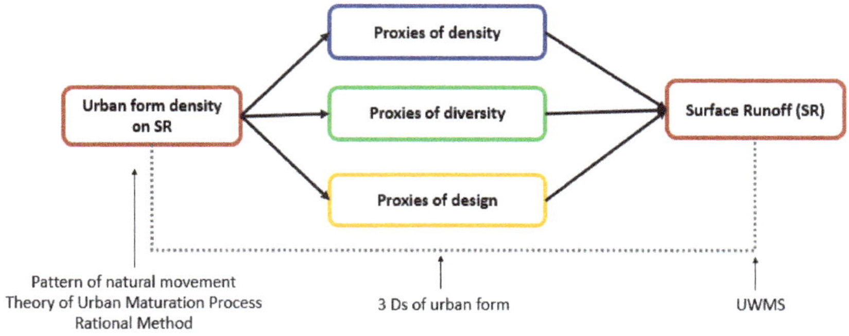

Figure 2. Proposed Conceptual Framework to analysing the relationship among urban form density and surface runoff. Source: Compiled by author.

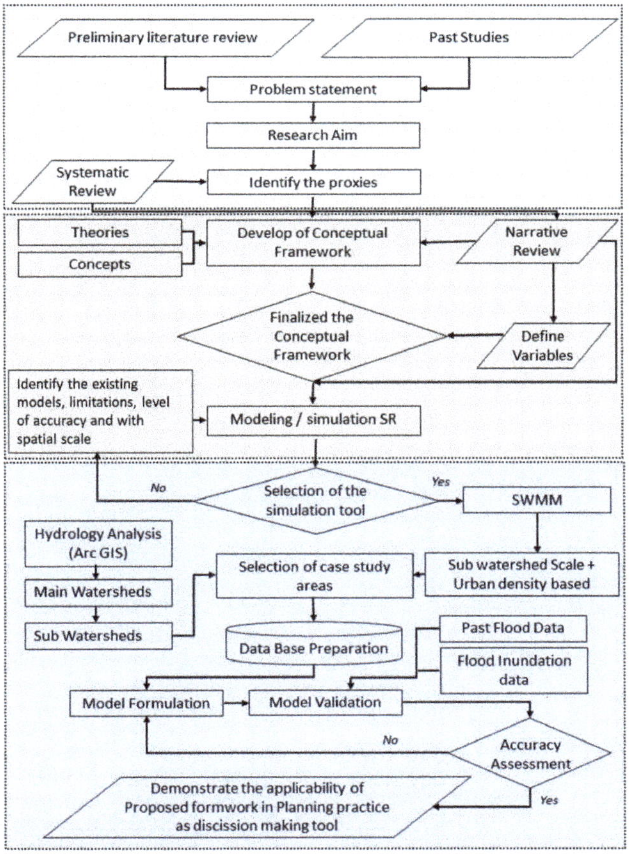

Figure 3. Methodological flow chart. Source: Compiled by author.

2.2. *Quantifying the Urban Form Density*

There are 13 sub-variables selected to quantify urban form density under the three main variables (density, diversity, and design). Table 3 summarizes the variables, quantification methods, and data collection sources.

Table 3. Quantification of variables.

Density-Based Key Variable	Measuring Variable	Equation/Method of Measure	Source
Proxies of density	Population density (PD)	$PD_x = \frac{Population_x}{Area_x}$	Census and statistics/Calculated by author
	Building density	Building density in a particular land plot/area	JICA database
	Road density	$RD = \frac{\Sigma(\text{Gross road area})}{\text{land area}}$	JICA database/Calculated by author
	FSI (FAR)	$FSI = \frac{\text{Gross Floor Area}}{\text{land area}}$	JICA database
	Building height	Sum of floors in selected land plot/area $S_n = (a1 + a2 + a3 + \ldots, a_n)$	JICA data/Calculated by author
Proxies of diversity	Level of accessibility	$CCi = (N - 1)/\Sigma dij$ (Closeness centrality of road segment)	JICA database/Calculated by author
	Land use mix (Mixed Use Index)	$MUI = -\sum_i P_i \left(\frac{\ln(P_j)}{\ln(J)}\right)$	JICA database
	Plot size	Extracted as mean plot size from survey department data	JICA database/survey department data
Proxies of urban design	Built-up coverage (BC)	$BC = \frac{\text{Ground Floor Plinth Area}}{\text{land area}} \times 100$	Satellite data/Calculated by author
	Open space ratio (OSR)	$OSR = \frac{\text{open space area}}{\text{land area}} \times 100$	Calculated by author
	Access road width	Extracted with google earth	OSM data/Google Earth measure
	Impervious surface coverage	The % of impervious area of the catchment	Satellite data/Calculated by author
	Drainage density	$DD = \frac{\Sigma(\text{dranage area})}{\text{land area}}$	Drainage data of the area—WSDB and GN level/Calculated by author

Source: Compiled by author. Abbreviations: FSI (FAR)—Floor Space Index or Flore Area Ratio; GN—Grama Niladari Divisions (that is the smallest administrative Divisions in Sri Lanka); JICA—Japan International Cooperation Agency; OSM—Open Street Map; WSDB—Water Supply and Drainage Board.

2.3. Selection of a Software Tools for Modelling Surface Runoff

To identify a simulation tool to model the surface runoff (SR) this study used both a systematic and a narrative review. Here, the existing modelling frameworks under different spatial scales, such as local level, site-specific level, and regional level were reviewed to verify the model accuracy. Further, the existing limitations of each model in practical usage and data requirements were also considered particularly referring to the Sri Lankan context. Table 4 represents the suitable model selection criteria used for this study.

By comparatively analyzing the existing flood simulation models, this study selected the SWMM modelling platform for modelling the surface runoff as per the above criteria.

The EPA SWMM (United States Environmental Protection Agency Storm Water Management Model) was selected to calculate the surface runoff in urban watersheds for this study by reviewing available surface runoff simulation approaches as a free and open-access flood inundation model [65]. It can be used under deterministic modelling scenarios to simulate water inflows, outflows, and storage within an urban sub-catchment area. Further, this model generates significant and accurate results on different spatial scales (i.e., local level, sub-watershed scale, neighborhood scale, and site scale). Furthermore, EPA SWMM has the capability to calculate runoff component functions as a collection of sub-catchment areas by adding land use dynamics and physical scenarios of urban form density. Among urban stormwater modelling, EPA SWMM 5.1 has recorded a reliable outcome in model calibration and verification [17,65]. This tool is used by several location-specific applications in worldwide planning and urban flood analysis, i.e., CSO-LTC (combined sewer overflows for long-term control plan by the United States Environmental Protection Agency) plans in Philadelphia, Cincinnati, Indianapolis, Seattle, New Haven, etc.) [53,66]. The result of SWMM is governed by the equation:

$$\frac{\partial Q}{\partial t} + gAS_f - 2V\frac{\partial A}{\partial t} - V^2\frac{\partial A}{\partial x} + gA\frac{\partial H}{\partial x} = 0 \quad (1)$$

where

Q = Discharge through the conduit
V = Velocity in the conduit
A = Cross sectional area of the flow
H = Hydraulic head (invert elevation plus water depth)
S_f = Friction slope [67]

Table 4. Selection of surface runoff (SR) simulation model (using pre-defined criteria).

Selection Criteria	HEC-RAS	SWMM	PC- SWMM	Urban BEATS	MIKE Flood	City Drain	3Di	2D RRI	DS	DEM Based	RS	Lidar/GIS	ML
Level of accuracy in local or watershed scale	√	√	√	x	√	x	√	x	x	√	x	√	√
Data availability in Sri Lankan context	√	√	√	√	√	√	x	x	√	√	√	x	√
Free and open-source application	√	√	x	x	x	x	√	√	√	√	√	x	√
Less calibration time	√	√	x	√	√	x	√	x	√	x	√	√	x
Used in urban planning subject area	√	√	√	x	√	√	x	√	√	√	√	√	√
Used for Urban flood modelling	x	√	√	x	√	√	√	√	√	x	√	√	√

Source: Compiled by author. Abbreviations: HEC-RAS—Horologic Engineering Center's River Analysis System; SWMM—Storm Water Management Model; PCSWMM—Personal Computer Storm Water Management Model; BEATS—Biophysical Environments and Technologies Simulator; MIKE—stormwater modeling software powered by Danish Hydraulic Institute (DHI); 3Di—three-dimensional flood model; 2D RRI—Two-Dimensional Rainfall-Runoff-Inundation; DS—Digitalwater Simulation; DEM—Digital Elevation Model; RS—Remote Sensing based; GIS—Geographic Information System; ML—Machine Learning.

2.4. Selection of Cases Study Areas

The case study areas were selected based on the type of density in the urban watershed. Three basic density types explained in the Spacemate density categorization [57] were considered. The Space matrix is a method to measure urban form densities that utilized nine density categories as depicted in Figure 4 based on floor space index (FSI), ground space index (GSI), and open space ratio (OSR). Those nine density categories are able to categorize the main three density groups (high, middle, and low-density). Hence, the three main density categorizations were directly adopted to validate the previously developed theoretical framework.

As the first step of case study area selection, the type of density layout of the urban watershed was selected as the process of creating urban layouts automatically using a computer-based procedural urban generation system with a set of rules and parameter values. Here, the key purpose is to develop a procedural generation system that creates urban layouts automatically while taking geometric urban parameters (such as road width, building orientation, road curvature, lot size, open space orientation, etc.) into account [68]. It is an open-source visual computing tool that helps to make decisions for urban planners in assessing the implementation of urban design layouts on expected flood risk within a limited time duration. The AI-based "Probabletrain Procedural City Generator" application was used to generate density-based procedural urban forms for this study. Table 5 depicts the set of parameters used for urban form density generation.

The second step of the case study areas was to select an entire urban watershed based on pre-derived urban form density types. The selected watershed was derived through hydrological analysis in the Arc GIS platform using a 12.5 m spatial resolution digital elevation model (DEM). The selected urban watershed is further subdivided into sub-catchment areas based on existing drainage networks and natural water flow patterns. Figure 5 indicates the procedural system layouts and the real-world layouts selected as the case studies to explore the relationship between urban form density and SR (surface runoff/urban flooding) in the Sri Lankan context. Table 6 depicts the characteristics of each selected density-based case study area.

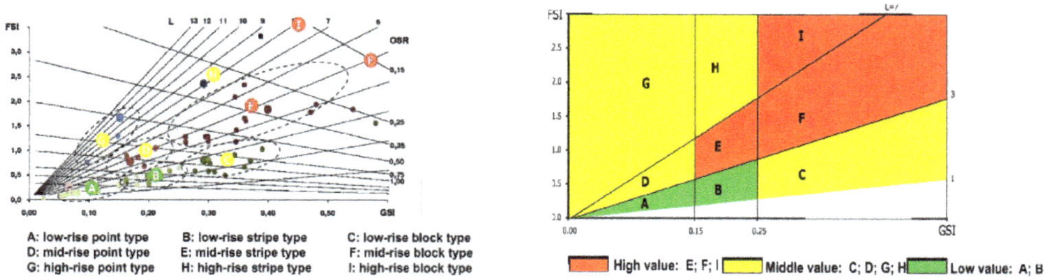

(a) (b)

Figure 4. Spacemate density categorization. Source: [57]; (**a**) Nine density categorization, (**b**) Three main density categorization.

Table 5. Input parameters for the parameterized urban city-generator model.

Parameter	High Density	Moderate Density	Low Density
Average street length	35–400 m	50–500 m	60–700 m
Major road width	12–20 m	12–15 m	12–15 m
Minor road width	6–10 m	6–10 m	6–8 m
Road curvature	0°–90°	0°–120°	0°–170°
Park coverage (green space)	0–20%	5–40%	5–98%
Buildings per lot	6–30	6–34	1–36
Lot size (in sq m)	250–2500	350–1400	600–11,000
Building front setback	0–5 m	0–35 m	0–30 m
Building rear setback	0–5 m	0–35 m	0–30 m
Building side setback	0–5 m	0–35 m	0–30 m

Source: Compiled by author.

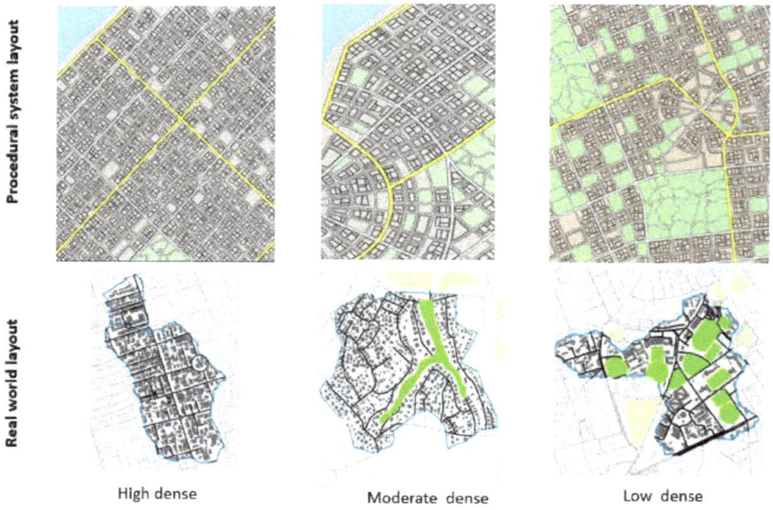

Figure 5. The procedural system layouts and the real-world layouts. Source: Compiled by author.

Figure 6, depicts the amount of surface runoff in selected case study areas. The surface runoff was simulated based on the actual highest recorded rainfall events occurred between 20 June 2021 and 25 June 2021 with the SWMM platform. There was an extreme rainfall event of 150–200 mm rainfall per 24 h. Accordingly, 15 min interval rainfall values were recorded and taken as input rainfall data at 4ONSE Weather Stations in the University of Moratuwa and Nagoda rainfall station by the Meteorological Department database.

Table 6. Characteristics of each selected density-based case study area.

	High Dense	Moderate Dense	Low Dense
Location	Bambalapitiya—CD	Nagoda hospital junction—KD	Colombo 7—CD
Land area	3.5×10^5 Sqm	5×10^5 Sqm	5.5×10^5 Sqm
Number of sub-catchments	53	51	51
Population density (persons per km)	257	15	5
Building density	59.52%	25.65%	16.52%
Open space	9.52%	62.47%	78.21%
Avg. number of floors	7	2	2
Avg. plot size (m)	758 Sqm	900 Sqm	2100 sqm
Land use mix	85.74%	14.31%	35.57%

Source: Compiled by author.

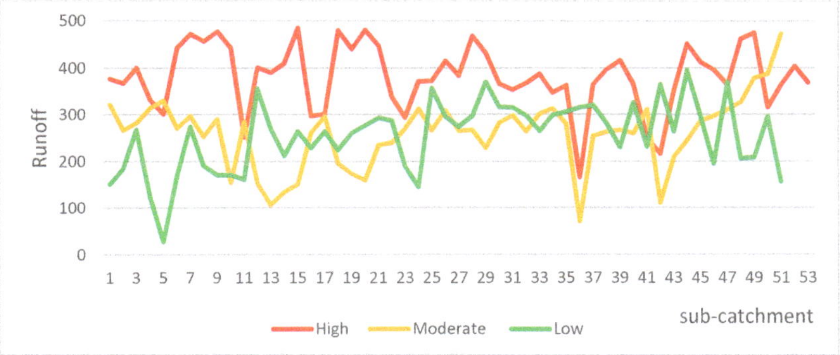

Figure 6. Amount of surface runoff in each sub-catchment of the selected case study areas—generated from SWMM. Source: Compiled by author.

3. Analysis and Results

The main aim of this study was to develop a spatial simulation framework to assess the impact of urban density on SR at the urban watershed scale. To achieve this aim, the developed framework was validated with selected case studies. As a first step of the analysis, Pearson correlation analysis was carried out to identify the correlation among selected individual density-based proxies. Next, the AI-based decision tree analysis was utilized to develop a model to determine the most influencing density-based parameter on surface runoff. The third stage was regression analysis utilized to validate the developed framework with real ground flood data. Table 7 indicates a summary of the analysis in each stage.

Table 7. Type of analysis with purpose in each stage.

Stage	Type of Analysis	Purpose
1	Correlation analysis	To identity the relationship between individual variables
2	Decision tree analysis	To measure the prediction probability and the level of accuracy of the pre-developed framework.
3	Regression analysis	Validation of the developed framework with real ground flood data (i.e., flood depth, inundation duration).

3.1. Correlation Analysis

The correlation analysis was carried out to identify how each independent urban form proxy affects SR in urban catchment areas. As per the results of correlation analysis, impervious coverage has a strong positive correlation as $R^2 = 0.92$ and the open space ratio (OSR) has a strong negative correlation $R^2 = (-0.846)$. Accessibility and road density also have strong correlations with the level of SR, as $R^2 = 0.873$ and $R^2 = 0.745$, respectively. Those factors (i.e., OSR, impervious coverage, accessibility, road density, and FAR) go hand in hand in an urban environment and these are the most influencing factors in increasing urban floods. Due to anthropogenic developments, the number of open spaces is converted to built-up areas then the infiltration rate is significantly reduced with impervious coverage. As a result of a high-intensity rainfall event, the urban areas are quickly inundated. Furthermore, the type of FAR, land use mix, built-up coverage, and access road width also moderately correlated with SR having a moderately strong correlation ($\pm 6.00 > r \pm 7.99 <$) ($p < 0.01$). The correlation matrix is shown in Figure 7 and it indicates the Pearson correlation between each density-based proxy in the 3Ds (i.e., proxies of density, diversity, and design).

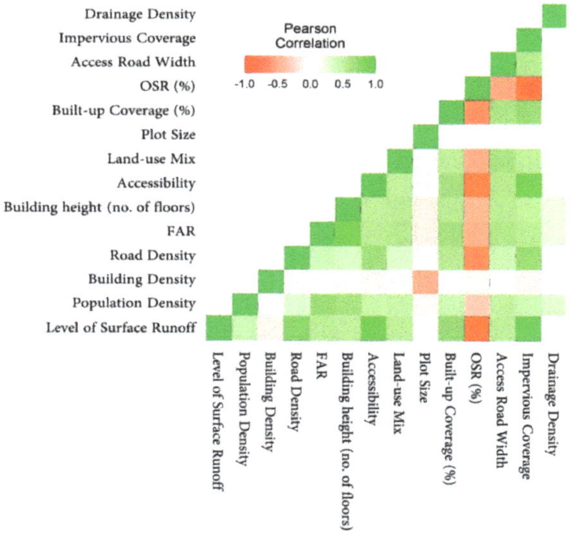

Figure 7. Correlation heat map.

3.2. Decision Tree Analysis

Decision tree analysis was carried out to measure the prediction probability and the level of accuracy of the pre-developed theoretical framework. Decision trees are machine learning approaches that discover the connections between predictors and target variable connections. In other words, depending on the frequencies of predictor variables, they assign a dataset to one of the specified classes [69]. The "Waikato Environment for Knowledge Analysis" (WEKA) application was used to perform a decision tree analysis to determine the potential flows of variables that could occur at various surface runoff levels. One of the common classification methods, the J48 Classifier, was utilized. It produced a decision tree that was created using C4.5 (an extension of ID3).

The viewer can see the decision tree using the Classification Table. By deleting the attributes that are not necessary and restarting the classification process, tree trimming can be conducted from the pre-process tab of the decision tree [69]. The model prediction accuracy is calculated utilizing the set of parameters (i.e., correctly classified instances, incorrectly classified instances, kappa statistic, mean absolute error, relative absolute error, root relative squared error). Three models were developed to make possible options to reduce the level of SR. As per the analysis, the output target is to make the level of SR low or very low. If the urban catchment has high or very high runoff generation that level can be reduced up to a moderate level (refer to Figures 8–10). Table 8 indicates the summary of accuracy in each derived model.

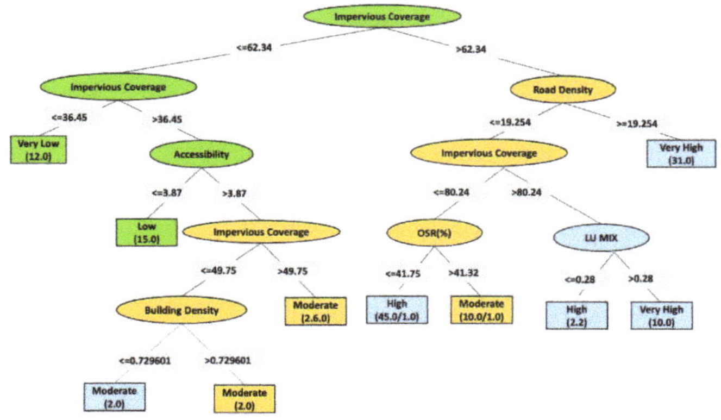

Figure 8. Decision Tree Analysis predicted model 1.

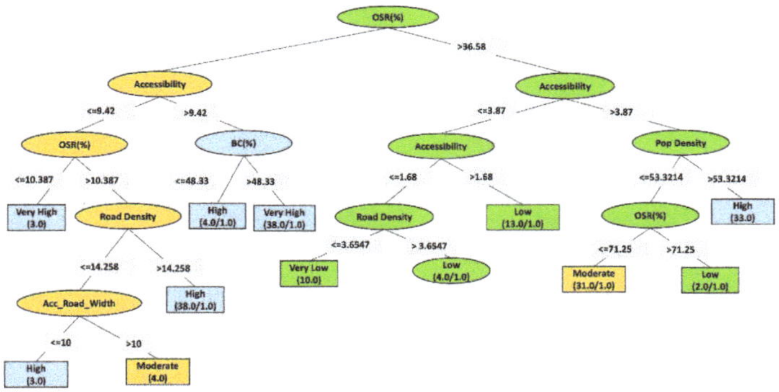

Figure 9. Decision Tree Analysis predicted model 2.

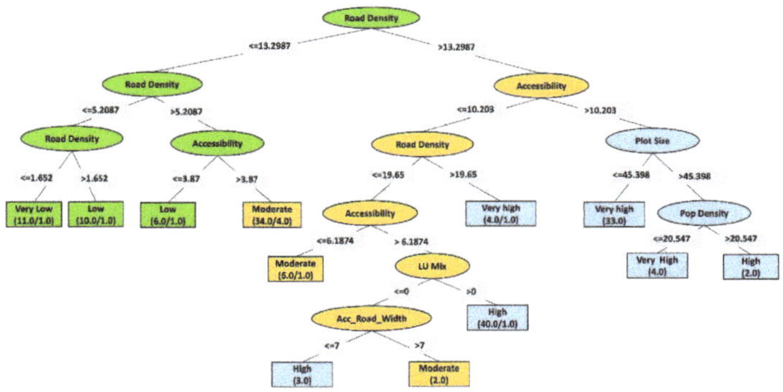

Figure 10. Decision Tree Analysis predicted model 3.

As an example, the model output illustrates how surface runoff was able to be reduced under each urban scenario. Three possible model options in the decision tree analysis to make the level of runoff under five grades (i.e., very low, low, moderate, high, and very high) by considering independent density variables were simulated. Among 13 independent density-determining variables the model selected three key variables to reduce the level of runoff in urban catchment areas: impervious coverage, open space ratio (OSR), and road density. Under those key variables the level of accessibility, population density, access road width, land use mix, built-up coverage (BC), and average plot size play a significant role to change the level of SR in urban catchment areas. In Figures 8–10, green indicates the most preferred regions to reduce the level of SR in complex urban catchment areas. The yellow indicates the feasible areas to reduce runoff level to moderate. Hence, those variables under the urban planning practices should be considered the minimum required values to make cities resilient to flooding. This provides a decision-making and guidance tool for designing future resilient cities or for managing existing urban areas by adjusting different density-based proxies.

Table 8. Model accuracy of decision tree analysis.

Parameters	Model 1 Accuracy	Model 2 Accuracy	Model 3 Accuracy
Correctly classified instances	98.7097%	94.8387%	93.5484%
Incorrectly classified instances	1.2903%	5.1613%	6.4516%
Kappa statistic	0.983	0.932	0.915
Mean absolute error	0.0097	0.034	0.0457
Relative absolute error	3.183%	11.1693%	14.9979%
Root relative squared error	3.183%	33.4472%	38.758%
Total number of instances	155	155	155

3.3. *Field Verification of the Simulated Results*

Finally, the results generated from the model were verified with real ground flood data (i.e., flood depth and flood inundation duration). In order to verify the prediction capability of the model that is based on GIS and SWMM platforms, this study carried out a comparative analysis of selected three case study locations in the Colombo Metropolitan Area of Sri Lanka with past flood occurrence data vs. simulated data. A total of 140 nodes were considered for accuracy testing. More than 88% ($R^2 > 0.88$) of the regions where the model predicted floods actually experienced ground flooding, as shown in Figure 11. The upper three images indicate actual flood conditions, and the latter three images indicate the model-generated flood result. The model has established a satisfactory accuracy level with ground flood sites and non-flood locations based on the aforementioned data set. The comparative result of the real ground flood and model results in three different case study areas is indicated in Figures 12 and 13. As a result, practitioners including disaster managers, planners, developers, engineers, and government and non-government entities can utilize this approach to reasonably accurately envision regions that may experience flooding in the future or present.

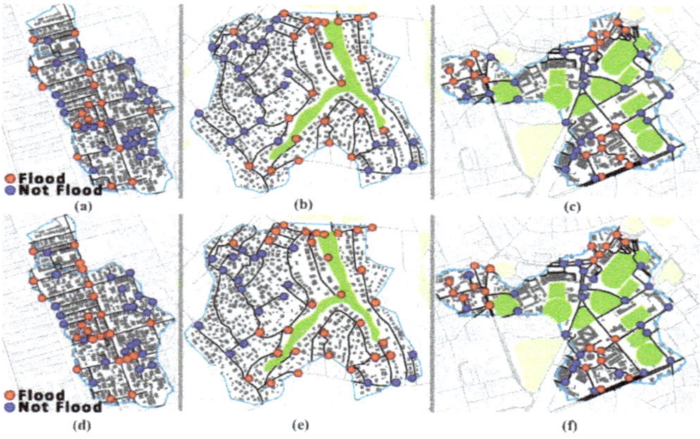

Figure 11. Real ground flood locations and model predicted flood locations: (**a**) actual flood Bambalapitiya; (**b**) actual flood Nagoda Hospital Junction; (**c**) actual flood Colombo-7; (**d**) model result for Bambalapitiya; (**e**) model result for Nagoda Hospital Junction; (**f**) model result for Colombo-7.

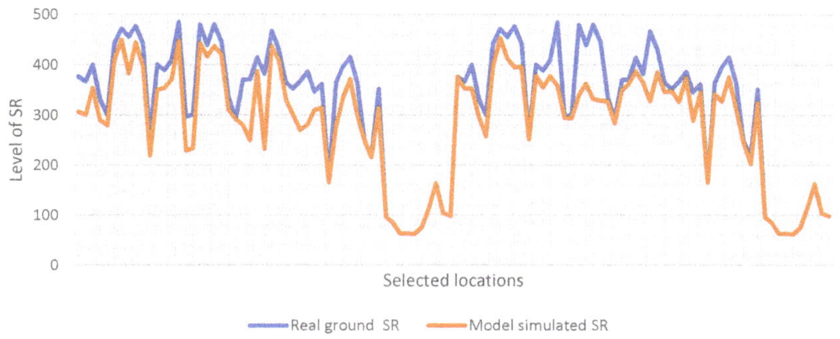

Figure 12. Change of surface runoff (SR) in real ground result and model result.

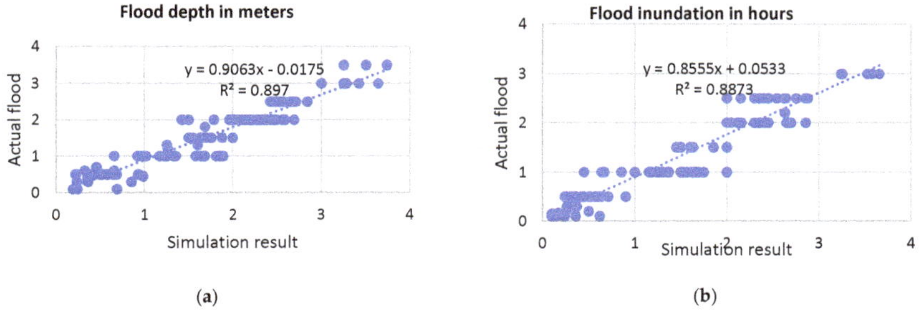

Figure 13. Level of accuracy verification: (**a**) flood depth; (**b**) inundation duration.

4. Discussion

The findings of this study indicate that urban form density has a considerable capability to manage surface runoff in an urban watershed as a standalone factor. Based on random occurrences, the decision tree generates models that resemble how trees offer different outcomes. This is conducted by examining the pattern of past occurrences impacted by various variables. Regression problems include, for instance, models that attempt to forecast actual importance for future predictions. Density classification has more than 90.00% model accuracy in predicting urban form densities, in the case of all 13 independent density parameters. Further, the model generated results that correspond to the real ground verifications of the simulated values. Hence it is promising that the planned interventions on urban density can be utilized to make urban areas resilient to flooding.

The developed evaluation framework on the level of surface runoff under distinct urban form densities has universal applicability to make cities resilient to urban flooding upon localization. The finding of this study reveals that the influence of all three types of density (3Ds) measuring proxies is important to managing SR the density-based parameters such as impervious coverage, OSR, and road density are the key factors incorporated with the level of accessibility, population density, and built-up coverage to determine surface runoff in the urban catchment. The finding of the study incorporates previous studies as urban design-based density factors have the highest significance on reducing surface runoff via urban design elements (i.e., urban water management strategies, low impact developments, BMP- Best Management Practices, etc.) [46,70]. The proxies of urban density also can be utilized to successfully manage the SR in urban catchments using sub-density parameters such as plot size, land use mix, and access road width [14].

Previous studies have identified the difference in urban morphological elements on the level of SR [26,40,41], but this study developed a quantitative evaluation mechanism of physical urban density as a standalone factor which helps elucidate the impact of density in a case-specific manner. The built-form density that incorporates natural factors has the highest impact on changing surface runoff in urban catchments as per the results revealed. The novelty of this study is that it contributes a holistic spatial framework to measure the built-form density by categorizing three density areas (i.e., 3Ds: density, diversity, and design) which can be applied to any urban context in the world. Hence, this application supports the decision-making processes in the field of urban flood management and planning practices.

5. Conclusions

This study has contributed with a qualitative technological-based framework to pre-evaluate disaster risk assessment by consolidating urban form densities with a set of dynamic parameters. It has the ability to compute and simulate a range of parameters within a user-friendly environment, and the ability to visualize it geospatially with different intensity levels numerically. Hence, this approach is capable of catering to the spatial change needs of land use policy planning and decision-makers. The usability of this framework can be further improved by incorporating existing policy regulations with expert opinion surveys in future research. Furthermore, this approach is only verified at the micro watershed scale and may be developed to manage at the macro watershed scale by changing density parameters for large catchment areas as future work. Nevertheless, more case studies (i.e., different land uses, different terrain conditions, different urban density management strategies, etc.) must be carried out to increase the accuracy level of this application. Therefore, such research may be very helpful to those who plan for land use, formulate policies and decisions, and work with implementing agencies. In conclusion, the research's findings can continue to be a valuable resource for stakeholder groups who are engaged in flood-related catastrophe management and control.

As itemized earlier, rapid urbanization and expansion of built-up area density have weakened the natural defense mechanisms increasing the probability of urban flooding. Empirical evidence revealed that disaster-resilient development is needed to be focused on supplementing the flood-resilient ecosystem services. This has become a critical challenge for decisionmakers partly due to the limited availability and validity of accurate methods to predict future and existing flood situations with urban expansion scenarios. Accordingly, the proposed spatial simulation approach suggested in this study has the ability to capture the thresholds of built-form density variations, as well as the desirable dynamics of land use changes and infrastructure supply which can be utilized for future development plans as an application of free and open source. In order to strengthen such efforts, this research has attempted to develop a theory-based simulation framework with the existing built-up scenarios and verified the accuracy of the simulated outcome.

Author Contributions: Conceptualization, N.W. and. C.A.; methodology, N.W. and N.D.; software, N.W. and A.J.; validation, C.A. and N.W.; formal analysis, N.W.; investigation, N.W.; resources, C.A.; data curation, N.W.; writing—original draft preparation, N.W.; writing—review and editing, C.A. and A.J.; visualization, N.W.; supervision, C.A. and A.J.; project administration, C.A.; funding acquisition, C.A. All authors have read and agreed to the published version of the manuscript.

Funding: This research received no external funding.

Institutional Review Board Statement: Not applicable.

Informed Consent Statement: Not applicable.

Data Availability Statement: Data sharing not applicable.

Conflicts of Interest: The authors declare no conflict of interest.

References

1. Zevenbergen, C.; Cashman, A.; Evelpidou, N.; Pasche, E.; Garvin, S.; Ashley, R. *Urban Flood Management*, 1st ed.; CRC Press: London, UK, 2010.
2. World Bank. *Land Use Planning for Urban Flood Risk Management*; World Bank: Washington, DC, USA, 2017.
3. United Nations Office for Disaster Risk Reduction. *Human Cost of Disasters an Overview of the Last 20 Years 2000–2019*; United Nations: New York, NY, USA, 2020.
4. United Nations; Department of Economic and Social Affairs; Population Division. World Urbanization Prospects: The 2018 Revision; 2019. Available online: https://www.un.org/development/desa/publications/2018-revision-of-world-urbanization-prospects.html (accessed on 1 December 2022).
5. Feng, B.; Zhang, Y.; Bourke, R. Urbanization impacts on flood risks based on urban growth data and coupled flood models. *Nat. Hazards* **2021**, *106*, 613–627. [CrossRef]
6. Kang, S.; Yeom, J.; Jung, J. Urban Form and Natural Hazards: Exploring the Dual Aspect Concept of Urban Forms on Flood Damage. *Sustainability* **2021**, *13*, 9007. [CrossRef]
7. Ferrari, A.; Viero, D.P. Floodwater pathways in urban areas: A method to compute porosity fields for anisotropic subgrid models in differential form. *J. Hydrol.* **2020**, *589*, 125193. [CrossRef]
8. Alexander, E.R. Density measures: A review and analysis. *J. Archit. Plan. Res.* **1993**, *10*, 181–202.
9. Nguyen, T.T.; Ngo, H.H.; Guo, W.; Wang, X.C.; Ren, N.; Li, G.; Ding, J.; Liang, H. Implementation of a specific urban water management—Sponge City. *Sci. Total Environ.* **2019**, *652*, 147–162. [CrossRef]
10. Wang, M.; Shao, Y.; Jiang, Q.; Xiao, L.; Yan, H.; Gao, X.; Wang, L.; Liu, P. Impacts of Climate Change and Human Activity on the Runoff Changes in the Guishui River Basin. *Land* **2020**, *9*, 291. [CrossRef]
11. Hoyer, J. (Ed.) Water Sensitive Urban Design: Principles and Inspiration for Sustainable Stormwater Management in the City of the Future. Berlin: Jovis-Verl. 2011. Available online: https://www.hcu-hamburg.de/fileadmin/documents/Research/Forschungsgruppen/REAP/WD_Publikationen/Hoyer_Dickhaut_Kronawitter_Weber_Manual_WSUD_2011.pdf (accessed on 1 December 2022).
12. Park, K.; Lee, M.-H. The Development and Application of the Urban Flood Risk Assessment Model for Reflecting upon Urban Planning Elements. *Water* **2019**, *11*, 920. [CrossRef]
13. Madusanka, S.; Abenayake, C.; Jayasinghe, A.; Perera, C. A Decision-Making Tool for Urban Planners: A Framework to Model the Interdependency among Land Use, Accessibility, Density, and Surface Runoff in Urban Areas. *Sustainability* **2022**, *14*, 522. [CrossRef]
14. Sharifi, A. Urban form resilience: A meso-scale analysis. *Cities* **2019**, *93*, 238–252. [CrossRef]
15. Owusu-Ansah, J.K. The influences of land use and sanitation infrastructure on flooding in Kumasi, Ghana. *GeoJournal* **2016**, *81*, 555–570. [CrossRef]
16. Kumar, M.; Sharif, M.; Ahmed, S. Impact of urbanization on the river Yamuna basin. *Int. J. River Basin Manag.* **2020**, *18*, 461–475. [CrossRef]
17. Abenayake, C.C.; Wijayawardana, P.N.P.; Jayasinghe, A.B.; Kalpana, L.D.C.H.N.; Dias, N.; Amaratunga, D.; Haigh, R. A GIS-Based Simulation Application to Model Surface Runoff Level in Urban Blocks. *FARU J.* **2020**, *7*, 56. [CrossRef]
18. Li, M.; Wang, Y.; Rosier, J.F.; Verburg, P.H.; van Vliet, J. Global maps of 3D built-up patterns for urban morphological analysis. *Int. J. Appl. Earth Obs. Geoinform.* **2022**, *114*, 103048. [CrossRef]
19. Schubert, J.E.; Sanders, B.F. Building treatments for urban flood inundation models and implications for predictive skill and modeling efficiency. *Adv. Water Resour.* **2012**, *41*, 49–64. [CrossRef]
20. Eini, M.; Kaboli, H.S.; Rashidian, M.; Hedayat, H. Hazard and vulnerability in urban flood risk mapping: Machine learning techniques and considering the role of urban districts. *Int. J. Disaster Risk Reduct.* **2020**, *50*, 101687. [CrossRef]
21. Zhang, H.; Cheng, J.; Wu, Z.; Li, C.; Qin, J.; Liu, T. Effects of Impervious Surface on the Spatial Distribution of Urban Waterlogging Risk Spots at Multiple Scales in Guangzhou, South China. *Sustainability* **2018**, *10*, 1589. [CrossRef]
22. Berghauser Pont, M.; Haupt, P. "Space, Density and Urban Form," urn:NBN:nl:ui:24-uuid:0e8cdd4d-80d0-4c4c-97dc-dbb9e5eee7c2, Netherlands. 2009. Available online: http://resolver.tudelft.nl/uuid:0e8cdd4d-80d0-4c4c-97dc-dbb9e5eee7c2 (accessed on 1 December 2022).
23. Zhao, C.; Weng, Q.; Hersperger, A.M. Characterizing the 3-D urban morphology transformation to understand urban-form dynamics: A case study of Austin, Texas, USA. *Landsc. Urban Plan.* **2020**, *203*, 103881. [CrossRef]
24. Nguyen, H.D.; Fox, D.; Dang, D.K.; Pham, L.T.; Viet Du, Q.V.; Nguyen, T.H.T.; Dang, T.N.; Tran, V.T.; Vu, P.L.; Nguyen, Q.-H.; et al. Predicting Future Urban Flood Risk Using Land Change and Hydraulic Modeling in a River Watershed in the Central Province of Vietnam. *Remote Sens.* **2021**, *13*, 262. [CrossRef]
25. Berling-Wolff, S.; Wu, J. Modeling urban landscape dynamics: A case study in Phoenix, USA. *Urban Ecosyst.* **2004**, *7*, 215–240. [CrossRef]
26. Piyumi, M.M.M.; Abenayake, C.; Jayasinghe, A.; Wijegunarathna, E. Urban Flood Modeling Application: Assess the Effectiveness of Building Regulation in Coping with Urban Flooding Under Precipitation Uncertainty. *Sustain. Cities Soc.* **2021**, *75*, 103294. [CrossRef]
27. Chen, C.; Gong, H.; Paaswell, R. Role of the built environment on mode choice decisions: Additional evidence on the impact of density. *Transportation* **2008**, *35*, 285–299. [CrossRef]

28. Khalaj, M.R.; Noor, H.; Dastranj, A. Investigation and simulation of flood inundation hazard in urban areas in Iran. *Geoenvironmental Disasters* **2021**, *8*, 18. [CrossRef]
29. Waqas, H.; Lu, L.; Tariq, A.; Li, Q.; Baqa, M.F.; Xing, J.; Sajjad, A. Flash Flood Susceptibility Assessment and Zonation Using an Integrating Analytic Hierarchy Process and Frequency Ratio Model for the Chitral District, Khyber Pakhtunkhwa, Pakistan. *Water* **2021**, *13*, 1650. [CrossRef]
30. Lin, J.; He, X.; Lu, S.; Liu, D.; He, P. Investigating the influence of three-dimensional building configuration on urban pluvial flooding using random forest algorithm. *Environ. Res.* **2021**, *196*, 110438. [CrossRef] [PubMed]
31. Liu, Y.; Bates, P.D.; Neal, J.C.; Yamazaki, D. Bare-Earth DEM Generation in Urban Areas for Flood Inundation Simulation Using Global Digital Elevation Models. *Water Resour. Res.* **2021**, *57*. [CrossRef]
32. Abdrabo, K.I.; Kantoush, S.A.; Saber, M.; Sumi, T.; Habiba, O.M.; Elleithy, D.; Elboshy, B. Integrated Methodology for Urban Flood Risk Mapping at the Microscale in Ungauged Regions: A Case Study of Hurghada, Egypt. *Remote Sens.* **2020**, *12*, 3548. [CrossRef]
33. Thoban, M.I.; Hizbaron, D.R. Urban resilience to floods in parts of Makassar, Indonesia. *E3S Web Conf.* **2020**, *200*, 01007. [CrossRef]
34. Ress, L.D.; Hung, C.J.; James, L.A. Impacts of urban drainage systems on stormwater hydrology: Rocky Branch Watershed, Columbia, South Carolina. *J. Flood Risk Manag.* **2020**, *13*, e12643. [CrossRef]
35. Mwangi, P.W.; Karanja, F.N.; Kamau, P.K.; Letema, S.C. Impact of urban forms on 3d built-up intensity expansion rate from aerial stereo-imagery. *ISPRS Ann. Photogramm. Remote Sens. Spat. Inf. Sci.* **2020**, *4*, 203–208. [CrossRef]
36. Papilloud, T.; Röthlisberger, V.; Loreti, S.; Keiler, M. Flood exposure analysis of road infrastructure—Comparison of different methods at national level. *Int. J. Disaster Risk Reduct.* **2020**, *47*, 101548. [CrossRef]
37. Khadiyanto, P.; Soetomo, S.; Hadi, S.P. Violation factors of the building coverage ratio: A study in Trimulyo Genuk, Semarang, Indonesia. *IOP Conf. Ser. Earth Environ. Sci.* **2020**, *490*, 012012. [CrossRef]
38. Ogato, G.S.; Bantider, A.; Abebe, K.; Geneletti, D. Geographic information system (GIS)-Based multicriteria analysis of flooding hazard and risk in Ambo Town and its watershed, West shoa zone, oromia regional State, Ethiopia. *J. Hydrol. Reg. Stud.* **2020**, *27*, 100659. [CrossRef]
39. Chen, J.; Li, Q.; Wang, H.; Deng, M. A Machine Learning Ensemble Approach Based on Random Forest and Radial Basis Function Neural Network for Risk Evaluation of Regional Flood Disaster: A Case Study of the Yangtze River Delta, China. *Int. J. Environ. Res. Public. Health* **2019**, *17*, 49. [CrossRef]
40. Albano, R. Investigation on Roof Segmentation for 3D Building Reconstruction from Aerial LIDAR Point Clouds. *Appl. Sci.* **2019**, *9*, 4674. [CrossRef]
41. Fahy, B.; Brenneman, E.; Chang, H.; Shandas, V. Spatial analysis of urban flooding and extreme heat hazard potential in Portland, OR. *Int. J. Disaster Risk Reduct.* **2019**, *39*, 101117. [CrossRef]
42. Ahmed, S.; Meenar, M.; Alam, A. Designing a Blue-Green Infrastructure (BGI) Network: Toward Water-Sensitive Urban Growth Planning in Dhaka, Bangladesh. *Land* **2019**, *8*, 138. [CrossRef]
43. Caparros-Midwood, D.; Dawson, R.; Barr, S. Low Carbon, Low Risk, Low Density: Resolving choices about sustainable development in cities. *Cities* **2019**, *89*, 252–267. [CrossRef]
44. Afifi, Z.; Chu, H.-J.; Kuo, Y.-L.; Hsu, Y.-C.; Wong, H.-K.; Zeeshan Ali, M. Residential Flood Loss Assessment and Risk Mapping from High-Resolution Simulation. *Water* **2019**, *11*, 751. [CrossRef]
45. Cai, T.; Li, X.; Ding, X.; Wang, J.; Zhan, J. Flood risk assessment based on hydrodynamic model and fuzzy comprehensive evaluation with GIS technique. *Int. J. Disaster Risk Reduct.* **2019**, *35*, 101077. [CrossRef]
46. Peng, Z.; Jinyan, K.; Wenbin, P.; Xin, Z.; Yuanbin, C. Effects of Low-Impact Development on UrbanRainfall Runoff under Different RainfallCharacteristics. *Pol. J. Environ. Stud.* **2018**, *28*, 771–783. [CrossRef]
47. Stetsenko, S.E.; Yastrebova, N.A. The Influence of Urban Planning and Building Factors on the Dustiness of the Urban Environment. *IOP Conf. Ser. Mater. Sci. Eng.* **2018**, *463*, 032031. [CrossRef]
48. Abo-El-Wafa, H.; Yeshitela, K.; Pauleit, S. The use of urban spatial scenario design model as a strategic planning tool for Addis Ababa. *Landsc. Urban Plan.* **2018**, *180*, 308–318. [CrossRef]
49. Kumar, B.; Bhaduri, S. Disaster risk in the urban villages of Delhi. *Int. J. Disaster Risk Reduct.* **2018**, *31*, 1309–1325. [CrossRef]
50. Sitzenfrei, R.; Zischg, J.; Sitzmann, M.; Bach, P. Impact of Hybrid Water Supply on the Centralised Water System. *Water* **2017**, *9*, 855. [CrossRef]
51. Majid, M.R.; Jamaludin, J.A.; Wan Ibrahim, W.Y. Estimation of residential impervious surface using gis technique. *Plan. Malays. J.* **2013**, *11*. [CrossRef]
52. I-soon, R.; Chaweewan, D.; Iamtrakul, P. Evaluation of Storm Surge Map for Safety Improvement in Bangkok Metropolitan Region, Thailand. *Lowl. Technol. Int.* **2011**, *13*, 19–26.
53. Chrysochoou, M.; Brown, K.; Dahal, G.; Granda-Carvajal, C.; Segerson, K.; Garrick, N.; Bagtzoglou, A. A GIS and indexing scheme to screen brownfields for area-wide redevelopment planning. *Landsc. Urban Plan.* **2012**, *105*, 187–198. [CrossRef]
54. Buitelaar, E.; Segeren, A. Urban Structures and Land. The Morphological Effects of Dealing with Property Rights. *Hous. Stud.* **2011**, *26*, 661–679. [CrossRef]
55. Bobkova, E. *Towards a Theory of Natural Occupation: Developing Theoretical, Methodolgical and Empirical Support for the Relation between Plot Systems and Urban Processes*; Chalmers University of Technology: Gothenburg, Sweden, 2019; ISBN 978-91-7905-196-9.
56. Marcus, L.; Colding, J. Toward an integrated theory of spatial morphology and resilient urban systems. *Ecol. Soc.* **2014**, *19*, 55. [CrossRef]

57. Ye, Y.; Van Nes, A. Measuring urban maturation processes in Dutch and Chinese new towns: Combining street network configuration with building density and degree of land use diversification through GIS. *J. Space Syntax* **2013**, *4*, 18–37.
58. Grimaldi, S.; Petroselli, A. Do we still need the Rational Formula? An alternative empirical procedure for peak discharge estimation in small and ungauged basins. *Hydrol. Sci. J.* **2015**, *60*, 67–77. [CrossRef]
59. Dempsey, N.; Brown, C.; Raman, S.; Porta, S.; Jenks, M.; Jones, C.; Bramley, G. Elements of Urban Form. In *Sustainable City Form*; Jenks, M., Jones, C., Eds.; Future City; Springer: Dordrecht, The Netherlands, 2008; Volume 2, pp. 21–51, ISBN 978-1-4020-8646-5.
60. Churchman, A. Women and the Environment: Questioned and Unquestioned Assumptions. In *Theoretical Perspectives in Environment-Behavior Research*; Wapner, S., Demick, J., Yamamoto, T., Minami, H., Eds.; Springer: Boston, MA, USA, 2000; pp. 89–106, ISBN 978-1-4613-7129-8.
61. Cervero, R.; Kockelman, K. Travel demand and the 3Ds: Density, diversity, and design. *Transp. Res. Part Transp. Environ.* **1997**, *Volume 2*(no. 3), 199–219. [CrossRef]
62. Kim, Y.-A.; Hipp, J.R. Density, diversity, and design: Three measures of the built environment and the spatial patterns of crime in street segments. *J. Crim. Justice* **2021**, *77*, 101864. [CrossRef]
63. Ye, Y.; Yeh, A.; Zhuang, Y.; van Nes, A.; Liu, J. "Form Syntax" as a contribution to geodesign: A morphological tool for urbanity-making in urban design. *URBAN Des. Int.* **2017**, *22*, 73–90. [CrossRef]
64. Carpio-Pinedo, J.; Ramírez, G.; Montes, S.; Lamiquiz, P.J. New Urban Forms, Diversity, and Computational Design: Exploring the Open Block. *J. Urban Plan. Dev.* **2020**, *146*, 04020002. [CrossRef]
65. Moravej, M.; Renouf, M.A.; Lam, K.L.; Kenway, S.J.; Urich, C. Site-scale Urban Water Mass Balance Assessment (SUWMBA) to quantify water performance of urban design-technology-environment configurations. *Water Res.* **2021**, *188*, 116477. [CrossRef] [PubMed]
66. Jang, S.; Cho, M.; Yoon, J.; Yoon, Y.; Kim, S.; Kim, G.; Kim, L.; Aksoy, H. Using SWMM as a tool for hydrologic impact assessment. *Desalination* **2007**, *212*, 344–356. [CrossRef]
67. Rossman, L.A. *Storm Water Management Model User's Manual, Version 5.0*; Environmental Protection Agency: Washington, DC, USA, 2010.
68. Bruwier, M.; Mustafa, A.; Aliaga, D.G.; Archambeau, P.; Erpicum, S.; Nishida, G.; Zhang, X.; Pirotton, M.; Teller, J.; Dewals, B. Influence of urban pattern on inundation flow in floodplains of lowland rivers. *Sci. Total Environ.* **2018**, *622–623*, 446–458. [CrossRef]
69. Abana, E.C. A Decision Tree Approach for Predicting Student Grades in Research Project using Weka. *Int. J. Adv. Comput. Sci. Appl.* **2019**, *10*. [CrossRef]
70. Rodrigues, M.; Antunes, C. Best Management Practices for the Transition to a Water-Sensitive City in the South of Portugal. *Sustainability* **2021**, *13*, 2983. [CrossRef]

urban science

Article

Mental Models for Assessing Impacts of Stormwater on Urban Social–Ecological Systems

Caitlyn B. O'Connor [1] and Phillip S. Levin [1,2,*]

[1] School of Marine and Environmental Affairs, University of Washington, Seattle, WA 98195, USA
[2] The Nature Conservancy, Seattle, WA 98121, USA
* Correspondence: pslevin@uw.edu

Abstract: Managing social–ecological systems that benefit both humans and nature is the central challenge of natural resource management. Integrating multiple perspectives into decision-making adds flexibility to social–ecological systems by reducing rigidity and promoting adaptability. Our objective was to assess expert perceptions of the structure, content, and function of the Puget Sound stormwater social–ecological system. We interviewed Puget Sound stormwater experts to document their mental models of the system and compared the network structure of expert maps. We also assessed differences among experts in the components of the social–ecological system which were included in mental models. Our analyses revealed differences between genders, as well as between managers, in how experts characterized the system. Notably, female participants tended to characterize the social–ecological system as one in which there were many system drivers generating multiple impacts across the system. The mental models of the scientists tended to include more resource units than those of the managers, which focused more on governance compared to those of the scientists. Finally, we incorporated the diverse input from mangers and scientists to create a single mental model to represent a consensus on the Puget Sound stormwater social–ecological system. This work highlights the fact that addressing the stormwater problem requires that we embrace the varied perspectives of scientists, managers, and stakeholders. We contend that incorporating the diverse perspectives of experts within the context of social–ecological systems provides a promising path towards a lasting and durable recovery for the ecosystem.

Keywords: mental model; Puget Sound; stormwater; social–ecological system; herring; expert elicitation

1. Introduction

Social–Ecological Systems (SES) are complex, adaptive systems that consist of diverse connections between people and their environments [1]. The SES approach to natural resource management emphasizes that people, communities, economies, societies, and cultures are embedded parts of the ecosystem, and that each part is shaped by, dependent on, and evolving with one another [1–3]. Given this interdependence between human and ecological well-being, it is vital to incorporate this connection during natural resource decision-making [4]. Indeed, managing social–ecological systems that benefit both humans and nature is a central challenge of natural resource management [1,5,6].

Relationships among components of an SES can be complex and non-linear, and can operate across multiple scales; as a result, a first step in natural resource decision-making must be to understand the constituents of SES components and their connections [7,8]. To this end, experts often play a key role in building an understanding of social–ecological processes (e.g., [9–11]), and decision-makers frequently seek input from a wide range of technical experts (e.g., [9,10,12,13]). Elicitation of expert knowledge can generate valuable information, particularly in data-poor situations that require rapid management action [14]. Expert opinion can provide information on possible consequences and tradeoffs of management action (e.g., [9]), and because experts are trained in a diversity of disciplines and hold positions that focus on different parts of the system, they bring a variety of perspectives to bear on issues [15]. Thus, it is both a challenge and an opportunity for natural resource management to understand and effectively use the diverse perspectives of experts [16].

Capturing mental models is an emerging approach used to integrate and share knowledge from diverse experts [17–20]. Mental models allow individuals to use their "fuzzy" logic to illustrate how they catalog, interpret, and assign meaning to their environment [21,22]. In this way, experts can indicate what they believe are the most critical components and causal relationships, and then determine the strength, directionality, and impact of these relationships [20]. The qualitative nature of mental models allows individuals to describe components of the system that are not well-known, and makes them able to incorporate relationships that have yet to be quantified [20]. As examples: (1) Stier and colleagues [12] used mental models to describe and compare varying conceptualizations of the pelagic food web in Haida Gwaii, Canada; (2) Henly-Shepard and colleagues [23] used participatory modeling workshops to develop mental models that represented, explored, and actively questioned community beliefs about the natural hazards faced by communities of the North Shore of O'ahu Hawai'i; and (3) Nayaki and colleagues [24] used mental models to compare the assumptions driving externally-generated bushmeat management with perceptions of bushmeat trade derived from local community members. In these examples, mental models have proven to be useful tools for aligning perceptions of diverse actors and improving success by promoting context-appropriate policies.

Herein, we use mental models as a tool to capture the perceptions of experts of the Puget Sound, USA, (Figure 1) social–ecological system, with a focus on urban stormwater management. Our objective of this project was to elicit the opinions of stormwater experts in order to fill a key knowledge gap about the linkages among biophysical and social dimensions of stormwater management, as well as to reveal the perceptions of experts regarding the factors and processes influencing the stormwater SES in Puget Sound. We define the Puget Sound stormwater SES as the resources, resource systems, actors, and governance engaged with managing urban stormwater pollution in Puget Sound. Specifically, we elicited mental models from diverse stormwater experts and asked whether the structure of mental models differed among experts with varying demographic or employment attributes (i.e., stormwater managers and scientists). We built a consensus mental model to highlight key components of the stormwater SES, and then characterized the mental models using an SES framework to examine whether experts varied in their perspectives on the Puget Sound stormwater SES structure.

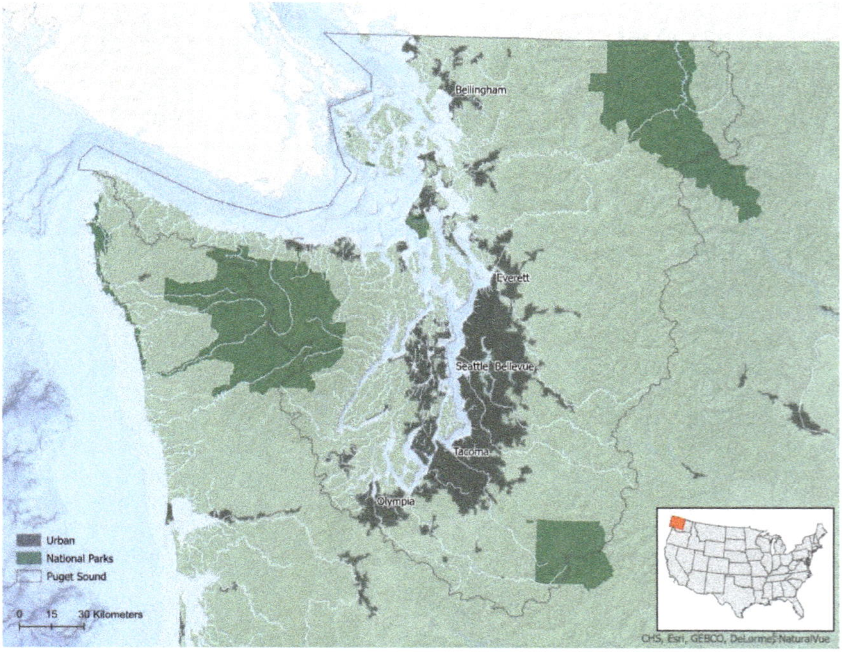

Figure 1. Map of Puget Sound, USA study region. Urbanized areas are shown in gray, National Parks are shown in dark green.

2. Materials and Methods

2.1. The Puget Sound Study System

Puget Sound encompasses 41,500 km^2 of upland, freshwater, estuarine, and marine habitats in Washington State, USA, and British Columbia, Canada, and supports a large (>4.2 million) and increasingly urban population ranging from Vancouver, British Columbia to Olympia, Washington [25] (Figure 1). With dozens of birds, mammals, fishes, plants, and invertebrates currently listed on state and federal endangered species lists, Puget Sound is also considered a hot-spot of extinction risk [26].

The Puget Sound region receives up to 1 m of precipitation annually, generating about 1.5 billion cubic meters of stormwater runoff [27]. This runoff is largely untreated, resulting in 544 fresh and marine waterbodies being designated as impaired or threatened by pollutants [27]. Stormwater impacts a diversity of species, from invertebrates [28] to marine mammals [29]. For example: (1) Tian and colleagues [30] recently demonstrated that a compound from tire rubber causes acute mortality in coho salmon (*Oncorhynchus kisutch*) when they migrate to urban creeks to spawn; (2) Pacific herring (*Clupea pallasii*) exposed to urban stormwater runoff suffer cardiac injury and reduced growth [31]; and (3) toxic contaminants in the blubber of southern resident killer whales ostensibly result in adverse health consequences, such as modifications in hormone levels, reproductive disruption or miscarriages, reduced immunity to diseases, neurotoxicity, neurobehavioral disruptions, and cancer [32]. Managing and mitigating stormwater impact is a priority in the Puget Sound region and beyond, but linkages among components of the biophysical and human dimensions of the stormwater SES are poorly understood [33].

2.2. Expert Elicitation of Mental Models

We conducted semi-structured interviews with stormwater experts to understand how experts perceived the Puget Sound Stormwater SES. Using stratified chain referral sampling (also known as snowball sampling) [34], we identified 25 Puget Sound stormwater experts.

To accomplish this, we identified individuals who were considered stormwater experts by local, state, or federal management agencies, and, following the interviews, we asked them for the names of others whom they considered to be experts. We defined a stormwater expert as someone who works professionally in stormwater policy, science, or management. Experts were described as having either scientific or management expertise (hereafter referred to as "scientists" or "managers"). There was no exchange of money or goods for participating in the interviews. Interviews lasted between 60 and 110 min.

Following Carley and Palmquist [35], we asked each expert to draw a network with the most critical components and interactions in the Puget Sound stormwater SES. We asked experts to consider key drivers of stormwater, impacts of stormwater, ways to mitigate stormwater, species, habitats, threats, and ecological relationships. We then asked participants to consider linkages between the components of the system and describe the strength of interactions, ranging from −2 (strongly negative) to +2 (strongly positive). We also asked a series of demographic questions to gather information that could potentially influence responses (e.g., age, years of experience, professional affiliation, and gender).

We constrained expert responses in two ways: (1) they had to include herring and stormwater in their model, and (2) due to computational efficiency, they could include no more than 20 components in their model. We focused on herring because they have been identified by the Puget Sound Partnership as a key indicator of ecosystem health [36], are a critical component of the Puget Sound food web [37], and play a vital role in the trophic transfer of contaminants in the food web [38].

2.3. *Analysis of Mental Models*

Network Structure

We transformed each expert drawing of the Puget Sound Stormwater SES into adjacency matrices in the form A(D) = [aij], where the variables vi are listed on the vertical axis and *vj* on the horizontal axis to form a square matrix [17]. Connections among variables were then coded in the square matrix (between −2 and 2).

We assessed the content and structure of the mental models by evaluating eight network descriptors: number of components, number of connections, number of drivers, number of receivers, centrality, complexity, number of connections per component, and density (Table 1).

Table 1. Structural metrics applied to matrix forms of fuzzy cognitive maps to quantify structural properties of each expert's perceived food web. Adapted from [12].

Mental Model, Structural Measurement	Description of Measure and Cognitive Inference
Components	Number of variables included in the model; higher number of concepts indicates more concepts in the mental model
Connections	Number of connections included between components; a higher number of connections indicates a higher degree of interaction between components in a mental model
Drivers	Components with only arrows out—this means that they are not affected by other components and have influence over other variables, and, consequently, over the entire system
Receivers	Components with only arrows in—this means they are impacted by other components, but have no effect on the system
Centrality	Absolute value of either (a) overall influence in the model (all + and − relationships indicated, for the entire model), or (b) influence of individual concepts, as indicated by positive (+) or negative (−) values placed on connections between components. Indicates (a) the total influence (positive and negative) in the system or (b) the conceptual weight/importance of individual concepts. The higher the value, the greater the importance of all concepts or the individual weight of a concept in the overall model
Complexity	Ratio of receiver variables to transmitter variables. Indicates the degree of resolution and is a measure of the degree to which outcomes of driving forces are considered. Higher complexity indicates more complicated systems.
Connections per component (C/N)	Number of connections divided by number of variables (concepts). The lower the C/N score, the higher the degree of connectedness in a system.
Density	Number of connections compared to number of all possible connections. The higher the density, the more potential management policies exist [17].

To test the null hypothesis that scientists and managers did not differ in the network structure of their mental models, we used *t*-tests to test for differences in the means of each of the eight network descriptors. We used a Bonferroni adjustment to modify the level of significance to account for multiple tests [39]. To examine the influence of years of experience on the structure of mental models, we used linear regression, with years of experience as the independent variable and network descriptors as dependent variables. We again adjusted *p*-values using a Bonferroni adjustment.

We also conducted a non-metric multidimensional scaling analysis (NDMS) using a Bray–Curtis dissimilarity matrix to further analyze patterns in the network structure of mental models. We used the number of components, number of connections, number of drivers, number of receivers, centrality, complexity, number of connections per component, and density (Table 1) as inputs for the analysis. The analysis was performed in R using the Vegan package [40].

2.4. Characterization of the Puget Sound Stormwater SES

We next investigated the degree to which experts emphasized different components of the Puget Sound SES. To accomplish this, we followed McGinnis and Ostrom [7] and classified each component that arose in mental models as follows: (1) actor, (2) resource system, (3) governance system, or (4) resource unit. We then examined the frequency at which participants emphasized different components of the SES. As with the structural network descriptors above, we used *t*-tests with Bonferroni adjustments to evaluate the null hypothesis that scientists and managers did not differ in the mean number of SES categories in mental models.

2.5. Development and Analysis of Aggregate Models

Following the approach of Özesmi and Özesmi [17] and Gray et al. [20], we created an aggregate mental model of the Puget Sound SES. Individual mental models were given equal weight in the aggregating process. Our first step was to group similar components by SES framework elements (actor, resource system, governance system, resource unit). Because individuals differ in the level of detail or components of their models, our next step was to qualitatively combine similar components to produce an aggregate model with about 20 components. We estimated interaction strengths in the aggregate model by averaging interaction strengths from individual mental models [20].

3. Results

3.1. Structural Characterization of the Mental Models

We elicited 25 individual mental models from experts with an average of 13.7 (SD 1.7) years of experience in stormwater science or management. Of the experts, 56% identified as female, and 44% as male. Individuals who identified as scientists comprised 40% of our subjects, while 60% described themselves as managers.

The mental models had an average of 18.04 (SE 0.53) components, with a mean of 31.44 (SE 1.68) connections. The average number of connections per component was 1.75 (SE 0.08), and that of complexity was 0.64 (SE 0.17). Individual mental models can be found in O'Connor, 2020 [41].

We were unable to detect an association between years of experience and eight network descriptors: number of components, number of connections, number of drivers, number of receivers, centrality, complexity, number of connections per component, and density (in all cases, $r^2 < 0.03$; $p > 0.05$).

In models generated by participants who identified as female, the average number of drivers (4.86, SE 0.75) was nearly double that of models created by males (2.45, SE 0.39; $t = 2.85$, adjusted $p = 0.02$), and the average number of receivers in female-created models (2.21; SE 0.41) was 2.4-fold that of participants who identified as male (0.91, SE 0.32; $t = 2.53$, adjusted $p = 0.02$). We did not detect differences between the genders in any of the other network descriptors. In models generated by scientists, the average number of receivers was more than twice that of managers (2.13 (SE 0.40) vs. 0.90 (SE 0.31); t = 2.42, adjust $p = 0.04$). We did not detect differences between scientists and managers in any of the other network descriptors.

The non-metric multidimensional scaling (NMDS) shows no evidence of any groupings of mental models based on the network descriptors we used (Figure 2). However, the spread of individuals across the multivariate space in the NMDS plot highlights the diversity of the mental models developed by the experts we interviewed.

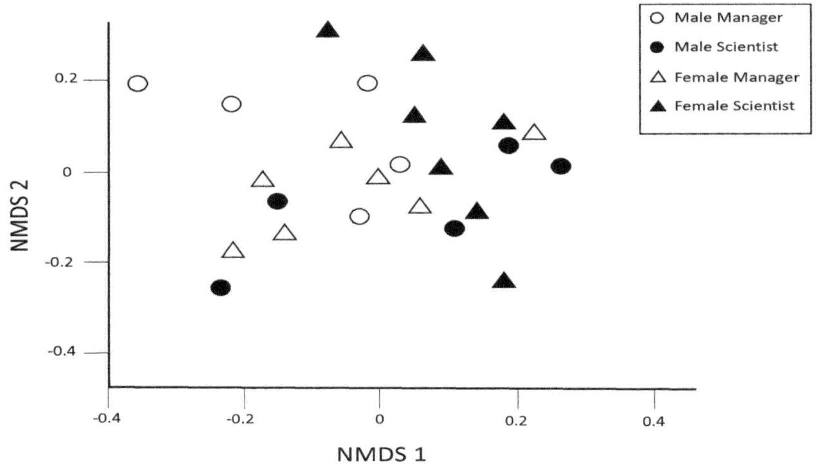

Figure 2. A plot of non-metric multidimensional scaling of individual fuzzy cognitive map-based network analysis. Each point represents a single expert and is derived from the eight metrics of model structure which we calculated from the fuzzy cognitive maps created by experts. Distance: Bray-Curtis; dimensions: 2 (2-dimensional plot represents the data structure well); stress: 0.14 (a stress level <0.2 is good); weak ties, 2 convergent solutions found after 20 tries.

3.2. *Aggregate Mental Model of the Puget Sound Social–Ecological System*

When we combined the 25 mental models elicited from stormwater experts, 4 ecological resource units emerged: salmon, herring, plankton, and southern resident killer whales (Figure 3; Figure A1). While some participants spoke of salmon generally (e.g., "salmon" or "Puget Sound salmon"), others listed specific species of salmon (e.g., Chinook salmon, Coho salmon, see also [41]). Similarly, some experts referred to plankton generally, while others specified zooplankton or phytoplankton. Most respondents included herring as a single node in their mental model; however, some separated different life stages (i.e., eggs, embryos, adults). Experts also included nutrients and stormwater as resource units in their models (Figure 3). In the resource unit sub-model, increased stormwater has negative impacts, both direct and indirect, on the food web. Nutrients, however, had mixed impacts on the food web—small increases in nutrients had a positive impact on plankton while large increases had negative effects.

The combined mental model characterized the resource system with nine components that represented the region's urban and adjacent rural areas. In the resource system sub-model, urban development is the primary driver (Figure 3). The model highlights that increased development directly increases stormwater by expanding impervious surfaces, and indirectly increases stormwater toxicity by raising the number of vehicles in the region. Additionally, the model underscores that increased roadways and other impervious surfaces result in more overflow events from combined wastewater–stormwater systems, resulting in increased toxics and nutrients entering the system. Development also impacts nutrients directly (e.g., from wastewater or septic systems) or indirectly through agriculture.

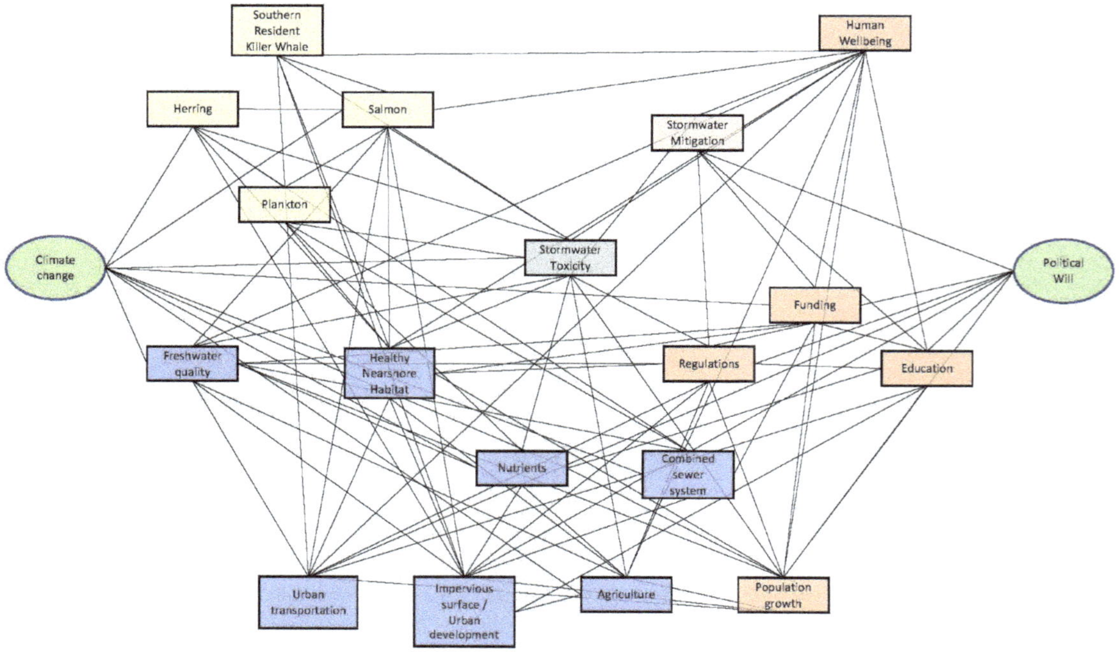

Figure 3. The aggregate mental model of stormwater experts showing connections among ecological resource units (yellow), the resource system (green), governance and actors (orange), and key externalities (blue). Details of the linkages among nodes can be found in Figure A1.

The governance and actor sub-model derived from our interviews included five additional components (Figure 3). In this sub-model, stormwater education was a key driver. Participants perceived that increased education would lead directly to more effective stormwater regulations, more funding for stormwater management, and increased use of green stormwater infrastructure to mitigate its negative effects on ecosystems and human well-being. Experts also identified funding as an important limitation to increasing green stormwater infrastructure in the Puget Sound region.

Finally, stormwater experts noted two key externalities in their mental models: climate change and political context (Figure 3). Study participants predicted that climate change would increase precipitation, leading to increased runoff of stormwater pollutants and nutrients. Unless mitigated, this would negatively impact human well-being and ecosystem health. Experts also noted that political decisions and political will to address would significantly impact the implementation of measures to mitigate stormwater; however, whether the political milieu would have a positive or negative effect was uncertain.

3.3. Characterization of the Social–Ecological System

When we organized mental models by elements of the Social–Ecological System (i.e., resource system, resource units, governance system, and actors), it became clear that managers and scientists emphasized different aspects of the SES (Figure 4); thus, a complete picture of the SES required us to include perspectives from both scientists and managers.

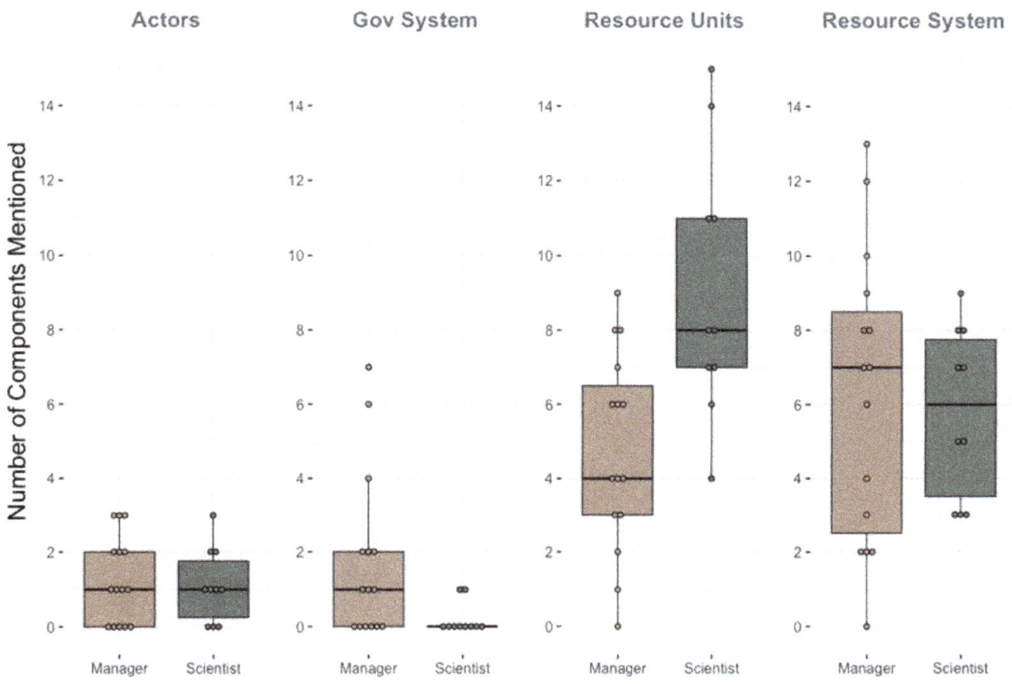

Figure 4. Box plot showing the number of Ostrom's SES components mentioned by each expert. The circles represent an amount mentioned by an expert. The top of the box represents the 75th percentile, the bottom of the box represents the 25th percentile, and the line in the middle represents the 50th percentile. The whiskers represent the highest and lowest values that are not outliers. The circles beyond the whiskers represent outliers.

On average, scientists included about twice the number of resource unit components than managers (t = 3.31; adjusted $p = 0.002$; Figure 4). In contrast, models created by managers included eight times the number of governance system components compared to scientists (t = 2.57, adjusted $p = 0.04$; Figure 4). We did not observe differences between scientists and managers in the number of actors or resource system components in the models (Figure 4).

We estimated centrality values of the components in two aggregate models: one created using only scientist input and a second created with only manager input. The rank order of the centrality values of components from the scientist model was correlated with those of managers (Spearman rank correlation, R = 0.68; Figure 5). Despite the overall correlation between models, managers and scientists appeared to differ in their perspectives on the importance of some model components (Table 2). Centrality of plankton, for example, ranked seventh in the scientist model, but was twentieth in the manager model (Table 2). Scientists also perceived agriculture as more important (centrality rank = 9) than managers did (centrality rank 19; Table 2). In contrast, the centrality of stormwater regulation ranked 10th in the manager model, but 17th in the scientist model (Table 2).

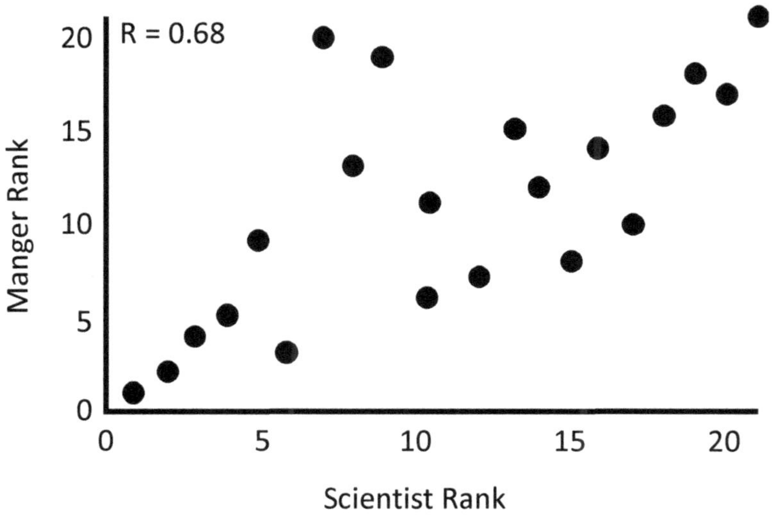

Figure 5. Spearman rank order correlation reveals a positive correlation between centrality of components in an aggregate model derived from stormwater managers and an aggregated model derived from stormwater scientists.

Table 2. Rank centrality scores for components in the mental model created by aggregating all stormwater experts (aggregate model); a model derived by aggregating models from stormwater scientists (scientist rank), and a model derived by aggregating models from stormwater managers (manager rank). Centrality rank is the overall influence in a model, with rank one being the most important and 21 being the least important.

Mental Model Component	Aggregate Rank	Scientist Rank	Manager Rank
Stormwater	1	1	1
Biotic Habitat	2	2	2
Management Practices	8	3	4
Stormwater Quantity	6	4	5
Salmon	4	5	9
Impervious Surface	3	6	3
Plankton	14	7	20
Herring	11	8	13
Agriculture	15	9	19
Freshwater Quality Health	9	10.5	6
Human Well-Being	10	10.5	11
Human Population	7	12	7
Orcas	16	13	15
Climate: Precipitation	13	14	12
Economy/Funding	5	15	8
Nutrients	17	16	14
Regulation	12	17	10
Transportation	18	18	16
Combined Sewer Overflows	20	19	18
Education	19	20	17
Politics	21	21	21

4. Discussion

People are drawn to places where land and water meet [6]. While cities emerge along coasts out of geographic and economic necessity, the land–water interface also provides leisure and recreational opportunities and meets critical cultural needs for a range of indigenous and non-indigenous communities [42–44]. While coastal zones are essential contributors to the delivery of ecosystem services, their growing population, geographical location, and frequent pattern of unsustainable land use has led to their degradation. The diversity of users and threats to coastal zones makes their management particularly challenging [45]. Herein, we elicited knowledge from Puget Sound stormwater specialists in the form of mental models. These mental models provided insight into the varying perspectives of stormwater professionals and highlighted the need to synthesize disparate perceptions to achieve a holistic view of the system.

To solve complex problems such as those associated with stormwater, decision-makers increasingly embrace the integration of knowledge from diverse experts into natural resource management (e.g., [11,46–49]). However, expert knowledge can be siloed, incomplete, variable, and biased [11,50–52]. Despite this, mental models make the implicit explicit, which provides a concrete way of examining the perspectives of experts, including what is fundamental and of value to them [20,49,53]. The usefulness of this information may justify and explain the behavior of individuals or support for certain management.

Our analyses revealed wide diversity in the network structure of mental models. In particular, experts who identified as male or as managers created mental models with fewer receivers than scientists or female participants. Thus, experts and scientists who identified as female tended to characterize the social–ecological system as one in which its drivers generate multiple impacts across the system (cf. [54]). Moreover, female experts also identified more drivers than males; thus, they perceive the Puget Sound system as one where some SES components are impacted by multiple factors (cf. [54]). For example, such experts see the node "Healthy Nearshore Habitat" as being affected by a diversity of direct threats (e.g., nutrients, stormwater pollution, freshwater quality) as well as a variety of indirect drivers (e.g., regulations, agricultural practices, transportation policy, education). The Puget Sound Partnership, the State agency charged with Puget Sound management, defines six management domains (healthy human population, vibrant quality of life, thriving species and food web, protected and restored habitat, abundant water quantity, and healthy water quality) [55]. Thus, the tendency of managers to build models with multiple impacts across the system may reflect the multiple objectives of the State. For example, managers often linked water quality, human community, and health objectives to each other and with ecological objectives. For instance, one participant noted that

> *"We want to improve stormwater for the health of Puget Sound and the health of people, so that leads to two questions we don't know. We don't know how much water quality would need to improve in order to help specific species, and we don't know how much nature in communities we would need to have a positive impact on several different aspect of human communities, whether it be individual health, or community cohesion, or improving the water into human communities"*

Our analysis of the models using Ostrom's SES framework revealed differences between the SES elements on which experts focused, and contained individual and group discourses that justified and explained the experts' behavior [53,56–59]. Managers were much more likely to emphasize aspects of governance in their models, while scientists were more likely to highlight resource units. This may be because scientists often focus on the ecological components of the system, while managers are required to meet regulatory standards. Our findings support the notion that incorporating a diverse range of expertise is necessary to fully conceptualize management plans for the Puget Sound stormwater SES. Therefore, to completely conceptualize the Puget Sound stormwater SES and to fully consider the potential consequences of different management actions or policies, managers and scientists must both be included to ensure all facets of the SES are considered.

Incorporating a diversity of perspectives into management may lead to outcomes that are enduring, because it makes knowledge structures less rigid and more adaptive to change [20,60–62]. However, including diverse perspectives can introduce some challenges. Indeed, knowledge diversity can lead to conflict and, sometimes, may even be counterproductive [15,63]. For example, diverse perceptions of the structure or function of social–ecological systems can lead to conflicts over where to intervene or where there are "leverage points" in a resource system [15,20,24]. Additionally, diverse perceptions of functional goals of management can lead to conflict over the appropriate management actions to take [64–66].

One means of overcoming such conflicts is participatory modeling—an approach for including a broad group of actors in the process of developing and implementing scientific models [67]. The work we conducted here is a necessary pre-cursor to participatory modeling approaches using a diversity of methodologies, including Bayesian Belief Networks (e.g., [9]), Qualitative Network Models (e.g., [68,69], and Fuzzy Cognitive Models (e.g., [12,21]). Moving from the static mental models we created here to more dynamic models that could be used to test the efficacy of alternative management strategies requires a more detailed understanding of the strength of the linkages among nodes (for Fuzzy Cognitive Models) or joint probability distributions (for Bayesian Networks) [70]. While such models will require additional effort and engagement, they have proven to be effective in reaching a consensus regarding the direction that management actions should take [22,71]. Importantly, our work highlights the fact that effective participatory modeling will require input from both scientists and managers to capture the complete social–ecological system. Thus, future work will advance more effectively when individuals and institutions who are skilled boundary spanners are engaged, as they will be able to foster transparent discussions and expose unconscious biases and assumptions [72,73]. Ultimately, as conservation scientists increasingly embrace and integrate community values, we expect better and more durable outcomes for both nature and humans.

5. Conclusions

The recognized importance of stormwater mitigation to the health of Puget Sound requires prompt research and action [33]. Ideally, conservation action is grounded in strong empirical science; however, conservation science, particularly that informing restoration at local scales, is often inelegant, ambiguous, and uncertain (e.g., [73]). Given the substantial repercussions regarding human and ecological well-being that conservation actions can have, in conjunction with limited conventional scientific information, it is clearly necessary to broaden participation and knowledge sources to include all those who can contribute. Equally important is that broadening project goals and outcomes to include community needs builds support for actions that benefit conservation.

In the face of a degraded Puget Sound ecosystem [74], our work highlights that addressing the stormwater problem requires that we embrace human as well as ecological processes, and innovative solutions leading towards transformative progress will most likely emerge from processes that include the varied perspectives of scientists, managers, and stakeholders. Moreover, it is clear that the diverse stormwater experts in the Puget Sound region have cogent views on system connections, and this shines a light on specific ecological and socioeconomic research that could inform future management decisions. Indeed, incorporating the diverse perspectives of regional experts within the context of the Puget Sound social–ecological system provides a promising path towards the lasting and durable recovery of Puget Sound. Rich, collaborative processes, though time- and resource-intensive, are critical for success in environmental management [49]. We highlight here that such an approach, built on genuine engagement with experts, yields a picture of the social–ecological system that is better positioned to advance the needs of both nature and humans.

Author Contributions: Conceptualization, C.B.O. and P.S.L.; methodology, C.B.O. and P.S.L.; data collection and analysis, C.B.O.; writing—original draft preparation, C.B.O.; writing—review and editing, P.S.L.; supervision, P.S.L.; project administration, P.S.L.; funding acquisition, P.S.L. All authors have read and agreed to the published version of the manuscript.

Funding: This research was funded by gift from the Boeing Company.

Data Availability Statement: Individual mental models summarized in this paper are available in graphical and tabular form here: https://digital.lib.washington.edu/researchworks/handle/1773/46013, accessed on 18 January 2023.

Acknowledgments: We are grateful to the staff at The Nature Conservancy in Washington, in particular the Science and Puget Sound teams, as well as the UW Interdisciplinary and Conservation Science Lab for their support. The manuscript was improved by the insightful comments from Emily Howe and Greg Bratman. We thank Ericka Hegeman for creation of the map used in Figure 1. Funding for this project was generously provided by the Boeing Company and the Nature Conservancy of Washington.

Conflicts of Interest: The authors declare no conflict of interest.

Appendix A. Interview Guide

Opening

(*Establish rapport*) My name is Caitlyn O'Connor and I am a graduate student at SEFS at UW. Based on your knowledge, skills, and abilities, we would like to interview you about stormwater in Puget Sound.

(*Introduction*) I would like to start by asking a few quick demographic questions and then I will ask you to draw a mental model of the Puget Sound stormwater to marine environment ecosystem.

(*Motivation*) I'm interested in learning what you believe are the drivers and effects behind the stormwater problem. I understand that your model is no means complete but I want to capture your experience and understanding to provide the start of better stormwater management.

(Privacy) Your privacy is important to me. Your name and this recording will not be linked unless you identify yourself in the recording. Only myself and my graduate advisor, Phillip Levin, will have access to your recordings.

(Timeline) The interview should take about 1 h. I would like to record this conversation to go back and clarify any of your responses as well as be able to draw out the key themes in your responses. Do you provide consent for me to record our discussion? Do you have any questions at this time?

Discuss Research Project

So, as we both know, urbanization is increasing and along with it, the amount of impervious surfaces. Of course, this means that when it rains, the water picks up contaminants that mostly go straight to the closest body of water. This polluted rainwater can harm aquatic life and is making our waterways an unhealthy place to live, work, and play. Today, I'd like to focus our discussion on stormwater in Puget Sound.

I am particularly interested in understanding how experts in stormwater (management or science) perceive this problem's structure, impacts, and solutions within this urban to marine ecosystem problem.

To look at this land–sea connection, I have decided to use herring as my indicator species. As you know, the Puget Sound Partnership has identified this as one of its vital signs because of its centrality in the food web.

As we move forward, I want to be clear that I am really interested in your perceptions of how the system is structured and functions. I expect that you will have a great deal of uncertainty about some components of the system—that's okay! Part of my work is understanding where people see key uncertainties and understanding similarities and differences among experts in this field. So, I'm interested in your opinion—whether or not there are quantitative data to back it up. I am looking to see what your experience tells us. How you see the system and the solutions. In essence, I'm investigating the scientists who study or manage stormwater, not the stormwater itself.

General Information

This is the part where I collect data on gender, years of experience, professional affiliation, training, and place of residence.

Educational background?
Highest degree, Major, and Where?
Who is your employer?
E.g. government, state, local, federal, university, consultant, etc.
How would you describe your role in stormwater management?
E.g. science, policy, management, communication
How long have you worked on this topic?
Birth year?
Preferred pronoun?

Transition into Mental Model Exercise

In this mental model exercise, I would like you to sketch out the most important players and interactions in the Puget Sound stormwater system—this could include key drivers of stormwater, the impacts of stormwater, and ways to mitigate stormwater—so anything like species, habitats, human activity, threats, predator–prey relationship, or factors affecting stormwater. You can focus on whatever you like or a combination of all.

I have three requirements.

You must include stormwater and herring.

You then get 18 more nodes. You can use as many or few of those 18 as you would like.

And you should draw arrows illustrating the interactions between the nodes. They can be positive or negative interactions—and you can illustrate these −−, −, +, ++. Arrows can go both ways, and they don't have to be symmetrical.

For example, seal predation might be strongly negative for salmon (−−), but salmon might only have a moderately positive interaction on seals (+) if seals eat lots of different kinds of fish.

Conceptual Model Activity

I would ask this for anything directly connected to stormwater and herring and would ask these similar questions.

How much stormwater needs to be treated to ensure a healthy Puget Sound?
I see that you put a (negative/0/positive) from (stormwater to herring/species), I'm wondering how much would you guess that I have to reduce this toxicity to change this negative to a zero?
Would you say 50% or would I have to get rid of all of it?
Like what is your ballpark guess?
How confident are you on a scale from 0 to 100%?
How would this change make the Puget Sound species respond?
How come?
Would you expect to see a response higher in some species rather than others?
Would some species decline if stormwater pollution decreased?
If they have other species on their mental model
Which species are most at risk?
What is the dynamic response of the food web?
How would you describe the difference between one negative/positive to two negative/positives?
Ask them to clarify what they mean by each relationship.
Ask them to define the node.

Closing

(summarize)

(*maintain rapport*) I appreciate the time you took for this interview.

Is there anything you would like to add?

Have we missed something you think is important?

What else should we talk about regarding this issue/topic?

(*action to be taken*) I should have all the information I need. Would it be alright to call/email you if I have any more questions?

Thanks again.

Appendix B

	Plankton	Herring	Salmon	Southern Resident Killer Whale	Impervious surface / Urban development	Funding	Stormwater mitigation	Transportation	Political will	Regulation
Plankton		0.73	1							
Herring	-0.5		0.68	0.5		0.5				
Salmon		-0.2		0.61		0.5				
Southern Resident Killer Whale			-0.5				1			
Impervious surface / Urban development		-0.67	-0.75	-0.5		0.5	0.67	0.5		1
Funding					0.75		0.75			0.83
Stormwater mitigation		0.5	0.75	0.5	-0.5					
Transportation			-0.5	-0.5						
Political will					0.5					-0.5
Regulation					-0.5	0.13	0.5			
Education					-0.5		0.75	-0.5	0.5	0.17
Population growth		-0.67	-0.5		0.83	-0.5		0.79		0.5
Human well-being		-0.5				0.5				0.5
Climate		-0.5	-0.5			-0.5				
Combined sewer system	-0.5	-0.5								
Agriculture										
Nutrients	0.5									
Healthy nearshore habitat	0.67	0.71	0.8	0.67						
Freshwater quality			0.83							
Stormwater toxicity	-0.57	-0.64	-0.69	-0.8		-0.5				0.5

	Education	Population growth	Human well-being	Climate	Combined sewer system	Agriculture	Nutrients	Healthy nearshore habitat	Freshwater quality	Stormwater toxicity
Plankton			1					1	1	
Herring			0.67					0.5		
Salmon			0.63					1		
Southern Resident Killer Whale			0.67							
Impervious surface / Urban development				0.5	0.5	-0.5	0.5	-0.6	-0.5	0.75
Funding	0.5	1	1		0.5				-0.5	-0.25
Stormwater mitigation			0.5	-0.75				0.75	0.67	-0.75
Transportation			-0.5	0.5				-0.5	-0.5	0.64
Political will										
Regulation		-0.5				-1		0.5	0.5	-0.75
Education		-0.17					-0.5			-0.5
Population growth	0.5		-1			0.75	0.5	-0.75	-0.5	0.6
Human well-being										
Climate					0.5	1		-0.4	-0.5	0.75
Combined sewer system								-0.5		0.5
Agriculture							1	-0.5	-0.75	0.6
Nutrients								-0.5	-1	-0.5
Healthy nearshore habitat			0.5	0.5			0.5			-0.5
Freshwater quality			0.5					0.75		
Stormwater toxicity			-0.7		0.5			-0.5	-0.71	

Figure A1. Matrix representation of the aggregate mental model of the Puget Sound stormwater social–ecological system shown in Figure 2. The aggregate model integrates information from all experts interviewed in the study. Numbers represent interaction strengths between nodes in the mental model and were estimated by averaging interaction strengths from individual mental models. See methods for more details.

References

1. Folke, C.; Biggs, R.; Norström, A.V.; Reyers, B.; Rockström, J. Social-Ecological Resilience and Biosphere-Based Sustainability Science. *Ecol. Soc.* **2016**, *21*, 43. [CrossRef]
2. Leach, M.; Rockström, J.; Raskin, P.; Scoones, I.; Stirling, A.C.; Smith, A.; Thompson, J.; Millstone, E.; Ely, A.; Arond, E.; et al. Transforming Innovation for Sustainability. *Ecol. Soc.* **2012**, *17*, 11. [CrossRef]
3. Clark, W.C.; Munn, R.E. *Sustainable Development of the Biosphere*; Cambridge University Press: Cambridge, UK, 1986.
4. Gray, S.; Sterling, E.J.; Aminpour, P.; Goralnik, L.; Singer, A.; Wei, C.; Akabas, S.; Jordan, R.C.; Giabbanelli, P.J.; Hodbod, J.; et al. Assessing (Social-Ecological) Systems Thinking by Evaluating Cognitive Maps. *Sustainability* **2019**, *11*, 5753. [CrossRef]
5. Ostrom, E. A General Framework for Analyzing Sustainability of Social-Ecological Systems. *Science* **2009**, *325*, 419–422. [CrossRef] [PubMed]
6. Levin, P.S.; Poe, M.R. *Conservation for the Anthropocene Ocean: Interdisciplinary Science for Nature and People*; Academic Press: London, UK, 2017.
7. McGinnis, M.D.; Ostrom, E. Social-Ecological System Framework: Initial Changes and Continuing Challenges. *Ecol. Soc.* **2014**, *19*, 30. [CrossRef]
8. Del Mar Delgado-Serrano, M.; Ramos, P. Making Ostrom's Framework Applicable to Characterise Social Ecological Systems at the Local Level. *Int. J. Commons* **2015**, *9*, 808–830. [CrossRef]
9. Rehr, A.P.; Williams, G.D.; Tolimieri, N.; Levin, P.S. Impacts of Terrestrial and Shoreline Stressors on Eelgrass in Puget Sound: An Expert Elicitation. *Coast. Manag.* **2014**, *42*, 246–262. [CrossRef]
10. Burgman, M.; Carr, A.; Godden, L.; Gregory, R.; McBride, M.; Flander, L.; Maguire, L. Redefining Expertise and Improving Ecological Judgment. *Conserv. Lett.* **2011**, *4*, 81–87. [CrossRef]
11. Martin, T.G.; Burgman, M.A.; Fidler, F.; Kuhnert, P.M.; Low-Choy, S.; Mcbride, M.; Mengersen, K. Eliciting Expert Knowledge in Conservation Science. *Conserv. Biol.* **2012**, *26*, 29–38. [CrossRef]
12. Stier, A.C.; Samhouri, J.F.; Gray, S.; Martone, R.G.; Mach, M.E.; Halpern, B.S.; Kappel, C.V.; Scarborough, C.; Levin, P.S. Integrating Expert Perceptions into Food Web Conservation and Management. *Conserv. Lett.* **2016**, *10*, 67–76. [CrossRef]
13. Dietz, T. Bringing Values and Deliberation to Science Communication. *Proc. Natl. Acad. Sci. USA* **2013**, *110*, 14081–14087. [CrossRef] [PubMed]
14. Morgan, D.L. *Integrating Qualitative and Quantitative Methods: A Pragmatic Approach*; SAGE Publications, Inc.: London, UK, 2014; ISBN 978-0-7619-1523-2.
15. Levin, P.S.; Gray, S.A.; Möllmann, C.; Stier, A.C. Perception and Conflict in Conservation: The Rashomon Effect. *Bioscience* **2020**, *71*, 64–72. [CrossRef]
16. Elsawah, S.; Guillaume, J.H.; Filatova, T.; Rook, J.; Jakeman, A.J. A Methodology for Eliciting, Representing, and Analysing Stakeholder Knowledge for Decision Making on Complex Socio-Ecological Systems: From Cognitive Maps to Agent-Based Models. *J. Environ. Manag.* **2015**, *151*, 500–516. [CrossRef]
17. Özesmi, U.; Özesmi, S.L. Ecological Models Based on People's Knowledge: A Multi-Step Fuzzy Cognitive Mapping Approach. *Ecol. Model.* **2004**, *176*, 43–64. [CrossRef]
18. Vasslides, J.M.; Jensen, O.P. Quantitative vs. Semiquantitative Ecosystem Models: Comparing Alternate Representations of an Estuarine Ecosystem. *J. Coast. Res.* **2017**, *78*, 287–296. [CrossRef]
19. Ziegler, J.P.; Jones, S.E.; Solomon, C.T. Local Stakeholders Understand Recreational Fisheries as Social-Ecological Systems but Do Not View Governance Systems as Influential for System Dynamics. *Int. J. Commons* **2019**, *13*, 1035–1048. [CrossRef]
20. Gray, S.; Chan, A.; Clark, D.; Jordan, R. Modeling the Integration of Stakeholder Knowledge in Social–Ecological Decision-Making: Benefits and Limitations to Knowledge Diversity. *Ecol. Model.* **2012**, *229*, 88–96. [CrossRef]
21. Gray, S.A.; Gray, S.; de Kok, J.L.; Helfgott, A.E.R.; O'Dwyer, B.; Jordan, R.; Nyaki, A. Using Fuzzy Cognitive Mapping as a Participatory Approach to Analyze Change, Preferred States, and Perceived Resilience of Social-Ecological Systems. *Ecol. Soc.* **2015**, *20*, 11. [CrossRef]
22. Gray, S.; Jordan, R.; Crall, A.; Newman, G.; Hmelo-Silver, C.; Huang, J.; Novak, W.; Mellor, D.; Frensley, T.; Prysby, M.; et al. Combining Participatory Modelling and Citizen Science to Support Volunteer Conservation Action. *Biol. Conserv.* **2017**, *208*, 76–86. [CrossRef]
23. Henly-Shepard, S.; Gray, S.A.; Cox, L.J. The Use of Participatory Modeling to Promote Social Learning and Facilitate Community Disaster Planning. *Environ. Sci. Policy* **2015**, *45*, 109–122. [CrossRef]
24. Nyaki, A.; Gray, S.A.; Lepczyk, C.A.; Skibins, J.C.; Rentsch, D. Local-Scale Dynamics and Local Drivers of Bushmeat Trade. *Conserv. Biol.* **2014**, *28*, 1403–1414. [CrossRef] [PubMed]
25. *Puget Sound Regional Council 2050 Forecast of People and Jobs*; Puget Sound Regional Council: Seattle WA, USA, 2018. Available online: https://www.psrc.org/planning-2050/vision-2050 (accessed on 18 January 2023).
26. Ruckelshaus, M.; Essington, T.; Levin, P. Puget Sound, Washington, USA. In *Ecosystem-Based Management for the Oceans*; McLeod, K., Leslie, H., Eds.; Island Press: Washington, DC, USA, 2009; pp. 201–226.
27. Baker, J.; Biedenweg, K.; Birkeland, C.; Christie, P.J.; Dunagan, C.; Francis, T.; Gaydos, J.; Genther, K.; Georgiadis, N.; Howe, E.; et al. *Puget Sound Factbook Version 3*; University of Washington: Tacoma, WA, USA, 2015.

28. James, C.A.; Lanksbury, J.; Khangaonkar, T.; West, J. Evaluating Exposures of Bay Mussels (*Mytilus trossulus*) to Contaminants of Emerging Concern through Environmental Sampling and Hydrodynamic Modeling. *Sci. Total. Environ.* **2019**, *709*, 136098. [CrossRef] [PubMed]
29. Krahn, M.M.; Hanson, M.B.; Baird, R.W.; Boyer, R.H.; Burrows, D.G.; Emmons, C.K.; Ford, J.K.; Jones, L.L.; Noren, D.P.; Ross, P.S.; et al. Persistent Organic Pollutants and Stable Isotopes in Biopsy Samples (2004/2006) from Southern Resident Killer Whales. *Mar. Pollut. Bull.* **2007**, *54*, 1903–1911. [CrossRef] [PubMed]
30. Tian, Z.; Zhao, H.; Peter, K.T.; Gonzalez, M.; Wetzel, J.; Wu, C.; Hu, X.; Prat, J.; Mudrock, E.; Hettinger, R.; et al. A Ubiquitous Tire Rubber–Derived Chemical Induces Acute Mortality in Coho Salmon. *Science* **2021**, *371*, 185–189. [CrossRef] [PubMed]
31. Incardona, J.P.; Carls, M.G.; Holland, L.; Linbo, T.L.; Baldwin, D.H.; Myers, M.S.; Peck, K.A.; Tagal, M.; Rice, S.D.; Scholz, N. Very Low Embryonic Crude Oil Exposures Cause Lasting Cardiac Defects in Salmon and Herring. *Sci. Rep.* **2015**, *5*, 13499. [CrossRef] [PubMed]
32. Mongillo, T.M.; Ylitalo, G.M.; Rhodes, L.D.; O'Neill, S.M.; Noren, D.P.; Hanson, B.M. Exposure to a Mixture of Toxic Chemicals: Implications for the Health of Endangered Southern Resident Killer Whales. *NOAA Tech. Memo.* **2016**, *107*, 1–118. [CrossRef]
33. Levin, P.S.; Howe, E.R.; Robertson, J.C. Impacts of Stormwater on Coastal Ecosystems: The Need to Match the Scales of Management Objectives and Solutions. *Philos. Trans. R. Soc. B Biol. Sci.* **2020**, *375*, 20190460. [CrossRef]
34. Bernard, H.R. *Social Research Methods*; Sage: Los Angeles, CA, USA, 2011.
35. Carley, K.; Palmquist, M. Extracting, Representing, and Analyzing Mental Models. *Soc. Forces* **1992**, *70*, 601–636. [CrossRef]
36. Puget Sound Partnership The 2022-2026 Action Agenda for Puget Sound; Puget Sound Partnership. Available online: https://www.psp.wa.gov/2022AAupdate.php/ (accessed on 13 January 2023).
37. Harvey, C.J.; Williams, G.D.; Levin, P.S. Food Web Structure and Trophic Control in Central Puget Sound. *Estuaries Coasts* **2012**, *35*, 821–838. [CrossRef]
38. West, J.E.; O'Neill, S.M.; Ylitalo, G.M. Time Trends of Persistent Organic Pollutants in Benthic and Pelagic Indicator Fishes from Puget Sound, Washington, USA. *Arch. Environ. Contam. Toxicol.* **2017**, *73*, 207–229. [CrossRef]
39. Cabin, R.J.; Mitchell, R.J. To Bonferroni or Not to Bonferroni: When and How Are the Questions. *Bull. Ecol. Soc. Am.* **2000**, *81*, 246–248.
40. Oksanen, J.; Blanchet, F.G.; Kindt, R.; Legendre, P.; Minchin, P.R.; O'hara, R.B.; Simpson, G.L.; Solymos, P.; Stevens, M.H.H.; Wagner, H. Package 'Vegan': Community Ecology Package; R Package Version 2.5-6; 2017. Available online: https://cran.r-project.org/web/packages/vegan/vegan.pdf (accessed on 18 January 2023).
41. O'Connor, C.B. *Variation in Perceptions of the Stormwater Social-Ecological System in Puget Sound: Insights for Management Across the Land-Sea Interface*; University of Washington: Seattle, WA, USA, 2020; ISBN 9798662579101.
42. Ghermandi, A.; Nunes, P.A.D. A Global Map of Coastal Recreation Values: Results from a Spatially Explicit Meta-Analysis. *Ecol. Econ.* **2013**, *86*, 1–15. [CrossRef]
43. King, O.H. Estimating the Value of Marine Resources: A Marine Recreation Case. *Ocean Coast. Manag.* **1995**, *27*, 129–141. [CrossRef]
44. Poe, M.R.; Norman, K.C.; Levin, P.S. Cultural Dimensions of Socioecological Systems: Key Connections and Guiding Principles for Conservation in Coastal Environments. *Conserv. Lett.* **2013**, *7*, 166–175. [CrossRef]
45. Safford, T.G.; Norman, K.C.; Henly, M.; Mills, K.E.; Levin, P.S. Environmental Awareness and Public Support for Protecting and Restoring Puget Sound. *Environ. Manag.* **2014**, *53*, 757–768. [CrossRef]
46. Farr, B.D.; Otto, C.M.; Szymczak, J.E. Expert Perspectives on the Performance of Explosive Detection Canines: Operational Requirements. *Animals* **2021**, *11*, 1976. [CrossRef]
47. Jalkanen, J.; Vierikko, K.; Moilanen, A. Spatial Prioritization for Urban Biodiversity Quality Using Biotope Maps and Expert Opinion. *Urban For. Urban Green.* **2020**, *49*, 126586. [CrossRef]
48. Tarancón, A.A.; Kim, Y.-S.; Padilla, T.; Fulé, P.Z.; Meador, A.J.S. Co-construction of Ecosystem Services Management in Tribal Lands: Elicit Expert Opinion Approach. *Weather. Clim. Soc.* **2020**, *12*, 487–499. [CrossRef]
49. Reed, M.S. Stakeholder Participation for Environmental Management: A Literature Review. *Biol. Conserv.* **2008**, *141*, 2417–2431. [CrossRef]
50. Hemming, V.; Hanea, A.M.; Walshe, T.; Burgman, M.A. Weighting and Aggregating Expert Ecological Judgments. *Ecol. Appl.* **2020**, *30*, e02075. [CrossRef]
51. Crawford, B.A.; Olds, M.J.; Maerz, J.C.; Moore, C.T. Estimating Population Persistence for At-Risk Species Using Citizen Science Data. *Biol. Conserv.* **2020**, *243*, 108489. [CrossRef]
52. McAndrew, T.; Wattanachit, N.; Gibson, G.C.; Reich, N.G. Aggregating Predictions from Experts: A Review of Statistical Methods, Experiments, and Applications. *WIREs Comput. Stat.* **2020**, *13*, e1514. [CrossRef] [PubMed]
53. Siqueiros-García, J.M.; Lerner, A.M.; Eakin, H.C.; Aguilar, B.H. A Standardization Process for Mental Model Analysis in Socio-ecological Systems. *Environ. Model. Softw.* **2018**, *112*, 108–111. [CrossRef]
54. Levy, M.A.; Lubell, M.N.; McRoberts, N. The Structure of Mental Models of Sustainable Agriculture. *Nat. Sustain.* **2018**, *1*, 413–420. [CrossRef]
55. Puget Sound Partnership Puget Sound Vital Signs. Available online: https://vitalsigns.pugetsoundinfo.wa.gov/ (accessed on 18 January 2023).

56. Alexandridis, K.; Takemura, S.; Webb, W.; Lausche, B.; Culter, J.; Sato, T. Semantic Knowledge Network Inference Across a Range of Stakeholders and Communities of Practice. *Environ. Model. Softw.* **2018**, *109*, 202–222. [CrossRef]
57. Hämäläinen, R.P. Behavioural Issues in Environmental Modelling—The Missing Perspective. *Environ. Model. Softw.* **2015**, *73*, 244–253. [CrossRef]
58. Jones, N.A.; Ross, H.; Lynam, T.; Perez, P. Eliciting Mental Models: A Comparison of Interview Procedures in the Context of Natural Resource Management. *Ecol. Soc.* **2014**, *19*, 13. [CrossRef]
59. Singer, A.; Gray, S.; Sadler, A.; Olabisi, L.S.; Metta, K.; Wallace, R.; Lopez, M.C.; Introne, J.; Gorman, M.; Henderson, J. Translating Community Narratives into Semi-Quantitative Models to Understand the Dynamics of Socio-Environmental Crises. *Environ. Model. Softw.* **2017**, *97*, 46–55. [CrossRef]
60. Folke, C. Traditional Knowledge in Social–Ecological Systems. *Ecol. Soc.* **2004**, *9*, 7. [CrossRef]
61. Ludwig, D.; Mangel, M.; Haddad, B. Ecology, Conservation, and Public Policy. *Annu. Rev. Ecol. Syst.* **2001**, *32*, 481–517. [CrossRef]
62. McLain, R.J.; Lee, R.G. Adaptive Management: Promises and Pitfalls. *Environ. Manag.* **1996**, *20*, 437–448. [CrossRef] [PubMed]
63. Varjopuro, R.; Gray, T.; Hatchard, J.; Rauschmayer, F.; Wittmer, H. Introduction: Interaction between Environment and Fisheries—The Role of Stakeholder Participation. *Mar. Policy* **2008**, *32*, 147–157. [CrossRef]
64. Levin, P.S.; Williams, G.D.; Rehr, A.; Norman, K.C.; Harvey, C.J. Developing Conservation Targets in Social-Ecological Systems. *Ecol. Soc.* **2015**, *20*, 6. [CrossRef]
65. Shelton, A.O.; Samhouri, J.F.; Stier, A.C.; Levin, P.S. Assessing Trade-Offs to Inform Ecosystem-Based Fisheries Management of Forage Fish. *Sci. Rep.* **2014**, *4*, 7110. [CrossRef] [PubMed]
66. Stave, K. Participatory System Dynamics Modeling for Sustainable Environmental Management: Observations from Four Cases. *Sustainability* **2010**, *2*, 2762–2784. [CrossRef]
67. Carey, M.P.; Levin, P.S.; Townsend, H.; Minello, T.; Sutton, G.R.; Francis, T.B.; Harvey, C.J.; Toft, J.E.; Arkema, K.K.; Burke, J.L.; et al. Characterizing Coastal Foodwebs with Qualitative Links to Bridge the Gap between the Theory and the Practice of Ecosystem-Based Management. *ICES J. Mar. Sci.* **2013**, *71*, 713–724. [CrossRef]
68. Reum, J.C.P.; McDonald, P.S.; Ferriss, B.E.; Farrell, D.M.; Harvey, C.J.; Levin, P.S. Qualitative Network Models in Support of Ecosystem Approaches to Bivalve Aquaculture. *ICES J. Mar. Sci.* **2015**, *72*, 2278–2288. [CrossRef]
69. Voinov, A.; Bousquet, F. Modelling with Stakeholders. *Environ. Model. Softw.* **2010**, *25*, 1268–1281. [CrossRef]
70. Goulding, R.; Jayasuriya, N.; Horan, E. A Bayesian Network Model to Assess the Public Health Risk Associated with Wet Weather Sewer Overflows Discharging into Waterways. *Water Res.* **2012**, *46*, 4933–4940. [CrossRef]
71. Francis, T.B.; Levin, P.S.; Punt, A.E.; Kaplan, I.C.; Varney, A.; Norman, K. Linking Knowledge to Action in Ocean Ecosystem Management: The Ocean Modeling Forum. *Elementa Sci. Anthr.* **2018**, *6*, 63. [CrossRef]
72. Bednarek, A.T.; Wyborn, C.; Cvitanovic, C.; Meyer, R.; Colvin, R.M.; Addison, P.F.E.; Close, S.L.; Curran, K.; Farooque, M.; Goldman, E.; et al. Boundary Spanning at the Science–Policy Interface: The Practitioners' Perspectives. *Sustain. Sci.* **2018**, *13*, 1175–1183. [CrossRef] [PubMed]
73. Carwardine, J.; Klein, C.J.; Wilson, K.A.; Pressey, R.L.; Possingham, H.P. Hitting the Target and Missing the Point: Target-Based Conservation Planning in Context. *Conserv. Lett.* **2009**, *2*, 4–11. [CrossRef]
74. Puget Sound Partnership State of the Sound Report. Olympia, Washington. 2019. Available online: www.stateofthesound.wa.gov (accessed on 18 January 2023).

urban science

Article

An Analysis of Urban Ethnic Inclusion of Master Plans—In the Case of Kabul City, Afghanistan

Fakhrullah Sarwari * and Hiroko Ono

Department of Civil Engineering and Architecture, University of the Ryukyus, Okinawa 903-0213, Japan
* Correspondence: k208678@eve.u-ryukyu.ac.jp or fakhrullahsarwari@yahoo.com

Abstract: This study examines the history of master planning in Kabul city and how the government approaches segregation through urban planning. There are five master plans made for Kabul city, starting in 1964, with the others being conceived in 1970, 1978, 2011, and 2018. The civil war exacerbated the ethnic segmentation in Kabul city. The city is ethnically divided mainly among the different ethnicities of Pashtun, Tajik, and Hazara, which live in three different zones. The urban planning literature and master plans for Kabul city are surveyed, starting from the 1960s with the first master plan to the 2018 Kabul urban design framework. The first three master plans were designed on technical rather than communitive rationalities, with authoritarian planning. However, the fourth master plan of 2011 was developed through engagement with citizens and addressed the ethnic segregation in the city in abstract ways. The fifth masterplan, Kabul urban design framework, was a step backward in participatory planning; it also ignored the ethnic segmentation in the city by unequally distributing the future economic zones, administrative and facilities hubs. The past master plans have ignored the ethnic segregation of the city; there is no detailed plan on how the city will approach segregation through urban planning.

Keywords: Kabul city; ethnicity; urban segregation; urban planning; master plan; inclusive planning

1. Introduction

The 'divided city' is a term that embraces a variety of phenomena in which cities are separated geographically by ethnicity, race, income, and age [1–4]. An alarming number of cities, from social and ethnic segregation in the western cities to civil war in Beirut or political division in Berlin, are susceptible to intense intercommunal conflict and violence, reflecting ethnic or nationalist fractures [1]. Cities such as Jerusalem, Belfast, Johannesburg, Nicosia, Algiers, Sarajevo, New Delhi, Beirut, Hong Kong, and Brussels are urban arenas penetrated by deep intergroup conflict. In some cases (such as Jerusalem and Belfast), cities are the focal point for unresolved nationalistic ethnic conflict [4]. These cities can be a battleground between "homeland" ethnic groups, each proclaiming the city as their own [5]. The legitimacy of a city's political structures and decision-making rules are challenged by ethnic groups seeking an equal or proportionate share of power [4]. Such a flash point city can act as a significant and independent obstruction to the success of the more extensive regional and national peace process [4].

Discrimination, disadvantage, preferences, and social networkism all seem to play a role in segregation [6,7]. The actions of members of minority groups are restricted by discrimination and prejudice by the majority group. Even though most nations prohibit discrimination in the housing and employment markets and the public acceptance of minorities has risen, discrimination persists in daily life [8,9].

An ethnic group is distinguished from or defined by race, religion, national origin, or some combination of these characteristics that contribute to a sense of peoplehood [10]. The group is also defined by its members' interaction with people from other collectivities within the framework of a social system [11]. However, the term does not apply to the sense of community brought about by a shared socioeconomic condition [12]. The group may function as a social unit due to an internal idea of peoplehood or because other groups view them as distinct entities [13,14].

The ethnic group can result from in-migration to the city [15]. Ethnic groupings are interest groups that compete with other groups for resources in the public arena [11]. Conflict makes people feel threatened; the threat could be physical violence [15] or assimilation, resulting in a loss of cultural identity. As a result, there is frequently a strong need for internal coherence to preserve the cultural history of the group, and the aggregation is perceived as always being defensive in some way [14].

Minorities are typically isolated in overly segregated cities, with their segregation linked to education, employment, poverty, safety, and health care issues. As a result, the spatial segregation of minorities is typically viewed as undesirable [16,17]. Furthermore, in the case of Afghanistan and other countries affected by terrorism, ethnically and religiously segregated settlements are also easy targets for terrorist attacks. For example, district 13 of Shia minorities in Kabul city has been a target of terrorist groups.

The most important and influential sources on urban segregation (whether discussed in terms of ethnic, racial, cultural, or economic terms) have their origins in the post-1950s U.S.A. [2]. However, segregation as a process is as old as the history of urbanization [18]. The study of urban segregation in Afghanistan and Kabul city has not gained any traction, and there are not enough studies on urban segregation in Kabul city.

Afghanistan is a multicultural nation. According to Barth, an ethnic group satisfies the following four requirements: it reproduces biologically, shares essential cultural values, creates a space for social interaction and communication and is characterized by its definitions and those of others [19]. The four significant ethnicities of Afghanistan constitute 90 percent of the population: Pashtun, Tajik, Hazara, and Uzbek, and other ethnicities include Turkman, Baloch, Nuristani, Pashai, and others [20]. Afghan ethnicity is a fluid concept, making it enormously challenging to estimate the size of an ethnic group there [21]. Almost 99% of Afghans are Muslims, of which 75–80% are Sunnis, predominantly of the Arian race; the second majority are Shiite Muslims (with some minorities being Sunnis and Ismailis) of Turko-Mongol origin [22,23].

The ethnic urban landscape will challenge urban planners and government policymakers to achieve inclusive and sustainable cities. District 13, a majority Hazara ethnicity, is connected to the Maidan Wardak, Bamiyan, and central provinces of Hazarajat; the Hazara people have preferred to settle in the western section of Kabul [24]. The Tajik people have preferred to settle to the north of Kabul due to its proximity to Parwan and other Tajik majority provinces; Pashtun to the south and east of Kabul due to its proximity to the Pashtun settlement provinces [25]. See Figure 1. Each ethnic territory is connected through a highway to its ethnic regions. Kabul city's ethnic segregation, which increased following the aftermath of the civil war, makes the city's urban segmentation a unique case study.

More research on Afghanistan has been done on the anthropological aspects and history of ethnic segmentation at the national level. Less focus has been on urban segregation and how government should approach it. Moreover, the research that is focused on Kabul city has mainly analyzed the ethnic division during and after the civil war of 1992–1996. Samimi studied the historic fabrics of Herat in a western province of Afghanistan. They found the concentration of indigenous inhabitants in less accessible, well-preserved sites and the new incomers in redeveloped areas [26]. However, there is no classification of new incomers' sub-ethnic groups or origins [27].

In another study by Christine Issa, ethnic groups in Kabul city interact closely through migration. Still, their most substantial linkages are formed through familial ties, ethnic group ties, and regional ties. Typically, immigrants join kin-based communities that have already settled in the city. Here, people can communicate with others who belong to the same group using a mutually-beneficial understanding method. They join relatively small groups for social welfare and cooperative systems, which they need for self-identification. As a result, they reside in a specific area of Kabul [25]. An interpretation of the map drawn by this study is shown in Figure 1. Moreover, Sarwari found that Kabul city is not just segregated by ethnicity but is further divided at the neighborhood level into sub-ethnic communities of geographical communities based on the rural district they migrated from [28].

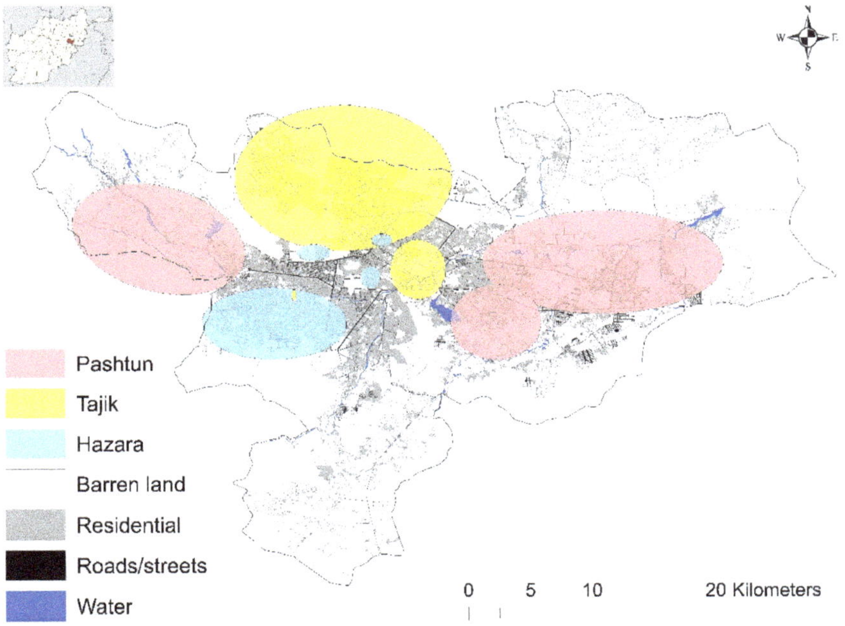

Figure 1. Kabul City Ethnic Map.

This research aims to provide a basis for urban planning and political discussion on segregation and planning for urban social sustainability in Kabul city. We conduct an extensive research overview of residential segregation. We aimed to discern if the government of Afghanistan has an urban plan for ethnic inclusion in the city by reviewing the past master plans. Because the master plan has been the only method of land-use planning for the city of Kabul, we compared the previous five master plans in this study. Furthermore, we aimed to find whether the city's segmentation has been a priority of urban policy. In doing so, we address the following main questions: What does recent research indicate about urban segregation in Kabul? Is segregation discussed in the Kabul city master Plan? What are the government's responses to segregation?

There are significant limitations in our study on segregation. Because segregation is an inevitably complex, fluid phenomenon, it can be challenging to determine what scales and variables are essential for addressing the topic. For example, mapping ethnic minority concentrations at the regional level may reveal very different findings from mapping minorities at the district or neighborhood level. A study by Sarwari found that D13 of Kabul city has a majority Hazara ethnicity, although, at the neighborhood level, it contains a mix of small communities of other ethnicities in the area [28]. Zooming out too far can obscure the most intense patterns of wealth and deprivation, neighborhood-level division, and the mix of different ethnicities living in a part of a segregated area. At the same time, a narrow focus on one neighborhood can miss wider urban or regional demographic patterns. Moreover, defining what constitutes a minority ethnicity in the country is a controversial topic because there has not been any proper population survey done on ethnic size in the country.

2. History of Master Planning Kabul

Afghanistan gained independence from the British in 1919. In 1925, the capital Kabul had a population of about 90,000. The 1940s and 1950s saw the foundation of the current Kabul city being built, a time when residential growth was actively occurring. After the 1950s, the street network was expanded, residential development continued, and Kabul, with a population of 380,000 in 1962, became the largest city in Afghanistan. With the increasing size and population of the city, the city needed the plan to guide its growth; hence, the first masterplan of Kabul city was created. A master plan is an overarching planning document and spatial layout which is used to structure land use development and establish a framework for city growth. Its scope can be as long as ten years [29–33].

There have been five master plans made for Kabul, starting in 1964, with the following plans being conceived in 1970, 1978, 2011, and 2018. Very little information is available for the first three masterplans, except a hand drawing in the Kabul municipality archives. Hence, it is hard to gather more information about the plans; however, researchers have digitized them [32–35]. Figure 2 shows the five master plans, and Table 1 shows comparisons of the master plans.

There has not been much research on urban planning history in Afghanistan. However, Calogero examined the politics of urbanization and various planning modes in Kabul. He classified planning into three categories: formal (concrete), informal (clay), and exceptionalist (mirror glass). He digitized the first three master plans, and the rationality of the plans was analyzed [33,36]. Calogero's study concludes that three decades of political turmoil and a century of modernization significantly weakened sovereignty.

Moreover, Beyer investigated Soviet urban planning, housing, and institution-building programs in Kabul throughout the 1960s. She examined Soviet technical assistance related to Afghanistan's housing and town planning projects and the competing coexistence of capitalism and communist development missions in Afghanistan. She concluded that the vision of Kabul city's first master plan and the expertise of international planners of the 1960s delivered an average experience of modern urban life for a minority of city residents until the progress was halted by conflict and war [29,36,37].

Mushkani has studied urban planning, the political system, and public participation in a century of urbanization in Kabul. The available urban planning literature concerning Afghanistan's urbanization process from 1919 to 2020 was investigated. In a century of urbanization in Kabul, the study identified urban planning patterns, the function of national, supranational, and multiplied Foucauldian powers in plan preparation and implementation, the plan's vision, and the approving authorities. Since the middle of the 20th century, decentralized supranational forces have governed urban planning; only in the early 21st century have residents begun to have a voice, and only in the context of unplanned settlement upgrading. Furthermore, citizens have not played a significant role in determining where they will live in the future; their perspectives are also neglected. Finally, during the past century of urbanization, the government has been the only institution in charge of approving urban plans, and technical rationality has dominated the urban regime [36].

Mushkani divided the past century of urbanization into three distinct paradigms: biopower, complementary, and sporadic urban planning. Biopower has progressively replaced brutal sovereign power, exerting constructive influence on the subject and administering and optimizing the individual's life through controls and inclusive regulations [38]. This planning mode started at the end of the 18th century and continued until the mid-20th century in Kabul. This paradigm change was evident in the implementation of many political, social, and economic reforms and the first significant urban development effort, which consisted of adopting a district-by-district development urban planning technique [36].

Complementary planning paradigm transformation occurred after the 1950s. Because of the rivalry between the two supranational Cold War superpowers, the East and West blocs, or the capitalist and communist blocs, and their intent to show their superior planning ability, some researchers referred to this paradigm as competitive planning. When the USSR invaded the nation, the complementary planning paradigm gradually evolved toward the East Bloc. The third paradigm emerged following the U.S. invasion of Afghanistan in 2001. Because too many simultaneous, frequently non-collaborative planning bodies were working for the country's rehabilitation, which was started and directed by centralized national and decentralized international powers, this paradigm is known as sporadic planning [36].

The first master plan was prepared in 1962 by Afghan experts with the support of advisors from the USSR. The plan expected 800,000 inhabitants in an area of 23,780 ha within 25 years [39]. The model did not show dedicated green space; however, the undeveloped mountainous areas and the belt along the Kabul River appear to have been dedicated open spaces. The 1964 master plan's future growth was a series of microregions assembled into four regions [33,37]. The microregion neighborhood comprises apartments housing 2500 to 5000 people, with essential services, local shops, a health center, a cinema, and a primary school [40]. Microregion One was completed in the 1960s, Two in the 1970s, and Three in the 1980s. Microregion Four was begun in the late 1980s; however, construction was abruptly abandoned in 1992 when the Najibullah regime was overthrown [32,33,37,41]. Figure 2a shows the first master plan.

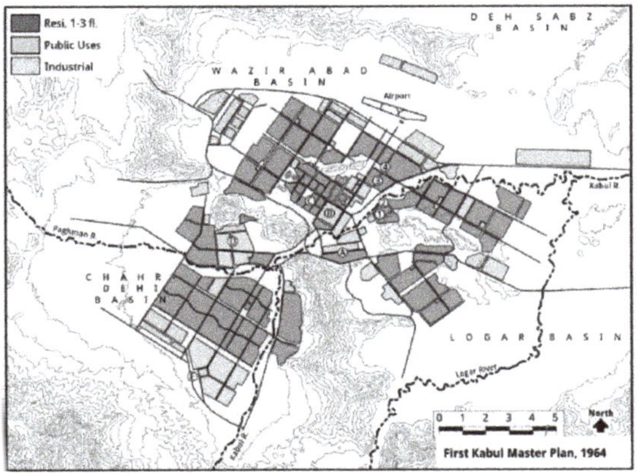

(**a**)

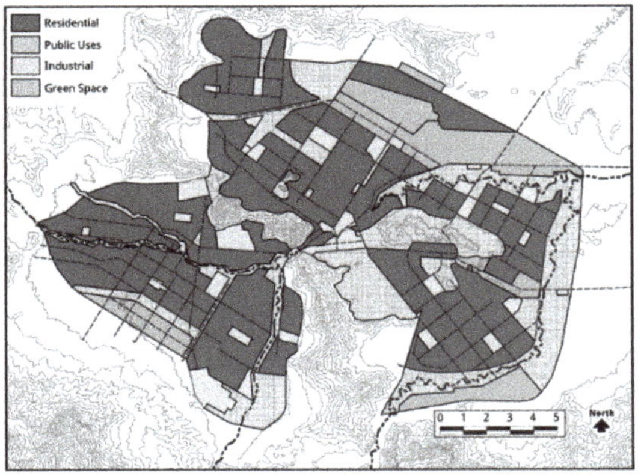

(**b**)

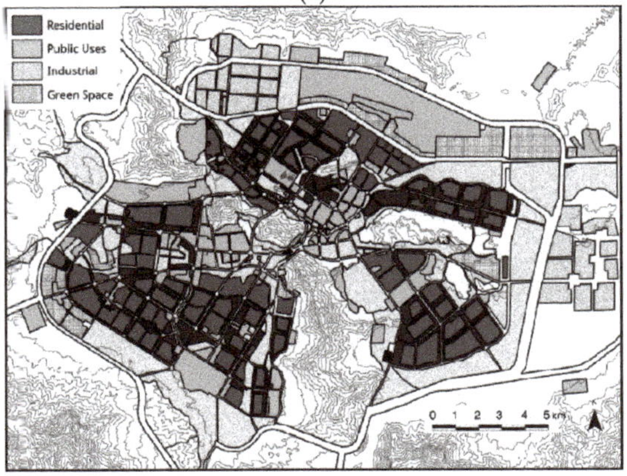

(**c**)

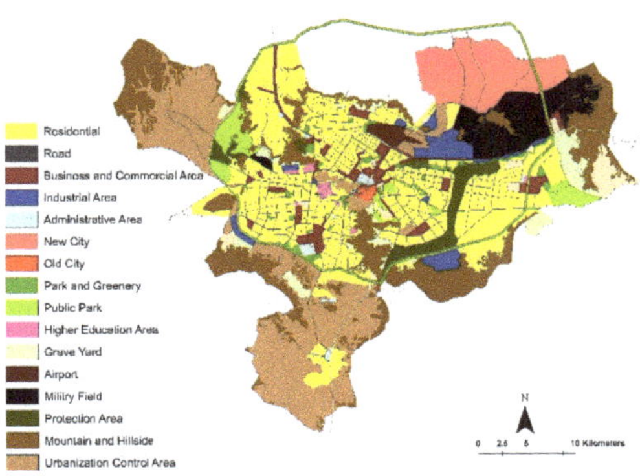

(**d**)

Figure 2. *Cont.*

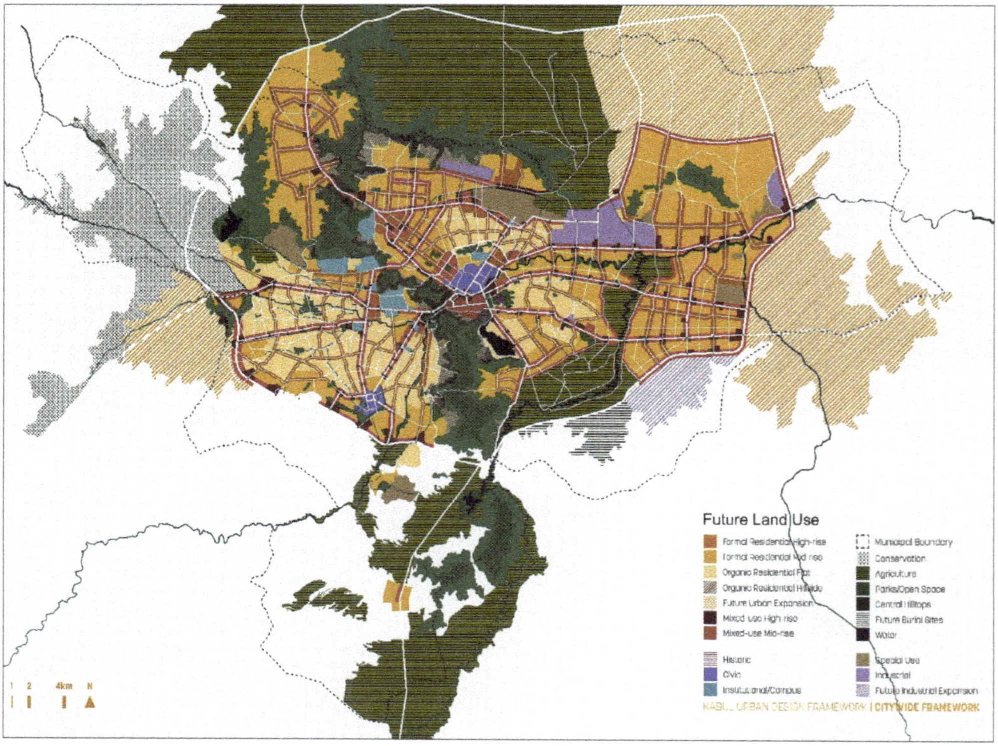

(**e**)

Figure 2. Kabul City Master Plans through the years: (**a**) First Master Plan of Kabul, 1964 (Calogero 2011); (**b**) Second Master Plan of Kabul, 1970 (Calogero 2011); (**c**) Third Kabul Master Plan (Calogero 2011), 1978; (**d**) Japan International Cooperation Agency (JICA) Master Plan, 2011; (**e**) Kabul Urban Design Framework (KUDF) 2018, Sasaki, Inc.

The second master plan Figure 2b was prepared in 1970 by Soviet experts and the United Nations Educational, Scientific and Cultural Organization (UNESCO). The plan covered 29,900 ha to accommodate 1.416 million residents [33,34,39,42]. It was designed to guide the growth of Kabul from 500,000 to about 800,000 people. As with contemporaneous Soviet master plans, substantial urban areas were set aside explicitly for green space and industry. In contrast to the first master plan, where all new residential development appeared to be based on microregions, this plan also included single-family housing districts similar to what Afghan planners had been doing from 1930 to 1961. Khair Khana, in the northeastern area, and Khushhal Khan Mena, were developed according to this plan in the 1970s as districts of single-family houses on the extreme northwest and west of Kabul [33].

Preparation of the third master plan started in 1976 and was approved in 1978. Figure 2c. The plan covered 32,330 ha for a population of two million in 2002 [33,42]. Three new features of this plan were essential. First, it promoted much higher residential densities to double the city's population without increasing the gross developed land area. Mid-rise densification only began in a few areas of Kabul after 2002 and only in private apartment districts or Shahrak. Second, most of the Logar riverway and part of the Kabul riverway were reserved as undeveloped aquifer recharge areas. To this day, the areas designated as aquifer recharge areas in the 1978 plan remain the primary sources from which the city pumps its urban water supply [33]. In 1999, a special decree was issued on implementing the Kabul master plan, which included changes to the third master plan. These changes were proposed by the Head of the Municipality and approved by the Head of the State. Eventually, a decision was taken to suspend the modified third master plan to look for a more responsive and implementable Kabul city plan [25,32,43].

The bloodless coup of the 1970s caused political unrest in Kabul. In 1979, Soviet forces invaded Afghanistan, and the invasion lasted until 1989. Many refugees entered the capital city during the civil war that followed the occupation, and Kabul's population reached 1.5 million in 1992. Kabul was the scene of a civil war that broke out following the fall of the communist government in 1992. As each ethnic group in the nation fought for government control, many people immigrated to Afghanistan's suburbs and other countries. Before the civil war, Kabul city was less segmented; however, the civil war caused the city to become segregated by ethnicity. The country's civil war and political unrest prevented the implementation of the master plan throughout the years; therefore, people erected homes informally instead. Informal settlements are defined as settlements which are built after 1978 without compliance with the third master plan and detail plans. The informal settlements occupied 76% of the existing residential area in 2008 [29,32,39,44,45].

International armies under the command of the United States invaded Afghanistan in 2001. The country saw a period of peace for a short time, and aides started pouring into the city; the city of Kabul saw a significant transformation as refugees from outside of Afghanistan returned to the nation and opted to reside there in large numbers, seeking jobs and opportunities. People from rural areas also moved to Kabul. As a result, the city's population dramatically increased. According to estimates, four million people live in the city, and 80 percent reside in informal settlements [46–49].

The Kabul city master plan of 1978 was revised by the Japan International Cooperation Agency (hereafter as JICA) at the request of the Kabul municipality. The fourth master plan was created in Japan and authorized by the president in 2012 using the previously-examined data from the Inter-continental Consultants and Technocrats study (2007–2008) and the Kabul Metropolitan Area Urban Development master plan (2008–2009), both financed by the JICA [4]. It suggested a population assumption of 3.7 million for the metropolitan region in the case of adequate infrastructure availability and projected as far ahead as 2025. The administration was unable to implement it [32]. See Figure 2d and Table 2.

The Kabul Urban Design Framework was created in 2018 by SASAKI, a Boston-based American company, in collaboration with the formerly-named Ministry of Urban Development and Housing Afghanistan (MUDH) in order to more sustainably guide the city's growth and draw private sector investment based on the vision of the president under the National Unity Government [50,51]. The urban framework serves as a bold road map, outlining how the president saw Kabul developing and expanding over the coming years. There are two corridor designs for key highways, Dar ul-Aman and Massoud boulevards, and a citywide framework [36,50]. See Figure 2e and Table 2.

After population growth and the government's failure to implement the master plan, Kabul's informal settlement has grown significantly. The majority favored relocating inside their ethnic groups, resulting in a divided city [25]. Thus, it has been divided among the different ethnic groups of the country; this has not just created a problem for the government in the distribution of resources, but it is also a problem for the social sustainability of the city's future.

Table 1. Master plans of Kabul.

Type	**1964**	**1970**	**1978**	**2011**	**2018**
Projected Population	0.8 million	1.2 million	2 million	6.7 million	8.8 million
Allowed floors	3	6	16	20	10+ floors
Participants	The French-led team of 15 expatriates	A UNDP-led team from 35 countries	USSR- led the team from C.Z., G.D.R., IN, and AU	JICA-led team with Afghanistan Government	American Sasaki Company-led with Afghanistan Government
Main Target	Focused building microregion housing	Apart from Microregions, they also include single-family housing, green space, and industrial area	Promotes much higher residen-tialdensities, riverways are reserved as undeveloped aquifer rechargeareas	Formulate a regional development plan focusing on harmonized development of the Dehsabz New city and the existing Kabul city.	Developing corridors, Specially for two main boulevards
Women inclusion	-	-	-	-	Civic institutions like education to physical interventions to create spaces for women in the city
Preservation of Heritage	-	-	-	Preserved Old city and the heritage buildings	Preserved Old city and heritage buildings, Including a few parks
Ethnic Inclusion	-	-	-	The plan tried to connect each ethnic settlement equally to the new Kabul city to minimize segregation in future	-

Table 2. Japan International Cooperation Agency (JICA) 2011, and Kabul Urban Design Framework 2018 Master Plans Chapters.

No	Kabul City Master Plan 2011	Kabul Urban Design Framework 2018
1	LAND USE PLAN AND LAND DEVELOPMENT STRATEGY • Procedure for land use planning . . . • Directions for physical development of Kabul city • Future urban structure of Kabul city • Land and built environment development strategy • Formulation of land use plan	Citywide Framework ❖ Design Concepts • Corridors as catalysts • Regenerate the central city • Expand to the east • Ring road as three zones • Integrate organic neighborhoods • Sustainable infrastructure • A network of higher education • Connect agriculture and the city • Cultural and ecological conservation • Create and cultivate public space • Empowering women in Kabul ❖ Citywide Systems • Growth & development • Landscape framework • Mobility • Infrastructure
2	TRANSPORT INFRASTRUCTURE DEVELOPMENT PLAN • Existing condition of urban transport infrastructure • Road traffic characteristics • Issues and strategy for transport Development in Kabul city • Traffic demand forecast • Road network development plan • Public transport and logistics development plan • Traffic management system development plan	Corridor Districts • Dar ul-Aman boulevard • Massoud boulevard
3	UTILITY INFRASTRUCTURE DEVELOPMENT PLAN • Water supply system development • Rainwater drainage system • Sewerage system • Power distribution system development plan • Telecommunication and I.C.T. • Solid waste management system development plan	Infrastructure Systems • Mobility • Water • Energy infrastructure • Solid Waste
4	PROJECT COST ESTIMATE • Total project cost • Project cost by sector • Project cost to be implemented by Kabul Municipality	Implementation strategies

3. Materials and Methods

The master plans of Kabul city were comparatively studied to find if ethnic segregation was considered in planning. We studied ethnic segregation research to find how other advanced segregated cities approached an ethnically segmented city. We studied the ethnicities through general cultural, anthropological, and social theories and then reviewed them in the case of Afghanistan. We also did a literature review on Afghanistan's ethnicities throughout the years and Kabul's urban community development history to determine how the city is ethnically divided into different zones.

We gathered data from Afghanistan organizations, such as Kabul Municipality District 13 land-use, UN-Habitat land-use for Kabul city, and Aerial imagery of Kabul city from Kabul Municipality and the Ministry of Urban Development and Land (MUDL). Data on the five master plans were acquired from the Ministry of Urban Development and

Land of Afghanistan and Kabul municipality. We combined the data into the Geographic information system (G.I.S.) with the data from our literature review; we created maps of Kabul city ethnic segregation and compared them with the master plans.

4. Result and Discussion

4.1. The First Three Master Pans

The first three master plans from 1962, 1965, and 1970 were developed during a period of soviet influence in Afghanistan. Hence, little data are available from this period. The Kabul city boundary was small at that time, with less segregation. With the passing years of wars and migration, the segmentation of the city increased [25]. Between the creation of the first master plan and the collapse of the Taliban government in Afghanistan in 2001, different regimes changed, and the capital Kabul went through turmoil; all the infrastructure was ruined [33,41], including the data for the city's development. There are little data available to discuss whether the planners have considered the importance of ethnic segregation in urban planning. However, the first three plans focused more on urban city center redevelopment, with more public housing in microregions [37]. In the 1978 plan, the western part of Kabul city was planned to be built as a medium high-rise residential, and it was planned to be developed using urban redevelopment; however, the western part of Kabul was an informal settlement zone for the Hazara ethnicity. These first three master plans developed following a hierarchical matrix that focused more on political than economic or social centralities [36]. During this same period, the western countries' approach to urban planning has been more incremental, in which public participation was critical [52]. However, in Kabul, none of these technical cooperation initiatives engaged citizen input at the decision-making and vision development stages; they might be characterized as authoritarian urban planning projects. With centralized planning, these cooperative instances aimed to systematize Kabul's future development based on technical rationality [4].

As per Mushkani, in the second paradigm, complementary planning, King Zahir gradually pushed for modernization. The supranational authorities of the East and West Blocs oversaw urban planning and urbanization and established institutions in architecture, urbanism, education, and even governance [36]. The master plan did not consider citizens' participation during plan preparation and implementation. Additionally, during the ratification process, locals were marginalized [36]. In this complimentary paradigm, the instances of the East and West blocs' involvement in the construction of urban space are pieces of a post-colonial narrative that sought to leverage sociopolitical and economic ties over technical support during the Cold War. They can also be studied further from the perspectives of modernity's exportation and production in culture and space, influenced by communist and capitalist political ideologies [53]. Several microregions and urban public parks are two evident results of the 1964 master plan as the formation of productive negotiation between participants in constructing urban space [54]. Hence, these historical studies of this era can show that the planning priority during this time was more political and centralized than the resident's ethnic inclusion.

4.2. JICA Master Plan 2011

The 2011 master plan by JICA addressed the problems of ethnic segregation in Kabul city. The plan addressed it as a problem and an opportunity as a potential source of dynamism and plural society: The city's future should be a planned development for mixed cultures and ethnicities for socioeconomic diversity. The approach was to equally connect each current ethnic settlement to the new city of Kabul Dehsabz. The city of Kabul draws visitors because it offers a variety of economical options. The plan stated that the new city in Dehsabz and the current Kabul city must jointly provide the broadest range of economic and employment opportunities with a complementary functional division between them [39].

The metropolitan area's regional artery transit system was suggested to address the demands that were anticipated to arise in tandem with regional growth. In order to promote the complementary growth of the segregated urban areas, it was planned to connect them, including the new urban areas that would be constructed in the new city and other outlying areas. The plan created numerous links between the old and modern Kabul cities for integrated growth of the capital region with a multi-centric urbanization design. It was intended to make it easier for the inter-regional traffic that moves through the Kabul municipality area, which was anticipated to grow as the Kabul municipality area expanded. It was intended to improve east-west and north-south connections without going through Kabul's center [39].

JICA, in collaboration with German and French companies, prepared the new Kabul city master plan; it was planned to provide housing for three million and was created collaboratively with the Kabul city master plan [32]. It was anticipated that the new metropolis would grow in tandem with Kabul. By reducing the strain of urbanization, the successful connection with the new city would enhance urban spaces in Kabul. The regional transportation network was expanded with a ring road and stronger east-west and north-south axes to achieve these criteria [39]. However, several issues with land ownership, infrastructure provision—particularly water supply and warlord predicaments—and a lack of political commitment helped to keep the development on paper [55].

There are currently no circular roads in Kabul; instead, the national and provincial highways that make up the primary arterial road network are radial roads that extend from the city center. Kabul city is divided into various segregated urban regions due to the topography and planned urbanization. Comparatively speaking, this urbanization plan is less effective at providing various urban services than a conurbation or urbanization along a corridor. To improve the effectiveness of urban areas, these segmented urban centers need to be appropriately connected [39]. The JICA plan was holistic and had a participatory approach toward the existing communities; however, the implementation never happened. The municipality took a long time to prepare and implement the neighborhood-detailed plan, partly due to a lack of institutional authority and political will, the absence of necessary urban regulations, an out-of-date land expropriation law, a lack of technical expertise, and warlord-related issues [42,56].

The focus of the JICA plan has been on developing a new city, connecting each ethnic settlement equally to the new city through a better route design, and making a ring road around Kabul city. However, there is no detailed plan for tackling ethnic segregation in the current city and the possible ethnic segmentation in the new city. It has been documented that the people of Afghanistan prefer to live among their kinship, tribe, and ethnicity [57,58]. We need an effective urban policy to develop a new city, and ethnic segregation should be a prime factor in developing a plan for a metropolitan area of Kabul.

4.3. Kabul Urban Design Framework (KUDF) 2018

The Kabul Urban Design Framework 2018, which is the current master plan of the city, differs from the JICA in two primary ways. First, as the name suggests, it focuses on the city's quality of urban design, leading to strategies that speak to regional issues but resolve them at the urban design scale. The second primary difference is that the Urban Design Framework proposes a growth strategy centered around the existing city. Growth is imagined as expanding the existing urban fabric rather than a new development in a satellite city. The design focuses on developing corridors in different city directions; the corridor is better for developing a citywide mix of cultures because people of different ethnicities invest in different parts of Kabul [35,50].

One significant difference in the 2018 plan has been the involvement of women's empowerment through urban planning. Many of these strategies are integrated into the more significant design concepts of this Urban Design Framework. This integration reflects the interconnectedness between a thriving Kabul and the success of women in the future. The plan has highlighted how critical it is to deliberately design for women in Kabul. These strategies range from policy proposals and improvements to civic institutions such as education to physical interventions to create spaces that recognize the unique needs of women in Afghanistan today [35]. Sasaki has identified four key areas to engage urban design. First, education: providing better schools and educational opportunities for women of all ages. Second, health and wellness: empowering women to lead more active lifestyles and providing access to adequate healthcare. Third, economic development: creating facilities to support women in the workforce and capacity-building to help women generate income. Fourth, accessibility: providing streets and transit networks where women can safely and comfortably travel across Kabul at all times of the day [35]. Hence, KUDF is an updated plan for designing a futuristic idea for women's safety and empowerment. Women, Business, and the Law 2019: A Decade of Reform employs eight indicators structured around women's interactions with the law as they begin, progress through, and end their careers. Afghanistan scored the lowest; it is hard for women to choose where to live and to own or rent immovable properties [59].

However, the plan ignored ethnic segregation in the city. Concerning public involvement, the framework is seen as a step backward from the 2011 master plan across the planning, designing, and decision-making processes. After the framework's approval in The High Council for Urban Development session, the president called for MUDH to provide Dari and Pashto translations of the framework. This symbolizes the totalitarian nature of the Afghan urban planning approach. A governmental institution was tasked to translate the framework of the signed master plan into local languages [36]. The framework's planned design for two main boulevards utterly disregarded the elements of the existing built environment by proposing to demolish the structures that front the streets and rebuild the intended corridors while the locals were not even aware of this intention [36,60]. Research has found that ethnicity is essential for the residents. Moreover, in the case of urban redevelopment, residents want to be relocated inside their current ethnic communities [28].

Figure 3 shows the future economic zones and significant facilities distribution per KUDF; the existing educational hub, which will also be the future of educational zones, government, and heritages, is towards the center and south of the city, partly overlapping with the Hazara ethnic settlement. Industrial and training, healthcare, new economies, agriculture, food processing, and ecology are planned to be developed towards the city's eastern side, which is occupied by a majority Pashtun ethnicity. Figure 3 shows that ethnic segregation was not a factor in developing the KUDF plan; the Tajik ethnic settlement has been ignored for equal distribution of future economies.

Future economic urban resources and facilities equal distribution for each ethnic settlement is crucial. The residents of each ethnicity can leave their ethnic settlement to visit other segregated areas for business and daily work to see each other and interact. In the previous republic government, unequal resource distribution was a significant factor in ethnic protest in Kabul city. Researchers argue that the distribution of resources can be a reason for interethnic conflict in urban areas. The role of urban policy in ethnically-polarized cities is problematic in that urban policymakers must contend with both the particular exigencies of daily urban life and broader ideological imperatives [4]. When ethnic and nationalist demands combine and have an enormous, persistent impact on distributional issues at the municipal level, this is known as urban "polarization," which is a more intense and intransigent kind of urban conflict [61,62]. One of the significant roles of urban policy in such circumstances is to ameliorate urban conflict through an acceptable allocation of urban resources across ethnic groups and neighborhoods [4].

In Kabul city, each ethnic settlement has been a representative of the country's ethnicity in general, any action towards the ethnically segregated areas will be taken as a political movement towards an ethnicity. Hence, the equal distribution of resources and urban planning is vital for each ethnicity so that they can see themselves as equal in the eye of the government. Political science theorists have de-emphasized applications to city governance and management, assuming that the city reflects the playing out of broader power distributions at a concrete level [4]. The study of urban policy provides the opportunity to connect broader political ideologies to specific urban territorial outcomes, which significantly affect group identity and perceived viability and, ultimately, the extent and manifestations of urban unrest and violence [4].

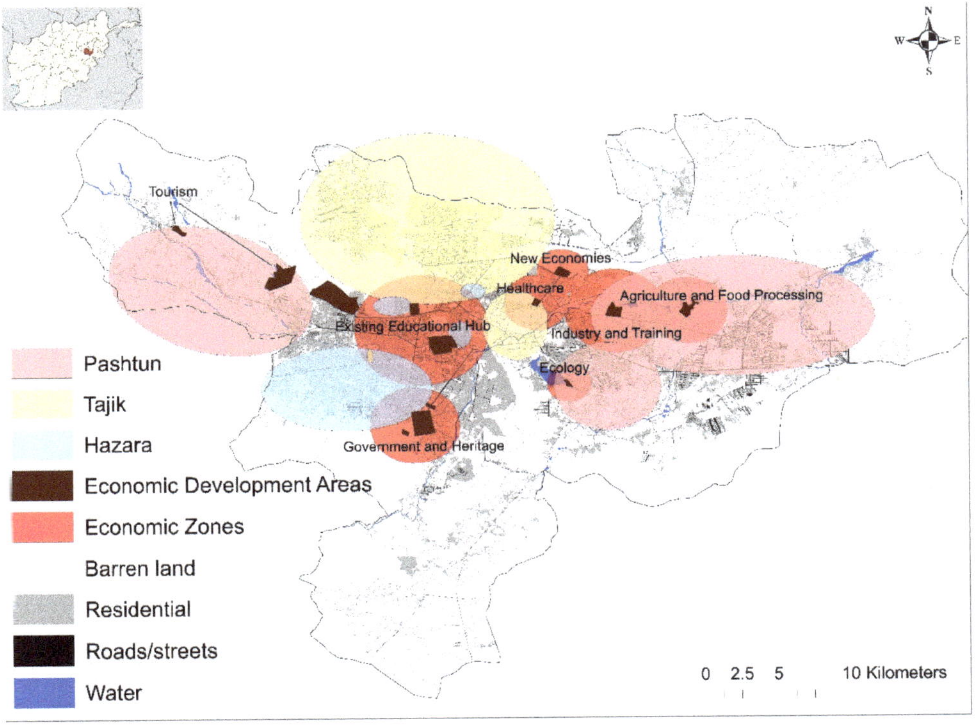

Figure 3. Intersection of Ethnic settlements buffer zones with existing and future facilities distributions according to KUDF.

Urban planning analysts have scrutinized the roles of urban professionals in local politics [62–65]. However, an urban policy most directly affects interethnic relations through its significant influence on the control of land and territoriality [66–69]. The land-use planning function of government is not a neutral allocator of advantage but rather constitutes, in most cities, a quiet distributive mechanism [70]. Hence, extending material benefits (urban services, social security insurance, and urban employment) may moderate intergroup material disparities [4].

KUDF has planned Kabul's future growth towards the east of the city for the following reasons: water resources that feed Kabul's aquifer tend to exist primarily to the west. To the north, a significant agricultural zone should be prioritized and protected. The south and north of the existing city feature steep mountains with limited opportunities for connectivity. All of these factors point to the east as the most attractive direction for development. Its relatively flat terrain, multiple points of access to the existing urban fabric, and water availability position it to absorb significant growth over the next 20 years [35]. The plan has focused chiefly on technical rationality, undermining the social impact of segregation and equal resource distribution. Without ethnic consideration and a proper plan for segregation, it will create more conflict and problems in implementing the project. Expanding to the east without a policy for de-segmentation will benefit one ethnicity, and the other two ethnic settlements will be isolated.

Kabul city urban policy planners should approach the city's redevelopment plan carefully, and the team leading the project should consist of diverse ethnicities. This is because when there is a single dominating ethnic group in control of the government apparatus, that ethnonational group's moral doctrines regarding sovereignty and cultural identity will merge with the state's urban policy. In other cases where a third-party overseer may govern the city or after the resolution of political conflict, the government is more likely to pursue a civic ideology that seeks to accommodate or transcend ethnonational ideologies [4]. Considering the history of Afghanistan and the interethnic conflict, and one of the ethnicities in control of the government, it will be challenging for urban planners to approach segregation in the city. If segregated areas are redeveloped through urban renewal for de-segmentation of the settlement, residents of the segregated area may consider it as ethnic cleansing or washing away the identity of their places.

Maintaining group identity is critical to interethnic relations in a polarized city and can be affected by urban government actions [4]. Ethnicity is the main reason for the national division in Afghanistan [71]. Studies have indicated more interethnic contact in areas with mixed ethnic groups, which is generally accompanied by knowledge spillover [72,73] and a decrease in ethnic prejudice [74]. Ethnic inclusion planning, which results in ethnicities interacting with each other daily, can help with the national peace process in Afghanistan. Urban accommodation without national peace would leave the city vulnerable and unstable, while national peace without urban accommodation would be unrooted in intergroup and territorial relations' practical and explosive issues [4]. However, it will be challenging for urban planners in Kabul—the paradox of maintaining ethnic identity and planning for social sustainability.

5. Conclusions

The first three master plans of 1964, 1970, and 1978 were developed during a more totalitarian regime; they focused on government-oriented planning without inclusive planning and public participation; they were designed based on technical rationality rather than communicative. The plans focused on microregions and urban renewal of the old city of Kabul. As the plans were more politically centrally oriented than toward social and economic centralities, they were eventually abandoned.

After the collapse of the communist regime in Afghanistan in 1992, Kabul city became the center of a civil war. Each ethnicity fought to control the government. Hence, the civil war exacerbated the ethnic segmentation in the city. Later, in 2001, with the United States-led invasion, Kabul city underwent massive reconstruction, and informal settlements grew as the government lacked institutional capacity. People migrated from rural areas to Kabul, and refugees returned to the city; most preferred settling among their ethnicities.

After the population increase in the city, the government of Afghanistan, with help from the Japan International Cooperation Agency (JICA), developed the new Kabul master plan in 2011. The plan has focused on connecting different parts of the city with a ring road and developing a new metropolitan city master plan for Kabul. The master plan significantly changed the city's traditional planning, engaging the citizens and social centrality. However, the plan has focused less on the segregation of Kabul city. It is planned to connect the current Kabul city ethnic settlement with the new Kabul city equally, to have an ethnically diverse new city, without any detailed plan. Because of a lack of institutional authority, political will, and required urban regulation, the Kabul municipality failed to implement it.

As a comprehensive plan for the city, Kabul's urban design framework (KUDF) ignored the city's segregation. The plan is a step backward from the 2011 plan regarding public participation. The framework ignores the existing built environment around the corridors, tearing down homes and communities. The future resource planning is not considered to be distributed equally across the city for each ethnic settlement; the result will be a more segregated city with unequal distribution of facilities and will enlarge the already existing inter-ethnic conflict of Kabul city. Urban planners and urban policymakers in the country should reconsider their approach. The past master plans ignored the critical factor of ethnic segregation in the city and how the government should approach that issue. There is no straightforward approach or urban policy for the segmentation of Kabul; this will make the city more polarized and dangerous for a sustainable future.

Urban policymakers should focus on ethnic inclusion in their planning because ethnicity has always been a sensitive issue for the citizens of Afghanistan. A city where different ethnicities can interact with each other daily through a better design is needed. More research is required on Afghanistan's ethnic segregation; the study needs to be continued at the regional and neighborhood levels because of the complexity of residential segmentation.

Author Contributions: F.S. and H.O. authors have contributed equally to the paper. All authors have read and agreed to the published version of the manuscript.

Funding: This research received no external funding.

Institutional Review Board Statement: Not applicable.

Informed Consent Statement: Not applicable.

Acknowledgments: We are thankful for the reviewers of this paper with insightful comments to improve this research. We are grateful to the Japan International Cooperation Agency for providing a scholarship for a master's degree in Japan and to the University of the Ryukyus for providing a tuition fee exemption during the Ph.D. of the Correspondence author. We want to thank the ministry of urban development and land (MUDL), Afghanistan, and Kabul Municipality for helping us gather the data. Moreover, we appreciate the help from our laboratory colleagues.

Conflicts of Interest: The authors declare no conflict of interest associated with this publication, and there has been no significant financial support for this work that could have influenced its outcome.

References

1. Scholz, D. Geteilte Stadte: Teilung Als Gegenstand Geographischer Forschung. *Geogr. Rundsch.* **1985**, *37*, 418–421.
2. Massey, D.S.; Denton, N.A. *American Apartheid: Segregation and the Making of the Underclass*; Harvard University Press: Cambridge, MA, USA, 1993.
3. McDaniel, A.; Goldsmith, W.W.; Blakely, E.J. Separate Societies: Poverty and Inequality in U.S. Cities. *Contemp. Sociol.* **1993**, *22*, 377. [CrossRef]
4. Bollens, S.A. Urban Policy in Ethnically Polarized Societies. *Int. Political Sci. Rev.* **1998**, *19*, 187–215. [CrossRef]
5. Esman, M.J. Two Dimensions of Ethnic Politics: Defense of Homelands, Immigrant Rights. *Ethn. Racial Stud.* **1985**, *8*, 438–440. [CrossRef]
6. Allen, J.P.; Turner, E. Black–White and Hispanic–White Segregation in U.S. Counties. *Prof. Geogr.* **2012**, *64*, 503–520. [CrossRef]
7. Johnston, R.; Poulsen, M.; Forrest, J. The comparative study of ethnic residential segregation in the U.S.A., 1980–2000. *Tijdschr. Econ. Soc. Geogr.* **2004**, *95*, 550–569. [CrossRef]
8. Meyer, S.G. *As Long as They Don't Move Next Door: Segregation and Racial Conflict in American Neighborhoods*; Rowman and Littlefield: Lanham, MD, USA, 2000.
9. Myers, S.L. Closed Doors, Opportunities Lost: The Continuing Costs of Housing Discrimination. By John Yinger. New York: Russell Sage Foundation, 1995. 452p. $29.95. *Am. Political Sci. Rev.* **1996**, *90*, 927–928. [CrossRef]
10. Gordon, M. *Assimilation in American Life: The Role of Race, Religion, and National Origins*; Oxford University Press: New York, NY, USA, 1964.
11. Cohen, A. (Ed.) *Introduction: The Lesson of Ethnicity*; Tavistock Publications: London, UK, 1974; ISBN 9781136418853.
12. Glazer, N. The Universilization of Ethnicity. *Encounter* **1975**, *44*, 8–17.
13. Chinoy, E. *Society*; Random House: New York, NY, USA, 1967.
14. Stern, D. Ethno-Ideological Segregation and Metropolitan Development. *Geoforum* **1990**, *21*, 397–409. [CrossRef]
15. Boal, F. *Ethnic Residential Segregation*; Herbert, D., Johnston, R., Eds.; Social Areas in Cities; John Wiley: Chichester, UK, 1978.
16. Cutler, D.M.; Glaeser, E.L. Are Ghettos Good or Bad? *Q. J. Econ.* **1997**, *112*, 827–872. [CrossRef]
17. Massey, D.S.; Condran, G.A.; Denton, N.A. The Effect of Residential Segregation on Black Social and Economic Well-Being. *Soc. Forces* **1987**, *66*, 29. [CrossRef]
18. Marcińczak, S.; Tammaru, T.; Novák, J.; Gentile, M.; Kovács, Z.; Temelová, J.; Valatka, V.; Kährik, A.; Szabó, B. Patterns of Socioeconomic Segregation in the Capital Cities of Fast-Track Reforming Postsocialist Countries. *Ann. Assoc. Am. Geogr.* **2015**, *105*, 183–202. [CrossRef]
19. Barth, F. (Ed.) *Ethnic Groups and Boundaries: The Social Organization of Cultural Difference*; George Allen & Unwin: London, UK, 1969.

20. United States Central Intelligence Agency. *Ethnolinguistic Groups in Afghanistan*; United States Central Intelligence Agency: Washington, DC, USA, 1997.
21. Khan, S.; Shah, I.A. Salience of Qawm, Ethnicity, in Afghanistan: An Overview. *Cent. Asia J. Univ. Peshawar* **2014**, *75*, 15–49.
22. Karimi, M.A. *"The West Side Story": Urban Communication and the Social Exclusion of the Hazara People in West Kabul*; University of Ottawa: Ottawa, ON, Canada, 2011.
23. Dittmann, A. Recent Developments in Kabul's Shar-e-Naw and Central Bazaar Districts. *ASIEN* **2007**, *104*, 34–43.
24. Sokefeld, M. (Ed.) *Spaces of Conflict in Everyday Life*, 1st ed.; Transcript Verlag: Bielefeld, Germany, 2015.
25. Issa, C. Architecture as a Symbol of National Identity in Afghanistan. Myth and Reality in the Reconstruction Process of Kabul. *Geogr. Rundsch. Int. Ed.* **2006**, *2*, 27–32.
26. Samimi, S.A.B.; Maraschin, C. Built Heritage and Urban Spatial Configuration: The Case of Herat, Afghanistan. *GeoJournal* **2022**, *2022*, 1–20. [CrossRef]
27. Samimi, S.A.B.; Ando, T.; Kawish, K. A Study on distribution of houses with domical vault roofs in Herat city—Afghanistan. *J. Archit. Plan. (Trans. A.I.J.)* **2018**, *83*, 2221–2228. [CrossRef]
28. Sarwari, F.; Ono, H. *A Study of Kabul City Urban Community Development*; Proceedings of the Architectural Institute of Japan, Kyushu; Issue 61, No. 718; March 2022. Available online: https://jglobal.jst.go.jp/en/detail?JGLOBAL_ID=202202258835983047 (accessed on 5 October 2022).
29. Beyer, E. Building Institutions in Kabul in the 1960s. Sites, Spaces and Architectures of Development Cooperation. *J. Archit.* **2019**, *24*, 604–630. [CrossRef]
30. Ghobar, M.M. *Afghanistan Dar Masir-i-Tarikh (Afghanistan in the Course of History)*; Government Press: Kabul, Afghanistan, 1967.
31. Gregorian, V. *The Emergence of Modern Afghanistan: Politics of Reform and Modernization, 1880–1946*; Stanford University Press: Redwood City, CA, USA, 1969.
32. Jica, J.I. *The Study for the Development of the Master Plan for the Kabul Metropolitan Area in the Islamic Republic of Afghanistan: Final Report, Executive Summary*; RECS International Inc.: Brussels, Belgium, 2009.
33. Calogero, P.A. *Planning Kabul: The Politics of Urbanization in Afghanistan*; University of California: Berkeley, CA, USA, 2011.
34. Arez, G.J.; Dittmann, A. *Kabul: Aspects of Urban Geography*; Peshawar Press: Peshawar, Pakistan, 2005.
35. Sasaki; Mudh. *Kabul Urban Design Framework: Executive Summary, Citywide Framework, Dar Ul-Aman Boulevard, Massoud Boulevard, Infrastructure Systems and Implementation Strategies*; Sasaki: Boston, MA, USA, 2018.
36. Mushkani, R.A.; Ono, H. Urban Planning, Political System, and Public Participation in a Century of Urbanization: Kabul, Afghanistan. *Cogent Soc. Sci.* **2022**, *8*, 2045452. [CrossRef]
37. Beyer, E. Competitive Coexistence: Soviet Town Planning and Housing Projects in Kabul in the 1960s. *J. Archit.* **2012**, *17*, 309–332. [CrossRef]
38. Burchell, G.; Gordon, C.; Miller, P. *The Foucault Effect: Studies in Governmentality*; University of Chicago Press: Chicago, IL, USA, 1991.
39. JICA. *Draft Kabul City Master Plan—Product of Technical Cooperation Project for Promotion of Kabul Metropolitan Area Development Sub Project for Revise the Kabul City Master Plan*; JICA: Tokyo, Japan, 2011.
40. French, R.A. Kyiv. 2022. Available online: https://www.britannica.com/place/Kyiv (accessed on 5 October 2022).
41. Esser, D. *Who Governs Kabul? Explaining Urban Politics in a Post-War Capital City*; Crisis States Research Paper: London, UK, 2009.
42. Habib, A.J.; Kidokoro, T. Institutional Framework for Collaborative Urban Planning in Afghanistan in View of the Transferring Process of International Urban Planning Systems. *Int. J. Built Environ. Sustain.* **2015**, *2*, 177–182.
43. Viaro, A. What Is the Use of a Master Plan for Kabul? In *Development of Kabul: Reconstruction and Planning Issues*; Mumtaz, B., Noschis, K., Eds.; Comportements: Lausanne, Switzerland, 2004; pp. 153–164.
44. Jardine, E. The Tacit Evolution of Coordination and Strategic Outcomes in Highly Fragmented Insurgencies: Evidence from the Soviet War in Afghanistan. *J. Strateg. Stud.* **2012**, *35*, 541–572. [CrossRef]
45. Kakar, H. The Fall of the Afghan Monarchy in 1973. *Int. J. Middle East Stud.* **1978**, *9*, 195–214. [CrossRef]
46. Government of the Islamic Republic of Afghanistan. *State of Afghan Cities*; Government of the Islamic Republic of Afghanistan: Kabul, Afghanistan, 2015; Volume 1.
47. Chaturvedi, V.; Kuffer, M.; Kohli, D. Analysing Urban Development Patterns in a Conflict Zone: A Case Study of Kabul. *Remote Sens.* **2020**, *12*, 3662. [CrossRef]
48. Hidayat, O.; Kajita, Y. Influences of Culture in the Built Environment; Assessing Living Convenience in Kabul City. *Urban Sci.* **2020**, *4*, 44. [CrossRef]
49. Shahraki, S.Z.; Hosseini, A.; Sauri, D.; Hussaini, F. Fringe More than Context: Perceived Quality of Life in Informal Settlements in a Developing Country: The Case of Kabul, Afghanistan. *Sustain. Cities Soc.* **2020**, *63*, 102494. [CrossRef]
50. Pieprz, D. *Extreme Urbanism: A View on Afghanistan, Session 1—Planning for Urban Afghanistan*; The Lakshmi Mittal and Family South Asia Institute at Harvard University: New Delhi, India, 2020.
51. Sasaki Associates, I. *Kabul Urban Design Framework*; Sasaki Associates Inc.: Kabul, Afghanistan, 2021; Available online: https://www.sasaki.com/projects/kabul-urban-design-framework/ (accessed on 10 October 2022).
52. Lane, M.B. Public Participation in Planning: An Intellectual History. *Aust. Geogr.* **2005**, *36*, 283–299. [CrossRef]
53. Lefebvre, H. *The Production of Space*; Wiley-Blackwell: London, UK, 1992.

54. Mushkani, R.A.; Ono, H. The Role of Land Use and Vitality in Fostering Gender Equality in Urban Public Parks: The Case of Kabul City, Afghanistan. *Habitat Int.* **2021**, *118*, 102462. [CrossRef]
55. Hamidi, H. Kabul New City: Afghanistan's Forgotten Development Dream. The Diplomat. 2020. Available online: https://thediplomat.com/2020/04/kabul-new-city-afghanistans-forgotten-development-dream/ (accessed on 10 October 2022).
56. Abdullaev, K.N. Warlordism and Development in Afghanistan. In *Beyond Reconstruction in Afghanistan: Lessons from Development Experience*; Montgomery, J.D., Rondinelli, D.A., Eds.; Palgrave Macmillan: London, UK, 2004.
57. Azoy, W.G. *Buzkashi: Game and Power in Afohanisfan*, 2nd ed.; Waveland Press: Prospect Heights, NY, USA, 2003.
58. Rasanayagum, A. Afghanistan: A Modern History; Monarchy, Despotism or Democracy? In *The Problems of Governance in Muslim Tradition*; I.B. Taurus Co., Ltd.: New York, NY, USA, 2005; p. 201.
59. International Bank for Reconstruction and Development. *Women, Business and the Law*; International Bank for Reconstruction and Development: Washington, DC, USA, 2019.
60. Sadid, B.A. Pathology of Kabul City Design Framework. *8am*. 2020. Available online: https://8am.media/eng/ (accessed on 30 October 2021).
61. Boal, F.W.; Douglas, J.N. *Integration and Division: Geographical Perspectives on the Northern Ireland Problem*; Academic Press: London, UK, 1982.
62. Benvenisti, M. *Conflicts and Contradictions*, 1st ed.; Villard: New York, NY, USA, 1986.
63. Friedmann, J. Planning in the Public Domain: Discourse and Praxis. *J. Plan. Educ. Res.* **1989**, *8*, 128–130. [CrossRef]
64. Friedmann, J. Why Do Planning Theory? *Plan. Theory* **2003**, *2*, 7–10. [CrossRef]
65. Forester, J. Planning in the Face of Power. *J. Am. Plan. Assoc.* **1982**, *48*, 67–80. [CrossRef]
66. Murphy, P.A. Regional Development Policy in New South Wales: Contemporary Needs and Options. *Aust. Q.* **1989**, *61*, 262. [CrossRef]
67. Yiftachel, O. *Planning a Mixed Region in Israel: The Political Geography of Arab-Jewish Relations in the Galilee*; Avebury: Aldershot, UK, 1992.
68. Gurr, T.R. Why Minorities Rebel: A Global Analysis of Communal Mobilization and Conflict since 1945. *Int. Political Sci. Rev.* **1993**, *14*, 161–201. [CrossRef]
69. Williams, R.M. The Sociology of Ethnic Conflicts: Comparative International Perspectives. *Annu. Rev. Sociol.* **1994**, *20*, 49–79. [CrossRef]
70. Harvey, D. *Social Justice and the City*; Edward Arnold: London, UK, 1973.
71. Roy, O. Afghanistan: Back to Tribalism or on to Lebanon? *Third World Q.* **1989**, *11*, 72. [CrossRef]
72. Audretsch, D.B.; Feldman, M. R&D Spillovers and the Geography of Innovation and Production. *Am. Econ. Rev.* **1996**, *86*, 630–640.
73. Glaeser, E.L. Learning in Cities. *J. Urban Econ.* **1999**, *46*, 254–277. [CrossRef]
74. Pettigrew, T.F.; Tropp, L.R. How Does Intergroup Contact Reduce Prejudice? Meta-Analytic Tests of Three Mediators. *Eur. J. Soc. Psychol.* **2008**, *38*, 922–934. [CrossRef]

urban science

MDPI

Article

Geographically Weighted Regression-Based Predictions of Water–Soil–Energy Nexus Solutions in Île-de-France

Walid Al-Shaar [1,*], Olivier Bonin [1], Bernard de Gouvello [2,3], Patrice Chatellier [4] and Martin Hendel [5,6]

1 LVMT—Laboratoire Ville Mobilité Transport, Université Gustave Eiffel, 77420 Champs sur Marne, France
2 CSTB—Centre Scientifique et Technique du Bâtiment, 77447 Marne-la-Vallée, France
3 LEESU—Laboratoire Eau Environnement et Systèmes Urbains, 77420 Champs-sur-Marne, France
4 IMSE—Instrumentation, Modélisation, Simulation et Expérimentation, Université Gustave Eiffel, 77420 Champs sur Marne, France
5 Département Santé Energie Environnement (SEN), ESIEE, Université Gustave Eiffel, 93162 Noisy le Grand, France
6 LIED—UMR8236 Laboratoire Interdisciplinaire des Energies de Demain, CNRS—Centre National de la Recherche Scientifique, Université Paris Cité, 75006 Paris, France
* Correspondence: walid.al-shaar@enpc.fr

Abstract: Due to global urbanization, urban areas are encountering many environmental, social, and economic challenges. Different solutions have been proposed and implemented, such as nature-based solutions and green and blue infrastructure. Taking into consideration exogenous factors that are associated with these solutions is a crucial question to assess their possible effects. This study examines the possible explanatory factors and their evolution until the year 2054 of several solutions in the Île-de-France region: wastewater heat-recovery, surface geothermal energy, and heat-mitigation capacities of zones. This investigation is performed by a series of statistical models, namely the ordinary least squares (OLS) and the geographically weighted regressions (GWR), integrated within a geographic information system. The main driving factors were identified as land use/land cover and population distribution. The results show that GWR models capture a large part of spatial autocorrelation. Apropos of prediction results, areas with low, medium, and high potential for implementing specific solutions are determined. Furthermore, the implementation capacities of solutions are compared with the demand depicted as the need for slowing down the effects of surface urban heat islands and the dependence on fossil energy. Moreover, the heat mitigation capacities are not at all times distinctively linked to human activities. Further investigations are needed to discover the remaining possible reasons, particularly air quality, water, vegetation, and climate change.

Keywords: water–soil–energy nexus; nature-based solutions; green and blue infrastructure; heat recovery; surface geothermal energy; geographically weighted regression; Île-de-France

1. Introduction

Due to rapid urbanization, European cities are encountering a lot of environmental, social, and economic challenges [1]. The European Commission [2] summarized these challenges as risk and disaster management, poverty and social equity, degradation of natural and green areas, degradation of water and air quality, impacts of urbanization on human health, climate change adaptation, provision of ecosystem services, cost-effective infrastructure (as the initial capital expenses and the cost of on-going operations represent about 3.8% of the global gross domestic product in the year 2013), and the sustainable development.

Nature-based solutions (NBS), as well as green and blue infrastructure (GBI), emerge as cost-effective solutions and answers for these challenges [3] and will result in multiple benefits at the environmental and socioeconomic level, as well as for society and for public health [2,4]. These solutions, seeking sustainable development, could be implemented by harnessing the beneficial hidden sides of nature and infrastructure to turn socioeconomic and environmental challenges into innovative benefits and convenience. Despite the low number of research papers discussing the participation of stakeholders in NBS in Europe up to the year 2020 (e.g., 76 publications in all European countries; 5 in France), the European Union Research and Innovation (R&I) agenda on nature-based solutions pointed out that "*Europe will become a world leader both in R&I and in the growing market for nature-based solutions*" [1,2]. To this end, understanding the effectiveness of these solutions is necessary before implementation; this requires a systemic approach that incorporates the technical measures' regulatory, governing, financial, business, social, and geographical sides. In gross, the benefits can be depicted particularly in terms of: (a) exhaustive energy consumption (EC) and the questions of renewable sources of energy, (b) mitigation of heat and environmental risks, and (c) the economic burden of operating, protecting, and maintaining the traditional non-natural infrastructure, particularly for water drainage and management. More precisely, these solutions, considered to be urban innovations, stem from interactions between different domains such as: (i) soil–energy interactions, for instance, the geothermic production [5–7]; (ii) wastewater–energy interactions, such as the fatal HR [5,8,9]; (iii) green spaces–air temperature interactions: urban cooling, and enhancing air quality [10,11]; (iv) soil–water interactions: water management, flood mitigation, and water recharge [12]; (v) soil–vegetation interactions: carbon storage [10,11], etc.

However, according to the scientific literature review, no systemic study has investigated all the possible interactions in the urban context, but only limited disciplinary approaches. Examples of these studies are those of NBS and GBI that focus on urban cooling and water management—the studies of local energy production (as fatal heat recovery (HR), geothermic production, and solar energy), and those examining the solutions to enhance air quality. Furthermore, almost all these solutions require space to be implemented, and this could lead to possible competition for space between these solutions. In addition, the existing territories are highly constrained by their histories, topographic specificities, and urban configurations: suggesting marginal evolution rather than a design from scratch. This spatial competition is also not well recognized or analyzed. The aforementioned spatial analysis is essential for decision support, especially when comparing the alternative solution in an integrated policy–science–society framework [1]. This paper identifies the elements of three interacting spheres that are relevant to study urban innovations: (a) soil: the historical actor in urban development, space allocation, vegetation, imperviousness, albedo; (b) water: a crucial element necessary for life, but also a possible threat (storms, floods, etc.), stock and flow processes; and (c) energy: a crucial element, hard to produce in an urban setting, hard to store (batteries) and to transport over large distances. It is noteworthy to mention that both water and energy must be saved in the context of sustainable development. In the context of this research, all the solutions that cross at least two dimensions of the water–soil–energy nexus (WSE nexus) are envisioned. Attention must be drawn to the fact that NBS and GBI are part of the WSE nexus. Figure 1 shows the most commonly known WSE interactions.

According to the literature review presented in the following subsection and to the best of the authors' knowledge, the links between existing WSE solutions and urban characteristics, as well as the potential for further implementation of WSE solutions, are still unclear. As a result, these relationships are not well recognized and understood by institutional, political, and ruling authorities and official decision-makers, especially when they enact energy/environment-based policies. As a consequence, this could generate suboptimal sustainable development decisions.

Therefore, this paper aims to analyze the links between existing WSE solutions and urban characteristics in conjunction with the assessment of the potential for further implementation of WSE solutions in the Île-de-France area. This analysis aims to provide a clear picture of WSE solutions–urban interactions for the governing bodies and local authorities. Several hypotheses are proposed for validation. Among these suppositions, it is hypothesized that the dense urban areas (with high population density) represent good candidates for the implementation of wastewater HR solutions. In the same direction, medium to low urban areas are suggested to represent good candidates for the implementation of surface geothermic solutions. The hypotheses are also extended to assume that the implementation of some WSE solutions (notably HR) is attributed, in general, to political decisions rather than to factors from the urban context. Regarding limitations, this paper analyzes only the WSE nexus in the urban context and the potential of implementing these solutions from a spatial context, particularly the renewable energy sources and the WSE solutions to reduce the land surface temperature.

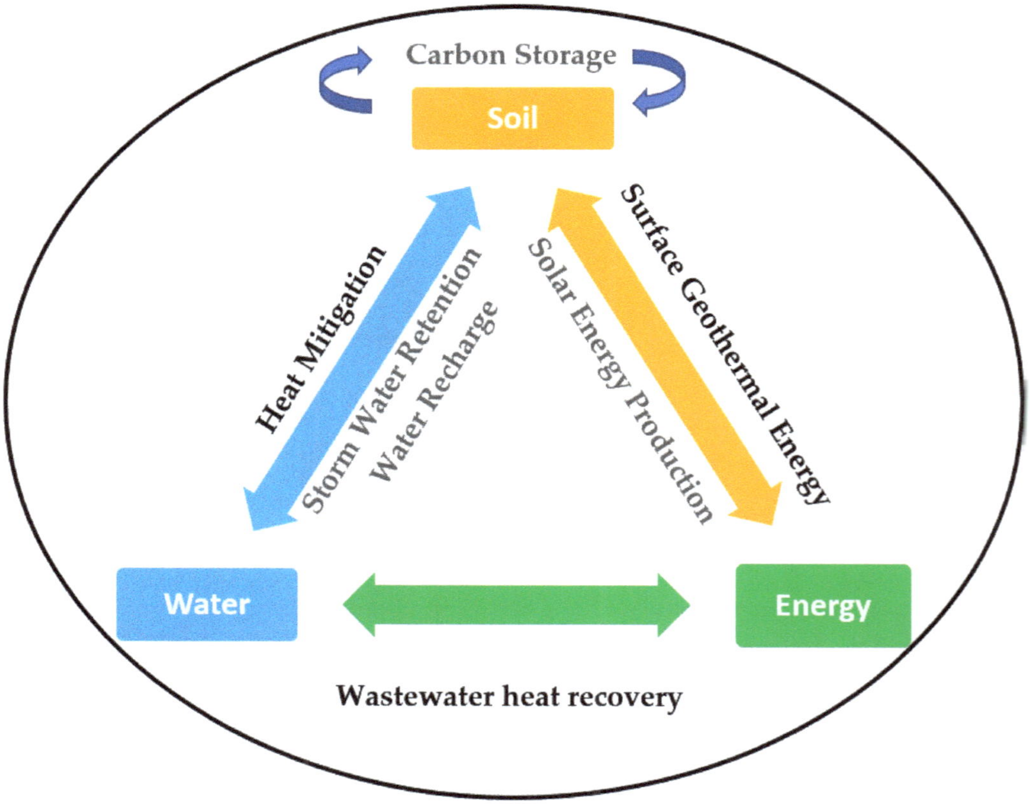

Figure 1. Water–soil–energy nexus. Source: own elaboration.

The solutions are designed to mitigate the risk of climate change, floods, and air pollution and to ensure that biodiversity protection is not investigated for further predictions. In particular, the impact of green roofs and vegetated facades on the quality and temperature of the air, as well as the effects of solar energy on fossil energy consumption, are not investigated due to limited available data and information about the explanatory variables. Several previous studies have investigated the different naturally and artificially established interactions between soil, water, energy, and vegetation. An overview of recent relevant studies is presented as follows. Various studies examined the effectiveness of operating different NBS (vegetation in particular) for better water management, ecosystem integrity, and biodiversity protection. For instance, Pander et al., Schindler et al., and Funk et al. [13–15] examined the effects of reconnecting rivers to floodplains, by removing barriers along the river course in the Danube floodplain in Germany and in different countries of Europe on reducing the soil erosion, flood mitigation, and water purification. Similarly, the effects of green infrastructure, such as (i) reforestation, (ii) green roofs, (iii) maintaining vegetation cover and good soil structure, and (iv) the construction of shallow water bodies with vegetation, such as wetlands, on water management have been analyzed in the studies of Perni and Martínez-Paz in Spain [16], Majidi et al. in Bangkok, Thailand [17]; Soana et al. in Italy [18], and Harrington et al. in Ireland [19], respectively. Furthermore, the importance of green corridors and their associated drainage capacities in protecting the rail infrastructure, particularly in the case of extreme weather events, were examined by Blackwood et al. [12]. In addition, the green infrastructures/infrastructure network, such as the green corridors, ensure the security of regional ecology by maintaining the ecosystem's integrity and conserving biodiversity [20,21]. Other studies examined the cost efficacy of NBS, in the manner of afforestation, in supporting biodiversity and protecting the ecosystem services, such as in the study by Seddon et al. [22], and in the vein of using high-albedo-pervious pavement material to slow down global warming and to mitigate heat and climate change as in the study of Majidi et al. [17]. Similarly, Blackwood et al. [12] explained how green corridors could support climate change adaptation and protect the transport infrastructure (e.g., rail services), specifically during extreme weather events.

Recent analyses were carried out to examine how to increase the sustainability of the use of matter and renewable energy [23]. For instance, the HR from hot commercial, industrial, and domestic wastewater to reuse for residential heating demands, using technologies such as heat pumps and heat exchangers, was examined in different studies [24–26]. Dürrenmatt and Wanner [27] indicated that the process of HR is explained by two phases, (1) the thermal conductivity between the wastewater and the pipe wall, which temporarily store the heat, and (2) the recovery of energy by heat transfer from the wall of the pipe with the help of a heat exchanger and a heat pump. The wastewater HR process could be implemented at different scales as the wastewater treatment plants [9,28], the sewer network level, and the building level [24]. The authors pointed out that the HR process could supply heat energy to individual buildings as well as to large communities. With a further detailed inspection, the wastewater treatment plants have a high potential to provide heat energy and feed urban areas, however, the efficiency of the system integration depends on the timeline grid of energy supply and demand as well as the spatial contiguity between the treatment plant and the beneficiaries [9,29]. On the other hand, surface geothermal energy (SGE) also represents a new way to reduce the consumption of fossil energy, particularly for home heating and cooling [6,7]. The SGE is used for air conditioning, such as cooling applications, as well as heating needs [7]. The authors explained the setting up of the system as the deployment of a ground source heat pump system composed of a horizontal ground heat exchanger connected to a reversible geothermal heat pump that is connected to a chilled ceiling panel system.

In order to analyze the links between existing WSE solutions and urban characteristics of the surrounding areas as well as to predict the potential for future implementation of WSE solutions, the following summarized sequence is respected: (1) choosing a terrain: part of the Île-de-France region; (2) examining some implemented WSE solutions (e.g., HR from hot wastewater, SGE, forest development . . .); (3) characterizing the intensity (e.g., HR) or the effectiveness (e.g., heat mitigation (HM)) of the WSE solutions; (4) setting-up a statistical model (geographically weighted regression GWR) between the WSE characteristics and the urban characteristic (e.g., population, infrastructures . . .); (5) assessing the potential for further implementation of WSE solutions with the help of predictions for urban characteristics in the horizon of the year 2054; and (6) analyzing the possibilities for implementing the WSE solutions against the spatial demand represented by the need for this solutions. The year 2054 was selected (a) since it represents, from the current year, a sufficient time horizon to implement and evaluate the strategies proposed in this research, and (b) since the land use is projected for this year using the Cellular Automata Markov Chain Model (CAMCM) based on available data. With regards to GWR, these models are frequently used to link air temperature [30] and the variation of the surface urban heat island [31] to their influencing factors, such as the distance from water bodies and the vegetation cover.

Nonetheless, and to the best of the author's knowledge, there is no research study that employs the GWR in holistically examining the WSE nexus with its driving factors.

For the brief, this paper aims to (1) analyze the extensive (i.e., forestry development) and intensive (e.g., HR of wastewaters) components of WSE solutions, and (2) identify bottlenecks (e.g., saturation of urbanization in the north: forests are very unlikely to be developed there) and perspectives for the Greater Paris region. The paper is organized as follows. After the introduction, the second Section addresses the selection of the study area, the used research methodology and the data collection methods. The third Section presents the structure and the characteristics of the used models. The fourth Section summarizes and discusses the results and the fifth Section summarizes the main concluding remarks of the study and its limitations, and proposes new topics for future research.

2. Materials and Methods

Examining the possible benefits of implementing solutions from the WSE nexus, as the relationships that could be established between energy production and consumption, usage and management of water and soils, is the main focus of this study, which was undertaken as part of a larger research effort, the "Wise Cities" project. This project examines the potential benefits of implementing solutions in this area both from the technical and managerial sides. It focuses mainly on the relationships between water and soil and between water and energy. This Section consists of two parts: the first one refers to the selection of the study area, and the second part presents the adopted research methodology, the needed data, and the data collection technique. The study area, which covers the most developed urban zone of the Île-de-France region, extends over 9261 square kilometers. As the envisioned work presented in this paper is the assessment of several water–soil–energy solutions, such as the fatal HR and the recovery of SGE, the area of interest, which covers a large area of the Île-de-France region, was selected because different types of these solutions have been implemented there in several places [5,32,33], and the required data are mostly available. The southeastern part of the Île-de-France region, which is outside the main agglomeration of Paris and for which the data are not available, is not included in the area of interest. Nonetheless, the study area is large enough to have proper data in order to be adopted to conduct the analysis. Regarding the analysis, the study area was selected to identify the key drivers of WSE solutions and to assess the possibility to predict their evolution. The predictions are envisioned for the horizon of the year 2054. Figure 2 shows the area of interest.

The methodology consists of predicting and analyzing the potential changes in some essential elements of the water–soil–energy nexus, such as the SGE, as well as recovering heat energy from wastewater and afforestation/reforestation to assess the possibility of implementing these concepts, especially in high-demand areas. Applying these measures intends, in general, to reach sustainable development as the main objective. In a more detailed way, the objectives within the WSE nexus are depicted by (i) reducing the need for fossil energy by developing natural and recycled sources of energy, such as the SGE and the HR from hot wastewater, (ii) enhancing the use of renewable sources of energy, and (iii) reducing the land surface temperature and limit the emergence of the surface urban heat island phenomenon. In this perspective, the main factors to be examined are (i) EC, (ii) SGE, (iii) HR from wastewater, and (iv) the capacity for HM. To this end, the identification of explanatory variables, as well as the use of statistical and regression models as the correlation analysis, ordinary least squares (OLS), geographically weighted regressions (GWR), spatial autocorrelation, and variance analyses (ANOVA), could give an overview of the significant explanatory variables of dependent variables, their effect sizes, the possibility to calculate spatial regressions, and the possibility to predict the future changes/evolutions of these variables. At greater length, the identification of explanatory variables is conducted through logical reasoning of the common driving factors. The correlation analysis, which is the part that comes next and represents the first data filter, is used to refine the data by keeping only the representative variable and removing the remaining factors among the observed collinear variables.

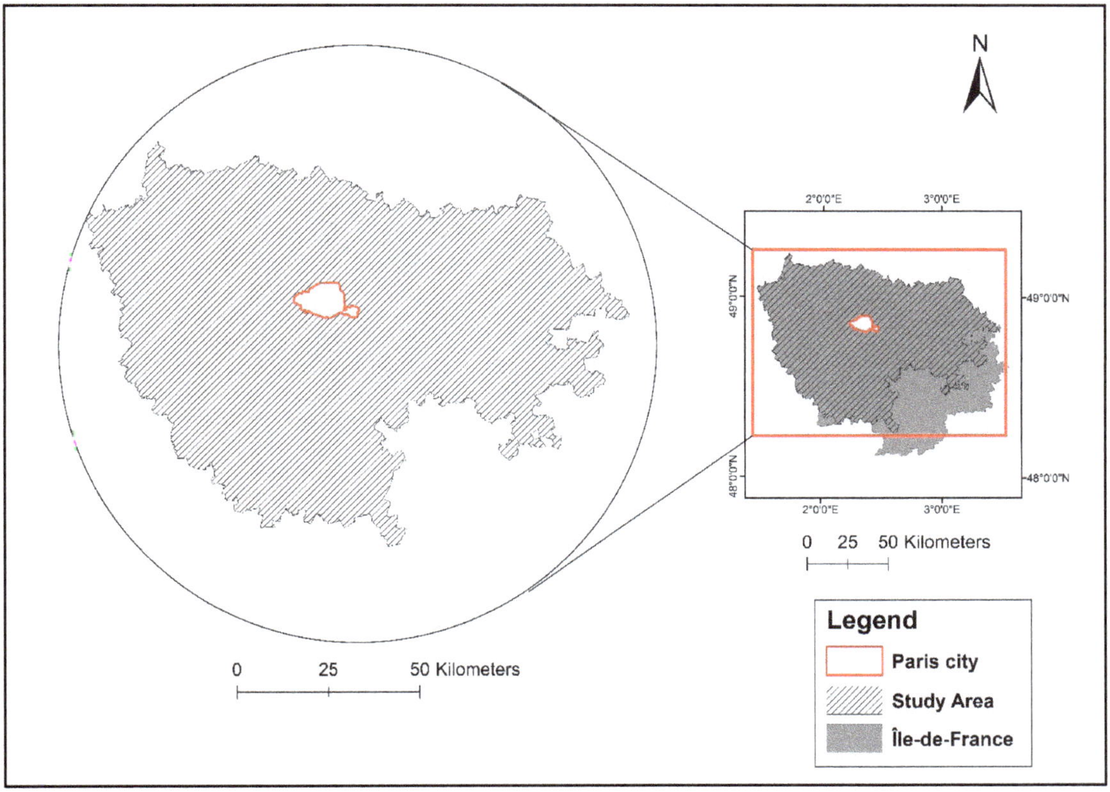

Figure 2. The selected study area.

The following step is the selection of the variables by conducting the second data refinement process presented by the ordinary least square regression model (OLS).

A particular variable can be modeled (or predicted) using the OLS, one of the general linear modeling techniques, if this variable can be explained (as a regressive dependence relationship) by other explanatory variables [34] as indicated in the following equation:

$$y_i = \beta_0 + \sum_{j=1}^{n} \beta_j X_{ij} + \varepsilon_i \tag{1}$$

where β_0, intercept; β_j, regression coefficients; X_{ij}, explanatory variables; ε_i, random errors with mean 0 (uncorrelated with one another).

Different trials are conducted to check the best-performing OLS model by checking the adjusted coefficient of determination (R2), as well as the multi-collinearity of variables and the overall multi-collinearity of the model, in addition to the spatial distribution of the standard residuals and their z-scores. The spatial autocorrelation is used to measure the correlation among residuals caused by their spatial location [35]. Usually, this test is used to check the existence of interactions between the residuals that are induced on the grounds of the spatial location of the observations. The spatial autocorrelation is a necessary measure to know whether the autocorrelation is significant or not. This latter concept could give information where the value of a residual is dependent or not on the values of neighboring residuals, so then the scale of the spatial dependence is determined by the geographic range within it the autocorrelation is significant. The following step is the application of the geographically weighted regression (GWR) in order to determine the regression relationship between the dependent variables and their explanatory variables, and also to establish a basis for the prediction process of future changes. The GWR is similar to the OLS model, however, the difference is depicted by taking the values of variables for each of the spatial features individually according to their spatial distribution. The GWR was developed as a solution for the problem indicating that the regression model estimated over an entire study area could not sufficiently cover local variations [35]. A particular variable can be modeled (or predicted) at different spatial spots using the GWR model based in a dependence-regressive way on several explanatory variables following Equation (2).

$$y_i = \beta_{0(u_i,v_i)} + \sum_{j=1}^{n} \beta_{j(u_i,\, v_i)}\, X_{ij} + \varepsilon_i \quad (2)$$

where u_i and v_i, spatial coordinates of observation I; β_0, intercept at point (u_i, v_i); β_j, regression coefficients at point (u_i, v_i); X_{ij}, the explanatory variables at point (u_i, v_i); ε_i, random error with mean 0.

The sequence of these processes, used to predict the changes in the dependent variables, is presented in Figure 3.

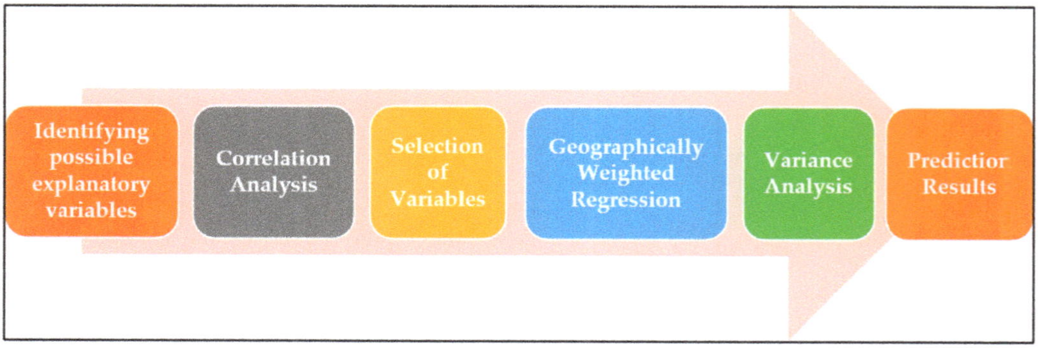

Figure 3. The structure of the methodology used.

Along the same lines and starting with the first part of identifying the possible explanatory variables, a structure of logical relationships is proposed to be analyzed. For instance, the wastewater HR and the SGE were hypothetically supposed to affect the EC in addition to the area of industrial land use and the demographic population. It is also hypothesized that the HR from wastewater is highly dependent on population and industrial areas where most of the hot wastewater is generated. It is also supposed that the SGE, which is usually implemented in the gardens of individual homes, is highly dependent on population and land use type. By way of explanation, the estate prices in industrial areas are usually less than in other urban zones. Moreover, the green areas were also supposed to affect the HM capacity of spatial zones, which could, in turn, affect the land surface temperature (LST) in addition to the consumption of energy and the areas of green zones. Figure 4 shows a structure of relationships between the aforementioned factors.

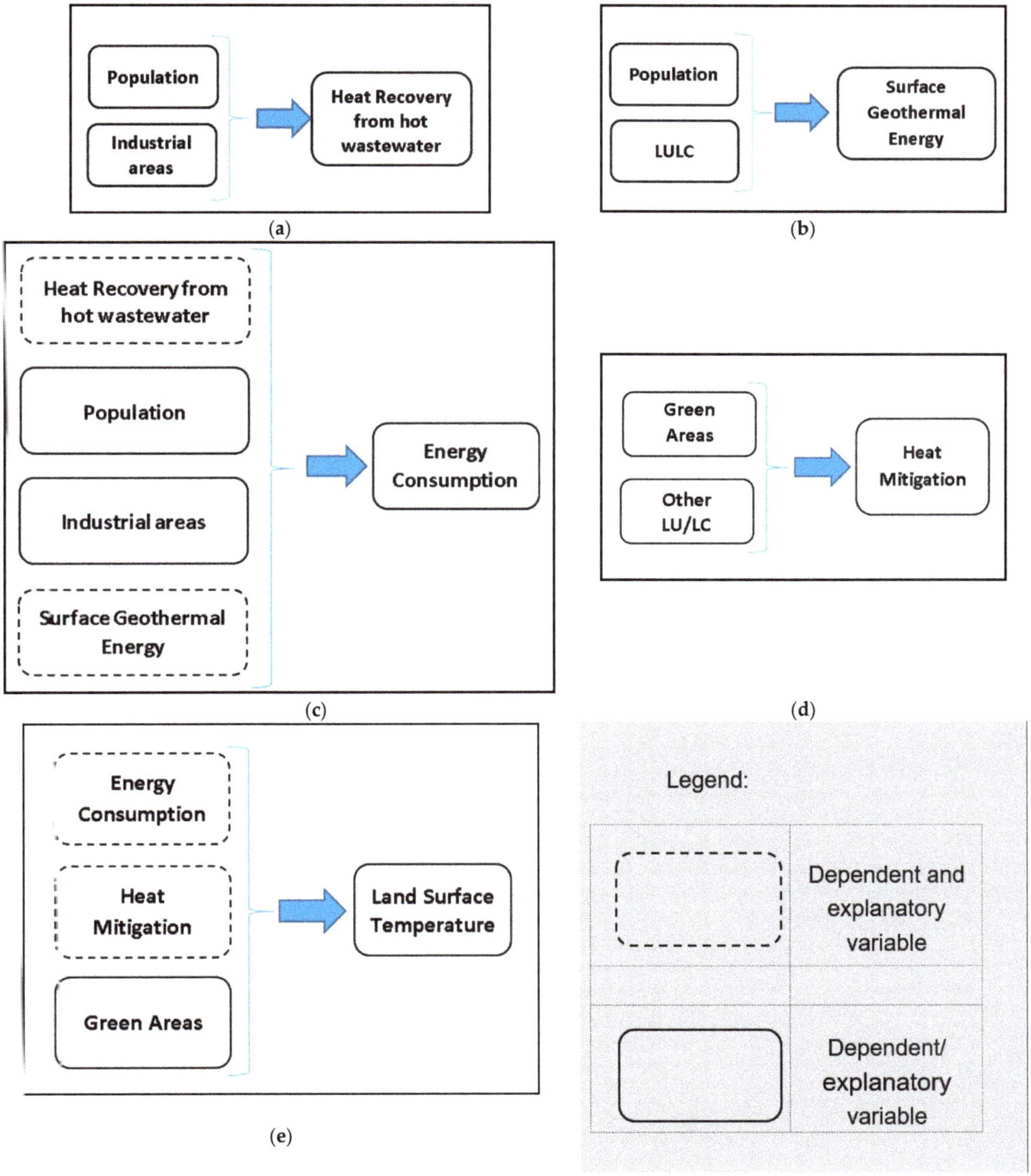

Figure 4. Structure of relationships between possible determining factors and dependent factors: (**a**) heat recovery from hot wastewater; (**b**) surface geothermal energy; (**c**) energy consumption; (**d**) heat mitigation; and (**e**) land surface temperature.

Accordingly, the data of (i) population, (ii) land use/land cover (LULC), (iii) SGE, (iv) HM index, (v) EC, (vi) HR from hot wastewater, and (vii) LST index were collected from different sources. The data of population for the year 2017 were collected from the population database of INSEE (2021) website. The Urban Atlas [36] provides the LULC maps for the Île-de-France area for the years 2006, 2012, and 2018. The data on wastewater heat recovery for the year 2015 indicates a concentric form of high capacities at the center with low capacity for the neighboring suburban areas. The potential of SGE available only for a small area in the Île-de-France region in the year 2022 was collected by digitizing the published distribution map of the *Bureau de Recherches Géologiques et Minières* [33]. In the same context, it is important to note that the data of SGE was extended by conducting a regressing projection of the ordinary least square (OLS) to cover the whole study area. The pattern of these data is mostly a ring and extends slightly to neighboring areas where the existence of many individual homes with private gardens where the SGE systems could be installed. The HM indexes for the Île-de-France region for the year 2016 were collected in a rasterized form from the Naturvation project [10]. These values were aggregated, by average, to the community's level. The pattern of these data follows that of the distribution of forests. The available data of EC for the year 2018, as well as that of HR from hot wastewater for the year 2015 in the Île-de-France region, were collected from the website of the Réseau d'Observation Statistique de l'Énergie [5]. The EC pattern shows a downward radial trend of distribution from high values at the center to low values in peripheral areas. The land surface temperature indexes for the year 2021 were collected from the "Ilots de Chaleur Urbains" data provided by *Institut Paris Région* [37]. The texture of the distribution of LST indexes during daytime is almost the opposite of that of HM. Similar to the EC pattern, the distribution of LST indexes at night follows a downward path of distribution from high indexes in the center to low indexes at the fringes. Figure 5 presents the maps of the collected data.

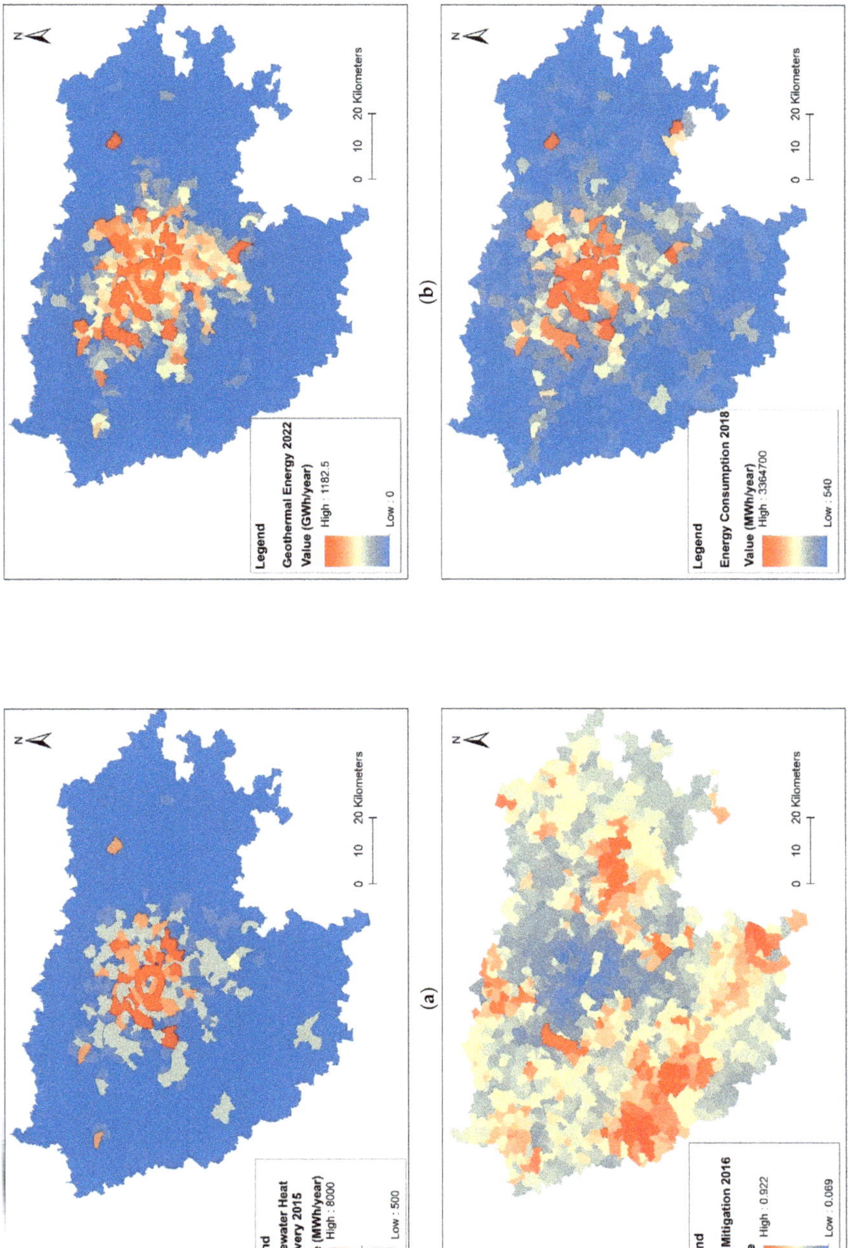

Figure 5. *Cont.*

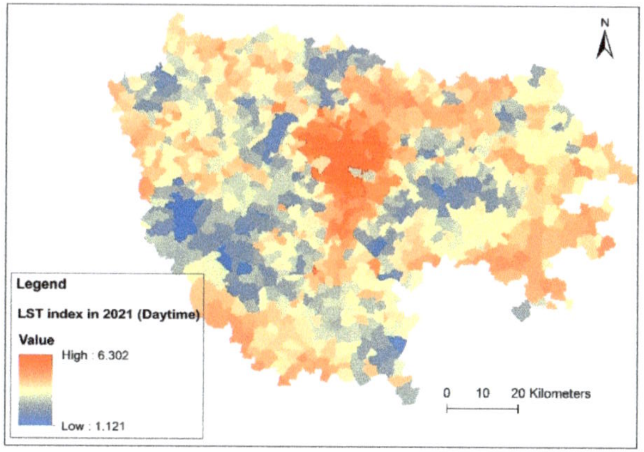

(e)

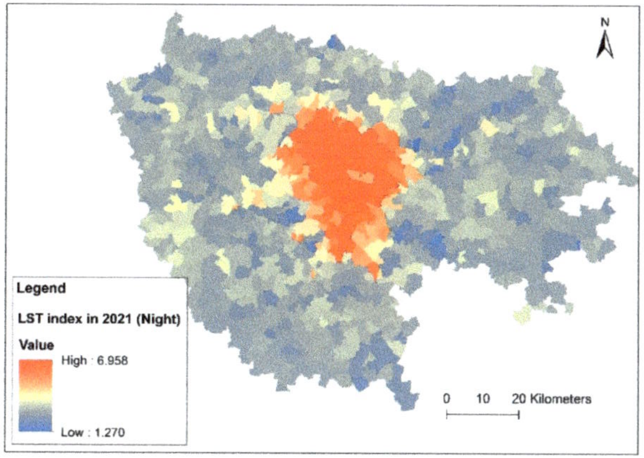

(f)

Figure 5. The mapped data of (**a**) wastewater heat recovery (2015); (**b**) surface geothermal energy (2022); (**c**) heat mitigation (2016); (**d**) Energy Consumption (2018); (**e**) daytime LST (2021); and (**f**) night time LST (2021).

The LULC maps of the years 2006, 2012, and 2018 were used to predict the LULC for the year 2054 using the Cellular Automata Markov Chain Model (CAMCM). The time span of the prediction is 36 years and is commonly used in the scientific literature for LULC predictions mainly because 36 is a multiple of 12 (the period extended between the years 2006–2018) and because it constitutes a relatively long-term horizon. The first phase of this prediction process is the validation of the data used. This is conducted by (a) employing the available mapped data of 2006 and 2012 to predict the LULC for the year 2018 via the CAMCM simulations performed in TerrSet 18 software, and by (b) comparing the actual and predicted LULC maps for the year 2018. The prediction model was validated through Cohen's kappa test conducted in TerrSet 18. The validation process showed high accuracy values of the predicted LULC for the year 2018. For instance, the calculated kappa values were all above 98%, indicating an almost perfect prediction according to Al-Shaar et al. [38]. In detail, the kappa values were 0.9919 for "Kappa for no information (Kno)", 0.9955 for "Kappa of grid cells level location (Klocation)", 0.9999 for "Kappa of stratum level location (KlocationStrata)" and 0.9896 for the "Overall kappa (Kstandard)". Subsequently, the LULC maps of the years 2006 and 2018 were the inputs to predict the LULC for the year 2054. Figure 6 shows the process of predicting the LULC maps for the year 2054.

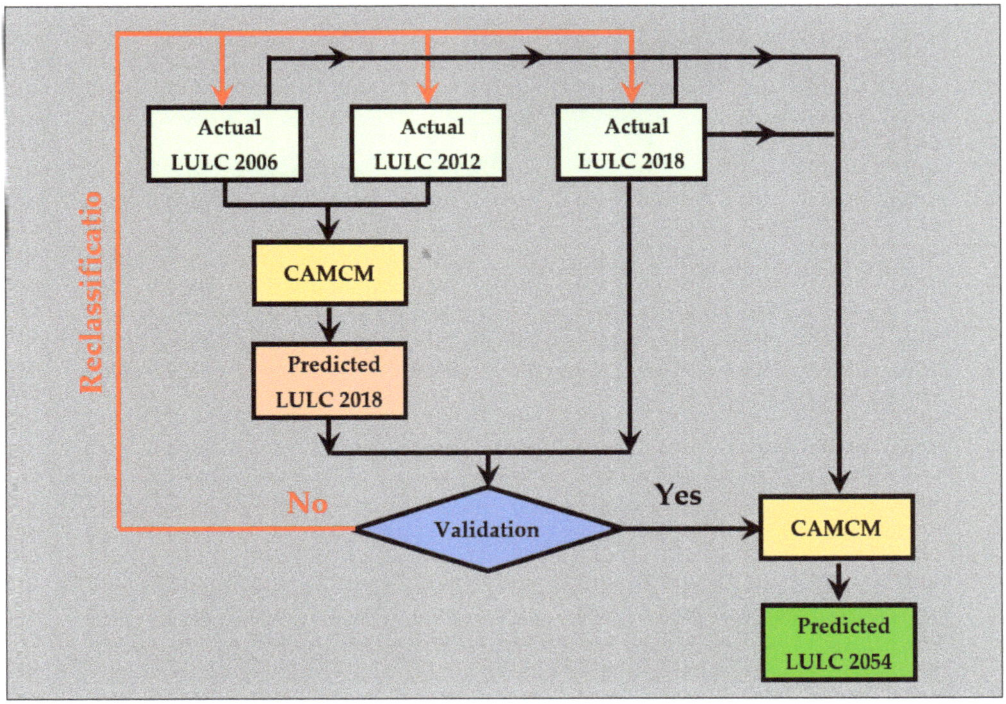

Figure 6. Process of predicting the LULC maps for the year 2054.

The changes of LULC between the years 2018 and 2054 showed (a) an increase of 5.52%, 17.7%, 1.25%, and 5%, respectively, in urban areas, industrial areas, forest, and wetlands, and the total area of roads and rail services; and (b) a decrease of 1.39%, 4.4%, and 50.9%, respectively, in the green urban areas, agriculture lands and bare soil zones. The land use/land cover distributions for the years 2018 and 2054 are presented in Figures A1 and A2 in Appendix A. The population data for the year 2054 were calculated based on the forecasts in Île-de-France, which were prepared by INSEE [39]. The population in Île-de-France for the year 2013 was 11,959,800 persons [39]. These forecasts show that the population in Île-de-France in the year 2050 will be 13,504,900 persons. A simple projection for the year 2054 was conducted and indicated a population size of 13,689,488 persons.

The population growth amounts in the study area communities are considered proportional to the urban growth rate in each community indicated by the predicted LULC distribution for the year 2054. Accordingly, the changes in population density between the years 2017 and 2054 show strong population growth in the North and Northeast of the study area. These changes are presented in Figure 7.

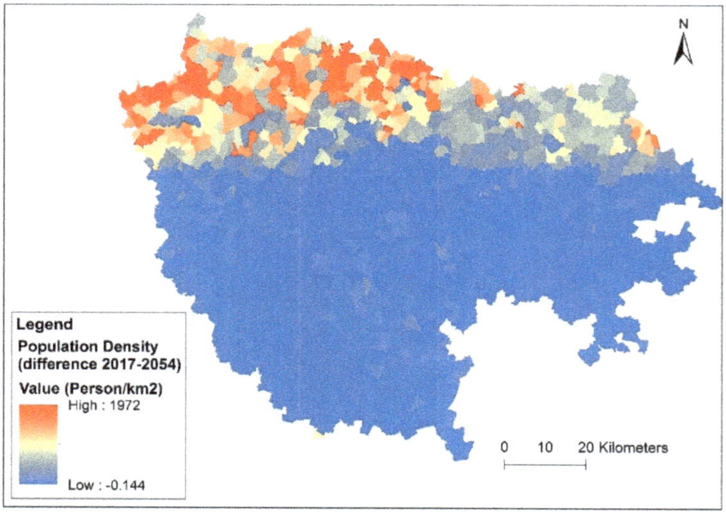

Figure 7. The predicted change of population density (2017–2054).

The current and projected data (to the year 2054) of population and LULC distributions are used in the statistical models, especially the GWR and ANOVA, to predict the evolution of SGE, hot wastewater HR and EC as well HM index, in addition to land surface temperature index.

3. Models Developed

This Section presents the findings obtained from the correlation analysis, the used OLS and GWR regression models, the spatial autocorrelation, and the variance analyses.

3.1. Correlation Analysis

The correlation analysis, which was carried out with R software, represents the refinement phase of the used data. This analysis is applied to support the following "selection of variables" phase by indicating what collinear variables could be reduced. This simplification is operated by keeping one representative variable and removing the remaining among the observed collinear variables. For instance, among the values of "carbon storage", "stormwater retention index", and HM index, only the HM index is used as one of the exploratory factors of dependent variables since the three aforementioned variables are all inter-correlated. It is important to indicate that the selection of the representative variable was performed based on several trials with the help of models used for the selection of variables, as indicated in the next sub-section. The correlation matrix, generated in R software, is presented in Figure A3 in Appendix B.

3.2. Selection of Variables

Ordinary Least Squares

The OLS regression model is the model used to select the variables. A derived OLS module called the exploratory regression (ER) was developed in ArcMap software. The ER runs all OLS models to cover all possible combinations of the explanatory variables, representing the input of the model. This ER model carried out in ArcMap 10.8 software indicates the coefficients of determination (R^2) for all combinations. The selected model is the one having the highest R^2 with the least number of variables. All the selected models have an R^2 above 70% except the HM and the night LST models, with 62% and 60%, respectively. In the second stage, the OLS regression is applied to the selected model to determine the variance inflation factor (VIF) for each variable as well as for the overall model. Checking the values of VIF is necessary to ensure that there is no problem of multicolinearity. All the VIF values of the selected models are less than 10, which indicates no multicolinearity problems [35]. The spatial autocorrelation analysis was carried out as the final stage of this process to check whether the GWR approach is needed. The Moran's I indexes ranged from 0.101 to 0.717, showing that the standard residuals are spatially auto-correlated. The z-scores of the spatial autocorrelations are all above 1.96, indicating the significance of the spatial autocorrelation (p-values < 0.05). Table 1 presents the selected variables and summarizes the results of OLS models.

Table 1. Selected variables and summary of ordinary least squares results.

Model	Used Variables		Adjusted R^2	Overall VIF	Residual Spatial Auto-correlation (p-Value)	Z-Score	Moran's I coefficient
	Variables	VIF					
Heat recovery from wastewater (year 2015)	Population 2017	3.21	0.75	1.3	<0.05	7.16	0.101
	Industrial areas 2018	2.01					
Surface Geothermal Energy (year 2022)	Population 2017	1.91	0.72	1.88	<0.05	2.58	0.286
	Urban areas 2018	1.86					
	Green Urban areas 2018	1.28					
	Agriculture areas 2018	1.45					
	Industrial areas 2018	1.45					
Energy Consumption (year 2018)	Population 2017	6.06	0.84	6.15	<0.05	16.62	0.228
	Industrial areas 2018	1.74					
	Heat recovery from wastewater 2015	4.24					
	Surface geothermal energy 2022	6.17					
Heat Mitigation (year 2016)	Urban areas 2018	2.23	0.62	3.32	<0.05	36.66	0.538
	Industrial areas 2018	3.03					
	Roads and rail 2018	3.32					
	Green urban areas 2018	1.44					
	Forests 2018	1.10					
	Agricultural areas 2018	1.17					

Table 1. *Cont.*

Model	Used Variables		Adjusted R^2	Overall VIF	Residual Spatial Auto-correlation (p-Value)	Z-Score	Moran's I coefficient
	Variables	VIF					
Daytime Land Surface Temperature (year 2021)	Heat mitigation 2016	2.65	0.79	2.65	<0.05	38.52	0.566
	Energy consumption 2018	1.81					
	Green urban areas 2018	1.40					
	Forests 2018	2.40					
	Agricultural areas 2018	1.27					
Nighttime Land Surface Temperature (year 2021)	Heat mitigation 2016	2.65	0.60	2.65	<0.05	48.79	0.717
	Energy consumption 2018	1.81					
	Green urban areas 2018	1.40					
	Forests 2018	2.40					
	Agricultural areas 2018	1.27					

3.3. *GWR Models (Consistency and Prediction Power)*

After checking the exogenous determining factors and the best combination models via the OLS models, the GWR regressions were applied to determine the values of regression relationships between the dependent variables and the driving variables according to their spatial distribution and local variations. The spatial features were taken into account individually. The regression coefficients calculated for the actual observations were afterward employed to conduct the projection for the year 2054 (using the LULC and population data of 2054). All the selected models have an R^2 above 83%.

The Moran's I indexes ranged from 0.025 to 0.250, showing that residual spatial autocorrelation is still present. However, the Moran' I coefficients are much lower, especially when data cover the whole area, such as that of SGE and HM.

The z-scores of the spatial autocorrelations are all above 1.96, indicating the significance of the spatial autocorrelation (p-values < 0.05) except for the data of SGE having a z-score of 1.75 corresponding to a significant p-value of 0.08.

Table 2 summarizes the results of GWR models as the coefficients of determination and spatial autocorrelation indicators.

Table 2. Coefficient of determination and spatial autocorrelation results of GWR models.

Model	Adjusted R^2	Residual Spatial Autocorrelation (p-Value and Z-Score)	Moran's I coefficient	Ratio: Moran's I (OLS)/Moran's I (GWR)
Surface geothermal energy 2022	0.987	($Z = 1.75, p = 0.08$)	0.025	11.44
Energy consumption 2018	0.851	($Z = 12.65, p < 0.05$)	0.172	1.33
Heat recovery from wastewater 2015	0.898	($Z = -3.13, p < 0.05$)	−0.046	−2.20
Heat mitigation 2016	0.832	($Z = 3.53, p < 0.05$)	0.051	10.55
Daytime LST intensity 2021	0.879	($Z = 11.72, p < 0.05$)	0.172	3.29
Nighttime LST intensity 2021	0.898	($Z = 17.05, p < 0.05$)	0.250	2.87

Regarding the residuals of Wastewater HR, the pattern of their distribution is a central shape located in and around Paris. This distribution shows several under and over-estimations, which could be explained as the lack of explanatory variables described by the local regulations corresponding to HR and a

For the SGE, the residuals are distributed, with under and over-estimations, in the suburbs around the center of the studied area, not located on fringes, which are characterized by the individual type of residences, such as individual homes with gardens.

For HM, the existence of forests is not fully sufficient. The continuity of the forests was found to be an important factor that could determine the accuracy of estimating the HM capacity of the zone. For instance, the HM capacity of the Saint-Germain forest was underestimated by the GWR model. This could refer to the fact that some areas in this forest are employed for some urban activities, such as the railroad terminal/train depot indicated in Figure 8a,b. Similarly, the EC were under and overestimated in a radial form from the center to the peripheries. For instance, the EC was overestimated in the community of Grandpuits because of the existence of a no longer functioning oil refinery (the red spot in the southeastern part of the study area, as shown Figure A4 in Appendix C). The underestimation of the nighttime LST index is concentrated around the center. In addition, the GWR model under and overestimated the nighttime LST in a dispersed radial form to peripheries (Figure A4 in Appendix C). It is worth noting that the HM and the existence of forests are not fully sufficient for GWR estimations (for instance, in the Saint-Germain forest, where some human activities such as the train terminal exist, the GWR underestimated the LST index at night time). These findings reveal the need to integrate additional data that could enhance the estimations and increase accuracy. The spatial distribution pattern of residuals for the estimated daytime LST index is random with slight under/overestimation. This indicates that estimations are nearly correct. Figure 8a illustrates the spatial distribution of standard residuals for the HM GWR model. The mapped residual distributions of GWR models are illustrated in Figure A4 in Appendix C.

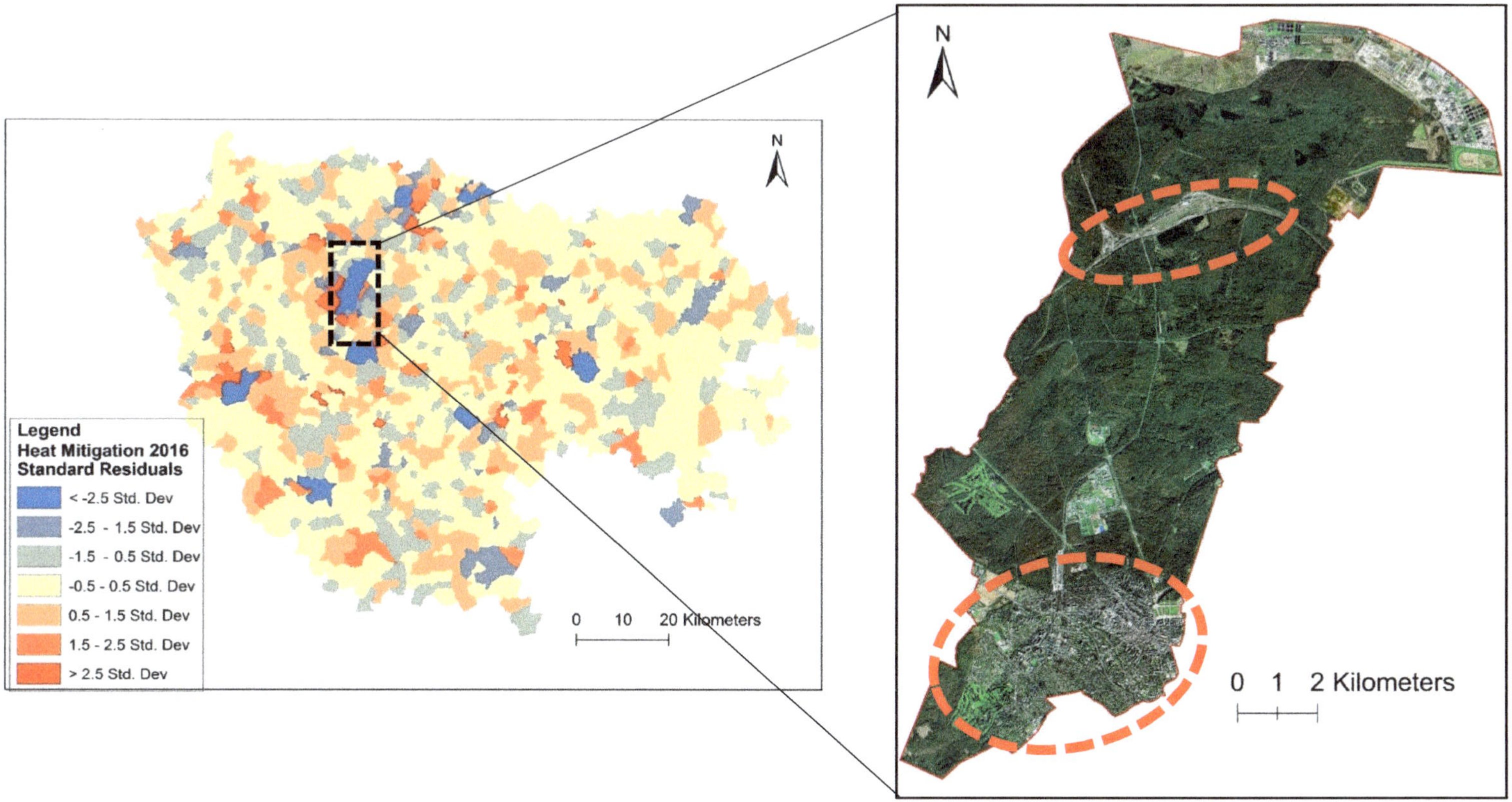

(**a**) (**b**)

Figure 8. (**a**) Spatial distribution of standard residuals for the HM GWR model, (**b**) the Saint-Germain Forest (red circles show urban development and activities in the Saint-Germain Forest).

3.4. Effect Size (Variance Analysis)

The variance analysis was carried out to identify the effect size of determining factors for each dependent variable. The effect size is calculated as the ratio of the "sum of squares" for each determining variable to the total of the "sum of squares" of all determining factors. The analysis shows that population is the main determining factor for HR, with a percentage of 99.66; the industrial areas have a slight effect. Regarding the SGE, the population is the factor having the most effect on power, with a percentage of 72.12. Urban areas and agriculture zones are the factors having medium to low effect powers, with percentages of 12.4 and 9.52, respectively. Population, HR, and industrial areas are the main factors affecting energy consumption, with percentages of 39.3, 33.19, and 24.61, respectively. The HM is mainly affected by the existence of forests, with a percentage of 86.02. With respect to the LST, the determining factors depend on the time of the day. While the HM and the EC are the main determining factors for LST in the daytime with percentages of 85.66 and 8.20, respectively, the LST at night is affected by HM, EC, the existence of agriculture areas and forests with percentages of 22.84, 35.38, 31.6 and 8.93, respectively. It is worth mentioning here that from day to night times, the effect of heat mitigation is reduced by around 63%, which is distributed as an increase in the effect of (i) energy consumption by 27%, (ii) agriculture areas by 29%, and (iii) forest by 9%. The effects of determining factors support the selection of solutions and plans as well as supporting and guiding the enactment of corresponding policies. This change of effects between day and night times needs to be further investigated to identify the reasons behind them. Table 3 presents the effect sizes of GWR determining factors.

Figure 9 shows the regression relationship structure among all dependent and exogenous variables. Effect sizes below 5% are indicated by disconnected lines in the regression relationship structure. Positive and negative regression relationships are indicated respectively by the signs of "+" and "−".

Table 3. The effect size of determining factors.

Model	Used Variables	
	Variables	**Effect Size (%)**
Heat recovery from wastewater	Population 2017	99.66
	Industrial areas 2018	0.34
Surface geothermal energy	Population 2017	72.12
	Urban areas 2018	12.40
	Green urban areas 2018	2.60
	Agriculture areas 2018	9.52
	Industrial areas 2018	3.36
Energy consumption	Population 2017	39.30
	Industrial areas 2018	24.61
	Heat recovery from wastewater 2015	33.19
	Surface geothermal energy 2022	2.90
Heat mitigation	Urban areas 2018	3.40
	Industrial areas 2018	0.79
	Roads and rail 2018	0.72
	Green urban areas 2018	4.22
	Forests 2018	86.02
	Agricultural areas 2018	4.85

Table 3. *Cont.*

Model	Used Variables	
	Variables	Effect Size (%)
Daytime land surface temperature	Heat mitigation 2016	85.66
	Energy consumption 2018	8.20
	Green urban areas 2018	3.93
	Forests 2018	0.07
	Agricultural areas 2018	2.14
Nighttime land surface temperature	Heat mitigation 2016	22.84
	Energy consumption 2018	35.38
	Green urban areas 2018	1.25
	Forests 2018	8.93
	Agricultural areas 2018	31.60

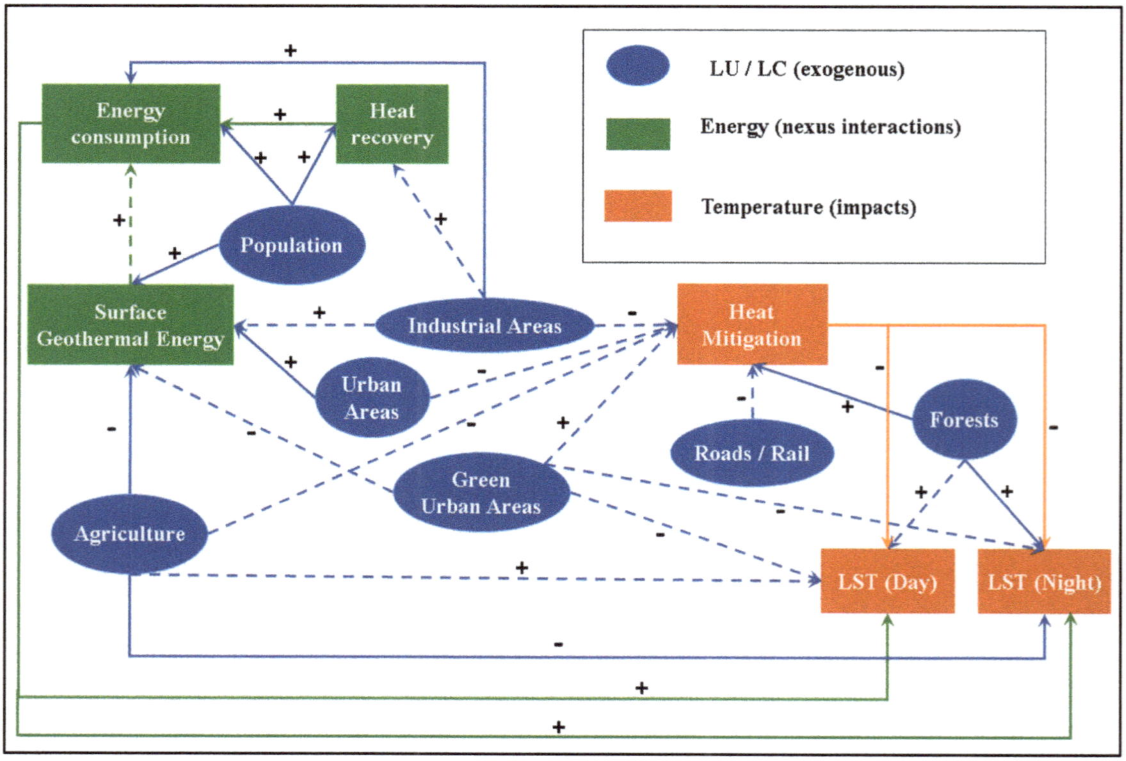

Figure 9. Regression relationship structure among all dependent and exogenous variables.

4. Results and Discussion

The predicted EC pattern for the year 2054 generally shows an increasing trend in the whole area, especially in the north and northwest part of the study area, where concentrated population growth occurs. It is worth noting that in some areas in proximity to the central zone, the energy consumption is expected to be reduced. This could refer to the individual behavior of reducing energy consumption and/or the effects of policies or other unidentified factors.

On the other hand, the expected potentials for HR and SGE are not in line with the forecasted EC, particularly in the southwest and southeast parts of the central zone and its neighboring areas. In these two zones, the potential to recuperate heat energy is lowered compared to the current period. In contrast, in other zones, the expected potentials for HR and SGE are compatible with the needs for the forecasted EC. For instance, the HR is expected to increase in the northern part of areas surrounding the center. Similarly, the SGE is expected to increase in the north and northwest parts of peripheral zones in the study area. A third important case of energy supply versus demand is notable. It is depicted, as in the case where the potential to recuperate energy from wastewater is high, nonetheless, the energy consumption is reduced. This forecast is expected in some areas of Paris where the HR will be intensified due to possible regulations or implementation of HR systems and accompanied by a decrease in energy consumption. The predicted changes in HM capacities between the years 2016 and 2054 show different increased and decreased values. What is important to point out is that some of the reduced capacities are accompanied by an increase in population density (2017–2054) such as in the northwest region of the study area. However, the reduced capacities of HM observed in the remaining areas that are not associated with new human settlements need to be further investigated, in future research, to identify the main causes of these predicted changes.

The texture of the distribution of the predicted LST indexes during the daytime is almost the opposite of that of HM. Similar to the EC pattern, the predicted distribution of LST indexes at night follows a downward path of distribution of high indexes at the center to low indexes at the fringes. Figure 10 shows the predicted change of (a) wastewater heat recovery (2015–2054); (b) surface geothermal energy (2022–2054); (c) heat mitigation (2016–2054); (d) energy consumption (2018–2054); (e) daytime LST (2021–2054); and (f) night time LST (2021–2054).

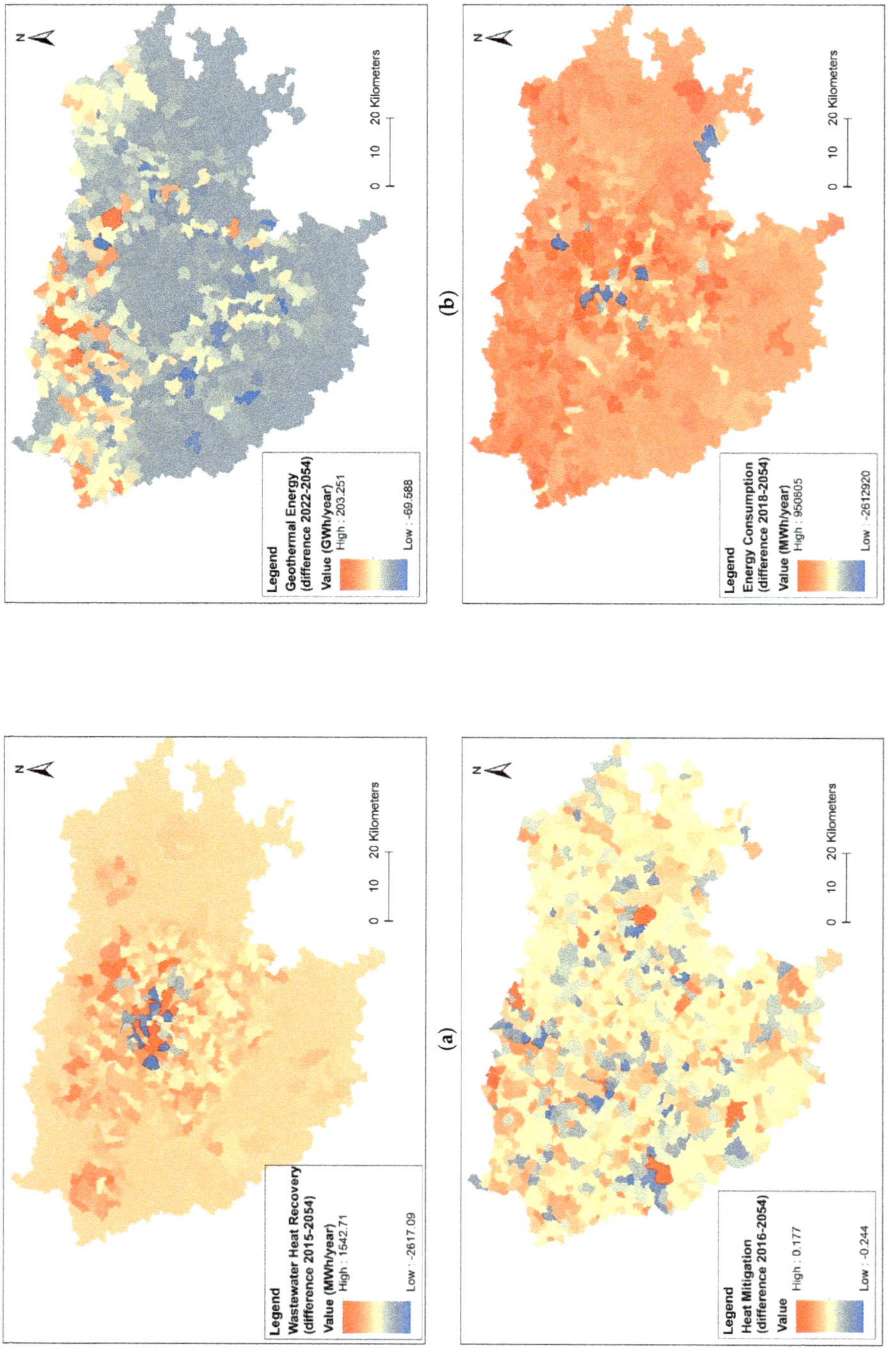

Figure 10. *Cont.*

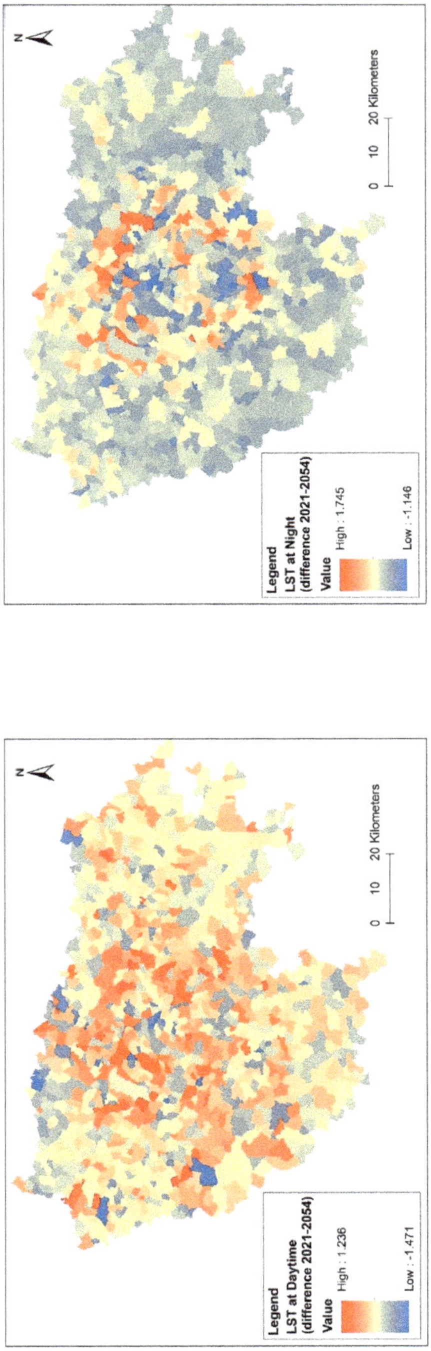

(e) (f)

Figure 10. The predicted change of (**a**) wastewater heat recovery (2015–2054); (**b**) surface geothermal energy (2022–2054); (**c**) heat mitigation (2016–2054); (**d**) energy consumption (2018–2054); (**e**) daytime LST (2021–2054); and (**f**) night time LST (2021–2054).

5. Conclusions

This paper investigates the trends and the solutions to manage the water–soil–energy nexus in the context of increasing urbanization. The examined solutions, integrated into the water–soil–energy nexus, are designed primarily to reduce the consumption of fossil energy by discovering and implementing new renewable sources of energy and for heat mitigation by examining the spatial possibilities for afforestation/reforestation. However, the effects of exogenous spatial driving factors of these solutions, in addition to their future spatial evolution are not holistically studied. Bearing in mind the spatial competition between different land use/land cover patterns, the analysis is elaborated by (a) determining the areas with low, medium, and high potential for implementing the solutions, as well as defining the type of solution to be implemented, and (b) by comparing the aforementioned implementation capacities with the demand depicted as the needs for slowing down the effects of the surface urban heat islands and warming, and reducing dependence on fossil energy. This study identifies the current key drivers of the SGE, the wastewater HR and the spatial capacity for HM in the study area, which covers a wide spatial extent in the Île-de-France region, in addition to their potential spatial changes until the year 2054. This methodology used the statistical analysis of OLS and GWR, combined with the geographic information system, based on data on land use/land cover as well as the distribution of population. The findings indicate that the spatial autocorrelation of GWR residuals is lesser than those of OLS models. The difference, introduced as the ratios, ranges from 1.33 to 11.44. These values are clearly observed particularly in the cases of SGE (11.44) and HM (10.55). On that account, GWR models explain the regressive relationships between key drivers and WSE solutions at the individual spatial level. In addition, these models predict the spatial evolution of the examined WSE solutions. In addition, variance analyses were conducted to quantify the influence of each driving factor. For instance, and with respect to LST, the key determinants change over the daytime. Whereas the HM and the EC are the main determining factors for daytime LST with effect sizes of 85.66% and 8.20%, respectively, the nighttime LST is affected by HM and EC in addition to the existence of agriculture areas and forests with effect sizes of 22.84%, 35.38%, 31.6%, and 8.93%, respectively. This change needs to be further investigated to identify the reasons behind it since the effects of determining factors support the selection of solutions and plans as well as supporting and guiding the enactment of corresponding policies. Regarding the prediction results, areas with the potential for implementing specific solutions are determined and classified according to their capacities. Along the same lines, these capacities are compared to the demand for reducing the dependence on fossil energy and slowing down the effects of surface urban heat islands. The predictions indicate three types of distribution regarding the energy consumption: (i) the best fit where the potential for implementing SGE or HR is elevated and associated with an increase in energy consumption as in the northern part of areas surrounding the center of Île-de-France, (ii) the medium pattern where the potential for implementing SGE or HR is elevated, however, the energy consumption is expected to decrease as in some area of Paris, and (iii) the worst case where the potential for implementing SGE or HR is low/null and the energy consumption is expected to increase as in the southwest and southeast parts of the central zone and its neighboring areas. With respect to the predicted change of HM capacities between the years 2016 and 2054, it is important to mention that in some areas the forecasted reduced capacities of HM are not associated with human activities. The reasons behind this change should be clarified by further research. Concerning the limitations, the solutions designed (a) to mitigate the risk of climate change, floods, air pollution, and temperature, (b) to protect biodiversity, and (c) to reduce the dependence on fossil energy, such as the green roofs and vegetated facades as well as the solar energy, were not inspected due to limited data and information about the explanatory variables.

Moreover, the impacts of air temperature on the consumption of fossil energy were not investigated. It would be interesting to clarify all these points in further research.

Author Contributions: Conceptualization, W.A.-S. and O.B.; methodology, W.A.-S. and O.B.; software, W.A.-S. and O.B.; validation, W.A.-S., O.B., B.d.G., P.C. and M.H.; formal analysis, W.A.-S., O.B., and B.d.G.; investigation, W.A.-S.; resources, O.B.; data curation, W.A.-S.; writing—original draft preparation, W.A.-S.; writing—review and editing, W.A.-S., O.B., B.d.G., P.C. and M.H.; visualization, W.A.-S.; supervision, O.B., B.d.G., P.C. and M.H.; project administration, O.B., B.d.G., P.C. and M.H; funding acquisition, O.B., B.d.G., P.C. and M.H. All authors have read and agreed to the published version of the manuscript.

Funding: This research conducted as part of the WISE Cities project (Water–soil–energy interactions for a future sustainable environment in cities), is funded by the I-SITE FUTURE, benefits from State aid managed by the ANR under the Programme d'Investissements d'Avenir (reference ANR-16-IDEX-0003) in addition to the contributions of the institutions involved.

Institutional Review Board Statement: Not applicable.

Informed Consent Statement: Not applicable.

Data Availability Statement: The data presented in this study are available on request from the corresponding author.

Conflicts of Interest: The authors declare no conflict of interest.

Appendix A

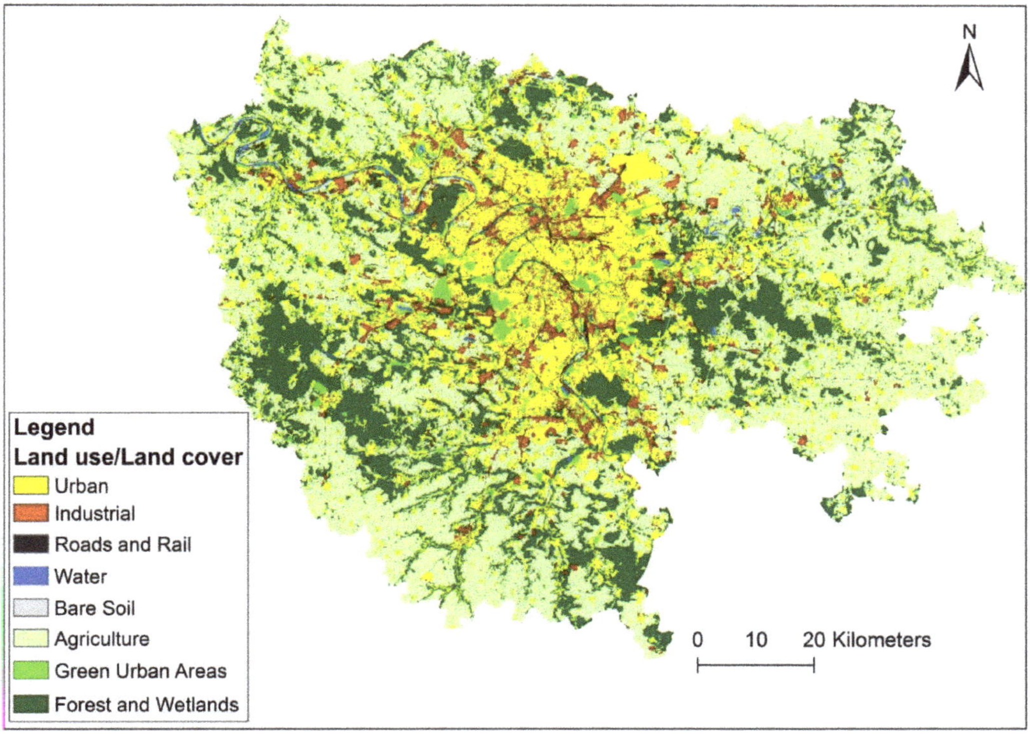

Figure A1. LULC map for the year 2018.

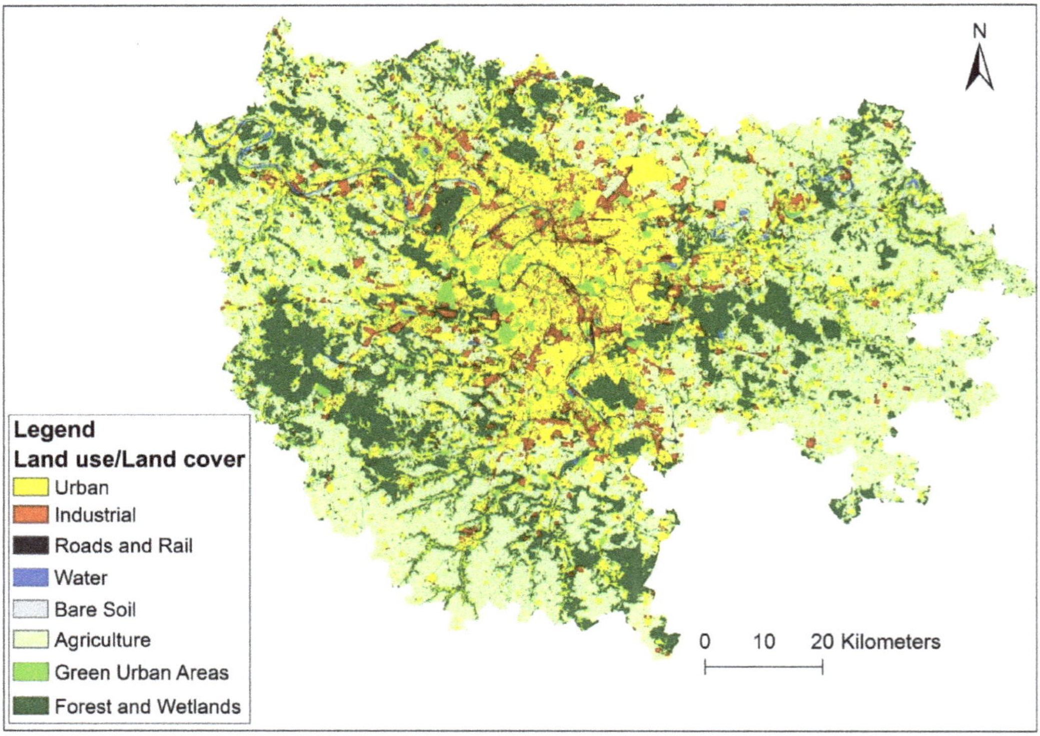

Figure A2. LULC map for the year 2054.

Appendix B

For the correlation analysis conducted in R software, the abbreviations corresponding to the used variables are listed below:

1. Actif_2017: number of persons working
2. Rev_Med_an: median revenue per year in each community
3. Area_km2: area of community
4. PopDen2017: population density of each community in the year 2017
5. DenActif2017: employment density of each community in the year 2017
6. T400m2_20: carbon Storage per 400 m^2 area for each community in the year 2020
7. H_Mit_i_16: heat Mitigation index in each community for the year 2016
8. SW_Ret_i20: stormwater retention index in each community for the year 2020
9. Urb_Gro_m2: growth of urban areas (m^2) between the years 2017 and 2054 in each community
10. P_Gro17_54: population growth (person) between the years 2017 and 2054 in each community
11. CF_Mwh2015: wastewater heat recovery (Mwh) in the year 2015 in each community
12. PopDen2054: population density of each community in the year 2054
13. Pop2054: population of each community in the year 2054
14. LST_ii_D21: daytime land surface temperature index in the year 2021 in each community
15. LST_ii_N21: nighttime land surface temperature index in the year 2021 in each community
16. Urb_m2: urban areas (m^2) in the year 2018 in each community
17. GreeUrb_m2: green urban areas (m^2) in the year 2018 in each community
18. Forest_m2: forest areas (m^2) in the year 2018 in each community

19. Rd_Rail_m2: areas of roads and rail lands (m^2) in the year 2018 in each community
20. BareSoil_m2: bare soil areas (m^2) in the year 2018 in each community
21. Water_m2: areas of water bodies (m^2) in the year 2018 in each community
22. Agric_m2: agriculture areas (m^2) in the year 2018 in each community
23. Indust_m2: industrial areas (m^2) in the year 2018 in each community
24. EC_Mwh2018: energy consumption (Mwh) in the year 2018 in each community
25. C_Stor-T20: carbon storage capacity (Ton) in the year 2020 in each community

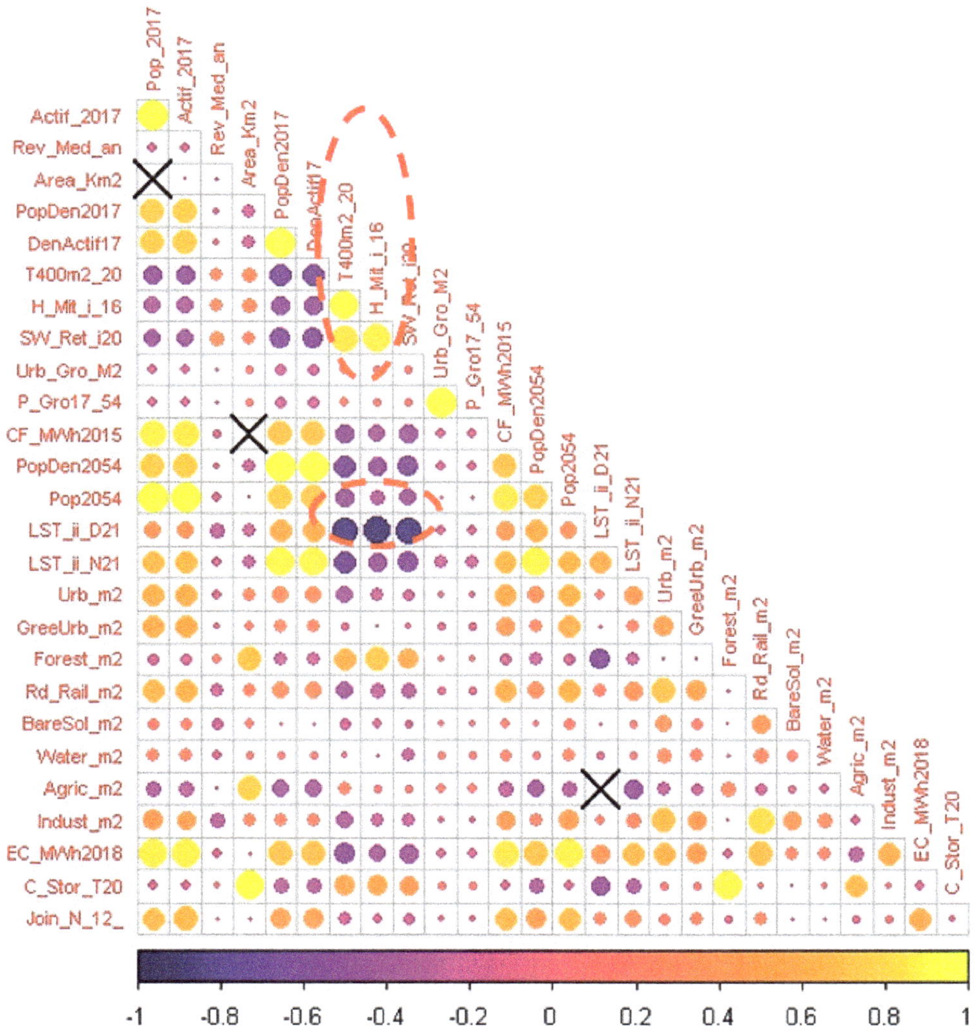

Figure A3. The correlation matrix of the used data (the X symbol indicates the non-correlation, and the two red circles show the strongest positive and negative correlations).

Appendix C

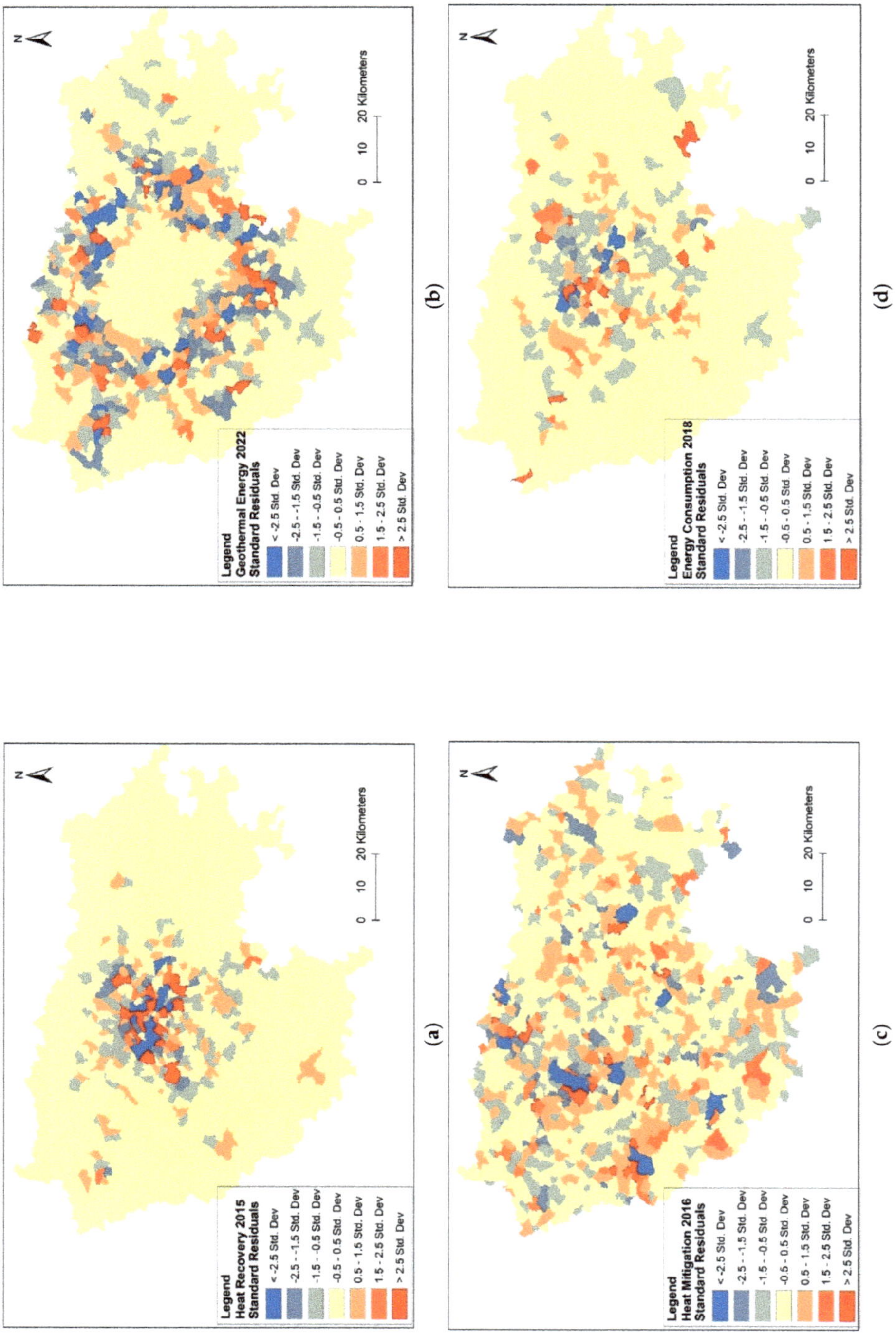

Figure A4. *Cont.*

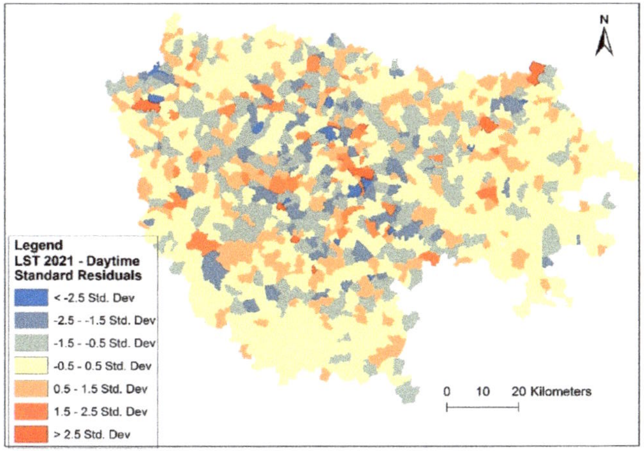

(e)

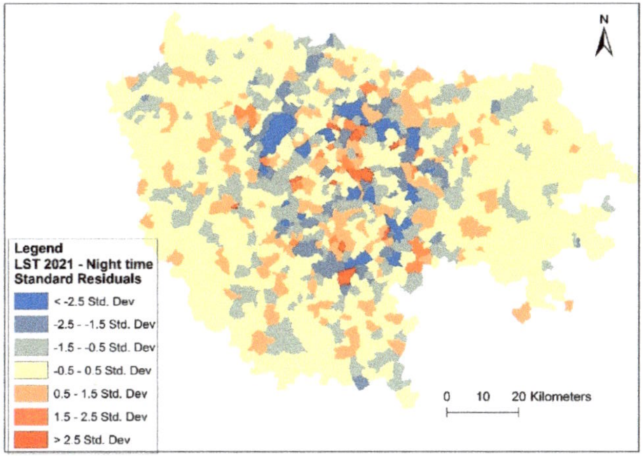

(f)

Figure A4. The GWR residual distributions of (**a**) wastewater heat recovery; (**b**) surface geothermal energy; (**c**) heat mitigation; (**d**) energy consumption; (**e**) daytime LST; (**f**) nighttime LST.

References

1. Ferreira, V.; Barreira, A.P.; Loures, L.; Antunes, D.; Panagopoulos, T. Stakeholders' Engagement on Nature-Based Solutions: A Systematic Literature Review. *Sustainability* **2020**, *12*, 640. [CrossRef]
2. Directorate-General for Research and Innovation (European Commission). *Towards an EU Research and Innovation Policy Agenda for Nature-Based Solutions & Re-Naturing Cities: Final Report of the Horizon 2020 Expert Group on 'Nature Based Solutions and Re Naturing Cities*; Publications Office of the European Union: Brussels, Belgium, 2015; ISBN 978-92-79-46051-7.
3. Dick, J.; Miller, J.D.; Carruthers-Jones, J.; Dobel, A.J.; Carver, S.; Garbutt, A.; Hester, A.; Hails, R.; Magreehan, V.; Quinn, M. How Are Nature Based Solutions Contributing to Priority Societal Challenges Surrounding Human Well-Being in the United Kingdom: A Systematic Map Protocol. *Environ. Evid.* **2019**, *8*, 37. [CrossRef]
4. World Bank. *World Bank Biodiversity, Climate Change, and Adaptation: Nature-Based Solutions from the World Bank Portfolio*; World Bank: Washington, DC, USA, 2008.
5. Réseau D'observation Statistique de L'énergie (ROSE). Energif | Consommations Enérgétiques Détaillées du Secteur Résidentiel. Available online: http://sigr.iau-idf.fr/webapps/cartes/rose/?op=d (accessed on 18 May 2022).
6. Stober, I.; Bucher, K. *Geothermal Energy: From Theoretical Models to Exploration and Development*; Springer International Publishing: Cham, Switzerland, 2021; ISBN 978-3-030-71684-4.
7. Naili, N.; Hazami, M.; Attar, I.; Farhat, A. Assessment of Surface Geothermal Energy for Air Conditioning in Northern Tunisia: Direct Test and Deployment of Ground Source Heat Pump System. *Energy Build.* **2016**, *111*, 207–217. [CrossRef]
8. Saagi, R.; Arnell, M.; Wärff, C.; Ahlström, M.; Jeppsson, U. City-Wide Model-Based Analysis of Heat Recovery from Wastewater Using an Uncertainty-Based Approach. *Sci. Total Environ.* **2022**, *820*, 153273. [CrossRef]
9. Spriet, J.; McNabola, A.; Neugebauer, G.; Stoeglehner, G.; Ertl, T.; Kretschmer, F. Spatial and Temporal Considerations in the Performance of Wastewater Heat Recovery Systems. *J. Clean. Prod.* **2020**, *247*, 119583. [CrossRef]
10. NATure-Based URban innoVATION Project (Naturvation) European Assessment Maps. Available online: https://naturvation.eu/assessment/maps (accessed on 7 March 2022).
11. Sowińska-Świerkosz, B.; García, J. What Are Nature-Based Solutions (NBS)? Setting Core Ideas for Concept Clarification. *Nat. Based Solut.* **2022**, *2*, 100009. [CrossRef]
12. Blackwood, L.; Renaud, F.G.; Gillespie, S. Nature-Based Solutions as Climate Change Adaptation Measures for Rail Infrastructure. *Nat. Based Solut.* **2022**, *2*, 100013. [CrossRef]
13. Pander, J.; Mueller, M.; Geist, J. Succession of Fish Diversity after Reconnecting a Large Floodplain to the Upper Danube River. *Ecol. Eng.* **2015**, *75*, 41–50. [CrossRef]
14. Schindler, S.; O'Neill, F.H.; Biró, M.; Damm, C.; Gasso, V.; Kanka, R.; van der Sluis, T.; Krug, A.; Lauwaars, S.G.; Sebesvari, Z.; et al. Multifunctional Floodplain Management and Biodiversity Effects: A Knowledge Synthesis for Six European Countries. *Biodivers. Conserv.* **2016**, *25*, 1349–1382. [CrossRef]
15. Funk, A.; Martínez-López, J.; Borgwardt, F.; Trauner, D.; Bagstad, K.J.; Balbi, S.; Magrach, A.; Villa, F.; Hein, T. Identification of Conservation and Restoration Priority Areas in the Danube River Based on the Multi-Functionality of River-Floodplain Systems. *Sci. Total Environ.* **2019**, *654*, 763–777. [CrossRef]
16. Perni, A.; Martínez-Paz, J.M. A Participatory Approach for Selecting Cost-Effective Measures in the WFD Context: The Mar Menor (SE Spain). *Sci. Total Environ.* **2013**, *458–460*, 303–311. [CrossRef]
17. Majidi, A.N.; Vojinovic, Z.; Alves, A.; Weesakul, S.; Sanchez, A.; Boogaard, F.; Kluck, J. Planning Nature-Based Solutions for Urban Flood Reduction and Thermal Comfort Enhancement. *Sustainability* **2019**, *11*, 6361. [CrossRef]
18. Soana, E.; Fano, E.A.; Castaldelli, G. The Achievement of Water Framework Directive Goals through the Restoration of Vegetation in Agricultural Canals. *J. Environ. Manage.* **2021**, *294*, 113016. [CrossRef]
19. Harrington, R.; O'Donovan, G.; McGrath, G. Integrated Constructed Wetlands (ICW) Working at the Landscape Scale: The Anne Valley Project, Ireland. *Ecol. Inform.* **2013**, *14*, 104–107. [CrossRef]
20. Benedict, M.A.; McMahon, E.T. Green Infrastructure: Smart Conservation for the 21st Century. *Renew. Resour. J.* **2002**, *20*, 12–17.
21. Liu, W.; Xu, H.; Zhang, X.; Jiang, W. Green Infrastructure Network Identification at a Regional Scale: The Case of Nanjing Metropolitan Area, China. *Forests* **2022**, *13*, 735. [CrossRef]
22. Seddon, N.; Chausson, A.; Berry, P.; Girardin, C.A.J.; Smith, A.; Turner, B. Understanding the Value and Limits of Nature-Based Solutions to Climate Change and Other Global Challenges. *Philos. Transact. R. Soc. B Biol. Sci.* **2020**, *375*, 20190120. [CrossRef]
23. European Commission. *European Commission Sustainable Europe Investment Plan European Green Deal Investment Plan*; European Commission: Brussels, Belgium, 2020.
24. Nagpal, H.; Spriet, J.; Murali, M.K.; McNabola, A. Heat Recovery from Wastewater—A Review of Available Resource. *Water* **2021**, *13*, 1274. [CrossRef]
25. Wärff, C.; Arnell, M.; Sehlén, R.; Jeppsson, U. Modelling Heat Recovery Potential from Household Wastewater. *Water Sci. Technol.* **2020**, *81*, 1597–1605. [CrossRef]
26. Schmid, F. Sewage water: Interesting heat source for heat pumps and chillers. In Proceedings of the HPT—Heat Pumping Technologies, Zürich, Switzerland, 22 May 2008.
27. Dürrenmatt, D.J.; Wanner, O. A Mathematical Model to Predict the Effect of Heat Recovery on the Wastewater Temperature in Sewers. *Water Res.* **2014**, *48*, 548–558. [CrossRef]

28. Cipolla, S.S.; Maglionico, M. Heat Recovery from Urban Wastewater: Analysis of the Variability of Flow Rate and Temperature in the Sewer of Bologna, Italy. *Energy Proced.* **2014**, *45*, 288–297. [CrossRef]
29. Kretschmer, F.; Simperler, L.; Ertl, T. Analysing Wastewater Temperature Development in a Sewer System as a Basis for the Evaluation of Wastewater Heat Recovery Potentials. *Energy Build.* **2016**, *128*, 639–648. [CrossRef]
30. Ivajnšič, D.; Kaligarič, M.; Žiberna, I. Geographically Weighted Regression of the Urban Heat Island of a Small City. *Appl. Geogr.* **2014**, *53*, 341–353. [CrossRef]
31. Wang, Z.; Fan, C.; Zhao, Q.; Myint, S.W. A Geographically Weighted Regression Approach to Understanding Urbanization Impacts on Urban Warming and Cooling: A Case Study of Las Vegas. *Remote Sens.* **2020**, *12*, 222. [CrossRef]
32. Eklipse. *EKLIPSE Draft Document of Work: Energy Request*; Eklipse Management Body: Leipzig, Germany, 2017; p. 43.
33. Bureau de Recherches Géologiques et Minières (BRGM). Grand Paris: Le Potentiel de la Géothermie de Surface Cartographié | BRGM. Available online: https://www.brgm.fr/fr/actualite/communique-presse/grand-paris-potentiel-geothermie-surface-cartographie (accessed on 19 June 2022).
34. Hutcheson, G.D.; Moutinho, L. *Statistical Modeling for Management*; Sage Publishing: Newbury Park, CA, USA, 2022; ISBN 978-0-7619-7011-8.
35. Loonis, V.; de Bellefon, M.-P. *Handbook of Spatial Analysis*; Insee—Eurostat: Montrouge, France, 2018; ISBN 978-2-11-139686-9.
36. Urban Atlas. Urban Atlas—Copernicus Land Monitoring Service. Available online: https://land.copernicus.eu/local/urban-atlas (accessed on 25 November 2021).
37. Institut Paris Region Ilots de chaleur Urbains (ICU): Classification des IMU en Zone Climatique Locale (LCZ), Aléas et Vulnérabilités à la Chaleur de Jour et de Nuit en Île-de-France. Available online: https://data-iau-idf.opendata.arcgis.com/datasets/ilots-de-chaleur-urbains-icu-classification-des-imu-en-zone-climatique-locale-lcz-al%C3%A9as-et-vuln%C3%A9rabilit%C3%A9s-%C3%A0-la-chaleur-de-jour-et-de-nuit-en-%C3%AEle-de-france/explore?location=48.671264,2.503150,9.00 (accessed on 20 August 2022).
38. Al-Shaar, W.; Adjizian Gérard, J.; Nehme, N.; Lakiss, H.; Buccianti Barakat, L. Application of Modified Cellular Automata Markov Chain Model: Forecasting Land Use Pattern in Lebanon. *Model. Earth Syst. Environ.* **2021**, *7*, 1321–1335. [CrossRef]
39. Institut National de la Statistique et des Etudes Economiques (INSEE) Les Résultats Des Recensements de La Population | Insee. Available online: https://www.insee.fr/fr/information/2008354 (accessed on 4 January 2022).

urban science

MDPI

Article

A Partial Least Squares Analysis of the Perceived Impact of Sustainable Real Estate Design upon Wellbeing

Anna Cortesi [1], Ioannis Vardopoulos [1,2,*] and Luca Salvati [3,*]

1 RICS Accredited Master of Science in Real Estate, School of Architecture, Land and Environmental Sciences, Neapolis University Pafos (NUP), Pafos 8042, Cyprus
2 School of Environment, Geography and Applied Economics, Harokopio University (HUA), 17671 Kallithea, Attica, Greece
3 Department of Economics and Law, University of Macerata, I-62100 Macerata, Italy
* Correspondence: ivardopoulos@post.com (I.V.); luca.salvati@unimc.it (L.S.)

Abstract: Improving communities and the urban built environment to promote good health, wellness, and wellbeing has become a top priority globally. This growing trend, evident also in the Sustainable Development Goals' urgent call for action, has a significant influence on the real estate sustainable development process, which is mostly expressed through design, and is understood as a key value creator in the real estate sector, for all dimensions of the build environment. In order to shed further light on this complex matter, with reference to the perceived impact of sustainable real estate design upon wellbeing, cross-sectional data collected through a survey (n = 150, RR = 75%) were used. The results, obtained from descriptive statistics, regression analysis, variables correlation, and partial least squares-structural equation modeling analysis that incorporated the assessment of measurement and structural models, suggest a positive correlation among the design elements and health, wellness, and wellbeing aspects. The findings are considered significant in terms of filling the gap in the currently published scholarly literature, further supporting the importance of interdisciplinary urban sustainability among real estate professionals.

Keywords: sustainability; health city science; built environment; real estate; design theory; user experience; urban wellbeing; SDGs

1. Introduction

Improving communities and the urban built environment in order to promote good health, wellness, and wellbeing (herein referred to as HWWb) has become a top priority globally [1,2]. This growing focus on developing healthy communities stems from the increased recognition of the physical and operational characteristics of personal environments (such as homes, workplaces, public spaces, schools, and transportation systems) and their significant influence upon HWWb [3,4], especially since humans have become an indoor and mostly sedentary species [5], spending approximately 90% of their time inside a building [6].

For the past few years, people have opted for a better lifestyle that incorporates the concept of communities [7], families and their values, mental [8] and physical health, and most importantly, their personal wellness. Academia has also made significant efforts to stress the impact of HWWb and how it can be incorporated and embedded into the notable aspects of people's lives [4,9]. HWWb, due to its diverse and complex nature, has been studied through various perspectives, covering fields that ranged from environmental and health sciences to social sciences, and is defined differently by various scholars in different disciplines [10–13]. As a term, it gained popularity after WWII, when it was used to describe a good life that focused more on issues such as employment, environment, visual arts, health, and housing [14]. In social sciences, for example, the term is defined through the concepts of employment, education, housing facilities, cultural values, community involvement, family ties, etc. [15], whereas, in environmental sciences, it is defined through the concepts of pollutions, waste management, climate change, etc. [16–18].

Thomas (2009) [19] argues that 'wellbeing' is a notion that is very hard to define and measure. The idea of 'wellbeing' stemmed from the impression of happiness, which led to the term 'objective wellbeing'. In ancient Greek literature, *ευτυχία*, happiness, meant a great life. A happy person was considered to be satisfied with his/her life and more focused on their religion over their life span. In the 18th century, this traditional concept of happiness started transforming into various different concepts, such as life satisfaction, quality of life, prosperity and wellbeing. Happiness was henceforth referred to as temporarily pleasing emotions. Life satisfaction, on the other hand, gained the meaning of the overall satisfaction of life in the long term. The concept of prosperity expresses the economic conditions that are tangible in nature, while the concept of 'wellbeing' is defined by Ruut Veenhoven as the overall quality of life with the underlying concepts of happiness and life satisfaction [20]. Dodge et al. (2012) [21], in defining 'wellbeing', took under consideration the following two specific aspects: the hedonic tradition (which emphasized the positive effect, happiness, low negative affect, and satisfaction with life) and the eudemonic tradition (which highlighted human development and positive psychological functioning). Their study concluded by providing a simple (as a basis for measurement) definition of 'wellbeing' that is universally applicable, conveying the multidimensional nature of the term to enable stakeholders and policymakers to advance their understanding.

HWWb is explained via psychological, philosophical, medical and health conceptualization. In the psychological conceptualization of 'wellbeing', the 'subjective wellbeing' indicator is used to examine the individual's perceived wellbeing. In philosophical conceptualization, wellbeing is examined in term of ethics and the nature of living of an individual. Wellbeing via health conceptualization is explained in terms of complete physical and mental health state of an individual. Gillett-Swan and Sargeant (2015) [22] gave a new perspective to 'wellbeing', as a process of accrual. The advantages of considering 'wellbeing' as an accrual process reside in the ability to build upon one's life experiences (psychological and physical) to inform the future direction of 'wellbeing'. Eger and Maridal (2015) [23] support the idea that the most effective factors that define HWWb are happiness, and satisfaction. Their study provides empirical support for the following six livability factors of HWWb: living standard, freedom, health, peace, personal and community relationships, and security. The results of this study confirmed the findings in the prior published scholarly literature, but also provided some new insights and paved the way for future research.

Since HWWb considerations have significantly increased, the literature shows that real estate has also turned its focus to this area [9,24,25]. Modern real estate projects are developing assets based on the Sustainable Development Goals [26,27], in particular goals 1 to 6, which directly (or indirectly) address HWWb. Real estate entities, developers, and construction companies are addressing HWWb-related issues, such as the need for outdoor activities, the need to improve vitamin D levels by sun exposure, the need of avoiding stress at work, the quality of the indoor environment, occupational safety, etc. [28–30]. Indoor air quality, ventilation, thermal comfort, water quality, moisture control, safety, and security, lighting, and views, noise control, and the limitation of dust and pests are among the elements considered most important for the inhabitants of any building [31].

HWWb is significantly influenced by the operation and the design of the communities where people live, work, play and learn. Within the real estate industry, the large impact of community development [32], transportation [33], urban design [34], and other development projects [35–38] might be viewed as positive or negative impacts as economic externalities that could be unmeasured, unconsidered, and unregulated. It was observed by Trowbridge et al. (2014) [24] that those externalities or lack of transparencies would lead to an increase in inefficiency for real estate investment, which is a main concern for promoting HWWb. Within the real estate industry, those externalities also limited the market incentives for innovation. The research concluded that within the real estate industry, HWWb metrics are required, as well as investments from multiple sectors, including health and care, in order to expand market adoption and enable more effective HWWb design considerations.

Mensah et al. (2016) [39] research's adds to this idea of community planning, especially urban design. The authors examined the relationship between quality of life and green spaces from different perspectives of life, such as social, economic and environmental perspectives, to better understand the different ways in which green spaces enhance human life. Their study concluded that green spaces help towards enhancing social, physical, emotional, psychological and material HWWb, which improves the quality of life of an individual. These results suggested that the governing and policy-making bodies should promote green spaces to provide high levels of quality of life to the citizens, and enable sustainable development of the economy [40,41].

Hogan et al. (2014) [42], in their attempt to optimize the process of co-design and deliberation by citizens, experts, and policy-makers, noted that there is a need to explore new policies and measures to improve HWWb. In addition, the authors argue that there is a need to establish a measure for the national HWWb and social progress, in addition to the economic activity measure, as reflected by the gross domestic product.

The recently arising theory for conscious cities has further shifted the real estate focus to HWWb-led design [43]. Design, understood from all dimensions of the built environment, including urban, landscape, architecture, interior design, and industrial design, is a key value creator in the real estate development process. Design impacts the way humans function [44] and how they occupy space. The capacity of a space to attract people depends heavily on its design [45], which may either provide a feeling of ontological security or social capital qualities, which are critical for promoting pro-social behavior and improving HWWb [46]. To enhance the living conditions and the usage of architectural spaces, while taking the environment and technology into consideration, the designers need to focus more on the psychological and physical impacts of the design on residents' needs, preferences, and expectations [47]. An impactful design can have a very strong effect on the residents' physical and mental state, i.e., their HWWb. Nevertheless, shifting the focus onto HWWb and experience does not necessarily mean compromising on design [48,49].

There is a significant relationship between HWWb and place, predicted by a mechanism of curiosity in which place is mobilized. The study by Philips et al. (2015) [50] addressed different questions of HWWb and place-mobilized curiosity, such as what forms curiosity would take when it is mobilized as practices of HWWb, and also how that curiosity might be supported and understood. Two sets of curious practices were identified. One emphasized places, while the other set of practices strongly emphasized the things associated with those places, highlighting collective, shared and interactive forms of curiosity. On the other hand, people might be curious about each other, which leads us to understand the association or relationship between places and HWWb. Nevertheless, the study notes that place, HWWb, and curiosity are interlinked in terms of objects, people and practices.

Steen (2016) [51] argues that design promotes human HWWb. The author discusses that design for HWWb projects is different from the projects of 'traditional' design with their aim to engage people in creative and meaningful activities so that they can flourish. Loftness at el. (2007) [52] presented three main ideas for healthy building designs, namely sustainable development, individual behavior for ensuring the air quality or environment indoors, and the latest building material trends to provide a healthier environment. Their research concluded that quality of life sustainable design consists of good infrastructure, higher durability, recyclability, and lower energy consumption.

An increasing value-beyond-value, as strictly defined by real estate, is being attached to the significance of the space in which people live, in terms of HWWb. As an example, one can refer to the expanded published scholarly literature that relates to HWWb and design of medical facilities and educational establishments [53–55]. Thus, in order to enhance sustainability, resilience, effectiveness, and performance at workplaces, educational institutes, hospitals, or residential buildings, HWWb-led design and architectural and technical solutions must be adopted. Supportive design and a positive environment are important for the occupants of a building. According to Loftness et al. (2007) [52], various design elements, such as colors, lighting, efficient use of space, etc., can have significant influence on the HWWb and the efficiency of the occupants /residents of a building. Yet, there is no empirical study, to the best of one's knowledge, that bears strong evidence of the relation among design and occupants /residents HWWb.

In order to address this gap, this study aims to obtain residents' perceptions, to address the following two research questions:

RQ1: What is the relationship between the design elements (lighting, ventilation, acoustics, color, texture, use of space, ergonomics and universal design) and all the dimensions of HWWb?

RQ2: What are the opinions of everyday people about the relationship between design and wellness?

2. Materials and Methods

2.1. Scope Determination

HWWb does not encompass merely the physical and mental state; rather, it is the embodiment of every dimension, including emotions, social life, and spirituality. This study, in order to frame HWWb, will use the Six Dimensions of Wellness Model originally offered by the National Wellness Institute (www.nationalwellness.org, accessed on 1 October 2022), namely intellectual, emotional, social, spiritual, occupational, and physical dimensions.

Physical Wellness: This dimension focuses on the need for regular physical activity [56]. When a person focuses on this aspect of their health, it encourages them to observe the other dimensions of wellness as well, including a focus on the quality of their diet and nutrition and avoiding harmful things, such as tobacco and drugs [57]. An individual can achieve peak wellness not by just physical activity, but also through healthy eating habits [58]. Personal care, building strength and medical self-care also contribute to the achievement of physical wellness [59]. An individual must be responsible and caring toward their own health and should know when to seek medical attention [60]. Usually, building a healthy and athletic-looking body leads to improved mental health and especially confidence of the individual [61,62]. This dimension provides higher self-esteem, self-determination, self-control and a sense of direction [63].

Emotional Wellness: This dimension relates to emotions, feelings and awareness and acceptance of those feelings [56]. It is focused around feeling positive about life [64]. Emotional wellness places great emphasis on emotional intelligence, i.e., managing and understanding one's own emotions and coping with stress through keeping in mind others' emotions as well [65]. An emotionally intelligent person understands the feelings and emotions of oneself, as well as those of the people around them [63]. This helps the individual to maintain healthy, satisfying relationships with oneself, as well as others. They make decisions by analyzing their feelings, thoughts, philosophies and behavior, as well as seeking appreciation of others' support and assistance [66]. Emotionally intelligent people have the ability to maintain relationships that are built on mutual understanding, commitment, trust and respect [65]. The ability to accept challenges and risks is a significant factor in emotional wellness. The conflict is considered as potentially healthy. Emotional wellness involves managing one's own life and taking responsibility for one's own actions [56,65].

Spiritual Wellness: Spiritual wellness is focused on the meaning and purpose of our existence [56,67]. It is related to soul searching [68]. It expands beyond human life to accepting and appreciating the natural forces of the universe [69]. It means creating harmony between one's emotions, feelings and the tumultuous journey of their life [70]. It involves accepting and owning one's experiences of self-doubt, despair, fear and disappointment, as well as the pleasure, joy and happiness [71]. It also involves keeping a positive balance between one's feelings, thus achieving inner peace and happiness and reflecting this through one's actions [72].

Intellectual Wellness: This is related to creativity [56]. An intellectually well person builds their knowledge and skills and shares these with others [63]. They cherish intellectual growth and discover the potential of sharing this gift with others [73]. A well person has many healthy habits, such as reading books and a continued pursuit toward learning new skills [74]. They are curious in nature and this curiosity keeps them chasing greater intellect, challenging their mind and encourages them to be more creative [75]. This becomes a significant part of their life.

Occupational Wellness: This dimension is related to life satisfaction and enrichment through one's career and work [56]. A person's occupational development impacts upon their attitude towards work [65,76]. If an individual can contribute to their occupation with their true skills and talents, this contribution helps them to achieve occupational wellness [63,77]. The contribution of personal values, enthusiasm and a passion for one's choice of profession, or career, and the feeling of reward for that effort is occupational wellness [30,78,79].

Social Wellness: This dimension recognizes an individual's contribution towards their environment and community [56]. A socially well person exhibits interdependence between nature and other people [80]. This person will focus on nature, the balance of nature, and also look to their environment to gain strength [81]. This strength helps them to achieve all other dimensions of wellness and most importantly, inner-peace [82]. It involves making healthy choices about life and living, communicating with others and contributing towards building a better environment for everyone [83].

2.2. Empirical Analysis

The literature review implies a link between HWWb and the role of design as the key value creator in the real estate development process, which must be understood from all dimensions of the built environment, including urban, landscape, building design and architecture, with an emphasis on interior design. In order to test this, a model was developed that includes two hypotheses, as presented in Figure 1.

HWWb	Design
• Physical Dimension • Spiritual Dimension • Intellectual Dimension • Social Dimension • Occupational Dimension • Others	• Lighting • Ventilation • Acoustics • Color • Texture • Use of Space • Ergonomics • Universal Design Principles • Incorporation of Nature • Art • Green Design Principles
H1: HWWb is dependent on the design	
H2: Dimensions of HWWb are associated with dimensions of design	

Figure 1. Hypotheses Model.

To prove these hypotheses correct or otherwise, cross-sectional data collected through a survey questionnaire were used. Cross-sectional analysis is the study of a group's attitudes, beliefs or opinion at a specific point in time [84]. The questionnaire used for this survey was developed based on the one used by Kathy F. Montgomery (2004) for her study on design and wellness [85]. Likert scale-based questions allowed respondents to indicate the degree to which they agree with the statements. A Likert scale asks for responses that range from strongly agree to strongly disagree. A Likert item is an anchored rating scale in which the anchors represent different levels of agreement or disagreement for a given parameter. For the scope of this study, the scale was organized into 5 score items, ranging from 5 (complete level of agreement) to 1 (complete level of disagreement), and respondents were invited to express their views using the entire scale. Five-point Likert scale survey questions are a widely applied measuring attitude method in urban science, as well as in other fields [86–91].

The questionnaire was created electronically and the link was sent using email. It should be noted that all candidates, technically, were ultimately interviewed by chance. The main purpose for distributing the questionnaire via email was to maximize the reach and number of responses. It is also a cost effective, easier, and quicker way to collect data. This mode of data collection also facilitated the compilation of responses into a database that tabulates the responses for each question. Convenient sampling was used in this survey. The emails of the residents were collected through LinkedIn and other social media public profiles. Later, the email was sent with the link to the questionnaire and the recipients were given 15 days to respond. The respondents filled in the survey of their own free will. An introductory cover letter that explained the purpose of the survey and how the findings would be used was attached to the front page of the email message. The cover letter was sent with the survey form. Instructions for completing the form were also included in the letter. After one week, a second reminder e-mail was sent. A final email was sent to all respondents upon completion. This message was to thank them for their participation and the time they spent in responding to the survey.

The survey was organized into categories. Section 1 asked for personal background and demographic information. Section 2 was comprised of questions that asked the respondent for their opinion on design and its impact on HWWb. Section 3 asked the respondents for their opinions about HWWb. The Six Dimension of Wellness Model was used to explain the term(s). Each dimension listed was supported by bullet points that together explain that dimension. This section and this definition were provided to the respondents to help them to consider the design elements that may impact the six dimensions of HWWb listed in Section 4. In Sections 3 and 4, respondents are asked to indicate the degree to which they think each dimension affects HWWb, and the degree to which each design element may impact the HWWb of occupants using that space. This is considered the most appropriate methodology for the current context.

3. Results

The data were collected at one time using a cross-sectional study approach. Initially, the survey questionnaires were distributed among 200 people. However, 150 responses were received because some respondents did not return the questionnaires or did not complete the questionnaires properly. Furthermore, incomplete questionnaires were also excluded, which resulted in 150 responses. Therefore, the response rate was 75%.

To understand composition of the sample, this study took two demographical variables. The first is years and the second is employment status. According to the analysis, 12% of the people were less than 20 years old. Around 13% had an age of between 21 and 25. Around 27% of the people were between 26 and 30 years. Around 25% of the people were aged between 31 and 35. In addition, around 23% of the people were above 35 years of age. In terms of employment status, around 6% of the people were employed and around 14% of the people were unemployed. Table 1 explains the details of the demographic profile of the survey respondents.

The descriptive statistics reveal interesting insights. As presented in Table 2, the mean values for 'texture' and 'lighting' are 2.75 and 2.70, respectively. This shows that the respondents prefer natural day lighting and that the texture adds to the overall aesthetic quality. On the other hand, the respondents consider 'art' and the 'green design principles' as the least important factors. On the HWWb side, the mean value of 'intellectual dimension' and 'occupational dimension' is 3.31 and 3.08, respectively, and these are the most dominant dimensions. The value range between −2 and +2 for skewness and kurtosis indicates that these data fulfill the normality conditions.

Table 1. Demographic Profile of the Survey Respondents.

		Frequency	Percent	Cumulative Percent
Age	Less than 20	18	12.0	12.0
	21–25	19	12.7	24.7
	26–30	40	26.7	51.3
	31–35	38	25.3	76.7
	Above 35	35	23.3	100.0
	Total	150	100.0	
Employment Status	Employed	129	86.0	86.0
	Unemployed	21	14.0	100.0
	Total	150	100.0	

Table 2. Descriptives.

Items	Minimum	Maximum	Mean	Std. Deviation	Skewness		Kurtosis	
	Statistic	Statistic	Statistic	Statistic	Statistic	Std. Error	Statistic	Std. Error
Lighting	1	5	2.70	1.309	−0.082	0.198	−1.347	0.394
Ventilation	1	5	2.62	1.224	0.140	0.198	−1.239	0.394
Acoustics	1	5	2.63	1.255	0.167	0.198	−1.232	0.394
Color	1	5	2.62	1.319	0.180	0.198	−1.314	0.394
Texture	1	5	**2.75**	1.254	−0.274	0.198	−1.399	0.394
Use of space	1	5	2.55	1.196	0.063	0.198	−1.304	0.394
Ergonomics	1	5	2.63	1.282	0.096	0.198	−1.290	0.394
Universal design principles	1	5	2.62	1.288	0.150	0.198	−1.319	0.394
Incorporation of nature	1	5	2.69	1.220	−0.155	0.198	−1.213	0.394
Art	1	5	2.41	1.050	0.268	0.198	−0.847	0.394
Green design principles	1	5	2.39	1.055	0.303	0.198	−0.842	0.394
Physical dimension	1	5	2.73	1.123	−0.077	0.198	−0.842	0.394
Spiritual dimension	1	5	2.68	1.149	−0.019	0.198	−0.943	0.394
Intellectual dimension	1	6	**3.31**	1.396	−0.381	0.198	−1.074	0.394
Social dimension	1	6	2.83	1.079	−0.103	0.198	−0.271	0.394
Emotional dimension	1	5	2.91	1.209	−0.201	0.198	−1.104	0.394
Occupational dimension	1	5	3.08	1.303	0.071	0.198	−1.092	0.394

A regression analysis was carried out in order to test H1. The full model regression analysis is presented in Tables 3–5.

Table 3. Regression Model Summary.

Model	R	R Square	Adjusted R Square	Std. Error of the Estimate
1	0.906 [a]	0.821	0.820	0.47782

[a] Predictors: (constant), ID.

Table 4. ANOVA [a].

Model		Sum of Squares	df	Mean Square	F	Sig.
1	Regression	154.690	1	154.690	677.547	0.000 [b]
	Residual	33.790	148	0.228		
	Total	188.479	149			

[a] Dependent variable: HWWb. [b] Predictors: (constant), ID.

Table 5. Full Model Regression Coefficients [a].

Model		Unstandardized Coefficients		Standardized Coefficients	t	Sig.
		B	Std. Error	Beta		
1	(Constant)	0.693	0.094		7.357	0.000
	ID	0.857	0.033	0.906	26.030	0.000

[a] Dependent variable: HWWb.

In Table 3, the regression model summary is presented. In this summary, the R-square value is 0.821, which indicates that around 82% of HWWb is predicted by the design elements. Thus, H1 is verified.

In Table 4 the significance value ($p < 0.01$) of the F-value (677.547) indicates that the regression is significant.

In Table 5, the unstandardized beta value is 0.857; however, the standardized coefficient beta value is 0.906, with a significance value of 0.000. This indicates that one unit of the design element will increase around 91% of HWWb.

In Table 6, and in order to provide answers for RQ1, a detailed analysis was conducted to examine which dimension of design elements affect which dimension of HWWb (see H2). According to the analysis, the 'physical dimension' is significantly predicted by 'color', 'use of space', and 'universal design principles'. The 'spiritual dimension is predicted by 'ergonomics'. The 'intellectual dimension' is predicted by 'art'. The 'social dimension' is predicted by 'color, 'universal design principles', and 'incorporation of nature'. The 'emotional dimension is predicted by 'incorporation of nature', 'art', and 'green design principles'. The 'occupational dimension is predicted by 'color', and 'art'.

Table 6. Regressions Coefficients.

Items	Physical Dimension		Spiritual Dimension		Intellectual Dimension		Social Dimension		Emotional Dimension		Occupational Dimension	
	β	Sig.	β	Sig.	β	Sig.	β	Sig.	β	Sig.	β	Sig.
Lighting	0.21	0.35	−0.02	0.92	0.18	0.51	−0.05	0.82	0.00	0.99	0.11	0.67
Ventilation	0.14	0.69	0.00	0.99	−0.55	0.18	−0.23	0.51	0.02	0.96	−0.09	0.81
Acoustics	0.05	0.89	−0.09	0.81	0.04	0.94	0.00	0.99	−0.33	0.47	−0.29	0.49
Color	0.45	0.04	0.27	0.23	0.34	0.21	0.96	0.00	0.07	0.80	0.43	0.07
Texture	0.18	0.30	0.19	0.28	−0.10	0.63	0.00	1.00	0.02	0.92	−0.09	0.62
Use of space	0.46	0.02	0.26	0.20	0.38	0.12	0.25	0.23	0.12	0.61	0.34	0.13
Ergonomics	0.08	0.79	0.59	0.04	0.19	0.57	0.18	0.53	0.28	0.40	0.22	0.47
Universal design principles	0.53	0.03	0.15	0.51	0.26	0.36	0.86	0.00	0.32	0.24	0.28	0.26
Incorporation of nature	0.18	0.29	0.11	0.52	0.56	0.01	0.77	0.00	0.58	0.00	0.35	0.05
Art	−0.36	0.24	−0.28	0.36	0.04	0.92	−0.38	0.22	0.83	0.02	0.28	0.40
Green design principles	0.02	0.96	0.01	0.97	0.02	0.96	0.11	0.71	−0.40	0.26	−0.08	0.81

Furthermore, and in order to understand the correlation between the variables of this study, a two-tailed Pearson correlation analysis was conducted. The results are presented in Table 7. The results indicate that the construct 'years' is insignificantly related to employment status ($\beta = 0.083$, $p > 0.05$), design ($\beta = 0.055$, $p > 0.05$) and HWWb ($\beta = 0.130$, $p > 0.05$). This shows that 'years' have no impact on other study constructs. Regarding employment status, the results are also insignificant with design ($\beta = 0.123$, $p > 0.05$) and HWWb ($\beta = 0.065$, $p > 0.05$). Regarding design and its correlation with HWWb, the correlation was found to be positively significant ($\beta = 0.906$, $p < 0.01$).

Table 7. Inter-Constructs' Correlation.

Sr.	Construct	1	2	3	4
1	Years	1			
2	Employment status	0.083	1		
3	Design	0.055	0.123	1	
4	HWWb	0.130	0.065	0.906	1

In partial least square structure equation modeling (PLS–SEM), both measurement models were evaluated to check the reliability and the validity of the constructs and methodology [92]. The reliability of the constructs was measured by assessing the composite reliability, as mentioned in Table 8. The average variance extracted values were above 0.5, which fulfills the criteria for validity. The average variance extracted values for both design elements and HWWb were 0.944 and 0.865, respectively. The internal consistency of the constructs was above the threshold value of 0.7 [93]. Therefore, it is considered that all the constructs fulfill the internal consistency of their items.

Table 8. Reliability and Average Variance Extracted.

Variable	Cronbach's Alpha	rho_A	Composite Reliability	Average Variance Extracted
Design	0.994	0.994	0.995	0.944
HWWb	0.969	0.969	0.975	0.865

For indicator reliability, the factor loading of the constructs was evaluated. The outer model presented in Figure 2 shows the factor loadings of both the constructs. Thus, no items of the constructs were deleted and all the items of the constructs were noted in the further analysis.

To assess the discriminant validity, the heterotrait-monotrait ratio of correlations was used [93–95]. Table 9 shows that the values for $HTMT_{.85}$ and $HTMT_{.90}$ are below 0.85 [96] and 0.90 [97], respectively. Hence, the discriminant validity is established.

Table 9. Heterotrait-Monotrait Ratio.

Variable	Design
Design	
HWWb	0.923

The model also evaluates the R square value of HWWb, which is 0.821 (Table 10). This indicates that interior design elements predict around 82% of wellness.

Table 10. R Square Value.

Construct	R-Square
HWWb	0.821

After evaluating the measurement model, the structure model was formulated (Figure 3).

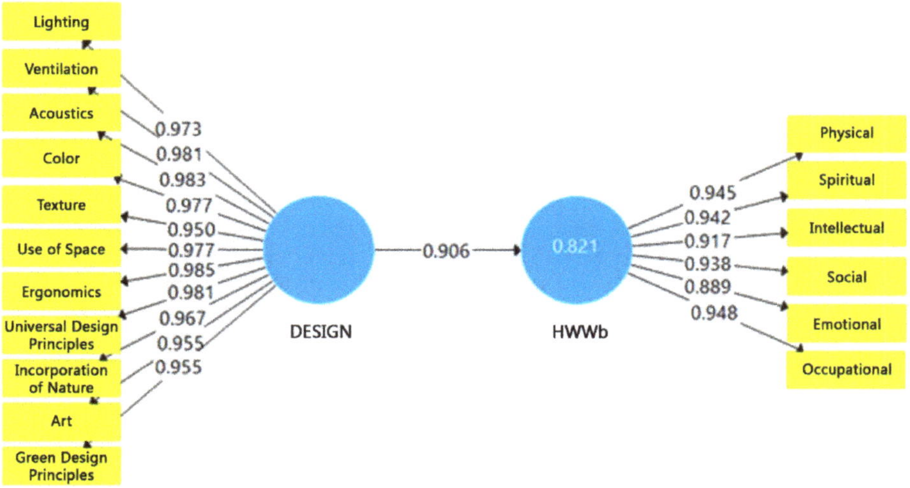

Figure 2. Measurement Model.

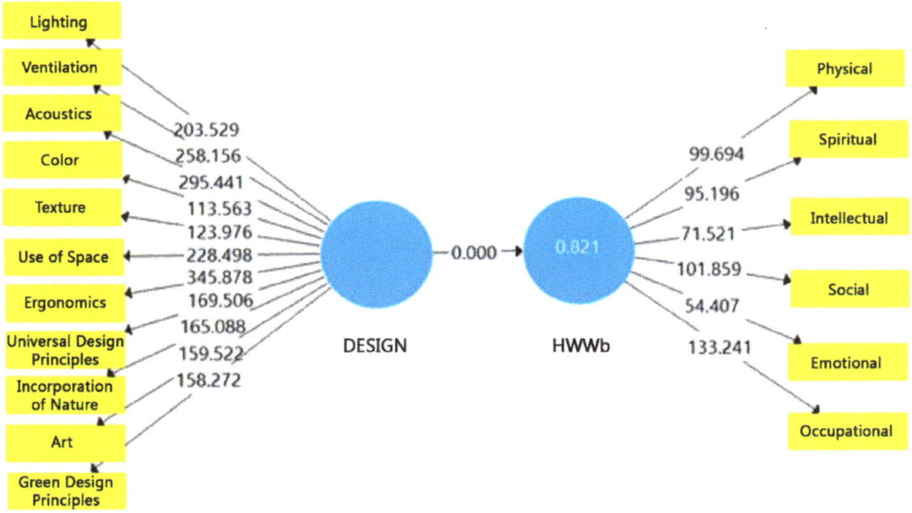

Figure 3. Structural Model.

In the structural model, other than the quality statistics and factor loadings, the path coefficient determined by significance and the T-value, using the bootstrap procedure [98], are also calculated. All the T-values greater than 1.645 and the significance value greater than 0.05 are considered to be a significant path [99]. The outer model in Figure 3 represents the T-values with all the indicators of the constructs, whereas the inner model represents the significance value between the construct, which is significant at a p-value less than 0.00. The path coefficient in Table 11 indicates that the relationship between design and HWWb is positively significant ($\beta = 0.91$, $t = 64.72$, $p < 0.01$).

Table 11. Path Coefficient.

Path	Original Sample	Sample Mean	Standard Deviation	T Statistics	*p* Values
Design → HWWb	0.91	0.91	0.01	64.72	0.00

Table 12 indicates the Q-square value. The Q-square value is assessed by the blindfolding technique in PLS–SEM [100,101]. This technique helps in assessing the predictive relevance of the structural model. In this technique, the resampling procedure is executed in a specified number of iterations to assess the data points of the endogenous construct. After that, the predictive value and the original value are compared. If the value difference is small, then it shows that the predictive relevance is greater [98]. However, the value should be greater than zero. Thus, the data presented in Table 12 indicate that the Q-square value of HWWb is 0.706, which is greater than the threshold of 0. This indicates that the model has good predictive relevance.

Table 12. Q-Square Value.

Construct	SSO	SSE	Q^2 (= 1 − SSE/SSO)
Design	1650	1650	
HWWb	900	264.948	0.706

4. Discussion and Conclusions

The survey responses provide meaningful insights into the role of design as a key value creator in the real estate development process. A total of 99% ('strongly agree' and 'agree') of the respondents believe that design has a substantial effect on the HWWb of the residents of a building, a finding that is consistent with the wider literature [102]. The respondents also indicated a clear preference for buildings that include design and planning considerations for the HWWb of the occupants. The responses to the following statement varied: 'HWWb is an important factor in the design of a corporate building'. A total of 57% of participants responded as 'neutral', while 36% agreed with the statement (23% responded as 'strongly agree' and 13% as 'agree'). In addition, 7% disagreed with the statement. These responses show that majority of people are ambivalent towards HWWb concerns in regard to the design of a corporate building. It is not viewed as important and they do not seem to care either way whether their workplace incorporates HWWb-led design or not.

In the detailed data analysis, the responses show that different dimensions of HWWb are predicted by different dimensions of design. The 'physical dimension' is significantly predicted by 'color', 'use of space', and 'universal design principles'. The 'spiritual dimension' is predicted by 'ergonomics'. The 'intellectual dimension' is predicted by 'art'. The 'social dimension' is predicted by 'color', 'universal design principles', and 'incorporation of nature'. The 'emotional dimension' is predicted by the 'incorporation of nature', 'art' and 'green design principles'. The 'occupational dimension' is predicted by 'color' and 'art'.

According to the results displayed in Table 2, the respondents consider that natural day lighting has a very positive effect on HWWb. They also state that texture adds to the aesthetic quality of the interior environment. Thus, when designers work on interiors, they must pay attention to the lighting, as well as aesthetic quality. This finding further supports Morales-Bravo and Navarrete-Hernandez's 2022 study [103], which demonstrates that natural lighting conditions have a major impact design on the perceived HWWb in residential spaces.

The least importance was given to the use of 'art' in the interior environments, although previous studies support the contribution of art and cultural development and community wellbeing [104], and the 'green design principles', which are considered design practices that conserve the natural environment. This is not in complete agreement with evidence found earlier in the published scholarly literature (for example, see [105]), thus offering further insights and posing further questions regarding HWWb and the design in the built environment. The current analysis also suggests that design predicts 82% of HWWb and 1 unit change in design will bring 91% change in HWWb. This is a significant predictor of the dependent variable.

As hypothesized in the model of this study, the relationship between design and HWWb is found to be positively significant, also concurring well with earlier attempts [106]. To obtain the results, several analyses, including descriptive statistics, regression analysis, variables correlation, and PLS–SEM that incorporates assessment of measurement and structural models, were conducted. The results conclusively explain that design elements are positively linked with HWWb.

Sustainable real estate development is directly related to HWWb [107]. However, since the sector, driven by the contemporary target market, has shifted its focus from 'luxury' to 'wellbeing', all stakeholders involved in the process need to better understand and comprehend, in a progressive and exponential way, all aspects around sustainable healthy development and design.

This study was limited to a small sample, which is, however, adequate to support the findings [91]. Future research could further expand the sample using data from real estate developers, professional designers and the residents/ occupants in order to further validate the arguments of the current research, compare the differences among these stockholders, and provide valuable insights for the real estate sector. Additionally, future research could study the effects of all the HWWb dimensions on all the dimensions of real estate development, considering them as separate and independent variables.

The results of the current research are significant in terms of filling a significant gap in the literature regarding HWWb in relation to real estate assets, further supporting the importance of interdisciplinary urban sustainability, as well as real estate professionals within the HWWb industry, such as those working in hotel retreats, spas, elderly care facilities, hospitals, and rehabilitation centers.

HWWb real estate is a rising market that has the ability to address the current urban concerns. It reflects a paradigm change that clearly prioritizes people's HWWb in the concept, design, construction, renovation, development and redevelopment of the built environment. Many components of the sustainable construction movement, the design-driven movements, and other similar endeavors are presently transformed in the new and forthcoming HWWb-focused real estate. As we look into the future of HWWb real estate, this study has contributed to enhancing our understanding of the new metrics to capture HWWb, in addition to the relationships among personal HWWb, the built environment, and community HWWb.

Author Contributions: A.C. conceived the original idea. I.V. encouraged A.C. to investigate health, wellness, and wellbeing aspects in the real estate sector, and supervised the findings of this work. A.C. developed the theoretical formalism, performed the analytic calculations and performed the numerical simulations, with the support of L.S. L.S. applied statistical techniques to analyze the data in order to verify the analytical methods. A.C. wrote the manuscript with support from I.V. L.S. took the lead in formulating the revised version. A.C., I.V. and L.S. contributed to the final version of the manuscript. I.V. supervised the project. All authors have read and agreed to the published version of the manuscript.

Funding: This research received no external funding.

Institutional Review Board Statement: Ethical review and approval were waived for this study. The survey was anonymous, gathering no sensitive data, and the participants gave consent to use their answers for research.

Informed Consent Statement: Informed consent was obtained from all subjects involved in the study.

Data Availability Statement: The data presented in this study are contained within this manuscript for reproducibility purposes.

Acknowledgments: We would like to thank all the people who have directly or indirectly helped us in carrying out this study.

Conflicts of Interest: The authors declare no conflict of interest.

References

1. Jevtic, M.; Matkovic, V.; Paut Kusturica, M.; Bouland, C. Build Healthier: Post-COVID-19 Urban Requirements for Healthy and Sustainable Living. *Sustainability* **2022**, *14*, 9274. [CrossRef]
2. Ho, T.P.; Stevenson, M.; Thompson, J.; Nguyen, T.Q. Evaluation of Urban Design Qualities across Five Urban Typologies in Hanoi. *Urban Sci.* **2021**, *5*, 76. [CrossRef]
3. Al Horr, Y.; Arif, M.; Kaushik, A.; Mazroei, A.; Elsarrag, E.; Mishra, S. Occupant Productivity and Indoor Environment Quality: A Case of GSAS. *Int. J. Sustain. Built Environ.* **2017**, *6*, 476–490. [CrossRef]
4. Krefis, A.; Augustin, M.; Schlünzen, K.; Oßenbrügge, J.; Augustin, J. How Does the Urban Environment Affect Health and Well-Being? A Systematic Review. *Urban Sci.* **2018**, *2*, 21. [CrossRef]
5. Kosec, Z.; Sekulic, S.; Wilson-Gahan, S.; Rostohar, K.; Tusak, M.; Bon, M. Correlation between Employee Performance, Well-Being, Job Satisfaction, and Life Satisfaction in Sedentary Jobs in Slovenian Enterprises. *Int. J. Environ. Res. Public Health* **2022**, *19*, 10427. [CrossRef]
6. Cincinelli, A.; Martellini, T. Indoor Air Quality and Health. *Int. J. Environ. Res. Public Health* **2017**, *14*, 1286. [CrossRef]
7. McCormack, G.R.; Frehlich, L.; Blackstaffe, A.; Turin, T.C.; Doyle-Baker, P.K. Active and Fit Communities. Associations between Neighborhood Walkability and Health-Related Fitness in Adults. *Int. J. Environ. Res. Public Health* **2020**, *17*, 1131. [CrossRef]
8. Mueller, M.A.E.; Flouri, E.; Kokosi, T. The Role of the Physical Environment in Adolescent Mental Health. *Health Place* **2019**, *58*, 102153. [CrossRef]
9. Kyricos, M. The Growing Phenomenon of Wellness Communities and Lifestyle Real Estate. *Int. J. Spa Wellness* **2018**, *1*, 144–151. [CrossRef]
10. Orii, L.; Alonso, L.; Larson, K. Methodology for Establishing Well-Being Urban Indicators at the District Level to Be Used on the CityScope Platform. *Sustainability* **2020**, *12*, 9458. [CrossRef]
11. Stagno, E. Investigating Relationship Between Built Environment and Health. In Proceedings of the International Symposium: New Metropolian Perspectives. Knowledge Dynamics and Innovation-Driven Policies Towards Urban and Regional Transition, Reggio Calabria, Italy, 24–26 May 2020; Bevilacqua, C., Calabrò, F., Della Spina, L., Eds.; Springer: Cham, Switzerland, 2021; Volume 2, pp. 285–296.
12. Kim, J.; de Leeuw, E.; Harris-Roxas, B.; Sainsbury, P. Four Urban Health Paradigms: The Search for Coherence. *Cities* **2022**, *128*, 103806. [CrossRef]
13. Kavouras, S.; Mitoula, R. Urban Development: Re-Thinking City Branding. The Role of Health and Safety. *Urban. Inf.* **2020**, *289*, 8–11.
14. Holmes, S. Assessing the Quality of Life—Reality or Impossible Dream? *Int. J. Nurs. Stud.* **2005**, *42*, 493–501. [CrossRef] [PubMed]
15. Vosko, L.F.; Basok, T.; Spring, C.; Candiz, G.; George, G. Understanding Migrant Farmworkers' Health and Well-Being during the Global COVID-19 Pandemic in Canada: Toward a Transnational Conceptualization of Employment Strain. *Int. J. Environ. Res. Public Health* **2022**, *19*, 8574. [CrossRef]
16. Albouy, D.; Graf, W.; Kellogg, R.; Wolff, H. Climate Amenities, Climate Change, and American Quality of Life. *J. Assoc. Environ. Resour. Econ.* **2016**, *3*, 205–246. [CrossRef]
17. Corburn, J.; Njoroge, P.; Weru, J.; Musya, M. Urban Climate Justice, Human Health, and Citizen Science in Nairobi's Informal Settlements. *Urban Sci.* **2022**, *6*, 36. [CrossRef]
18. Abdelaziz Mahmoud, N.S.; El Samanoudy, G.; Jung, C. Simulating the Natural Lighting for a Physical and Mental Well-Being in Residential Building in Dubai, UAE. *Ain Shams Eng. J.* **2022**, *14*, 101810. [CrossRef]
19. Thomas, J. *Current Measures and the Challenges of Measuring Children's Wellbeing*; Office for National Statistics: Newport, UK, 2009.
20. Frisch, M.B. Ruut Veenhoven: Pioneer in Empirical Research on Happiness. *Appl. Res. Qual. Life* **2013**, *8*, 539–542. [CrossRef]
21. Dodge, R.; Daly, A.; Huyton, J.; Sanders, L. The Challenge of Defining Wellbeing. *Int. J. Wellbeing* **2012**, *2*, 222–235. [CrossRef]
22. Gillett-Swan, J.K.; Sargeant, J. Wellbeing as a Process of Accrual: Beyond Subjectivity and Beyond the Moment. *Soc. Indic. Res.* **2015**, *121*, 135–148. [CrossRef]
23. Eger, R.J.; Maridal, J.H. A Statistical Meta-Analysis of the Wellbeing Literature. *Int. J. Wellbeing* **2015**, *5*, 45–74. [CrossRef]
24. Trowbridge, M.J.; Pickell, S.G.; Pyke, C.R.; Jutte, D.P. Building Healthy Communities: Establishing Health And Wellness Metrics For Use Within The Real Estate Industry. *Health Aff.* **2014**, *33*, 1923–1929. [CrossRef] [PubMed]
25. De Toro, P.; Nocca, F.; Buglione, F. Real Estate Market Responses to the COVID-19 Crisis: Which Prospects for the Metropolitan Area of Naples (Italy)? *Urban Sci.* **2021**, *5*, 23. [CrossRef]
26. Mironiuc, M.; Ionașcu, E.; Huian, M.C.; Țaran, A. Reflecting the Sustainability Dimensions on the Residential Real Estate Prices. *Sustainability* **2021**, *13*, 2963. [CrossRef]

27. Ionașcu, E.; Mironiuc, M.; Anghel, I.; Huian, M.C. The Involvement of Real Estate Companies in Sustainable Development—An Analysis from the SDGs Reporting Perspective. *Sustainability* **2020**, *12*, 798. [CrossRef]
28. MacNaughton, P.; Satish, U.; Laurent, J.G.C.; Flanigan, S.; Vallarino, J.; Coull, B.; Spengler, J.D.; Allen, J.G. The Impact of Working in a Green Certified Building on Cognitive Function and Health. *Build. Environ.* **2017**, *114*, 178–186. [CrossRef]
29. Gullett, L.R.; Alhasan, D.M.; Jackson, W.B.; Jackson, C.L. Employment Industry and Occupational Class in Relation to Serious Psychological Distress in the United States. *Int. J. Environ. Res. Public Health* **2022**, *19*, 8376. [CrossRef]
30. Kavouras, S.; Vardopoulos, I.; Mitoula, R.; Zorpas, A.A.; Kaldis, P. Occupational Health and Safety Scope Significance in Achieving Sustainability. *Sustainability* **2022**, *14*, 2424. [CrossRef]
31. Cedeño Laurent, J.G.; Williams, A.; Oulhote, Y.; Zanobetti, A.; Allen, J.G.; Spengler, J.D. Reduced Cognitive Function during a Heat Wave among Residents of Non-Air-Conditioned Buildings: An Observational Study of Young Adults in the Summer of 2016. *PLoS Med.* **2018**, *15*, e1002605. [CrossRef]
32. Bencardino, M.; Granata, M.F.; Nesticò, A.; Salvati, L. Urban Growth and Real Estate Income. A Comparison of Analytical Models. In Proceedings of the Computational Science and Its Applications—ICCSA 2016, Beijing, China, 4–7 July 2016; Gervasi, O., Murgante, B., Misra, S., Rocha, A.M., Torre, C.M., Tania, D., Apduhan, B.O., Stankova, E., Wang, S., Eds.; Springer: Cham, Switzerland, 2016; pp. 151–166.
33. Salvati, L.; Rontos, K.; Morelli, V.G. Urban Sprawl and Implications for Sustainable Transportation: Analysing Changing Commuting Patterns in a Mediterranean City Region. *Int. J. Sustain. Soc.* **2015**, *7*, 333. [CrossRef]
34. Pyrilli, D.; Savvides, A.L.; Fokaides, P.A. The Impact of Urban Design on the Realization of the Zero Energy Building Target Through On-Site Energy Production: A Case Study. *Curr. Sustain. Energy Rep.* **2017**, *4*, 72–86. [CrossRef]
35. Vardopoulos, I. Industrial Building Adaptive Reuse for Museum. Factors Affecting Visitors' Perceptions of the Sustainable Urban Development Potential. *Build. Environ.* **2022**, *222*, 109391. [CrossRef]
36. Tsilika, E.; Vardopoulos, I. The FIX-up Mix-up; Undue Facadism or Adaptive Reuse? Examining the Former FIX Brewery Transformation into the National Museum of Contemporary Art in Athens. *Archnet-IJAR Int. J. Archit. Res.* **2022**. [CrossRef]
37. Vardopoulos, I.; Tsilika, E.; Sarantakou, E.; Zorpas, A.; Salvati, L.; Tsartas, P. An Integrated SWOT-PESTLE-AHP Model Assessing Sustainability in Adaptive Reuse Projects. *Appl. Sci.* **2021**, *11*, 7134. [CrossRef]
38. Vardopoulos, I.; Theodoropoulou, E. Does the New 'FIX' Fit? Adaptive Building Reuse Affecting Local Sustainable Development: Preliminary Results. In Proceedings of the The IAFOR Conference on Heritage & the City (HCNY2018), New York, NY, USA, 7–9 November 2018; pp. 114–997.
39. Mensah, C.A.; Andres, L.; Perera, U.; Roji, A. Enhancing Quality of Life through the Lens of Green Spaces: A Systematic Review Approach. *Int. J. Wellbeing* **2016**, *6*, 142–163. [CrossRef]
40. Bianconi, F.; Clemente, M.; Filippucci, M.; Salvati, L. Regenerating Urban Spaces: A Brief Commentary on Green Infrastructures for Landscape Conservation. *TeMA J. Land Use Mobil. Environ.* **2018**, *11*, 107–118. [CrossRef]
41. Clemente, M.; Bianconi, F.; Filippucci, M.; Salvati, L. Regenerating Urban Spaces under Place-Specific Social Contexts: A Commentary on Green Infrastructures for Landscape Conservation. *Int. J. Soc. Sci.* **2017**, *VI*, 18–31. [CrossRef]
42. Hogan, M.J.; Johnston, H.; Broome, B.; McMoreland, C.; Walsh, J.; Smale, B.; Duggan, J.; Andriessen, J.; Leyden, K.M.; Domegan, C.; et al. Consulting with Citizens in the Design of Wellbeing Measures and Policies: Lessons from a Systems Science Application. *Soc. Indic. Res.* **2015**, *123*, 857–877. [CrossRef]
43. Palti, I.; Bar, M. A Manifesto for Conscious Cities: Should Streets Be Sensitive to Our Mental Needs? *The Guardian* 2015. Available online: https://www.theguardian.com/cities/2015/aug/28/manifesto-conscious-cities-streets-sensitive-mental-needs (accessed on 1 October 2022).
44. Irvine, K.N.; Suwanarit, A.; Likitswat, F.; Srilertchaipanij, H.; Ingegno, M.; Kaewlai, P.; Boonkam, P.; Tontisirin, N.; Sahavacharin, A.; Wongwatcharapaiboon, J.; et al. Smart City Thailand: Visioning and Design to Enhance Sustainability, Resiliency, and Community Wellbeing. *Urban Sci.* **2022**, *6*, 7. [CrossRef]
45. Gehl, J. *Life between Buildings: Using Public Space*; Reinhold: New York, NY, USA, 1987.
46. Holy-Hasted, W.; Burchell, B. Does Public Space Have to Be Green to Improve Well-Being? An Analysis of Public Space across Greater London and Its Association to Subjective Well-Being. *Cities* **2022**, *125*, 103569. [CrossRef]
47. Anastasiadou, P.; Sarantakou, E.; Maniati, E.; Tsilika, E. Exploring Stakeholders' Perspectives on Hotel Design. In *Transcending Borders in Tourism Through Innovation and Cultural Heritage, Proceedings of the 8th International Conference, IACuDiT, Hydra, Greece, 1–3 September 2021*; Springer Proceedings in Business and Economics; Katsoni, V., Şerban, A.C., Eds.; Springer: Cham, Switzerland, 2022; pp. 239–255.
48. Palti, I. Defining Conscious Cities. *J. Urban Des. Ment. Health* **2016**, *1*, 1. Available online: https://www.urbandesignmentalhealth.com/journal1-ipeditorial.html (accessed on 1 October 2022).
49. Bessoudo, M. Health, Wellness, and Experience in the Built Environment: From Green Buildings to Conscious Cities. *Conscious Cities Anthol.* **2017**, *2017*. [CrossRef]
50. Phillips, R.; Evans, B.; Muirhead, S. Curiosity, Place and Wellbeing: Encouraging Place-Specific Curiosity as a 'Way to Wellbeing'. *Environ. Plan. A Econ. Space* **2015**, *47*, 2339–2354. [CrossRef]
51. Steen, M. Organizing Design-for-Wellbeing Projects: Using the Capability Approach. *Des. Issues* **2016**, *32*, 4–15. [CrossRef]
52. Loftness, V.; Hakkinen, B.; Adan, O.; Nevalainen, A. Elements That Contribute to Healthy Building Design. *Environ. Health Perspect.* **2007**, *115*, 965–970. [CrossRef] [PubMed]

53. Shajahan, A.; Culp, C.H.; Williamson, B. Effects of Indoor Environmental Parameters Related to Building Heating, Ventilation, and Air Conditioning Systems on Patients' Medical Outcomes: A Review of Scientific Research on Hospital Buildings. *Indoor Air* **2019**, *29*, 161–176. [CrossRef] [PubMed]
54. Setyowati, E.; Harani, A.R.; Falah, Y.N. Green Building Design Concepts of Healthcare Facilities on the Orthopedic Hospital in the Tropics. *Procedia Soc. Behav. Sci.* **2013**, *101*, 189–199. [CrossRef]
55. Pilosof, N.P. Building for Change: Comparative Case Study of Hospital Architecture. *HERD Health Environ. Res. Des. J.* **2021**, *14*, 47–60. [CrossRef]
56. Wickramarathne, P.D.V.C.; Phuoc, J.C.; Albattat, A.R.S. A Review of Wellness Dimension Models: For the Advancement of the Society. *Eur. J. Soc. Sci. Stud.* **2020**, *5*, 185–198. [CrossRef]
57. Sallis, J.F.; McKenzie, T.L.; Beets, M.W.; Beighle, A.; Erwin, H.; Lee, S. Physical Education's Role in Public Health. *Res. Q. Exerc. Sport* **2012**, *83*, 125–135. [CrossRef]
58. Zaidi, U. Health and Rehabilitation Science Specialities, Physical Activity and Dimensions of Wellness among the Students of PNU. *Heliyon* **2020**, *6*, e03204. [CrossRef]
59. Al-Hazzaa, H.M. Physical Inactivity in Saudi Arabia Revisited: A Systematic Review of Inactivity Prevalence and Perceived Barriers to Active Living. *Int. J. Health Sci.* **2018**, *12*, 50–64.
60. Kaveh, M.H.; Ostovarfar, J.; Keshavarzi, S.; Ghahremani, L. Validation of Perceived Wellness Survey (PWS) in a Sample of Iranian Population. *Malays. J. Med. Sci.* **2016**, *23*, 46–53. [CrossRef] [PubMed]
61. Kirkham-King, M.; Brusseau, T.A.; Hannon, J.C.; Castelli, D.M.; Hilton, K.; Burns, R.D. Elementary Physical Education: A Focus on Fitness Activities and Smaller Class Sizes Are Associated with Higher Levels of Physical Activity. *Prev. Med. Rep.* **2017**, *8*, 135–139. [CrossRef] [PubMed]
62. Yuan, Y.; Ji, X.; Yang, X.; Wang, C.; Samsudin, S.; Omar Dev, R.D. The Effect of Persistence of Physical Exercise on the Positive Psychological Emotions of Primary School Students under the STEAM Education Concept. *Int. J. Environ. Res. Public Health* **2022**, *19*, 11451. [CrossRef] [PubMed]
63. Stoewen, D.L. Dimensions of Wellness: Change Your Habits, Change Your Life. *Can. Vet. J./Rev. Vet. Can.* **2017**, *58*, 861–862.
64. Randall, R. Emotional Wellness Needs: Older Adults in Rural Communities. *J. Fam. Consum. Sci.* **2009**, *101*, 33–37.
65. Strout, K.A.; Howard, E.P. Five Dimensions of Wellness and Predictors of Cognitive Health Protection in Community-Dwelling Older Adults: A Historical COLLAGE Cohort Study. *J. Holist. Nurs.* **2015**, *33*, 6–18. [CrossRef]
66. Lee, A.H.; Denizci Guillet, B.; Law, R. Tourists' Emotional Wellness and Hotel Room Colour. *Curr. Issues Tour.* **2018**, *21*, 856–862. [CrossRef]
67. Lalchali, P.; Sdrali, D.; Mitoula, R.; Apostolopoulos, C. Exploring Visitor Motivations at Religious Tourism Sites towards Sustainability on the Region of West Thessaly, Greece. *Tourismos* **2019**, *14*, 171–199. [CrossRef]
68. Ingersoll, R.E. Refining Dimensions of Spiritual Wellness: A Cross-Traditional Approach. *Couns. Values* **1998**, *42*, 156–165. [CrossRef]
69. Smith, D.; Louw, M. Conceptualisation of the Spiritual Life Dimension: A Personal and Professional Leadership Perspective. *SA J. Hum. Resour. Manag.* **2007**, *5*, 19–27. [CrossRef]
70. Odrovakavula, L.; Mohammadnezhad, M. "Everything Else Is Going to Be Ok If Your Spiritual Wellness Is Well". A Qualitative Exploration of Wellness amongst Secondary School Students in Fiji. *Int. J. Qual. Stud. Health Well-Being* **2021**, *16*, 2001895. [CrossRef] [PubMed]
71. Delaney, C. The Spirituality Scale. *J. Holist. Nurs.* **2005**, *23*, 145–167. [CrossRef] [PubMed]
72. Purdy, M.; Dupey, P. Holistic Flow Model of Spiritual Wellness. *Couns. Values* **2005**, *49*, 95–106. [CrossRef]
73. Syed, S.; Rehman, R.; Hussain, M.; Shaikh, S. Intellectual Wellness in Medical University Teachers: Gender Based Comparison. *J. Pak. Med. Assoc.* **2017**, *67*, 782–784.
74. Strout, K.A.; Howard, E.P. The Six Dimensions of Wellness and Cognition in Aging Adults. *J. Holist. Nurs.* **2012**, *30*, 195–204. [CrossRef]
75. Horton, B.W.; Snyder, C.S. Wellness: Its Impact on Student Grades and Implications for Business. *J. Hum. Resour. Hosp. Tour.* **2009**, *8*, 215–233. [CrossRef]
76. Grzegorzewska, M.; Kirschke, P. The Impact of Certification Systems for Architectural Solutions in Green Office Buildings in the Perspective of Occupant Well-Being. *Buildings* **2021**, *11*, 659. [CrossRef]
77. Fu, Y.; Wang, H.; Sun, W.; Zhang, X. New Dimension to Green Buildings: Turning Green into Occupant Well-Being. *Buildings* **2021**, *11*, 534. [CrossRef]
78. Bhattacharyya, N.; Chakrabarti, D. Design Development Scopes towards Occupational Wellness of Women Workers: Specific Reference to Local Agro Based Food Processing Industries in NE India. *Work* **2012**, *43*, 403–409. [CrossRef]
79. Theodoropoulou, E.; Vardopoulos, I.; Sardianou, E.; Mitoula, R.; Kavouras, S. Sustainable Development: Setting the Curricula for Environmental and Occupational Safety and Health Skills and Education. In Proceedings of the 2019 International Institute of Engineers and Researchers International Conference on Natural Science and Environment, Florence, Italy, 19–20 December 2019; pp. 22–26.
80. Schwartz, S.A. Social Values, Social Wellness: Can We Know What Works? *Explore* **2012**, *8*, 89–91. [CrossRef] [PubMed]
81. Roscoe, L.J. Wellness: A Review of Theory and Measurement for Counselors. *J. Couns. Dev.* **2009**, *87*, 216–226. [CrossRef]

82. Khattak, A.; Khan, W.; Pervez, Z.; Iqbal, F.; Lee, S. Towards A Self Adaptive System for Social Wellness. *Sensors* **2016**, *16*, 531. [CrossRef] [PubMed]
83. Luque-Suárez, M.; del Carmen Olmos-Gómez, M.; Castán-García, M.; Portillo-Sánchez, R. Promoting Emotional and Social Well-Being and a Sense of Belonging in Adolescents through Participation in Volunteering. *Healthcare* **2021**, *9*, 359. [CrossRef] [PubMed]
84. Creswell, J.W.; Guetterman, T.C. *Educational Research: Planning, Conducting, and Evaluating Quantitative and Qualitative Research*, 6th ed.; Pearson: London, UK, 2018; ISBN 9780131367395.
85. Montgomery, K. Understanding the Relationship between the Design of the Workplace Environment and Wellness. M.S. Thesis, Texas Tech University, Lubbock, TX, USA, 2004.
86. Pazhuhan, M.; Shahraki, S.Z.; Kaveerad, N.; Cividino, S.; Clemente, M.; Salvati, L. Factors Underlying Life Quality in Urban Contexts: Evidence from an Industrial City (Arak, Iran). *Sustainability* **2020**, *12*, 2274. [CrossRef]
87. Karytsas, S.; Vardopoulos, I.; Theodoropoulou, E. Factors Affecting Sustainable Market Acceptance of Residential Microgeneration Technologies. A Two Time Period Comparative Analysis. *Energies* **2019**, *12*, 3298. [CrossRef]
88. Zanganeh Shahraki, S.; Ahmadifard, N.; Farhadikhah, H.; Fotouhi Mehrabani, B.; Haydari, A.; Abdali, Y.; Abbasi Fallah, V.; Farhadi, E.; Cividino, S.; Vinci, S.; et al. Spatial Planning, Urban Governance and the Economic Context: The Case of 'Mehr' Housing Plan, Iran. *Land* **2020**, *9*, 169. [CrossRef]
89. Karytsas, S.; Vardopoulos, I.; Theodoropoulou, E. Factors Affecting Residents' Attitude toward Sustainable Tourism Development. *Tourismos* **2019**, *14*, 1–40.
90. Christina, P.; Asimina, K.; Anastasios, M.; Luca, S. Assessing School Teachers' Perception of Disasters: Insights from a Socio-Environmentally Stressed Mediterranean Area (Attica, Greece). *Int. J. Disaster Risk Reduct.* **2022**, *79*, 103134. [CrossRef]
91. Vardopoulos, I.; Stamopoulos, C.; Chatzithanasis, G.; Michalakelis, C.; Giannouli, P.; Pastrapa, E. Considering Urban Development Paths and Processes on Account of Adaptive Reuse Projects. *Buildings* **2020**, *10*, 73. [CrossRef]
92. Hair, J.; Hult, T.; Ringle, C.; Sarstedt, M. *A Primer on Partial Least Squares Structural Equation Modeling*; Sage Publications: Thousand Oaks, CA, USA, 2014; ISBN 1452217440.
93. Hair, J.; Ringle, C.; Sarstedt, M. The Use of Partial Least Squares (PLS) to Address Marketing Management Topics. *J. Mark. Theory Pract.* **2011**, *19*, 135–138. [CrossRef]
94. Fornell, C.; Larcker, D.F. Evaluating Structural Equation Models with Unobservable Variables and Measurement Error. *J. Mark. Res.* **1981**, *18*, 39. [CrossRef]
95. Henseler, J.; Ringle, C.M.; Sarstedt, M. A New Criterion for Assessing Discriminant Validity in Variance-Based Structural Equation Modeling. *J. Acad. Mark. Sci.* **2015**, *43*, 115–135. [CrossRef]
96. Kline, R.B. *Principles and Practice of Structural Equation Modeling*; Guilford Press: New York, NY, USA, 2015.
97. Gold, A.H.; Malhotra, A.; Segars, A.H. Knowledge Management: An Organizational Capabilities Perspective. *J. Manag. Inf. Syst* **2001**, *18*, 185–214. [CrossRef]
98. Sarstedt, M.; Ringle, C.M.; Smith, D.; Reams, R.; Hair, J.F. Partial Least Squares Structural Equation Modeling (PLS-SEM) A Useful Tool for Family Business Researchers. *J. Fam. Bus. Strateg.* **2014**, *5*, 105–115. [CrossRef]
99. Hair, J.F., Jr.; Sarstedt, M.; Matthews, L.M.; Ringle, C.M. Identifying and Treating Unobserved Heterogeneity with FIMIX-PLS: Part I—Method. *Eur. Bus. Rev.* **2016**, *28*, 63–76. [CrossRef]
100. Cohen, J. *Statistical Power Analysis for the Behavioral Sciences*; Routledge: New York, NY, USA, 2013; ISBN 9781134742707.
101. Sullivan, G.M.; Feinn, R. Using Effect Size—Or Why the *p* Value Is Not Enough. *J. Grad. Med. Educ.* **2012**, *4*, 279–282. [CrossRef]
102. Gillis, K.; Gatersleben, B. A Review of Psychological Literature on the Health and Wellbeing Benefits of Biophilic Design. *Buildings* **2015**, *5*, 948–963. [CrossRef]
103. Morales-Bravo, J.; Navarrete-Hernandez, P. Enlightening Wellbeing in the Home: The Impact of Natural Light Design on Perceived Happiness and Sadness in Residential Spaces. *Build. Environ.* **2022**, *223*, 109317. [CrossRef]
104. Wiseman, J.; Brasher, K. Community Wellbeing, Art and Culture: Challenges and Opportunities for Local Communities and Local Governments. In Proceedings of the Arts and Local Goverment Conference, Prahran, Australia, 24–27 July 2007.
105. Thatcher, A.; Milner, K. Changes in Productivity, Psychological Wellbeing and Physical Wellbeing from Working in a "green" Building. *Work* **2014**, *49*, 381–393. [CrossRef]
106. Andreucci, M.B.; Russo, A.; Olszewska-Guizzo, A. Designing Urban Green Blue Infrastructure for Mental Health and Elderly Wellbeing. *Sustainability* **2019**, *11*, 6425. [CrossRef]
107. Kempeneer, S.; Peeters, M.; Compernolle, T. Bringing the User Back in the Building: An Analysis of ESG in Real Estate and a Behavioral Framework to Guide Future Research. *Sustainability* **2021**, *13*, 3239. [CrossRef]

MDPI AG
Grosspeteranlage 5
4052 Basel
Switzerland
Tel.: +41 61 683 77 34

Urban Science Editorial Office
E-mail: urbansci@mdpi.com
www.mdpi.com/journal/urbansci

www.ingramcontent.com/pod-product-compliance
Lightning Source LLC
LaVergne TN
LVHW070503061126
851858LV00011B/286